Casebook on the Law of Persons and Family Law

Second Edition

Vonnisbundel oor die Persone- en Familiereg

Tweede Uitgawe

Casebook on
the Law of Persons
and Family Law

Second Edition

Vonnisbundel oor
die Persone- en
Familiereg

Tweede Uitgawe

by/deur

DSP CRONJÉ Hons-BA (Stell), LLB (Unisa) LLM LLD (RAU)
Professor in Private Law, University of South Africa
Professor in Privaatreg, Universiteit van Suid-Afrika

J HEATON BLC LLB (Pret), LLM (Unisa)
Associate Professor in Private Law, University of South Africa
Medeprofessor in Privaatreg, Universiteit van Suid-Afrika

Butterworths
Durban

Butterworth Publishers (Pty) Ltd

Reg No 91/05175/07

© 1994

First edition 1990
Reprinted 1991, 1992, 1993
Second edition 1994
Reprinted 1995, 1996

ISBN 0 409 02081 8

Durban

8 Walter Place, Waterval Park
Mayville 4091

Johannesburg

Grayston 66, 2 Norwich Close
Sandton 2196

Cape Town

3 Gardens Business Village, Hope Street
Cape Town 8001

Printed and bound by Colorgraphic, Durban

Preface/Voorwoord

In order to save on space and costs we have decided to publish the English and Afrikaans version of this Casebook in a single volume. The summary of the facts of each case and the notes thereon are given in both languages while the extract from the case is obviously given only in the language in which the case was reported. The reference of the case and remarks on the judgment are also given in the language of the reported decision.

As far as the extracts are concerned, we tried to give too much detail rather than too little. On occasion we have corrected obvious spelling and printing errors in the extracts.

Reported judgments up to and including the June 1994 edition of the South African Law Reports have been considered for inclusion in this Casebook.

Ten einde plek en koste te bespaar, het ons besluit om die Engelse en Afrikaanse weergawe van hierdie Vonnisbundel in een boek uit te gee. Die feite-opsomming van, asook die aantekening by, elke beslissing word in albei tale gegee terwyl die uittreksel uit elke saak natuurlik verskaf word in die taal waarin die saak gerapporteer is. Die saakverwysing en opmerkings by die saak word ook verskaf in die taal waarin die beslissing gerapporteer is.

Wat die uittreksels betref, het ons probeer om eerder te veel as te min te gee. Ons het by geleentheid opvallende spel- en drukfoute in die uittreksels reggestel.

Beslissings tot en met die Junie 1994-uitgawe van die Suid-Afrikaanse Hofverslae is oorweeg vir insluiting in hierdie Vonnisbundel.

Table of Contents / Inhoudsopgawe

DIVERSE FACTORS WHICH INFLUENCE STATUS
DIVERSE FAKTORE WAT STATUS BEÏNVLOED

THE ENGAGEMENT
DIE VERLOWING

REQUIREMENTS FOR THE CONCLUSION OF A VALID MARRIAGE
GELDIGHEIDSVEREISTES VIR DIE SLUITING VAN 'N HUWELIK

ADMINISTRATION OF THE JOINT ESTATE
BEHEER OOR DIE GEMEENSKAPLIKE BOEDEL

The requirement of joint consent / Die vereiste van gesamentlike toestemming

Protection of the spouses / Beskerming van die gades

THE MARRIAGE OUT OF COMMUNITY OF PROPERTY
DIE HUWELIK BUITE GEMEENSKAP VAN GOED

Requirements for the creation of a valid antenuptial contract / Vereistes vir die totstandkoming van 'n geldige huweliksvoorwaardeskontrak

Termination, cancellation and amendment of the antenuptial contract / Beëindiging, kansellasie en wysiging van die huweliksvoor- waardeskontrak

Marriage settlements / Huweliksbevoordelings

ALTERATION OF THE MATRIMONIAL PROPERTY SYSTEM
WYSIGING VAN DIE HUWELIKSGOEDEREBEDELING

Section 21(1) of the Matrimonial Property Act / Artikel 21(1) van die Wet op Huweliksgoedere

Extra-judicial amendment / Buitegeregtelike wysiging

THE GROUNDS FOR DIVORCE
DIE EGSKEIDINGSGRONDE

FORFEITURE OF PATRIMONIAL BENEFITS
VERBEURING VAN VERMOËNSREGTELIKE VOORDELE

REDISTRIBUTION OF ASSETS IN TERMS OF SECTION 7(3) OF
THE DIVORCE ACT 70 OF 1979
HERVERDELING VAN BATES INGEVOLGE ARTIKEL 7(3) VAN
DIE WET OP EGSKEIDING 70 VAN 1979

MAINTENANCE OF THE SPOUSES
ONDERHOUD VAN DIE GADES

Nasciturus

The interests of the unborn child

Succession
Maintenance
Personality interests
Protection of life

Nasciturus

Die belange van die ongebore kind

Erfreg
Onderhoud
Persoonlikheidsregte
Beskerming van lewe

Succession   Erfreg

[1] EX PARTE BOEDEL STEENKAMP*

1962 3 SA 954 (O)

Capacity of a *nasciturus* to inherit

The testator, *inter alia*, bequeathed the residue
of his estate in equal shares to his daughter
and her children of the first generation "wat
by datum van dood in die lewe is ..." At
the time of the testator's death his daughter
had two children. At that stage, however, the
daughter was pregnant and subsequently gave
birth to a son (Paul Johannes). The executor
applied that the court should establish
whether only those grandchildren already
born at the testator's death could inherit or
whether the child born after his death could
also share in the inheritance. The court held
that he could inherit.

Bevoegdheid van 'n *nasciturus* om te erf

Die testateur se testament het onder andere
die volgende bepaling bevat: "Ek bemaak die
restant van my boedel in gelyke dele aan my
dogter ... en haar kinders van die eerste
geslag wat by datum van dood in die lewe
is ..." Die testateur se dogter het ten tyde
van sy dood twee kinders gehad. Sy was op
daardie stadium egter swanger en het later
die lewe aan 'n seun (Paul Johannes) geskenk.
Die eksekuteur het aansoek gedoen dat die
hof moes bepaal of net die kleinkinders kon
erf wat tydens die testateur se dood reeds
gebore was en of die kind wat na sy dood
gebore is ook in die erfenis kon deel. Die
hof het beslis dat hy kon erf.

DE VILLIERS R: [956] Dit is gemene saak dat 'n kind *in ventre matris* vir die doeleindes
van erflating vermoed word lewendig te wees mits dit later gebore word en mits dit tot
die voordeel van sodanige kind is. *Voet*, 1.5.5, word soos volg deur *Gane* vertaal:

> "Still by a fiction of law they (kinders in *ventre matris*) are regarded as already born
> whenever it is a question of their advantage" ...

Dit is egter duidelik ... dat die vermoedes geskep in *Voet*, 1.5.5 en 28.5.12 en 13, moet
wyk indien dit blyk uit die testament as 'n geheel dat die testateur 'n ander bedoeling
het.

Mnr *van Heerden*, wat opgetree het as *kurator-ad-litem* namens Gerda en Daniel Johannes
[die twee kinders wat reeds gebore was], het aangevoer dat die woorde gebesig deur die
testateur, naamlik "wat by datum van dood in die lewe is" die vermoede geskep in *Voet*,
1.5.5, weerlê en daarop dui dat die testateur slegs die kinders van sy dogter wou bevoordeel
wat by sy dood reeds gebore en in die lewe is. Mnr *Linde* wat as *kurator-ad-litem* opgetree
het vir Paul Johannes [die *nasciturus*], het daarenteen aangevoer dat die aangehaalde woorde
nie genoeg is in die lig van die bepalings van die testament as 'n geheel, om die vermoede
geskep in *Voet*, 1.5.5, te weerlê nie.

Na my mening moet mnr *Linde* gelyk gegee word. Al word dit [957] aanvaar dat mnr
van Heerden gelyk gegee moet word dat die testateur deur die gebruik van die woorde
"wat by datum van dood in die lewe is" bedoel dat kleinkinders wat na sy dood verwek

---

* This case has been taken from *Erfreg Vonnisbundel/
Casebook on the Law of Succession*, 1993 by D S P Cronjé
and Anneliese Roos with permission of the publisher,
the University of South Africa.

* Hierdie saak is oorgeneem uit *Erfreg Vonnisbundel/
Casebook on the Law of Succession*, 1993 deur D S P Cronjé
en Anneliese Roos met die toestemming van die uitgewer, die Universiteit van Suid-Afrika.

en gebore word nie deel in die erfenis nie, beteken dit nog nie dat hy ook daardeur bedoel dat kleinkinders wat reeds voor sy dood verwek is, maar na sy dood gebore word nie sal erf nie . . .

[DE VILLIERS R het na die uitspraak van die House of Lords in *Elliot v Lord Joicey* 1935 AC 209 verwys en voortgegaan:]

Dit wil my voorkom, indien ek dit reg verstaan, dat die *ratio decidendi* van bogemelde outoriteite is dat, selfs indien dit onthou word dat 'n verwysing na kinders "in lewe" of "gebore" op 'n besondere tydstip in normale taalgebruik 'n kind *in ventre matris* uitsluit, die gebruik van sodanige woorde in die onderhawige omstandighede en in die afwesigheid van enige ander aanduiding wat die testateur se bedoeling heeltemal duidelik maak, nie genoeg is om die baie sterk natuurlike vermoede te weerlê dat die testateur bedoel het dat 'n kind *in ventre matris* as reeds gebore of in lewe beskou moet word nie . . .

[958] In die onderhawige geval moet in die lig van die baie sterk vermoede vervat in *Voet*, 1.5.5 (en wat deur hom as 'n fiksie beskryf word) dit veronderstel word dat die testateur die natuurlike drang sou gehad het om 'n kleinkind *in ventre matris* te bevoordeel net soos kleinkinders wat reeds gebore is by sy dood.

Die gebruik van die woord "in lewe" moet nie te letterlik opgeneem word nie en beskou word as 'n noodwendige aanduiding dat die testateur daardeur bedoel om die vermoede te weerlê nie, maar eerder, aangesien dit tot die voordeel van Paul Johannes is, dat hy die vermoede beklemtoon. Kyk byvoorbeeld na die saak van *Ex parte Odendaal*, 1957 (2) SA 15 (O), waar die Hof nie die woorde "by die dood" letterlik vertolk het nie en ook na die saak van *In re Estate van Velden* [(1901) 18 SC 31], waar 'n testateur die waarde van twee-derdes van sy boedel aan die "children born of our marriage" vererf het. In laas-genoemde saak het die Hof beslis dat 'n kind van die testateur se huwelik *in ventre matris* by sy dood geregtig was om te erf saam met die kinders reeds gebore by sy dood. Die woord "born" het nie verhoed dat die Hof uitvoering gee aan die vermoede van *Voet*, 1.5.5, nie.

Dit word beveel dat wat die restant van die testateur se boedel betref Paul Johannes beskou moet word as in lewe by die dood van die testateur en geregtig is om gelykop te erf met sy moeder . . . en met sy suster en broer . . .

Note

If the testator had in this case left the residue of his estate to his daughter and her children, there would have been no doubt that the son she was expecting at the time of the testator's death would also have shared in the inheritance, as it was clearly to the grandson's benefit that he was regarded as having been born at the date of the death of the testator. The question is now whether the words in the will "kinders . . . wat by datum van dood in die lewe is" did not rebut the presumption that the testator also wished to benefit children born later.

As a result of the use of these words one could perhaps argue that the decision is not correct. The *ratio* for the rule that a *nasciturus* can inherit if he is later born alive, is that the testator presumably intended also to benefit members of the class concerned who have already been conceived

Aantekening

Indien die testateur in die onderhawige saak bepaal het dat die restant van sy boedel aan sy dogter en haar kinders bemaak word, sou daar geen twyfel gewees het dat die seun wat sy dogter ten tyde van die testateur se dood verwag het ook kon erf nie. Dit was immers duidelik tot die kleinseun se voordeel dat hy beskou moes word as reeds gebore op die datum van dood van die testateur. Die vraag is egter of die woorde in die testament "kinders . . . wat by datum van dood in die lewe is" nie die vermoede weerlê het dat die erflater ook later geborenes wou bevoordeel nie.

Weens die gebruik van hierdie woorde sou 'n mens moontlik kon aanvoer dat die beslissing nie korrek is nie. Die *ratio* vir die reël dat 'n *nasciturus* kan erf as hy later gebore word, is dat die erflater vermoedelik bedoel het om reeds verwekte, maar

but have not yet been born. Now, if the basis for benefiting the unborn really is the intention of the testator, then an indication that only children or grandchildren who are alive at the time of the death of the testator should inherit, is certainly a strong enough indication that the testator in this case did not want to benefit the unborn child. What could the restriction in the will otherwise have meant? Nevertheless, we think that the decision is correct simply because the reason why the testator had not made provision for the *nasciturus* was because he had never considered the possibility that his daughter might be expecting a child at the time of his death. In other words, all the court did was to interpret the will in accordance with what the testator himself would have done had he considered his daughter's pregnancy. We can find nothing wrong with such an interpretation.

The decision, however, is on the one hand a clear illustration of the unwillingness of the courts to act to the prejudice of *nascituri*, and on the other hand makes it clear that a testator who wishes a *nasciturus* not to inherit will have to express his intention very clearly.

nog ongebore, lede van die betrokke klas by die bevoordeling in te sluit. Nou, as die grondslag vir bevoordeling van ongeborenes werklik die wil van die erflater is, dan is 'n aanduiding dat slegs kinders of kleinkinders moet erf wat op die datum van die erflater se dood in die lewe is, tog seker 'n sterk genoeg aanduiding dat die erflater in hierdie geval nie die ongeborenes wou bevoordeel nie. Wat sou die insluiting van sodanige beperking in die testament immers andersins kon beteken? Nogtans meen ons dat die beslissing korrek is, eenvoudig omdat die rede waarom die testateur nie vir die *nasciturus* voorsiening gemaak het nie, was omdat hy nooit aan die moontlikheid gedink het dat sy dogter tydens sy dood verwagtend sou wees nie. Al wat die hof met ander woorde gedoen het, was om die testament so uit te lê dat dit in ooreenstemming was met wat die testateur sou bepaal het as hy sy dogter se swangerskap voorsien het. Met sodanige uitleg kan ons geen fout vind nie.

Die beslissing is egter enersyds 'n duidelike illustrasie van die howe se onwilligheid om tot die nadeel van *nascituri* op te tree, en andersyds is dit uit hierdie uitspraak duidelik dat 'n testateur wat wil hê dat 'n *nasciturus* nie moet erf nie sy bedoeling baie duidelik sal moet uitdruk.

Maintenance   **Onderhoud**

[2] CHISHOLM V EAST RAND PROPRIETARY MINES LTD

1909 TH 297

Nasciturus — the right of a child to claim damages for the negligent killing of his father while he was still *in ventre matris*

The plaintiff's husband was employed by the defendant. He was killed due to the negligence of another employee of the defendant. The plaintiff was expecting a child when her husband was killed. She claimed damages from the defendant and the question arose whether the child had an independent right of action, apart from the mother, against the person who had killed his father. The court

Nasciturus — die reg van 'n kind om skadevergoeding te eis vir die nalatige veroorsaking van sy vader se dood terwyl hy nog *in ventre matris* was

Die eiseres se man was in diens van die verweerder. Hy is gedood deur die nalatigheid van 'n ander persoon wat in die verweerder se diens was. Die eiseres was swanger toe haar man dood is. Sy het nou skadevergoeding van die verweerder geëis, en die vraag het ontstaan of die kind 'n aksiegrond, onafhanklik van dié van sy moeder, gehad het om skadevergoeding te eis van die persoon

held that he did have an independent right of action.

wat sy vader gedood het. Die hof het beslis dat hy wel 'n onafhanklike aksiegrond het.

MASON J: [301] One of the first questions which arises is whether the compensation to be awarded must include such a provision for the child as the father would have made for it. That depends, again, on the further question whether the child has an independent right of action apart from the mother against a person responsible for the death of the father. The case of *Jameson's Minors v C.S.A.R.* ([1908] T.S. 575) answers that question affirmatively. The well-known principle that a posthumous child is to be considered as born at the death of the father, if such a fiction will be to its advantage (Voet, 1,5,5), places this infant in the same position as other children . . .

Note

A person's dependants have a personal right to claim maintenance from him. If he is then killed due to the negligence of a third person, the latter infringes the dependants' personal right with the result that they may claim damages from the third party for their loss of maintenance. In this case the child's father was killed before the child was born and the question arose whether he had a right to claim damages from the third party for the loss of maintenance. The court extended the *nasciturus* fiction to the law of delict and held that the child had an independent right of action, apart from his mother, against the person responsible for his father's death. See also *Pinchin v Santam Insurance Company Ltd* [3]; *Christian League of Southern Africa v Rall* [4]; Van der Vyver and Joubert 63.

Aantekening

'n Persoon se afhanklikes het 'n persoonlike reg om onderhoud van hom te eis. As hy dan gedood word deur die nalatigheid van 'n derde maak sodanige derde inbreuk op die afhanklikes se persoonlike reg met die gevolg dat hulle skadevergoeding van die derde party mag eis vir hulle verlies aan onderhoud. In hierdie saak is die kind se vader gedood voor die kind se geboorte en die vraag het ontstaan of hy skadevergoeding van die derde party kon eis vir sy verlies aan onderhoud. Die hof het die *nasciturus*-fiksie uitgebrei na die gebied van die onregmatige daad en beslis dat die kind, onafhanklik van sy moeder se eis, 'n aksie kon instel teen die persoon wat sy vader se dood veroorsaak het. Sien ook *Pinchin v Santam Insurance Company Ltd* [3]; *Christian League of Southern Africa v Rall* [4]; Van der Vyver en Joubert 63.

Personality interests   Persoonlikheidsregte

[3]   PINCHIN V SANTAM INSURANCE CO LTD

1963 2 SA 254 (W)

Nasciturus — the right to claim damages for injuries sustained pre-natally

A woman who was six months pregnant was involved in a motor accident. The driver of the other car was insured with the defendant. As a result of the accident the mother suffered a substantial loss of amniotic fluid. The pregnancy continued normally but the baby was subsequently born with cerebral palsy, as a result of which he would never be able to take care of himself. Negligence on the

Nasciturus — die reg om skadevergoeding te eis vir beserings wat voor geboorte opgedoen is

'n Vrou wat ses maande verwagtend was, is in 'n motorongeluk beseer. Die bestuurder van die ander motor is deur die verweerder verseker. As gevolg van die ongeluk het die vrou heelwat vrugwater verloor. Die swangerskap het normaal voortgegaan maar die kind is later met ernstige serebrale letsels gebore wat beteken het dat hy nooit in staat sou wees om vir homself te sorg nie. Na-

part of the driver of the other car was admitted. The father claimed special damages on behalf of his child and damages for patrimonial loss in his own name. The medical witness for the plaintiff maintained that with the loss of the amniotic fluid the woman's uterus had contracted considerably. As a result of this the placental site had also contracted and consequently the child had suffered from anoxia, that is lack of oxygen, which is a well-known cause of cerebral palsy. The medical witness for the defendant, however, rejected this theory entirely. It was common cause between the parties that a *foetus* can be deprived of two-thirds of its blood supply and not suffer anoxia. According to the medical witness for the defendant the damage to the placenta could not have been so severe that two-thirds of the blood supply to the *foetus* could have been shut off for a sufficiently long period to cause anoxia. The court held that the child did have an action to recover for pre-natal injuries but found that it had not been proved in this case that the brain damage was caused by the accident and consequently absolution from the instance was ordered.

latigheid deur die ander bestuurder is erken. Die kind se vader het namens die kind genoegdoening en in sy eie naam skadevergoeding geëis. Die mediese getuie vir die eiser het aangevoer dat die verlies van die vrugwater die vrou se baarmoeder laat saamtrek het. As gevolg hiervan het die plasenta ook saamgetrek wat daartoe gelei het dat die kind te min suurstof gekry het wat 'n alombekende oorsaak van serebrale gestremdheid is. Die mediese getuie vir die verweerder het hierdie teorie egter geheel en al verwerp. Dit was gemene saak tussen die partye dat twee derdes van 'n *foetus* se bloedtoevoer afgesny kan word sonder dat dit tot 'n suurstoftekort lei. Volgens die mediese getuie vir die verweerder kon die skade aan die plasenta nie so ernstig gewees het dat twee derdes van die bloedtoevoer na die *foetus* vir 'n lang genoeg tydperk afgesny kon gewees het om 'n suurstoftekort te kon veroorsaak het nie. Die hof het beslis dat 'n kind wel 'n aksie om skadevergoeding vir voorgeboortelike beserings het maar dat daar nie bewys is dat die breinskade deur die ongeluk veroorsaak is nie en het gevolglik absolusie van die instansie beveel.

HIEMSTRA J: [254] This case presents a problem which is *res nova*, not only in our case law, but also, as I understood the evidence, in the field [255] of gynaecology and neurology. The legal question is whether an action lies for pre-natal injury to a *foetus*. The medical question is whether there is in this case a chain of causation between an injury sustained by the pregnant mother and the fact that the child suffers from cerebral palsy ...

The legal question is crisply: Does a person have an action in respect of injury inflicted on him while he was still a *foetus* in his mother's womb? ...

[HIEMSTRA J referred to an article by Versfeld in the 1960 *Acta Juridica* 2 and proceeded:]

This merely poses the further question – when is man created, at birth or at conception, or when he starts to move within the womb?

The Roman Law has given an answer in *D*.1.5.7:

"A child in its mother's womb is cared for just as if it were in existence, whenever its own advantage is concerned; but it cannot benefit anyone else before it is born."

And in *D*.1.5.26:

"Those who are unborn are, by almost every provision of the Civil Law, understood to be already in existence; for estates legally descend to them, and if a pregnant woman is taken by the enemy, her child has the right of *postliminium* ..." [to regain most of its rights].

In *D*.50.16.231:

> "When we say that a child, who is expected to be born, is considered as already in existence, this is only true where his rights are in question, but no advantage accrues to others unless they are actually born."

The reason why these passages are not always regarded as decisive of the issue, is that all commentators have related them to the law of succession and to the question of *status* — whether freedman or slave. Not one has extended their operation to the field of delict. Glück *Erläuterung der Pandekten*, 11, p. 69 (1.5.114) links these passages only with succession and *status*. So does *Voet*, 1.5.5. Grotius *Inleiding*, 1.3.4, says merely that a child in the womb is regarded as born if it is to its advantage, and not when it would be to its disadvantage. Van der Keessel, *Praelectiones*, comments on this purely in relation to the law of succession. So does *Schorer*. None of them however expressly limit it to the right of succession and none contend that the *foetus* can be a bearer of rights and obligations. The position is merely that the vesting of rights is kept suspended until the *nasciturus* is born. It is in the more modern law that greater guidance in regard to this action can be found ...

[256] The question is purely this: Does the fiction, which is clearly part of our law, apply outside the law of property, and does it include the law of delict?

McKerron thinks it does (*Law of Delict*, 5th ed. p. 139):

> "It remains only to note that provided there is sufficient evidence of causal connection between the act complained of and the resultant harm, there would appear to be no valid reason why a child should not be entitled to recover in respect of injuries inflicted before birth."

He relies on two very weighty authorities. The first is a decision of the Supreme Court of Canada, *Montreal Tramways Co v Léveillé*, (1933) 4 D.L.R. 337 ... The second is an article by Professor Winfield ... in the *Cambridge Law Journal*, vol 8, p. 76, in which the *Léveillé* case is fully discussed ...

[HIEMSTRA J discussed these authorities as well as the position in America and proceeded:]

[259] The point remains whether the fiction having its origins in *D*. 1.5.7. and 26 must with any good reason be limited to the law of property. Why should an unborn infant be regarded as a person for the purposes of property but not for life and limb? I see no reason for limiting the fiction in this way, and the old authorities did not expressly limit it. It is probably because the state of medical knowledge at the time did not make it possible to prove a causal link between pre-natal injury and a post-natal condition, that it did not occur to them to deal with this situation. Would there be an action in the case of *dolus*? It seems impossible to deny it. If one can visualise a mind so evil as to allow the intentional administration of a drug like thalidomide, in order to produce a misshapen infant, our law would be archaic and inflexible if it should refuse an action. Once it is conceded in the case of *dolus* [intent; fraud], there is no ground in principle to deny it in a case of *culpa* [negligence]. Foreseeability creates no difficulty. It is not unforeseeable that a pregnant mother may be travelling on the highway ...

[260] I hold that a child does have an action to recover damages for pre-natal injuries. This view is based on the rule of the Roman law, received into our law, that an unborn child, if subsequently born alive, is deemed to have all the rights of a born child, whenever this is to its advantage. There is apparently no reason to limit this rule to the law of property and to exclude it from the law of delict.

Such an action will encounter difficulties of proof, but that cannot be a reason for denying a right ...

[HIEMSTRA J then analysed the facts and proceeded:]

[263] In the result the likelihood that the loss of fluid led to the cerebral palsy is not

stronger than the opposite contention. That means that plaintiff's case has not been proved on a balance of probabilities ...

The order is: Absolution from the instance ...

Note

The important point in this case is that a child does have an action to recover damages for pre-natal injuries, although it was found that it had not been proved in this case that the brain damage was caused by the accident and consequently the action was refused.

Some authors are of the opinion that it was unnecessary to invoke the *nasciturus* fiction in these circumstances (see for example Joubert 1963 *THRHR* 295 *et seq*). The *nasciturus* fiction, it is maintained, was applied to a case in which it was never used at common law and for which it was never intended. At common law it was applied in cases relating to succession and to the status of the child. It is argued further that the question arising in this case can be solved without bringing the *nasciturus* maxim into the issue, for it can be said that the defect from which the child suffered after birth was caused by the driver of the car's action before the child's birth. The fact that the defect only manifested itself after birth makes no difference: the child is now a person suffering from a defect resulting from the delict committed by the driver of the car. According to this view it is therefore unnecessary to base the child's action for damages on the *nasciturus* fiction.

Boberg, on the other hand, argues convincingly that the *nasciturus* rule must be applied to give an action for pre-natal injury. He points out that the child does not suffer damage only at birth but that "the damage has all been done before ever the child enters this world. He does not *suffer* ... damage on birth: he simply *continues to suffer* the damage which he already sustained *en ventre sa mère*" (17 fn 11, Boberg's accentuation). In other words, when the child started to suffer damage he was not a person and therefore the *nasciturus* rule has to be applied to give him an action for pre-natal injury.

The question of whether a *nasciturus* has an action for pre-natal injuries has been considered by the court only once and, although there can be no doubt that an action will be given to him, it is difficult to ascertain at this stage what the basis of the action will be.

Aantekening

Die belangrike aspek wat in hierdie saak beslis is, is dat 'n kind wel 'n aksie het om skadevergoeding vir voorgeboortelike beserings te eis, alhoewel in hierdie saak bevind is dat die breinskade nie deur die ongeluk veroorsaak is nie en gevolglik is die aksie van die hand gewys.

Sommige skrywers is van mening dat dit onnodig is om in hierdie omstandighede van die *nasciturus*-fiksie gebruik te maak (sien byvoorbeeld Joubert 1963 *THRHR* 295 ev). Die *nasciturus*-fiksie, so word aangevoer, is hier toegepas op 'n geval waarvoor dit nooit in die gemenereg gebruik is nie en waarvoor dit ook nooit bedoel was nie. In die gemenereg is dit toegepas in gevalle met betrekking tot die erfreg en die status van die kind. Daar word verder aangevoer dat die vraag wat in hierdie saak ter sprake gekom het, opgelos kan word sonder byhaling van die *nasciturus*-fiksie deur te sê dat die gebrek waaraan die kind na sy geboorte gely het, veroorsaak is deur die handeling van die motorbestuurder voor die kind se geboorte. Die feit dat die gebrek eers na sy geboorte blyk, maak geen verskil nie: die kind is nou 'n persoon wat as gevolg van die motorbestuurder se onregmatige daad aan 'n gebrek ly. Volgens hierdie siening is dit dus nie nodig om die kind se aksie om skadevergoeding op die *nasciturus*-fiksie te baseer nie.

Boberg aan die ander kant redeneer oortuigend dat die *nasciturus*-reël wel toegepas moet word om 'n aksie vir voorgeboortelike beserings te verleen. Hy wys daarop dat die kind nie eers by sy geboorte skade ly nie, maar dat "the damage has all been done before ever the child enters this world. He does not *suffer* ... damage on birth: he simply *continues to suffer* the damage which he already sustained *en ventre sa mère*" (17 vn 11, Boberg se beklemtoning). Met ander woorde, toe die kind begin het om skade te ly, was hy nie 'n persoon nie en daarom moet die *nasciturus*-reël toegepas word om hom 'n aksie vir voorgeboortelike beserings te gee.

Die vraag of 'n *nasciturus* 'n aksie vir voorgeboortelike beserings het, is nog net een keer deur die hof oorweeg en hoewel daar ongetwyfeld 'n

See also *Christian League of Southern Africa v Rall* [4]; *Chisholm v East Rand Proprietary Mines Ltd* [2]; Van der Merwe 1963 *THRHR* 291; Joubert 1963 *THRHR* 295; Meyer 1963 *SALJ* 447.

On the distinction between the *nasciturus* fiction and the *nasciturus* rule, see *Christian League of Southern Africa v Rall* [4].

aksie aan hom verleen sal word, is dit moeilik om op hierdie stadium te bepaal wat die basis van die aksie sal wees.

Sien ook *Christian League of Southern Africa v Rall* [4]; *Chisholm v East Rand Proprietary Mines Ltd* [2]; Van der Merwe 1963 *THRHR* 291; Joubert 1963 *THRHR* 295; Meyer 1963 *SALJ* 447.

Oor die onderskeid tussen die *nasciturus*-fiksie en die *nasciturus*-reël, sien *Christian League of Southern Africa v Rall* [4].

Protection of life   Beskerming van lewe

[4]   CHRISTIAN LEAGUE OF SOUTHERN AFRICA V RALL

1981 2 SA 821 (O)

Nasciturus — protection of the *foetus* against abortion

The applicant applied for the appointment of a *curator ad litem* to represent the interests of the respondent's daughter's unborn child in all matters concerning the proposed abortion of the child that had allegedly been conceived by rape. The applicant was an organisation which had as one of its objectives the promotion of the Christian faith, morals and ethics and alleged that the protection of human life and the care of the well-being of unborn children were pertinent to those Christian morals and ethics. Accordingly, it was a matter of the utmost importance to the applicant that any abortion performed under the Abortion and Sterilization Act 2 of 1975 should be procured with the recognition and protection of the rights of the unborn child. The application was dismissed.

Nasciturus — beskerming van die *foetus* teen aborsie

Die applikant het aansoek gedoen om die aanstelling van 'n *curator ad litem* om die belange van die ongebore kind van die respondent se dogter te verteenwoordig in alle aangeleenthede rakende die voorgenome aborsie van die kind. Die kind is na bewering deur verkragting verwek. Die applikant was 'n organisasie wie se doelstellings die bevordering van die Christelike geloof, sedes en etiek ingesluit het en daar is beweer dat die beskerming van die menslike lewe en versorging van die welsyn van ongeborenes met die Christelike sedes en etiek verband gehou het. Dit was gevolglik vir die applikant van die uiterste belang dat enige aborsie wat ingevolge die Wet op Vrugafdrywing en Sterilisasie 2 van 1975 uitgevoer word met die nodige erkenning en beskerming van die belange van die ongebore kind sou geskied. Die aansoek is van die hand gewys.

LC STEYN R: [827] Die applikant se belang in die aangeleentheid is uiters vaag. Daar word ook nie eers *prima facie* aangetoon dat die *nasciturus* in wie se belang die aansoek gebring word op enige wyse skakel met die applikant organisasie of met enige van die verenigings waarmee hulle affiliasie het nie. Daar word nie eers beweer dat hulle enige lede in daardie betrokke distrik het nie.

In die omstandighede het applikant geen regsbelang aangetoon op grond waarvan hulle *locus standi in judicio* het nie.

5.1 Die aanvanklike vraag waarop egter uitsluitsel gegee moet word is of daar regsgronde bestaan vir die aanstelling van 'n kurator *ad litem* om 'n *foetus* te verteenwoordig in sake of aangeleenthede wat op die beëindiging van die moeder se swangerskap betrekking het.

5.2 In ons reg is 'n ongebore vrug of *nasciturus* nie 'n regsubjek nie, en word hy dit eers by sy lewendige geboorte, en kan dus nie die draer van regte wees, wat namens hom afgedwing kan word voor daardie tydstip nie.

5.3 By wyse van die *nasciturus*-fiksie word egter aan die ongebore vrug beskerming verleen reeds in die Romeinse reg soos duidelik blyk uit *Digesta* 1.5.7:

> "A child in its mother's womb is cared for just as if it were in existence, whenever its own advantage is concerned; but it cannot benefit anyone else before it is born."

In die Romeins-Hollandse reg was dit ook algemeen erken; *Voet* 1.5.5 (*Gane* se vertaling) lees soos volg:

> "Still by fiction of law they are regarded as already born whenever it is a question of their advantage."

In die huidige Suid-Afrikaanse reg word die *nasciturus*-fiksie ook aangewend om die belange van die ongebore vrug te beskerm.

[828] Die aanwendingsveld vind toepassing onder andere ten opsigte van testamentêre erfopvolging en word by 'n bemaking aan kinders verwekte ongeborenes ingesluit. Dit is ook toegepas in *Ex parte Boedel Steenkamp* 1962 (3) SA 954 (O) [1] waar die erflating moes gaan na kinders wat by datum "van dood in die lewe is" . . .

Wat betref beskerming van die verwekte ongeborene se reg tot eiendom het die fiksie ook erkenning geniet, bv, onder andere, in *Ex parte Muller and Others* 1946 OPD 117. Art 33 (1) van die Algemene Regswysigingswet 62 van 1955 gee ook uitdruklik die bevoegdheid aan die Hooggeregshof om namens ongeborenes (selfs onverwektes) toe te stem tot vervreemding of beswaring van eiendom. Hierna het dit algemene gebruik geword dat die Hof vir ongebore belanghebbendes kurators *ad litem* aanstel om hulle belange te behartig. Die *nasciturus*-fiksie is ook in *Chisholm v East Rand Proprietary Mines Ltd* 1909 TH 297 [2] toegepas deur 'n aksie namens 'n kind te erken vir verlies aan onderhoud waar die vader nalatiglik gedood is, terwyl die kind nog 'n ongebore vrug of *foetus* was.

In *Pinchin and Another NO v Santam Insurance Co Ltd* 1963 (2) SA 254 (W) [3] beslis HIEMSTRA R dat, namens 'n kind wat reeds gebore is, op grond van onregmatige daad geëis kan word tov beserings opgedoen in *ventre matris* voor geboorte . . .

5.4 Daar is egter voldoende gesag dat met die Aquiliaanse aksie skadevergoeding verhaal kan word namens 'n kind na geboorte, ten aansien van 'n onregmatige daad wat voor geboorte gepleeg is, wat tot gevolg het dat die kind na geboorte skade ly . . .

[STEYN R het na McKerron *Law of Delict* 5e uitg 139 verwys en voortgegaan:]

Tot dieselfde effek is die volgende skrywers, wat van mening is dat HIEMSTRA R op grond van die beginsels by onregmatige daad, en sonder gebruik van die *nasciturus*-fiksie sodanige vordering kon erken het. W A Joubert 1963 *THRHR* te 295; Van der Merwe en Olivier *Die Onregmatige Daad in die Suid-Afrikaanse Reg* 3de [829] uitg te 52–57; P C Smit *Die Posisie van die Ongeborene in die Suid-Afrikaanse Reg met Besondere Aandag aan die Nasciturus Leerstuk* te 292–293.

Ek vereenselwig my met hierdie skrywers tov die aspek dat namens 'n kind na geboorte geëis kan word tov skade hom nalatiglik aangedoen in *ventre matris* as ongeborene. In die *Pinchin*-saak was daar egter gehandel met 'n eis ingevolge art 11 van Wet 29 van 1942 waar die verpligting om te vergoed berus op skade gely as gevolg van "bodily injury to *any person*", wat moontlik die toepassing van die *nasciturus*-beginsel nodig gemaak het.

5.5 Dit is gemene saak dat op die huidige stand van ons reg, die *nasciturus*-fiksie nog nie uitgebrei is om die veld te dek waarop nou gevra word dat dit aangewend moet word nie ... ,

Ek is van mening dat die toepassing van die *nasciturus*-fiksie nie die ongeborene met enige regspersoonlikheid beklee nie. Dit [830] verseker slegs dat voordele wat die ongebore vrug na geboorte mag toeval *in suspenso* gehou word tot sy geboorte. *P C Smit* aw te 172–199; en *Pinchin*-saak *supra* te 260B.

Waar die ongebore vrug nie lewend gebore word nie is daar geen sprake van enige regte wat hom toeval nie en kleef geen regte aan hom, op grond waarvan gesê kan word dat hy 'n regsubjek is nie. *P C Smit* aw te 214–217. Waar die ongebore vrug se "regte" met hom sterf, is daar ook geen ruimte vir die uitbreiding van die *nasciturus*-fiksie tot die beskerming teen vrugafdrywing nie.

In die omstandighede is ek geensins tevrede gestel dat die *nasciturus*-fiksie verder uitgebrei behoort te word nie.

Die Wet op Vrugafdrywing en Sterilisasie 2 van 1975, wat die belange van die ongebore vrug of *foetus* strafregtelik met die nodige sanksies beskerm, laat ook, ingeval van die beweerde verkragting van die moeder, vrugafdrywing slegs toe as aan die bepaalde voorskrifte voldoen word ...

[STEYN R het na artikel 6(4) van die wet verwys en voortgegaan:]

By hierdie verrigtinge voor die landdros is daar na my mening geen ruimte of behoefte vir die verskyning van 'n kurator *ad litem* namens die ongeborene nie, wie se belange behartig word deur die landdros ... Dit sou 'n vrou die onnodige koste van bestrede verrigtinge wat tydsaam [is] en gepaard gaan met koste, veroorsaak. Die applikant het ook op hierdie aspek nie voldoende gronde voorgelê vir die aanstelling van 'n kurator *ad litem* by sodanige verrigtinge ingevolge art 6(4) van die gemelde Wet nie.

Vir hierdie redes het ek applikant se aansoek van die hand gewys ...

Note

This decision is criticised by Van der Vyver (1981 *THRHR* 305–314); Du Plessis (1990 *TSAR* 44 51–54) and Van der Vyver and Joubert (69). These authors are of the opinion that the court should be allowed to appoint a *curator ad litem* to represent the interests of an unborn child in all matters relating to its proposed abortion, since it is after all the child's right to life which is at stake and consequently it has a special interest in the matter. Du Plessis pleads for "preventive protection" for the unborn child in cases like these. See also *G v Superintendent, Groote Schuur Hospital* 1993 2 SA 255 (C) 259D–E, where Seligson AJ expresses "doubts about the correctness of that decision [ie the decison in *Rall*] insofar as it holds that there is no scope for the extension of the *nasciturus* doctrine so as to provide protection for an unborn foetus against abortion". He continues by saying that "there is much to be said for recognising that an unborn child has a legal right to representation, or an interest capable of protection, in

Aantekening

Hierdie beslissing word gekritiseer deur Van der Vyver (1981 *THRHR* 305–314); Du Plessis (1990 *TSAR* 44 51–54) en Van der Vyver en Joubert (69). Hierdie skrywers is van mening dat dit vir die hof geoorloof behoort te wees om vir 'n ongeborene 'n kurator aan te stel om na sy belange om te sien by alle verrigtinge wat op sy voorgenome aborsie betrekking het, aangesien dit per slot van sake sy reg op lewe is wat op die spel is en die ongeborene daarom 'n besondere belang by die aangeleentheid het. Du Plessis pleit vir "preventive protection" (dit wil sê voorkomende beskerming) vir die ongebore kind in hierdie soort gevalle. Sien ook *G v Superintendent, Groote Schuur Hospital* 1993 2 SA 255 (K) 259D–E, waar Seligson Wn R sy twyfel oor die korrektheid van die *Rall*-beslissing uitspreek "insofar as it holds that there is no scope for the extension of the *nasciturus* doctrine so as to provide protection for an unborn foetus against abortion". Hy sê verder dat "there is much to be said for recognising that an unborn

circumstances where its very existence is threatened".

Authors like Van der Vyver and Joubert, are of the opinion that, whenever its interests are at issue, the *nasciturus* becomes a legal subject before it is born. In this respect one must distinguish between the *nasciturus* fiction and the *nasciturus* rule. According to the *nasciturus* fiction the *foetus* is regarded as having been born at the time of conception whenever it is to its advantage. According to the *nasciturus* rule, on the other hand, the *foetus* is regarded as a legal subject from the date of its conception whenever its interests are at issue (Van der Merwe 1963 *THRHR* 291 *et seq*). In the case under discussion the court endorsed the view that the *nasciturus* is not a legal subject. See further on this matter Bedil 1981 *SALJ* 462–466; Davel 1981 *De Jure* 361–363.

See also *Pinchin v Santam Insurance Co Ltd* [3]; *Chisholm v East Rand Proprietary Mines Ltd* [2].

child has a legal right to representation, or an interest capable of protection, in circumstances where its very existence is threatened".

Outeurs soos Van der Vyver en Joubert is van mening dat die *nasciturus* voor geboorte 'n regsubjek is wanneer sy belange op die spel kom. In hierdie verband moet 'n mens onderskei tussen die *nasciturus*-fiksie en die *nasciturus*-reël. Volgens die *nasciturus*-fiksie word daar geag dat die *foetus* reeds by verwekking gebore was wanneer dit tot sy voordeel is. Volgens die *nasciturus*-reël aan die ander kant, word die *foetus* vanaf bevrugting as 'n regsubjek beskou wanneer sy belange op die spel kom (Van der Merwe 1963 *THRHR* 291 ev). In die onderhawige saak was die hof ook van mening dat die *nasciturus* nie 'n regsubjek is nie. Sien verder oor hierdie aangeleentheid Bedil 1981 *SALJ* 462–466; Davel 1981 *De Jure* 361–363.

Sien ook *Pinchin v Santam Insurance Co Ltd* [3]; *Chisholm v East Rand Proprietary Mines Ltd* [2].

Presumption of death

Requirements of presumption of death
Effect of presumption of death
Presumption regarding sequence of death

Vermoede van dood

Vereistes van vermoede van dood
Effek van vermoede van dood
Vermoede oor volgorde van oorlye

Requirements of presumption of death   **Vereistes van vermoede van dood**

[5]   RE BEAGLEHOLE★

1908 TS 49

Presumption of death

A testator left a small sum of money to a beneficiary. The executor in the estate of the testator had paid the money to the master of the supreme court because the beneficiary could not be traced. The executor now applied for an order authorising the master to pay out to him the money for distribution amongst the remaining heirs in the estate of the testator. It was alleged that the beneficiary had not been heard of for over fifteen years, and that it was presumed that he was dead at the time that the money was paid to the master and that such payment had therefore been made in error. The court refused to express a presumption of death.

Vermoede van dood

'n Testateur het 'n klein bedraggie geld aan 'n begunstigde nagelaat. Die eksekuteur van die testateur se boedel het die geld aan die meester van die hooggeregshof oorbetaal omdat die begunstigde nie opgespoor kon word nie. Die eksekuteur het nou aansoek gedoen om 'n bevel wat die meester sou magtig om die geld aan hom uit te betaal vir verdeling onder die ander erfgename van die testateur. Daar is aangevoer dat daar vir meer as vyftien jaar niks van die begunstigde gehoor is nie, en dat vermoed is dat hy reeds dood was toe die geld aan die meester oorbetaal is en dat sodanige betaling dus foutiewelik gemaak was. Die hof het geweier om 'n vermoede van dood uit te spreek.

INNES CJ: [51] I am satisfied that it was not a hard and fast rule of the Roman-Dutch law that the court was bound to presume death after the lapse of any fixed period of years. Some writers did hold that view. And various terms were suggested — seven years, nine years, fifteen years, and so on. But the weight of authority seems to have been in favour of leaving the question [52] in each case to the discretion of the judge. Schorer (*Note* 45) is of that opinion; and Voet (10.2.20), who discusses the subject at considerable length, says the matter is entirely one for the discretion of the judge. In coming to a conclusion, he adds the judge should take into consideration the age of the absent person at the date of disappearance, his position in life, his occupation, whether he was exposed to any special risk or danger and so on; and taking all these circumstances into consideration he should deal with each case upon its merits. In any event the practice was, in cases where an order of division was granted, to direct the heirs to give security, because they were considered as being in the position of fiduciaries. That was the rule of the Roman-Dutch law, and I think it was a sound, common-sense one. It left full discretion to the judge; it laid down the lines upon which that discretion should be exercised, and it gave him power to safeguard the interests of the absent person by requiring due security.

But then it is urged that I should follow on this point not the Roman-Dutch, but the English law. Mr *Morice* [for the applicant] argued that I was bound to follow the English rule, because the question was one of evidence, and our law of evidence is, by statute,

★ This case has been taken from *Erfreg Vonnisbundel/ Casebook on the Law of Succession*, 1993 by D S P Cronjé and Anneliese Roos with permission of the publisher, the University of South Africa.

★ Hierdie saak is oorgeneem uit *Erfreg Vonnisbundel/ Casebook on the Law of Succession*, 1993 deur D S P Cronjé en Anneliese Roos met die toestemming van die uitgewer, die Universiteit van Suid-Afrika.

the law of England. But I am satisfied that our Evidence Proclamation does not cover a case of this kind, and that I am not bound to follow the English rule ... [53] but the Roman-Dutch rule ...

This man has been absent for fifteen years. He was thirty-one years old when last heard of, so that if alive now he would only be forty-six. He was exposed to no special peril; he did not follow a dangerous occupation. He was a miller, living somewhere in the south of England; but for fifteen years he has not communicated with his relatives. What strikes me is that it would have been possible to have made more accurate inquiries as to what had become of him. It is not as if he went away to a foreign country. He was last heard of next door to where he [54] had formerly lived. If he was a miller, surely it would have been easy to ascertain from the persons who employed him what became of him and, when and where he was last heard of. Information on those points should have been laid before the Court; but it is not forthcoming, and I do not think, in the exercise of my discretion, that I should make any order. True, the period of absence has been considerable, and the amount in dispute is not large. But if I make this order it will be used as a precedent in some cases in which probably the amount in dispute is very large, and I think we should be careful before we divide the estates of absent persons. There will be no order on the application.

Note

Initially our law followed the English ruling according to which an order presuming the death of a person was granted after an absence of seven years (*In re Booysen* 1880 Foord 187) but as appears from the above decision, at the moment no fixed period of time is required.

A person's death is not lightly presumed and it is therefore required that the applicant bring all the relevant facts and circumstances to the attention of the court (*Ex parte Parker* 1947 3 SA 285 (C)). The length of a person's absence is of course a very important factor and it can even be decisive, but it is certainly not the only factor. Mere absence for a long period, without other facts pointing to the probability of death, is not sufficient evidence on which to base a presumption of death (*In re Cuthbert* 1932 NPD 615; *Ex parte Estate Russell* 1926 WLD 188; *Ex parte Heard* 1947 1 SA 236 (C); *Ex parte Pieters* [6]; *Ex parte Govender* 1993 3 SA 721 (D)). On several occasions the courts have refused to pronounce a presumption of death in spite of the fact that the person concerned had been absent for a period of twenty years and longer (see for example *Ex parte Verster* 1956 1 SA 409 (C); *Ex parte Pieters* [6] and cases quoted there). On the other hand a presumption of death can be pronounced after a short absence if the probability of death is very strong (*Dempers and Van Ryneveld v SA Mutual Co* (1908) 25 SC 162; *Ex parte Alexander* 1956 2 SA 608 (A); *Ex parte Rungasamy* 1958 4 SA 688 (D)).

Aantekening

Die reël van die Engelse reg waarvolgens 'n vermoede van dood na 'n afwesigheid van sewe jaar uitgespreek word, het aanvanklik ook by ons gegeld (*In re Booysen* 1880 Foord 187) maar soos uit bostaande uitspraak blyk, word tans geen bepaalde tydperk as vereiste gestel nie.

'n Vermoede van dood word nie ligtelik uitgespreek nie. Daarom word van 'n applikant vereis om al die relevante feite en omstandighede van die geval onder die aandag van die hof te bring (*Ex parte Parker* 1947 3 SA 285 (K)). Die lengte van 'n persoon se afwesigheid is natuurlik 'n baie belangrike faktor en dit kan selfs van deurslaggewende belang wees, maar dit is sekerlik nie die enigste faktor nie. Blote afwesigheid vir 'n lang periode sonder ander feite wat op vermoedelike dood dui, is nie genoeg om 'n vermoede van dood te fundeer nie (*In re Cuthbert* 1932 NPA 615; *Ex parte Estate Russell* 1926 WPA 118; *Ex parte Heard* 1947 1 SA 236 (K); *Ex parte Pieters* [6]; *Ex parte Govender* 1993 3 SA 721 (D)). Verskeie gevalle het al in die regspraak voorgekom waar 'n vermoede van dood nie uitgespreek is nie ten spyte daarvan dat die betrokke persoon vir 'n tydperk van twintig jaar en langer weg was (sien byvoorbeeld *Ex parte Verster* 1956 1 SA 409 (K); *Ex parte Pieters* [6] en sake daar aangehaal). Daarteenoor kan 'n vermoede van dood uitgespreek word na 'n kort afwesigheid indien die waarskynlikheid van dood baie sterk is (*Dempers and Van Ryneveld v SA Mutual Co* (1908) 25 SC 162;

Only the supreme court of the area where the missing person was domiciled at the time of his disappearance has jurisdiction to pronounce or cancel an order presuming his death. Such an order is binding on the whole world (*Ex parte Welsh: In re Estate Keegan* 1943 WLD 147).

Ex parte Alexander 1956 2 SA 608 (A); *Ex parte Rungasamy* 1958 4 SA 688 (D)).

Net die hooggeregshof in die gebied waar die vermiste persoon ten tyde van sy verdwyning gedomisilieer was, het jurisdiksie om 'n vermoede van dood ten opsigte van hom uit te spreek of op te hef. Sodanige bevel is bindend op die hele wêreld (*Ex parte Welsh: In re Estate Keegan* 1943 WPA 147).

[6]   EX PARTE PIETERS

1993 3 SA 379 (D)

Presumption of death

The applicant's father disappeared in 1975. Subsequently his mother died and left a sum of money to his father which was deposited to his credit in the Guardian's Fund. The applicant then applied for an order presuming the death of his father, and in the alternative, an order against the master of the supreme court to effect payment to the children of the said money on their providing security therefor. A rule *nisi* was granted to which there was no response. At the time of the application, the applicant's father would have been seventy-three. There was no evidence before the court to suggest that he was physically or mentally ill, nor was there any indication of emotional stress, financial embarrassment or any other factor which may have thrown light on the reason for his disappearance. On the morning after he had been paid his salary, he told the applicant, with whom he stayed, that he intended visiting his daughter to repay her some money, and left the balance of his salary with the applicant. He kept his identity document and bank savings book at his daughter's home. He never arrived there. The court did not express a presumption of death but authorised the master to distribute the money equally between the applicant and his brothers and sisters without the necessity of their providing security.

Vermoede van dood

Die applikant se vader het in 1975 verdwyn. Toe sy moeder later oorlede is, het sy 'n bedrag geld aan sy vader nagelaat, welke geld tot sy krediet in die Voogdyfonds inbetaal is. Die applikant het aansoek gedoen dat 'n vermoede van dood ten opsigte van sy vader uitgespreek word, en in die alternatief dat die meester van die hooggeregshof gemagtig word om die geld aan die kinders uit te betaal teen die verskaffing van die nodige sekuriteit. Die hof het 'n bevel *nisi* verleen waarop daar geen reaksie was nie. Die applikant se vader sou ten tyde van die aansoek drie en sewentig jaar oud gewees het. Daar was geen getuienis voor die hof dat hy liggaamlik of geestelik siek was, dat hy aan spanning onderworpe was, finansiële probleme gehad het of enige ander aanduiding wat lig op sy verdwyning kon werp nie. Die oggend nadat hy sy salaris ontvang het, het hy aan die applikant, by wie hy gewoon het, gesê dat hy sy dogter gaan besoek om sekere geld aan haar terug te betaal. Die res van sy salaris het hy by die applikant gelaat. Hy het sy identiteitsdokument en spaarboekie altyd by sy dogter gehou. Hy het nooit by haar huis opgedaag nie. Die hof het nie 'n vermoede van dood uitgespreek nie maar het die meester gemagtig om die geld gelykop tussen die applikant en sy broers en susters te verdeel sonder dat dit vir hulle nodig was om sekuriteit te verskaf.

ALEXANDER J: [380] This matter raises the question under what circumstances the Court will presume the death of a person who has disappeared for many years, unaccompanied, however, by any indication that through misadventure, or the like, he may have died prematurely ...

[ALEXANDER J referred to the application by one of the missing person's children and proceeded:]

[381] A rule *nisi* was granted with publication to be effected in the *Government Gazette* and the *Sunday Times*. There has been no further word from any source. This is now the return day, when the question of *onus* may assume a different dimension. As pointed out by FAGAN JA in *Ex parte Alexander and Others* 1956 (2) SA 608 (A) at 611D, a *prima facie* case will suffice for the issue of a rule *nisi* but 'a decision as to the sufficiency or otherwise of the information submitted to support a presumption of death will have to be made by the Court ... on the return day'. It may be that the absence of any response to the rule is a further factor to be taken into account, although, as pointed out by Hoffmann and Zeffertt in *The South African Law of Evidence* 4th ed at 557, '(i)n many cases it will be clear that a lack of response to the rule will add nothing to the probative value of the evidence ...'. Nevertheless it is always implicit in the issuing of a rule that someone may come forward with relevant information. When, however, nothing has eventuated, the only question at the end of the day is whether what has been put up, coupled with the absence of any additional facts, is sufficiently cogent, as a matter of probability, to presume that death has taken place — compare *Ex parte Heard* 1947 (1) SA 236 (C) at 239 *in fine* ...

[382] The argument for the applicant ... goes thus. Mr Pieters [the missing person] had a job, he had a home, he had children who cared for him and, judging by the pattern of his last known movements, there is absolutely nothing to indicate that he was surreptitiously bent on taking on a new life, bereft of money, his personal documents and his family. He must therefore be dead. A persuasive argument at first blush, but it is one still to be measured against the fact that no clue as to his disappearance has come to light, nor is there anything to show why his body, if indeed he is dead, has not been found.

These particular considerations have loomed large where the Courts have been called on to deal with similar cases in the past.

The remarks of LANSDOWN J in *In re Cuthbert* 1932 NLR 615 at 616 echoed what by then had already been a long-established approach. See *Re Beaglehole* 1908 TS 49 [5]; *Re Nicholson* 1908 TS 870; *In re Widdicombe* 1929 NLR 311; *Ex parte Estate Russell* 1926 WLD 118. He said: 'I know of no rule of law or practice which would require the Court to presume death merely from the lapse of years alone ...' The circumspection which underlies this attitude has been consistently followed since: see *Ex parte Heard* (*supra*); *Ex parte Verster and Another* 1956 (1) SA 409 (C); *Ex parte Rookminia: In re Sardha* 1964 (4) SA 163 (D). It seems that there will always be a reluctance to assume that death alone will serve to explain a disappearance when the pointers to the conclusion are minimal and rest on little else save conjecture.

But having stated the general rule of thumb there are notable exceptions. It may prove the case that the intervening effluxion of time has made it extremely unlikely that the person in question would still be alive. So, for instance, in *Ex parte Engelbrecht* 1956 (1) SA 408 (E) the Court was inclined to presume death when the man had been missing for 35 years and by then would have been 93. Even then, however, a rule *nisi* was issued. Only four years unexplained absence was the position in *Ex parte Rungasamy* 1958 (4) SA 688 (D), but the lady concerned was 83 or 84 years of age, was known to be in frail health, and she had ceased to collect her old age pension. The Court was prepared to presume death, but *ex abundante cautela* issued a rule.

As noted earlier, Mr Pieters would by now be close to 73. He may well have passed his allotted three score years and ten, but in this day and age that would surely be no cause for undue surprise. And least of all when there is nothing to show that when last seen he was in failing health. On the contrary he was still actively employed as a cleaner which, one assumes, entails a fair amount of physical effort. I would be hard pressed on these facts to find a helpful analogy in either *Engelbrecht* or *Rungasamy*.

There is the further exception, which again on the facts, finds little sustenance, viz that Mr Pieters probably met his death by accident, suicide or homicide. The Law Reports abound with such instances where the missing body can be attributed to such causes: murder at the hands of the Nazis in Poland — *Ex parte Chodos* 1948 (4) SA 221 (N); irresistible pointers to drowning — *In re B R C Cook* 1907 NLR 315; *In re Labistour* 1908 NLR 227; *Ex parte Dorward* 1933 NPD 17; suicide — *Ex parte Holden* 1954 (4) SA 128 (N).

Nothing, however, surfaces on these papers to suggest that Mr Pieters has taken his own life or become the victim of some accident or attack. As a matter of probability any such reason seems remote when no information could be gleaned from the police, hospitals or mortuary. Nor can it readily be imagined, much less inferred, that he was waylaid by some thugs en route to his daughter, who not only killed him but did away with his body.

The mystery as to the whys and wherefores of his disappearance persist, but that in itself cannot serve as a basis for excluding all explanations, save that of death. I must, with some regret, decline to confirm the rule.

The Master, however, raises no objection to the moneys in the Guardian's Fund being distributed among Mr Pieters' six children. They, however, total only R6 148,14. The amount each will receive is so small that should the Court so order, he would be prepared to dispense with their providing security ...

In the result:

1. ... [N]o order is made presuming William Emmanuel Pieters ... to be dead.
2. The Master is authorised to distribute the amount of R6 148,14 presently held in the Guardian's Fund ... equally between [the missing person's children] without the necessity of their providing security *de restituendo*.

Note	Aantekening
See the note on *Re Beaglehole* [5] and *Ex parte Govender* 1993 3 SA 721 (D).	Sien die aantekening by *Re Beaglehole* [5] en *Ex parte Govender* 1993 3 SA 721 (D).

Effect of presumption of death	Effek van vermoede van dood

[7] IN RE KANNEMEYER: EX PARTE KANNEMEYER

(1899) 16 SC 407

Presumption of death	Vermoede van dood
Louis Kannemeyer left Cape Town for New York in 1871 when he was nineteen years old. He was heard of again in 1875 but since that time he had not been seen or heard of	In 1871, toe hy negentien jaar oud was, het Louis Kannemeyer Kaapstad verlaat en na New York vertrek. In 1875 is weer van hom gehoor maar sedertdien het nie een van sy

by any of his relatives or friends, notwith-standing enquiries made by them to find him. His mother died in 1873 and Louis inherited an amount of £900 from her. In 1890 an application was made to court for the payment of this money to his next-of-kin, but the application was refused. Nine years later, on a renewed application to have the money paid out, the court held that it could not declare him to be dead but that his inheritance could be distributed amongst his next-of-kin upon their giving their personal undertaking to the master of the supreme court that they would restore to Louis Kannemeyer the capital sums received by them respectively, should he be found to be alive.

familielede of vriende hom weer gesien of van hom gehoor nie, ten spyte daarvan dat hulle navraag oor hom gedoen het. Sy moeder is in 1873 oorlede en Louis het £900 van haar geërf. In 1890 is by die hof aansoek gedoen om die geld aan sy naasbestaandes uit te betaal maar die aansoek is van die hand gewys. Nege jaar later is die aansoek herhaal. Die hof het toe beslis dat dit nie die bevoegdheid het om Kannemeyer dood te verklaar nie, maar dat sy erfporsie onder sy naasbestaandes verdeel kon word indien hulle persoonlik teenoor die meester van die hooggeregshof sou onderneem om die bedrae wat hulle onderskeidelik ontvang het aan Louis Kannemeyer terug te betaal indien later bevind sou word dat hy nog leef.

DE VILLIERS CJ: [408] In my opinion it is in the highest degree probable that Louis Kannemeyer is dead, but there is no legal presumption to that effect. The Court cannot, therefore, declare him to be dead or order executors to be appointed of his estate. If his inheritance is to be distributed amongst his next-of-kin, they must give security to the Master for the repayment of the money in case he should hereafter be found to be alive. If the probability of death had been less than it is, it would have been desirable to have substantial security other than that of the next-of-kin themselves, but after an absence of twenty-eight years, during the last twenty-four of which he has never been heard of, notwithstanding the efforts made to find him, such strictness is unnecessary and may be dispensed with. The Court will direct the executor to distribute the inheritance amongst those persons who would be his heirs *ab intestato* in case he were dead upon their giving their [409] personal undertaking to the Master of the Supreme Court that they will restore to Louis Kannemeyer the capital sums respectively received by them in case he should hereafter be found to be alive . . .

BUCHANAN J and MAASDORP J concurred.

Note

It is evident from this decision that the courts are sometimes too hesitant to express a presumption of death. Van der Vyver and Joubert (426) ascribe this to the fact that the courts do not distinguish clearly between a declaration and a presumption of death. In the case under discussion, for example, it was found that it was "in the highest degree probable" that the person concerned was dead, but the court stated that "there is no legal presumption to that effect. The Court cannot, therefore, declare him to be dead . . ." Van der Vyver and Joubert correctly point out that a court cannot declare a person to be dead; it can only express a presumption of death and

Aantekening

Dit wil voorkom of die howe soms te huiwerig is om 'n vermoede van dood uit te spreek. Van der Vyver en Joubert (426) skryf dit toe aan die feit dat die howe nie duidelik tussen 'n verklaring en 'n vermoede van dood onderskei nie. In die onderhawige saak is byvoorbeeld gesê dat dit "in the highest degree probable" was dat die betrokke persoon dood was "but there is no legal presumption to that effect. The Court cannot, therefore, declare him to be dead . . ." Van der Vyver en Joubert wys tereg daarop dat 'n hof nie 'n persoon dood kan verklaar nie; die hof kan net 'n vermoede van dood uitspreek en dit kan gedoen word as die hof op 'n oorwig van waar-

this the court can do if it is convinced on a preponderance of probabilities that the person is dead. In the case under discussion it would appear as though this was indeed the position.

From this case it is, however, also clear that although the court may not be prepared to express a presumption of death, it may nonetheless order that the missing person's estate be administered and his property be divided amongst his heirs, provided that they furnish security for the return of the property, or its value, should the missing person reappear (see further *In re Cuthbert* 1932 NPD 615; *Ex parte Davids* 1948 1 SA 1018 (W); Barnard, Cronjé and Olivier 31).

Berger v Aiken 1964 2 SA 396 (W) is an example of a case where persons in respect of whom presumptions of death had been expressed, reappeared.

skynlikheid daarvan oortuig is dat die persoon dood is. Dit wil voorkom of dit in die onderhawige saak wel die geval was.

Uit hierdie saak is dit egter ook duidelik dat alhoewel die hof nie bereid mag wees om 'n vermoede van dood uit te spreek nie, dit in 'n gegewe geval wel bereid mag wees om te beveel dat die vermiste persoon se boedel beredder en onder sy erfgename verdeel word, indien die erfgename sekuriteit stel vir teruggawe van die voordele of die waarde daarvan as die verdwene persoon sou terugkeer (sien ook *In re Cuthbert* 1932 NPA 615; *Ex parte Davids* 1948 1 SA 1018 (W); Barnard, Cronjé en Olivier 32).

Berger v Aiken 1964 2 SA 396 (W) is 'n voorbeeld van 'n geval waar persone ten opsigte van wie 'n vermoede van dood uitgespreek is, weer hulle opwagting gemaak het.

Presumption regarding sequence of death

Vermoede oor volgorde van oorlye

[8]   EX PARTE GRAHAM*

1963 4 SA 145 (D)

Presumption regarding sequence of death

In terms of her will, a woman of fifty left her estate to her adopted son of sixteen. The will also provided that should the son predecease the testatrix the whole estate was to devolve on her mother. The testatrix and her son were both killed in an air disaster in which all the passengers and crew perished. The executrix awarded the whole estate to the testatrix's mother, but the registrar of deeds first required an order of the court declaring that the adopted son died before or simultaneously with the testatrix before he would transfer any immovable property

Vermoede oor die volgorde van oorlye

'n Vrou van vyftig het haar boedel in haar testament aan haar aangenome seun van sestien bemaak. Die testament het verder bepaal dat as die seun voor die testatrise sou sterf, die hele boedel na haar moeder moes gaan. Die testatrise en haar seun het albei in 'n vliegongeluk gesterf waarin al die passasiers en lede van die bemanning omgekom het. Die eksekutrise het die hele boedel aan die testatrise se moeder toegeken, maar die registrateur van aktes wou eers 'n hofbevel hê wat verklaar het dat die seun voor of gelyktydig met die testatrise gesterf het voor-

---

* This case has been taken from *Erfreg Vonnisbundel/ Casebook on the Law of Succession*, 1993 by D S P Cronjé and Anneliese Roos with permission of the publisher, the University of South Africa.

* Hierdie saak is oorgeneem uit *Erfreg Vonnisbundel/ Casebook on the Law of Succession*, 1993 deur D S P Cronjé en Anneliese Roos met die toestemming van die uitgewer, die Universiteit van Suid-Afrika.

to the mother. The executrix then applied for an order declaring that the testatrix and her son had died simultaneously. The order was granted.

dat hy die onroerende goed aan die moeder wou oordra. Die eksekutrise van die boedel het toe aansoek gedoen om 'n verklarende bevel dat die testatrise en haar seun gelyktydig gesterf het. Die hof het die aansoek toegestaan.

WARNER J: [145] In the case of *Nepgen NO v Van Dyk NO*, 1940 EDL, 123 at p 130, it was said that there was no presumption as to which of two [146] people predeceased each other. That was a case of a motor accident in which two people met their deaths ... There is nothing in the judgment to show that there was any relationship between the two people.

In *Ex parte Martienssen*, 1944 CPD 139, an order was granted presuming the deaths of a mother aged 63 and her daughter aged 27 to have been simultaneous. It was clear in that case that it would make no difference whether the daughter was presumed to have died after or simultaneously with the mother and the court was referred to the Roman Law which indicated that in Roman Law there are certain presumptions to which I shall refer later in dealing with certain passages in Voet's *Commentary on Pandects*.

There are two other cases in which an order presuming simultaneous deaths was made, the first *Ex parte Bagshaw*, 1942 (2) PH F77, where a mother and two children died as a result of the ship upon which they were travelling being torpedoed and, from the available report, it does not appear that any authorities were referred to. The other case is *Ex parte Chodos*, 1948 (4) SA 221 (C), where a mother and daughter were presumed to have died as a result of being shot in Poland in 1942. Death was presumed to have been simultaneous and there was no reference to any presumptions, the order being granted because, apparently, it would make no difference. It does not appear from the report that any judgment was given.

Voet 34.5.3, does refer to certain presumptions after making the statement that, generally speaking, where people die together in a single catastrophe, no one is deemed to have survived another, unless such is proved. The first presumption is that where a freed man and his son die together, it is presumed in case of doubt, that the son died first. The reason he gives is that thereby the freed man's estate will go to the patron. Obviously, no such presumption can have any application today. The second one is the Roman Law presumption referred to in *Martienssen's* case which is that where a father or mother and son die together in one catastrophe, the son will be presumed to have died first if he is under the age of puberty on the ground that he

"was less able to put up a struggle and was indeed weaker that his parents in strength of body and determination."

If the son is over the age of puberty, he is presumed to have died after the parent

"on the ground that then death would have overtaken each according to the usual course of mortality."

(*Gane's* translation, vol 5 p 265). These presumptions have not been followed in the cases to which I have referred and if they formed part of the Roman-Dutch Law, I do not believe that it is either necessary or desirable slavishly to follow such completely artificial reasoning in these modern times. In any event, it must be remembered that the general rule is that there is no presumption.

It seems to me that the approach adopted in *Nepgen v Van Dyk* is the proper one. There the Court examined the facts to see if there was any evidence to support a conclusion that the deaths were not simultaneous. In the present case, we are concerned with the crash of an aircraft and the evidence is that the aircraft crashed in a swamp and [147] was extensively damaged with debris being strewn around over a large area. All the passengers and crew were killed and, in many instances, the identification of the bodies was impossible. It seems to me that in such circumstances the probabilities are overwhelming that the passengers did, in fact, die simultaneously and consequently any presumptions that there may be are excluded. In any event, there is no ground for believing that death would have overtaken them in the usual course of mortality. I consequently make an order that the testatrix and her son are presumed to have died simultaneously . . .

Note

A beneficiary can inherit from a deceased person only if he survives the deceased. Therefore if a person dies before another or simultaneously with him he cannot inherit from him. Where several persons lose their lives in the same disaster (*commorientes*) it may be important to determine which of them died first, in order to establish whether one inherited from the other. The artificial presumptions of the common law which came into operation where members of the same family perished in such circumstances are no longer accepted in our law. The general presumption of English law that the oldest person died first, irrespective of whether the people concerned were members of the same family, is also not applicable in our law. The general rule today is that if the sequence in which people died cannot be proved on a balance of probabilities, there is no presumption either of survival or of simultaneous death. In other words the time of death of the deceased persons today is a question of fact which is established without the aid of presumptions (Van der Merwe and Rowland 19; Lee and Honoré 363). Unless there is evidence to the contrary the courts will, however, find that *commorientes* died simultaneously (Boberg 26; Hahlo and Kahn *The Union of South Africa — The Development of its Laws, and Constitution* 348). As Barnard, Cronjé and Olivier (32) rightly point out, if there are no witnesses to testify that one person died before the other, the court can do nothing else but find that they died simultaneously.

See also Blackwell 1963 *SALJ* 132.

Aantekening

'n Persoon kan net van 'n erflater erf as hy leef ten tyde van die erflater se dood. As 'n persoon dus voor 'n ander of tesame met hom sterf, kan hy nie van hom erf nie. Waar verskeie persone in dieselfde ramp sterf (*commorientes*), kan dit van belang wees om te bepaal wie van hulle eerste gesterf het ten einde vas te stel of die een van die ander geërf het. Die kunsmatige vermoedens wat in die verband in die gemenereg gegeld het as lede van dieselfde gesin in sodanige omstandighede gesterf het, is nie meer in ons reg van toepassing nie. So ook nie die algemene vermoede van die Engelse reg dat die oudste persoon eerste gesterf het, afgesien daarvan of die betrokke persone lede van een gesin was of nie. Die algemene reël vandag is dat as die volgorde waarin die persone dood is nie op 'n oorwig van waarskynlikheid bewys kan word nie, daar geen vermoede van óf oorlewing óf gelyktydige dood is nie. Die tydstip van die oorledenes se dood is met ander woorde vandag 'n feitlike vraag wat sonder die hulp van vermoedens vasgestel word (Van der Merwe en Rowland 19; Lee en Honoré 363). Tensy daar getuienis tot die teendeel is, sal die howe egter beslis dat die persone gelyktydig gesterf het (Boberg 26; Hahlo en Kahn *The Union of South Africa — The Development of its Laws, and Constitution* 348). Soos Barnard, Cronjé en Olivier (33) tereg aantoon, kan die hof eintlik niks anders doen as om te verklaar dat hulle gelyktydig om die lewe gekom het as daar geen getuies is om aan te dui dat die een persoon voor die ander gesterf het nie.

Sien ook Blackwell 1963 *SALJ* 132.

Domicile

Domicile of choice

Factum requirement
Animus requirement
Persons not free to choose where to reside
Domicile of a prohibited immigrant

Domisilie

Domisilie van keuse

Factum-vereiste
Animus-vereiste
Persone wat nie vrylik kan kies waar om te woon nie
Domisilie van 'n verbode immigrant

Factum requirement   *Factum*-vereiste

[9]   COOK V COOK

1939 CPD 314

The *factum* requirement for establishing a domicile of choice

The plaintiff was born in Natal, married there in 1928 and the couple lived in Natal until 1935. The husband then moved to Johannesburg in search of work and remained there until 1938. He thereupon decided to go to Cape Town because he had heard that the prospects of obtaining employment there were better than in Johannesburg. He arrived in Cape Town on 9 January 1939 and obtained employment on a weekly basis on 12 January. He had never lived in the Cape before but had friends there. His wife had refused to join him in Cape Town. A week after his arrival in Cape Town the plaintiff commenced with the institution of divorce proceedings against his wife and the Cape court had to decide whether he was domiciled within its jurisdiction. It was held that he was not and absolution from the instance was ordered.

Die *factum*-vereiste vir die vestiging van 'n domisilie van keuse

Die eiser is in Natal gebore, is in 1928 daar getroud en hy en sy vrou het tot in 1935 in Natal gewoon. Die man het hierna op soek na werk na Johannesburg verhuis en tot 1938 daar gebly. Hy het toe besluit om na Kaapstad te gaan omdat hy verneem het dat werksvooruitsigte daar beter was as in Johannesburg. Hy het op 9 Januarie 1939 in Kaapstad aangekom en op 12 Januarie op 'n weeklikse basis werk gekry. Hy het nooit voorheen in Kaapstad gewoon nie maar het vriende daar gehad. Sy vrou het geweier om saam met hom Kaap toe te verhuis. 'n Week na sy aankoms in Kaapstad het die eiser met die instel van egskeidingsverrigtinge teen sy vrou begin en die Kaapse hof moes beslis of hy binne die hof se jurisdiksie gedomisilieer was. Daar is beslis dat hy nie daar gedomisilieer was nie en die hof het absolusie van die instansie beveel.

DE VILLIERS J: [315] He [the plaintiff] left Johannesburg purely in the hope of obtaining work in Cape Town and intended, if he obtained employment, to settle down at the Cape. He has no home or residence of his own in the ordinary sense of the term at Cape Town and is simply living with friends. A week after he arrived in Cape Town he consulted an attorney with a view to setting restitution proceedings [i e divorce proceedings] in train. A summons was duly issued on the 13th February. It will seem, therefore, that a month after arriving at Cape Town he invoked the aid of this Court to adjudicate upon his matrimonial affairs, the initial steps having been taken a week after his arrival here. Upon this review of the facts the question that falls for determination is whether this Court can be said to have jurisdiction to entertain this action.

I am prepared to accept his evidence to the effect that in Johannesburg he gave expression to an intention to move to Cape Town. In my view the residence is of the slenderest description, while the expression of intention amounts to little more than an intention to settle at Cape Town if he found work here.

In order to determine whether he could be said to have acquired [316] a domicile within the jurisdiction of the Court, the Court must be satisfied both as to the *factum* of residence and the *animus*; and the *onus* of proving that he has acquired a fresh domicile rests upon him: see *Webber v Webber* (1915, A.D. 239). I do not think that any minimum period of residence can be laid down. The length of residence, however, is of assistance in determining whether a Court can accept the expression of his intention to found a new domicile within the jurisdiction of this Court. The correct legal approach to the question for determination has been very well put by *Voet* (5.1.97): "But whenever it is not quite clear where a person has fixed his domicile, and whether he has any intention of not leaving again, resort must be had to the probabilities of the case, gathered from the various surrounding circumstances, although they may not all be equally strong, or each considered by itself, equally conclusive, but much weight is attached to them in the opinion of a careful and experienced judge." *Voet's* views have been adopted by the Appellate Division in *Webber v Webber* (1915, A.D. at p. 242), where INNES, CJ, dealt with this question in the following terms: "The principles regulating domicile, founded as they are upon the civil law, have been developed in England and in Holland upon very similar lines. The Roman-Dutch law recognised that any person, being *sui juris*, could acquire a domicile of choice in a new country by establishing his actual residence in that country with the intention of making it his permanent home: *Cens. For.* (Pt. 1, 3, 125); Voet *Ad Pand.* (5.1.98, etc.). Both elements (*factum et animus*) were essential; intention without residence, and residence without intention were alike ineffective. And it also adopted the rule that the burden of proving a change of domicile lay upon the person alleging it ..."

The question of the duration of residence, is dealt with very clearly by KINDERSLEY, VC, in *Cockrell v Cockrell* (25 Law Journal, Chancery, at p. 732). His Lordship there emphasised that length of residence is one of the first things that should be considered when a question of domicile arises: "Length of time is considered one of the *criteria*, or one of the *indiciae*, from which the intention to acquire a new domicile is to be inferred, and, it is considered a very material ingredient in the consideration of the question." In most of the authorities the duration of the residence was lengthy, generally a period of years.

[317] In the present case the residence has been of extremely short duration. I am asked to say that on the evidence this short period of residence is confirmatory of the expression by the plaintiff of his intention to make Cape Town his permanent home. I agree that the *factum* and the *animus manendi* are inter-related, and, that from the *factum* of residence an inference of intention to reside permanently can be drawn. It should, however, be borne in mind that the evidence of a plaintiff who gives evidence of his intention to change his domicile is usually accepted with considerable reserve; and as was pointed out by LORD CAIRNS in *Bell v Kennedy* (1868, LR 1 Sc. and Div. at p. 313), such evidence requires to be carefully weighed in the light of all the circumstances of the case (see Halsbury, vol. 6, Hailsham ed., sec. 246). Judges have in the past frequently had occasion to remark that this branch of the law was firmly established, but that the real difficulty was to be found in the application of the law to combinations of circumstances which frequently varied.

The inter-relation of *factum* and *animus* has been elucidated in a very helpful manner by the speech of VISCOUNT DUNEDIN in *Bowie v Liverpool Royal Infirmary* (1930, AC 588): "It has again and again been laid down that a change of domicile from the domicile of origin must be made *animo et facto*. The *factum* is the bare fact of residence within the new domicile. No amount of assertion of change will be effectual if unaccompanied by actual residence. How then is the *animus* to be proved? It may be proved by assertion of one sort or another; it may also be inferred from the *factum* of residence, but in order to be so inferred the colour and the characteristics of the residence as deduced from the whole story of what has happened must be taken into account." In the same case LORD McMILLAN made the following pertinent remarks: "The real question in the case is whether this prolonged residence in England was accompanied by an intention on the part of the deceased to choose England as his permanent home in preference to the country of his birth. The law requires evidence of volition to change. Prolonged actual residence is an important item of evidence of such volition, but it must be supplemented by other facts and circumstances indicative of intention. The residence must answer a qualitative as well as a quantitative test."

Applying these pronouncements to the facts put in evidence before me by the plaintiff, I can come to no other conclusion than [318] that the plaintiff has failed to establish residence either qualitatively or quantitatively. His actual residence is of the most slender description, while his evidence as to volition is clearly dictated by fact that he was dissatisfied with the conditions obtaining in his sphere of employment in Johannesburg and hoped that by coming to Cape Town he would be able to make a more regular livelihood.

The result is that in my view plaintiff has failed to prove that he was domiciled within the jurisdiction of this Court at the time when he invoked its assistance. There must, in consequence, be absolution from the instance.

Note

In order to acquire a domicile of choice in a particular place a person must actually reside there (the *factum* requirement), his residence must be lawful and he must have the *animus manendi*, that is the intention to remain in that place. It must, however, be noted that although these requirements must at some stage exist simultaneously, they need not come into existence simultaneously. It is therefore quite possible that a person may settle in a certain place and only later form the intention of residing there permanently (Kahn 41; Boberg 69).

A person who wishes to acquire a domicile of choice in a specific place must personally reside in that place. He cannot satisfy the *factum* requirement through the residence of, for example, his wife and children (*Shapiro v Shapiro* 1914 WLD 38; *Clayton v Clayton* 1922 CPD 125; Kahn 40; Van der Vyver and Joubert 100).

Aantekening

Ten einde 'n domisilie van keuse op 'n betrokke plek te verkry, moet die persoon hom daadwerklik daar vestig (die *factum*-vereiste), sy verblyf moet wettig wees en hy moet die *animus manendi* hê, dit wil sê hy moet die bedoeling hê om op daardie plek te bly woon. Daar moet egter op gelet word dat alhoewel hierdie vereistes op een of ander stadium tegelyk moet bestaan, hulle nie tegelyk hoef te ontstaan nie. Dit is dus goed moontlik dat 'n persoon eers op 'n plek gaan woon en dan later die bedoeling vorm om hom permanent daar te vestig (Kahn 41; Boberg 69).

'n Persoon wat 'n domisilie van keuse op 'n spesifieke plek wil vestig, moet self op die betrokke plek woon. Hy kan nie aan die *factum*-vereiste voldoen deur, byvoorbeeld, die verblyf van sy vrou en kinders nie (*Shapiro v Shapiro* 1914 WPA 38; *Clayton v Clayton* 1922 KPA 125; Kahn 40; Van der Vyver en Joubert 100).

Animus requirement   *Animus*-vereiste

[10]   Eilon v Eilon

1965 1 SA 703 (A)

Domicile of choice

The appellant and the respondent were married in Israel in 1947. They both obtained teaching posts at a school in a town in Israel called Ntanya where they also acquired a flat.

Domisilie van keuse

Die appellant en die respondent is in 1947 in Israel getroud. Hulle het albei onderwysposte by 'n skool in 'n Israeliese dorp genaamd Ntanya beklee. Hulle het ook 'n

In 1956 they moved to South Africa with their minor children. The respondent took up a teaching post under the Jewish Board of Education in Cape Town. This arrangement was made through an organisation called the Jewish Agency which operated from Jerusalem. It was the policy of the Jewish Agency to send Hebrew teachers to different parts of the world to teach Hebrew in Jewish schools. The teachers went abroad for a fixed period generally from two-and-a-half to five years. The Jewish Agency was usually unwilling to grant an extension beyond this five year period. The Agency subscribed to Zionist beliefs according to which Jews were encouraged to settle in Israel. It was not the policy of the Jewish Agency to allow the teachers to remain abroad permanently. The respondent never applied for South African citizenship but in 1959 he successfully gained permanent residence status in this country. Subsequently, he arranged for his children to be educated in South Africa. The respondent's initial two-and-a-half year contract of employment was renewed a few times by the Jewish Board in Cape Town. When the parties had been living in South Africa for approximately five years they went to Israel on holiday during which the respondent sold the flat in Ntanya and bought another flat as well as a plot of land in the said town. After the spouses returned to South Africa, the respondent became involved in an adulterous affair and, presumably because of that, the Jewish Board of Education in Cape Town refused to renew his teaching contract and gave him a single air ticket to return to Israel. He secretly tried to convert this ticket into a return ticket. In June 1963 the respondent applied to the Johannesburg Jewish Board of Education for a post as an inspector of Jewish schools. He was appointed but his contract was cancelled forthwith, presumably because of information received from the Cape Town Board. In July 1963 the respondent returned to Israel where he was employed by the Israeli Min-

woonstel in daardie dorp aangeskaf. In 1956 het hulle saam met hulle minderjarige kinders na Suid-Afrika verhuis. Die respondent het 'n onderwysbetrekking by die "Jewish Board of Education" in Kaapstad gekry. Hierdie reëling is getref deur 'n organisasie genaamd die "Jewish Agency" wat in Jerusalem werksaam was. Dit was die Jewish Agency se beleid om Hebreeuse onderwysers na verskillende dele van die wêreld te stuur om Hebreeus in Joodse skole te doseer. Die onderwysers het vir 'n bepaalde periode na die buiteland gegaan, gewoonlik van twee en 'n half tot vyf jaar. Die Jewish Agency was gewoonlik onwillig om die tydperk tot meer as vyf jaar te verleng. Die Jewish Agency het die Zionistiese beginsels onderskryf waarvolgens Jode aangemoedig word om hulle in Israel te vestig. Dit was nie die Jewish Agency se beleid om onderwysers toe te laat om permanent in die buiteland te woon nie. Die respondent het nooit om Suid-Afrikaanse burgerskap aansoek gedoen nie maar het in 1959 suksesvol aansoek gedoen om permanente verblyf in Suid-Afrika. Die respondent het reëlings getref dat sy kinders in Suid-Afrika opgevoed moes word. Die respondent se aanvanklike dienskontrak van twee en 'n half jaar is 'n paar keer deur die Jewish Board in Kaapstad hernu. Toe die partye reeds vir 'n tydperk van byna vyf jaar in Suid-Afrika gewoon het, is hulle met vakansie na Israel. Gedurende hierdie vakansie het die respondent die woonstel in Ntanya verkoop en 'n ander woonstel in Ntanya asook 'n stuk grond gekoop. Die gades het na Suid-Afrika teruggekeer. Die respondent het in 'n owerspelige verhouding betrokke geraak en vermoedelik as gevolg hiervan het die Jewish Board in Kaapstad geweier om sy kontrak te hernu en het hulle vir hom 'n enkel-vliegkaartjie terug na Israel gegee. Hy het in die geheim probeer om hierdie enkelkaartjie in 'n retoerkaartjie te omskep. In Junie 1963 het die respondent by die Johannesburgse Jewish Board of Education aansoek gedoen om 'n pos as inspekteur van

istry of Education. At the date of the trial he was still thus employed. The appellant instituted a divorce action against the respondent in the Cape Provincial Division and the court had to adjudicate on the matter of the respondent's domicile at the time of the institution of the action. The court a quo found that the appellant had failed to establish respondent's domicile within the area of the court's jurisdiction at the time of institution of the action. On appeal the majority of the judges confirmed this finding. A minority of the judges of appeal held that the appellant had proved that the respondent was domiciled within the area of the court's jurisdiction.

Joodse skole. Hy is aangestel maar sy kontrak is summier gekanselleer, vermoedelik as gevolg van inligting wat vanaf die Jewish Board in Kaapstad verkry is. In Julie 1963 het die respondent na Israel teruggekeer waar hy deur die Israeliese Departement van Onderwys in diens geneem is. Op die datum van die geding was hy steeds daar in diens. Die appellant het 'n egskeidingsaksie teen die respondent aanhangig gemaak in die Kaapse Provinsiale Afdeling en die hof moes beslis oor die vraag waar die respondent ten tyde van die instel van die aksie gedomisilieer was. Die hof a quo het beslis dat die appellant nie daarin geslaag het om te bewys dat die respondent ten tyde van die instel van die aksie binne die jurisdiksiegebied van die hof gedomisilieer was nie. Teen hierdie beslissing is na die Appèlhof geappelleer waar die meerderheidsbeslissing die bevinding van die hof a quo bevestig het. In 'n minderheidsuitspraak is egter bevind dat die appellant wel bewys het dat die respondent binne die hof se jurisdiksiegebied gedomisilieer was.

WILLIAMSON JA [dissenting]: [705] A decision in this matter requires in the first place a determination of the question as to where the respondent was domiciled in October, 1962, when his wife, the appellant, instituted action against him in the Cape Provincial Division for a divorce and other relief ... [A]t the time of the institution of action by the appellant they had both had their home in that city for close on seven years. The requisite of residence in relation to the acquisition of a domicil in South Africa was therefore clearly satisfied. The difficulty is as to whether the respondent ever formed such an intention to remain in South Africa as would convert that residence into domicil. The learned trial Judge cited as the basis of his approach to the legal requirements of such an intention the decision of this Court in Johnson v Johnson, 1931 AD 391; in particular he referred to the judgment of DE VILLIERS, CJ, in that case where at p. 398 thereof the learned Chief Justice said that he agreed with Westlake, Private International Law, 4th ed. para. 264, when that author said that as a result of the English cases

"the intention for acquiring a domicil of choice excludes all contemplation of any event on the occurrence of which the residence would cease".

"This statement,"

[706] continued the learned Chief Justice,

"satisfies the test of Voet's 'propositum illic perpetuo morandi'" [with the purpose to stay there permanently].

The reference to Voet is to 5.1.98, translated in Gane, Selective Voet, vol. 2 p. 115 as follows:

"It is certain that domicil is not established by the mere intention and design of the head of a household, nor by mere formal declaration without fact or deed; nor by the mere getting ready of a house in some country; nor by mere residence without the purpose to stay there permanently . . ."

Whilst the above passage from *Westlake* may be a correct summary of the effect of the English decisions prior to 1904, the year of publication of the said 4th edition, I do not find actual support for its rigid interpretation of the word "permanently" in the particular passage of *Voet* or in any other passage in that work or in the reference to the *Hollandsche Consultatien* III, 217 also quoted by DE VILLIERS, CJ.

The above phraseology adopted by the author *Westlake*, has given rise to difficulty not only in England, the Private International Law of which country he was expounding, but by virtue of the aforesaid statement by DE VILLIERS CJ, also in South Africa. It was discussed in some detail by CENTLIVRES, CJ, in *Ley v Ley's Executors*, 1951 3 SA 186 (AD) at p 195, in a passage quoted *in extenso* in the judgment of the learned Judge *a quo* and in the judgment of my Brother POTGIETER in this Court. In my view it is more than doubtful whether any such rigid requirement in relation to the "permanence" of the residence sufficient to found a new domicil of choice ever formed part of the Roman-Dutch Law principles of Private International Law. References to *Voet* 5.1.92 and 94 certainly indicate that he did not treat the question of "permanence of residence" for domicil upon the basis that any contemplation of a possible move would negative the existence of the required *animus manendi* or *morandi* . . .

[WILLIAMSON JA referred to some English authorities and proceeded:]

[708] I think that the phraseology used in the summary by LANGTON J, in *Gulbenkian's* case, [*Gulbenkian v Gulbenkian* [1937] 4 All ER 618] . . . namely [709] that "permanent residence" involves only

"a present intention to reside permanently . . . an intention unlimited in period but not irrevocable in character",

can be accepted as doing no violence to the principles of our own law . . . I would therefore approach the problem of the present respondent's domicil in October, 1962, upon the basis that at any rate the above interpretation by LANGTON J, of the present position in English Law is also our law. In other words I think the enquiry is whether, on a balance of probabilities, the appellant showed that in October, 1962, the respondent then had a present intention to reside permanently in South Africa in the sense that he had no intention of limiting the period of such residence; the enquiry does not involve, in my view, a scrupulous and solicitous investigation as to whether perhaps in the future he might not in certain circumstances decide to remove his permanent home to Israel . . .

There were five specific points mentioned by the learned Judge which in his view operated to negative any inference that the respondent did form an intention to stay in South Africa. The first was the fact that, when he failed to get a renewal of his teaching contract, he did [710] return to Israel. Secondly, whilst the parties acquired no fixed property in South Africa, they did during their stay in this country continue to hold property, and even acquire further property, in Israel and did employ some of their savings in this country for that purpose. Thirdly, an abandonment of his domicil in Israel, would postulate on the part of the respondent a disloyalty to the ideals of Zionism. Fourthly, he retained his Israeli citizenship. Fifthly, he had parents and brothers and sisters alive in Israel.

It is clear that each of these factors could and should properly be taken into consideration in deciding whether the respondent ever intended to settle in South Africa. But they must be considered of course in the light of all the circumstances, of the evidence of the appellant and of the other factors I shall mention. One circumstance which should be borne in mind is that the respondent's previous source of income (and his wife's source also) was what they earned as teachers of Hebrew in Jewish schools. To cut himself off from that source might have been an unnecessarily foolish act. The parties had managed to get to South Africa in 1956 under the aegis of the Jewish Agency; *inter alia* the Agency actively engages itself in despatching "missionaries" in the form of teachers of Hebrew all over the world; it also seems to be regarded by the local Jewish Boards of Education as the best source of supply of such teachers. There were obvious reasons why the respondent should remain to all outward appearances a loyal "missionary" ...

To turn to the above five factors said to indicate that the respondent was unlikely to have considered settling permanently in South Africa, it seems to me that the last one mentioned, the presence of parents and brothers and sisters in Israel, is of very little weight. Thousands of people annually are migrating permanently from one country to another leaving relatives behind. It may be a factor to be considered in some cases of very closely knit families; it may again be of no significance at all. There is no suggestion, even in the respondent's affidavit, that this was a factor influencing him to return to Israel. The appellant in fact gave evidence that he actually wanted to induce some of his relatives to come out to South Africa from Israel. The fourth factor is, in my view, of little significance. There was positive evidence by the appellant that the respondent felt he could not change his citizenship because it might have caused unpleasantness if a man in his position publicly abandoned his Israeli citizenship. The third factor similarly is not a matter which in the case of the respondent can really carry [711] much weight. There is uncontroverted evidence that the Agency has suffered many "defections" from the ranks of its "missionary" teachers, particularly in America. And, as I have already said above, I cannot be satisfied that the respondent is so highly principled that he would never consider deserting the Agency if it suited his inclinations and pocket to do so. I also have no doubt, in the light of matters I shall mention later, that he would "act out" as long as possible the part of a loyal and faithful servant of the Agency and of Israel.

The second of the factors mentioned by CORBETT J, viz the assets held in Israel and the lack of assets in South Africa, is certainly a matter of substance to be thrown into the balance when the probabilities are weighed. In assessing the weight to be attached to this factor it must be remembered that the parties had acquired an asset of value in Israel before they ever actually considered coming to South Africa ...

[WILLIAMSON JA considered the evidence on the manner in which the investment was made and concluded that the spouses' conduct in investing in property in Israel did not render it improbable that they had decided to stay in South Africa. He proceeded:]

There is also to be considered the often anomalous position of a Jew in the Diaspora in relation to the ideal of rebuilding Zion and his domicil in another country. There must be many thousands of Jews who have no intention of ever departing from the countries in which they are settled and who yet feel an urge to assist in and to participate in the growth of the new Zion.

I come lastly to the factor mentioned first by the learned Judge, viz the actual return of the respondent in 1961 to Israel. The fact [712] that he did return after he had learned that the doors of the Jewish Boards of Education in South Africa seemed to be closed to him, precluded, in the learned Judge's view, a state of mind which excluded any contemplation of an event upon the occurrence of which the respondent would leave South Africa; it was perfectly consistent, he considered, with an attitude upon the part of the respondent that he would stay on in the Republic as long as he could renew his teaching appointments under the Jewish Board of Education. This is of course so; but it could be equally consistent with the conduct of a man who had become anxious to settle in the

Republic but who changed his mind again when he was caught in adultery on April 18, 1963, by a wife who was suing him for restitution of conjugal rights and making other serious claims on him. The respondent's conduct in the months immediately prior to being trapped in adultery were much more consistent with that of a man who wanted to remain in the Republic, even if it meant his overstaying the last possible extension of time which would be allowed him by the Jewish Agency ...

[WILLIAMSON JA analysed the evidence relating to the respondent's conduct during these months and proceeded:]

[714] It is not required, nor is it to be expected, that at some particular date a layman should come to a fixed and settled intention to stay and to abandon his previous domicil. It is usually an almost unperceived or subconscious development of the mind, culminating in a general attitude that

"this place is my home and I have no present intention of leaving it".

In the respondent's case there was of course a possible fixed event which might have changed his attitude, viz his actual recall to Israel by the Jewish Agency. But the fact remains that he in the meantime may well have equivocated so as not to prejudice his employment; it does not mean that he necessarily continued to contemplate leaving his home here at any given time or at all ...

[WILLIAMSON JA discussed the accuracy of the appellant's evidence on the question whether the spouses regarded South Africa as their permanent home. He concluded that appellant's evidence was supported by a number of facts, namely the respondent's conduct between November 1962 and July 1963; his obvious keenness to remain in South Africa for as long as possible; his arrangements for the education of his children to be continued in South Africa; his interest in South African primitive life; his efforts to stay on in South Africa indefinitely even after he was no longer considered a "missionary" for the Jewish Agency and his distortion and suppression of certain facts such as his effort to exchange his single air ticket for a return ticket. WILLIAMSON JA proceeded:]

[716] On the evidence of the appellant, supported by the facts I have mentioned, I think it was established on a balance of probabilities that the respondent had decided to make his home indefinitely in South Africa ... By his residence here and by his decision to remain here indefinitely, South Africa became, in the circumstances, his place of domicil ...

[717] In the circumstances the appeal should be allowed with costs and the judgment of the Court below set aside; the matter should, in my view, be remitted for that Court to deal with the claim for divorce and other consequential relief ...

[RUMPFF JA, in a separate judgment, concurred with WILLIAMSON JA.]

POTGIETER AJA: [719] The *onus* of proving that a domicile of choice has been acquired rests on the party who asserts it and this *onus* is discharged by a preponderance of probabilities. (See *Webber v Webber*, 1915 AD 239, and *Ley v Ley's Executors and Others*, 1951 (3) SA 186 (AD)).

In the case of *Johnson v Johnson*, 1931 AD 391 at p 398, DE VILLIERS CJ, indicated what has to be proved in order to discharge this *onus* in the following terms:

"Both in the Roman law and in our own and the English law a person *sui juris* is free to choose for himself a domicile of choice *animo et facto* by establishing for himself in fact a residence in the territory in question, combined with an *animus manendi* in that territory — Westlake, *Private International Law*, 4th ed. para 256."

Appellant therefore had to prove the two requirements, namely residence in the court's area and an intention of settling there permanently.

On the evidence adduced at the trial there is no doubt that appellant has proved that respondent resided in Cape Town for about seven years and had been residing there when action was instituted.

The question is whether the learned Judge *a quo* was correct in holding, as he did, that appellant had not discharged the *onus* of proving that, at the commencement of the proceedings, respondent acquired a domicile of choice, which domicile he still retained at that time. In other words whether respondent had decided to make Cape Town his permanent home. In *Johnson's* case, *supra*, DE VILLIERS CJ, cited with approval the following passage in Westlake, *Private International Law*:

"... intention necessary for acquiring a domicile of choice excluded all contemplation of any event on the occurrence of which the residence would cease".

The learned Judge came to the conclusion that this statement satisfied the test of *Voet*, 5.1.98, who requires a *propositum illic perpetuo morandi*. It seems quite clear, however, that the words "excludes all contemplation" can never mean and were never intended to mean that the *de cujus* has excluded from his mind all possibility that in future he might leave the country. In *Ley's* case CENTLIVRES CJ, deals with the meaning of the *dictum* in *Johnson's* case. It appears from his judgment, and especially at p 193 thereof, that in his view this *dictum* was merely intended to emphasise the necessity of proving a fixed and deliberate intention to abandon one domicile and to acquire a new one. He certainly did not understand the *dictum* to mean that intention of permanent residence is not proved if it is contingent upon an unforeseen event. He quotes with approval at p 194 the following remarks of BRAMWELL B, in *Attorney-General v Pottinger*, 30 LJ Excl 284 at p 292:

"But is it to be said that a contingent intention of that kind defeats the intention which is necessary to accompany the *factum* in order to establish a domicile? Most assuredly not. There is not a man who has not contingent intentions to do something that would be very much to his benefit if the occasion arises. But if every such intention or expression of opinion prevented a man having a fixed domicile, no man would ever have a domicile at all except his domicile of origin."

He further explains the meaning of the words "excludes all contemplation" as follows:

"As I understand the expression, it means that if the state of mind of the *de cujus* is something like this, 'I may settle here permanently, and anyhow I'll stay for a time; but perhaps I'll move to another country' the intention required to establish a domicile is not present. But if his state of mind is like this, 'I shall settle here', that is enough, even though it is not proved that if he had been asked, 'Will you never move elsewhere?' he might not have said something like, 'Well, never is a long day. Who knows? I might move if I change my mind or if circumstances were to change.' Any doubt actually present to his mind as to whether he will move or not will according to *Westlake's* statement exclude the intention to settle permanently, but the possibility that, if the idea of a move in the future had been suggested to him, he might not at once have scouted it does not amount to contemplation of an event on which the residence would cease. It is only the former that has to be disproved by the person alleging a change of domicile ..."

[721] In my judgment, having regard to these authorities, the *onus* of proving a domicile of choice is discharged once physical presence is proved and it is further proved that the *de cujus* had at the relevant time a fixed and deliberate intention to abandon his previous domicile, and to settle permanently in the country of choice. A contemplation of any certain or foreseeable future event on the occurrence of which residence in that country would cease, excludes such an intention. If he entertains any doubt as to whether he will

remain or not, intention to settle permanently is likewise excluded. That appears to be in accordance with our common law. I do not understand *Voet*, 5.1.89, and *Vromann*, Bk 1, Civ 1, in any other sense ...

It remains then to apply these legal principles to the facts of the instant case ...

[I]t seems to me to be highly improbable, in the circumstances of this case, that, in the period of two-and-a-half years' stay in South Africa, the respondent would already have decided to sever his bonds with Israel, where he had lived for over twenty years ...

There are, to my mind, strong indications which point to a contrary intention on the part of the respondent. The whole system under which teachers contract to teach abroad is essentially one which provides for temporary employment there and I can find nothing in the evidence to [722] convince me that respondent, in spite of the temporary nature of his employment, made up his mind to turn his back on Israel and to settle permanently in South Africa ...

An important factor which to my mind weighs heavily against appellant is the fact that respondent invested fairly large sums of money in Israel, whereas no fixed property was acquired in this country nor did he make any long-term investments here ...

[POTGIETER AJA also referred to the fact that the respondent had applied for permanent residence in South Africa and that he had returned to South Africa after his holiday. He concluded:]

[723] The result is that, although there are some indications in appellant's favour, the evidence does not show that respondent ever made up his mind to settle permanently in this country. It may equally well be that at all relevant times he contemplated that he would at some foreseeable future date return to Israel, or, in any event, entertained a doubt as to whether he would return or not.

I accordingly come to the conclusion that the finding of the Judge *a quo* that appellant had not discharged the *onus* of proving that at the time of the institution of the proceedings respondent had acquired a domicile of choice in this country, is correct ...

STEYN CJ and WESSELS JA concurred in the judgment of POTGIETER AJA.

Note

Domicile has always been very important for establishing jurisdiction in a divorce action. At common law the only court which had jurisdiction to entertain a divorce action was the court in the area of which the spouses were domiciled at the time of institution of the proceedings (*Le Mesurier v Le Mesurier* [1895] AC 517 (PC); Hahlo 4 ed 539). As a wife at that stage followed her husband's domicile, the common law rule signified that she could only institute a divorce action against her husband at the court of his domicile. This created great difficulties for a wife who was not resident where her husband was domiciled — see for example *Nefler v Nefler* 1906 ORC 7.

Aantekening

Domisilie was nog altyd baie belangrik by die beantwoording van die vraag of 'n hof jurisdiksie in 'n egskeidingsgeding het. In die gemenereg was die hof, in wie se jurisdik-siegebied die gades ten tyde van die instel van die geding gedomisilieer was, die enigste hof wat jurisdiksie gehad het om hulle eg-skeidingsgeding aan te hoor (*Le Mesurier v Le Mesurier* [1895] AC 517 (PC); Hahlo 4e uitg 539). Aangesien 'n getroude vrou op daardie stadium haar man se domisilie ge-volg het, het hierdie gemeenregtelike reël beteken dat sy slegs 'n egskeidingsaksie teen haar man aanhangig kon maak in die hof van sy domisilie. Dit het groot probleme ver-oorsaak vir 'n vrou wat nie woonagtig was

The wife's position was alleviated somewhat by section 1(1) of the Matrimonial Causes Jurisdiction Act 22 of 1939; section 6 of the Matrimonial Affairs Act 37 of 1953 and section 21 of the General Law Amendment Act 70 of 1968. The latter provisions were in effect when *Eilon v Eilon* was decided and did not assist a wife whose husband was not domiciled in South Africa. Sections 6 and 21 were repealed by section 2(1)(b) of the Divorce Act 70 of 1979.

In 1992 the jurisdictional requirements for instituting a divorce action were changed once more when the Domicile Act 3 of 1992 came into operation. Section 6 of the Domicile Act amended section 2 of the Divorce Act so that the same requirements apply in respect of husband and wife. A court now has jurisdiction in a divorce action if the parties are or either of them is:

(a) domiciled in the area of jurisdiction of the court on the date on which the action is instituted; or

(b) ordinarily resident in the area of jurisdiction of the court on the date on which the action is instituted and the parties have or one of them has been ordinarily resident in the Republic for a period of not less than one year immediately prior to that date.

Next we discuss the *animus* requirement for acquiring a domicile of choice. The *animus* requirement has been interpreted strictly in some cases and more leniently in others. The different interpretations of the *animus* requirement have created much uncertainty as to what exactly a person's intention must be before he can comply with the *animus* requirement.

In *Johnson v Johnson* 1931 AD 391 the *animus* requirement was interpreted very strictly (see the quotation in *Eilon's* case 719–720) while the interpretation of the *animus* requirement in *Ley v Ley's Executors* 1951 3 SA 186 (A) was more lenient (see the quotation in *Eilon's*

waar haar man gedomisilieer was nie — sien byvoorbeeld *Nefler v Nefler* 1906 ORC 7.

Daar is 'n mate van verligting vir die vrou gebring deur artikel 1(1) van die Wet op Regsbevoegdheid in Matrimoniële Regsake 22 van 1939; artikel 6 van die Wet op Huweliksaangeleenthede 37 van 1953 en artikel 21 van die Algemene Regswysigingswet 70 van 1968. Laasgenoemde bepalings was in werking toe *Eilon v Eilon* beslis is en was nie vir die vrou wie se man nie in Suid-Afrika gedomisilieer was van enige hulp nie. Hierdie bepalings is herroep deur artikel 2(1)(b) van die Wet op Egskeiding 70 van 1979.

In 1992 het die jurisdiksievereistes vir die instel van 'n egskeidingsgeding weer eens verander toe die Wet op Domisilie 3 van 1992 in werking getree het. Artikel 6 van die Wet op Domisilie het artikel 2 van die Wet op Egskeiding gewysig sodat dieselfde vereistes nou vir sowel die man as die vrou geld. 'n Hof het nou jurisdiksie in 'n egskeidingsgeding indien die partye of enigeen van hulle:

(a) op die datum waarop die geding ingestel word in die regsgebied van die hof gedomisilieer is, of

(b) op die datum waarop die geding ingestel word gewoonlik in die regsgebied van die hof woonagtig is en vir minstens een jaar onmiddellik voor daardie datum gewoonlik in die Republiek woonagtig was.

Ons gee nou aandag aan die *animus*-vereiste vir die verkryging van 'n domisilie van keuse. Die *animus*-vereiste is in sommige sake streng en in ander meer toeskietlik uitgelê. Die verskillende interpretasies van die *animus*-vereiste het baie onsekerheid teweeggebring oor presies wat 'n persoon se bedoeling moet wees voordat hy aan die *animus*-vereiste kan voldoen.

In *Johnson v Johnson* 1931 AA 391 is die *animus*-vereiste baie streng uitgelê (sien die aanhaling in die *Eilon*-saak 719–720) terwyl die interpretasie daarvan in *Ley v Ley's Executors*

case 720). The majority judgment in *Eilon v Eilon* complies with the strict interpretation of the *animus* requirement, whereas the minority judgment complies with the more lenient interpretation. The precedent system stipulates that the majority judgment must be followed. The majority judgment requires a "fixed and deliberate intention" to settle permanently at the specific place (721). "A contemplation of any certain or foreseeable future event on the occurrence of which residence ... would cease excludes such an intention" (721). Therefore, according to the majority decision in *Eilon*, a person cannot comply with the *animus* requirement if he at all doubts whether he will remain at the specific place where he has settled, nor can he do so if he contemplates an event which will occur or might foreseeably occur and which will cause him to leave the place he has settled at. This interpretation of the *animus* requirement was generally accepted as being too strict (see eg Kahn 48–49), and on 1 August 1992 (when the Domicile Act came into operation) the *animus* requirement as set out in *Eilon* was replaced with a more flexible test. Section 1(2) of the Domicile Act provides that a domicile of choice is acquired by a person who is lawfully present at a particular place and who "has the intention to settle there for an indefinite period".

The position of persons who, at common law, could not acquire domiciles of choice but were given domiciles of dependence by operation of law, namely wives, children and insane persons, has also been amended by the Domicile Act. Section 1(1) of the act provides that "[e]very person who is of or over the age of 18 years, and every person under the age of 18 who by law has the status of a major, excluding any person who does not have the mental capacity to make a rational choice, shall be competent to acquire a domicile of choice, *regardless of such a person's sex or marital status*" (our emphasis). Therefore, a wife no longer automatically follows her husband's domicile and a child of 18 years

1951 3 SA 186 (A) meer toeskietlik was (sien die aanhaling in die *Eilon*-saak 720). Die meerderheidsuitspraak in *Eilon v Eilon* is in ooreenstemming met die streng interpretasie van die *animus*-vereiste terwyl die minderheidsuitspraak in ooreenstemming is met die meer toeskietlike benadering. Die meerderheidsuitspraak moet ingevolge die presedentestelsel nagevolg word. Die meerderheidsuitspraak vereis 'n "fixed and deliberate intention" om permanent op die bepaalde plek te vestig (721). "A contemplation of any certain or foreseeable future event on the occurrence of which residence ... would cease excludes such an intention" (721). Ingevolge die meerderheidsuitspraak in – *Eilon* voldoen 'n persoon dus nie aan die *animus*-vereiste nie indien hy enigsins twyfel of hy gaan bly op die besondere plek waar hy hom gevestig het. Hy sal ook nie aan die *animus*-vereiste voldoen nie indien hy voorsien dat 'n gebeurtenis mag plaasvind of moontlik mag plaasvind wat sal veroorsaak dat hy die besondere plek sal verlaat. Dit is algemeen aanvaar dat hierdie interpretasie van die *animus*-vereiste te streng is (sien byvoorbeeld, Kahn 48–49), en op 1 Augustus 1992 (toe die Wet op Domisilie in werking getree het) is die *animus*-vereiste soos gestel in *Eilon* deur 'n meer toeskietlike toets vervang. Artikel 1(2) van die Wet op Domisilie bepaal dat 'n domisilie van keuse verkry word deur 'n persoon wat wettig op 'n bepaalde plek aanwesig is en wat "die bedoeling het om hom vir 'n onbepaalde tydperk daar te vestig".

Die posisie van persone wat ingevolge die gemenereg nie 'n domisilie van keuse kon verwerf nie en aan wie daar deur regswerking 'n domisilie van afhanklikheid toegeken is, naamlik getroude vrouens, kinders en kranksinniges, is ook deur die Wet op Domisilie verander. Artikel 1(1) van die wet bepaal: "Elke persoon wat 18 jaar oud of ouer is, en elke persoon onder die ouderdom van 18 jaar wat regtens die status van meerderjarigheid het, uitgesonderd 'n persoon wat

or more (and a child below 18 who has been declared a major) no longer automatically follows his natural guardian's domicile. In respect of a child who cannot acquire his own domicile of choice, that is, generally speaking, a child below the age of 18, section 2(2) of the act provides that, "[i]f, in the normal course of events, a child has his home with his parents or with one of them, it shall be presumed, unless the contrary is shown, that the parental home concerned is the child's domicile." Section 1(1) of the act clearly states that a person "who does not have the mental capacity to make a rational choice" cannot acquire a domicile of choice. Thus, an insane person is still precluded from establishing such a domicile. In terms of section 2(1) of the act he (like any other person "not capable of acquiring a domicile of choice") is domiciled at the place "with which he is most closely connected". (In respect of the domicile of soldiers, diplomats, prisoners and other persons who are not free to choose where they want to reside see the note on *Naville v Naville* [11]. In respect of the requirement of lawful presence see the note on *Smith v Smith* [12].)

Although the Domicile Act has introduced certainty in most areas of the law of domicile, cognisance must still be taken of the sometimes unclear and conflicting common law rules in respect of domicile, for the Domicile Act does not operate with retroactive effect (sections 8(2) and (3)). The act regulates the law of domicile only as from the date of its commencement. Therefore the *Eilon* case, and all the other cases on domicile which were decided before 1 August 1992, remain important.

For a discussion of the Domicile Act see Davel 1993 *De Jure* 400 and Jordaan and Davel 32 *et seq.*

nie oor die geestesvermoë beskik om 'n rasionele keuse te maak nie, is bevoeg om 'n domisilie van keuse te verkry, *ongeag so 'n persoon se geslag of huwelikstaat*" (ons beklemtoning). Gevolglik volg 'n vrou nie meer outomaties haar man se domisilie nie en 'n kind van 18 jaar en ouer (en 'n kind onder 18 wat meerderjarig verklaar is) volg nie meer outomaties sy natuurlike voog se domisilie nie. In verband met 'n kind wat nie sy eie domisilie van keuse kan vestig nie, dit is, oor die algemeen gesproke, 'n kind onder 18 jaar, bepaal artikel 2(2) dat, "[i]ndien 'n kind in die gewone gang van sake sy tuiste by sy ouers of by een van hulle het" daar vermoed word "dat die betrokke ouerhuis die kind se domisilie is, tensy die teendeel bewys word". Artikel 1(1) van die wet verklaar onomwonde dat 'n persoon "wat nie oor die geestesvermoë beskik om 'n rasionele keuse te maak nie", nie 'n domisilie van keuse kan vestig nie.

'n Kranksinnige persoon is dus nog steeds nie in staat om so 'n domisilie te vestig nie. Ingevolge artikel 2(1) van die wet is hy (net soos enige ander persoon "wat nie bevoeg is om 'n domisilie van keuse te verkry . . . nie") gedomisilieer op die plek "waaraan hy die nouste verbonde is". (Sien die aantekening by *Naville v Naville* [11] in verband met die domisilie van soldate, diplomate, gevangenes en ander persone wat nie vry is om te kies waar hulle wil woon nie. Sien die aantekening by *Smith v Smith* [12] in verband met die vereiste van wettige aanwesigheid.)

Alhoewel die Wet op Domisilie sekerheid bewerkstellig het oor die meeste aspekte van die reg rakende domisilie, moet daar steeds gelet word op die soms onduidelike en botsende gemeenregtelike reëls rakende domisilie want die Wet op Domisilie geld nie met terugwerkende krag nie (artikel 8(2) en 8(3)). Die wet reël die reg met betrekking tot domisilie slegs vanaf die datum van die inwerkingtreding daarvan. Die *Eilon*-saak, en al die ander sake wat voor 1 Augustus 1992

in verband met domisilie beslis is, bly dus steeds van belang.

Vir 'n bespreking van die Wet op Domisilie sien Davel 1993 *De Jure* 400 en Jordaan en Davel 32 ev.

| Persons not free to choose where to reside | Persone wat nie vrylik kan kies waar om te woon nie |

[11]   NAVILLE V NAVILLE

1957 1 SA 280 (C)

Domicile of a diplomat

A Swiss consul who was stationed in Cape Town instituted an action for restitution of conjugal rights against his wife in the Cape Provincial Division. The consul was due to retire at the end of the following year and had already been stationed in Cape Town for six years. He sold his house in Switzerland about two years prior to the institution of the present action. At the time of selling the house he arranged with the Swiss authorities to have his pension paid to him in Cape Town and he indicated to them that he considered Cape Town to be his permanent home and that he intended to remain there. The Swiss authorities undertook not to transfer him until he retired and furthermore agreed to discharge him at Cape Town. The consul stated that he intended to resign if he was transferred. He averred that he had acquired a domicile of choice in Cape Town and that he could therefore institute his application in the Cape Provincial Division. The application was granted.

Domisilie van 'n diplomaat

'n Switserse konsul wat in Kaapstad gestasioneer was, het in die Kaapse Provinsiale Afdeling 'n aksie vir die herstel van huweliksregte teen sy vrou aanhangig gemaak. Die konsul sou aan die einde van die volgende jaar aftree. Hy was alreeds vir ses jaar in Kaapstad gestasioneer. Omtrent twee jaar voor die aanvang van die aksie het hy sy huis in Switserland verkoop. Op die stadium toe hy sy huis verkoop het, het hy met die Switserse owerhede ooreengekom dat sy pensioen in Kaapstad aan hom uitbetaal sou word en hy het dit aan hulle duidelik gemaak dat hy Kaapstad beskou as die plek waar sy permanente woning is en dat hy in Kaapstad wou bly woon. Die Switserse owerhede het onderneem om hom nie voor sy aftrede te verplaas nie en hulle het verder onderneem dat hy in Kaapstad uit diens kon tree. Die konsul het verklaar dat hy sou bedank indien hy verplaas sou word. Hy het beweer dat hy 'n domisilie in Kaapstad verwerf het en dat hy dus sy aansoek in die Kaapse Provinsiale Afdeling kon instel. Die aansoek is toegestaan.

DE VILLIERS JP: [281] He [the plaintiff] has satisfied me that this [ie to remain in Cape Town] is his intention and that he had formed that intention not less than two years ago. On the facts I accept that that is what he intends to do, and he has made the arrangements necessary to enable him to carry out that intention as soon as he does retire. If indeed he is transferred elsewhere prior to his retirement, his intention is to resign his position, which apparently, he is free to do.

The only difficulty that stands in his way is whether he can be said to be domiciled here whilst still in the service of the Swiss Government. Ordinarily he would be liable to be transferred anywhere and the question arises as to whether he could (a) form an intention to change his domicile and (b) give effect to that intention whilst still in the service of his Government here.

In other words, whilst still in the employ of his Government is he a free agent in the matter of changing his domicile?

This is a question on which our Courts have in the past given decisions which are far from harmonious. In *Baker v Baker*, 1945 A.D. 708 a similar question arose although upon quite different facts . . .

[282] SCHREINER JA thought there was a strong body of judicial opinion favouring the view that the sailor or soldier is not debarred from acquiring a domicile in the country in which he was stationed. He did not, however, express a definite decision on this point because on the facts of that case the plaintiff was not seeking to establish a domicile of choice in the country in which he was stationed, for in fact, he had at no time been stationed in South Africa. He therefore left the matter open.

That was the position until *Nicol v Nicol*, 1948 (2) SA 613 (C), where OGILVIE THOMP-SON J, had to decide whether or not there was an absolute legal bar against a member of the fighting services acquiring, during the period of his service, a domicile of choice in the country where he is stationed on service. Whether, in fact, such a domicile of choice had been established will depend upon the facts of the case. In *McMillan v McMillan*, 1943 TPD 345, MURRAY J, with whom GREENBERG, JP, concurred, held that although such a person could form an intention to change his domicile during the period of his service, it only became operative as, and when he became a free agent, ie after he had been discharged and was no longer under any disability in regard to his freedom of action.

With this view OGILVIE THOMPSON J, disagreed feeling that it went unduly far. After considering various other authorities he decided that there was no absolute bar against a soldier acquiring a domicile in the country where he is stationed provided he is able to establish it by satisfactory proof.

This decision has been followed subsequently and is at any rate by inference approved by MURRAY, J, himself in *Van Rensburg v Ballinger*, 1950 (4) SA 427 (T) at pp. 437 and 438 . . .

Members of the fighting services would appear to be in no different position from persons who reside abroad in pursuance of their duties as public servants of their Government. The matter is thus put by Cheshire *Private International Law*, (1952) 4th ed p. 168:

> "If a person resides abroad in pursuance of his duties as a public servant of his own Government, as, for example, an ambassador, a military or naval officer, a colonial judge, or a consul or if he is a servant under contract to go where sent, the inference to be drawn from the cause of the residence is that no change of domicil is intended. In such cases the existing domicil is retained unless there are additional circumstances from which a contrary intention can be collected."

In a footnote the learned author relies upon the cases I have already [283] cited: . . . *Sellars v Sellars* [1942 SC 206]; *Baker v Baker*; *Nicol v Nicol* as well as *Ex parte Glass et Uxor*, 1948 (4) SA 379 (W).

I am of the opinion, therefore, that a consul of a foreign Government who has been stationed in Cape Town on service is not precluded from obtaining a domicile of choice in Cape Town whilst on such service. Whether he has so acquired a new domicile must

depend on the facts of the case. He must satisfy the Court that there has been, on his part, a final and deliberate intention of abandoning his former domicile and establishing a new one.

On the facts presently before me the plaintiff has sufficiently, in my view, satisfied the requirements of such proof.

He is therefore entitled to a restitution order in terms of which his wife will be ordered to return to him on or before 17th December, 1956, and failing compliance, to show cause on 27th December, 1956, why a decree of divorce should not be granted.

Note

Uncertainty existed at common law as to whether persons who are not free to choose where they want to reside could acquire a domicile of choice. Soldiers, diplomats, public servants and employees of foreign governments or firms were initially thought to be incapable of acquiring a domicile of choice at the place where they were stationed or where they were in public service or in employment. It was argued that, since these people are not free to choose where they are to be sent but are stationed at a particular place or transferred to a particular place by their employer, they could not comply with the *animus* requirement for acquiring a domicile of choice – they could not really form the intention to stay on at that place. Although a more lenient approach was sometimes adopted towards compliance with the *animus* requirement by such employees, the position in respect of the establishment of a domicile of choice by them remained unclear.

The question is whether the Domicile Act 3 of 1992 removed the uncertainty which existed at common law. The answer is not clear because the act does not expressly deal with this situation. Generally speaking, section 1 of the act provides that every person who is of or over the age of 18 years can acquire a domicile of choice if that person is "lawfully present" at the place concerned and "has the intention to settle there for an indefinite period". There is, however, no indication whether this rule applies to persons who are not free to choose where they want to reside. It is however submitted that, like any other person, the above categories of persons should be competent to establish a domicile of choice within the limitations of their capacity. (See further Davel 1993 *De Jure* 403.)

Briefly summarised, the common law position is as follows:

Aantekening

Ingevolge die gemenereg was dit onseker of persone wat nie vrylik kan kies waar hulle wil woon nie 'n domisilie van keuse kan vestig op die plek waar hulle woon. Die standpunt is aanvanklik gehuldig dat soldate, diplomate, staatsamptenare en werknemers van buitelandse regerings of firmas nie 'n domisilie van keuse kan vestig op die plek waar hulle gestasioneer is of waar hulle werk nie. Aangesien hierdie persone nie vrylik kan kies waarheen hulle gestuur word nie, maar op 'n bepaalde plek gestasioneer word of deur hulle werkgewer na 'n bepaalde plek oorgeplaas word, is geargumenteer dat hulle nie aan die *animus*-vereiste vir vestiging van 'n domisilie van keuse kan voldoen nie – hulle kan nie werklik die bedoeling vorm om op daardie plek te bly woon nie. Soms is weliswaar 'n meer toeskietlike benadering gevolg ten opsigte van voldoening aan die *animus*-vereiste deur sulke werknemers, maar die posisie rakende die vestiging van 'n domisilie van keuse deur hulle het onseker gebly.

Die Wet op Domisilie 3 van 1992 het die onsekerheid wat bestaan het nie uit die weg geruim nie aangesien dit hierdie aangeleentheid nie uitdruklik aanspreek nie. In die algemeen gesproke bepaal die wet in artikel 1 dat elke persoon wat 18 jaar oud of ouer is 'n domisilie van keuse kan vestig indien daardie persoon "wettig" op die betrokke plek aanwesig is en "die bedoeling het om hom vir 'n onbepaalde tydperk daar te vestig." Die wet bevat egter geen aanduiding of hierdie reël ook geld ten opsigte van persone wat nie vrylik kan kies waar hulle wil woon nie. Daar word egter aan die hand gedoen dat bogenoemde kategorieë van persone, net soos enige ander persoon, bevoeg is om 'n domisilie van keuse binne die perke van hulle bevoegdheid te vestig. (Sien verder Davel 1993 *De Jure* 403.)

Die gemeenregtelike posisie kan kortliks soos volg

In respect of a soldier, the court in *Baker v Baker* 1945 AD 708 held that a domicile of choice can be acquired at the place where the soldier is *not* stationed. The court declined to give an answer to the question of whether a soldier can acquire a domicile of choice at the place where he *is* stationed, but *obiter dicta* contained in the case have been interpreted as authority for the view that a soldier can acquire a domicile of choice at the place where he is stationed (see for example *Moore v Moore* 1945 TPD 407 and *Nicol v Nicol* 1948 2 SA 613 (C)). (In respect of the acquisition of a domicile of choice by a soldier, see further *Naville v Naville* at 282.)

In respect of diplomats, public servants and employees of foreign governments or firms there are *obiter dicta* in *Ex parte Quintrell* 1922 TPD 14 16; *Fozard v Fozard* 1923 CPD 62 63 and *McMillan v McMillan* 1943 TPD 345 349–350 which suggest that such an employee can acquire a domicile of choice since he is normally not transferred as often as a soldier. However, in *Bothma v Bothma* 1940 1 PH B9 (O) and *Carvalho v Carvalho* 1936 SR 219, where the court dealt with the acquisition of a domicile of choice by a civil servant, it was held that since such an employee is unable to exercise a choice as to where he resides, he cannot acquire a domicile of choice but retains his last domicile.

The decisions in which it was held that a person who can be transferred by his employer cannot acquire a domicile of choice at the place to which he has been transferred have been described as outdated ("verouderd") (Van der Vyver and Joubert 108) and "manifestly wrong" (Kahn 62). The position as reflected in *Naville v Naville* is probably the correct one. A diplomat or any other public servant or an employee of a foreign firm should have the capacity to acquire a domicile of choice if he has a firm and final intention of settling at a specific place (Barnard, Cronjé and Olivier 47; Van der Vyver and Joubert 108; Kahn 62). The fact that he has been sent to the specific place by his employer should not render him incapable of complying with the *animus* requirement for acquisition of a domicile of choice.

Similarly, a soldier should not be precluded from acquiring a domicile of choice at the place where he is stationed. The general rule in section 1 of the Domicile Act should be made expressly applicable to these persons.

opgesom word:

Met betrekking tot 'n soldaat het die hof in *Baker v Baker* 1945 AD 708 beslis dat 'n domisilie van keuse verkry kan word op 'n plek waar die soldaat *nie* gestasioneer is nie. Die hof het egter geen antwoord gegee op die vraag of 'n soldaat 'n domisilie van keuse kan vestig op die plek waar hy wel gestasioneer *is* nie. *Obiter dicta* in die saak is egter al uitgelê as gesag vir die siening dat 'n soldaat 'n domisilie van keuse kan vestig op die plek waar hy gestasioneer is (sien byvoorbeeld *Moore v Moore* 1945 TPD 407 en *Nicol v Nicol* 1948 2 SA 613 (K)). (Sien verder *Naville v Naville* 282 in verband met die vestiging van 'n domisilie van keuse deur 'n soldaat.)

In verband met diplomate, staatsamptenare en werknemers van buitelandse regerings of firmas is daar *obiter dicta* in *Ex parte Quintrell* 1922 TPA 14 16; *Fozard v Fozard* 1924 KPA 62 63 en *McMillan v McMillan* 1943 TPA 345 349–350 wat daarop dui dat sodanige werknemer wel 'n domisilie van keuse kan vestig aangesien hy gewoonlik nie so dikwels as 'n soldaat verplaas word nie. In *Bothma v Bothma* 1940 1 PH B9 (O) en *Carvalho v Carvalho* 1936 SR 219, waar die hof te doen gehad het met die verkryging van 'n domisilie van keuse deur 'n staatsamptenaar, is egter beslis dat so 'n werknemer nie 'n domisilie van keuse kan vestig nie aangesien hy nie 'n keuse kan uitoefen oor waar hy wil bly nie en dat hy sy laaste domisilie behou.

Die uitsprake waarin daar beslis is dat 'n persoon wat deur sy werkgewer verplaas kan word nie 'n domisilie van keuse kan vestig op die plek waarheen hy verplaas word nie, is al beskryf as "verouderd" (Van der Vyver en Joubert 108) en "manifestly wrong" (Kahn 62). Die posisie soos deur *Naville v Naville* weergegee word, is waarskynlik korrek. 'n Diplomaat of enige ander staatsamptenaar, of 'n werknemer van 'n buitelandse firma, behoort die bevoegdheid te hê om 'n domisilie van keuse te verkry indien hy 'n vaste bedoeling het om hom op 'n spesifieke plek te vestig (Barnard, Cronjé en Olivier 49; Van der Vyver en Joubert 108; Kahn 62). Die feit dat sy werkgewer hom na daardie plek gestuur het, behoort dit nie vir hom onmoontlik te maak om aan die *animus*-vereiste te voldoen nie.

Insgelyks behoort daar geen beletsel te wees teen die vestiging van 'n domisilie van keuse deur 'n soldaat op die plek waar hy gestasioneer is nie. Die algemene reël in artikel 1 van die Wet op

The same should apply in respect of a prisoner. At common law the view was widely held that a prisoner could not acquire a domicile of choice at the place where he was incarcerated but retained the last domicile he had before imprisonment (Boberg 74; Barnard, Cronjé and Olivier 47; Kahn 53). The view that the prisoner could not acquire a domicile of choice at the place of his imprisonment was based on two arguments: Firstly, that the prisoner was not at that place of his own free will, and secondly, that in the case of a prisoner other than a prisoner serving a long or a life sentence, the imprisonment would be of too short a duration to enable the prisoner to form the *animus* required for the acquisition of a domicile of choice at the place of his imprisonment. In *Nefler v Nefler* 1906 ORC 7 it was, strangely enough, held that a prisoner for life will of necessity acquire a domicile of choice at the place of his imprisonment. (Barnard, Cronjé and Olivier 47 describe it as a domicile of choice by operation of the law.) *Nefler's* decision cannot be supported, for there is no reason why, in the case of a prisoner for life, the ordinary principles for the acquisition of a domicile of choice should be deviated from. If any prisoner, including a long-term prisoner or a prisoner for life, does not comply with the *animus* requirement because he has not, through the exercise of his *free will*, formed the intention to remain *permanently* at the place of his imprisonment, he cannot be said to have acquired a domicile of choice at the place of his imprisonment. He should not automatically be awarded a domicile of choice at a particular place merely because he is incarcerated there. However, if a prisoner complies with the *animus* requirement by *forming the intention* to remain permanently at the place of his imprisonment, he should be able to acquire a domicile at that place (Barnard, Cronjé and Olivier 47; Boberg 74; Kahn 53–54; Van der Vyver and Joubert 105). If a prisoner does in fact decide to remain permanently at the place of his imprisonment even after his release, he should immediately acquire a domicile of choice at that place – even before he is released from prison (Boberg 74; Kahn 53; Van der Vyver and Joubert 105).

Kahn (53) submits that *Nefler* should not be interpreted as though life-imprisonment automatically confers a domicile of choice upon the

Domisilie behoort uitdruklik op hierdie persone van toepassing gemaak te word.

Dieselfde behoort vir gevangenes te geld. In die gemenereg is die standpunt algemeen gehuldig dat 'n gevangene nie 'n domisilie van keuse kan vestig op die plek waar hy sy gevangenisstraf uitdien nie en dat hy die laaste domisilie behou wat hy voor die aanvang van sy gevangenisstraf gehad het (Boberg 74; Barnard, Cronjé en Olivier 49; Kahn 53). Die standpunt dat 'n gevangene nie 'n domisilie van keuse kan vestig op die plek waar hy sy gevangenisstraf uitdien nie, het op twee argumente berus: Eerstens is aangevoer dat die gevangene nie uit vrye keuse op die plek van sy gevangehouding verkeer nie, en tweedens dat 'n gevangene wat nie lewenslange of langtermyngevangenisstraf uitdien nie, nie lank genoeg aangehou word om die nodige *animus* te vorm wat vir vestiging van 'n domisilie van keuse op die plek waar die gevangenisstraf uitgedien word, vereis word nie. In *Nefler v Nefler* 1906 ORC 7 is, eienaardig genoeg, beslis dat 'n lewenslange gevangene noodwendig 'n domisilie van keuse verwerf op die plek waar hy sy straf uitdien. (Barnard, Cronjé en Olivier 49 beskryf dit as 'n domisilie van regsweë.) Die beslissing in *Nefler* kan nie aanvaar word nie. Daar is geen rede waarom daar in die geval van 'n lewenslange gevangene van die gewone beginsels vir die verkryging van 'n domisilie van keuse afgewyk moet word nie. Indien enige gevangene, insluitende 'n lewenslange of langtermyngevangene, nie aan die *animus*-vereiste voldoen nie, aangesien hy nie deur die uitoefening van sy *eie vrye wil* die bedoeling gevorm het om *permanent* op die plek te bly waar hy sy gevangenisstraf uitdien nie, kan daar nie gesê word dat hy daar 'n domisilie van keuse gevestig het nie. 'n Domisilie van keuse behoort nie outomaties aan hom toegeken te word op 'n bepaalde plek bloot omdat hy daar in die tronk opgesluit is nie. Indien 'n gevangene egter aan die *animus*-vereiste voldoen deur *die bedoeling te vorm* om permanent te bly woon op die plek waar hy sy gevangenisstraf uitdien, behoort hy in staat te wees om daar 'n domisilie van keuse te vestig (Barnard, Cronjé en Olivier 49; Boberg 74; Kahn 53–54; Van der Vyver en Joubert 105). Indien 'n gevangene inderdaad besluit om selfs na sy vrylating permanent te bly woon op die plek waar hy sy gevangenisstraf uitdien, behoort hy onmiddellik daar 'n domisilie van keuse te verwerf – selfs voor sy vrylating uit die gevangenis (Bo-

prisoner. He is of the opinion that the court in that case merely assumed jurisdiction *ad misericordiam* (to relieve the misery) without finally deciding the matter of a domicile of choice of such a prisoner. Nowadays it would, however, not be necessary for the court to assume such jurisdiction as the legislature alleviated the problems of a wife who found herself in a position similar to the plaintiff's in the *Nefler* case – see the note on *Eilon v Eilon* [10] regarding jurisdiction in divorce actions.

As far as the plaintiff's claim for restitution of conjugal rights in *Naville* is concerned, it should be noted that current divorce law does not provide for such a claim. One of the grounds upon which a divorce could be obtained in terms of the old divorce law (which was repealed by the Divorce Act 70 of 1979) was malicious desertion. Proceedings for a divorce on the ground of malicious desertion consisted of two actions merged into one: in the preliminary action the plaintiff applied for an order for restitution of conjugal rights on which the court issued a rule *nisi* calling upon the defendant to restore conjugal rights by a certain date. If he did not do so by the specified date, the court dissolved the marriage on the return date of the rule *nisi*. (Hahlo 4 ed 407–408). Section 14 of the Divorce Act 70 of 1979 repealed the court's authority to order restitution of conjugal rights with the result that such an order can no longer be issued.

berg 74; Kahn 53; Van der Vyver en Joubert 105). Kahn (53) voer aan dat die uitspraak in *Nefler* nie beteken dat lewenslange gevangenisstraf veroorsaak dat 'n gevangene outomaties 'n domisilie van keuse in die gevangenis verkry nie. Hy meen dat die hof in daardie saak bloot jurisdiksie *ad misericordiam* (om die ellendige situasie te verlig) aanvaar het sonder om finaal te beslis oor die probleem van die domisilie van keuse van so 'n gevangene. Deesdae sal dit in elk geval nie meer vir die hof nodig wees om op so 'n wyse jurisdiksie te aanvaar nie aangesien die wetgewer die probleme wat vir 'n vrou soos die eiseres in die *Nefler*-saak bestaan het, uit die weg geruim het – sien die aantekening by *Eilon v Eilon* [10] oor jurisdiksie in egskeidingsaksies.

Vir sover dit die eiser in *Naville* se eis om herstel van huweliksregte aangaan, moet daarop gelet word dat die huidige egskeidingsreg geen voorsiening maak vir so 'n eis nie. Een van die egskeidingsgronde ingevolge die ou egskeidingsreg (wat deur die Wet op Egskeiding 70 van 1979 herroep is) was kwaadwillige verlating. 'n Egskeidingsgeding wat gebaseer was op kwaadwillige verlating het bestaan uit twee aksies wat in een aksie saamgevoeg is: in die voorlopige aksie het die eiser 'n bevel tot herstel van huweliksregte gevra waarop die hof 'n bevel *nisi* uitgereik het wat die verweerder beveel het om teen 'n bepaalde datum huweliksregte te herstel. Indien hy dit nie teen die vasgestelde datum gedoen het nie, is die huwelik op die keerdatum van die bevel *nisi* deur die hof ontbind. (Hahlo 4e uitg 407–408). Artikel 14 van die Wet op Egskeiding 70 van 1979 het die hof se bevoegdheid om 'n bevel tot die herstel van huweliksregte uit te reik, herroep sodat geen sodanige bevel meer uitgereik kan word nie.

Domicile of a prohibited immigrant   **Domisilie van 'n verbode immigrant**

[12] SMITH V SMITH

1962 3 SA 930 (FC)

Domicile of a prohibited immigrant

The respondent sued her husband in the High Court of Southern Rhodesia (now Zim-

Domisilie van 'n verbode immigrant

Die respondent het haar man in die Hoërhof van Suid-Rhodesië (nou Zimbabwe) gedag-

babwe) for a declaration of nullity of their marriage. She alleged that the parties were domiciled in Southern Rhodesia which allegation was never disputed. The High Court issued the declaration of nullity and the husband appealed against the declaration. When the appeal came before the Federal Supreme Court the court *mero motu* (of its own accord) raised the issue of the parties' domicile. From the evidence it appeared that the husband's residence in Southern Rhodesia was unlawful. The court *a quo* was unaware of this fact. The Federal Court remitted the case to the High Court for further evidence and a finding on the matter of the parties' domicile. On further evidence the High Court found that the husband would have established a domicile in Southern Rhodesia had it not been for the fact that his residence there was illegal. The High Court declared that if it had been aware of the husband's illegal residence, it would have held that the husband could not have acquired a domicile in Southern Rhodesia. The appeal was resumed in the Federal Court. The appeal was allowed.

vaar om nietigverklaring van hulle huwelik. Sy het beweer dat die partye in Suid-Rhodesië gedomisilieer was, welke bewering nooit betwis is nie. Die Hoërhof het die huwelik nietig verklaar en die man het teen hierdie beslissing na die Federale Hooggeregshof geappelleer. Hierdie hof het die aangeleentheid van die gades se domisilie *mero motu* (uit eie beweging) geopper. Uit die getuienis het geblyk dat die man se verblyf in Suid-Rhodesië onwettig was. Die hof *a quo* was onbewus van hierdie feit. Die Federale Hooggeregshof het die saak na die Hoërhof terugverwys vir die aanhoor van verdere getuienis en 'n bevinding oor die partye se domisilie. Na die aanhoor van verdere getuienis het die Hoërhof bevind dat die man wel 'n domisilie in Suid-Rhodesië sou gevestig het as dit nie was vir die feit dat sy verblyf daar onwettig was nie. Die Hoërhof het verklaar dat indien dit van die man se onwettige verblyf bewus was, dit sou beslis het dat die man nie 'n domisilie in Suid-Rhodesië kon gevestig het nie. Die appèl is voortgesit in die Federale Hof. Die appèl was suksesvol.

BRIGGS ACJ: [932] There is no doubt that in England mere liability to be deported as an alien does not make it impossible to acquire a domicile of choice ... Our law is to the same effect. In *Joosub v Salaam*, 1940 TPD 177, the point directly in issue was not domicile, but whether the respondent was an *incola*. He had no right to remain permanently in the Union, but it seemed probable that [933] he would later obtain that right. It was held that he should be regarded as an *incola*. GREENBERG JP said, at p.180,

"Thus where a statute (or the common law for that matter) makes it unlawful for a person to live in a country, his residence in that country even though he intends to reside there permanently, does not create a domicile there. (*Hassen Mia v Immigrants' Appeal Board*, 1915 NPD 620; *Essop v Commissioner of Immigration*, 1932 AD 223). And if the particular requisite of domicile which is affected by this consideration is also a requisite in the case of an *incola*, then the illegality of residence may be equally relevant. But I do not think that this disqualification applies to a person who lawfully enters a country but who by reason of his being an alien may be deported either if he commits a crime or merely because for reasons of policy his presence is deemed undesirable." ...

The *dictum* of GREENBERG JP is not a governing authority, but it must carry great weight. He proceeds to refer ... to the common law right of a sovereign power to expel any alien, and concludes that the mere possibility of expulsion cannot preclude the existence of an *animus manendi* sufficient to bring into being either domicile or the status of *incola* ...

There is also a class of cases, which similarly require to be distinguished, where the illegality of entry or residence has been expressly or impliedly condoned by the authorities ...

In such a case there is no continuing illegality at the time when domicile comes into question. *Van Rensburg v Ballinger*, 1950 (4) SA 427 (T), falls in the same category... "Temporary residence" on certain conditions was permitted by the authorities, and after 22 years of such residence it was held that common-law domicile was established...

The Court referred to the difference between entry as a final act and residence as a continuing one. It was then said that the case was "directly covered" by *Joosub v Salaam*, *supra*, which the Court recognised as authoritative on the question of common law domicile, as well as on status of an *incola*. The Court also distinguished cases such as *Ex parte Donelly*, 1915 WLD 30, and *Ex parte MacLeod*, 1946 CPD 312, where a domicile of choice has been acquired, but was held to be subsequently extinguished by actual expulsion and a lawful order forbidding return...

In [934] *MacLeod's* case the Court quoted with approval an article in the 1934 *South African Law Journal* by Mr Walter Pollak, QC. I quote at somewhat greater length (pp. 19–20)

> "A difficult question arises when a domicile of choice in the Union or in one of its Provinces is alleged. As a result of legislation the entry into and the residence in the Union of certain classes of persons is prohibited. A person falling within a prohibited class may, however, have succeeded in evading the vigilance of the immigration officials and may in fact be residing in the Union with the *animus manendi*. Is such person domiciled in the Union? The question has several times been raised in connection with domicile under the Immigration Acts, and the answer has always been in the negative. Apart from domicile under the Immigration Acts the question has apparently only been raised in *Abelheim v Abelheim* [1918 SR 85], where the entry of the husband into Southern Rhodesia was contrary to the Immigration Act, but RUSSELL, J, held that he had nevertheless acquired a domicile there. It is submitted that the correct view is that which is expressed in the immigration cases, and that a person cannot acquire a domicile of choice in the Union in the teeth of the law. A similar question arises when a person who has acquired a domicile of choice in the Union is deported. Can such person retain such domicile by showing that he intends to return to the Union, even though his return would be illegal? It is submitted that he does not retain such domicile. To put it briefly, when a domicile of choice in the Union or in one of its Provinces is alleged, the residence must be lawful and the *animus manendi* or the *animus revertendi* must be capable of being carried into effect without transgressing the law."

The learned author's interpretation of *Abelheim's* case differs from mine, but he supports my view that on his interpretation the case must have been wrongly decided...

There is a third category of cases which must shortly be distinguished, but which may be of importance by way of analogy. Some persons by the nature of their employment are not free to choose their place of residence. Serving soldiers and sailors and prisoners are examples. There are many decisions and some conflict on the question whether such persons can acquire a domicile of choice. These cases depend on a physical and legal compulsion to proceed to and live in a certain place and to leave it if ordered. I consider the case of highest authority on this question to be *McMillan v McMillan*, 1943 TPD 345, and believe the correct view to be that in such a case the necessary *animus manendi* coupled with "residence as a free agent" cannot ordinarily be shown, though in special cases the facts may establish a domicile of choice. The question in every case depends on the facts...

[BRIGGS ACJ then referred to some authorities and proceeded:]

[935] The learned Judge [in the court *a quo*], in his report on the remitted proceedings said,

"In the absence of clear authority the matter falls to be decided by the application of fundamental principles. It is a fundamental principle of our law that legal rights may not be acquired by unlawful means. Although the acquisition of a domicile of choice is not normally regarded as the acquisition of a privilege conferring rights and benefits under the law it does in my view have this effect. The acquisition confers among other rights the right now under consideration – the right to sue in this Court. Such a right can only be acquired by lawful means." . . .

[936] I think the learned Judge's reasoning is entirely correct, and I would respectfully adopt it . . .

My conclusion is that it is not possible under our law for a person *sui juris* to acquire a domicile of choice in this country if his initial entry and his residence at all times thereafter have both always been unlawful in terms of the Immigration Act, 1954. The condonation cases may appear to provide an exception to this principle, but on the view I take they do not. Nor do the precarious residence or service cases. I think such authority as is in point supports my view; but, if there were none, I should unhesitatingly express the same opinion. I should formulate the proposition in this way. Acquisition of a domicile of choice requires both residence and *animus manendi*. Not every kind of *de facto* residence will suffice. It must usually be residence of one's free will or, at least, if it is not, the residence can be of no value as evidence of an *animus manendi*. The *animus manendi* must be both genuine and honest. An intention to persist indefinitely in a course of unlawful conduct may be genuine: but it cannot be honest. Fears that the worst may happen do not necessarily preclude a sufficient *animus*. But knowledge that one is residing only in defiance of the law, and will so continue indefinitely, makes it impossible to have an *animus manendi* of the requisite quality. I think also that the matter may properly be put in another way. The *animus manendi*, though it does not require an absolute intention to reside permanently, must at least be an unconditional intention to reside for an indefinite period. It would not be enough if a chronic invalid were to come to this country and say, "I will settle here if the climate suits my health", if he died a few days later. There would at least have to be a trial period, after which the unconditional intention might come into existence. In this case the intention of the appellant, putting it at the highest, can only have been, "I will stay in Rhodesia if I can escape the attention of the authorities, whose statutory duty is to deport me, and who will at once do so if they learn the true facts about me." I think a conditional or provisional intention of this kind cannot in law amount to the *animus manendi* necessary to establish a domicile of choice. If these propositions have not yet been held to be part of our law, they should, I think, be so held now.

[937] I would allow the appeal and order that the judgment of nullity be set aside for want of jurisdiction . . .

QUÈNET FJ and BEADLE CJ concurred.

Note

This case established that an illegal immigrant cannot acquire a domicile of choice in the country he entered illegally. He cannot acquire a domicile of choice even if he intends to settle permanently at a specific place, since the residence relied on for the acquisition of a domicile of choice must be lawful.

In accordance with the same principle a person who has been deported cannot retain his domicile

Aantekening

Uit hierdie saak is dit duidelik dat 'n onwettige immigrant nie 'n domisilie van keuse kan vestig in die land wat hy onwettig binnegekom het nie. Die verblyf waarop vir die verwerwing van 'n domisilie van keuse gesteun word, moet wettige verblyf wees. Gevolglik kan sodanige persoon nie 'n domisilie van keuse vestig nie selfs al het hy die bedoeling om hom permanent op die bepaalde plek te vestig.

of choice in the country from which he has been deported either, because any *animus revertendi* which he might have will be unlawful and will therefore be of no legal effect (*Ex parte MacLeod* 1946 CPD 312; *Drakensbergpers Bpk v Sharpe* 1963 4 SA 615 (N)). Only when the deported person's return is no longer illegal, that is when he is allowed to return to South Africa, can he re-establish a domicile of choice in this country because only then would he be able to have lawful residence in the country (*Ex parte MacLeod*).

However, where the authorities have permitted a prohibited immigrant to stay in the country, his residence in the country is lawful and accordingly he can acquire a domicile of choice – *Van Rensburg v Ballinger* 1950 4 SA 427 (T). In *Van Rensburg's* case the defendant was a prohibited immigrant who arrived in South Africa in 1928 and was granted a temporary residence permit. His residence permit was extended by the Minister of the Interior (now the Minister of Home Affairs) for an unspecified period of time. The minister informed him that he could stay permanently if his behaviour was satisfactory. After that the defendant resided in South Africa continuously for approximately twenty-two years. In holding that the defendant had acquired a domicile of choice in South Africa the court stated:

> "In the present case, as in the alien cases, residence persists and is lawful, the only difficulty is the possibility of the right of termination and, as the alien cases show, domicile is lost only when the higher authority has actually invoked that right of termination. The individual is, in fact, to quote the phrase used, the master of his own destiny. He can decide to have his home in the particular place and he can carry that decision into effect ...

> I have come to the conclusion on general principles that the power of a higher authority to terminate a person's residence in a particular area cannot *per se* affect the question whether that person intended to make his permanent abode there. If the power of termination is actually exercised, then naturally with the disappearance of physical residence the domicile thus acquired is brought to an end. Until such termination the only effect of the possibility of that power of deportation being exercised by a higher authority is that the person may (I do not say he must) be taken to realise the

Op grond van dieselfde beginsel kan 'n gedeporteerde persoon ook nie sy domisilie van keuse behou in die land waaruit hy gedeporteer word nie aangesien enige *animus revertendi* wat hy mag hê ongeldig sal wees, en gevolglik geen regskrag sal hê nie (*Ex parte MacLeod* 1946 KPA 312; *Drakensbergpers Bpk v Sharpe* 1963 4 SA 615 (N)). Slegs wanneer die gedeporteerde persoon se terugkeer nie meer onwettig is nie, dit wil sê wanneer hy toegelaat word om na Suid-Afrika terug te keer, kan hy 'n domisilie van keuse in hierdie land vestig aangesien hy eers dan wettige verblyf in die land kan hê (*Ex parte MacLeod*).

Waar die owerhede egter 'n verbode immigrant toegelaat het om in die land te bly, is sy verblyf wettig en kan hy gevolglik 'n domisilie van keuse verwerf – *Van Rensburg v Ballinger* 1950 4 SA 427 (T). In die *Van Rensburg*-saak was die verweerder 'n verbode immigrant wat in 1928 in Suid-Afrika aangekom het en aan wie 'n tydelike verblyfpermit uitgereik is. Sy verblyfpermit is vir 'n onbepaalde tydperk deur die Minister van Binnelandse Sake verleng. Die minister het hom in kennis gestel dat hy permanent in Suid-Afrika kon bly indien sy gedrag bevredigend was. Daarna het die verweerder vir omtrent twee en twintig jaar ononderbroke in Suid-Afrika gebly. In sy beslissing dat die verweerder wel 'n domisilie van keuse in Suid-Afrika verwerf het, het die hof verklaar:

> "In the present case, as in the alien cases, residence persists and is lawful, the only difficulty is the possibility of the right of termination and, as the alien cases show, domicile is lost only when the higher authority has actually invoked that right of termination. The individual is, in fact, to quote the phrase used, the master of his own destiny. He can decide to have his home in the particular place and he can carry that decision into effect ...

> I have come to the conclusion on general principles that the power of a higher authority to terminate a person's residence in a particular area cannot *per se* affect the question whether that person intended to make his permanent abode there. If the power of termination is actually exercised, then naturally with the disappearance of physical residence the domicile thus acquired is brought to an end. Until such termination the only effect of the possibility of that power of deportation being exercised

precarious character of his residence and consequently may not be held to have formed the intention of making his permanent home in such area..." (441).

The common-law principle that for a domicile of choice to be established, residence at the particular place must be lawful, was confirmed by section 1(2) of the Domicile Act 3 of 1992.

In respect of the remarks made in *Smith v Smith* (at 937) about the acquisition of a domicile of choice by a chronic invalid, the case of *GRE Insurance Ltd v Chisnall* 1982 1 SA 387 (Z) can be cited. In *Chisnall*'s case a person who was confined to a wheelchair as a result of a motor vehicle accident left Zimbabwe to receive medical treatment in the United States of America. When he left Zimbabwe he applied for emigrant status so that he could receive his pension abroad and seek employment in the United States to pay for his medical treatment. In letters to his attorney however, he made it clear that he wished eventually to return to Zimbabwe. When he had been living in the United States for only a few months a dispute arose, *inter alia* about where he was domiciled at that time. The court held that the injured person did not establish a domicile of choice in the United States but retained his domicile in Zimbabwe. One of the reasons advanced by the court for its decision was that the purpose of the injured person's stay in the United States was medical treatment and the improvement of his medical condition. The conclusion one reaches from this case and the remarks in *Smith* in this regard is that a person cannot establish a domicile of choice at a particular place if the reason for his being there is merely medical treatment or the improvement of his health.

See also the note on *Eilon v Eilon* [10] about jurisdiction in a divorce action.

by a higher authority is that the person may (I do not say he must) be taken to realise the precarious character of his residence and consequently may not be held to have formed the intention of making his permanent home in such area..." (441).

Die gemeenregtelike beginsel dat 'n domisilie van keuse nie gevestig kan word tensy die persoon se verblyf op die bepaalde plek wettig is nie, is deur artikel 1(2) van die Wet op Domisilie 3 van 1992 bevestig.

In verband met die opmerkings wat in *Smith v Smith* (937) gemaak is oor die verkryging van 'n domisilie van keuse deur 'n chroniese invalide kan ook gelet word op *GRE Insurance Ltd v Chisnall* 1982 1 SA 387 (Z). In *Chisnall* se saak het 'n persoon wat as gevolg van 'n motorongeluk aan 'n rolstoel gekluister was, Zimbabwe verlaat om mediese behandeling in die Verenigde State van Amerika te ondergaan. Toe hy Zimbabwe verlaat het, het hy aansoek gedoen om emigrasiestatus sodat hy sy pensioen in die buiteland kon ontvang en in die Verenigde State werk kon soek om vir sy mediese behandeling te betaal. In briewe aan sy prokureur het hy dit egter duidelik gemaak dat hy later weer na Zimbabwe wou terugkeer. Nadat hy 'n paar maande in die Verenigde State gewoon het, het 'n dispuut ontstaan oor, onder andere, die vraag waar hy toe gedomisilieer was. Die hof het beslis dat die beseerde persoon nie 'n domisilie van keuse in die Verenigde State gevestig het nie maar sy domisilie in Zimbabwe behou het. Een van die redes wat die hof vir sy beslissing aangevoer het, was dat die doel van die beseerde persoon se verblyf in die Verenigde State was om mediese behandeling te ondergaan en sy gesondheidstoestand te verbeter. Die gevolgtrekking wat 'n mens uit hierdie saak en uit die opmerkings in hierdie verband in *Smith* kan maak, is dat 'n persoon nie 'n domisilie van keuse op 'n bepaalde plek kan vestig indien die rede vir sy verblyf daar bloot die behandeling of verbetering van sy gesondheidstoestand is nie.

Sien ook die aantekening by *Eilon v Eilon* [10] oor jurisdiksie in 'n egskeidingsgeding.

Extra-marital children

Proof of paternity
Parental authority
Legitimation of extra-marital children

Buite-egtelike kinders

Bewys van vaderskap
Ouerlike gesag
Wettiging van buite-egtelike kinders

Proof of paternity   **Bewys van vaderskap**

[13] VAN LUTTERVELD V ENGELS

1959 2 SA 699 (A)

Rebuttal of the presumption *pater est quem nuptiae demonstrant*

Weerlegging van die vermoede *pater est quem nuptiae demonstrant*

The respondent sued the appellant for lying-in expenses and maintenance for a child which had been born to her on 27 June 1956 and of which she alleged the appellant to be the father. The respondent was married to someone else when she met the appellant, but this marriage was unhappy from the start as her husband had a very low sex drive, while she wished to have a child of her own. The respondent met the appellant in March 1955. They fell in love and since April or May 1955 they had had sexual intercourse regularly until 1 February 1956. According to medical evidence the child was conceived on or about 21 October 1955 whereas the respondent and her husband had completely stopped having sexual intercourse with each other in February 1955. The respondent's husband confirmed this evidence although he thought that the last time he had sexual intercourse with his wife was in March or April 1955. He also admitted that his sex drive was low. The respondent and her husband were divorced on 1 May 1956 as a result of her adultery with the appellant. The appellant admitted that he had sexual intercourse with the respondent only once and that he had then practised *coitus interruptus*. The respondent's application was successful in the magistrate's court and an appeal against this decision to the Transvaal Provincial Division was turned down. An appeal against this decision to the Appellate Division was also unsuccessful.

Die respondent het die appellant gedagvaar vir die betaling van kraamkoste en onderhoud vir 'n kind aan wie sy op 27 Junie 1956 geboorte geskenk het en van wie sy beweer het dat die appellant die vader was. Die respondent was met iemand anders getroud toe sy die appellant ontmoet het, maar hierdie huwelik was van die begin af ongelukkig aangesien haar man nie 'n baie sterk seksdrang gehad het nie, terwyl sy baie graag 'n kind van haar eie wou hê. Die respondent het die appellant in Maart 1955 ontmoet. Hulle het op mekaar verlief geraak en vanaf April of Mei 1955 tot 1 Februarie 1956 gereeld seksueel met mekaar verkeer. Volgens mediese getuienis is die kind om en by 21 Oktober 1955 verwek. Op hierdie stadium het seksuele omgang tussen die respondent en haar man reeds heeltemal opgehou. Die laaste keer wat hulle seksueel met mekaar verkeer het, was in Februarie 1955. Die respondent se man het hierdie getuienis bevestig alhoewel hy van mening was dat seksuele omgang tussen hulle die laaste keer in Maart of April 1955 plaasgevind het. Hy het ook erken dat sy seksdrang nie baie sterk was nie. Die respondent en haar man is op 1 Mei 1956 as gevolg van haar owerspel met die appellant geskei. Die appellant het erken dat hy een keer seksueel met die respondent verkeer het en dat hy toe *coitus interruptus* toegepas het. Die respondent se aansoek het in die landdroshof geslaag en 'n appèl teen hierdie beslissing na die Transvaalse Provinsiale Afdeling het misluk. 'n Appèl teen hierdie beslissing na die Appèlafdeling was ook onsuksesvol.

VAN BLERK AR: [702] Die enigste grond waarop die appèl steun is dat die regsvermoede, *pater est quem nuptiae demonstrant*, wat die partye tereg toegee hier van toepassing is, nie weerlê is nie. Kragtens art. 101 (3) van die Algemene Regswysigingswet, 1935 [sien nou artikel 3 van die Wet op Bewysleer in Siviele Sake 25 van 1965], kan hierdie presumpsie weerlê word deur getuienis van respondent en haar eggenoot dat hul geen geslagsverkeer met mekaar gehad het nie gedurende die tydperk wat die kind verwek is.

Die verskil van mening wat daar blykens sekere gewysdes bestaan het oor watter standaard van bewys van toepassing is vir die weerlegging van die regsvermoede is uit die weg geruim deur 'n aantal beslissings in hierdie Hof, waarvolgens dit duidelik gestel is dat in alle siviele sake die bewyslas deur 'n oorwig van waarskynlikhede gekwyt kan word . . .

Maar hierdie reël moet egter toegepas word met inagneming van die algemene on-waarskynlikheid van die voorval wat beweer word . . . Die redelike gemoed word, by-voorbeeld, nie lig oortuig dat iemand hom aan onkuisheid of oneerlike gedrag besondig nie want daarin is 'n algemene onwaarskynlikheid geleë. In die onderhawige geval word oorspel beweer, maar dit word deur die betrokke partye erken, desondanks egter bly die regsvermoede nog staan (*Voet,* 1.6.8) en kan dit met die oog op die getuienis wat in hierdie saak aangevoer is slegs weerlê word deur bewys van geslagsonthouding; 'n aangeleentheid waarvan uit die aard van die saak net respondent en haar eggenoot direk kan getuig, soos hulle ook gedoen het. Al het appellant erken dat hy die vader is, dan is dit nog geen bewys van sy vaderskap nie, want so 'n erkenning kan slegs gebaseer wees op 'n vermoede aan sy kant omdat hyself geen sekerheid daaromtrent kon gehad het nie.

[703] 'n Regsvermoede is, soos APPÈLREGTER KOTZÉ sê in *Kunz v Swart,* 1924 AD 618 op bl. 681, gegrond op die waarskynlikhede en die lewenservaring. Dit is seker teen die instelling van die natuur, en daarom nie waarskynlik nie, dat 'n jong egpaar van die ouderdomme van respondent en haar eggenoot in die afwesigheid van fisiese beletsels vir nege maande lank saam in een slaapkamer sal slaap sonder om uiting te gee aan hul geslagsdrange. Volgens die getuienis van respondent en haar eggenoot was die sekslewe klaarblyklik nie normaal nie en as hul getuienis teen dié agtergrond beskou word, dan val dit makliker te begryp dat daar wel onthouding was, veral as respondent se liefdes-verhouding met appellant in gedagte gehou word. Respondent se eggenoot was wat homself betref tevrede met die toestand van onthouding. Sy gebrek aan seksdrang verklaar dit. Respondent weer het nie meer behoefte gehad om haar tot haar man te wend nie want sy het geluk en bevrediging gevind in haar verhouding en intieme lewe met appellant. Laasgenoemde, wat klaarblyklik 'n ongeloofwaardige getuie was, se verklaring, dat hy slegs op een geleentheid met respondent geslagsverkeer gehad het, is verwerp en respondent is geglo dat sy gedurende die tydperk van onthouding van geslagsverkeer met haar man gereeld geslagtelike omgang met appellant gehad het.

Dit was seker nie maklik vir respondent se man om sy swak seksdrang te kom bely nie, en dit is nouliks denkbaar dat reggeaarde ouers sy eie kind sal bastardiseer. Dit is moeilik om te begryp wat die respondent en haar man sou kon beweeg het, en wat hul daarby kon voor gehad het, om valselik te getuig. Sy wou graag 'n kind van haar eie gehad het en hul was finansieel gerieflik daaraan toe. Om aan appellant, nog 'n afhanklike min-derjarige, die vaderskap op te sweer kon niks by gehaal word nie.

As die getuienis van respondent en haar eggenoot in die lig van hierdie omstandighede beskou word, dan, in afwesigheid van ander getuienis wat daaraan afding, val dit nie moeilik om, soos die landdros gedoen het, aan te neem dat hul die waarheid praat nie.

[704] Daar is geen rede nie om in te gryp teen die landdros se benadering van die saak en sy beoordeling van die getuienis. Die aanvaarding van die getuienis van respondent en haar eggenoot was geregverdig en onder die omstandighede van die geval was daar voldoende bewys aangevoer om die regsvermoede te weerlê.

Die appèl word van die hand gewys . . .

STEYN AR; DE BEER AR; HALL Wn AR en SMIT Wn AR het saamgestem.

Note

It is clear from this case that it is not necessary for the husband to prove that he could not have had sexual intercourse with his wife during the time that conception could have taken place, for example because he was abroad. It is sufficient if he shows on a balance of probabilities that he in fact did not have intercourse with his wife, and the onus on him is no heavier than in any other civil case (*R v Isaacs* 1954 1 SA 266 (N); Boberg 324 fn 18). In *Van Lutterveld's* case husband and wife slept in the same room during the relevant period and still the presumption was found to be rebutted.

Aantekening

Dit is uit hierdie saak duidelik dat die man nie hoef te bewys dat hy nie geslagsverkeer met sy vrou kon gehad het op die tydstip toe die kind verwek kon gewees het nie, byvoorbeeld omdat hy in die buiteland was. Dit is voldoende as hy op 'n oorwig van waarskynlikheid bewys dat hy inderdaad nie seksueel met sy vrou verkeer het nie, en die bewyslas op hom is nie swaarder as in enige ander siviele geding nie (*R v Isaacs* 1954 1 SA 266 (N); Boberg 324 vn 18). In *Van Lutterveld* se saak het die man en vrou op die betrokke tydstip in dieselfde kamer geslaap en nogtans is bevind dat die vermoede weerlê is.

[14] MAYER V WILLIAMS

1981 3 SA 348 (A)

Corroboration of the mother's evidence in paternity cases

The appellant was the complainant at an enquiry in terms of section 5 of the Maintenance Act 23 of 1963. She alleged that the respondent was the father of her child, which he denied. The magistrate found that he was the father and accordingly he was ordered to pay maintenance for the child. The respondent appealed against this decision to the Cape Provincial Division where the magistrate's decision was overruled and the maintenance order set aside. The appellant appealed against this decision to the Appellate Division. The appeal was successful.

Stawing van die moeder se getuienis in vaderskapsake

Die appellant was die klaagster in 'n ondersoek ingevolge artikel 5 van die Wet op Onderhoud 23 van 1963. Sy het beweer dat die respondent die vader van haar kind was maar hy het dit ontken. Die landdros het bevind dat hy wel die vader was en hy is gevolglik gelas om onderhoud vir die kind te betaal. Die respondent het teen hierdie beslissing na die Kaapse Provinsiale Afdeling geappelleer waar die landdros se bevinding omvergewerp is en die onderhoudsbevel tersyde gestel is. Die appellant het teen hierdie beslissing na die Appèlhof geappelleer. Die appèl was suksesvol.

TRENGOVE JA: [351] [I]t was incumbent upon the appellant to prove on a balance of probabilities that the respondent was the father. The question which we now have to consider is whether the magistrate erred in finding that this *onus* had been satisfactorily discharged.

Before dealing with the evidence, and the magistrate's evaluation thereof, it is necessary to refer to the general approach of our Courts to the question of the sufficiency of evidence in a case of this nature. Section 16 of the Civil Proceedings Evidence Act 25 of 1965 provides that "judgment may be given in any civil proceedings on the evidence of any single competent and credible witness".

On the face of it, this section appears to deal exhaustively with the sufficiency of evidence in all civil cases. However, our Courts have, for many years, said that in seduction and paternity cases a woman's testimony against a man's requires corroboration. No matter how cogent the woman's evidence may be, corroboration was necessary as a matter of law. In *Wiehman v Simon NO* 1938 AD 447 at 450 this Court approved of the following statement of STRATFORD J in *Mackay v Ballot* 1921 TPD 430 at 432: "In paternity cases *the law* requires that the mother's story cannot prevail against the defendant's denial unless it is corroborated. By corroboration I understand that some evidence must be given in addition to the woman's which *in some degree,* is consistent with her story and inconsistent with the innocence of the defendant."

(My italicising of the words "the law".) Although this *dictum* has been followed and applied in many paternity cases ever since, doubts have, in more recent years, been raised as to whether it is a correct statement of our law . . .

In my view the time has arrived to dispense with the rule as formulated in *Mackay v Ballot (supra).* I have come to this conclusion for the following reasons:

(a) the rule is based on a misunderstanding of Roman-Dutch procedure in actions of this nature (see *Davel v Swanepoel* [1954 1 SA 383 (A) at 388]; FP van den Heever *Breach of Promise and Seduction in SA Law* at 51–59; Schmidt *Bewysreg* at 48);

(b) it seems to me to be an anomaly that
"in any field of investigation a greater certainty of proof may be required where civil rights are in issue than when a person is being tried criminally".
(See *R v W* [1949 3 SA 772 (A)] at 779–780);

(c) the rule as formulated is, in my view, inappropriate in our modern system of civil trial procedure. (See FP van den Heever (*op cit* at 59); Hoffmann *SA Law of Evidence* 2nd ed at 410); and

(d) the rule appears to have been excluded by the provisions of s 16 of Act 25 of 1965.

I am of the opinion, therefore, that courts should no longer, as a matter of law, insist upon corroboration of the evidence of complainants in paternity or seduction cases.

[352] There can, nevertheless, be no doubt whatever that, in a case of this nature, there is always a need for special caution in scrutinising and weighing the evidence of the complainant (see *R v J* 1966 (1) SA 88 (SRA) at 90). Experience has shown that it is essential for the purpose of doing justice between the parties in this class of case – where allegations of paternity are so easily made and with such difficulty rebutted, and where there is often a strong temptation either to conceal the identity of the real father or to impose liability upon the person who is best able to bear it – that the evidence of the complainant should be approached with caution. As a rule of practice the trial court should, therefore, always warn itself of the inherent danger of acting upon the testimony of the complainant in a paternity case.

In *S v Snyman* 1968 (2) SA 582 (A) at 585 this Court refers to the cautionary rule of practice which has been evolved to assist the courts in sexual cases in criminal proceedings, and which requires:

"(a) the recognition by the court of the inherent danger aforesaid (ie of relying upon the testimony of a complainant in a sexual case); and

(b) the existence of some safeguard reducing the risk of wrong conviction, such as corroboration of the complainant in a respect implicating the accused, or the absence of gainsaying evidence from him, or his mendacity as a witness."

In my view there is no reason why the rule as formulated above should not also be applied

– *mutatis mutandis* – in respect of the evidence of complainants in paternity disputes in civil proceedings . . .

[TRENGOVE JA analysed the evidence and proceeded:]

To conclude. This is a not clear-cut case. However, after having carefully considered all the evidence, and the arguments advanced on behalf of the respondent, I am not persuaded that the magistrate erred in finding that the appellant had established, on a balance of probabilities, that the respondent was the father of her child.

[353] The appeal is, accordingly, upheld . . .

JANSEN JA; KOTZÉ JA; JOUBERT JA and HOLMES AJA concurred.

Note

On this case see also Van der Vyver and Joubert (217). These authors stress the importance of the application of the cautionary rule. They point out that a woman may have various motives for naming an innocent man as the father of her child, such as revenge for an injustice done to her, love for the man or because of his wealth or status. They mention further that it can be very difficult to establish the truth in the cross-examination of the woman.

It is suggested that more use should be made of blood tests in this regard. See further *Seetal v Pravitha* [15]; *M v R* [16]; *S v L* [17]; Skeen 1981 *SALJ* 459; Noble 1981 *THRHR* 441; Van der Merwe 1981 *TSAR* 287.

Aantekening

Sien oor hierdie saak ook Van der Vyver en Joubert (217). Hierdie skrywers beklemtoon die belangrikheid van die toepassing van die versigtigheidsreël. Hulle wys daarop dat 'n vrou verskeie motiewe mag hê om 'n onskuldige man as die vader van haar kind aan te wys, byvoorbeeld uit wraak vir 'n onreg wat haar aangedoen is, weens liefde vir die man, of vanweë die man se rykdom of status. Hulle meld ook dat dit baie moeilik kan wees om die waarheid in kruisondervraging van die vrou vas te stel.

Daar word voorgestel dat in hierdie verband meer van bloedtoetse gebruik gemaak moet word. Sien verder *Seetal v Pravitha* [15]; *M v R* [16]; *S v L* [17]; Skeen 1981 *SALJ* 459; Noble 1981 *THRHR* 441; Van der Merwe 1981 *TSAR* 287.

[15]   SEETAL V PRAVITHA

1983 3 SA 827 (D)

The use of blood tests where paternity is disputed

The applicant was the husband of the first respondent. The second respondent was the *curator ad litem* who was appointed to represent the child. The applicant sued the first respondent for divorce on the ground of her alleged adultery. This action was awaiting trial. The first respondent had a son aged four years who was conceived after the first respondent had married the applicant and while they were living as husband and wife. Never-

Die gebruik van bloedtoetse waar vaderskap betwis word

Die applikant was die eerste respondent se man. Die tweede respondent was die *curator ad litem* wat aangestel is om die kind te verteenwoordig. Die applikant het die eerste respondent om 'n egskeiding gedagvaar op grond van haar beweerde owerspel. Hierdie geding was nog hangende. Die eerste respondent het 'n seun van vier jaar gehad wat verwek is nadat die respondent met die applikant getroud is en terwyl hulle as man en

theless, the applicant was convinced that someone else was the father of the child although he had no idea of the identity of that person. Therefore, the only reason for the allegation of adultery was his conviction that someone else was the father. For the same reason he sought an additional order declaring the child illegitimate. The applicant's denial of paternity was based only on the child's physical features. These, he contended, were so unlike his own that the child could not possibly have been his offspring. In order to obtain more information the applicant wanted samples taken of his own, the first respondent's and the child's blood for tests in order to reveal whether he could or could not be the child's father. The result would then be available for use at the trial of the divorce action. The respondent refused to let any sample of blood be taken either from herself or from the child. The reasons for her refusal were at this stage not known to the court. The application was refused.

vrou saamgewoon het. Die applikant was nietemin daarvan oortuig dat iemand anders die kind se vader was alhoewel hy nie 'n benul gehad het van wie die persoon was nie. Sy oortuiging dat iemand anders die kind se vader was, het egter verklaar waarom hy sy vrou van owerspel beskuldig het aangesien geen ander redes daarvoor aangevoer is nie. Dit het ook die verdere bevel wat hy aangevra het verduidelik, naamlik dat die kind buite-egtelik verklaar moet word. Die applikant se ontkenning van vaderskap het alleenlik op die kind se voorkoms berus. Hy het beweer dat die kind so min na hom gelyk het dat hy net nie van hom kon afstam nie. Ten einde meer inligting te bekom, wou hy hê dat bloedmonsters van hom, die eerste respondent en die kind getoets moes word ten einde aan te toon of hy die kind se vader kon wees al dan nie. Die resultaat sou dan in die egskeidingsgeding gebruik kon word. Die respondent het geweier om enige bloedmonster van haar of van die kind te laat neem. Die redes vir haar weiering was op hierdie stadium nie aan die hof bekend nie. Die aansoek is van die hand gewys.

DIDCOTT J: [830] The question which concerns me . . . is whether the Court can, and if so whether it should, compel the first respondent to co-operate with the applicant so that the blood test which he has in mind may be performed . . .

Unlike a number of places, South Africa has no legislation which governs the question. Section 37 of the Criminal Procedure Act 51 of 1977 allows samples of blood to be collected from persons facing criminal charges and from others whose condition is thought relevant to such, and that is often done to test intoxication, for instance, most familiarly when drivers of motor vehicles are suspected of it. There is no statutory counterpart, however, in civil proceedings . . .

[831] The applicant contended . . . that I had the inherent power to grant him the order he sought . . .

The Supreme Court's inherent power to regulate its own procedure and that to be followed by the litigants appearing before it was invoked by Mr *Yacoob* [for the applicant]. That the power exists is plain. It has been recognised for a long time . . .

[833] It was . . . not enough for Mr *Yacoob* to point to the bearing which evidence of a blood test might very well have on the result of the impending trial, and to the applicant's inability to obtain the evidence unless the Court made the test possible by ordering the required samples of blood to be provided. While these features of the case were essential to his argument, while he could not have reached first base without them, they are not in themselves decisive, but must be measured against any objections there are to requisitions of blood in cases like this . . .

[DIDCOTT J referred to *E v E* 1940 TPD 333 where the application to have a child subjected to a blood test was refused. He then gave a detailed review of cases decided on this matter in Scotland, Canada, Australia, the United States of America and England and proceeded:]

[860] A South African Court can thus find a mass of foreign teaching by which to be guided, and perhaps perplexed. What line should it take?

Blood tests on adults will be considered first.

The objection that a blood test is intrinsically likelier in many cases to yield evidence which assists the other side than it is to produce a result helpful to the person tested is not one that appeals to me greatly. As has been pointed out, the discovery of documents or obedience to a subpoena *duces tecum* can have the selfsame consequence. Nor does the enforcement of an order for a test seem a problem significantly more intractable or delicate, when the person who must comply remains stubborn, than it is to enforce in such circumstances a variety of orders which are commonplace. These, I believe, are inadequate answers to the contention that, since tests may well show for certain where the truth lies, the interests of justice call for them.

That such is an attractive argument in favour of compulsory blood tests can scarcely be denied. Yet it loses some of its allure when it in turn is examined closely. The blemishes of oversimplification and exaggeration are then noticeable.

To say without qualification that the law demands the discovery of the truth is not, I venture to suggest, to tell the truth about the law. A truer statement would be that, concerned as it often is with means no less than ends, the law requires the truth to be ascertained in ways it allows. In criminal trials here, to give but one instance, it does not permit evidence to be led of confessions obtained by force or made to policemen of junior rank. Such confessions happen sometimes to be [861] true. But that does not matter. The Court will not hear them, and it would not even if their truth could in some manner be demonstrated. The result, when there is no other evidence, may be the acquittal of a guilty man, of one who is a veritable menace to society. Public policy, however, stands firmly between the Court and the search for the truth, preventing the Court from learning that. It insists that the truth shall not emerge in certain ways and, if they are the only ways which can be found, that the truth shall not emerge at all.

To take a few drops of blood from someone against his will is not, to be sure, as serious a matter as beating a confession out of him. The two are not even comparable. The extraction of a blood sample is a minor procedure. It is done all the time for routine purposes. The discomfort it causes is negligible. So is the risk to health that is run. The rare case when there is reason to believe in an element of danger need not detain one. Judicial compulsion is then unthinkable.

Yet a blood test on somebody without his consent is unquestionably an invasion of his privacy. And the invasion is no less such because on just about every occasion the test is otherwise innocuous. This strikes me as the only objection to compulsory blood tests which has substance. It is, I feel, a very real one.

It must be admitted, on the other hand, that the privacy of the individual is not in law absolutely inviolable. Were subpoenas *duces tecum* and the discovery of documents innovations instead of practices to which we had grown accustomed, many lawyers would surely balk at the threat to privacy inherent in requisitions of personal correspondence and the like. Nor, to take another example, has the law ever protected the privacy of the confessional, of the psychiatrist's couch, of the physician's consulting room, against the disclosure in litigation of secrets told there. In all these instances the truth is pursued ruthlessly.

In the end the debate about compulsory blood tests amounts, as I see it, to a showdown between the two ideas, these two ideas which cannot satisfactorily be reconciled, the idea that the truth should be discovered whenever possible and the idea that personal privacy should be respected. Both are important. Neither, however, is sacrosanct. Each, as it happens, gets sacrificed, the first on some occasions, the second on others . . .

[862] I turn next to blood tests on children, a different matter altogether, I believe.

What makes the difference is the nature of the problem, which concerns not compulsion so much as consent. No longer is one dealing with an adult who might have consented to a blood test on himself but has not, and considering as a result whether the Court should compel him to be tested. The enquiry has now to do with a child incapable in the first place of either giving or withholding consent, with a consent which can be given or withheld only by another acting on his behalf. No issue of compulsion really arises in such a case. Should the person whose consent is required decline to furnish it, a Court determined to overrule him has no occasion to compel him to give it or the child to be tested without it. The Court simply exercises the power of an upper guardian, as we call it here, by supplying its own consent . . .

A South African Court, like an English one, can thus consent on a child's behalf to the removal from him of a blood sample which is wanted for diagnostic or therapeutic purposes. There is no reason, once that is the case, why it should not lay claim to the authority its English counterpart has to grant the requisite consent when the sample is required for forensic purposes instead. When I speak of a Court here, it goes without saying, I refer to the Supreme Court alone . . .

I consider it equally clear that, in order to investigate paternity, a South African Court can authorise a blood test on a child despite any [863] objection to one registered by the parent caring for and controlling the child, and that it can therefore overrule the objection . . .

The Court will not flinch in an appropriate case, after all, from reversing the refusal of the parent concerned to allow a test on the child which is diagnostic or therapeutic. In both situations, indeed whenever it acts as upper guardian, it will pay keen attention to parental attitudes and attach due weight to the reasons for such. These do not, however, bind it.

In this country, as it happens, it is difficult to see how the question whether a child's blood should be tested can ever arise in Court unless one or another adult having or claiming a say in the matter has objected to the proposal and the Court is approached to adjudicate upon the ensuing dispute, either by overruling the objection and sanctioning the test or by upholding the objection and issuing an interdict which prohibits a test. The explanation is that, once such is not the case and the adults are all of one mind, they will see to it themselves that the test is done. There is nothing to stop them. There is no occasion for any of them to come to Court, and nobody else to do so . . .

Having reached the conclusion that a South African Court handling a case like the present one can effectively consent on a child's behalf to a blood test on him, I come now to the important question of its touchstone for the decision whether or not to do so in a given instance . . .

Once the *rationale* for an order requiring a blood test on a child is [864] grasped, once it is accepted that what the Court does in essence when it grants the order is to consent to the test on the child's behalf, I do not see how the conclusion can be avoided . . . that it must act in the interests of the child and take account of nothing else. That is what happens when the Court consents on a child's behalf to the sale of his immovable property. Competing interests may well be involved in that situation, the private interests of those who wish to buy, perhaps even the public interests should some useful development be planned. The Court cares nothing for any of this. The child alone is its responsibility...

This boils down to the problem whether the interests of a child whose paternity has been questioned are best served by ascertaining it...

According to LORD DENNING MR [in *B v B and E* [1969] 3 All ER 1106 1108 BC], it is "nearly always" in a child's interests for the truth about his paternity to emerge. I beg to differ. I think the statement facile. One is talking of personal matters, not of contracts *uberrimae fidei*. To be told of certain things does some of us [865] no good. Not every patient is better off for learning that he has terminal cancer. Not every husband is better off for learning that his wife was once unfaithful. Nor does every child benefit from the discovery that his true father is not the one he has always supposed he had. The problem does not lend itself to generalisations. Its solution depends on the particular child, on his particular circumstances, on the particular facts of the litigation concerning his paternity...

I turn to the case before me. I am not satisfied that it would benefit the first respondent's child were I to allow a blood test on him. Indeed, I believe that it would not.

There are no great doubts about the child's paternity which need in his interests to be resolved, and the reasons for those which the applicant says he entertains could hardly be weaker. Whatever may be thought nowadays about the stigma of illegitimacy, a topic on which any confident assertion would be unwise in a heterogeneous society like ours with its variety of cultures and religions, it must amount to some handicap at least for the child to be declared a bastard. Were that to happen, what is more, the child would be left with no identifiable father. The applicant's attitude may tend to make him an unsatisfactory one, and it certainly will should he fail to prove yet persist in maintaining that the child is not his...

[866] Whether he likes it or not, however, what will be forthcoming still is money. His obligation to support the child financially will endure. The child would have no substitute to whom to turn, on the other hand, if such support were withdrawn because illegitimacy was established. That would be a hardship, and a substantial one...

The application is dismissed...

Note	**Aantekening**
See the note on *S v L* [17].	Sien die aantekening by *S v L* [17].

[16]   M v R

1989 1 SA 416 (O)

The use of blood tests where paternity is disputed	**Die gebruik van bloedtoetse waar vaderskap betwis word**
The applicant and the respondent met each other in July 1978 and from then onwards they had sexual intercourse on a regular basis. The respondent said she was a virgin when they met but the applicant denied this alle-	Die applikant en die respondent het mekaar in Julie 1978 ontmoet. Hulle het van toe af gereeld seksuele omgang met mekaar gehad. Die respondent het beweer dat sy 'n maagd was toe hulle ontmoet het maar die applikant

gation. He averred that the respondent had another boyfriend at the time, which she denied. In January 1979 she informed the applicant she was pregnant and the child, S, was born in April 1979. For eight years the applicant paid maintenance for the child. He was then informed by the respondent that she intended claiming an increased amount of maintenance from him. Subsequently, the applicant applied for an order compelling the respondent and the child to subject themselves to blood tests in order to attain certainty on whether he could or could not be the child's father. The application was opposed by the respondent. Three years after the child's birth the respondent had married R and the child accepted and loved R as his own father. The respondent and R were planning to tell the child during the coming year that the applicant was his father. The court felt that it was of crucial importance for the child's development and happiness that clarity as regards the applicant's paternity should be reached and granted the order.

het hierdie bewering ontken. Hy het aangevoer dat die respondent op daardie tydstip 'n ander kêrel gehad het, maar sy het dit ontken. In Januarie 1979 het sy die applikant meegedeel dat sy swanger was en die kind, S, is in April 1979 gebore. Die applikant het agt jaar lank onderhoud vir die kind betaal. Die respondent het hom toe in kennis gestel dat sy van voorneme was om 'n verhoogde bedrag onderhoud van hom te vra. Hierop het die applikant aansoek gedoen om 'n bevel om die respondent en die kind te verplig om hulle aan bloedtoetse te onderwerp ten einde sekerheid te verkry oor die vraag of hy die kind se vader kon wees al dan nie. Die respondent het die aansoek teengestaan. Drie jaar na die kind se geboorte het die respondent met ene R getrou en die kind het R as sy eie vader aanvaar en liefgehad. Die respondent en R was van plan om die kind in die komende jaar te vertel dat die applikant sy vader was. Die hof was van mening dat dit van die grootste belang vir die kind se ontwikkeling en geluk was dat duidelikheid oor die applikant se vaderskap verkry moes word en het die aansoek toegestaan.

KOTZE R: [420] Die Hooggeregshof is die oppervoog van alle minderjariges binne sy gebiedsgrense en is geregtig en verplig om in te gryp wanneer en slegs as sodanige ingreep in hul beste belang sal wees. In hierdie opsig wens hierdie Hof, met respek, saam te stem met die toeligting wat daar in hierdie verband in *Seetal v Pravitha and Another NO* 1983 (3) SA 827 (D) [15] aangetref word . . .

Die Hooggeregshof sal . . . ingryp en so 'n bevel uitvaardig [dws dat die kind aan 'n bloedtoets onderwerp moet word] wanneer dit die minderjarige se belange tot voordeel sal strek en die vraag is vervolgens watter faktore in hierdie verband 'n rol gegun sal word . . .

[KOTZE R het weer eens na DIDCOTT R se uitspraak in *Seetal v Pravitha* verwys en vervolg:]

[421] [E]k kan, met respek, nie saamstem met 'n stelling wat wil sê dat die oppervoog net op die kind se onmiddellike omstandighede en op niks anders in die oorweging van sy beslissing moet let nie. So 'n lineêre beskouing van die kind ter wille van die kind ignoreer die eise van die werklikheid en die interafhanklikheid en wisselwerking wat tussen die buite-egtelike kind en sy gesins- en bloedgenote bestaan en in werking tree. So 'n benadering sal, na my beskeie mening, nie 'n korrekte oplossing kan bied vir 'n geval waar beide die onwettige kind en sy moeder of selfs ook die beweerde vader almal minderjarig is en direk op die Hof se oppervoogdyskap aanspraak maak nie. Ook nie in 'n geval waar die verlening van so 'n bevel wat beide die kind en die moeder verplig om hulle aan die neem van bloedmonsters te laat onderwerp, geringe onmiddellike voor-

deel vir die kind maar terselfdertyd ernstige lewensgevaar vir die moeder, wat aan 'n besonderse siekte ly, sal inhou nie. Dit ignoreer verder ander objektiewe oorwegings en ideale soos die strewe dat die waarheid aan die lig gebring moet word en die feit dat elke individu 'n hoë premie op sy reg op privaatheid plaas.

Dit is my mening dat die toets dieselfde moet wees as wat in ouers se bewaringaansoeke oor kinders toegepas word, te wete dat die minderjarige se belang nie die enigste nie maar wel die deurslaggewende of oorheersende rigsnoer, waarteenoor alle ander oorwegings 'n ondergeskikte rol speel, moet wees. (Vergelyk *Fletcher v Fletcher* 1948 (1) SA 130 (A).) En so 'n toets beteken dan dat hoe nader die faktore aangaande die kind se belange aan 'n toestand van ewewigtigheid, oor die vraag of die aansoek toegestaan moet word of nie, kom, hoe groter sal die rol van hierdie ander faktore word, soos voorgeskryf in die woorde van SCHREINER AR in *Fortune v Fortune* 1955 (3) 348 (A) op 354:

> "... (W)here there is an approximately even balance of the factors relating to the minor's interests, the Judge would be obliged to add the other considerations to one scale or the other and so reach his conclusion."

Die tweede aspek is die vraag of die omstandighede van die onderhawige geval verg dat daar, nieteenstaande die teenstand van respondente, deur die Hof, as oppervoog, ingegryp moet word ...

[422] S se kurator *ad litem*, wat deur my aangestel is, se argumente ... is met baie meer erns deur my bejeën [as dié van die moeder]. Die belangrikste is die volgende. Eerstens dat S, in navolging van DIDCOTT R se woorde in die *Seetal*-uitspraak, "will be left with no identifiable father" as die bloedtoetse bewys dat applikant nie die vader is nie. Daar is, na my mening, twee antwoorde hierop. Die een is dat S tans vir mnr R, klaarblyklik met laasgenoemde se samewerking, as sy vader beskou en liefhet. As voormelde gevolg intree kan mnr R moontlik oorweeg om vir hom aan te neem. Maar in elk geval sal so 'n gevolg ook vermy kan word deur respondente. Sy moet dan net sê wie die regte vader is. Tweedens dat bloedtoetse geweier moet word omdat dit die moontlikheid inhou dat S die onderhoud wat hy nou ontvang, kan verloor. Hierdie argument is waarskynlik van DIDCOTT R ontleen waar hy die volgende in die *Seetal*-uitspraak 866A gesê het:

> "The child would have no substitute to whom to turn, on the other hand, if such support were withdrawn because illegitimacy was established. That would be a hardship, and a substantial one."

Dit is egter my beskeie mening dat waar geld verkeerdelik van 'n man, wat werklik nie die vader is nie, afgedwing word dit nie 'n "voordeel" is wat deur die Hof in ag geneem en beskerm moet word nie.

'n Goeie argument, teen die toestaan van die regshulp, wat deur respondente se advokaat voorgelê is, is dat applikant nie nou na verloop van nege jaar toegelaat moet word om 'n bestel, wat hy self help skep het, te poog omver te werp nie. Dit is 'n faktor wat baie swaar by my geweeg het en eers na ernstige bepeinsing het die faktor hierna genoem ook hierdie beswaar, tesame met al die ander, oorheers.

[423] Respondente en mnr R is voornemens, so berig die kurator *ad litem,* om op grond van mediese advies vir S (wat tot hiertoe vir mnr R as vader aanvaar) gedurende die jaar wat voorlê mee te deel dat applikant sy vader is. Gestel nou dat hulle dit doen en dit sal daarna deur middel van 'n hofgeding deur applikant of andersins vir S voorgehou word, dat applikant nie werklik sy vader is nie sal dit, na my mening, soveel skade aan hierdie kind se gees veroorsaak dat dit te alle koste vermy moet word. 'n Gevoel van sekuriteit is, na my beskeie mening, een van die grootste behoeftes vir 'n kind se geluk en iets wat te alle tye gekoester moet word ...

Dit is dus, na my mening, van deurslaggewende belang vir S se ontwikkeling en geluk dat daar nou, voordat iets vir hom van 'n ander "vader" as mnr R vertel word, met soveel sekerheid as wat moontlik kan, deur middel van bloedtoetse, bepaal word wat die werklike toestand is.

Die derde vraag wat ontstaan is weer eens een van jurisdiksie. Dit wel die vraag of dit binne hierdie Hof se regsbevoegdheid val om S se moeder (respondente) te dwing om haar teen haar sin, aan die neem van bloedmonsters te onderwerp. Sonder so 'n bevel sal daar nie voldoende sin in wees om 'n monster van S se bloed te laat neem nie. Monsters van al drie die betrokkenes se bloed word benodig om by 'n absolute betroubare resultaat uit te kom. Dit val dadelik op dat hier 'n gebied van botsende ideale en belange betree word. Aan die een kant die strewe na die waarheid wat deur ondersoek van die bloedmonsters blootgelê kan word en aan die ander kant die reg van privaatheid van die party wat nie tot die neem van bloedtoetse wil toestem nie. Dit is bekende reg dat die Hooggeregshof, as Hof van eerste instansie, se regsbevoegdheid uit drie bronne, te wete die gemene reg, wetgewing en inherente regsbevoegdheid, ontspring . . .

Die gemene reg het nie bloedtoetse geken nie en daar is geen statuut wat 'n siviele Hof magtig om partye te dwing om hulle aan bloedtoetse te onderwerp nie. In art 2 van die Wet op Status van Kinders 82 van 87, is daar met 'n bewysregtelike reëling, wat soos volg lees, volstaan:

"Indien daar by geregtelike verrigtinge waarby die vaderskap van 'n kind in geskil geplaas is, by wyse van getuienis of andersins aangevoer word dat 'n party by daardie verrigtinge, nadat hy deur die ander party by daardie verrigtinge daartoe versoek is, weier om homself te onderwerp of, indien hy die ouerlike gesag oor daardie kind voer, om daardie kind te laat onderwerp aan die neem van 'n bloedmonster ten einde wetenskaplike toetse betreffende die vaderskap van daardie kind te doen, word vermoed, totdat die teendeel bewys word, dat so 'n weiering daarop gemik is om die waarheid aangaande die vaderskap van daardie kind te verberg."

[424] Daar is ongelukkig daarmee volstaan nieteenstaande die Regskommissie se besef eerstens, dat daar in hierdie verband 'n behoefte aan 'n reëling bestaan en tweedens, dat 'n blote bewysregtelike reëling nie hierdie duisternis van onsekerheid sal besweer nie; alles soos blyk uit die volgende passasies van die verslag van die Suid-Afrikaanse Regskommissie, Projek 38, *Ondersoek na die Regsposisie van Buite-egtelike Kinders* 1985 wat hierdie stukkie wetgewing voorafgegaan het:

"Bladsy 70:   Alhoewel die wetgewing in hierdie geval geklee word in terme van die bewysreg, blyk dit uit bogaande dat sodanige wetgewing in werklikheid as aanduiding geneem sal kan word dat die Wetgewer as beleid aanvaar het dat die reg op privaatheid of die reël teen selfinkriminasie die knie moet buig voor die waarheid.

Bladsy 72:   Die Kommissie is egter van mening dat die bevredigendste oplossing te vind is in wetgewing wat die party op indirekte wyse dwing om uit eie beweging mee te werk om ouerskap deur bloedtoetse te bepaal. Dit hou die voordeel in dat dit onnodig is om die Hof te dwing om die arena te betree deur van die Hof te verwag om 'n bevel uit te reik dat partye hulle aan bloedtoetse moet onderwerp, maar dit plaas ook nie 'n demper op die regsontwikkeling ten opsigte van die bevoegdheid van 'n Hof om bloedtoetse te beveel in gevalle waar dit wenslik mag wees nie."

Ten laaste word daar geëindig by die vraag of hierdie Hof deur middel van sy inherente jurisdiksie so 'n bevel kan en moet uitreik . . .

[KOTZE R het na *E v E* 1940 TPA 333 en *Seetal v Pravitha* verwys en vervolg:]

[425] Hierdie Hof kom tot die gevolgtrekking dat dit binne sy inherente regsbevoegdheid val om S se moeder te verplig om haar aan die neem van bloedmonsters te onderwerp en dat sy ook gedwing moet word om so te doen. Dit wel spesiaal uit hoofde van die volgende faktore wat die Hof se beslissing onderlê:

(1) Soos hierintevore aangetoon is, is dit in S se belang dat betroubare inligting nou dringend bekom moet word om uitsluitsel te verkry oor die vraag of applikant werklik sy vader is of nie.

(2) Hedendaagse bloedanalises is sonder twyfel 'n betroubare hulpmiddel om 'n geskil oor vaderskap uit die weg te help ruim. Daar dien voor hierdie Hof 'n beëdigde verklaring van 'n Professor AR Rabson wat verbonde is aan die Suid-Afrikaanse Instituut vir Mediese Navorsing van die Universiteit van die Witwatersrand. Hy beoog die volgende toetse om by die hiernavermelde resultate uit te kom:

> "The question whether the applicant is the natural father of the particular child may be assessed by tissue typing the white blood cells of the child, his mother and the applicant and by looking at the red cell blood groups and various enzymes in the blood of the said three parties. If certain blood groups or tissue types are present on the child's cells but are not present on the applicant's cells, the applicant is conclusively excluded from being the biological father. If, on the other hand, certain blood groups and tissue types are present on the cells of the child and the applicant, then these tests do not exclude the applicant from being the biological father and a statistical probability of such a man being the father can be given and could be as high as 99,9%."

[426] Hierdie toetse staan, sover ek weet, kortweg bekend as die HLA stelsel van weefseltipering . . .

(3) Die resultaat van die voorgenome bloedanalises sal in 'n geregshof as toelaatbare getuienis ontvanklik wees. Sien *Ranjith v Sheela and Another NO* 1965 (3) SA 103 (D) en *Van der Harst v Viljoen* 1977 (1) SA 795 (K).

(4) Die publieke belang en elke regterlike amptenaar se angstige ideaal is, om sover dit menslik moontlik is, in elke regsgeskil altyd by die waarheid uit te kom. In die onder-hawige verband het ons reg vanuit die ou jare die bewysregtelike reël geërf dat 'n man se erkenning van byslaap die regsvermoede skep dat hy die vader van die kind is (sien *S v Swart* 1965 (3) SA 454 (A)) mits sodanige byslaap binne die gestasieperiode plaasgevind het. (Sien art 1 van Wet 82 van 1987.) Hierdie bewysregtelike reëling het verseker, so glo mens graag, die waarheidsideaal in menige gevalle tot sy reg laat kom maar dit sal onrealisties wees om te ontken dat dit al die jare steeds 'n saadjie van misbruik tot onwaarheid in sigself gedra het . . .

[Dit] wil . . . my tog voorkom dat daar goeie redes moet bestaan vir 'n weiering om in siviele sake gebruik te wil maak van getuienis wat, normaalweg, 'n baie groot waarborg vir die waarheid inhou. Soveel te meer waar dit toelaatbaar is om kragtens arts 37(3) en 225(2) van die Strafproseswet 51 van 1977, bloedmonsters in kriminele sake af te dwing. Dit is algemeen bekend dat die Westerse wêreld op die vooraand van 'n kennisrevolusie en midde in 'n ruimte-eeu van dramatiese tegnologiese ontwikkeling staan. HLA weef-seltipering van bloed is in tyd opgevolg deur die sogenaamde "DNA-vingerafdruk" waar nie net die bloed nie maar ook die speeksel, semen en stukkies huid ontleed word en die uitslae hiervan word reeds al in sommige lande in kriminele sake gebruik . . .

Daar word nie uit die oog verloor dat die neem van 'n bloedmonster wat normaalweg in effek kwalik iets meer as 'n naaldeprik is, tegnies as 'n inbreukmaking op die reg op privaatheid, soos bedoel in die persoonlikheidsgoederereg, aangeslaan kan word nie. Dit val egter swaar op die oor [427] om te hoor dat 'n moeder op haar reg op privaatheid

kan vasskop wanneer haar kind, wat in liggaam en welsyn intiem met haar eie liggaam en self verbind is, se belange verg dat haar reg op privaatheid ter wille van groter belange moet swig . . .

Gevalle waar dit reeds al geverg is dat die reg op privaatheid van die eie liggaam moet wyk voor die groter ideaal om die waarheid te dien is ook nie onbekend aan ons reg nie. Vergelyk die bepalings van Hooggeregshofreël 36 waar verpligte mediese ondersoeke geverg kan word van eisers wat vergoeding vir liggaamlike beserings vorder.

Die doel van bloedontledings in vaderskapeise is om getuienis te verkry oor iets wat reeds gebeur het. Die aard is soortgelyk aan handskrifontledings . . .

[428] 'n Bevel wat bloedontledings afdwing val, na my beskeie mening, wel binne die toelaatbare . . . Dit het nie te doen met die totstandkoming van die skuldoorsaak self nie en op sigself bring dit ook nie enige regsgevolg tot stand nie. Dit is 'n blote getuienisbron wat 'n Hof kan help om die waarheid te laat seëvier en in daardie sin dan 'n prosesregtelike aangeleentheid.

(5) Respondente het vir S die lewenslig laat aanskou. Sy is sy voog . . . Sy is verplig om sy belange op die hart te dra en behoort nie teenstrydig daarmee op te tree nie. Selfs nie eers wanneer haar eie wense in die proses geskaad gaan word nie. Die teenkant van die regte voortvloeiende uit haar voogdyskap is pligte en die voorregte se teenkant is verantwoordelikhede . . .

Haar subjektiewe beskouing oor haar eie en S se beste belange moet wyk voor die Hof, as oppervoog, se objektiewe beskouing van S se beste belange en sy is verplig om haar samewerking daartoe te verleen . . .

Note

See the note on *S v L* [17].

Aantekening

Sien die aantekening by *S v L* [17].

[17]   S v L

1992 3 SA 713 (E)

The use of blood tests where paternity is disputed

The appellant was the mother of a ten-year-old child, L, of whom she alleged the respondent was the father. Since the birth of the child the respondent had from time to time paid maintenance to the appellant for the child. However, he alleged that despite these payments of maintenance, he had never admitted paternity of the child. He admitted that he had intercourse with the appellant at the time when the child was conceived, but contended that he was not the only one to do so. During 1988 the appellant applied to the maintenance court for an increase in the

Die gebruik van bloedtoetse waar vaderskap betwis word

Die appellant was die moeder van 'n tien jaar oue kind, L, van wie sy beweer het dat die respondent die vader was. Die respondent het vanaf die kind se geboorte van tyd tot tyd aan die appellant onderhoud vir die kind betaal. Hy het egter beweer dat hy, ten spyte van die betaling van die onderhoud, nooit erken het dat hy die kind se vader was nie. Hy het erken dat hy met die appellant geslagsverkeer gehad het toe die kind verwek is maar het aangevoer dat hy nie die enigste was nie. Gedurende 1988 het die appellant by die onderhoudshof om verhoging van die

amount of maintenance to be paid by the respondent. The application was opposed by the respondent, who requested that the appellant and the child subject themselves to blood tests in order to establish whether the respondent was indeed the father of the child. Although the appellant had previously consented to such tests, she now refused to do so. The respondent then applied to the supreme court for an order compelling the appellant and the child to submit themselves to the required tests. The order was granted. The appellant appealed against this order to the full bench. The basis on which the respondent claimed the relief was that he averred that the tests were required to place medical evidence before the court to support his denial of paternity. The appeal was allowed.

onderhoud aansoek gedoen. Die respondent het die aansoek teengestaan en versoek dat die appellant en die kind hulle aan bloedtoetse onderwerp ten einde vas te stel of hy inderdaad die vader van die kind was. Alhoewel die appellant vroeër tot sodanige toetse ingestem het, het sy nou geweier om dit te doen. Die respondent het toe by die hooggeregshof aansoek gedoen om 'n bevel ten einde die appellant en die kind te verplig om hulle aan die toetse te onderwerp. Die respondent het geslaag in die hof *a quo* maar die appellant het teen hierdie bevel na die volbank geappelleer. Die respondent het sy eis gebaseer op die feit dat die toetse nodig was om hom in staat te stel om mediese getuienis voor die hof te plaas ter ondersteuning van sy ontkenning van vaderskap. Die appèl het geslaag.

MULLINS J: [715] In regard to the possible effect on the child of the results of such tests, he [the respondent] says that it will provide certainty whether he is the father or not, and that if he is shown not to be the father, appellant will still have a claim against one Lottering, whom respondent alleges also to have been intimate with appellant during the relevant period. Respondent states baldly that the 'bloedweefseltoetse' ought not themselves to have any harmful or prejudicial effects on the child.

The papers are totally lacking in any information regarding the precise nature of the proposed tests, whether samples of only blood or also of other tissue are required, the quantity of such samples, the method of obtaining such samples, and the pain and other consequences attendant thereon. Furthermore the respondent merely makes the bald allegation that such tests will determine whether he is the father of the child or not. Respondent's occupation is not apparent from the papers, but I am satisfied that he has no expert knowledge to support such an allegation. We were referred in argument to various authorities and articles in which the value of such tests is discussed, and these certainly suggest that modern technology is able with a high degree of probability to exclude a particular individual from being the father of a child and, with a lesser degree of probability, to confirm whether he is the father.

In this regard BURGER AJ [in the court *a quo*] stated in his judgment as follows:

'Die applikant het nie enige verklarings ingehandig om te bewys wat met bloed- en weefseltoetse bereik kan word nie, maar betoog dat die Hof geregtelike kennis daarvan kan neem. Daar was in die saak *Van der Harst v Viljoen* 1977 (1) SA 795 (K) volledige getuienis gelei oor hierdie aangeleentheid, dié getuienis was nie betwis nie. Dieselfde inligting verskyn ook in handboeke (sien Schäfer *Family Law Service J78,* en Boberg *The Law of Persons and the Family* op 332 voetnota 31), en dit word tans na my mening algemeen aanvaar. Die applikant se aansoek is op hierdie veronderstelling baseer en indien die respondent nie saamstem nie kon sy dit maklik in geding gestel het. Hierdie feite is so welbekend in die moderne samelewing dat 'n hof geregtelike kennis behoort te neem dat bloed- en weefseltoetse bewyswaarde het.

Dit is welbekend dat as gevolg van die navorsing wat met orgaanoorplantings gepaard gaan, daar voortdurend gevorder word met die tipering van 'n persoon se bloed en weefsel. In die verlede voor 1950 kon die bloedtoetse net in beperkte gevalle die vermeende vader uitskakel. Maar die toetse was in 1977 sover gevorder dat tot in 99,85% van die gevalle die vermeende vader, as hy verkeerd aangewys is, uitgesluit kan word (sien *Van der Harst v Viljoen* 1977 (1) SA 795 (K) en *Family Law Service* deur Schäfer J78 op 30, vir 'n meer volledige uiteensetting).

Omrede dat die persentasie van die gevalle wat die vermeende vader weens die ver-beterde tegnieke uitgeskakel kan word, so hoog is, volg dit dat, as hy nie uitgesluit kan word nie, daar 'n waarskynlikheid is dat hy wel die ware vader is. Hoe groter die persentasie, hoe groter is die waarskynlikheid. Anders as in die verlede waar die toetse net in belang van die vermeende vader was en gedien het om [hom] uit te sluit, het dit nou positiewe bewyswaarde en kan die ander party ook bevoordeel. Hierdie feit regverdig heroorweging van die riglyne wat in vroeëre beslissings neergelê is.'

[716] I have my doubts whether the learned Judge *a quo* was correct in taking judicial notice of the fact that there has been such development in the technique of blood testing that blood tests can now exclude a man as the father of a child with a 99,85% probability of correctness, and the corollary that, if he is not excluded as the father, he probably is the father. While such evidence may well have been adduced in other cases, or have appeared in legal or scientific articles, I am doubtful whether such technique has 'advanced to a certain degree of general recognition (that its) trustworthiness may be judicially noticed as too notorious to need comment'. Wigmore on *Evidence* 3rd ed vol III at 190; *S v Mthimkulu* 1975 (4) SA 759 (A) at 763H–765B. That the results of blood tests are admissible in evidence is clear. But details of the whole process of the taking of the samples, the process of testing such samples, the potential results of such tests, and the conclusions to be drawn therefrom, should in my view be properly proved in each specific case.

A similar view was adopted in *Nell v Nell* 1990 (3) SA 889 (T), where, at 894F–I LE ROUX AJ stated:

'Op die stukke voor my is daar geen aanduiding oor wat hierdie sogenaamde weef-seltoetse behels nie. Ek weet gevolglik nie hoeveel van die menslike liggaam verwyder word of vanwaar dit verwyder word nie. Moontlik behels dit slegs 'n bloedtoets maar hieroor kan ek nie seker wees nie. Om onder hierdie omstandighede die applikant sy spreekwoordelike pond vleis toe te laat, kom vir my kras voor. Geen bevel word deur die applikant gevra teen die minderjarige nie. (Ek mag hier meld dat dit om daardie rede is dat ek nie aangedring het op die aanstelling van 'n kurator *ad litem* nie.) Gesien die respondente se houding, is ek tevrede dat die applikant 'n Hofbevel sal benodig om die minderjarige te onderwerp aan hierdie klas van toets. Indien daardie regshulp later geweier word, dien hierdie bevel, indien ek dit sou toelaat, geen doel nie. Verder is daar geen mediese getuienis voor my, dat dit nodig is ten einde vaderskap te bepaal, om toetse op die moeder uit te voer nie. Ek is verwys na sekere getuienis gelewer in die saak van *M v R* 1989 (1) SA 416 (O) op 425H–J [16]. Vir soverre ek geregtig is om my te vereenselwig met getuienis gelewer in 'n ander saak, blyk dit allermins daaruit dat die moeder enige rol te speel het in die vergelyking tussen die bloed- of veselgroepe van die vader en die kind.'

I should mention that in *Nell's* case it appeared from the papers that the mother had been requested by the applicant to arrange to take a day's leave from her employment, as it was anticipated a day would be required to complete the necessary tests. This suggests that the taking of the necessary samples may not consist of merely a pin-prick to draw a small quantity of blood, as is suggested in other cases.

I am, however, for the purposes of the present appeal, prepared to assume that the respondent has established that the blood tests he seeks will provide evidentiary material which will assist the maintenance court in determining whether the respondent is the father of L or not. This assumption (which I make with considerable hesitation) leaves it open for the appeal to be decided on the main issues with which we are faced.

As already stated, it is not in issue in the present case that expert evidence of tests based upon blood or tissue samples are admissible in evidence, particularly when paternity is in issue. See for example *Ranjith v Sheela and Another NO* 1965 (3) SA 103 (D); *Van der Harst v Viljoen* 1977 (1) SA 795 (C). In those cases the necessary blood samples were voluntarily [717] provided, and there is no doubt that the expert evidence of the results of genetic tests of such samples contributed in a large degree to the Courts' findings, and in reaching a just decision in those cases.

There have, however, been a number of cases in which the power of the Court to order a child, its mother, and the alleged father, to submit themselves to the taking of blood or tissue samples from their bodies has been considered. Cases to which we were referred included *Eynon v Du Toit* 1927 CPD 76; *E v E and Another* 1940 TPD 333; *Seetal v Pravitha and Another NO* 1983 (3) SA 827 (D) [15]; *Cerebos Food Corporation Ltd v Diverse Foods SA (Pty) Ltd and Another* 1984 (4) SA 149 (T) at 172C–173B; *M v R* 1989 (1) SA 416 (O); *Nell v Nell (supra)*. Regrettably the issue does not as yet appear to have received the attention of the Appellate Division.

In *Eynon v Du Toit (supra)*, which was a claim for damages for personal injuries, the Court held that it had no power to make an order directing a plaintiff to submit himself to a medical examination required by the defendant, although it pointed out that he would be unwise not to submit himself to such examination. There is of course now a procedure provided by Rule of Court 36(1), sanctioned in terms of s 43(3) of the Supreme Court Act 59 of 1959, requiring a plaintiff to submit to such an examination.

The question of a blood test to determine paternity first arose in *E v E and Another (supra)*. The mother was prepared to submit to such a test, but refused to allow a blood sample to be taken from the child, who was in her custody. The Court held, at 336, that the 'order which he seeks has no reference to the paternal relationship or the welfare of the child. He seeks an order from the Court which will in effect enable him to exercise rights against an adverse party to a suit'. The Court held, on the authority of *Eynon v Du Toit*, that this was a right to which he was not entitled. Although not specifically stated in the judgment, it appears that the Court was not prepared to interfere with the decision of the mother, as custodian of the child, to refuse to allow a blood sample to be taken from her child.

In *Seetal v Pravitha and Another NO (supra)* DIDCOTT J exhaustively reviewed local and overseas authorities relating to the power of the Court to order blood tests to determine disputed paternity issues, and considered as separate issues the power of the Court to order blood tests on adults, ie a parent, and on a minor child.

In regard to adults, DIDCOTT J weighed up at length the merits and demerits of judicial interference in the personal privacy and bodily integrity of the individual against the search for truth, but in the result found it unnecessary to decide whether the Court had the power to make the order sought. He was able to avoid (I am sure he did not evade) the issue, because of his findings on the facts of that case that 'it would not benefit the ... child were I to allow a blood test on him'. This factual finding was based on the learned Judge's conclusion that a South African Court 'can effectively consent on a child's behalf to a blood test'. I shall revert to this view, and the reasons given therefor, after referring to the other authorities referred to above.

In *Cerebos Food Corporation Ltd v Diverse Foods SA (Pty) Ltd and Another* (*supra* at 172C–173B) reference was made, in a completely [718] different context, to the three preceding decisions on blood tests referred to above, but no additional principle emerges therefrom.

M v R (*supra*) was, however, a case, on facts very similar to the present case, where the Court followed *Seetal's* case in regard to the power of a Court to order a blood test to be taken from a minor 'wanneer dit die minderjarige se belange tot voordeel sal strek' (at 420I). The Court went further, however, and came to the conclusion that, in respect of adults, the Supreme Court had the inherent power to regulate its procedures, and that this includes an order that a mother be required to submit to a blood test.

Lastly in *Nell v Nell* (*supra*) LE ROUX AJ came to the conclusion, contrary to the views in *M v R*, that the ordering of blood tests was not purely a procedural matter which entitled the Court, in the exercise of its inherent powers to regulate its own procedure, to order submission to a blood test. As he was not satisfied that it was not a matter of substantive law, in terms of which there was no authority to make such an order, the relief sought was refused.

A tally of the aforegoing decisions reveals the following differences of opinion. The Court has no power to order any individual, adult or minor, to undergo a blood test against his will. *Eynon v Du Toit* (*supra*). The Court has no power to order a mother against her will to allow a blood sample to be taken from her child. *E v E* (*supra*). The Court left open the question whether it could order a blood sample to be taken from an adult, but held that the Court has the power to consent on a child's behalf to a blood test if it is in the interests of the child. *Seetal v Pravitha and Another NO* (*supra*) [15]. The Court can order blood samples from adults in accordance with its inherent powers to regulate its own procedures, and has the power to order a blood sample from a child when it will be to the child's benefit to do so. *M v R* (*supra*) [16]. The ordering of the taking of blood samples is not purely a procedural matter, and the Court has no power to create a principle of substantive law which would infringe the rights of privacy of the individual. *Nell v Nell* (*supra*).

In the absence of any clear and definitive authority which satisfies me that I should follow one or other of the above views, I can but do my best, at the risk of further confusing such an important issue, to justify my own conclusions. This involves raising certain additional views to those so painstakingly researched and set out in the aforementioned judgments.

The value of blood tests in determining disputed issues of paternity has not escaped the attention of the Legislature. In October 1985 the South African Law Commission prepared an extensive report (Project 38) into the legal position of illegitimate children. This included, at 60–72, a full consideration of the value of blood tests and the means whereby such tests could resolve disputed paternity issues. The Commission recommended (at 72) that legislation should be introduced 'indirectly compelling parties to co-operate of their own accord to determine parentage by means of blood tests'.

This recommendation was presumably the basis for the enactment of ss 1 and 2 of the Children's Status Act 82 of 1987, which read as follows:

'1.   If in any legal proceedings at which it has been placed in issue whether any particular person is the father of an extra-marital child it is proved by way of a judicial admission or otherwise that he had sexual intercourse with the [719] mother of that child at any time when that child could have been conceived, it shall, in the absence of evidence to the contrary, be presumed that he is the father of that child.

2. If in any legal proceedings at which the paternity of any child has been placed
    in issue it is adduced in evidence or otherwise that any party to those proceedings,
    after he has been requested thereto by the other party to those proceedings, refuses
    to submit himself or, if he has parental authority over that child, to cause that
    child to be submitted to the taking of a blood sample in order to carry out scientific
    tests relating to the paternity of that child, it shall be presumed, until the contrary
    is proved, that any such refusal is aimed at concealing the truth concerning the
    paternity of that child.'

It is in my view an inescapable conclusion from the provisions of s 2 that the Legislature
was not satisfied that there were legal means available to compel a party to submit to a
blood test, but it does not necessarily follow therefrom that the Court does not have the
power to compel the taking of blood tests.

The appellant in the present case cannot prevent respondent from raising as an issue, in
the maintenance court proceedings which she has brought, that he is not the father of
L. The fact that appellant refuses to agree to the blood tests will in those proceedings
necessitate her rebutting the presumption that she is seeking to conceal the truth concerning
the paternity of the child. Section 2 does not, however, create a presumption that the
man who had placed paternity in issue, *in casu* the respondent, is not the father of the
child. Nevertheless the presumption is one which appellant will have to overcome and
prima facie, insofar as the maintenance court proceedings are concerned, it would appear
to be more in the interests of appellant and L if the presumption were avoided by appellant
agreeing to the taking of blood samples.

On the other hand, however, respondent has to avoid the presumption, in terms of s 1,
that he is the father of L and this in view of his admitted intercourse with appellant at
the time when L could have been conceived. On the papers before us respondent seeks
to suggest that the aforesaid Lottering is the father of L but appellant denies intercourse
with Lottering.

It may be noted that s 1 of Act 82 of 1987 provides for the presumption created therein
to operate 'in the absence of evidence to the contrary' whilst the presumption in s 2
operates 'until the contrary is proved'. The presumptions, which may conflict in the
maintenance court proceedings, will have to be considered by the tribunal hearing the
maintenance application and I have been careful not to prejudge the very issue which
the maintenance court will have to decide, but a reference to the section is necessary and
relevant to enable the parties to appreciate their positions, and that of L, in the maintenance
court proceedings.

Insofar as respondent is concerned, and after considering all the authorities and the
persuasive reasoning in each of them, I am not satisfied that an order that she submit
herself to a blood test is a procedural matter, nor am I persuaded that this Court has the
power to make such an order.

Furthermore the order sought is to obtain evidence to be used in the maintenance court.
That court is a creature of statute, its procedure being, in terms of s 15 of the Maintenance
Act 23 of 1963, that applicable to [720] magistrates' courts. The maintenance court clearly
has no inherent power to order blood tests, and I know of no authority which entitles
the Supreme Court, under the guise of its own inherent powers, to regulate the procedure
of inferior courts. *Universal City Studios Inc and Others v Network Video (Pty) Ltd* 1986 (2)
SA 734 (A) at 754G.

I revert to the views of DIDCOTT J in *Seetal's* case *supra* at 862E regarding blood samples
from minors that,

'(s)hould the person whose consent is required declined to furnish it, a Court determined to overrule him has no occasion to compel him to give it or the child to be tested without it. The Court simply exercises the power of an upper guardian, as we call it here, by supplying its own consent.'

I must take the risk of being labelled an iconoclast in questioning whether the Court can 'simply... supply its own consent' in its capacity of upper guardian of minors.

It is not in dispute in the present case that appellant is the sole legal guardian of L, with all the rights and powers of a guardian. It is not suggested that she did not, *qua* guardian, have the legal right to refuse to allow L to be subjected to blood tests. It is implicit from the terms of s 2 of the Children's Status Act 82 of 1987 that the Legislature recognises that a parent having parental authority over the child may refuse to cause that child to be submitted to blood tests, with the concomitant presumption arising from such refusal. Nor is it suggested that her said refusal is *mala fide*, or motivated for improper purposes, or even that it is unreasonable. Respondent seeks such blood tests solely and specifically for the purpose of obtaining evidence which he hopes will disprove his alleged paternity of L.

The provisions of the Criminal Procedure Act 51 of 1977 apart, the Court has no *statutory* power or authority to order blood tests to be taken, whether of adults or minors. The Legislature in enacting Act 82 of 1987 followed the recommendation of the Law Commission which specifically recommended that legislation should indirectly, and not directly, seek to compel parties to submit to blood tests. In such context, the word 'compel' is not entirely appropriate. The sanction, namely that a presumption is created that the refusal to submit to blood tests is with the intention of concealing the truth regarding parentage, can have persuasive, but not compulsive, effect.

It was stated in the Law Commission report at para 7.31, on the authority of *Seetal v Pravitha and Another NO* 1983 (3) SA 827 (D), that

'(a) Court may as upper guardian overrule a guardian's objection in this regard. The Court held that it should act purely in the interests of the child in taking a decision, since it would be consenting to the taking of blood tests on the child's behalf.'

This statement, in my view, is open to question.

It is not proposed to examine in detail the history in Roman-Dutch law of the Court's powers as upper guardian of minors. Suffice it to say that in Holland the power appears to have been exercised solely for the purpose of the appointment of guardians to minors. See Wessels on *History of Roman-Dutch Law* at 423–4; Hahlo and Kahn on *The Union of South Africa-The Development of its Laws and Constitution* at 369.

[721] The Courts in South Africa have continued to act as upper guardian of minors in disputed issues related to custody. In *Calitz v Calitz* 1939 AD 56 at 63–4 [19] it was held that the Court will as upper guardian interfere with a father's custody *stante matrimonio* only on special grounds such as, for example, danger to the child's life, health or morals. See also *Van der Westhuizen v Van Wyk and Another* 1952 (2) SA 119 (GW).

In later cases it was held that these three grounds for interference were not exclusive, and the Court would exercise its powers *relating to custody* when the interests of the minor required it. *Bam v Bhabha* 1947 (4) SA 798 (A); *Short v Naisby* 1955 (3) SA 572 (D); *September v Karriem* 1959 (3) SA 687 (C); *Ex parte Van Dam* 1973 (2) SA 182 (W) [20]; *Ex parte Kommissaris van Kindersorg, Krugersdorp: In re JB; Ex parte Kommissaris van Kindersorg, Oberholzer: In re AGF* 1973 (2) SA 699 (T); *Goodrich v Botha and Another* 1952 (4) SA 175 (T); *Petersen en 'n Ander v Kruger en 'n Ander* 1975 (4) SA 171 (C) [145]. All of these cases related to questions of custody, and not interference with the day to day parental power and control.

The Courts have also assumed the power, as upper guardian, to act in the interests of a minor who has no guardian. Leave to marry was granted in *Ex parte Kropf* 1936 WLD 28 where the minor had no guardian. Leave to marry is now regulated by statute.

The Full Bench of the Transvaal Provincial Division in *Coetzee v Meintjies* 1976 (1) SA 257 (T) came to the conclusion, however, that the Supreme Court acts as upper guardian of minors (*a*) where the minor has no guardian, or (*b*) where the guardian neglects his duty, or (*c*) where the parents are unable to agree as to what is best in the interests of the child (eg disputed custody cases). At 261B–D the Court held:

> 'Ons is van oordeel dat wanneer die natuurlike voog in staat is om sy funksies te vervul en dit ook inderdaad doen, daar geen ruimte vir ingryping deur die oppervoog is nie.... (D)ie Hof sal ingryp as hy sy plig nie doen nie.'

In my view the powers of the Supreme Court are not unlimited, but are circumscribed as set out above. In *Nugent v Nugent* 1978 (2) SA 690 (R) at 692A it was stated that

> '(t)he exercise of parental power is, however, always subject to the right of the Court as upper guardian of the children to interfere so as to ensure and enforce what is in the best interests of the children'.

If this was intended to mean that the Court can interfere with a decision made by the guardian of the child merely because it disagrees with that decision, the statement is not supported by authority and I disagree therewith. *Nugent's* case involved a dispute as to the religious upbringing of children of divorced parents, and on the facts the Court, while assuming it had the power to do so, declined to interfere with the custodian parent's decision. In my view, however, the Court does not have the power to interfere with the decision of the custodian parent as to the religious faith of the children, unless such parent neglects his or her duty in this regard. Such a decision, as in the present case, is an incidence of the custodian parent's day to day control.

My conclusion from all the authorities I have referred to is that the Court does not in the present case, as upper guardian of minors, have the power to interfere with a decision of the appellant as guardian that the child should not undergo blood tests. She has given reasons for her [722] decision, and even if this Court might have come to a different decision, the Court does not have the power to interfere.

I come to the question of the interests of L. I have already said that insofar as the maintenance proceedings themselves are concerned it would *prima facie* appear to be more in the interests of appellant and L if the presumption created in s 2 of Act 82 of 1987 were avoided by appellant agreeing to the taking of blood samples. However, assuming that the Court has the power to make an order for the taking of blood samples and that it could overrule appellant's decision in that regard simply on the basis of the interests of L, I am not satisfied that such an order by the Court would necessarily be in L's overall interests.

According to appellant's answering affidavit, L knows she is illegitimate, particularly as appellant has never married. At all times L has recognised respondent as her father and his photograph is next to her bed. L knows that respondent has been paying maintenance for her, and she has a close familial contact with respondent's son from his present marriage and with other members of respondent's family. She is an intelligent child and appellant feels it will create a feeling of insecurity if she is subjected to tests, the purpose of which will probably be apparent to her. The *curator ad litem* also opposed the granting of the order sought by the respondent.

Finally, I am not convinced that blood tests should be ordered simply on the basis that they will provide certainty or at least a considerable degree of certainty as to the paternity of L and that the Court's prime objective should be the ascertainment of the truth. There are many situations where the Courts, applying principles such as estoppel or waiver, close their eyes to the truth, and grant relief because parties to litigation themselves place a different complexion on the facts to what they truly are. This is a fascinating field of jurisprudence which it is not necessary in the present case to consider in more detail. It was touched on in *Seetal v Pravitha* (*supra* at 860H–861A and 864H–865C) [15].

I am therefore of the view that it was not proved by respondent on a balance of probabilities that the interests of L require that this Court, as upper guardian of minors, should order that appellant or L submit themselves to the tests sought by respondent, even if this Court had the power to make the order sought . . .

[723] The appeal succeeds . . .

JENNETT J concurred.

ERASMUS J: The facts of the application are set out in the judgment of MULLINS J. I agree with his final conclusion, but would arrive there by a different route – one which does not affect the Court's jurisdiction. I would, with respect, if possible avoid a judgment which could inhibit legal development regarding the power of the Court to order blood tests for forensic or therapeutic purposes. This objective can be achieved on the basis of the conclusion to which I have come, viz that respondent should not have approached the Supreme Court, as there was an adequate alternative remedy available to him in the maintenance court. This conclusion involves analysis of the applicable statutory provisions against the background of the common law.

Previously, prior to the enactment of ss 1 and 2 of the Children's Status Act 82 of 1987, the common law as propounded in *S v Swart* 1965 (3) SA 454 (A) obtained, ie that where a woman claimed maintenance for her illegitimate child, an admission of intercourse, no matter when it had occurred, by the man indicated by the mother, created a presumption that the man was the father and it placed an *onus* on him to prove that he could not be the father. The man was required to rebut this presumption on the balance of probability. The effect was that a man who admitted sexual intercourse with the woman was usually in an untenable position in a disputed paternity suit. Proof of intercourse by the woman with another man or men did not avail him. In practical terms the only defences open to him were proof of sterility or negative blood tests. There existed, however, no legal machinery whereby he could compel the taking of blood samples. This position served to provide many illegitimate children with a source of support, but it would be unrealistic to assume that such source was invariably the real father of the child. The acceptability of the approach in the *Swart* case in modern society was questioned on a number of grounds . . . *Inter alia*, it gave rise to the criticism that the courts were less interested in biological fatherhood than in providing legal fathers for illegitimate children (Thomas 'Investigation into the legal position of illegitimate children' 1985 *De Rebus* at 337). The effect of such an approach was not only inequitable as far as the man was concerned, but was not necessarily in the true interests of the child. The Law Commission found in its study (*supra* at para 7.15) that fathers who accept their illegitimate children are far more likely to fulfil their duty of support, than are men who are in doubt as to whether the child is theirs. The psychological benefits to the child of certainty as to the identity of its biological father are obvious (see the comments of KOTZÉ J in *M v R* 1989 (1) SA 416 (O) at 423A–D [16]).

[724] In terms of the *Swart* decision, as applied in *Mahomed v Shaik* 1978 (4) SA 523 (N) at 525H–526D, proof of sexual intercourse amounted to virtually incontrovertible proof of paternity (Van der Vyver and Joubert *Persone- en Familiereg* 3rd ed at 217–18). This unsatisfactory position probably flowed from the then lack of scientific means of proving consanguinity. This problem has in recent times been overcome by advancement in the

field of blood tissue typing, leading to significant increase in the probative value of these tests in establishing paternity. These developments have not gone unnoticed by the Courts . . .

[725] In view of the Courts' recognition of the reliability achieved in the field of blood tissue typing, the Legislature, in passing the Children's Status Act in 1987, was obviously satisfied that it could safely relax the *Swart* presumption of paternity by taking a firm stand in favour of scientific proof of biological paternity. The relevant provisions, ss 1 and 2 of the Act, provide as follows:

'1.   *Presumption of paternity in respect of extra-marital children*
If in any legal proceedings at which it has been placed in issue whether any particular person is the father of an extra-marital child it is proved by way of a judicial admission or otherwise that he had sexual intercourse with the mother of that child at any time when that child could have been conceived, it shall, in the absence of evidence to the contrary, be presumed that he is the father of that child.

2.   *Presumption on refusal to submit to taking of blood samples*
If in any legal proceedings at which the paternity of any child has been placed in issue it is adduced in evidence or otherwise that any party to those proceedings, after he has been requested thereto by the other party to those proceedings, refuses to submit himself or, if he has parental authority over that child, to cause that child to be submitted to the taking of a blood sample in order to carry out scientific tests relating to the paternity of that child, it shall be presumed, until the contrary is proved, that any such refusal is aimed at concealing the truth concerning the paternity of that child.'

The lawmaker chose his words carefully: First, the presumption of paternity in terms of s 1 operates only upon proof that sexual intercourse took place '*at a time when the child could have been conceived*'.

Second, the presumption of paternity operates only '*in the absence of evidence to the contrary*'. In other words, where there is evidence to the contrary, the presumption does not operate, or ceases to operate. Note that the word 'evidence' as opposed to 'proof' is used. Schmidt *Bewysreg* 3rd ed at 136-7 comments as follows:

[726] 'Die woorde "by ontstentenis van *getuienis* tot die teendeel" is betekenisvol. Hoewel in *Holloway v Stander* 1969 (3) SA 291 (A) van 'n weerleggingslas en weerleggingsbewys gepraat word, word ook in dieselfde verband na 'n bewyslas verwys. Ander uitsprake het sterk in die rigting beweeg om 'n volle bewyslas op die betrokke man te plaas, en wel 'n las om te bewys dat hy nie vader *kon* gewees het nie. Artikel 1 stel dit egter nou duidelik dat slegs 'n weerleggingslas op die man rus. Die vermoede word weerlê sodra hy getuienis voorlê wat aantoon dat hy nie die vader van die kind is nie.'

'Evidence' is not defined, nor is it limited or qualified. It therefore bears its usual, wide, meaning. It follows that any acceptable 'evidence to the contrary', direct or circumstantial, suffices to undo the presumption. Circumstantial evidence is a wide concept and may be found in conduct on the part of the mother indicating that the man whom she charges with paternity is possibly not the father of the child, for example (relevant here) a refusal on her part to undergo blood testing without good reason for her refusal. This example of 'evidence to the contrary' is in s 2 raised to a presumption that she is concealing the truth of paternity of the child.

Third, in marked contrast to the s 1 presumption, the s 2 presumption operates '*until the contrary is proved*' – the standard *onus* of proof in civil suits. The two presumptions are contradictory and logically cannot operate simultaneously. This apparent contradiction disappears if one reads the two sections together, as one must: the difference in the nature of the *onus* raised in the two presumptions becomes immediately significant and forces the conclusion that the stronger s 2 presumption overrides the weaker s 1 presumption.

Fourth, the s 2 presumption operates where it is adduced in evidence that *'any party to the proceedings'* has refused to submit to the taking of a blood test. The presumption therefore operates against both the man or the woman who refuses to co-operate.

Fifth, the presumption raised in terms of s 2 is that *'any such refusal is aimed at concealing the truth of the paternity of the child'*. The wording of what is presumed determines the nature of the evidence required in rebuttal thereof. Had s 2 provided that a refusal gives rise to a presumption that the man was not the father of the child the woman could presumably have rebutted the presumption by means of proof of intercourse with the alleged father. On the wording of s 2, however, the refusal must relate to considerations other than the 'truth of the paternity of the child', such as valid medical or religious objections to the act of furnishing blood (JMT Labuschagne 'Biogenetiese Vaderskap: Bewysregtelike en Regspluralistiese Problematiek' 1984 *De Jure* at 342). The fact that the woman has a strong *prima facie* case relates to the 'truth concerning the paternity of the child' and accordingly does not serve to rebut the presumption. To hold that the woman can justify her refusal on the basis of a strong case would mean that the man could do the same for the reason that she has a weak case. Such finding would destroy the elaborate scheme constructed by the Legislature. Unacceptable aspects of the *Swart* situation would be restored and largely defeat the prime object of the Legislature, viz to place paternal obligation on the basis of blood relationship. It follows that men who would have been liable to maintenance on application of the *Swart* approach will now escape such [727] obligations. This latter consequence accords with the view that it is not 'in the interests of the child' that the woman should succeed in her action against a man who is not the child's procreator. This point of view is expressed as follows by BURGER AJ in his judgment in the Court *a quo*:

> 'Die argument dat die dogter benadeel kan word omdat sy nie meer geregtig sal wees op onderhoud as dit bewys word dat die applikant nie haar vader is nie, is nie suiwer nie. In daardie geval was sy nooit regtens daarop geregtig nie, en wat 'n mens nie op geregtig is nie kan jy nie voorhou as benadeling nie.'

This statement accords with the view expressed by KOTZE J in *M v R* (*supra* at 422H–I [16]) to the effect that support paid under compulsion by a man who is not the father is not an 'advantage' to the child of which the Court can take cognisance or should protect.

Sections 1 and 2 of the Act achieve the objectives of the Law Commission's key re-commendations from which they obviously flow:

> '7.12   From the point of view of equity and jurisprudence the presumption of paternity should come into operation only on proof or admission of intercourse at a time relevant to conception, and the presumption should be linked to an *onus* of rebuttal. The Commission recommends accordingly...

> 7.44   The Commission is, however, of the opinion that the most satisfactory solution is to be found in legislation indirectly compelling the parties to co-operate of their own accord to determine parentage by means of blood tests. This has the advantage of making it unnecessary to force the court to enter the arena by expecting it to issue an order for parties to submit to blood tests, while not inhibiting legal development regarding the power of a court to order blood tests in cases where this is deemed desirable. The disadvantages of expecting the court to make an order, namely that costs will be pushed up and that proceedings will be drawn out, are also avoided. It is possible to compel parties in such an indirect

way by creating a presumption that a party's intention in refusing is to conceal the truth regarding parentage. The presumption should be rebuttable that this is not the case.'

The compulsion contained in the Act is the real risk of failure to prove (or disprove) parentage which flows from a refusal to co-operate in the test without good and sufficient reason for the refusal. This means that the man in a fatherhood suit can bring pressure to bear on the woman by placing the fact of her refusal to co-operate before the tribunal. She will either have, or not have, good reason for her refusal. In either event little or nothing would be gained from an application to the Supreme Court to order blood tests: if she does not have good reason to refuse, the presumption operates to place the man in (almost) as strong a position as he would have been had he been armed with a favourable blood test; if, on the other hand, the woman does have good reason for her refusal, the Supreme Court (assuming that it has the necessary powers) would presumably refuse to order the tests.

The Legislature has placed presumptive proof of fathership on a sound basis. Litigants can in effect achieve the benefits of blood tissue typing without the Court having to order either of them to submit to blood tests. In consequence, the legislation will promote greater accuracy in establishing the identity of the biological father, and should discourage false accusations and denials of paternity. A woman facing the possible challenge of a blood test will not lightly bring a false paternity suit. If she [728] is certain of her case, she will have nothing to fear from the tests and should in the interests of the child willingly furnish the necessary blood samples. On the other hand, where she has difficulty proving sexual intercourse, her hand has been strengthened as she can now with confidence challenge the man whom she knows to be the father to submit to tests. The corollary is that the man who is falsely accused, or who has doubts as to whether he was responsible for the woman's pregnancy, can effectively challenge her to submit to the tests. The operation of the two presumptions will lead to the truth except only where the mother refuses without good reason a request for blood samples made by the biological father, or where he likewise refuses such request. One can only hope that the former will seldom if ever occur, while in the latter case the man will have only himself to blame for the consequences of his refusal. This position caters satisfactorily for the run of the mill case (such as the present).

On close analysis of the wording of ss 1 and 2 it becomes clear that within the scheme constructed by the Legislature there is in most cases (of which the present is one) no need for any of the parties to approach the Supreme Court for a blood test order. This in my view is the main reason why the Court a quo should not have granted the application. There are additional considerations. By rendering unnecessary applications to the Supreme Court for the ordering of tests, costs are saved and proceedings are expedited. Further costs may be saved in that where a party proceeds on the basis of the s 2 presumption, the statutory recognition now afforded blood tests probably renders it unnecessary for such party to produce expert evidence at the trial in regard to the nature and the reliability of blood tests, or what the taking of a blood sample involves. Avoidance of costs and delay further indicate that the court is the proper and only forum in which to raise the whole issue of blood tests. Furthermore, in my view, the trial court that is required to adjudicate on the question of paternity is best able to decide, in the full context of the case, whether the woman has good reason to refuse her co-operation. Also, her reason for refusal will be better tested in a trial than on paper in an application. Finally, even assuming that the Supreme Court has the power to make an order in regard to proceedings in the maintenance court before which the paternity enquiry is pending (in which regard I have substantial doubt), such practice should in my view be avoided. The Act clearly discourages applications to the Supreme Court for the ordering of blood tests. It is certainly most undesirable that such applications become part and parcel of paternity disputes. The Supreme Court should not lightly intervene in the proceedings of another court, in order to grant a party a procedural remedy which it does not have in terms of the lower court's rules of practice. Even if it does have such powers, it should exercise them only in special or exceptional circumstances. No such circumstances exist here, especially as respondent has an alternative effective remedy in the maintenance court . . .

[729] I find therefore that the respondent should not have approached the Supreme Court for relief, but should have remained in the maintenance court, and there adduced proof of appellant's refusal to submit herself and the child to the taking of blood samples and tested her reasons for refusal. (He may still do so.)

I would therefore allow the appeal . . . and make an order in the terms set out by MULLINS J.

Note

In the past, blood tests were not often used in South Africa in paternity disputes, since the courts held that they could not compel the mother and the child to submit to such tests (E v E 1940 TPD 333), and as the position in this regard was certain it is understandable that the matter seldom came before the courts. However, where a blood test was submitted to voluntarily the results thereof were accepted as proof in paternity cases. In, for example, Ranjith v Sheela 1965 3 SA 103 (D), the parties were married and although the opportunity for sexual intercourse between them existed, the husband maintained that he did not have intercourse with his wife at the time when the child was conceived. Blood tests were thereupon performed on the husband, wife and child and these tests were accepted as sufficient proof that the husband could not have been the father of the child. In Van der Harst v Viljoen 1977 1 SA 795 (C) the plaintiff averred that the defendant had had sexual intercourse with her. The defendant denied this. The results of blood tests done on the defendant, his parents, the plaintiff and the child, however corroborated her evidence and showed an overwhelming probability that the defendant was the father of the child. Again this evidence was accepted.

As is mentioned in S v L the whole question of blood tests in regard to paternity disputes was also considered by the South African Law Commission and the commission's recommendations formed the basis of sections 1 and 2 of the Children's Status Act 82 of 1987. Since the coming into operation of this act there has been a marked increase in the litigation on blood tests, and the courts have rightly decided the matter with ref-

Aantekening

Bloedtoetse is in die verlede nie dikwels in vaderskapsake in Suid-Afrika gebruik nie aangesien die howe beslis het dat hulle nie die bevoegdheid gehad het om die moeder en die kind te verplig om hulle daaraan te onderwerp nie (E v E 1940 TPA 333), en aangesien die regsposisie in die verband seker was, is dit verstaanbaar dat die aangeleentheid nie juis voor die howe gekom het nie. Waar die partye hulle egter vrywillig aan 'n bloedtoets onderwerp het, is die uitslag daarvan wel in vaderskapsake as bewys aanvaar. In, byvoorbeeld, Ranjith v Sheela 1965 3 SA 103 (D) was die partye getroud en alhoewel die geleentheid vir geslagsverkeer tussen hulle bestaan het, het die man beweer dat hy nie op die tydstip toe die kind verwek is met sy vrou geslagsgemeenskap gehad het nie. Bloedtoetse is toe op die man, vrou en kind uitgevoer en die uitslag daarvan is as voldoende bewys aanvaar dat die vrou se man nie die vader van die kind kon wees nie. In Van der Harst v Viljoen 1977 1 SA 795 (K) het die eiseres beweer dat die verweerder geslagsverkeer met haar gehad het. Die verweerder het dit ontken. Die uitslag van bloedtoetse wat op die verweerder, sy ouers, die eiseres en die kind uitgevoer is, het haar getuienis egter gestaaf en oorweldigend aangetoon dat die verweerder die vader van die kind was. Weer eens is hierdie getuienis aanvaar.

Soos wat in S v L aangetoon is, het die Suid-Afrikaanse Regskommissie ook aan die hele aangeleentheid van bloedtoetse in verband met vaderskapsgeskille aandag gegee, en het die kommissie se aanbevelings die grondslag gevorm van artikels 1 en 2 van die Wet op die Status van Kinders 82 van 1987. Na die inwerkingtreding

erence to the criterion of whether the ordering of blood tests would be in the child's best interests. As we have seen above, the Free State court found that it would have been in the child's best interests to order him and his mother to undergo blood tests in *M v R* [16], but in *Nell v Nell* 1990 3 SA 889 (T); *S v L* and *O v O* 1992 4 SA 137 (C) the Transvaal, Eastern Cape and Cape Divisions found that the taking of blood tests would not have been in the child's best interests.

Unfortunately the position in respect of the ordering of blood tests is now more uncertain than it was before the Children's Status Act came into operation. We would like to point out the following:

At the moment it is uncertain whether a court can order a child to undergo a blood test. JUDGE MULLINS held in *S v L* that the court, as upper guardian of minors, does not have the power to interfere with the decision of the mother (as guardian of the child) that the child should not undergo blood tests, even if the court would have come to a different decision (721-722). In *O v O* at 139HI, on the other hand, the Cape court was of the opinion that the court, in the exercise of its power as upper guardian, is entitled to authorise a blood test on a minor despite objections by the custodian parent. This was also the view taken in *Seetal v Pravitha* at 862-864 [15]. In *M v R* [16] the court went even further and ordered a child to undergo a blood test (420DE).

Uncertainty also prevails on the question of whether the court can order an adult to submit to a blood test. In *M v R* the court ruled that it may do so since the supreme court has the inherent power to regulate its own procedures. On this basis it was argued that the court could order an unwilling adult to submit to a blood test because the court is empowered to search for and collect evidence, which is a procedural matter. If the results of blood tests are therefore necessary for trial purposes, the court can order the person concerned to undergo the tests. However, in *Nell v Nell* 1990 3 SA 889 (T) LE ROUX AJ felt that to order a person to submit to a blood test was not merely a procedural matter because such order also affects principles of substantive law in that it is a violation of the person's bodily integrity. (See also *Seetal v Pravitha* 832BD; Zeffertt 1990 *SALJ* 582). The court does not have the

van hierdie wet was daar 'n opmerklike vermeerdering in litigasie oor bloedtoetse, en die howe het heeltemal tereg beslis dat die beste belang van die kind moet bepaal of 'n persoon gelas gaan word om hom aan 'n bloedtoets te onderwerp. In *M v R* [16] het die Vrystaatse hof bevind dat dit in die beste belang van die kind sou wees dat bloedtoetse op hom en sy ma uitgevoer word, maar in *Nell v Nell* 1990 3 SA 889 (T); *S v L* en *O v O* 1992 4 SA 137 (K) het die Transvaalse, Oos-Kaapse en Kaapse afdelings beslis dat die neem van bloedtoetse nie in belang van die kind sou wees nie.

Ongelukkig is die vraag of 'n persoon gelas kan word om hom aan 'n bloedtoets te onderwerp nou meer onseker as wat dit voor die inwerkingtreding van die Wet op die Status van Kinders was. Ons wil graag op die volgende wys:

Op die oomblik is dit onseker of 'n hof 'n kind kan verplig om 'n bloedtoets te ondergaan. MULLINS R het in *S v L* beslis dat die hof, as oppervoog van minderjariges, nie die bevoegdheid het om met die moeder, as voog van die kind, se beslissing in te meng dat die kind nie bloedtoetse moet ondergaan nie, selfs al sou die hof tot 'n ander beslissing geraak het (721-722). In *O v O* op 139HI daarenteen was die Kaapse hof van mening dat die hof, in die uitoefening van sy bevoegdheid as oppervoog, wel bevoeg is om 'n minderjarige te gelas om hom aan 'n bloedtoets te onderwerp ongeag die besware van die ouer wat die bewaring van die kind het. Dit was ook die opvatting in *Seetal v Pravitha* op 862-864 [15]. In *M v R* [16] het die hof nog verder gegaan en 'n kind verplig om 'n bloedtoets te ondergaan (420DE).

Daar heers ook onsekerheid oor die vraag of die hof 'n volwassene kan verplig om 'n bloedtoets te ondergaan. In *M v R* het die hof beslis dat dit wel daartoe bevoeg is aangesien die hooggeregshof die inherente bevoegdheid het om sy eie prosedure te reël. Op grond hiervan is aangevoer dat die hof 'n onwillige volwassene kan verplig om 'n bloedtoets te ondergaan omdat die hof getuienis mag insamel wat 'n prosedure-aangeleentheid is. As die uitslag van bloedtoetse dus in 'n verhoor benodig word, mag die hof die betrokke persoon gelas om die toetse te ondergaan. In *Nell v Nell* was LE ROUX Wn R egter van mening dat dit nie net 'n prosedure-aangeleentheid was om 'n

power to create substantive law. The judge was of the opinion that it could be very difficult to draw the dividing line between substantive and procedural law, and where it cannot be done a remedy is probably not available. (On the difference between substantive and procedural law see Zeffertt 1990 *SALJ* 579 *et seq.*) This was also the court's view in *S v L* at 719.

The decision in *Nell v Nell* is rather disappointing and the reasons put forward by the court for refusing to grant the order are not very convincing (see Keyser 1990 *Annual Survey* 12). The same applies to the decision in *S v L*.

Reference can also be made to *O v O* in which FRIEDMAN JP states that there "is no statutory nor common-law power enabling the Court to order an adult to allow a blood sample to be taken for the purpose of establishing paternity" (139IJ). In this case it was not necessary to decide the question as the court found that the taking of blood tests would not have been in the child's interests.

A further uncertain point is whether a judge can take judicial notice of the technique and results of blood testing. In the judgment of the court *a quo* in *S v L* BURGER J thought that he could do so, but in the decision of the full bench in this case MULLINS J doubted whether this approach was correct (715–716). However, whether the latter view is correct is rather doubtful since the value of blood tests is so generally recognised today that judicial notice can in our view be taken thereof. See, for example, *Ex parte Emmerson* 1992 3 SA 987 (W), in which a pregnant woman applied for an order authorising the performance of certain tests on skin, blood and muscle samples of a man who had been killed in a motor accident. She maintained that the deceased was the father of her unborn child and with a view to a later claim for maintenance against the deceased's estate, the tests were necessary to prove the deceased's paternity of the child. The order was granted but because of the extreme urgency of the matter the court gave no reasons for the order.

Whether blood tests will indeed in future play a bigger role in cases where the paternity of a child is disputed is not clear. This is very unsatisfactory because, as was pointed out above, blood tests can with near certainty establish who the father of a child is.

persoon te verplig om 'n bloedtoets te ondergaan nie omdat sodanige bevel ook beginsels van die substantiewe reg raak aangesien dit 'n inbreukmaking op die persoon se liggaamlike integriteit daarstel. (Sien ook *Seetal v Pravitha* 832BD; Zeffertt 1990 *SALJ* 582). Die hof het nie die bevoegdheid om substantiewe reg te skep nie. Die regter was van mening dat dit baie moeilik kan wees om 'n skeidslyn tussen substantiewe- en prosesreg te trek en waar dit nie gedoen kan word nie is 'n remedie waarskynlik nie beskikbaar nie. (Oor die verskil tussen substantiewe- en prosesreg, sien Zeffertt 1990 *SALJ* 579 ev.) Dit was ook die opvatting in *S v L* op 719.

Die beslissing in *Nell v Nell* is teleurstellend en die redes wat die hof vir weiering van die bevel aanvoer, is nie baie oortuigend nie (sien Keyser 1990 *Annual Survey* 12). Dieselfde geld vir die beslissing in *S v L*.

Verder kan ook na *O v O* verwys word. In die saak sê FRIEDMAN RP "[t]here is no statutory nor common-law power enabling the Court to order an adult to allow a blood sample to be taken for the purpose of establishing paternity" (139IJ). In hierdie saak was dit nie nodig om die aangeleentheid te beslis nie aangesien die hof bevind het dat die neem van bloedtoetse nie in belang van die kind sou wees nie.

'n Verdere aangeleentheid waaroor onsekerheid bestaan, is of 'n regter geregtelik kan kennis neem van die uitslag van bloedtoetse en die tegniek van hoe sulke toetse uitgevoer word. In die uitspraak van die hof *a quo* in *S v L* was BURGER R van mening dat hy dit wel kon doen, maar in die volbankbeslissing in hierdie saak het MULLINS R getwyfel of hierdie benadering korrek was (715–716). Of laasgenoemde siening korrek is, is egter te betwyfel aangesien die waarde van bloedtoetse vandag so algemeen erken word dat na ons mening wel geregtelik daarvan kennis geneem kan word. Sien byvoorbeeld *Ex parte Emmerson* 1992 3 SA 987 (W) waarin 'n swanger vrou aansoek gedoen het om 'n bevel dat magtiging verleen word om sekere toetse uit te voer op vel-, bloed- en spiermonsters van 'n man wat in 'n motorongeluk gedood is. Sy het beweer dat die oorledene die vader van haar ongebore kind was en die toetse was nodig ten einde sy vaderskap te bewys met die oog op 'n latere eis om onderhoud uit sy boedel. Die hof het die bevel verleen

Furthermore, in the case where one party refuses to undergo blood tests the courts usually find that it will not be in the child's interests if blood tests were to prove that a man who is paying maintenance for the child is not his father with the result that he will lose the maintenance. This surely also applies where the parties voluntarily submit to the taking of the tests. Yet, in the case of voluntary submission to blood tests there is no objection to the results of these tests being used to prove or disprove paternity.

Section 2 of the Children's Status Act creates a presumption against a person who refuses to submit himself, or a child over which he has parental authority, to the taking of blood tests to establish the paternity of the child.

In *S v L* ERASMUS J was of the opinion that the respondent should not have approached the supreme court for an order requiring the mother and child to submit themselves to blood tests. He should have stayed in the maintenance court and there adduced proof of her refusal, and if the refusal was without adequate reason he could rely on the presumption in section 2 of the Children's Status Act 82 of 1987, namely that her refusal "is aimed at concealing the truth concerning the paternity of that child". This may mean that a man in whose favour the presumption operates will not have to pay maintenance for a child but it still would not resolve with certainty the question of whether or not he is the child's father.

From the above it is clear that the provincial divisions of the supreme court take diverse views on the role of blood tests to determine paternity and as the matter has not as yet been considered by the appellate division, it is rather difficult to tell what the attitude of the courts will be in future. It is submitted that the paramount consideration should still be whether the taking of blood tests would be in the interests of the child, but as medical science can today by means of blood tests establish almost certainly whether a man is the father of a child, it is submitted that more use ought to be made of blood tests in cases where the paternity of a child is in dispute (see also Darroll 1965 *SALJ* 322; Boberg 332). It is therefore understandable that the decision in *M v R* was widely acclaimed (see eg Du Plessis 1990 *THRHR* 285; Zeffertt 1990 *SALJ* 579; Lind 1989 *BML* 173).

maar, omdat die aangeleentheid so dringend was, is geen redes vir die bevel verskaf nie.

Of bloedtoetse in die vervolg inderdaad 'n groter rol gaan speel in gevalle waar die vaderskap van 'n kind betwis word, is op hierdie stadium onseker. Dit is 'n onbevredigende toedrag van sake aangesien, soos hierbo daarop gewys is, deur middel van bloedtoetse byna met sekerheid vasgestel kan word wie die vader van 'n kind is.

Verder is dit so dat waar die een party weier om bloedtoetse te ondergaan, die howe gewoonlik bevind dat dit nie in belang van die kind sal wees as bloedtoetse sou bewys dat 'n man wat vir die kind onderhoud betaal nie sy vader is nie, met die gevolg dat hy die onderhoud sal verloor. Maar dit is tog sekerlik ook die geval waar die partye hulle vrywillig aan die neem van bloedtoetse onderwerp. In sodanige geval is daar egter geen beswaar dat bloedtoetse vir die bewys van vaderskap gebruik word nie.

Artikel 2 van die Wet op die Status van Kinders skep 'n vermoede teen die persoon wat weier om homself, of 'n kind oor wie hy ouerlike gesag voer, aan die neem van bloedtoetse te onderwerp ten einde die vaderskap van die kind vas te stel.

In *S v L* was ERASMUS R van mening dat die respondent nie die hooggeregshof moes genader het om 'n bevel dat die moeder en kind hulle aan bloedtoetse moes onderwerp nie. Hy moes in die onderhoudshof gebly het en daar bewys van haar weiering gelewer het, en as die weiering sonder voldoende rede was, kon hy op die vermoede in artikel 2 van die Wet op die Status van Kinders 82 van 1987 gesteun het, naamlik dat haar weiering "daarop gemik is om die waarheid aangaande die vaderskap van daardie kind te verberg." Dit mag beteken dat die man ten gunste van wie die vermoede werk nie onderhoud vir 'n kind hoef te betaal nie, maar dit kan nie vir hom sekerheid bring of hy die kind se vader is al dan nie.

Uit bostaande is duidelik dat die provinsiale afdelings van die hooggeregshof verskil oor watter rol bloedtoetse by die bepaling van vaderskap moet speel, en aangesien die aangeleentheid nog nie deur die appèlhof oorweeg is nie, is dit moeilik om te sê watter houding die howe in die toekoms gaan inneem. Sekerlik moet die belangrikste oorweging steeds wees of die neem van

What is, however, clear is that any person who approaches the court for an order compelling someone to submit himself to a blood test would be well advised to submit full details to the court of exactly what the test entails (apart from *S v L* see also *Nell v Nell*).

bloedtoetse in belang van die kind sal wees, maar aangesien die mediese wetenskap vandag byna met sekerheid deur middel van bloedtoetse kan vasstel of 'n man die vader van 'n kind is, word aan die hand gedoen dat in die toekoms meer van bloedtoetse gebruik gemaak behoort te word waar die vaderskap van 'n kind in geskil is (sien ook Darroll 1965 *SALJ* 322; Boberg 332). Dit is daarom verstaanbaar dat die beslissing in *M v R* wye byval gevind het (sien byvoorbeeld Du Plessis 1990 *THRHR* 285; Zeffertt 1990 *SALJ* 579; Lind 1989 *BML* 173).

Wat egter baie duidelik is, is dat enige persoon wat die hof om 'n bevel nader ten einde iemand anders te verplig om hom aan 'n bloedtoets te onderwerp, volle besonderhede aan die hof moet voorlê van presies wat die toets behels (sien afgesien van *S v L* ook *Nell v Nell*).

[18] MITCHELL V MITCHELL

1963 2 SA 505 (D)

Period of gestation

The plaintiff sought an order of divorce against his wife (first defendant) on the ground of her adultery. He also claimed an order declaring that he was not the father of the child born to his wife on 3 October 1962. It appeared from the plaintiff's evidence that his wife had left him on 17 November 1961. Since that date he had seen her once and only from a distance. The last occasion on which he had sexual intercourse with his wife was approximately one week before 17 November. The only medical evidence presented was that of a medical superintendent who, although a registered medical practitioner, was not a gynaecologist. He was of the opinion that it was impossible that the child born to the wife could have been conceived as early as 16 November, as that would have meant that the period of gestation was approximately 320 days. In an affidavit the wife admitted that she had

Swangerskapsduur

Die eiser het op grond van sy vrou (eerste verweerder) se owerspel 'n egskeidingsgeding teen haar ingestel. Hy het ook om 'n bevel aansoek gedoen wat verklaar dat hy nie die vader van die kind aan wie sy vrou op 3 Oktober 1962 geboorte geskenk het, was nie. Dit het uit die eiser se getuienis geblyk dat sy vrou hom op 17 November 1961 verlaat het. Sedert daardie datum het hy haar net een keer op 'n afstand gesien. Die laaste keer wat hy seksueel met haar verkeer het, was ongeveer een week voor 17 November. Die enigste mediese getuienis is deur 'n mediese superintendent gelewer. Hy was weliswaar 'n geregistreerde mediese praktisyn maar nie 'n ginekoloog nie. Hy was van mening dat dit onmoontlik was dat die kind aan wie die vrou geboorte geskenk het reeds op 16 November verwek kon gewees het. Dit sou beteken het dat die swangerskapsduur ongeveer 320 dae was. Die vrou het in 'n be-

committed adultery with a man whom she refused to name and that he was the father of the child. The *curator ad litem* (second defendant) appointed to represent the child denied the plaintiff's right to the order sought, on the ground that the *pater est quem nuptiae demonstrant* presumption was against him. The court held that the plaintiff was entitled to a decree of divorce but refused to grant a declaratory order bastardising the child.

ëdigde verklaring erken dat sy owerspel gepleeg het met 'n man wie se naam sy geweier het om te noem en dat hy die vader van die kind was. 'n *Curator ad litem* (tweede verweerder) is aangestel om die kind se belange te verteenwoordig. Hy het betwis dat die eiser op die bevel geregtig was aangesien die *pater est quem nuptiae demonstrant*-vermoede teen hom gegeld het. Die hof het die egskeidingsbevel toegestaan maar geweier om die kind buite-egtelik te verklaar.

MILLER J: [506] I have no reason to suspect the genuineness of first defendant's admissions against herself and such admissions, considered together with the other facts and circumstances ... satisfy me that first defendant committed adultery and that plaintiff is entitled to a decree of divorce.

Different considerations arise, however, in connection with plaintiff's claim for a declaration that he is not the father of the child born to his wife *stante matrimonio*. The presumption of paternity can, of course, be rebutted, and notwithstanding that the effect of the order sought would be to bastardise the child, I am prepared to accept that the presumption may be rebutted by clear evidence showing, to the cautious mind, a preponderance of probabilities ... The evidence against the second defendant in this case is not necessarily co-extensive with that against first defendant, for the latter's admissions of her adultery are not necessarily admissible against a third party. The child is a party to these proceedings, through his *curator-ad-litem*, but notwithstanding what I have found in regard to first defendant's adultery I am not prepared to accept the evidence of first defendant's admission made to others as evidence against the child, but only as evidence [507] against herself. And in so far as the first defendant's affidavit is concerned, I am not prepared to consider that evidence in connection with the claim for an order bastardising the child, since the first defendant was not cross-examined or available for cross-examination, on behalf of the child, on her evidence contained in the affidavit.

In the result, the only evidence on which plaintiff may properly rely for the further relief sought by him is that his wife gave birth to a normal child approximately 320 days after the last occasion on which he had sexual intercourse with her and that an opinion was expressed by the medical superintendent that this fact made it impossible for him to be the father of the child. It is not necessary for me to say what the position would be if such an opinion were expressed by a gynaecologist. On the very frank admission of the medical superintendent himself, he is not and does not hold himself out to be an expert in regard to such matters and his reference to the recorded facts in medical literature was equivocal and obviously not the result of thorough research.

If I were to accept that a period of gestation of 320 days was so inordinately lengthy as to make it impossible for the plaintiff to be the father of the child, I would be taking judicial cognisance of something which I do not think a mere Judge has any claim to know as a clear and well-established fact. It may be that judicial notice may be taken of the fact that the normal period of gestation is approximately nine months, but it is a far cry from that to say that a period of ten months, or eleven months, is so lengthy as to be impossible or very highly improbable ...

[MILLER J referred to the English case of *Preston-Jones v Preston-Jones* [1951] 1 All ER 127 and proceeded:]

[508] In *Williams v Williams*, 1925 TPD 538, TINDALL, J (as he then was) refused, without medical evidence, to hold that the eleventh month was beyond the period of gestation. The period in issue in that case was 322 days (see at p 542). I am not aware of any case in South Africa where an adverse inference was drawn without strong medical or other evidence in respect of a period approximating to that in issue in this case, although in *Barker v Barker*, 1 Menz 245, an inference of adultery was drawn, apparently without any medical evidence, where the period was fifteen months.

I am not satisfied that the plaintiff has made out a case for a declaration bastardising the child and I am not prepared to make the order sought on the evidence before me. In the circumstances, however, I am prepared to give the plaintiff the opportunity of placing further medical or other evidence before me, if he is so advised. Leave is therefore granted to him to set the matter down for further hearing on a date to be arranged with the Registrar and upon due notice to the *curator-ad-litem* whose appointment as such is effective until the termination of this case.

As against first defendant there will be a decree of divorce . . .

Note

There is no fixed gestation period in our law today. The courts make a decision on an *ad hoc* basis, relying on medical evidence as to when conception could possibly have taken place. The normal period of gestation is more or less 270 days, but it is evident from the case under discussion that the courts are very reluctant to declare a child illegitimate. Notwithstanding the fact that in this case the wife admitted that she had committed adultery and that the other man was the father of the child, the court held that there was insufficient evidence to rebut the presumption *pater est quem nuptiae demonstrant*.

See also *Gradidge v Gradidge* 1948 1 SA 120 (D) where it was held that the husband of the mother could not have been the father of a child born to her 206 days after the husband's return from active service overseas. See further Boberg 324 fn 18; Van der Vyver and Joubert 211.

Aantekening

In ons huidige reg word 'n vasgestelde swangerskapsduur nie aanvaar nie. Die howe beslis van geval tot geval met behulp van mediese getuienis wanneer verwekking waarskynlik plaasgevind het. Die normale swangerskapsduur is ongeveer 270 dae maar dit is uit die onderhawige saak duidelik dat die howe nie baie geneë is om 'n kind buiteegtelik te verklaar nie. Ten spyte van die feit dat die vrou in hierdie saak erken het dat sy owerspel gepleeg het en dat die ander man die vader van die kind was, het die hof beslis dat daar nie genoeg getuienis was om die vermoede *pater est quem nuptiae demonstrant* te weerlê nie.

Sien ook *Gradidge v Gradidge* 1948 1 SA 120 (D) waarin beslis is dat die man van 'n vrou nie die vader van 'n kind kon wees waaraan sy geboorte geskenk het 206 dae nadat hy van die oorlog teruggekeer het nie. Sien verder Boberg 324 vn 18; Van der Vyver en Joubert 211.

Parental authority   Ouerlike gesag

[19]   CALITZ V CALITZ

1939 AD 56

Right of a father to the custody of his minor child

The appellant's wife sued him for judicial separation and for the custody of their

Reg van 'n vader op die bewaring van sy minderjarige kind

Die appellant se vrou het hom gedagvaar om geregtelike skeiding en vir die bewaring van

daughter, aged two years and three months. In the court *a quo* it was found that grounds for a separation had not been established. The wife had left her husband with no intention of returning. The appellant, on the other hand, wished his wife to return and was prepared to take her back. In the court *a quo* the judge stated that he did not find that the appellant was not a fit and proper person to have the custody of the child. The judge found, however, that, taking everything into consideration, the interests of the child would be best served by awarding custody to the mother. Her husband appealed against this decision and the decision of the court *a quo* was reversed.

hulle dogtertjie wat twee jaar en drie maande oud was. In die hof *a quo* is bevind dat gronde vir 'n geregtelike skeiding nie bewys is nie. Die vrou het haar man verlaat met die bedoeling om nie weer terug te keer nie. Die appellant wou hê dat sy vrou moes terugkeer en was ook bereid om haar terug te neem. In die hof *a quo* het die regter gemeld dat hy nie bevind het dat die appellant nie 'n geskikte persoon was om die bewaring van die kind aan toe te ken nie. Die regter het egter bevind dat, alles inaggenome, dit in die beste belang van die kind sou wees om die bewaring aan die moeder toe te ken. Haar man het teen die beslissing geappelleer en die beslissing van die hof *a quo* is omvergewerp.

TINDALL JA: [61] Although the *patria potestas* of the Roman Law was not recognised in the Roman-Dutch Law and the parental power belongs to the mother as well as the father (*Voet* 1.6.3), there is no doubt that under our law, at any rate as it exists today in the Union, the rights of the father are superior to those of the mother . . .

[63] In my judgment the Court has no jurisdiction, where no divorce or separation authorising the separate home has been granted, to deprive the father of his custody except under the Court's powers as upper guardian of all minors to interfere with the father's custody on special grounds, such for example as danger to the child's life, health or morals . . .

[64] The non-existence of the common home, brought about as it has been by the wife's unlawful desertion is not a factor which a Court of law can allow to operate in her favour on the question of the custody of the child. As the learned Judge found that she had no just ground for leaving her husband, her duty is to return to him and look after the child under his roof.

That being the position, it is clear that the Court was not entitled to deprive the husband of the custody. The learned Judge held that he was a fit and proper person to have the custody. The father had done nothing which entitled the Court in the exercise of its powers as upper guardian to hold that he had forfeited his right to the custody of the child. The fact that the child, being of tender years, would be better looked after by the mother did not, under the circumstances, justify the order made . . .

Naturally the Court does not regard with unconcern the prospect of a female child of 2¼ years being without the care of its mother. It lies, however, with the mother to avoid that misfortune in the present case by returning to her husband.

The result is that the appeal is allowed . . .

DE WET JA; WATERMEYER JA and CENTLIVRES AJA concurred.

Note

As a general rule a parent cannot be deprived of the custody of his or her legitimate minor child except upon divorce, or where, in the opinion of the court, special grounds of the kind referred to in *Calitz's* case exist (see the judgment of

Aantekening

As 'n algemene reël kan 'n ouer nie die bewaring van sy of haar binne-egtelike minderjarige kind ontneem word nie behalwe na 'n egskeiding, of waar daar na die mening van die hof spesiale gronde bestaan om dit te doen soos wat in die

SCHREINER JA in *Bam v Bhabha* 1947 4 SA 798 (A) 809). The grounds stated by TINDALL JA in *Calitz's* case, viz "danger to the child's life, health and morals" are, however, not the only grounds which would justify interference by the court with the parents' powers (*Bam v Bhabha; Short v Naisby* 1955 3 SA 572 (D); *September v Karriem* 1959 3 SA 687 (C); *Petersen v Kruger* [145]; Boberg 413; Van der Vyver and Joubert 622–623). Good reasons will have to be advanced before the court will intervene but this requirement cannot be precisely defined. Each case must, therefore, be considered on its own merits (*Short v Naisby* 575). Whether a court will interfere or not will always depend on whether such intervention will be in the best interests of the child.

The same principles apply when it has to be decided whether to interfere with the parental authority of the mother of an illegitimate child (*Rowan v Faifer* 1953 2 SA 705 (E) 711).

The remedies available at common law to interfere with the exercise of parental power are seldom resorted to today, since much of the field is now covered by legislation. See, for example, section 5 of the Matrimonial Affairs Act 37 of 1953 and the Child Care Act 74 of 1983. See further *Ex parte Van Dam* [20]; Spiro 259 331 *et seq*; Boberg 420; Van der Vyver and Joubert 623 *et seq*.

It must be remembered that different rules apply in respect of guardianship of legitimate children and illegitimate children. A mother is the guardian of her illegitimate child. In terms of the common law, a father was the only guardian of his legitimate child. During the life of the father, the mother of a legitimate child had no powers of guardianship over the child, although in exceptional circumstances guardianship could be conferred on her by the court.

However, the Guardianship Act 192 of 1993, which came into operation on 1 March 1994, amended the law. In section 1(1), the act confers guardianship on the mother of a legitimate child, which guardianship is "equal to that which a father has under the common law." In terms of section 1(2) of the act, the parents of a legitimate child may exercise their powers of guardianship independently and without each other's consent, except in respect of those legal acts for which the consent of both parents is expressly required by the section. These are:

Calitz-saak die geval was (sien die uitspraak van SCHREINER AR in *Bam v Bhabha* 1947 4 SA 798 (A) 809). Die gronde wat deur TINDALL AR in *Calitz* se saak genoem is, naamlik "danger to the child's life, health or morals", is egter nie die enigste gronde op grond waarvan 'n hof in die uitoefening van ouerlike gesag kan inmeng nie (*Bam v Bhabha; Short v Naisby* 1955 3 SA 572 (D); *September v Karriem* 1959 3 SA 687 (K); *Petersen v Kruger* [145]; Boberg 413; Van der Vyver en Joubert 622–623). Daar sal goeie redes aangetoon moet word voordat die hof sal inmeng, maar hierdie vereiste kan nie presies omskryf word nie. Elke saak moet gevolglik op sy eie meriete beoordeel word (*Short v Naisby* 575). Of 'n hof sal inmeng al dan nie sal altyd daarvan afhang of sodanige inmenging in die belang van die kind sal wees.

Dieselfde beginsels geld wanneer besluit moet word of met die ouerlike gesag van die moeder van 'n buite-egtelike kind ingemeng moet word (*Rowan v Faifer* 1953 2 SA 705 (OK) 711).

Daar word vandag selde gebruik gemaak van die gemeenregtelike remedies om met die uitoefening van ouerlike gesag in te meng, aangesien daar tans wetgewing bestaan wat 'n groot deel van die gebied dek. Sien byvoorbeeld artikel 5 van die Wet op Huweliksaangeleenthede 37 van 1953 en die Wet op Kindersorg 74 van 1983. Sien verder *Ex parte Van Dam* [20]; Spiro 259 331 ev; Boberg 420; Van der Vyver en Joubert 623 ev.

Daar moet in gedagte gehou word dat verskillende reëls geld met betrekking tot die voogdy oor binne-egtelike kinders en buite-egtelike kinders. 'n Moeder het voogdy oor haar buite-egtelike kind. Ingevolge die gemenereg was die vader die enigste voog van sy binne-egtelike kind. Terwyl die vader geleef het, het die moeder van 'n binne-egtelike kind geen voogdyskap oor die kind gehad nie, alhoewel daar wel in uitsonderlike gevalle deur die hof voogdyskap aan haar toegeken kon word.

Die Wet op Voogdy 192 van 1993, wat op 1 Maart 1994 in werking getree het, het die reg egter gewysig. In artikel 1(1) beklee die wet die moeder van 'n binne-egtelike kind met voogdyskap, welke voogdyskap "gelykwaardig [is] aan dié wat 'n vader kragtens die gemene reg . . . het." Ingevolge artikel 1(2) van die wet kan die ouers van 'n binne-egtelike kind hulle voogdy selfstandig en sonder mekaar se toestemming uitoefen, behalwe ten opsigte van daardie regshandelinge waarvoor die artikel uitdruklik die toestemming van albei ouers vereis. Hierdie regshandelinge is:

(a) the contracting of a marriage by the child;

(b) the adoption of the child;

(c) the removal of the child from the Republic by one of the parents or by another person;

(d) the application by one of the parents for a passport in which the child is specified as a child of the applicant;

(e) the alienation or encumbrance of immovable property or any right to immovable property belonging to the child.

The act also amends section 5 of the Matrimonial Affairs Act 37 of 1953 and section 72 of the Administration of Estates Act 66 of 1965 to provide that only if a parent of a legitimate child has been appointed by the court as the sole guardian of the child, or if he is the sole surviving parent of the child, can he appoint somebody to act as guardian in his place after his death. A father who is not the sole guardian of his child can therefore no longer appoint somebody to act as guardian jointly with the child's mother after his death. Upon the death of the first-dying parent, the surviving parent therefore becomes the sole guardian of the child, unless the surviving parent has, by court order, been deprived of his or her rights of guardianship.

Under the old divorce law the courts could grant orders for judicial separation. Such an order meant that the marriage continued to exist but that the spouses were no longer bound to cohabit. Neither of the spouses could, however, enter into another marriage. Section 14 of the Divorce Act 70 of 1979 abolished orders for judicial separation. Consequently this remedy no longer exists in our law.

(a) die sluit van 'n huwelik deur die kind;

(b) die aanneming van die kind;

(c) die verwydering van die kind uit die Republiek deur een van die ouers of 'n ander persoon;

(d) die aansoek deur een van die ouers om 'n paspoort waarin die kind aangedui word as kind van die applikant;

(e) die vervreemding of beswaring van onroerende goed of 'n reg op onroerende goed wat aan die kind behoort.

Die wet wysig ook artikel 5 van die Wet op Huweliksaangeleenthede 37 van 1953 en artikel 72 van die Boedelwet 66 van 1965 en bepaal dat 'n ouer van 'n binne-egtelike kind slegs iemand kan aanstel om na sy dood in sy plek as voog op te tree indien daardie ouer deur die hof as alleenvoog van die kind aangestel is, of as hy die enigste oorlewende ouer van die kind is. 'n Vader wat nie die enigste voog van sy kind is nie, kan dus nie meer iemand aanstel om na sy dood saam met die kind se moeder as voog op te tree nie. By die dood van die eerssterwende ouer word die langslewende ouer gevolglik die enigste voog van die kind, tensy die langslewende ouer deur middel van 'n hofbevel van sy of haar voogdyskap ontneem is.

Volgens die ou egskeidingsreg kon die howe bevele tot geregtelike skeiding gee. Sodanige bevel het beteken dat die huwelik voortbestaan het, maar die gades was nie verplig om saam te woon nie. Geeneen van die gades kon egter 'n volgende huwelik sluit nie. Artikel 14 van die Wet op Egskeiding 70 van 1979 bepaal egter nou dat die howe nie meer sulke bevele kan gee nie. Hierdie remedie bestaan gevolglik nie meer in ons reg nie.

[20] EX PARTE VAN DAM

1973 2 SA 182 (W)

Father of an illegitimate child appointed guardian of the child

Vader van 'n buite-egtelike kind aangestel as voog van die kind

The applicant was formerly married and a child was born of this marriage. The parties

Die applikant was voorheen getroud en 'n kind is uit die huwelik gebore. Die partye were then divorced and custody of the child was given to the mother. Despite the divorce the parties continued to live together and a child was born of this extra-marital relationship. The mother would not remarry the applicant and wished to terminate their joint life. The children had lived a family life with their parents up till then and both parents desired to allow for the future relationship of the children with their father. In order to realise this they entered into an agreement in terms of which the mother was to have custody of both children, whilst the applicant was to pay maintenance for them and have reasonable access to them. The applicant was also to be the guardian of both children and the mother was to support him in the application for his appointment as such. The applicant then applied for an order appointing him guardian of the two children, that is, also of the child born out of wedlock, and to have the agreement between him and the children's mother made an order of court. The order was granted.

is toe geskei en bewaring van die kind is aan die moeder toegesê. Ten spyte van die egskeiding het die partye voortgegaan om saam te woon. Uit hierdie buite-egtelike verhouding is ook 'n kind gebore. Die moeder wou nie weer met die applikant trou nie en wou hulle verhouding beëindig. Tot op daardie stadium het die kinders as gesin saam met hulle ouers gewoon en albei ouers wou vir die toekomstige verhouding tussen die kinders en hulle vader voorsiening maak. Ten einde dit te bewerkstellig, het hulle 'n ooreenkoms aangegaan waarvolgens die moeder die bewaring van albei kinders sou hê, terwyl die applikant onderhoud vir hulle sou betaal en 'n reg van redelike toegang tot hulle sou hê. Die applikant sou ook die voog van albei kinders wees. Die moeder sou sy aansoek om as voog aangestel te word ondersteun. Die applikant het toe aansoek gedoen om as voog oor die twee kinders aangestel te word, dit wil sê ook oor die buite-egtelike kind, asook om die ooreenkoms tussen hom en die kinders se moeder 'n bevel van die hof te maak. Die bevel is toegestaan.

MARGO J: [182] On the question of guardianship, the applicant's position in relation to the legitimate child may be stated simply. In our law the father is the natural guardian of a legitimate child . . .

[183] In regard to the illegitimate child, the rule in our law is that generally speaking the mother and not the father is the natural guardian. *Dhanabakium v Subramanian and Another*, 1943 AD 160, *per* TINDALL, JA, at p 166.

In this case the provisions of the modern statutes on the judicial change of natural guardianship do not appear to be applicable. Sec 5 (1) of the Matrimonial Affairs Act, 37 of 1953, judged in the context of sec 5 itself and of the Act as a whole, does not seem to deal with the custody or guardianship of an illegitimate child. That is also *Hahlo's* view, [*The South African Law of Husband and Wife* 3 ed] at p 451. Sec 60 of the Children's Act, 33 of 1960, is clearly not applicable.

The question of whether the mother's guardianship of the *illegitimate* child can be transferred to the father by the Court must therefore be decided by reference to the common law. This particular aspect does not appear to have been examined specifically by the Roman-Dutch writers to whom I have referred. Nor have I found any direct authority in our case law on the position relative to illegitimate children . . .

[MARGO J then discussed the circumstances under which a father will be deprived of his guardianship over his legitimate children and proceeded:]

[184] So much then for the common law on changes in the guardianship of legitimate children. Authority is not plentiful on the corresponding position in regard to illegitimate

children. In *Rowan v Faifer*, 1953 (2) SA 705 (E), GARDNER, JP, at p 710A–E, after referring to the earlier cases on the custody of illegitimate children, held *obiter* that, although the father of an illegitimate child has no right to custody, he has *locus standi* to appear on the question of custody. GARDNER, JP, obviously did not intend to convey that such a father could never be given custody, for it is clear that, in a proper case, the Court as the upper guardian of all minors might find that the father is best fitted to have custody.

In *Rowan's* case, GARDNER, JP, at p 711, referred to the power of the Court, in the absence of a decree of divorce or order of separation, to deprive the natural guardian of legitimate children of custody, where there are special grounds for doing so. GARDNER, JP, then went [185] on to say that there appeared to be no reason why the Court should not act similarly in the case of illegitimate children.

In my view the same reasoning applies to guardianship. Since the Court has the power in a proper case to deprive the natural guardian of legitimate children of his guardianship, and to vest it in another, there appears to be no reason why the Court should not act similarly in the case of illegitimate children. See *Hahlo, supra op cit* at p 451, where the learned author suggests that, although sec 5 of the Matrimonial Affairs Act of 1953 does not apply to illegitimate children, that would not prevent the Court from dealing with the custody or guardianship of an illegitimate child under the ordinary rules of the common law. Spiro on *The Law of Parent and Child,* 3rd ed p 426, expresses a similar view. He goes so far as to say that if the interests of the minor illegitimate child so demand, custody if not even guardianship may be awarded to the natural father.

In the present case the mother and natural guardian of the illegitimate child wishes to renounce and surrender her guardianship on the ground that it would be in the best interests of the child that the applicant should be the guardian. It is plainly not competent for a natural guardian to renounce guardianship in favour of a third person at will. Guardianship is a duty much more than it is a right.

However there are special circumstances in the present case and I am satisfied that it will be in the best interests of the child that the applicant as its father and *de facto* guardian hitherto should continue to occupy a position of parental authority.

I have accordingly come to the conclusion that the applicant has made out a case for the order he seeks on the guardianship of the illegitimate child.

It is unnecessary to define the guardianship to be conferred on the applicant other than to identify it as the guardianship of a natural guardian who does not have custody of the child . . .

Note

The court as upper guardian of all minors (both legitimate and illegitimate) will always act in the best interests of the child (see also *B v P* [22] at 115–116). In the special circumstances of *Van Dam's* case, the court found that it would be in the interests of the illegitimate child that his father be appointed his guardian. Section 5 of the Matrimonial Affairs Act 37 of 1953 deals with the guardianship and custody of legitimate children only. In terms of this section the court may, at the request of either parent of a minor whose parents are divorced or are living apart, issue any

Aantekening

Die hof, as oppervoog van alle minderjariges (binne-egtelik sowel as buite-egtelik), tree altyd in die beste belang van die kind op (sien ook *B v P* [22] op 115–116). In die spesiale omstandighede van *Van Dam* se saak het die hof bevind dat dit in die buite-egtelike kind se belang sou wees dat sy vader as sy voog aangestel word. Artikel 5 van die Wet op Huweliksaangeleenthede 37 van 1953 het slegs te doen met die voogdy en bewaring van binne-egtelike kinders. Ingevolge hierdie artikel mag die hof, op aansoek van enigeen van die ouers van 'n minderjarige wie se ouers

order which it may deem fit in regard to the custody or guardianship of, or access to the minor. The court is authorised specifically to grant to either parent the sole guardianship or custody of the minor if, in the court's opinion, it would be in the interests of such minor to do so. As this section does not apply to illegitimate children, the common-law principles are still applied in all matters regarding the guardianship and custody of illegitimate children (see also *Calitz v Calitz* [19]).

In terms of section 60 of the Children's Act 33 of 1960 either parent could have been deprived of his parental power. This section was repealed by the Child Care Act 74 of 1983. The Child Care Act does not contain a provision exactly corresponding to section 60 of the Children's Act (see in this regard Heaton 54 fn 64).

If the mother of an illegitimate child is unmarried and a minor, the guardianship of the child vests in the guardian of the mother, but the mother will have the custody of the child. If the mother is under the age of twenty-one but acquires the status of a major, the guardianship and custody of the child vest in the mother. In all these instances the court may, however, direct otherwise (section 3 of the Children's Status Act 82 of 1987).

Where a person acts as guardian of a child whilst he is under the impression that he is the child's natural guardian, although he is not, the court can ratify his acts if such acts were done in the interests of the child (*Yu Kwam v President Insurance Co Ltd* 1963 1 SA 66 (T)).

geskei is of apart woon, 'n bevel uitvaardig wat die hof goedvind met betrekking tot die voogdy of bewaring van of toegang tot die minderjarige. Die hof word uitdruklik gemagtig om aan een ouer die uitsluitlike voogdy of bewaring van die minderjarige toe te ken as dit na die hof se mening in die kind se belang is om dit te doen. Aangesien hierdie artikel nie op buite-egtelike kinders van toepassing is nie is dit steeds die beginsels van die gemenereg wat geld met betrekking tot alle aangeleenthede rakende die voogdy en bewaring van buite-egtelike kinders (sien ook *Calitz v Calitz* [19]).

Ingevolge artikel 60 van die Kinderwet 33 van 1960 kon enige ouer van sy ouerlike gesag ontneem word. Hierdie artikel is deur die Wet op Kindersorg 74 van 1983 herroep. Die Wet op Kindersorg bevat nie 'n bepaling wat presies met artikel 60 van die Kinderwet ooreenstem nie (sien in die verband Heaton 54 vn 64).

Indien die moeder van 'n buite-egtelike kind ongetroud en 'n minderjarige is, berus die voogdy oor die kind by die moeder se voog, maar die bewaring van die kind berus by die moeder self. Indien die moeder onder die ouderdom van een en twintig jaar is maar die status van 'n meerderjarige verkry, berus die voogdy oor en die bewaring van die kind by die moeder. In al hierdie gevalle kan die hof egter anders gelas (artikel 3 van die Wet op die Status van Kinders 82 van 1987).

Waar 'n persoon as voog van 'n kind optree menende dat hy die voog is, maar dit in der waarheid nie is nie, kan die hof sy optrede as voog ratifiseer as dit in belang van die kind is (*Yu Kwam v President Insurance Co Ltd* 1963 1 SA 66 (T)).

[21]   F v L

1987 4 SA 525 (W)

A father's right of access to his illegitimate child

The first and second respondents were married to each other. Shortly after their marriage the first respondent gave birth to a child.

'n Vader se reg op toegang tot sy buite-egtelike kind

Die eerste en tweede respondente was met mekaar getroud. Kort na hulle huwelik het die eerste respondent geboorte aan 'n kind

The applicant alleged that he was the father of the child because he had had sexual intercourse·with the first respondent during the time when conception could have taken place. The first respondent admitted this but alleged that she also had sexual intercourse with the second respondent during that period. The applicant applied for an order declaring that he was the natural father of the child and that he was entitled to a right of reasonable access to the child. The application was rejected.

geskenk. Die applikant het aangevoer dat hy die vader van die kind was omdat hy gedurende die tydperk waarin bevrugting kon plaasgevind het, geslagsverkeer met die eerste respondent gehad het. Die eerste respondent het dit erken maar beweer dat sy gedurende daardie tydperk ook geslagsverkeer met die tweede respondent gehad het. Die applikant het nou aansoek gedoen om 'n verklarende bevel dat hy die natuurlike vader van die kind was en dat hy op 'n reg van redelike toegang tot die kind geregtig was. Die aansoek is van die hand gewys.

HARMS J: [526] The *causa* for the relief sought is the allegation that he [the applicant] is the natural father of the child. It is not alleged, nor was it argued, that any of the relief sought is in the interest of the child ...

The first objection taken on behalf of the respondents to the present application is that the applicant has no *prima facie* right which would entitle him to relief in the action and that, for that reason, the application should be dismissed. In order to determine the correctness of this objection it is necessary to consider the legal relationship between a natural father and his illegitimate child. The natural father has a duty to maintain his illegitimate offspring and the child has a right of maintenance against the father. That is trite. It is also trite that in common law no other rights and duties between them were recognised.

According to Van Leeuwen *Rooms-Hollands Recht* so-called "speelkinderen" are considered as if they have no father. In a footnote he adds that, except for children of noblemen, illegitimate children are *quoad* their father considered as strangers.

The applicant's counsel submitted, however, that in modern South African law it has always been accepted that the father of an illegitimate child is entitled to reasonable access. The textbooks quoted by counsel refer, in support of this modern rule, to two cases, namely *Matthews v Haswari* 1937 WLD 110 and *Wilson v Ely* 1914 WR 34.

In *Matthews'* case a mother claimed the return of her illegitimate child from the father who had removed the child from her custody. The father resisted the application on the basis that the mother was not fit to have custody. In view of the factual disputes the matter was referred to trial. At the end of the order a rider was added that the father was entitled to reasonable access to the child. It is not clear whether this order as to access was interim or final. This part of the order was not explained nor justified in the course of the judgment.

Accordingly, I am of the view that this part of the order cannot qualify as a precedent. *Wilson v Ely* was reported in the Weekly Reporter. It is hardly an acceptable source of law because the judgment is merely summarised. However, the facts were that the applicant and the respondent were married according to Muslim rites, had four children and thereafter the applicant left the respondent. She placed one child in the care of a school. The respondent removed the child because "it had come to him voluntarily and in_rags and tatters". The return of the child [527] was ordered to the mother, and it was said that in the circumstances of the case the father was entitled to access as it was his duty to provide maintenance.

The "circumstances" obviously refer to the allegation that the welfare of the child was in danger and the Court left the door open to the father to bring new facts to its attention in that regard. The statement that the duty to maintain gave rise to a right of access was not based on logic or authority. A right of access is not a *quid pro quo* for payment of maintenance.

Furthermore, a duty to maintain can exist quite independently from parental authority or right to access. I am consequently not prepared to consider this case as authority for any legal principle . . .

In any event, these . . . cases are irreconcilable with binding authority. In *Edwards v Fleming* 1909 TH 232 it was held that the mother of an illegitimate child is its guardian and that the guardianship can be interfered with if the welfare of the child is in danger. In *Docrat v Bhayat* 1932 TPD 125 a father claimed, as of right, custody of his illegitimate child after the death of the mother. It was held that the father had no *locus standi* but the Court proceeded to consider whether the father would not be a better custodian than the *de facto* custodian. Both these cases were quoted with approval in *Dhanabakium v Subramanian and Another* 1943 AD 160 at 166.

The decision in *Rowan v Faifer* 1953 (2) SA 705 (E) was critical of *Docrat's* case but is distinguishable because it was really concerned with the so-called right of a father to bring to the Court's attention the fact that the mother's custody jeopardised the child's welfare (cf *Ex parte Van Dam* 1973 (2) SA 182 (W) [20]).

As indicated, that is not the applicant's case. I am therefore not concerned, in the present case, with the so-called rights of a natural father where the child's welfare is in jeopardy. If authority is needed for the proposition that access to a child is an incidence or consequence of parental authority, reference may be made to, for instance, Boberg *Law of Persons and the Family* chap 20 and Van der Vyver and Joubert *Persone- en Familiereg* at 610.

A father acquires parental authority over his natural children in three ways, namely birth from a valid marriage, secondly, legitimation and, thirdly, adoption. (See *Voet* 1.6.4.) A mother, on the other hand, acquires her parental authority by reason of birth. She cannot make a bastard (Van der Linden *Koopmanshandboek* 1.4.2).

The applicant did not acquire parental authority over the child. He could therefore not have acquired any of the incidents of parental authority and he cannot acquire them by having the child declared his natural offspring. (Cf Arntzenius *Institutiones* 2.3.26.) The conclusion therefore is that the applicant has no *prima facie* right of access to the child.

[528] It follows that the applicant is not entitled to institute action to have this right determined . . .

I now turn to consider separately the applicant's right to a declaratory order that he is the natural father of the child. As I understand the applicant's papers, the declaratory order was only sought in order to create an entitlement to a right of access.

Applicant's counsel submitted, however, that the applicant is entitled to know whether he is the child's father or not, even if he is not entitled to access. The question is then whether a natural father has the right to bastardise his child who is, by virtue of at least two legal presumptions, deemed to be the child of another. The curious situation existing in this case is that different presumptions apply.

Firstly, according to the presumption of *pater est quem nuptiae demonstrant*, the second respondent is presumed to be the father. By virtue of the presumption of fatherhood following upon an admission of sexual intercourse, it is presumed that both the applicant and the second respondent are the father of the child. However, the law gives the mother the right to choose or appoint the father in such a case. (See VAN DEN HEEVER J as

quoted in *MacDonald v Stander* 1935 AD 325.) The first respondent has chosen the second respondent as father. Her selection is presumably irrevocable. I know of no principle that gives the jilted lover the right to interfere with her choice nor do I believe it to be in the public interest to create such a right. It may be otherwise if it were in the interests of the child. *In casu* the welfare of the child is not an issue.

The effect of the declaratory order sought may not only be devastating for the child, but will have serious legal consequences for the child. It will deprive the child of an existing right of maintenance, not only against his present father but against any paternal grandparent ...

In the absence of any authority or principle pointing in another direction I conclude that the applicant has no *prima facie* right to have himself declared the natural father of his illegitimate child. The submission that he wishes to know if he might have a duty to maintain the child is of no merit. Having regard to his admission of intercourse, the question whether he is in fact the natural father is an irrelevant consideration. He is, in law, liable to maintain the child unless his liability is destroyed by the choice exercised by the mother in selecting the second respondent as father.

Assuming that I were wrong in concluding that the applicant has no right to know, the applicant has another hurdle to overcome. The grant of a declaratory order is a discretionary matter. The applicant must, therefore, at least have given some facts which would tend to indicate that a trial Court would be prepared to consider to exercise its discretion in his favour. The applicant did not do so. As a matter of fact I am unable to visualise why any Court should come to his assistance in the exercise of its discretion. I therefore conclude that the applicant has not *prima facie* established that the trial Court will exercise its discretion in his favour to consider his application for a declaratory order ...

[529] The application is dismissed ...

Note	Aantekening
The right of access of a father in respect of his illegitimate child is currently one of the most controversial aspects of private law.	Die reg van toegang van 'n vader tot sy buite-egtelike kind is tans een van die mees kontroversiële aspekte van die privaatreg.
It was formerly suggested, on the basis of the authority of *Matthews v Haswari* 1937 WLD 110 and *Wilson v Ely* 1914 WR 34, that the father of an illegitimate child has a right of reasonable access to that child (Spiro 458; Boberg 334). However, in *Douglas v Mayers* 1987 1 SA 910 (Z) and *F v B* 1988 3 SA 948 (D) it was held that the father of an illegitimate child does not have an inherent right of access to his illegitimate child. Nevertheless, like any other third party, he has a right to apply for access and it will be granted if he can satisfy the court that it is in the best interests of the child to do so. It must be pointed out that in the *Douglas* case it was found that it would not have been in the best interests of the child to grant a right of reasonable access to the father (see also *F v B*).	Op gesag van *Matthews v Haswari* 1937 WPA 110 en *Wilson v Ely* 1914 WR 34 is die mening vroeër uitgespreek dat die vader van 'n buite-egtelike kind 'n reg op redelike toegang tot die kind het (Spiro 458; Boberg 334). In *Douglas v Mayers* 1987 1 SA 910 (Z) en *F v B* 1988 3 SA 948 (D) is egter beslis dat die vader van 'n buite-egtelike kind nie 'n inherente reg op toegang tot sodanige kind het nie. Net soos enige ander derde party mag hy egter om toegang aansoek doen en dit sal aan hom verleen word as hy die hof kan oortuig dat dit in die beste belang van die kind is. Daar moet egter op gewys word dat in die *Douglas*-saak bevind is dat dit nie in die beste belang van die kind sou wees dat 'n reg op redelike toegang aan die vader verleen word nie (sien ook *F v B*).
Although these cases held that the best interests of the child is the paramount consideration in	Alhoewel in hierdie sake beslis is dat die beste belang van die kind die hoofoorweging is om te bepaal of 'n reg van toegang aan die vader verleen

deciding whether or not to allow access by the father, they added further qualifications which resulted in the father of an illegitimate child having a very difficult onus to discharge in order to be successful in his attempt to obtain a right of access. According to *Douglas v Mayers* the father of an illegitimate child will not be given a right of access "unless there is some *very strong ground compelling* [the court] to do so" (914, our emphasis). In *F v B* it was held that the court will allow the father access to the child only "in *exceptional cases* in which considerations relating to the interests of the child *compel* it to do so" (950, our emphasis).

These additional qualifications were rejected in the decision of the full bench of the Transvaal Provincial Division in *B v P* [22]. In this case, it was held that the father only has to prove on a preponderance of probability that access would be in the best interests of the child (117, see also *Van Erk v Holmer* [23] 647).

An example of a situation where a right of access should be awarded to the father because such access would clearly be in the best interests of the child is provided by the facts in *Wilson v Ely*. In this case, the parties were married by Muslim rites. Under South African law, however, such a marriage is invalid. The parties lived together for a long time before they separated (see also *Davids v Davids* 1914 WR 142; *Docrat v Bhayat* 1932 TPD 125; *Matthews v Haswari*). It is submitted that in a case like this the court would grant a right of reasonable access to the father even if the additional qualifications in *Douglas v Mayers* and *F v B* were to be applied.

In *Van Erk v Holmer* [23] VAN ZYL J sought to radically alter the position in respect of a father's right of access to his illegitimate child. Although he was bound by the full bench decision in *B v P*, VAN ZYL J (sitting as a single judge) held that, although the common law is silent on the right of the father of an illegitimate child to have access to his child, this does not mean that he has no such right. VAN ZYL J held that, just as there is no justification for distinguishing between legitimate and illegitimate children, so there is no justification for distinguishing between the fathers of legitimate and illegitimate children. He further emphasised that, although payment of maintenance is not a *quid pro quo* for

moet word, is verdere vereistes neergelê wat die effek gehad het dat die vader van 'n buite-egtelike kind 'n baie swaar bewyslas gehad het om te kwyt ten einde 'n reg van toegang tot sy kind te verkry. Volgens *Douglas v Mayers* word geen reg van toegang aan die vader van 'n buite-egtelike kind verleen nie "unless there is some *very strong ground compelling* [the court] to do so" (914, ons beklemtoning). In *F v B* is beslis dat die hof slegs toegang aan die vader sal verleen "in *exceptional cases* in which considerations relating to the interests of the child *compel* it to do so" (950, ons beklemtoning).

Hierdie bykomende vereistes is verwerp in die volbankbeslissing van die Transvaalse Provinsiale Afdeling in *B v P* [22]. In hierdie saak is beslis dat die vader slegs hoef te bewys dat toegang op 'n oorwig van waarskynlikheid in die beste belang van die kind sal wees (117, sien ook *Van Erk v Holmer* [23] 647).

Wilson v Ely is 'n voorbeeld van 'n geval waar 'n reg van toegang aan die vader toegeken behoort te word aangesien sodanige toegang duidelik in die beste belang van die kind sal wees. In hierdie saak is die partye volgens die Moslemgeloof getroud. 'n Huwelik wat op so 'n wyse gesluit is, is egter ingevolge die Suid-Afrikaanse reg ongeldig. Die partye het vir 'n lang tyd saamgewoon voordat hulle verhouding beëindig is (sien ook *Davids v Davids* 1914 WR 142; *Docrat v Bhayat* 1932 TPA 125; *Matthews v Haswari*). Daar word aan die hand gedoen dat die hof in sodanige geval 'n reg van redelike toegang aan die vader sal toeken, selfs al word die addisionele vereistes van *Douglas v Mayers* en *F v B* toegepas.

In *Van Erk v Holmer* [23] het VAN ZYL R gepoog om die posisie in verband met 'n vader se reg van toegang tot sy buite-egtelike kind radikaal te wysig. Alhoewel hy gebonde was aan die volbankuitspraak in *B v P*, het VAN ZYL R (wat as enkelregter gesit het) beslis dat, alhoewel die gemenereg swyg omtrent die vader se reg van toegang tot sy buite-egtelike kind, dit nie beteken dat die vader nie sodanige reg het nie. VAN ZYL R het beslis dat, net soos daar geen regverdiging bestaan om 'n onderskeid te maak tussen binne- en buite-egtelike kinders nie, daar geen regverdiging is om tussen die vaders van binne- en buite-egtelike kinders te onderskei nie. Hy het verder beklemtoon dat, alhoewel betaling van on-

exercise of a right of access, it is manifestly unfair to compel the father of an illegitimate child to pay maintenance and to deny him the right to see his child. VAN ZYL J concluded that "the time has arrived for the recognition by our Courts of an inherent right of access by a natural father to his illegitimate child" (649), which right would be removed "only if the access should be shown to be contrary to the best interests of the child" (650).

Although this decision was lauded by many, FLEMMING DJP and SPOELSTRA J, sitting as single judges in S v S [24] and B v S 1993 (2) SA 211 (W), respectively, emphatically rejected it and considered themselves bound by B v P. (In B v S SPOELSTRA J held, incorrectly, that the decision in B v P was that the court had to be satisfied that "a very strong and compelling ground" existed, which would render access in the best interests of the child).

In the light of the uncertainty about whether a father has (or should have) an inherent right of access to his illegitimate child, the South African Law Commission decided to investigate the position with a view to possible legal reform. Their *Working Paper 44* Project 79 *A Father's Rights in respect of his Illegitimate Child* contained two different proposals in respect of the father's right of access: The first recommended the retention of the current position, namely that the father does not have an inherent right of access but may obtain such a right on application to the supreme court. The second recommended that the father be given an inherent right of access, which could be removed or restricted by the court. It is understood that the final report of the Law Commission will be published soon. It remains to be seen which of the two options will be contained in the final report and how that option will be embodied in the draft legislation which is customarily attached to the Law Commission's final reports.

Further on the right of access of the father of an illegitimate child see Boberg 1988 *BML* 35; Jordaan 1988 *THRHR* 392; Ohannessian and Steyn 1991 *THRHR* 254; Eckard 1992 *TSAR* 122; Sonnekus and Van Westing 1992 *TSAR* 232; Clark 1992 *SAJHR* 565; Hutchings 1993 *THRHR* 310; Labuschagne 1993 *THRHR* 414; Kruger, Blackbeard and De Jong 1993 *THRHR* 696; Goldberg 1993 *SALJ* 261 and 416.

derhoud nie 'n *quid pro quo* vir die uitoefening van 'n reg van toegang is nie, dit duidelik onregverdig is om die vader van 'n buite-egtelike kind te dwing om onderhoud te betaal en hom dan 'n reg van toegang te ontsê. VAN ZYL R het tot die slotsom gekom dat "the time has arrived for the recognition by our Courts of an inherent right of access by a natural father to his illegitimate child" (649), welke reg weggeneem sal word "only if the access should be shown to be contrary to the best interests of the child" (650).

Alhoewel hierdie uitspraak groot byval gevind het, het FLEMMING ARP en SPOELSTRA R, wat as enkelregters gesit het, dit onderskeidelik in S v S [24] en B v S 1993 2 SA 211 (W) verwerp en hulleself gebonde geag aan B v P. (In B v S het SPOELSTRA R verkeerdelik gemeen dat die hof in B v P bevind het dat dit net 'n reg van toegang sal verleen as dit oortuig is dat daar "a very strong and compelling ground" bestaan wat aandui dat toegang in die beste belang van die kind sal wees.)

In die lig van die onsekerheid rondom die vraag of 'n vader 'n reg van toegang tot sy buite-egtelike kind het (of moet hê), het die Suid-Afrikaanse Regskommissie besluit om die posisie te ondersoek met die oog op regshervorming. Hulle *Werkstuk 44* Projek 79 *'n Vader se Regte ten opsigte van sy Buite-egtelike Kind* het twee verskillende voorstelle met betrekking tot die vader se reg van toegang bevat: Die eerste was dat die bestaande posisie behou word. Hiervolgens het die vader nie 'n inherente toegangsreg nie maar hy kan sodanige reg verkry deur by die hooggeregshof daarom aansoek te doen. In die tweede plek is voorgestel dat 'n inherente reg van toegang aan die vader toegeken word, welke reg deur die hof weggeneem of beperk kan word. Na verneem word, sal die regskommissie se finale verslag binnekort verskyn. Ons sal moet wag en sien welke van die twee opsies in die finale verslag opgeneem word en hoe daardie opsie in die voorgestelde wetgewing, wat gewoonlik saam met die regskommissie se finale verslae gepubliseer word, beliggaam word.

Oor die reg van toegang van die vader van 'n buite-egtelike kind sien verder Boberg 1988 *BML* 35; Jordaan 1988 *THRHR* 392; Ohannessian en Steyn 1991 *THRHR* 254; Eckard 1992 *TSAR* 122; Sonnekus en Van Westing 1992 *TSAR* 232; Clark

On a different point it should be noted that in *F v L* HARMS J mentioned that the child was deemed the mother's husband's child by virtue of at least two presumptions. In this regard it may be mentioned that the presumption of fatherhood which follows upon an admission of sexual intercourse with the child's mother actually applies only when the mother is *unmarried. In casu* where the mother was married, only the presumption of *pater est quem nuptiae demonstrant* should therefore have been applicable. It is further suggested that the viewpoint that the mother has the right to choose the father where sexual intercourse is admitted (or proved) by more than one man with the mother, should be reconsidered. Today sophisticated blood tests are available which can be used in this regard, and it would surely be more satisfactory for all parties concerned if the father's identity could be established by a more objective test than the mother's choice. (See in this regard *Seetal v Pravitha* [15]; *M v R* [16]; *S v L* [17].)

1992 *SAJHR* 565; Hutchings 1993 *THRHR* 310; Labuschagne 1993 *THRHR* 414; Kruger, Blackbeard en De Jong 1993 *THRHR* 696; Goldberg 1993 *SALJ* 261 en 416.

In verband met 'n heeltemal ander aspek het HARMS R genoem dat die kind op grond van twee vermoedens geag is om die kind van die moeder se man te wees. In hierdie verband kan daarop gewys word dat die vermoede van vaderskap wat ontstaan as geslagsgemeenskap met die moeder erken word eintlik net van toepassing is waar die moeder *ongetroud* is. Aangesien die moeder *in casu* getroud was, behoort net die vermoede *pater est quem nuptiae demonstrant* van toepassing te gewees het. Daar word verder aan die hand gedoen dat die opvatting dat die moeder die man kan aanwys waar meer as een man geslagsverkeer met haar erken (of dit bewys word), heroorweeg behoort te word. Daar bestaan vandag gesofistikeerde bloedtoetse wat in die verband aangewend kan word, en dit sal sekerlik baie meer bevredigend vir al die betrokke partye wees as die man se identiteit met 'n meer objektiewe toets as die moeder se keuse vasgestel kan word. (Sien in die verband *Seetal v Pravitha* [15]; *M v R* [16]; *S v L* [17].)

[22]   B v P

1991 4 SA 113 (T)

A father's right of access to his illegitimate child

The appellant was the father of an illegitimate child. When the child was born in 1979 the appellant and respondent were living together. In 1984 they ceased living together and the child had been living with her mother ever since. The mother permitted the appellant to see the child and take her to his home until February 1989, but since then she had refused to let him see or speak to the child. He then applied for an order declaring that he was entitled to reasonable access to the child. The application was dismissed in the court *a quo*. On appeal to the full bench

'n Vader se reg op toegang tot sy buiteegtelike kind

Die appellant was die vader van 'n buiteegtelike kind. Toe die kind in 1979 gebore is, het die appellant en die respondent saamgewoon. In 1984 het hulle opgehou om saam te woon en die kind het sedertdien by haar moeder gewoon. Die moeder het die appellant tot Februarie 1989 toegelaat om die kind te besoek en haar na sy huis te neem, maar sedertdien het sy geweier dat hy die kind sien of met haar praat. Hy het toe aansoek gedoen om 'n verklarende bevel dat hy op redelike toegang tot die kind geregtig is. Die aansoek is in die hof *a quo* van die hand gewys.

it was held that the applicant had to prove on a preponderance of probability that the access was in the best interests of the child and that it would not unduly interfere with the mother's right of custody. The court's decision will, in any particular case, depend on the facts thereof and as there was a dispute on the facts of this case which could not be resolved on the papers before the court, the matter was referred back for the hearing of oral evidence on whether access to the child should be granted to the applicant.

In appèl na die volbank is beslis dat die applikant op 'n oorwig van waarskynlikheid moet bewys dat die toegang in belang van die kind is en dat dit nie op 'n onbehoorlike wyse met die moeder se reg van bewaring sal inmeng nie. Die hof se beslissing sal in elke geval van die feite van die saak afhang en aangesien daar in hierdie saak 'n feitegeskil was wat nie op die stukke voor die hof opgelos kon word nie, is die aangeleentheid terugverwys vir die aanhoor van mondelinge getuienis oor die vraag of toegang tot die kind aan die applikant verleen moes word.

KIRK-COHEN J: [114] The guardianship and custody of an illegitimate child are vested in the mother and the father has no right of access: see F v L ([21] at 527H–J) . . . and F v B ([1988 3 SA 948 (D)] at 950E).

The judgment in *Matthews v Haswari* 1937 WLD 110 is not, as has been suggested, authority for the proposition that the father of an illegitimate child has a right of access to such child. In that case the mother of an illegitimate child sought an order that the father return the child to her. There was a dispute of fact on the affidavits whether it would be in the child's best interests to be with the mother or the father – the father alleging that the mother was not fit to have custody. SCHREINER AJ held at 110:

'Being an illegitimate child the legal custody, until some special order of Court is made, rests with the applicant, the mother.'

It is implicit in this judgment that the father of such a child could be awarded custody in the event of it being proved that it was in the child's best interests to be placed in his custody.

In the order granted (at 113) the following was included, *pendente lite*:

'The respondent is entitled to reasonable access to the child and to take it out on two afternoons each week.'

It does not appear whether this part of the order was made by consent or incorporated by the Court simply as a temporary measure. If the latter, it apparently was not argued that the father had a right of access. The learned Judge certainly did not so decide; such a contention would run contrary to the legal disability of the father of an illegitimate child as considered by the learned Judge in his judgment.

I am of the view that the judgment in F v L (*supra* at 526G–H) is correct and that the *pendente lite* order in *Matthews'* case is not authority for the proposition that the latter enjoys a right of access.

[115] Thus, in certain circumstances, the father of an illegitimate child, like other parties, may approach the Court for an order limiting the mother's right of custody by granting him access to his child and, in an appropriate case, the Court may deprive a mother of her custody . . .

In *Matthews'* case *supra* at 111 SCHREINER AJ referred to the main or paramount consideration as the interests of the child itself. This approach is echoed in the judgments in *Douglas v Mayers* and F v B (*supra*). Yet, in the former case, there is a qualification – namely that the Court will only interfere if 'there is *some very strong ground compelling it to do so'* (my italicising). In *F v B* the Court also qualified the paramount consideration by stating that access will only be granted 'in *exceptional* cases in which considerations relating to the interests of the child *compel* it to do so' (my italicising).

The *onus* of proof in all civil litigation, including issues of custody and access, is discharged on a preponderance of probability. See *Van Oudenhove v Gruber* 1981 (4) SA 857 (A) at 867D–E and *Ley v Ley's Executors and Others* 1951 (3) SA 186 (A) at 191H–193A.

What then is the significance of the words italicised in both passages above? They do not alter the *onus* of proof, but they are used to qualify and restrict the main and paramount consideration to which I have referred. It seems that the words in question in both cases emanate from the passage quoted from *Nicolson v Nicolson* 6 Sc LR 692, referred to in *Calitz v Calitz* 1939 AD 56 at 64 [19]. It must be borne in mind, however, that in *Calitz's* case the Appellate Division was considering the custody of a legitimate child only where no divorce or separation order had been granted. The Appellate Division held that in such circumstances it had no jurisdiction to deprive the father of the custody of his child, except in exceptional cases, such as where there was a danger to life, health or morals. (The headnote refers to 'special grounds'.)

There is no justification for introducing or applying that test, relating as it does to particular circumstances, to the issue of access to an illegitimate child. It would be untenable to suggest that the Court, as upper guardian, will assist a legitimate child, whose parents are in the process of becoming [116] divorced or are divorced, on the basis of what is in the best interests of that child, but an illegitimate child only if there is danger to life, health or morals.

Where divorce proceedings are pending, or after divorce, and the custody of, or access to, legitimate children is in issue

'. . . the Court is primarily concerned with the welfare of the children, that is the paramount consideration. In *Bailey v Bailey* 1979 (3) SA 128 (A) at 135H TRENGOVE JA said the following:

"Just as in custody cases, so also in disputes arising out of custody orders, the welfare of the children is the predominant consideration which should weigh with the Court (*Shawzin v Laufer* 1968 (4) SA 657 (A) at 662G–H). In *Du Preez v Du Preez* 1969 (3) SA 529 (D) MILLER J referred to the effect of the burden upon an applicant to show 'good cause' for a variation of a custody order, and at 532C–G of the report he made the following observations with which I respectfully agree, namely:

'But when the paramountcy of the child's welfare in such a conflict between the parents is borne in mind, it is obvious that the burden upon the applicant (who in this instance happens to be the non-custodian parent) dare not be magnified. She may be held to have shown good cause for variation of the order, even if no new facts or circumstances have arisen in the interim, provided it appears clearly to the Court that the child's interests would be better served by varying the order than by maintaining the *status quo*. If this should appear to be the case, the Court ought not to hesitate to vary its order, however inadequate her explanation might be for consenting to the order in the first place, or however adamantly the respondent may insist that the limitation is one which he, as custodian parent, deems to be desirable. This is not to say that the opinion and desires of the custodian parent are to be ignored or brushed aside; indeed, the Court takes upon itself a grave responsibility if it decides to override the custodian parent's decision as to what is best in the interests of his child and will only do so after the most careful consideration of all the circumstances, including the reasons for the custodian parent's decision and the emotions or impulses which have contributed to it.'

> Where it is said in the above passage that it must appear 'clearly' to the Court that it would be in the interests of the minor to vary the order, it simply means that the Court must be satisfied on a balance of probabilities that the order should be varied (see also *Manning v Manning* 1975 (4) SA 659 (T) at 661D–E)."
>
> In applications for the variation of custody orders, the Court, whilst not losing sight of the paramount consideration, nevertheless, will have regard to the rights of the custodian parent.'...

[117] [T]he Court acts according to what is in the best interests of the children in question. The Court, as upper guardian of illegitimate minors, would apply the same procedure and the same standards. Thus, the additional qualifications imported into *Douglas v Mayers* and *F v B (supra)* and applied by the Court *a quo*, are based upon a different consideration dealt with in *Calitz's* case [19] and are, with respect, inapplicable to the issue of when access should be granted to an illegitimate child.

I approach the problem as follows: the paramount consideration is what is in the best interests of the illegitimate child. The other consideration is the right of the custodian parent which, in the case of an illegitimate child, is not subject to the right of access by the non-custodian parent. In regard to the paramount consideration, the following passage from the judgment in *Dunscombe v Willies* 1982 (3) SA 311 (D) at 315H–316A, although dealing with different circumstances, is apposite:

> 'I prefer, though this may be a difference of phraseology only, to think of the matter as being a question of the rights of the children, viz their right to have access to the non-custodian parent. It is in their interests, generally speaking, even where a family has broken up, that they should continue to have a sound relationship with both parents. Not infrequently, and perhaps more frequently than has been thought in the past, it is sometimes in the interests of the children to deprive them completely of access to the non-custodian parent.'

My conclusion is that the Court's approach, when considering an application such as this, will be similar to that in *Oudenhove v Gruber (supra)*; an applicant must prove on a preponderance of probability that the relief sought, i e access, is in the best interests of the illegitimate child (the paramount consideration) and that such relief will not unduly interfere with the mother's right of custody. The Court's decision in any particular case will depend upon the facts thereof...

[KIRK-COHEN J then set out the facts and proceeded:]

[119] Whether the child has refused to see her father on the grounds alleged or has been influenced by the respondent, or whether the respondent has terminated all contact between father and child because of the advice given to her by the magistrate or the officials at the children's court, is in dispute and this dispute cannot be resolved on paper.

On the same footing is the allegation that the respondent is not acting in the best interests of the child, but is being unduly influenced by her father.

In conclusion, the appellant has made out a *prima facie* case justifying the orders hereinafter set forth...

I make the following orders:...

The matter is referred for the hearing of oral evidence on a date to be determined by the Registrar on the following issues:
whether access to the child T should be granted to the applicant; and,
if so, what such access should be...

LABUSCHAGNE J and DE VILLIERS J concurred.

Note

Aantekening

See the note on *F v L* [21].

Sien die aantekening by *F v L* [21].

[23] VAN ERK V HOLMER

1992 2 SA 636 (W)

A father's right of access to his illegitimate child

The applicant (father) and the respondent (mother) lived together from February 1988 to January 1991. During January 1989 a child was born of this relationship. Initially the parties had the intention of marrying each other, but as time passed the applicant became less and less enthusiastic about marrying the respondent. This factor contributed to the breakdown of the relationship and the respondent left the applicant when the child was about two years old. That was the last time the applicant had any contact with the child. Since then, the respondent had refused to allow him to visit or see the child. It appeared to the family advocate, to whom the matter had been referred, that this refusal had arisen from the bitterness felt by the respondent towards the applicant because of his failure to marry her. In this way she was attempting to punish him and did not consider whether or not her conduct in doing so was in the best interests of the child. The applicant applied for an order that he be granted reasonable access to the child. When the matter first came before the court, it was referred to the family advocate who recommended that the applicant should be granted a defined right of access. The parties thereupon settled the matter on the basis that the applicant should be granted a right of reasonable access to the child. This agreement was made an order of the court. Because of the importance of the matter the court furnished reasons for its accepting the family advocate's recommendation.

'n Vader se reg op toegang tot sy buite-egtelike kind

Die applikant (vader) en die respondent (moeder) het vanaf Februarie 1988 tot Januarie 1991 saamgewoon. Gedurende Januarie 1989 is 'n kind uit hierdie verhouding gebore. Aanvanklik het die partye die bedoeling gehad om met mekaar te trou, maar met verloop van tyd het die applikant al minder en minder lus gehad om hom in 'n huwelik te begewe. Dit het bygedra tot die verbrokkeling van die verhouding en die respondent het die applikant verlaat toe die kind ongeveer twee jaar oud was. Dit was die laaste keer wat die applikant enige kontak met die kind gehad het, aangesien die respondent sedertdien geweier het om hom toe te laat om die kind te besoek of selfs te sien. Volgens die gesinsadvokaat het dit geblyk dat hierdie weiering gespruit het uit haar verbitterdheid omdat die applikant nie met haar wou trou nie. Sy het op dié wyse gepoog om hom te straf en het haar nie daaraan gesteur of haar gedrag in belang van die kind was nie. Die applikant het toe aansoek gedoen om 'n bevel dat 'n reg van redelike toegang aan hom toegestaan word. Toe die aangeleentheid die eerste keer voor die hof gekom het, is dit na die gesinsadvokaat verwys wat aanbeveel het dat 'n omskrewe reg van toegang aan die applikant verleen word. Die partye het daarop die aangeleentheid geskik en in die skikkingsooreenkoms ooreengekom dat die applikant 'n reg van redelike toegang sou verkry. Hierdie ooreenkoms is 'n bevel van die hof gemaak. Aangesien dit so 'n belangrike aangeleentheid was, het die hof redes verskaf waarom hy die gesinsadvokaat se aanbeveling aanvaar het.

[VAN ZYL J gave a detailed discussion of the position at common law and the court cases in which the matter was considered and also referred to legal literature on the subject. He then proceeded:]

VAN ZYL J: [647] The fact that the common law says nothing about a father's right of access to his illegitimate child does not justify the inference that such right does not or cannot exist. I have been unable to find any common law discussion of a non-custodian parent's rights of access to a *legitimate* child; yet no one would presume to say that no such right exists. The emphasis throughout is on guardianship and parental power. The question of access appears simply not to have been considered.

What is significant in the common law is that the maxim relating to a mother's not bastardising her illegitimate child is clearly based on her cognate or blood relationship with the child. Similarly, the father's duty to maintain a child born out of wedlock is based on his paternity and hence on his cognate biological relationship with the child. This makes nonsense of the fiction that the father is regarded as not being related to the child. Should he be no relation he should have neither rights nor duties in respect of the child. The illogicality is borne out by the fact that the father is subject to marriage impediments with regard to the child in so far as there is a blood relationship between them, regardless of whether the child is legitimate or illegitimate.

It is true that *Wilson v Ely* 1914 WR 34 and *Matthews v Haswari* 1937 WLD 110 do not constitute authority that an inherent right of access should be afforded the father of an illegitimate child. I furthermore agree with HARMS J in *F v L and Another* 1987 (4) SA 525 (W) at 527B [21] that a right of access is not a *quid pro quo* for the payment of maintenance. I do not believe, however, that access to a child should always or necessarily be regarded as an incidence of parental authority. In the case of legitimate children it can be so regarded, but it is certainly not so in cases where access has been granted to the father of an illegitimate child on the ground that it is in the child's best interests. By granting access under such circumstances it cannot be said that a Court is conferring parental authority upon the father.

The case of *Douglas v Mayers* 1987 (1) SA 910 (ZH) is a Zimbabwean precedent which has only persuasive authority in a South African court. This was apparently not considered in *F v B* 1988 (3) SA 948 (D). I must in any event respectfully disagree with the reasoning prompting the Court to hold that the father of an illegitimate child has no inherent right of access to the child. It does not follow from the fact that access may encroach upon or curtail custodial rights, and that such rights should not be interfered with unless the interests of the child require it, that the father should not, and does not, have an inherent right of access to his illegitimate child.

I respectfully associate myself with the criticism in *B v P* 1991 (4) SA 113 (T) [22] regarding the *onus* of proof required by the Court in the *Douglas v Mayers* and *F v B* cases and likewise welcome the Court's emphasis on the rights of the child rather than on those of the parent. Unfortunately the [648] Court uncritically accepted the finding in *F v L and Another* (*supra*) that the father of an illegitimate child does not have an inherent right of access to the child. I believe, with great respect, that in none of these cases was consideration given to the important principle enunciated by Hahlo and Kahn *The South African Legal System and its Background* [(304)] ... This is, to my mind, a case where the old authorities do not advert to the relevant legal issue and where there is no legislation, precedent or custom in point. It hence falls to the Judge to decide the case in accordance with the principles of reasonableness, justice, equity and, I would add, the *boni mores* or public policy, which cannot be ignored in these times of change ...

The Law Commission, in its report on the legal position of illegitimate children [Project 38 1985, par 8.16 *et seq*], took due cognisance of the changing *mores* of our time and of the social realities existing in South Africa in supporting the notion that the father of an illegitimate child should have an inherent right of access to the child. Yet not one of the said cases referred to the report or, for that matter, to the criticism spelt out in the legal literature available to them. I believe that the arguments supporting the Law Commission's contentions are cogent and worthy of consideration.

The criticism of *Boberg* [1988 *BML* 35] in his cited contributions can likewise not be faulted to the extent that he calls for the application of justice, equity and public policy in accordance with the 'social realities of our times'. I agree with the learned author that the arguments usually directed against granting access to the father of an illegitimate child are no different from those which are generally present in the case of access to a legitimate child, yet which are certainly not sufficient to support an application to deprive him of his access. This being so, the question may justifiably be asked why a father's access should depend on whether he was lawfully married to the child's mother or not.

Similarly one cannot but agree with *Ohannessian* and *Steyn* in their cited article [1991 *THRHR* 254] that the approach of our Courts has led to unfairness and injustice. A 'socially and legally equitable solution' in accordance with the precepts of justice, equity, reasonableness and public policy is certainly called for. The very interests of the child, which constitute a predominant or paramount consideration in evaluating matters such as access, demand that no distinction should be drawn between a legitimate and an illegitimate child. Modern day circumstances are radically different from those subsisting in earlier times, when cohabitation was far less frequent than today and was frowned upon as morally unacceptable. Social *mores* and attitudes have changed considerably. In South Africa in particular legally binding marriages in accordance with Christian precepts are not the only lasting unions between a man and a woman. In addition the emphasis on the child's rights rather than on those of the parents requires that the child should have the opportunity to bind and form a lasting relationship with both parents, regardless of whether or not one or the other is married [649] to a third party. Only if this should be against the interests of the child should it be denied.

I do not support the restrictions on access suggested by *Clark* and *Van Heerden* in their cited article [*Questionable Issue: Illegitimacy in South Africa*]. To require that the father of an illegitimate child should be granted access to the child only if he can prove that he has acknowledged and voluntarily undertaken the duties of a father is unfounded and places an unjustifiable burden of proof upon the father. Furthermore the authors do not give an acceptable explanation for their opinion that there are 'serious risks' in granting 'automatic' rights to fathers. Why should it be any more difficult for the mother to approach the Court than it is for the father?

In establishing whether public policy requires a new approach to and fresh outlook upon existing law one must, I believe, take cognisance of what the general public's views are on the subject. A thought-provoking article by Margaret McAllister and Narieke Brand, 'Fighting to be a Father', appeared in the *Fair Lady* issue of 24 April 1991. Linda Shaw was responsible for two similar contributions in the *Sunday Times* of 1 December 1991 ('The Unwanted Daddies') and 15 December 1991 ('In the Best Interests of the Child'). These are only examples of what I understand to be numerous appeals for a reconsideration of the father's relationship with his illegitimate child.

In my view public policy dictates that, just as there should be no distinction between a legitimate and an illegitimate child, just so there is no justification for distinguishing between the fathers of such children. By this I do not propose that they should be equated with each other in one fell swoop. Certain parental rights have been legislatively enacted and will require amendments to such legislation to provide for more extended rights. It is the least of these rights – the 'booby prize' as *Boberg* calls it (*op cit*) – namely the right of access, which public policy requires should be inherently available to all fathers. In time to come further extensions may be required and public policy will no doubt play a role in regard thereto. At this stage, however, it is unnecessary to speculate on the nature and extent of the further rights which may call for consideration.

Perhaps one of the strongest motivations for an improvement in the legal position of the unmarried father is what is perceived as the gross injustice which occurs when a father is compelled to pay maintenance for a child whom he may never be able to see or visit, despite his being prepared to commit and devote himself entirely to the interests of the child. This is not simply a plea for a *quid pro quo* but a proper recognition of a biological father's need to bind and form a relationship with his own child and the child's interest that he or she should have the unfettered opportunity to develop as normal and happy a relationship as possible with both parents. This is not only in the interest of the child but it is in fact a right which should not be denied unless it is clearly not in the best interests of the child.

In view of the aforegoing considerations I believe the time has indeed arrived for the recognition by our Courts of an inherent right of access by a natural father to his illegitimate child. That such right should be recognised is amply justified by the precepts of justice, equity and reasonableness and by the demands of public policy. It should be removed [650] only if the access should be shown to be contrary to the best interests of the child.

When these principles are applied to the facts in the instant case there is little doubt that the respondent, the mother of the child, has come nowhere near proving that the granting of access to the applicant, the child's father, will be in conflict with the child's best interests. On the contrary her denial of access to the applicant appears to have been substantially motivated by her personal animosity towards the applicant and did not take any account of the child's interests and the importance of maintaining a parental relationship which had subsisted from the child's birth for a period of two years. I therefore had no hesitation in accepting the Family Advocate's recommendation that access should be granted to the applicant. Making the agreement relating to reasonable access an order of Court followed as a matter of course.

Note	Aantekening
See the note on *F v L* [21].	Sien die aantekening by *F v L* [21].

[24] S v S

1993 2 SA 200 (W)

A father's right of access to his illegitimate child	'n Vader se reg op toegang tot sy buiteegtelike kind
The applicant (father) and the respondent (mother) engaged in an intimate relationship while both of them were still involved in other relationships. As a result of the relationship between them, the respondent fell pregnant. When this happened she termin-	Die applikant (vader) en die respondent (moeder) het 'n intieme verhouding aangeknoop terwyl albei nog in 'n ander verhouding betrokke was. As gevolg van die verhouding tussen die applikant en die respondent het die respondent swanger geword. Toe dit

ated her relationship with her other boyfriend. The applicant, however, refused to terminate his other relationship. Nevertheless, the respondent moved in with the applicant, but by the time the child was born, the parties were no longer living together. After the child's birth the applicant showed very little interest in the child. He saw her only twice, and then only in passing. The applicant initially denied paternity and refused to pay maintenance for the child but after the respondent had approached the maintenance court and blood tests had been performed the applicant paid maintenance for the child. The applicant thereafter applied to the supreme court for an order allowing him to have access to his child. At the time of the application the applicant was unemployed but was still paying maintenance for the child. The respondent was at that stage living with her previous boyfriend, who was, for all intents and purposes, the father of the child. According to the respondent, the applicant was seeking access merely as a *quid pro quo* for the payment of maintenance and not because he really desired to see the child. The court rejected the application for access.

gebeur, het sy haar verhouding met haar ander kêrel beëindig. Die applikant het egter geweier om sy ander verhouding te beëindig. Desnieteenstaande het die respondent by die applikant ingetrek maar op die stadium toe die kind gebore is, het die partye nie meer saamgewoon nie. Na die kind se geboorte het die applikant baie min belangstelling in die kind getoon. Hy het haar net twee keer in die verbygaan gesien. Die applikant het aanvanklik vaderskap ontken en geweier om onderhoud vir die kind te betaal, maar nadat die respondent die onderhoudshof genader het en bloedtoetse gedoen is, het hy onderhoud betaal. Die applikant het toe by die hooggeregshof aansoek gedoen om 'n bevel wat hom toegang tot sy kind sou verleen. Ten tyde van die aansoek was die applikant werkloos maar hy het nog steeds onderhoud vir die kind betaal. Die respondent het op daardie stadium by haar vorige kêrel gewoon en hy was vir alle praktiese doeleindes die vader van die kind. Volgens die respondent wou die applikant bloot toegang hê as 'n *quid pro quo* vir die betaling van onderhoud en nie omdat hy werklik begerig was om die kind te sien nie. Die hof het die aansoek om toegang van die hand gewys.

FLEMMING DJP: [202] That applicant is entitled to some access if he has a legal right to access, but not otherwise, is not simply a result of shifting of *onus* of proof ... Parental authority vests in the respondent so that it is she and not the Court which has the power to decide [who is to have access to her child]; and then her decisions involve the exercise of a discretion. Mainly because of her daily custody and care, she has advantages over a Court greater than that which a trial Court enjoys above a Court of appeal. She knows her child, its reactions, the applicant and his true character and all other sensitivities of the matter ... Compare the *Simleit* case ([*Simleit v Cunliffe* 1940 TPD 67] at 79) on judicial intervention only if it is established that the custodian's discretion is

'not being properly exercised in the interests of the children and that in all the circumstances the interests of the children make intervention necessary or desirable'.

[FLEMMING DJP cited other cases on judicial intervention in respect of the custodian's discretion and proceeded:]

[203] Does applicant have a 'right to access'? As the only decision favouring applicant is *Van Erk v Holmer* 1992 (2) SA 636 (W) [23], I must focus on that decision.

At best for applicant there are also, *inter alia, Douglas v Mayers* 1987 (1) SA 910 (ZS); *F v L and Another* 1987 (4) SA 525 (W) [21] including the 'binding authority' mentioned at 527D–F; *W v S and Others (1)* 1988 (1) SA 475 (N); *F v B* 1988 (3) SA 948 (D); *J v O* [(case 1407/90 (W)]; and a Full Bench decision, *B v P* 1991 (4) SA 113 (T) [22]. After the *Van Erk* order in October 1991, Judges at least thrice regarded themselves as bound by the Full Bench: STREICHER J in *T v V* (case 2840/91); ROUX J in *K v G* (case 10433/92); and DANIELS J in *B v V* (case 91/35144).

A principle known as *stare decisis* is part of our legal system. It entails that a single Judge must abide by a previous decision unless he is convinced that it is clearly wrong, and that he is essentially fully bound by a decision of a Full Bench of his own Division. I am not convinced that those cases were all wrongly decided. Nor do I have the right to deviate from the Full Bench decision in *B v P*. I must therefore analyse whether the *Van Erk* decision breached the *stare decisis* principle or found a legitimate opening for its conclusion and, if so, whether it is correct. That [204] in our law access is an incident of parental authority was decided *inter alia* in *F v L* (*supra*). See at 527G–H; compare also the *Douglas* case at 914C–D. That is sound in logic and based on principle. But the *Van Erk* case, at 647F, despite quoting Boberg *The Law of Persons and the Family* at 642H, reads:

> 'I do not believe, however, that access to a child should always or necessarily be regarded as an incidence of parental authority.'

Reason in principle or on authority was not advanced for regarding *F v L* as clearly wrong. Nor to justify the *dictum*. The basis of rights when it is known where parental authority vests (and the only question is whether another has a concurrent right in the form of a right to access), circumstances for which *F v L* recognised a basis which does not extend to an unmarried father, cannot be qualified by reason of the totally different situation when the Court has the very intent of acting against the wrong exercise of custodial rights by creating, by its order, rights which never previously existed. (In the latter case custody may be shifted to a third party who may, as in *September v Karriem* 1959 (3) SA 687 (C), be the natural father.)

In this case, as in the *Van Erk* case, the full parental power vested in the mother; there was no parental authority in the father. (This approach underlies s 3 of the Children's Status Act 82 of 1987, which governs parental authority when the mother is a minor.) As initially explained, the mother as a natural consequence has the right to create own access to the child and to control access by others. The father has nothing which corresponds.

In any event the recognition, wrong in my view, of a basis other than parental authority for a right of access, could overcome only being tied to a basis which would be invalid for the father. The question remained: on what authority can it be said that alongside the mother's uncurtailed rights the father, like a divorced father, has a concurrent and to some extent competing right? Where did the ruling law recognise an 'inherent right' of access?

Prior to the *Van Erk* decision it was settled law that the father of an extra-marital child has no such a right . . . The *Van Erk* judgment accepts as much and then moves to a 'fresh outlook', seeing 'no justification for distinguishing between fathers' and deciding that 'the time has indeed arrived for the recognition by our Courts of an inherent right of access by a natural father to his illegitimate child'. See at 649 at C, E and I . . . Recent times have seen some debate on what the law should be but, whatever the position may have been in common law, there has undeniably been unanimity on what the law is. So much so that, in *J v O* at pp 17–18, it was said with reference to *F v L* [21]:

> 'It is somewhat surprising that, notwithstanding the unambiguous language used by HARMS J in the passage I have quoted – as also the language used generally in the course of that judgment – an argument can still be advanced to the effect that the criterion, when the natural father seeks access to his child, is the interests of the child. I must re-emphasise that the mother of an illegitimate child is the sole [205] guardian and custodian of that child. In that capacity she has the exclusive right to exercise

parental authority over such child. In the exercise of such right and duty she may decide with whom that child shall consort and who shall have access to such child. It is her duty and right primarily to decide whether the natural father may have access to the child and, if so, on what terms.'

I therefore believe that the *stare decisis* principle barred the conclusion reached in the *Van Erk* case [23].

My next difficulty with being swayed by the *Van Erk* case arises from the inapplicability of its crucial tool for legitimating its end-conclusion, the 'important principle enunciated by *Hahlo and Kahn*'. See at 648A–D. The principle, quoted at 643I, is that a Court can design the law to suit justice when it is 'bereft of binding legislation, precedent or modern custom'. (In passing I note a probable injustice to suggest – at 648A was said 'in none of these cases was consideration given' – that so many Judges in so many cases all overlooked that principle. They probably regarded the law as settled by older authorities so that there would be no need for using that principle.) But, quite apart from non-judicial authorities, we are not 'bereft of ... precedents'. The *Van Erk* judgment itself mentions 'precedents'.

Nor could the old authorities or professors of the law of our century be regarded as neutral on the point. If searches for the existence of a specific entitlement produce no trace thereof, it normally constitutes safe reason for inferring that no such right exists. That no single authority can be found anywhere to the effect that a father has a right of access to an extra-marital child is a strong indication that no such right exists. However, that reasoning was not followed in the *Van Erk* case. It was concluded that the total absence of recognition is a sign that no consideration was given to the matter... Illegitimacy has been known through the ages. There must have been fathers desiring access and seeking opinions. They, and students, would have caused lawyers and professors to think about the issue. The impact of illegitimacy was in fact often attended to. To debit hundreds of capable lawyers through the centuries with such a blatant oversight is, I suggest, not acceptable.

I need not decide whether the old authorities did not provide an answer which in itself barred use of the principle mentioned by *Hahlo and Kahn*. Perhaps they also tied the matter to familial or parental authority...

Before leaving the key parts in the structure of the *Van Erk* judgment, I quote one instance to convey that silence on other issues does not imply assent. It is no 'assumption' that an illegitimate child is not related to its father. Like a maxim, it is a short-hand way of sketching the crux of the law's approach. Lee and Honoré *Law of Property, Family Relations and Succession* 2nd ed at 162 grasps correctly when saying: 'ie the legal consequences of the natural relationship between him and his father ... are reduced to the minimum'. It is not a denial of the facts. The law's acknowledgement of the (complete set of) facts is the reason why one man and no other must pay maintenance; can legitimate the child by marrying its mother, etc.

[206] It is, however, more important to turn to remarks about public policy, fairness and desirability which, even when they fail to give direction to legal rules, can influence discretion. I number only because I mention independent aspects:

1. When public policy is not involved in the application of known law to particular facts; when the question is rather whether the law should be as it is, there is really no room for judicial initiative. The law must be applied even when a Judge believes that the law requires revision or is in an undesirable state. It is alien to a Judge's functions or powers to act as an alternative for Parliament. That is salutary because the state of the law should not be determined by the preference of one single individual. Also because a Judge is not equipped in terms

of material, methods, access or time to ascertain the true preferences and desirabilities which operate in society. Members of the community know to make
representations elsewere than to Judges.

2. The report in project 38 [South African Law Commission Project 38 *Investigation
   into the Legal Position of Illegitimate Children* October 1985] is not risk-free. The
   author suddenly, without stating reasons, when referring to Spiro *Law of Parent
   and Child,* begins to refer to a 'right' of access. That embracing is inconsistent
   with the view against giving parental authority to the father. See paras 8.30 and
   11.1. With such accuracy on law and logic, care is not out of place about
   desirabilities.

3. The ascertainment of public views is a process fraught with risks of error. Risks
   are increased by relying on magazines striving for circulation, persons who
   represent the fringes of opinion, etc... The many cases that came before this
   Division since *Van Erk's* case certainly show that there is also a mother's side to
   the matter. It is not always simply emotional or resistance born of spitefulness.
   Inter alia, but not only, the mother is faced therewith that the child is born into
   this world with a problem which, unless it has no sensitivity, the child will be
   facing over many years; that a child has a willingness and tendency to accept
   as father figure the male who actually daily lives with the mother; that the
   natural father chose not to similarly make a joint home; that the immediate
   availability of a real-life father figure and the peaceful stability of family living
   of the new grouping are important to the child, etc. Even if the mothers are
   not vocal, the problems of crisis management and long term development of the
   child must be duly considered.

4. The particular issue touches society as such. It may well have been a reaction
   of societies that the existing legal approach is the only means (perhaps in modern
   times not always effective) of putting pressure on the natural father to seriously
   consider the situation, also the plight of the (expecting) mother and the totally
   helpless result. To destroy that pressure would then be a cut into the nerve system
   of the operation of society...

[207] 5. In so far as it is suggested that the established law is unduly sectarian in that it
   is based upon Christian views (at 644E–F and 648I), I think that a wrong impression is given. Firstly, there is no necessary logic therein that because a rule has
   a known origin it is contrary to public policy or is bad or unjust. Secondly, the
   approach of our law is no more Christian than it is Muslim or indigenous. In
   each case the legal approach is maintained because of an underlying view on
   what is fair and good. The English and the Scottish law was (and even after
   conventions on human rights, is) that the father has no 'inherent right' of access.
   The facts of a case may entitle him to access – which if not conceded is declared
   by a court order. The German and Dutch systems regard the mother as sole
   parent but the natural father may obtain an order which gives him something
   of a supervisory capacity. I do not have adequate research possibilities about
   sources outside Europe but my impression is that although sections do differ on
   what should bring about a valid 'marriage', there is fair similarity of views about
   where a father stands in relation to his extra-marital child; views which would
   render the decision in *B v P* [22] rather liberal and is to the opposite effect of
   the *Van Erk* approach. The Law Commission's Project 38 cared about Muslim
   views. In para 8.26 it is indicated that on those views the father of an illegitimate
   child has no parental rights. Our indigenous legal systems are reflected by Clark
   and Van Heerden (at 43 in *Questionable Issue: Illegitimacy in South Africa*), in reliance

upon *Zwani v Dhlamini* 1951 NAC 353 (NE) as being that 'the natural father has no rights to the child'. Those systems basically follow the pattern that it is only the mother's family (rather than the mother herself) who has rights and duties in regard to the child until the crucial step marking acceptance of the child into the father's family by 'marriage' or a lesser step, variable amongst groups, normally created by negotiation plus payment. Compare 1991 *Acta Iuridica* at 43, 44. No doubt the possibility exists to protect whatever rights are created by indigenous law. Compare (1983) XVI No 1 *CILSA* at 47, 48; JC Bekker in *Seymour's Customary Law in South Africa* (1989) at 231; (1973) 90 *SALJ* at 4–11.

6. The undesirability of giving the law the content preferred by a single individual, even a Judge, is highlighted by divergent views of other legal systems, commissions of enquiry on some of those systems, and views of authors . . .

[FLEMMING DJP cited some examples and concluded that the] weight of opinion is against the conceding of an inherent right which may be denied only if it is 'clearly' not 'in the best interests of the child' (at 649I, 650A) . . .

It may, of course, be that Parliament (or the Appellate Division if it finds room to override preceding authority and has certainty about what the law should be) may change the law. Until that eventuates, the background for applying views about the interests of the extra-marital child is:

[208] Firstly, Courts have taken a wide view on *locus standi* in regard to asking orders about the custody of children. This approach is often more evident in practice than in reported judgments but that the father of an extra-marital child has *locus standi* is settled in this Division by *B v P* at 115A [22].

Secondly, in the absence of official interference with parental authority in the form of taking away portion of such rights, the mother exclusively has parental authority over her child born out of wedlock. She has sole control over to whom the child has access and who has access to the child.

Thirdly, in deciding whether or not to interfere with the discretion exercised by the mother as custodian parent, the Court will approach the matter on the basis that due weight should be given to the fact that the mother and not the Court is vested with the discretion. The Court should not allow mere own preferences to prove a vitiated discretion or a discretion which is to the detriment of the child . . . At the end of the day it must be satisfied that an order will not constitute undue 'interference with the mother's right' (*B v P* at 117F). Subject to such matters as degree of proof (cf *W v S and Others (1)*), the Court responds on the basis that the child has a right that the parent must exercise its discretion in the best interests of the child. (Differently put: the parent has a duty to make decisions on that basis. But perhaps the child has a legal right about access . . .) The best interests of the child is the yardstick. But, unlike a custody dispute between spouses or ex-spouses, the issue is not which of two parents it is best to choose to benefit the child most. The issue is whether it is established that the interests of the child require that there must be access *to* a specific person (someone who has no parental authority). Otherwise, as pointed out at p 24 in *O v J*, the position in regard to legitimate and extra-marital children is equated.

Fourthly, just as the Court can force the custodian mother to permit access between the child and someone who is important to the child's development in terms of religion, education and general balance, the Court can enforce access to someone who is important to the child's emotional development. The Court will not protect only non-interference with the child's Sunday school or secular education or violin lessons; it will not look at participation in sporting activities and Boy Scouts only. It can also compel the mother to allow visits to somebody between whom and the child there is a bond of affection such as a grandfather, friend, or natural father with whom the child has been living for nine years. (I mention a time factor not as a guideline but to emphasise that I mention an illustration.)

It is neither possible nor advisable to attempt to define when and with what cogency existing bonds between natural father and extra-marital child should be a factor. Or, if none exists, in which circumstances it is desirable that (a) the child be informed that the person with whom he lives is not his genetical father and (b) ties with the biological father be developed.

How are the best interests of the extra-marital child approached?

I think there is substance in views in England – where there are also more recent decisions which are not in full consonance with the cases quoted at 645 in the *Van Erk* case . . .

[FLEMMING DJP referred to some English authorities and proceeded:]

[209] Regarding the best interests of the child as the predominant consideration does not mean that it figures as the first item on a list but may be ousted by the joint or several importance of other facts. It is the end of the day measure for the soundness of the decision of the parent.

What is in a child's best interests may not be cluttered by preconceived notions about the fairness of the law. The views about policy and about views of communities stated in the *Van Erk* case may not operate through the back door. Firstly, there is the lack of cogency with which I have dealt. Secondly, they wrongly and unnecessarily blinker assessment of what is good for the specific child in his specific situation in his specific community. Two further considerations were wrongly embraced in the *Van Erk* case. The father's duty to maintain stands whether it is good or bad that he has contact with the child. It is widely accepted that neither the law nor the child or its mother owes the father anything in return. It is then wrong to acknowledge a 'gross injustice' (at 649) which is relevant to what is best in regard to access. What is *fair*-to-a-father is distinct from what is *good*-for-the-child. The rights of a child are not broadened but are rather burdened by axiomatic greater choice given to a distinct party – also if he is a genetic father. Secondly, tolerating discussion of fairness to the father in terms of 'booby prize' or better postulates that something is due. Why should the father get any prize? For the joy brought by a drunken one night stand without any emotional involvement? For seduction? Or inadequate safety of technique? Is the rapist entitled (by law in terms of the *Van Erk* case or otherwise by 'fairness') to visit the resultant child so that the law gives at least a booby prize?

Nor is it acceptable to approach the matter with preconceived views about desirabilities attached to specific facts. Facts are rarely truly identical, the interplay with other facts will vary, and the importance of any given fact is not a constant. That is true also of the need of a child to know who his parent is and to bond with him . . .

When respondent had to decide what access she should permit, she had to ascertain what such access has to offer the child in terms of her moral, [210] emotional, social, religious and educational development . . . Not only the scope but the depth thereof is important. The main factors governing scope and depth would be the potential but also the expected extent of realising the potential. The latter is influenced by the expected duration and stability of the father's attention. That is affected by the make-up of the father, his true reasons for desiring access, the prospects of his being distracted (also by new employment, new associations or children), all of which is often loudly spoken on by past behaviour.

Respondent also had to decide what existing good is threatened and what harm will be caused by permitting access. The prevention of confusion with the child; the protection of a new 'family unit' which has developed and its stability, and harm to the sense of security given to the child are legitimate factors.

Respondent had to weigh the potential harm of refusing access. Had the facts been appropriate she would have had to seriously weigh the bonding which in fact developed between child and genetic father. Had the child been older it may have become a factor that the child *de facto* requires to know that applicant is biologically related or that the child did display a need to contact him. I again do not claim to have exhausted all possibilities.

It makes sense, accordingly, that relevant insights can be gleaned from, for example, the willingness or not of the father to set up a home for the child or, if that is refused by the mother, to give financial support . . . It tends to reflect upon *bona fide* concern for the child and willingness to be a *real* father and not merely a biologically-tied or cheque-book 'father'. Similarly with the time elapsed before access is earnestly sought. Thirdly, I also understand a tendency that if the mother has settled into a 'family' set-up, provided it has a prospect of stability, the chance of access for a natural father who up to then did not have meaningful access, tends to weaken. All the more if the child is bonding or has bonded with the *de facto* male head of the new 'family'. . .

[T]he facts are such that I am unconvinced that respondent is wrong in her scepticism or in her conclusion about what now is in the best interests of the child . . .

The application is dismissed . . .

Note	Aantekening
See the note on *F v L* [21].	Sien die aantekening by *F v L* [21].

[25]   L v J

1985 4 SA 371 (C)

A man is not obliged to maintain an AID child who was conceived without his consent	'n Man is nie verplig om 'n KIS-kind te onderhou wat sonder sy toestemming verwek is nie
The plaintiff, while married to the defendant, had herself artificially inseminated with the sperm of an unknown donor without her husband's consent. The marriage broke down irretrievably and the parties were divorced. The plaintiff, *inter alia*, claimed maintenance for the child from the defendant. The court held that there was no obligation upon him to maintain the child.	Die eiseres het, terwyl sy met die verweerder getroud was, haar kunsmatig laat insemineer met die sperm van 'n onbekende skenker sonder haar man se toestemming. Die huwelik het onherstelbaar verbrokkel en die partye is geskei. Die eiseres het onder andere onderhoud vir die kind van die verweerder geëis. Die hof het beslis dat daar geen verpligting op hom gerus het om die kind te onderhou nie.

BERMAN J: [377] Now whatever the nature of the relationship may be between a husband and the child born (with his consent) to his wife as a result of her having been artificially inseminated with the sperm of an unknown donor and whatever the status of such a child may be (and the only reported case thereon in our law reports is *V v R* 1979 (3)

SA 1006 (T)), it seems to me to admit of no doubt that where there has been no consent to resort being had by the wife from her husband to such insemination (AID), the child is illegitimate...

And it is also clear that no duty is imposed on a husband to provide maintenance for the child of his wife if he is not that child's natural father, the sole difference between the cases where the child is born by AID or out of an adulterous relationship is that in the former case no accusation of adultery can be levelled against the wife – the child's legitimacy, or rather illegitimacy, remains unaffected by his or her mother having undergone medical treatment or having enjoyed the thrills of illicit passion. The obligation in our law to provide maintenance (apart from where such an obligation has been created by statute, as in the case of adoption) is based on consanguinity, so that inasmuch as a husband is not obliged in law to support his step-child (see *S v MacDonald* 1963 (2) SA 431 (C) at 432F (and the old authorities there cited) and *Joffe v Lubner* 1972 (4) SA 521 (C) at 523-4) he can certainly not be obliged to support a child born to his wife by AID without his consent...

[378] *MacDonald's* case *supra* provides no authority for the proposition that any duty to continue – after divorce – to support a wife's child born to her as a result of AID undertaken without her husband's consent can be acceptably based on the mere fact that the husband has treated the child as his own "as an inevitable concomitant with the maintenance of the household" while he had the *consortium* of the child's mother; see "Case of a Sterile Father" by JD van der Vyver 1979 *SALJ* at 437...

Nor do any considerations of public policy dictate that a man in defendant's position bears any obligation to maintain, upon divorce, the child of his wife, born *stante matrimonio* to her by AID undertaken without his consent...

It follows that I hold that no legal obligation rests on defendant to support [the child]...

Note

In *V v R* 1979 3 SA 1006 (T) it was held that a child procreated by means of artificial insemination with the semen of a third party donor which took place at the request of the wife with the consent of her husband is an illegitimate child, and that only the mother's consent is required for the adoption of the child. The judge also expressed the view *obiter* that the husband who consented to the artificial insemination of his wife must be responsible for the child's maintenance.

This position has now been changed by the Children's Status Act 82 of 1987. Section 5(1)(a) of this act provides that if a married woman is artificially inseminated with the semen of a third party donor, any child born of that woman as a result of such insemination shall for all purposes be deemed the legitimate child of the woman and her husband if both of them have consented to such insemination. In terms of section 5(1)(b) it will be presumed that both the wife and her husband have consented to the insemination, until the contrary is proved.

Aantekening

In *V v R* 1979 3 SA 1006 (T) is beslis dat 'n kind wat op versoek van 'n vrou deur kunsmatige bevrugting verwek is deur gebruikmaking van die semen van 'n derde party, en waartoe haar man toegestem het, 'n buite-egtelike kind is, en dat net die moeder se toestemming nodig is vir die aanneming van die kind. Die regter het ook *obiter* die mening uitgespreek dat 'n man wat tot die kunsmatige bevrugting van sy vrou toegestem het vir die onderhoud van die kind verantwoordelik moet wees.

Hierdie posisie is nou deur die Wet op die Status van Kinders 82 van 1987 verander. Artikel 5(1)(a) bepaal dat as 'n getroude vrou kunsmatig bevrug word met die semen van 'n derde party, 'n kind wat as gevolg van sodanige kunsmatige bevrugting uit die vrou gebore word vir alle doeleindes as die binne-egtelike kind van daardie vrou en haar eggenoot geag word indien albei van hulle tot die bevrugting toegestem het. Ingevolge artikel 5(1)(b) word vermoed dat sowel die vrou as haar man tot die bevrugting toegestem het, tot die teendeel bewys word. Hieruit kan 'n mens

From this one can deduce that if a woman has herself artificially inseminated without her husband's consent, the child will be illegitimate and that her husband will not be liable for support of the child.

Although *L v J* was decided before the Children's Status Act came into operation, the judgment in this case accords with the provisions of the act.

aflei dat as 'n vrou haar sonder haar man se toestemming kunsmatig laat bevrug die kind buiteegtelik sal wees en dat haar man nie aanspreeklik sal wees vir die kind se onderhoud nie.

Alhoewel *L v J* beslis is voor die Wet op die Status van Kinders in werking getree het, is die uitspraak in die saak in ooreenstemming met die bepalings van die wet.

[26] LAMB V SACK

1974 2 SA 670 (T)

Maintenance of an illegitimate child

This case concerned a dispute between the mother (appellant) and father (respondent) of an illegitimate child about the payment of the child's maintenance. The respondent lodged a complaint with the maintenance officer in terms of which he sought to have his contribution reduced. The appellant lodged a counterclaim asking for the respondent's contribution to be increased. An enquiry by the maintenance court resulted in the reduction of the respondent's monthly contribution. The appellant appealed against this order. The respondent's attitude on appeal was that he was being required to make a much bigger contribution towards the maintenance of the child than he was legally obliged to do. He submitted that, although the duty of support ordinarily rests upon both parents, the natural father of an illegitimate child is, as a matter of public policy, never called upon to make more than a nominal contribution towards the maintenance of such child unless the mother is indigent. The respondent's argument was rejected and the appellant's claim for increased maintenance was granted.

Onderhoud van 'n buite-egtelike kind

Hierdie saak het te doen gehad met 'n geskil tussen die moeder (appellant) en vader (respondent) van 'n buite-egtelike kind in verband met die betaling van onderhoud vir die kind. Die respondent het 'n klagte by die onderhoudsbeampte ingedien om sodoende te poog om 'n vermindering van sy bydrae te verkry. Die appellant het 'n teeneis ingestel en versoek dat die respondent se bydrae verhoog word. Die onderhoudshof het 'n ondersoek ingestel wat daartoe gelei het dat die respondent se maandelikse bydrae verminder is. Die appellant het teen hierdie bevel geappelleer. In appèl het die respondent aangevoer dat van hom vereis word om 'n groter bydrae tot die kind se onderhoud te maak as waartoe hy regtens verplig is. Hy het aangevoer dat hoewel die onderhoudsplig normaalweg op albei ouers rus daar, ooreenkomstig openbare beleid, nooit van die vader van 'n buite-egtelike kind vereis word om meer as 'n nominale bydrae tot die onderhoud van sodanige kind te maak nie tensy die moeder hulpbehoewend is. Die respondent se argument is verwerp en die appellant se eis om verhoogde onderhoud is toegestaan.

TRENGOVE J: [671] The general principle, according to the authorities, is that the duty of supporting a child is a duty common to both parents, according to their respective means, and it makes no difference whether such child is born in or out of wedlock ... As far as the general principle is concerned I need do no more than to refer to the well-known cases of *Farrell v Hankey*, 1921 TPD 590; *Van der Westhuizen v Rex*, 1924 TPD 370;

Herfst v Herfst, 1964 (4) SA 127 (W) [143]. In *Farrell v Hankey*, MASON, J, in referring to the parents' duty of support said at p 596 of his judgment:

"The Roman-Dutch authorities are quite clear that the burden of supporting the children, whether before or after a divorce, is a burden common to the two spouses, the only qualification being that it is distributable between them according to their means."

In *Van der Westhuizen v Rex*, at p 373, FEETHAM, J, after pointing out that under the English common law a father was under no civil liability to maintain either his legitimate or illegitimate children, proceeded to say:

[672] "Under the Roman-Dutch law, on the other hand, a father is bound to support and maintain his illegitimate as well as his legitimate children."

The basis upon which the obligation in regard to a child's maintenance attaching to both parents jointly is apportioned *inter se*, is set out very clearly in the following passage in the judgment of TROLLIP, J, in *Herfst v Herfst*, at p 130, namely:

"The general principles are that a child of divorced parents is entitled to be maintained by them, and they are correspondingly obliged to provide it with everything that it reasonably requires for its proper living and upbringing according to their means, standard of living and station in life. That obligation attaches to both parents jointly, but, *inter se*, their respective shares of that obligation are apportioned according to the financial resources and circumstances of each of them."

Although the learned Judge was here dealing specifically with rights of a child of divorced parents to maintenance, it seems to me to be clear that according to the Roman-Dutch law authorities, these principles apply with equal force to the apportionment, *inter se*, of the respective shares of the joint obligation, which also rests upon the natural parents of an illegitimate child, to support such child (cf *Voet*, 25.3.5; De Groot, *Inleiding*, 3.58.8, and Van Leeuwen, *RHR*, 1.13.7).

At this stage it is necessary to refer to the case of *A v M*, 1930 WLD 292. The respondent, as I have mentioned, based his argument on the fact that he was not obliged to make more than a nominal contribution towards the maintenance of his illegitimate child on the case of *A v M*, and particularly on the following passage in the judgment, by BARRY, J, at p 293, namely:

"The question that the Court has to determine is the amount of maintenance that has to be paid for this illegitimate child. The plaintiff has admitted that she was generously treated by the defendant, and claims that an amount of £15 should be awarded her by the Court. The question that I have to consider is what is a fair amount in the circumstances and, as pointed out by the Roman-Dutch authorities, it is a matter which is left largely to the discretion of the Court. *Voet*, in a passage to which the Court was referred (book 25, title 3, sec 6), does not indicate the basis on which the Court is to calculate the amount of maintenance. He points out that the burden of maintaining a child is common both to the father and the mother unless one of them is indigent and that burden applies whether the children are born in lawful wedlock or not. If the father is indigent and the mother has means, then the burden falls upon her. It would appear from what he says that the burden falls on the father and mother according to their means. He does not appear to draw a distinction between the amount of maintenance in the case of legitimate and illegitimate children, but from the cases to which the Court was referred I think a principle can be gathered where the Court orders maintenance in the case of illegitimate children. Taking those cases as a guide, it appears that in each case a small amount has been awarded for such maintenance. I take it that the reason is that the policy of the law is to discourage illicit relations. At the same time the Court is careful to see that something is paid by the father so as not to throw the whole burden of maintenance upon the mother, and in the case where the mother is indigent it would be unjust to leave an innocent illegitimate child destitute. It was said that the defendant was comparatively rich, but I do not think his social condition and means is a guide in a case of this kind because I think that a distinction must be drawn between legitimate and illegitimate children. In the case of legitimate children the amount of maintenance would, it seems to me, depend on the condition in life of the parents, but it does not follow that, because maintenance in that case depends on the condition in life of the parents, the same rule is applicable in the case of illegitimate children, the reason being that the Courts will not encourage illicit relations."

Although this passage appears to lend support to the propositions advanced by the respondent, I do not believe that the learned Judge really intended it to have that effect. Looking at the passage in the [673] context of the judgment as a whole, I doubt very much whether the learned Judge intended to convey that, as a matter of legal principle, the burden of supporting an illegitimate child rests mainly on the mother and that the natural father of the child, whatever his financial resources may be, was not under any legal obligation to pay anything more than a small or nominal amount towards maintenance of the child, unless the mother was indigent. However, if this is what the learned Judge, in fact, intended to express in the passage under consideration, I must respectfully disagree with his views. As regards the apportionment of the contributions which parents are obliged to make towards the support of their children, the Roman-Dutch authorities, as I have already mentioned, do not appear to draw any distinction whatever between legitimate and illegitimate children. I have not, furthermore, been able to trace any case, subsequent to *A v M*, in which the views expressed by the learned Judge on this particular issue have been followed or adopted. In my judgment, there is no valid reason why the ordinary rule, namely, that the burden of support, resting on both parents jointly, is distributable *inter se* according to their respective means and income, should not also apply in respect of the natural parents of illegitimate children. This approach appears to me to be in accordance with the principles of our law on the subject and it is also consistent with, what I believe to be, the benevolent attitude of our modern society to the so-called illegitimate child. I am also not persuaded that the application of this principle for the purpose of determining what the natural father's contribution towards the maintenance of his illegitimate child should be, would in any way tend to encourage or promote illicit relations; on the contrary, it might possibly even have the opposite effect. I must, therefore, reject the submission made by the respondent on this issue . . .

[TRENGOVE J then discussed the individual circumstances and financial position of the parties and concluded:]

[674] To sum up, the position of the parties, broadly stated, appears to be as follows: The respondent, after making allowance for his monthly expenses, has a net income of about R450 per month and the appellant, if she were to take up employment, would probably be able to earn from R120 to R150 per month. On this basis the actual net income of the respondent and the potential income of the appellant are in the ratio of 3 to 1. This seems to me to be a fair and just basis upon which to make an apportionment, *inter se*, of the amount of R102 which the child is entitled to receive from its parents in respect of maintenance. I have accordingly come to the conclusion that the respondent should be ordered to contribute an amount of R75 per month towards the maintenance of the child.

In the result the appeal succeeds . . .

VAN WYK DE VRIES J concurred.

Note

There is no justification in modern law for the view that a father may pay less maintenance for his illegitimate child than for his legitimate child. All children should be treated on an equal basis as far as their right to maintenance against their father is concerned (see Boberg 279 fn 2). The views expressed by BARRY J in *A v M* 1930 WLD 292 were therefore rightly rejected by TRENGOVE J in the case under discussion. See also *Tate v Jurado* 1976 4 SA 238 (W).

Aantekening

In the moderne reg is daar geen regverdiging vir die opvatting dat 'n vader minder onderhoud vir sy buite-egtelike kind mag betaal as vir sy binne-egtelike kind nie. Alle kinders behoort op 'n gelyke grondslag behandel te word vir sover dit hulle eis op onderhoud teenoor hulle vader aangaan (sien Boberg 279 vn 2). Die opvattinge van BARRY R in *A v M* 1930 WPA 292 is gevolglik met reg deur TRENGOVE R in die onderhawige saak verwerp. Sien ook *Tate v Jurado* 1976 4 SA 238 (W).

[27]   MOTAN V JOOSUB

1930 AD 61

The duty of paternal grandparents to support their son's illegitimate child

The appellant was married to the respondent's son by Mohammedan rites. She and the respondent's son had four children who were still minors at the time the action came before the court. As the union between the appellant and the respondent's son did not constitute a valid marriage, their children were illegitimate. The appellant claimed maintenance for the children from the respondent. She averred, *inter alia*, that the respondent, being the paternal grandfather of the children, was liable to support his son's illegitimate children. The respondent, however, denied any liability. Subsequently, the appellant excepted against this plea but the exception was dismissed and it was held that the paternal grandfather of illegitimate children was under no duty to support them. The appellant appealed against this decision but the appeal was rejected.

Die plig van grootouers aan vaderskant om hulle seun se buite-egtelike kind te onderhou

Die appellant is ingevolge die Mohammedaanse geloof met die respondent se seun getroud. Sy en die respondent se seun het vier kinders gehad wat nog minderjarig was toe die aksie deur die hof aangehoor is. Aangesien daar geen geldige huwelik tussen die appellant en die respondent se seun tot stand gekom het nie, was hulle kinders buite-egtelik. Die appellant het onderhoud vir die kinders van die respondent geëis. Sy het onder andere beweer dat die respondent, as grootvader aan vaderskant, aanspreeklik was vir die onderhoud van sy seun se buite-egtelike kinders. Die respondent het aanspreeklikheid ontken. Die appellant het eksepsie teen hierdie verweer aangeteken. Die eksepsie is van die hand gewys en daar is beslis dat buite-egtelike kinders se grootvader aan vaderskant onder geen verpligting staan om die kinders te onderhou nie. Die appellant het teen hierdie beslissing appèl aangeteken maar die appèl is van die hand gewys.

WESSELS JA: [65] There is no doubt that this question belongs to the *jus controversum* [controversial points of law]. It will therefore be advisable briefly to trace the development of our law in this respect in order to ascertain which is the better view. The Roman law has been exhaustively considered by Glück in his *Commentary on the Digest* (vol 28, sec 1288a), where he proves that it never was part of the civil law that a paternal grandfather was obliged to support the illegitimate children of his son. I may state that almost all the modern commentators whom I have consulted agree with his conclusions ...

[66] The Roman law, however, compelled the mother of an illegitimate child and also the mother's father to provide for it ... (D 25 3. *lex* 5; 4 and 5). The only obligation of maintenance, therefore, recognised by the Roman law is between the illegitimate children on the one part and the mother and the mother's ascendants on the other part. There is no text in the *Corpus Juris* which lays any obligation on the paternal grandfather to support the illegitimate children of his sons.

According to *Glück* the Canon law placed no obligation for maintenance on the grand-parents. It only mentions the parents of the illegitimate child. It however placed all illegitimate children on the same footing as *naturales liberi* [natural illegitimate children], and the Civil law, so modified, was accepted in Holland as well as in many parts of Europe in the days of *Van Leeuwen*. We will now consider whether the Roman-Dutch law extended the obligation for the maintenance of illegitimate children to the paternal grandfather ...

[WESSELS JA analysed a number of Roman-Dutch texts and concluded that Roman-Dutch law did not place any liability on the paternal grandfather to maintain his son's illegitimate child. He proceeded:]

[70] I now come to Mr *de Villiers'* [for the appellant] argument that we ought to draw no distinction between the maternal and the paternal grandfather. They are both bound to the illegitimate child of their daughter or son respectively *nexu sanguinis* [by a bond of blood relationship] and therefore the same duty lies upon both. From an ethical point of view there is much to be said for this contention, and the Civilians may have taken this view if there were no great practical difficulties in the way. But there are. The father of the mother of an illegitimate child knows full well that it is his daughter's child, and if called upon to pay for its support, the proof of the *nexus sanguinis* is at hand. If, however, the paternal grandfather is called upon to pay, he may perhaps be sufficiently certain in those cases where the woman is the concubine of his son, where they live together as man and wife, but in no other case can he be certain. He must either accept the word of the mother or trust to the worldly wisdom of his son. He is called upon to prove a negative where he has no real means of repelling the claim. To hold, therefore, that the paternal grandfather is liable to maintain every illegitimate child of his son would be to cast upon him a burden which it may be difficult for him to remove by proof. In these circumstances it appears to me to be the more correct view ... that no such liability as we are considering lies upon the paternal grandfather ...

In our opinion the view taken by the lower court is the correct view, and the appeal must therefore be dismissed ...

DE VILLIERS CJ; CURLEWIS JA and STRATFORD JA concurred.

Note

After an analysis of Roman-Dutch law Van den Heever in his book (69–70) concluded that there is indeed authority for holding the paternal grandparents of an illegitimate child liable for the support of the child. He submits that "[this] decision is so patently wrong that it should be reconsidered" (70). Davel (462–468) is of the same opinion. Boberg (341 fn 53) points out that it is illogical to argue (as WESSELS JA did) that the

Aantekening

Na 'n ontleding van die Romeins-Hollandse reg het Van den Heever in sy boek (69–70) tot die gevolgtrekking gekom dat daar wel gesag vir die standpunt bestaan dat die grootouers aan vaders-kant aanspreeklik is om hulle seun se buite-egtelike kind te onderhou. Hy reken dat "[this] decision is so patently wrong that it should be reconsidered" (70). Davel (462–468) huldig die-selfde mening. Boberg (341 vn 53) wys daarop paternal grandfather cannot be certain that the child is in fact his son's. Before any liability to support a grandchild can be placed on a grandparent, it must in any event first be proved that that person is in fact the grandparent of the child.

dat dit onlogies is om te redeneer (soos wat WESSELS AR gedoen het) dat die grootvader aan vaderskant nie seker kan wees dat die kind inderdaad sy seun s'n is nie. Voordat enige aanspreeklikheid vir onderhoud op 'n grootouer geplaas kan word, moet immers eers bewys word dat daardie persoon inderdaad die grootouer van die kind is.

Legitimation of extra-marital children

Wettiging van buite-egtelike kinders

[28]   POTGIETER V BELLINGAN

1940 EDL 264

Legitimatio per rescriptum principis

The applicant and the respondent were "married" in April 1939. In the "marriage certificate" the respondent was described as a bachelor. A child was born, of this "marriage". In November 1939 the respondent was arrested on a charge of bigamy. The applicant was confronted with the fact that the respondent, at the time of his "marriage" to her, was a married man. She now applied, *inter alia,* for the "marriage" to be declared null and void and for an order declaring the child born of the "marriage" legitimate. Both orders were granted.

Legitimatio per rescriptum principis

Die applikant het in April 1939 met die respondent "in die huwelik getree". In die "huweliksertifikaat" is die respondent as 'n oujongkêrel aangedui. 'n Kind is uit hierdie "huwelik" gebore. In November 1939 is die respondent op 'n aanklag van bigamie in hegtenis geneem. Die applikant het toe vir die eerste keer gehoor dat hy ten tyde van sy "huwelik" met haar 'n getroude man was. Sy het nou onder andere aansoek gedoen dat die "huwelik" nietig verklaar word en dat die kind wat uit die "huwelik" gebore is, binne-egtelik was. Albei bevele is toegestaan.

GANE J: [267] But I should also mention a later passage in the same title, 25.7.14, where it appears to me that *Voet* indicates a way out of the present difficulty. *Voet* is there dealing with the question of legitimation by the Princeps or Sovereign. *Voet* says in that section that the Princeps will only grant an order for legitimation of children where there are no other legal children, at least so far as the order may purport to make the children concerned the heirs of their father; but he adds that the Princeps may so far legitimate the children *ut macula nativitatis aboleatur* – in order that the stain of their nativity may be wiped out. The procedure of legitimation by the Princeps or Sovereign is unknown in South Africa; I think it may be said to be for practical purposes obsolete. I think that the Supreme Court of the country now exercises the power, somewhat rarely no doubt, which formerly resided in the Princeps . . .

Note

Hahlo and Kahn (*The Union of South Africa The Development of its Laws and Constitution* 357) and Spiro (23) agree with the view of the court in this case, viz that a child cannot be legitimised

Aantekening

Hahlo en Kahn (*The Union of South Africa The Development of its Laws and Constitution* 357) en Spiro (23) stem saam met die opvatting van die hof in hierdie saak, naamlik dat 'n kind nie meer

any more by an order of the Sovereign in South Africa. Pont (1958 *Acta Juridica* 134; 1959 *SALJ* 448 *et seq*), however, is of the opinion that the court erred in this case. He advocates the re-introduction of this method of legitimation and considers that the Department of Home Affairs should be the competent authority to deal with such matters.

in Suid-Afrika deur 'n bevel van die owerheid binne-egtelik verklaar kan word nie. Pont (1958 *Acta Juridica* 134; 1959 *SALJ* 448 ev) is egter van mening dat die hof in hierdie saak gefouteer het en hy bepleit die herinstelling van hierdie metode van wettiging. Hy meen dat die Department van Binnelandse Sake met hierdie bevoegdheid beklee moet word.

Age

Contractual capacity of minor
Termination of minority

Ouderdom

Minderjarige se kontrakteerbevoegdheid
Beëindiging van minderjarigheid

Contractual capacity of minor   Minderjarige se kontrakteerbevoegdheid

[29]   PLEAT v VAN STADEN

1921 OPD 91

Misrepresentation by a minor	Wanvoorstelling deur 'n minderjarige

The defendant's brother bought oxen on credit from the plaintiff for £408. The defendant agreed to stand surety for his brother. The plaintiff asked the defendant whether he was of age and the latter said he was. Consequently, a promissory note to the value of £408 was signed by the defendant and his brother. The purchase price of the oxen was not paid and subsequently the plaintiff sued the defendant for provisional sentence on the promissory note. The defendant defended himself against the claim by relying on his minority at the time when he signed the note. The court *a quo* was satisfied that the defendant was a minor and ordered the plaintiff to proceed with the principal case. The plaintiff then declared that the defendant had induced him to enter into the agreement by misrepresenting himself as a major. The plaintiff further alleged that the defendant had been allowed by his father to buy and sell in his own name and for his own account and had therefore been emancipated by his father. The defendant averred that he had signed the promissory note because the plaintiff stated that he was merely signing as a witness to the contract of sale regarding the oxen. The defendant further alleged that he did not buy the cattle nor did he receive any value for the promissory note and that the plaintiff was fully aware of the defendant's age. The claim was granted.

Die verweerder se broer het osse vir £408 van die eiser op krediet gekoop. Die verweerder het onderneem om borg te staan vir sy broer. Die eiser het vir die verweerder gevra of hy mondig was en die verweerder het bevestigend geantwoord. Die verweerder en sy broer het toe 'n skulderkenning ten bedrae van £408 onderteken. Die koopprys van die osse is nie betaal nie en die eiser het die verweerder vir voorlopige vonnis gedagvaar. Die verweerder het die eiser se eis teengestaan deur hom te beroep op sy minderjarigheid ten tyde van die ondertekening van die skulderkenning. Die hof *a quo* was tevrede dat die verweerder wel minderjarig was en het die eiser beveel om met die hoofgeding voort te gaan. Die eiser het beweer dat die verweerder hom oorreed het om die ooreenkoms aan te gaan deur hom as 'n mondige persoon voor te doen. Die eiser het verder beweer dat die verweerder se vader hom toegelaat het om in sy eie naam en op sy eie rekening te koop en te verkoop en dat sy vader hom dus geëmansipeer het. Die verweerder het beweer dat hy die skulderkenning onderteken het omdat die eiser gesê het dat hy bloot as getuie tot die koopkontrak van die osse teken. Die verweerder het verder beweer dat hy nooit die osse gekoop het nie en nooit enige waarde op grond van die skulderkenning gekry het nie en dat die eiser bewus was van sy ouderdom. Die eis is toegestaan.

WARD J: [94] There are two answers to the defendant's plea of minority. The one is that, as he represented that he was a major, he cannot avail himself of that plea, and the second is that he had been tacitly emancipated and was therefore liable. It may be convenient to take the second ground first, namely, tacit emancipation.

The plaintiff in his declaration (para 8) states that at the date of the purchase in question in this case the defendant had been allowed by his father and natural guardian to trade and do business and to buy and sell on his own account and had thus been tacitly emancipated, and, in reply to a request for particulars the plaintiff states that the defendant had (a) his own bank account, (b) that he purchased goods at the store of Jacobsohn & Cohen, of Kroonstad, and kept a running account there, (c) that he sold eight oxen to one Mervis and also 17 heifers and three cows to one Hotz and (d) a motor-car through Stainer, an auctioneer; and also that he had had certain dealings with a certain Sher.

Now the plaintiff does not allege that he had any knowledge of any of these transactions when the cattle were sold and the promissory note sued upon was taken, but I take it if tacit emancipation had already taken place and the defendant was in the position of a major, the plaintiff would be entitled to sue defendant, though when the transaction took place, he was ignorant of the facts which would go to show such emancipation . . .

[WARD J then analysed the evidence regarding the acts from which the court was asked to infer emancipation and concluded that the defendant had not been emancipated. He proceeded:]

[97] There remains the further and much more difficult question: Is the defendant liable on the ground that when he was asked by the plaintiff if he was of age he replied in the affirmative? – and I may state here that I find as a fact that such question was put and such answer given . . . The authority is very meagre in our Courts, but what little there is seems to be that a minor who makes a false representation as to his age is not protected by his minority from responsibility . . .

[WARD J referred to some cases and common law authorities and proceeded:]

[98] *Domat* states the law as follows: "If a minor has given out that he is of age, and by producing a false certificate of the registry of his christening, or by some other way, has made people believe that he is a major, he cannot be relieved against those acts into which he shall have engaged anyone by this surprise." And he adds in a footnote: "This rule is to be understood only of the cases where the creditor has had just reason to believe that the minor was of age. For if there was no more than a *bare declaration* of the minor's, who pretended to be of age, the creditor ought to blame himself for his credulity."

[99] My difficulty in deciding this case arises from the apparently perfunctory way in which the plaintiff endeavoured to ascertain whether the defendant was of age or not. The plaintiff admits that the defendant appeared "baie jonk" and a "bietje jonk," but the only question he puts to him is "are you of age?" The transaction involved a considerable sum of money (£408), and the defendant's father lived only fifteen miles from Kroonstad, where the transaction took place, and one would have expected that the plaintiff would have verified the defendant's statement as to his being a major by enquiries from the defendant's father, with whom he was in the habit of having business transactions. *Voet* (4.4.43 . . .) does not however seem to regard the duty of the creditor dealing with a minor in the same strict way that *Domat* does. The passage from *Voet* is summarised by *Nathan* (Vol I, paragraph 198, p 126) as follows: "Restitution on the ground of minority will be refused if a person is held, in interpretation of law, to be a major at the time of entering into the contract, when, for instance, he has fraudulently represented himself as a major to the person with whom he has contracted if the other acted *bona fide* and under a genuine mistake . . . If a minor acts fraudulently and represents himself as a major to one, who knows that in reality he is a minor, the person so contracting with the minor cannot avail himself of the minor's fraud, as he was aware of the deceit. The proof of knowledge on the person contracting with the minor that the minor pretending to be a major was in reality a minor, will be on the minor, since fraud on the part of the other person will not be presumed unless such person is a blood relation of the minor's, for then the presumption is that he was aware of the minor's age." Now has the defendant in this case established that the plaintiff was not deceived by his (the defendant's) mis-representation and that the plaintiff believed all the time that the defendant was a minor? It appears that the minor when this representation was made was between sixteen and

seventeen years of age. I have already pointed out how the age of the defendant could have been placed beyond all doubt, without much difficulty, and considerations of this kind are not without their weight, but I do not think that they are conclusive. Other facts are proved which should be taken into account in the endeavour to ascertain the state of plaintiff's mind. The defendant sold cattle to a Mr Hotz – the transaction seems to have been a perfectly honest one. On that occasion Mr Hotz asked the defendant if he was of age, and he states, that defendant replied that he was, and apparently Mr Hotz was satisfied and purchased some of the cattle. Then again, the evidence as to the opening by the defendant of an ordinary account at the National Bank, Kroonstad, is of importance. The accountant at that bank was called as a witness, and states that he queried the opening of this account on the ground that defendant was a minor, but on investigations he was satisfied that the defendant was entitled to open the account. If no reasonable man could believe from the defendant's appearance that he was a major, then that would be strong evidence that the plaintiff could not have believed him to be such, and the transaction should be set aside, but if other persons, equally interested in the defendant's age also took him to be, and dealt with him as a major, then there is no inherent difficulty in accepting the plaintiff's evidence that, when he took the promissory note sued on in this case, he did believe defendant to be a major. The plaintiff swears that he believed the defendant when he told him that he was a major. The evidence led for the defence has not convinced me that he is swearing falsely on this point, and I think judgment should be for the plaintiff ...

MCGREGOR J: It may be convenient at the outset to dispose of the contention advanced for the plaintiff that the defendant was emancipated. It may be conceded that there are passages in the evidence that lend some colour to such a contention. The defendant to some extent carried on for himself: bought and sold and opened a banking account in his own name. But while he may have been, to a greater or less extent, intellectually emancipated (if such an expression be permissible), I am of opinion, on the evidence of record, that he cannot be regarded as emancipated in law ...

[101] The next question is, what legal consequences flow from the circumstance that defendant knowingly made the false statement in question. *Voet* was relied on by the plaintiff's counsel to show that a false statement like that before us displaced the privilege flowing from the minority. In Bk 4 (T 4, para 43) he states that *restitutio in integrum* is not granted because of minority where the minor has falsely represented himself as of full age to the person with whom he was contracting, and who in good faith and in fact was under a misapprehension; the reason being that the law did not come to the aid of persons *fallentibus ac dolosis malitia in mentientibus aetatem supplente* [who act fraudulently and deceitfully as malice in liars makes up for age]. This passage is referred to elsewhere in his Commentaries (27.9.13) where we are told that even a sale of immovable property should be held good which a minor had made without leave of the Court or intervention of his tutor, in the case where he passed himself off as a major and so deceived the purchaser, who was ignorant of the facts by reason of honest mistake. Without enquiring whether this result would necessarily follow under our present practice, the reference indicates how seriously the jurist regards the deception. Other authorities are found supporting *Voet*, eg, Van Leeuwen *Censura Forensis*, 4.43.7; *Huber*, 4.40.17; *Gail* (11.65, s 1) ...
All this seems to be founded on the Roman law ...

[MCGREGOR J then discussed Roman law and also analysed English law on this point. He proceeded:]

[104] It now remains for us to enquire whether the plaintiff is precluded from founding on the defendant's misrepresentation, on the ground that he was not misled thereby. Now on this point plaintiff deposed that he accepted the defendant's statement. To the question why he enquired into the age, he replied, "Hy het vir my gelyk baie jonk ... Ek het

gevra want ek het gedink hy is beetjie jonk. Ek wou weet of hy meerderjarig is." Further on he says, "Ek het verstaan hy is mondig. Ek het eerlik gedink hy is mondig." And again, "Hy het gesê hy is lank al mondig, en ek het hom aangeneem."

Now if plaintiff was minded to sell the cattle to the defendant, minor or no minor, why ask the question? It may of course be suggested that he wished to have a formal statement as to age, "to serve as occasion might require" – in explanation of his conduct or defence of his contract. But it does not appear that there was any impending or present necessity to sell the cattle then and there, and to this particular youth, nor is it averred that he took advantage of the youth's immaturity to snatch an unfair advantage out of the transaction. Mr *Fischer* [for the defendant] argued strenuously that plaintiff must have known that the purchaser was a minor: But I do not think that the defendant has established that . . .

Now while the boy looks young (and he was only in his seventeenth year at the time), a person's appearance (though an element in the case) is not always decisive; and the defendant in Court gave the answers, and perhaps possesses the intelligence, of a person older than what he actually is. Nor ought one to lose sight of the fact that he had been in the way of doing an appreciable amount of business and that the bank [105] apparently allowed him to open a banking account in the way a person of full age does – apparently treating him as such; and that the accountant of the bank stated that if the defendant said he was of age, he would believe him. Hotz, one of the witnesses, before paying defendant a substantial amount asked him whether he was twenty-one. "I asked that because he looked to me so young." That was in January, 1920. It seems a fair inference that Hotz accepted defendant's answer that day, for he paid him the money.

Now on this specific matter, where the one party made a false statement, material to the matter in hand, it is for him I think to establish that the other party was not deceived if he wishes to escape the liability entailed by his misstatement. *Voet* says: "If a minor fraudulently passes himself off for a major, or even says he is a major to a person who is not ignorant of his being a minor, but who cleverly pretends that he is ignorant, the minor, however, fraudulently is still to be listened to", but he adds, "the proof of the knowledge is upon the minor; since fraud is not to be presumed . . . and he affirms who says that there was knowledge of his age." (*Voet* 4.4.43, Sampson's trans.) And . . . I might cite an observation by JESSEL, MR in the case of *Redgrave v Hurd* where he says: "If a man is induced to enter into a contract by a false representation, it is not a sufficient answer to him to say: If you had used due diligence you would have found out that the report was untrue." (45 LTR at p 488). This remark seems substantially in accord with our own law too, having regard to the way *Voet* states the proposition, viz, that the *onus probandi* is on the person who deceived. In Bell's *Commentaries* (Vol 1, Bk II, Part II, c VIII, sec III, Edition of 1870) there is this note (at p 131): "*Kennedy v Weir* (1665, M 11658). The bond in this case bore majority, which was held a good objection, unless the minor could prove the creditor's knowledge of his minority, or that he was fraudulently induced to insert majority in the bond." I am of opinion that the defendant has not here established that his misstatement did not in fact deceive.

If the above reasoning is sound, it follows that the defendant cannot in this case escape liability by reason merely of his undoubted minority.

Note

See the note on *Louw v MJ & H Trust* [31].
It must be borne in mind that the father is no

Aantekening

Sien die aantekening by *Louw v MJ & H Trust* [31].

longer the only natural guardian of a legitimate child – see the note on *Calitz v Calitz* [19].

Dit moet in gedagte gehou word dat die vader nie meer die enigste natuurlike voog van 'n binne-egtelike kind is nie – sien die aantekening by *Calitz v Calitz* [19].

[30] FOUCHÉ v BATTENHAUSEN & CO

1939 CPD 228

Misrepresentation by a minor

While still a minor, the defendant (appellant) bought a car from plaintiff (respondent) in terms of a hire purchase agreement. Before the minor entered into the contract his father discussed the possibility of exchanging a Dodge car for a Chevrolet with a garage owner (a Mr Van der Mescht). The father promised that he would pay a deposit on the car and that his son would pay the balance of the purchase price in instalments. The minor subsequently phoned his father and asked him to send him the Dodge. When the defendant received the Dodge he took it to Van der Mescht's garage and a hire purchase agreement was entered into. A Mr Van der Walt, acting as the garage owner's agent, discussed the terms of the contract with the defendant. The defendant phoned his father to consult him on the terms of the contract and was then taken to the garage owner's attorney. The defendant misrepresented himself as a major. The garage owner's attorney thought that the defendant looked somewhat young but he and Mr Van der Walt were convinced by the defendant's explicit assurance that he was of age. The contract was finalised and the Chevrolet was delivered to the defendant's father. The latter was also informed of the total amount of £115 which was due in terms of the contract. Subsequently the defendant fell in arrears with his payments and the plaintiff claimed the return of the Chevrolet and payment of the arrear instalments. The defendant relied on his mi-

Wanvoorstelling deur 'n minderjarige

Terwyl hy nog minderjarig was, het die verweerder (appellant) 'n motor op huurkoop van die eiser (respondent) gekoop. Voordat die minderjarige die kontrak gesluit het, het sy vader die moontlikheid om 'n Dodge-motor vir 'n Chevrolet in te ruil, met 'n motorhawe-eienaar (ene mnr Van der Mescht) bespreek. Die vader het onderneem om die deposito op die motor te betaal en dat sy seun die res van die koopprys in paaiemente sou afbetaal. Die minderjarige het daarna sy vader geskakel en gevra dat die Dodge na hom toe gestuur word. Toe die verweerder die Dodge ontvang, het hy dit na Van der Mescht se motorhawe geneem en 'n huurkoopooreenkoms gesluit. Ene mnr Van der Walt, wat as die motorhawe-eienaar se verteenwoordiger opgetree het, het die bepalings van die kontrak met die verweerder bespreek. Die verweerder het sy vader geskakel om hom oor die bepalings te raadpleeg en daarna is hy na die motorhawe-eienaar se prokureur toe. Die verweerder het bedrieglik voorgegee dat hy meerderjarig was. Die verweerder het vir die prokureur ietwat jonk voorgekom maar hy en mnr Van der Walt het die verweerder se uitdruklike versekering dat hy meerderjarig was, geglo. Die kontrak is gefinaliseer en die Chevrolet is aan die verweerder se vader gelewer. Hy is ook ingelig dat die totale bedrag van £115 nog ingevolge die kontrak verskuldig was. Die verweerder het agterstallig geraak met sy betalings en die eiser het teruggawe van die Chevrolet en betaling van die agterstallige paaiemente

nority at the time of entering into the contract and lodged a counterclaim for *restitutio in integrum*. In the magistrate's court the plaintiff's claim was allowed and the defendant's claim in reconvention was also allowed. The defendant appealed against this order. His appeal was dismissed.

geëis. Die verweerder het hom op sy minderjarigheid ten tyde van kontraksluiting beroep en 'n teeneis om *restitutio in integrum* ingestel. In die landdroshof is die eiser se eis toegestaan asook die verweerder se eis in rekonvensie. Die verweerder het appèl aangeteken teen hierdie bevel. Sy appèl is van die hand gewys.

DAVIS J: [232] The ... statement of the facts is, I think, amply sufficient to show that the magistrate was quite correct in his finding that the defendant's father, though he was not at first aware of the precise terms of the contract, subsequently approved of it with full knowledge of all its material terms. The father originally commissioned the son to procure a car (he clearly wanted it for himself and not for the son). The son did so and though there is no proof that the father knew all the material terms of the contract at once, yet he did know them before he confirmed the son's contract. In my opinion if a guardian knows that a minor has obtained a car under a hire purchase agreement, knows that another car has been traded in and the amount of the difference which has to be paid, the amount of the deposit and the amount of the monthly payments, then even if the guardian was told nothing of the other terms of the written document, the contention that his approval was given upon insufficient data would not be justified, more especially where, as here, the other terms appear to be the usual ones to be found in documents of this character ...

[I]n addition the evidence here is that the father was not merely told the principal terms but, as the son says, was broadly told the contents of the whole contract. I have no doubt whatever that this is sufficient to validate any approval that he gave. Mr *Hockly* [for the appellant], relied upon the case of *Baddeley v Clarke* (1923, NPD 306). There a minor had bought a motor-bicycle on the hire-purchase system. I cite from the headnote: "There was evidence that the father knew that his son possessed and used the cycle, but not that he knew of the terms upon which the boy had it, or knew that it had been purchased." It will at once be seen how different the circumstances were from those in the present case.

[233] It only remains to add that this confirmation by the guardian with knowledge of the terms is of the same effect as if he had originally interposed his authority – *Voet* (26.8.1) ...

That this contract, for the acquisition of a car to be used by the father on his farm and in his business, entered into by a minor earning £5 a month as a cleaner on the railway, was for that son's benefit was not found by the magistrate nor contended before us. On the contrary, it was seriously to his detriment.

In speaking of the privileges given to a minor in certain circumstances to annul or resile from a contract entered into with the authority of his guardian – *inter alia*, if he were damnified thereby – MASON JP says in *Skead v Colonial Banking and Trust Co Ltd* (1924, TPD 497 at p 500): "These privileges he exercises by means of an action for restitution *in integrum*, there is weighty authority for holding that relief upon this ground, from a contract duly made with the consent of his guardian for value received can only be obtained by such action (*Breytenbach v Frankel and Another* (1913 TPD 300 and 1913 AD 390)." I have examined the authorities referred to and they seem to bear out this statement. It is true that the learned Judge-President then goes on: "But the same reasons, perhaps, do not apply to a defence raised by a minor on the same grounds." I am not sure that I quite understand what is meant: certainly *Voet* (4.4.12) seems to draw no distinction whether a minor is plaintiff or defendant and to regard an *exceptio*, or defence, of minority as merely another form of the claim for *restitutio*. See also *Grotius* (1.8.8). It is unnecessary, however, here to consider whether there is any real difference at all, for in the present case what the defendant seeks, both by his plea and by his claim in reconvention, is a *restitutio in integrum*. The plaintiff's claim is not only for the payment of money, to which the defendant might answer: "I was a minor; the contract damnified me and I now refuse to pay." It is a claim [234] also for the return of a car, and to this portion of the claim the defendant replies: "I will return your car if you return to me mine," though it is not disputed that the ownership in the Dodge car had passed to plaintiff, whereas the plaintiff also continued to be owner of the Chevrolet car.

The next point to be considered is how far defendant's right to *restitutio* is affected by his fraud in describing himself as a major. It was argued that this was immaterial, because the fraud did not induce the true contract, which was an anterior verbal one made with Van der Walt, the written instrument being only a memorandum of that verbal contract – *Goldblatt v Fremantle* (1920, AD 123); *Woods v Walters* (1921 AD 303). The simple answer to this contention is that on the pleadings it is common cause that the contract was a written one. No application was made to amend: if it had been, attention would have been drawn to what may well merely be somewhat loose expressions of the witness Van der Walt and they might have been corrected. Certainly, a verbal hire purchase agreement in relation to a motor car would, I think, be very unusual.

It is unnecessary to consider whether the statement of the law in Wessels, *Contract*, pars 830 *et seq* to the effect that the minor's fraud will only debar him from seeking *restitutio in integrum*, but will not prevent him from defending an action, is correct, for here, as I have shown, the defendant is in fact seeking *restitutio*. To this, upon all the authorities, his fraud is a bar – see, for instance C 2.43.2, *Voet* 4.4.43, and 27.9.13, Van Leeuwen *Censura Forensis* 1.4.43.7, *Gail* 2 obs 65 1, *Christinaeus* 2 dec 131, *Domat* 4.6.2.7, Huber *Hed Rechts* 4.40.17, Pothier, *Pandects* 4.4.43.

But Mr *Hockley*, while not denying the correctness of this proposition, urged that it could have no application to a case where the defrauded party has acted upon the mere word of the minor, and he cited a footnote to the passage in *Domat* referred to above, which is to the following effect: "This rule is to be understood only of the cases where the creditor has had just reason to believe that the minor was of age. For if there was no more than a bare declaration of the minor's, who pretended to be of age, the creditor ought to blame himself for his credulity." This note is fully dealt with in the judgments in the case of *Pleat v Van Staden* (1921, OPD 91) [29]. I agree with the conclusion there come to that it is in accordance neither with the weight of Roman-Dutch [235] authority nor with the decisions of our own courts. In the present case it is not suggested that the minor's fraud did not really deceive both plaintiff's attorney and his representative – as they say that it did – and no ground was put forward as to why they could, or should, not have been so deceived.

I come to the conclusion therefore that the magistrate's decision was right and that the appeal must be dismissed with costs.

HOWES J concurred.

Note

See the note on *Louw v MJ & H Trust* [31].

It must be borne in mind that the father is no longer the only natural guardian of a legitimate

Aantekening

Sien die aantekening by *Louw v MJ & H Trust* [31].

Dit moet in gedagte gehou word dat die vader

child – see the note on *Calitz v Calitz* [19].

nie meer die enigste natuurlike voog van 'n binne-egtelike kind is nie – sien die aantekening by *Calitz v Calitz* [19].

[31] Louw v MJ & H Trust

1975 4 SA 268 (T)

Misrepresentation by a minor

At the age of twenty the appellant bought a motorcycle from the respondent. The appellant subsequently reclaimed R338 which he had paid to the respondent on the ground that the payment was made in pursuance of a contract of sale which could not be enforced against him because he was a minor at the time when the contract had been concluded. The respondent disputed liability for repayment, *inter alia*, on the ground that the appellant had induced the respondent to enter into the agreement by misrepresenting that, although he was only twenty years of age, he was an orphan and self-supporting and that he was therefore tacitly emancipated. The respondent filed a counterclaim for payment of two instalments which were in arrears (amounting to R69) and R298,45 being the value of some parts stolen off the motor cycle. It was alleged that the theft of the parts was due to the appellant's failure to observe the obligation imposed by the contract to keep the motorcycle in good order, repair and condition or alternatively that the theft was due to the appellant's negligence. The court *a quo* found that the appellant had misrepresented himself to be emancipated and that he was therefore bound by the contract. It was further held that the theft of the motorcycle parts was due to the appellant's lack of care and that he was liable for the value of the parts. In addition it was ordered that the appellant should pay the respondent the two arrear instalments. On appeal it was ar-

Wanvoorstelling deur 'n minderjarige

Toe die appellant twintig jaar oud was, het hy 'n motorfiets by die respondent gekoop. Die appellant het later 'n bedrag van R338 wat hy reeds aan respondent betaal het, teruggeëis op grond daarvan dat die betaling gemaak is ingevolge 'n koopkontrak wat nie teen hom afgedwing kon word nie omdat hy ten tyde van die sluiting van die kontrak minderjarig was. Die respondent het aanspreeklikheid vir terugbetaling van die bedrag ontken, onder andere op grond daarvan dat die appellant die respondent deur 'n wanvoorstelling oorreed het om die kontrak met hom aan te gaan. Die appellant het voorgegee dat, alhoewel hy net twintig jaar oud was, hy 'n weeskind was wat selfonderhoudend was en dus stilswyend geëmansipeer was. Die respondent het 'n teeneis ingestel vir die betaling van twee agterstallige paaiemente (wat R69 bedra het) en vir R298,45 synde die waarde van sekere onderdele wat van die motorfiets gesteel is. Daar is beweer dat die diefstal van die onderdele toe te skryf was aan die appellant se versuim om die kontraktuele plig na te kom om die motorfiets in 'n goeie, werkende toestand te hou, of in die alternatief dat die diefstal aan die appellant se nalatigheid te wyte was. Die hof *a quo* het bevind dat die appellant 'n wanvoorstelling gepleeg het deur voor te gee dat hy geëmansipeer was en dat hy dus aan die kontrak gebonde was. Die hof het verder beslis dat die diefstal van die motorfiets se onderdele toe te skryf was aan die appellant

gued on behalf of the appellant that, in the light of his knowledge that the appellant was a minor, the respondent should not have accepted the appellant's representation that he was emancipated without an extensive enquiry as to the truth of that averment. Alternatively it was argued that a minor's contract cannot be enforced against him even if it was induced by misrepresentation and that the minor was accordingly entitled to *restitutio in integrum*. The court of appeal dismissed the argument relating to verification by the respondent of the information given to him by the minor. The court held that the minor was not liable on the contract but dismissed the claim for *restitutio in integrum*. It further dismissed the counterclaim for the payment of the two instalments which were in arrears as well as the payment of the value of the stolen parts.

se gebrek aan sorg en dat hy vir die waarde van die onderdele aanspreeklik was. Verder is ook beveel dat die appellant die twee agterstallige paaiemente aan die respondent moes betaal. In appèl is namens die appellant aangevoer dat, aangesien die respondent bewus was van die appellant se minderjarigheid, hy nie die appellant se bewering dat hy geëmansipeer was, moes aanvaar sonder dat hy 'n uitgebreide ondersoek na die waarheid daarvan ingestel het nie. In die alternatief is beweer dat, selfs indien 'n minderjarige deur die pleeg van 'n wanvoorstelling iemand oorreed om 'n kontrak met hom te sluit, daardie kontrak steeds nie teenoor die minderjarige afdwingbaar is nie en dat die minderjarige gevolglik op *restitutio in integrum* geregtig is. Die hof het die argument verwerp dat die respondent 'n ondersoek moes ingestel het na die inligting wat die minderjarige aan hom verskaf het. Die hof het verder beslis dat die minderjarige nie op grond van die kontrak aanspreeklik was nie maar het die eis om *restitutio in integrum* van die hand gewys. Die hof het verder ook die teeneis vir betaling van die agterstallige paaiemente sowel as vir betaling van die waarde van die gesteelde onderdele verwerp.

ELOFF J: [269] It will be convenient firstly to discuss the question posed by the argument that respondent should have been put on its enquiry on being informed that [270] appellant was a minor, and that it was under a duty to secure verification of the representation that he was emancipated . . .

The related question whether a person induced to enter into a contract with a minor is entitled to act on his say-so that he is of age has been dealt with in our law. *Domat*, 4.6.2.7, states:

"For if there was no more than a mere declaration of the minor, who pretended to be of age, the creditor ought to blame himself for his credulity."

In the case of *Pleat v Van Staden*, 1921 OPD 91 [29], WARD, J, declined, as appears from p 99 of the report, to accept this as a correct statement of the law, and expressed preference for the contrary view propounded by *Voet* in 4.4.43. In a concurring judgment MCGREGOR, J, also relied on *Voet* and supported the main judgment in expressing dissent from the opinion expressed by *Domat*. These views were endorsed in the subsequent case of *Fouché v Battenhausen & Co*, 1939 CPD 228 at p 234 [30]. I should add that Gail in *Pract Obs*, vol II, 65 p 1, also deals with the related problem of whether a creditor can rely on the statement by a minor that he is of age and concludes that he is entitled to do so except if he had good reason to believe that he was dealing with a minor, as there he could guess from his appearance or in some other way.

I respectfully agree with the opinions expressed on the point under discussion in these two cases. Admittedly they deal with the simple situation where a minor represents that he is of age and not with a case such as the present where a person admits his minority but claims that he is emancipated. Counsel for the appellant contended that justification for a different approach in the latter type of situation lies therein that it should be assumed that a minor might attempt to contract without the consent of his guardian, and that the person with whom he deals and who knows that he is under 21 cannot without verification accept his statement that he is emancipated.

In my view there is no foundation for the existence of such an assumption, either in principle or in logic. Of course if the minor does not appear to be a person who could be self-supporting the party to whom he states that he is emancipated may have difficulty in proving that he was or could reasonably have been misled.

In the present case, however, the facts as found by the magistrate reveal that, so far from having reasons to doubt appellant's statement, respondent's manager got verification for that part of it that appellant was in employment. That *per se* goes far to show that appellant might well be self-supporting. There was nothing to engender any doubt in the mind of the respondent's manager that the appellant was in fact emancipated. In my opinion the magistrate correctly found that appellant induced respondent to believe and that respondent was entitled to believe that the appellant was emancipated at the stage when he entered into the contract.

I now turn to the question whether, in view of appellant's fraud, he became bound by the contract . . .

[ELOFF J then referred to *Edelstein v Edelstein* [33] where it was said that an unassisted minor is not bound by his contracts and proceeded:]

[271] The Court did not have to consider whether, in addition to the exceptions mentioned, there was the case where the minor falsely represented himself to have legal capacity. That issue was dealt with in a number of decisions by our Courts.

In the case of *J.C. Vogel & Co v Greentley*, (1903) 24 NLR 252, it was held by the CHIEF JUSTICE:

> "I think however there can be no doubt that, under Roman-Dutch law, where the minor represents himself to be of age, and by virtue of the representation enters into a contract, he is generally bound by that representation. It is right it should be so, otherwise it would give scope for fraud of a very serious description indeed."

On the strength of the view taken of the law the Court enforced a contract against a minor who had fraudulently represented himself to be a major. No authorities were quoted in support of the conclusion reached.

Vogel's case was followed in *Pleat's* case [29], *supra*, where a minor's contract was enforced because of his fraudulent representation that he was of age. Certain authorities, presently to be discussed, were relied upon.

In the Cape DE VILLIERS, CJ, said *obiter* in the case of *Cohen v Sytner*, (1897) 14 SC 13, that:

> "When a minor incurs a debt by representing that he is of full age he is bound."

No authority seems to have been quoted in support of the *dictum*.

Next there is the decision in the case of *Auret v Hind*, 4 EDC 283, wherein the Court seems to have assumed, although in view of its finding on the facts it was unnecessary to do so, that a minor is bound by a contract entered into by him where he deceives the other party into believing that he was a major. Reliance was placed on English authority for this proposition.

In *Fouché v Battenhausen* [30], *supra*, the Court considered but found it unnecessary to decide whether a minor's contract which was entered into by reason of his inducement that he was of age bound him.

This Court has not, so far as I am aware, pronounced on the point. We were urged by counsel for respondent to follow the decisions to which I have referred. Now, in *Fouché's* case, as I have said, the point was left open. The decision in *Auret's* case was *obiter*, and it was based on English law . . .

[272] I do not think that I need say any more about *Auret's* case. The view expressed in *Vogel's* case is emphatic enough, but its value is questionable since no authority is quoted. The only decision which supports respondent's contention which does reflect an examination of Roman and Roman-Dutch law authorities is *Pleat's* case [29] . . .

[ELOFF J analysed some of the old authorities and proceeded:]

[273] [T]he only Roman-Dutch or Roman law authorities which seem to support the contention reached in *Pleat's* case is the passage of doubtful validity from *Voet*, 27.9.13. Nor is there any authority – apart from those to which I have referred – which says that a minor's contract is valid in the circumstances under discussion.

There are, to my mind, cogent reasons why such a contract should be held to be invalid. As is pointed out by Wessels in *The Law of Contract in South Africa*, 2nd ed, para 831, if one were to consider his contract to be valid if induced by his fraud one places it in the power of the minor to bind himself effectively by his contract. To permit this will frustrate the motivation of the rule rendering a minor's contract invalid, and is in my view inconsistent with the rationale expounded in *Edelstein's* case [33].

We were referred by counsel for the respondent to a criticism of the views expressed by *Wessels* made by De Wet and Yeats in their book *Kontraktereg en Handelsreg*, 3rd ed at p 54. They say that, while the main principle certainly exists in order to protect a minor, if he has reached an age where he can represent himself to be a major he should suffer the consequences of his conduct rather than the other contracting party. To my mind this argument loses sight of the fact that the minor is liable in delict and, should the other party suffer a loss by reason of the minor's fraud, he can always [274] recover those losses by an action or counterclaim. I should mention that the learned authors, while recognising that *Van Leeuwen* [*Censura Forensis*], 1.4.43.7 and *Voet*, 4.4.43, discourse solely on *restitutio in integrum*, state that in consequence these authorities nevertheless keep the minor to his contract by declining him restitutionary relief. With respect that seems to me to be a *non sequitur* and is not what *Van Leeuwen* and *Voet* say. There is a vast difference in precluding a minor from reclaiming that with which he parted in pursuance of his contract and in keeping him bound to the contract. The present case presents an illustration of the difference in consequence, which I have in mind. Here, if the minor is not bound by his contract, the respondent cannot claim, as it has claimed, that he should pay any arrear instalments. To that extent the minor's contract is invalid and he is not bound by it, but he does suffer the consequence that he may not reclaim the amounts which he paid in pursuance of the contract.

I accordingly come to the conclusion that the above-stated *dicta* in *Pleat's* case [29], (*supra*, *Vogel's* case, *supra*, *Cohen's* case, *supra*, and *Auret's* case, *supra*), are incorrect and that the true view is that a minor's contract is void even if he misrepresented his contractual capacity, either by holding himself out as being of age or by pretending that he had become emancipated. On this view of the law the respondent was not entitled to claim enforcement of the contract as it did in its counterclaim and the magistrate should not have entered judgment in favour of the respondent in respect of the two unpaid instalments.

As far as the appellant's main claim is concerned I am of the view that it should have failed, not for the reason that the contract was void, but because of the fact that in consequence of his fraud the appellant is not entitled to *restitutio in integrum*. In my discussion of the issue as to the validity or otherwise of the contract I referred to a large number of authorities which enunciate the principle that in circumstances such as those found by the magistrate the minor is not entitled to claim restitutionary relief. That is also the effect of the judgment in *Fouché's* case [30], *supra*, with which I respectfully agree . . .

[I]n the result it seems to me that the plaintiff's claim should have been disallowed on the basis that he fraudulently held himself out to have in effect become emancipated . . .

[ELOFF J further held that, as far as the stolen parts were concerned, the evidence as recorded was insufficient to justify a finding against the appellant. He proceeded:]

[275] For these reasons I conclude that the magistrate – albeit for the wrong reason – correctly absolved respondent from the instance on the main claim. As regards the counter-claim he erred in giving judgment in favour of respondent in regard to the arrear instalments and he erred on the facts in finding the appellant guilty of negligence.

In my judgment the appeal should be allowed to the extent that in relation to the counterclaim the magistrate's judgment should be altered to one of absolution from the instance on the claim for R298,45, and to judgment for plaintiff [appellant] on the claim for R69 . . .

F S STEYN J concurred.

Note

When a minor fraudulently misrepresents himself to be a major or to be emancipated or to have his guardian's consent to contract, two principles of law come into conflict: the first is that a minor should be protected against his own immaturity of judgment and the second is that an innocent party should not be allowed to suffer because of a fraudulent misrepresentation by another (Christie 283). The prevalent view is that a minor should incur some liability if he makes a fraudulent misrepresentation regarding his capacity to enter into contracts. There is, however, no unanimity as to the basis of his liability. The minor could be held liable contractually or delictually.

(i) The minor could be held liable on the contract. This basis for liability is advocated *inter alia* by Van der Vyver and Joubert (156–157) and De Wet and Van Wyk (63). These authors base their opinions on *Vogel v Greentley* (1903) 24 NLR 252; *Pleat v Van Staden* [29] and *Fouché v Battenhausen* [30].

In the first place, those who are in favour of contractual liability of a minor who misrepresents himself, attach much weight to the fact that Roman-Dutch authorities de-

Aantekening

Indien 'n minderjarige bedrieglik voorgee dat hy meerderjarig of geëmansipeerd is of dat hy sy voog se toestemming het om te kontrakteer, kom twee regsbeginsels in botsing met mekaar: die eerste is dat 'n minderjarige beskerm moet word teen sy eie onrype oordeelsvermoë en die tweede is dat 'n onskuldige party nie moet skade ly as gevolg van die bedrieglike wanvoorstelling deur 'n ander nie (Christie 283). Die algemeen aanvaarde mening is dat die minderjarige wel aanspreeklikheid moet opdoen as hy op 'n bedrieglike wyse voorgegee het dat hy kontrakteerbevoegdheid het. Daar is egter geen eenstemmigheid oor die basis van sy aanspreeklikheid nie. Die minderjarige kan kontraktueel of deliktueel aanspreeklik gehou word.

(i) Die minderjarige kan op grond van die kontrak aanspreeklikheid opdoen. Hierdie grondslag vir aanspreeklikheid word onder andere deur Van der Vyver en Joubert (156–157) en De Wet en Van Wyk (63) bepleit. Hierdie skrywers baseer hulle standpunt op *Vogel v Greentley* (1903) 24 NLR 252; *Pleat v Van Staden* [29] en *Fouché v Battenhausen* [30].

nied the minor *restitutio in integrum* if he fraudulently misrepresented himself. They argue that since the minor could not claim *restitutio in integrum*, it is implied that his contract is valid. As those opposing the theory that the minor is contractually liable point out, the contract which a minor enters into without the necessary consent of his guardian simply does not bind the minor (Boberg 600–601; Barnard, Cronjé and Olivier 83; Hawthorne *Family Law Service* par E51; also compare Christie 284). It is therefore unnecessary for the minor to apply for *restitutio in integrum* if he seeks to reclaim whatever he has performed in terms of the contract. He can simply reclaim his performance with the *rei vindicatio* or, in the case of a monetary performance, with a *condictio*. The fact that he is denied the remedy of *restitutio in integrum* does not mean that the minor's contract is valid because of his misrepresentation. It only means that he is denied a remedy which he in any event does not need (Boberg 601; Barnard, Cronjé and Olivier 84). (Also see the note on *Wood v Davies* [37].)

It should be noted that in *Louw v MJ & H Trust* it was held that the minor's misrepresentation did not render him liable on the contract but precluded him from obtaining *restitutio in integrum* so that he could not recover any performance he had already given in terms of the contract. The court was correct when it stated that "[t]here is a vast difference in precluding a minor from reclaiming that with which he parted in pursuance of his contract and in keeping him bound to the contract" (274). As pointed out above, denial of *restitutio in integrum* does not mean that the minor is bound by the contract. The refusal of *restitutio in integrum* in *Louw's* case can therefore be justified. However, since the minor was not bound by the contract he should have been allowed to recover his money by means of a *condictio*. The minor cannot not be bound to the contract and at the same time be denied the right to reclaim that which he has performed in terms of the unenforceable contract.

In the second place, the proponents of con-

In die eerste plek heg diegene wat ten gunste daarvan is dat die minderjarige kontraktuele aanspreeklikheid opdoen as hy 'n bedrieglike wanvoorstelling pleeg baie waarde aan die feit dat die Romeins-Hollandse skrywers geweier het om *restitutio in integrum* toe te staan aan 'n minderjarige wat 'n wanvoorstelling gepleeg het. Hulle redeneer dat aangesien die minderjarige nie *restitutio in integrum* kan verkry nie, dit geïmpliseer word dat sy kontrak geldig is. Die teenstanders van die opvatting dat die minderjarige kontraktueel gebonde is, wys egter tereg daarop dat die kontrak wat 'n minderjarige sonder die nodige toestemming van sy voog aangaan hom doodeenvoudig glad nie bind nie (Boberg 600–601; Barnard, Cronjé en Olivier 85–86; Hawthorne *Family Law Service* par E51; vergelyk ook Christie 284). Dit is dus onnodig vir die minderjarige wat teruggawe wil eis van dit wat hy reeds ingevolge die kontrak gepresteer het, om aansoek te doen om *restitutio in integrum*. Hy kan eenvoudig teruggawe eis van dit wat hy reeds gepresteer het deur gebruik te maak van die *rei vindicatio* of, in die geval van 'n geldelike prestasie, van 'n *condictio*. Die feit dat die minderjarige die remedie van *restitutio in integrum* ontneem word, beteken gevolglik nie dat die kontrak geldig is as gevolg van sy wanvoorstelling nie. Dit beteken bloot dat 'n remedie hom ontneem word wat hy in elk geval nie nodig gehad het nie (Boberg 601; Barnard, Cronjé en Olivier 87). (Sien ook die aantekening by *Wood v Davies* [37].)

'n Mens moet daarop let dat in *Louw v MJ & H Trust* beslis is dat die minderjarige se wanvoorstelling nie tot gevolg het dat hy kontraktuele aanspreeklikheid opdoen nie maar bloot dat hy nie *restitutio in integrum* kan verkry nie sodat hy nie dit wat hy reeds ingevolge die kontrak gepresteer het, kan terugeis nie. Die hof het tereg bevind dat: "[t]here is a vast difference in precluding a minor from reclaiming that with which he parted in pursuance of his contract and in keeping him bound to the contract" (274). Soos wat hierbo aangedui is, beteken weerhouding van *restitutio in integrum* nie dat die minderjarige deur die kontrak gebind word nie. Die weiering om *restitutio in integrum* in

tractual liability argue that the fraudulent minor can be held contractually liable by application of the rules relating to estoppel. By means of estoppel the minor can be held to the impression he has created, that is the impression that he has the capacity to enter into the contract. He would therefore not be able to rely on his minority to escape contractual liability.

A number of authors correctly submit that a minor who has committed a fraudulent misrepresentation should not be held liable on the basis of the contract he had entered into as that would enable the minor to change his status through misrepresentation (Boberg 610; Barnard, Cronjé and Olivier 85; Hawthorne *Family Law Service* par E51). This point of view was also expressed in *Louw's* case where it was stated that: "if one were to consider his contract to be valid if induced by his fraud one places it in the power of the minor to bind himself effectively by his contract. To permit this will frustrate the motivation of the rule rendering a minor's contract invalid, and is in my view inconsistent with the rationale expounded in *Edelstein's* case" (273).

(ii) The minor could be held liable in delict. Boberg (600 fn 66 609); Barnard, Cronjé and Olivier (85) and Hawthorne *Family Law Service* (par E51) support such liability. Delictual liability was also accepted by the court in *Louw v MJ & H Trust* (see 273 of the case). Since delictual liability does not carry with it all the criticism that has been raised against contractual liability, it is suggested that a minor who misrepresents himself should be held liable only on the basis of his delict and should not incur contractual liability (Boberg 609; Barnard, Cronjé and Olivier 85).

The minor would be liable only if, firstly, he made a fraudulent misrepresentation regarding his "mondigheid" or his capacity to enter into the contract, secondly, if the other party to the contract was induced to contract by the misrepresentation and, thirdly, if the other contracting party suffered damage as a result of the misrepresentation (Boberg 610; Barnard, Cronjé and Olivier 86; Hawthorne

Louw se geval toe te staan, kan dus geregverdig word. Aangesien die minderjarige nie deur die kontrak gebonde was nie, moes hy egter wel toegelaat gewees het om sy geld met 'n *condictio* terug te eis. Daar kan nie bevind word dat die minderjarige nie aan die kontrak gebonde is nie en terselfdertyd gesê word dat hy nie dit wat hy reeds ingevolge die onafdwingbare kontrak gepresteer het, mag terugeis nie.

In die tweede plek steun die voorstanders van die opvatting dat die minderjarige wat 'n bedrieglike wanvoorstelling pleeg kontraktueel gebonde is op estoppel. Die minderjarige word gebonde gehou aan die skyn wat hy geskep het dat hy die bevoegdheid gehad het om die kontrak te sluit. Hy kan dus nie kontraktuele aanspreeklikheid vermy deur hom op sy minderjarigheid te beroep nie.

'n Aantal skrywers redeneer tereg dat 'n minderjarige wat 'n bedrieglike wanvoorstelling gepleeg het nie aanspreeklik gehou moet word op grond van die kontrak wat hy gesluit het nie, aangesien dit die minderjarige in staat sou stel om sy status te verander deur 'n wanvoorstelling te pleeg (Boberg 610; Barnard, Cronjé en Olivier 87; Hawthorne *Family Law Service* par E51). Hierdie mening is ook in die saak onder bespreking uitgespreek waar gesê is dat: "if one were to consider his contract to be valid if induced by his fraud one places it in the power of the minor to bind himself effectively by his contract. To permit this will frustrate the motivation of the rule rendering a minor's contract invalid, and is in my view inconsistent with the rationale expounded in *Edelstein's* case" (273).

(ii) Tweedens kan die minderjarige deliktueel aanspreeklik gehou word. Boberg (600 vn 66 609); Barnard, Cronjé en Olivier (88) en Hawthorne *Family Law Service* (par E51) is voorstanders van sodanige aanspreeklikheid. Deliktuele aanspreeklikheid is ook deur die hof in *Louw v MJ & H Trust* erken (sien 273 van die saak). Hierdie opvatting is nie aan soveel kritiek blootgestel nie en ons wil ook aan die hand doen dat 'n minderjarige wat 'n bedrieglike wanvoorstelling pleeg slegs op grond van delik aanspreeklik gehou be-

Family Law Service par E51). Although the other contracting party apparently is not obliged to investigate the averment made or the impression created by the minor that he has the capacity to enter into the contract (*Pleat v Van Staden* [29]; Boberg 610 fn 90; Barnard, Cronjé and Olivier 85–86; Christie 283), the other party will not be able to rely on the minor's misrepresentation if no reasonable person in his position would have believed that the minor had the necessary capacity (Christie 284; also see Boberg 611–612; Barnard, Cronjé and Olivier 86; Reinecke 1964 *THRHR* 133; Van der Walt 1984 *Obiter* 100).

It must be borne in mind that the father is no longer the only natural guardian of a legitimate child – see the note on *Calitz v Calitz* [19].

hoort te word en nie kontraktuele aanspreeklikheid behoort op te doen nie (Boberg 609; Barnard, Cronjé en Olivier 88).

Die minderjarige sal slegs aanspreeklik wees indien hy 'n bedrieglike wanvoorstelling oor sy mondigheid of bevoegdheid om te kontrakteer gepleeg het, indien die ander kontrakparty deur die wanvoorstelling oorreed is om die kontrak aan te gaan en indien die ander party skade gely het as gevolg van die wanvoorstelling (Boberg 610; Barnard, Cronjé en Olivier 88–89; Hawthorne *Family Law Service* par E51). Alhoewel daar skynbaar geen plig op die ander kontrakparty rus om ondersoek in te stel na die minderjarige se bewering of skyn wat hy skep dat hy bevoeg is om die kontrak te sluit nie (*Pleat v Van Staden* [29]; Boberg 610 vn 90; Barnard, Cronjé en Olivier 88; Christie 283), sal die ander kontrakparty nie op die minderjarige se wanvoorstelling kan steun nie indien geen redelike persoon in sy posisie sou geglo het dat die minderjarige wel die nodige bevoegdheid gehad het nie (Christie 284; sien ook Boberg 611–612; Barnard, Cronjé en Olivier 88; Reinecke 1964 *THRHR* 133; Van der Walt 1984 *Obiter* 100).

Dit moet in gedagte gehou word dat die vader nie meer die enigste natuurlike voog van 'n binne-egtelike kind is nie – sien die aantekening by *Calitz v Calitz* [19].

[32]   NEL V DIVINE, HALL & CO

(1890) 8 SC 16

"Benefit" theory

The defendant bought a number of goods from the plaintiff while still a minor. The defendant gave half the goods to her sister and used the other half herself. The plaintiff alleged that the defendant was liable for the purchase price of the goods as she benefited from the contract. The plaintiff's claim was disallowed in the magistrate's court. The

"Benefit"-teorie

Terwyl sy nog 'n minderjarige was, het die verweerderes 'n aantal artikels by die eiser gekoop. Die verweerderes het die helfte van die artikels aan haar suster gegee en die ander helfte self gebruik. Die eiser het beweer dat die verweerderes vir die koopprys van die artikels aanspreeklik was aangesien sy voordeel getrek het uit die kontrak. Die eiser se

plaintiff appealed against this decision. The appeal was allowed.

eis is in die landdroshof van die hand gewys. Die eiser het teen hierdie beslissing geappelleer. Die appèl is toegestaan.

DE VILLIERS CJ: [18] The simple question is whether to an action brought against a person of full age for goods purchased during his minority without his parents' or tutors' consent and without proof that it was for his benefit that the articles were bought, the plea of minority affords a valid defence. If the contention be correct that an unemancipated minor, having a parent or tutor alive, labours under an absolute incapacity to enter into any contract, without such parent's or tutor's consent, it is clear that even with proof that the contract was for the minor's benefit, it could not be enforced against him. That no such incapacity, however, exists, is evident when it is borne in mind that a person who contracts with a minor is bound to abide by his part of the contract if the minor insists upon it (*Voet* 26.8.3), and that the minor himself becomes bound if after attaining majority he ratifies the contract (*Voet* 26.8.4). The earliest authority that I am aware of for the proposition that the minor's benefit may afford a test as to the validity of his contracts is the Rescript of *Antoninus Pius*, as quoted in the *Code* [2.37.1]. There he says: "Since you yourself admit that the contract was entered into with Zenodora before she became of age and it could not be proved to the praetor that she had been enriched (*locupletiorem factam esse*) by means of that contract, you must understand that she has properly obtained a *restitutio in integrum*." I do not understand the phrase "that she has been enriched" to mean merely that she has had the best of the bargain, but that, considering the position in life and the other circumstances of the case, the contract was for her benefit. That *Voet* so understood the rescript appears from his references to it in his commentaries (4.4.13) and (26.8.2).

The burthen of proving that an obligation has been incurred by a minor for his benefit lies upon the person who seeks to enforce it. In the present case, as to one half of the articles purchased, the defendant's counsel admits that it was [19] for her benefit that the articles should have been purchased, but as to the other half, which were given by her to her sister, he contends that the purchase was wholly unnecessary and against her interest. Whatever may be said as to the morality of such a defence there is no doubt as to its being a good one in law. The appeal must be allowed . . .

SMITH and BUCHANAN JJ concurred.

Note

This decision has been critised by virtually all the authors who have commented on it (see for example Van der Vyver and Joubert 150; Barnard, Cronjé and Olivier 89; Coertze 1939 *THRHR* 280 *et seq*; Hamman 1949 *THRHR* 229-230; Van Reenen 1956 *THRHR* 158 *et seq*; Conradie 1964 *SALJ* 63 *et seq*). However, the "benefit" theory was applied in many cases (see for example *De Beer v Estate De Beer* 1916 CPD 125; *Du Toit v Lotriet* 1918 OPD 99; *Silberman v Hodkinson* 1927 TPD 562) before it was first rejected by the Transvaal Provincial Division in *Tanne v Foggitt* 1938 TPD 43. In 1952 the Appellate Division settled the issue in *Edelstein v Edelstein* [33] in which it re-

Aantekening

Hierdie uitspraak is gekritiseer deur feitlik al die skrywers wat daarop kommentaar gelewer het (sien byvoorbeeld Van der Vyver en Joubert 150; Barnard, Cronjé en Olivier 89; Coertze 1939 *THRHR* 280 ev; Hamman 1949 *THRHR* 229-230; Van Reenen 1956 *THRHR* 158 ev; Conradie 1964 *SALJ* 63 ev). Die "benefit"-teorie is egter in baie sake nagevolg (sien byvoorbeeld *De Beer v Estate De Beer* 1916 KPA 125; *Du Toit v Lotriet* 1918 OPA 99; *Silberman v Hodkinson* 1927 TPA 562) voordat dit vir die eerste keer deur die Transvaalse Provinsiale Afdeling in *Tanne v Foggitt* 1938 TPA 43 verwerp is. In 1952 het die Appèlhof die aangeleentheid finaal beslis toe dit in *Edelstein v*

jected the "benefit" theory completely. See the note on *Edelstein v Edelstein*.

Edelstein [33] die "benefit"-teorie heeltemal verwerp het. Sien die aantekening by *Edelstein v Edelstein*.

[33]   EDELSTEIN V EDELSTEIN

1952 3 SA 1 (A)

The antenuptial contract of a minor entered into without the necessary assistance

The appellant's parents were divorced when she was six years old and the custody of the minor children of the marriage was awarded to the mother. In 1918, at the age of nearly twenty, the appellant was married with the consent of both her parents. Before their marriage the parties entered into an antenuptial contract in which community of property, community of profit and loss and the marital power were excluded. Furthermore, the bridegroom promised certain gifts to the bride and some of these promises were fulfilled. The appellant was assisted in the execution of the contract by her mother but not by her father. All persons concerned were apparently under the impression that, since the custody of the minor children had been awarded to the mother, only her assistance was required to enable the appellant to enter into a valid antenuptial contract. The appellant's husband died in 1947. He left a will in which the appellant was one of the beneficiaries. The executors of his estate framed the liquidation and distribution account on the basis that the marriage had been out of community of property, and the appellant, in the *bona fide* belief that she had been so married, accepted the benefits under the will. Subsequently, on being advised that the antenuptial contract was invalid, she applied to the court for an order declaring that she had been married to her late husband in community of property, and directing the executors to amend the liquidation and

Die huweliksvoorwaardeskontrak van 'n minderjarige wat sonder die nodige bystand gesluit is

Die appellant se ouers is geskei toe sy ses jaar oud was en die bewaring van die minderjarige kinders uit die huwelik is aan die moeder toegestaan. In 1918, toe die appellant amper twintig jaar oud was, het sy met die toestemming van albei haar ouers in die huwelik getree. Voor die huwelik het die partye 'n huweliksvoorwaardeskontrak aangegaan waarin gemeenskap van goed, gemeenskap van wins en verlies en die maritale mag uitgesluit is. Verder het die bruidegom sekere geskenke aan die bruid beloof en sommige van die beloftes is ook inderdaad uitgevoer. Die appellant is by sluiting van die kontrak deur haar moeder bygestaan maar nie deur haar vader nie. Al die partye wat betrokke was, was skynbaar onder die indruk dat die moeder se bystand voldoende was om 'n geldige huweliksvoorwaardeskontrak daar te stel, aangesien die bewaring van die minderjarige kinders aan haar toevertrou is. Die appellant se man is in 1947 oorlede. Hy het 'n testament nagelaat waarin die appellant een van die bevoordeeldes was. Die eksekuteurs van sy boedel het aanvaar dat die huwelik buite gemeenskap van goed gesluit was en het die likwidasie- en distribusierekening dienooreenkomstig opgestel. Aangesien die appellant *bona fide* geglo het dat sy aldus getroud was, het sy die voordele ingevolge die testament aanvaar. Sy is later meegedeel dat die huweliksvoorwaardeskontrak ongeldig was en sy het toe by die hof aansoek gedoen om 'n bevel dat sy binne

distribution account by awarding her one half of the net value of the joint estate. The only opposing party was the Commissioner of Inland Revenue. His sole interest in the proceedings was the fact that the amount of death duties payable would have been less if the request was granted. The application failed in the court *a quo* but an appeal against this decision was successful.

gemeenskap van goed met haar man getroud was en dat die eksekuteurs die likwidasie- en distribusierekening moes wysig deur aan haar die helfte van die netto waarde van die gemeenskaplike boedel toe te ken. Die enigste opponerende party was die Kommissaris van Binnelandse Inkomste. Al belang wat hy in die verrigtinge gehad het, was die feit dat die boedelbelasting minder sou wees indien die aansoek toegestaan sou word. Die aansoek is in die hof *a quo* van die hand gewys maar 'n appèl teen hierdie beslissing het geslaag.

VAN DEN HEEVER JA: [9] It is difficult to gather the crisp *ratio decidendi* [that is of the judgment of the court *a quo*], but I think it may fairly be stated to have been the following: contracts entered into by minors without the assistance of their guardians are invalid except in so far as the minors have benefited thereby . . .

[10] It was assumed in the Court *a quo* and before us that where upon divorce the custody of a minor child is awarded to the mother, the father remains the child's natural guardian for the purpose of assisting it in the performance of juristic acts and that the mother alone is incapable of doing so. That assumption was, I think, correct. An order awarding the custody of a minor to the mother merely suspends in the interests of the minor certain of the incidents of parental authority . . . (*Landmann v Mienie*, 1944 OPD 59; D 43.30.3.5).

Respondent cannot rely upon the ante-nuptial contract itself to rebut the presumption that the marriage was in community since it is on the face of it invalid for lack of capacity of the contracting party against whom it is sought to be used. The only three Roman-Dutch authorities who to my knowledge deal directly with this subject are Lybrechts (*Redeneerend Vertoog*, 1.7.5), Arntzenius (*Instit Jur Belg*, 2.5.15 and 2.5.90(8)), and Van der Keessel (*Dictata ad Grot* 2.12.3). All three maintain that an ante-nuptial contract entered into by a minor without the assistance of his guardian is *ipso iure* void and a nullity.

Mr *Retief* [for the Commissioner] strenuously argued that the contract of an unassisted minor cannot be null and void since it is capable of ratification and since there are authorities, cited to us, to the effect that minors may obtain *restitutio in integrum*. As to the former, it is unsafe to classify transactions into those which are voidable and those which are void and then to draw conclusions from the classification. Such a proceeding begs the question . . .

Moreover our authorities speak of a contract being null and void in one direction of its operation and valid in another. *Voet* (27.6.1) observes:

[11] "From the principles of the law it is clear that a minor who contracts without the assistance of his guardian can render others under an obligation to himself, but does not himself become obliged to them . . . On the minor's side a contract entered into without the assistance of his guardian is *ipso iure* null and void."

The second argument advanced on this point can have no relevance to this enquiry. Restitution presupposes a binding contract; therefore one concluded by a minor with the assistance of his guardian. The question is whether an unassisted minor is bound by his contract.

Practically all our authorities – and Mr *Pollak* [for the appellant] has referred us to a number – state that, save for certain exceptions and then only to a certain extent, a contract entered into by a minor without the assistance of his guardian is not binding upon the minor. In his *Dictata ad Grot* (1.8.5 and 3.1.26) Van der Keessel mentions two exceptions: *Voet* 14.5.4 *in fine* and Groenewegen, *de Legib Abrogat ad C* 4.26.2 and 9. *Groenewegen* in the passages cited deals with the father's liability in respect of his son's acts as guardian of a third person, which is irrelevant to our inquiry. *Voet* deals with the *beneficium competentiae*. He undoubtedly has in mind contracts entered into by a minor with the assistance of his natural guardian, for he says the minor may be sued *in solidum* on his contract, even if he rejects his paternal inheritance, but may obtain *restitutio in integrum* if he has been prejudiced by the contract. However, even if we assume that *Voet* thought that a minor, who unassisted concluded a contract, could be relieved from the consequent obligations only by *restitutio in integrum*, it is clear that Van der Keessel (*ad Grot* 3.1.26) does not agree with him, but is in concord with the general opinion of Roman-Dutch authorities. He observes that *Voet's* proposition reflects Roman, not Roman-Dutch law. He points out that in Rome a minor who was *sui iuris* and had attained the age of puberty could at his option accept a tutor or not; if not, he was bound by all his contracts save money loans (*Senatusconsultum Macedonianum*). In Roman-Dutch law the judgment of a minor is considered immature throughout his minority and he is consequently not bound by his contracts.

It follows that in this case the ante-nuptial contract could not *per se* exclude community of property. Mr *Retief* contended, however, that the appellant was bound by the ante-nuptial contract because it was for her benefit. If the contention is sound, every ante-nuptial contract to which an unassisted minor is a party and in which a few shillings are settled upon the minor would be binding. It is unnecessary, however, to examine the alleged benefits, since the proposition is based upon a misunderstanding of the authorities.

In as far as his *dictum* is relevant Grotius (*Inleyd* 1.8.5) remarks:

> "Die minderjarige weezen ... mogen ook zichzelve niet verbinden ... maar zyn alle handelingen, by dezelve aangegaan ... buiten rechtsdwang, als verlaten van de Burgerlyke wet, uitgenomen dat zy iets mogen bedingen [12] t'hunnen voordeel en ook aangesproken mogen worden, voor zoo veel zy by de handelinge verrykt zouden mogen zyn."

In 3.1.26 of the same work he observes:

> "Doch de burgerlike wet houdt van onwaarde alle verbintenissen van onmondigen ... uitgezonderd voor zover zy zouden mogen zyn gebaat."

It will be observed that *Grotius* does not say that in the exceptional cases mentioned by him the contract of a minor is valid. He approaches the matter from the point of view of obligations. In general, he states, a minor cannot assume an obligation; if he purports to do so, the obligation is not enforceable. *Grotius* mentions two relevant exceptions: (1) a minor may validly stipulate for an advantage and (2) he is obliged in so far as he has been enriched. What is meant by the former is perfectly clear from our authorities: an unassisted minor cannot validly make a promise to perform; he may, however, stipulate for a performance by the other party to the transaction. The type of stipulation appears from Van der Keessel (*Dictata ad Grot* 1.8.5): an unassisted minor may validly accept a donation or stipulate that a valid claim against himself be not enforced. The other exception is that a minor is under an obligation to make restitution to the other party to the extent to which he has been enriched. His obligation does not arise *ex contractu* but *ex lege* and the other party's remedy is condiction. The minor is not even obliged to restore whatever he has received pursuant to the contract, but only so much as still remains in his possession at the time of the action or the surrogates of such residue (*in rem versa*, Grot 3.30.3). *Grotius* himself translated the phrase "voor zoo veel zy zyn gebaat" as *in quantum locupletiores facti sunt*, a phrase which has frequently been explained in the *Pandects* and in our institutional writers (*cf* D 5.3.25.11). It never meant that the minor was bound by the contract whenever in a vague and general way it could be said to have been to his benefit. (See *Tanne v Foggitt*, 1938 TPD 43, and the observation of TINDALL, JA, in *Dhanabakium v Subramanian and Another*, 1943 AD 160 at p 167). It means that the other party to such a contract may recover from the minor so much as at the time of action the minor's estate is enriched by the transaction.

In the earliest cases in the Cape and one decision in the Transvaal the undoubtedly correct rule of our law was applied, namely that the contract of a minor is invalid unless he is assisted by his guardian (*Gantz v Wagenaar*, 1 Menz 92; *Riggs v Calff*, 3 Menz 76; *Groenewald v Rex*, 1907 TS 47).

There is, however, a long line of decisions in our Courts based on a misunderstanding as to the meaning of the expression *quatenus locupletior factus est*. In *Nel v Divine Hall & Co*, 8 SC 16 [32], DE VILLIERS, CJ, considered C 2.37.1, and *Voet* 4.4.13 and 26.8.2 and came to the conclusion that *locupletior facta est* meant that "considering the position in life of the minor and the other circumstances of the case the contract was for her benefit," and held that if that be so, the minor is bound by her contract...

[VAN DEN HEEVER JA analysed C 2.37.1 and *Voet* 4.4.13 and 26.8.2. He concluded that the decision in *Nel v Divine Hall & Co* [32] rested on an incorrect interpretation of these texts. He proceeded:]

[14] The statement of the law by DE VILLIERS, CJ, has been accepted in a number of cases...

This Court is not bound by those decisions but the question arises, in how far have they modified our law in this regard? No principle capable of practical and logical application emerges from them. What standard of measurement is one to adopt in determining whether the contract was for the benefit of the minor?...

I have difficulty in applying the alleged rule to the ante-nuptial contract in this case. The normal matrimonial proprietary regime in this country is community of property. The basis of community is the Frankish notion of *conlaboratio*; in other words, whatever spouses acquire during the marriage they do by reason of their combined but specialised efforts. The deceased could not successfully have conducted his bag and bottle business if his wife had not cooked the dinner and minded the children. Most couples are relatively poor when they marry and amass some substance during the marriage. In consideration of promises to give her a few hundred pounds the bride agreed to become a housewife and to waive her rights to the yield of the joint efforts of both spouses for the whole of her married life. Promises cannot enrich; only [15] fulfilled promises can do so. But how is one to measure whether in these circumstances the contract was in some general and nebulous sense for the benefit of the minor?...

The alleged rule is incapable of practical application unless it means that Courts can review the contracts of unassisted minors and confirm or annul them at discretion. If *communis error facit ius* [common error makes law] it must at least give birth to some definable legal rule. That is not the case here and in my opinion the cases to which I have referred were either wrongly decided or decided correctly for the wrong reasons. The object of the law in regarding the contracts of minors as unenforceable is to protect them against their own immaturity of judgment. This object would be frustrated if a minor were bound by his contract whenever the other contracting party has been astute enough to promise or grant the minor some small immediate advantage...

Then Mr *Retief* contended that, when appellant attained her majority and retained the assets given her pursuant to the ante-nuptial contract, she ratified it. This is a startling proposition. Our law is clear: once a particular proprietary matrimonial regime is established at the marriage it may not ... be altered except by an order of court in certain circumstances ...

As was pointed out in *De Beer v Estate de Beer*, 1916 CPD 125 such a wife had no capacity to ratify, since at marriage she passed out of the guardianship of her father and entered into that of her husband. Mr *Retief* sought to surmount this difficulty by contending that she ratified with the assistance of her husband. The argument is untenable: first, the husband would have contracted with himself; [16] secondly, it is clear that until his death the husband thought that the ante-nuptial contract was valid and could not have considered assisting his wife in its ratification; thirdly, it would have amounted to an unlawful alteration of the proprietary regime.

Finally Mr *Retief* contended that, since the will of appellant's late husband was drafted on the understanding that the ante-nuptial contract was valid and since she took benefits under the will, she has thereby ratified the ante-nuptial contract. The suggestion is remarkable. It amounts to this that if a *falsa causa* induced a testator to make a testamentary disposition, the *falsa causa* being the erroneous belief that the beneficiary had concluded a certain contract with the testator, the beneficiary by accepting a bequest under the will becomes bound by an imaginary contract. It seems to me that this argument is manifestly unsound. If by "adiating" under the will appellant is precluded from maintaining that the joint estate should devolve in a manner different from that provided in the will, her act will have economic consequences but cannot alter the fact that during the subsistence of the marriage the appellant had the status and expectations of a wife married in community of property. We are not concerned with the devolution of the property but with the question what was the matrimonial proprietary regime, which cannot retrospectively have been altered merely because appellant by a new dispositive act has renounced her rights ...

In my judgment, therefore, the appeal is allowed ...

CENTLIVRES CJ and HOEXTER JA concurred.

Note

In this case the "benefit" theory was rejected completely. The "benefit" theory, as expounded in *Nel v Divine Hall & Co* [32] and followed in a number of cases, held that a minor who entered into a contract without the necessary assistance would be bound by that contract if it was beneficial to him. The mere fact that the unassisted minor could obtain some benefit from the contract would, according to the "benefit" theory, make it enforceable against him. *Edelstein's* case authoritatively laid down that an unassisted minor cannot incur contractual liability in terms of a contract which encumbers him, but that he can be held liable on the basis of undue enrichment.

With regard to the statement by VAN DEN HEEVER JA (15) that the spouses' matrimonial property regime may not be altered, it should be noted that section 21(1) of the Matrimonial Property Act 88 of 1984 has changed the common law position.

Aantekening

In hierdie saak is die "benefit"-teorie heeltemal verwerp. Die "benefit"-teorie, soos uiteengesit in *Nel v Divine Hall & Co* [32] en gevolg in 'n hele aantal sake, het bepaal dat 'n minderjarige wat sonder die nodige bystand 'n kontrak gesluit het, wel aan die kontrak gebonde was indien die kontrak vir hom voordelig was. Die blote feit dat hy 'n voordeel uit die kontrak verkry het, het volgens die "benefit"-teorie veroorsaak dat die kontrak teenoor die minderjarige afdwingbaar was. In *Edelstein* se saak is gesaghebbend beslis dat 'n minderjarige wat nie die nodige toestemming tot kontraksluiting gehad het nie, geen kontraktuele aanspreeklikheid kan opdoen ingevolge 'n kontrak wat enige verpligting op hom lê nie, maar dat hy wel op grond van ongeregverdigde verryking aanspreeklik gehou kan word.

Met betrekking tot VAN DEN HEEVER AR se stelling (15) dat die gades se huweliksgoederebedeling nie verander kan word nie, moet daarop

Another very important point which was decided in *Edelstein's* case is that the antenuptial contract of an unassisted minor cannot be ratified after the marriage has been entered into. It is the one exception to the rule that the minor, upon becoming a major (or within a reasonable period thereafter), or his guardian, can ratify a contract which the minor had entered into without the necessary assistance, with the result that the contract then becomes fully enforceable. Also see Spiro 1952 *SALJ* 430; Hahlo 1952 *SALJ* 251.

It must be borne in mind that the father is no longer the only natural guardian of a legitimate child – see the note on *Calitz v Calitz* [19].

gelet word dat artikel 21(1) van die Wet op Huweliksgoedere 88 van 1984 die gemeenregtelike posisie gewysig het.

'n Ander baie belangrike aangeleentheid wat in *Edelstein* se saak beslis is, is dat die huweliksvoorwaardeskontrak wat 'n minderjarige sonder die nodige bystand gesluit het nie na huweliksluiting geratifiseer kan word nie. Dit is die een uitsondering op die reël dat 'n minderjarige, wanneer hy mondigheid bereik (of binne 'n redelike tyd daarna), of sy voog, 'n kontrak wat die minderjarige sonder die nodige bystand aangegaan het, kan ratifiseer met die gevolg dat dit dan ten volle afdwingbaar word. Sien ook Spiro 1952 *SALJ* 430; Hahlo 1952 *SALJ* 251.

Dit moet in gedagte gehou word dat die vader nie meer die enigste natuurlike voog van 'n binne-egtelike kind is nie – sien die aantekening by *Calitz v Calitz* [19].

[34]   VAN DYK V SAR & H

1956 4 SA 410 (W)

A guardian's assistance to a minor who enters into a contract

The applicant attained majority on 6 May 1955. Before he reached the age of twenty-one he entered into a contract of employment as a railway policeman with the South African Railways and Harbours. The applicant's father gave his unconditional written consent to his son's joining the Railway Police. However, the applicant and his father were both unaware of any particular terms of the contract of employment and accepted that the employment would be subject to the usual terms and conditions of service. It later appeared that the contract included a term which prohibited the applicant from terminating his service with the Railway Police for a period of three years from the date he joined. When the applicant became aware of this term he applied to court *inter alia* for

'n Voog se bystand aan 'n minderjarige wat 'n kontrak sluit

Die applikant het op 6 Mei 1955 meerderjarig geword. Voor hierdie datum het hy 'n dienskontrak met die Suid-Afrikaanse Spoorweë en Hawens gesluit ingevolge waarvan hy as spoorwegpolisieman in diens geneem is. Die applikant se vader het onvoorwaardelik skriftelik toegestem dat sy seun by die spoorwegpolisie kon aansluit. Die applikant en sy vader was onbewus van enige spesifieke bepalings van die dienskontrak en hulle het aanvaar dat die kontrak aan die gewone diensvoorwaardes onderworpe was. Dit het later geblyk dat die kontrak 'n bepaling bevat het wat die applikant verbied het om die spoorwegpolisie se diens binne drie jaar vanaf sy datum van aansluiting te verlaat. Toe die applikant van hierdie bepaling bewus word, het hy onder andere by die hof aansoek gedoen dat die dienskontrak tersyde gestel word.

an order setting aside the contract of employment. The applicant argued that the contract was not binding upon him as he did not have the necessary assistance to enter into the contract since his father was not present at the time when the contract was signed. Furthermore, he maintained that his father did not approve of all the terms of the contract as he was unaware of the specific terms it contained. The application was dismissed.

Die applikant het beweer dat die kontrak hom nie gebind het nie aangesien hy nie die nodige toestemming tot kontraksluiting gehad het nie omdat sy vader nie teenwoordig was toe die kontrak aangegaan is nie. Hy het verder aangevoer dat sy vader ook nie toegestem het tot al die bepalings van die kontrak nie aangesien hy nie van al die spesifieke bepalings bewus was nie. Die aansoek is van die hand gewys.

WILLIAMSON J: [412] There is a strange lack of authority in our law as to what exactly constitutes "assistance" of a minor in entering into a contract. It has been suggested in some authorities that, for instance, the parent or guardian should be present. In fact, *Voet* says so but quite obviously that is not a modern day approach to it and never has been the approach of our Courts.

In the case of *De Deer v Estate De Beer*, 1916 CPD 125, it was held that an ante-nuptial contract that had been entered into by a minor was of no force and effect because the parent had not consented to the ante-nuptial contract although the parent had specifically consented to the marriage. But in that case KOTZE, J, who presided, held that there was no assistance for the simple reason that in fact there was no evidence that the father had ever consented. He mentioned that the father, of course, had not been present when the contract was executed and that the father had not brought his mind to bear on it at all but quite obviously, he did contemplate the position that the father or guardian might give consent without being present if that consent was clearly proved.

Now, in my view, on these papers presently before me, the father gave consent in unequivocal terms to his son joining the Police Force and that written consent, proved as it is in the case, would be, in my opinion, ordinarily, good assistance, sufficient to make the contract a binding contract.

It could, of course, be shown that the father did not actually consent to a specific contract because of his attention not being drawn to certain terms. I do not think that for a father to give his assistance, it is necessary for him to know specifically all the terms or that his attention should be drawn to all the terms. It is sufficient if he gives his mind specifically enough to the contract, to know the type of contract which his ward is proposing to enter into and the type of contract in respect of which he is giving his assent. In this case, he gave his consent to the son joining the Police Force. He says that he meant him to join subject to the ordinary service conditions.

Now, whether as a fact the father knew of this one condition that service must last for three years or not, to me is immaterial. It was not an extraordinary term; it was quite a normal sort of term in a contract whereby a person is taken into service and trained for a particular occupation. In my view, a guardian must be taken to know and would ordinarily, of course, know that a person being taken into a trade or an occupation requiring special training, would be required to continue in service for some specific period. Obviously, he would not be allowed to enter into a contract to learn or to be trained with the right to terminate immediately after he has got such training, and I cannot see anything abnormal or extraordinary in the provision which is now [413] being put into these contracts as a result of Parliament's provision in the Railways and Harbours Service Act for a minimum period of three years' service.

The contract of a minor in these cases, of course, is subject to the ordinary rules of capacity; he must be assisted; he could set aside the contract on any basis on which the

contract could be set aside ordinarily; the form of contract is immaterial; the attestation in itself would be, in my view, a contract of service and this appears from the case of *Broodryk v Smuts, NO,* 1942 TPD 47. In this present case it was an ordinary contract of service with no conditions other than reasonable conditions for the type of service. The father did not choose to examine all the conditions, but he did consent to his son joining, as he says, under the usual conditions and in my view, nothing but usual conditions are incorporated. In the circumstances, the father has sufficiently assisted the son so as to make the contract binding upon the applicant . . .

In my view, the petition as it appears before me, showing no ground for relief on the basis sought, must be dismissed . . .

Note

A minor's contract is valid and enforceable against him if he obtained his guardian's assistance to the contract (see for example *Skead v Colonial Banking & Trust Co Ltd* 1924 TPD 497; *Marshall v National Wool Industries Ltd* [36]; *Wood v Davies* [37]. The guardian's assistance may be in the form of being present at the execution of the contract and consenting thereto; or of giving his consent prior to the minor entering into the contract; or of ratifying the contract after the minor has concluded it (see for example *Skead v Colonial Banking & Trust Co Ltd; Marshall v National Wool Industries Ltd; Wood v Davies; Baddeley v Clarke* 1923 NPD 306; *Fouché v Battenhausen & Co* [30]).

How much knowledge of the terms of the contract a guardian is supposed to have before he can be said to have assisted the minor is not quite clear. It is established beyond doubt that the guardian need not be familiar with all the terms of the contract and that his knowledge of the broad terms of the contract and his failure to object to the contract is sufficient (see for example *Fouché v Battenhausen* [30]). In *Baddeley v Clarke* it was held that the guardian must have at least some idea of the transaction the minor has entered into before he can be said to have ratified the contract. In the latter case the minor bought a motorcycle on hire purchase. The minor's father (the plaintiff) knew that his son had the motorcycle but was unaware of the fact that the minor had entered into a hire purchase agreement. When the minor failed to pay an instalment on the motorcycle the defendant repossessed it and refused to pay back the money the minor had already paid in terms of the hire purchase agreement. The plaintiff sued the defendant for repayment of the money paid by the minor. The defendant averred that the plaintiff had ratified the contract but the court found no such

Aantekening

'n Minderjarige se kontrak is geldig en afdwingbaar teenoor hom indien hy sy voog se bystand tot kontraksluiting gehad het (sien byvoorbeeld *Skead v Colonial Banking & Trust Co Ltd* 1924 TPA 497; *Marshall v National Wool Industries Ltd* [36]; *Wood v Davies* [37]). Die voog se bystand kan op verskillende wyses gegee word: hy kan teenwoordig wees ten tyde van die kontraksluiting en sy toestemming daartoe verleen; of hy kan voor die kontrak gesluit word sy toestemming verleen; of hy kan die kontrak ratifiseer nadat die minderjarige dit reeds gesluit het (sien *Skead v Colonial Banking & Trust Co Ltd; Marshall v National Wool Industries Ltd; Wood v Davies; Baddeley v Clarke* 1923 NPA 306; *Fouché v Battenhausen & Co* [30]).

Die presiese omvang van die kennis wat die voog van die bepalings van die kontrak moet hê voordat daar gesê kan word dat hy die minderjarige bygestaan het, is nie heeltemal duidelik nie. Dit staan vas dat die voog nie van al die bepalings van die kontrak bewus hoef te wees nie en dat kennis van die breë bepalings van die kontrak en 'n versuim om beswaar teen die kontrak aan te teken, voldoende is – sien byvoorbeeld *Fouché v Battenhausen* [30]. In *Baddeley v Clarke* is beslis dat die voog ten minste 'n begrip moet hê van die transaksie wat die minderjarige aangegaan het voordat daar gesê kan word dat hy die kontrak geratifiseer het. In laasgenoemde saak het die minderjarige 'n motorfiets op huurkoop gekoop. Die minderjarige se vader (die eiser) was bewus daarvan dat sy seun die motorfiets in sy besit gehad het maar hy was onbewus daarvan dat sy seun 'n huurkoopooreenkoms aangegaan het. Toe die minderjarige versuim om een paaiement te betaal, het die verweerder die motorfiets teruggeneem en geweier om die bedrae wat die minderjarige reeds ingevolge die kontrak betaal het

ratification and issued judgment for the plaintiff. The court per TATHAM J explained the position regarding the knowledge required for ratification as follows:

"The most that can be said to have been proved against the plaintiff is that he knew that the motor bicycle was in the possession of his son. But there is nothing in the evidence from which we are entitled to infer that he had any knowledge whatever of the terms upon which it had been acquired; or even that the son had acquired it by purchase. That being so, there cannot be said to have been any ratification by the plaintiff of the contract, or such knowledge in him and such conduct with knowledge, as would amount to consent . . ." (309).

DOVE-WILSON JP added:

"Before it can be established that he consented to the contract there must be clear and satisfactory proof that he was aware of its conditions, and there is none. It cannot therefore be held that he consented . . ." (310).

From *Van Dyk's* case it seems that the guardian need not know of the terms of the contract, but merely what type of contract the minor has entered into.

Boberg (578) submits that the question whether the guardian assisted the minor should be answered with reference "not [to] whether the terms of a contract were the usual ones but whether the guardian consented to them. This he could not have done unless he knew of them . . . [I]t is not necessary that the guardian's attention be drawn to every aspect of a transaction before he can consent to it, but he should, at least, be acquainted with every term that is material in the sense that it imposes obligations upon the minor or is otherwise onerous to him." This is the correct approach; the standard laid down in *Van Dyk's* case is too lenient.

It must be borne in mind that the father is no longer the only natural guardian of a legitimate child – see the note on *Calitz v Calitz* [19].

aan hom terug te betaal. Die eiser het die verweerder gedagvaar vir terugbetaling van die bedrae wat die minderjarige reeds betaal het. Die verweerder het beweer dat die eiser die kontrak geratifiseer het maar die hof het bevind dat daar geen sodanige ratifikasie was nie en het ten gunste van die eiser beslis. Die hof het per monde van TATHAM R die posisie rakende die mate van kennis wat vir ratifikasie vereis word soos volg verduidelik:

"The most that can be said to have been proved against the plaintiff is that he knew that the motor bicycle was in the possession of his son. But there is nothing in the evidence from which we are entitled to infer that he had any knowledge whatever of the terms upon which it had been acquired; or even that the son had acquired it by purchase. That being so, there cannot be said to have been any ratification by the plaintiff of the contract, or such knowledge in him and such conduct with knowledge, as would amount to consent . . ." (309).

DOVE-WILSON RP het bygevoeg:

"Before it can be established that he consented to the contract there must be clear and satisfactory proof that he was aware of its conditions, and there is none. It cannot therefore be held that he consented . . ." (310).

Uit *Van Dyk* se saak lyk dit asof die voog glad nie eers hoef te weet wat die bepalings van die kontrak is nie maar slegs hoef te weet watter soort kontrak die minderjarige aangegaan het.

Boberg (578) redeneer dat die vraag of die voog die minderjarige bygestaan het, nie beantwoord moet word met verwysing na "whether the terms of a contract were the usual ones but whether the guardian consented to them. This he could not have done unless he knew of them . . . [I]t is not necessary that the guardian's attention be drawn to every aspect of the transaction before he can consent to it, but he should, at least, be acquainted with every term that is material in the sense that it imposes obligations upon the minor or is otherwise onerous to him." Hierdie benadering is korrek; die standaard wat in *Van Dyk* se saak neergelê is, is nie streng genoeg nie.

Dit moet in gedagte gehou word dat die vader nie meer die enigste natuurlike voog van 'n binne-egtelike kind is nie – sien die aantekening by *Calitz v Calitz* [19].

[35] STUTTAFORD & CO V OBERHOLZER

1921 CPD 855

Ratification by a minor upon reaching majority

Shortly before he reached majority, the defendant, without his guardian's assistance, bought a motorcycle in terms of a hire purchase agreement. The defendant reached the age of twenty-one on 26 March 1921. After this date the defendant continued to use the motorcycle as if it was his own property. On 27 May 1921 the plaintiff sued the defendant for payment of arrear instalments on the motorcycle. On 10 June 1921 the defendant filed a plea in which he set up his minority at the time of entering into the contract as a defence to the plaintiff's claim. In reconvention the defendant claimed, *inter alia,* repayment of the amounts he had already paid in terms of the hire purchase agreement. In the meantime he still continued to use the motorcycle. In the court *a quo* the defendant's plea of minority was upheld. The plaintiff appealed against this decision and his appeal was upheld.

Ratifikasie deur 'n minderjarige by die bereiking van meerderjarigheid

Kort voordat hy meerderjarig geword het, het die verweerder, sonder die bystand van sy voog, 'n motorfiets op huurkoop gekoop. Die verweerder het op 26 Maart 1921 meerderjarigheid bereik. Na hierdie datum het die verweerder aangehou om die motorfiets te gebruik asof dit sy eiendom was. Op 27 Mei 1921 het die eiser die verweerder gedagvaar vir betaling van agterstallige paaiemente op die motorfiets. Op 10 Junie 1921 het die verweerder 'n verweerskrif teen die eiser se eis ingedien waarin hy hom op sy minderjarigheid ten tyde van die kontraksluiting beroep het. Die verweerder het in rekonvensie onder andere terugbetaling geëis van die bedrae wat hy reeds ingevolge die huurkoopooreenkoms betaal het. Die verweerder het steeds voortgegaan om die motorfiets te gebruik. In die hof *a quo* was die verweerder se beroep op sy minderjarigheid suksesvol. Die eiser het teen hierdie beslissing geappelleer en sy appèl is gehandhaaf.

GARDINER J: [857] As I say he [the defendant] attained his majority on the 26th March and if he wished to set up the fact that he entered into the contract during minority as a defence to any action which might be brought, one would have expected him to have put it forward at once, but he continued to use the cycle *and even after the 10th June he went about on it and continued to use it as his own* [our emphasis]. Whatever may be said as to the conduct of the defendant between the 26th March and the 10th June when he filed his plea, on the latter date he knew his legal position, and he knew that minority was a defence to the contract . . . He was, therefore, perfectly well aware of his legal position on the 10th June . . .

Now it seems to me that this is pre-eminently a case in which the maxim: "A man cannot both approbate and reprobate," can be applied. It is not open to him to repudiate a contract and then immediately afterwards to continue as if he adopted it. The magistrate has held in effect that there must be an express agreement made after [858] majority in order to effect an obligation, and he relies for this view on the case of *Van der Byl & Co v Solomon* (1877, Buch 25). In that case the late CHIEF JUSTICE quoted from Story on *Contracts* where indeed it is said that there must be an express promise, voluntarily and deliberately made by the infant upon arriving at the age of majority. But then *Story* goes on to say: "No act or word which does not unequivocally imply a new and primary promise by the infant himself will be sufficient to create a liability on his executory contract." Therefore, he contemplates that there may be ratification by something else than an express promise, namely, by acts. Now it was not necessary for the purposes of that case for the Court to concur entirely with every word that *Story* said, and although the CHIEF JUSTICE said: "*Story's* views appear to me to be quite consistent with our law," I do not think that I am bound by every word *Story* has said in the passage cited. It seems to me that there may be ratification by deed just as well as by word, and it also seems to me that when a person, after attaining his majority, continues to use an article, the subject of the contract, as his own with full knowledge of his legal position, he must be taken to ratify the contract entered into during minority in respect of such article, even if he does not do so in express language. He cannot approbate and reprobate, and acts and not words must be taken to govern the case. If this were held not to be ratification I can very well conceive that a person might go on, after reaching his majority, using the subject matter of the contract until that subject matter became useless, and the plaintiff would have no redress. It seems to me that that would be a most inequitable view to arrive at, and one which we could not uphold. The appeal must be allowed . . .

VAN ZYL J concurred.

Note

When a minor, after reaching majority, ratifies a contract which he entered into without the necessary assistance while still a minor, it becomes completely valid and enforceable with retrospective effect (see also *De Canha v Mitha* 1960 1 SA 486 (T)). After ratification the position is as if the minor had the necessary assistance when he initially entered into the contract.

As is evident from the case under discussion, ratification can be express or implied and can take place "by deed just as well as by word" (858).

The extent of knowledge of his rights which is required of the erstwhile minor before he can be said to have ratified the contract, is not clear. (See Boberg 590; Barnard, Cronjé and Olivier 89; Christie 289.) There is authority for the view that "[t]here can be no ratification where there is not a full knowledge of the *exact state* of things" (*De Beer v Estate De Beer* 1916 CPD 125 128; our emphasis). On the other hand it has been suggested that knowledge of the legal position and his right to repudiate the contract, can be imputed to the person when he reaches majority (see Boberg 590 fn 34; Barnard, Cronjé and Olivier 89; Christie 289). From the *Stuttaford* case it appears as if there must be at least some knowledge of the legal position before the erstwhile minor can be said to have ratified the contract.

Aantekening

Indien 'n minderjarige na sy meerderjarigwording 'n kontrak ratifiseer wat hy as minderjarige sonder die nodige bystand aangegaan het, word daardie kontrak terugwerkend heeltemal geldig en afdwingbaar (sien ook *De Canha v Mitha* 1960 1 SA 486 (T)). Na ratifikasie is die posisie dieselfde asof die minderjarige die nodige bystand gehad het toe hy oorspronklik die kontrak gesluit het.

Soos uit die onderhawige saak blyk, kan ratifikasie uitdruklik of stilswyend plaasvind "by deed just as well as by word" (858).

Dit is onseker hoeveel kennis die voormalige minderjarige van sy regte moet hê voordat daar gesê kan word dat hy die kontrak geratifiseer het. (Sien Boberg 590; Barnard, Cronjé en Olivier 92; Christie 289.) Daar is gesag vir die standpunt dat "[t]here can be no ratification where there is not a full knowledge of the *exact state* of things" (*De Beer v Estate De Beer* 1916 KPA 125 128; ons kursivering). Aan die ander kant is daar al aan die hand gedoen dat kennis van die regsposisie en van sy reg om die kontrak te repudieer aan die persoon toegedig kan word wanneer hy meerderjarigheid bereik (sien Boberg 590 vn 34; Barnard, Cronjé en Olivier 92; Christie 289). Uit die *Stuttaford*-saak wil dit voorkom asof die voormalige minderjarige ten minste 'n mate van kennis van die regsposisie moet hê voordat daar gesê kan word dat hy die kontrak geratifiseer het.

[36] MARSHALL V NATIONAL WOOL INDUSTRIES LTD

1924 OPD 238

Personal liability of a guardian who assists a minor who enters into a contract

An agent of the respondent company sold 250 shares in the company to the appellant and 250 shares to his son. The appellant's son was a minor at the time of the sale but the appellant was present when the contract was entered into and he knew that his son was buying shares in the company. The appellant's son experienced financial difficulties and could not pay the full purchase price of the shares. About two years after the execution of the contract the respondent issued summons for the unpaid amount against the appellant's son. By this time the appellant's son had reached majority. He defended the action and relied on his minority at the time of entering into the contract. The respondent then obtained leave to join the appellant as a co-defendant with his son. The action against the appellant's son was subsequently withdrawn and the appellant was left as the only defendant in the matter. In the court *a quo* the magistrate ordered the father to pay the unpaid amount of the purchase price of the shares which his son had bought. He appealed against this decision. The appeal was upheld.

Persoonlike aanspreeklikheid van 'n voog wat 'n minderjarige by kontraksluiting bystaan

'n Verteenwoordiger van die respondent-maatskappy het 250 aandele in die maatskappy aan die appellant en 250 aandele aan sy seun verkoop. Ten tyde van die aankoop was die appellant se seun minderjarig maar die appellant was teenwoordig toe die kontrak gesluit is en hy was bewus daarvan dat sy seun aandele in die maatskappy gekoop het. Die appellant se seun het finansiële probleme ondervind en kon nie die volle koopprys van die aandele betaal nie. Omtrent twee jaar na die sluiting van die kontrak het die respondent die appellant se seun gedagvaar vir die uitstaande bedrag. Teen hierdie tyd het die appellant se seun reeds meerderjarigheid bereik. Hy het die aksie verdedig en het op sy minderjarigheid ten tyde van kontraksluiting gesteun. Die respondent het toestemming verkry om die appellant as medeverweerder by sy seun te voeg. Die aksie teen die appellant se seun is later teruggetrek en die appellant het as enigste verweerder in die geding oorgebly. In die hof *a quo* het die landdros die vader beveel om die uitstaande koopprys van die aandele wat sy seun gekoop het, te betaal. Hy het teen hierdie uitspraak geappelleer. Die appèl was suksesvol.

DE VILLIERS JP: [239] The magistrate bases his judgment on the ground that, though the son signed the application form for the 250 shares, in respect of which the action was brought, "the whole contract was made with the father, and that the transaction so far as the son was concerned was purely nominal and was never seriously regarded by the father." Now it seems to me impossible to support the judgment on this ground. If it had been proved that the company and the father while mutually intending to make a contract as between themselves, had disguised their intention by feigning to make a contract between the company and the son, the court might possibly have gone behind the form and have given effect to the real intention of the parties. But there is not even a suggestion that the parties disguised their real intentions, nor is there a suggestion of any reason or motive why the parties or either of them should wish to disguise their intentions or should wish to conclude a contract between the father and the company under the guise of a contract between the son and the company. Quite on the contrary, as the father was willing to take shares, he must have thought that it was desirable to own shares, and there would be no reason why he should wish to disguise his own shareholding behind his son's name . . .

[240] [T]he contract was entered into solely between the company and the son . . .

[242] It seems to me therefore that the magistrate's finding is not supported by the evidence when he says that "the transaction so far as the son was concerned was purely nominal and was never seriously regarded by the father." Even if we were to suppose what was not the case, viz, that the father had not seriously regarded the contract in his son's name, or had thought himself morally or even legally responsible to pay the instalments on his son's shares, that would not have made him liable, for the company chose to contract with the son and to hold the son liable as the sole contracting party; in those circumstances the father could only become liable by contracting or undertaking to become liable in lieu of or in addition to the son. But there is no evidence to show that the father ever made such a contract with or gave such an undertaking to the company . . .

It seems to me, therefore, that the magistrate's judgment cannot be supported on the grounds set forth in his reasons for judgment.

[243] It is, however, sought to support the magistrate's judgment on an alternative ground. It is said to be a proposition of Roman-Dutch Law that a father, who authorises his minor son to contract, becomes liable himself on the contract . . .

Now it is obvious that, if a father authorises his minor son to contract on his (the father's) behalf, the father will be liable on the contract as any principal is liable on his agent's contract. But will the father be liable on his son's contract if he has merely interposed his consent as father and natural guardian to a contract which the son makes for his own benefit and on his own behalf? On general principles one would say that the father would not be liable, no more than an ordinary guardian would be. It seems therefore that the subject for enquiry is what is the nature of the authority (*jussus*) which will in law make the father liable; is it an authority to the son to contract on the father's behalf, or is the father also liable if he merely authorises the son to contract on his (the son's) own behalf? . . .

[DE VILLIERS JP analysed a number of texts on Roman law and proceeded:]

[244] There is therefore reason to think that the *jussus* was not a mere assistance to the son to bind himself, but an authority or *mandatum* to him to bind the father . . .

[DE VILLIERS JP analysed other authorities and proceeded:]

[245] It thus appears that, whatever form the *jussus* took in the Roman Law . . . its essence was that the father signified his consent to be bound by the son's contract. The son in effect became the father's agent and could thus bind the father as well as himself by the contract. No doubt the agency was not a true agency in its simplest modern form, for, if it were, the son would not be liable at all on the contract; but it was a common feature also in other forms of agency in the Roman Law that the agent was bound as well as the principal . . .

[I]t seems clear enough that in the Roman Law the *jussus* on which the father became liable was a mandate authorizing the son to bind the father by the contract, even though the contract might be made in the son's name.

Coming now to the Roman-Dutch Law, we find several authorities laying down that the father is liable upon his minor son's contract if entered into by the father's *jussus*, but it is here even clearer that the father's liability, when it exists, is simply that of a principal for an agent. It must be borne in mind that now the son is no longer as a rule liable (as he was in the Roman Law) upon contracts entered into by him without his father's consent. (*Van der Linden*, 1.4.1). Two cases can thus arise under Roman-Dutch Law: (1) the father may merely interpose his consent or [246] assistance to a contract entered into by the son on his own behalf, in which case one would expect that the son alone would be bound; and (2) the father may give authority (*jussus*) to the son to contract on behalf of the father, in which case one would expect that the father alone would be bound. This appears to be the sense in which the Roman-Dutch Law is understood by the authorities . . .

[DE VILLIERS JP then analysed some Roman-Dutch authorities and concluded:]

[248] [T]he bulk of authority supports the view that the father is liable on his minor son's contract if he has authorised the son to contract on his behalf, not if he has merely interposed his consent and assistance as natural guardian to a contract entered into by the son on his own behalf. That view is also supported by principle and by equity, and by the analogy of the case of a guardian and his ward. If the father were liable on the obligations arising under such a contract of his son, to which he has merely interposed his consent as natural guardian, he would be entitled also to the rights and *lucrum* [benefits] accruing under such a contract; which he clearly is not, for the profits under such a contract belong to the son by modern Roman-Dutch Law. The same view is also supported by the fact that no case has yet arisen in South Africa in which it has been sought to hold the father liable by reason of his having merely interposed his consent to a contract entered into by the son on the son's own behalf. It is admitted that in all such cases the action has been brought by or against the son, or by or against the father, in his capacity as natural guardian, never by or against the father in his individual capacity.

In the present case the furthest that the evidence goes is that the father consented to the son entering into the contract on the son's own behalf; there is no evidence to show, nor is it suggested, that the father authorised the son to contract on behalf of and as the agent of the father, nor is the action founded on agency, and in dealing with the first part of the case I have attempted to show why I think that the true intention of the company and the father and the son was that a contract should be concluded between the company and the son as an individual, not as agent for his father. The father cannot therefore be held liable.

The appeal must be allowed . . .

BLAINE J: [249] Certainly a son could be rightly said to have his father's authority to conclude a contract, although he merely had the latter's consent to do so; but on principle this authority should be limited to the purpose for which it is given, namely to furnish the minor, under direction of the law, with what is lacking in his capacity to enter into a valid contract on his own behalf.

[250] It seems clear, therefore, that the consent referred to is simply required for the formation of the contract by the son and cannot be legitimately extended so as to make the father personally liable thereon.

If authority and consent in this connection are to be treated as interchangeable terms having one and the same meaning, then a father could never give the necessary assistance to his minor son to contract – even in cases where the minor's interests clearly demanded this – without thereby making himself personally liable *in solidum*. This certainly is a startling proposition, which does not commend itself as being fair and equitable, so that it is not surprising that it has apparently never previously required investigation in South African courts. But now that the question has been fully gone into, I am satisfied that both on principle and authority no personal liability attaches to a father in respect of a contract made by his minor son, merely on the ground that it has been entered into with his knowledge and consent, and this is all that is established against the father by the evidence in this case . . .

Note

In assisting the minor the guardian supplements the minor's limited capacity to act so that the minor's contract becomes completely valid and enforceable. Consequently the guardian should not incur any liability under the contract the minor enters into (Boberg 580–581). The minor is the party to the contract and he incurs contractual liability – not his guardian. (See also *Dreyer v Sonop Bpk* 1951 2 SA 390 (O)).

It must be borne in mind that the father is no longer the only natural guardian of a legitimate child – see the note on *Calitz v Calitz* [19].

Aantekening

Wanneer die voog sy bystand aan die minderjarige verleen, vul hy die minderjarige se beperkte handelingsbevoegdheid aan sodat die minderjarige se kontrak heeltemal geldig en afdwingbaar kan wees. Die voog behoort gevolglik geen aanspreeklikheid op te doen ingevolge die kontrak wat deur die minderjarige aangegaan word nie (Boberg 580–581). Die minderjarige is die kontrakparty en hý doen kontraktuele aanspreeklikheid op – nie sy voog nie. (Sien ook *Dreyer v Sonop Bpk* 1951 2 SA 390 (O)).

Dit moet in gedagte gehou word dat die vader nie meer die enigste natuurlike voog van 'n binne-egtelike kind is nie – sien die aantekening by *Calitz v Calitz* [19].

[37]   WOOD V DAVIES

1934 CPD 250

Restitutio in integrum

While the plaintiff was still a minor he inherited a sum of £10 000. The will in terms of which he inherited the money provided that the money would remain in trust and that the plaintiff would only be entitled to interest on the capital. On the plaintiff's death the capital would devolve on the plaintiff's legitimate children. During the plaintiff's minority his father (in his capacity as guardian of the plaintiff) purchased a house on behalf of the plaintiff. There was no money at hand to pay the purchase price of the house and the parties agreed that the purchase price of £1 750 would be payable in instalments. The value of the property was no more than £1 550. Until the plaintiff's majority the instalments were paid out of the interest on the sum inherited by him. During his minority the plaintiff lived with his parents on the property. When he reached the age of majority a considerable amount of the purchase price was still unpaid. The instalments would absorb most of the interest payable to the plaintiff in terms of the will.

Restitutio in integrum

Terwyl die eiser nog 'n minderjarige was, het hy 'n bedrag van £10 000 geërf. Die testament ingevolge waarvan hy die geld geërf het, het bepaal dat die geld in trust gehou moes word en dat die eiser slegs op die rente van die kapitaal geregtig sou wees. By die eiser se dood sou die kapitaal op sy binne-egtelike kinders vererf. Gedurende die eiser se minderjarigheid het sy vader (in sy hoedanigheid as die eiser se voog) 'n huis namens die eiser gekoop. Daar was nie geld om die koopprys van die huis te betaal nie en die partye het ooreengekom dat die koopprys van £1 750 by wyse van paaiemente betaalbaar sou wees. Die waarde van die eiendom was nie meer as £1 550 nie. Die paaiemente is tot en met die eiser se meerderjarigwording uit die rente op die bedrag wat hy geërf het betaal. Tot op hierdie stadium het die eiser saam met sy ouers in die huis gewoon. Toe hy meerderjarig geword het, was 'n substansiële deel van die koopprys nog uitstaande. Die paaiemente sou die meeste van die rente in beslag neem wat ingevolge die testament

The plaintiff claimed cancellation of the contract entered into on his behalf and claimed repayment of the amounts he had already paid in terms of the contract. He alleged that the contract was prejudicial to him. His claim was granted.

aan die eiser betaalbaar was. Die eiser het tersydestelling van die kontrak wat namens hom aangegaan is, asook terugbetaling van die bedrae wat hy reeds ingevolge die kontrak betaal het, geëis. Hy het beweer dat die kontrak vir hom nadelig was. Sy eis is toegestaan.

SUTTON J: [255] I shall first consider the question whether the plaintiff's father in his capacity as natural guardian had authority to enter into the contract. It is contended on behalf of the plaintiff that he had no authority on two grounds.

It is said that in his capacity as natural guardian (1) the father could not validly contract on behalf of the minor to buy property beyond the funds actually in hand; (2) he had no authority to make a contract which was to endure beyond majority and which was to impose on the minor, on becoming a major, heavy and substantial liabilities...

The rights and duties of natural guardians must ... be sought in the general law. In *Van Rooyen v Werner* (9 J 425), DE VILLIERS, CJ, traces the history of our law relating to the paternal power. He sums up their position as follows:– Firstly as to the father, he is the natural guardian of [256] his legitimate children until they attain majority. He has the right to administer their property. In *Van der Byl and Co v Solomon* (1877, Buch 25 at p 27) he says: "Now although a father, as the natural guardian, has the administration of his minor children's property his powers are not unlimited. He may employ their income for their sustenance, education and such like purposes, and may place their money into appropriate investments."

The duty of the Board of Executors as trustee of the fund of £10 000 was to invest the money in proper security and to pay over the interest half-yearly to the beneficiary. During his minority his father as natural guardian was entitled to receive his interest and to administer it for the benefit of the minor. *Prima facie* a minor is liable on a contract duly made with the sanction and within the authority of his guardian...

[A]ssuming that a natural guardian has the power to invest the funds of his ward in immovable property in my view he has only such authority where he has funds in hand for that purpose. In my opinion though he has the right to administer the property of his ward he exceeds his authority when he purchases immovable property for the purchase of which he has not funds in hand. His duty is to lay out the funds of the ward which are not required for the necessary uses of the ward. His function is to invest surplus income and no more. I cannot regard the purchase of this property as an investment by the guardian on behalf of his ward.

[257] I now come to deal with the question whether this contract was bad in law because it imposed obligations which extended beyond the minority of the ward...

In *Du Toit v Lotriet* (1918, OPD 99), MAASDORP, CJ, said: "Now the rule of law applicable to a case of this sort is that as a general rule the power of a guardian to deal with the property or affairs of his ward is limited to the period of his guardianship and ceases with the termination thereof. If however in order to the proper utilisation of such property and the beneficial administration of such affairs it is necessary to enter into contracts which whilst commencing during such guardianship unavoidably extend to a moderate period beyond in accordance with the customs of the country ... the ward will be bound by such contract until the termination thereof." See also McGREGOR, J, at pp 110 and 111, and WARD, J, at p 117.

In *Skead v Colonial Banking and Trust Co Ltd* (1924, TPD 497 at p 503): "Of course care must be taken by guardians who undertake contracts which impose a liability after a minor's majority. But in this particular case the liability was of a comparatively small character, and the minor desired the insurance, and there were a good many reasons for thinking that it was desirable in his interests that he should be insured."

I do not think that a hard and fast rule can be laid down. Each case must depend upon its particular circumstances. In the above case the Court upheld a contract of insurance which imposed liabilities upon the minor after he attained his majority. The present case, however, goes far beyond that one. The effect of the contract was to deprive the ward of the free use of a considerable portion of his income after he attained majority, it restricted the [258] enjoyment of his proprietary rights after he attained majority and I therefore think the father exceeded his authority as natural guardian in entering into the contract.

For these reasons I am of opinion that plaintiff must succeed in his action.

I now come to deal with the question whether plaintiff is entitled to claim *restitutio in integrum* on the ground that the contract has prejudiced him. In *Van der Byl and Co v Solomon* (1877, Buch 25 at p 27), DE VILLIERS, CJ, says: "But I can find no authority for holding that he may bind them to the purchase of land for the payment of which he has no funds of theirs in hand. I do, however, find authority for the view that minors will be relieved by means of *restitutio in integrum* against contracts made to their prejudice either by themselves together with ("nevens") their guardians or by their guardians alone . . .

Maasdorp's *Institutes* (vol III, 2nd ed, p 63) in treating of *restitutio in integrum* in the case of minors, says: "The relief here treated of applies to contracts entered into by minors with the consent of their guardians, and with the due observance of all the other essentials of contract, but from which the minor has suffered some serious loss, damage or prejudice, for which there exists no other complete remedy."

Voet (IV.1.11; Sampson's Trans, p 10) says: "Restitution is, however, not to be promiscuously granted to everyone who applies for it, and alleges grounds for relief, but only after inquiry whether the grounds are true and just or are sufficiently weighty. For in the first place it is not to be granted if there has been a small injury done (*levis laesio*) . . . But what comes under the designation of trivial (*minimae*) seems to be mainly left to the discretion of the Judge, the damage being considered not by itself and in itself, but proportionately to the whole transaction in which it occurs." . . . The *onus* of proving loss is on the plaintiff . . . A good deal of evidence was directed to the value of the property purchased at the time of the contract in 1929 . . .

[SUTTON J analysed the evidence regarding the value of the property and concluded that the purchase price was at least £200 more than the actual value of the property. He proceeded:]

[259] The minor was therefore prejudiced to the extent of £200. In my opinion that was serious and substantial prejudice to him.

[260] Not only was the purchase price excessive but the minor did not require the property. At the time of the purchase he was at boarding-school and did not need a dwelling house then, or when he left school. In reality the property was purchased as a home for the family of the minor though incidently for the minor as well. The result of the purchase is that he is now saddled with a property which he cannot sell and which has depreciated in value since 1929.

There was also potential prejudice to the minor in clause 8 of the contract for in the event of the insolvency of the seller he would have lost the property as well as his payments under the contract. There was also potential prejudice to the minor in clause 10 of the contract for it provided that should the purchaser fail to pay one instalment on due date then the seller should have the right to cancel the sale and retain the amounts paid as rent...

Another ground of serious prejudice to the plaintiff is that the contract contemplated and imposed liabilities on him after he attained his majority and so hampered him in the free administration of his income after the attainment of his majority... It is said that the minor has had a *quid pro quo*, that he has had occupation of the property. That is so, but then he did not require it. It is also said that the purchase has been the means of the minor saving a portion of his income. That may also be the case, but *non constat* that it could not have been more usefully employed.

For these reasons I come to the conclusion that the plaintiff is entitled to *restitutio in integrum* and that there must be an order for the cancellation of the contract of sale, and for the return of the payments made on his behalf under the contract together with interest. The defendant however is entitled to be placed in *statu quo*, see *Voet* (4.1.22, Sampson's Trans, p 16). Plaintiff has had occupation of the property purchased since May 1st, 1929, and he must account to defendant for the use and occupation of the property, since that day...

[261] In my opinion an allowance of £12 per month for the period from May 1st to December 31st, 1929; of £11 per month for the year 1930 and £10 per month thereafter is a fair and reasonable amount for the use and occupation of the property by the plaintiff. Defendant is entitled to receive credit from the plaintiff for these several amounts together with interest thereon at a rate of 6 per cent per annum from the first day of each month in which each monthly sum would have been payable had it accrued as rent.

There will therefore be judgment in favour of the plaintiff...

The defendant is however to receive credit from the plaintiff for the use and occupation of the property...

Note

As Boberg (512) points out, it is difficult to see why SUTTON J did not conclude his judgment when he found that: "the father exceeded his authority as natural guardian in entering into the contract" (258). If the father did not act within the limits of his authority the contract could be set aside for that reason and the minor could reclaim his payments with a *condictio*. (In this regard also see the note on *Louw v MJ & H Trust* [31].) He would then not need *restitutio in integrum* as *restitutio in integrum* is really only necessary in the case where the minor is contractually bound (Christie 276–277; Barnard, Cronjé and Olivier 84; Boberg 509 fn 68; Van der Vyver and Joubert 159).

However, the minor is not prohibited from applying for *restitutio in integrum* if he is not bound by the contract but he would have to satisfy a

Aantekening

Boberg (512) wys daarop dat dit moeilik is om in te sien waarom SUTTON R nie sy uitspraak afgesluit het toe hy bevind het dat "the father exceeded his authority as natural guardian in entering into the contract" nie (258). Indien die vader nie binne die perke van sy bevoegdheid opgetree het nie, kon die kontrak om daardie rede ter syde gestel word en kon die minderjarige sy paaiemente met 'n *condictio* teruggeëis het. (Sien in hierdie verband ook die aantekening by *Louw v MJ & H Trust* [31].) Hy sou dan nie *restitutio in integrum* nodig gehad het nie aangesien *restitutio in integrum* net werklik nodig is in die geval waar die minderjarige kontraktueel gebonde is (Christie 276–277; Barnard, Cronjé en Olivier 87; Boberg 509 vn 68; Van der Vyver en Joubert 159).

Die minderjarige word egter nie verbied om aansoek te doen om *restitutio in integrum* indien hy nie aan die kontrak gebonde is nie, maar hy sal

more onerous burden of proof if he applies for *restitutio in integrum* than if he merely reclaimed his performance with the *rei vindicatio* or a *condictio*. In order to be successful in a claim for *restitutio in integrum* the minor would have to prove that the contract was prejudicial to him from its inception. It would, however, not be necessary for him to prove this if he merely claimed back the performance he rendered in terms of a contract which his guardian, without having the necessary authority, entered into (Christie 276–277; Boberg 508 509 fn 67; Barnard, Cronjé and Olivier 91; Van der Vyver and Joubert 159).

Du Toit v Lotriet 1918 OPD 99 is another example of a case where the court unnecessarily ordered *restitutio in integrum*. In this case the minor's guardian entered into a leasing agreement in terms of which the lease would have commenced after the minor reached majority. The court held that the contract was invalid since a contract which binds the minor only after he reaches majority falls outside the scope of the guardian's authority. The court ordered *restitutio in integrum* but this was unnecessary as the contract could simply have been set aside on the ground of the guardian's lack of authority.

It should be noted that, since the minor who claims *restitutio in integrum* has to prove that the contract was prejudicial to him *from its inception*; a change of circumstance which occurs after entering into the contract would not entitle the minor to *restitutio in integrum* – see *Skead v Colonial Banking & Trust Co Ltd* 1924 TPD 497. In this case the minor took out an endowment policy with the consent of his father. However, he could not pay the premiums. After the minor reached majority he claimed *restitutio in integrum* but the court refused his claim as his inability to pay the premiums was not due to the fact that the contract was prejudicial to him but to the fact that he became a spendthrift. MASON, JP put it thus:

"[T]he contract for insurance was made by the father in the *bona fide* belief that it was for the son's benefit and as the only means of saving, without any idea that his son would develop into a spendthrift. There can be no doubt the policy was worth the money and that defendant has had and still has the benefit of the policy in question . . .

There seems good reason also for thinking that, if the defendant had not become a spendthrift,

hom dan van 'n swaarder bewyslas moet kwyt as wat nodig sal wees indien hy bloot sy prestasie met die *rei vindicatio* of 'n *condictio* terugeis. Om suksesvol te wees met 'n eis om *restitutio in integrum* sal die minderjarige moet bewys dat die kontrak vanaf die sluiting daarvan vir hom nadelig was terwyl dit nie bewys hoef te word indien hy bloot die prestasie terugeis wat hy gelewer het ingevolge 'n kontrak wat sy voog sonder die nodige bevoegdheid gesluit het nie (Christie 276–277; Boberg 508 509 vn 67; Barnard, Cronjé en Olivier 94; Van der Vyver en Joubert 159).

Du Toit v Lotriet 1918 OPA 99 is nog 'n voorbeeld van 'n geval waar dit onnodig was dat die hof *restitutio in integrum* beveel het. In hierdie geval het die minderjarige se voog 'n huurkontrak ("leasing agreement") gesluit wat eers in werking sou tree nadat die minderjarige meerderjarigheid bereik het. Die hof het beslis dat die kontrak ongeldig was aangesien die voog nie bevoeg was om 'n kontrak te sluit wat eers in werking sou tree nadat die minderjarige meerderjarig geword het nie. Die hof het *restitutio in integrum* beveel maar dit was onnodig aangesien die kontrak bloot ter syde gestel kon word op grond van die voog se gebrek aan bevoegdheid.

'n Mens moet daarop let dat aangesien die minderjarige wat *restitutio in integrum* eis, moet bewys dat die kontrak *vanaf die sluiting daarvan* vir hom nadelig was; dit beteken dat 'n verandering in omstandighede wat plaasvind nadat die kontrak gesluit is, nie die minderjarige op *restitutio in integrum* geregtig sal maak nie – sien *Skead v Colonial Banking & Trust Co Ltd* 1924 TPA 497. In hierdie saak het die minderjarige met sy vader se toestemming 'n uitkeerpolis gesluit. Hy kon egter nie die premies betaal nie. Nadat die minderjarige meerderjarig geword het, het hy *restitutio in integrum* geëis maar die hof het sy eis van die hand gewys aangesien sy onvermoë om die premies te betaal nie daaraan te wyte was dat die kontrak vir hom nadelig was nie maar aan die feit dat hy 'n verkwister geword het. MASON RP het dit soos volg gestel:

"[T]he contract for insurance was made by the father in the *bona fide* belief that it was for the son's benefit and as the only means of saving, without any idea that his son would develop into a spendthrift. There can be no doubt the policy was worth the money and that defendant has had

this insurance would have been a beneficial contract. Under these circumstances, can he repudiate it? Are those who, with the guardian's sanction, make with a minor a contract which all parties are justified in considering to be for his benefit, to be subject to the risk of the contract being set aside because subsequent circumstances arise which render the performance of the contract by the minor disadvantageous to him? That seems rather a serious proposition, to make those who thus contract with minors insurers of the contracts for the minors' benefit . . .

The authorities . . . are clear that accident is not a ground for restitution; the *Digest* (4.4.11 (4)), indeed, puts it in this manner: It is not the occurrence of loss but unadvised heedlessness that favours restitution . . ." (500–501).

It must be borne in mind that the father is no longer the only natural guardian of a legitimate child – see the note on *Calitz v Calitz* [19].

and still has the benefit of the policy in question . . .

There seems good reason also for thinking that, if the defendant had not become a spendthrift, this insurance would have been a beneficial contract. Under these circumstances, can he repudiate it? Are those who, with the guardian's sanction, make with a minor a contract which all parties are justified in considering to be for his benefit, to be subject to the risk of the contract being set aside because subsequent circumstances arise which render the performance of the contract by the minor disadvantageous to him? That seems rather a serious proposition, to make those who thus contract with minors insurers of the contracts for the minors' benefit . . .

The authorities . . . are clear that accident is not a ground for restitution; the *Digest* (4.4.11 (4)), indeed, puts it in this manner: It is not the occurrence of loss but unadvised heedlessness that favours restitution . . ." (500–501).

Dit moet in gedagte gehou word dat die vader nie meer die enigste natuurlike voog van 'n binne-egtelike kind is nie – sien die aantekening by *Calitz v Calitz* [19].

Termination of minority   **Beëindiging van minderjarigheid**

[38]   MEYER V THE MASTER

1935 SWA 3

"Mondigheid" versus majority

When the petitioner was fourteen years and four months old he inherited a sum of money from his mother in terms of her will which provided that the money had to be deposited with the master of the supreme court "op ons kinders hier voornoemd se name . . . tot hulle meerderjarig is." As soon as he reached the age at which he could marry, the petitioner did so but he did not live with his wife subsequent to the marriage. He then contended that he became a major as a result of his marriage and applied for the money

Mondigheid teenoor meerderjarigheid

Toe die petisionaris veertien jaar en vier maande oud was, het sy moeder in haar testament 'n som geld aan hom bemaak onderworpe aan die bepaling dat die geld by die meester van die hooggeregshof gedeponeer moes word "op ons kinders hier voornoemd se name . . . tot hulle meerderjarig is." Toe hy die ouderdom bereik het waarop hy kon trou, is die petisionaris getroud maar hy het nooit sedert die huwelik met sy vrou saamgeleef nie. Hy het beweer dat hy op grond van sy huwelik meerderjarig geword het en

to be paid out to him. The petitioner was unable to manage his own affairs and the claim was opposed by the master of the supreme court. It was clear that the real person who wanted to lay his hands on the money was the petitioner's father. The petitioner's brother had also married a few years earlier when he was sixteen years of age and his money was paid out to him. He was divorced two years later. The application was refused.

aansoek gedoen dat die geld aan hom uitbetaal word. Die petisionaris was nie daartoe in staat om sy eie sake te bestuur nie en die eis is deur die meester van die hooggeregshof teengestaan. Dit was duidelik dat die petisionaris se vader die eintlike persoon was wat die geld in die hande wou kry. Die petisionaris se broer is ook 'n paar jaar vantevore getroud toe hy sestien jaar oud was en sy geld is aan hom uitbetaal. Twee jaar later is hy geskei. Die aansoek is van die hand gewys.

VAN DEN HEEVER R: [5] My oortuiging is dat die aansoek van die hand gewys moet word en dit op drie gronde ...

Mnr Bond [vir die applikant], het betoog dat die woorde "meerderjarig" en "mondig" dieselfde betekenis het ...

Die woord "meerderjarig" is self-verklarend; dit dui aan 'n leeftydsgrens ... Gedurende die tydperk van minderjarigheid is hy ten volle regsbevoegd, maar is sy handelingsbevoegdheid in groter of minder mate beperk, na gelang van die klas minderjariges waarin hy sorteer. Sodra hy egter die bepaalde leeftydsgrens oorskry erlang hy tewens ook volle handelingsbevoegdheid en derhalwe sy volle status ...

Dat die woord "meerderjarig" dikwels taamlik los gebruik word moet mens toegee ...

In die meeste gevalle kan een uitdrukking net sowel vir die ander dien, daar die [6] regsgevolge van die twee toestande vrywel dieselfde is. Slegs waar die teenstelling van een en die ander begrip beklemtoon word is die bepaalde benamings van gewig.

Die woord "mondig" is natuurlik afgelei van "munt" of "mundium"; so kan mens ontmondig word maar nie minderjarig nie. M.a.w. meerderjarigheid is slegs een, en daarby 'n bepaalde wyse van moontlike mondigwordig t.w. deur verloop van tyd tot die oorskryding van die by wet bepaalde leeftydsgrens ...

[VAN DEN HEEVER R het na verskeie Romeins-Hollandse skrywers verwys en vervolg:]

Ten laaste, Grotius konstateer in sy Inleyd Boek I deel 6 n 4: "De onbestorven kinderen [die kinders wie se ouers nog leef] werden mondig door huwelick ofte handlichtinge ..." Meerderjarig word hulle slegs deur verloop van tyd. Ook vertel Grotius (1.10.3) dat 'n minderjarige deur middel van *venia aetatis* mondig word. Ons weet egter uit bedoelde teks sowel as uit Voet Comment ad Pandect 26.1.5 dat die handelingsbevoegdheid wat deur die huwelik, deur handligting of deur *venia aetatis* verkry word meer beperk is as die omvang van die bevoegdheid wat uit meerderjarigheid vloei ...

In die breë sin beduie die woord "mondig" in Afrikaans die genus en "meerderjarig" die species. Mans word mondig deur meerderjarigheid, huwelik, handligting, *venia aetatis* ens. Die erflaatster het in hierdie geval 'n bepaalde soort van mondigwording [8] as voorwaarde van uitbetaling gestel; ek moet veronderstel dat sy dit bewus gedaan het en bedoel het wat sy gesê het. Daarby kom nog dat die voorwaarde klaarblyklik ingevoeg is ter beskerming van die seun. Aan die voorwaarde moet derhalwe 'n ruime werking toegeken word. As mens nog boonop in aanmerking neem dat die kapasiteit of bevoegdheid wat uit huwelik, handligting of *venia aetatis* voortvloei meer beperk is as die wat op letterlike meerderjarigheid volg, soos ek reeds aangetoon het, dan moet mens sê dat die voorwaarde, waaraan die erflaatster in die onderhawige testament die uitbetaling van hierdie legaat onderhewig gemaak het, nie deur die huwelik van die legataris verwesenlik kan word nie maar slegs deur sy oorlewing van die wettelike leeftydsgrens ...

[9] Die tweede grond waarop ek die aansoek van die hand wys is die volgende:

Indien die huwelik 'n minderjarige mondig maak dan doen hy dit nie steeds en onbeperk nie maar slegs indien, en onder sulke beperkings as, die hedendaagse verteenwoordiger van die [10] Weeskamer [dit is die meester van die hooggeregshof] dit raadsaam ag . . .

[VAN DEN HEEVER R het na De Groot 1.10.2; Voet 4.4.5 en Loenius *Decis* 124 verwys en vervolg:]

Dit is dus duidelik dat in 'n geskikte geval dit nie nodig was om 'n gehuude bestorwe kind te *ontmondig* nie, maar dat die betrokke gesag desondanks die beperking op sy bevoegdheid, d.i. sy onmondigheid *kon verleng*. Ek weet van geen wysiging wat hierin aangebring is nie . . . [D]ie redes waarom die Meester weier om uit te betaal (d.w.s. die onmondigheid verleng) [is] van die gewigtigste. Soos duidelik uit die voorgelegde stukke blyk is die petisionaris onbevoeg om sy eie sake te behartig en kan die beheer nie aan sy vader toevertrou word nie. Op hierdie grond ook – veral daar petisionaris se enigste bate 'n som geld in die voogdyfonds is – beaam ek heeltemal die handelwyse van die Meester en is nie gereed nie om sy beslissing te vernietig of te wysig.

[As derde grond waarop VAN DEN HEEVER R die aansoek van die hand gewys het, het hy die omstandighede van die huwelik ondersoek. Hy het tot die gevolgtrekking gekom dat die vader die eintlike petisionaris was en sy seun slegs 'n houtpop. Die huwelik was niks anders nie as 'n set van die vader om die besittings van sy minderjarige seun in die hande te kry. Hy vervolg:]

[13] Waar die ouderlike *consensus* as oorsaak aangedui word, verg die reël natuurlik 'n *consensus* wat nie bedrieglik is nie, soos in hierdie geval, en beoog dit werklike selfmondigheid sowel as die seun se bekwaamheid daartoe, wat hier nie die geval is nie . . .

[I]nwilliging van die partye is nog steeds 'n onmisbare voorwaarde van 'n ware huwelik. Indien die vader sy seun beweeg het om in te stem met die verrigting van 'n onbeduidende formaliteit wat na twee jaar weer verhelp kon word twyfel ek daaraan of die seun werklik ingewillig het.

Maar dis nie eintlik op daardie grond wat ek my beslissing baseer nie.

Indien die seun 'n *per se* beperkte mondigheid erlang het, of indien die Meester geregtig was om die onmondigheid van die petisionaris te verleng dan is petisionaris nog nie volmondig nie en *cadit quaestio* [die vraag verval]. Indien hy egter mondig is uit hoofde van die huwelik dan is dit hom toerekenbaar dat hy hom vereenselwig het met die set van sy vader. Dan het hy die instelling van die huwelik geminag deur 'n skynhuwelik aan te gaan om sodoende sy erfnis ontydig in die hande te kry. Deur meinedige verklarings en vereenselwiging daarmee het hy die proses van die Hof misbruik en geminag. Ek is nie geneig om die gesag van die Hof te verleen om die oënskynlike regsgevolge van 'n klugspel te verwesenlik nie, om sodoende die werklike petisionaris in sy bedrieglike voornemens behulpsaam te wees, sodat hy deur aanspraak op die letter van die wet sy gees verkrag. Ook daarom word die aansoek van die hand gewys as skandaleus. Insover die Meester se beslissing, [14] om die onmondigheid van petisionaris te verleng, die goedkeuring van die Hof as oppervoogd vereis, word dit hierby verleen . . .

Note

There is no English translation for the concept of "mondigheid". Majority ("meerderjarigheid") refers to a specific age (that is twenty-one years) that one must reach and is one way of becoming "mondig" but there are also other ways in which "mondigheid" can come about, for example by

Aantekening

Meerderjarigheid ("majority") verwys na 'n spesifieke ouderdom (naamlik een en twintig jaar) wat 'n mens moet bereik en is een manier waarop 'n mens mondig kan word. Daar is egter ook ander wyses waarop dit kan geskied, byvoorbeeld deur huweliksluiting soos in die onderhawige

marriage as is illustrated in the case under discussion. In other words all major persons are "mondig" but not all "mondiges" are majors.

In some instances a person must be twenty-one years of age before he can perform a certain function, for example a person who becomes "mondig" before he has reached the age of twenty-one years cannot be appointed guardian (Van der Keessel *Theses Selectae* 112 114; Grotius 1.7.6; Voet 26.1.5; Van Leeuwen *Censura Forensis* 1.1.16.13; *Dhanabakium v Subramanian* 1943 AD 160; *Nokoyo v AA Mutual Insurance Association Ltd* 1976 2 SA 153 (E)). For further examples, see Van der Vyver and Joubert 140–141.

saak geïllustreer word. Alle meerderjarige persone is met ander woorde mondig maar nie alle mondiges is meerderjarig nie.

In sommige gevalle moet 'n mens die ouderdom van een en twintig jaar bereik voordat hy 'n sekere funksie kan vervul, byvoorbeeld 'n persoon wat mondig word voor hy een en twintig jaar oud is, kan nie as voog aangestel word nie (Van der Keessel *Theses Selectae* 112 114; De Groot 1.7.6; Voet 26.1.5; Van Leeuwen *Censura Forensis* 1.1.16.13; *Dhanabakium v Subramanian* 1943 AA 160; *Nokoyo v AA Mutual Insurance Association Ltd* 1976 2 SA 153 (OK)). Vir verdere voorbeelde, sien Van der Vyver en Joubert 140–141.

[39] EX PARTE VAN DEN HEVER

1969 3 SA 96 (OK)

Release of a minor from tutelage

The applicant applied to court for an order releasing his minor brother, Ignatius Michael van den Hever, from tutelage and affording him full capacity to act ("volle handelingsbevoegdheid"). Ignatius would have reached the age of majority on 10 March 1970. The brothers' parents were both deceased. The applicant was a farmer and the testamentary executor of his deceased mother's estate. In terms of the will of the brothers' parents, Ignatius inherited an undivided share in certain immovable property as well as other assets. Ignatius assisted applicant in his farming operations from the beginning of 1968 until 1 March 1968 when he took up independent farming operations on the immovable property to which he was entitled by virtue of his parents' will. Applicant sold stock to the value of R26 000 to Ignatius on credit. The only debts Ignatius had were the R26 000 he owed applicant and R7 000 he borrowed from the bank as operating capital. In his affidavit applicant stated that Ignatius was a conscientious farmer; that he had proved himself to be a hardworking and re-

Ontslag van 'n minderjarige uit voogdy

Die applikant het by die hof aansoek gedoen om 'n bevel dat sy minderjarige broer, Ignatius Michael van den Hever, uit voogdy ontslaan word en volle handelingsbevoegdheid aan hom toegeken word. Ignatius sou op 10 Maart 1970 meerderjarig geword het. Die broers se ouers was albei oorlede. Die applikant was 'n boer en die testamentêre eksekuteur van sy oorlede moeder se boedel. Ingevolge die testament van die broers se ouers, het Ignatius 'n onverdeelde aandeel in sekere onroerende eiendom sowel as ander bates geërf. Ignatius het die applikant vanaf die begin van 1968 tot 1 Maart 1968 in sy boerderybedrywighede bygestaan en daarna selfstandig gaan boer op die onroerende eiendom wat hom ingevolge sy ouers se testament toegekom het. Die applikant het vee ter waarde van R26 000 op krediet aan Ignatius verkoop. Die enigste skuld wat Ignatius gehad het, was die R26 000 wat hy aan die applikant geskuld het en R7 000 wat hy as bedryfskapitaal by die bank geleen het. In sy beëdigde verklaring het die applikant verklaar dat Ignatius 'n baie knap boer was,

sponsible young man and that he was capable of conducting independent farming operations. Applicant also alleged that his brother would suffer loss if the cash to which he was entitled had to be kept in the Guardian's Fund as the Fund paid a very low rate of interest and further that Ignatius' limited capacity to act restrained him in his farming activities. Ignatius associated himself with everything applicant stated and also alleged that his minority restrained him in his farming activities. The affidavits of farmers from adjacent farms corroborated the allegations regarding Ignatius' responsibility and farming abilities. Ignatius' maternal grandfather, who was appointed as his testamentary guardian, also submitted an affidavit in which he stated that it was impractical and very difficult for him to fulfil his duties as testamentary guardian as he was eighty-three years old and lived approximately two hundred miles from Ignatius' farm. He further stated that he was satisfied that Ignatius was sufficiently responsible and independent to be able to conduct his own farming operations. The application for release from tutelage was granted.

dat hy hom bewys het as 'n hardwerkende en verantwoordelike jong man en dat hy in staat was om selfstandig te boer. Die applikant het ook beweer dat sy broer 'n verlies sou ly indien die kontant waarop hy geregtig was in die Voogdyfonds gehou moes word aangesien die Fonds 'n baie lae rentekoers betaal het en verder dat Ignatius se beperkte handelingsbevoegdheid sy boerderybedrywighede aan bande gelê het. Ignatius het hom vereenselwig met alles wat die applikant verklaar het en het ook beweer dat sy minderjarigheid hom in sy boerderybedrywighede aan bande gelê het. Die beëdigde verklarings van boere in die onmiddellike omgewing het die bewerings rakende Ignatius se verantwoordelikheid en vermoë om te boer bevestig. Ignatius se grootvader aan moederskant, wat as sy testamentêre voog aangestel is, het ook 'n beëdigde verklaring ingedien waarin hy gesê het dat dit vir hom onprakties en baie moeilik was om sy pligte as testamentêre voog na te kom aangesien hy drie en tagtig jaar oud was en omtrent twee honderd myl van Ignatius se plaas af gewoon het. Hy het verder verklaar dat hy tevrede was dat Ignatius verantwoordelik en selfstandig genoeg was om sy eie boerderybedrywighede te kon bedryf. Die aansoek om ontslag uit voogdy is toegestaan.

KANNEMEYER R: [97] Die vraag is of die Hof die bevoegdheid het om 'n minderjarige van voogdyskap te ontslaan. En dit lei tot die verdere vraag: wat presies beteken 'n bevel van so 'n aard, wat is die verskil tussen dit en *venia aetatis*? Dat die Hooggeregshof geen bevoegdheid het om *venia aetatis* aan 'n minderjarige te verleen nie, ly geen twyfel nie: *In re Cachet*, 15 SC 5; *Ex parte Moolman*, 1903 TS 159. Maar daar is, in die Kaap Provinsie, 'n reeks gewysdes waarin die Hof aan minderjariges "ontslag uit voogdyskap" verleen het. In *In re Cachet, supra*, het die Hof geweier om *venia aetatis* te verleen, maar gesê:

[98] "But it does seem to be for the interest of this minor that he should be declared of such an approved state as to be entitled to have paid to him the inheritance coming to him under his mother's will. The Court will only be consulting the minor's interest in granting that part of the prayer of the petition; and an order will also be granted discharging the minor from tutelage."

In *Ex parte Louw*, 1920 KPA 7, lui die samevatting

"decree of *venia aetatis* granted in favour of a minor of the age of 20 years to enable him to carry on farming operations".

Die aansoek was wel vir *venia aetatis* maar die bevel van die Hof het die betaling van geld uit die Voogdyfonds gemagtig en verklaar

"that the petitioner be released from tutelage".

In *Ex parte Estate van Schalkwyk*, 1927 KPA 268, was die aansoek vir ontslag uit voogdyskap. Die Weesheer het verslag gedoen

"that it would be to the advantage of the heirs that the assets in the estate be not realised, that the minor should accept the bequest made by his father and that the minor should be discharged from tutelage and authorised to pass the mortgage bond as proposed"

en die Hof het 'n bevel ooreenkomstig die Weesheer se verslag uitgereik. *Ex parte Smit*, 1929 (1) PH F40, was ook 'n aansoek om *venia aetatis* maar die Hof het 'n bevel gegee

"that the applicant be released from tutelage".

In *Ex parte Curling*, 1952 (1) PH M13, is 'n soortgelyke bevel toegestaan. In *Ex parte Velkes*, 1963 (3) SA 584 (K), is die Hof se bevoegdheid om so 'n bevel toe te staan vir die eerste keer deur 'n Hof in twyfel getrek, maar al in 1937, in die *Tydskrif vir Heedendaagse Romeins-Hollandse Reg* op bl 194 het professor Coertze gesê:

"As die Kaapse Hof dus besluit dat hy geen reg het om *venia aetatis* te verleen nie, dan het dit ook geen reg om die meerderjarigheid te vervroeg nie 'to discharge the minor from tutelage', want *venia aetatis* is juis 'n offisiële meerderjarigheidsvervroeging waaraan daardie Hof meedoen. Waar die Kaapse Hof dus aan hierdie bevoegdheid kom moet nog ontdek word."

De Wet en Yeats, *Kontraktereg en Handelsreg*, 3de uitg, bl 57, meld dat

"alhoewel die Kaapse Hof nêrens verklaar wat hierdie ontslag uit voogdyskap presies beteken nie, kan dit nouliks iets anders beteken as dat die minderjarige nou dieselfde status verkry as iemand aan wie *venia aetatis* verleen is".

Lee, *Introduction to Roman Dutch Law*, 5de uitg, bl 44, is van mening dat ontslag uit voogdyskap

"is not *venia aetatis*, though it seems to come very near to it"

maar hy verduidelik nie wat die verskil wel is nie. As daar geen verskil is tussen *venia aetatis* en ontslag uit voogdyskap nie dan kan die Hof nie sy gebrek aan bevoegdheid om *venia aetatis* te verleen ontduik nie, deur om dieselfde status onder 'n ander naam te verleen nie.

Die uitspraak in *Cachet* se saak, *supra*, is baie kort maar ek is oortuig dat DE VILLIERS, HR, en BUCHANAN en MAASDORP, RR, sou nooit

"an order discharging the minor from tutelage"

verleen het nie onmiddellik nadat hulle geweier het om *venia aetatis* te verleen, tensy hulle tevrede was dat daar wel 'n verskil tussen die twee is.

Myns insiens is daar 'n verskil. *Venia aetatis* is 'n vervroeging van mondigheid wat die reg om vaste eiendom te vervreem of te verband kan insluit terwyl die ontslag uit voogdyskap nie meer as emansipasie is nie, en emansipasie gee nooit 'n minderjarige die reg om vaste eiendom te vervreem of te verband nie. Hy bly 'n minderjarige. Daar is onsekerheid of 'n minderjarige aan wie *venia aetatis* verleen is, gemagtig is om sonder toestemming van sy ouers te trou, maar dit is duidelik dat 'n geëmansipeerde minderjarige toestemming van sy ouers [99] of die Hof moet hê. *Venia aetatis* is 'n vergunning van owerheidsweë, emansipasie is 'n gevolg van òf uitdruklike òf stilswyende toestemming van 'n minderjarige se ouers. Ek kan geen aanduiding vind dat *venia aetatis* herroepbaar is nie, maar emansipasie is aan ouerlike toestemming onderworpe en die toestemming is herroepbaar: *Ex parte Keeve*, (1928) 12 PH M51; Spiro, *Law of Parent and Child*, 2de uitg, bl 162; *Lee, op cit*, bl 39. Ons praat van stilswyende handligting maar dit kan uitdruklik

wees. Die gebruik van die woord stilswyend is, waarskynlik om die verskil te beklemtoon tussen die hedendaagse handligting wat informeel plaasvind deur òf die uitdruklike òf die stilswyende ouerlike toestemming op die een kant en die outydse prosedure waaronder die vader van die minderjarige 'n verklaring van emansipasie voor die Hof gemaak het. Daaronder was dit nie die Hof wat handligting verleen het nie; dit was nog die vader maar hy het dit *coram legi loco* gedoen vir doeleindes van bekendmaking. Sien 44 *SALJ*, bl 316. Gevolglik, waar 'n minderjarige geen ouers of voog het nie kan die Hof, na my mening, in sy hoedanigheid as oppervoog, in 'n toepaslike geval, 'n minderjarige emansipeer of ontvoog. Dit, na my beskeie mening, is wat die Hof in *Cachet* se saak gedoen het, en wat ek in die onderhawige saak gevra word om te doen. Ek is oortuig dat dit in die minderjarige se belang sal wees as hy gemagtig is om sy boerdery voort te sit sonder om deur sy minderjarigheid gestrem te word en dat ek 'n toepaslike bevel behoort toe te staan. Ek is nie bereid om meer te doen as om hom van voogdyskap te ontslaan nie. Hy vra ook dat "volle handelingsbevoegdheid" aan hom verleen word, maar om dit te doen sou hom in staat stel, byvoorbeeld, om vaste eiendom te koop of vervreem . . .

Note

The distinction which KANNEMEYER J tried to draw (98–99) between *venia aetatis* and release from tutelage is not entirely satisfactory. Zeffertt (1969 *SALJ* 407 409) has described this equation of release from tutelage with a type of judicial emancipation which has the same effect as emancipation of a minor by his guardian, as "unconvincing" and an "oversimplification". De Wet and Yeats (3 ed 57) state that release from tutelage "kan . . . nouliks iets anders beteken as dat die minderjarige nou dieselfde status verkry as iemand aan wie *venia aetatis* verleen is." Hahlo and Kahn (*The Union of South Africa: The Development of its Laws and Constitution* 364) are also of the opinion that release from tutelage has "very much the same practical effect as *venia aetatis*."

Whether one accepts KANNEMEYER J's distinction or not, the question remains whether the court does in fact have the power to order "release from tutelage". Coertze (1937 *THRHR* 190 *et seq*) and De Wet and Yeats (3 ed 57) are of the opinion that the court does not have such a power. Coertze argues that release from tutelage as a legal institution never formed part of the Roman-Dutch law that was received into our law; that this institution fell into disuse as early as the end of the eighteenth century and that release from tutelage was granted by administrative organs and not by the court.

Spiro (248), however, points to the fact that the supreme court, in its capacity as upper guardian of all children, may always give its consent on behalf of the minor's parent and suggests that it

Aantekening

Die onderskeid wat KANNEMEYER R tussen *venia aetatis* en ontslag uit voogdy probeer maak (98–99), is nie heeltemal bevredigend nie. Zeffertt (1969 *SALJ* 407 409) het hierdie onderskeid en die gelykstelling van ontslag uit voogdy met 'n soort judisiële emansipasie wat dieselfde gevolge het as emansipasie van 'n minderjarige deur sy voog, as onoortuigend en 'n oorvereenvoudiging beskryf. De Wet en Yeats (3e uitg 57) reken dat ontslag uit voogdy "nouliks iets anders [kan] beteken as dat die minderjarige nou dieselfde status verkry as iemand aan wie *venia aetatis* verleen is." Hahlo en Kahn (*The Union of South Africa: The Development of its Laws and Constitution* 364) is ook van mening dat ontslag uit voogdy "very much the same practical effect as *venia aetatis*" het.

Of 'n mens nou KANNEMEYER R se onderskeid aanvaar of nie, bly die vraag steeds of die hof inderdaad die bevoegdheid het om "ontslag uit voogdy" te beveel. Coertze (1937 *THRHR* 190 ev) en De Wet en Yeats (3e uitg 57) is van mening dat die hof nie sodanige bevoegdheid het nie. Coertze voer aan dat ontslag uit voogdy as 'n regsfiguur nooit deel gevorm het van die Romeins-Hollandse reg wat in ons reg geresipieer is nie; dat dié regsfiguur reeds teen die einde van die agtiende eeu in onbruik verval het en dat ontslag uit voogdy deur administratiewe organe toegestaan is en nie deur die howe nie.

Spiro (248) wys egter op die feit dat die hooggeregshof, in sy hoedanigheid as oppervoog van alle kinders, altyd toestemming kan verleen in die plek van die kind se ouer en hy spreek die mening uit dat KANNEMEYER R "for this or

"must be for this or a similar reason that KAN-NEMEYER J . . . distinguished the release from tutelage and *venia aetatis* and construed the former as a revocable emancipation." Boberg (379 fn 31) also finds "a certain logical appeal in the learned judge's invocation of the court's power as upper guardian of minors to justify judicial emancipation of minors."

It appears as if the "release from tutelage" that was ordered in *Ex parte Van den Hever* was not really the Roman-Dutch "release from tutelage" and, in our view, should not have been called that. It was rather a type of emancipation by means of which the court, acting in its capacity of upper guardian of all minors, emancipated the minor.

Since the coming into operation of the Age of Majority Act 57 of 1972, the debate about the court's power to order release from tutelage and *venia aetatis* has lost much of its relevance. Although the act did not expressly repeal *venia aetatis* and release from tutelage, it appears that they have been replaced by the statutory provision. (Boberg 383; Barnard, Cronjé and Olivier 96; Van der Vyver and Joubert 139; Spiro 1973 *SALJ* 50; *contra* Van Aswegen 1981 *Codicillus* 32–33).

a similar reason . . . distinguished the release from tutelage and *venia aetatis* and construed the former as a revocable emancipation." Boberg (379 vn 31) vind ook "a certain logical appeal in the learned judge's invocation of the court's power as upper guardian of minors to justify judicial emancipation of minors."

Dit lyk asof die "ontslag uit voogdy" wat in *Ex parte Van den Hever* toegestaan is, nie werklik dieselfde as die Romeins-Hollandse "ontslag uit voogdy" was nie en na ons mening moes dit ook nie in hierdie saak so genoem gewees het nie. Dit was eerder 'n soort emansipasie waardeur die hof, in sy hoedanigheid as oppervoog oor alle minderjariges, die minderjarige geëmansipeer het.

Sedert die inwerkingtreding van die Wet op die Meerderjarigheidsouderdom 57 van 1972 het die debat oor die hof se bevoegdheid om ontslag uit voogdy en *venia aetatis* te verleen baie van sy relevansie verloor. Al het die wet nie *venia aetatis* en ontslag uit voogdy uitdruklik herroep nie, wil dit tog voorkom asof die statutêre bepalings hulle vervang het (Boberg 383; Barnard, Cronjé en Olivier 100; Van der Vyver en Joubert 139; Spiro 1973 *SALJ* 50; *contra* Van Aswegen 1981 *Codicillus* 32–33).

[40] EX PARTE BOTES

1978 2 SA 400 (O)

Declaration of a minor to be a major

About six months before the applicant reached the age of majority, his application to be declared a major in terms of the Age of Majority Act 57 of 1972 came before the court. The applicant had inherited a third of certain immovable property which was not yet registered in his name and he wanted to enter into a redistribution agreement in terms of which he would waive all his rights in respect of the immovable property and would obtain a cash amount of R30 000. The applicant had no intentions of farming and was qualifying as an hotelkeeper. The only evidence as to the applicant's maturity and re-

Meerderjarigverklaring van 'n minderjarige

Die applikant se aansoek om meerderjarigverklaring ingevolge die Wet op die Meerderjarigheidsouderdom 57 van 1972 het omtrent ses maande voordat hy meerderjarig sou word voor die hof gekom. Die applikant het 'n derde van sekere onroerende eiendom geërf maar dit was nog nie op sy naam geregistreer nie. Hy wou 'n herverdelingsooreenkoms aangaan ingevolge waarvan hy afstand sou doen van al sy regte op die onroerende eiendom en 'n kontantbedrag van R30 000 sou ontvang. Die applikant het geen voornemens gehad om ooit te boer nie en was besig om as 'n hotelhouer te kwalifiseer. Die enigste

sponsibility came from his mother who declared that the applicant was responsible, that
he achieved above average marks at school,
that he was always well-behaved and that he
showed good business sense. It was not clear
how he showed such business sense. The application was refused.

getuienis oor die applikant se volwassenheid
en verantwoordelikheid was van sy moeder
afkomstig. Sy het verklaar dat die applikant
verantwoordelik was, dat hy op skool bo ge-
middeld gepresteer het, dat hy hom altyd
goed gedra het en dat hy goeie besigheidsvernuf aan die dag gelê het. Dit was nie
duidelik hoe hy hierdie besigheidsvernuf getoon het nie. Die aansoek is van die hand
gewys.

FLEMMING R: [401] Die genoemde Wet [Wet op die Meerderjarigheidsouderdom 57
van 1972] toon heelwat ooreenstemming met die inhoud van hoofstuk 89 van die Vrystaatse
Wetboek wat mondigverklaring in hierdie provinsie tot 1972 beheers het. Volgens art 6
daarvan, moes die Hooggeregshof rapporteer daaromtrent of die toestaan van so 'n bevel
wenslik sou wees of onwenslik sou wees. Die Wetboek het nie voorskrifte bevat wat die
maatstawwe vir uitoefening van die Staatspresident se daaropvolgende diskresie omskryf
nie, maar dit kan met redelike veiligheid afgelei word dat die Staatspresident ook na
gelang van die wenslikheid tot 'n besluit sou kom. Na aanleiding van dié neergelegde
maatstaf is in *Ex parte Akiki* 1925 OPD 211 die volgende gesê:

> "The mere fact that an applicant is thoroughly capable of managing his own affairs,
> and of successfully carrying on the business or calling by means of which he proposes
> to earn his livelihood, is not sufficient to establish a claim to *venia aetatis* ... However
> inconvenient or irksome it may be for capable and energetic young men to await for
> the day of majority before enjoying the privileges and becoming subject to the burdens
> of full age, the Court should not be expected to come to their assistance on such
> grounds, in the absence of evidence that without such aid they would suffer serious
> detriment or loss, which, in all probability, could not be remedied or recovered on
> their reaching full age."

Die onderhawige Wet rig ook nie die Hof se diskresie in soveel woorde nie. Die inhoud
van art 3 (*g*) is egter 'n voldoende aanduiding dat die diskresie uitgeoefen moet word na
gelang van die wenslikheid van toestaan van die aansoek of die noodsaaklikheid daarvan.
Die feit dat die Wetgewer na sowel wenslikheid as noodsaak verwys, mag aanduidend
wees van die Wetgewer se begeerte om 'n laer oortuigingsmaatstaf voor te skryf as die
"some pressing *necessity*" wat volgens die *Akiki*-beslissing geverg was. (Vgl PQR Boberg
in 1975 *SALJ* 183 op 190.) Selfs op daardie benadering kan die applikant tegemoetgekom
word slegs indien hy 'n mate van "wenslikheid" aantoon.

Die aangehaalde gedeelte uit die *Akiki*-beslissing bly in daardie verband van toepassing
minstens in die opsig dat dit onvoldoende is vir die applikant om bloot aan te toon dat
hy in staat is om sy sake te beheer. Die vermoë daartoe (vgl art 3 (*b*) van die Wet) is wel
die grondslag en gevolglik 'n voorvereiste vir toestaan van die regshulp maar iets daarnaas
moet getoon word voordat die toestaan van die regshulp as "wenslik" beskou kan word.
Daar is geen aanduiding in die Wet dat dit beoog was dat 'n meerderjarigverklaring
verkry kan word deur elke minderjarige bo die ouderdom van 18 jaar wat kan aantoon
dat hy verantwoordelik genoeg en kundig genoeg is om sy eie sake te beheer nie. *Venia
aetatis* is soos in die gemenereg nie bedoel om 'n kategorie van verantwoordelike minderjariges te skep wat die Hof genader het teenoor ander wat die Hof nie genader het
nie. Dit is bedoel om in gevalle waar die handhawing van die normale maatstaf vir

meerderjarigheid (wat tot 'n mate arbitrêr vasgestel is op [402] 21-jarige ouderdom) onreg en onaanvaarbare benadeling en ongerief vir 'n bepaalde individu sou veroorsaak, voorkomende verligting te verleen ...

Die feit dat 'n minderjarige vryelik geëmansipeerd kan word, kan nie 'n ander benadering tot die onderhawige Wet regverdig nie. Emansipasie kan wel lei daartoe dat selfs 'n onbekwame minderjarige regtens gebonde staan aan sy optrede ... Emansipasie rus in die hande van die voog (*Grand Prix Motors WP (Pty) Ltd v Swart* 1976 (3) SA 221 (K) [43]) wat nie aan enige statutêre of ander oorwegings gebonde is by die veroorlowing daarvan al dan nie. Dit is 'n heeltemal selfstandige regsverskynsel wat nie in verband met die Wetgewende bedoeling by die onderhawige Wet gebring kan word nie.

Dit is na my mening onvoldoende om die nodige "wenslikheid" te skep dat daar 'n transaksie is wat applikant wil sluit maar as minderjarige nie kan sluit nie. Vir so 'n nie-herhalende probleem, is ander oplossings beskikbaar soos, bv, spesifieke toestemming deur die Hof. Indien die benadering anders was, sou 'n minderjarige wat onroerende eiendom wil verkoop maar nie die nodige feite kan aantoon om die Hof se sanksionering te verkry nie, 'n bevel van meerderjarigverklaring verkry en daarna ongehinderd voortgaan met 'n transaksie wat die Hof nie sou goedkeur nie. Hy sou trouens (volgens art 7) van die Wet "vir alle doeleindes" meerderjarig wees en gevolglik as meevallertjie selfs 'n huwelik kon sluit. Ek glo nie dat die Wetgewer beoog het dat 'n beperkte probleem met betrekking tot kontraktuele bevoegdheid die grondslag moet vorm waarom die minderjarige vryelik kontrakte kan sluit nie. In hierdie geval beoog die applikant 'n herverdelingsooreenkoms waarvolgens hy sy regte met betrekking tot onroerende eiendom laat vaar. Die applikant sou gevolglik die Hof se toestemming (vgl *Rabie v Die Meester van die Hooggeregshof en 'n Ander* 1960 (3) SA 848 (T) op 850H) moes verkry wat verleen sou word alleen nadat die Hof tevrede gestel is omtrent die beskerming van die minderjarige se eie belange. In die geval van 'n herverdelingsooreenkoms is andersins die toestemming van die Meester nodig.

Tydens argument is aangevoer dat die beoogde herverdelingsooreenkoms nie in die aansoek genoem is as die rede waarom meerderjarigverklaring wenslik is of aangevra word nie. As dit die geval is, berus die applikant se aansoek op die voormelde betreklik karige gegewens afkomstig van sy moeder met wie hy vir geruime tyd nie saamwoon nie weens sy militêre diensplig en opleiding te Johannesburg. Op die sterkste vir die applikant toon dit dat hy net so bevoeg is om sy sake te hanteer as 'n meerderjarige. Hierbo is reeds aangedui dat iets meer as dit nodig is voordat die Hof die applikant kan tegemoetkom. Die "belang van die aansoeker" waarna art 3 (*g*) van die onderhawige Wet verwys, moet nie gevind word in die blote verwydering van die beperking teen vrye optrede nie. Hierdie beperking mag die applikant dalk nie aanstaan nie en mag selfs van tyd tot tyd vir hom lastig wees. Elke minderjarige ondervind [403] hierdie lastighede tot meerdere of mindere mate. Regtens is die oorheersende logika egter dat dit in belang van die minderjarige beoog word dat die beskerming bestaan ondanks die amper noodwendige lastigheid wat dit uit subjektiewe oogpunt vir die minderjarige meebring. Die blote feit dat sulke lastighede inderdaad ondervind word, kan gevolglik nie voldoende basis wees daarvoor dat dit in die applikant se belang sal wees dat hy nie die beskerming geniet nie. Slegs indien die lastighede in sulke omstandighede in so 'n verband of so dikwels voorkom dat dit in die bepaalde omstandighede (en gesien die potensiële nadele wat so 'n stap mag meebring) oortuig dat die verwydering van die belemmernisse van soveel waarde is dat dit die belang van voortbestaan van die minderjarige se beskerming oorskadu, kan meerderjarigverklaring geregverdig word en sou dit "in belang van die aansoeker" wees soos in art 3 (*g*) van die Wet bedoel word ...

In die omstandighede word die aansoek afgewys.

Note

In *Ex parte Botes* and *Ex parte Smith* [41] the court considered a declaration of majority in terms of the Age of Majority Act 57 of 1972 to be *venia aetatis*. Spiro (247–248) is apparently of the same view. Van der Vyver and Joubert (140) indicate that the statutory provision is not the same as *venia aetatis*:

– *venia aetatis* is granted by the executive while the court issues a declaration of majority in terms of the act;

– *venia aetatis* does not confer full majority on the minor (he still cannot alienate or encumber immovable property unless the order expressly provides for this, and it is uncertain whether he can get married without parental consent) while a declaration of majority allows the minor to act as a major for all purposes;

– *venia aetatis* is revocable while a declaration of majority cannot be revoked.

When the Age of Majority Act was promulgated it was welcomed as an act introducing "certainty, uniformity and clarity" (D'Oliviera 1973 *SALJ* 68) and widening the scope of the discretion of the court by not setting the strict requirement of pressing necessity that was set in *Ex parte Akiki* 1925 OPD 211 (Boberg 383; Spiro 1973 *SALJ* 53). Although the act does not expressly prescribe the criteria the court should apply when exercising its discretion whether or not to declare a minor a major, the opinion is widely held that the requirement that the declaration of majority has to be necessary or desirable in the interest of the applicant, should form the basis for the exercise of the court's discretion (Boberg 383; Beck 1979 *De Rebus* 528; Spiro 1973 *SALJ* 53; Van Aswegen 1981 *Codicillus* 34). Unfortunately, the decisions in *Ex parte Botes* and *Ex parte Smith* brought little certainty, uniformity and clarity and did not move away from the strict approach advanced in *Ex parte Akiki*. Both decisions seem to require something more than mere necessity or desirability in the interest of the minor. (*Contra* Van Aswegen 1981 *Codicillus* 35 who submits that the judgment in *Ex parte Botes* might be interpreted in such a way that pressing necessity is not required.) The abovementioned decisions did not give effect to the intention of the legislature and consequently "the law has essentially remained the same" as before the coming into operation of the Age of Majority Act (Beck 1979 *De Rebus* 569).

Aantekening

In *Ex parte Botes* en *Ex parte Smith* [41] het die hof 'n meerderjarigverklaring ingevolge die Wet op die Meerderjarigheidsouderdom 57 van 1972 beskou as *venia aetatis*. Spiro (247–248) huldig skynbaar dieselfde mening. Van der Vyver en Joubert (140) dui aan dat die statutêre bepaling nie dieselfde is as *venia aetatis* nie:

– *venia aetatis* word deur die uitvoerende gesag toegestaan terwyl die hof 'n meerderjarigverklaring ingevolge die wet uitreik;

– *venia aetatis* verleen nie volle meerderjarigheid aan die minderjarige nie (hy kan nie onroerende eiendom vervreem of beswaar tensy die bevel dit uitdruklik magtig nie, en dit is onseker of hy sonder ouerlike toestemming mag trou) terwyl 'n meerderjarigverklaring die minderjarige in staat stel om vir alle doeleindes as 'n meerderjarige op te tree;

– *venia aetatis* kan herroep word terwyl 'n meerderjarigverklaring nie herroep kan word nie.

Toe die Wet op die Meerderjarigheidsouderdom gepromulgeer is, is dit verwelkom as 'n wet wat "certainty, uniformity and clarity" (D'Oliviera 1973 *SALJ* 68) sou bring en wat die omvang van die hof se diskresie sou verbreed deur nie die streng vereiste van dwingende noodsaaklikheid te stel wat in *Ex parte Akiki* 1925 OPA 211 vereis is nie (Boberg 383; Spiro 1973 *SALJ* 53). Alhoewel die wet nie uitdruklik die kriteria voorskryf wat die hof moet toepas in die uitoefening van sy diskresie wanneer hy moet besluit of hy 'n minderjarige meerderjarig gaan verklaar of nie, is die algemene standpunt dat die vereiste dat die meerderjarigverklaring in die belang van die applikant noodsaaklik of wenslik moet wees die basis vir die uitoefening van die hof se diskresie moet vorm (Boberg 383; Beck 1979 *De Rebus* 528; Spiro 1973 *SALJ* 53; Van Aswegen 1981 *Codicillus* 34). Ongelukkig het die beslissings in *Ex parte Botes* en *Ex parte Smith* weinig sekerheid, eenvormigheid en duidelikheid gebring en het hulle nie weg beweeg van die streng benadering wat in *Ex parte Akiki* voorgestaan is nie. Albei beslissings vereis skynbaar iets meer as bloot net dat die meerderjarigverklaring in belang van die applikant noodsaaklik of wenslik moet wees. (*Contra* Van Aswegen 1981 *Codicillus* 35 wat meen dat die beslissing in *Ex parte Botes* so geïnterpreteer kan word dat dwingende noodsaaklikheid nie vereis

The courts are loath to use the power to declare a minor a major, presumably because of the drastic nature of the declaration: the minor becomes a major "for all purposes". Barnard, Cronjé and Olivier (98) submit that the courts might be more willing to issue a declaration of majority if they were empowered to make a qualified or conditional order.

Ex parte Botes and *Ex parte Smith* were both decided in the Orange Free State Provincial Division and are therefore not binding on the other divisions of the supreme court. It is hoped that the other courts will not follow these two decisions when they are called upon to exercise their discretion to issue a declaration of majority.

word nie.) Hulle het nie gevolg gegee aan die bedoeling van die wetgewer nie en gevolglik het die regsposisie wesenlik dieselfde gebly as wat dit was voor die inwerkingtreding van die Wet op die Meerderjarigheidsouderdom (Beck 1979 *De Rebus* 569).

Die howe is waarskynlik huiwerig om die bevoegdheid te gebruik om 'n minderjarige meerderjarig te verklaar omdat die verklaring so 'n drastiese uitwerking het: die minderjarige word "vir alle doeleindes" 'n meerderjarige. Barnard, Cronjé en Olivier (102) spreek die mening uit dat die howe dalk meer geneë sal wees om 'n meerderjarigverklaring uit te reik indien hulle die bevoegdheid het om 'n gekwalifiseerde of voorwaardelike bevel uit te vaardig.

Ex parte Botes en *Ex parte Smith* is albei in die Oranje Vrystaatse Provinsiale Afdeling beslis en bind gevolglik nie die ander afdelings van die hooggeregshof nie. Hopelik sal die ander howe nie hierdie twee beslissings navolg wanneer hulle hulle diskresie om 'n meerderjarigverklaring uit te reik, moet uitoefen nie.

[41] EX PARTE SMITH

1980 2 SA 533 (O)

Declaration of a minor to be a major

On 31 January 1980 the applicant applied for a declaration of majority. His application was heard on 7 February 1980. He would have celebrated his twenty-first birthday on 22 July 1980. The applicant's father supported his application. The applicant had his own farm but lived with his parents on their farm which was only thirteen kilometres away from his own place. He had a good relationship with his father and often consulted him when he had to make important decisions. The court rejected the application.

Meerderjarigverklaring van 'n minderjarige

Op 31 Januarie 1980 het die applikant aansoek gedoen om meerderjarig verklaar te word. Sy aansoek is op 7 Februarie 1980 aangehoor. Hy sou op 22 Julie 1980 sy een en twintigste verjaardag vier. Die applikant se vader het sy aansoek gesteun. Die applikant het sy eie plaas gehad maar het saam met sy ouers op hulle plaas gewoon. Sy eie plaas was slegs dertien kilometer van sy ouers se plaas geleë. Hy het 'n goeie verhouding met sy vader gehad en het hom dikwels geraadpleeg wanneer hy belangrike besluite moes neem. Die hof het die aansoek van die hand gewys.

BETHUNE WN R: [534] Die verlening van *venia aetatis* deur die owerheid het sy oorsprong in die Romeinse Reg, waarskynlik as gevolg van die probleme wat soms ontstaan het omdat voljarigheid destyds eers op die ouderdom van 25 jaar bereik is. In die Oranje-

Vrystaat is die prosedure wat gevolg moes word gereël in OVS Wetboek, hoofstuk 89. In die ander provinsies was daar geen soortgelyke wetgewing nie, maar is *venia aetatis* tog in 'n paar gevalle deur die owerhede toegestaan. Daarbenewens het die Kaapse Howe ook in gepaste gevalle applikante uit voogdy ontslaan.

Hoofstuk 89 van die OVS Wetboek is deur Wet 57 van 1972 herroep. Dit bring nou mee dat daar eenvormigheid in al die provinsies van die Republiek en Suidwes-Afrika is vir die meerderjarigverklaring van minderjariges. Die besluit of die aansoek toegestaan behoort te word is nou in die hande van die Howe in plaas van die owerheid. Deur hierdie Wet is ons gemene reg in belangrike opsigte verander maar daar is nog steeds die vermoede dat die Wet, sover doenlik, so uitgelê moet word dat sy bepalings so min moontlik van die bestaande reg afwyk.

Art 6 van Hoofstuk 89 van die OVS Wetboek het bepaal:

"After inquiry the High Court or Circuit Court Judge, as the case may be, shall report to the State President, whether in the opinion of the said Court or Judge [535] it is desirable or not to grant *venia aetatis* to the applicant, and the State President shall grant or refuse *venia aetatis*, according to such report."

As die bepalings van art 4 van hoofstuk 89 vergelyk word met die bepalings van art 3 van Wet 57 van 1972 dan is dit duidelik dat die inligting waarop die Hof sy aanbeveling gemaak het in wese dieselfde is as die inligting waarkragtens die Howe nou 'n verklaring moet maak. Dit is so dat art 3 (*g*) spesifiek melding maak van

"of dit in die belang van die aansoeker noodsaaklik of wenslik is om die aansoek toe te staan"

terwyl die vorige wetgewing gemeld het

"whether in the opinion of the Court or Judge it is desirable or not to grant *venia aetatis* to the applicant".

Myns insiens behoort hierdie verskil in bewoording nie 'n wesenlike verskil in die Hof se benadering te maak nie. Uiteraard het die Hof onder die vorige wetgewing ook die belange van die minderjarige in gedagte gehad.

Waar 'n Volbank van hierdie Hof in *Ex parte Akiki* 1925 OPA 211 die vereiste van 'n bykomstige "pressing necessity" neergelê het is dit nie gedoen uit hoofde van die destydse wetgewing nie want die Wet het slegs melding gemaak van wenslikheid. Die herroeping van hoofstuk 89 raak gevolglik nie die algemene benadering van hierdie Hof nie. Na my mening het hierdie Hof in *Ex parte Botes* [40] tereg verwys na die maatstaf soos neergelê in *Ex parte Akiki*.

In der waarheid behoort die Hof na my mening onder die huidige Wetgewing nog meer omsigtig as voorheen te wees alvorens 'n aansoek toegestaan word aangesien die uitwerking van 'n bevel kragtens art 7 van die Wet wyer is as die verlof wat die owerheid voorheen toegestaan het. Dit is duidelik uit die uitspraak van REGTER BLAINE dat die Hof in *Akiki* se saak nie die verlening van *venia aetatis* sou aanbeveel het nie as dit sou meebring dat die applikant daardeur die reg sou verkry het om sy vaste eiendom te verkoop of te verpand.

Elke aansoek moet natuurlik op sy eie meriete beoordeel word. In die geval van *Baron Marius van Schalkwyk* [A318/76] was die applikant 'n dienspligtige gestasioneer te Pretoria terwyl sy weduwee moeder in die distrik van Bloemfontein woonagtig was. Hy het geen vaste eiendom besit nie. Dit is moontlik dat hierdie twee faktore die deurslag gegee het vir die toestaan van die aansoek. Aangesien dit 'n onbestrede aansoek was, was daar geen redes vir die bevel gegee nie.

In die onderhawige geval is 'n plaas ter waarde van R68 000 (volgens applikant se vader) alreeds in die naam van die applikant aangekoop vir 'n bedrag van R57 800. Alhoewel dit nie duidelik gestel is in die stukke nie, neem ek aan dat die applikant se vader se toestemming vir die koopkontrak verkry is. Indien nie, kan dit maklik verkry word want dit blyk duidelik uit die vader se eedsverklaring dat die koop hom welgeval het. In die stukke voor my is daar geen geswore waardasie van die plaas nie en ek weet ook nie welke waarde in die oordragsdokumente verstrek is nie.

Die applikant woon tans saam met sy ouers op die plaas "Vooruitzicht" en die aangekoopte plaas is minder as 13 kilometer daarvandaan geleë. Hy raadpleeg sy vader gereeld aangaande belangrike besluite en al die aanduidings is dat daar geen wrywing tussen vader en seun bestaan nie. Onder daardie omstandighede vind ek dit moeilik om te begryp [536] waarom sy vader nie vir die volgende vier en 'n half maande kan voortgaan om hom by te staan by die aangaan van kontrakte nie.

Die aansoekdoener meld dat hy "waarskynlik in die toekoms" sal oortrek na die aangekoopte plaas. Hierdie vae waarskynlikheid is onvoldoende rede om die aansoek toe te staan. In ieder geval is die twee plase so na aan mekaar geleë dat dit geen werklike probleme behoort te veroorsaak indien die seun sou verhuis nie.

'n Ander rede wat vir die aansoek gegee is, is dat indien die aansoek nie toegestaan sou word nie, 'n aansoek aan hierdie Hof gerig sal moet word vir bekragtiging van die aankoop van die plaas en verlof tot registrasie van 'n verband oor die plaas vir die volle koopprys daarvan. Volgens die applikant sal die koste van laasgenoemde aansoek ongeveer R750 bedra teenoor die koste van ongeveer R300 van hierdie aansoek. Geen verduideliking word verstrek aangaande die verskil van R450 nie. Dit mag wees omdat die Hof in die eersgenoemde geval gewoonlik aandring op 'n geswore waardasie van die eiendom en soms aandring op 'n verslag van 'n *curator ad litem*. Hoe dit ookal sy, kan ek nie insien dat waar 'n Hof by 'n aansoek om 'n meerderjarigverklaring bewus is dat een van die gevolge van sodanige aansoek sal wees dat die minderjarige homself onmiddellik gaan verbind as verbandgewer vir 'n aansienlike bedrag, die Hof tevrede sal wees met minder inligting as wat hy andersins sou verlang het by 'n aansoek om verlof om 'n verband te registreer nie.

In ieder geval is, na my mening, die moontlike besparing van 'n paar honderd rand nie 'n rede om 'n aansoek vir 'n meerderjarigheidsbevel te regverdig indien 'n minder ingrypende prosedure tot die applikant se beskikking is nie.

Onder die omstandighede word die aansoek van die hand gewys.

Note

See the note on *Ex parte Botes* [40].

Aantekening

Sien die aantekening by *Ex parte Botes* [40].

[42] DICKENS V DALEY

1956 2 SA 11 (N)

Emancipation of a minor

The respondent, a minor, entered into a contract of lease with the appellant. The respondent drew a cheque in favour of the appellant in pursuance of the contract, but

Emansipasie van 'n minderjarige

Die respondent, 'n minderjarige, het 'n huurkontrak met die appellant aangegaan. Die respondent het op grond van die kontrak 'n tjek ten gunste van die appellant getrek maar

the cheque was dishonoured on presentation as payment had been stopped by the respondent. The appellant subsequently sued the respondent for payment in the magistrate's court. In a special plea the respondent admitted to drawing the cheque but averred that he was a minor and, as such, had no *locus standi in iudicio* or capacity to contract and that the appellant's claim was, accordingly, unenforceable. The appellant contended that the respondent was emancipated and was therefore liable on the cheque. He relied on the fact that the respondent had been living with his mother and stepfather for the past twelve years; that he had contributed to his board and lodging; that he had been working as a clerk for four years; that his father had not exercised any control over him (except for the drawing up of an affidavit which the minor required to obtain a passport) and that he had administered his own bank account. The magistrate ordered absolution from the instance. The appellant appealed against this decision and the appeal was allowed.

die tjek is gedishonoreer toe dit vir betaling aangebied is aangesien die respondent betaling daarvan gestop het. Die appellant het die respondent toe vir betaling in die landdroshof gedagvaar. In 'n spesiale pleit het die respondent erken dat hy die tjek getrek het maar hy het aangevoer dat hy 'n minderjarige was en as sodanig nie *locus standi in iudicio* of die bevoegdheid gehad het om te kontrakteer nie en dat die appellant se eis gevolglik onafdwingbaar was. Die appellant het beweer dat die respondent geëmansipeer was en gevolglik op grond van die tjek aanspreeklik was. Hy het gesteun op die feit dat die respondent vir die afgelope twaalf jaar by sy moeder en stiefvader gewoon het; dat hy tot sy losies bygedra het; dat hy vir vier jaar as 'n klerk werksaam was; dat sy vader geen beheer oor hom uitgeoefen het nie (behalwe vir die aflê van 'n beëdigde verklaring wat die minderjarige nodig gehad het om 'n paspoort te bekom) en dat hy sy eie bankrekening gehad het. Die landdros het absolusie van die instansie beveel. Die appellant het teen hierdie beslissing geappelleer en die appèl het geslaag.

SELKE J: [13] I . . . agree that various of the common law authorities are not clear about the precise effect of tacit emancipation, and that some of the cases in our own Courts appear to be based on, or to expound, views which make the cases at first sight difficult to reconcile.

The result is that the subject of emancipation and its effects seems, on the face of it, rather formidable . . .

Such consideration as I have been able to give to the subject inclines me to suppose that some, at least, of the seeming differences of view – anyhow in the decided cases – result from the fact that the word "emancipation" has not always been given precisely the same meaning – that at times it has been regarded as indicating the complete release of a minor from *potestas* and, at other times, no more than the idea of a father's or guardian's consenting to, or acquiescing in, the minor's or ward's engaging in some particular occupation, business or enterprise without assistance. If this is so, then to that extent, the confusion may rightly be attributed to terminological inexactitude.

In the present instance, it seems to me clear that the respondent's father has either tacitly released the respondent altogether from *potestas*, or, without releasing him completely, has allowed the respondent to engage unassisted in the ordinary activities of every-day life – by which I mean to work as an employee in a business, to receive and dispose of his own salary, to run a banking account, and draw cheques – all free of paternal control and supervision. In these circumstances, notwithstanding that the respondent boards voluntarily in his mother's house – for which board, however, he pays – I think it is quite clear that the respondent's father has abrogated any claim to have the respondent still in his *potestas* so far as concerns the issue by respondent of cheques drawn by him on his own banking account. For these reasons, it seems to me that the magistrate was wrong in upholding the special plea . . .

BROKENSHA J: [14] The magistrate's conclusion as to the legal position on the facts was set out by him as follows:

> "In the case of *Ambaker v African Meat Co*, 1927 CPD 326, it was held that a minor who traded on his own behalf with the consent of his parents became tacitly emancipated, but was only emancipated to the extent of contracts in connection with that particular business and if a minor is allowed by his parents to engage in business on behalf of another he may be tacitly emancipated but merely so as to bind himself as far as contracts between himself and his principals for whom he trades are concerned.

> See also Wessels on *Contracts*, Vol 1, p 262. At para. 827 *Wessels* says:–

> 'Whether a minor has or has not been emancipated is a question of fact to be decided from the circumstances of each case. Residence away from his parents is not essential.'

> It is possible that the facts before the court coupled with an assertion by defendant that he was emancipated would be sufficient proof of his total emancipation. Without such an assertion it was held that the facts presented were not proof of defendant's total emancipation. For these reasons absolution from the instance was granted."

Appellant filed lengthy grounds of appeal, but the main submission made by Mr *Muller*, who appeared for him before us, was the ground that the magistrate should have held respondent was tacitly emancipated in all respects save where the law in any event requires a person under the age of twenty-one years to be assisted by his guardian or the Court . . .

[BROKENSHA J analysed the facts and proceeded:]

[15] The subject of emancipation has been considered by the writers on Roman-Dutch Law, and in many decisions in the South African Courts. Wille, in the *Principles of South African Law*, at p 85 (3rd ed), says this:

> "The chief doubt arises as to whether the contractual capacity of an emancipated minor is absolute or relative. Many authorities say that his legal capacity is relative only, and not absolute, that is, he acquires legal capacity only as regards transactions arising out of the business in question; this means that he can bind himself on contracts made by himself with persons in connection with his business, and that he can sue and be sued on such contracts, but that he cannot bind himself on contracts not connected with the business. Other authorities, however, are to the effect that, apart from the cases mentioned above, an emancipated minor acquires full legal capacity." . . .

In an interesting survey on the subject by Dr Hahlo in the *South African Law Journal*, 1943, at p 289, the learned writer says at p 298:

> "A tacitly emancipated minor becomes altogether free from the power of his parents, save that he still requires their consent if he desires to get married. And he acquires full legal capacity, provided that he may not be appointed as a guardian to others and that he may not alienate or pledge immovables without leave of the Court."

Whether a minor has been emancipated or not is a question of fact depending upon the circumstances of each case. Some of the facts to be considered, according to the authorities, are the relation between the minor and his guardian; whether or not he is living with them; the nature of his occupation and the length of time for which the occupation has been carried on.

In the case of *Dama v Bera*, 1910 TPD 928, DE VILLIERS, JP, with whom WESSELS, J, concurred, said at p 929:

> "Emancipation, after all, is a question of fact, which must be decided by the Court having regard to the circumstances of each particular case. Undoubtedly if the facts are that the minor lives away from his parent, and carries on business apart from them, the presumption is very strong that he is emancipated."

In that case the magistrate found the respondent had been emancipated [16] and gave judgment in her favour. An appeal was dismissed. The facts were that the respondent was an Indian girl close upon twenty-one years old. She had been earning her own livelihood for four or five years. She resided with her mother and step-father and paid them portion of her earning for board and lodging.

In the case of *Ambaker v African Meat Co*, which was relied upon by the magistrate, the Court held that the plaintiff had not discharged the *onus* of proving that the defendant had been tacitly emancipated.

In the case of *Van Rooyen v Werner*, 9 SC 425, DE VILLIERS, CJ, dealt with the question of the father's right to administer the property of his minor children, and at p 429 he said:

> "He" (that is the father) "has the right to administer their property, but he may lose that right by allowing them to live apart from him, and openly to exercise some trade or calling. Until they have thus been virtually emancipated, or until they become majors, either by marriage, or by attaining the age of twenty-one years, he has the management of their property, except such property as has been left to them by others and placed under a different administration."

For the respondent, Mr *Milne* relied upon the fact that the respondent was living with his mother and step-father, and that he did not run a business on his own, but was in employment as a clerk, as factors showing that the respondent has not been emancipated . . .

It seems to me quite clear from the evidence that respondent's father, who was his guardian, had abandoned his right of control over the respondent in regard to the latter's mode of life and such operations as he undertook to maintain himself. When he gave his consent to his son obtaining a passport, he exercised an obligation upon him as father and guardian of the respondent, but did not raise any objection to his son proceeding overseas with his employer for business purposes.

It seems to me, the question whether the respondent is emancipated or not is not dependent, as the magistrate seems to hold, upon the fact whether there has been an assertion by the respondent himself. The question is whether, on the facts and circumstances, the respondent's father has emancipated him, and, in my view, on the facts in this case, the answer must be that the father has done so.

Under modern conditions, I think it would be an unjustified restriction in the interpretation of the law to say that a minor of over twenty years of age who, so far as his father is concerned, has complete freedom of action with regard to his mode of living and earning his livelihood, and operates a banking account, is not to be held liable on cheques issued by him, unless such cheques be given in regard to the business which he may be carrying on.

I cannot see that there should be any difference in the contractual status of the respondent, whether he were carrying on a business on his own account or living and working as the respondent does. It seems to me it is too narrow an interpretation to say that emancipation only applies in regard to the transactions of such business as the minor may be carrying on. If that is the position, then a minor carrying on a business on his own account would be entitled to enter into contracts, apparently of any magnitude, in regard to that business and be liable [17] thereon, but if he entered into a contract not connected with the business, for instance, the purchase of furniture for a bachelor flat, then he would be entitled to repudiate liability on the ground that he was a minor.

For these reasons I come to the conclusion that the magistrate erred in granting absolution from the instance. In my view, the appeal should be allowed . . .

Note

In terms of the common law a father, as natural guardian, could emancipate his legitimate child. Unless guardianship had been awarded to her, a mother could not emancipate her legitimate child (see for example *Grand Prix Motors WP (Pty) Ltd v Swart* [43]). The Guardianship Act 192 of 1993 does not expressly provide that a mother now has the capacity to emancipate her legitimate child. However, because section 1(1) of the act provides that a woman is the guardian of her legitimate child and that such guardianship is "equal to that which a father has under the common law in respect of his minor children", it seems that the mother may indeed now grant emancipation. On the equal guardianship exercised by parents of a legitimate child, see also the note on *Calitz v Calitz* [19].

Whether a minor has been emancipated or not is a question of fact depending upon the circumstances of each case (*Dama v Bera* 1910 TPD 928; *Venter v De Burghersdorp Stores* 1915 CPD 252). Factors which will be taken into account include the fact that the minor is living apart from his parents; that he is carrying on a trade or calling for his own account and the number of years before the minor reaches majority (*Le Grange v Mostert* (1909) 26 SC 321; *Dama v Bera; Venter v De Burghersdorp Stores; Pleat v Van Staden* [29]; *Ahmed v Coovadia* 1944 TPD 364). In *Venter v De Burghersdorp Stores* it was held that a minor's physical appearance and the opinions formed as to his age on the basis of his appearance cannot be taken into account to determine whether he has been emancipated. The court held that a minor who entered into a few transactions, owned a few sheep which were kept with his father's flocks, owned a horse, saddle and bridle, had twice bought a bicycle and was occasionally paid for small tasks he did for his father, was not emancipated.

Emancipation cannot take place without the consent of the minor's guardian (*Grand Prix Motors*

Aantekening

Ingevolge die gemenereg kon 'n vader as natuurlike voog sy binne-egtelike kind emansipeer. Tensy voogdy aan die moeder toegeken is, kon sy dit nie doen nie (sien byvoorbeeld *Grand Prix Motors WP (Pty) Ltd v Swart* [43]). Die Wet op Voogdy 192 van 1993 bepaal nie uitdruklik of 'n moeder nou die bevoegdheid het om haar binne-egtelike kind te emansipeer nie. Aangesien artikel 1(1) van die wet bepaal dat 'n vrou voog is van haar binne-egtelike kind en sodanige voogdy "gelykwaardig [is] aan dié wat 'n vader kragtens die gemene reg ten aansien van sy minderjarige kinders het", skyn dit egter asof die moeder wel nou emansipasie kan verleen. Oor die gelyke voogdy wat die ouers van 'n binne-egtelike kind het, sien ook die aantekening by *Calitz v Calitz* [19].

Of 'n minderjarige geëmansipeer is al dan nie, is 'n feitlike vraag wat beantwoord moet word na aanleiding van die omstandighede van elke saak (*Dama v Bera* 1910 TPA 928; *Venter v De Burghersdorp Stores* 1915 KPA 252). Faktore wat in aanmerking geneem word, sluit in dat die minderjarige nie by sy ouers woon nie; dat hy sy eie besigheid bedryf of beroep beoefen en hoeveel jaar nog moet verloop voordat hy meerderjarig word (*Le Grange v Mostert* (1909) 26 SC 321; *Dama v Bera; Venter v De Burghersdorp Stores; Pleat v Van Staden* [29]; *Ahmed v Coovadia* 1944 TPA 364). In *Venter v De Burghersdorp Stores* is beslis dat die minderjarige se voorkoms en menings wat op grond daarvan oor sy ouderdom gevorm word, nie in ag geneem kan word om te bepaal of hy geëmansipeer is nie. Die hof het beslis dat 'n minderjarige wat 'n paar transaksies aangegaan het, 'n paar skape besit het wat saam met sy pa se kuddes geloop het, 'n perd, saal en toom besit het, twee maal 'n fiets gekoop het en af en toe betaal is vir klein takies wat hy vir sy pa verrig het, nie geëmansipeer was nie.

Emansipasie kan nie sonder die toestemming van

WP (Pty) Ltd v Swart [43]; Watson v Koen h/a BMO 1994 2 SA 489 (O)). Abandonment of the minor by his guardian cannot constitute such consent (Grand Prix Motors WP (Pty) Ltd v Swart).

As pointed out by SELKE J in Dickens v Daley, there is uncertainty as to the exact effect of emancipation (13). The Roman-Dutch writers described emancipation as a means of terminating minority (see Boberg 383–388; Spiro 249–250; Van der Vyver and Joubert 151–153; Van der Vyver 1979 THRHR 309 in this regard) but it appears as if emancipation, in the form in which it appears today, is only a type of general consent which enables the minor to enter into certain legal transactions.

Hahlo (1956 Annual Survey 93) was of the opinion that Dickens v Daley showed that "the question in each case ought to be what degree of legal independence the parent or guardian conferred upon the minor. If the facts show that he gave him authority for a certain business or occupation only, the minor's legal capacity will be accordingly restricted. If, on the other hand, the facts show that the parent or guardian intended, in the words of BROKENSHA J, to give the minor 'complete freedom of action with regard to his mode of living and earning his livelihood', the minor will be able to enter unassisted into all kinds of legal transactions (saving marriage and alienation and hypothecation of immovable property), and not only into transactions connected with the business or occupation he happens to be carrying on." Barnard, Cronjé and Olivier (100) and Van der Vyver and Joubert (155) share Hahlo's point of view. (See also Watson v Koen h/a BMO where it was accepted – without deciding it – that there can be general and wide emancipation relating to all the contracts entered into by a minor.)

Palmer (1968 SALJ 24) criticised the decision in Dickens v Daley as failing to distinguish between the effects of discarding parental authority and the granting of authority to the minor to act independently, thereby enabling a minor whose guardian shows a total lack of concern for the minor's welfare to enhance his legal status. (For criticism on Palmer's approach, see Boberg 400.)

D'Oliviera (1973 SALJ 57) correctly points out that the court in Dickens v Daley was not con-

die minderjarige se voog plaasvind nie (Grand Prix Motors WP (Pty) Ltd v Swart [43]; Watson v Koen h/a BMO 1994 2 SA 489 (O)). Om die minderjarige eenvoudig aan homself oor te laat, kan nie sodanige toestemming daarstel nie (Grand Prix Motors WP (Pty) Ltd v Swart).

SELKE R het tereg in Dickens v Daley daarop gewys dat daar onsekerheid oor die presiese effek van emansipasie bestaan (13). Die Romeins-Hollandse skrywers het emansipasie beskryf as 'n wyse van beëindiging van minderjarigheid (sien in hierdie verband Boberg 383–388; Spiro 249–250; Van der Vyver en Joubert 151–153; Van der Vyver 1979 THRHR 309) maar dit lyk asof emansipasie, in die vorm waarin dit vandag voorkom, 'n soort algemene toestemming is wat die minderjarige in staat stel om sekere regshandelinge aan te gaan.

Hahlo (1956 Annual Survey 93) was van mening dat Dickens v Daley aangedui het dat "the question in each case ought to be what degree of legal independence the parent or guardian conferred upon the minor. If the facts show that he gave him authority for a certain business or occupation only, the minor's legal capacity will be accordingly restricted. If, on the other hand, the facts show that the parent or guardian intended, in the words of BROKENSHA J, to give the minor 'complete freedom of action with regard to his mode of living and earning his livelihood', the minor will be able to enter unassisted into all kinds of legal transactions (saving marriage and alienation and hypothecation of immovable property), and not only into transactions connected with the business or occupation he happens to be carrying on." Barnard, Cronjé en Olivier (104) en Van der Vyver en Joubert (155) deel Hahlo se standpunt. (Sien ook Watson v Koen h/a BMO waar aanvaar is – sonder om dit te beslis – dat daar algemene en wye emansipasie kan bestaan met betrekking tot alle kontrakte wat 'n minderjarige aangaan.)

Palmer (1968 SALJ 24) kritiseer die uitspraak in Dickens v Daley omdat dit volgens hom nie 'n onderskeid tref tussen die gevolge wat afstanddoening van ouerlike gesag het en die verlening van die bevoegdheid aan die minderjarige om onafhanklik op te tree nie. Sodoende word 'n

cerned with absolute reaching of majority but only with the capacity of the minor to enter into contracts. He further points out that there is a difference between holding that emancipation confers capacity to contract and holding that it releases the minor from parental authority.

minderjarige wie se voog 'n totale gebrek aan belangstelling in die minderjarige se welvaart toon, in staat gestel om sy regstatus te verhoog. (Vir kritiek op Palmer se benadering sien Boberg 400.)

D'Oliviera (1973 *SALJ* 57) wys tereg daarop dat die hof in *Dickens v Daley* nie met absolute verkryging van meerderjarigheid gemoeid was nie maar slegs met die bevoegdheid van 'n minderjarige om kontrakte te sluit, en dat daar 'n verskil bestaan tussen emansipasie wat kontrakteerbevoegdheid toeken en emansipasie wat die minderjarige van ouerlike gesag vrystel.

[43]   GRAND PRIX MOTORS WP (PTY) LTD V SWART

1976 3 SA 221 (K)

Emancipation of a minor

On 28 September 1973, when she was eighteen years of age, the plaintiff entered into a hire purchase agreement for the purchase of a motor car from defendant. When she had paid an amount of R571,30 in terms of the contract, she returned the motor car and claimed repayment of the R571,30 she had already paid for the car. She based her claim on the fact that she was a minor at the time when she entered into the contract and that she was therefore not bound by it. The defendant averred that the plaintiff was bound as she was emancipated at the time when she entered into the contract and could, therefore, have validly concluded the contract without assistance from her guardian. The plaintiff's father had left his family in 1968 and neither the plaintiff nor her mother had any idea what became of him. In 1972 the plaintiff's mother obtained a divorce and custody of the minor children was awarded to her. In 1973, after finishing school, the plaintiff started working as a probation nurse and she lived in the nurses' home. She used her salary as she thought fit and her mother ex-

Emansipasie van 'n minderjarige

Op 28 September 1973, toe sy agtien jaar oud was, het die eiseres 'n huurkoopooreenkoms gesluit ingevolge waarvan sy 'n motor van die verweerder gekoop het. Toe sy 'n bedrag van R571,30 ingevolge die kontrak betaal het, het sy die motor teruggegee en terugbetaling geëis van die R571,30 wat sy reeds vir die motor betaal het. Sy het haar eis gebaseer op die feit dat sy 'n minderjarige was toe sy die kontrak gesluit het en dat sy dus nie aan die kontrak gebonde was nie. Die verweerder het beweer dat die eiseres wel gebonde was aangesien sy geëmansipeer was toe sy die kontrak gesluit het en dat sy gevolglik geldig kon kontrakteer sonder die bystand van haar voog. Die eiseres se vader het sy gesin in 1968 verlaat en nóg die eiseres nóg haar moeder het geweet wat van hom geword het. In 1972 het die eiseres se moeder 'n egskeiding verkry en bewaring van die minderjarige kinders is aan haar toegeken. In 1973, nadat sy haar skoolloopbaan voltooi het, het die eiseres as 'n leerlingverpleegster begin werk. Sy het in die verpleegsterstehuis gewoon. Sy het haar salaris na goeddunke

ercised no control over her finances or her actions. The plaintiff's mother only found out about the hire purchase agreement five weeks after the plaintiff had entered into the agreement. She informed her daughter that she did not approve of the transaction. When she was given forms to fill in regarding the hire purchase agreement, she refused to complete them. She told the plaintiff to return the car to the defendant. In the court *a quo* the magistrate found that these facts did not constitute emancipation and the court accordingly decided in favour of the plaintiff. The defendant appealed against this decision but the decision was confirmed on appeal.

gebruik en haar moeder het geen beheer oor haar finansies of optrede uitgeoefen nie. Die eiseres se moeder het eers vyf weke nadat die eiseres die huurkoopooreenkoms aangegaan het daarvan uitgevind. Sy het die eiseres meegedeel dat sy nie ten gunste van die transaksie was nie. Toe sy vorms gegee is om in te vul in verband met die koop het sy geweier om dit te doen. Sy het die eiseres aangesê om die motor aan die verweerder terug te besorg. In die hof *a quo* het die landdros bevind dat hierdie feite nie emansipasie daargestel het nie en die hof het gevolglik ten gunste van die eiseres beslis. Die verweerder het appèl aangeteken teen hierdie beslissing maar die appèl het misluk.

GROSSKOPF WN R: [222] Die vraag voor ons is . . . of die landdros behoort te bevind het dat eiseres geëmansipeer was en daardeur die bevoegdheid gehad het om die kontrak aan te gaan. Die bewyslas om emansipasie te bewys, het op die verweerder gerus. Sien *Cohen v Sytner*, (1897) 14 SC 13 te bl 15–16; *Ambaker v African Meat Co*, 1927 KPA 326 te bl 327, en *Ochberg v Ochberg's Estate*, 1941 KPA 15 te bl 36 . . .

[GROSSKOPF WN R het die feite van die saak uiteengesit en vervolg:]

[223] Die vraag is dan of eiseres se omstandighede, soos hierbo uiteengesit, sodanig was dat sy onder ouerlike toestemming die gewraakte kontrak kon sluit. Emansipasie van minderjariges is 'n onderwerp waaroor daar heelwat in ons reg geskryf is . . . Dat dit 'n gewilde onderwerp vir akademiese bespreking is, is maklik verstaanbaar. Die Appèlhof het hom nog nie hieroor uitgespreek nie, terwyl die gemeenregtelike bronne en Hofbeslissings neig om onduidelik of teenstrydig te wees op heelparty fundamentele aspekte.

In die onderhawige geval het die landdros hom beroep op De Wet en Yeats, *Kontraktereg en Handelsreg*, 3de uitg, bl 55, en die beslissings in *Ambaker* se saak en *Ochberg* se saak, albei *supra*, vir die stelling dat emansipasie hedendaags erken word slegs waar 'n minderjarige selfstandig handel dryf, en dan ook slegs met betrekking tot ooreenkomste wat in verband staan met sy besigheid. Indien hierdie 'n korrekte stelling van die regsposisie is, *cadit quaestio* [die vraag verval] – eiseres het nie handel gedryf nie, en in elk geval het die kontrak wat sy geteken het geen verband gehad met haar werk as leerlingverpleegster nie.

In sy betoog het mnr *Farlam* [namens die appellant] die juistheid van die landdros se benadering aangeveg. Daarbenewens het hy betoog dat niks in ons pad staan om van *Ambaker* en *Ochberg* se sake, albei *supra* – elk 'n beslissing van twee Regters van hierdie Afdeling – af te wyk nie, aangesien die betrokke passasies blote *obiter dicta* is.

Myns insiens is dit nie nodig om op hierdie betoog in te gaan nie, aangesien daar 'n meer basiese rede is waarom daar nie emansipasie in die huidige geval kan wees nie. In sommige gewysdes en bronne (sien bv *Dickens v Daley*, 1956 (2) SA 11 (N) te bl 13 [42]; *Boberg*, [1975 SALJ* 183] te bl 193 ev, word die mening uitgespreek dat daar twee verskillende regsinstellings is wat albei deur die woord "emansipasie" aangedui word, nl, eerstens, [224] volkome ontslag uit die ouerlike mag, en tweedens, algemene toestemming deur die voog tot 'n bepaalde klas transaksies. In watter van hierdie twee vorms emansipasie ook al mag voorkom is dit egter myns insiens duidelik dat dit net kan ontstaan uit die optrede van die minderjarige se natuurlike voog. (Oor die posisie waar daar nie 'n natuurlike voog is nie, hoef ek my nie uit te laat nie, aangesien dit nie hier ontstaan nie. Sien egter die bespreking in *Boberg, op cit* te bl 201–2). Dit is die natuurlike voog wat deur sy toestemming, uitdruklik of stilswyend, aan die minderjarige die bevoegdheid verleen om op sy eie op te tree. Sien *Voet*, 1.7.12; *Venter v De Burghersdorp Stores*, 1915 KPA 252 te bl 256; *Ambaker* se saak, *supra* te bl 327; I van Zyl Steyn, " 'n Paar Aspekte van die Emansipasie van Minderjariges", (1927) 44 *SALJ* 313 te bl 323; PJ Conradie, "Iets oor Beperkte Handligting", (1946) 63 *SALJ* 25 te bl 33–4; *Boberg, op cit* te bl 196. Waar, soos hier, die minderjarige se ouers geskei is en toesig aan die moeder verleen is, bly die vader die natuurlike voog van die minderjarige en is die moeder nie bevoeg om die minderjarige op haar eie by te staan by die verrigting van regshandelinge nie. Sien *Edelstein v Edelstein, NO and Others*, 1952 (3) SA 1 (AA) te bl 10 [33]. Dat in so 'n situasie die vader se optrede en nie dié van die toesighebbende moeder nie, ter sake is om te bepaal of emansipasie plaasgevind het, volg eintlik vanself. Dit word ook gestaaf deur *Dickens v Daley* [42], *supra*, te bl 13E–G en 16D–G.

In die onderhawige geval het eiserés se vader luidens die getuienis in alle waarskynlikheid geen kennis van haar omstandighede gehad nie. Uiteraard kan daar dus geen basis wees om te bevind dat hy toestemming, uitdruklik of stilswyend, tot eiseres se onafhanklike leefwyse verleen het nie. Sy verlating van sy gesin toe eiseres 13 jaar oud was, en sy verdwyning 'n jaar later, kan na my mening klaarblyklik nie vertolk word as dade van handligting nie. Mnr *Farlam* het betoog dat dit egter wel vertolk kan word as 'n delegasie aan eiseres se moeder van die reg om toe te stem tot eiseres se emansipasie. Myns insiens is die blote feite van verlating en verdwyning, sonder enige inligting omtrent die omstandighede waaronder dit geskied het, nie genoeg om die afleiding te maak waarvoor mnr *Farlam* betoog nie. Daarbenewens sou dit my verbaas as so 'n delegasie regsgeldig kan plaasvind – 'n vraag waaroor dit egter nie nodig is om 'n mening uit te spreek nie, aangesien 'n gepoogde delegasie na my mening nie bewys is nie.

Daar mag betoog word dat die resultaat wat aldus bereik word, tot onbevredigende resultate kan lei waar 'n minderjarige se vader kontak met hom of haar verloor het – iets wat hedendaags meer dikwels voorkom. Daar moet egter in gedagte gehou word dat dit die beskerming van minderjariges teen hul eie onrypheid is wat onderliggend is aan die reël dat hul kontrakte onafdwingbaar is (sien *Edelstein* se saak [33], *supra* te bl 15). Die vader se afwesigheid verminder nie die minderjarige se behoefte aan beskerming nie. Wanneer die vader se afwesigheid vir die minderjarige probleme skep vanweë sy eie gebrek aan handelingsbevoegdheid is daar verskillende maniere waarop sodanige probleme te bowe gekom kan word. So, bv, kan die moeder ingevolge art 5 van die Wet op Huweliksaangeleenthede, 37 van 1953, aansoek doen om uitsluitlike voogdy oor die minderjarige, of kan die minderjarige self in 'n gepaste geval aansoek doen ingevolge die Wet op die Meerderjarigheidsouderdom, 57 van 1972, om 'n bevel waardeur hy meerderjarig verklaar word.

Dit is wel waar dat daar op hierdie gebied van die reg omstandighede mag [225] ontstaan waar die beskerming van minderjariges nie allesoorheersend is nie en die regte van onskuldige derdes ook beskerming mag verdien, bv waar die skyn verwek word dat die minderjarige meerderjarig is, of dat hy geëmansipeer is, of dat sy moeder, wat toestemming tot 'n kontrak verleen het, sy natuurlike voog is. Wat die regsposisie is by 'n botsing tussen die behoefte aan beskerming van, aan die een kant, 'n minderjarige, en, aan die ander kant, 'n onskuldige persoon wat te goeder trou onder die omstandighede hierbo genoem met die minderjarige gekontrakteer het, hoef nie hier oorweeg te word nie. Sulke omstandighede bestaan nie in hierdie geval nie. Verweerder was onder geen misverstand oor die feit dat die gepoogde kontrak gesluit was met 'n agtienjarige leerlingverpleegster nie – hierdie inligting verskyn op die getekende kredietinformasie-vorm . . .

Daar is geen aanduiding dat verweerder vir eiseres as geëmansipeer beskou het nie, of enige rede gehad het om haar as sodanig te beskou nie. Eiseres se moeder het inderdaad nie toestemming tot die kontrak gegee nie – 'n moontlike wanindruk dat sy eiseres se voogdesse was, is dus nie ter sake nie.

Weens die voorgaande meen ek dat die landdros se beslissing korrek was . . .

Om die redes hierbo uiteengesit word die appèl van die hand gewys . . .

FAGAN WN R het saamgestem.

Note

See the note on *Dickens v Daley* [42].

Aantekening

Sien die aantekening by *Dickens v Daley* [42].

[44]   SESING v MINISTER OF POLICE

1978 4 SA 742 (W)

Emancipation

The plaintiff sued the Minister of Police and a policeman (the defendants) for damages for bodily injuries suffered in a shooting incident on 21 December 1974. The defendants raised the special plea that the plaintiff was a minor at the time when the summons was issued and that he therefore did not have *locus standi in iudicio* to sue. The plaintiff averred that he was tacitly emancipated prior to the summons being issued. The court had to decide, *inter alia*, whether the plaintiff was emancipated, and if so, to what extent. The court found that the plaintiff was not emancipated but gave him leave to argue some other basis upon which the action could be preserved.

Emansipasie

Die eiser het die Minister van Polisie en 'n polisieman (die verweerders) gedagvaar vir skadevergoeding vir liggaamlike beserings wat hy opgedoen het in 'n skietvoorval op 21 Desember 1974. Die verweerders het die spesiale pleit geopper dat die eiser 'n minderjarige was op die stadium toe die dagvaarding uitgereik is en dat hy dus geen *locus standi in iudicio* gehad het om aksie in te stel nie. Die eiser het beweer dat hy stilswyend geëmansipeer is voordat die dagvaarding uitgereik is. Die hof moes onder andere beslis of die eiser geëmansipeer was, en indien wel, wat die omvang van sy emansipasie was. Die hof het bevind dat die eiser nie geëmansipeer was nie maar het aan hom toestemming verleen om die een of ander grond aan te dui ingevolge waarvan die aksie voortgesit kon word.

MARGO J: [744] The . . . inquiry is whether the plaintiff was emancipated prior to [745] 18 April 1975, that is the date of institution of the action, and, if so, whether that emancipation was sufficiently wide in extent to cover the institution of this action. The *onus* of proving tacit emancipation rests upon the person who alleges it. *Ochberg v Ochberg's Estate and Another* 1941 CPD 15 *per* SUTTON J at 36. The relevant facts here are that the plaintiff was born out of wedlock. There is evidence that his mother has become an alcoholic. He went to work in 1972 after leaving school and his evidence amounts to this, that since then he alone has had control of his employment and his earnings. He says that he chose to live with his grandmother until her death. However, his uncle, Mr Makoro, says that he lived with his father. I find nothing improbable in the plaintiff's evidence on this aspect of the case. In the Black townships of Johannesburg, where the plaintiff was born, where he grew up and where he now lives, many a young man goes to work and becomes, to a greater or lesser extent, independent of parental control and influence at a relatively early age. The demands of schooling were small in the plaintiff's case. He gave up at the standard 3 level. His parents parted long ago, according to Mr Makoro, and there was no sustained family abode. When he was tried in 1971, his brother assisted him. At the later trial his father was present. His father gave the consent to treatment when he was admitted to hospital on the first occasion after he had been shot. That may have been because he was seriously injured and unable to attend to the matter himself. The fact that one's next-of-kin signs the consent to treatment in such circumstances is not necessarily inconsistent with having been emancipated. In this regard it is to be noted that, on the occasion of the second admission to hospital on 18 April 1975, the plaintiff furnished the further particulars himself. He gave his father as next-of-kin, but named himself as "the breadwinner or person responsible for the support of the patient", and reflected "the total family income" as being his own income. On all the evidence I consider the plaintiff has shown that in his employment and the enjoyment of his earnings he is free from any control by his parents.

However, in the sad tale of the plaintiff's life, there is no evidence of tacit emancipation by some action or conduct on the part of his father or his mother. His mother is his natural guardian by reason of his birth out of wedlock. See *Dhanabakium v Subramanian and Another* 1943 AD 160 *per* TINDALL JA at 166. The indications are that his mother neglected her responsibilities, probably because of her own incapacity, and thus the plaintiff has perforce had to fend for himself. It seems to me that there is an important distinction between the case in which a minor is allowed to manage his own affairs, free from parental *potestas*, on the one hand, and on the other hand the case in which the minor is left to survive as best he can because of the desertion and neglect of his natural guardian. See *Grand Prix Motors (Pty) Ltd v Swart* 1976 (3) SA 221 (C) [43] *per* GROSSKOPF AJ at 224D–F; see also Vernon Palmer on "Absolute Emancipation" 1968 *SALJ* 24 at 25. There is no justification for depriving a minor of the law's protection merely because his parents have failed in their duties and left him to face life alone and unassisted. Tacit emancipation can only be effected by the express or implied consent of the guardian. See *Voet* 1.7.12; the *Grand Prix Motors* case *supra* at 224 and the authorities there cited; *Ex parte Van den Hever* 1969 (3) SA 96 (E) [39] *per* KANNEMEYER J [746] at 99 and the authorities there cited; Wessels on *Contract* 2nd ed paras 824–826; Hahlo and Kahn *The Development of the Laws and Constitution of the Union of South Africa* at 365. In the absence of any evidence at all on this aspect of the matter, there is no proof of one of the essentials of tacit emancipation.

Another difficulty arises out of the limited evidence on the extent to which the plaintiff has been left to control his own affairs. In this regard there is a conflict of authority on the concepts of absolute emancipation and relative emancipation.

There is authority in the decided cases for the view that tacit emancipation gives the minor full capacity, equivalent to that of a major. See *Cairncross v De Vos* 1876 Buch 5; *Nangle v Mitchell* 1904 EDC 56; *Dickens v Daley* 1956 (2) SA 11 (N) [42]. These were all claims against an emancipated minor on contract. The only case I have found of a claim by an emancipated minor *ex delicto* is *Bosch v Titley* 1908 ORC 27, where it was taken for granted by the Court that a minor who had been tacitly emancipated had *locus standi* to sue for defamation. However, as Margaret Donaldson on *Minors in Roman-Dutch Law* points out, in para 162, the general weight of opinion is against this view of absolute emancipation. In *Riesle and Rombach v McMullin* 10 HCG 381 the Court held that an emancipated minor could contract only within the scope of the business in respect of which he is emancipated. In *Ambaker v African Meat Co* 1927 CPD 326 BENJAMIN J said at 327 *in fine*:

> "A person is tacitly emancipated when he is allowed by his guardian to carry on business on his own behalf, but he is only tacitly emancipated to the extent of contracts by or in connection with that particular business. He is not emancipated beyond that . . ."

This is followed in the *Ochberg* case *supra per* SUTTON J at 37, and in *Ahmed v Coovadia* 1944 TPD 364 *per* SCHREINER J at 366, and *per* NESER AJ at 367–8. SCHREINER J said this, *loc cit*:

> "It seems to me that this view is in accordance with common sense – that a father may assign a small business to his minor child intending that the child should be able to conduct that business effectively, and therefore to enter into contracts in connection with it, while at the same time he may never intend that the child shall be wholly independent of him and that in matters quite unconnected with the business, as for instance his marriage, the child shall be regarded as entirely emancipated."

The modern writers who support this view of relative emancipation include *Wessels* (*op cit* para 824); *Hahlo and Kahn* (*loc cit*); De Wet and Yeats *Kontraktereg en Handelsreg* 3rd ed at 55; *Donaldson* (*supra* para 162); Conradie 1946 *SALJ* 25; Vernon Palmer 1968 *SALJ* 24; D'Oliviera 1973 *SALJ* at 58–60.

Prof Boberg in 1975 *SALJ* at 205, and in his recent work *The Law of Persons and the Family* at 392–3 and at 403, points to the fact that the issue has not yet been authoritatively decided. In 1975 *SALJ* at 193 *et seq* and at 205, *Boberg* suggests that our Courts have confused two distinct institutions, namely tacit emancipation, which terminated the parental power and irrevocably conferred full majority status, and general authority, which, being no more than advance consent to enter into transactions of a certain kind, had no effect on the parental power and could be revoked at will. This view was accepted by GROSSKOPF AJ in the *Grand Prix Motors* case [43] *supra* at 223 *in fine*-224. See also *Dickens v Daley* [42] (*supra* at 13).

[747] It is generally assumed that *locus standi in judicio* is a concomitant of emancipation. See the comment and authorities collected in Boberg *The Law of Persons and the Family* at 689–690, and particularly in footnote 25 on 689. If the correct view of the law is that emancipation is equivalent to full majority, then full *locus standi* would result, but if there is such a thing as relative emancipation, then the *locus standi* conferred thereby would only be *pro tanto*, that is, in relation to matters falling within the scope of the emancipation.

On the facts of this case I do not have to choose between the conflicting authorities, or to decide whether I am bound by the Transvaal Provincial Division decision in *Ahmed v Coovadia* (*supra*) to the exclusion of decisions such as *Dickens v Daley* (*supra*) [42]. The evidence tendered in this case did not go beyond proving that the plaintiff lived apart from his mother, and accepted and engaged in employment of his own choice and had complete control over his earnings. On the approach favoured by *Boberg*, that is not proof of tacit emancipation. At best, it would amount to a general authority. Alternatively, and on the other approach, the evidence at best proved nothing more than emancipation for the limited purpose of engaging in employment, which would not empower the plaintiff to engage in litigation in an unconnected matter. Hence, on either of the legal bases examined above, the plaintiff has not proved his case.

It follows that the special plea must succeed. Had I been free to do so, I would have explored the possibility of enabling the action to continue on some basis, such as that the plaintiff is now a major, or that a summons issued by an unassisted minor is not necessarily a nullity... However... I am confined to deciding the specific issues raised in the pleadings...

However, instead of dismissing the action now, I think it right and proper, in the interests of justice, to allow to the plaintiff the opportunity of arguing some basis upon which the action can be preserved, and I propose to make provision for that in my order...

[748] The special plea succeeds, but the plaintiff is given leave to set the matter down for a further hearing on the form of relief to be granted...

Note

See the note on *Dickens v Daley* [42].

Aantekening

Sien die aantekening by *Dickens v Daley* [42].

Diverse factors which influence status

Insanity

Inability to manage own affairs

Prodigality

Drunkenness

Sex

Diverse faktore wat status beïnvloed

Geestesongesteldheid

Onvermoë om eie sake te behartig

Verkwisters

Dronkenskap

Geslag

Insanity   **Geestesongesteldheid**

[45] LANGE V LANGE

1945 AD 332

What constitutes insanity

The appellant married the defendant in
March 1940. In December 1942 the defendant was admitted to a mental hospital. In
May 1944 the appellant applied for an order
declaring her marriage to the defendant to
be null and void on the ground that the defendant was insane at the date of the marriage. From the evidence it was clear that
the defendant suffered from *dementia praecox*
and heard imaginary voices. On the day of
their marriage, for example, before entering
the magistrate's office where they were married, he stopped on the steps and listened to
the voices to get their consent before he was
willing to be married. The application was
dismissed in the court *a quo*. An appeal against
this decision was successful.

Wat onder kranksinnigheid verstaan word

Die appellant is in Maart 1940 met die verweerder getroud. In Desember 1942 is die
verweerder in 'n inrigting vir sielsiekes opgeneem. In Mei 1944 het die appellant aansoek gedoen om 'n bevel dat haar huwelik
met die verweerder nietig verklaar word op
grond daarvan dat die verweerder kranksinnig was toe die huwelik aangegaan is. Dit
was uit die getuienis duidelik dat die verweerder aan 'n vorm van skisofrenie gely
het en nie-werklike stemme gehoor het. Op
hulle huweliksdag het hy byvoorbeeld op die
trappe van die landdroskantoor waar hulle
getroud is, gaan staan en eers na die stemme
geluister om hulle goedkeuring te verkry
voordat hy bereid was om in die huwelik te
tree. Die aansoek is in die hof *a quo* van die
hand gewys maar 'n appèl teen hierdie beslissing het geslaag.

TINDALL JA: [341] Before considering whether the evidence was sufficient to discharge
the *onus*, it is necessary to consider what proof is required to establish that a marriage is
invalid on the ground that one of the parties thereto was suffering from mental disorder
at the time. As stated by INNES, CJ, in *Pheasant v Warne* (1922, AD 481, at pp 487, 488),
a consenting mind is essential to contractual validity. *Voet* (23.2.6) states that "the consent
of the parties to the marriage is such an essential that a flaw in the consent renders a
marriage *ipso jure* void; which happens when a marriage is contracted by an insane person."
I use the term "insane person" as a translation of the Latin *furiosus*. See also *Voet* (27.10.2),
the passage quoted in *Molyneux v Natal Land & Colonization Co* (1905, AC 555). There are
various types of insanity, but whatever types may be intended to be included in the
statement that an insane person cannot contract a valid marriage, the reason for the
invalidity is the absence of the consenting mind. [See also] Brouwer (*de Jure Connub*
2.4.29) . . .

In *Pheasant v Warne*, INNES, CJ, stated at p 488:

"And running through all the statutory definitions of mental disorder, so far as these
definitions affect civil liability, there will be found the test – whether the person
concerned is incapable of managing his affairs. It is in essence the test of the early
writers, though modern science may enable us to give it a more extended and effective
application. And a court of law called upon to decide a question of contractual liability
depending upon mental capacity must determine whether the person concerned was

or [342] was not at the time capable of managing the particular affair in question – that is to say whether his mind was such that he could understand and appreciate the transaction into which he purported to enter. If he was, then due effect must be given to his intention as manifested; if he was not, then the *animus* which the law requires could not have been present and the transaction must be declared null and void."

I doubt whether this statement was intended to convey that mental disorder in a contracting party does not invalidate the contract unless that party was, owing to such disorder, unable to understand and appreciate the transaction into which he entered. It is noteworthy that, in spite of the wide language used by INNES, CJ, in the passage just quoted, in framing the terms of the order remitting the case for further hearing, the learned CHIEF JUSTICE phrased it in these terms: "The defendant to be permitted to file a plea that at the date of the alleged contract of sale he was mentally incapable of assenting thereto." It is clear, of course, that if, owing to mental disease, a contracting party does not understand or appreciate the nature of the matter, the contract will be void; for he could not be held to have consented to obligations the nature of which he could not understand. But the converse is not necessarily true. As pointed out by DE VILLIERS, JP, in *Estate Rehne v Rehne* (1930, OPD 80, at p 87), where a party enters into a transaction under the influence of an insane delusion the transaction would not be validated merely because that party understood the transaction and intended to enter into it. It seems to me that a party's consent may be motivated or influenced by an insane delusion caused by mental disease, and that, where this is proved to be the case, it cannot truly be said that his mind was a consenting mind . . .

The behaviour of the defendant described by these two witnesses [ie the plaintiff and a friend], when it is considered in the light of the subsequent [343] history of the defendant and the medical evidence . . . leaves no doubt in my mind that at the time of his marriage the defendant already had *dementia praecox*; he was then subject to delusions of persecution and to auditory hallucinations and the delusions and hallucinations were caused by disease of the mind. The defendant's mental state in December, 1942, which was undoubtedly that of a person suffering from *dementia praecox*, was not recent or sudden in its inception; the evidence shows that it was of slow growth. It had begun as far back as 1938 or earlier, and the question is whether by the time of the marriage in March, 1940, it had developed to such an extent that the defendant was not capable of consenting validly to the contract of marriage . . .

[T]he defendant must have understood the nature of the contract and have appreciated the nature of the obligations he was undertaking. But the question is whether his volition was not influenced by his mental disease and more particularly by the auditory hallucinations from which he suffered. Of course it cannot be demonstrated that his volition was so influenced. Whether it was or was not is a matter of inference; but it is legitimate to draw an inference on a balance of probabilities. The evidence above mentioned, and especially that as to his behaviour before entering the magistrate's office to be married, seems to me to render it highly [344] probable that his volition was so influenced. It is true that the incident made little impression at the time on the plaintiff, who seems to have given her evidence very candidly. But that she should have treated it lightly then is readily intelligible; it is only in the light of the defendant's subsequent history that the significance of the symptom in question can be measured.

I have come to the conclusion on the evidence that the plaintiff established that the defendant's volition in entering into the marriage was influenced by auditory hallucinations caused by mental disease. This is not a case where the delusion was unconnected with the transaction in question . . . The case is not free from difficulty; indeed, it is an illustration of the truth of the remark of LORD LANGDALE in *Snook v Watts* (50 ER

757) that "there is no subject, I conceive, more difficult to investigate and satisfactorily to adjudicate upon in courts of justice than the state of a man's mind, with reference to his sanity or insanity, for the purpose of determining whether he is legally bound or answerable for his acts". But on the whole I am of opinion that the plaintiff's claim ought to have succeeded.

The appeal is allowed . . .

GREENBERG JA and DAVIS AJA concurred.

Note

The important aspect of this decision is that the court declared the marriage null and void although it was found that the defendant at the time of his marriage understood the nature of the contract and appreciated the nature of the obligations he was undertaking. It was held that a person is insane not only if he cannot understand the nature of the transaction in question because of a mental disease, but also if he understands the nature and consequences of his juristic acts but is motivated or influenced by insane delusions caused by mental illness. On account of the defendant's insanity the marriage was consequently annulled. See Barnard, Cronjé and Olivier 106.

See in this regard also *Estate Rehne v Rehne* 1930 OPD 80. In this case a deceased person had made certain donations to his one son before his death. After his death these donations were set aside since it was found that the donations were made while the deceased was under the influence of insane delusions.

See also *Theron v AA Life Assurance Association Ltd* 1993 1 SA 736 (C) where the court set aside a life insurance contract entered into by a person who was mentally retarded to such an extent that he lacked the fairly sophisticated level of understanding which is necessary to grasp the terms of a life insurance contract. The court held that there are three elements which must be considered when it is alleged that a person lacked capacity to contract on the ground of a mental disability.

(i) The person's understanding and appreciation of the transaction entered into must be established. If his mental condition was such that the *animus* required by the law for the specific transaction could not have been present, the transaction is void.

(ii) The person must have the mental capacity to understand and appreciate at a level which

Aantekening

Die belangrike aspek van hierdie beslissing is dat die hof die huwelik nietig verklaar het alhoewel bevind is dat die verweerder tydens die huweliksluiting die aard van die kontrak verstaan het en ook die aard van die verpligtinge wat hy onderneem het begryp het. Daar is bevind dat 'n persoon nie net kranksinnig is as hy die aard van die betrokke regshandeling as gevolg van 'n geestesiekte nie begryp nie, maar ook as hy die aard en gevolge van sy regshandelinge verstaan maar onder die invloed van, of aangedryf deur, kranksinnige delusies, veroorsaak deur 'n geestesiekte, handel. Op grond van die verweerder se kranksinnigheid is die huwelik gevolglik nietig verklaar. Sien Barnard, Cronjé en Olivier 110.

Sien in die verband ook *Estate Rehne v Rehne* 1930 OPA 80. In hierdie saak het 'n oorledene voor sy dood sekere skenkings aan sy een seun gemaak. Na sy dood is hierdie skenkings nietig verklaar aangesien daar bevind is dat die skenkings gedoen is toe die oorledene onder die invloed van kranksinnige delusies was.

Sien ook *Theron v AA Life Assurance Association Ltd* 1993 1 SA 736 (K) waarin die hof 'n lewensversekeringskontrak ter syde gestel het omdat die kontrak gesluit is deur 'n persoon wat dermate verstandelik vertraag was dat hy nie die redelik gesofistikeerde vlak van begrip gehad het wat nodig is om die bepalings van 'n lewensversekeringskontrak te begryp nie. Die hof het beslis dat daar drie elemente is wat oorweeg moet word indien beweer word dat 'n persoon as gevolg van 'n geestesprobleem nie die bevoegdheid gehad het om 'n kontrak te sluit nie.

(i) Daar moet vasgestel word of die persoon die betrokke transaksie begryp het. Indien sy geestesprobleem van so 'n aard was dat die *animus* wat deur die reg vir die betrokke transaksie vereis word nie aanwesig kon wees nie, is die transaksie nietig.

(ii) Die persoon moet die geestesvermoë hê om

is sufficient to enable him to manage the particular affair.

(iii) The person must be able to make rational decisions about the nature of the transaction he is entering into and the nature of the obligations he is undertaking, and his volition must not be influenced by his mental problem.

See further *Prinsloo's Curators Bonis v Crafford and Prinsloo* [46]; *Pheasant v Warne* 1922 AD 481; *Levin v Mechanich* 1931 EDL 32; *Uys v Uys* 1953 2 SA 1 (E).

te kan begryp op 'n vlak wat hom in staat stel om die besondere aangeleentheid te behartig.

(iii) Die persoon moet in staat wees om rasionele besluite te neem oor die aard van die transaksie wat hy besig is om aan te gaan en die verpligtinge wat hy besig is om op homself te neem, en sy wilsvryheid moet nie deur sy geestesprobleem beïnvloed word nie.

Sien verder *Prinsloo's Curators Bonis v Crafford and Prinsloo* [46]; *Pheasant v Warne* 1922 AA 481; *Levin v Mechanich* 1931 OD 32; *Uys v Uys* 1953 2 SA 1 (OD).

[46] PRINSLOO'S CURATORS BONIS V CRAFFORD AND PRINSLOO

1905 TS 669

Marriage entered into by a person declared to be of unsound mind

In July 1903 the court declared one Prinsloo to be of unsound mind and curators were appointed to his estate. In April 1905 while the order was still in force, Prinsloo married a lady by the name of Crafford (the defendant). The curators of Prinsloo's estate now applied for an order declaring the said marriage to be null and void, or, in the alternative, for an order setting aside the marriage in so far as it affected his property. The defence was raised that at the time the marriage was entered into Prinsloo was perfectly sane and of sound mind, and, consequently, that the marriage was valid and that, as an ordinary consequence of marriage, it was one in community of property. Mrs Prinsloo claimed in reconvention for an order asking the court to declare the marriage valid and in community of property. She further prayed for an order declaring Prinsloo to be sane and of sound mind, and removing the plaintiffs from their position as *curators bonis*. The court held that the marriage was valid and

Huwelik aangegaan deur 'n persoon wat kranksinnig verklaar is

In Julie 1903 is ene Prinsloo deur die hof kranksinnig verklaar en kurators is aangestel om sy boedel te administreer. In April 1905 toe die bevel nog van krag was, het Prinsloo met 'n vrou met die naam Crafford (die verweerderes) in die huwelik getree. Die kurators van Prinsloo se boedel het hierop aansoek gedoen om 'n bevel dat die huwelik nietig verklaar word, of in die alternatief, dat die huwelik nietig verklaar word vir sover dit sy eiendom raak. Die verweer teen die aksie was dat Prinsloo by sy volle verstand was toe die huwelik aangegaan is, en dat die huwelik gevolglik geldig was en dat een van die normale gevolge van 'n huwelik ingetree het, naamlik dat die huwelik binne gemeenskap van goed was. Mevrou Prinsloo het in rekonvensie aansoek gedoen om 'n bevel dat die huwelik geldig was en dat dit binne gemeenskap van goed was. Sy het verder aansoek gedoen dat die hof moes verklaar dat Prinsloo by sy volle verstand was en dat die eisers van hulle posisie as *curators bonis*

that it was a marriage in community of property.

onthef moes word. Die hof het beslis dat die huwelik geldig was en dat dit binne gemeenskap van goed gesluit was.

SOLOMON J: [671] Now the first important question which arises in this case is as to what was the effect of the order which was made by the High Court in July, 1903, declaring Prinsloo to be of unsound mind and appointing *curators bonis* to his estate. It has been argued by Mr *Ward* on behalf of the plaintiffs that the effect of that order was to change the status of Prinsloo – that it was a judgment *in rem*, and that it deprived him of the power to enter into a contract of any nature whatsoever. Mr *Ward* contends that so long as the order stands – until it has been superseded by another order of court – there is a conclusive presumption that Prinsloo is insane, and that there can be no inquiry as to what his state of mind was at the time of the transaction which is challenged. Mr *Ward*, however, has quoted no authority which will support that proposition ... and the authorities which have been quoted by Mr *Gregorowski* are conclusive on this point – that the order has not the effect which was contended for by Mr *Ward*. On the contrary, they show clearly that there is no conclusive presumption that a person who has been declared to be insane [672] by order of court must be deemed to be insane so long as the order is in force, but that it is still open to any such person, or to any person with whom he enters into a transaction of any nature whatsoever, to satisfy the Court that at the time when the transaction was entered into he was sane. I need not refer in detail to the passages which have been quoted from Voet, because he is perfectly clear on this point, that where a person has been declared to be insane, and where curators have been appointed to take charge of his property, if a lucid interval supervenes he thereupon *ipso facto* again acquires the right to dispose of his property and to enter into contracts with regard to that property, and that his capacity to do so continues until insanity again supervenes, when the order of curatorship revives, and he once more becomes subject to his curators ...

In effect it seems to me that the result of the authorities is this: that an order declaring a person to be of unsound mind is conclusive proof of the fact that at the time the order was made such person was insane, and consequently that an order of that nature merely shifts the onus of proof. For there is no doubt a presumption that when a person has been declared to be of unsound mind he continues to be of unsound mind, but it is open to him at any time to bring evidence to satisfy the Court that subsequent to the date of the order he became sane, and that consequently a contract entered into by him after the order was a valid contract, inasmuch as it was entered into by him at a time when he was in full possession of his faculties. The only effect, therefore, as far as I can see, is that such an order shifts the onus of proof. If in the ordinary course any transaction is challenged on the ground of insanity, the onus of proof is on the person challenging it to satisfy the Court that the person was insane at the time when the transaction was entered into, because the ordinary presumption is that [673] a person is sane. But after an order of this nature it appears to me that the onus is shifted upon the person who has been declared insane, and that it is necessary for him to satisfy the Court that he was sane at the time when the transaction was entered into.

If that is the state of the law on this question, then the whole point which we have to consider is whether it has been proved to our satisfaction that at the time when this marriage was contracted – on the 25th April, 1905 – Gert Cornelius Prinsloo was of sound mind. In other words, we have to be satisfied that his state of mind at that time was such that he was able to understand the nature of the contract into which he entered and to appreciate properly the duties and responsibilities which were created by that contract. Now on that question I have not the slightest doubt whatsoever. After all, the contract of marriage is a very simple one, and it does not require any very high degree of intelligence to understand the nature of the contract; and no one who was in Court, and who heard Prinsloo give his evidence yesterday, could have any possible doubt that he was of sufficiently sound mind and understanding to realise the nature of the obligation into which he was entering, and to appreciate the duties and responsibilities created by that contract . . .

[SOLOMON J then analysed the evidence and proceeded:]

[675] I find then that it has been established that Prinsloo is a perfectly sane and sound-minded person at present, that he is in the same condition now as at the time when this marriage was entered into, and that we are therefore bound to come to the conclusion that the marriage is a valid marriage, and consequently that the ordinary consequences of a marriage must follow, and that the marriage is one in community of property. That being so, on the claim in the action in convention, asking the Court to declare the marriage null and void or to set aside the marriage in so far as it affects the property of the co-defendant, there must be judgment for the defendant. On the claim in reconvention the judgment of the Court is that the Court declares the marriage to be of full force and effect and to be a marriage in community of property, and the Court further declares that Prinsloo is of sound mind and is able to take charge of his own property, and therefore we remove the plaintiffs from their position as *curators bonis* . . .

WESSELS and BRISTOWE JJ concurred.

Note

An insane person has absolutely no capacity to act and any legal transaction he enters into is void *ab initio* (Voet 27.10.3; Grotius 3.1.19; Van Leeuwen *Rooms-Hollands-Regt* 2.7.8; *Lange v Lange* [45]). The fact that a person has been declared insane and a curator has been appointed to him does not, as such, affect his capacity to act (Barnard, Cronjé and Olivier 104). The important question is whether he was *in fact* insane when the transaction was entered into. If he was, the transaction is void whether he has been declared a lunatic or not. As is clear from *Prinsloo's* case, certification is, however, important as far as the onus of proof is concerned. See also *Vermaak v Vermaak* 1929 OPD 13; *Mitchell v Mitchell* 1930 AD 217; *Levin v Mechanich* 1931 EDL 32.

Aantekening

'n Kranksinnige persoon is geheel en al handelingsonbevoeg en enige regshandeling wat hy aangaan, is *ab initio* nietig (Voet 27.10.3; De Groot 3.1.19; Van Leeuwen *Rooms-Hollands-Regt* 2.7.8; *Lange v Lange* [45]). Die feit dat 'n persoon kranksinnig verklaar is en 'n kurator vir hom aangestel is, raak nie op sigself sy handelingsbevoegdheid nie. (Barnard, Cronjé en Olivier 108). Die belangrike vraag is of hy *inderdaad* ten tyde van die aangaan van die handeling kranksinnig was. Was hy kranksinnig, is die handeling nietig of hy kranksinnig verklaar is al dan nie. Soos uit *Prinsloo* se saak blyk, is sertifisering egter van belang vir sover dit die bewyslas aangaan. Sien ook *Vermaak v Vermaak* 1929 OPA 13; *Mitchell v Mitchell* 1930 AA 217; *Levin v Mechanich* 1931 OD 32.

Inability to manage own affairs   Onvermoë om eie sake te behartig

[47] EX PARTE KLOPPER: IN RE KLOPPER

1961 3 SA 803 (T)

Appointment of a *curator* to an adult

This case dealt with an application for the appointment of a *curator bonis*. First the ap-

Aanstelling van 'n *curator* vir 'n volwassene

Hierdie saak het gehandel oor 'n aansoek om

pointment of a *curator ad litem* was applied for. The application was made by the respondent's son and supported by respondent's wife, that is the applicant's mother. The respondent opposed the application. He was a wealthy man who until 1955 successfully managed his affairs. He then suffered a stroke after which his wife managed his affairs for four years. In 1959 he resumed active control of his affairs, although he occasionally suffered from epileptic fits. The applicant maintained that due to and as a result of the stroke, the respondent was unable to manage his affairs. The application was dismissed.

die aanstelling van 'n *curator bonis*. Eers is aansoek gedoen om die aanstelling van 'n *curator ad litem*. Die aansoek is deur die respondent se seun gedoen en hy is deur die respondent se vrou, dit wil sê die applikant se moeder ondersteun. Die respondent het die aansoek teengestaan. Hy was 'n welgestelde man wat tot 1955 sy sake suksesvol behartig het. Hy het toe 'n beroerteaanval gehad en sy vrou het vier jaar lank sy sake bestuur. Vanaf 1959 het hy weer sy eie belange behartig. Hy het van tyd tot tyd epileptiese aanvalle gekry. Die applikant het beweer dat die respondent as gevolg van die beroerteaanval nie daartoe in staat was om sy eie sake te behartig nie. Die aansoek is van die hand gewys.

GALGUT J: [GALGUT J dealt with the evidence and proceeded:] [804] On these affidavits I am of the view that it has not been shown that the respondent is unable to manage his affairs. The medical evidence gives ground for no more than suspicion. There is no doubt that certain material facts were not mentioned in the petition. The fact that the son was prepared to take from the father, during the time when the father was seriously ill, a guarantee, for the large sum mentioned in the answering affidavit is, in my view, something which should have been set out in the petition. The petition should have made mention of the fact that the father, since he resumed control of his own affairs, had farmed successfully; there should have been some mention made [805] of the reasons why the animosity between the son and wife and the father had continued to grow. The affidavits filed by the respondent are from responsible people and there can be no doubt that they have no reason to believe that he cannot manage his affairs. There is nothing on the papers to suggest that he is giving away his assets; that he is squandering his money or that he is likely to farm at a loss. Nowhere is it suggested that he, by his conduct, will cause any diminution of his assets. In all these circumstances it seems to me that the probabilities are that he is able to manage his affairs. It may be that he is quick tempered or eccentric and it may be that he suffers from fits on occasions but this does not mean that he is not capable of managing his affairs.

For the applicant it was argued that it was not necessary to show on a balance of probabilities that there was need for the appointment of a *curator-ad-litem*. It was urged that the procedure is tantamount to a judicial enquiry into the state of the respondent's capacity to take care of himself or of his property with a view to protecting him against loss; it was, therefore, only necessary to show *prima facie* that the respondent could not manage his affairs; if a Court is of the view that the circumstances are such as to cause it to believe that it might be necessary for the protection of the respondent to appoint a curator it should do so. It seems to me that this submission goes far too far. The authorities to which I have been referred are not *in pari materia*. Most of them deal with the position in regard to the appointment of a *curator bonis*. Others deal with the position of the appointment of a *curator-ad-litem* for a specific purpose but not as a preliminary step to the appointment of a *curator bonis*. As I read the authorities a Court will not appoint a *curator bonis* until it is absolutely satisfied that the patient has to be protected against loss which would be caused because the patient is unable to manage his affairs. I do not propose to deal with the authorities quoted to me. Some of them have been referred to by HERBSTEIN, J, in *Ex parte Kotze*, 1955 (1) SA 665 (C) at p 666. The learned Judge in that case came to the conclusion that before the Court could interfere with the right of an adult to control his own affairs the Court had to be satisfied after a proper enquiry into the mental condition of the alleged patient that interference by the Court was justified. In that case the following *dictum* from *Mitchell v Mitchell*, 1930 AD 217 at p 224 was cited with approval:

> "Before a *curator-ad-litem* is appointed to a person of full age there must be an enquiry into the mental state of the person concerned at the time of the appointment."

The facts in *Mitchell's* case were very different from those before me but I quote these two cases only to show how careful a Court will be before it will appoint a *curator-ad-litem* to an adult. No authority has been cited to show that the rule of *onus* should be different in an application for the appointment of a *curator-ad-litem* which is opposed than in any other opposed application. It is for the applicant to satisfy the Court on a balance of probabilities that such a step is necessary. In my view in this case the probabilities seem to me to lie with the respondent. He has in fact been conducting his affairs successfully [806] for the past year or more and has not squandered or dissipated any of his assets.

In the result the application fails and is dismissed ...

Note

The appointment of a curator to a person may involve a serious violation of a person's rights and liberties (*Mitchell v Mitchell* 1930 AD 217; *Martinson v Brown; Gray v Armstrong* 1961 4 SA 107 (C); *Ex parte Hill* 1970 3 SA 411 (C)). The court is therefore very reluctant to appoint a curator to an adult who is *compos mentis*. The courts attach considerable importance to the fact that the person concerned consents to be placed under curatorship (*Mitchell v Mitchell; Ex parte De Villiers* 1943 WLD 56; *Ex parte Berman: In re Estate Dhlamini* 1954 2 SA 386 (W); *Ex parte Derksen* 1960 1 SA 380 (N); *Ex parte Thomson: In re Hope v Hope* 1979 3 SA 483 (W)). A person's consent, however, is not binding on the court. In other words, a person can be placed under curatorship whether he consents thereto or not. In each case the court will have to be convinced on a balance of probabilities that the appointment is necessary (see in this regard Van der Vyver and Joubert 368-369). Where a person consents it is obvious that he must be able to understand the proceedings (*Ex parte Van Dyk* 1939 CPD 202; *Ex parte Bell* 1953 2 SA 702 (O)).

Note that the court in *Klopper's* case rejected the argument that in an application for a *curator ad litem* it was sufficient if a *prima facie* case was made out. In this instance too it must be proved on a balance of probabilities that the appointment of a *curator ad litem* is necessary.

Aantekening

Die aanstelling van 'n kurator oor 'n persoon kan ernstige inbreuk op die regte en vryheid van sodanige persoon maak (*Mitchell v Mitchell* 1930 AA 217; *Martinson v Brown; Gray v Armstrong* 1961 4 SA 107 (K); *Ex parte Hill* 1970 3 SA 411 (K)). Die hof is gevolglik baie huiwerig om 'n kurator aan te stel oor 'n volwasse persoon wat *compos mentis* is. Die howe heg baie waarde aan die feit dat die betrokke persoon toestem om onder kuratele geplaas te word (*Mitchell v Mitchell; Ex parte De Villiers* 1943 WPA 56; *Ex parte Berman: In re Estate Dhlamini* 1954 2 SA 386 (W); *Ex parte Derksen* 1960 1 SA 380 (N); *Ex parte Thomson: In re Hope v Hope* 1979 3 SA 483 (W)). 'n Persoon se toestemming is egter nie deurslaggewend nie. Met ander woorde 'n persoon kan onder kuratele geplaas word of hy nou daartoe toestem al dan nie. In elke geval moet die hof op 'n oorwig van waarskynlikheid oortuig word dat die aanstelling nodig is (sien in die verband Van der Vyver en Joubert 368-369). Waar 'n persoon toestem, is dit vanselfsprekend dat hy in staat moet wees om die verrigtinge te verstaan (*Ex parte Van Dyk* 1939 KPA 202; *Ex parte Bell* 1953 2 SA 702 (O)).

Let daarop dat die hof in *Klopper* se saak die argument verwerp het dat by 'n aansoek om 'n *curator ad litem* dit voldoende is as 'n *prima facie* saak uitgemaak word. Ook in hierdie geval moet dit op 'n oorwig van waarskynlikheid bewys word dat die aanstelling van 'n *curator ad litem* nodig is.

[48]   PIENAAR V PIENAAR'S CURATOR

1930 OPD 171

Marriage entered into by a woman declared incapable of managing her own affairs	**Huwelik aangegaan deur 'n vrou wat onbevoeg verklaar is om haar eie sake te behartig**

Before the plaintiff married his wife she was suffering from chronic mental and physical disorders which rendered her incapable of managing her own affairs. One of her relatives then applied to court to have her placed under curatorship. The court granted the order declaring her to be incapable and unfit to manage her own person and affairs and appointed the defendant as curator to her person and property. While the order was still in force she married the plaintiff in community of property without the consent of the defendant. Subsequently, the plaintiff, by virtue of the community of property effected, claimed an order compelling the defendant to hand over to him the assets which until then had belonged to his wife. The defendant excepted to the plaintiff's declaration. However, the exception was dismissed, in other words, the court held that the wife could have married without the curator's consent.	Voordat die eiser met sy vrou getroud is, het sy aan chroniese geestelike en fisiese ongesteldheid gely, wat daartoe gelei het dat sy nie in staat was om haar eie sake te behartig nie. 'n Familielid van haar het toe by die hof aansoek gedoen dat sy onder kuratele geplaas word. Die hof het die aansoek toegestaan en verklaar dat sy nie daartoe in staat was om haar eie persoon en sake te bestuur nie en het die verweerder as kurator oor haar persoon en goed aangestel. Terwyl die bevel nog gegeld het, het die vrou sonder die toestemming van die verweerder binne gemeenskap van goed met die eiser getrou. Die eiser het nou as gevolg van die gemeenskap van goed wat tussen hom en sy vrou tot stand gekom het, aansoek gedoen om 'n bevel om die verweerder te verplig om die goed wat tot op daardie stadium aan sy vrou behoort het, aan hom te oorhandig. Die verweerder het eksepsie aangeteken teen die eiser se deklarasie. Die eksepsie is van die hand gewys, met ander woorde die hof het beslis dat die vrou sonder haar kurator se toestemming in die huwelik kon tree.

DE VILLIERS JP: [173] Mr *Hoexter* contends on behalf of the defendant that a person who has been declared incapable of managing her own affairs and been placed under curators of the person and property, cannot [174] marry without the curator's consent, even if she is able to understand the nature of the contract of marriage and is mentally and physically capable of entering into such contract; and secondly, that, even if she can so marry, the marriage is without community of goods. Mr *Hoexter* relies strongly on the analogy of the *prodigus*. It certainly appears from the authorities quoted by him that, where the Court has declared a person to be a *prodigus* and has interdicted him from the management of his own property, and has appointed a curator to his estate, such person cannot enter into a marriage without his curator's consent, or at any rate not into a marriage in community of goods. – Kersteman, *Rechtsg Woord s.v.* "Curateele", and "Trouwbeloften", pp 90 and 554; Voet (23.1.3); Brouwer *De Jure Conn* (1.4.18). It seems to me, however, that the analogy cannot be followed in this case, as the position is vitally different. It is not difficult to understand why a declared prodigal should be under restrictions as to marriage in community, for he has been interdicted from the administration of his estate ("*bonis interdictum*", "het bewind zijner goederen ontnomen," *Voet* (27.10.6.7); Lybrecht, *Red Vert* (pt I, p 516)), and the sole administration has been vested in the curator. It could therefore well be held to follow that, on his marriage without the curator's consent, his estate would not fall into the community. The position is not the same in the case of persons to whom curators are appointed on the ground of insanity or by reason of some other mental or physical defect or incapacity, such as feeblemindedness, lack of understanding, blindness, deafness, dumbness, chronic disease. To all these persons curators may be appointed by the Court – *Voet* (27.10.13) – to assist them in performing legal acts at such times as, and to the extent to which, their particular form of incapacity renders such assistance necessary, but the persons mentioned are not interdicted or deprived of the administration of their property, as the *prodigus* is. The mere fact that such a person has been declared insane or incapable of managing his affairs, and that a curator is appointed to such person, does not deprive him of the right of administering his own property and entering into contracts and other legal dispositions to the extent to which he may *de facto* be capable, mentally and physically, of so doing. Such mental or physical capacity may vary from day to day, but at all times it remains a question of fact. The object of appointing a curator is merely to assist the person in question in performing legal acts [175] to the extent to which such assistance is from day to day, in varying degrees, necessary. Thus even a person who has been declared insane and to whose estate a curator has been appointed can dispose of his property and enter into contracts whenever he is mentally capable of doing so – *Voet* (27.10.3, 4), and can therefore enter into a valid marriage in community of goods at any time when he is mentally capable of doing so – *Prinsloo's Curators v Crafford* (1905, TS 669) [46]. The same principle applies *a fortiori* to the person who has not been declared insane, but has merely been declared incapable of managing his affairs and to whom a curator has on that account been appointed. Here again the curator is merely appointed to assist the person in making legal dispositions in so far as such assistance is necessary, according to the nature of the incapacity in question, but the person still retains his contractual and legal capacities and the administration of his property to the full extent to which he is from time to time mentally or physically able to exercise them. The point is stated clearly by *Voet* (27.10.13): "It has also been thought proper that curators should be appointed to persons who on account of some physical defect are unable to manage their affairs, and on that account need the assistance of another in their affairs; such as deaf persons and dumb persons and persons ailing from a chronic disease. In the case of such persons, however, the curator will not assist with his advice or authority and assistance in business matters save in so far as such persons may be impeded by such physical defect from managing and administering their own affairs as they think fit; almost in the same way as a curator appointed to a lunatic is only a curator in name during any lucid interval in which the lunatic may manage his own affairs." It is clear, therefore, that these cases differ from that of the interdicted prodigal. In all these instances the person who has been declared insane or otherwise incapable, retains his contractual and legal capacities and his administration of his own affairs to the extent to which he is from day to day capable of exercising them. If at any time he is not legally competent to perform a legal act, that incompetence flows from the physical or mental incapacity which prevents him from understanding or from giving his *consensus*, and not from the fact that he has been declared incapable and had a curator appointed to him. It seems to me, therefore, that Mr *Hoexter's* argument founded upon the [176] analogy of the *prodigus* cannot be accepted. The same may be said about his parallel argument founded upon the analogy of a minor... There is again this vital difference that a minor, like the *prodigus*, has not the administration of his own property, and has no contractual capacity as a general rule, whereas the person to whom a curator is appointed on the ground of some mental or physical incapacity retains the administration of his property in the manner above described. Lastly, Mr *Hoexter* has relied upon the fact that in the present

case (differing from the case of Prinsloo, *ubi supra*, and from the case of *Mitchell v Mitchell and Others* 1930, AD 217), Mrs Pienaar [the plaintiff's wife] has had a curator to her person appointed as well as a curator to her property. It does not seem to me that the difference is material. It appears that the distinction between a curator to the person and a curator to the property was known to Roman-Dutch lawyers – Hoola van Nooten, *Vad Recht* (vol II, p 596), but I have not found that any distinct line is drawn between the functions of the one and the other . . . It seems, however, that no distinction was drawn between the legal capacity of the adult ward in the one case and the other. Thus the passages of *Voet* to which reference has been made above – *Voet* (27.10.5; 27.10.13) – deal with the case of a person to whom any curator has been appointed, without drawing any distinction between curators to the person and curators to the estate. In any case it seems to me that, if the appointment of a curator to the property does not deprive the adult ward of contractual capacity and the administration of property as above described, it follows *a fortiori* that the appointment of a curator to the person will not do so. Leaving on one side, then, the case of a prodigal who has been interdicted from the administration of his property, it seems to me that, where a person has been declared incapable of managing his affairs on account of some mental or physical incapacity or defect, and a curator of the person or property, or both, has been appointed to such person, he may nevertheless administer his property or enter into any contract or other legal disposition which he may from time to time be *de facto* capable, mentally or physically, of entering into, including a contract of marriage in community of goods. It [176] follows that the plaintiff's declaration discloses a cause of action, as it alleges that at all times Mrs Pienaar was "capable of understanding the nature of marriage and the responsibilities created thereby," which I understand as an allegation that she had at the time of her marriage the necessary mental capacity to contract, or at any rate the necessary mental capacity to enter into the contract of marriage. The exception is therefore dismissed . . .

Note

This case clearly illustrates that the fact that a *curator bonis* has been appointed to a person does not mean that the person has been deprived of his capacity to act (see also *Mitchell v Mitchell* 1930 AD 217; *De Villiers v Espach* 1958 3 SA 91 (T)). Such a person can manage his own affairs when his mental and physical abilities allow him to, although, as a question of fact, his capacity to do so may differ from day to day.

Note the difference between the capacity to act of a person placed under curatorship due to a mental or physical defect, and that of a minor, a prodigal, and an insane person. Generally speaking, a minor has limited capacity to act and may not enter into certain transactions without the necessary assistance (see, for example, *Edelstein v Edelstein* [33]). A prodigal's capacity to act is restricted by a court order, the effect of which is that the prodigal's legal position becomes analogous to that of a minor. Like the minor he has limited capacity to act and may consequently not enter independently into juristic acts by which duties are imposed upon him, but he may without

Aantekening

Uit die uitspraak is dit duidelik dat die feit dat 'n *curator bonis* vir 'n persoon aangestel is nie beteken dat die persoon se handelingsbevoegdheid hom ontneem is nie (sien ook *Mitchell v Mitchell* 1930 AA 217; *De Villiers v Espach* 1958 3 SA 91 (T)). Sodanige persoon kan sy eie belange behartig as hy geestelik en liggaamlik bevoeg is om dit te doen. Hierdie bevoegdheid mag van dag tot dag verskil maar dit bly 'n feitlike vraag.

Let op die verskil tussen die handelingsbevoegdheid van 'n persoon wat weens 'n geestelike of fisiese gebrek onder kuratele geplaas is en dié van 'n minderjarige, 'n verkwister, en 'n kranksinnige persoon. In die algemeen gesproke het 'n minderjarige beperkte handelingsbevoegdheid en mag hy sekere transaksies nie sonder die nodige bystand aangaan nie (*Edelstein v Edelstein* [33]). 'n Verkwister se handelingsbevoegdheid word deur 'n hofbevel beperk. Die gevolg van sodanige bevel is dat die verkwister, wat handelingsbevoegdheid betref, in 'n posisie analoog aan die van 'n minderjarige kom. Net soos die minderjarige het hy beperkte handelingsbevoegdheid en hy mag

assistance enter into any transaction which improves his condition without placing duties upon him (Voet 27.10.9; *Phil Morkel Bpk v Niemand* [49]). Transactions initially entered into without assistance by the minor or the prodigal may be ratified. An insane person, on the other hand, has no capacity to act. Any transaction he enters into is void *ab initio* and may not be ratified (see *Prinsloo's Curators Bonis v Crafford and Prinsloo* [46]).

On the question whether a declared prodigal may enter into a valid marriage without his curator's consent, the *consensus* of opinion among modern South African writers is that the curator's consent is not necessary. The marriage will apparently be in or out of community of property, depending on whatever is to the prodigal's advantage (Hahlo 67; Barnard, Cronjé and Olivier 149–150; Boberg 177; Van der Vyver and Joubert 362–363. See also *Mitchell v Mitchell* 1930 AD 217; *Ex parte Hamer* 1946 OPD 163).

gevolglik nie regshandelinge selfstandig aangaan waardeur hy verpligtinge op hom neem nie, maar hy mag sonder bystand enige handeling aangaan waardeur hy sy posisie verbeter sonder om self verpligtinge op te doen (Voet 27.10.9; *Phil Morkel Bpk v Niemand* [49]). 'n Handeling wat die minderjarige of die verkwister aanvanklik sonder die nodige bystand aangegaan het, kan later geratifiseer word. 'n Kranksinnige persoon daarenteen is geheel en al handelingsonbevoeg. Enige handeling wat hy aangaan, is *ab initio* nietig en kan nie geratifiseer word nie (sien *Prinsloo's Curators Bonis v Crafford and Prinsloo* [46]).

Oor die vraag of 'n verklaarde verkwister 'n geldige huwelik sonder sy kurator se toestemming mag aangaan, is moderne Suid-Afrikaanse skrywers van mening dat die kurator se toestemming nie nodig is nie. Of die huwelik binne of buite gemeenskap van goed sal wees, sal vermoedelik afhang van wat tot die verkwister se voordeel sal wees (Hahlo 67; Barnard, Cronjé en Olivier 153–154; Boberg 177; Van der Vyver en Joubert 362–363. Sien ook *Mitchell v Mitchell* 1930 AA 217; *Ex parte Hamer* 1946 OPA 163).

Prodigality   **Verkwisters**

[49]   PHIL MORKEL BPK V NIEMAND

1970 3 SA 455 (K)

Capacity of a prodigal to act

On 21 October 1965 the appellant sold certain goods to the respondent in terms of a hire purchase agreement. When the respondent failed to pay his monthly instalments, the appellant sued him for the outstanding balance. The respondent then averred that he had been declared a prodigal in 1958, that since then he had no capacity to act and could therefore not have concluded a valid contract. He offered to return the goods against repayment of all the instalments paid by him. The appellant admitted that the respondent had been declared a prodigal but contended that he was nevertheless bound by

Handelingsbevoegdheid van 'n verkwister

Op 21 Oktober 1965 het die appellant sekere goedere ingevolge 'n huurkoopooreenkoms aan die respondent verkoop. Toe die respondent nie sy maandelikse paaiemente betaal het nie, het die appellant hom vir die uitstaande balans gedagvaar. Die respondent voer toe aan dat hy in 1958 tot verkwister verklaar is, dat hy sedertdien nie handelingsbevoegdheid gehad het nie en gevolglik nie 'n geldige kontrak kon sluit nie. Hy het aangebied om die goedere terug te gee teen terugbetaling van al die paaiemente wat hy betaal het. Die appellant het erken dat die respondent tot

the contract since it was ratified by his curator. The question which then had to be
decided was whether a prodigal was in the
position of a minor in which case an agreement he had entered into could be ratified,
or whether he was in the position of an insane person in which case the agreement
could not be ratified. In the court *a quo* the
magistrate held that the agreement could not
be ratified. On appeal it was held that the
contract of a prodigal could be ratified by
his curator.

verkwister verklaar is maar het aangevoer
dat hy nogtans aan die kontrak gebonde was
aangesien dit deur sy kurator geratifiseer is.
Die vraag wat toe beslis moes word, was of
'n verkwister in die posisie van 'n minderjarige was, in welke geval 'n kontrak wat hy
aangegaan het wel geratifiseer kon word, en
of hy in die posisie van 'n kranksinnige persoon was, in welke geval die ooreenkoms nie
geratifiseer kon word nie. In die hof *a quo*
het die landdros beslis dat die ooreenkoms
nie geratifiseer kon word nie. In appèl is
beslis dat die kontrak van 'n verkwister wel
geratifiseer kon word.

VAN WINSEN R: [456] Mnr *Burger*, namens appellant, het in hierdie Hof in oorweging
gegee dat 'n verkwister, wat sy handelingsbevoegdheid betref, gelykstaan aan 'n minderjarige, en dat ooreenkomste deur hom aangegaan vir bekragtiging deur sy voog vatbaar
is. Mnr *Vivier* het, inteendeel, aangevoer dat 'n verkwister op dié gebied deur die reg in
dieselfde posisie geplaas word as 'n kranksinnige wat weens sy verstandelike gebrek nie
kan deelneem nie aan die vorming van die *consensus* wat ten grondslag van 'n ooreenkoms
lê. Gevolglik kan 'n verkwister, ondanks sy oënskynlike toetrede tot 'n kontraktuele
verhouding, niks in die lewe roep wat vir bekragtiging deur sy kurator vatbaar is nie.

Indien dit juis is dat die omvang van die handelingsbevoegdheid van 'n verkwister in
alle opsigte dieselfde is as dié van 'n minderjarige dan moet die appèl slaag, want 'n
ooreenkoms deur 'n minderjarige aangegaan is vir bevestiging deur sy voog vatbaar. *Voet*
27.8.1 en 3; Van Leeuwen, *Censura Forensis*, 1.1.17.10; *Fouche v Battenhausen & Co*, 1939
CPD 228 op bl 235 [30]. Moet die verkwister, inteendeel, wat sy handelingsbevoegdheid
betref, in alle opsigte gelyk gestel word aan 'n kranksinnige, dan kan die appèl nie slaag
nie, want laasgenoemde se skynbare toetrede tot 'n ooreenkoms besit geen regswerking
nie, en daar word selfs nie 'n gebrekkige ooreenkoms, wat vir bevestiging vatbaar is, in
die lewe geroep nie. *Institutiones*, 3.19.8; *Dig*, 44.7.1.12; *De Groot*, 3.1.19; *Voet*, 27.101.7.

Nadere ondersoek na die posisie van die verkwister en sy handelingsbevoegdheid volgens
die substantiewe Romeinse en Romeins-Hollandse reg word derhalwe geverg ...

[VAN WINSEN R bespreek die verkwister se posisie in die Romeinse en Romeins-
Hollandse reg en gaan dan voort:]

[458] Dit is dus duidelik dat die verkwister onder kuratele sekere regte en verantwoordelikhede besit wat 'n kranksinnige ... [459] nie het nie, en is gevolglik van die kranksinnige in alle sodanige opsigte te onderskei ...

Dit wil dus voorkom dat die ou skrywers soos *De Groot, Van der Linden* en *Van Leeuwen*
òf geen verskil getrek het tussen die regsposisie van minderjariges, kranksinniges en
verkwisters en die twee laasgenoemdes op dieselfde grondslag geplaas het as minderjariges,
òf waar hul – meer korrek – wel 'n verskil getrek het tussen verkwisters en kranksinniges,
hul eersgenoemdes eerder as minderjariges as kranksinniges behandel het ...

Ons hedendaagse Suid-Afrikaanse skrywers huldig die mening dat die [460] handelingsbevoegdheid van 'n verkwister van dié van 'n kranksinnige verskil. *Wessels*, band 1, para
713, sê:

> "The contract of a prodigal is not void like that of a lunatic but voidable like that of
> an infant. Thus a prodigal can make a valid contract, provided he improves his con-
> dition, even though he has not obtained the consent of his curator."

De Wet en Yeats, *Kontraktereg*, bl 49, beskryf die verkwister, anders as die kranksinnige, as beperk handelingsbevoeg. Hy besit die reg om sonder toestemming van sy kurator kontrakte aan te gaan waaruit hy slegs voordeel put of hom van verpligtings bevry. Kyk ook Mackeurtan, *Sale*, 3de uitg, bl 109, waar die skrywer sê dat 'n kontrak van 'n verkwister "is voidable at the instance of the curator". (Vgl Lee, *Introduction to Roman Dutch Law*, 2de uitg, op bl 113).

Ons Howe het, tot op hede, insake hierdie vraagstuk nog geen uitsluitsel gegee nie.

Uit die voorgaande oorsig van ons regsbronne is dit duidelik dat daar 'n hemelsbreë verskil is tussen die perke op die handelingsbevoegdheid van 'n kranksinnige en die perke op dié van 'n verkwister.

By die onder-kuratelestelling deur die Hof van 'n kranksinnige konstateer die Hof die bestaan van geestesgebreke by hom. Sy handelingsonbevoegdheid is egter aan die bestaan van sodanige gebreke te wyte en nie aan die bevel van die Hof nie. In die geval egter van 'n verkwister is die perke op sy handelingsbevoegdheid toe te skrywe aan die bevel van die Hof ... Die oorsaak van die handelingsonbevoegdheid van 'n kranksinnige is dat weens sy geestesgebrek hy nie 'n behoorlike wilsuiting kan vermag nie en dus nie aan die *consensus* wat nodig is by die skepping van 'n verbintenis kan deelneem nie. Die Hof lê die handelingsbevoegdheid van 'n verkwister aan bande nie omdat hy nie normaalweg aan die skepping van 'n verbintenis kan deelneem nie, maar omdat die nodige oordeel by hom ontbreek om te weet aan watter verbintenisse hy behoort deel te neem. Beskerming bly die doel in geval van beide *currandi* maar die oorsaak vir die beskerming is verskillend. Die oorsaak in geval van 'n verkwister is dieselfde as dié wat by die minderjarige geld, naamlik onoordeelkundigheid. Nòg by die verkwister nòg by die minderjarige ontbreek die vermoë tot behoorlike wilsuiting of deelname aan verbintenisskepping. Daar is dus geen rede in logika nie waarom kontrakte deur 'n verkwister aangegaan nie ewe vatbaar vir bekragtiging deur sy kurator moet wees as in geval van 'n minderjarige se kontrakte nie. Na my mening is so 'n gevolgtrekking ook te rym met die reg soos hierbo uiteengesit. Gevolglik staan dit appellant regtens vry om op respondent se pleit te repliseer dat laasgenoemde se kurator die bedoelde huurkoopkontrak bekragtig het.

Die appèl slaag dus ...

BEYERS RP het saamgestem ...

Note

See the note on *Pienaar v Pienaar's Curator* [48].

Aantekening

Sien die aantekening by *Pienaar v Pienaar's Curator* [48].

Drunkenness   **Dronkenskap**

[50]   VAN METZINGER V BADENHORST

1953 3 SA 291 (T)

The influence of drunkenness on a person's capacity to act

The plaintiff acted as estate agent in a transaction between the defendant and a third

Die invloed van dronkenskap op 'n persoon se handelingsbevoegdheid

Die eiser het as eiendomsagent opgetree in 'n transaksie tussen die verweerder en 'n derde

person in terms of which certain immovable property was sold by the defendant to the third party. The plaintiff subsequently claimed his commission from the defendant who admitted that he and the third party signed a contract of sale but he contended that he was under the influence of intoxicating liquor and therefore did not know that he had signed the contract nor what its contents were. Furthermore the defendant averred that the contract was in conflict with his instructions to the plaintiff and that he would never have signed a contract with such provisions if he had been sober. The magistrate found that although the defendant had been drinking, he was not under the influence to such an extent that he was unable to enter into the contract. On appeal this decision was confirmed.

persoon ingevolge waarvan sekere onroerende goed deur die verweerder aan die derde party verkoop is. Die eiser het nou sy kommissie van die verweerder geëis. Die verweerder het erken dat hy en die derde party 'n koopkontrak onderteken het maar hy het beweer dat hy onder die invloed van drank was en dat hy nie besef het dat hy die kontrak onderteken het of wat die inhoud daarvan was nie. Hy het verder beweer dat die kontrak gebots het met sy opdrag aan die eiser en dat hy nooit 'n kontrak met sodanige inhoud sou gesluit het as hy nugter was nie. Die landdros het bevind dat alhoewel die verweerder gedrink het, hy nie in so 'n mate onder die invloed van drank was dat hy nie in staat was om die kontrak aan te gaan nie. 'n Appèl teen hierdie beslissing het misluk.

RUMPFF R: [293] Dit is nodig om stil te staan by die invloed van dronkenskap op die handelingsbevoegdheid van 'n persoon. Iemand wat so onder invloed van drank is dat hy nie weet wat hy doen nie is volgens ons reg onbevoeg om 'n kontrak te sluit. Grotius druk dit as volg uit – *Inleidinge*, 3.14.5:

"Uit het gunt hier vooren in 't ghemeen is ghezeit kan genoeg verstaen werden, dat oock droncke luiden niet bequaem en zijn om haer selve te verbinden: te weten die door dronckenschap haers verstands onmachtich zijn geworden . . ."

Sien ook *Voet* 18.1.4, en Pothier *Oblig* § 49 (vertaling Evans) wat lui:

"It is evident that drunkenness, when it goes so far as absolutely to destroy the reason, renders a person in this state, so long as it continues, incapable of contracting since it renders him incapable of consent."

So ook Van der Linden *Koopmans Handboek* 1.14.3:

"Die zoo dronken zyn dat zy het gebruik der reden geheel verloren hebben, zyn ook onbekwaam om te contracteeren."

Uit wat hier aangehaal is volg dit dat dronkenskap as sodanig van so 'n aard moet wees dat die betrokke persoon nie net makliker oortuigbaar is nie of meer gewillig is om 'n kontrak te sluit nie maar hy moet nie weet dat hy 'n kontrak aangaan nie of hy moet geen benul hê van die bepalings van die kontrak nie. Volgens Engelse Reg is 'n persoon wat weens dronkenskap sy rede verloor het *non compos mentis*. Tog skynbaar kan hy 'n kontrak aangegaan in so 'n toestand later bekragtig wanneer hy nugter word. Indien daar geen totale verlies van rede is nie weens drank sal die Hof geen verligting gee nie tensy die beskonkene tot drank uitgelok is of sy dronkenskap misbruik is om 'n onbillike voordeel uit hom te kry. – Story *Equity Commentaries on Equity Jurisprudence,* 3de ed, bl 96, Leake *Contracts,* 8ste ed, bl 435.

Daar is 'n verskil tussen die Suid-Afrikaanse Reg en die Engelse Reg. In ons Reg is die kontrak nietig indien aangegaan deur 'n persoon *non compos mentis.* In die Engelse Reg word die kontrak aangegaan deur 'n beskonkene, wat sy rede verloor het, as vernietigbaar beskou. Die bevinding van WAARNEMENDE HOOFREGTER BEAUMONT in *Good-*

man v Pritchard, 28 NLR 227 te bl 231, in hierdie verband is te verkies bo die stelling van Wessels in sy *Law of Contracts,* deel I, para 704 . . .

In al die omstandighede van die saak en gesien die feit dat die bewyslas op verweerder gerus het is ek nie oortuig dat die magistraat die waarskynlikhede in hierdie saak verkeerd beoordeel en 'n verkeerde uitspraak gegee het nie.

Na my mening moet die appèl afgewys word . . .

MURRAY J het saamgestem.

Sex   **Geslag**

[51]   W v W

1976 2 SA 308 (W)

Marriage between persons of the same sex

Huwelik tussen persone van dieselfde geslag

The plaintiff was born and registered as a male. She also had the body of a male but felt herself to be a woman "encased in a male body" and was homosexual in the sense that she was sexually attracted to persons of the male sex. She then underwent a so-called sex-change operation, the purpose and effect of which was the construction of an artificial vagina as well as the insertion of a prosthesis which gave her the appearance of having a woman's breasts. After the operation, which was regarded as a success, the plaintiff considered herself a female and passed as such in society. The sex description in her birth certificate was altered so as to reflect the change of sex. She then entered into a properly solemnised marriage with the defendant, who was aware of the operation. They had normal sexual relations although the plaintiff was not able to bear children. The defendant then committed adultery and the plaintiff instituted an action for divorce. The court held that the plaintiff failed to prove that the marriage to the defendant was valid and ordered absolution from the instance.

Die eiseres is as 'n manlike persoon gebore en geregistreer. Sy het ook 'n manlike liggaam gehad maar het haarself as 'n vrou "encased in a male body" beskou. Sy was homoseksueel in die sin dat sy seksueel aangetrokke gevoel het tot persone van die manlike geslag. Sy ondergaan toe 'n sogenaamde geslagsveranderingsoperasie. Die doel en effek hiervan was om haar van 'n kunsmatige vagina te voorsien en om haar borste deur middel van plastiese chirurgie te vergroot sodat sy die voorkoms van 'n vrou gehad het. Die operasie is as 'n sukses beskou. Na die operasie het die eiseres haarself as 'n vrou beskou en sy is ook as sodanig in die gemeenskap aanvaar. Haar geslagsbeskrywing is ook op haar geboortesertifikaat verander om die geslagsverandering weer te gee. Sy het hierna 'n huwelik met die verweerder aangegaan. Die huwelik is behoorlik voltrek en die verweerder was bewus van die operasie. Die partye het 'n normale seksuele verhouding gehad alhoewel die eiseres nie kinders sou kon hê nie. Die verweerder pleeg toe owerspel en die eiseres het 'n aksie om egskeiding ingestel. Die hof het beslis dat die eiseres nie bewys het dat haar huwelik met die verweerder geldig was nie en absolusie van die instansie beveel.

NESTADT J: [310] Marriage being the union of a man and a woman, two persons of the same sex cannot contract a valid marriage. (*Hahlo*, [*The SA Law of Husband and Wife*] p 66; *Corbett v Corbett*, (1970) 2 All ER 33 (PDA) at p 48). Accordingly, whether the parties in this case contracted a valid marriage depends on whether the plaintiff (at the time of the marriage) was a woman . . .

The determination of the present matter depends, I consider, on the resolution of the following: What was the sex of the plaintiff prior to the operation; if "she" was a male, then the further issue that arises is whether it has been proved that such operation changed the plaintiff's sex to that of a female. If it did not then it must follow that the marriage was invalid.

This type of problem involving, as it does, the question of what is sex and what are the criteria for determining a person's sex, has not so far as I am aware previously been dealt with or encountered (save for the unreported case of *Jonker v Jonker,* to which I shall later refer) in our case history, although it has been in that of other countries. Of course, over a very large area, the law is indifferent to sex (*Corbett v Corbett, supra*). However, in a number of respects what one's sex is, is legally relevant. An example that [311] comes to mind, besides the validity of marriage, is the case of adultery and rape where the sex of the participants is by definition an essential determinant. So too a change of sex (if it can be achieved) obviously has legal consequences of a fundamental nature: it may amount to conduct justifying a divorce on the grounds of constructive desertion (*Hahlo,* p 395); a change of sex may affect the provisions of a will, eg a bequest by a testator to "my son" who in the meantime has undergone surgery to become a "woman"; it may affect typically male obligations by law, such as compulsory military training ("Transsexualism and the Law" by SA Strauss (1970) 3 *CILSA* 348 at p 349); if the father of children underwent the operation, would such children cease to have a father?

I agree with the observation of the learned author of the article referred to in the previous paragraph that it is not for the jurist to solve the problem of what a person's sex is. It is essentially a question of fact in regard to which the Courts ought to be guided by the opinions of experts in the field of medicine . . .

[NESTADT J discussed *Corbett v Corbett* [1970] 2 All ER 33 (PDA) and proceeded:]

[312] In essence what the Court in *Corbett's* case decided was the following: the respondent, prior to the operation, was, applying biological criteria, a male; according to the medical evidence the sex of a person cannot be changed by surgical means; accordingly, the respondent was a male when "she" purported to marry the applicant and the marriage was therefore void. Other than an acknowledgment of the principle that marriage is essentially a relationship between a man and a woman, and that, in determining a person's sex for the purpose of deciding on the validity of a marriage, biological criteria are to be applied, the decision was one of fact . . .

To return to the facts of the present matter, the first question that arises concerns what sex the plaintiff was prior to the operation. In the absence of any medical evidence I must do my best on the facts deposed to by the parties themselves. These facts reveal, I consider, that biologically the plaintiff was a male. I refer in this regard to the plaintiff's admission that she was registered as a male, that she had a male body, that she was a homosexual in the sense indicated and that she underwent a "sex-change" operation. Indeed, I did not understand counsel for the plaintiff to dispute this, save to point out that psychologically the plaintiff regarded herself as a woman. There is however no evidence (nor, one imagines, could there be) to justify a finding that merely on this basis the plaintiff was a woman. I therefore find that prior to the operation the plaintiff was a male.

Mr *Trengove's* main submission was that the operation which the plaintiff underwent changed her sex to that of a female. During the course of his argument in this regard he relied on *Jonker's* case (WLD 25 February; Case No 248/70). In this matter, which was an undefended action for a restitution order, the plaintiff's husband testified that the defendant was born [313] a male, but that, prior to the parties' marriage, she had undergone an operation which changed her to a person of the female sex. Without hearing any further evidence in this regard, THERON, J, granted the restitution order prayed for. The learned Judge obviously considered himself bound by the assertion that the defendant had become, and was at the time of the marriage, a female. For the reasons which follow I consider that the evidence does not go to this length in the present matter, and that *Jonker's* case is accordingly distinguishable on the facts.

I do not think I am adopting too technical an approach when I say that the plaintiff's evidence does not show that the operation converted her into a female. What it did was to artificially supply her with certain of the attributes of a woman, namely breasts and a vagina-like cavity. This, however, so it was argued, taking into account the fact that the plaintiff was (always) a transsexual and thus psychologically a woman, was sufficient; that in her post-operative state, and, in particular, because of her ability to have sex with the defendant, she was capable of fulfilling the essential role of a woman in marriage (and this, despite her inability to procreate) and that it would be anomalous to classify the plaintiff as male when she had the physical and psychological attributes of a female and was socially accepted as, and looked like, a woman . . .

[NESTADT J referred to certain criticisms of *Corbett's* case and proceeded:]

[314] To accede to the argument set out above would, in my view, be to subvert the requirement of our law that a valid marriage requires the parties to be of the opposite sex. It seeks to overcome the impliedly admitted impossibility of changing one's sex by the argument that post-operatively the patient is no longer an effective male but is, on the contrary, now capable of having sexual intercourse with a male in the normal manner. It is open to doubt whether the latter proposition is correct. In *Corbett's* case, *supra*, ORMROD, J, (at p 49) held that if necessary he would have been prepared to hold that the respondent was physically incapable of consummating the marriage because he did not think that sexual intercourse, using the artificial cavity, could be described as ordinary or natural coitus. In the view I take of the matter, it is unnecessary (even if I were able to in the absence of medical evidence) to decide this point. The issue is not whether, after the operation, the plaintiff was an effective male, nor whether she looked like a female (which she does), nor whether society has accepted her as a female, nor whether she is capable of having sex with a male; the issue is whether the plaintiff at the time of the marriage was a woman.

I find no justification, however desirable it may be or may not be, for finding that a person in the position of the plaintiff was a woman when she married the defendant where, on the evidence, she was a male prior to her operation but which the evidence does not reveal had changed her sex. Imitation cannot be equated with actual transformation. If what I may call this pseudo-type of woman is, for the purposes of marriage, properly to be regarded as a female, then, in the absence of medical evidence justifying such a finding, the intervention of the Legislature would be necessary.

Reference to the Legislature provides me with the opportunity of dealing with a further argument advanced on the basis of the provisions of sec 7B of the Births, Marriages and Deaths Registration Act, 81 of 1963. This section which was inserted by sec 1(1) of Act, 51 of 1974 reads:

> "Alteration of sex description of person in his birth register. – The Secretary may, on the recommendation of the Secretary for Health alter, in the birth register of any person who had undergone a change of sex, the description of the sex of such person

and may for this purpose call for such medical reports and institute such investigations as he may deem necessary".

It was submitted that contrary to what was held in *Corbett's* case, *supra,* the notion that a person can undergo a change of sex has thus been accepted in South African law. It would appear as if the Legislature does recognise the factual possibility of a change of sex. How, if in fact, cases to come confirm that a change of sex is not possible, the section will be interpreted lies beyond the scope of this judgment. Dealing with the amendment, Professor *Hahlo* in 1974 *Annual Survey of South African Law,* p 60, states:

> "Since a true change of sex, transforming a full man into a full woman or *vice versa,* is not possible, the question whether a change of sex as envisaged in sec 7B has taken place will presumably be determined in accordance with generally accepted 'conventional' criteria".

Suffice to say that I do not consider that the section can or does assist the plaintiff in proving that she changed her sex.

[315] It remains for me to deal with the argument that the marriage certificate was in itself sufficient to prove that the marriage was valid. In terms of sec 42(3) of Act 81 of 1963, a marriage certificate (and other types of certificates)

> "shall, in all courts of law ... be *prima facie* evidence of the particulars set forth therein".

This means that a judicial official must accept the particulars as correct until he is convinced that he cannot rely upon them. Whether such a conviction is justified must depend on the evidence which refutes or throws doubt upon the contents of the certificates. (*R v Chizah,* 1960 (1) SA 435 (AD)). Included in the presumption thus created would be all the essentials for the conclusion of a valid marriage including the capacity of the parties (Schmidt, *Die Bewysreg,* p 110). A further (common law) presumption which is relevant in this regard is the presumption of the validity of a marriage flowing from evidence of the ceremony and subsequent cohabitation (*Ex parte L (also known as A),* 1947 (3) SA 50 (C)). The presumptions referred to may of course be rebutted. In *Ex parte L, supra,* OGILVIE-THOMPSON, AJ, dealing with the common law presumption referred to, stated (at p 57):

> "Any presumption which might otherwise have applied on this point is in my view conclusively rebutted by the circumstances that the Court is actually aware that neither of these ministers was in fact at the relevant date a duly appointed marriage officer. The case is therefore not one which can be decided on a presumption; it must be decided on the actual evidence before the Court. This latter is fatal to the petitioner's contention".

Similar considerations apply in the present matter. The evidence indicates that the plaintiff was a male prior to the operation; there is no evidence that the operation changed the plaintiff's sex. Accordingly, I am of the view that the presumptions referred to have been rebutted and, therefore, do not avail the plaintiff.

My conclusion is that the plaintiff was a male prior to her operation and that, in the absence of proof that such operation changed her sex, she has failed to prove that her marriage to the defendant was valid.

It follows that there must be absolution from the instance on the plaintiff's claim for a divorce and division of the joint estate ...

Note

The Births, Marriages and Deaths Registration Act 81 of 1963 has been repealed and replaced by the Births and Deaths Registration Act 51 of

Aantekening

Die Wet op die Registrasie van Geboortes, Huwelike en Sterfgevalle 81 van 1963 is deur die Wet op Registrasie van Geboortes en Sterftes 51

1992. The replacement act contains many of the provisions of its predecessor. It does not, however, contain a provision similar to section 7B. A person who has had a sex change can therefore no longer have his altered sex registered on his birth certificate. The South African Law Commission is currently investigating the legal consequences of sexual realignment. It is hoped that the omission of a provision similar to section 7B will be addressed by the commission.

The present position seems to be that although sex change operations are allowed, a change of sex is not recognised in our law. One sympathizes with the transsexual who finds himself in a tragic position. If any relief is to be brought for him it should, however, be done by the legislature (see Taitz 1980 *SALJ* 76; Thomas 1980 *SALJ* 82; Barnard, Cronjé and Olivier 162. See also Strauss 1967 *SALJ* 214; Kahn 1981 *SALJ* 111; Van Oosten 1988 *Codicillus* 7.)

W's case has been criticised by Lupton (1976 *SALJ* 385 *et seq*) but the criticism does not seem to be fully justified (see Taitz 1980 *SALJ* 75).

In *W's* case NESTADT J was prepared to annul the marriage provided the summons, on notice to the defendant, was appropriately amended. In *Simms v Simms* 1981 4 SA 186 (D) where the facts were similar to those in *W's* case, the court declared the marriage null and void.

van 1992 herroep en vervang. Die nuwe wet bevat baie van die bepalings van sy voorganger. Dit bevat egter nie 'n bepaling soortgelyk aan artikel 7B nie. 'n Persoon wat 'n geslagsverandering ondergaan het, kan dus nie meer sy veranderde geslag op sy geboortesertifikaat laat aanteken nie. Die Suid-Afrikaanse Regskommissie is tans besig met 'n ondersoek na die regsgevolge van geslagsverandering. Hopelik sal die weglating van 'n bepaling soortgelyk aan artikel 7B deur die kommissie aangespreek word.

Die huidige posisie skyn te wees dat alhoewel geslagsveranderingsoperasies toegelaat word, 'n geslagsverandering nie deur die reg erken word nie. 'n Mens het simpatie met die transseksuele persoon wat hom werklik in 'n tragiese situasie bevind. Enige verbetering in sy posisie kan egter net deur die wetgewer bewerkstellig word (sien Taitz 1980 *SALJ* 76; Thomas 1980 *SALJ* 82; Barnard, Cronjé en Olivier 166. Sien ook Strauss 1967 *SALJ* 214; Kahn 1981 *SALJ* 111; Van Oosten 1988 *Codicillus* 7).

W se saak is deur Lupton gekritiseer (1976 *SALJ* 385 ev). Die kritiek skyn egter nie heeltemal geregverdig te wees nie (sien Taitz 1980 *SALJ* 75).

In *W* se saak was NESTADT R bereid om die huwelik nietig te verklaar mits die dagvaarding na kennisgewing aan die verweerder behoorlik gewysig sou word. In *Simms v Simms* 1981 4 SA 186 (D) was die feite soortgelyk aan die in *W* se saak en het die hof die huwelik nietig verklaar.

The engagement

Requirements for a valid engagement
Termination of the engagement
Consequences of breach of promise

Die verlowing

Geldigheidsvereistes vir 'n verlowing
Beëindiging van die verlowing
Gevolge van troubreuk

Requirements for a valid engagement   Geldigheidsvereistes vir 'n verlowing

[52]   THELEMANN V VON GEYSO

1957 3 SA 39 (W)

Breach of promise to marry which was induced by misrepresentation

The plaintiff mistakenly believed that she was pregnant as a result of sexual intercourse with the defendant. It was on account of her innocent misrepresentation in this regard that the defendant promised to marry her. Later it became clear that the plaintiff was not pregnant and the defendant refused to marry her. The plaintiff then sued defendant for damages for breach of promise. The defendant put the plaintiff's misrepresentation forward as a defence. The claim was dismissed.

Verbreking van 'n verlowing waar die verlowingsooreenkoms deur wanvoorstelling teweeggebring is

Die eiseres het verkeerdelik geglo dat sy swanger was as gevolg van geslagsgemeenskap met die verweerder. Op grond van hierdie onskuldige wanvoorstelling het die verweerder beloof om met haar te trou. Toe dit later blyk dat die eiseres nie swanger was nie het die verweerder geweier om met haar te trou. Die eiseres het hom toe aangespreek vir skadevergoeding op grond van troubreuk. Die verweerder het die eiseres se wanvoorstelling as 'n verweer geopper. Die,eis is van die hand gewys.

HIEMSTRA J: [39] There is authority that fraudulent misrepresentation justifies rescission of a promise because there is little prospect of a happy marriage if the parties commence their association with deceit (Brouwer, *De Jure Connubiorum,* 1.19.2, quoted by Hahlo *Husband and Wife,* on p 21). I find that there was no fraudulent misrepresentation here because plaintiff impressed me favourably as to character, and if she wanted to [40] deceive, she could have kept the pretence up much longer than she did, in order to induce him to commit himself more deeply. The matter must rest on innocent misrepresentation. In this regard Professor Hahlo says on p 21:

> "There is no authority on the question whether a contract of engagement may be rescinded by one of the parties on the ground of innocent misrepresentation, eg the man promised marriage after the woman told him, mistakenly but *bona fide,* that she was pregnant by him. It is submitted, though not without doubt, that the contract may not be rescinded on this ground."

The ground on which *Brouwer* recognises the right of a party to resile in case of fraudulent pretence of pregnancy is the broad one that the marriage is bound to be miserable. This ground in my opinion also applies where pregnancy was mistakenly believed to exist. If an unwilling bridegroom has been led to the altar because of this belief, he will not be converted into an enthusiast for matrimony when the mistake is discovered. Van den Heever on *Breach of Promise and Seduction* states on p 28:

> "It is not possible exhaustively to enumerate the just causes for breaking off an engagement; within the principles laid down the Courts have a wide discretion."

On the conclusion of fact as stated above, I hold that the promise was not binding ...

The overall picture is one from which defendant emerges with little credit. The plaintiff however acted unwisely in granting him her favours without making sure that he wanted to marry her. Adult females must protect themselves against such depredations by the male. The law cannot give them redress in matters where they are able to look after themselves . . .

The plaintiff's case is dismissed . . .

Note

The importance of the decision in this case is that the court held that any contract of engagement which was induced by misrepresentation was voidable; the fact that the misrepresentation was innocent is immaterial.

Aantekening

Die belang van die uitspraak in hierdie saak is dat die hof beslis het dat enige verlowingskontrak wat as gevolg van 'n wanvoorstelling tot stand gekom het, vernietigbaar is; die feit dat die wanvoorstelling onskuldig was, is irrelevant.

[53]   FRIEDMAN V HARRIS

1928 CPD 43

Promise by a married person to marry another

The plaintiff was seduced by the defendant when she was twenty years old. She then claimed damages from him on the ground of the seduction but he settled the matter by paying her a sum of £1 000 in cash. The defendant thereafter induced the plaintiff to return the money still in her possession by promising the plaintiff that when he obtained a divorce from his wife, he would marry her. He declared that the divorce proceedings had already been commenced. He further promised the plaintiff that, if he did not obtain the divorce, he would refund her the money. The plaintiff, relying on these representations, repaid £800 to the defendant. He gave £20 back to her. Later it became apparent that the defendant had not commenced divorce proceedings against his wife. The plaintiff thereafter claimed a refund of the £780 but the defendant refused to give it to her. She instituted an action to recover the money. The defendant excepted to her claim on the ground that it was bad in law in that the cause of action was illegal, *contra bonos mores* and against public policy. The

'n Belofte deur 'n getroude persoon om met 'n ander te trou

Die eiseres is deur die verweerder verlei toe sy twintig jaar oud was. Sy het op grond van die seduksie skadevergoeding van hom geëis maar hy het die aangeleentheid geskik deur 'n bedrag van £1 000 aan haar te betaal. Op grond van 'n belofte dat hy met haar sou trou sodra hy van sy vrou geskei is, het die verweerder die eiseres oorgehaal om die gedeelte van die £1 000 wat sy nog in haar besit gehad het aan hom terug te betaal. Hy het beweer dat die egskeidingsgeding teen sy vrou reeds aanhangig gemaak is. Hy het verder belowe om die geld aan die eiseres terug te betaal indien hy nie 'n egskeiding sou verkry nie. Die eiseres het hierdie bewerings geglo en £800 aan die verweerder terugbetaal. Hy het £20 aan haar teruggegee. Dit het later geblyk dat die verweerder nie 'n egskeidingsgeding teen sy vrou aanhangig gemaak het nie. Die eiseres het toe die £780 van die verweerder teruggeëis maar hy het geweier om dit te betaal. Sy het toe aksie ingestel om die geld van hom te verhaal. Die verweerder het eksepsie aangeteken teen haar eis op grond daarvan dat dit regtens onge-

exception was allowed and the plaintiff's claim failed.

grond, *contra bonos mores* en in stryd met die openbare belang was. Die eksepsie is gehandhaaf en die eiseres se eis het misluk.

BENJAMIN J: [45] The contract that [the claim] was founded on was an undertaking by the defendant to marry the plaintiff in consideration of her paying him the sum of £1 000, or, if he should not marry her to return the £1 000. He could only undertake to marry the plaintiff if he obtained a divorce from his wife, he at that time being, as was well known to the plaintiff, a married man. This is therefore an undertaking on the defendant's part to obtain a divorce and then to marry the plaintiff. Now, such an undertaking is clearly illegal under our law as being *contra bonos mores*. There are two cases in our courts in which that point has been specifically considered. I might refer to the later case of *Staples v Marquard* (1919, CPD at page 181), a decision by the present JUDGE-PRESIDENT, the headnote of which is: "The promise by a married man to marry another woman when his existing marriage shall have been dissolved is against public policy. The ratification of such a promise, though made after dissolution of marriage, cannot be pleaded as a cause of action." That case virtually follows a similar decision by the late JUDGE-PRESIDENT in this Division in the case of *Kiely v Dreyer* (1916, CPD 603). I might just refer to a passage in the judgment by the late JUDGE-PRESIDENT where he says: "The contract of marriage is the most serious and important one that can be entered into, the most far-reaching consequences to the community and the State ensue on its completion; the law in most civilised communities rightly regards it with great respect, if not reverence, and that a bargain should be made with a third party to receive money in order to bring about its dissolution is repugnant to the fundamental principles on which our common society has been built up, and ought to remain established." In my opinion it does not matter whether the exception be that the contract is against public policy or is *contra bonos mores*, for such a contract is both, and the exception is a sound one. I approve in every respect of the statement there made. The sanctity of marriage must not be lightly interfered with and contracts with other parties to interfere with such sanctity are certainly [46] *contra bonos mores* and illegal. If that be so, a well-known maxim of law becomes applicable to the present case. The present case is a claim to recover, or to obtain a refund of, an amount of money paid by a third party to a husband to induce him to bring about a divorce. Such a contract, as I have already said, is *contra bonos mores* and illegal. Now, the maxims which apply in such a case as this are expressed in the words: "*In pari delicto potior est conditio defendentis, in pari delicto potior est conditio possidentis.*" [In a case of equal wrong by both parties, the defendant is in the stronger position, in a case of equal wrong by both parties, the possessor is in the stronger position]. Now, the *defendens* or the *possidens* of the present case is the defendant. He has received the sum of £800 and has already refunded £20, still remaining in possession of £780. That amount the plaintiff seeks to recover, but she can only found her claim on an illegal and immoral contract, and, that being so, the maxims which I have just cited would apply. The position of the defendant is that he would be entitled to remain in possession of the money which he now has. No action to recover possession of that money will lie at the instance of any one setting up such an illegal or immoral contract. I therefore think that the exception raised by the defendant is a good one, but, at the same time, if the facts alleged in this declaration are true, one cannot express otherwise than the greatest repugnance at the position taken up by the defendant. It may be a sound position in law, but it is a most repugnant one to set up in a court of morals . . .

[I]n the circumstances I very reluctantly give effect to the exception which has been taken that the plaintiff's declaration is bad in law, as showing no ground of action entitling her to recover the £780 for which she sues. The exception must be allowed . . .

LOUWRENS J concurred.

Note

For a contract of engagement to be valid, both parties must have the capacity to marry each other at the time when the promise to marry is made. A person who is already married does not have the capacity to marry anybody else and therefore any engagement he purports to enter into will be invalid. He can only enter into a valid contract of engagement once his marriage has been dissolved. Any purported contract of engagement entered into by a married person is *contra bonos mores* and void *(Duncan v Willson* (1906) 27 NLR 624; *Claassen v Van der Watt* 1969 3 SA 68 (T)). The fact that the purported contract of engagement is invalid means that no damages can be claimed for breach of promise to marry *(Duncan v Willson; Viljoen v Viljoen* [54]; *Claassen v Van der Watt*).

Aantekening

'n Verlowingskontrak kan alleenlik geldig wees as albei die partye die bevoegdheid het om met mekaar te trou op die tydstip wat hulle beloof om met mekaar in die huwelik te tree. 'n Getroude persoon is onbevoeg om met 'n ander persoon te trou en gevolglik is enige verlowing wat hy voorgee om te sluit, ongeldig. Hy kan slegs 'n geldige verlowingskontrak aangaan nadat sy huwelik ontbind is. Enige verlowingskontrak wat 'n getroude persoon sluit, is *contra bonos mores* en nietig *(Duncan v Willson* (1906) 27 NLR 624; *Claassen v Van der Watt* 1969 3 SA 68 (T)). Die feit dat die verlowingskontrak ongeldig is, beteken dat geen skadevergoeding op grond daarvan verhaal kan word indien die belofte om te trou nie gestand gedoen word nie *(Duncan v Willson; Viljoen v Viljoen* [54]; *Claassen v Van der Watt*).

[54] VILJOEN V VILJOEN

1944 CPD 137

Promise by a married person to marry another

The plaintiff alleged that the defendant agreed to marry her, professing to be unmarried, and that it was only on the day fixed for the wedding that he told her he was married. She now claimed satisfaction from the defendant. The defendant contended that the plaintiff knew he was married but his evidence was not accepted. The court awarded the plaintiff satisfaction for *contumelia* (insult).

Belofte deur 'n getroude persoon om met 'n ander te trou

Die eiseres het beweer dat die verweerder ingestem het om met haar te trou, dat hy voorgegee het dat hy ongetroud was en dat hy eers op die dag wat hulle sou trou aan haar gesê het dat hy getroud was. Sy het nou genoegdoening van hom geëis. Die verweerder het beweer dat die eiseres geweet het dat hy getroud was maar sy getuienis is nie aanvaar nie. Die hof het aan die eiseres genoegdoening vir *contumelia* (belediging) toegestaan.

SUTTON J: [137] This is not an action for breach of promise of marriage. It could not be such an action, because a married man cannot make a valid promise of marriage to anybody. An action for breach of promise of marriage cannot be founded on such a promise as he [the defendant] now admits he made and of which there is abundant evidence, because at the time he made that promise, he was a married man. The action is founded on the deceit which he practised on this woman, and the *injuria* suffered by her. There is authority to show that such an action will lie. The matter was gone into in the case of *Duncan and Willson* (27 NLR 624), where damages [138] was awarded against a married man, the plaintiff being unaware that the defendant was at the time a married man. Ordinarily in a case of breach of promise of marriage, the elements which the Courts would take into consideration in assessing damages are the monetary loss which the plaintiff has sustained, the financial position of the defendant, the social position of the parties and the extent to which the feelings of the plaintiff have been wounded.

In this case I cannot award any damages for breach of contract. In the view I take of the law I can only give damages for the *injuria* suffered by the plaintiff, for *contumelia*, for the insult that this man not only proposed to this woman and was accepted by her, but made love to her and so on ...

I am satisfied that she was not aware that he was a married man. I accept her evidence, which she gave clearly. I do not accept anything the defendant has said ...

It is clear from the evidence that ... he represented himself to the Rev Steenkamp as a bachelor, as he did all along to the plaintiff's family, a decent respectable family of a much better class than he is. He is one of those men who prefer to take a woman to the door of the church, but not over the threshold. It was not until the morning of the wedding that he for the first time told her he was a married man. It is quite clear from the undated letter he wrote that he actually allowed her to make all the arrangements for the wedding, to arrange for the reception and insert advertisements in the papers, to have the banns called and so on. He was quite prepared to do that, well knowing he was not in a position to marry her. His agreement to marry her, and all his subsequent conduct while remaining with her on the footing of an engaged woman was an injury to her feelings. It was a serious injury he inflicted upon her, but it does not seem to me there would be any point in awarding heavy damages. The position in life of the parties does not warrant it.

In the circumstances, I give judgment for £150 ...

Note

The innocent party may only institute an action against the married party if she was unaware at the time of the making of the promise that he was married (*Duncan v Willson* (1906) 27 NLR 624). If she knew that he was married she is barred from bringing the action (*Claassen v Van der Watt* 1969 3 SA 68 (T)). The engagement is void because a married man cannot make a valid promise of marriage (Voet 23.1.2,8; Grotius 1.5.2). The action can therefore not be based on the contract, but must, instead, be based on the *iniuria* suffered by the plaintiff. In other words, it is an infringement of a personality interest. The court can therefore only award her satisfaction for the *contumelia* but no damages for any patrimonial loss.

See also *Friedman v Harris* [53].

Aantekening

Die onskuldige party kan het 'n aksie instel teen die getroude party as sy onbewus was van die feit dat hy getroud was toe hy beloof het om met haar te trou (*Duncan v Willson* (1906) 27 NLR 624). As sy geweet het dat hy getroud was, het sy geen aksie nie (*Claassen v Van der Watt* 1969 3 SA 68 (T)). Die verlowing is nietig omdat 'n getroude man nie 'n geldige verlowingskontrak kan aangaan nie (Voet 23.1.2,8; De Groot 1.5.2). Die aksie kan gevolglik nie op die kontrak gebaseer word nie, dit moet gebaseer word op die *iniuria* wat teenoor haar gepleeg is. Met ander woorde dit is die aantasting van 'n persoonlikheidsreg. Die hof kan gevolglik net genoegdoening vir die *contumelia* toeken maar nie enige vergoeding vir vermoënskade wat gely is nie.

Sien ook *Friedman v Harris* [53].

| Termination of the engagement | Beëindiging van die verlowing |

[55] SCHNAAR V JANSEN

(1924) 45 NLR 218

Breach of promise to marry – *justa causa*

The plaintiff was engaged to the defendant. After they became engaged, the defendant discovered that one of the plaintiff's uncles was married to an African woman, that another had been hanged for the murder of his wife and that her brother had been convicted of housebreaking and theft. The defendant then repudiated the engagement. The plaintiff sued him for breach of promise. The defendant admitted breach of promise but averred that the abovementioned circumstances rendered it impossible for him to comply with his promise to marry the plaintiff and that his repudiation of the contract was justified. The plaintiff excepted to the defendant's plea and the exception was allowed, as was the claim.

Troubreuk – *justa causa*

Die eiseres was verloof aan die verweerder. Nadat hulle verloof geraak het, het die verweerder uitgevind dat een van die eiseres se ooms met 'n Swart vrou getroud was, dat 'n ander oom vir die moord op sy vrou gehang is en dat haar broer skuldig bevind is aan inbraak en diefstal. Die verweerder het die verlowingskontrak toe gerepudieer. Die eiseres het hom op grond van troubreuk aangespreek. Die verweerder het erken dat hy die verlowing verbreek het maar het beweer dat bogenoemde omstandighede dit vir hom onmoontlik gemaak het om met die eiseres te trou en dat sy terugtrede uit die kontrak daardeur geregverdig is. Die eiseres het teen hierdie verweer eksepsie aangeteken en die eksepsie is gehandhaaf. Die eis is toegestaan.

DOVE-WILSON JP: [219] [The defendant] does not even allege that the plaintiff was aware of the circumstances, or, that, knowing them, she concealed them from him; and, of course, they are circumstances for which the plaintiff cannot be said to be responsible. No decisions of the South African Courts have been cited in support of this plea, and I am not surprised. I should be surprised to find that there was any decision that the discovery, subsequent to the engagement, that the relatives of one of the parties were not such as the other would desire, would give the other the right to break off the contract. If a man engages himself to a woman without having satisfied himself as to her relatives he takes the risk of their being unsatisfactory. And even if it can be said that there is an authority in the institutional writers supporting such a plea, the fact that it has never been appealed to and applied in the Courts is sufficient warrant for regarding it as obsolete and no longer the common law of South Africa, especially as the discovery after engagement by one of the parties that the other has objectionable relations is not unlikely to have happened frequently. The matters alleged may be relevant to the question of damages, but they afford no absolute justification for the breach of the promise. The exception must be allowed.

CARTER J concurred; TATHAM J concurred in a separate judgment.

Note

It is suggested that the court's finding that the circumstances of this case did not warrant the defendant's resiling from the contract is incorrect. Any grounds which, in the light of human

Aantekening

Daar word aan die hand gedoen dat die hof se bevinding dat die omstandighede van hierdie saak nie regverdiging gebied het vir die verweerder se terugtrede uit die kontrak nie, verkeerd is.

experience, may render the proposed marriage an unhappy one and which the party resiling from the contract only discovers after the conclusion of the engagement, should justify unilateral repudiation of the contract of engagement. If a party to an engagement discovers facts which in his opinion make it impossible for him to marry the person to whom he is engaged, it appears unfair to hold him liable on the ground of his breach of promise.

Another point which arises in connection with *Schnaar v Jansen* is the question of how much personal information a person has to reveal to his future spouse. It is unnecessary to provide the other party with full information but if one of the parties, voluntarily or in reply to questions, gives information, that information must be the truth (Hahlo 51). An engagement is a contract which requires the utmost good faith and there would be little chance of a happy marriage if the parties gave each other false personal information. Van der Vyver and Joubert (477) accept *Schnaar v Jansen* as authority for the statement that in ordinary circumstances a fiancé need not supply the other party with information on his family background and that the other party would have to ask about these matters if he were interested in them. However, Van den Heever (26) correctly submits that "a party with a skeleton in his cupboard is obliged to disclose it", whether such information relates to family background or any other matter. It is submitted that, if a party knows or foresees that a certain fact concerning himself or his background would be of importance to the other party, he is obliged to provide the other party with that information. With regard to the question of which facts would be regarded as material, Van der Vyver and Joubert (478) submit that one should look at what the reasonable man would do. Would the reasonable man not have entered into the engagement, had he known of the specific facts, these facts should be regarded as material. If these facts are withheld from the other party, this would be misrepresentation and would enable the misled party to resile from the contract.

See also *Krull v Sangerhaus* [56].

If a contract of engagement was induced by misrepresentation, the party who breaks off the engagement is not liable on the ground of breach of promise – see *Thelemann v Von Geyso* [52].

Enige gronde wat, gesien in die lig van menslike ondervinding, die voorgenome huwelik ongelukkig kan maak en waarvan die party wat uit die kontrak terugtree eers na die verlowing bewus word, behoort eensydige terugtrede uit die verlowingskontrak te regverdig. Dit lyk onregverdig om 'n verloofde wat feite ontdek wat dit vir hom onmoontlik maak om met sy verloofde te trou op grond van sy verbreking van die verlowing aanspreeklik te hou.

'n Ander aspek wat in *Schnaar v Jansen* ter sprake gekom het, is die vraag hoeveel persoonlike inligting 'n persoon aan sy verloofde moet openbaar. Dit is onnodig om die ander party volledig in te lig maar indien een van die partye, vrywillig of in antwoord op vrae, inligting verskaf, moet daardie inligting die waarheid wees (Hahlo 51). 'n Verlowing is 'n kontrak wat die hoogste trou verg en die kanse op 'n gelukkige huwelik sal uiters skraal wees indien die partye mekaar van vals persoonlike inligting voorsien. Van der Vyver en Joubert (477) aanvaar *Schnaar v Jansen* as gesag vir die stelling dat 'n verloofde normaalweg nie die ander party van inligting oor sy familie-agtergrond hoef te voorsien nie en dat die ander party oor hierdie aangeleentheid navraag sal moet doen indien hy daarin geïnteresseerd is. Hierteenoor stel Van den Heever (26) egter tereg voor dat "a party with a skeleton in his cupboard is obliged to disclose it", of sodanige inligting nou met familie-agtergrond te doen het of nie. Ons wil aan die hand doen dat 'n party verplig is om inligting oor hom of sy agtergrond aan die ander party te verskaf indien hy weet, of voorsien, dat sodanige inligting vir die ander party van wesenlike belang is. Met betrekking tot die vraag welke feite as wesenlik beskou moet word, stel Van der Vyver en Joubert (478) voor dat die redelike man as maatstaf gebruik moet word. Indien die redelike man nie die verlowing sou gesluit het indien hy van die betrokke feite bewus was nie, moet hierdie feite as wesenlik beskou word. Indien hierdie feite vir die ander party verberg word, is dit wanvoorstelling en sal die misleide party die reg hê om uit die kontrak terug te tree.

Sien ook *Krull v Sangerhaus* [56].

Indien 'n verlowingskontrak deur wanvoorstelling teweeggebring is, is die party wat die verlowing beëindig nie op grond van troubreuk aanspreeklik nie – sien *Thelemann v Van Geyso* [52].

[56] KRULL V SANGERHAUS

1980 4 SA 299 (E)

Breach of promise to marry – *justa causa*

The plaintiff sued the defendant for damages, *inter alia*, in respect of breach of promise to marry. The defendant admitted his agreement to get married and his repudiation thereof, but claimed that the repudiation was as a result of a disagreement between the parents of the plaintiff and of the defendant on the arrangements for the wedding reception. The plaintiff and the defendant also became involved in the dispute, plaintiff siding with her parents and defendant siding with his parents. He contended that his repudiation of the agreement was justified. The plaintiff excepted to the defendant's defence. The exception was upheld.

Troubreuk – *justa causa*

Die eiseres het die verweerder onder andere vir skadevergoeding weens troubreuk gedagvaar. Die verweerder het die ooreenkoms om te trou sowel as sy repudiëring daarvan erken, maar aangevoer dat die repudiëring die gevolg was van 'n geskil tussen die ouers van die eiseres en die verweerder omtrent die reëlings van die huweliksonthaal. Die eiseres en die verweerder het ook in die geskil betrokke geraak; die eiseres het haar ouers se kant gekies en die verweerder sy ouers s'n. Die verweerder het aangevoer dat sy repudiëring van die ooreenkoms geregverdig was. Die eiseres het eksepsie aangeteken teen hierdie verweer en die eksepsie is gehandhaaf.

EKSTEEN J: [301] In view of the fact that the defendant, in the present instance, has admitted that he had repudiated the agreement to marry and pleaded that his repudiation had been justified and therefore lawful, Mr *Jardine,* who appeared on his behalf, conceded, in my view correctly, that the *onus* of proving such justification rested on him. It was also not disputed that it was incumbent on the defendant to plead the grounds upon which he relies to prove such justification . . .

It was common cause at the argument of the exception that an agreement to marry is a contractual relationship of considerable importance to the parties, so much so that its unjustifiable repudiation may attract, and often does attract, both contractual and delictual damages. (Wessels *Law of Contract in South Africa* 2nd ed para 3195.) The unilateral repudiation of such an agreement by one of the parties could only be lawful if done for just cause. *Voet* at 23.1.13–16 deals with the circumstances which may constitute just cause for repudiation, and it is clear from his treatment of the subject that where a disagreement between the parties is relied upon for a repudiation of the agreement it must be of so serious a nature as

"to interfere wholly or partially with the aims of marriage or with its anticipated harmony and happiness".

(*Voet* 23.1.15, *Gane's* translation.) He then goes on to mention certain features which in his view would constitute a just cause, such as incapacity to procreate; that one of the parties suffers from a repulsive disease, or from insanity, or has become "infamous as a result of crime"; that an

"unjust and causeless dislike has been conceived on one side or the other such as to inspire a fear of savagery";

that one of the parties deceived the other as to the dowry;

"or some other like cause sufficiently serious in the discretion of the Judge, has appeared".

(*Ibid.*)

[302] At 23.1.18 he remarks that:

"The bond of betrothal, like that of every other pledge given, is inviolable; and the expectation of marriage is not to be rashly broken off or violated."

It is clear from these authorities that, although the Courts may have a wide discretion in determining what would constitute just cause for the unilateral repudiation of an agreement to marry (Van den Heever *Breach of Promise and Seduction* at 28), such cause, in order to be regarded as *justa*, must be of a sufficiently serious nature as to warrant the breach of so "inviolable" a pledge. *Van den Heever (op cit)* expresses the view that the objection of the parents to the marriage of their adult children would be a "hollow excuse" for repudiation and would not be upheld by a Court.

In my view, therefore, where, as in the present case, the defendant relies on a *justa causa* for his alleged lawful repudiation, it must appear from his pleadings that the circumstances are of such a serious nature as to constitute a *justa causa*. The mere allegation of a disagreement between the parents about the arrangements for the reception seems to me to be far too frivolous a circumstance to warrant a repudiation. The further allegation that the parties themselves became somehow involved in this dispute without any allegation of any unlawful or unreasonable conduct on the part of the plaintiff does not seem to take the defendant's case any further.

Mr *Jardine* submitted that the mere reference to a disagreement between the parents must imply a sufficiently serious circumstance as possibly to render the intended marriage an unhappy and disharmonious one, and that the seriousness of the allegation should be left for fuller elucidation at the trial and not be dealt with on exception. As I have pointed out, however, the defendant, in order to plead a lawful defence, must plead such circumstances as would constitute a *justa causa*. The mere reference to a disagreement between the parents on a trivial aspect of the wedding arrangements, involving the parties in an undisclosed way, without any further particularity as to the seriousness of the disagreement, or the degree of involvement of the parties themselves, does not constitute a *justa causa*, nor, for that matter, does the plea suggest that it does. I am therefore of the view that the plea does not, in the circumstances, disclose a defence and that it is therefore bad in law...

In the result, therefore, the exception to the plea to plaintiff's claim in respect of the alleged breach of contract to marry... is upheld and these paragraphs are struck out...

McCREATH AJ concurred.

Note

Either party to an engagement may unilaterally terminate it if his repudiation is based on a *justa causa* or good cause. It would be impossible to give a comprehensive definition of all the circumstances that would constitute a good cause for such a repudiation (Hahlo 53; Lee and Honoré 11). It is however generally accepted that such a cause must be of a sufficiently serious nature as to warrant a repudiation of the agreement.

Any circumstance which arises after the engagement has been entered into which will seriously jeopardise the chances of a happy marriage will be a good ground for repudiation, for example impotence, sterility, a serious physical or mental

Aantekening

Enigeen van die partye by 'n verlowing mag dit eensydig opsê as die repudiëring op 'n *justa causa* of goeie grond gebaseer is. Dit sou onmoontlik wees om 'n omvattende definisie te gee van al die omstandighede wat 'n goeie grond vir sodanige repudiëring daarstel (Hahlo 53; Lee en Honoré 11). Daar word egter algemeen aanvaar dat die rede van so 'n ernstige aard moet wees dat dit opsegging van die ooreenkoms regverdig.

Enige omstandigheid wat na die sluiting van die verlowing ontstaan wat die kanse op 'n gelukkige huwelik ernstig mag benadeel, sal 'n goeie grond vir beëindiging van die verlowing daarstel, byvoorbeeld as een van die gades gedurende die

defect or illness which develops during the existence of the engagement, or if one of the parties discovers that the other has a criminal record, or is an alcoholic or drug addict. The case under discussion offers a good example of circumstances which do not constitute a good cause. It is also clear from this case that the court has a wide discretion in determining what constitutes a good cause. See further Hahlo 53–55; Lee and Honoré 11–12.

See also *Schnaar v Jansen* [55].

bestaan van die verlowing impotent of steriel raak, of 'n ernstige fisiese gebrek of geestesiekte ontwikkel, of as een van die partye agterkom dat die ander een 'n kriminele rekord het, of 'n alkoholis is of aan verdowingsmiddels verslaaf is. Die onderhawige saak bied 'n goeie voorbeeld van omstandighede wat nie 'n *justa causa* daarstel nie. Hierdie saak illustreer ook duidelik dat die hof 'n baie wye diskresie het om te bepaal wat 'n goeie grond daarstel. Sien verder Hahlo 53–55; Lee en Honoré 11–12.

Sien ook *Schnaar v Jansen* [55].

Consequences of breach of promise

Gevolge van troubreuk

[57]   GUGGENHEIM V ROSENBAUM

1961 4 SA 21 (W)

Breach of promise to marry – damages

In 1943 the plaintiff was divorced at Reno in the American state of Nevada. At that stage she was domiciled in the state of New York. While she resided in New York she met the defendant who was on a visit to the United States. The defendant was domiciled in South Africa. They fell in love and in New York the defendant asked the plaintiff to marry him. It was agreed that the marriage would take place in South Africa. The plaintiff gave up her flat, sold her motor car and some of her furniture, had the rest of her furniture stored and gave up her employment. When she arrived in Cape Town early in February 1960 the defendant met her and repeated his promise to marry her. Later that month the parties moved to Johannesburg where the defendant lived. In Johannesburg the defendant refused to marry the plaintiff. The plaintiff sued the respondent for £7 185 damages for breach of promise to marry. In reply the defendant pleaded two special defences:

(i) that the plaintiff's divorce could not be recognised in terms of South African law since she and her husband were

Troubreuk – skadevergoeding

In 1943 is die eiseres te Reno in die Amerikaanse staat Nevada geskei. Op daardie stadium was sy in die staat New York gedomisilieer. Terwyl sy in New York gewoon het, het sy die verweerder ontmoet toe hy op 'n besoek aan Amerika was. Die verweerder was in Suid-Afrika gedomisilieer. Hulle het op mekaar verlief geraak en die verweerder het die eiseres in New York gevra om met hom te trou. Hulle het ooreengekom dat die huwelik in Suid-Afrika sou plaasvind. Die eiseres het haar woonstel opgesê, haar motor en sommige van haar meubels verkoop, die res van haar meubels laat opberg en uit haar werk bedank. Sy het vroeg in Februarie 1960 in Kaapstad gearriveer. Die verweerder het haar daar ontmoet en sy belofte om met haar te trou herhaal. Later daardie maand het die partye na Johannesburg vertrek waar die verweerder woonagtig was. In Johannesburg het die verweerder geweier om met die eiseres te trou. Die eiseres het die verweerder weens troubreuk vir £7 185 skadevergoeding gedagvaar. In antwoord op die eiseres se eis het die verweerder twee spesiale verwere geopper:

divorced in a state in which they were not domiciled. The defendant's promise to marry the plaintiff was therefore void as being *contra bonos mores* on the ground that the plaintiff was still legally married; and

(ii) that the law of the state of New York had to be applied to the matter. New York law did not allow the plaintiff to recover damages for breach of promise and the plaintiff's claim for damages should therefore be rejected.

The plaintiff's claim for damages was allowed but the amount was reduced.

(i) dat die eiseres se egskeiding nie ingevolge die Suid-Afrikaanse reg erken kon word nie aangesien sy en haar man geskei is in 'n staat waar hulle nie gedomisilieer was nie. Die verweerder se belofte om met die eiseres te trou was dus *contra bonos mores* en gevolglik nietig aangesien die eiseres steeds wettig getroud was; en

(ii) dat die reg van die staat New York op die aangeleentheid toegepas moes word en dat die eiseres nie ingevolge die New Yorkse reg skadevergoeding kon verhaal op grond van die verbreking van die verlowingskontrak nie. Dus moes haar eis van die hand gewys word.

Die eiseres se eis om skadevergoeding is toegestaan maar die bedrag is verminder.

TROLLIP J: [TROLLIP J discussed the law applicable to the defendant's first special defence and concluded that the plaintiff was effectively divorced on 14 September 1943 and that the engagement between the plaintiff and defendant was therefore valid. As regards the defendant's second special defence TROLLIP J held that South African law governed the matter. He proceeded:]

[33] Consequently, the plaintiff is entitled to recover such damages as she has been able to prove and as the law allows her to recover.

The plaintiff claims general damages and particular items of actual and prospective loss and expenditure which she alleges were and will be caused by the defendant's breach of promise. Included under the latter items were the losses she said she had sustained in giving up her apartment and disposing of many of her assets. In regard to these items, it was contended by Mr *Schwarz* [for the plaintiff], that if it was held that she had failed to prove the actual loss that she had suffered, the Court could nevertheless take into account, in fixing the amount of general damages, that she has sustained some unascertained but appreciable loss in those respects. Furthermore, Mr *Schwarz* contended that because [34] of certain imputations against the plaintiff's character made by the defendant or on behalf of the defendant during the course of the trial, the *injuria* involved in the breach of promise was aggravated and therefore the general damages should accordingly be substantially increased.

In view of the amount and the nature of the claims for damages and the above-mentioned contentions, it is necessary to give close attention to the rules of our law governing the award of damages for breach of promise.

In English law, the breach of promise is regarded as being "attended with some of the special consequences of a personal wrong" (*Finlay v Chirney* (1888) 20 QBD 494 at p 504), in consequence of which the plaintiff is presumed to have suffered damage as a result of the breach of promise itself. In nature and effect the damages are like those in libel actions ...

The ordinary damages (ie other than any specific monetary loss which must be specially claimed) are not measured by any fixed standard but are almost entirely in the discretion of the jury (*Halsbury*, 3rd ed vol 19 p 773 para 1235). Like libel too (see Spencer Bower on *Actionable Defamation*, 2nd ed p 156) the damages which can be awarded are not necessarily compensatory but may also be of "a vindictive and uncertain kind ... to punish the defendant in an exemplary manner" (*Finlay's* case *supra*; *Quirk v Thomas*, 1916 (1) KB 516 at p 338). Consequently, it follows logically that "the conduct of the parties may properly be considered in aggravation ... of damages" (*Halsbury, ibid* para 1236) and I think that that conduct would most probably include the conduct of the defendant at the trial itself as in libel actions ...

In pure Roman-Dutch Law the action for damages for breach of promise "remained rather undeveloped" (Van den Heever on *Breach of Promise* p 37) because the usual remedy was an order for specific performance of the marriage, but where it did lie it was to recover the plaintiff's *id quod interest* (ie the actual and prospective loss) as in ordinary actions for damages for breach of contract (*Van den Heever, ibid; McCalman v Thorne*, 1934 NPD 86 at pp 90, 91 and counsel's argument at pp 87–8, where the authorities are canvassed; *Davel v Swanepoel*, 1954 (1) SA 383 (AD) at p 387G–H). Mere breach of promise itself did not give rise to an *injuria* which would have entitled the plaintiff to include a claim for damages for personal wrong in her action; if the breach, however, was committed in circumstances that also constituted *injuria*, then doubtless she could have included such a claim as a separate cause of action (cf *Jockie v Meyer*, 1945 AD 354 at pp 367–8).

[35] Melius de Villiers on *Injuries* at p 26 says:

"A breach of contract is not, in its nature, an injury. The duty of fulfilling one's contracts is one that does not arise from the respect due to the other parties thereto ... So also, a breach of promise of marriage is not necessarily an injury. The favourable inclination of a man towards a woman may turn to aversion from numerous other causes than those which reflect upon her character, and there may be cases where a breach of promise of marriage may be occasioned by reasons which are strictly honourable. It might, however, be an injury when a person wilfully enters into an engagement to marry another which he does not intend keeping with the object of exposing that other to ridicule, or when he justifies his action by giving reasons for his conduct which are slanderous and untruthful."

It will therefore be seen that fundamentally Roman-Dutch Law differed from English law; but the early decisions of our Courts seem to have followed English law implicitly without any reference to or enquiry into Roman-Dutch Law (see, for example, *Triegaardt v Van der Vyver*, 1910 EDL 44; *Radloff v Ralph*, 1917 EDL 86). In 1934, for the first time a full argument was addressed to a Court, the NPD (HATHORN J and CARLISLE AJ) in *McCalman's case, supra*, on the Roman-Dutch Law, and the difference between it and English law; and the Court was urged to follow the former and accordingly to award damages only for pecuniary loss and none for *injuria*, as the *injuria* had not been specifically pleaded and the damages therefor claimed as a separate cause of action. It is a pity that the Court did not take the opportunity of establishing the action firmly on a Roman-Dutch Law basis. It held in effect that under the influence of English law the action had developed in our law into a unified or composite one comprising both contractual and delictual elements ...

It was further held (p 92) that there was no need, as a matter of practice and pleading, to separate the delictual from the contractual damages claimed in the action. Damages for both could be claimed in one lump sum.

McCalman's case has been followed in Natal (*Mymenah v Cassim Rahim*, 1943 NPD 229; *Combrink v Koch*, 1946 NPD 512) and it probably set the pattern for breach of promise cases in South Africa. In consequence, the delictual damages and the prospective loss in the contractual damages are now usually claimed in a lump sum as general damages, and any monetary loss is claimed and pleaded as special contractual damage. That was done in this case and no attempt was made in the pleadings or at the hearing to separate the delictual from the contractual general damages. That was probably due to *McCalman's* case.

Now *McCalman's* case appears to hold that the breach of contract itself gives rise not only to the contractual damages but also to the [36] delictual damages; in other words, that the mere breach of contract *ipso jure* constitutes an *injuria*. If it does mean that then, with great respect, I disagree with that part of it. I think that the plaintiff, in order to recover delictual damages, must prove not merely that the breach was wrongful but also that it was injurious or contumelious. Otherwise there would be an unnecessary subversion of the wholesome principle of Roman-Dutch Law set out in De Villiers on *Injuries,* quoted above. I think that that is also the effect of the view expressed so well and forcibly by the late Mr JUSTICE VAN DEN HEEVER at pp 30–31 in his *Breach of Promise. Inter alia* he said:

"It is submitted that those decisions of our Courts which seem to imply that breach of promise must necessarily contain a delictual element are unconsciously based on English principles and have no support in Roman-Dutch Law. Unless a person who breaks off an engagement commits an actionable wrong 'the feelings of the plaintiff and the moral suffering she has undergone' are irrelevant to the question of damages . . . The notion that a woman necessarily loses social position or 'face' when an engagement is broken off in non-injurious circumstances seems to me to reflect the morals of a by-gone age when espousals constituted an inchoate marriage and repudiation was equiv-alent to malicious desertion."

Consequently, contrary to what was held in *McCalman's* case, I think that it is generally advisable to separate in the composite action the contractual and the delictual elements and the damages claimed for each. That would conduce to clarity of thinking in assessing the general damages because each of the elements is governed by its own special principles that might be confused if not separately considered. For example, damages might be awardable for the contractual but not for the delictual remedy or *vice versa,* as it appears from what I have just said above; the former has to be proved with that degree of precision required in breach of contract whilst the latter is in the Court's discretion; the latter is, whereas the former is not, subject to aggravation or mitigation according to the contumely of the defendant's conduct; and so on. Consequently, unless the two elements are kept well separated there is a risk of confusion with consequent injustice, as, for example, of mitigating the plaintiff's prospective loss because the defendant's conduct has not been contumelious, or of claiming aggravation of damages for the defendant's subsequent conduct when there is no delictual liability at all. I am therefore constrained to disagree with *McCalman's* case in that respect too, and to say that in my view, although the modern action for breach of promise is a composite one, combining both contractual and delictual elements, as a general rule these elements should be clearly separated in the pleadings and in the assessment of damages so as to avoid confusion.

These further points relating to damages are also relevant in the present case. In regard to contractual damages, both the prospective loss of the benefits of the marriage and the actual monetary loss or expenditure incurred or to be incurred can be awarded. The latter must either flow directly from the breach of promise or must be reasonably supposed to have been within the contemplation of the parties at the time the contract was entered into as a probable consequence of the breach. Therefore, expenditure reasonably incurred prior to the breach in contemplation of the promised marriage taking place and which is rendered useless by the breach can obviously be [37] recovered. Expenditure or loss incurred or to be incurred after the breach can also be awarded if the above requisites are present, but only if such damage is not covered by an award of prospective loss. A duplication of damages in this respect must be safe-guarded against (*Van den Heever* at p 38).

In regard to delictual damages, these can, I think, be aggravated by any further contumelious or injurious conduct by or on behalf of the defendant at the trial itself but only if such conduct is a continuation of or is directly connected with the contumelious or injurious conduct involved in the actual breach of promise, and is not an entirely separate and distinct *injuria* (cf *Salzmann v Holmes*, 1914, AD 471 at pp 481–2; *Black v Joseph*, 1931 AD 132 at pp 145, 146, 148–9) . . .

[TROLLIP J then applied these principles to the damages claimed by the plaintiff under separate headings:

(1) Loss on sale of motor car: The court rejected the plaintiff's claim as she did not succeed in proving that the car had been sold below its market value.

(2) Loss on disposal of her furniture: The court rejected this claim too on the basis of lack of proof that the furniture was sold below its market value.

(3) The cost of packing and storing the plaintiff's belongings: The plaintiff proved these expenses and was awarded damages to the amount of R187.

(4) Loss of earnings: The court found that the plaintiff was supported by the defendant for a period of time and subsequently found employment in Johannesburg and that plaintiff did not prove that her income in Johannesburg was lower than that which she had in America. The plaintiff's claim was therefore rejected.

(5) Loss of plaintiff's apartment: The court rejected the plaintiff's claim as she could not prove that she would have to pay a higher rental for a similar apartment once she returned to New York.

(6) The cost of returning to New York: The court held that plaintiff could not claim this item of damages as it would amount to duplication of damages if she was awarded the cost of return fare to New York as well as the prospective loss for which she was indemnified under (7) *infra*.

(7) Prospective loss: Under this head the court held:]

[40] The probability is that the parties would have married with an ante-nuptial contract, excluding community of property and profit and loss. In the absence of proof to the contrary it must be assumed against the plaintiff that no marriage settlement would have been made on her in the ante-nuptial contract. It appears from the evidence, however, that the defendant is a man of some affluence and occupies a position in life that is superior to her own. She would therefore as his spouse, though married out of community of property and profit and loss, have derived material benefits from the marriage by way of status, maintenance, gifts, and otherwise, which she has now lost as a result of his breach of promise. The defendant's own letters adduced in evidence for example mentions possible trips to America, Europe and Kenya that they might have taken together after they were married. For the loss of all these benefits she is entitled to be compensated (*Van den Heever*, p 40; *Davel v Swanepoel*, 1954 (1) SA 383 (AD) at p 386 A–B and at p 387 F–H). I think that her loss under this heading is substantial. It is correct, as Mr *Morris* [for the defendant] contended, that the evidence shows that the marriage would probably not have lasted very long, and that is a factor that must abate the loss to some extent; but I think that its force is somewhat lessened by this fact. The evidence shows that it would probably have been the defendant who would have deserted the plaintiff, and on the divorce the plaintiff would therefore probably have obtained either alimony or a lump sum payment in lieu thereof by virtue of the provisions of sec 10 of the Matrimonial Affairs Act, 1953. The possibility of her getting married again must also be taken into account. She is, however, now

nearly 44 years old which reduces her chances of marriage, but as I mentioned at the commencement of this judgment, she carries her age well and the possibility of her remarrying cannot consequently be ruled out altogether.

Taking all the circumstances into consideration, I assess her loss under this heading at R2 000 ...

[TROLLIP J then proceeded to deal with the delictual damages to be awarded to the plaintiff:]

The enquiry is first whether the defendant's breach of promise was committed in a manner or in circumstances [41] that constituted it injurious or contumelious. Unfortunately, probably owing to *McCalman's* case, specific attention was not given to this aspect of the case either in evidence or in argument. The reasons the defendant gave for refusing to implement his promise were not fully investigated in evidence or cross-examination but I think that on the balance of probabilities shown by all the evidence adduced, the defendant must have stated that he refused to marry the plaintiff at the final stage of their relationship because he had never promised to do so. In his attorney's letter dated the 5th April, 1960 ... in answer to the plaintiff's claim for damages, it was stated that the defendant denied that he had ever agreed to marry the plaintiff. That was also the attitude that was taken up by the defendant in his pleadings and evidence in the case. I think, therefore, that it can be inferred that that was his attitude at all times relevant to this action. This is therefore not the kind of case where the defendant acknowledges the promise to marry but breaks the engagement in a sensible and non-contumelious manner in the interests of both parties (cf *Van den Heever* p 30; *Mocke v Fourie,* 3 CTR 313). Here the defendant promised to marry the plaintiff; caused her to uproot herself from New York and come to South Africa in contemplation of the promised marriage; and thereafter cast her out and refused to marry her by maintaining that he had not made any promise to marry her at all. I think that that constitutes injurious or contumelious conduct for which the plaintiff is entitled to damages. No specific evidence was, however, adduced to prove the extent of the injury to her feelings, her pride, or her reputation. She seemed to be more concerned during the trial with her contractual damages. But I think that it can be inferred that her feelings and pride were hurt at the time. However, although it is true that she is relatively unknown in Johannesburg and she intended returning to New York after the conclusion of the trial, she will suffer some humiliation on returning to her circle of friends in New York after all the elaborate steps she had taken to wind up her affairs there in order to leave for South Africa to get married. On the other hand, she is a mature level-headed woman who has suffered somewhat similarly before when her marriage broke up, so the effect on her feelings and pride of the defendant's breach is not likely to have been as severe as it would have been on a younger unsophisticated person. I think in all the circumstances that the damages for the *injuria* should be R500 which I award.

It remains to consider whether those damages should be increased by reason of the statements concerning the plaintiff made by or on behalf of the defendant at various times during the course of the trial. These statements were to the effect that the plaintiff was a blackmailer, a fabricator of evidence, a person who cunningly schemed to ensnare him into matrimony, that she drank to excess and surrendered her virtue easily. None of those statements were proved to be true and on the evidence [42] I heard they are without any foundation at all. Should they therefore inflate the damages awarded under this head? None of them had anything to do with the actual breach of promise itself. The defendant did not at the time of the breach, or in his pleadings, or in his evidence in the case, seek to justify his breach of promise because of the plaintiff's character. I do not think that I need canvass the actual or possible reasons for the making of the statements, save to say that they had no direct connection with the actual breach of promise. Consequently I do not think that those statements can be used to inflate the delictual damages. See *Salzmann's* and *Black's* cases, *supra*. The above statements are *prima facie* defamatory of the plaintiff but they would constitute a separate and distinct *injuria* for which the plaintiff could sue separately if she is so minded . . .

The conclusion I have therefore come to is that there should be judgment for the plaintiff in the sum of R2 687 (two thousand six hundred and eighty-seven rand) . . .

Note

If a breach of promise to marry occurs, the plaintiff can make use of two remedies, namely an action for patrimonial loss, which is based on breach of the contract of engagement, and an action for delictual damages, which is based on the delict of *iniuria*. These two claims should be pleaded and argued separately. In South African law the two claims have, however, been merged into one composite action in which damages are claimed without properly distinguishing between contractual and delictual damages (*McCalman v Thorne* 1934 NPD 86). In *Guggenheim v Rosenbaum* this approach was correctly criticised by TROLLIP J (36). He suggested that it would, at the very least, be "advisable to separate in the composite action the contractual and the delictual elements and the damages claimed for each . . . because each of the elements is governed by its own special principles that might be confused if not separately considered."

M v M 1991 4 SA 587 (D) is a recent case in which a contractual claim for breach of promise and a delictual claim (this time a claim for seduction) were again merged into one. The court awarded a single global figure to the plaintiff (who acted on behalf of his minor daughter). It held that as there was some overlapping between the breach of promise and the seduction it would be impractical to allocate separate figures to each head. The decision and the practice of "rolling into one" a claim for breach of promise and a claim for seduction is criticised by Bekker 1992 *THRHR* 484 488. (On *M v M* see also Robinson 1991 *Obiter* 138.)

As regards contractual damages TROLLIP J held in *Guggenheim's* case (36) that: "both the prospective loss of the benefits of the marriage and the actual monetary loss or expenditure incurred or to be incurred can be awarded." This statement by TROLLIP J does not accord with the general rule applicable to contractual damages.

Aantekening

By verbreking van 'n verlowingskontrak kan die eiser van twee remedies gebruik maak: Hy kan eerstens 'n aksie vir vermoënsregtelike skade instel wat op die kontrakbreuk gebaseer is, en tweedens kan hy deliktuele skadevergoeding eis, welke aksie op die delik *iniuria* gebaseer is. Hierdie twee eise behoort in die pleitstukke van mekaar geskei te word. In die Suid-Afrikaanse reg het die twee aksies egter in een saamgestelde aksie vervaag ingevolge waarvan skadevergoeding geëis word sonder dat behoorlik tussen kontraktuele en deliktuele skadevergoeding onderskei word (*McCalman v Thorne* 1934 NPA 86). In *Guggenheim v Rosenbaum* is hierdie benadering tereg deur TROLLIP R (36) gekritiseer. Hy het voorgestel dat, op die allerminste, "it is . . . advisable to separate in the composite action the contractual and the delictual elements and the damages claimed for each . . . because each of the elements is governed by its own special principles that might be confused if not separately considered."

M v M 1991 4 SA 587 (D) is 'n onlangse saak waarin 'n kontraktuele eis op grond van troubreuk en 'n deliktuele eis (hierdie keer 'n eis vir seduksie) weer eens in een aksie saamgevoeg is. Die hof het 'n globale bedrag aan die eiser (wat namens sy minderjarige dogter opgetree het) toegeken. Die hof het beslis dat aangesien daar 'n mate van oorvleueling was tussen die troubreuk en die seduksie dit onprakties sou wees om aparte bedrae onder elke hofie toe te ken. Die uitspraak en die praktyk om 'n eis vir troubreuk en 'n eis vir seduksie "in een te rol" word gekritiseer deur Bekker 1992 *THRHR* 484 488. (Oor *M v M* sien ook Robinson 1991 *Obiter* 138.)

Vir sover dit kontraktuele skadevergoeding betref, het TROLLIP R in die *Guggenheim*-saak (36) beslis dat "both the prospective loss of the benefits of the marriage and the actual monetary loss or expenditure incurred or to be incurred can be

The general rule in the law of contract is that the innocent party is entitled to positive interest in the event of breach of contract, that is such compensation as is necessary to place him in the position he would have been in if the breach of contract had never occurred. In other words he must be placed in the financial position he would have been in had the marriage taken place. If this rule was applied in the *Guggenheim* case the plaintiff would have received compensation only for the lost benefits of the marriage and the expenses she had to incur because the marriage did not take place. According to this rule TROLLIP J should have awarded her the cost of her return fare to New York (which he denied her) and her "prospective loss", ie the loss she suffered because she did not get married to the defendant and could therefore not share in his wealth. The amount to be awarded under "prospective loss" would, however, be reduced by factors such as the probable duration of the intended marriage and the plaintiff's chances of getting married to somebody else. If the general rule of placing the plaintiff in the position she would have been in if the marriage had taken place, was applied, TROLLIP J would not have compensated the plaintiff for expenses she had to incur to enable her to get married to the defendant. She would then not have been compensated for the cost of packing and storing her belongings. By the same token she would also not have been successful if she had claimed compensation for the buying of a trousseau, the printing of wedding invitations, for expenses incurred for the wedding reception or for any other expenses incurred in preparation for the marriage. By allowing compensation for expenses which were incurred in preparation of the marriage, the court allowed the plaintiff to claim not only positive interest but also negative interest, ie to be placed in the financial position she would have been in if the contract was never entered into. TROLLIP J therefore placed the plaintiff partially in the position she would have been in if the marriage had taken place and partially in the position she would have been in if the contract of engagement had never been entered into.

From the *Guggenheim* case it appears that the general rule of awarding positive interest when breach of contract occurs, does not apply to breach of

awarded." Hierdie stelling van TROLLIP R is nie in ooreenstemming met die algemene reël wat by die toekenning van skadevergoeding by kontrakbreuk geld nie.

Die algemene reël in die kontraktereg is dat die onskuldige party by kontrakbreuk op positiewe interesse geregtig is, dit wil sê sodanige vergoeding as wat nodig is om hom te plaas in die posisie waarin hy sou gewees het indien die kontrakbreuk nooit plaasgevind het nie. Hy moet met ander woorde in die posisie geplaas word waarin hy sou gewees het indien die huwelik wel voltrek is. As hierdie reël in die *Guggenheim*-saak toegepas was, sou die eiseres slegs vergoeding kon ontvang het vir die verlore voordele van die huwelik en die uitgawes wat sy aangegaan het omdat die huwelik nie plaasgevind het nie. Ingevolge hierdie reël moes TROLLIP R haar reiskoste terug na New York aan haar toegeken het (wat hy geweier het om te doen) asook haar "toekomstige verlies", dit is die verlies wat sy gely het omdat sy nie met die verweerder getrou het nie en dus nie in sy rykdom kon deel nie. Die bedrag wat onder "toekomstige verlies" toegeken word, sal egter verminder word aan die hand van faktore soos die waarskynlike duur van die voorgenome huwelik en die moontlikheid dat die eiseres met iemand anders sou trou. Indien die algemene reël wel toegepas was, dit wil sê dat die eiseres geplaas moet word in die posisie waarin sy sou gewees het indien die huwelik wel plaasgevind het, moes TROLLIP R nie die eiseres vergoed het vir die uitgawes wat sy aangegaan het om die sluiting van die huwelik tussen haar en die verweerder moontlik te maak nie. Sy sou dan nie vergoed kon word vir die onkoste wat sy in verband met die verpakking en berging van haar meubels aangegaan het nie. Sy sou insgelyks ook nie vergoeding kon eis vir uitgawes soos die aankoop van 'n bruidsuitset, die druk van huweliksuitnodigings, uitgawes wat ten opsigte van die huweliksonthaal aangegaan is of vir enige ander uitgawes wat met die oog op die huwelik aangegaan is nie. Deur vergoeding toe te ken vir uitgawes wat aangegaan is met die oog op die huwelik, het die hof die eiseres toegelaat om nie net positiewe interesse te eis nie maar ook negatiewe interesse, dit wil sê om geplaas te word in die posisie waarin sy sou gewees het indien die verlowing nooit gesluit was nie. TROLLIP R het dus die eiseres gedeeltelik geplaas in die posisie waarin sy sou gewees het indien die hu-

promise to marry. It appears that damages *sui generis* is awarded when breach of a contract of engagement takes place. The plaintiff is awarded positive interest as well as negative interest.

As regards delictual damages it is important to note the emphasis the court placed on the fact that the mere breach of the contract of engagement is not sufficient to justify a claim for delictual damages. The breach of contract of engagement does not in itself constitute an *iniuria* – "the plaintiff, in order to recover delictual damages, must prove not merely that the breach was wrongful but also that it was injurious or contumelious" (36). In this case the respondent's denial that he ever promised to marry the plaintiff constituted such injurious or contumelious conduct and this entitled the plaintiff to compensation. See also Hahlo and Kahn 1961 *SALJ* 355; Bekker 1974 *THRHR* 403; 1975 *THRHR* 52.

welik wel voltrek was en gedeeltelik in die posisie waarin sy sou gewees het indien die verlowing nooit gesluit is nie.

Dit blyk dus uit die *Guggenheim*-saak dat die algemene reël ingevolge waarvan positiewe interesse op grond van kontrakbreuk toegeken word, nie toepassing vind indien 'n verlowingskontrak verbreek word nie. Dit blyk dat skadevergoeding by die verbreking van 'n verlowingskontrak *sui generis* toegeken word. Die eiser kry positiewe sowel as negatiewe interesse.

Vir sover dit deliktuele skadevergoeding betref, moet gelet word op die klem wat die hof geplaas het op die feit dat die blote verbreking van 'n verlowingskontrak nie voldoende is om 'n eis op grond van delik te regverdig nie. Die kontrakbreuk self is nie 'n *iniuria* nie – "the plaintiff, in order to recover delictual damages, must prove not merely that the breach was wrongful but also that it was injurious or contumelious" (36). In hierdie geval het die verweerder se ontkenning dat hy ooit belowe het om met die eiseres te trou sodanige krenkende of beledigende gedrag daargestel wat die eiseres op vergoeding geregtig gemaak het. Sien ook Hahlo en Kahn 1961 *SALJ* 355; Bekker 1974 *THRHR* 403; 1975 *THRHR* 52.

[58] BULL V TAYLOR

1965 4 SA 29 (A)

Action for damages for breach of promise and seduction

In 1956 when the appellant and the respondent were respectively sixteen and twenty years of age, they agreed to marry each other. On the basis of the understanding that they would get married, they lived together on intimate terms and built up what might be termed joint assets. Towards the end of 1962 a date was set for their marriage but when the arrangements for the marriage were all made the respondent repudiated the engagement. The appellant then sued the respondent for damages on the grounds of breach of promise to marry and seduction. As dam-

'n Eis om skadevergoeding op grond van troubreuk en seduksie

In 1956 toe die appellant en die respondent onderskeidelik sestien en twintig jaar oud was, het hulle ooreengekom om met mekaar te trou. Op grond van die verstandhouding dat hulle sou trou, het hulle intiem met mekaar begin saamleef en het hulle saam bates opgebou wat 'n mens gemeenskaplike bates sou kon noem. Teen die einde van 1962 het hulle op 'n datum vir hulle huwelik ooreengekom maar toe die reëlings klaar getref was, het die respondent die verlowing gerepudieer. Die appellant het die respondent daarop aangespreek vir die betaling van ska-

ages for breach of promise she claimed certain expenses relating to the setting up of a home, costs she incurred for the wedding arrangements and loss of the prospective benefits of the marriage. The appellant alleged that the respondent had seduced her some months after the parties had agreed to marry each other. The respondent admitted the promise to marry but averred that it was made at a later date than that alleged by the appellant. He also admitted that sexual intercourse took place between them but alleged that this occurred prior to the promise to marry and that it took place without his having induced it or having persuaded the appellant. He admitted that he had repudiated the engagement but pleaded that the appellant's behaviour justified his repudiation. In a counterclaim he sued for the return of certain immovable property registered by him in the appellant's name. The court *a quo* dismissed the claim for damages holding that the appellant had failed to prove that she had been seduced by the respondent and that, although the respondent had repudiated the engagement contract, the appellant had failed to prove that she had suffered any damages in consequence thereof. The court ordered a division of the joint assets, including the immovable property registered in the appellant's name. The appellant appealed against this decision. The appeal was successful.

devergoeding op grond van die verbreking van die verlowing en seduksie. As skadevergoeding het sy sekere uitgawes geëis wat sy aangegaan het om huis op te sit, onkoste wat sy met die oog op die huwelik aangegaan het en verlies van die voordele van die huwelik. Die appellant het beweer dat die respondent haar verlei het 'n paar maande nadat hulle ooreengekom het om te trou. Die respondent het erken dat hy beloof het om met die appellant te trou maar het beweer dat die belofte gemaak is op 'n later datum as wat die appellant beweer het. Hy het ook erken dat geslagsgemeenskap tussen hulle plaasgevind het maar het beweer dat dit plaasgevind het nog voor die partye verloof geraak het en dat hy nie die appellant daartoe oorgehaal het nie. Hy het erken dat hy die verlowing gerepudieer het maar het beweer dat die appellant se gedrag sy repudiëring geregverdig het. In 'n teeneis het hy teruggawe geëis van sekere onroerende eiendom wat hy op die appellant se naam laat registreer het. Die hof *a quo* het die eis om skadevergoeding verwerp en het beslis dat die appellant nie bewys het dat sy deur die respondent verlei is nie en dat, alhoewel die respondent die verlowing gerepudieer het, die appellant nie bewys het dat sy as gevolg daarvan skade gely het nie. Die hof het gelas dat die gemeenskaplike bates, insluitende die onroerende eiendom wat in die naam van die appellant geregistreer was, verdeel moes word. Die appellant het appèl aangeteken teen hierdie beslissing. Die appèl het geslaag.

BEYERS JA: [33] It is clear from the evidence that the appellant's case is not that she was induced to have intercourse with the respondent on the strength of an offer of marriage. She was, as she says, "prepared" to have intercourse with him because of the understanding that they would one day be married. No doubt she acquiesced more readily on that account but that is not to say she was induced by the offer of marriage to have intercourse with him. This view, it seems to me, is consistent with the allegation in her declaration that "relying on the promise to marry aforesaid, she allowed respondent to seduce her". In all likelihood the respondent's offer of marriage, made some months before the first act of intercourse, was a genuine offer. Although he has not given evidence to this effect, his subsequent conduct, as testified to by the appellant, suggests that he genuinely intended to marry her one day. The learned trial Judge, in his treatment of the appellant's evidence, appears to have viewed the matter in this light.

I consider, however, that in holding that the requirements for seduction were absent, he took too narrow a view of the evidence – even on the assumption that a "leading astray" is an essential element in seduction. In saying that the intercourse took place because the parties had reached a stage in their love-making where they could no longer contain themselves, he has inferred a spontaneity on the appellant's part which is not justified on the evidence. He has not, it seems to me, approached the evidence, as he ought to have done, on the basis that "seduction is presumed on the part of the man" – *Bensimon v Barton*, 1919 AD 13; see also Van den Heever, *Breach of Promise and Seduction*, at p 45:

> "Virtue is presumed until the contrary is proved; consequently the presumption is that the woman fell as a result of the man's seductive efforts."

The appellant says "he showed and expressed, his feelings, and I had my feelings". Testifying, as she was, to events which took place eight years earlier, she could not be expected to remember precisely what [34] overtures the respondent made to her, and with what blandishments he coaxed her and persuaded her to submit to his advances, and finally to his embraces. The fact that she may "very readily and with very little persuasion" have succumbed to his solicitations is no defence (*Scholtemeyer v Potgieter*, 1916 TPD 188 at p 196).

While it may be an overstatement to say that the respondent took advantage of the appellant's youth, the disparity in their ages is an important factor in the case. He was at the time almost a grown man (twenty years of age); she was a young girl of sixteen, not yet out of school.

The most authoritative definition of seduction which I have been able to find is that which appears in *Bensimon v Barton, supra*. It is there stated, by INNES, CJ, at p 23, that the remedy is available to a virgin who has been seduced – that is, who has parted with her virtue at the solicitation of a man. In an earlier passage the learned CHIEF JUSTICE refers to the opinion of *Voet*, 47.10.7 – in discussing the Civil Law – that a man was liable to an action who by blandishment or solicitation assailed the chastity of a female or procured a chaste woman to become unchaste.

The appellant does not say in what manner the respondent "showed his feelings", but I have no doubt that, in doing so, he solicited or induced her to co-operate in the performance of the sexual act. The presumption is that she "fell as a result of the man's seductive efforts". The respondent has not rebutted this presumption, neither by giving evidence nor by pointing to anything in the appellant's evidence which might serve in lieu thereof.

The learned trial Judge held the view that for seduction to be present there had to be something akin to a leading astray. He no doubt had in mind the words of HATHORN, JP, in *Dhai v Vawda*, 1940 (1) PH J 11, a case which is referred to in *Pillai v Pillai*, 1963 (1) SA 542 (N) at p 553, to the effect that

> "the underlying idea of seduction in its ordinary sense, and I think in its legal sense as well, is leading astray".

I have no quarrel with this definition of seduction, provided it is understood that the "leading astray" is a leading astray of a woman from the paths of virtue, and that this, and not the means – deceitful or otherwise – by which it is achieved, is the essential feature of seduction ...

Accepting that to constitute seduction something akin to a leading astray, in the sense mentioned above, must be present, it seems to me that that element is not lacking in the present case. The evidence discloses no grounds for suggesting that appellant was at the relevant date a sexually precocious teenager who actively encouraged respondent to have intercourse with her. Quite apart from the above-mentioned presumption, on the evidence the probabilities all point towards appellant [35] having succumbed to the blandishments

of the respondent, her senior by four then important years. A man who has sexual relations with a virtuous young school-girl can surely not be heard to say that he has not led her astray. That the respondent in the present case did indeed lead the appellant astray is evidenced by the latter's subsequent behaviour. After the first act of intercourse she used occasionally to stop at his home on her way to school, there to have further intercourse with him. It could in these circumstances be said of her, as it was of the plaintiff in *De Stadler v Cramer*, 1922 CPD 16 at p 19, that she

"has thus gone still further along the wrong path into which he has led her".

In my opinion the appellant has proved that she was seduced, and is entitled to damages on that account . . .

[BEYERS JA then analysed the evidence to establish whether the respondent's repudiation of the engagement was shown to be justified and concluded that it was not. He proceeded:]

[36] In dismissing the appellant's claim for damages arising from the breach of the contract of marriage, the Court held

(a)   that the mere fact of a repudiation of a marriage is not in itself a contumelious act giving rise to damages;

(b)   that there was no *contumelia* [insult] present in the manner in which the respondent acted in repudiating the marriage; and

(c)   that the appellant had suffered no patrimonial loss as a result of the breach.

Before discussing these findings it is necessary to say something about the manner in which the wedding date first came to be postponed and then to be cancelled altogether.

[The learned Judge then analysed the evidence and proceeded:]

I am quite satisfied in my mind that the appellant was genuinely hurt and embarrassed on account of the last-minute defection on the part of the bridegroom. In the circumstances I consider that there was an element of *contumelia* in the manner in which the respondent broke his promise to the appellant.

I now turn to the question of damages.

Wessels, *Law of Contract*, paras 3191 *et seq*, deals with damages for breach of contract and states the general principle in these terms:

"In the case of a breach of contract we are not concerned with the mental or bodily sufferings of the creditor. The action for damages in such a case is intended to place the creditor as much as possible in the same position as regards his property as he would have been in if the contract had been performed . . . Hence the damages must be in satisfaction of some pecuniary loss . . ."

In para 3195 the learned author states:

"Cases of breach of promise to marry have been advanced in support of the view that moral and intellectual damages are often awarded by our courts. This class of case is, however, *sui generis*, for a breach of promise to marry is not only a breach of contract, but a substantial wrong done to the injured party, and the [37] damages are awarded both for loss in property and as a *solatium* to the feelings of wounded pride of the plaintiff.

In the usual breach of promise case there is an underlying element of fraud and deceit. It should be regarded as an action both *ex contractu* and *ex delicto*."

These passages are quoted with approval by TINDALL, JA, in *Jockie v Meyer*, 1945 AD 354 at pp 366, 367.

The authorities are agreed that the remedy is *sui generis*. See Van den Heever, *Breach of Promise and Seduction*, p 29:

"It is a remedy *sui generis* having features in common with an action on contract and an action in delict;"

Triegaardt v Van der Vyver, 1910 EDL 44; *McCalman v Thorne*, 1934 NPD 86.

There is, however, a difference of opinion as to whether a breach of the contract *ipso jure* constitutes an *injuria*, or whether it becomes such only if there is an element of *contumelia* present in the breach. Counsel for the appellant referred to *McCalman v Thorne, supra*, as authority for the former of these propositions. In that case CARLISLE, AJ, citing with approval the decision in *Radloff v Ralph*, 1917 EDL 168, pointed out at p 91 that

"The heads of damages stated in *Radloff's* case can be traced to two sources: first, the ordinary measure for breach of contract, which comprises (a) any monetary loss sustained by the plaintiff, (b) what may be called the prospective loss, where for instance the defendant is in a good financial position and through his or her breach of contract has deprived the plaintiff of the opportunity of any participation therein; and second, the ordinary measure for *injuria* arising out of *contumelia* suffered by the plaintiff, for in civilised society in South Africa the wrongful putting an end to of a betrothal contract by one party is, in ordinary cases, regarded as an impairment of the personal dignity or reputation of the other party and is thus an *injuria*. Here regard will be had to the wounded feelings of the plaintiff and the social position of the parties."

The Court held that so long as damage for *injuria* forms part of the plaintiff's claim under our law, it is unnecessary, if damages are claimed for *contumelia*, that they should be expressly sued for as such.

In *Guggenheim v Rosenbaum* (2), 1961 (4) SA 21 (W) [57], TROLLIP, J, at p 35, after dealing fully with *McCalman's* case, reached the following conclusion:

"*McCalman's* case has been followed in Natal (*Mymenah v Cassim Rahim*, 1943 NPD 299; *Combrink v Koch*, 1946 NPD 512) and it probably set the pattern for breach of promise cases in South Africa. In consequence, the delictual damages and the prospective loss in the contractual damages are now usually claimed in a lump sum as general damages, and any monetary loss is claimed and pleaded as special contractual damage. That was done in this case and no attempt was made in the pleadings or at the hearing to separate the delictual from the contractual general damages. That was probably due to *McCalman's* case.

Now *McCalman's* case appears to hold that the breach of contract itself gives rise, not only to contractual damages but also to the delictual damages; in other words, that the mere breach of contract *ipso jure* constitutes an *injuria*. If it does mean that then, with great respect, I disagree with that part of it. I think that the plaintiff, in order to recover delictual damages, must prove not merely that the breach was wrongful but also that it was injurious or contumelious."

I am not sure whether TROLLIP, J, has not read into *McCalman's* case something which is not there. However that may be, the view expressed by him in *Guggenheim's* case has the clear support of the two eminent writers referred to by him in his judgment. The first of these, Melius de Villiers on *Injuries*, says at p 26:

"A breach of contract is not, in its nature an injury. The duty of fulfilling one's contracts is one that does not arise from the respect due to the other parties thereto . . . So also, a breach of promise of marriage is not necessarily an injury. The favourable inclination of a man towards a woman may turn to aversion from numerous other causes than those which reflect upon her character and there may be cases where a breach of promise of marriage may be occasioned by reasons [38] which are strictly honourable. It might, however, be an injury when . . ."

The view of the other authority, Van den Heever, *Breach of Promise and Seduction*, is to the same effect. At pp 30, 31, the learned author says:

"It is submitted that those decisions of our Courts which seem to imply that breach of promise must necessarily contain a delictual element, are unconsciously based on English principles and have no support in Roman-Dutch law. Unless a person who breaks off an engagement commits an actionable wrong 'the feelings of the plaintiff and the moral suffering she has undergone' are irrelevant to the question of damages ... The notion that a woman necessarily loses social position or 'face' when an engagement is broken off under non-injurious circumstances seems to me to reflect the morals of a bygone age ... On the other hand an engagement may be broken off under such humiliating circumstances as to constitute a grave injury, ... for example, where defendant unjustifiably breaks off the engagement when all the arrangements for the wedding have been made and the invitations are out; where the defendant wilfully fails to appear at the wedding and shames the bride before the assembled congregation; where on the eve of the marriage the bridegroom marries another."

In saying, in *Davel v Swanepoel*, 1954 (1) SA 383 (AD) at p 387, that

"In hierdie geval tree die deliktiese element in die verstoting van eiseres sterk na vore,"

VAN DEN HEEVER, JA, was not, as suggested by counsel for the appellant, speaking in general terms. He was dealing with the facts of that particular case, in which substantial damages were awarded for breach of promise, because

"verweerder het eiseres aan 'n lyntjie gehou en sonder om die verlowing te beëindig met 'n ander vrou in die huwelik getree".

In other words, it was a clear case of *contumelia* amounting to an *injuria*. In *Jockie v Meyer, supra* at p 367, TINDALL, JA, after setting out the terms of para 3191 of Wessels, *Law of Contract, op cit*, adds the following:

"The learned author mentions breach of promise to marry, which, he states, is *sui generis* and is not only a breach of contract but a substantial wrong done to the injured party, the damages being awarded both for loss in property and as a *solatium* to the feelings of the plaintiff. Dealing with cases where damages for inconvenience suffered, as, for instance, where a contract of marriage has been broken ... the writer states (secs 3196, 3197) that the inconvenience and discomfort constitute an injury to the person of the passenger and that, although these actions are couched in contract, they contain an element of tort *as soon as the bodily sufferings of the passenger come into play*, the true *damnum* in a contract being a compensation for patrimonial loss."

The words italicised by me suggest that damages are not automatically awarded for a breach of these contracts, and that the mental or bodily sufferings, as the case may be, have to be proved before damages are awarded.

It is, however, not necessary for me to commit myself to either of the two propositions mentioned above, because in the present case it makes no difference whichever view one favours. The appellant has sued for general damages as well as for patrimonial loss, and, having proved *contumelia* on the part of the respondent, is entitled to delictual damages.

In the result the appellant is entitled to damages both for the seduction and for breach of contract ...

As far as the seduction is concerned the appellant is entitled to be compensated for the loss of her virginity, and for her diminished chances of making a suitable marriage. In considering what might be a [39] suitable match for her regard must be had to her social standing. She is the daughter of a middle class working family, living, as far as can be gathered from her evidence, in humble, but decent, circumstances. In my opinion a sum of R250 will be a fair award of damages under this head.

The appellant is entitled, as damages for breach of promise, to a *solatium* for her feelings of wounded pride, as well as to compensation for patrimonial loss. As to the former, the appellant was engaged to the respondent for seven or eight years. These were important years in her life. When the respondent rejected her she was no longer a young woman. By casting her aside after all those years, when she was on the very threshold of marriage, the respondent dealt her pride a shattering blow. The Court must, however, also take into account the financial standing of the man she hoped to marry. The respondent is not a man of means, and in this instance, too, I consider that R250 will be fair and adequate compensation for the hurt she has suffered . . .

The trial Court ordered a division of [the parties' joint] assets, and included in the list the Norwood property registered in the appellant's name.

As stated above, the respondent is not a man of means. In 1963 he was in receipt of a salary of R160 per month, with prospects of later earning R180 per month. The appellant was earning R120 per month at the time, and intended to continue working after she was married. In these circumstances I consider that the trial Court rightly held that:

"Approached from a purely material point of view . . . a girl with her earning capacity suffers no financial loss by losing an opportunity of marrying a man whose maximum earning capacity is R180 per month."

As far as actual and prospective patrimonial loss is concerned, the appellant persists only in her claim to the Norwood property. The appellant would have been the undisputed owner of this property had the parties been married, because it was their intention to marry without community of property. In my view the appellant has at least clearly proved that, had the marriage supervened, she would have acquired and retained, as a benefit of the marriage, the notional sum representing the difference between the value of this property and the mortgage bond thereon. The appellant accepts liability for the existing mortgage bond. In terms of the trial Court's judgment, however, this property has to be divided, along with the other assets. In this way the appellant will lose a one-half interest in the property. In my opinion, the respondent having wrongfully repudiated the contract, the appellant is entitled to be awarded the full ownership of this property under her claim for loss of prospective benefits.

The appeal is accordingly upheld . . .

VAN BLERK JA, OGILVIE THOMPSON JA, WILLIAMSON JA and POTGIETER AJA concurred.

Note

In this case BEYERS JA (38) declined to decide whether the mere unjustified repudiation of the contract of engagement constituted an *iniuria* or whether an element of *contumelia* (affront or insult) should also be present. Whichever approach is adopted, it is clear that the defendant's conduct and motives in breaking off the engagement will be taken into consideration in calculating the damages to be awarded to the injured party. Conduct which took place after the breaking off of the engagement could also be considered (*Guggenheim v Rosenbaum* [57]). On the other hand the amount of damages might be reduced if the defendant's motives in terminating the engagement

Aantekening

In hierdie uitspraak wou BEYERS AR (38) geen bevinding maak nie oor die vraag of blote ongeregverdigde verbreking van 'n verlowingskontrak 'n *iniuria* daarstel en of daar ook 'n element van *contumelia* (belediging) teenwoordig moet wees. Welke benadering ook al gevolg word, is dit duidelik dat die verweerder se gedrag en sy motief vir die verbreking van die verlowing in ag geneem sal word by die berekening van die bedrag skadevergoeding wat aan die benadeelde party toegeken sal word. Selfs gedrag wat na die verbreking van die verlowing plaasvind, kan in ag geneem word (*Guggenheim v Rosenbaum* [57]). Aan die ander kant kan die bedrag verminder

were not justified, as long as they were not dishonourable or unreasonable, for example if he broke off the engagement only because his parents disapproved of his fiancée and he discovered that he did not love her enough to marry her in the face of parental opposition (*Smit v Jacobs* 1918 OPD 30). See also *M v M* 1991 4 SA 587 (O) where it was held that the celebration of a Hindu marriage by the parties was a mitigating circumstance as it meant that the parties' living together did not amount to a "totally illicit liaison" (602EF).

As regards the seduction of the appellant, Bekker (426–427) emphasises that the question of whether the woman has in fact been seduced remains a factual one. The woman has a presumption of chastity which operates in her favour. In accordance with this presumption it is presumed that the woman led a chaste life until she had sexual intercourse with the man and that she was seduced by him. If the man does not bring evidence to rebut this presumption he cannot escape liability. Bekker is of the opinion that the Appellate Division in *Bull v Taylor* may have assumed too much in favour of the appellant but he agrees with the finding that the respondent did not rebut the presumption. The respondent's failure to lead evidence on the matter as well as the appellant's young age led the court to hold that the presumption was not rebutted.

See also the note on *Guggenheim v Rosenbaum* [57].

word indien die verweerder se motief vir die verbreking van die verlowing ongeregverdig was, solank dit net nie oneerbaar of onredelik was nie, byvoorbeeld as hy die verlowing verbreek het slegs omdat sy ouers nie van sy verloofde gehou het nie en hy ontdek het dat hy nie lief genoeg vir haar was om met haar te trou terwyl dit nie sy ouers se goedkeuring weggedra het nie (*Smit v Jacobs* 1918 OPA 30). Sien ook *M v M* 1991 4 SA 587 (O) waar beslis is dat die bestaan van 'n Hindu-huwelik tussen die partye 'n faktor is wat die bedrag skadevergoeding verminder omdat sodanige huwelik beteken dat die partye se samewoning nie op 'n "totally illicit liaison" neergekom het nie (602EF).

Vir sover dit die seduksie van die appellant aangaan, beklemtoon Bekker (426–427) dat die vraag of die vrou verlei is 'n feitlike vraag bly. Die vrou het 'n vermoede van kuisheid wat in haar guns tel. Ingevolge hierdie vermoede word vermoed dat die vrou 'n kuis lewe gelei het totdat sy geslagsgemeenskap met die man gehad het en dat sy deur hom verlei is. Indien die man geen getuienis aanvoer wat hierdie vermoede weerlê nie, kan hy nie aanspreeklikheid ontsnap nie. Bekker is van mening dat die Appèlhof in *Bull v Taylor* dalk te veel in die guns van die appellant aanvaar het maar hy stem saam met die bevinding dat die respondent nie die vermoede weerlê het nie. Die feit dat die respondent versuim het om getuienis oor die aangeleentheid te lei asook die appellant se jeugdige ouderdom het tot gevolg gehad dat die hof beslis het dat die vermoede nie weerlê is nie.

Sien ook die aantekening by *Guggenheim v Rosenbaum* [57].

Requirements for the conclusion of a valid marriage

Capacity to act
Consensus
Marriage must be lawful
Formalities

Geldigheidsvereistes vir die sluiting van 'n huwelik

Handelingsbevoegdheid
Wilsooreenstemming
Geoorloofdheid
Formaliteite

Capacity to act   Handelingsbevoegdheid

[59]   ALLCOCK V ALLCOCK

1969 1 SA 427 (N)

Court consenting to the marriage of a minor where the parents refused

The applicant, a minor, brought an application in terms of section 25(4) of the Marriage Act 25 of 1961, requesting permission to marry and asking for an appropriate order in regard to the execution of an antenuptial contract. The applicant would have come of age in eleven months' time and her fiancé was a major. The reason why the couple wished to marry before the applicant turned twenty-one was that she had just completed her training as a nurse and was shortly to sit for her final examination after which she would be entitled to a leave of absence. She would then have been employed in a hospital and would only have been able to take leave after a year. The applicant's parents refused to consent to the marriage and although they had repeatedly been asked for their reasons for refusing, they had given no answer other than that they would not consent. The applicant, her fiancé and his parents, who approved of the proposed marriage, all endeavoured to obtain their co-operation, but to no avail. Notice of the application and copies of the affidavits and other documents had been served upon both parents of the applicant (the respondents) but neither had filed any affidavit in reply or had communicated with the registrar or appeared at the hearing. After the judge interviewed the couple in chambers the court granted the application.

Hof verleen toestemming tot die huwelik van 'n minderjarige waar die ouers dit geweier het

Die applikant, 'n minderjarige, het ingevolge artikel 25(4) van die Huwelikswet 25 van 1961 aansoek gedoen om toestemming om in die huwelik te tree, asook dat 'n gepaste bevel met betrekking tot die verlyding van 'n huweliksvoorwaardeskontrak uitgevaardig word. Die applikant sou oor elf maande meerderjarig word en haar verloofde was reeds meerderjarig. Die rede waarom die partye voor die applikant se een en twintigste verjaardag wou trou, was omdat sy so pas haar verpleegstersopleiding voltooi het en binnekort haar finale eksamen sou skryf waarna sy op verlof geregtig sou wees. Daarna sou sy by 'n hospitaal in diens geneem word en sou eers weer oor 'n jaar verlof kon kry. Die applikant se ouers het geweier om tot die huwelik toe te stem en alhoewel hulle herhaaldelik gevra is om watter redes hulle geweier het, het hulle geen antwoord gegee nie behalwe dat hulle nie hulle toestemming sou verleen nie. Die applikant, haar verloofde en sy ouers, wat ten gunste van die voorgenome huwelik was, het gepoog om hulle samewerking te verkry maar sonder sukses. Albei die applikant se ouers (die respondente) is verder kennis gegee van die aansoek en afskrifte van die beëdigde verklarings en ander dokumente is op hulle bestel, maar nie een van hulle het 'n beëdigde verklaring ingedien, of met die registrateur in verbinding getree, of die hofverrigtinge bygewoon nie. Nadat die regter 'n onderhoud met die paartjie in sy kamers gevoer het, het hy die aansoek toegestaan.

MILLER J: [427] The applicant... [and] [h]er fiancé appear to be responsible and thoroughly decent young people who have been on terms of close friendship for nearly four years and who are firmly resolved to marry one another...

[428] Sub-sec (4) of sec 25 of the Marriage Act, 25 of 1961, requires a Judge not to grant consent to a marriage to which the parent or guardian of a minor has refused consent,

> "unless he is of the opinion that such refusal of consent by the parent, guardian [429] . . . is without adequate reason and contrary to the interests of such minor".

Prior to the passing of the Act, the Courts entertained similar applications by minors and granted leave to marry where they were satisfied that the parents' refusal of consent was "*mala fide* or frivolous or senseless" (*Paton v Paton*, 1929 TPD 776) and where they regarded such refusal as "grossly unreasonable". (*Ex parte E*, 1946 (1) PH M19 and *D v D*, 1946 (1) PH M20). In *C en 'n Ander v Van T*, 1965 (2) SA 239 (O), the Court had occasion to consider an application brought in terms of sec 25(4) and concluded (at p 242) that that section conferred on the Court " 'n onbelemmerde diskresie" to decide, in all the circumstances of the case, whether the parental refusal to grant consent would "vir alle praktiese doeleindes" unreasonably prejudice the minor and that if it would so prejudice the minor the Court ought to give its consent to the marriage "afgesien daarvan of die weiering *mala fide*, beuselagtig, sinneloos of hoogs onredelik is". The learned Judge, however, prefaced his conclusion with the observation that sec 25(4) still extended full recognition to the objections of a parent or guardian to the proposed marriage of a minor "ingevolge die norme soos deur die erkende Romeins-Hollandse regsbeginsels openbaar".

While I agree that the terms of sec 25(4) do not provide, nor envisage, that the Court may interfere only if the parents' refusal was *mala fide* or frivolous or senseless or grossly unreasonable, with respect, I cannot agree that the Court may interfere by the exercise of an unfettered discretion in regard to whether the minor will be unreasonably prejudiced by the parental refusal. The section requires a Judge to apply his mind to two factors:

(i) whether the parental refusal is "without adequate reason" and (ii) whether it is contrary to the interests of the minor. Unless he is of the opinion both that the parental refusal is without adequate reason and that such refusal is contrary to the interests of the minor, he shall not grant consent to the proposed marriage. I take the words "of the opinion" in this context to be virtually synonymous with "is satisfied", but with the reservation that the Judge need be satisfied not necessarily beyond reasonable doubt but on the preponderance of probabilities (cf the observations of SCHREINER, JA, in *Fletcher v Fletcher*, 1948 (1) SA 130 (AD) at p 145). The use of the word "adequate" to qualify "reason" in the formulation of the first requirement for the grant of judicial consent, is of some significance. "Adequate," I think, conveys something less than a full measure. The dictionaries give many meanings of the word but in its context in sec 25(4), it seems to me that "adequate reason" suggests sufficient reason to justify the parental refusal of consent. (In the Afrikaans text of the Act, which is not the signed text, the words "genoegsame rede" are used). A parent may refuse consent for reasons which, although not conclusive, nor very convincing to the mind of the Judge, nevertheless cannot be said by him to constitute inadequate grounds for the parental decision. He may consider that were he in the parents' place, he would have consented to the marriage but unless he is able to go further and, with conviction, stigmatise the parent's reason or ground for refusal as inadequate, or without sufficient substance, he will not, as I see the matter, override them. To this extent the Judge's discretion is indeed circumscribed; it is still true that

> [430] "the mere fact that the Court holds a different opinion about the advisability of a marriage"

is not sufficient to justify intervention, (*per* GREENBERG, J, as he then was, in *Paton v Paton, supra* at p 778) and that the Court will not "lightly interfere" in cases of this nature or lightly "pass the father by". (*Per* WESSELS, J, as he then was, in *A v B*, 1906 TS 958 at p 961). A heavy responsibility rests upon a Court which is asked to interpose its consent to the marriage of a minor to which the minor's parents are sufficiently strongly opposed to cause them firmly to refuse their consent; the Court will at all times be conscious of the superior advantages which the parents have over it in the matter of so personal and intimate a decision, but this will not deter it from overruling the parents where it is satisfied both as to the inadequacy of the parents' reasons and the interests of the minor.

Returning now to the facts of this case, the question whether the parental refusal is without adequate reason is nebulous where the Court is left completely in the dark concerning the reasons for such refusal. Conflicting considerations beset the matter. One tends to assume that responsible parents, concerned for their daughter's welfare and happiness, would not, without reason, withhold consent to her marriage. But one also tends to assume that in such a case they would frankly disclose their grounds or reasons to the Court which is being asked to interpose its consent for theirs. The silence which the applicant's parents have from beginning to end observed in regard to this issue, is puzzling . . . There may indeed be factors which properly weighed with the parents but which, for obscure reasons of their own, they decided not to divulge. This possibility, however, is insufficient to displace, or to weaken, my belief that on the undisputed facts deposed to in the affidavits and on what I have seen of and heard from the applicant and her fiancé, there is everything to be said for their being permitted to marry and nothing of substance to be said against it. This is not a case of a very young girl, in her teens, wishing to marry a man whom she has only very recently met and of whom she can know very little. The applicant's friendship with her fiancé has survived several years, she appears to be a responsible and worthy young woman and the man of her choice equally responsible and worthy and the only obstacle to the fulfilment of their natural desire to be married is the impenetrable wall of silence which her parents have erected between them and her. I have considered the fact that in 11 months' time the applicant could marry without consent but this is insufficient reason to justify refusal of the application, for it is of considerable practical importance to her to be married at a time which is opportune for both her and her fiancé and it would, I have no doubt, be against her interests to require her, when no objection in principle can be discerned to the proposed marriage, to defer it.

For these reasons the application was granted . . .

Note	Aantekening
See the note on *B v B* [60].	Sien die aantekening by *B v B* [60].

[60]   B v B

1983 1 SA 496 (N)

Court consenting to the marriage of a minor where the parents refused	**Hof verleen toestemming tot die huwelik van 'n minderjarige waar die ouers dit geweier het**
The applicant was a young girl less than seventeen years of age. She wished to marry one Moodley who was twenty-two years old. Her parents opposed the application mainly for two reasons: (a) the applicant was too	Die applikant was 'n jong meisie wat nog nie heeltemal sewentien jaar oud was nie. Sy wou met ene Moodley, wat twee en twintig jaar oud was, in die huwelik tree. Haar ouers

young and (b) the applicant was a Muslim while Moodley was a Hindu. The applicant's parents tried everything in their power to prevent the applicant from seeing Moodley. In the end she left home and went to live in the house occupied by Moodley and his parents. His parents approved of the match. Moodley then converted to the Islamic faith. There seemed to be no doubt that the couple were genuinely in love and had a real desire to marry. The applicant brought an *ex parte* application in terms of section 25(4) of the Marriage Act 25 of 1961 for a rule calling upon her parents to show cause why she should not be granted leave to marry Moodley. The court confirmed the rule. In other words the application was successful.

het die aansoek hoofsaaklik om twee redes teengestaan: (a) die applikant was te jonk en (b) die applikant was 'n Moslem en Moodley was 'n Hindoe. Die applikant se ouers het alles in hulle vermoë gedoen om die applikant te verhoed om met Moodley in aanraking te kom. Op die ou end het sy hulle huis verlaat en by Moodley en sy ouers gaan woon. Sy ouers het die verhouding goedgekeur. Moodley het toe die Moslem-geloof aanvaar. Dit het voorgekom asof die paartjie waarlik lief was vir mekaar en 'n werklike begeerte gehad het om te trou. Die applikant het by wyse van 'n *ex parte* aansoek ingevolge artikel 25(4) van die Huwelikswet 25 van 1961 aansoek gedoen om 'n bevel wat haar ouers opgeroep het om redes aan te voer waarom toestemming nie aan haar verleen moes word om met Moodley te trou nie. Die hof het die bevel bekragtig, met ander woorde die applikant was suksesvol.

MILNE DJP: [MILNE DJP analysed the evidence and proceeded:]

[500] Section 25(4) of the Marriage Act 25 of 1961 is in the following terms:

> "If the parent, guardian or commissioner of child welfare in question refuses to consent to a marriage of a minor, such consent may on application be granted by a Judge of the Supreme Court of South Africa: provided that such a Judge shall not grant such consent unless he is of the opinion that such refusal of consent by the parent, guardian or commissioner of child welfare is without adequate reason and contrary to the interests of such minor."

In *C en 'n Ander v Van T* 1965 (2) SA 239 (O) the Court concluded that the section conferred on the Court " 'n onbelemmerde diskresie" to decide whether the parental refusal to grant consent would unreasonably prejudice the minor, and that if it would so prejudice the minor the Court ought to give its consent to the marriage "afgesien daarvan of die weiering *mala fide*, beuselagtig, sinneloos of hoogs onredelik is". In *Allcock v Allcock and Another* 1969 (1) SA 427 (N) at 429 [59] MILLER J, as he then was, held that the Court did not have an unfettered discretion in regard to whether the minor will be unreasonably prejudiced by the parental refusal. He held that the section requires a Judge to apply his mind to two factors:

> "(i) whether the parental refusal is 'without adequate reason' and (ii) whether it is contrary to the interests of the minor. Unless he is of the opinion both that the parental refusal is without adequate reason and that such refusal is contrary to the interests of the minor, he shall not grant consent to the proposed marriage".

He further held that, having regard to the use of the word "adequate" (the Afrikaans text uses the word "genoegsame rede"), the Judge would not be able to grant consent, even if he would have consented to the marriage were he in the parents' place, but would have to be able to go further "and, with conviction, stigmatise the parent's reason or ground for refusal as inadequate, or without sufficient substance ...".

Prima facie the wording of s 25(4) does indeed indicate that the Legislature postulated two separate requirements, namely that the parental refusal was without adequate reason and also that the refusal was contrary to the interests of the minor. With very real respect, however, I [501] must confess that I have some difficulty in interpreting the legislation in this manner. I find it difficult to imagine circumstances in which the Court, having found that it was clearly contrary to the interests of such minor to refuse to allow the minor to marry, would nevertheless find that the parents' refusal was not without adequate reason. It might be suggested that such a situation could arise where, for example, the marriage would have the result of breaking the relationship between the parents and the minor. The Court, however, in coming to the conclusion as to whether the refusal would be contrary to the interests of the minor, would have to take the fact of such a break into account. If it came to the conclusion that, despite the obvious undesirability of such a break occurring, it was nevertheless in the interests of the minor for the minor to be allowed to marry, would it be obliged to refuse to grant its consent because the parents' reason for such refusal was that the parent had such a strong antipathy to the proposed spouse that marriage would bring about such a break? One can envisage such an antipathy existing on grounds which, while not wholly irrational, might nevertheless be such that the Court would come to the conclusion that it was still in the best interests of the minor to allow the minor to marry. If the Court comes to the conclusion that it is clearly in the interests of the minor to marry, but the parent refuses to consent on the ground that the applicant has been brought up in the Catholic Faith and is a Catholic, whereas the man she proposes to marry is Jewish, would the Court be *bound* to refuse its consent? I respectfully agree with the learned Judge when he says that the words "adequate reason" suggest "sufficient reason to justify the parental refusal of consent". The difficulty is, however, to determine the criteria which are applicable in determining whether or not the parental refusal is justified. The effect of the decision in *Allcock's* case appears to be this: if a reasonable parent could in the circumstances of the particular case under consideration come to the conclusion that he should withhold his consent, then, even though the Court might itself conclude that in those circumstances such consent should not be withheld and that it would be plainly in the interests of the minor to allow her or him to marry, it must refuse its consent. Perhaps one might with considerable diffidence suggest that the two requirements of the subsection are really complementary and cannot be considered separately. With equal diffidence it seems to me that the Judge must apply his mind to *all* the circumstances. He must apply his mind to the reasons for the parental refusal and must of course be "at all times conscious of the superior advantages which the parents will have over it in the matter of so personal and intimate a decision". (*Allcock's* case at 430B.) But the Court must ultimately decide, having weighed up the reasons for the parental refusal, whether by its own objective standards there is "sufficient reason to justify the parental refusal" and in doing so it must, it seems to me, be of paramount importance whether it will be in the best interests of the minor to allow the minor to marry.

I have no doubt that it would be in the best interests of the applicant to allow her to marry Moodley and that the parents' refusal to consent is contrary to her interests. She has formed what is obviously a strong [502] and lasting relationship with a young man with good prospects who will be able to look after her more than adequately. It is true that there is a religious difference and that the applicant is a devout Muslim. I accept Mr *Meskin's* [for the respondents] submission that it cannot be said that in the circumstances Moodley has, at this stage, genuinely converted to the Muslim faith. What does seem perfectly clear is that the difference is not likely to produce any friction or difference between the parties. I say this because the lengths to which Moodley has gone, including undergoing circumcision, indicate that his previous religious beliefs could not have been particularly strong and that he is prepared to go to considerable lengths to adjust to the applicant's religious beliefs. This is not the situation which arises where, for example, a strong Catholic seeks to marry a person who is a strong Anglican or a staunch adherent to the Jewish faith. Both Sheik Najaar and Mr Bawa [both witnesses] spoke of the profound change which has come about in the Muslim community over the past 15 to 20 years with the education and consequent "liberation" of Muslim women. It is this change that has brought about the situation that the fact that a Muslim girl has had sexual relations with a non-Muslim is no longer likely to depreciate her prospects of marrying a Muslim. In the circumstances it cannot be said that the applicant would be likely to be ostracised or that the married life of herself and Moodley would be prejudiced by the fact that she has chosen to marry a person who was, originally at any rate, a Hindu but now professes the Muslim faith. It is true that the applicant is a very young girl. One is not, however, looking at the situation which would arise where a young girl, who is living with her parents and attending school, is seeking to break out of the cocoon as it were and embark upon marriage with a person with whom she has only had romantic experience. The applicant has known the man she wishes to marry for close on three years. They have had an intimate relationship over a very long period and in fact she has been living in his parents' house with him for the past five months. Their relationship has withstood the very great impact of parental opposition and all the upset associated with a Court case.

Assuming, however, that I am incorrect in my interpretation of s 25(4) and that the law is correctly stated in *Allcock's* case, I am of the view that the parents' reason for refusal is without sufficient substance. In my view it fails to take account of the realities of the situation, by which I mean the pliability of Moodley with regard to religious matters and his willingness to adapt to the Muslim faith, and, furthermore, that the refusal fails to take into account or to give sufficient weight to the well-established and comparatively well-tried relationship that has grown up between the applicant and Moodley.

In the result the rule is confirmed . . .

Note

It is submitted that MILNE DJP is correct when he suggests, albeit with diffidence, that the two requirements, viz that the refusal must be contrary to the interests of the minor and without adequate reason, are complementary, in other words they must not be considered separately.

The court will not lightly exercise its power to override the refusal of a parent or guardian to consent to the marriage of his minor child. It will always give earnest consideration to the objection raised by the parents, especially where it appears that they are acting in the interests of the minor. See in this regard, for example, *De Greeff v De Greeff* 1982 1 SA 882 (O). In this case a nineteen-year-old woman wanted to marry a man of thirty two years of age. Her parents refused to consent to the marriage because they were concerned about the age difference between

Aantekening

Daar word aan die hand gedoen dat MILNE ARP korrek is waar hy voorstel, alhoewel hy dit met huiwering doen, dat die twee vereistes, naamlik dat die weiering teen die belange van die minderjarige moet wees en dat dit sonder genoegsame rede moet geskied, komplementêr is, met ander woorde nie afsonderlik oorweeg moet word nie.

Die hof sal nie die ouer of voog se weiering om tot die huwelik van sy minderjarige kind toe te stem ligtelik omverwerp nie. Die hof sal altyd ernstige oorweging aan die besware van die ouers skenk, veral waar dit blyk dat hulle in die belang van die minderjarige optree. Sien in hierdie verband byvoorbeeld *De Greeff v De Greeff* 1982 1 SA 882 (O). In hierdie saak wou 'n negentienjarige meisie met 'n man van twee en dertig trou. Haar ouers het geweier om tot die huwelik toe te stem aangesien hulle besorg was oor die ou-

her and her proposed husband and about the man's alcohol problems (he had received treatment the previous year for alcohol abuse). The court refused to consent to the marriage because it held that the parents' refusal was not contrary to the interests of the minor.

The mere fact that the minor is pregnant is insufficient to convince the court that her parents' refusal to consent is without sufficient reason and contrary to her interests (*Ex parte F* 1963 1 PH B9; *Kruger v Fourie* 1969 4 SA 469 (O)).

The court may make its consent to the marriage of a minor conditional upon the execution of an antenuptial contract (*Ex parte Blumenfield and King* 1939 WLD 352; *Ex parte Reitz* 1941 OPD 124; *C v T* 1965 2 SA 239 (O)).

See also *Allcock v Allcock* [59].

If the minor's parents are deceased and no guardian has been appointed for him, the minor must first seek the consent of the commissioner of child welfare in terms of section 25(1) of the Marriage Act 25 of 1961. The minor may not by-pass the commissioner by approaching the supreme court in terms of section 25(4) of the same act for permission to marry. The court may only be approached by the minor if the commissioner refuses consent (*Ex parte Balchund* 1991 1 SA 479 (D)).

derdomsverskil tussen haar en haar voorgenome man en oor die man se alkoholprobleem (hy het die vorige jaar behandeling ontvang vir drankmisbruik). Die hof het geweier om tot die huwelik toe te stem aangesien dit beslis het dat die ouers se weiering nie strydig was met die minderjarige se belange nie.

Die blote feit dat die minderjarige swanger is, is onvoldoende om die hof te oortuig dat haar ouers se weiering sonder rede en strydig met haar belange is (*Ex parte F* 1963 1 PH B9; *Kruger v Fourie* 1969 4 SA 469 (O)).

Die hof mag sy toestemming aan die minderjarige om in die huwelik te tree aan die verlyding van 'n huweliksvoorwaardeskontrak onderworpe maak (*Ex parte Blumenfield and King* 1939 WPA 352; *Ex parte Reitz* 1941 OPA 124; *C v T* 1965 2 SA 239 (O)).

Sien ook *Allcock v Allcock* [59].

Indien die minderjarige se ouers oorlede is en geen voog vir hom aangestel is nie, moet die minderjarige eerstens die toestemming van die kommissaris van kindersorg vra ingevolge artikel 25(1) van die Huwelikswet 25 van 1961. Die minderjarige mag nie die kommissaris omseil deur ingevolge artikel 25(4) van die wet by die hooggeregshof aansoek te doen om te trou nie. Die hof mag slegs deur so 'n minderjarige genader word indien die kommissaris sy toestemming weier (*Ex parte Balchund* 1991 1 SA 479 (D)).

Consensus   **Wilsooreenstemming**

[61] MARTENS V MARTENS

1952 3 SA 771 (W)

Action for a declaration of nullity of a marriage where a man married a woman merely to enable her to enter South Africa

Prior to 1947, the defendant had met a certain Mr Holden in Greece. She wished to come to South Africa to live with him although he was a married man. In order that the defendant might enter South Africa it was necessary for her to come to this country

Aansoek om nietigverklaring van 'n huwelik waar 'n man met 'n vrou getrou het net om haar in staat te stel om Suid-Afrika binne te kom

Voor 1947 het die verweerderes 'n sekere mnr Holden in Griekeland ontmoet. Sy wou na Suid-Afrika kom om by hom te woon alhoewel hy getroud was. Die verweerderes kon Suid-Afrika egter net binnekom as sy hierheen gekom het om in die huwelik te

to be married. Obviously Mr Holden could not marry her. He therefore persuaded the plaintiff, a friend of his, to act as husband in the marriage ceremony. On 5 November 1947 the plaintiff and the defendant were married before a magistrate. Immediately after the marriage the defendant went to live with Mr Holden and had been with him ever since. They had two children. The plaintiff could not speak Greek and the defendant could not speak English. In fact after the marriage ceremony they did not speak to or see each other until November 1951. In October 1950 the plaintiff wrote a letter to the defendant, asking her to be his wife. This she refused to do. An action for restitution of conjugal rights was then brought by the plaintiff but the order was refused. Some time after this Mr Holden obtained a divorce from his wife. On 20 November 1951 the plaintiff went to see the defendant to ask her to live with him. She again refused. The plaintiff then instituted action for a declaration of nullity of the marriage or for the granting of a restitution order. The court dismissed the action for a declaration of nullity but granted a restitution order.

tree. Mnr Holden kon vanselfsprekend nie met haar trou nie en hy het die eiser, wat 'n vriend van hom was, omgepraat om met haar in die huwelik te tree. Op 5 November 1947 is die eiser en die verweerderes voor 'n landdros getroud. Die verweerderes het onmiddellik na die huwelik saam met mnr Holden vertrek en het sedertdien saam met hom gewoon. Hulle het twee kinders gehad. Die eiser kon nie Grieks praat nie en die verweerderes kon nie Engels praat nie. Na die huwelikseremonie het hulle in werklikheid nooit met mekaar gepraat of mekaar gesien voor November 1951 nie. In Oktober 1950 het die eiser die verweerderes in 'n brief versoek om sy vrou te wees maar sy het geweier. Hy het toe om 'n bevel vir die herstel van huweliksregte aansoek gedoen maar die aansoek is van die hand gewys. 'n Tyd hierna is mnr Holden van sy vrou geskei. Op 20 November 1951 is die eiser na die verweerderes om haar te versoek om by hom te kom woon maar sy het weer geweier. Die eiser het hierop aansoek gedoen om die nietigverklaring van die huwelik of om 'n bevel vir die herstel van huweliksregte. Die hof het die aansoek om nietigverklaring van die huwelik verwerp maar het die bevel vir die herstel van huweliksregte toegestaan.

CLAYDEN J: [774] I do not consider it necessary to consider the authorities which have been put before me by Mr *Schreiner* [for the plaintiff], because the evidence in this case indicates to me that the parties here were not intending merely to go through a form of marriage. Both of them say that they got married because they thought that they could easily be divorced afterwards. This shows, I consider, that they fully realised that there would be a binding marriage needing divorce to dissolve it. This is not a case where the parties did not intend the ceremony to have the effect of making them married. By their contemplation of a later divorce it is obvious that they intended that very thing. What might be the legal position if it was shown that despite the ceremony the parties did not really intend the ceremony to have the effect of making them husband and wife . . . need not, I consider, be investigated, because the facts do not show that position . . .

[775] In the present case it seems to me that the facts show that the parties did intend that the defendant should become the wife of the plaintiff. That was the very object of the ceremony, so that she could remain in the country, and that object was brought about with a realisation by both contracting parties that there would be need for divorce to end the marriage. As explained later, any agreements contrary to the relationship of marriage must be disregarded. The action for a declaration of nullity of marriage must be dismissed.

It remains to consider the action for an order for restitution of conjugal rights. When previously the plaintiff sued, the action was dismissed by DE VILLIERS, J, on two grounds. The judgment is unreported, given in this Court on the 29th November, 1950. It sets out the facts and then proceeds:

"Under these circumstances it does not seem to me that there was any desertion at all, and if it can be said to amount to desertion in law, it certainly was not malicious, as it was agreed upon beforehand that no effect would be given to the marriage, the parties having no desire or intention of honouring the marriage.

The whole scheme was solely for the purpose of conferring Union domicile on the defendant to prevent her from being deported.

The scheme was in fraudem legis and was collusive. The parties are now, through the plaintiff, in effect asking the court to assist them in their scheme.

To my mind this amounted to an abuse of the institution of marriage and the present action is an abuse of the process of the Court."

None of the authorities which are before me in this regard were apparently put before the Court on that occasion. [In] [t]he case of Weintraub v Weintraub [1921 CPD 595]... although there was an agreement that there should be no marital relationship before the Jewish ceremony and although that ceremony had not taken place, an order for restitution of conjugal rights was granted. Van Oosten v Van Oosten, 1923 CPD 409, was a case where the husband and the wife had, prior to marriage, lived together and had children. To a declaration claiming an order for restitution of conjugal rights the wife pleaded that they were married merely to legitimise the children born to them and that at the time of the marriage they verbally agreed that they would not live together. An exception was taken to this plea, and VAN ZYL, J, at p 411, says:

"Such an agreement, as a matter of fact, goes towards undermining the very object of a contract of marriage; one of the natural results of marriage is that the parties after marriage should live together. It defeats the whole object of marriage if it were to be arranged prior to the marriage that the parties should not live together. I think, therefore, that that part [776] of the plea, if it is intended to be relied upon as a defence, should be struck out."

Washkansky v Washkansky, 1940 CPD 238, was a case similar to the present one. It appeared that at the time of the marriage the plaintiff was an alien in the Union on a temporary permit, that the parties had never lived together, and that the marriage was merely one of convenience to enable the plaintiff to evade the provisions of the Immigration Laws of the Union. Giving judgment SUTTON, J, said:

"In this case the defendant has appeared. He is in default and he has not asked to cross-examine the witness Prins, and it is clear from her evidence that he is really living with her and that there has been adultery. In the circumstances there must be a decree of divorce."

And later:

"The consequence is, now, that the marriage has been put to an end, that the Immigration laws have been successfully evaded. It may be that that was quite lawful, but there it is. It is just as well that some publicity should be given to this matter. The decree of divorce will be granted but no order made as to costs."

Because there is, in my view, a valid marriage, the parties to that marriage are obliged to accord to each other the rights of marriage and I quite agree with decisions to the effect that agreements to the contrary, except of course recognised deeds of separation, are invalid. Even those deeds, of course, are terminable at will. Had those authorities been put before DE VILLIERS, J, I feel sure that his reliance on the agreement to justify the refusal of the defendant to give conjugal rights to the plaintiff would not have been given as a reason. With respect I feel obliged, on the authorities cited, to take the contrary view. The evidence shows quite clearly that defendant takes up the view that in no circumstance will she ever become a wife in more than name. It seems to me that if I decide that there is a legal marriage then I must give that marriage its legal consequences.

The other ground for refusing relief is that to grant relief would be to allow abuse of the process of Court by lending the Court to the furtherance of a scheme to evade the laws of the land. There is of course no doubt that the Court will not lend its procedure to a scheme to evade the Immigration laws. In a case such as the present the obtaining of a dissolution of the marriage was a part of the original scheme to allow the defendant to enter the country and to live in adultery with Mr Holden. The position has, however, to be judged from the attitude which should be adopted towards the plaintiff, and not that which should be adopted towards Mr Holden. The plaintiff appeared to me to be a man of weak character who would easily be persuaded to any course of action. The question is whether he is to be condemned forever to an undissoluble marriage with a wife who will never be his wife. It seems to me that in the decision whether or not the action which is brought is an abuse of the process of the Court, the degree of culpability of the plaintiff, the passage of time and the possible repentance and change of attitude of the plaintiff must be elements.

[777] It is as a matter of public policy that the Courts will not lend themselves to schemes to evade the law, but the Courts should not, I consider, be relentless; and if there are countervailing considerations of public policy, as there now here are, and if the facts show that the person approaching the Court has been stupid in his disregard of the law rather than defiant, that he has in no way acted for his own advantage, and, when the error of his way has been made clear to him, he has done what lies within his power to comply with the law, then there is, I think, room for a decision that what was once an abuse of the process of Court is no longer such. Since the judgment was given in this Court in 1950 time has passed, but in addition to that the evidence shows that the plaintiff has made an effort to make of the marriage in form a marriage in fact. That that effort was doomed to failure cannot affect the attitude which the Court should adopt towards him, provided the Court is satisfied that his acts were genuine. The evidence of the plaintiff is that after he was refused relief in 1950 he came to realise that he must accept this marriage as a marriage and that he then approached the defendant to try to persuade her to become his wife. Had this evidence been given in regard to a time much nearer to the marriage I should have been most doubtful of it, but the character of the plaintiff, as it appeared when he gave his evidence, made it seem not improbable that he might have come to the conclusion that on his part he could have tolerated life with this wife whom he had married to help his friend. His evidence that if he should be divorced he intends to marry another casts some doubt upon this, but he seems truthful, and I can see no reason to reject his sworn evidence as to his intention when he approached his wife in November.

Without in any way casting doubt on the correctness of the decision in 1950 it seems to me that the altered circumstances since that time are such that it can be said that the plaintiff no longer makes abuse of the process of the Court in asking that his wife should become his wife.

The defendant is therefore ordered to restore conjugal rights to the plaintiff on or before the 16th day of February, 1952, failing which to show cause on the 26th February, 1952, why a decree of divorce should not be granted and why the custody of the children should not be awarded to the defendant . . .

Note

It is evident from this case that if a man and a woman enter into a marriage in order to evade the immigration laws without the intention of establishing a proper marriage relationship, this does not prevent a valid marriage from coming into existence. The reason for this is because the parties did in fact have the intention of entering into a valid marriage. The marriage can therefore not be annulled but can only be terminated by divorce. The agreement between the parties not to live together is *contra bonos mores* as it defeats the object of marriage. For this reason it is void but the voidness of the term does not affect the validity of the marriage (see also *Washkansky v Washkansky* 1940 CPD 238).

The reason why the plaintiff in this case applied for a restitution order was because this was the only way in which he could obtain a divorce in terms of the divorce procedure which applied before the Divorce Act 70 of 1979 came into operation: if conjugal rights were not restored by the defendant, the court would grant a decree of divorce. On the divorce procedure followed in divorce actions before the Divorce Act came into operation, see *Naville v Naville* [11].

Aantekening

Dit is uit hierdie saak duidelik dat as 'n man en 'n vrou in die huwelik tree ten einde die immigrasiewette te omseil sonder dat hulle die bedoeling het dat daar 'n werklike huweliksverhouding tussen hulle tot stand sal kom, dit nie verhoed dat 'n geldige huwelik tot stand kom nie. Dit is so omdat die partye inderdaad die bedoeling gehad het om 'n geldige huwelik aan te gaan. Die huwelik kan gevolglik nie nietig verklaar word nie maar kan net deur egskeiding beëindig word. Die ooreenkoms wat die partye aangegaan het om nie saam te woon nie is *contra bonos mores* aangesien dit teen die wese van die huwelik indruis. Om hierdie rede is dit dan ook nietig maar die nietigheid van die bepaling beïnvloed nie die geldigheid van die huwelik nie (sien ook *Washkansky v Washkansky* 1940 KPA 238).

Die rede waarom die eiser in hierdie saak om die herstel van huweliksregte aansoek gedoen het, was omdat dit die enigste wyse was waarop hy 'n egskeiding kon verkry ingevolge die egskeidingsprosedure wat voor die inwerkingtreding van die Wet op Egskeiding 70 van 1979 gegeld het: as die verweerder nie huweliksregte herstel het nie sou die hof 'n egskeiding toestaan. Oor die egskeidingsprosedure wat voor die inwerkingtreding van die Wet op Egskeiding gegeld het, sien *Naville v Naville* [11].

[62]   SMITH V SMITH

1948 4 SA 61 (N)

Consent to marriage induced by fear and duress

The plaintiff applied for an order declaring her marriage to the defendant null and void. At the time of her marriage she was a minor and she contended that she entered into it "against her will through fear induced by threats made by, and under duress and pressure by, her father and her mother and the defendant such as to render the free exercise of her own will impossible." Although the plaintiff originally wished to marry the de-

Toestemming tot huweliksluiting verkry deur vreesaanjaging en dwang

Die eiseres het aansoek gedoen dat haar huwelik met die verweerder nietig verklaar word. Ten tyde van die huweliksluiting was die eiseres minderjarig en sy het beweer dat die huwelik gesluit is "against her will through fear induced by threats made by, and under duress and pressure by, her father and her mother and the defendant such as to render the free exercise of her own will impossible." Alhoewel die eiseres vroeër met die

fendant and became engaged to him, her feelings for him underwent a change and she fell in love with a certain McConnell. Initially the plaintiff did not tell this to her parents because of fear of her father, and when she eventually informed them that she was no longer willing to marry the defendant, both her parents and the defendant insisted that she should go through with the marriage. Both her father and the defendant assaulted her on more than one occasion and she was threatened and bullied to such an extent that when the marriage took place she was reduced to a state of mind which rendered her quite incapable either of consenting to the marriage, or of resisting further the coercion of her parents and the defendant. The evidence showed further that the plaintiff was in a dazed and acutely distressed condition throughout the marriage ceremony. After the marriage the couple lived with the plaintiff's parents for a few weeks. The plaintiff then ran away with McConnell and they lived together as man and wife. Later she also gave birth to McConnell's child. The application was granted.

verweerder wou trou en aan hom verloof geraak het, het haar gevoel vir hom verander en sy het verlief geraak op 'n sekere McConnell. Aanvanklik het die eiseres, uit vrees vir haar vader, niks hiervan aan haar ouers vertel nie, en toe sy hulle later in kennis gestel het dat sy nie langer bereid was om met die verweerder te trou nie, het albei haar ouers en die verweerder daarop aangedring dat sy met die huwelik moes voortgaan. Haar vader sowel as die verweerder het haar verskeie keer aangerand en sy is in so 'n mate gedreig en getreiter dat toe die huwelik plaasgevind het sy in so 'n geestestoestand was dat sy nie in staat was om tot die huwelik toe te stem of die dwang wat deur haar ouers en die verweerder op haar uitgeoefen is verder te weerstaan nie. Die getuienis het verder aangetoon dat die eiseres gedurende die huweliksseremonie verdwaas en uiters ontsteld voorgekom het. Na die huwelik het die paartjie vir 'n paar weke by die eiseres se ouers gewoon waarna die eiseres met McConnell weggeloop het. Hulle het as man en vrou saamgeleef en die eiseres het later ook aan McConnell se kind geboorte geskenk. Die aansoek is toegestaan.

SELKE J: [66] Though it may be that there is no South African decision exactly in point, it is noteworthy that *Voet* 23:2:6 in emphasising that consent is an essential of marriage, classes amongst the factors negativing consent the mental incompetence of one who is drunk; and he also mentions, as a potentially vitiating or nullifying factor, fear, provided that it is such as would affect the mind of a man of courage and resolution. It is true that he goes on to say, of these [67] and kindred grounds of avoidance, that in his time they hardly applied "(*vix pertinent*)" to marriages, as distinct from betrothals, marriages, unlike betrothals, being conducted with publicity and formalities, either in a Church or in a Court of Law. I understand him, by this, to suggest that, consequently, it was very difficult to prove that the requisite consent was lacking, and I think that in making these remarks he seems... to have had in mind difficulties in the way of proof, rather than principles of substantive law...

Voet's statement (at 23:2:6) about the quality of the fear necessary to nullify a seeming consent must, I think, be read with his remarks (at 4:2:2) about the necessity of taking into account the age, the sex, and the circumstances, of the person alleged to have been intimidated. Van der Linden, in his "*Institutes*" (Bk. 1, Chap 14, sec 2), remarks that in estimating the probable effect of allegedly intimidating conduct, the Court must have regard to the circumstances both of the persons and the things concerned, and take account of the fact that, for example, a fear which would not be sufficient to disturb the mind of a person of mature years or a soldier, might easily suffice in the case of a woman or an old man. In this relation, the remarks of BUTT, J, in *Scott v Sebright* (LR 12 PD at p 24) are very apposite. He says,

> "It has sometimes been said that in order to avoid a contract entered into through fear, the fear must be such as would impel a person of ordinary courage and resolution to yield to it. I do not think that is an accurate statement of the law. Whenever from natural weakness of intellect or from fear – whether reasonably entertained or not – either party is actually in a state of mental incompetence to resist pressure improperly brought to bear, there is no more consent than in the case of a person of stronger intellect and more robust courage yielding to a more serious danger"...

I take it – but the point was not specifically raised or debated before us – that the legal position in cases of this kind is that [68] unless and until the Court declares the purported marriage a nullity, the union must be regarded as a valid one. Seeing, therefore, that there is nothing to compel a person in the position of the present plaintiff to take steps to have the union declared null and void, it seems to follow that such a person could, by conduct subsequent to the ceremony, in effect affirm or acquiesce in the union. That looks as though the proper view is that such a union is voidable, and not *ipso jure* void, although I do not know that that appears clearly from the Common Law authorities. But assuming that it is voidable – and I mention this point merely to show that the Court did not lose sight of it – the Court took the view that notwithstanding that the plaintiff admitted that she and the defendant lived together as man and wife from the day of the ceremony until August 14th 1947, when she ran away with McConnell, her conduct in thus living with the defendant ought not to be construed as an affirmation or acquiescence in her marriage with defendant, such as to overcome the effect of the original want of consent, because during the whole time plaintiff and defendant lived together as husband and wife, she was residing in her father's house, where she had resided, so far as appears, all her life, and, thus, between July 6th [the date of the marriage] and August 14th, she presumably remained throughout subject to the same influences as were responsible for her going through the ceremony of marriage.

Further, it seems clear that the effect of a Court's order declaring a marriage null and void for want of consent is retro-active to the time of the marriage ceremony, and that, thus, the facts that on August 14th, 1947, the plaintiff ran away with McConnell and has ever since lived with him as his wife, and now has a child by him, constitute no bar to her being granted the relief for which she asks in this action...

HATHORN JP and BROOME J concurred.

Note

A marriage that is annulled for want of consent is void *ab initio*. It produces none of the legal incidents of marriage (Hahlo 103), for example the children of such a marriage would be illegitimate and the spouses would not be able to claim maintenance from each other. For this reason the sexual relations which the plaintiff had with McConnell did not amount to adultery and therefore constituted no bar against the action for annulment.

This case also illustrates that it is immaterial whether the duress emanates from the other party to the marriage or a third party (Lee and Honoré 37; Hahlo 50 84). Van der Vyver and Joubert

Aantekening

'n Huwelik wat weens gebrek aan wilsooreenstemming nietig verklaar word, is *ab initio* nietig. Dit het in geen opsig die regsgevolge van 'n huwelik nie (Hahlo 103). Die kinders wat uit so 'n huwelik gebore word sal byvoorbeeld buite-egtelik wees en die partye sal ook nie onderhoud van mekaar kan eis nie. Om hierdie rede het die geslagsverkeer wat die eiseres met McConnell gehad het ook nie op owerspel neergekom nie en was dit gevolglik nie 'n beletsel teen die aksie om nietigverklaring nie.

Uit hierdie saak is verder duidelik dat dit nie saak maak of die vreesaanjaging van die ander huweliksparty of van 'n derde party afkomstig

(498–499) suggest in this regard that the marriage should only be voidable as a result of the unlawful conduct of the other spouse unless the duress resulted in an *incapacity to act* on the part of the coerced spouse. Threats brought to bear on the victimised spouse by persons other than the other spouse only, and of which the other spouse was not aware should therefore not affect the validity of the marriage. It is suggested that the first view is correct since in principle it makes no difference from where the duress emanates if the result is that the coerced person enters into a marriage to which he has not consented of his own free will.

The action to have the marriage set aside can only be brought by the coerced spouse (Hahlo 83; Lee and Honoré 37).

is nie (Lee en Honoré 37; Hahlo 50 84). Van der Vyver en Joubert (498–499) doen in dié verband aan die hand dat die huwelik net vernietigbaar behoort te wees as gevolg van die onregmatige optrede van die ander gade tensy die vreesaanjaging *handelingsonbevoegdheid* van die gedwonge persoon tot gevolg gehad het. As die vreesaanjaging net deur ander persone as die ander eggenoot gepleeg is en hy nie daarvan bewus was nie behoort dit gevolglik nie die geldigheid van die huwelik te beïnvloed nie. Daar word aan die hand gedoen dat die eerste standpunt die korrekte is aangesien dit in beginsel geen verskil maak waar die vreesaanjaging vandaan kom as die gevolg daarvan is dat die gedwonge persoon 'n huwelik aangaan waartoe hy nie uit sy eie vrye wil toegestem het nie.

Net die gedwonge eggenoot kan aansoek doen om die huwelik ter syde te laat stel (Hahlo 83; Lee en Honoré 37).

Marriage must be lawful   **Geoorloofdheid**

[63] ISMAIL V ISMAIL

1983 1 SA 1006 (A)

Validity of a marriage celebrated and terminated according to tenets and customs of Muslim faith

The parties' marriage was celebrated and terminated according to the tenets and customs of the Muslim faith. The appellant (plaintiff) claimed payment of arrear maintenance as well as maintenance for a specified period after termination of the marriage, delivery of a deferred dowry, and delivery or payment of the value of two sets of jewellery which the respondent had given to her, but which she had returned to him for safe keeping. The plaintiff did not claim that a valid civil marriage existed between the parties. She based her case on the alleged existence of certain customs and on contract. The respondent excepted to the appellant's particulars of claim on the grounds that they did not disclose a cause of action in that the

Geldigheid van 'n huwelik wat volgens die leerstellinge en gewoontes van die Moslem-geloof aangegaan en ontbind is

Die partye se huwelik is aangegaan en ontbind ooreenkomstig die leerstellinge en gewoontes van die Moslem-geloof. Die appellant (eiseres) het betaling van agterstallige onderhoud sowel as onderhoud vir 'n bepaalde periode na ontbinding van die huwelik geëis, asook lewering van 'n bruidskat wat nog nie betaal was nie, en lewering, of betaling van die waarde, van twee stelle juweliersware wat die respondent aan haar gegee het maar wat sy aan hom teruggegee het vir veilige bewaring. Die eiseres het nie beweer dat 'n geldige burgerlike huwelik tussen die partye tot stand gekom het nie. Sy het haar saak gebaseer op sekere gewoontes wat na bewering bestaan het en op kontrak. Die respondent het eksepsie aangeteken teen

customs relied upon by the appellant were *contra bonos mores*, unreasonable and in conflict with laws which could not be altered by agreement. The exception was upheld by the court *a quo* and the appellant appealed against this decision. The appeal was unsuccessful except in so far as the jewellery was concerned.

die appellant se besonderhede van eis op grond daarvan dat hulle nie 'n eisoorsaak geopenbaar het nie, aangesien die gewoontes waarop die appellant gesteun het *contra bonos mores*, onredelik, en in stryd met wette was wat nie deur ooreenkoms verander kon word nie. Die eksepsie is deur die hof *a quo* gehandhaaf en die appellant het teen hierdie beslissing geappelleer. Die appèl was onsuksesvol behalwe met betrekking tot die juweliersware.

TRENGOVE JA: [1017] The central issue in this appeal is whether the proprietary consequences of such a marriage and its termination, according to Muslim custom, are enforceable at law . . .

[1019] In opening the appeal, plaintiff's counsel was at pains to emphasize that it was not part of plaintiff's case that the alleged conjugal union between the parties constituted a valid civil marriage. He submitted, however, that the Court should not on that account refuse to give effect to proprietary stipulations flowing from the union. This union can obviously not be regarded as a valid civil marriage. Two requirements were lacking. Firstly, under our law, a marriage is the legally recognised voluntary union for life of one man and one woman to the exclusion of all others while it lasts (see Hahlo [1020] *The SA Law of Husband and Wife* 4th ed at 28 and the authorities cited in footnote 1). Within South Africa the monogamous concept of marriage is fundamental. In the instant case the union was, *ex facie* the pleadings, a polygamous one even though there may have been "a tacit *consensus* between plaintiff and defendant to the effect that their marriage would be monogamous". Their tacit understanding cannot affect the inherent nature of their relationship. Under our law a marriage is regarded as polygamous if it is celebrated under tenets which allow the husband to take another wife during its subsistence, whether he does so or not. A potentially polygamous union is equated with a *de facto* polygamous union (see *Seedat's Executors v The Master (Natal)* 1917 AD 302 at 308). It furthermore appears from the pleadings that the requisite formalities were not observed although this is not a factor which has a bearing on the point at issue. The union between the parties was not solemnized by a marriage officer as envisaged by ss 2, 3 and 11 of Act 25 of 1961, nor was it solemnized in the presence of both parties as required by s 29(2) of the Act.

Plaintiff's counsel submitted, however, that her cause of action was based on the alleged existence of certain customs, and on contract, and that the question for consideration was, therefore, not whether her marriage was valid but whether, *ex facie* the pleadings, the said customs and the contract were *per se* either *contra bonos mores*, unreasonable, or in conflict with laws which are unalterable by agreement. I do not agree with this approach to the problem. In my view the claims should not be viewed in isolation. The tenets of the Muslim faith appear to govern all aspects of the marriage relationship. Plaintiff's claims, namely for payment of arrear maintenance and deferred dowry, and for the return of the marital gifts, flow from, and are by their very nature intrinsic to, the conjugal union entered into between parties. In considering whether these claims are enforceable or not, the Court must have regard to the very close and intimate connection between the customs and the contract in question and the underlying conjugal union. Counsel conceded that, statutory exceptions apart, our Courts have persistently refused to give recognition and effect to polygamous unions on the grounds of public policy or as being *contra bonos mores* (see eg *Bronn v Fritz Bronn's Executors and Others* (1860) 3 Searle 313 at

318; *Ngqobela v Sihele* (1893) 10 SC 346 at 352; *Kaba v Ntela* 1910 TS 964 at 969; *Seedat's Executors v The Master (Natal)* (supra at 308–309); *Docrat v Bhayat* 1932 TPD 125 at 127). Counsel contended, however, that we are living in a constantly changing world, that the attitude of society towards polygamous unions has in recent years become more tolerant, and that we have by statute been extending our recognition of such unions. There was no longer any valid reason, he said, for refusing to give effect to the proprietary consequences of such a union as they are not part of the invariable consequences of a marriage and are of no concern to anyone but the parties themselves. A number of arguments were advanced in support of this general proposition.

Plaintiff's counsel relied, firstly, on the provisions of s 3(1) and s 11 of Act 25 of 1961. The Act consolidates and amends the laws relating [1021] to the solemnization of marriages and matters incidental thereto. The word "marriage" is not defined in the Act, but it is quite clear from the context of the Act as a whole that it means a marriage under the common law, that is, a marriage which is designed to create a monogamous union. In my view the provisions of ss 3(1) and 11 do not assist plaintiff's case. Referring to s 3(1), counsel contended that the Legislature has taken cognisance of the existence of Muslim marriages by providing for the appointment of marriage officers for the purposes of solemnizing marriages according to Mohammedan rites. In my view, the section does not accord any recognition whatever to polygamous unions and, if the purport of counsel's submission is that it does, I cannot accept it. Section 3(1), in so far as it is material, provides as follows:

> "The Minister . . . may designate any minister of religion of, or any person holding a responsible position in, any religious denomination or organization to be . . . a marriage officer for the purpose of solemnizing *marriages according to Christian, Jewish or Mohammedan rites or the rites of any Indian religion*."

(My italics.)

The words which I have italicised clearly relate only to the form of the marriage ceremony, not to the essentials of the marriage as such. The section, for example, enables a Muslim male and a Muslim female to have their marriage solemnized according to Muslim rites by an Imam [the person who performs a Muslim marriage] who has been designated a marriage officer; but, if the marriage is intended to be a monogamous marriage, the Imam, officiating at such a marriage, will also have to comply with all the prescribed formalities pertaining to the solemnization of marriages under the Act such as, for example, the provisions of s 29(2) which require, *inter alia*, that a marriage be solemnized in the presence of the parties themselves.

Counsel for plaintiff sought to rely on s 11 as giving "some form of recognition" to the solemnization of a marriage ceremony in accordance with Muslim rites because such a ceremony "does not purport to effect a valid marriage". Section 11 reads as follows:

> "(1) A marriage may be solemnized by a marriage officer only.
> (2) Any marriage officer who purports to solemnize a marriage which he is not authorized under this Act to solemnize or which to his knowledge is legally prohibited, and any person not being a marriage officer who purports to solemnize a marriage, shall be guilty of an offence . . .
> (3) Nothing in ss (2) contained shall apply to any marriage ceremony in accordance with the rites or formalities of any religion, *if such ceremony does not purport to effect a valid marriage*."

(My italics).

Counsel submitted, quite rightly, that the marriage ceremony, in the instant case, fell within the ambit of s 11(3). It follows, as counsel said, that although the Imam who officiated at the ceremony was not a marriage officer, he was, nevertheless, not guilty of an offence under s 11(2) because the ceremony did not purport to effect a valid marriage. I cannot, however, accept counsel's further submission, namely that in consequence of the aforegoing the polygamous union between the parties and the customs incidental thereto are not to be regarded as being *contra bonos mores*, or unreasonable, or in conflict with the rules of law which are unalterable by agreement. The mere fact that [1022] the Legislature has not prohibited polygamous unions, recognised as marriages under the tenets of the Muslim faith, does not mean that it also approves of such unions or that the consequences thereof are legally enforceable. The effect of the aforementioned section is simply that parties entering into such a union commit no criminal offence, just as a man and a woman commit no crime by agreeing to live together, but that is a far cry from recognising and giving legal effect to such unions and the consequences thereof . . .

[1023] It was also contended on plaintiff's behalf that the Legislature in this country has given increasing recognition to polygamous unions, and [1024] certain of the consequences thereof, and that this should be regarded as a spur to the Courts to exercise a formative jurisdiction in respect of related matters. The statutory provisions on which counsel relied are conveniently summarised in *Hahlo* (*op cit* at 39–42) and the appendix thereto at 604–611. I do not consider it necessary to refer to these provisions in any detail. A perusal of the various provisions reveals that, whereas the Legislature has extended very wide and comprehensive recognition to Black customary unions (see, eg, chap V of the Black Administration Act 38 of 1927), it has refrained from doing so in the case of customary polygamous unions of other ethnic or religious groups, such as the Muslim community. As to the latter groups, the Legislature has, in a number of general statutes, and for specific purposes, recognised polygamous unions, obviously because it was considered expedient to do so (see, eg, s 21(13) of Insolvency Act 24 of 1936 and s 1 of Income Tax Act 58 of 1962 *sv* "married persons"). Except for Black customary unions, I have not found any indication, in any of the statutory provisions to which we have been referred, that the Legislature either expressly or impliedly approves of polygamy; or, as INNES CJ said in *Seedat's* case, the existence of statutes in which such polygamous unions are recognised is no indication of "the tolerance of polygamy as part of the general South African system."

To sum up thus far. Having considered all the arguments presented on plaintiff's behalf, I have come to the conclusion that we would not be justified in deviating from the long line of decisions in which our Courts have consistently refused, on grounds of public policy, to recognise, or to give effect to the consequences of, polygamous unions contracted in South Africa, statutory exceptions apart. The concept of marriage as a monogamous union is firmly entrenched in our society and the recognition of polygamy would, undoubtedly, tend to prejudice or undermine the status of marriage as we know it; and from a purely practical point of view it would, in my view, also be unwise to accord recognition to polygamous unions for the simple reason that all our marriage and family laws – and to some extent also our law of succession – are primarily designed for monogamous relationships . . . Furthermore, in view of the growing trend in favour of the recognition of complete equality between marriage partners, the recognition of polygamous unions solemnized under the tenets of the Muslim faith may even be regarded as a retrograde step; *ex facie* the pleadings, a Muslim wife does not participate in the marriage ceremony; and while her husband has the right to terminate their marriage unilaterally by simply issuing three "talaaqi", without having to show good cause, the wife can obtain an annulment of the marriage only if she can satisfy the Moulana [a high-ranking ecclesiastical office-bearer of the Muslim creed] that her husband has been guilty of misconduct. While this may be consistent with the tenets of the Muslim faith, it is entirely foreign to our notion of a conjugal relationship. I also mention, in passing, that it seems unlikely that the non-recognition of polygamous unions will cause any real hardship to the members of the Muslim [1025] community, except, perhaps, in isolated instances. According to the pleadings, only about 2 per cent of all Muslim males in South Africa have more than one wife. This means that approximately 98 per cent of all Muslim males have either contracted valid civil marriages or *de facto* monogamous unions. And, in the case of the latter, the parties have for many years had the right to convert their *de facto* monogamous unions into *de jure* monogamous unions. They had the option of doing so under the Indians' Relief Act 22 of 1914 (which was repealed by the General Law Amendment Act 57 of 1975) and they can still do so by entering into valid civil marriages under Act 25 of 1961. In the result, I have come to the conclusion that the polygamous union between the parties in the instant case must be regarded as void on the grounds of public policy.

As was mentioned earlier in this judgment, plaintiff's counsel contended that her claims were enforceable at law because the claims and the grounds on which they were based were *per se* innocuous. However, it is also quite clear from the pleadings, as I mentioned previously, that the claims (except for the claim for the return of the jewellery to which I shall presently refer) are based on a custom or a contract which arises directly from, and is intimately connected with, the polygamous relationship entered into by the parties. It follows from this that, if the polygamous relationship is regarded as void on the grounds of public policy, the custom or the contract which flows from this relationship is also vitiated. See *Ngqobela v Sihele* (*supra* at 352) and *Kaba v Ntela* (*supra* at 269) – in each instance the Court held that no action could be brought for the recovery of "lobola" cattle because they had been paid in respect of a Black customary union, ie a polygamous union. I should mention that the Courts have since been precluded, by s 11 of Act 38 of 1927, from declaring that the custom of "lobola" or "bogadi" is repugnant to the principles of public policy. [These provisions are now embodied in section 1 of the Law of Evidence Amendment Act 45 of 1988.] The principle enunciated in the aforementioned cases, nevertheless, still holds good as far as the consequences of polygamous unions between other members of our community are concerned.

In my judgment, the customs and the contract in question are contrary to public policy and are, consequently, unenforceable. They may equally well be regarded as being *contra bonos mores,* as was alleged by defendant in his notice of exception. Although the phrase *contra bonos mores* is ordinarily used with reference to conduct which is regarded as immoral or sexually reprehensible, it really has a far wider meaning (cf *Grotius* 3.1.42–43; Van der Linden *Koopmans Handboek* 1.14.2; Aquilius "Immorality and Illegality in Contract" 1941 *SALJ* vol 58 at 337). *Mores* or *boni mores* (Dutch: "zeden" or "goede zeden"; English: "morals" or "morality" and Afrikaans: "sedes" or "goeie sedes") can be defined as meaning

> "the accepted customs and usages of a particular social group that are usually morally binding upon all members of a group and are regarded as essential to its welfare and preservation" . . .

[1026] I would not regard a polygamous union solemnized under the tenets of the Muslim faith, and the customs related thereto, as being *contra bonos mores,* in the narrower sense in which the expression is ordinarily used, ie as immoral (see *Ngqobela v Sihele* (*supra* at 352) and *Docrat v Bhayat* (*supra* at 127)), but such a union can be regarded as being *contra bonos mores* in the wider sense of the phrase, ie as being contrary to the accepted customs and usages which are regarded as morally binding upon all members of our society or, as INNES CJ said in *Seedat's* case at 309,

> "as being fundamentally opposed to our principles and institutions" . . .

[As far as the claim for the return of the jewellery was concerned, TRENGOVE JA held that this claim was founded on a contract of deposit. This contract was an entirely unrelated and independent contract and therefore not affected by the considerations which vitiated the plaintiff's other claims. He proceeded:]

[1027] In the result, plaintiff's appeal succeeds only in respect of the cause of action on which the claim for the return of the jewellery is founded. As to the other claims the appeal fails . . .

RABIE CJ; KOTZÉ JA; BOTHA JA and VAN WINSEN AJA concurred.

Note	Aantekening
Marriages celebrated according to Muslim customs are not recognised as valid, firstly because such marriages are potentially polygamous and secondly because they are not celebrated in accordance with the provisions of the Marriage Act 25 of 1961 (Hahlo 32).	Huwelike wat volgens die Moslem-geloof aangegaan word, word nie as wettig beskou nie, eerstens omdat sodanige huwelike potensieel poligaam is, en tweedens omdat hulle nie ooreenkomstig die bepalings van die Huwelikswet 25 van 1961 aangegaan is nie (Hahlo 32).
For criticism of this decision, see Kerr 1984 *SALJ* 445 *et seq* and Kaganas and Murray 1991 *Acta Juridica* 116 123–125.	Vir kritiek op hierdie beslissing, sien Kerr 1984 *SALJ* 445 ev en Kaganas en Murray 1991 *Acta Juridica* 116 123–125.
The underlying reasons for not recognising Muslim and Hindu marriages are the same as those grounding non-recognition of the customary marriages of Blacks. In the light of the recommendation by the South African Law Commission that customary marriages of Blacks should receive complete recognition (*Report* Project 51 *Marriages and Customary Unions of Black Persons* 1986), it is clear that recognition of (potentially) polygamous Muslim and Hindu marriages must also be considered. The Law Commission has, fairly recently, launched an investigation into the recognition of aspects of Islamic family law and succession. It has not yet published a working paper or report on its investigation. It seems that Hindu family law is not yet receiving the Law Commission's attention.	Die onderliggende rede vir die nie-erkenning van Moslem- en Hindu-huwelike is dieselfde as die wat nie-erkenning van die gebruiklike huwelike van Swartes ten grondslag lê. In die lig van die aanbeveling van die Suid-Afrikaanse Regskommissie dat die gebruiklike huwelike van Swartes ten volle erken moet word (*Verslag* Projek 51 *Huwelike en Gebruiklike Verbindings van Swart Persone* 1986) is dit duidelik dat die erkenning van (potensieel) poligame Moslem en Hindu-huwelike ook oorweeg moet word. Die Regskommissie het, redelik onlangs, 'n ondersoek ingestel na die erkenning van aspekte van Islamitiese familiereg en erfreg. Geen werkstuk of verslag is nog oor die ondersoek gepubliseer nie. Dit skyn asof die familiereg van die Hindu's nog nie die Regskommissie se aandag geniet nie.

Formalities	**Formaliteite**

[64] SANTOS V SANTOS

1987 4 SA 150 (W)

Marriage solemnised by a foreign vice-consul in South Africa	Huwelik deur 'n buitelandse vise-konsul in Suid-Afrika voltrek
The plaintiff instituted an action for divorce against the defendant. The marriage had been solemnised in the Portuguese consulate in	Die eiser het 'n egskeidingsaksie teen die verweerder aanhangig gemaak. Die huwelik is in die Portugese konsulaat in Johannesburg

Johannesburg by the Portuguese vice-consul. The parties were both domiciled in South Africa at the time. The defendant averred that the marriage had been solemnised by a person not authorised to solemnise marriages in South Africa and consequently denied that the parties were lawfully married. By agreement between them the court was asked to decide *in limine* (that is in the beginning of the case) whether the marriage was valid according to South African law. The court held that it was not.

deur die Portugese vise-konsul. Die partye was op daardie stadium albei in Suid-Afrika gedomisilieer. Die verweerder het beweer dat die huwelik deur 'n persoon voltrek is wat nie die bevoegdheid gehad het om huwelike in Suid-Afrika te voltrek nie en het gevolglik ontken dat die partye wettig getroud was. Die partye het ooreengekom om die hof te versoek om *in limine* (dit is aan die begin van die saak) te beslis of die huwelik ingevolge die Suid-Afrikaanse reg geldig was. Die hof het beslis dat dit ongeldig was.

GROSSKOPF J: [151] Under South African law the formal validity of a marriage is determined by the law of the place where the marriage is solemnized, ie the *lex loci celebrationis*. That is in accordance with the general principle of *locus regit actum* [the place governs the act].

It is ... common cause that the vice-consul [152] who solemnized the marriage was not a marriage officer in terms of the provisions of the Marriage Act 25 of 1961.

Section 11(1) of the Marriage Act provides that

"a marriage may be solemnized by a marriage officer only".

A marriage which is solemnized in South Africa by a person who is not a marriage officer is, generally speaking, not a valid marriage under our law...

Mrs *Cassim,* who appeared for the plaintiff in this case, submitted that the provisions of the Act would not apply to a marriage celebrated in an embassy or a consulate of a foreign country in South Africa inasmuch as such place ought to be regarded as an extension of that foreign country's area of jurisdiction. Mrs *Cassim* contended that it should make no difference, therefore, whether the marriage was celebrated in the Portuguese consulate in Johannesburg or in Portugal itself.

The rule of diplomatic immunity had, in the past, been based on the notion of extraterritoriality, ie that the premises of a diplomatic mission in the receiving State represented an extension of the territory of the sending State ... According to modern writers on international law the fiction of extraterritoriality has been discarded ...

The fiction of extraterritoriality originally gave rise to the rule that an embassy marriage is valid if concluded within the precincts of a foreign embassy between two subjects of that foreign State, and according to the forms held valid by such State ...

[GROSSKOPF J referred to the views of a few writers on the Conflict of Laws and the position in England in this regard and proceeded:]

[153] Section 10 of our Marriage Act 25 of 1961 also allows the solemnization of a marriage in accordance with the provisions of the Act in a country outside the Republic of South Africa between South African citizens who are domiciled in the Republic. Such a marriage may be solemnized by a diplomatic or consular officer in the service of the Republic of South Africa who has been designated as a marriage officer in terms of the Act. The Marriage Act 1961, however, has no corresponding provision enabling a foreign diplomatic or consular officer to solemnize a marriage between subjects of that foreign State in accordance with the laws of that State in its embassy or consulate in South Africa ...

[154] Had the Legislature intended to accord recognition to foreign embassy or consular marriages in South Africa it would undoubtedly have made provision for it in the Marriage Act 25 of 1961. Equally, there is no indication that South African law has followed the practice of the United Kingdom and other countries in Western Europe of according recognition to foreign embassy or consular marriages by custom . . .

The view that embassy or consular marriages solemnized by foreign officials in South Africa are invalid, could, however, lead to the anomalous result that the marriage between the parties may be completely valid according to Portuguese law, and a valid judgment of a Portuguese Court may consequently be transmitted to South Africa for enforcement, despite the fact that the marriage is regarded as invalid according to South African law. The Reciprocal Enforcement of Civil Judgments Act 9 of 1966 is not yet in force, but the Reciprocal Enforcement of Maintenance Orders Act 80 of 1963 is in operation and may present problems for the defendant in this regard. Despite this possible anomaly I am not prepared to declare the marriage between the parties a valid marriage.

[155] In my judgment the marriage between the parties is invalid . . .

Note

On this case see Therion 1985 *De Rebus* 353 and Van Warmelo 1988 *THRHR* 102.

Aantekening

Sien oor hierdie saak Therion 1985 *De Rebus* 353 en Van Warmelo 1988 *THRHR* 102.

[65] EX PARTE DOW

1987 3 SA 829 (D)

Marriage not solemnised in compliance with section 29(2) of the Marriage Act 25 of 1961

The applicant applied for an order declaring his marriage null and void *ab initio*. His wife supported the application. The marriage had been solemnised by a duly designated marriage officer. Section 29(2) of the Marriage Act provides that: "A marriage officer shall solemnise any marriage in a church or other building used for religious service, or in a public office or private dwelling-house, with open doors and in the presence of the parties themselves and at least two competent witnesses . . ." In this case, however, the entire ceremony had taken place in the front garden of a dwelling house. The fact that the marriage was not solemnised *in* the house was the only defect alleged. The application was dismissed.

Huwelik nie voltrek ooreenkomstig artikel 29(2) van die Huwelikswet 25 van 1961 nie

Die applikant het aansoek gedoen om 'n verklarende bevel dat sy huwelik *ab initio* nietig was. Sy vrou het die aansoek ondersteun. Die huwelik is deur 'n behoorlik aangestelde huweliksbevestiger voltrek. Die hele seremonie het egter in die voortuin van 'n woonhuis plaasgevind terwyl artikel 29(2) van die Huwelikswet bepaal dat: " 'n Huweliksbevestiger 'n huwelik [moet] voltrek in 'n kerk of 'n ander gebou wat vir godsdiensoefening gebruik word of in 'n openbare kantoor of private woonhuis, met oop deure en in die teenwoordigheid van die partye self en minstens twee bevoegde getuies . . ." Die feit dat die huwelik nie *in* die huis voltrek is nie was die enigste defek wat beweer is. Die aansoek is van die hand gewys.

BROOME J: [831] In considering what are the objects sought to be achieved, it is necessary to trace the changes that have taken place in the formalities required for the conclusion of a valid marriage. In Roman law marriages were contracted by consent evinced by word or act in any way whatever. See *Voet* 23.2.2 and *Bronn v Fritz Bronn's Executors and Others* 3 Searle 313 at 319. Hahlo in his *South African Law of Husband and Wife* 5th ed describes at 6 onwards how, when in the Middle Ages marriage in Western Europe passed under the jurisdiction of the Church, it became the practice for the parties to declare their consent to marry before a priest who would confer the Church's blessing on the couple. However, he adds, "it was the consent of the parties, and not the blessing by the priest, which brought the marriage into existence". As early as 1215 the Fourth Lateran Council prescribed the publication of banns "in order to do away with the evils and abuses inherent in a system that permitted clandestine (ie secret) marriages". However, a contravention of these rules did not affect the validity of the marriage, and the evil of clandestine marriages continued until the Church Council of Trent in 1563 prescribed that henceforth a marriage was to be invalid unless banns had been published and the parties had declared their consent to marry before a priest and no fewer than two witnesses. This form of marriage before a priest or marriage officer and witnesses became the standard form. See also *Bronn's* case *supra* at 323–4.

I have not been referred to, nor have I found, any reference to the reason or need for the ceremony to take place indoors . . .

[BROOME J then quoted the requirements as regards the time and place of the ceremony from the old provincial legislation before the Marriage Act 25 of 1961 came into operation, and proceeded:]

[832] Substantially similar provisions were enacted in the Marriage Act 25 of 1961.

In my view the object of these provisions was essentially to ensure that marriages took place in public, that the public were to be informed of intended marriage so that any objections could be raised, and that a register to which the public had access be kept. The constant reference to open doors is an indication that the public were to be permitted access to every marriage ceremony, the mischief being clandestine marriages. See also *Voet* 23.2.3 (*Gane's* translation vol 1 at 36–7) where there is also reference to, "in a private house" in the passage dealing with the dispensation in the need for three public callings of banns in the passage:

> "*Marriage in private houses.* It is the same if, when the triple calling has already been completed, ill health of the betrothed man or woman does not at all allow of a journey to the church or court or other place publicly appointed for the entering into of marriages; and for that reason it is requested that it may be allowed to conduct the formalities of marriage in a private house before a meeting of the neighbours. One who calls banns would not act with wisdom in Holland if he thinks that such a course is to be essayed without the consent of the magistracy, as can be gathered from enactments which have been made by the States of Holland."

I have not been able to ascertain the basis for, or object of, the requirement that a marriage must be solemnized *in* a private dwelling as opposed to at, or in the precincts of, a private dwelling.

[833] As I say, it seems to me that the object of these provisions is to avoid clandestine marriages.

Since its enactment the Marriage Act 25 of 1961 has been amended quite drastically in that the Marriage Act Amendment Act 51 of 1970 repealed ss 13–21 inclusive. These were the sections which provided for the publication of banns, proof thereof, the publication of notice of intention to marry, the issue of special licences to marry without the publication of banns or notice of intention to marry, the marriage officer by whom the marriage could be solemnized and the lapse of banns, etc after three months. It follows that there has been a complete abolition of the provisions which previously served to inform the public of an intended marriage.

A marriage is such an important contract and relationship, and the consequences of a decree of nullity can be so far-reaching, that I do not consider that the Legislature intended non-compliance with the two-letter word "in" to be visited with nullity. Indications which support my view are to be found in s 22, for instance, which in its original form provided that if the provisions relating to the publication of banns and notice of intention to marry, or to the issue of a special marriage licence, were not strictly complied with owing to an error committed in good faith by either of the parties, or to an error by the person who made the publication or issued the licence, the marriage shall be as valid and binding as it would have been if the provisions had been strictly complied with. Section 24 provides that no marriage officer shall solemnize a marriage to which a minor is party unless the necessary consent is obtained, but s 24A then provides that the marriage shall not be void, but may be dissolved by a Court on grounds of want of consent if application is made by a parent of the minor before he attains the age of 21 and then only if the Court is satisfied that the dissolution of the marriage is in the interests of the minor or minors. Similarly, s 26 provides for the prohibition of marriages of boys under 18 or girls under 15 except with permission from the Minister or consent of a Judge, but then it proceeds in ss (2) to provide that, if no such consent has been obtained, the Minister may direct that it shall for all purposes be a valid marriage. The point I am attempting to make is that in cases where there would seem to me to be far more compelling reason to treat a marriage as void *ab initio* the statute does not do so. I treat this as an indication that the Legislature did not intend strict compliance with the provision that a marriage be solemnized *in* a private dwelling house, and that where, as in this case, the parties were competent to marry, that is there was no legal impediment to their marriage, the ceremony was performed by a marriage officer and all concerned *bona fide* intended and believed it to be a valid marriage, the objects of the Act have been achieved despite the fact that the marriage was solemnized in the garden outside the house and not inside the house with open doors.

The application is dismissed.

Note

From this case it seems that a marriage is not void if the provisions of section 29(2) are not complied with although the provisions are couched in imperative language. This decision is to be welcomed since only a material defect should render a marriage void *ab initio*. A material defect would be, for example, if the formalities regarding the proper identification of the parties were not complied with, if there was no *consensus* between the parties and if the participation of the state and community to the marriage had been disregarded, for example if the marriage officer was not competent, or there were not at least two witnesses present at the marriage (Lee and Honoré 32). On the other hand it must be pointed out that the wording of the section and the act as a whole, strongly indicate the legislature's in-

Aantekening

Dit blyk uit hierdie saak dat nie-voldoening aan die bepalings van artikel 29(2) nie tot nietigheid van die huwelik lei nie ten spyte daarvan dat die bepalings in gebiedende taal geklee is. Hierdie beslissing word verwelkom aangesien net 'n wesenlike gebrek tot die nietigverklaring van 'n huwelik *ab initio* behoort te lei. 'n Wesenlike gebrek sou byvoorbeeld wees as die formaliteite met betekking tot die behoorlike identifikasie van die partye nie nagekom is nie, as daar nie *consensus* tussen die partye bestaan het nie en as die deelname van die staat en die gemeenskap aan die huwelik verontagsaam is, byvoorbeeld omdat die huweliksbeampte nie bevoeg was nie of daar nie ten minste twee getuies by die huwelik teenwoordig was nie (Lee en Honoré 32). Aan die ander kant moet tog daarop gewys word dat die

tention that non-fulfilment of these provisions will result in the marriage being null and void. And since it is quite conceivable that a marriage may be solemnised in circumstances where the decision in *Dow* may not be applicable (for example in a submarine or an airborne aeroplane) it is suggested that in order to ensure the validity of their marriages, persons who wish to get married in strange and unusual places also go through an ordinary ceremony which complies with the explicit provisions of the act.

On *Ex parte Dow* see also Labuschagne 1988 *TSAR* 578 and Robinson 1990 *THRHR* 433.

bewoording van die artikel en die wet as geheel sterk op die bedoeling van die wetgewer dui dat nie-nakoming van hierdie bepalings nietigheid van die huwelik tot gevolg sal hê. En aangesien dit goed moontlik is dat 'n huwelik in omstandighede voltrek kan word waar die beslissing in *Dow* se saak nie van toepassing sal wees nie (byvoorbeeld in 'n duikboot of 'n vliegtuig wat in die lug is), word aan die hand gedoen dat persone wat op eienaardige plekke wil trou, ook 'n gewone seremonie volgens die duidelike voorskrifte van die wet deurloop, ten einde die geldigheid van hulle huwelike te verseker.

Oor *Ex parte Dow* sien ook Labuschagne 1988 *TSAR* 578 en Robinson 1990 *THRHR* 433.

Void and voidable marriages

Consequences of a void marriage
Grounds for the voidability of a marriage
The putative marriage

Nietige en vernietigbare huwelike

Gevolge van 'n nietige huwelik
Gronde vir vernietigbaarheid van 'n huwelik
Die putatiewe huwelik

Consequences of a void marriage   Gevolge van 'n nietige huwelik

[66]   ARENDSE V ROODE

1989 1 SA 763 (C)

Satisfaction (*solatium*) awarded to the bona fide party to a void marriage

The plaintiff entered into "marriage" with the defendant while she was unaware that he was still married to someone else. Before they were "married" the defendant had told the plaintiff that he was a divorced man. At the time of the "marriage" the plaintiff was still a virgin. Approximately nine months after she was "married" to the defendant his first wife informed the plaintiff's mother of the defendant's true marital status. When the plaintiff discovered that the defendant had committed bigamy by marrying her, she was so shocked that she suffered a kind of paralysis and could not work for two months. The plaintiff instituted an action to have her "marriage" to the defendant declared void. She also claimed R10 000 for impairment of her *dignitas,* R10 000 for impairment of her *fama* and R5 000 for seduction. The court allowed the plaintiff's claim for a declaration of nullity of the marriage as well as her claim for satisfaction but awarded her only R6 500.

Genoegdoening (*solatium*) toegeken aan die bona fide party by 'n nietige huwelik

Die eiseres het met die verweerder "getrou" terwyl sy onbewus was daarvan dat hy steeds met iemand anders getroud was. Voor hulle "getroud" is, het die verweerder die eiseres vertel dat hy 'n geskeide man was. Op die stadium toe die partye in die "huwelik" getree het, was die eiseres nog 'n maagd. Omtrent nege maande na die eiseres met die verweerder "getroud" is, het sy eerste vrou die eiseres se moeder ingelig omtrent die verweerder se ware huwelikstatus. Toe die eiseres uitvind dat die verweerder bigamie gepleeg het deur met haar te trou, was sy so geskok dat sy 'n soort verlamming gekry het en twee maande lank nie kon werk nie. Die eiseres het 'n aksie ingestel om haar "huwelik" met die verweerder nietig te laat verklaar. Sy het ook R10 000 vir krenking van haar *dignitas,* R10 000 vir krenking van haar *fama* en R5 000 op grond van seduksie geëis. Die hof het die eiseres se aansoek om nietigverklaring van die huwelik toegestaan asook haar eis om genoegdoening maar het slegs R6 500 aan haar toegeken.

HODES AJ: [765] The only reported judgment of which I am aware in which a claim for damages arising from bigamy has been considered is that of GOLDSTONE J in *Snyman v Snyman* 1984 (4) SA 262 (W). I am, with due respect, in agreement with GOLDSTONE J and with Hahlo *The South African Law of Husband and Wife* 5th ed at 107 that an action for damages under the *actio injuriarum* lies against a defendant who by his deceit took advantage of a plaintiff's innocence and induced her to enter into a marriage which the defendant knew, but the plaintiff did not know, to be null and void because he was already married.

As in *Snyman's* case *supra,* in the present case there was both *injuria* and *contumelia* attendant upon the unlawful conduct of defendant.

It was clear from her testimony in the witness-box and from what I saw of her that plaintiff is a sensitive woman and that she has been and remains affected deleteriously by defendant's wrongful and unlawful conduct.

It does not, however, appear from the evidence before me that there has been any noteworthy impairment of plaintiff's reputation.

Taking into account all the relevant facts set forth above, including the extent to which plaintiff has suffered anguish and humiliation as a result of defendant's behaviour, plaintiff's social standing and financial circumstances, defendant's financial circumstances and the attitude of defendant and whether he has shown any repentance or concern for plaintiff, I am of the view that an amount of R5 000 would be an appropriate award of damages under the *actio injuriarum*.

Plaintiff also claims damages for seduction. This claim does not fall within the ambit of the *actio injuriarum*, but is an action *sui generis*. Van den Heever *Breach of Promise and Seduction in South African Law* at 42–3 and *Carelse v Estate De Vries* (1906) 23 SC 532 at 539.

That a plaintiff who had been seduced may recover compensation for the loss of her virginity and the consequent impairment of her marriage prospects is clear. *Bull v Taylor* 1965 (4) SA 29 (A) at 38–9 [58].

In deciding what compensation should be awarded a seduced plaintiff for the loss of her virginity and for the diminished chances of her making a suitable marriage, a court should, in my view, take into account, *inter alia*, plaintiff's social standing and financial position as well as that of defendant. Taking into account these factors as well as all other relevant [766] facts and circumstances, I am of the view that an award of R1 500 in respect of the claim based upon seduction would be appropriate.

Based upon the aforegoing I have come to the conclusion that I should order defendant to pay to plaintiff a total amount of R6 500 as and for damages.

Grounds for the voidability of a marriage	Gronde vir vernietigbaarheid van 'n huwelik

[67]   STANDER v STANDER

1929 AD 349

***Stuprum* is not a ground for declaring a marriage void**	***Stuprum* is nie 'n grond vir nietigverklaring van 'n huwelik nie**
The appellant claimed that his marriage was void and applied for an order to have it annulled. Before he entered into marriage with the respondent she had given birth to another man's child. At the time when he married her the appellant was unaware of this fact. He claimed that his wife's *stuprum* followed by the birth of a child before the marriage was a ground for nullity. The court *a quo* rejected his claim and refused to declare the marriage void. He appealed against this decision but the decision was upheld.	Die appellant het beweer dat sy huwelik nietig was en aansoek gedoen dat dit ter syde gestel word. Voordat hy met die respondent getrou het, het sy geboorte geskenk aan 'n ander man se kind. Toe hy met haar getrou het, was die appellant onbewus van hierdie feit. Hy het beweer dat sy vrou se *stuprum* gevolg deur die geboorte van 'n kind voor die huwelik 'n grond vir nietigverklaring van die huwelik was. Die hof *a quo* het sy eis verwerp en geweier om die huwelik nietig te verklaar. Hy het teen hierdie beslissing geappelleer maar die beslissing is gehandhaaf.

WESSELS JA: [351] We are asked to say that by our law a husband is entitled to have his marriage set aside on the ground that his wife had had illicit intercourse with another man, unknown to him, prior to the marriage, or if the Court is not prepared to go so far, that it should adopt the principle that the marriage can be set aside where the wife has had a child as the consequence of illicit intercourse prior to the marriage, that such child is alive, and that the husband was ignorant of this at the time of the marriage . . .

[353] There is strong authority for the proposition that the Roman-Dutch lawyers did not consider that pre-marriage stuprum alone on the part of a wife was sufficient to enable a husband to set aside the bond . . .

[WESSELS JA discussed some old Roman-Dutch law authorities and proceeded:]

[354] We may safely say . . . that it was not part of the general Roman-Dutch law that pre-marriage stuprum entitled the husband to repudiate his wife.

Suppose, however, that a child had been born previous to the marriage, of whom some other man was the father, and if this fact were unknown to the husband, could he in such a case claim to set aside the marriage upon discovery of the truth? . . .

[WESSELS JA analysed other texts and some cases and proceeded:]

[355] It seems . . . that the decision of the Natal Court in the considered judgment of *Shaw v Shaw* (26 NLR 392) is correct, and that stuprum, unaccompanied by a condition of pregnancy at the date of the celebration of the marriage is not sufficient to entitle a plaintiff to a decree of nullity of marriage. It is difficult to see, if this is the correct view, how the birth of a child can make any difference. The birth of a child before marriage is no doubt conclusive proof of stuprum, but it can have no greater effect because such a child can never be regarded as the child of the husband . . .

[356] In these circumstances this Court cannot extend the husband's right to have the marriage set aside . . .

The appeal is therefore dismissed . . .

DE VILLIERS ACJ and STRATFORD JA concurred.

Note

Sexual intercourse with a third party before a marriage does not affect the validity of the marriage (*Gabergas v Gabergas* 1921 EDL 279; *Reyneke v Reyneke* 1927 OPD 130).

From the case under discussion it appears that pre-marital sexual intercourse with a third party resulting in the birth of a child before the marriage is entered into also does not affect the validity of the marriage.

Only if the bride is pregnant with the child of another man at the time when she enters into the marriage, will her *stuprum* constitute a ground for annulment of the marriage. In such an instance it is not the *stuprum* as such which affects the validity of the marriage but the wife's pregnancy with another man's child. (See for example *Horak v Horak* (1860) 3 Searle 389; *Reyneke v Reyneke; Smith v Smith* 1936 CPD 125; *X v X* 1939 2 PH B65 (O). See also *Van Niekerk v Van Niekerk*

Aantekening

Geslagsgemeenskap met 'n derde party voor die sluiting van 'n huwelik het geen effek op die geldigheid van die huwelik nie (*Gabergas v Gabergas* 1921 OD 279; *Reyneke v Reyneke* 1927 OPA 130).

Uit die onderhawige saak blyk verder dat voorhuwelikse geslagsgemeenskap met 'n derde party wat voor sluiting van die huwelik tot die geboorte van 'n kind aanleiding gegee het, ook geen uitwerking op die geldigheid van die huwelik het nie.

Die bruid se *stuprum* kan net 'n grond vir nietigverklaring van die huwelik daarstel indien sy ten tyde van huweliksluiting swanger is met 'n ander man se kind. In so 'n geval is dit nie die *stuprum* as sodanig wat 'n invloed op die geldigheid van die huwelik het nie maar die feit dat sy ten tyde van huweliksluiting swanger is met 'n ander man se kind. (Sien byvoorbeeld *Horak v Horak* (1860)

[70]; Hunt 1962 *SALJ* 426; 1963 *SALJ* 94; Van der Vyver and Joubert 496; Hahlo 122–123; Barnard, Cronjé and Olivier 176–177; Lee and Honoré 38.) If the wife is pregnant with another man's child at the time when she enters into marriage and her husband is unaware of this fact, the marriage is voidable. The husband can then have it set aside when he discovers the pregnancy (*Horak v Horak; Walters v Walters* 1911 TPD 42; *Reyneke v Reyneke; Smith v Smith; Vereen v Vereen* 1943 GW 50; *X v X*). Hahlo (122) submits that the husband would, however, not be able to have the marriage set aside on this ground if "the child was conceived respectably in the lady's first marriage bed".

If the husband knew of his wife's pregnancy at the time of marriage or if he subsequently discovers it and condones it, he cannot have the marriage set aside (*Kilian v Kilian* 1908 EDC 377).

Hahlo also submits (123) that the fact that the wife was unaware of her pregnancy at the time of marriage does not affect her husband's right to claim annulment of the marriage, nor does he lose his right if his wife aborts or if the child is still-born.

The fact that the husband too had sexual intercourse with his wife before they were married in no way affects his right to have the marriage set aside, provided she was pregnant with the child of another man at the time of marriage and the husband was unaware of her condition (*Reyneke v Reyneke; Smith v Smith*).

3 Searle 389; *Reyneke v Reyneke; Smith v Smith* 1936 KPA 125; *X v X* 1939 2 PH B65 (O). Sien ook *Van Niekerk v Van Niekerk* [70]; Hunt 1962 *SALJ* 426; 1963 *SALJ* 94; Van der Vyver en Joubert 496; Hahlo 122–123; Barnard, Cronjé en Olivier 180–181; Lee en Honoré 38.) Indien die vrou ten tyde van huweliksluiting swanger is met 'n ander man se kind en haar man onbewus daarvan is, is die huwelik vernietigbaar. Die man kan die huwelik dan ter syde laat stel wanneer hy van die swangerskap bewus word (*Horak v Horak; Walters v Walters* 1911 TPA 42; *Reyneke v Reyneke; Smith v Smith; Vereen v Vereen* 1943 GW 50; *X v X*). Hahlo (122) doen aan die hand dat die man nie die huwelik op hierdie grond ter syde kan laat stel nie indien "the child was conceived respectably in the lady's first marriage bed".

Indien die man ten tyde van die huwelik bewus was van sy vrou se swangerskap of hy later daarvan bewus word en dit kondoneer, kan hy nie die huwelik laat nietig verklaar nie (*Kilian v Kilian* 1908 OD 377).

Hahlo (123) doen ook aan die hand dat die feit dat die vrou ten tyde van huweliksluiting onbewus was van haar swangerskap geen invloed behoort te hê op haar man se bevoegdheid om die huwelik ter syde te laat stel nie. Insgelyks behoort hy ook nie sy bevoegdheid te verloor nie indien die vrou 'n miskraam het of indien die kind doodgebore word.

Die feit dat die eggenoot self met sy vrou geslagsgemeenskap gehad het voor hulle getroud is, het geen effek op sy reg om die huwelik ter syde te laat stel nie, solank sy maar ten tyde van die huweliksluiting swanger was met 'n ander man se kind en die man onbewus daarvan was (*Reyneke v Reyneke; Smith v Smith*).

[68]   W v W

1959 4 SA 183 (C)

Impotence as a ground for the annulment of a marriage

The parties were married out of community of property. The plaintiff (wife) instituted action for judicial separation against the de-

Impotensie as 'n grond vir die nietigverklaring van 'n huwelik

Die partye was buite gemeenskap van goed getroud. Die eiseres het aksie ingestel teen die verweerder vir geregtelike skeiding en

fendant and she asked for the implementation of the terms of the antenuptial contract and for substantial maintenance. The defendant, in a counterclaim, sought an order for restitution of conjugal rights, and failing compliance therewith, a decree of divorce and forfeiture of the benefits conferred on the plaintiff by the antenuptial contract. The defendant then applied for an amendment of his plea and counterclaim. He averred that at the time of marriage he had been, and still was, impotent and that the marriage had never been consummated. He said further that at the time of marriage he was unaware of his incapacity. Shortly after the marriage he received medical treatment which proved to be ineffective and ultimately the doctor advised him that his condition was incurable. He accordingly claimed that the marriage was voidable, and asked for an annulment thereof and for an order declaring the antenuptial contract of no force and effect. He stated further that he had been unaware of the fact that his own impotence could possibly afford him ground for claiming nullity of the marriage. The amendment was allowed.

gevra vir die implementering van die bepalings van die huweliksvoorwaardeskontrak asook vir aansienlike onderhoud. In 'n teeneis het die verweerder aansoek gedoen om 'n bevel vir die herstel van huweliksregte, en as nie daaraan voldoen sou word nie, om 'n egskeiding en die verbeuring van die voordele waarop die eiseres ingevolge die huweliksvoorwaardeskontrak geregtig was. Die verweerder het toe aansoek gedoen om 'n wysiging van sy pleit en teeneis. Hy het aangevoer dat hy ten tyde van die huweliksluiting impotent was en nog steeds was, en dat die huwelik nooit deur byslaap volvoer is nie. Hy het verder beweer dat hy ten tyde van die huweliksluiting onbewus was van sy onvermoë. Kort na die huweliksluiting het hy mediese behandeling ontvang maar dit was onsuksesvol, en uiteindelik het die dokter hom meegedeel dat sy toestand nie genees kon word nie. Hy het gevolglik aangevoer dat die huwelik vernietigbaar was en om nietigverklaring daarvan aansoek gedoen, asook om 'n bevel dat die huweliksvoorwaardeskontrak ongeldig was. Hy het verder aangevoer dat hy onbewus daarvan was dat sy impotensie as rede vir hom kon dien om om nietigverklaring van die huwelik aansoek te doen. Die wysiging is toegelaat.

BLOCH J: [186] Actions for nullity of marriage are, for reasons of delicacy and sensitivity, not frequently instituted. And when they are, the initiative would reasonably be expected to be taken, as it has been, by the potent spouse. It must in the nature of things be a rare occurrence where, the potent spouse being willing to continue the marriage relationship, the impotent partner would take proceedings for annulment and voluntarily make public his incapacity. The impotent spouse would moreover have found much to discourage him from taking action in two assumedly relevant interwoven principles, viz: firstly that it is only the "aggrieved" or "injured" or "victimised" marriage partner who can be heard to complain, and secondly that no one can take advantage of his own wrong. Each of these merits investigation.

Both partners to a marriage are entitled to expect sexual intercourse as one of the fundamental incidents of a marriage. Where this is impossible by reason of impotence in one spouse existing at the time of the marriage and continuing thereafter and shown to be irremediable both spouses are equally aggrieved except in the case where the impotent spouse knew, before the marriage, of his impotence, where the potent spouse entered into the marriage with knowledge of the other's incapacity, and where by reason of the age of the parties – or of the one against whom complaint is made – it must reasonably have been anticipated that the marital function could no longer be performed. (See Brouwer *De Jure Connubiorum*, 2.4.18.) Assuming, however, ignorance of his condition on the part of the impotent spouse why should it be supposed that he is not "aggrieved" at finding himself (as well as the other partner) deprived of something which he was entitled to expect? And why, on principle and as a matter of equity, should it be required of him, merely because his potent partner desires a continuance of the married status, that he should be held to it and suffer its financial disadvantages without its physical benefits? To say that he must suffer the marriage to continue because he has committed a wrong against his potent partner and cannot take advantage of his own wrong seems to [187] me to afford no answer. What was the wrong? On the assumption of his ignorance of his condition he did not deceive her; or if he did he did it innocently and equally deceived himself. And if the impotence of the spouse is psychological and not absolute but only relative to the other spouse – *quoad hanc* or *quoad hunc* as it is expressed – the task of apportioning "blame" becomes as impossible as it was in the unusual case of *G v G*, 25 TLR 328, where non-consummation was due to physical causes – the male's generative organ being unusually large and the female's unusually small.

But even if one considers the case of absolute impotence – not due to an obvious malformation or defect for in that case it might well and probably would be found, as in the old case of *Norton v Seton*, (1819) 3 Phill. 147, that the spouse seeking redress on the ground of his own impotence should be non-suited because he knew or must be held to have known of his incapacity at the time he contracted the marriage – the attributing of wrongdoing or blameworthiness to the *incapax* spouse who married in ignorance of his condition seems to me to be entirely arbitrary and without either moral or legal justification. See in this context the views expressed in *F v F*, 1945 SC at pp 208 and 212, and particularly the opposite observation of LORD MONCRIEFF:

> "As the impotent spouse he may have suffered even more than his more fortunate partner from the endurance of that merely ostensible marriage. He has suffered in like manner as a victim and not as a delinquent."

See also *Harthan v Harthan*, 1948 (2) AER at p. 644. Ritterhusius *Ad Novellas*, 4.7.10, writing early in the seventeenth century expresses remarkably similar views. Writing in the context of an action by the husband against the impotent wife, he says (freely translated):

> "This must be taken note of, that in a marriage dissolved for such a reason there must be restoration of the dowry without any diminution, and any donation in respect of the marriage must remain with the husband. The reason is that there was no fault here of anyone but rather a calamity. And there ought to be no penalty where there is no fault (*culpa*). Nor ought an affliction to be added to a person already afflicted."

Before embarking on a detailed consideration of the authorities I should consider another general point, viz. whether it is against public policy to allow the remedy of nullity at the instance of the impotent spouse. The Canon Law, reflecting contemporary thought and morality at a time when the institution of marriage was regarded as more properly falling within the jurisdiction of spiritual than of temporal courts and when its sanctity and indissolubility was more jealously entrenched than in modern times, permitted such an action. (*Corpus Juris Canonici* (1622), Decretals of Pope Gregorius 2:19:4 and 4:15:1.) The climate of public opinion and morality does not appear to me to have sharpened but rather to have become more temperate towards unhappy and frustrated partners locked in matrimony. So far from public policy to-day favouring the maintenance of a marriage where one of its essential conditions is incapable of performance it seems to me to lean in the opposite direction. Certainly in the case where impotence is only relative a dissolution which would enable both partners to seek sexual fulfilment in another marriage would not be discouraged. And where the impotence is absolute and the potent, but not the impotent, party is willing to continue the relationship it is difficult to see why public policy should make the happiness and wish [188] of the former prevail against the un-

happiness and frustration of the latter, unless it be to penalise him for a "wrong" which in reality he has not committed. (See the views of LORD MURRAY in *SG v WG,* 1933 SC 735, adopted with approval in *F v F, supra* at pp 207–8.) . . .

Neither counsel, nor the Court, has found any decision in our Courts dealing directly with the right of an impotent spouse to sue for nullity, and I approach the matter firstly, for such guidance as they may afford, with a consideration of a number of overseas decisions where the same problem has in relatively recent years enjoyed detailed and elaborate attention . . .

[BLOCH J then considered the position in Scotland, Ireland and England where the matter has been finally settled in favour of the right of the impotent spouse to sue by the Court of Appeal in *Harthan v Harthan* [1948] 2 All ER 639 (A). He then surveyed modern writers on our law as well as our old authorities, but not much assistance was to be gained from the latter sources. He proceeded:]

[192] Wessels's *History of the Roman-Dutch Law* pp 137–143 indicates that even after the Reformation the Canon Law was frequently quoted and relied upon by the Roman-Dutch jurists, and that it had a profound effect upon matrimonial law. The *Decretals of Gregorius* cited earlier herein are, in no authority that I have been able to consult, expressed to be in conflict with local decision or custom. It seems to me that the mere absence of reference in our classical authorities to the right given by Canon Law to the impotent spouse, and the understandable assumption which underlies them that the potent spouse would be the one to be expected to make complaint does not afford sufficient ground for declaring that right to be non-existent. Modern authorities in England and Scotland have founded largely on the provisions of the Canon Law and as those provisions are in my view entirely consistent with modern legal thought (and some, as I have indicated, which is not so modern) and as moreover they are not in conflict with what I conceive to be the public policy of our day they should be followed. In my judgment, accordingly, a spouse irremediably impotent at the time of marriage, who entered into such marriage in ignorance of such impotence, is competent to bring an action to have the marriage declared null on the ground of such impotence . . .

[194] The amendment will be allowed . . .

Note

It must be noted that a party may only have the marriage set aside if he had no knowledge of the other party's impotence at the time of the marriage and his ignorance must also be reasonable, for example a young woman who marries a man of eighty five years of age should realise that he might be impotent and should therefore not be able to obtain an annulment of the marriage on the ground of his impotence (*Joshua v Joshua* 1961 1 SA 455 (GW)). If the plaintiff knew of the defendant's impotence but believed on reasonable grounds that he would recover from that disability, the plaintiff is not debarred from obtaining a decree of nullity (*Smith v Smith* 1963 2 SA 194 (SR)). It is not required that the impotent spouse must have acted fraudulently and *bona fides* on his part is no defence (Hunt 1963 *SALJ* 107). It is irrelevant whether the inability is due to physi-

Aantekening

'n Mens moet daarop let dat 'n party net 'n huwelik tersyde kan laat stel as hy ten tyde van die huweliksluiting nie kennis gedra het van die ander party se impotensie nie en sy onkunde moet ook redelik wees. So behoort 'n jong vrou wat met 'n man van vyf en tagtig jaar trou daarmee rekening te hou dat hy moontlik impotent mag wees en daarom behoort sy nie nietigverklaring van die huwelik op grond van sy impotensie te verkry nie (*Joshua v Joshua* 1961 1 SA 455 (GW)). As die eiser geweet het van die verweerder se impotensie maar op redelike gronde geglo het dat hy van sy onvermoë sou herstel, word die eiser nie verhinder om nietigverklaring van die huwelik te verkry nie (*Smith v Smith* 1963 2 SA 194 (SR)). Dit is nie 'n vereiste dat die impotente gade bedrieglik moes gehandel het nie en *bona fides* aan sy kant is nie 'n verweer nie (Hunt 1963

cal or psychological factors (*Joshua v Joshua* 1961 1 SA 455 (GW)).

The impotence must be incurable and it must exist at the time of marriage (*Joshua v Joshua*; *Hunt v Hunt* 1940 WLD 55). Impotence that develops afterwards is not a ground for annulment but it may lead to irretrievable breakdown of the marriage grounding an action for divorce (Hahlo 119).

The marriage is voidable, not void, because the potent spouse can decide to abide by the marriage and then the marriage remains valid and binding (*Wells v Dean-Willcocks* 1924 CPD 89; Hahlo 119; Hunt 1963 *SALJ* 107). The right to have the marriage annulled is lost by acquiescence (Hahlo 120; Lee and Honoré 38).

It is sufficient to support a claim for nullity if the defendant is impotent as regards the plaintiff although he is not impotent as to others (*Smith v Smith* 1963 4 SA 729 (SR)).

The onus is on the plaintiff to prove the impotence (*Hunt v Hunt*; Hahlo 119; Lee and Honoré 38).

It would seem as though the old authorities allowed only the potent spouse to institute the action (Hahlo 121; Hunt 1963 *SALJ* 107). Be this as it may it seems reasonable that this relief is also extended to the impotent spouse (Hunt 1963 *SALJ* 107; Lee and Honoré 38; Van der Vyver and Joubert 494; Boberg 1959 *Annual Survey* 39).

It must however be stressed that the action is barred to the impotent spouse, if at the time of the marriage, he knew of his own impotence, or if the impotence could reasonably have been foreseen, for example because of old age. (See in this regard *B v B* 1964 1 SA 717 (T) and *D v D* 1964 3 SA 598 (E).) Hahlo (121–122) submits further that the impotent spouse would be precluded from asking for an annulment where it would be unjust in the circumstances, for example if his condition can be cured and he refuses to undergo treatment.

B v B and *D v D* were both actions by husbands for the annulment of their respective marriages on the ground of their own impotence. In *D's* case the applicant failed but in *B v B* the applicant succeeded in obtaining an annulment of his marriage although he was eighty years old at the time of the marriage. This decision is criticised

SALJ 107). Dit is irrelevant of die impotensie aan fisiese of sielkundige faktore te wyte is (*Joshua v Joshua* 1961 1 SA 455 (GW)).

Die impotensie moet ongeneeslik wees en dit moet ten tyde van huwelikssluiting bestaan (*Joshua v Joshua*; *Hunt v Hunt* 1940 WPA 55). 'n Huwelik kan nie op grond van impotensie wat later ontwikkel nietig verklaar word nie maar dit mag tot onherstelbare verbrokkeling van die huwelik lei en sodoende 'n egskeidingsgrond vorm (Hahlo 119).

Die huwelik is vernietigbaar en nie nietig nie aangesien die potente gade hom met die toedrag van sake kan versoen in welke geval die huwelik as 'n geldige huwelik bly voortbestaan (*Wells v Dean-Willcocks* 1924 KPA 89; Hahlo 119; Hunt 1963 *SALJ* 107). 'n Gade verbeur sy bevoegdheid om die huwelik nietig te laat verklaar as hy in die situasie berus (Hahlo 120; Lee en Honoré 38).

Dit is voldoende vir 'n eis om nietigverklaring as die verweerder impotent is ten opsigte van die eiser alhoewel hy nie met betrekking tot ander persone impotent is nie (*Smith v Smith* 1963 4 SA 729 (SR)).

Die onus om die impotensie te bewys, rus op die eiser (*Hunt v Hunt*; Hahlo 119; Lee en Honoré 38).

Dit wil voorkom asof die ou skrywers die bevoegdheid om die aksie in te stel net aan die potente gade verleen het (Hahlo 121; Hunt 1963 *SALJ* 107). Hoe dit ook al mag sy lyk dit heeltemal redelik om die aksie ook ter beskikking van die impotente gade te stel (Hunt 1963 *SALJ* 107; Lee en Honoré 38; Van der Vyver en Joubert 494; Boberg 1959 *Annual Survey* 39).

Daar moet egter beklemtoon word dat die aksie nie deur die impotente gade ingestel kan word as hy ten tyde van die huwelikssluiting van sy eie impotensie geweet het of as die impotensie redelikerwys voorsienbaar was nie, byvoorbeeld op grond van hoë ouderdom. Sien in hierdie verband *B v B* 1964 1 SA 717 (T) en *D v D* 1964 3 SA 598 (OK). Hahlo (121–122) doen verder aan die hand dat die impotente gade ook nie om nietigverklaring van die huwelik sal kan aansoek doen waar dit in die omstandighede van die geval onbillik sou wees om dit te doen nie, byvoorbeeld as sy toestand genees kan word en hy weier om behandeling te ondergaan.

In sowel *B v B* as *D v D* het mans op grond van

by Hahlo in 1964 *SALJ* 146 427. See also 1964 *Annual Survey* 62 and 1965 *SALJ* 261.

See the note on *Naville v Naville* [11] for a discussion of the concept "restitution of conjugal rights".

Under the old divorce law the courts could have granted orders for judicial separation. Such an order meant that the marriage continued to exist but that the spouses were no longer compelled to cohabit. Naturally neither of the spouses could enter into another marriage. Section 14 of the Divorce Act 70 of 1979 abolished orders for judicial separation.

hulle eie impotensie om nietigverklaring van hulle onderskeie huwelike aansoek gedoen. In *D v D* het die applikant misluk maar in *B v B* was die applikant suksesvol en is sy huwelik nietig verklaar alhoewel hy ten tyde van die huweliksluiting reeds tagtig jaar oud was. Hierdie beslissing word gekritiseer deur Hahlo in die 1964 *SALJ* 146 427. Sien ook die 1964 *Annual Survey* 62 en die 1965 *SALJ* 261.

Sien die aantekening by *Naville v Naville* [11] vir 'n bespreking van die begrip "herstel van huweliksregte".

Die howe kon ingevolge die ou egskeidingsreg bevele tot geregtelike skeiding gee. Sodanige bevel het beteken dat die huwelik voortbestaan het maar die gades was nie verplig om langer saam te woon nie. Geeneen van die partye kon egter 'n ander huwelik sluit nie. Artikel 14 van die Wet op Egskeiding 70 van 1979 het die uitreiking van bevele tot geregtelike skeiding afgeskaf.

[69] VENTER V VENTER

1949 4 SA 123 (W)

Sterility as a ground for the annulment of a marriage

The plaintiff (husband) claimed a decree of nullity of his marriage with the defendant on the ground that at the time of the marriage she was "without the knowledge and suspicion of the plaintiff . . . permanently incapable of procreating offspring." The evidence clearly established that the defendant at the time of the marriage, by reason of an operation which had been performed on her, was not capable of bearing children. It was also established that the plaintiff did not know this. The plaintiff's evidence also showed that the defendant was aware of her state. The claim was, however, not based on knowledge on the part of the defendant that she was sterile or concealment of this fact from the plaintiff. The court ordered absolution from the instance.

Steriliteit as 'n grond vir die nietigverklaring van 'n huwelik

Die eiser (man) het aansoek gedoen om die nietigverklaring van sy huwelik met die verweerderes op grond daarvan dat sy ten tyde van die sluiting van die huwelik "without the knowledge and suspicion of the plaintiff was permanently incapable of procreating offspring." Die getuienis het duidelik aangetoon dat die verweerderes ten tyde van die sluiting van die huwelik nie kinders sou kon voortbring nie as gevolg van 'n operasie wat op haar uitgevoer was. Dit was ook duidelik dat die eiser nie hiervan bewus was nie. Die eiser se getuienis het verder aangetoon dat die verweerderes van haar toestand bewus was. Die eiser het egter nie sy aksie op die verweerderes se kennis van haar toestand of die verberging daarvan vir hom gebaseer nie. Die hof het absolusie van die instansie beveel.

CLAYDEN J: [125] In considering whether in Roman-Dutch law inability to procreate in one party existing at the time of the marriage is a ground upon which the other party to the marriage can ask for a declaration that the marriage is null and void I have I think to consider the matter on a broad basis, and not to confine myself to the particular facts of this case. This particular case is an exceptional one. But if there is a general rule that a decree of nullity will be granted because there never was in a marriage a chance of the procreation of children the effect will be that any marriage by persons who are past the child-bearing age may at any time be set aside. Moreover with modern medical knowledge it may now be discovered, years after a marriage, that one or other of the parties to it was at the time of the marriage sterile, quite unknown to themselves. Yet if the general rule exists such a marriage could be avoided. These cases could be dealt with by the rule of the law excluding them from its general operation as exceptions to it. But for this to be the case there would, I think, have to be some reason to apply the rule in the one case and not in the other. Or they could be dealt with because the basis for the grant of relief was never wide enough to cover such a case; so that there is no need to speak of an exception to the general rule . . .

[CLAYDEN J then considered the Roman-Dutch authorities in regard to the objects of marriage to see to what extent emphasis was placed on the procreation of children as one of the purposes of marriage. He concluded:]

[128] In the light of these passages in the Roman-Dutch law, I do not think that it can be said that the procreation of children is so essential an element of marriage that, where it cannot come about, there is no marriage. A general rule that a marriage can be annulled if one of the parties were incapable of procreating at the time of the marriage might lead to the setting aside of many a marriage of old persons. It is clear that the law does not allow that. But the authorities, *Voet*, for example, do not discuss that position as an exception to a general rule.

By several of the authors who discuss the matter fully there is put forward a basis for relief which, while making full allowance for the procreation of children as a principle aim of marriage, of itself excludes the cases in which there should not be relief. That is that a person who knows of his or her incapacity to procreate, but does not disclose it at the time of marriage, is contracting that marriage in a sense fraudulently. If this be the basis of relief, the case of the person past child-bearing age is met; for the person marrying such a person is not deceived. And the case of subsequent discovery of a pre-marital sterility is met; for there was no knowledge of it. And the procreation of children as a hope of marriage is retained; for neither party knows that there is no hope . . .

[CLAYDEN J referred to Christinaeus *Practicarum Quaestionum* (Pt I, Decis 338); Brouwer *De Jure Connubiorum* Bk 2 cap ult (33) 20; Van Leeuwen *Censura Forensis* 1.15.5 and Voet 24.2.15 and proceeded:]

[129] But before I could come to the conclusion that the true basis for relief in a case such as the present may be the concealment of her inability by the defendant, it is necessary to consider the authorities to which I have been referred as showing that mere sterility, existing before marriage, is a ground for a declaration that the marriage is void. Generally in regard to these authorities there are two matters to be mentioned. The one is that some of them relate not to the declaring void of a marriage, but to the avoidance of a promise to marry. The other is that at times it seems quite uncertain whether the authors are referring to impotence or sterility . . .

[CLAYDEN J discussed the common-law authorities and proceeded:]

[131] From the mere use by some of these authorities of words which can mean incapacity to procreate I should not, I think, decide that that incapacity of itself justifies the declaring

void of a marriage. There is so often a change from the phrase which can indicate sterility to the phrase which can only indicate impotence, that there is doubt whether the phrases such as "onbekwaam tot voortteelen", or *"impotentia generandi"*, are not meant in the sense of incapacity to procreate because of impotence. And when, in addition to this, it is found that *Christinaeus, Brouwer, Van Leeuwen,* and probably *Voet,* assuming that he is speaking of sterility, and not impotence, make the knowledge of the sterile spouse at the time of marriage the important factor, it seems to me that I cannot say that a declaration of nullity can be made merely because the defendant in this case was sterile before marriage, unknown to her husband.

In the course of argument the suggestion was made by me that perhaps an allegation of knowledge of her condition by the wife was necessary. But because of the general rule that a marriage cannot be set aside on the ground of fraud, as to which see *Voet* (24.2.15), no amendment was asked for. I come to the conclusion, however, that without some such allegation the relief sought [132] cannot be granted. Just as the case of *stuprum* [pre-marital sexual intercourse] discussed by *Voet* in 24.2.15 is a case where the fraud of the wife may affect the marriage, because of the difficulty of investigating the true position before marriage, so it seems to me that in a case of pre-marital sterility the true basis of relief may be the concealment of sterility by one party to the marriage.

In the present case, if relief were sought on the basis pleaded with the additional allegation, which is, I think, necessary, it would be necessary to serve a notice of amendment to the summons. I think it proper, therefore, to make an order of absolution from the instance in this case.

Note

It is clear from the decisions in *Venter v Venter* and *Van Niekerk v Van Niekerk* [70] that the courts are not in agreement on the question of whether sterility (*impotentia procreandi*) unaccompanied by the inability to have sexual intercourse (*impotentia coeundi*) is a ground for annulment of a marriage (Hahlo 120). In *Venter's* case it was held that if one of the parties at the time of marriage fraudulently concealed that he was sterile, the other may have the marriage annulled. In *Van Niekerk's* case, on the other hand, it was held that the mere fact of sterility renders the marriage voidable, regardless of whether it was fraudulently concealed or not. This, however, applies only to those cases where the procreation of children was an express or implied object of the marriage. The common-law authors do not always distinguish clearly between *impotentia procreandi* and *impotentia coeundi* so that they are not of much assistance in deciding the matter (Van der Vyver and Joubert 496; Van der Walt 1960 *THRHR* 221. On the old authorities see also Scholtens 1961 *SALJ* 159 *et seq*). It would, however, seem as though sterility unaccompanied by impotence was not a ground for annulment of a marriage in Roman-Dutch law (Scholtens 1961 *SALJ* 169; Hahlo 121; Van

Aantekening

Dit is duidelik uit die beslissings in *Venter v Venter* en *Van Niekerk v Van Niekerk* [70] dat die howe nie eensgesind is oor die vraag of steriliteit (*impotentia procreandi*) 'n grond vir nietigverklaring van 'n huwelik daarstel as dit nie met die onvermoë om seksuele omgang te hê (*impotentia coeundi*) gepaard gaan nie (Hahlo 120). In *Venter* se saak is beslis dat as een van die partye by huweliksluiting bedrieglik verswyg dat hy of sy onvrugbaar is, die ander party bevoeg is om die huwelik nietig te laat verklaar. Hierteenoor is in *Van Niekerk* se saak beslis dat die blote feit van steriliteit die huwelik vernietigbaar maak, afgesien daarvan of dit bedrieglik verswyg is of nie. Dit geld egter net in daardie gevalle waar die voortbring van kinders 'n uitdruklike of stilswyende oogmerk van die huwelik was. Die gemeneregskrywers onderskei nie altyd duidelik tussen *impotentia procreandi* en *impotentia coeundi* nie sodat hulle nie van veel hulp is by die oplossing van die probleem nie (Van der Vyver en Joubert 496; Van der Walt 1960 *THRHR* 221. Sien oor die ou bronne ook Scholtens 1961 *SALJ* 159 ev). Dit wil egter voorkom asof steriliteit wat nie met impotensie gepaard gegaan het nie, nie 'n grond vir nietigverklaring van 'n huwelik in die

der Walt 1960 *THRHR* 221). The approach in *Venter's* case is therefore preferred to that in *Van Niekerk's* case. On policy grounds too this seems to be the better view (Hahlo 121; Van der Vyver and Joubert 496. *Contra* De Vos 1962 *Acta Juridica* 157, who agrees with the decision in *Van Niekerk's* case).

See also Hunt who subscribes to the view that sterility is not a ground for the annulment of a marriage, but who does not think that fraudulent concealment of sterility should make any difference since it is, according to him, no worse than the fraudulent concealment of an illness such as cancer (1963 *SALJ* 109).

On impotence as a ground for the annulment of a marriage, see *W v W* [68] and *Joshua v Joshua* 1961 1 SA 455 (GW).

Romeins-Hollandse reg gevorm het nie (Scholtens 1961 *SALJ* 169; Hahlo 121; Van der Walt 1960 *THRHR* 221). Die benadering in die *Venter*-saak word daarom bo dié in die *Van Niekerk*-saak verkies. Ook op grond van beleidsoorwegings skyn dit die beter standpunt te wees (Hahlo 121; Van der Vyver en Joubert 496. *Contra* De Vos 1962 *Acta Juridica* 157 wat met die beslissing in die *Van Niekerk*-saak saamstem).

Sien ook Hunt wat saamstem met die opvatting dat steriliteit nie 'n grond vir die nietigverklaring van 'n huwelik daarstel nie. Hy dink egter nie dat bedrieglike verswyging van steriliteit enige verskil moet maak nie aangesien dit volgens hom nie erger as die verswyging van 'n siekte soos kanker is nie (1963 *SALJ* 109).

Sien *W v W* [68] en *Joshua v Joshua* 1961 1 SA 455 (GW) oor impotensie as 'n grond vir die nietigverklaring van 'n huwelik.

[70]   VAN NIEKERK V VAN NIEKERK

1959 4 SA 658 (GW)

Sterility as a ground for the annulment of a marriage

The plaintiff (husband) instituted divorce proceedings against the respondent (wife). He then applied for an amendment of the summons so as to enable him to claim an order declaring the marriage to be null and void on account of the respondent's pre-marital sterility. She had two children of a former marriage but then had an operation performed on her, with her consent, as a result of which she was permanently incapable of having more children. The plaintiff was unaware of this condition but it was known to the respondent who fraudulently concealed it from the plaintiff. The respondent opposed the application on the ground that sterility unaccompanied by impotence was no ground for the annulment of a marriage irrespective of whether or not the respondent knew of the fact at the time of marriage and con-

Steriliteit as 'n grond vir die nietigverklaring van 'n huwelik

Die eiser (man) het egskeidingsverrigtinge teen die respondent (vrou) ingestel. Hy het toe aansoek gedoen om wysiging van die dagvaarding ten einde hom in staat te stel om aansoek te doen om nietigverklaring van die huwelik op grond daarvan dat die respondent voor sluiting van die huwelik steriel was. Sy het twee kinders uit 'n vorige huwelik gehad maar het toe met haar toestemming 'n operasie ondergaan wat tot gevolg gehad het dat sy nie weer kinders sou kon voortbring nie. Die eiser was onbewus van hierdie toedrag van sake maar die respondent het daarvan geweet en het dit bedrieglik vir die eiser verswyg. Die respondent het die aansoek teengestaan op grond daarvan dat steriliteit wat nie met impotensie gepaard gaan nie, nie 'n grond vir die nietigverklaring van 'n huwelik daarstel nie ongeag of die respon-

cealed it from the plaintiff, and that the plaintiff sought to claim a declaration of nullity of the marriage on the ground of fraud. The application for the amendment of the summons was granted.

dent ten tyde van die huweliksluiting daarvan geweet het en dit vir die eiser verberg het, en dat die eiser gepoog het om nietigverklaring van die huwelik op grond van bedrog te verkry. Die aansoek om wysiging van die dagvaarding is toegestaan.

WESSELS J: [661] I propose dealing now with Mr *Zietsman's* [for the applicant] contention that in our law permanent and incurable pre-marital sterility (*impotentia procreandi*) is a ground for having the marriage set aside.

There appears to be a singular dearth of authority in South Africa on this point. The only case dealing pertinently with the matter to which we were referred by counsel is *Venter v Venter*, 1949 (4) SA 123 (W) [69] . . .

In *Venter's* case CLAYDEN, J (as he then was), decided that pre-marital sterility did not provide a basis for setting aside the marriage, adding (without deciding that point) that in a case of pre-marital sterility the true basis of relief might be the concealment of sterility by one party to the marriage . . .

[662] Two questions seem to arise for consideration. The first is concerned with a determination of the ends (the *causae finales*) of marriage, the second with the legal consequences flowing from a failure of one or more of these causes at the time of the marriage. I specifically refer to a failure at the time of the marriage inasmuch as a subsequent failure and its effect on the continued existence of the marriage clearly fall outside the scope of the present enquiry.

[WESSELS J referred to some definitions of marriage in order to determine whether the procreation of children is an end of marriage. He concluded that]

there can be no doubt but that the procreation and rearing of children is an end of marriage. It is not only an end of marriage but also one of the main purposes of life itself. The urge towards self-preservation and reproducing the species is of vital and fundamental importance. While it is true that children may be procreated where there is no marriage, social conditions require that they should only be procreated where a man and a woman are joined in marriage.

[663] The procreation of children is obviously not the only purpose of marriage. In this regard I . . . adopt the following statement of the late VAN DEN HEEVER JA, in his monograph on *Breach of Promise and Seduction in South African Law* (p 20):

"Adopting the principles of the Canon law Roman-Dutch law regarded the teleological causes or *causae finales* of marriage to be: . . . (1) sexual intercourse, (2) the procreation of children, (3) mutual aid and assistance, (4) cohabitation and the enjoyment of each other's society for life and (5) the avoidance of illicit intercourse." . . .

[WESSELS J then investigated impotence as a ground for setting aside a marriage. He concluded that]

[665] [t]he logical justification for the existence of this ground for setting aside a marriage would seem to be the fact that sexual intercourse is so essential an element of marriage that where it cannot come about there is no marriage, ie, the remaining purposes or causes are in contemplation of law insufficient to support the marriage unless the parties themselves are content to regard them as sufficient.

At this stage I should like to refer to another common law ground for setting aside a marriage on account of a circumstance existing at the time of the marriage, ie, the pregnancy of the wife at the time of the marriage as a result of pre-marital intercourse with a man other than her husband. In this case, too, the true basis for relief does not appear to be the immoral pre-marital conduct of the wife or her deception in concealing her pregnancy (circumstances might conceivably arise when she honestly believes that the illicit intercourse did not result in pregnancy).

In *Fietze v Fietze,* 1913 EDL 170, an action founded on this ground, there is reference to fraud on the defendant's part. It is not clear to me why that course was taken. In *Smith v Smith*, 1936 CPD 125, DAVIS, J (at p 126) states the position as follows:

"... the arrival into the family of a child who will be the child of one spouse and not of the other brings in its train immense possibilities of tragedy and dissension and difficult questions as to maintenance and discipline. I am quite satisfied that that is the true and proper reason for our law on this subject."

In *Horak v Horak,* 3 SC 389, there is a reference in the head-note to error and fraud. At p 399 it is, however, stated that the judgment,

"is rested entirely upon the conjunction of the two facts of deflowerment and pregnancy whereby one of the great, if not the great object of marriage – procreation of children – is defeated."

The basis for the relief was thus not fraud but pre-marital circumstances resulting in a failure of one of the final causes of marriage, namely, the procreation of children. See also *Stander v Stander,* 1929 AD 349 at p 355 [67]; *Vereen v Vereen and Another,* 1943 GWLD 50; *Reyneke v Reyneke,* 1927 OPD 130; *Pansegrouw v Pansegrouw,* 1910 OPD 51.

The true basis on which relief is granted on the two grounds referred to above (ie impotence and pre-marital pregnancy) would thus seem to be the one spouse's error as to certain qualities of the other spouse. The mistake is regarded as fundamental because the qualities to which it relates in turn relate to the essential (and not incidental) ends of marriage. Impotence must necessarily result in the failure of sexual intercourse and the procreation of children as ends of marriage and would probably give rise to illicit sexual intercourse on the part of the potent spouse. Pregnancy on the part of the wife results in at least a temporary failure of procreation of children as an end of marriage and might furthermore, throughout the marriage, seriously jeopardise the chances of harmonious cohabitation and the enjoyment of each other's society.

[666] To sum up:

1 Post-nuptial failure of any one or more of the final causes of marriage owing to the unlawful conduct of one spouse entitles the innocent spouse to relief.

2 Where the element of unlawful conduct is absent even a total failure of the final causes of marriage does not provide a basis for relief ... The parties are bound to honour the marriage vow of taking each other "for better or for worse".

3 If *Venter's* case, *supra,* correctly states our law, it follows that a spouse's mistake as to the qualities of the other spouse existing at the time of the marriage only provides a basis for relief where the mistake relates to the potency of the man or woman (restricted to *potentia coeundi*) or to the woman's condition of being pregnant by another man. I have already ventured the opinion that a mistake of this nature is regarded as fundamental on account of the relationship between the qualities concerned and the appropriate final causes of marriage. In both cases the absence of the quality thought to exist inevitably results in an immediate failure of one or more of the causes of marriage. In the case of *impotentia coeundi* the failure is necessarily permanent, but in the case of pre-marital pregnancy the only inevitable consequence is a temporary failure of pro-

creation as an end of marriage. Its effect on the other causes of marriage are neither inevitable nor necessarily permanent.

A mistake as to other qualities (eg age, race, nationality, religion, social standing, financial circumstances, pre-marital chastity, etc) does not provide a basis for relief, not even where fraud is an element ... These mistakes are not regarded as fundamental, notwithstanding the fact that in individual cases a mistake eg as to religion or pre-marital chastity, may seriously affect the marriage. It cannot, however, be said that a failure of one or more of the causes of marriage must inevitably flow from such a mistake. It follows from what I have said that a mistake as to *potentia procreandi* seems to be the one exception to the rule that a mistake as to a quality which must inevitably result in a failure of at least one of the causes of the marriage (ie one of a fundamental nature) entitles the aggrieved party to relief.

In *Venter's* case CLAYDEN, J, proceeded to consider the opinions of various authors on Roman-Dutch law and states his conclusion as follows at p 128:

> "In the light of these passages in the Roman-Dutch law, I do not think it can be said that the procreation of children, is so essential an element of marriage that where it cannot come about, there is no marriage."

It follows then that at the time the rule relating to impotence was introduced the distinction between *impotentia coeundi* and *impotentia procreandi* and their relationship with the final causes of marriage was given effect to, the first-mentioned incapacity alone being regarded as of such fundamental importance as to entitle an aggrieved party to relief. This pre-supposes that the various recognised final causes of marriage can be listed in order of essentiality. One can only conclude that sexual intercourse tops the list and that the remaining causes are all to be [667] bracketed together as "not so essential" or else to be placed in some as yet undetermined order of essentiality. This approach casts doubt on the logical basis of the rule relating to pre-marital pregnancy suggested above. The temporary failure of procreation resulting from pre-marital pregnancy viewed with alarm in *Horak's* case, *supra,* cannot be more serious than the total failure flowing from incurable sterility. (It must be remembered that the woman is not being punished for indulging in illicit intercourse.) The "immense possibilities of tragedy and dissension" referred to by DAVIS, J, in *Smith's* case, *supra* at p 126, are also present where the bride of one day for the first time introduces her one-month-old illegitimate child to her unsuspecting husband.

It is also to be noted that immediately after the marriage this "list" becomes legally insignificant. The causes are all dealt with on a basis of parity where there is a failure flowing from the unlawful conduct of one spouse ...

In *Venter's* case, *supra,* CLAYDEN, J, refers to certain consequences which might follow from the rule that sterility unaccompanied by impotence provides a basis for relief. He mentions, eg, that any marriage by persons who are past the child-bearing age may be set aside. The answer seems to be that in a large number of cases it could be held that the plaintiff knew of or was not concerned with the probable failure of procreation. He also states,

> "moreover with modern medical knowledge it may now be discovered, years after a marriage, that one or other of the parties to it was at the time of the marriage sterile, quite unknown to themselves".

Firstly, I doubt whether many of such cases would ever arise for decision. Secondly, the question is not the desirability or otherwise of recognising such a rule, but whether it in fact exists. In order to determine whether it exists regard must be had to times when medical knowledge was in its infancy.

In *Venter's* case, *supra* at pp 126 and 127, CLAYDEN, J, refers to several definitions of marriage put forward by various writers on Roman-Dutch law ...

[668] None of these definitions refer in detail to the teleological causes of marriage. In so far as any one cause is specifically mentioned, it appears more often to be the procreation of children ...

In so far as the reference to *Voet*, 23.2.28, is concerned it would seem that the repeal by *Justinian* of the prohibition in the Julian and Papian law against marriage by elderly persons justifies a conclusion that it was recognised that there were other reasons for marriage in addition to the procreation of children, but certainly not a conclusion that procreation was not an end of marriage or one of lesser importance than the others referred to in the passage referred to.

In *Baxter v Baxter*, 1946 AC 274, VISCOUNT JOWITT, LC, adopts a definition in Lord Stair's, *Institutions* (1681 ed. Bk 1, tit. 4 para. 6) which is as follows:

> "So then, it is not the consent of marriage as it relateth to the procreation of children that is requisite; for it may consist, though the woman be far beyond that date; but it is the consent, whereby ariseth that conjugal society, which may have the conjunction of bodies as well as of minds, as the general end of the institution of marriage in the solace and satisfaction of man."

It seems to me that *Lord Stair's* view is not very different from that put forward by *Voet* in the passage referred to above (23.2.28). One feels constrained to observe that in our law a marriage may be validly contracted even where by reason of advanced age the desire for sexual intercourse has waned completely.

In considering procreation as an end of marriage I think one should not over-emphasise the momentary miracle of fertilisation. Seen in its proper perspective procreation relates not only to the begetting of children, but also to their maintenance and education within the family circle. In this sense, I think, procreation is not only a most important end of marriage, but also the most important single factor contributing to "the solace and satisfaction of man".

For the reason set out above I conclude that the begetting and rearing of children is a final cause of marriage which, if it is not to be regarded as the principal end of the institution of marriage, at the time of the marriage ranks on a basis of parity with the other ends thereof. During the subsistence of the marriage the emphasis may shift from one cause to another at the instance of the parties, but in contemplation of law they remain of equal importance (as I attempted to indicate above).

CLAYDEN, J, purported to derive assistance from his conclusion that the procreation of children was not "so essential an element of marriage that, where it cannot come about, there is no marriage", in interpreting the scope and effect of the Roman-Dutch law relating to impotence. In my view it was necessary for him to go one step further, namely, to hold that sexual intercourse (unrelated to procreation) is so essential an element of marriage that, where it cannot come about, there is no marriage. I have already stated it as my opinion that such a conclusion cannot be justified.

[669] It is necessary now to consider whether in Roman-Dutch law pre-marital sterility afforded a basis for relief to an aggrieved party where the element of deceit is absent and where the condition does not flow from *impotentia coeundi* ...

[WESSELS J considered the opinions of Roman-Dutch authors and proceeded:]

[670] In my opinion the somewhat loose language employed by those authorities which I was able to consult can possibly be explained by the fact that at the time they were

writing Roman-Dutch law was not concerned with subtle distinctions between the capacity to consummate and the capacity to procreate in granting relief where at the time of the marriage it appears that there is no chance of off-spring. It is highly probable that in most cases where natural and full intercourse was possible fertilisation would follow. Having regard to the extent of medical knowledge on the subject available at the time, it would have been difficult for any spouse to prove that the other was at fault where there was a failure of off-spring notwithstanding their apparent ability to have natural and full intercourse. In the case of *impotentia coeundi*, however, proof of the fact that one party was responsible for the failure of the off-spring was readily available, because that defect must inevitably result in incapacity to procreate.

If there had in fact been any such distinction one would have expected some of the authorities to refer to it. None of those that I was able to consult deal with this distinction in any way.

Nor does there seem to be any warrant for holding that [671] Roman-Dutch law drew a deliberate distinction between sterility resulting from impotence on the one hand and from other causes on the other hand.

In my opinion it is the more acceptable explanation that where the Roman-Dutch law authorities state that sterile people may not marry they in fact mean that people who are incapable of procreating children may not marry. Impotent persons would automatically fall within the prohibited class, since impotence necessarily involves sterility. Where language is employed which is perhaps more appropriate to the act of intercourse, the authorities would have in mind the fact that the impotence involves sterility and that the impotent constitute a special class of sterile person.

I am thus driven to the conclusion that in Roman-Dutch law *impotentia procreandi* (whether or not it flowed from *impotentia coeundi*) was a ground for setting aside a marriage if the defect existed at the time of the marriage, and that this is still our law to-day. Notwithstanding the references in some of the older authorities to fraud, it appears from the cases cited above in which marriages were set aside on the ground of impotence that fraud is not an essential element. There seems to be no reason based on public policy why this rule should not be recognised by our Courts at the present time. For the reasons referred to above the rule will not affect marriages between elderly people. In so far as other marriages are concerned medical science is no doubt in a position to determine at an early stage of the marriage why there is a failure of off-spring notwithstanding the apparent ability of the parties to have full and natural intercourse and whether the position can be remedied.

If I am wrong in my conclusion, and if in fact the Roman-Dutch law drew a distinction between *impotentia coeundi* and *impotentia procreandi* along the lines suggested in *Venter's* case, *supra*, the further question remains whether the fraudulent conduct imputed to defendant in this case if proved entitles plaintiff to relief.

Marriages have been set aside on the ground of fraud under our law, but in so far as I have been able to ascertain only in cases where the fraud results in the absence of real and valid consent on the part of the plaintiff to contract a marriage with the defendant ...

I have already referred to the fact that there is no indication in our law that fraud relating to any particular quality of the party concerned provides a basis for relief. (Where the fraud relates to the quality of potence or absence of pregnancy, the plaintiff need not rely on fraud as a basis for claiming the setting aside of the marriage.)

The Courts should not, I take it, display over-eagerness in adding to the grounds upon which a marriage may be set aside. It is the function of the lawgivers to step in where it is desirable in the public interest to modify or add to the grounds upon which a marriage may be set aside.

[672] I am, however, satisfied that, if I should be wrong in my conclusion stated above in regard to the scope of the impotence rule, the fraudulent conduct of a party in relation to his or her ability to procreate off-spring provides a basis upon which a marriage may be set aside.

The fraud would relate to a matter of substance, inasmuch as the inability to procreate inevitably results in the failure of one of the ends of marriage. The failure of children in these circumstances must of necessity have an important effect on the fulfilment of the remaining causes of marriage.

If the impotence rule was in fact restricted to *impotentia coeundi* it would seem that it might have been so restricted not by reason of any fundamental importance accorded to the transient solace resulting from intercourse, but by reason of the then existing practical inability of relating sterility to a cause other than impotence. In the case of latent sterility the failure of children was no doubt related to divine intervention ...

The advance of medical science now makes it possible not only to cause sterility by artificial means, but also to relate sterility to causes other than impotence ...

In addition those authorities to which CLAYDEN, J, refers and which I was able to consult would appear to support a conclusion that fraud in relation to pre-marital sterility provides a basis for relief. This is also the conclusion stated by *Van den Heever* at p 20 of his monograph to which I have already referred.

In the result I am of the opinion that the application for the amendment of plaintiff's summons and declaration should be granted ...

DE VOS HUGO J: In this matter I agree with the conclusion arrived at by my Brother WESSELS that the application to amend the summons and declaration should be allowed ...

[673] There is no lack of authority in Roman-Dutch law or indeed in our law that the procreation of children is one of the principal objects, if not the principal object, of marriage ...

[674] In view of the fact that procreation is such an important foundation of marriage one would expect to find that the inability to procreate on the part of one of the spouses would be a ground for annulment of the marriage. The writers on the Roman-Dutch law leave one in no doubt that this is indeed the case ...

In view of what these authorities say I have come to the conclusion [675] that pre-marital inability to procreate is a ground for annulment of the marriage ...

In my opinion the rule that a marriage can be annulled on the ground of pre-marital inability to procreate should be confined to those cases in which the procreation of children is an explicit or implied object of the marriage and in which the woman at least is of child-bearing [676] age ...

The second ground on which applicant seeks leave to claim annulment is fraud, that is, fraud consisting in concealment by the defective spouse of his or her inability from the able spouse. I agree with CLAYDEN, J, that this is a good ground and one for which there is sufficient Roman-Dutch authority ...

For these reasons I agree that the application should be allowed.

Note	**Aantekening**
See the note on *Venter v Venter* [69].	Sien die aantekening by *Venter v Venter* [69].

The putative marriage   Die putatiewe huwelik

[71] MOOLA V AULSEBROOK

1983 1 SA 687 (N)

Due solemnisation as requirement for a putative marriage

The applicant (wife) and her deceased husband had gone through a marriage ceremony solemnised in accordance with Islamic rites by a priest who was not a properly appointed marriage officer. Neither the applicant nor her husband knew that they had to be married by a duly appointed marriage officer. The spouses lived together in monogamy as husband and wife from the date of the marriage until the husband's death. They had seven children. When the husband died his will was invalid and his estate therefore had to devolve intestate. The applicant applied for an order declaring the children to be legitimate to enable them to inherit intestate from their father. The application was based on the argument that the marriage between the parents of the children was a putative marriage even though the statutory requirements regarding the marriage formalities had not been complied with and that the children born of such a marriage should be declared legitimate. The application was granted.

Nakoming van formaliteitsvereistes as vereiste vir 'n putatiewe huwelik

Die applikant (vrou) en haar oorlede man is ooreenkomstig die Islamitiese geloof in die huwelik bevestig deur 'n priester wat nie 'n behoorlik aangestelde huweliksbevestiger was nie. Nòg die applikant nòg haar man was bewus daarvan dat hulle deur 'n behoorlik aangestelde huweliksbevestiger in die huwelik bevestig moes word. Vanaf die dag van hulle huweliksluiting tot by die man se dood het die gades in 'n monogame verhouding as man en vrou saamgeleef. Hulle het sewe kinders gehad. By die man se dood het dit geblyk dat sy testament ongeldig was en sy boedel moes gevolglik intestaat vererf. Die applikant het aansoek gedoen dat die kinders binne-egtelik verklaar word ten einde hulle in staat te stel om intestaat van hulle vader te erf. Die aansoek is gebaseer op die argument dat die huwelik tussen die ouers van die kinders 'n putatiewe huwelik was al is die statutêre vereistes vir sluiting van 'n huwelik nie nagekom nie en dat die kinders wat uit sodanige huwelik gebore is binne-egtelik verklaar moes word. Die aansoek is toegestaan.

FRIEDMAN J: [689] [The question] whether or not the children of a union, which had not been solemnised in conformity with our statutory requirements, but which was *bona fide* regarded by one or both of the parties as a valid marriage, could be considered to be the issue of a putative marriage and therefore legitimate ... was left open expressly by the Appellate Division on the only occasion that the question was raised before it. This was in the case of *Bam v Bhabha* 1947 (4) SA 798 (A). The only time this question has been considered directly was in the case of *Ramayee v Vandiyar* 1977 (3) SA 77 (D), a judgment of DIDCOTT J. DIDCOTT J answered the question in the affirmative holding, *inter alia*, that he was bound by the decision of the Full Court in *Ex parte Soobiah and Others: In re Estate Pillay* 1948 (1) SA 873 (N). PAGE J had doubts as to whether or not *Ex parte Soobiah* was binding in the present situation and, even if it was binding, he believed it appropriate for the legal requirements of a putative marriage to be considered once again by the Full Court ...

[690] In order to avoid any misconceptions as to what I shall say later, it is necessary to make certain preliminary observations. A so-called "putative marriage" is not a marriage. Nor does the recognition by a Court of a union as meeting the requirements of a putative marriage convert that union into a valid marriage. The parties to such a union are not and do not become "husband" and "wife" within the legally recognised meaning of those words. Normally, of course, an invalid marriage has none of the legal consequences of a valid one. But where the invalid marriage meets the requirements of the concept of a putative marriage, certain, but not all, of the consequences of a valid marriage will result. These consequences can broadly speaking be classified under two main headings, namely property rights and children ... The first category probably has very little practical significance since similar results can no doubt be achieved by purely contractual considerations without resort to the concept of a putative marriage. I have in mind in this regard those cases dealing with the creation or formation of tacit universal partnerships between persons, who although unmarried, live together as husband and wife. The true importance of the concept of putative marriage lies therefore in the fact that children of such a union are legitimate with all the legal advantages of legitimate children. I interpolate here to point out that it is something of an open question whether the children of a putative marriage become legitimate only when declared by the Court to be such or whether they are legitimate and the Court's order is merely declaratory of an existing fact (see *Hahlo* (*op cit* at 495)). The latter would appear to be the better view (Conradie 1947 *SALJ* at 382; cf *Vather v Seedat and Another* 1974 (3) SA 389 (N)); but as nothing turns on this question in the present case I prefer to leave it an open one.

The concept of a putative marriage was unknown to the Roman law. In Roman law, illegitimate children could only be legitimated by the subsequent marriage of their parents or by imperial rescript, which, in turn, would only be resorted to in very special cases (*Voet* 25.7.13). The concept of a putative marriage was an invention of Canon law ...

[691] Consequently it applied only to unions contracted, as Professor Lee puts it in the article to which I have referred (at 39), "*in facie ecclesiae* [in the church] with all due solemnities and (as required by the Lateran Council) after publication of banns". That was the sole scope of its application. The Canon law had no application to what it regarded as clandestine marriages. In these circumstances, by its very nature, the concept of a putative marriage could only apply to those unions which, although formally correct, were invalid by reason of a defect of capacity, eg marriages within the prohibited degrees, bigamous marriages etc.

Once, however, the Canon law principle was taken over by the Courts of Holland as part of the legal system of Holland and, more particularly, once the principle is accepted as being part of our law, its scope falls to be regarded against an entirely different background. Our law, of course, recognises that marriages can be contracted in a variety of ways which do not always or necessarily involve compliance with the formalities and ceremonies prescribed by any particular religion or indeed by any religion at all. In addition, they are solemnised by a marriage officer who may or may not be a priest or [692] minister of religion. When, therefore, one applies the concept of a putative marriage to a system in which a marriage might be contracted in a variety of ways and in a variety of forms, not all of which are necessarily the same as those recognised by the Canon law which developed the principle, it is apparent that one is applying it to a system in which invalidities may result not only from defects in capacity but also from defects in form (eg a defect in the appointment of the marriage officer or the fact that the marriage ceremony is performed by a person who is not a marriage officer); types of defects which, in short, did not arise under the Canon law. It seems to me that the application of the concept to the different system of law necessarily involves widening and adapting the scope of the concept to deal with the various types of invalidities which may arise out of the requisites for a valid marriage of that system. Were it otherwise our law would apply a different principle depending upon whether the marriage was or was not contracted according to the formalities stipulated by the Canon law under which the concept was developed, a result which I believe cannot be correct.

Our Courts have had little difficulty in applying the concept to cases where marriages have been invalid because of an absence of the necessary formal legal requirements...

It is of interest to note that other systems of law which have taken over the concept of putative marriages from the Canon law and enshrined it in their civil codes appear to have dropped the requirement of "due solemnisation"...

[693] Assuming the requirement to be one which still exists, it seems to me, as I have already said, that all that is required is that the union be contracted openly and in accordance with rituals and ceremonies not inconsistent with our law; that is to say, there must be some formal and solemn ceremony by means of which the parties give open expression to their desire to marry and by means of which they manifest their intention to marry and not simply to enter into what I might call a clandestine union. That requirement was clearly met in the present case (as, of course, were all the other requirements)... [A]ll that was lacking in the present case to have made the union between the first applicant and the deceased a valid marriage was the fact that the priest who solemnised the marriage was not apparently a duly appointed marriage officer. That defect, in my view, is not one which thereby removes the union from the scope of the putative marriage concept...

There is, however, in conclusion a further consideration which appeals to me. The concept of a putative marriage was one which, to my mind, originated not only (as *Hahlo* put it at 494 footnote 70) "as a device to mitigate the harshness of annulment to an innocent spouse" but also, and more particularly, to mitigate the harshness of that annulment to children born of the union. Until the union is annulled or until the parties are made aware the union is invalid, it is their intention, in procreating children, to procreate legitimate children; or where only one of the parties is ignorant of the defect in the union, that at any rate is his or her intention. The concept of a putative marriage is designed to preserve that intention and to permit the children who, after all, were entirely innocent in the matter, to benefit from it (cf *H (wrongly called C) v C* 1929 TPD 992 at 995 *per* TINDALL AJP)...

[The children born of the marriage between their parents were therefore legitimate as they were born of a putative marriage.]

MILNE JP and KRIEK J concurred.

Note

In this case the court had to decide whether or not a putative marriage can come into existence if the marriage was not duly solemnised. At common law due solemnisation was a prerequisite for a putative marriage. Whether it is still a requirement is unclear. In *Bam v Bhabha* 1947 4 SA 798 (A) this question was left unresolved although the Appellate Division implied that it viewed due solemnisation as a requirement. There are, however, many cases which are authority for the view that as long as the marriage was "con-

Aantekening

In hierdie saak moes die hof beslis of 'n putatiewe huwelik tot stand kan kom indien die huwelik nie behoorlik in ooreenstemming met die formele vereistes bevestig is nie. Ingevolge die gemenereg is behoorlike bevestiging vereis vir 'n putatiewe huwelik. Of dit vandag nog vereis word, is onduidelik. In *Bam v Bhabha* 1947 4 SA 798 (A) is hierdie vraag oopgelaat alhoewel die Appèlhof te kenne gegee het dat dit behoorlike bevestiging as 'n vereiste beskou. Daar is egter baie sake wat gesag is daarvoor dat solank die

tracted openly and in accordance with rituals and ceremonies not inconsistent with our law" it can be putative (*Moola v Aulsebrook* at 693; see also *Ex parte Azar* 1932 OPD 107; *Ex parte L (also known as A)* 1947 3 SA 50 (C); *Ex parte Soobiah: In re Estate Pillay* 1948 1 SA 873 (N); *Ex parte Reynolds* 1970 1 SA 658 (T); *Vather v Seedat* 1974 3 SA 389 (N)). But in *Ngubane v Ngubane* [74] at 774 a full bench of the Transvaal supreme court adopted the common-law position that a putative marriage cannot come into existence in the absence of "a marriage ceremony performed by a marriage officer". In *Solomons v Abrams* [72] FLEMMING DJP not only considered himself bound by the decision in *Ngubane*, but in addition thought the approach in *Ngubane* to be the better one. It should, however, be noted that the issues in *Ngubane* and in *Solomons* were different: In *Solomons*, due solemnisation was at issue because the priest who officiated at the marriage ceremony was not a duly appointed marriage officer. Because the marriage in *Ngubane*'s case had been duly solemnised by a properly appointed marriage officer, the issue of due solemnisation was not discussed in any detail in that case. The case dealt with the status of children born out of a putative marriage and the question of whether the *mala fide* party can apply for an order declaring such children to be legitimate. The court did not deliver a considered judgment about the requirement of due solemnisation because the issue did not arise at all; it merely referred to due solemnisation in passing. Whether the judgment can properly be construed as authority for the statement that due solemnisation is required is therefore doubtful. Furthermore, the weight of modern opinion seems to be in support of relaxation or abandonment of the requirement of due solemnisation (see *LAWSA* vol 16 *Marriage* par 41; Van der Vyver and Joubert 520; *Wille's Principles* 175).

Formerly an illegitimate child could not inherit intestate from his father and paternal blood relations. Nor could the father and paternal blood relations inherit intestate from the illegitimate child. This position has now been changed by the Intestate Succession Act 81 of 1987. In terms of section 1(2) of this act illegitimate children may inherit intestate from both their parents (and from more distant blood relations) and both parents (and more distant blood relations) may inherit intestate from such illegitimate children.

huwelik "openly and in accordance with rituals and ceremonies not inconsistent with our law" gesluit is, dit putatief kan wees (*Moola v Aulsebrook* op 693; sien ook *Ex parte Azar* 1932 OPA 107; *Ex parte L (also known as A)* 1947 3 SA 50 (N); *Ex parte Soobiah: In re Estate Pillay* 1948 1 SA 873 (N); *Ex parte Reynolds* 1970 1 SA 658 (T); *Vather v Seedat* 1974 3 SA 389 (N)). In *Ngubane v Ngubane* [74] op 774 het 'n volbank van die Transvaalse hooggeregshof egter die gemeenregtelike posisie aanvaar dat daar geen putatiewe huwelik kan wees tensy daar "a marriage ceremony performed by a marriage officer" was nie. In *Solomons v Abrams* [72] het FLEMMING DJP hom nie alleen gebonde geag aan die beslissing in *Ngubane* nie, maar ook gemeen dat die benadering in *Ngubane* meer korrek is. Daar moet egter op gelet word dat die geskilpunte in *Ngubane* en in *Solomons* verskillend was: In *Solomons* was behoorlike bevestiging ter sprake omdat die priester wat by die seremonie opgetree het nie 'n behoorlik aangestelde huweliksbevestiger was nie. Aangesien die huwelik in die *Ngubane*-saak deur 'n behoorlik aangestelde huweliksbevestiger voltrek is, is die aangeleentheid van behoorlike bevestiging nie in daardie saak in enige besonderhede bespreek nie. Die saak het gehandel oor die status van kinders wat uit 'n putatiewe huwelik gebore word en oor die vraag of die *mala fide*-party aansoek kan doen om 'n bevel wat sulke kinders binne-egtelik verklaar. Die hof het geen oorwoë uitspraak gelewer oor die vereiste van behoorlike bevestiging nie aangesien die probleem glad nie in die saak ontstaan het nie; die hof het bloot in die verbygaan daarna verwys. Dit is gevolglik te betwyfel of die uitspraak as gesag kan dien vir die stelling dat behoorlike bevestiging vereis word. Verder is die moderne standpunt oorwegend ten gunste daarvan dat die vereiste van behoorlike bevestiging verslap word of dat heeltemal daarmee weggedoen word (sien *LAWSA* vol 16 *Marriage* par 41; Van der Vyver en Joubert 520; *Wille's Principles* 175).

Voorheen kon 'n buite-egtelike kind nie intestaat van sy vader en vaderlike bloedverwante erf nie en die vader en vaderlike bloedverwante kon ook nie intestaat van die buite-egtelike kind erf nie. Hierdie situasie is nou gewysig deur die Wet op Intestate Erfopvolging 81 van 1987. Ingevolge artikel 1(2) van hierdie wet mag buite-egtelike kinders intestaat van albei hulle ouers erf (en ook van verdere bloedverwante) en albei ouers (en verdere bloedverwante) mag intestaat van sodanige buite-egtelike kinders erf.

[72]   SOLOMONS V ABRAMS

1991 4 SA 437 (W)

A marriage ceremony performed by a marriage officer is a requirement for the recognition of a putative marriage

The applicant and the respondent had entered into a union under Islamic law. The parties *bona fide* believed that they were married according to Islamic law. There was no evidence that they attempted or intended to comply with the Marriage Act 25 of 1961 nor did they make any attempt to establish what those requirements were. They did not think that the priest who solemnised the union was a marriage officer, nor did they think that they had contracted a civil marriage. The priest did not hold himself out as authorised to create a civil marriage or as purporting to create such a marriage. He issued a document with the heading "Marriage Certificate (under Islamic Law)". It was not stated that he signed the certificate in the capacity as a marriage officer; it stated instead that he was authorised by the parties to solemnise the marriage. The applicant sought an order declaring that the union between the parties was a putative marriage and that the children born thereof were legitimate. The application was dismissed.

'n Huwelikseremonie wat deur 'n huweliksbeampte voltrek word, is 'n vereiste vir die bestaan van 'n putatiewe huwelik

Die applikant en die respondent het 'n huweliksverbintenis ingevolge die Islamitiese reg aangegaan. Die partye het *bona fide* geglo dat hulle ingevolge die Islamitiese reg getroud was. Daar was geen getuienis voor die hof dat hulle gepoog of bedoel het om aan die vereistes van die Huwelikswet 25 van 1961 te voldoen nie en hulle het ook geen poging aangewend om vas te stel wat die vereistes was nie. Hulle het nie gedink dat die priester wat die seremonie voltrek het 'n huweliksbevestiger was nie en hulle was ook nie van mening dat hulle 'n burgerlike huwelik gesluit het nie. Die priester het nie voorgegee dat hy die bevoegdheid gehad het om 'n burgerlike huwelik te voltrek of dat hy inderdaad sodanige huwelik voltrek het nie. Hy het 'n dokument uitgereik met die opskrif "Marriage Certificate (under Islamic Law)". Daarop is nie aangedui dat hy die sertifikaat in sy hoedanigheid van 'n huweliksbevestiger onderteken het nie. In plaas daarvan het dit aangedui dat die partye hom gemagtig het om die huwelik te voltrek. Die applikant het aansoek gedoen dat die verbintenis tussen die partye 'n putatiewe huwelik was en dat die kinders wat daaruit gebore is binne-egtelik was. Die aansoek is van die hand gewys.

FLEMMING DJP: [438] The method of obtaining relief which was chosen has its own hurdle. It consists of the common-law proposition that only a ceremony which was duly solemnised can be regarded as a putative marriage and the person who purported to do so in this case was not a marriage officer ... [439] The proposition has critical importance because of its acceptance by a Full Bench, whose decision binds me sitting as a single Judge. In *Ngubane v Ngubane* 1983 (2) SA 770 (T) at 773, 774 [74] a requirement for the law's recognition of a putative marriage was said to be a 'marriage ceremony performed by a marriage officer'.

Even if, as counsel suggests, I may consider whether the decision of the Full Bench is clearly wrong, I am neither convinced that it is wrong nor that it would have been different if it had considered the aspects which guided a Full Bench in Natal. I concisely mention aspects to justify this view.

Firstly, it is a matter of law that a 'putative marriage' was recognised only when parties in good faith complied with the prescribed solemnities but were not permitted by law to marry each other ...

It is in the nature of a Court in this country that it cannot abolish or alter a legal concept which has become embedded ...

Secondly, the Court in the *Ngubane* case may have doubted whether the decisions relied upon in [*Ramayee v Vandiyar* 1977 (3) SA 77 (D)] ought to have been convincing. Before explaining that comment, it is convenient to distinguish three levels of protecting the ... *bona fides* of parties. These are:

(a) The parties may do everything required by law to create a valid marriage but despite proper solemnising thereof, the marriage is a prohibited one.

(b) Parties equally do whatever the law requires (depending on the contents of the law from time to time, that could include publication of banns, conducting the ceremony with open doors, appearing before someone who is legally authorised to solemnise marriages) but find that their efforts were in vain. Thus although the marriage is permissible, their best efforts could not achieve the desired result because the purported marriage officer was not authorised to act as such.

(c) The parties make no attempt to comply with the civil law. They may even, as I understand the present case, make no attempt to establish what those requirements are.

The common law protected (a). Protection to (b) was given by the aforementioned s 6(2) [of the Marriage Act, which permits retrospective appointment as a marriage officer of a person who was not a duly appointed marriage officer at the time of the wedding]. The present parties fall under (c) ...

[440] [C]ounsel also relied on the decision in *Moola and Others v Aulsebrook NO and Others* 1983 (1) SA 687 (N) [71]. It is true that that decision was probably available in the law reports only after the *Ngubane* case was argued. I do not believe that this entitles a single Judge in this Division to deviate from the *Ngubane* decision. The *Aulsebrook* decision did not decide that insistence that the marriage be contracted 'palam et sollemniter' [openly and in compliance with the necessary formalities] has fallen away. See 693A ...

The reference in the *Moola* case to equitable and fair considerations occurs after the conclusion of the Court had already been stated at 693F–G. It is good if Courts are concerned about such matters. Sight must, though, not be lost of considerations such as the recognisable principles of law, the policy of law, the social impact, legislation and its policy, or the interest of third parties. Thus, to illustrate, if a child 'becomes' legitimate, all grandparents have a duty to maintenance but also a right to maintenance against that child. It is not clear that a putative marriage only removes disabilities for the legitimate children and that it does not become the equivalent of a proper marriage, for example, with reference to rights to claim for loss of support of a spouse or liability for household necessaries. I must accentuate the policy of the legislation. Whatever the Legislature might find appropriate in 1991, its 1961 views governed the passing of the Marriage Act, 1961. It had its set of views on what is socially desirable, what will create certainty, and perhaps even [441] religiously based views. If a Court is to recognise any 'formal and solemn ceremony by means of which the parties give open expression to their desire to marry...' (at 693C), consequences arise which cannot be lightly regarded as having the blessing of the Marriage Act, 1961 or the general policy of the law. The parties may then, instead of getting married according to law, prefer to make a 'solemn' declaration (provided it is a ritual or constitutes a 'ceremony'?) before any third party who is known not to be a marriage officer, and after acceptable evidence of cohabitation and repute, acquire the same advantages and disadvantages that arise from a marriage. Alongside the marriage governed by law would arise a truly consensual marriage. It is true that the need for a *bona fide* belief in having become married will still exist – but only a belief of being 'married per ritual'. I believe that the common law's protection (extended, perhaps, by the assistance of ss 6(1) and 6(2) of the Marriage Act) extends to cases where parties *bona fide* believe that they have become married in accordance with the law. The *Moola* case tolerates a belief of getting married in accordance with any ritual or ceremony which has to some extent become 'customary' (at 691D–E) and is openly done. That is the very distinction on which the *dictum* in the *Ngubane* case is of importance. I am not convinced that it would have been differently decided according to the reasoning which was found appealing in the *Moola* case. In the alternative, the Full Bench may have thought that the protection of parties in the case where the marriage officer is not in fact duly appointed as such at least finds its basis and scope of protection defined by ss 6(1) and 6(2) of the Marriage Act.

In the present case the parties did not think that the moulana (priest) was a marriage officer. Their evidence is not that they thought that they had become spouses in a 'civil marriage'. There is no evidence of attempting or intending to comply with the requirements of the Marriage Act, 1961. The moulana did not hold himself out as authorised to create a civil marriage or as purporting to create such a marriage. He issued a document with the heading: 'Marriage Certificate (under the Islamic Law)'. That clearly creates a contrast with the law of the land. Subject to the Arabic script, the certificate shows some resemblance to the large registers kept by marriage officers in the 1960's. It does not state that he signed in the capacity as a marriage officer but it states, 'I, M S Banoo, being duly authorised *by the parties* do hereby solemnize the marriage'. The parties *bona fide* believed that they were married according to Islamic law; they did not try to prove that they believed that they were 'married' in the sense in which a lawyer or a laymen, who knows that marriages are governed by law, would use the word.

I do not believe that in view of the historically recognisable policy and the terms of the Marriage Act, matters would be any different if by a self-devised 'ceremony' or 'customary' ritual, the officiating officer proceeds to pronounce to the parties that they are married and the parties believe him, irrespective of whether such officer is a priest, a headman in a kraal, the leader of a section of a 'weerstandsbeweging', or any other grouping.

The refusal to deviate from the *Ngubane* decision determines the outcome of the application.

[442] The declaratory orders sought by applicant are refused...

Note	**Aantekening**
See the note on *Moola v Aulsebrook* [71].	Sien die aantekening by *Moola v Aulsebrook* [71].

[73]   M v M

1962 2 SA 114 (GW)

Consequences of a putative marriage	Gevolge van 'n putatiewe huwelik
After his wife's death, the defendant married his stepdaughter (plaintiff). The plaintiff believed that she had entered into a valid marriage and was unaware of the fact that the marriage was invalid as the parties were within the prohibited degrees of relationship. She subsequently found out about the deficiency of the marriage and claimed, *inter alia,* an order declaring the marriage to be void. She also applied for an order declaring the children born of the marriage to be legitimate and that the assets she brought into the marriage be returned to her. The court granted the plaintiff's application.	Die verweerder het na sy vrou se dood met sy stiefdogter (eiseres) in die huwelik getree. Die eiseres het geglo dat sy 'n geldige huwelik gesluit het en was onbewus daarvan dat die huwelik nietig was omdat die partye binne die verbode grade van verwantskap aan mekaar verwant was. Sy het later uitgevind dat die huwelik ongeldig was en toe onder andere aansoek gedoen dat dit nietig verklaar word. Sy het verder aansoek gedoen dat die kinders wat uit die huwelik gebore is binne-egtelik verklaar word en dat die bates wat sy in die huwelik ingebring het aan haar teruggegee word. Die hof het die eiseres se aansoek toegestaan.

DE VOS HUGO R: [116] As albei of een van die partye *bona fide* glo dat die huwelik geldig is dan is dit 'n gewaande huwelik *(matrimonium putativum)* – vide H *(wrongly called C) v C,* 1929 TPD 992 op bl 994; *Ex parte L (also known as A),* 1947 (3) SA 50 (C) op bl 58.

In *H v C, supra,* is beslis dat kinders gebore uit 'n gewaande huwelik wettig is. Hierdie sienswyse is gevolg in 'n menigte ander beslissings waaronder genoem kan word *Ex parte Azar,* 1932 OPD 107; *Ex parte L, supra; Potgieter v Bellingan,* 1940 EDL 264 en *Prinsloo v Prinsloo,* 1958 (3) SA 759 (T).

Ten spyte van die bevinding, wat blykbaar heeltemal ongekwalifiseerd gemaak is, dat kinders uit 'n gewaande huwelik gebore wettig is, loop die beslissings tog uiteen wat betref die ongekwalifiseerdheid van die wettigverklaring van die kinders. So bv is daar wettigverklaring met voorbehoude in *H v C, supra; Potgieter v Bellingan, supra;* en *Lionel v Hepworth,* 1933 CPD 481. Dan is daar gevalle waarin wettigverklaring sonder voorbehoud geskied het: *Ex parte Azar, supra; Ex parte L, supra; Ex parte Soobiah and Others: In re Estate Pillay,* 1948 (1) SA 873 (N) op bl 883.

In die gevalle waarin daar 'n gekwalifiseerde wettigverklaring van die kinders gemaak is, was die hoofoorweging die feit dat alle belanghebbendes nie voor die Hof was nie en selfs in die gevalle waarin daar 'n ongekwalifiseerde wettigverklaring gemaak is met die uitsondering van *Ex parte Azar, supra,* het die Hof tog aandag aan die vraag gegee of die belanghebbendes nie daardeur benadeel sal word nie. Logies beskou is hierdie sienswyse moeilik te regverdig want as die kinders van 'n gewaande huwelik wettig gebore is dan kan die belange van ander niks aan hierdie feit verander nie ... [117] Die belange van die kinders wat uit die gewaande huwelik gebore is word tog seker die beste gedien deur te verklaar dat hulle wettig-gebore is. Dit is bloot erkenning van hul wettige status. Die groot voordeel hiervan is dat hulle dan by versterf gelyklik van albei ouers erf. Ek is nie bewus van enige nadeel wat so 'n verklaring vir hulle kan inhou nie. Kinders wat meer moeilikheid gee is kinders wat 'n beter erfenis sou bekom het as dit nie was dat die kinders uit die gewaande huwelik as erfgename bykom nie. Kinders van die kant van die eggenoot wat te goeder trou in die gewaande huwelik was het niks te kla nie omdat hulle teen die erflater geen regskending kan inbring as gevolg waarvan hulle erfdeel verminder kan word nie. Kinders van die kant van die erflater wat nie te goeder trou was nie het ook geen grond om te kla nie want as hulle erfdeel verminder word as gevolg van 'n regskendende daad deur die erflatende eggenoot wat te kwader trou was dan is dit 'n klag wat teen die oortredende eggenoot geldend gemaak moet word en seker nie teen die kinders van die onskuldige eggenoot en tot hulle nadeel nie. Hulle kan nie net die goeie uit die hand van die erflater ontvang en nie ook die nadelige gevolge van sy onregmatige handelinge nie. Ewemin kan die kinders uit die gewaande huwelik kla as ander kinders van die erflater wat te kwader trou in die gewaande huwelik was met hulle die erfenis deel . . . want ook hulle ontvang die goeie en die kwaaie uit die hand van die oortredende erflater. Wat hier van die kinders van die eggenotes van die gewaande huwelik gesê is, geld *a fortiori* ook vir verder verwyderde erfgename.

M.i. moet die bede vir die wettigverklaring van die kinders in die onderhawige geval slaag . . .

[Met betrekking tot die vrou se eis om teruggawe van dit wat sy in die huwelik ingebring het, vervolg DE VOS HUGO R:]

Die eiseres vra ook dat die goed wat sy in die huwelik ingebring het aan haar teruggegee moet word. Op grond van wat WAARNEMENDE REGTER OGILVIE THOMPSON (soos hy toe was) in *Ex parte L, supra* op bl 59, sê is dit 'n beskeie eis. 'n Gewaande huwelik het gemeenskap van goed tot gevolg sodat daar by nietigverklaring van die huwelik verdeling van die gemeenskaplike boedel kan wees. Die eiseres vra minder as dit. Haar eis slaag dus . . .

Note

This case deals with the patrimonial consequences of a putative marriage and with the status of the children born of such a marriage.

As far as the status of the children is concerned, the main question is whether or not these children are legitimate. *Bam v Bhabha* 1947 4 SA 798 (A) is the only reported Appellate Division decision on this point. However, the majority of the court left the matter open and did not express any opinion on it. The court decided the matter in its capacity as upper guardian of all children and held that it would be in the child's best interests to be placed with its mother. (SCHREINER JA, however, held that the child was illegitimate but this decision was based on the court's finding that there was no marriage (putative or otherwise) between the child's parents). This decision is therefore of no assistance in answering the question whether the children born of a putative marriage are legitimate or not. Nowadays it is, however, generally accepted that such children are legitimate, and in *M v M* this view was applied. (See also *H v C* 1929 TPD 992; *Ex parte Azar* 1932 OPD 107; *Ex parte L (also known as A)* 1947 3 SA 50 (C); *Ex parte Soobiah: In re*

Aantekening

Hierdie saak handel oor die vermoënsregtelike gevolge van 'n putatiewe huwelik asook oor die status van die kinders wat uit sodanige huwelik gebore word.

Wat die status van die kinders betref, is die belangrikste vraag of hulle binne-egtelik is of nie. *Bam v Bhabha* 1947 4 SA 798 (A) is die enigste gerapporteerde uitspraak van die Appèlafdeling wat oor hierdie aangeleentheid handel. Die meerderheid van die hof het die vraag egter oopgelaat en het geen mening daaroor uitgespreek nie. Die hof het in sy hoedanigheid as oppervoog van alle minderjariges oor die aangeleentheid beslis en het bevind dat dit in belang van die kind sou wees om in die sorg van haar moeder geplaas te word. (SCHREINER AR het egter beslis dat die kind buite-egtelik was maar hierdie beslissing het berus op die hof se bevinding dat daar geen huwelik (putatief of andersins) tussen die kind se ouers tot stand gekom het nie.) Hierdie beslissing is dus van geen hulp by beantwoording van die vraag of die kinders wat uit 'n putatiewe huwelik gebore word binne-egtelik is of nie. Deesdae word egter algemeen aanvaar dat sodanige kinders binne-egtelik is, en in *M v M* is hierdie standpunt

Estate Pillay 1948 1 SA 873 (N); *Rampatha v Chundervathee* 1957 4 SA 483 (N); *Prinsloo v Prinsloo* 1958 3 SA 759 (T); *Naicker v Naidoo* 1959 3 SA 768 (D); *Khan v Khatija* 1959 2 PH B26 (D); *Shields v Shields* 1959 4 SA 16 (W); *Vather v Seedat* 1974 3 SA 389 (N); *Moola v Aulsebrook* [71]; *Ngubane v Ngubane* [74].) The children are legitimate by virtue of the fact that their parents were parties to a putative marriage and not by virtue of the court order declaring them to be legitimate. They are born legitimate and the court simply issues a declaratory order. As the court put it in the case under discussion (117): "Dit is bloot erkenning van hul wettige status."

See also *Moola v Aulsebrook* [71] and *Ngubane v Ngubane* [74].

As far as the patrimonial consequences of a putative marriage are concerned, a distinction has to be drawn between the claim of the *bona fide* party and that of the *mala fide* party.

If both parties were *bona fide* and they did not enter into an antenuptial contract they will be deemed to have been married in community of property (Hahlo 115; Barnard, Cronjé and Olivier 180). Van der Vyver and Joubert 521 are of the opinion that the court will in such an instance view the matter as if the parties had entered into a universal partnership and that they intended to share equally in the proceeds of the partnership. (See also Joubert *Family Law Service* A64 and Barnard, Cronjé and Olivier 180.) If only one of the parties was *bona fide*, community of property will occur if the *bona fide* party will benefit thereby (Hahlo 115; Van der Vyver and Joubert 521; Barnard, Cronjé and Olivier 180; Joubert *Family Law Service* A64). In the case under discussion the plaintiff could therefore have claimed that community of property existed between her and the defendant.

Where the parties entered into an antenuptial contract and they were both *bona fide* the antenuptial contract will, according to Hahlo (115), be binding upon both of them. Joubert (*Family Law Service* A64) is, however, of a different opinion. He argues that the antenuptial contract will be invalid irrespective of whether one or both parties were *bona fide* (see also Van der Vyver and Joubert 521), but that the *bona fide* party will be able to claim any benefits due to him in terms of the antenuptial contract. Whichever opinion

toegepas. (Sien ook *H v C* 1929 TPA 992; *Ex parte Azar* 1932 OPA 107; *Ex parte L (also known as A)* 1947 3 SA 50 (K); *Ex parte Soobiah: In re Estate Pillay* 1948 1 SA 873 (N); *Rampatha v Chundervathee* 1957 4 SA 483 (N); *Prinsloo v Prinsloo* 1958 3 SA 759 (T); *Naicker v Naidoo* 1959 3 SA 768 (D); *Khan v Khatija* 1959 2 PH B26 (D); *Shields v Shields* 1959 4 SA 16 (W); *Vather v Seedat* 1974 3 SA 389 (N); *Moola v Aulsebrook* [71]; *Ngubane v Ngubane* [74].) Die kinders is binne-egtelik op grond van die feit dat hulle ouers 'n putatiewe huwelik gesluit het en nie op grond van die hof se verklaring dat hulle binne-egtelik is nie. Hulle word binne-egtelik gebore en die hof reik dus bloot 'n verklarende bevel uit. Dit is soos volg gestel in die saak onder bespreking (117): "Dit is bloot erkenning van hul wettige status."

Sien ook *Moola v Aulsebrook* [71] en *Ngubane v Ngubane* [74].

Met betrekking tot die vermoënsregtelike gevolge van 'n putatiewe huwelik moet 'n onderskeid getref word tussen die aanspraak van die *bona fide* party en dié van die *mala fide* party.

Indien albei partye *bona fide* was en geen huweliksvoorwaardeskontrak gesluit het nie, sal geag word dat hulle binne gemeenskap van goed getroud is (Hahlo 115; Barnard, Cronjé en Olivier 184). Van der Vyver en Joubert 521 huldig die mening dat die hof in sodanige geval die aangeleentheid sal beskou asof die partye 'n universele vennootskap aangegaan het en beoog het om gelykop in die opbrengs van die vennootskap te deel. (Sien ook Joubert *Family Law Service* A64 en Barnard, Cronjé en Olivier 184.) Indien net een van die partye *bona fide* was, sal gemeenskap van goed intree slegs indien dit tot voordeel van die *bona fide* party strek (Hahlo 115; Van der Vyver en Joubert 521; Barnard, Cronjé en Olivier 184; Joubert *Family Law Service* A64). In die onderhawige saak sou die eiseres dus daarop aanspraak kon maak dat gemeenskap van goed tussen haar en die verweerder ingetree het.

Indien die partye 'n huweliksvoorwaardeskontrak gesluit het en beide *bona fide* was, is Hahlo (115) van mening dat die huweliksvoorwaardeskontrak hulle albei sal bind. Joubert (*Family Law Service* A64) is egter 'n ander mening toegedaan. Hy voer aan dat die huweliksvoorwaardeskontrak ongeldig sal wees ongeag of een of beide partye *bona fide* was (sien ook Van der Vyver en Joubert 521), maar dat die *bona fide* party wel

one accepts, it is clear that the *bona fide* party can lay claim to the benefits conferred upon him by virtue of the antenuptial contract (Hahlo 115; Van der Vyver and Joubert 521; Barnard, Cronjé and Olivier 180; Joubert *Family Law Service* A64. See also Lee 1954 *Butterworths South African Law Review* 40). The *mala fide* party will, however, not be able to claim any benefits under the antenuptial contract and if any such benefits had already been conferred upon him he would have to return those (Van der Vyver and Joubert 521).

enige voordeel sal kan eis wat hom ingevolge die huweliksvoorwaardeskontrak toekom. Afgesien van welke een van hierdie menings ook al aanvaar word, is dit duidelik dat die *bona fide* party die voordele wat hom ingevolge die huweliks-voorwaardeskontrak toekom, sal kan vorder (Hahlo 115; Van der Vyver en Joubert 521; Barnard, Cronjé en Olivier 184; Joubert *Family Law Service* A64. Sien ook Lee 1954 *Butterworths South African Law Review* 40). Die *mala fide* party sal egter geen aanspraak kan maak op enige voordele wat hom ingevolge die huweliksvoorwaardes-kontrak toekom nie en indien enige sodanige voordele reeds aan hom toegeval het, sal hy dit moet teruggee (Van der Vyver en Joubert 521).

[74] NGUBANE V NGUBANE

1983 2 SA 770 (T)

The status of children born of a putative marriage

When the appellant (husband) and the respondent (wife) entered into marriage the respondent was unaware of the fact that the appellant was already a party to a valid marriage. The respondent claimed an order declaring their marriage to be void. The appellant conceded that the marriage was void *ab initio*. He pleaded, however, that the marriage was putative and applied for an order declaring the children born of the marriage to be legitimate. The court *a quo* declared the marriage void but declined to make a finding on the legitimacy of the children on the ground that the parent applying for the order had not been a *bona fide* party to the marriage. The appellant appealed against that part of the court order which did not declare the children to be legitimate. The appeal was successful.

Die status van kinders gebore uit 'n putatiewe huwelik

Toe die appellant (man) en die respondent (vrou) in die huwelik getree het, was die respondent onbewus daarvan dat die appellant alreeds met iemand anders getroud was. Die respondent het aansoek gedoen om 'n bevel dat die huwelik nietig verklaar word. Die appellant het erken dat die huwelik *ab initio* nietig was. Hy het egter aangevoer dat die huwelik putatief was en het aansoek gedoen dat die kinders wat uit die huwelik gebore is binne-egtelik verklaar word. Die hof *a quo* het die huwelik nietig verklaar maar geweier om te beslis of die kinders binne-egtelik was op grond daarvan dat die ouer wat om die bevel aansoek gedoen het, nie die *bona fide* party tot die huwelik was nie. Die appellant het geappelleer teen die gedeelte van die hofbevel wat die kinders nie binne-egtelik verklaar het nie. Die appèl het geslaag.

GORDON J: [771] The president [of the court *a quo*], in his reasons, stated *inter alia*:

"The only question to decide on a balance of probabilities was whether the defendant acted *bona fide* when he married the plaintiff. See Hahlo *The South African Law of Husband and Wife* 4th ed at 496:

'Where both parties acted *bona fide*, application to have the children declared legitimate may be made by either spouse. When only one party was *bona fide*, that party alone can apply.' "...

[772] It is clear from his reasons that the president refrained from making an order as to whether the marriage was putative and the children legitimate because of his finding that the parent applying for the order was not a *bona fide* party to the "marriage". He relied for this on the above-quoted passage in *Hahlo* (at 496)...

[773] As regards the passage in *Hahlo* relied on by the president, I doubt whether the learned author intended to convey that a court would legally be precluded, under any circumstances, from determining legitimacy of children simply because the party seeking an order of legitimacy was not a *bona fide* party to the "marriage". None of the authorities referred to by the author in support of what is stated in the passage would appear to support such a proposition and neither counsel were able to refer to any authority which did. In a later passage, *Hahlo* refers to the fact that a court has *mero motu* declared children to be offspring of a putative marriage and hence legitimate. *Hahlo* (*supra* at 495–496) says:

"According to our institutional writers, the children of a putative marriage *are* legitimate, and that this is so in modern law too finds support in *Prinsloo v Prinsloo* 1958 (3) SA 759 (where the Court declared the child legitimate *mero motu*)."

In *Ex parte L (also known as A)* 1947 (3) SA 50 (C) OGILVIE THOMPSON AJ says at 58:

" ... In *H (wrongly called C) v C* 1929 TPD 992 it was held that, despite some (authority) to the contrary, the weight of Roman-Dutch authority was in favour of the view that the issue of a putative marriage is legitimate; and that our Courts will, in a proper case, so declare such an issue. As the marriage with which the Court was in that case concerned was a bigamous marriage, the Court went on to point out that, on the authorities, a declaration of legitimacy may be made provided one of the putative spouses *bona fide* believed the marriage to be lawful ..."

In Lee and Honoré *SA Law of Property, Family Relations and Succession,* the following appears (para 396):

"The Court has declined in some cases to make a declaration of legitimacy where the children were not represented: *Lionel v Hepworth* 1933 CPD 481; *Potgieter v Bellingan* 1940 EDL 264 [28]. The reasons for such refusal do not appear to be convincing. In *Potgieter's* case the Court appears to have thought that the declaration of legitimacy of the issue of a putative marriage is an example of the prerogative of the *princeps* (see para 398). But the Canon law (which in this respect appears to be the law of South Africa) is quite explicit on the point: once a purported marriage is found to be putative, the legitimacy of the children is an inevitable result. A declaration of legitimacy, if one follows, is no more than a judicial recognition of an existing fact. Absence of such a declaration cannot make a legitimate child illegitimate, nor is such a child illegitimate until it has been pronounced legitimate."

In *Bam v Bhabha* 1947 (4) SA 798 (A) SCHREINER JA says at 809:

"Although the recognition of the legitimacy of the children born of putative marriages may rest primarily on the consideration of fairness to the children (considerations which are not thought sufficient in the case of the children of other extra-marital unions) I am not satisfied that there is sufficient reason for distinguishing, for present purposes, between the case of a legitimate child who is the offspring of a valid subsisting marriage and a legitimate child who is the offspring of an invalid but putative marriage."

There is thus ample authority for the proposition that where *one* of the parties to a marriage is *bona fide* then, provided the other conditions are satisfied, the marriage *is* putative and the children *are* legitimate for all purposes as if they are offspring of a valid and subsisting marriage. The "other conditions" referred to relate to acceptable [774] evidence of cohabitation and repute and of a marriage ceremony performed by a marriage officer . . .

It is my view that a court, in an appropriate case, is not precluded from determining issues of a putative marriage and legitimacy, merely because the party applying for an order in this regard is not a *bona fide* party to the "marriage". In my view the present case was one where these issues should not have been left in the air. It was clearly in the interests of the children that an appropriate order be made. On the facts it was common cause that one of the parties was *bona fide*, and that the "marriage" was performed by a marriage officer. It is also common cause that the parties had lived together as a married couple and that their children were accepted as being the offspring of a valid marriage. On the evidence, then, the marriage was legally a putative one, with the consequence that the children *are* legitimate. An appropriate order could and should have been made on application by either party or, in the absence of such application, then *mero motu*, despite the fact that there was no *curator ad litem* representing the children. To this extent, then, the appeal succeeds . . .

LE ROUX J concurred.

Note

The importance of this case is that it clarifies the position regarding the *locus standi* of the *mala fide* party to a putative marriage to apply for a declaratory order regarding the status of the children born of such a marriage.

The references in this case to Hahlo are to the fourth edition of his *The South African Law of Husband and Wife*. In the fifth edition of this work, Hahlo (114) makes it quite clear that the court order declaring a child born of a putative marriage to be legitimate is merely declaratory. It does not alter the status of the child. There is therefore no reason why the *mala fide* party to the putative marriage cannot apply for the order.

The declaratory order regarding the status of the children can therefore be issued at the instance of either party to the putative marriage, whether that party was *bona fide* or not. The order can also be sought by any other interested person, such as the child himself (Hahlo 114; Joubert *Family Law Service* A65; Van der Vyver and Joubert 520). See further Bedil 1984 *SALJ* 231.

See also *M v M* [73]; *Moola v Aulsebrook* [71].

Aantekening

Die belang van hierdie saak is daarin geleë dat dit die posisie opklaar rakende die *locus standi* van die *mala fide* party tot 'n putatiewe huwelik om aansoek te doen om 'n verklarende bevel rakende die status van die kinders wat uit sodanige huwelik gebore is.

Die verwysings in hierdie saak na Hahlo is na die vierde uitgawe van sy *The South African Law of Husband and Wife*. In die vyfde uitgawe van hierdie werk stel Hahlo (114) dit duidelik dat die hofbevel wat 'n kind wat uit 'n putatiewe huwelik gebore is binne-egtelik verklaar bloot verklarend is. Dit verander nie die status van die kind nie. Daar bestaan dus geen rede waarom die *mala fide* party tot die putatiewe huwelik nie ook om die bevel aansoek kan doen nie.

Die verklarende bevel rakende die status van die kinders kan dus toegestaan word op grond van die aansoek van enige van die partye tot die putatiewe huwelik, of daardie party nou die *bona fide* party was of nie. Enige ander persoon wat 'n belang by die aangeleentheid het, kan ook om die bevel aansoek doen, byvoorbeeld die kind self (Hahlo 114; Joubert *Family Law Service* A65; Van der Vyver en Joubert 520). Sien verder Bedil 1984 *SALJ* 231.

Sien ook *M v M* [73] en *Moola v Aulsebrook* [71].

The invariable consequences of marriage

Consortium omnis vitae
Reciprocal maintenance
Matrimonial home

Die onveranderbare gevolge van die huwelik

Consortium omnis vitae
Wedersydse onderhoud
Gades se woning

Consortium omnis vitae

Consortium omnis vitae

[75]   GROBBELAAR V HAVENGA

1964 3 SA 522 (N)

Action for enticement

The plaintiff claimed satisfaction for non-patrimonial damage which he allegedly suffered as a result of the enticement of his wife and the alienation of her affection from him by the defendant. The court ordered absolution from the instance; in other words the plaintiff was unsuccessful.

Aksie weens afrokkeling

Die eiser het genoegdoening geëis vir nadeel wat hy na bewering gely het weens die afrokkeling van sy vrou en die vervreemding van haar gevoelens teenoor hom deur die verweerder. Die hof het absolusie van die instansie beveel; met ander woorde die eiser was onsuksesvol.

HARCOURT J: [525] I am unable to accept Mr *Leon's* [for the defendant] contention that the true gist of the cause of action in cases such as this is for the loss of affection of the wife. It is true that this aspect may have loomed large in certain cases, but basically, as was said by LORD JUSTICE SCRUTTON in the case of *Place v Searle*, (1932) 2 KB 497 at p 512,

"... a husband has a right to the *consortium* of his wife, and the wife to the *consortium* of her husband, and ... each has a cause of action against a third party who, without justification, destroys that *consortium*".

As is remarked by Prof Hahlo in his work, *South African Law of Husband and Wife*, 2nd ed at p 109, the action for enticement protects the *consortium* existing between spouses against intentional destruction by a third party ...

The decision in *Searle's* case was specifically approved by the House of Lords in the case of *Best v Samuel Fox & Co Ltd*, (1952) 2 All ER 394, and this concept of *consortium* is, as I appreciate it, an abstraction comprising the totality of a number of rights, duties and advantages accruing to spouses of a marriage. It was, in my judgment, well described by LORD JUSTICE BIRKETT in *Best's* case in the Court of Appeal, (1951) 2 KB 639 at p 665, as follows:

"Companionship, love, affection, comfort, mutual services, sexual intercourse – all belong to the married state. Taken together, they make up the *consortium;* but I cannot think that the loss of one element, however grievous it may be, as it undoubtedly is in the present case, can be regarded as the loss of the *consortium* within the meaning of the decided cases. Still less could any impairment of one of the elements be so regarded. *Consortium*, I think, is one and indivisible. The law gives a remedy for its loss, but for nothing short of that."

Now this was approved by the House of Lords in *Best's* case when it proceeded as far as that tribunal. Thus LORD PORTER in his speech said the following:

"As however BIRKETT and COHEN, LJJ, decided the case in the Court of Appeal on a different ground, namely that *consortium* is one and indivisible and the wife has not lost it as a whole, and as LORD JUSTICE ASQUITH agreed with this contention, I think it desirable that I should express a tentative opinion on it. My Lords, I think there is much to be said for this view and, indeed, I find it difficult to draw the boundary between what is and what is not loss of *consortium* or to divide it into its component parts."

A more definite expression of view was given by LORD GODDARD where at pp 399 to 400, he delivered himself as follows:

"But as all the members of the Court of Appeal dealt with this matter and it was elaborately argued at the Bar, I think one ought to express an opinion, and I am in agreement with the Court of Appeal. *Consortium* seems to me to be essentially an abstraction. Where the exercise of a profession or the call of duty involves prolonged absence abroad of one of the spouses there is not an interruption of *consortium,* nor is there because one of them may become a permanent invalid to be waited on and nursed by the other. Again, there may be loss of affection, but, provided the spouses continue to live together as man and wife, it seems to me that it still exists however different life may be from the days of the honeymoon. Sexual relations are, doubtless, a most important part of the marriage relation, but, if age or illness or even disinclination impairs the potency of either of the spouses who continue to live together as [526] husband and wife, I do not think the *consortium* is affected. It would be only if on this account one of them withdrew and decided to live apart."

Now, the case of *Place v Searle* was quoted with approval in the case of *Rosenbaum v Margolis,* 1944 WLD 147 at p 151, and was referred to with apparent approval in the case of *Woodiwiss v Woodiwiss,* 1958 (3) SA 609 (D) at p 616. This last-mentioned case also specifically referred to *Best's* case, *supra,* as authority for the formulation therein of the cause of action in such cases. Thus, as was said at p 617:

"It seems that the plaintiff in these cases must prove that the third party has acted, and done so successfully, with the deliberate object of enticing the wife to leave her husband and thus deprive him of her *consortium* (*Pearce v Kevan,* pp 914–915; *Best v Samuel Fox & Co,* (1952) 2 AER 394 HL)."

In *Pearce v Kevan,* here specifically referred to with approval, SELKE, J, propounded the position as follows:

"As I understand it, the law material for the purposes of my decision may be stated briefly as follows: It is the duty of a wife to reside and consort with her husband, and any third person, who intentionally causes her to violate this duty, commits a wrong against the husband for which the latter is entitled to recover damages unless the third person acted from lawful motives, eg to protect her from her husband's ill-treatment, real or genuinely supposed. It is obvious that there must be a causative connection between the conduct of the third person and the dereliction by the wife of the duties she owes her husband, and the law as I have endeavoured to state it potentially embraces the conduct of a man who, whatever his immediate objects may be, perseveres in behaving towards another man's wife in a way which he realises is having the effect of alienating her affections from her husband, and which ultimately produces that result, and brings about an estrangement."

The emphasis in all these cases on the aspects of *consortium* renders it impermissible, in my view, to take the narrow view contended for by Mr *Leon* . . .

In my view . . . it suffices to say that however lacking in affection the plaintiff and his wife may have been, and I express no view in this regard, they consorted with each other, shared a common home and a common bank account and other activities which may properly be held to be comprised in the term *consortium* . . . Furthermore, the plaintiff, in my judgment, had a legal right to be protected in his enjoyment of that *consortium.* In addition, it also seems to me that, on the legal side, there are allegations in the declaration that, as a result of the defendant's alleged conduct, the plaintiff has been injured in his dignity, good name and reputation. These are proper items of claim in a case such as the present, as I appreciate the judgment in *Pearce v Kevan, supra* at pp 914–5.

As to the question of causation, the plaintiff in this case relies upon a cause of conduct spread over a period. In such circumstances as was said by MILNE, J, as he then was, in *Woodiwiss's* case:

> "When it comes, then, to proving that the latter deliberately enticed the wife away without his having implored or adjured her to do so, one can well imagine that, over a period of many months, a hundred or a thousand things may have been said or done to produce the desired result. It might take a plaintiff much time and cause him much labour and expense to procure the requisite evidence. At a stage where he has not collected all of it (he might never have to collect it all, as might be the case where the matter was suitably compromised out of Court) but has gathered enough to produce in him a *bona fide* [527] and reasonable belief that he has a good case and starts his action accordingly, I doubt whether he should be required to give detailed particulars even to the extent of his existing knowledge." ...

[528] At the outset it seems to me desirable to examine the state of the marriage which existed between the plaintiff and his wife, since this is not only relevant to the nature of the *consortium* which the plaintiff was then enjoying, but also as affecting the probabilities concerning the actions of the actors in this somewhat sordid matrimonial drama. It is also directly relevant to the credibility of the plaintiff, who claimed [529] that his marriage was an exceptionally happy one, and the plaintiff's wife, who claimed that it was almost exactly the reverse, in truth a cat and dog existence which had tested her endurance almost to breaking point. It is also relevant in regard to the motivation of the plaintiff's wife in leaving the plaintiff, and any possible causative responsibility on the defendant's part for such departure.

[The learned HARCOURT J then analysed the evidence and proceeded:]

Here there is no affirmative evidence of active enticement by the defendant, and the inferential proof is no more, in my view, than a resort to the barren logical fallacy of *post hoc, ergo propter hoc* [after this; therefore in consequence of this]. Any value to be attached to such inference is also greatly diminished because of the facts, which I found established, that the plaintiff's wife was thoroughly unhappy, and apparently poised on the brink of marital infidelity when she met the defendant. Viewing the totality of the evidence as a whole, I am quite unable to conclude that the defendant has acted, and done so successfully, in enticing away the plaintiff's wife. I find no more than that mentioned by MILNE, J, as being insufficient in *Woodiwiss's* case, where he says:

> "It would not be enough for the plaintiff to prove that the first defendant left him after frequent and continued association with the second defendant, or even in consequence of such association, for a wife might leave her husband of her own sweet will, in order to make herself more accessible to the other man, especially if he had, up till then, had some scruples about breaking up a happy home."

In truth, I would find difficulty in even going so far as to hold that the plaintiff's wife left him *in consequence of* her association with the defendant. Still less can I find that there was any coaxing or talking over or persuasion by the defendant as required by LUDORF, J, in *Van den Berg v Jooste*, 1960 (3) SA 71 (W) at p 73. Thus, in my view, the plaintiff has failed to discharge the *onus* upon him. Since there is a theoretical possibility that the plaintiff may procure further evidence and, particularly, because I am not convinced of the truthfulness of the defendant's evidence relative to his attraction to the plaintiff's wife at the commencement of their association, I think that the proper order should be for one of absolution from the instance ...

Note

A spouse has a claim on the ground of enticement if the *consortium omnis vitae* between the spouses has been infringed by a third party's enticing the other spouse away. *Consortium omnis vitae* is therefore the central issue in an action based on enticement, adultery or harbouring. In this case *consortium omnis vitae* was explained as being "an abstraction comprising the totality of a number of rights, duties and advantages accruing to spouses of a marriage" (525). This explanation was accepted and expanded on in *Peter v Minister of Law and Order* 1990 4 SA 6 (E). In *Peter* the court stated that "intangibles, such as loyalty and sympathetic care and affection, concern etc; as well as the more material needs of life, such as physical care, financial support, the rendering of services in the running of the common household or in a support-generating business, etc" are included under *consortium omnis vitae* (9G–H). (See also 10C where the court emphasised that the "matrimonial *consortium* embraces not only the non-material aspects of marriage, but also the material aspects thereof".)

On the meaning of *consortium omnis vitae* see further Barnard, Cronjé and Olivier 182 *et seq* 256 *et seq*; Church 1979 *THRHR* 376 379; Church and Parmanand 1987 *CILSA* 230 232–235; Robinson 1991 *THRHR* 508.

It must be emphasised that, in order to be successful in an action based on enticement, the plaintiff must prove that the enticer actively incited or persuaded the plaintiff's spouse to leave him resulting in the alienation of her affection for him (*Van den Berg v Jooste* 1960 3 SA 71 (W); *Wassenaar v Jameson* [76]). He must also prove that the third party acted intentionally, that is with the specific purpose of persuading her to desert the plaintiff, and by so doing deprived him of the *consortium* (*Woodiwiss v Woodiwiss* 1958 3 SA 609 (D); Barnard, Cronjé and Olivier 188). Damages may be claimed for pecuniary loss as well as for injured feelings (Hahlo 145; Barnard, Cronjé and Olivier 188; Lee and Honoré 42).

Both the husband and the wife can institute the action although the wife's action was only recognised in later decisions (*Rosenbaum v Margolis* 1944 WLD 147; *Foulds v Smith* 1950 1 SA 1 (A)).

See also *Wassenaar v Jameson* [76].

Aantekening

'n Gade het 'n eis op grond van afrokkeling indien daar as gevolg van afrokkeling deur 'n derde inbreuk gemaak is op die *consortium omnis vitae* tussen die gades. *Consortium omnis vitae* is dus van kardinale belang by 'n aksie op grond van afrokkeling, sowel as in 'n aksie op grond van owerspel of herberging. In die onderhawige saak is die begrip *consortium omnis vitae* verduidelik as "an abstraction comprising the totality of a number of rights, duties and advantages accruing to spouses of a marriage" (525). Hierdie verduideliking is bevestig en uitgebrei in *Peter v Minister of Law and Order* 1990 4 SA 6 (OK). In *Peter* het die hof verklaar dat "intangibles, such as loyalty and sympathetic care and affection, concern etc; as well as the more material needs of life, such as physical care, financial support, the rendering of services in the running of the common household or in a support-generating business, etc" onder *consortium omnis vitae* ingesluit word (9G–H). (Sien ook 10C waar die hof beklemtoon het dat die "matrimonial *consortium* embraces not only the non-material aspects of marriage, but also the material aspects thereof".)

Oor die betekenis van *consortium omnis vitae* sien verder Barnard, Cronjé en Olivier 186 ev 265 ev; Church 1979 *THRHR* 376 379; Church en Parmanand 1987 *CILSA* 230 232–235; Robinson 1991 *THRHR* 508.

Daar moet beklemtoon word dat die eiser, ten einde suksesvol te wees in sy aksie op grond van afrokkeling, moet bewys dat die afrokkelaar die eiser se gade daadwerklik aangehits of omgepraat het om hom te verlaat en dat sy as gevolg daarvan haar liefde vir hom verloor het (*Van den Berg v Jooste* 1960 3 SA 71 (W); *Wassenaar v Jameson* [76]). Hy moet ook bewys dat die derde party opsetlik gehandel het, dit wil sê met die bewuste oogmerk om haar te oorreed om die eiser te verlaat en hom sodoende van die *consortium* te beroof (*Woodiwiss v Woodiwiss* 1958 3 SA 609 (D); Barnard, Cronjé en Olivier 192). Vergoeding kan vir vermoënskade sowel as vir gekrenkte gevoelens geëis word (Hahlo 145; Barnard, Cronjé en Olivier 192; Lee en Honoré 42).

Die man sowel as die vrou kan die aksie instel alhoewel die vrou se aksie eers in later beslissings erken is (*Rosenbaum v Margolis* 1944 WPA 147; *Foulds v Smith* 1950 1 SA 1 (A)).

Sien ook *Wassenaar v Jameson* [76].

[76] WASSENAAR V JAMESON

1969 2 SA 349 (W)

Interdict to prevent spouse from committing adultery

The applicant applied for an order interdicting the respondent from committing adultery with, meeting, corresponding, visiting, or in any way communicating with the applicant's wife. The applicant's wife and the respondent, who was also married, were prominent golfers. During a golf tournament they fell in love with each other and committed adultery. This threatened to break up the applicant's marriage but a reconciliation was affected between the applicant and his wife. Both the applicant's wife and the respondent undertook not to associate with each other again. The applicant and his wife then lived together for three years, he contended that the reconciliation was complete and that they lived happily together. Their second child was conceived shortly after the reconciliation and was born during this period. The applicant's wife, however, said that although she made every effort to make the reconciliation happy, and pretended to the applicant that she was happy, these were the three most miserable years of her life, for she was still in love with the respondent. She then again met the respondent and their former liaison was renewed. They went to Durban together and committed adultery once again. When she returned to Johannesburg she did not return to her husband but stayed with friends and said that she had no intention of returning to him and that she wanted to marry the respondent whenever that became possible. The applicant, who wanted to save his marriage, averred that the respondent was the cause of its threatened break-up, that his wife was merely infatuated with the respondent, and that if the respondent were interdicted from seeing, communicating and consorting with her, that infatuation would pass and they would be reconciled and

Interdik om gade te verbied om owerspel te pleeg

Die applikant het aansoek gedoen om 'n interdik om die respondent te verbied om met die applikant se vrou owerspel te pleeg, haar te ontmoet, met haar te korrespondeer, haar te besoek, of op enige wyse met haar in verbinding te tree. Die applikant se vrou en die respondent, wat ook getroud was, was vooraanstaande gholfspelers. Hulle het gedurende 'n gholftoernooi op mekaar verlief geraak en owerspel gepleeg. Dit het tot die dreigende verbrokkeling van die applikant se huwelik gelei maar 'n versoening is tussen die applikant en sy vrou bewerkstellig. Sowel die applikant se vrou as die respondent het onderneem om nie weer met mekaar in verbinding te tree nie. Die applikant en sy vrou het daarna vir drie jaar saamgewoon. Die applikant het beweer dat die versoening heeltemal geslaagd was en dat hulle gelukkig was. Hulle tweede kind is kort na die versoening verwek en is in hierdie tydperk gebore. Die applikant se vrou het egter beweer dat hoewel sy alle moontlike pogings aangewend het om die versoening te laat slaag en aan die applikant voorgegee het dat sy gelukkig was, dit die ongelukkigste drie jaar van haar lewe was, aangesien sy nog steeds vir die respondent lief was. Sy het die respondent toe weer ontmoet en hulle vorige verhouding is hervat. Hulle is saam Durban toe en het weer owerspel gepleeg. Nadat sy van Durban na Johannesburg teruggekeer het, het sy nie na haar man teruggekeer nie maar by vriende gebly en gesê dat sy nie van voornemens was om na hom terug te gaan nie en dat sy met die respondent wou trou sodra dit moontlik word. Die applikant, wat sy huwelik wou red, het beweer dat die respondent die oorsaak van die dreigende verbrokkeling daarvan was, dat sy vrou net op die respondent verlief was, en as die respondent verbied sou

happy again as had happened in the past. The court refused the interdict.

word om haar te sien, met haar te kommunikeer, of met haar te assosieer, die verliefdheid sou verbygaan en hulle versoen sou raak en weer gelukkig sou wees soos wat in die verlede gebeur het. Dit hof het geweier om die interdik toe te staan.

TROLLIP J: [351] [B]efore I can grant an interim interdict I have to be satisfied that the relevant legal requisites for such an interdict have been fulfilled . . .

The first enquiry is what delict has the applicant proved that the respondent has committed, and will continue to commit against him, for it is only on that basis that any interim or final interdict can be granted. It is essential, in my view, to embark upon this enquiry at the outset, in order to clarify the real and true issues in this case.

It is common cause that the respondent and the applicant's wife have committed adultery. That is a delict by the respondent against the applicant, and *prima facie* it would appear from the papers that further acts of adultery will probably be committed in future. Mr *Cilliers* [for the applicant] [352] maintained that applicant had also proved, at any rate *prima facie* at this stage, that the respondent had also enticed the applicant's wife away from him, or, as it is sometimes put, had alienated her affections for the applicant, and would continue to do so in the future. That would of course be a delict *vis-à-vis* the applicant, but has the applicant proved, even *prima facie*, that the respondent has committed such a delict?

According to the authorities, in order to prove such a delict, the applicant has to show not merely that his wife left him for the respondent, but that the respondent actually induced her to leave him, ie actively caused her to leave him, or, as was stated in *Van den Berg v Jooste*, 1960 (3) SA 71 (W), that he had coaxed her away from the applicant, that he had talked her over, or that he had persuaded her to leave the applicant, and as a result thereof she had lost her affection for him. That is usually a very formidable *onus* to discharge.

There is no need to canvass the facts in detail on this aspect. It suffices to say that the applicant alleges several acts of enticement on the part of the respondent, but they are all derived from what his wife is alleged to have told him. That constitutes hearsay evidence against the respondent, who in any event denies them. That, therefore, does not constitute even *prima facie* proof against the respondent . . .

Mr *Cilliers*, however, stated that the applicant's case on this aspect rests upon circumstantial evidence; but, even assuming the truth of all the applicant's allegations to the effect that their marriage was happy until the respondent appeared on the scene, and that thereafter her affections for him waned and ceased, and she left him, it cannot be inferred therefrom, even *prima facie* in my view, that the respondent was guilty of enticing her away. Such an attachment between a wife and third party usually arises and continues quite spontaneously and voluntarily, without any coaxing, persuading, or wooing on the latter's part. Indeed, in the present case it would appear that, so far from requiring any coaxing, persuading, or wooing from the respondent, the applicant's wife was not only a willing, but an enthusiastic party to the renewed liaison right from its very inception.

The applicant has therefore not proved *prima facie*, and in my view will not be able to prove . . . that the respondent has been guilty of any enticement or alienation of affections. That aspect therefore falls away. I need not consider, therefore, whether such a delict can beget an interdict such as is claimed in the present case.

I now turn to consider the only remaining aspect which concerns the adultery. Mr *Philips* [for the respondent] has cogently contended that our law does not recognise the remedy of interdict against committing adultery. That such an interdict cannot be obtained against the wife follows from *Ex parte AB*, 1910 TPD 1332, which decided that

"adultery by one spouse does not constitute a tort in respect of which the other spouse can claim compensation from the guilty spouse".

As the defending spouse, therefore, does not thereby commit a tort [delict], the innocent spouse could not get an interdict against him or her, but it does not necessarily follow that an interdict cannot be granted against the co-respondent. Mr *Philips*, apart from advancing reasons that such [353] a remedy should not be recognised, has pointed out that no case has been found in the researches of either counsel in which such an interdict has been granted here, in the United Kingdom, or the United States of America. That is indeed a strong indication that such a remedy is not accorded by the law...

Nevertheless, I have some difficulty in seeing why, as adultery by a third party constitutes an *injuria* to the innocent spouse, the remedy of interdict in appropriate cases should not in principle lie, for as Mr *Cilliers* contended, *ubi ius ibi remedium* [where there is a right there is a remedy]. However, I am diffident, with the limited time I have had at my disposal, to rule affirmatively that such a remedy is available...

Fortunately I find it unnecessary to decide that question. I shall assume in the applicant's favour that such a remedy is available to him.

It is clear that the Court has a discretion to grant or refuse an interdict, for it is an extraordinary remedy. That discretion is wider in the case of an interim than in a final interdict. It seems to me that, if available, an interdict against a third party committing adultery with the claimant's spouse should only be granted in very special or exceptional circumstances, for these reasons: (1) it is obviously an unusual or novel remedy, for so far it is unheard of; (2) it interferes with, and restricts the rights and freedom that the third party ordinarily has of using and disposing of his body as he chooses; (compare *Ex parte AB, supra* at pp 30 and 39); (3) it also affects the relationship of the third party with the claimant's spouse, who is and cannot be a party to the interdict, and therefore indirectly interferes with, and restricts her rights and freedom of, using and disposing of her body as she chooses; (4) it attempts to regulate conduct between the third party and the claimant's spouse, which springs from human emotions and passion. This differentiates it from other, ordinary relationships; (5) its enforcement gives rise to practical difficulties. These were mentioned in argument, and they need not be amplified here; (6) if adultery is subsequently committed, the claimant is not without remedy, for he has the remedies of divorce and damages.

The above were all reasons advanced by Mr *Philips* in his able argument about why the law should not recognise, and does not recognise, a remedy by way of interdict. On the assumption I have made the law does recognise such a remedy, but those reasons that I have set out above would undoubtedly induce the Court to be slow to grant that remedy.

In the present case there are no special or exceptional circumstances that would warrant this Court... granting such an interdict. There are only two circumstances that are relevant, and were relied upon.

Firstly, the applicant submits that an interdict would probably save his marriage and restore his wife's *consortium* to him. But the facts are [354] completely against that. They show that the marriage has probably broken up irretrievably...

[TROLLIP J set out the wife's evidence in regard to her attitude towards the marriage with the applicant and proceeded:]

Now, that shows in my view that according to the applicant's wife the marriage is now firmly on the rocks . . .

Mr *Cilliers* argued that in 1965 the parties did become reconciled, and the same could happen again, but I think that that incident is against the applicant. What the applicant's wife says in effect is that she genuinely attempted a reconciliation during that period, but that it failed, and that strengthens her in her attitude never to attempt it again. That being so there is no purpose in granting the interdict in trying to save the marriage, because the marriage is irretrievably lost.

The second circumstance relied upon by Mr *Cilliers* is that the applicant should not be subjected to the insult or humiliation of the respondent's continuing to commit adultery with his wife. That argument is not without substance, but its force is considerably weakened by the fact that, firstly, as already mentioned, his marriage has already broken up irretrievably, and his wife has left him. So that if they now commit adultery the insult or humiliation must of necessity be considerably lessened, especially as it has not been shown that the respondent enticed the applicant's wife away from him. Secondly, that much of that insult and humiliation is caused by his wife herself, who, as I have already said, is and would probably continue to be, judging by her affidavit, an enthusiastic party to the commission of any further adultery. Thirdly, [355] the applicant would be able to recover damages for such further adultery from the respondent.

There is no suggestion in the papers that the respondent could not afford to pay those damages. In that regard Mr *Cilliers* submitted that it would be wrong to relegate the applicant merely to his right to claim damages, thereby enabling the respondent virtually to purchase the right to commit adultery with the applicant's wife at the expense of insulting or humiliating the applicant.

In view of the fact that the applicant's marriage has now irretrievably broken up, and that he has irretrievably lost his wife's *consortium*, I do not think it is wrong to relegate him to his claim for damages.

It was also mentioned in the papers that the applicant had suffered patrimonial loss from the defection of his wife. In so far as that has resulted from his wife's leaving him, as the respondent has not been shown to be responsible for enticing her away, he would not be liable therefor, but, if he is, the applicant has his remedy for damages against the respondent, and that is not a ground, therefore, for granting him an interdict.

I have therefore come to the conclusion that on the papers the applicant would not be entitled to a final interdict, and is therefore not entitled to have the matter referred to evidence or trial, and is not entitled to any interim interdict. The application is therefore dismissed . . .

Note

It is clear from this case that the times when a husband could control his wife's personal life are past (Hahlo 132; 1969 *SALJ* 268; Lee and Honoré 49; Van der Vyver and Joubert 242). The only remedies available to the innocent spouse are an action for divorce against the spouse who has committed a breach of his matrimonial duties and an action in delict against the third party on the grounds of adultery or enticement as the case may be. With this action he can claim damages for patrimonial loss as well as for his injured

Aantekening

Dit is uit hierdie saak duidelik dat die dae toe 'n man sy vrou se persoonlike lewe kon beheer verby is (Hahlo 132; 1969 *SALJ* 268; Lee en Honoré 49; Van der Vyver en Joubert 242). Die enigste regsmiddele wat vir die onskuldige gade beskikbaar is, is 'n aksie om egskeiding teen die gade wat nie sy huweliksverpligtinge nagekom het nie en 'n deliktuele aksie teen die derde party op grond van owerspel of afrokkeling afhangende van wat die geval mag wees. Met hierdie aksie kan hy vergoeding eis vir vermoënskade

feelings (Hahlo 1969 *SALJ* 271; Van der Vyver and Joubert 682 *et seq*; Lee and Honoré 40 *et seq*).

As far as this case is concerned reference must also be made to *Amra v Amra* 1971 4 SA 409 (D) and *Osman v Osman* 1983 2 SA 706 (D). In the *Amra* case the court granted the applicant an order restraining her husband from entering into a marriage with another woman according to Muslim rites, but refused to grant her an interdict restraining her husband from committing adultery. In *Osman's* case the court, however, did not follow *Amra's* case but refused the wife's application for an interdict restraining her husband from entering into a marriage by Islamic rites with another woman.

Some authors feel that the actions for adultery and enticement should be abolished as it is difficult to reconcile their continued existence with the new approach of the Divorce Act 70 of 1979 (Lee and Honoré 43 and especially Sonnekus 216 *et seq* 276 *et seq*).

See also *Grobbelaar v Havenga* [75].

sowel as vir die skending van sy gevoelslewe (Hahlo 1969 *SALJ* 271; Van der Vyver en Joubert 682 ev; Lee en Honoré 40 ev).

Wat hierdie saak betref moet ook melding gemaak word van *Amra v Amra* 1971 4 SA 409 (D) en *Osman v Osman* 1983 2 SA 706 (D). In die *Amra*-saak het die hof 'n interdik aan die applikant verleen wat haar man verbied het om met 'n ander vrou ingevolge die Moslem-geloof te trou, maar het geweier om 'n interdik aan haar te verleen wat haar man verbied het om owerspel te pleeg. In die *Osman*-saak het die hof egter nie *Amra* se saak gevolg nie maar het die vrou se aansoek om 'n interdik om haar man te verbied om met 'n ander vrou ingevolge die Moslem-geloof te trou, geweier.

Sommige skrywers is van mening dat die aksies weens owerspel en afrokkeling afgeskaf moet word omdat dit moeilik is om hulle voortbestaan met die nuwe benadering van die Wet op Egskeiding 70 van 1979 te versoen (Lee en Honoré 43 en veral Sonnekus 216 ev 276 ev).

Sien ook *Grobbelaar v Havenga* [75].

| Reciprocal maintenance | Wedersydse onderhoud |

[77] PLOTKIN V WESTERN ASSURANCE CO LTD

1955 2 SA 385 (W)

Reciprocal duty of support

The plaintiff was married out of community of property. His wife was seriously injured in a collision. A car and motorcycle collided and the motorcycle then ran into the plaintiff's wife. At the time of the collision the plaintiff's wife assisted him in his business. The plaintiff claimed damages from the insurers of the vehicles involved in the collision on the ground that the collision deprived him of his wife's assistance in his business. One of the defendants excepted to the plaintiff's claim on the ground that it disclosed no cause of action. It was contended on behalf of the excipient that a husband can only claim for damages suffered through the

Wedersydse onderhoudsplig

Die eiser was buite gemeenskap van goed getroud. Sy vrou is ernstig beseer in 'n botsing tussen 'n motor en 'n motorfiets. Die motor en die motorfiets het gebots en die motorfiets het toe die eiser se vrou getref. Ten tyde van die botsing het die eiser se vrou hom in sy sakeonderneming bygestaan. Die eiser het skadevergoeding geëis van die versekeraars van die voertuie wat in die botsing betrokke was op grond daarvan dat die botsing hom sy vrou se bystand ontneem het. Een van die verweerders het teen die eiser se eis eksepsie aangeteken op grond daarvan dat dit geen eisoorsaak geopenbaar het nie. Daar is ten behoewe van die eksipiënt aan-

loss of assistance rendered by his wife if she was under a legal duty to render such assistance, and that a wife who was married out of community of property was under no obligation to assist her husband in his business. The exception was dismissed.

gevoer dat 'n man net skadevergoeding kan eis vir skade wat hy as gevolg van die verlies van sy vrou se dienste gely het as daar 'n regsplig op haar gerus het om die dienste te lewer, en dat 'n vrou wat buite gemeenskap van goed getroud is nie verplig is om haar man in sy besigheid by te staan nie. Die eksepsie is van die hand gewys.

RAMSBOTTOM J: [389] It is clearly correct that an action of this sort lies only when the person who was killed or injured was under a legal duty to assist the plaintiff . . .

The question, then, is whether a wife, married out of community of property, owes a legal duty to assist him in his business if such assistance is "essential to the upkeep and maintenance of the joint household" subsisting between them, as is alleged in the declaration [of plaintiff].

[RAMSBOTTOM J then analysed case law dealing with a husband's right to claim damages for injuries to his wife. His analysis included *Abbott v Bergman* 1922 AD 53 and *Union Government v Warneke* 1911 AD 657. He proceeded:]

[393] With great respect, I think that in *Abbott v Bergman* the Appellate Division decided that a husband can recover damages suffered by him as the result of non-fatal injuries to his wife "under similar circumstances" to those in which he can recover where his wife has been killed, in accordance with the decision in *Warneke's* case. As far as loss of services is concerned, the "similar circumstances" are that the wife must owe a legal duty to the husband to render the services and the husband must have a right to demand those services. The right of the husband to claim as damages expenses incurred by him for the medical and hospital treatment of his injured wife stands on a different footing and need not now be considered. I think that *Abbott's* case, read, as it must be, with *Warneke's* case decided that if it is shown that the husband has a legal right to demand the services of his wife and has, through the negligence of the defendant been deprived of those services to his pecuniary loss, he has a cause of action whether the marriage is in or out of community of property. In *Warneke's* case, INNES, JA, mentioned that there was no allegation [394] that the marriage was not in community, but that circumstance was not mentioned by any of the other learned Judges and clearly had no bearing on the decision. The essential fact which is necessary to create a cause of action seems to me to be that the husband has a legal right to the services of his wife . . . On the allegation contained in the declaration the plaintiff's wife has suffered no patrimonial loss for which she herself could sue . . .

The person who has suffered loss is the husband, and if he had a legal right to demand the services of his wife in his business, I think he is entitled to sue for patrimonial loss suffered through being deprived of that right through the negligence of a wrongdoer.

The allegation in the declaration is that the assistance of the plaintiff's wife in the plaintiff's business was essential to the upkeep and maintenance of the joint household and for that reason the plaintiff had a legal right to demand his wife's assistance in his business. No authority was quoted to the effect that in the circumstances alleged a husband married out of community of property has no right to demand his wife's assistance in his business.

In my opinion, if the allegations in the declaration are true, as they must be assumed to be, that is, if the assistance of the plaintiff's wife in his business was "essential to the upkeep of the joint household", then the plaintiff had a legal right to demand that assistance.

I think that the statement in *Shanahan v Shanahan*, (1907) 28 NLR 15, that "it is the duty of husband and wife, both according to their means, to contribute towards the support of the marriage"

[395] has been accepted as being a correct statement of our law; see *inter alia Warneke's case, supra* at p 668; *Gildenhuys v Transvaal Hindu Educational Council*, [1938 WLD 260]; *Davis v Davis*, 1939 WLD 108; *Rousseau v Cloete*, 1952 (3) SA 703 (C). The duty of support rests primarily upon the husband, but if the husband's earnings are insufficient and if the assistance of the wife is necessary to support the joint household, whether there are children or not, I think that it is her legal duty to render such assistance. The form that such assistance will take must depend upon the circumstances. If she has separate property, she may have to contribute from her income or even from her capital. If she is able to earn money and contribute from her earnings, it may be her duty to assist in that way. Or it may be her duty to contribute by assisting her husband in his business. An example that was mentioned during the argument illustrates what I mean. A working tailor may be unable by his unaided efforts, or with paid assistance, to earn enough to support himself and his wife; the wife is skilled in sewing and finishing garments, and if both work in the business, they can earn enough to support both. In such circumstances I think it is the legal duty of the wife to contribute by rendering services in her husband's business. That duty is one of the consequences of marriage and does not depend upon whether the marriage was in or out of community. If the marriage is out of community of property and the business is the property of the husband, the income earned by the business, though produced by their combined efforts, is his property. The services rendered by the wife are not performed in terms of a partnership, unless a partnership has been entered into (see *Fink v Fink and Another*, 1945 WLD 226), they are rendered in the performance of a duty to contribute towards the support of the marriage. The wife's contribution instead of being a direct contribution of money is a contribution of services which enable her husband to earn an income with which to support the household.

The plaintiff alleges that the assistance of his wife in his business was essential for the maintenance of the joint household. If that is the fact, then, in my opinion the plaintiff had a legal right to such assistance. If he has been deprived of that right through the negligence of a wrongdoer, and in consequence has suffered pecuniary loss, he has the right to sue for damages.

The exception, therefore, fails and is dismissed ...

Note

Note that a husband or wife whose spouse is injured or killed by the wrongful act of a third person can only claim for the loss of services which that spouse rendered, for example assisting him or her in his or her shop, if that spouse was under a legal duty to render those services (see also *Abbott v Bergman* 1922 AD 53; *De Harde v Protea Assurance Company Ltd* 1974 2 SA 109 (E); *Witham v Minister of Home Affairs* 1989 1 SA 116 (ZHC); Hahlo 139). Note further that a husband or wife whose spouse has been killed by the wrongful act of a third party may claim damages for patrimonial loss but not for loss of *consortium*, that is for the loss of the deceased person's comfort and society (*Union Government v Warneke* 1911

Aantekening

Let daarop dat 'n man of vrou wie se gade deur die onregmatige optrede van 'n derde party beseer of gedood word net skadevergoeding vir die verlies van dienste wat daardie gade gelewer het, byvoorbeeld deur hom of haar in sy of haar winkel te help, kan eis as daar 'n regsplig op daardie gade gerus het om die dienste te lewer (sien ook *Abbott v Bergman* 1922 AA 53; *De Harde v Protea Assurance Company Ltd* 1974 2 SA 109 (OD); *Witham v Minister of Home Affairs* 1989 1 SA 116 (ZHC); Hahlo 139). Let verder daarop dat 'n man of vrou wie se gade deur die onregmatige handeling van 'n derde party gedood is, skadevergoeding vir vermoënskade mag eis maar nie vir die verlies van *consortium* nie, dit wil sê nie vir

AD 657; *Abbott v Bergman* 1922 AD 53; Hahlo 145).

die verlies van die oorledene se liefde en bystand nie (*Union Government v Warneke* 1911 AA 657; *Abbott v Bergman* 1922 AA 53; Hahlo 145).

[78]   CHAMANI V CHAMANI

1979 4 SA 804 (W)

A wife who deserts her husband is not entitled to maintenance

The applicant, who had deserted her husband (respondent), applied for a contribution towards her costs in matrimonial proceedings in which she claimed custody of the spouses' children pending the outcome of divorce proceedings. The applicant had at no time offered to return to the respondent. The respondent opposed the application. As the duty to contribute towards matrimonial costs forms part of the duty of support, the court had to decide whether the respondent's duty of support had been terminated by the applicant's desertion. If this was the case, the respondent could no longer be held liable for a contribution towards the applicant's costs. It was contended on behalf of the applicant that a husband's duty to support his wife is not terminated by her desertion. It was further argued that, even if she could no longer claim a contribution towards her costs on the basis of the respondent's duty to support her, the respondent would still be liable as he had a duty to contribute towards any litigation (not only matrimonial proceedings) his wife engaged in. It was further contended that a contribution towards her costs should be ordered as the litigation involved the spouses' children and the respondent had a duty to support his children. The application was dismissed.

'n Vrou wat haar man verlaat het, is nie op onderhoud geregtig nie

Die applikant het haar man (die respondent) verlaat. Sy het toe aansoek gedoen dat haar man 'n bydrae maak tot die koste van 'n geding waarin sy om die bewaring van hulle kinders aansoek gedoen het, hangende die uitslag van die egskeidingsgeding tussen hulle. Die applikant het nooit aangebied om na die respondent terug te keer nie. Die respondent het die aansoek teengestaan. Aangesien die plig om tot die koste van 'n huweliksgeding by te dra deel van die onderhoudsplig vorm, moes die hof beslis of die respondent se onderhoudsplig beëindig is toe die applikant hom verlaat het. As dit wel beëindig is, kon hy nie meer aanspreeklik wees om 'n bydrae tot die applikant se koste te maak nie. Daar is ten behoewe van die applikant aangevoer dat 'n man se onderhoudsplig nie deur sy vrou se verlating beëindig word nie. Daar is verder beweer dat selfs al was sy nie op grond van die respondent se onderhoudsplig op 'n bydrae tot haar koste geregtig nie, die respondent nog steeds aanspreeklik was aangesien hy verplig was om by te dra tot enige litigasie (nie net huweliksgedinge nie) waarin sy vrou betrokke raak. Daar is verder aangevoer dat hy 'n bydrae tot haar koste moes maak omdat die partye se kinders in die geding betrokke was en die respondent verplig was om sy kinders te onderhou. Die aansoek is van die hand gewys.

NESTADT J: [806] What is clear is that the husband's obligation to make a contribution towards his wife's matrimonial costs is based on his duty of support. (Hahlo *The SA Law of Husband and Wife* 4th ed at 113, 520; Boberg *The Law of Persons and the Family* at 251; *Barass v Barass* 1979 (1) SA 245 (R) at 247). One of the authorities cited in support is *Lyons v Lyons* 1923 TPD 345. At 346 MASON JP says:

> "The cases in which an indigent wife, married out of community of property – and this is a case where the marriage is out of community – has been held entitled to a contribution from the husband for costs are quite numerous. On what basis are those contributions ordered? It seems to me the only logical basis is that such contributions should be regarded as one of the necessaries accompanying married life, just as the supply of alimony. It is so called in Scotch law and in many English cases."

In so far as the learned Judge regards the wife's costs of legal proceedings as a household necessary, it may be that this is not quite correct. As pointed out by Prof Hahlo writing in 1954 *Annual Survey of SA Law* at 59, whilst a husband's duty of support and the wife's power to bind her husband in respect of household necessaries overlap to a large extent, they do not always coincide and it has been recognised that, though the costs of a lawsuit are not household necessaries, they fall within the duty of support as between spouses. (See too *Boezaart & Potgieter v Wenke* 1931 TPD 70 at 83; *Von Broembsen v Von Broembsen* 1948 (1) SA 1194 (O).) This, however, is by the way. Counsel's proposition was that once a wife had forfeited her right to support she could no longer claim a contribution towards costs and that the defendant in the present matter, ie the wife, by virtue of her desertion of the plaintiff, coupled with her failure to restore conjugal rights to him, was in this position.

I agree with this argument. A wife who has deserted her husband cannot claim support from him. (Hahlo (*op cit* at 114 and authorities there [807] cited).) It follows from this that the wife in the present matter cannot claim a contribution towards her costs. She has been held to have been the deserting party . . .

This conclusion does not, however, dispose of the matter. The question arises whether the wife cannot succeed in her application for a contribution towards costs on some other basis. Two were suggested. The one was that there existed a duty to contribute towards a wife's costs not only in matrimonial actions but in any litigation against the husband, especially involving minor children of the marriage. But the obstacle in the way of her succeeding and to which I have earlier referred, viz that, being the deserting party, she has no claim against her husband for support, still remains . . .

[808] The other basis on which it was submitted by counsel for the applicant, that a contribution towards costs should be ordered, rested on the father's duty of support towards the minor children. There is authority that the necessary costs of litigation by or against a child are included in a parent's duty of support. (*Meyer v Mohammed* 1930 CPD 301; Boberg (*op cit* at 259).) If this principle is not to be confined to litigation involving a third party, then could it serve as justification for a parent having to contribute towards or indeed pay the costs of a child involved in litigation against the parent? *Lalla v Lalla and Another* 1973 (2) SA 561 (D) is authority that the answer is no. The applicant, a minor daughter of the respondents, applied for an order giving her consent to marry. The Court had referred the dispute for the hearing of oral evidence. The applicant had applied for a contribution from one or other of her parents to enable her to continue with the application. It was held that there was no principle that the costs of the litigation were to be met as a matter of right, whatever the outcome of the litigation, by the respondent. The application was refused. During the course of his judgment SHEARER J at 564–565 said:

> "The conclusion to be drawn from these authorities is, I think, that the grant of a contribution in cases where the marriage is out of community of property is an equitable extension of the Roman-Dutch practice relating to contributions where spouses were

married in community of property and only applies to litigation affecting the matrimonial status ... The position of a minor, however, is not analogous, for the right of contribution in actions against the parents was recognized neither by Roman law nor Roman-Dutch law."

It is unnecessary to express an opinion as to whether the effect of this decision would be to bar a contribution towards costs in every type of litigation by a minor against his parents. Suppose, eg, a father, during or after the dissolution of a marriage, refuses to maintain his minor child, and the custodian mother on behalf of the child brings a claim for such maintenance. She and the child are indigent and he is opulent. To enable the claim properly to be presented could the father not be ordered to make a contribution towards costs? The matter before me is not such a case. The issue of custody for the determination whereof the mother requires a contribution, can hardly be said to be the children's litigation, however it may affect their interests. It is a claim by the mother. My conclusion is that Mr *Goldsmid's* [for the respondent] opposition to the applications is well founded and it is refused.

Note

This case was decided before the Divorce Act 70 of 1979 came into operation and as the guilt principle in this act has been replaced by the marital breakdown principle, it is uncertain whether this decision still represents the law (Hahlo 424). In terms of section 7 of the act the court has a discretionary power to award maintenance; it is no longer only the "innocent" spouse who can claim maintenance on divorce. The duty of support between spouses *stante matrimonio*, however, is regulated by common law rules. In terms of these rules a wife who deserts her husband cannot claim maintenance from him. Sinclair (1979 *Annual Survey* 77) points out that the new legislation has altered the criteria for entitlement to a decree of divorce. Even if the wife's conduct has caused the marriage to break down, she may prove that she is entitled to a divorce on the ground of the irretrievable breakdown of the marriage and she may then also be entitled to maintenance as a divorced woman. Sinclair submits that on this basis it may be arguable that a deserting wife, who is still a wife, may be entitled to a contribution to her costs *pendente lite* to enable her to prosecute her action for divorce. She suggests that the legislation supersedes the common law requirement that a woman must be innocent to be entitled to support *stante matrimonio*. (Also see Sinclair 1981 *SALJ* 96–98.) This view was followed in *Carstens v Carstens* 1985 2 SA 351 (SE).

Aantekening

Hierdie saak is beslis voor die Wet op Egskeiding 70 van 1979 in werking getree het en aangesien die skuldbeginsel in hierdie wet deur die verbrokkelingsbeginsel vervang is, is dit onseker of hierdie beslissing nog steeds geld (Hahlo 424). Die hof het ingevolge artikel 7 van die wet 'n diskresionêre bevoegdheid om onderhoud toe te staan; dit is nie meer net die "onskuldige" gade wat by egskeiding onderhoud kan eis nie. Die onderhoudsplig tussen gades *stante matrimonio* word egter deur die gemenereg gereël. Ingevolge hierdie reëls kan 'n vrou wat haar man verlaat het nie onderhoud van hom eis nie. Sinclair (1979 *Annual Survey* 77) wys daarop dat die nuwe wetgewing die kriteria verander het op grond waarvan 'n egskeiding verkry kan word. Selfs al was dit die vrou se optrede wat daartoe gelei het dat die huwelik verbrokkel het, mag sy bewys dat sy op 'n egskeiding geregtig is op grond van die onherstelbare verbrokkeling van die huwelik en dan mag sy as 'n geskeide vrou ook op onderhoud geregtig wees. Sinclair doen aan die hand dat daar op hierdie basis geredeneer kan word dat 'n vrou wat haar man verlaat, en nog steeds sy vrou is, op 'n bydrae tot haar koste *pendente lite* geregtig mag wees om haar in staat te stel om die egskeidingsaksie deur te voer. Sy doen aan die hand dat die wetgewing die gemeenregtelike vereiste vervang het dat 'n vrou onskuldig moet wees ten einde *stante matrimonio* op onderhoud geregtig te wees. (Sien ook Sinclair 1981 *SALJ* 96–98). Hierdie siening is nagevolg in *Carstens v Carstens* 1985 2 SA 351 (SOK).

[79] RELOOMEL V RAMSAY

1920 TPD 371

Liability for household necessaries

The defendant (Dr Ramsay) and his wife were married out of community of property. The defendant went to England and left his wife and children behind in Potchefstroom. There was no disagreement between the spouses at that time and they were therefore not living apart in the legal sense. The defendant gave his wife a very meagre allowance of £15 per month to spend while he was away. During his absence his wife lived beyond her allowance. On the defendant's return the plaintiff demanded payment for the debts which the defendant's wife had incurred in his absence. The defendant refused to pay and the plaintiff sued him in the magistrate's court. The defendant averred that the goods which the plaintiff had supplied to his wife were not necessaries of life, that his wife had no right to pledge his credit and that as their marriage was out of community of property he was not liable for the debts she incurred. The magistrate's court allowed the plaintiff's claim for payment for several items which he had provided to the defendant's wife but refused to allow his claim for payment for silk and other materials as the court did not consider them to be household necessaries. The plaintiff appealed against this decision. The appeal was upheld and the defendant was ordered to pay for the dress material as well.

Aanspreeklikheid vir huishoudelike benodigdhede

Die verweerder (dr Ramsay) en sy vrou was buite gemeenskap van goed getroud. Die verweerder het na Engeland vertrek en sy vrou en kinders in Potchefstroom agtergelaat. Op daardie stadium was daar geen geskil tussen die gades nie en hulle het dus nie in die juridiese sin van die woord apart gewoon nie. Die verweerder het sy vrou 'n skamele toelaag van £15 per maand gegee om mee uit te kom terwyl hy weg was. Gedurende sy afwesigheid het sy vrou haar toelaag oorskry. By die verweerder se terugkeer het die eiser betaling geëis vir die skuld wat die verweerder se vrou in sy afwesigheid aangegaan het. Die verweerder het geweier om te betaal en die eiser het hom in die landdroshof gedagvaar. Die verweerder het beweer dat die items wat aan sy vrou gelewer is nie noodsaaklik was nie en dat sy vrou geen reg gehad het om hom te bind vir skuld waarvoor sy krediet aangegaan het nie. Hy het verder aangevoer dat hy nie vir enige skuld wat sy aangegaan het aanspreeklik gehou kon word nie aangesien hulle buite gemeenskap van goed getroud was. Die eiser het in die landdroshof geslaag ten opsigte van 'n hele aantal items wat hy aan die verweerder se vrou verskaf het maar sy eis vir die betaling van sekere sy- en ander materiaal is van die hand gewys omdat die hof van mening was dat dit nie huishoudelike benodigdhede was nie. Die eiser het teen hierdie beslissing geappelleer. Die appèl het geslaag en die verweerder is beveel om ook vir die materiaal te betaal.

WESSELS JP: [373] The whole question in this appeal . . . turns on whether the magistrate was right in considering that the crêpe-de-chine and silk bought by Mrs Ramsay from the appellant was not a necessary, as understood by courts of law . . .

[374] As there is some difference of opinion as regards the legal principles upon which our decision should be based, it will be advisable to review our law with regard to the

binding effect of a wife's purchase of necessaries. The first question to decide is: What are necessaries? Now the magistrate is clearly wrong when he speaks of necessaries of life, as if a wife is only entitled to purchase necessaries of life without her husband's consent. By our law necessaries are considered to be such things as are required for the household of the spouses in accordance with their status, their mode of living in the past, the usual customs of the place where they live, and the means of the husband. What will be regarded by the Court as a necessary in the case of spouses who move in the best society of the place in which they live will not be regarded as a necessary in the case of a couple of humble origin and of narrow means. Rodenburg mentions a case where gems and costly linens were considered necessaries: *De Jur Conj* 2.1.20 . . .

Silk dresses are not necessaries of life, but they may have been necessaries in the legal sense for the wife of a doctor in Potchefstroon, with a fair practice, living in a large house, and whose wife had been allowed to wear such dresses during the time that her husband was actually in the town. It was suggested in the cross-examination of Mrs Ramsay that she dressed very extravagantly and that Dr Ramsay protested against this extravagance. This would go to show that Mrs Ramsay was allowed to appear to the public of Potchefstroom as a well-dressed woman. It is true that a husband can determine how he and his wife ought to live, but then he must take steps to see that in outward appearances she conforms to the standard of living he wishes to set for the household. His protestations are not enough; he must see that his wishes are carried out. Mrs Ramsay tells us that she [375] was in the habit of wearing silk dresses, and that before her husband left Potchefstroom she had dealt with the plaintiff and her husband had paid the accounts. She had bought silk material for dresses from this very plaintiff before her husband's departure and he had paid the account. This is not denied, and the magistrate seems to have accepted Mrs Ramsay's testimony upon this point . . .

I take it therefore that whilst Dr Ramsay was actually at Potchefstroom there was nothing out of the way in Mrs Ramsay having a couple of silk dresses. In other words, considering her husband's station in life, his allowing her to buy silk material for dresses, his means and his outward mode of life, silk dresses may be regarded as a necessary for Mrs Ramsay. The magistrate, however, seems to think that after Dr Ramsay left Potchefstroom Mrs Ramsay was not entitled to bind her husband by buying silk dresses, both because (1) "it was possible to obtain dress materials which will wear better at far less cost," and (2) "because her husband was living apart from his wife and had provided her with money." I shall take the last reason first.

A wife is not living apart from her husband, in a legal sense merely, because the husband is temporarily absent. The temporary absence of a husband on a journey makes no difference to the status of the wife or to her rights to buy necessaries. It may be that when her husband is absent, and the means of the couple contracted, a wife who buys very expensive articles is acting unreasonably, but it does not follow that a tradesman who is accustomed to see her wear silk dresses and from whom she has bought such articles, is not entitled to supply her with these during her husband's temporary absence. It might make a difference if the tradesman is fully conversant with the facts, or even perhaps if he is put upon his enquiry, but in this case there is no evidence that the plaintiff was even aware of Dr Ramsay's absence.

The fact that a wife may buy less costly things is irrelevant to our enquiry, because if her station in life and her past method of living would justify her in buying silk dresses, and if her [376] husband allowed her to wear such clothing, then she can bind her husband. *Voet*, 23.2.46; Rodenburg, *De Jure Conj*, 2.1.20.

This brings us to an important question in our enquiry. Is, in our law, the right of the wife to bind her husband's credit based on agency or not? In *Du Preez v Cohen Bros* (1904,

TS 157) I expressed the view that the capacity of a wife to bind her husband's credit for necessaries was not based on agency but was an incident that flowed from marriage. As the correctness of this view has been questioned, I have thought it advisable once more to consult the authorities upon that point. Now *Grotius* says (*Introd RD Law*, 1.5.23): "Other women (ie, women not traders) may only transact business connected with the household, and may to that extent bind themselves and their husbands; nor can the husband prevent this unless he interdict the wife judicially from the management and give public notice of the same." The fact that the husband cannot prevent his wife from binding him in her purchases for the household excludes all idea of agency, for if the relationship of principal and agent exists the former can always determine what the authority of the latter shall be. According to *Grotius,* the husband can only prevent his wife from pledging his credit by a judicial act. If modern circumstances exact a modification of this rule we should at least require a public notice on the part of the husband or, at any rate, a notice to the individual trader, and until the husband takes that step the law allows his wife to bind him so long as she purchases goods of the nature of food and clothing of such a kind as are usually bought by the wife who manages the particular household. This is what the old authorities say, though no doubt we have given to this an extended meaning in accordance with modern requirements. Thus false teeth have been held to be a necessary and a wife was held entitled to bind her husband's credit in such a case. *Brudo v Chamberlain* (1912 TPD 131).

Grotius is not the only authority who states that the husband cannot prevent the wife from binding his credit for household necessaries . . .

[WESSELS JP referred to other authorities and proceeded:]

[377] Our law assumes that a husband does not intend to worry himself about household matters such as the purchase of foodstuffs and clothing, and therefore *quoad* these the wife has the capacity – not the authority – to bind her husband.

The wife therefore, according to our law, has a greater capacity for binding her husband's credit than she has in English law, where her right is based solely on agency. Her right is of course not unlimited. She can only bind her husband's credit if her purchases are reasonable (*justus modus*), and whether they are reasonable or not depends, according to our law, on certain outward manifestations, of which, in a rough and ready way, the person who supplies her can judge, namely, *regionis mores, mariti conditionem, opes, consuetudo praeteriti temporis, debiti similis frequens in praeteritum agnitio. Voet,* 23.2.46; *Arntzenius,* p 264 [the prevailing customs, the duration of the marriage, the spouses' means, the number of times they have incurred similar debts].

It is, according to all our authorities, the Court which has to judge whether the wife's purchases are or are not reasonable, taking all the circumstances into consideration. It is nowhere said, in any of the authorities I have consulted, that the Court must take into consideration the fact that the husband has given his wife money to buy food and clothing. Our law looks at the subject not only from the point of view of the husband but also from that of the shopkeeper . . .

How can the shopkeeper tell that a wife was given money to buy a dress but that she spent it on a race course? The trader looks to the usual mode of life, he considers how she is dressed, what she had bought, and what her husband has allowed her to buy. He takes into consideration her husband's social standing and the customs of the place where the couple live, and from these he judges whether the purchase is or is not [378] reasonable. The shopkeeper's knowledge of any particular circumstances connected with the spouses can, no doubt, be taken into consideration by the Judge in order to decide whether the purchase was or was not reasonable and whether the shopkeeper ought or ought not to have given credit to the wife. Further, however, I do not think the law allows the Court to go. I do not think therefore that the claim of the plaintiff can be repelled, even though it be shown that Dr Ramsay had given her money or the means of obtaining money wherewith to buy clothing. No doubt if it can be shown that Mrs Ramsay had ample store of silk and other dresses, and that she had no need to purchase more, that would be an element in determining whether the purchase was or was not reasonable ...

Now in this case it appears to me that *prima facie* there is nothing unreasonable in the wife of a well-to-do doctor purchasing silk material ... especially if we consider the fact that Mrs Ramsay had bought such material before at the same shop and that it was paid for by her husband ...

If this was so, the plaintiff was *prima facie* entitled to succeed in his claim, and it became the duty of the defendant to show that neither his past mode of living, his social status, the customs of Potchefstroom, nor his means, justified his wife in buying silk dresses. This he did not attempt to prove. It is true he attempted to show that his wife had ample dresses before he left Potchefstroom and that therefore it was unreasonable for her to buy more. But of this there is no proof. There is an assertion on his part that this was so but, when challenged, he could not make it good. He says he told her to provide herself with dresses for 18 months, but he does not say that she carried out his instructions. She denies the whole story, and none of the shopkeepers he refers to bears him out. Nor did the magistrate accept this as a proven fact ...

[379] It makes no difference in a claim for necessaries whether the husband and wife are married in community of property or not. In either case it is the duty of the husband to pay for the upkeep of the household, including his wife's clothes. In both cases the wife acts as the manageress of the household and in both cases as such she can bind her husband. If she is married by antenuptial contract she may also be held liable in certain cases, but the mere fact of her being married by antenuptial contract does not free the husband of his obligation to pay. I have already pointed out that the magistrate errs when he thinks that the parties were living apart; they were not. If they had been separated, either voluntarily or otherwise, they might be regarded as living apart, and then no doubt the husband might escape payment, but this does not apply when there is a mere temporary absence on the part of the husband.

It has also been argued that personal credit was given to the wife and therefore the husband is not liable. There is no proof of this assertion – on the contrary, the proof is all the other way. The mere fact that Mrs Ramsay's name appears in the books is no proof, for she was the person with whom the plaintiff came in contact, and it is therefore quite reasonable that he should put her name in his books without any intention thereby to look to her and to her alone.

In all the circumstances of the case I think the magistrate was wrong in thinking that the silk bought for dresses and blouses and children's clothing was not *prima facie* a necessary within the meaning of the law, and he was wrong in thinking that the fact that the husband was temporarily absent changed the character of what might have been a necessary had the husband not gone abroad temporarily.

I am of opinion that the appeal must be upheld and that there should be judgment for the plaintiff for the amount claimed ...

BRISTOWE J concurred in a separate judgment. GREGOROWSKI J dissented in a separate judgment.

Note

At common law a wife, in her capacity as manageress of the joint household, could bind her

Aantekening

Ingevolge die gemenereg kon 'n vrou, in haar hoedanigheid as bestuurder van die gemeenskap-

husband and herself by contracts for household necessaries. She had this power regardless of whether the marriage was in or out of community of property and regardless of whether or not the marital power operated in the marriage (*Excell v Douglas* [81]). Nowadays each spouse has the power to bind the other or the joint estate (if the marriage is in community of property) by contracts for household necessaries. The rules in respect of household necessaries therefore apply to all marriages and to both spouses.

As was pointed out in *Reloomel v Ramsay* the power to purchase household necessaries is not based on agency. It is a legal incident of marriage. Therefore one spouse cannot revoke the other's power. A notice by one spouse to a trader that the other may not purchase household necessaries on credit or that that spouse will not be liable for the other's debts can constitute no more than a warning to the trader that he should make further enquiries before supplying the other spouse with goods. If the trader does not do so and gives credit to the other spouse, he does so at his own risk.

In the case under discussion the court set out how one should determine whether a particular item is a household necessary. The court emphasised that factors such as the spouses' standard of living, their means, the customs of the people in their area, etc must be considered.

A problem which arises in this regard is the approach which one should take to these factors. Should they be viewed objectively or subjectively? Under the objective test the court weighs all the relevant facts of the case and then decides whether the goods were in fact household necessaries. Under the subjective test the court takes into account what the trader who sold the goods to the spouse knew or could reasonably have been expected to know. In *Voortrekkerwinkels (Ko-operatief) v Pretorius* [80], for example, the court applied the objective test and did not pay any attention to what the dealer knew or could reasonably have been expected to know about the situation of the parties, for example the number of articles of clothing which the wife and children had, etc. In *Reloomel v Ramsay,* on the other hand, the subjective test was accepted and the court held that "[t]he shopkeeper's knowledge of any particular circumstances connected with the spouses [could] . . . be taken into consideration by

like huishouding, haar man en haarself bind deur middel van kontrakte vir huishoudelike benodigdhede. Sy het hierdie bevoegdheid gehad ongeag daarvan of die huwelik binne of buite gemeenskap van goed was en ongeag daarvan of die maritale mag in die huwelik gegeld het of nie (*Excell v Douglas* [81]). Tans het elke gade die bevoegdheid om die ander gade of die gemeenskaplike boedel (as die huwelik in gemeenskap van goed is) te bind deur middel van kontrakte vir huishoudelike benodigdhede. Die reëls in verband met huishoudelike benodigdhede geld dus in alle huwelike en ten opsigte van albei gades.

Soos wat in *Reloomel v Ramsay* uitgewys is, is die bevoegdheid om huishoudelike benodigdhede aan te koop nie geleë in verteenwoordiging nie. Dit is 'n natuurlik gevolg van die huwelik en daarom kan die een gade nie die ander se bevoegdheid herroep nie. 'n Kennisgewing deur die een gade aan 'n handelaar dat die ander gade nie huishoudelike benodigdhede op krediet mag aankoop nie, of dat daardie gade nie aanspreeklik sal wees vir die skulde van die ander gade nie, is niks meer nie as 'n waarskuwing aan die handelaar dat hy eers verder navraag moet doen voordat hy die ander gade van goedere voorsien. Indien hy dit nie doen nie handel hy op eie risiko.

In die onderhawige saak het die hof uiteengesit hoe 'n mens te werk moet gaan om te bepaal of 'n bepaalde item 'n huishoudelike benodigdheid is of nie. Die hof het beklemtoon dat faktore soos die gades se lewenstandaard, hulle vermoëns, die gewoontes van die mense in hulle gebied, ens oorweeg moet word.

'n Probleem wat in hierdie verband opduik, is welke benadering 'n mens tot hierdie faktore moet volg. Moet hulle objektief of subjektief beoordeel word? Ingevolge die objektiewe toets sal die hof alle relevante feite van die saak oorweeg en dan besluit of die items inderdaad huishoudelike benodigdhede was. Ingevolge die subjektiewe toets sal die hof in ag neem wat die handelaar van wie die gade die betrokke items verkry het, geweet het of wat redelikerwys van hom verwag kon word om te geweet het. In *Voortrekkerwinkels (Ko-operatief) v Pretorius* [80] is die objektiewe toets byvoorbeeld toegepas en het die hof geen ag geslaan op dit wat die handelaar geweet het of wat redelikerwys van hom verwag kon word om te geweet het omtrent die posisie van die gades nie, byvoorbeeld die hoeveelheid klere wat die vrou

the Judge" (378; see also 375 and 377). There is as yet no certainty as to which of these two tests will be applied in future. Yeats submits (45) that in cases where there is doubt, the subjective test should be applied since this is more favourable towards the trader. It would be very unfair towards the trader to always apply the objective test. How could he know, for example, that the spouses already have a sufficient stock of the particular item which appears to him to be a household necessary? (See also De Vos 1951 *SALJ* 424.)

Some authors criticise the subjective and objective tests as applied in our case law. Boberg 205–206 fn 99 rejects these tests and argues that the trader's knowledge and the supply of goods in the household should not affect the issue whether the one spouse has the contractual capacity to bind the other or the joint estate for household necessaries.

en kinders gehad het, ens. In *Reloomel v Ramsay* daarenteen is die subjektiewe toets toegepas en het die hof beslis dat "[t]he shopkeeper's knowledge of any particular circumstances connected with the spouses [could] . . . be taken into consideration by the Judge" (378; sien ook 375 en 377). Daar is nog geen sekerheid oor welke van die twee toetse in die toekoms toegepas gaan word nie. Yeats (45) doen aan die hand dat in geval van twyfel die subjektiewe toets toegepas moet word aangesien dit meer tegemoetkomend vir die handelaar is. Dit sou baie onregverdig wees teenoor die handelaar indien die objektiewe toets altyd toegepas sou word. Hoe sou hy byvoorbeeld kon weet dat die gades reeds 'n voldoende voorraad van die betrokke item het wat vir hom soos 'n huishoudelike benodigdheid voorkom? (Sien ook De Vos 1951 *SALJ* 424.)

Sommige skrywers kritiseer die subjektiewe en objektiewe toetse soos wat hulle in ons regspraak toegepas is. Boberg 205–206 vn 99 verwerp hierdie toetse en argumenteer dat kennis aan die kant van die handelaar en die hoeveelheid goedere wat reeds in die huishouding is, nie die vraag of die een gade die kontraktuele bevoegdheid gehad het om die ander of die gemeenskaplike boedel te bind, behoort te beïnvloed nie.

[80] VOORTREKKERWINKELS (KO-OPERATIEF) BPK V PRETORIUS

1951 1 SA 730 (T)

Liability for household necessaries

The respondent's wife unlawfully deserted him in April 1948 taking the three minor children of the marriage with her. In May 1948 she purchased certain clothing and groceries from the appellant on the respondent's account. The respondent was unaware of the fact that his wife had purchased these goods on his account. The appellant claimed payment for the goods from the respondent. It appeared from the evidence that, prior to May 1948, the respondent had conducted a credit account with the appellant. The

Aanspreeklikheid vir huishoudelike benodigdhede

Die respondent se vrou het hom in April 1948 op onregmatige wyse verlaat en het hulle drie minderjarige kinders met haar saamgeneem. In Mei 1948 het sy klerasie en kruideniersware op die respondent se rekening by die appellant gekoop. Die respondent was nie daarvan bewus dat sy vrou hierdie aankope op sy rekening gedoen het nie. Die appellant het betaling vir die goedere van die respondent geëis. Uit die getuienis het geblyk dat die respondent voor Mei 1948 'n rekening

amounts involved were usually small and the respondent's wife never bought on credit but only made small cash purchases. The purchases she made during May 1948 were on credit and were substantial. When his wife left him the respondent did not inform the appellant of his wife's desertion and also did not instruct the appellant not to supply his wife with goods on credit. The respondent's wife and children had sufficient clothing at the time when the wife purchased the goods on credit and the respondent therefore averred that the articles which his wife had bought on credit were not necessaries. The appellant relied on a letter which the respondent's attorney had sent to the appellant in reply to his demand for payment. In the letter it was stated, *inter alia*, that the respondent's wife had deserted him and that the respondent was willing to pay for any necessaries which his wife had bought. The appellant contended that this letter constituted ratification of the wife's purchases, or an admission of liability, or an abandonment of respondent's right to refuse payment for credit purchases made by his wife after her desertion of him. The respondent denied liability on two grounds, viz (a) that such goods as were supplied were not necessaries; and (b) that the goods were supplied to his wife after she had unlawfully deserted him and were not supplied to his household for which he would be liable. The court *a quo* upheld the second defence and rejected the appellant's claim. The appellant appealed against this decision but the appeal was dismissed.

by die appellant gehad het. Die bedrae wat betrokke was, was gewoonlik klein en die respondent se vrou het nooit op rekening gekoop nie maar het net klein kontantaankope gedoen. Die aankope wat sy gedurende Mei 1948 gedoen het, was op rekening en die bedrag was redelik groot. Toe sy vrou hom verlaat het, het die respondent nie die appellant daarvan in kennis gestel nie en hy het ook nie aan die appellant opdrag gegee om geen goedere op rekening aan sy vrou te verskaf nie. Die respondent se vrou en kinders het genoeg klere gehad op die stadium toe die kredietaankope gedoen is en die respondent het beweer dat die goedere wat sy vrou aangekoop het dus nie noodsaaklik was nie. Die appellant het gesteun op 'n brief wat die respondent se prokureur in antwoord op die appellant se eis om betaling aan die appellant gestuur het. In die brief is onder andere gesê dat die respondent bereid was om te betaal vir enige huishoudelike benodigdhede wat sy vrou aangeskaf het. Die appellant het aangevoer dat hierdie brief 'n ratifikasie van die vrou se aankope was, of dat dit 'n erkenning van aanspreeklikheid was, of dat dit daarop neergekom het dat die respondent afstand gedoen het van sy reg om betaling te weier vir kredietaankope wat sy vrou gedoen het nadat sy hom verlaat het. Die respondent het aanspreeklikheid op twee gronde ontken, naamlik (a) dat die goedere wat aan die vrou verskaf is nie huishoudelike benodigdhede was nie; en (b) dat die goedere aan sy vrou verskaf is nadat sy hom kwaadwillig verlaat het en dat die goedere nie aan sy huishouding, waarvoor hy aanspreeklik was, verskaf is nie. Die hof *a quo* het die tweede verweer gehandhaaf en die appellant se eis van die hand gewys. Die appellant het teen hierdie beslissing geappelleer maar die appèl is van die hand gewys.

MURRAY J: [734] I have come to the conclusion that there is no reason to interfere with the magistrate's judgment. For in my view the matter can be decided on a relatively simple question of fact. A wife's right to bind her husband in the purchase of articles on credit is limited to those articles which are necessary for the use of the joint household or of individual members thereof. There appears to be some difference of judicial opinion as to the degree of *onus* resting on the tradesman to show that what he supplied constituted necessaries. But I shall take the position most favourable to appellant, which appears to be that set out in the majority judgments in *Reloomel v Ramsay* 1920 TPD 371 [79] and assume that having regard to the station in life of the parties and the other circumstances mentioned by WESSELS JP (*loc cit* at p 377), the articles supplied were of the character and *prima facie* of the quantity reasonably required for the household, and that to such extent the *onus* was satisfied by appellant. But I do not think that this concludes the matter. As indicated by WESSELS JP (*loc cit* at p 378), and BRISTOWE J (*loc cit*, p 381) it is still open to the husband to show that in view of the amount of articles already possessed by the household or its members, the articles purchased were in fact not necessary. This may be an unfortunate result for a tradesman but he must take this risk when he relies on merely an implied authority to bind the husband, and in this particular case the appellant has only itself to thank if (as the wife says) she had never previously purchased goods from it on credit.

In the present case the wife gave evidence that the articles in question were required for herself and the children. She gave a certain amount of detail to support this, more particularly in [735] regard to the children. She admitted she had never told respondent she wished to buy these articles. As against this the respondent produced the somewhat general evidence of one Greyling that the wife and children were properly dressed in April and May, 1948. In addition he stated that the wife had a large wardrobe full of clothing including three new dresses and sufficient underclothing. The children also were in possession of sufficient clothing and shoes. He used to make purchases at other stores as well. These articles . . . he concedes, might have been necessary later on, but were not such at the time.

It is true that there is no specific finding of fact by the magistrate on this point, but there is no doubt that on the question of desertion he disbelieved her with good reason and believed respondent. In the circumstances I can see no reason why the respondent's statement should not be accepted in regard to the adequacy of the clothing possessed by the wife and children in April, 1948, and I have come to the conclusion that these articles . . . were shown not to be necessaries.

Even apart from this aspect of the case, the appellant's contentions, in my view, cannot be upheld. My consideration of them will be brief in view of the conclusion I have already stated. In the first place I see no reason to interfere with the magistrate's finding that the respondent's wife deserted him without just cause. If so (*vide Janion v Watson & Co*, 6 NLR 234, and *Bing and Lauer v Van der Heever*, 1922 TPD 279) such desertion terminates her right to bind respondent for her credit purchases.

Secondly I see no reason to differentiate between purchases made for the wife's use and those for the use of the children. Appellant relied on the case of *Fillis v Joubert Park Private Hospital (Pty) Ltd*, 1939 TPD 234. But there is an important distinction in that in the last-mentioned case the wife on divorce was given the custody of the children and was in consequence entitled to obtain necessaries for the children not covered by the maintenance paid to her by her former husband. I do not consider that this decision applies to the case where a husband is wrongfully deserted and the children taken from his household, and means that the wife can enjoy an implied authority to conduct the duty of maintaining the children at his expense, a duty which he is supposedly still prepared to discharge himself.

Thirdly, if it be true . . . that she had never previously purchased on credit, but only on cash, from plaintiff, I can see no duty resting on respondent . . . to warn appellant of the possibility of her buying on credit.

Finally there is the reliance placed by the appellant on the letter of 8th September...
[736] I am unable to construe that letter as either a definite undertaking on respondent's part to pay for what a Court of Law should find to be necessaries, or as an abandonment of his legal position as made clear to the appellant's manager verbally, and as reiterated in the letter – viz that his wife had deserted him and so he could not be held liable. Respondent was not (as far as I can judge) fully and specifically cross-examined as to the meaning, in the circumstances, of the letter. But he stated in evidence: "Ek sou die items betaal het wat ek as nodig beskou." That is to my mind what the letter conveyed, in the light of his previous attitude. I cannot see that he could have meant, or be taken to have meant, that he surrendered the power he had previously exercised of observing economy and himself deciding what purchases were necessary. His meaning was to give the matter further attention when he had seen the details and then to do what he considered fair both to himself and to appellant.

The appeal must be dismissed...

DE WET J concurred.

Note

See the note on *Reloomel v Ramsay* [79].

Aantekening

Sien die aantekening by *Reloomel v Ramsay* [79].

[81] EXCELL V DOUGLAS

1924 CPD 472

Liability for household necessaries when there is no joint household

The defendant and his wife were married in community of property. They agreed to live apart. For the duration of the separation the husband paid his wife an allowance. In 1923 a court ordered him to pay his wife £20 per month. A number of years after their separation, the wife bought clothes on credit. When she refused to pay for the goods the storekeeper requested the defendant to pay for them. He denied liability on the ground that the spouses were living apart and that he was paying his wife a monthly allowance. The court *a quo* held that a husband would indeed be liable for household necessaries bought by his wife while they were living apart owing to an agreement between them, as the duty to support one's spouse lasts for as long as the marriage does. The defendant appealed against this decision on the ground that there was no common household be-

Aanspreeklikheid vir huishoudelike benodigdhede waar daar geen gemeenskaplike huishouding bestaan nie

Die verweerder en sy vrou was binne gemeenskap van goed getroud. Hulle het ooreengekom om apart te woon. Gedurende die tyd wat hulle apart gewoon het, het die man 'n toelaag aan sy vrou betaal. In 1923 het 'n hof hom beveel om maandeliks 'n bedrag van £20 aan sy vrou te betaal. 'n Paar jaar nadat hulle apart begin woon het, het die vrou klere op krediet gekoop. Toe sy weier om daarvoor te betaal, het die winkelier die verweerder vir betaling aangespreek. Hy het aanspreeklikheid ontken op grond van die feit dat hy en sy vrou apart gewoon het en dat hy haar maandeliks 'n toelaag betaal het. Die hof *a quo* het beslis dat 'n man inderdaad aanspreeklik is vir huishoudelike benodigdhede wat sy vrou gekoop het terwyl die gades ingevolge 'n ooreenkoms tussen hulle apart

tween the parties and that the wife had no authority to pledge his credit. The appeal was upheld.

gewoon het aangesien die onderhoudsplig voortduur solank as wat die huwelik bestaan. Die verweerder het teen hierdie beslissing geappelleer op grond daarvan dat daar geen gemeenskaplike huishouding tussen die gades bestaan het nie en dat die vrou nie magtiging gehad het om hom te bind vir goed wat sy op krediet gekoop het nie. Die appèl was suksesvol.

VAN ZYL J: [475] The question as to when and how far a wife can bind her husband by her contracts is dealt with by a large number of Roman Dutch Law writers, and has often been discussed in our Courts. See, for instance, the authorities cited and discussed by WESSELS JP and GREGOROWSKI J (who arrived at different conclusions) in their judgments in the case of *Reloomel v Ramsay* (1920 TPD 371 [79]). For the purpose of the present case we need only concern ourselves with the law relating to contracts entered into by wives for necessaries. It is clear from Grotius (*Introduction to Roman Dutch Law* 1.5.23, *Voet* 23.2.46), and other Roman Dutch authorities that a wife can transact business connected with the household, and may to that extent bind herself and her husband.

In the case above referred to WESSELS JP came to the conclusion, after considering the authorities, that the capacity of a wife to bind her husband's credit in her purchases for the household was not based on agency, but was an incident which flowed from marriage. He came to this conclusion mainly on the statement of *Grotius* and *Voet* that the husband cannot prevent his wife entering into such contracts unless he interdicts her judicially from the management of the household and gives public notice thereof. In the same case GREGOROWSKI J however, came to the conclusion that in such cases the wife acts as the agent of the husband under his implied authority, and he based his view upon the statement of *Voet* (23.2.46) that the contract of the wife in the household management binds herself and her husband "as though established by the consent of the husband who tacitly relinquishes the household affairs and entrusts them to his wife."

Whether, however, this right of a wife to bind her husband's credit in her purchases for the household is based on agency or is [476] to be taken as an incident flowing from marriage, it seems to be generally accepted that it is a right which exists irrespective of whether the parties are married in community of property or not. None of the authorities, as far as I could find, suggest that there would be any difference in the right of the wife in that regard if she and her husband were married without community of property, and it seems to me quite natural that that should be so, because, whether the parties are married in community or out of community, it is one of the essentials of marriage that there should be a living together of the spouses in community of life, that is to say, that they should have a common household. Although by antenuptial contract the spouses may each retain the ownership and management of their separate property, they nevertheless by marriage become partners in the maintenance and upkeep of a household in keeping with their means and station in life. They each have their respective rights and duties in regard to such a household. The husband as such is primarily liable to pay the expense connected with the upkeep of the household but as a rule he does not worry himself about household affairs. The wife, on the other hand, usually runs the household and buys the necessary foodstuffs and clothing for it, and she does so in her capacity as wife and binds herself and her husband by her contracts. The wife's right, however, is not unlimited. She can only bind her husband's credit if her purchases are reasonable, and, broadly speaking, the authorities are agreed that the question whether these purchases are reasonable or not, will depend upon the husband's means and social standing, and upon the custom of the place where they live and also upon what has actually been done by the spouses in the past.

It is, however, only when husband and wife are actually living together that the above standard can be taken as a safe guide by tradesmen in their dealings with the wife. When husband and wife are living apart other considerations may have to be taken into account in order to determine, not only what is reasonable, but also whether the wife is in a position to bind her husband in any respect whatever. There will, for instance, in that case not be a household, for the magistrate is, in my opinion, mistaken when he says that marriage *ipso facto* creates a household. I think the position is rather this, that it is an essential condition of marriage (upon the fulfilment of which either party is entitled to insist) that there should be a household, that is to say, that [477] there should be a living together of the spouses in community of life. Thus if either of the spouses at any time after marriage refuses to live with the other, such refusal will entitle the other spouse to institute an action for the enforcement of such living together and if the refusal is persisted in, a dissolution of the contract of marriage may be claimed by the other spouse. The fact remains, however, that this living together is not always insisted upon by either spouse and that spouses often, for some reason or other live apart while their marriage continues to exist. In such a case there will not be a household. It is, however, well established law that there will, in that event, be a right in the wife to claim maintenance from her husband if she can show that he left her without cause, or that, by his conduct, he made living with him impossible or intolerable. That right is an incident which flows from the ... marriage pure and simple, and the wife can enforce it by action against her husband, but her further right to bind her husband's credit would seem, according to the authorities above referred to, to require something further, to wit the actual fulfilment of the basic condition of marriage under which either spouse can claim from the other that there should be a living together in community of life. It is, however, not necessary to decide this point. In the case of *Coetzee v Higgins* (5 EDC 352) it was held that even where a wife lived apart from her husband she could bind his credit as it was shown that it was his and not her fault that they were living apart.

On the other hand, the authorities are agreed that if the spouses are living apart, owing to the misconduct of the wife or to her having left her husband without cause, she will not be able to claim maintenance from her husband (see *Voet* 24.2.18; *Van Leeuwen Cens For* 1.1.15.19, and *Bing and Lauer v Van der Heever* (1922, TPD 274). In such a case it would seem that the wife will not be able to bind the husband's credit, and tradesmen will not be able to recover from the husband on the wife's contracts...

It seems to me that where husband and wife are living apart, the least that can be said is that the presumption is against [478] the wife being able to bind her husband by her contracts. It will not be enough merely to show that the contract is for necessaries and is reasonable, but the circumstances under which they live apart will also have to be gone into ...

[VAN ZYL J referred to the fact that in the present case the spouses had been living apart by agreement and that the husband had given his wife a fixed allowance and proceeded:]

I think here the defendant must be taken to have fulfilled the claim his wife had upon him for maintenance. Fraser (*Husband and Wife* 2.8.2, page 636, second edition), says that, according to the law of Scotland, where husband and wife live apart by mutual consent and the wife is possessed, either from her husband or from other sources, of adequate means of support according to her situation, the law gives no remedy against the husband. This seems to me to be a sound principle and not inconsistent with our law. It should further in the present case, be borne in mind that (1) Mrs Excell had not previously been in the habit of purchasing from the plaintiff on the defendant's account, but had actually been out of the country for more than ten years, and (2) Mrs Excell could not furnish the plaintiff with the defendant's address when asked for the same. Under these circumstances the plaintiff should, if her intention had been to hold the defendant liable for his wife's purchases, have made enquiries before she supplied Mrs Excell. Thus if she was in ignorance of what the position between the defendant and his wife was she should not be allowed to take advantage of that ignorance seeing that she had only herself to blame for it.

On the other hand, if she knew what the position between the defendant and his wife was, she should not, if she had wished to hold the defendant liable, have supplied anything until she had first obtained the defendant's consent to her supplying his wife on [479] his account. As already indicated above, the Court . . . not only fixed the allowance which the defendant had to pay his wife for the future, but in effect also held that . . . he had up till then adequately supported his wife . . . If in addition to, or in spite of that, Mrs Excell could, by buying at shops on the credit of her husband, bind him, she would in effect be getting more than she was entitled to, because she could in that way leave her shop accounts to be settled by her husband while she was in full enjoyment of an adequate allowance made to her by him. Where spouses live together a husband might become bound in that way even though he allowed his wife an adequate allowance but he should not, in my opinion, become so bound where they live apart . . .

The appeal should accordingly, in my opinion, be allowed . . . and judgment altered in the court below to judgment for the defendant . . .

WATERMEYER J: [480] It has been argued on behalf of the plaintiff that the husband's obligation to pay springs from his duty to support his wife; once he has married her he is bound to support her and supply her with clothes and consequently if she buys then he is bound to pay the tradesman who supplies them . . . If the argument is sound then the obligation is not contractual but quasi-contractual (see *Voet* 44.7.5) and would only arise if nothing has occurred at the time the goods were supplied to put an end to the husband's duty to support his wife.

[481] The application of the principle, however, presents certain difficulties. For example, a husband is not bound to maintain his wife if she has left him without lawful cause. See *Voet* (24.2.18), and Van Leeuwen *Cens For* (1.1.15.19). Consequently a tradesman who supplies goods to a wife living apart from her husband does so at his peril because his right to recover from the husband is based upon the continued existence of the husband's duty to support his wife which in turn may depend on the merits of the matrimonial dispute. If the wife was wrong in leaving her husband the tradesman can't recover (as was decided in *Bing and Lauer v Van der Heever* (1922 TPD 279), and if she was right then he can; *Coetzee v Higgins* (*ubi sup*). This can hardly be said to be a satisfactory result from the tradesman's point of view. How is he to know the merits of the matrimonial dispute? Also there may be difficulty in determining the merits in an action to which the wife is no party. So far as the present case is concerned it is not necessary to go into the question of a quasi-contractual obligation any further because in any event such an obligation towards the tradesman by the husband can only come into existence if his duty to support his wife is owed and unfulfilled. If it is not owed at the time that the tradesman supplied goods to the wife then no quasi-contractual obligation can arise and if it is fulfilled then it seems to me that the position is the same as if it is not owed . . .

It seems to me therefore that if the husband is fulfilling his duty by providing his wife with maintenance when they are living apart then a tradesman who supplies such a wife with necessaries on credit has no quasi-contractual claim against the husband . . .

[482] In the present case the husband had discharged his duty of supporting his wife . . . and if the defendant were held liable for clothes purchased by his wife on credit she would in effect be getting a larger amount in maintenance than she is entitled to under the Court's order. I think therefore that the plaintiff has failed to establish any case against the defendant based upon a quasi-contract . . .

There remains the question whether the defendant's wife had any power or authority to make a binding contract between the plaintiff and the defendant . . .

[483] [I]t is clear that a wife has power or authority to make contracts in the management of the common household . . .

[WATERMEYER J then referred to the writings of some of our common law writers and proceeded:]

[484] It seems to me from the authorities quoted that those who give reasons for the rule all say that the right springs from the fact that a husband in general allows his wife to manage his household and thus must be taken to consent to being bound by her contracts in the management of the household . . .

It would seem therefore that when the parties are living apart and there is no common household the reason given for holding the husband bound by the wife's contracts ceases to apply and consequently as she is not managing his household she cannot contract on his behalf. There are two cases reported in our Courts which support this view: *Janion v Watson* (6 NLR 234) and *Bing and Lauer v Van der Heever* (1922 TPD 279). In both those cases it was held that a wife who had left her husband without cause could not bind him by contract because there was no common household.

These cases recognise that the bare fact of marriage is not sufficient to impose upon the husband liability for his wife's contracts in household matters but that a further requirement is the existence of a common household . . .

[485] In my opinion therefore seeing that there was no common household the defendant's wife had no power or authority in the present case to bind her husband to the plaintiff by contract and consequently the plaintiff's action whether based upon contract or quasi-contract must fail . . .

I agree that the appeal should be allowed . . . and judgment entered in the court below for the defendant . . .

Note

This case deals with the basis of a spouse's liability for goods purchased by the other spouse on credit while there is no common household between the parties. One spouse has the capacity to bind the other and, if the marriage is in community of property, the joint estate, for household goods only if three requirements are met:

(i) There must be a valid marriage between the parties.

(ii) The parties must share a common household.

(iii) The goods in question must be household necessaries.

If these requirements are met, the basis upon which one spouse can bind the other is contractual in nature.

Aantekening

Hierdie saak handel oor die grondslag waarop een gade aanspreeklik is vir goedere wat deur die ander gade op krediet aangekoop is terwyl die gades nie 'n gemeenskaplike huishouding gehad het nie. Die een gade het die bevoegdheid om die ander gade en die gemeenskaplike boedel (indien die huwelik binne gemeenskap is) te bind vir huishoudelike benodigdhede slegs indien aan drie vereistes voldoen word:

(i) Daar moet 'n geldige huwelik tussen die partye wees.

(ii) Die gades moet 'n gemeenskaplike huishouding hê.

(iii) Die betrokke goedere moet huishoudelike benodigdhede wees.

As was pointed out in the case under discussion, once the common household between the parties comes to an end, one spouse can no longer bind the other in contract for household necessaries. The reason is that one of the requirements for contractual liability is absent, viz a common household. However, the other spouse may nevertheless be held liable on some other basis.

Undue enrichment and *negotiorum gestio* have been suggested as bases for liability where there is no joint household. Hahlo (209) supports the view that *negotiorum gestio* is the basis of liability. He submits that the trader who provides goods on credit after the termination of the common household fulfils the duty of support on behalf of the spouse who has to render support and therein acts as a *negotiorum gestor*. However, *negotiorum gestio* will not necessarily be the basis of a spouse's liability. If the spouse who is liable for support forbids the trader from providing goods on credit to the other spouse, *negotiorum gestio* cannot be the basis of liability since a person can always forbid another to act as *gestor* on his or her behalf. (For criticism of *negotiorum gestio* as the basis of liability see further Neethling 1970 *THRHR* 280; Barnard, Cronjé and Olivier 193.) Some authors therefore argue that *negotiorum gestio* is not the true basis of liability. They submit that undue enrichment will normally be the basis of liability. They argue that when the trader provides the spouse with goods which are required for maintenance, the spouse who is obliged to render support is unduly enriched at the expense of the trader. The spouse who is obliged to render support can therefore be held liable on the basis of undue enrichment. It is submitted that the correct position is, as Boberg (202 fn 88) points out, that either *negotiorum gestio* or undue enrichment can be the basis of liability. The facts of each particular case will determine which one will provide the correct remedy.

Excell v Douglas makes it quite clear that, irrespective of the basis on which the action is instituted, liability can arise only if the spouse who is sued for payment is under a duty to support the other spouse. In other words, once the common household comes to an end, the basis of liability is no longer the contractual power to purchase household necessaries, but the duty of support. Thus the spouse who purchases on credit

Indien aan hierdie vereistes voldoen word, is die grondslag waarop die een gade die ander een kan bind kontraktueel van aard.

Soos wat in die onderhawige saak uitgewys is, kan die een gade nie meer die ander gade kontraktueel vir huishoudelike benodigdhede bind indien die gemeenskaplike huishouding tot 'n einde gekom het nie. Die rede is dat een van die vereistes vir kontraktuele aanspreeklikheid afwesig is, naamlik 'n gemeenskaplike huishouding. Die ander gade kan egter steeds op 'n ander basis aanspreeklik gehou word.

Daar is al aan die hand gedoen dat ongeregverdigde verryking of *negotiorum gestio* die basis vir aanspreeklikheid is waar daar geen gemeenskaplike huishouding is nie. Hahlo (209) steun die standpunt dat *negotiorum gestio* die grondslag van aanspreeklikheid is. Hy doen aan die hand dat die handelaar wat goedere op krediet voorsien nadat die gemeenskaplike huishouding tot 'n einde gekom het die onderhoudsplig namens die onderhoudspligtige gade vervul en sodoende as *negotiorum gestor* optree. *Negotiorum gestio* sal egter nie noodwendig die grondslag van aanspreeklikheid wees nie. Indien die gade wat onderhoudspligtig is die handelaar verbied om goedere op krediet aan die ander gade te lewer, kan *negotiorum gestio* nie die basis van aanspreeklikheid wees nie aangesien 'n persoon altyd 'n ander kan verbied om namens hom of haar as *gestor* op te tree. (Vir kritiek op *negotiorum gestio* as die grondslag van aanspreeklikheid, sien verder Neethling 1970 *THRHR* 280; Barnard, Cronjé and Olivier 198.) Gevolglik argumenteer party skrywers dat *negotiorum gestio* nie die ware basis van aanspreeklikheid is nie. Hulle doen aan die hand dat ongeregverdigde verryking gewoonlik die grondslag van aanspreeklikheid sal vorm. Hulle redeneer dat wanneer die handelaar die gade van goedere voorsien wat vir onderhoud benodig word, die onderhoudspligtige gade ongeregverdig verryk word ten koste van die handelaar. Die onderhoudspligtige gade kan dus op grond van ongeregverdigde verryking aanspreeklik gehou word. Daar word aan die hand gedoen dat die korrekte posisie is, soos wat Boberg (202 vn 88) aandui, dat òf *negotiorum gestio* òf ongeregverdigde verryking die basis van aanspreeklikheid kan vorm. Die feite van elke besondere saak sal bepaal welke een die korrekte remedie sal wees om te gebruik.

will only be able to bind the other spouse to the extent to which that other spouse is obliged to support him or her.

When the spouses are living apart, the question of matrimonial guilt plays an important role because it determines whether one spouse is obliged to support the other. If, for example, a wife who cannot support herself leaves her husband without reason, she forfeits her right to be maintained by him. If she buys goods on her husband's credit he will not be liable for settlement of those accounts. But if she leaves him because he has made life with him intolerable, he will be liable for goods purchased by her on his credit.

When the spouses do not share a common household and the one buys goods on the other's credit, it has to be ascertained whether, as happened in the case under discussion, the spouse who is liable for support has already discharged his or her duty of support towards the other spouse. If support has already been provided, for example by way of an adequate allowance, the spouse who is liable for support cannot be forced to discharge the duty twice by holding him or her liable for goods purchased by the other spouse on credit.

Excell v Douglas maak dit heel duidelik dat, wat ookal die grond is waarop die aksie ingestel word, aanspreeklikheid slegs kan ontstaan indien die gade wat vir betaling gedagvaar word, verplig is om die ander gade te onderhou. Met ander woorde, sodra die gemeenskaplike huishouding tot 'n einde kom, is die basis van aanspreeklikheid nie meer die kontraktuele bevoegdheid om huishoudelike benodigdhede aan te koop nie, maar die onderhoudsplig. Gevolglik sal die gade wat krediet-aankope doen slegs die ander gade kan bind tot die mate wat daardie ander gade teenoor hom of haar onderhoudspligtig is.

Wanneer die gades apart woon, speel die skuld-faktor 'n belangrike rol want dit bepaal of die een gade onderhoudspligtig is teenoor die ander. Byvoorbeeld, indien 'n vrou wat haarself nie kan onderhou nie haar man sonder rede verlaat, verloor sy haar reg om deur hom onderhou te word. Indien sy goedere op haar man se krediet aankoop, sal hy nie aanspreeklik wees nie. Maar as sy haar man verlaat omdat hy die lewe saam met hom ondraaglik gemaak het, sal hy aanspreeklik wees vir goedere wat sy op sy krediet aankoop.

Wanneer die gades nie in 'n gemeenskaplike woning bly nie en die een goedere op die ander een se krediet aankoop, moet vasgestel word of, soos in die onderhawige saak gebeur het, die onderhoudspligtige gade nie alreeds in die onderhoudsplig teenoor die ander gade voldoen het nie. Indien onderhoud alreeds verskaf is, byvoorbeeld deur die verskaffing van 'n genoegsame toelaag, kan die onderhoudspligtige gade nie gedwing word om die onderhoudsplig 'n tweede keer te kwyt deur hom of haar aanspreeklik te hou vir goedere wat die ander gade op krediet gekoop het nie.

[82] CLARK & CO V LYNCH

1963 1 SA 183 (N)

Effectiveness of a notification by one spouse to third parties that he or she will not accept liability for the other spouse's debts

The defendant and his wife, to whom he was married out of community of property,

Die effektiwiteit van 'n kennisgewing deur die een gade aan derdes dat hy of sy nie aanspreeklikheid vir die ander gade se skuld sal aanvaar nie

Die verweerder en sy vrou, met wie hy buite gemeenskap van goed getroud was, het oor-

agreed to live apart. When the spouses separated the defendant notified the plaintiff (a
storekeeper who had previously supplied the
joint household with household necessaries)
that he would no longer accept any liability
for any credit the plaintiff might give to his
wife. The plaintiff knew that the spouses had
separated. Later the spouses again set up a
common household, of which fact the plaintiff was also aware. Thereafter the defendant's wife bought certain household items
from the plaintiff on credit. When the defendant was asked to pay for these items he
denied any liability, relying, *inter alia*, on the
notice he had sent to the plaintiff and the
fact that the items were supplied for the
benefit of his wife's minor children by a
former marriage for whose upkeep their
father paid his wife an allowance. The defendant further relied on the fact that he had
made sufficient funds available to his wife
to make it unnecessary for her to buy on
credit. In the court *a quo* it was held that the
defendant was not liable. The plaintiff appealed against this decision. His appeal was
successful.

eengekom om apart te woon. Toe die gades
apart gaan woon het, het die verweerder die
eiser ('n winkelier, wat voorheen huishoudelike benodigdhede aan die gemeenskaplike
huishouding verskaf het) in kennis gestel dat
hy nie langer aanspreeklikheid aanvaar vir
enige krediet wat die eiser aan sy vrou sou
gee nie. Die eiser het geweet dat die gades
apart gewoon het. Later het die gades weer
begin saamwoon en hiervan was die eiser ook
bewus. Daarna het die verweerder se vrou
sekere huishoudelike items op rekening by
die eiser gekoop. Toe die eiser die verweerder
vir betaling aanspreek, het die verweerder
alle aanspreeklikheid ontken. Hy het onder
andere gesteun op die kennisgewing wat hy
aan die eiser gestuur het asook op die feit
dat die goedere tot voordeel van sy vrou se
minderjarige kinders uit 'n vorige huwelik
gelewer is vir wie se onderhoud hulle vader
'n toelaag aan sy vrou betaal het. Die verweerder het verder gesteun op die feit dat
hy voldoende fondse tot sy vrou se beskikking gestel het sodat dit vir haar onnodig
was om op krediet te koop. In die hof *a quo*
is beslis dat die verweerder nie aanspreeklik
was nie. Die eiser het teen hierdie beslissing
geappelleer. Sy appèl het geslaag.

JAMES J: [185] I am satisfied that the wife's right to bind her husband in respect of
household necessaries is one of the consequences of marriage which takes place as soon
as the common household is established. See Hahlo *Law of Husband and Wife,* p 112 and a
notification to a supplier that the husband had withdrawn his wife's right to pledge his
credit has no legal effect, so long as the wife and husband live in a common household
and the articles supplied are in fact necessaries for their household. The giving of the
notice may be a factor in deciding whether the articles supplied are necessaries or not,
but it does not have the effect of overriding sec 3 of the Matrimonial Affairs Act, 37 of
1953, which makes a husband and wife married out of community of property jointly
and severally liable for all debts incurred by either spouse in respect of necessaries for
the joint household.

In his judgment the magistrate placed great reliance on the fact that the plaintiff had
been notified that the defendant would not be responsible for his wife's debts and held
that the plaintiff acted in an irresponsible and unconcerned manner in his dealings with
the wife. But in view of the fact that the defendant and his wife again set up a common
household in November, 1960, that reliance is ill-founded. The real question for determination is whether the goods supplied were household necessaries.

Now in general, the items supplied to the defendant's wife during the period now in dispute were the general sort of articles that a normal household would need, such as butter and eggs, groceries, soap and so forth . . .

In general, I think, it can fairly be said that . . . the goods supplied were the normal sort of things which would be supplied to an average household and did not contain anything which would not be regarded as household necessaries in the type of joint establishment run by the defendant and his wife.

The defendant in his evidence did not dispute that the goods supplied were the sort which would normally fall under household necessaries but maintained that some, if not all the goods, were bought for the use [186] of his wife's minor children and that his wife had undertaken that she would not hold him responsible for their upkeep as she was receiving an allowance from their father for this purpose.

If I understand Mr *Pistorius* [for the defendant] correctly, he contended that goods bought by the defendant's wife and consumed by those minor children could not be regarded as necessaries supplied to the joint household and that the *onus* was upon the plaintiff to establish what part of the necessaries it supplied were used by the joint household rather than by the wife's minor children. I am unable to agree with this contention. In my view it offends against the true conception of a household. In the *Shorter Oxford Dictionary* a household is defined as

> "the inmates of a house collectively; an organised family including servants or attendants dwelling in a house".

The word cannot be limited in my opinion to the husband and wife and the children born of their marriage. It extends to all persons who are part of the organised family establishment centering round the man and his wife living together in a joint home. The wife has power to bind her husband in respect of all those matters reasonably incidental to that organised family establishment whether the articles furnished are consumed or used by the husband or the wife, their children or their servants or any one else who is living with them either permanently or temporarily as part of the joint establishment of the marriage partners. See also Hahlo *Law of Husband and Wife*, p 113.

Once it is established, as it is established in the present case, that the wife's children by a former marriage were living in the joint household of their mother and the defendant, then in principle the defendant will be liable for the debts contracted by his wife in purchasing articles for these children if they may properly be regarded as household necessaries, in the same way as he would be liable for such debts for similar articles purchased for the use of the children born of the marriage between himself and his wife living in the joint household. This does not mean that he is under an obligation generally to maintain his stepchildren. It is simply an obligation which arises out of the fact that a joint household has been set up.

Lastly, the defendant contended that he was not obliged to pay the plaintiff's account for necessaries because he had provided his wife with money to buy goods for cash and his wife in addition had R50 per month from the father of her children to cover their maintenance. The defendant does not here make out the case that the goods furnished by the plaintiff were not necessaries on the grounds that the common household was already fully stocked with such goods and no further goods were needed.

It is unnecessary, therefore, to express an opinion as to whether such a defence would be a valid one. It received approval in *Voortrekkerwinkels (Ko-operatief) Beperk v Pretorius,* 1951 (1) SA 730 (T) [80], and *Smith v Phillips,* 1931 OPD 107 at p 113, amongst other cases, but the validity of such a defence has been challenged in an article by Wouter de Vos in the 1951 *SA Law Journal* at p 424.

The defendant in fact relies on the fact that his wife had been provided with sufficient funds to make it unnecessary to purchase goods on credit. In my view this is not a sound contention. As was said by WESSELS JP in *Reloomel v Ramsay*, 1920 TPD 371 at p 337 [79]:

[187] "It is nowhere said in any of the authorities that I have consulted that the Court must take into consideration the fact that the husband has given his wife money for food and clothing. Our law looks at the subject not only from the point of view of the husband but also from that of the shopkeeper."

And at p 378 he says:

"I do not think, therefore, that the claim of the plaintiff can be repelled even though it be shown that Dr Ramsay has given her money or the means of obtaining money to buy clothing."

I agree, with respect, with this statement of the law . . .

In my judgment the appeal must be allowed . . .

HENNING J concurred.

Note

See the note on *Reloomel v Ramsay* [79] with regard to the effect of one spouse's notice that he or she will not accept liability for debts incurred by the other with regard to household necessaries.

Aantekening

Sien die aantekening by *Reloomel v Ramsay* [79] oor die effek van een gade se kennisgewing dat hy of sy nie aanspreeklikheid aanvaar vir skuld wat die ander gade vir huishoudelike benodigdhede aangaan nie.

[83] SHER V SHER

1978 4 SA 728 (W)

Reciprocal duty of support – enforcement

A divorced wife claimed R2 130 arrear maintenance together with interest thereon and the costs of the proceedings from her ex-husband. She instituted her action in the supreme court. It was contended on behalf of the respondent (the ex-husband) that the applicant should have brought her application in the maintenance court and not in the supreme court; that the applicant had launched her application in the supreme court with a view to defeating respondent's right

Wedersydse onderhoudsplig – afdwinging

'n Geskeide vrou het R2 130 agterstallige onderhoud tesame met rente daarop sowel as die koste van die geding van haar gewese man geëis. Sy het haar aksie in die hooggeregshof aanhangig gemaak. Namens die verweerder (haar gewese man) is aangevoer dat die applikant haar aansoek in die onderhoudshof moes gebring het en nie in die hooggeregshof nie; dat die applikant haar aansoek in die hooggeregshof gebring het ten einde die respondent se reg te verydel om

to convert the proceedings into an investigation regarding the provision of support to the applicant in terms of the Maintenance Act 23 of 1963, and that the supreme court procedure was needlessly more time consuming and expensive than the procedure which is available under the Maintenance Act. The application was granted.

die verrigtinge ingevolge die Wet op Onderhoud 23 van 1963 in 'n ondersoek na die verskaffing van onderhoud aan die applikant te omskep, en dat die hooggeregshofprosedure onnodig meer tyd neem en duurder is as die prosedure ingevolge die Wet op Onderhoud. Die aansoek is toegestaan.

MELAMET J: [729] It was contended on behalf of the respondent that it was not competent for the applicant to have brought the application in this Court and that the proper *forum* was the maintenance court, and I would refer to the following authorities in support of such contention: *Althaus v Jordan* (WLD 27 May 1977, unreported decision by KING AJ); *Troskie v Troskie* 1968 (3) SA 369 (W) at 371; *Davis v Davis* 1947 (3) SA 111 (W) at 115; Boberg *The Law of Persons and Family* at 293; Hahlo *The South African Law of Husband and Wife* 4th ed at 117. Although all these authorities indicate that the proper *forum* for disputes of this nature is the maintenance court, none suggest, and I am of the view correctly so, that this Court has lost or abrogated its jurisdiction in this regard. It is competent to bring an application for variation or suspension of a maintenance order in this Court but it is a procedure which is actively discouraged by virtue of the fact that procedure in the former court is cheaper and more expeditious. Applications are discouraged normally by refusing to allow a successful applicant his costs. In the absence of what has been described as good and sufficient circumstances or reasons or special reason a [730] Supreme Court will not allow a successful applicant his or her costs. In the case of *Troskie (supra)* the Court refused to entertain the application but that was because the applicant attempted to use the provisions of Rule 45(12) to enforce a maintenance order, such procedure obviously being incorrect.

In the present instance the applicant has on two occasions gone before the maintenance court, in 1971 and 1976. She has followed the correct procedure. In the respect of the latter order the respondent noted an appeal which was dismissed in September 1977. Within a matter of weeks the respondent brought an application for an enquiry under the Maintenance Act before a magistrate. The magistrate refused to make an order in the enquiry. On the same date the applicant commenced criminal proceedings which the prosecutor applied to convert into an enquiry. The order was granted and in the course thereof the respondent was acquitted. The enquiry was subsequently abandoned by the prosecutor with the consent of the respondent.

The applicant was . . . entitled in my view to approach this Court for relief. There are good and sufficient circumstances warranting the seeking of relief in this Court. As set out above this Court has jurisdiction to grant relief and I am of the view that there is no reason why the respondent should not be ordered to pay, in one lump sum, the full amount of arrear maintenance. On the facts set out and in the exercise of my discretion I have come to the conclusion that the applicant is entitled to the costs of the application . . .

In the result the respondent is ordered to pay the applicant:

(a) the sum of R2 130;

(b) interest on the said sum . . .

(c) costs of the application.

Note

Although this case dealt with divorced spouses the principles set out in this case can also be

Aantekening

Alhoewel die partye in hierdie saak geskei was, kan die beginsels wat in die saak uiteengesit word

applied to applications where the spouses are still married to each other.

net so goed toegepas word in gevalle waar die gades getroud is.

Matrimonial home   Gades se woning

[84] LOVELL V LOVELL

1980 4 SA 90 (T)

Ejectment of a spouse from the matrimonial home

Pending a divorce action between the parties the wife applied for an order ejecting her husband from the spouses' matrimonial home. The spouses had two children who were both younger than five years. At the time of the application the applicant and the children were living with friends. The applicant alleged that the respondent had assaulted her. The matrimonial home was registered in the applicant's name and had been donated to her by the respondent. The house was located on a secluded piece of land some six acres in size. The respondent kept a number of aviaries on the property. He averred that he needed to stay in the house to care for the birds and that he was a businessman who used the house for his business purposes. Furthermore he often had to make repairs to the house. In answer to this the applicant offered to allow the respondent access to the property for business purposes, to care for the birds and to look after the house. The respondent further alleged that the applicant could easily find suitable alternative accommodation. He also denied that he had assaulted the applicant and averred that she abused alcohol and had assaulted him. The application was granted.

Uitsetting van 'n gade uit die gemeenskaplike woning

Hangende 'n egskeidingsaksie tussen die partye het die applikant aansoek gedoen om 'n bevel dat haar man uit die gades se gemeenskaplike woning gesit word. Die partye het twee kinders gehad wat albei jonger as vyf jaar was. Ten tyde van die aansoek het die applikant en die kinders by vriende gewoon. Die applikant het beweer dat die respondent haar aangerand het. Die gemeenskaplike woning was in die naam van die applikant geregistreer en is deur die respondent aan haar geskenk. Die huis was geleë op 'n afgeleë stuk grond wat ongeveer ses akker groot was. Die respondent het 'n aantal voëlhokke op die eiendom aangehou. Hy het beweer dat hy in die huis moes bly om die voëls te versorg en dat hy 'n sakeman was wat die huis vir sakedoeleindes gebruik het. Verder moes hy dikwels herstelwerk aan die huis doen. In antwoord hierop het die applikant aangebied om die respondent toegang tot die eiendom te verleen sodat hy die voëls kon versorg, sy sakebelange kon behartig en na die huis kon omsien. Die respondent het verder beweer dat die applikant maklik geskikte alternatiewe woonplek kon kry. Hy het ook ontken dat hy die applikant aangerand het en het beweer dat sy drank misbruik en hom aangerand het. Die aansoek is toegestaan.

VAN DER WALT J: [92] It is clear that the parties should not be together. The only issue is should the respondent then be ejected from the matrimonial home. That is a very drastic remedy. I have been referred to two judgments. I have not had the opportunity of reading any more in the time at my disposal. The judgment of *Badenhorst v Badenhorst*

1964 (2) SA 676 (T), a judgment by VIEYRA J in which he indicates the extraordinary nature of an ejectment order in these circumstances and, whilst granting an ejectment order in that case, Mr *Goldstein* [for the respondent] has sought to distinguish that judgment on the facts because the husband only infrequently returned to the matrimonial home, in that case being a farmer farming elsewhere. I have also been referred to the ... judgment by my Colleague BOTHA in the matter of *Buchholtz v Buchholtz* [1980 3 SA 424 (W)] where in matrimonial proceedings an ejectment order was granted against the husband.

In neither of those two cases did the children play a prominent part and as far as I can see from *Buchholtz's* judgment no children were mentioned in that case.

In my view and as appears from both judgments each case depends on its own facts and one must see what is an equitable solution to a problem created not by the Court but by the parties themselves. They are to blame for their own situation in which they find themselves and, in seeking relief from the Court, they should not complain should the Court make an order which does not suit either the one or the other, or inconveniences either the one or the other. The Court in these cases, and I think [93] properly, should have regard to the interest of the children which in my view is paramount, the Court being upper guardian of the children, and the children's interest should play a great part in determining what solution the Court arrives at eventually.

With these factors in mind, in my view, it is important that the children, not being school-going children, should be returned to their home, albeit a home on a large piece of ground, secluded, and in the words of Mr *Goldstein*, not the best place for them to be because of the dangerous situation that the seclusion creates. I am not persuaded that that is a valid argument. If they are to be returned to their home, it must of necessity follow that their mother should return with them, because children of this age should be with their mother and there is no dispute about that. If they return to the common home with their mother, it is obvious that the father cannot also stay there, because that creates an impossible situation, and to perpetuate that situation, at least until the end of this action, will only lead to a situation which could involve the children, and, if it does so, it would work to their detriment.

I therefore propose granting the relief sought ...

Note

During the subsistence of the marriage, both spouses are entitled to live in the matrimonial home, irrespective of whether they are married in or out of community of property and irrespective of which spouse owns or rents the matrimonial home. The owning or renting spouse may not, as a rule, eject the other spouse without providing him or her with suitable alternative accommodation; nor may the other spouse eject the owning or renting spouse (*Badenhorst v Badenhorst* 1964 2 SA 676 (T); *Owen v Owen* 1968 1 SA 480 (E); *Whittingham v Whittingham* 1974 2 SA 636 (R)).

The right to occupy the matrimonial home does not arise because the owning or renting spouse confers it on the other spouse. The right is an invariable consequence of marriage. In *Badenhorst v Badenhorst*, for example, the court held that:

Aantekening

Gedurende die bestaan van die huwelik het albei gades 'n reg om in die gemeenskaplike woning te bly. Dit geld ongeag of hulle binne of buite gemeenskap van goed getroud is en ongeag welke gade die woonplek besit of huur. Die gade wat die eienaar of huurder is, mag, in die reël, nie die ander gade uitsit sonder om geskikte alternatiewe akkommodasie aan hom of haar te verskaf nie; en die gade wat nie die eienaar of huurder is nie mag ook nie die een wat die eienaar of huurder is, uitsit nie (sien *Badenhorst v Badenhorst* 1964 2 SA 676 (T); *Owen v Owen* 1968 1 SA 480 (OK); *Whittingham v Whittingham* 1974 2 SA 636 (R)).

Die reg om die gades se gemeenskaplike woning te bewoon, ontstaan nie omdat die gade wat die eienaar of huurder is dit aan die ander gade toeken nie. Die reg is een van die onveranderbare

"[A] wife has no right to seek to eject her husband from the matrimonial home merely because the property belongs to her. Because he is her husband he has rights flowing from the marriage which in relation to that property put him in a category differing *toto coeli* from that of a stranger. The wife's right to eject him must therefore flow from considerations which to a great extent must depend on the merits of the matrimonial dispute."

This point of view was also expressed in *Du Plessis v Du Plessis* 1976 1 SA 284 (W) where the court emphasised (287) that "other factors affecting the matrimonial relationship" had to be considered.

Because ejectment is an extraordinary remedy it will not lightly be granted (see further *Badenhorst v Badenhorst; Du Plessis v Du Plessis* and *Oosthuizen v Oosthuizen* 1986 4 SA 984 (T)). In the case under discussion it was the interests of the children which moved the court to make the order. The interests of the children will no doubt always play an important role in deciding whether an order for ejectment should be granted, but there are other circumstances (such as assault) which also justify the making of an ejection order. It is suggested that the mere fact that it would be more convenient for the applicant if the other spouse were ejected from the matrimonial home would not constitute sufficient reason to convince the court to grant the order.

One spouse can protect his right to undisturbed occupation of the matrimonial home against interference by the other spouse. If there is a threat of interference an interdict can be applied for (see *Buck v Buck* 1974 1 SA 609 (R); *Du Plessis v Du Plessis; Glass v Glass* 1980 3 SA 263 (W)). If the right to occupy the matrimonial home has already been interfered with the prejudiced spouse may apply for a mandament van spolie (see *Rosenbuch v Rosenbuch* 1975 1 SA 181 (W); *Oglodzinski v Oglodzinski* 1976 4 SA 273 (D); *Coetzee v Coetzee* 1982 1 SA 933 (C); *Manga v Manga* 1992 4 SA 502 (ZSC); *Ross v Ross* 1994 1 SA 865 (SE)).

gevolge van huweliksluiting. In *Badenhorst v Badenhorst* het die hof byvoorbeeld beslis dat:

"[A] wife has no right to seek to eject her husband from the matrimonial home merely because the property belongs to her. Because he is her husband he has rights flowing from the marriage which in relation to that property put him in a category differing *toto coeli* from that of a stranger. The wife's right to eject him must therefore flow from considerations which to a great extent must depend on the merits of the matrimonial dispute."

Hierdie mening is ook in *Du Plessis v Du Plessis* 1976 1 SA 284 (W) gehuldig waar die hof beklemtoon het (287) dat "other factors affecting the matrimonial relationship" in ag geneem moet word.

Aangesien uitsetting 'n buitengewone remedie is, sal die hof dit nie maklik toestaan nie (sien verder *Badenhorst v Badenhorst; Du Plessis v Du Plessis* en *Oosthuizen v Oosthuizen* 1986 4 SA 984 (T)). In die onderhawige saak was dit die belange van die kinders wat die hof daartoe beweeg het om die bevel toe te staan. Die belange van die kinders sal ongetwyfeld altyd 'n belangrike rol speel as die hof moet besluit of die bevel toegestaan moet word al dan nie, maar daar is ook ander omstandighede (byvoorbeeld aanranding) wat verlening van 'n uitsettingsbevel mag regverdig. Dit word aan die hand gedoen dat die blote feit dat dit vir die applikant meer gerieflik sou wees indien die ander gade uit die woning gesit word, nie voldoende rede sou wees om die hof te oortuig om 'n uitsettingsbevel toe te staan nie.

Die een gade kan sy reg op ongehinderde okkupasie van die gades se gemeenskaplike woning teen inbreuk deur die ander gade beskerm. Indien daar 'n dreigende inbreuk is, kan om 'n interdik aansoek gedoen word (sien *Buck v Buck* 1974 1 SA 609 (R); *Du Plessis v Du Plessis; Glass v Glass* 1980 3 SA 263 (W)). Indien die inbreuk reeds plaasgevind het, kan die benadeelde gade aansoek doen om 'n mandament van spolie (sien *Rosenbuch v Rosenbuch* 1975 1 SA 181 (W); *Oglodzinski v Oglodzinski* 1976 4 SA 273 (D); *Coetzee v Coetzee* 1982 1 SA 933 (K); *Manga v Manga* 1992 4 SA 502 (ZSC); *Ross v Ross* 1994 1 SA 865 (SO)).

The marriage in community of property

The nature of universal community of property
Cases where community of property does not arise
Assets falling outside the joint estate
Joint liabilities

Die huwelik binne gemeenskap van goed

Die aard van algehele gemeenskap van goed
Gevalle waar gemeenskap van goed nie intree nie
Bates wat buite die gemeenskaplike boedel val
Gemeenskaplike laste

The nature of universal community
of property

Die aard van algehele gemeenskap
van goed

[85] ESTATE SAYLE V COMMISSIONER FOR INLAND REVENUE

1945 AD 388

The nature of universal community of property

A husband who was married in community of property with retention of the marital power donated property out of the joint estate to a third party. In terms of sections 4(e) and (f) of the Death Duties Act 29 of 1922 the donation was a *donatio inter vivos* and as such it was subject to estate duty since it took place within a period of two years prior to the husband's death. It was argued on behalf of the executor of the deceased estate (appellant) that only half of the value of the donation formed part of the deceased's estate and that the other half was part of the wife's half of the joint estate, and that death duties should therefore only be levied on the half that formed part of the deceased's estate. On behalf of the respondent it was argued that the total value of the donation formed part of the deceased's estate. In the court *a quo* it was held that the whole amount of the donation was taxable as the whole amount formed part of the husband's estate. An appeal was lodged against this decision. The appeal was successful.

Die aard van universele gemeenskap van goed

'n Man wat binne gemeenskap van goed met behoud van die maritale mag getroud was, het eiendom uit die gemeenskaplike boedel aan 'n derde party geskenk. Die skenking was ingevolge artikels 4(e) en (f) van die Sterfrechten Wet 29 van 1922 'n *donatio inter vivos* en as sodanig was dit aan boedelbelasting onderworpe aangesien dit minder as twee jaar voor die man se dood plaasgevind het. Daar is namens die eksekuteur van die bestorwe boedel (appellant) aangevoer dat slegs die helfte van die waarde van die skenking in die oorledene se boedel geval het terwyl die ander helfte die vrou se helfte van die gemeenskaplike boedel toegekom het. Boedelbelasting moes dus net gehef word op die helfte wat in die oorledene se boedel geval het. Namens die respondent is aangevoer dat die totale waarde van die skenking in die oorledene se boedel geval het. In die hof *a quo* is beslis dat die totale waarde van die skenking in die man se boedel geval het en dat die hele bedrag gevolglik belasbaar was. Daar is teen hierdie beslissing geappelleer en die appèl was suksesvol.

WATERMEYER CJ: [395] [T]he important point for our purposes is to know the effect of community, when introduced by marriage, upon the ownership of the property of the spouses. As to this, it seems to me that there can be no doubt in our law. The Dutch writers whom I have consulted seem to be unanimous in the view that in Holland such property was owned by the spouses in common, in equal undivided shares...

[396] This view has also been accepted without question in several decisions in our Courts. See, for example, *Chiwell v Carlyen* (14 SC at p 65); *Rosenberg v Dry* (1911, AD 679); *Union Government v Leask's Executors* (1918, AD 447); and also by MILLIN J in *Gratus'* case (1943, TPD 162 at p 166) [*Commissioner for Inland Revenue v Gratus*].

Mr *Horwitz* [for the appellant], in support of his contention that the husband was the owner of the property belonging to the spouses, referred to the Scotch law of *communio bonorum*. But a reference to Fraser's book on *Husband and Wife* (Part 2, Ch 9) will show how the Scotch *communio bonorum* arose. It originated in Germanic customs, was adopted in France and subsequently in Scotland, but *Fraser* points out that the nature of the *communio* became entirely changed after being adopted in France. Among the Germans it had been a proper partnership in which the two associates had equal rights and the wife's consent was required for an alienation of her property ... but when adopted in France the wife's right was reduced to "an eventual or casual right to a half or a third of the movables and conquest heritage belonging to the husband at his death." In this form, the *communio* was adopted in Scotland. It seems, therefore, that Mr *Horwitz'* first contention cannot be supported.

Mr *Horwitz'* second contention is really dependent on the marital power and not on community of property ... The marital power is the guardianship of the husband over his wife, which includes the power of administration and alienation of her property, whether such property be her half share of the joint estate or property of which she is the sole owner ... Mr *Horwitz* pointed to the very wide and extensive powers of alienation which the husband can exercise over his wife's property to her detriment and without reference to her. Undoubtedly such powers are nearly as wide as those of an owner ... But [397] they do not include all those of an owner; the law does not allow him to commit a fraud upon his wife (see *Voet* 23.5.54), *Rodenburgh* (1.2.10), and he cannot dispose of her property by will, and if a judicial separation takes place the Court can make orders which are inconsistent with the idea of his ownership. For the purposes of this case the important point to notice is that the marital power was not dependent upon the existence of community of property between the spouses. It was independent of community and if it was not excluded by antenuptial contract the husband acquired on marriage the wide powers of dealing with his wife's property which have been mentioned by Mr *Horwitz*, whether community existed or not. He could, for instance, make gifts out of his wife's property even against her will and thereby diminish her estate.

In the light of what I have said, let us now turn back to the provisions of sec 3(4)(*e*) and (*f*) of Act 29 of 1922. This is a section dealing with estate duty, which is intended to be a tax upon the property left by a deceased person on his death, provided the value of his estate exceeds a certain amount. By sec 3(4) there are brought into the estate, for taxation purposes, things which ordinarily would not be regarded as assets belonging to his estate. Among these are property which he has given away by a *donatio mortis causa* [a gift which will take effect on the donor's death], or by *donatio inter vivos* [a gift between the living] taking effect within two years before his death. The purpose of those sub-sections seems to be to impose, in estates above a certain value, a tax upon the amount whereby the property of the deceased has been diminished by donations *mortis causa* or by donations *inter vivos* made within two years of his death. Sec 3(4)(*f*) does not impose a tax upon all donations made by a deceased person within two years of his death, but merely brings the value of such donations into his estate in order to determine the value of the estate for purposes of taxation. It was not, in my opinion, intended to bring into his estate, under those sub-sections, property which in fact never belonged to him at all.

I return now to Mr *Horwitz'* argument. His contention was that, though in law a *donatio inter vivos* only takes place when the donor gives out of his own property, yet when community of property exists the husband's power to give away the property of the joint estate is so absolute that he virtually gives as owner and consequently he is making a *donatio inter vivos*. A somewhat [398] similar line of reasoning led MILLIN J to a similar conclusion in *Gratus'* case. He said:

"The husband is in no sense the wife's agent in the disposal of property held in common. In the disposal of any asset he disposes of the whole of it in his own right and not of a one-half interest in his own right and of the other half interest as representing his wife. The transaction is one and indivisible and it is a transaction by a principal in respect of property of which he has the right of disposal. Thus, where there is a donation by a husband of property belonging to the joint estate the donation is made by him and by no one else."

But this legal power of disposition, whatever may have been the position centuries ago in Holland ... now-a-days only belongs to the husband because the wife has impliedly or expressly agreed on marriage that he should have it ... and when he exercises it by giving away property of the joint estate, he does not diminish the value of his own estate by the whole amount of the gift but only by one-half. The true test for determining whether his gratuitous disposition is a *donatio inter vivos* made by him is not whether he has the legal authority to make it, however he may have acquired such authority, but whether his gratuitous disposition has the effect of enriching the donee at his expense. In so far as it does it is a *donatio* by him, in so far as it does not it is not.

That this is the true test will be realised if the case of a marriage out of community of property in which the marital power is not excluded be considered. In such a case the husband may have no property at all and the wife may have ample. The husband has power to give away her property. If he does so within two years of his death, is that a *donatio* made by him in terms of sec 3(4)(*f*) of Act 29 of 1922? It is in fact liberality exercised by him entirely at the expense of his wife and consequently it is not in law a *donatio* by him at all. If it were, and if it were made within two years of his death, then, though his estate has no assets and was never in any way diminished by his liberality, his executor would be primarily liable for estate duty on the value of such gift, provided the gift of his wife's property was large enough to create a liability for estate duty.

I do not think that the Act was intended to bring about such a result. The purpose of sec 3(4)(*f*) was ... to bring [399] back into the estate of a deceased person only the value of such property as was actually given away out of it within two years before the death of the deceased, and not the value of property which was never owned by the deceased.

For these reasons I think the judgment of the trial Court, following the decision of the case of *Gratus*, was wrong and that the appeal should succeed ...

TINDALL JA; FEETHAM JA; GREENBERG JA and DAVIS AJA concurred.

Note

The legal nature of community of property has led to much debate. There are three main theories in this regard, viz:

(i) that the joint estate forms a separate legal *persona*;

(ii) that the husband is the sole owner of the joint estate and that the wife merely has a claim to share in the estate upon its dissolution;

(iii) that the spouses are joint owners of the joint estate in undivided equal shares.

The latter theory is the one which is generally accepted today and which was confirmed in *Estate*

Aantekening

Die regsaard van gemeenskap van goed het al tot heelwat bespreking aanleiding gegee. Daar is drie belangrike teorieë in dié verband, naamlik:

(i) dat die gemeenskaplike boedel 'n afsonderlike regspersoon is;

(ii) dat die man die alleeneienaar van die gemeenskaplike boedel is en dat die vrou net 'n reg het om by die verdeling van die boedel daarin te deel;

(iii) dat die gades mede-eienaars van die gemeenskaplike boedel is in onverdeelde gelyke aandele.

Laasgenoemde teorie is die een wat vandag al-

Sayle v CIR. It was recently again accepted in *Ex parte Menzies* 1993 3 SA 799 (C).

With regard to the statements which were made in this case regarding the husband's marital power it must be borne in mind that, since the substitution of section 11 of the Matrimonial Property Act 88 of 1984 by section 29 of the General Law Fourth Amendment Act 132 of 1993, the marital power no longer forms part of our law.

On the legal nature of community of property see also *De Wet v Jurgens* [89] and *Nedbank v Van Zyl* [90].

gemeen aanvaar word en wat ook in *Estate Sayle v CIR* bevestig is. Dit is onlangs weer in *Ex parte Menzies* 1993 3 SA 799 (K) aanvaar.

Met betrekking tot die stellings wat in hierdie saak oor die man se maritale mag gemaak is, moet in gedagte gehou word dat die maritale mag sedert die vervanging van artikel 11 van die Wet op Huweliksgoedere 88 van 1984 deur artikel 29 van die Vierde Algemene Regswysigingswet 132 van 1993 nie meer deel vorm van ons reg nie.

Oor die regsaard van gemeenskap van goed, sien ook *De Wet v Jurgens* [89] en *Nedbank v Van Zyl* [90].

Cases where community of property does not arise

Gevalle waar gemeenskap van goed nie intree nie

[86]   SPERLING V SPERLING

1975 3 SA 707 (A)

The proprietary consequences of a marriage are determined by the law of the domicile of the husband at the time of the marriage

Die vermoënsregtelike gevolge van 'n huwelik word bepaal deur die reg van die man se domisilie ten tyde van huwelikssluiting

In 1954 two German citizens who were domiciled in East Germany were married there. At that time their marriage was out of community of property in terms of East German law. In 1965, however, East German law relating to the proprietary consequences of a marriage changed to provide for a kind of community of property. In 1957 the parties moved to South Africa and acquired a domicile in this country. Later the wife instituted matrimonial proceedings against her husband in South Africa. The question then arose as to whether the spouses were married in or out of community of property. It was common cause that the parties' matrimonial property rights had to be determined according to the law of the country where the husband was domiciled at the time of the marriage. The court *a quo* held that the law as amended in 1965 should be applied to the spouses' matrimonial property regime and

In 1954 het twee Duitse burgers wat in Oos-Duitsland gedomisilieer was daar met mekaar getrou. Op daardie stadium was hulle huwelik ingevolge die Oos-Duitse reg buite gemeenskap van goed. In 1965 is die Oos-Duitse huweliksgoederereg egter gewysig om vir 'n soort gemeenskap van goed voorsiening te maak. In 1957 het die partye na Suid-Afrika gekom en hier 'n domisilie verwerf. Later het die vrou in Suid-Afrika 'n huweliksgeding teen haar man aanhangig gemaak. Die vraag het toe ontstaan of die partye binne of buite gemeenskap van goed getroud was. Dit was gemene saak dat die vermoënsregtelike gevolge van die huwelik bepaal moes word deur die reg van die land waar die man ten tyde van huwelikssluiting gedomisilieer was. Die hof *a quo* het beslis dat die Oos-Duitse reg soos gewysig in 1965 op die gades se huweliksgoederebedeling toegepas moes word en dat die gades gevolglik binne ge-

that the spouses were therefore married in community of property. An appeal was lodged against this decision and it was argued that the law of the husband's domicile, as that law was at the time of the marriage, should be applied. The appeal was dismissed.

meenskap van goed getroud was. Daar is teen hierdie beslissing geappelleer en die argument is geopper dat die reg van die land van die man se domisilie toegepas moes word soos wat dit by huweliksluiting was. Die appèl is van die hand gewys.

CORBETT JA: [716] [T]he problem is one of that branch of our law known as Private International Law. The claims of the parties to the matrimonial property... are to be classified as relating to the proprietary consequences of marriage. In a case such as this, where no antenuptial contract has been entered into, the ... rule is that the proprietary consequences of a marriage are to be determined by reference to the law of the domicile of the husband at the time of the marriage (*Frankel's Estate and Another v The Master and Another*, 1950 (1) SA 220 (AD)), sometimes referred to, for the sake of brevity, as "the law of the matrimonial domicile"...

The position is not affected by a subsequent change of domicile ... nor is any distinction drawn in this regard between movable and immovable property or between property brought into the marriage or after-acquired property (*Shapiro v Shapiro*, 1904 TS 673; *Union Government (Minister of Finance) v Larkan*, 1915 CPD 681 at p 685). What is termed the "unity principle" is applied.

This much is reasonably clear. What is not so clear is the legal position when changes occur in the *lex causae* [the system of law governing the suit], after the date of the marriage. Does a South African Court which is seized of a dispute between spouses relating to the proprietary consequences of their marriage and which is referred by our [717] rules as to choice of law to a foreign *lex causae*, apply the foreign law as it stood at the time of the marriage, or the law as it is at the time of reference, or the law in some intermediate state? That, in a nutshell, is the problem here; and it is given reality by the fact that the subsequent change in the law which occured in 1965 was made to operate retrospectively in that it applied to all existing marriages, even though entered into before 1965...

[721] I am of the view that, when the South African rule of Private International Law prescribes that the proprietary consequences of a foreign marriage must be determined in accordance with the law of the matrimonial domicile, that reference should, in general, be to the whole law of the *lex causae*, including its transitional law. It is true that formulations of the choice of law rule generally speak of the "law of the domicile of the husband at the time of the marriage". I do not think, however, that by this mode of formulation it was intended to convey that the reference was to be to the law of the *lex causae* frozen, as it were, at the date of the marriage. If that were so, some quaint anomalies would result. To take the background of the present case: suppose that the parties had come to settle in South Africa in, say, 1968, instead of 1957. If our choice of law rule referred only to the state of the East German law at the moment of marriage, one would arrive at the situation that, practically speaking, the proprietary consequences of their marriage would have been out of community (in the sense of the East German law current in 1954) from 1954 until 1965 and in community (in the sense of the 1965 law) from 1966 to 1968; and after 1968 would have reverted to being out of community. This would hardly be consonant with either comity or common sense...

[722] [I]f in this case the *lex causae* is to be applied in its entirety, then clearly the proprietary rights of the parties upon the dissolution of their marriage must be adjudged in accordance with the 1965 law...

[723] The need for certainty in regard to the property rights of married persons was emphasised in *Frankel's* case, *supra* at pp 221I–221J, 239–40, the main reason given being

that third parties, such as creditors, should know where they stand. In that case the Court, accordingly, rejected the proposition that the matrimonial property régime should be governed by the intended matrimonial domicile, as opposed to the actual domicile of the husband at the time of the marriage. Similar considerations have also led our Courts to adopt the principle of immutability in preference to the one of mutability ...

Admittedly, if one takes the law of the matrimonial domicile as embracing the transitional rules, one can have the situation, as in this case, where the matrimonial property régime is altered overnight by foreign legislation. This could affect the interests of existing creditors of the spouses. Of course, the same result could occur ... if spouses were merely resident in this country when the law of the [724] matrimonial domicile was altered; but that is not a complete answer. It must be accepted that this is a disadvantage inherent in an acceptance of the transitional law. On the other hand, the number of creditors who would actually have placed reliance on the former state of the law of the foreign matrimonial domicile must be limited ...

Upon a review of the position as a whole I have come to the conclusion that there is no decisive consideration of public policy which impels one, in a case such as this, to ignore changes in the *lex causae*, enacted with retroactive effect, after the parties have acquired a new domicile in this country; and that in fact the balance of justice and convenience favour an adherence to the general principle that a reference to a foreign *lex causae* includes the transitional law thereof. I hold, therefore, that the trial Judge correctly approached the proprietary claims of the parties on the basis that the 1965 law applied ...

[725] The appeal is dismissed ...

RUMPFF CJ; HOLMES JA; MULLER JA and GALGUT AJA concurred.

Note	Aantekening
Our common law dictates that all marriages are automatically contracted in community of property. Because of this rule, it is presumed that every marriage is in community of property (see *Edelstein v Edelstein* [33]). This presumption operates unless the contrary is proved. The presumption cannot be rebutted merely by stating that the marriage is not in community of property. Some evidence must be brought to prove that the marriage is out of community of property (*Brummund v Brummund's Estate* 1993 2 SA 494 (NmHC)).	Ons gemenereg bepaal dat alle huwelike outomaties binne gemeenskap van goed is. As gevolg van hierdie reël word vermoed dat alle huwelike binne gemeenskap van goed is (sien *Edelstein v Edelstein* [33]). Hierdie vermoede geld tensy die teendeel bewys word. Die vermoede kan nie weerlê word bloot deur te sê dat die huwelik nie binne gemeenskap van goed is nie. Getuienis moet aangevoer word om te bewys dat die huwelik buite gemeenskap van goed is (*Brummund v Brummund's Estate* 1993 2 SA 494 (NmHC)).
One of the ways in which the presumption can be rebutted is by proving that the spouses were married according to some foreign legal system which dictates that community of property does not apply automatically, for example English law, which provides that marriage is automatically out of community of property. The law of the country of the husband's domicile at the time of entering into the marriage determines the patrimonial consequences of the marriage; in other words the husband's *lex loci domicilii* at the time of entering into marriage determines whether the	Een van die maniere waarop die vermoede weerlê kan word, is om te bewys dat die gades getroud is ingevolge die een of ander buitelandse regstelsel waarvolgens gemeenskap van goed nie outomaties intree nie, byvoorbeeld die Engelse reg, wat bepaal dat die huwelik outomaties buite gemeenskap van goed is. Die reg van die plek waar die man ten tyde van huweliksluiting gedomisilieer is, bepaal wat die vermoënsregtelike gevolge van die huwelik is; met ander woorde die man se *lex loci domicilii* ten tyde van huweliksluiting bepaal of die huwelik binne of buite gemeenskap van goed is (*Frankel's Estate v The*

marriage is in or out of community of property (*Frankel's Estate v The Master* 1950 1 SA 220 (A)). In the case under discussion, this rule had to be applied because the spouses were married in Germany. The spouses were held to have been married in community of property because German law provided that a kind of community of property would operate in their marriage.

See Barnard, Cronjé and Olivier 203 for a discussion of the cases in which community of property will not arise.

Master 1950 1 SA 220 (A)). In die onderhawige saak moes hierdie reël toegepas word omdat die gades in Duitsland getroud is. Die gades was binne gemeenskap van goed getroud omdat die Duitse reg bepaal het dat 'n soort gemeenskap van goed in hulle huwelik gegeld het.

Sien Barnard, Cronjé en Olivier 209 vir 'n bespreking van die gevalle waar gemeenskap van goed nie intree nie.

Assets falling outside the joint estate

Bates wat buite die gemeenskaplike boedel val

[87] VAN DER MERWE V VAN WYK

1921 EDL 298

A usufruct does not form part of the joint estate

The applicant, a woman who was married in community of property, acquired the usufruct of certain property during the existence of her marriage. When her husband died the question arose as to whether his executor could sell the right of usufruct as an asset in the joint estate. The applicant applied for an interdict restraining the executor of her deceased husband's estate from dealing with the right of usufruct. An *interim* interdict was granted. The applicant later moved to have the interdict made final and her application was granted.

'n Vruggebruik vorm nie deel van die gemeenskaplike boedel nie

Die applikant, 'n vrou wat binne gemeenskap van goed getroud was, het gedurende die bestaan van haar huwelik 'n vruggebruik oor sekere eiendom verkry. Na haar man se dood het die vraag ontstaan of sy eksekuteur die vruggebruik as 'n bate van die gemeenskaplike boedel kon verkoop. Die applikant het aansoek gedoen om 'n interdik ten einde die eksekuteur van haar man se boedel te belet om oor die vruggebruik te beskik. 'n Tussentydse interdik is toegestaan. Die applikant het daarna om 'n finale interdik aansoek gedoen en haar aansoek was suksesvol.

SAMPSON J: [301] Now usufructus is a personal servitude, and the Roman law drew a distinction in regard to its alienation, between the right and the fruit of a usufructus . . .

[SAMPSON J discussed some of the opinions expressed by our Roman and Roman-Dutch law authors and proceeded:]

[302] From a perusal of these authorities, it becomes evident that a usufruct is such a personal right, that it cannot be ceded to anyone but the owner of the property over which the usufruct exists, and consequently it is not a right which can by operation of law, in a marriage in community, be transferred to the community. That being so, it never vested in the community, and though deceased spouse participated in the fruits during marriage, he never became a part owner of the right of usufruct, and his executor cannot claim a half-share in it on behalf of his estate, and must be interdicted from doing so. Even if such a claim were valid, it is quite clear that the usufruct could not be sold

and transferred as a right to a stranger, though no doubt the fruits could be sold or leased . . .

[304] [I]t appears to me that the executor has no power to sell the life interests of the applicant, and the rule must be made absolute . . .

GRAHAM JP and HUTTON J concurred.

[88] BARNETT V RUDMAN

1934 AD 203

Fideicommissary property does not form part of the joint estate

The respondents, Mr and Mrs Rudman, were married in community of property. During the subsistence of the marriage Mrs Rudman became the registered owner of a farm subject to a *fideicommissum* in favour of her sisters. Thereafter Mr Rudman became insolvent and the joint estate was sequestrated. The appellants purchased from the trustee of the insolvent estate all the rights of the estate in and to the said farm. They claimed that the right to possession, use and enjoyment of the farm had formed part of the joint estate and that, by virtue of the purchase, they were entitled to these rights during the continuance of the respondents' marriage. The respondents, however, remained on the farm and refused to give possession to the appellants whereupon the latter applied to the court for an order of ejectment. The court *a quo* refused the application and an appeal to the Appellate Division was unsuccessful.

Fideikommissêre goed vorm nie deel van die gemeenskaplike boedel nie

Die respondente, mnr en mev Rudman, was binne gemeenskap van goed getroud. Gedurende die bestaan van die huwelik het mev Rudman die geregistreerde eienaar van 'n plaas geword onderworpe aan 'n *fideicommissum* ten gunste van haar susters. Mnr Rudman het hierna insolvent geraak en die gemeenskaplike boedel is gesekwestreer. Die appellante het al die regte van die insolvente boedel op die plaas van die kurator gekoop. Hulle het daarop aanspraak gemaak dat die reg om die plaas te besit, te gebruik en te geniet deel van die gemeenskaplike boedel gevorm het en dat hulle op grond van die koopkontrak vir die duur van die respondente se huwelik op hierdie regte geregtig was. Die respondente het egter op die plaas bly woon en geweier om besit daarvan aan die appellante af te staan. Die appellante het toe by die hof om 'n uitsettingsbevel aansoek gedoen. Hulle was onsuksesvol in die hof *a quo* en 'n appèl na die Appèlhof het ook misluk.

DE VILLIERS JA: [206] The rule of the Roman-Dutch law is concisely stated in van den Berg's *Ned. Adv. Boek* (Vol. 4 cons. 38): "*Goederen de welke fideicommis subject zyn komen niet in de conjugale gemeenskap, maar alleen de vrugten van de selve.*" (Goods subject to *fideicommissum* do not fall into the conjugal community but only the fruits thereof). Now it is common cause that the actually gathered physical fruits of fideicommissary land fall into the community, but the parties disagree as to the right of use and enjoyment of such land. The appellants contend that the interest of the fiduciary (ie, his burthened ownership) is to be analysed into two elements, viz (1) his "bare legal ownership" and (2) his "right of use and enjoyment," that is to say, the right to occupy, use, and enjoy the property, and to gather the fruits thereof, and to produce fruits therefrom. They further contend that when Roman-Dutch writers state that fideicommissary goods are excluded from the community, they mean that the bare legal ownership merely is excluded, but that the beneficial right of "use and enjoyment" falls into the community. The respondents on the other hand contend that the Roman-Dutch writers in saying that fideicommissary goods are excluded from the community, mean that the goods (*bona, goederen*) themselves are excluded from the community, and not merely the bare legal ownership; and that the "right of use and enjoyment" is excluded from the community, and that only the gathered physical fruits of the property (and the rents in the case of leased property) fall into the community. In the court below the learned Judge adopted the contention of the respondents. Now the crucial point in the appellant's contention is that the fiduciary's interest should be analysed into the two elements of "bare legal ownership" and "right of use and enjoyment". Mr *Hoexter* has insisted on the propriety and necessity of this analysis in the course of his able argument on behalf of the appellants. His argument takes this form: (1) The fiduciary's interest must be analysed into the two elements, "bare legal ownership" and [207] "right of use and enjoyment." (2) The fiduciary can lawfully alienate his right of use and enjoyment, but not his bare legal ownership. (3) The reason why fideicommissary property is excluded from community is because it is not alienable; (4) therefore only the bare right of ownership is excluded from the community, while the right of use and enjoyment falls into the community. Now in my opinion this argument fails in its very first link. Such an analysis of the fiduciary's interest, if made by this Court, would be in the nature of an afterthought, and would not reflect the Roman-Dutch rule. The Roman-Dutch writers state the rule very simply, plainly and tersely, viz that goods, "goederen," "bona," subject to *fideicommissum* do not fall into the matrimonial community. They invariably refer to the concrete physical goods themselves as being excluded from the community. They do not refer to the fiduciary's rights in those goods, and still less do they analyse his rights as Mr *Hoexter* proposes to do ...

[DE VILLIERS JA referred to a series of Roman-Dutch authors who state categorically that fideicommissary goods do not fall into the joint estate and proceeded:]

It is clear therefore that Roman-Dutch writers state simply that the goods, *goederen, bona,* themselves are excluded from the community, and none of them refers to, or analyses into constituent elements, the rights which the fiduciary holds in the goods. On the contrary, to say, as the Dutch writers do, that the goods (*goederen, bona*) are excluded from the community, is equivalent to saying that all the rights of the fiduciary in and to the goods are so excluded "save as to the fruits" [208] (*vrugten*). Mr *Hoexter's* argument therefore fails at the outset. It is accordingly unnecessary to consider the further links of his argument. I may say however, a few words with regard to the third link of his argument, viz "that the reason why fideicommissary property is excluded from community is because it is inalienable." There certainly are two writers who state that the reason for excluding fideicommissary goods from the community is because they are not freely alienable, viz Coren (*Cons.* 25) and Matthaeus (*Paroem* No 2, para 50). Coren remarks that a spouse can only bring into the community such goods (*bona*) as he can freely, and at his pleasure, alienate to another inasmuch as bringing goods into the community is a form of alienation, and that therefore goods (*bona*) subject to *fideicommissum* cannot be brought into the community as they cannot be so alienated and are consequently not considered to be absolutely in the ownership of the fiduciary (*absolute in dominio heredis*). Matthaeus' *Paroemia* is to the same effect. These authorities, however, do not advance Mr *Hoexter's* contention, for clearly the two authors apply the doctrine of "inalienability" to the fideicommissary goods, (*bona*) themselves, that is to say to the entire right and interest which the fiduciary has in the goods. They regard the fideicommissary goods themselves as being not freely alienable, and they do not analyse the fiduciary's rights into bare ownership and "right of use and enjoyment." Other authors adopt a different theoretical basis, and suggest that the reason why fideicommissary goods are excluded from the community is because they are in a sense *res alienae*... It is apparent here also that these authors apply the doctrine of *res aliena* to the fideicommissary goods themselves [209] and that no analysis of the fiduciary's rights into "bare ownership" and "use and enjoyment" enters into their speculations. They therefore do not assist Mr *Hoexter's* contention. In any case all these reasonings as to the theoretical basis of the rule of law cannot alter the rule of law which is positively stated as I have shown above, viz that the fideicommissary goods themselves are excluded from the community. Mr *Hoexter's* contention therefore, which I have thus far examined, fails in my opinion. He has, however, advanced a second argument. I am not clear whether this argument was intended by him as a separate contention, or merely as supporting his first argument. I shall deal with it as an independent contention, as I have already held that his first argument falls to the ground. This second argument is that although Roman-Dutch writers state that goods (*goederen, bona*) subject to *fideicommissum* are excluded from community, yet they add that the fruits (*vrugten, fructus*) of those goods fall into the community and he contends that by *vrugten* and *fructus* they mean not only physical fruits in the ordinary sense, but also the right to the use, possession and enjoyment of the fideicommissary property. This contention must, however, clearly be held to fail. Mr *Hoexter* does indeed quote, mainly from modern writers and dictionaries, to show that the Roman Law term *fructus* is, or was, sometimes used in a wide or secondary sense, as including not only physical fruits, but the right of using and enjoying the *res* itself; but he does not attempt to show that Roman-Dutch writers, in speaking of the *vrugten* or *fructus* of fideicommissary property as being excluded from community of goods, used these words in that wide and secondary sense. On the contrary it is clear that they use the words *vrugten* and *fructus* in their ordinary meaning, viz the physical products or produce of the fideicommissary thing (and the rents in the case of leased property)...

[DE VILLIERS JA again quoted from some Roman-Dutch authors and proceeded:]

[210] Now the ordinary meaning of the words "vrugten," "fructus," as used by writers on Roman-Dutch law, is the physical fruits or products of the land or other property, (or the rents in the case of leased land). That this is so is apparent, for instance, from the entire title (Bk 7, Tit 1) in which *Voet* deals with *fructus* in relation to the rights of a usufructuary; and in Book 41.1.28 *Voet* states in express terms that "fructus" consists of the three classes of (1) natural fruits which produce themselves without human care or culture, such as grass, timber, trees; (2) industrial fruits, which are produced with the aid of human care and culture, such as cereal crops; and (3) civil fruits, which are acquired not by nature but by law, such as rents and interest. This clearly is the meaning to be attached to the words "fructus," "vrugten," when Roman-Dutch writers lay down that the *fructus* or *vrugten* of fideicommissary property fall into the community of goods, and their meaning is not that the "right of use and enjoyment" of the fideicommissary property falls into the community. If this conclusion is correct, it disposes of the case but I wish to point out that the conclusion is strongly supported by the fact that even these *fructus* or *vrugten*, ie the physical products of fideicommissary land, do not fall into the community of property until they are gathered. Thus Wesel (*Tract de Con Com* No 2, para 143) lays down that the fruits gathered (*redacti*) from fideicommissary property, will become part of the community of property. Matthaeus (*Paroemia* No 2, para 25) states that the fruits of fideicommissary property fall into the community when they are separated from the soil, (*afgezonderd en gesepareerd*), but that fruits which still hang or stand form part of the soil. So also *Voet* (23.4.32) states that in the case of a usufruct, belonging to one spouse, the fruits gathered during the marriage fall into the community; and in other passages *Voet* states that *fructus pendentes* are part of the soil, and are therefore immovables, but when separated they become movables; and that fruits of the land only acquire the proper and distinct nature of fruits on separation from the soil, for while they are hanging they are considered not as fruits but as part of the soil. (*Voet* 1.8.13; and 7.1.28). The same

propositions are stated by Damhouder (*Prax Rer Civ Ch* 104, para 10) and by Bockelman (*Ad Pand* 6.1.9). So also Coren (*Cons* 25) states that "though fideicommissary property is excluded from the community, there [211] is nothing to prevent the fruits of such property from coming into community, for the fiduciary heir takes them and makes them his own, and can freely dispose of them." It appears, therefore, that when Roman-Dutch writers state that the *vrugten, fructus,* of fideicommissary land fall into the community, they mean that the physical products of the land fall into the community, and that even these only fall into the community when gathered and separated from the soil. It follows all the more, that the rights of use and enjoyment of the land are not *fructus* or *vrugten* of the land in this context, for they are neither physical products nor can they be "gathered" or "separated from the soil." These rights of use and enjoyment therefore do not fall into the community. To sum up, then, I come to the conclusion that when a spouse married, with community of goods, owns land subject to *fideicommissum*, only the gathered physical fruits (and the rents if the land is let) fall into such community, and that all other rights (eg the right of gathering fruits, the right of occupying the land, the right of using it for producing fruits) are excluded from the community. It follows that the decision of the learned Judge, FISHER, J, must be confirmed and the appeal dismissed . . .

STRATFORD ACJ and GARDINER, AJA concurred.

BEYERS JA concurred in a separate judgment.

[89]   BADENHORST V BEKKER

1994 2 SA 155 (N)

Effect of insolvency on separate assets of one spouse in a marriage in community	**Die effek van insolvensie op die aparte bates van 'n gade wat binne gemeenskap getroud is**

The applicant and her husband were married in community of property. In 1985 he had been declared insolvent and in consequence thereof the joint estate had been sequestrated. In 1992 the applicant's father died. In his will he left certain assets to the applicant. The will excluded these assets from the spouses' joint estate and provided that the assets would be "vry van die skulde" of her husband. The respondents, who were the trustees of the insolvent joint estate, claimed these assets. The applicant applied for a declaratory order that she was entitled to the assets. If granted, the order would mean that the assets could not be used to pay the creditors of the insolvent joint estate. The issue before the court, therefore, was whether effect could be given to the testator's wish that

Die applikant en haar man was binne gemeenskap van goed getroud. Die man is in 1985 insolvent verklaar en gevolglik is die gemeenskaplike boedel gesekwestreer. In 1992 is die applikant se vader oorlede. Hy het in sy testament sekere bates aan haar nagelaat. Die testament het hierdie bates van die gades se gemeenskaplike boedel uitgesluit en bepaal dat die bates "vry van die skulde" van haar man sou wees. Die respondente, wat die kurators van die insolvente gemeenskaplike boedel was, het hierdie bates opgeëis. Die applikant het aansoek gedoen om 'n verklarende bevel dat sy op die bates geregtig was. Indien die bevel toegestaan sou word, sou dit beteken het dat die bates nie gebruik kon word om die skuldeisers van die insolvente gemeenskaplike boedel te betaal nie. Die

the excluded assets be placed beyond the grasp of the creditors of the insolvent joint estate. The court held that effect could not be given to his wishes and that the excluded assets could be used in payment of the claims of the creditors of the joint estate.

vraag waaroor die hof moes beslis, was of gevolg gegee kon word aan die erflater se wense, naamlik dat die uitgeslote bates buite bereik van die skuldeisers van die insolvente gemeenskaplike boedel geplaas moes word. Die hof het beslis dat daar nie aan sy wense gevolg gegee kon word nie en dat die uitgeslote bates wel gebruik kon word om die eise van die skuldeisers van die gemeenskaplike boedel te betaal.

McLAREN R: [159] Die applikante se vader kon bates aan haar bemaak of skenk op so 'n wyse dat die bates nie deel sou uitmaak van die gemeenskaplike boedel nie en ook nie onderworpe sou wees aan Badenhorst se maritale mag nie. (*Erasmus v Erasmus* 1942 AD 265; *Cuming v Cuming and Others* 1945 AD 201.) Gerieflikheidshalwe verwys ek voortaan na bates wat op so 'n wyse deur 'n erflater bemaak is of deur 'n skenker geskenk is as 'uitgeslote bates'.

Ek oorweeg eerstens die effek van daardie gedeelte van die testament wat bepaal dat die applikante die uitgeslote bates erf 'vry van die skulde van' Badenhorst. Dit is duidelik dat 'n erflater nie regsgeldig kan bepaal nie dat 'n erflating nie vir beslaglegging vatbaar sal wees nie of dat dit, indien die begunstigde se boedel gesekwestreer word, nie deel sal vorm van sy insolvente boedel nie. (*Zeederberg v Zeederberg's Trustee and Another* (1864-67) 5 Searle 266 op 270, 274; *Pritchard's Trustee v Estate Pritchard* 1912 CPD 87 op 95; *Vorster v Steyn NO en Andere* 1981 (2) SA 831 (O) op 832E-833C.) Ek is derhalwe van mening dat indien die applikante se uitgeslote bates andersins vatbaar is vir beslaglegging ter voldoening van Badenhorst se skuld, die gemelde bepaling geen regskrag het nie.

Die vraag bly dus steeds wat die regsposisie is ten opsigte van uitgeslote bates indien een van die gades die bates erf nadat die gemeenskaplike boedel gesekwestreer is, maar voordat die gades gerehabiliteer is.

Die antwoord op hierdie vraag moet, myns insiens, eers in die bepalings van die Insolvensiewet 24 van 1936 ('die Wet') gesoek word.

Die sekwestrasie van die gemeenskaplike boedel van gades getroud binne gemeenskap van goed het tot gevolg dat albei insolvent word en onderwerp word aan al die gevolge van sekwestrasie. (*De Wet NO v Jurgens* 1970 (3) SA 38 (A) op 48B [90]; *Ex parte Geeringh* 1980 (2) SA 788 (O) op 789H; *Acar v Pierce and Other Like Applications* 1986 (2) SA 827 (W) op 830B-C.) Die Wet bevat geen voorskrif wat pertinent die lotgeval van uitgeslote bates behandel nie. Artikel 20(1)(a) van die Wet bepaal:

[160] 'Die sekwestrasie van die boedel van 'n insolvent het ten gevolge dat die insolvent se boedel ophou om aan hom te behoort en oorgaan op die Meester totdat 'n kurator aangestel is en na aanstelling van 'n kurator, op hom.'

Artikel 20(2)(a) van die Wet lui:

'By die toepassing van subart (1) omvat die boedel van 'n insolvent alle goedere van die insolvent op die dag van die sekwestrasie, met inbegrip van goedere of die opbrings daarvan, wat op grond van 'n lasbrief tot beslaglegging in hande van 'n balju of geregsbode is.'

Op die algemene reël wat in art 20(1)(a) vervat is, bestaan daar verskeie uitsonderings. Dit is onnodig om hierdie uitsonderings te bespreek, behalwe om aan te dui dat daar geen gesag in ons regspraak is wat onomwonde verklaar dat uitgeslote bates nie op die kurator oorgaan nie. (Vergelyk Mars *The Law of Insolvency in South Africa* 8ste uitg op 191-

205; Smith *The Law of Insolvency* 3de uitg op 87–100; Meskin *Insolvency Law* para 5.3.)

Die applikante se uitgeslote bates het haar toegeval na die sekwestrasie van die gemeenskaplike boedel.

Artikel 20(2)(*b*) van die Wet bepaal:

> 'By die toepassing van subart (1) omvat die boedel van 'n insolvent alle goedere wat gedurende die sekwestrasie deur die insolvent mag verkry word of aan hom mag toeval, vir sover art 23 nie anders bepaal nie.'

Die uitsonderings op die algemene reël wat in art 20(2)(*b*) vervat is, word uitvoerig in art 23 van die Wet behandel. Dit is weereens nie nodig om hierdie uitsonderings te bespreek nie, behalwe om aan te toon dat uitgeslote bates nie daaronder val nie. *Mars* (*op cit* 184–90); *Smith* (*loc cit*); *Meskin* (*op cit* paras 5.13, 5.14).

Die applikante se uitgeslote bates kan nie tuisgebring word onder enige van die gemelde uitsonderings nie en val derhalwe binne die kader van art 20(1)(*a*) en 20(2)(*b*) van die Wet. Enige bepaling van die gemene reg dat uitgeslote bates nie op die kurator van die insolvente gemeenskaplike boedel oorgaan nie, is myns insiens strydig met die bepalings van die Wet en het geen regskrag nie. (*Cornelissen NO v Universal Caravan Sales (Pty) Ltd* 1971 (3) SA 158 (A) op 170B–C.)

Hahlo *The South African Law of Husband and Wife* 5de uitg op 166 sê:

> 'The Insolvency Act 1936 does not deal explicitly with the position where there are, together with the community estate, separately owned assets of the wife. Where spouses are married out of community, the wife's separate estate vests in the trustee of her husband's insolvent estate under s 21(1), but the wife can claim under s 21(2) the release, *inter alia*, of any property which she had brought into the marriage or acquired during the marriage by a title valid as against her husband's creditors. Presumably the same applies, *mutatis mutandis*, where the marriage is in community, to separately owned assets of the wife.'

Dit behoef seker geen betoog nie dat art 21 van die Wet slegs van toepassing is op gades wat buite gemeenskap van goed getroud is. (*Smith* (*op cit* op 109).)

Steun vir *Hahlo* se standpunt word uitgespreek deur Van Aswegen 'Die Insolvente Gade en die Wet op Huweliksgoedere 88 van 1984' *De Rebus* Junie 1986 op 273.

Na my mening is art 21(1) van die Wet hoegenaamd nie vatbaar vir die [161] toepassing wat *Hahlo* en *Van Aswegen* voorstaan nie. Die artikel verwys na 'n eggenoot 'wie se boedel nie gesekwestreer is nie' en hy word beskryf as 'n 'solvente eggenoot'. Die gevolg van die sekwestrasie van die gemeenskaplike boedel is juis dat elkeen van die gades as 'n insolvent beskou word. (*De Wet* (*supra*); *Geeringh* (*supra*); *Acar* (*supra*).)

Ek mag fouteer in my vertolking van die tersaaklike bepalings van die, Wet en dit is derhalwe nodig om die status van uitgeslote bates in die gemene reg en ons regspraak te oorweeg.

Volgens die gemene reg was daar slegs een boedel waarop skuldeisers beslag kon lê en het die uitsluiting van bates slegs *inter coniuges* [tussen die gades] werking gehad. (*Voet* 23.4.50, 42.1.33; De Groot *Inleidinge* 1.5.22; Van Wyk *The Power to Dispose of Assets of the Universal Matrimonial Community of Property* (ongepubliseerde proefskrif, Leiden, 1976) op 60; Yeats 'Die Algehele Huweliksgemeenskap van Goedere' 1944 *THRHR* op 162–3; De Vos 'Aanspreeklikheid van die Vrou Getroud in Gemeenskap van Goedere vir Gemeenskapskulde na Ontbinding van die Huwelik' 1954 *THRHR* op 137–8; Lee en Honoré *Family, Things and Succession* 2de uitg para 82.) . . .

[McLAREN R het vervolgens 'n hele aantal tersaaklike sake geanaliseer en tot die gevolgtrekking gekom dat die sake nie gesag is vir die stelling dat daar nie op uitgeslote

bates beslag gelê kan word ter voldoening aan eise van skuldeisers van die gemeenskaplike boedel nie. Die een saak waarin uitdruklik verklaar word dat uitgeslote bates nie deur die kurator van 'n insolvente gemeenskaplike boedel aangewend kan word vir die betaling van skuld nie (*Ex parte Oberholzer* 1967 1 PH C7 (GW)) het McLAREN R as verkeerd verwerp. Hy toon aan dat die gesag nie die gevolgtrekking in *Ex parte Oberholzer* steun nie. Ook *Van Wyk v Groch* 1968 3 SA 240 (OK), waarin KOTZE R die mening gehuldig het "dat die afsonderlike eiendom van 'n getroude vrou ten opsigte waarvan die maritale mag uitgesluit is, onvatbaar is vir beslaglegging deur 'n skuldeiser van die man", is deur McLAREN R verwerp as ongestaaf en/of gebaseer op foutiewe gesag. Binne die konteks van laasgenoemde saak verwerp McLAREN R ook Hahlo se standpunt dat daar nie op uitgeslote bates beslag gelê kan word nie. Hy gaan dan voort:]

[168] Na my mening gaan *Hahlo* se argument dat daar nie op uitgeslote bates beslag gelê kan word nie, 'for otherwise the exclusion would make little sense', nie op nie. Die gevolge van die uitsluiting van 'n bate van die gemeenskaplike boedel is dat die begunstigde gade nie daardie bate met die ander gade hoef te deel nie wanneer die huwelik ontbind en, indien die man se maritale mag ook uitgesluit is, dat sy vrou gedurende die huwelik die uitsluitlike beheer oor die bate het.

Dit is duidelik dat *Hahlo* nie die vraag na die status van uitgeslote bates ondersoek het met verwysing na die vraag of die begunstigde gade ook 'n skuldenaar is en die algemene beginsels van die eksekusiereg nie . . .

[McLAREN R verwys daarna na ander outeurs wat botsende standpunte huldig oor die vraag of uitgeslote bates vir beslaglegging van skulde van die gemeenskaplike boedel vatbaar is. Hy vervolg:]

[170] Gesien die onsekerheid van die status van uitgeslote bates wanneer die gemeenskaplike boedel gesekwestreer word, is dit wenslik om sekere beginsels in oënskou te neem.

Die algemene reël is dat 'n skuldeiser op enige bate van sy skuldenaar beslag kan lê ter voldoening van sy vordering. (*Johannesburg Municipality v Cohen's Trustee* 1909 TS 811 op 818; *Gibson v Howard* 1918 TPD 185 op 186.)

Op hierdie algemene reël bestaan daar verskeie uitsonderings. (Kyk, byvoorbeeld, art 67 van die Wet op Landdroshowe 32 van 1944, en Jones en Buckle *The Civil Practice of the Magistrates' Courts in South Africa* 7de [171] uitg band 1 op 240-1. Vergelyk ook art 65D(4)(*a*) van Wet 32 van 1944 [die Wet op Landdroshowe].) Die uitsonderings bestaan klaarblyklik uit hoofde van gemeenskapsoorwegings.

Dit is teen hierdie agtergrond dat daar vasgestel moet word of die applikante 'n skuldenaar is van die skuldeisers wat vorderings teen die insolvente boedel bewys het. Dit wil vir my voorkom asof die onsekerheid wat daar heers ten aansien van die status van uitgeslote bates wanneer die gemeenskaplike boedel gesekwestreer word, grotendeels toegeskryf kan word aan die versuim om te bepaal of die betrokke gade 'n skuldenaar van die insolvente gemeenskaplike boedel se skuldeisers is.

In hierdie verband sê *Lee en Honoré* (*op cit* para 82 n 3) die volgende:

'The precise nature and implications of this community of debts are matters of some difficulty and uncertainty in our present law . . . This is due to the fact that our Courts (mostly unconsciously) vacillate between two entirely different approaches. The first approach treats the spouses as joint debtors with the result that the community can be described as a complex of joint assets and joint debts. During the existence of the community such debts can be recovered from *all* the assets of *both* spouses and, logically, both spouses should at dissolution of the community be liable for the full amount of all joint debts still unpaid at that stage . . . The second approach does not regard the spouses as joint debtors, but teaches that a "joint" debt is actually the debt of the spouse

incurring it, although the liability for the performance rests on the joint estate (and the private estate of *that* spouse) ... Our old authorities apparently subscribed to the first approach and taught that the exclusion of assets from the joint estate has no effect on the rights of creditors; joint debts can therefore be recovered from all the assets of both spouses ...'

In *Nedbank Ltd v Van Zyl* 1990 (2) SA 469 (A) op 476B–E [91] is die volgende gesê:

'The legal position in regard to contractual debts incurred by husband and wife where they are married to one another in community of property was authoritatively stated by this Court in *De Wet NO v Jurgens* 1970 (3) SA 38 (A) as follows (at 47D–F):

"Dit blyk duidelik dat die man en die vrou se skulde gemeenskaplike skulde is wat uit die gemeenskaplike boedel betaalbaar is. Hulle is dus eintlik medeskuldenaars. Dit is wel waar dat die man gewoonweg verantwoordelik is vir die betaling van skulde, maar dit beteken nie dat net hy skuldenaar is nie. Betalings word van hom geëis omdat hy in beheer van die boedel is, en hy word in die Hof aangespreek omdat, behalwe in sekere uitsonderingsgevalle, slegs hy voor die Hof gedaag kan word. Wanneer hy skulde betaal, betaal hy dit uit die gemeenskaplike boedel, en wanneer hy 'n vonnisskuld nie betaal nie, word eksekusie teen die bates in die gemeenskaplike boedel gehef."

On the facts of this case it is not necessary to consider what the position is with regard to so-called "private debts" (see Lee and Honoré *Family, Things and Succession* 2nd ed paras 82–4).'

Ook in die onderhawige geval is daar geen sprake daarvan nie dat die vordering van enige een van die skuldeisers 'n sogenaamde 'privaatskuld' is nie.

Van Wyk (*op cit* op 57) bespreek die teorie, naamlik dat die gades getroud binne gemeenskap van goed nie medeskuldenaars is nie en sê (op 64) dat *De Wet* (*supra*) gesag teen die aanvaarding van hierdie teorie is. *Nedbank* (*supra* op 476G–H, 477C en 478J–479A) maak dit baie duidelik dat gades getroud binne gemeenskap van goed medeskuldenaars is.

Ek kom derhalwe tot die gevolgtrekking dat, aangesien die applikante 'n medeskuldenaar is van die skuldeisers in die insolvente gemeenskaplike boedel, haar uitgeslote bates ook aangewend kan word ter delging van die vorderings teen die boedel. Hierdie gevolgtrekking is onversoenbaar met *Oberholzer* (*supra*) en ek verskil eerbiediglik van daardie beslissing.

Na my mening staan die *obiter* verwysing deur VAN HEERDEN R in *Geeringh* (*supra* op 789G–H) na die 'aparte boedel' van 'n vrou wat terselfdertyd 'n insolvent is as gevolg van die sekwestrasie van die gemeenskaplike boedel, nie in die weg van my slotsom nie. (Vergelyk *Sonnekus* ([1986 *TSAR* 92] op 98).)

Die resultaat mag onbillik voorkom, maar dit is myns insiens 'n onafwendbare gevolg van die applikante se huwelik binne gemeenskap van goed ...

Die aansoek word van die hand gewys ...

Note

There are, as was indicated in the case under discussion, conflicting views on the issue of whether the excluded assets of one spouse are protected against creditors of the joint estate. It is generally accepted that the excluded assets of one spouse can be attached in respect of debts of the joint estate which were incurred by that spouse. The dispute therefore is really only about the

Aantekening

Soos wat in die onderhawige saak aangedui is, is daar teenstrydige menings oor die vraag of die uitgeslote bates van die een gade beskerm is teen skuldeisers van die gemeenskaplike boedel. Dit word algemeen aanvaar dat die uitgeslote bates van die een gade vatbaar is vir beslaglegging ter delging van skulde van die gemeenskaplike boedel wat aangegaan is deur daardie gade. Die dis-

question of whether these assets can be attached in respect of debts which were incurred by the other spouse and which bind the joint estate. The decision in the case under discussion, namely that those assets can be attached and that they can, in the case of insolvency, be used to pay the creditors of the joint estate, corresponds with the recommendations made by the South African Law Commission in its *Working Paper 41* Project 63 *Review of the Law of Insolvency: Voidable Dispositions and Dispositions that may be set aside and the Effect of Sequestration on the Spouse of the Insolvent* 1991. The Law Commission considers it desirable that the exclusion of assets from a joint estate should be effective only as between the spouses and that it should not affect creditors (par 4.28), and that, in the case of insolvency, the insolvent estate should encompass the joint assets of the spouses as well as their excluded assets (par 4.33). On this case see further Nagel and Boraine 1993 *De Jure* 457; Sonnekus 1994 *TSAR* 143.

puut gaan dus eintlik net om die vraag of op hierdie bates beslag gelê kan word ter delging van skulde wat die ander gade aangegaan het en wat die gemeenskaplike boedel bind. Die beslissing in die onderhawige saak, naamlik dat wel op sodanige bates beslag gelê kan word en dat hulle in die geval van insolvensie ook aangewend kan word om skuldeisers van die gemeenskaplike boedel te betaal, is in ooreenstemming met die aanbevelings van die Suid-Afrikaanse Regskommissie in sy *Werkstuk 41* Projek 63 *Hersiening van die Insolvensiereg: Vervreemdings wat Nietig is of ter syde gestel kan word en die Uitwerking van Sekwestrasie op die Insolvent se Gade* 1991. Die Regskommissie ag dit wenslik dat die uitsluiting van bates uit 'n gemeenskaplike boedel slegs tussen die gades moet geld en dat dit nie skuldeisers affekteer nie (par 4.28) en dat, in die geval van insolvensie, die insolvente boedel die gemeenskaplike bates sowel as die uitgeslote bates van die gades moet insluit (par 4.33). Sien oor hierdie saak verder Nagel en Boraine 1993 *De Jure* 457; Sonnekus 1994 *TSAR* 143.

Joint liabilities   **Gemeenskaplike laste**

[90]   DE WET V JURGENS

1970 3 SA 38 (A)

Nature of the liability of spouses for their joint debts

Aard van die aanspreeklikheid van gades vir hulle gemeenskaplike skuld

The respondent was married in community of property. Her husband committed adultery with a woman named Shaw. Shaw's conduct affected the respondent to such an extent that she had to receive medical treatment. The respondent, with her husband's consent (which was necessary because she was subject to the marital power), claimed damages for injury to personality as well as for medical expenses from Shaw. Her husband was declared insolvent before the amount of damages was paid to the respondent. When the amount was eventually paid to the respondent, the curator of the insolvent estate (appellant) claimed the amount as he contended

Die respondent was binne gemeenskap van goed getroud. Haar man het owerspel gepleeg met 'n vrou genaamd Shaw. Shaw se optrede het tot gevolg gehad dat die respondent se gesondheid benadeel is en sy mediese behandeling moes ontvang. Die respondent het, met haar man se bystand (wat nodig was omdat sy aan die maritale mag onderworpe was), vergoeding vir persoonlikheidsnadeel sowel as vir mediese onkoste van Shaw geëis. Haar man is insolvent verklaar voordat die bedrag vergoeding aan die respondent uitbetaal is. Toe die bedrag uiteindelik aan die respondent betaal is, het die kurator van die insolvente boedel (appellant) geëis dat die be-

that it fell within the insolvent estate. The argument was that the respondent was an insolvent because her husband was an insolvent and that the damages fell within the insolvent estate. The court *a quo* held that the respondent was an insolvent but that the damages did not fall within the insolvent estate as it was excluded by section 23(8) of the Insolvency Act 24 of 1936. The curator appealed against this decision. It was argued on behalf of the appellant that a wife who is married in community of property, does not become an insolvent in terms of the Insolvency Act merely because her husband's estate has been sequestrated. The respondent therefore did not enjoy the protection of section 23(8) of the Insolvency Act. The argument then ran that the damages fell within the insolvent joint estate and that the executor could claim it. Alternatively it was argued that if the wife was an insolvent, the damages awarded to her were not excluded from the insolvent estate in terms of section 23(8) of the Insolvency Act which meant that the executor could claim it. On behalf of the respondent it was argued that she was an insolvent and that the damages were compensation for personal injury and were therefore excluded from the insolvent estate in terms of section 23(8) of the Insolvency Act. The appeal was dismissed.

drag aan hom oorbetaal moes word aangesien hy beweer het dat die bedrag in die insolvente boedel geval het. Daar is naamlik aangevoer dat die respondent 'n insolvent was omdat haar man 'n insolvent was en dat die vergoeding in die insolvente boedel geval het. Die hof *a quo* het beslis dat die respondent 'n insolvent was maar dat die vergoeding nie in die insolvente boedel geval het nie omdat dit deur artikel 23(8) van die Insolvensiewet 24 van 1936 uitgesluit was. Die kurator het teen hierdie beslissing geappelleer. Namens die appellant is aangevoer dat 'n vrou wat binne gemeenskap van goed getroud is, nie ook 'n insolvent ingevolge die Insolvensiewet word, bloot omdat haar man se boedel gesekwestreer is nie. Die respondent kon dus nie aanspraak maak op die beskerming van artikel 23(8) van die Insolvensiewet nie. Daar is beweer dat dit tot gevolg gehad het dat die vergoeding in die insolvente gemeenskaplike boedel geval het en dat die kurator daarop beslag kon lê. In die alternatief is aangevoer dat, indien die vrou 'n insolvent was, die vergoeding nie deur artikel 23(8) van die Insolvensiewet van die insolvente boedel uitgesluit was nie, wat beteken het dat die kurator daarop beslag kon lê. Namens die respondent is aangevoer dat sy wel 'n insolvent was en dat hierdie vergoeding vergoeding vir persoonlike letsel was wat deur artikel 23(8) van die Insolvensiewet van die insolvente boedel uitgesluit is. Die appèl is van die hand gewys.

RABIE WN AR: [45] Art 23(8) van die Insolvensiewet (hierna "die Wet" genoem) lees soos volg in die getekende Afrikaanse teks:

> "Die insolvent kan vergoeding van verlies of skade wat hy hetsy voor of na die sekwestrasie van sy boedel mag gely het weens belastering of persoonlike letsel, tot sy eie voordeel invorder: Met dien verstande dat hy nie sonder toestemming van die hof 'n aksie teen die kurator van sy boedel kan instel nie op grond van kwaadwillige vervolging of laster." . . .

Hierdie sub-artikel laat twee vrae ontstaan, die antwoord waarop die uitslag van die appèl sal bepaal, nl (i) of die respondente 'n "insolvent" is soos in die sub-artikel bedoel, en (ii) of, indien sy wel 'n "insolvent" is, sy skade gely het weens "persoonlike letsel" soos in [die] sub-art bedoel.

Ek behandel eers die eerste vraag. In art 2 van die Wet word "insolvent", wanneer dit as selfstandige naamwoord gebruik word, omskrywe as

" 'n skuldenaar wie se boedel onder sekwestrasie is en omvat, na gelang van die samehang, ook so 'n skuldenaar voor die sekwestrasie van sy boedel".

"Skuldenaar" word in dieselfde artikel omskryf as

" 'n persoon of vennootskap of die boedel van 'n persoon of vennootskap wat 'n skuldenaar volgens die gewone betekenis van die woord is, met uitsondering van 'n regspersoon, maatskappy of ander vereniging van persone wat kragtens die Wet op Maátskappye gelikwideer kan word".

Die appellant se hoofbetoog in hierdie verband is, kort gestel, die volgende: by 'n huwelik in gemeenskap van goed is die man in volle beheer van die boedel; hy het die alleenreg om die bates in die boedel te vervreem; hy betaal ook die skulde van die boedel en die vrou se [46] regte is van so 'n beperkte aard dat sy vóór ontbinding van die gemeenskap geen ware of effektiewe eiendomsreg t.o.v. die boedel het nie. Gevolglik, lui die betoog, kan die vrou nie as skuldenaar beskou word nie . . .

Ek kan nie met appellant se betoog saamstem nie. By 'n huwelik in gemeenskap van goed is die man en die vrou, behalwe in uitsonderingsgevalle wat hier nie ter sprake is nie, gesamentlike eienaars van die gemeenskaplike boedel . . . By die aangaan van so 'n huwelik word nie slegs die bates nie, maar ook die skulde, gemeen . . .

Hierdie gemeenwording van skulde geld nie alleen vir die voorhuwelikse skulde van die man en die vrou nie, maar ook vir skulde wat staande huwelik aangegaan word deur die man, of deur die vrou waar sy die nodige bevoegdheid daartoe het . . .

[47] Dit blyk duidelik dat die man en die vrou se skulde gemeenskaplike skulde is wat uit die gemeenskaplike boedel betaalbaar is. *Hulle is dus eintlik medeskuldenaars* [ons kursivering]. Dit is wel waar dat die man gewoonweg verantwoordelik is vir die betaling van skulde, maar dit beteken nie dat net hy skuldenaar is nie. Betalings word van hom geëis omdat hy in beheer van die boedel is, en hy word in die Hof aangespreek omdat, behalwe in sekere uitsonderingsgevalle, slegs hy voor die Hof gedaag kan word. Wanneer hy skulde betaal, betaal hy dit uit die gemeenskaplike boedel, en wanneer hy 'n vonnisskuld nie betaal nie, word eksekusie teen die bates in die gemeenskaplike boedel gehef. In hierdie omstandighede kan m.i. nie gesê word dat net die man as skuldenaar beskou moet word nie . . .

[48] [N]a my mening moet die sekwestrasie van die gemeenskaplike boedel noodwendig meebring dat die man sowel as die vrou insolvent word. Die vrou het nie 'n afsonderlike boedel ten opsigte waarvan 'n sekwestrasiebevel uitgereik kan word nie. (Kyk, bv, *Ex parte Vally*, 1930 CPD 304; *Edges v Goldin*, 1946 TPD 98 op bl 100; *Davids v Pullen and Others*, 1958 (2) SA 405 (C) op bl 408). Die man en die vrou het saam één boedel en as dit gesekwestreer word, kan die een nie insolvent wees en die ander solvent nie . . .

[RABIE WN AR het die bewoording van die bepalings van die Insolvensiewet 24 van 1936 ontleed om te bepaal of die vergoeding wat aan die vrou uitbetaal is wel in die insolvente boedel val of nie. Op grond van sy ontleding het hy tot die gevolgtrekking gekom dat dit vergoeding weens "persoonlike letsel" was soos bepaal in artikel 23(8) van die betrokke wet en dat dit gevolglik nie in die insolvente boedel val nie omdat vergoeding weens persoonlike letsel statutêr uitgesluit is van die insolvente boedel.]

[53] My mening is derhalwe dat die beslissing van die Hof *a quo* korrek was en dat die appèl nie kan slaag nie . . .

STEYN HR; VAN BLERK AR; BOTHA AR en TROLLIP AR het saamgestem.

Note	Aantekening
In the case under discussion the spouses were simply regarded as co-debtors in respect of joint	In die onderhawige saak is die gades eenvoudig as medeskuldenaars beskou ten opsigte van ge-

debts (47) but it has also been said that the spouses remain separate debtors although the debt has to be paid out of the joint estate, unless the spouse who incurred the debt has sufficient separate property to cover it (see for example *Santam Versekeringsmaatskappy Bpk v Roux* 1978 2 SA 856 (A)). Certainty that the spouses are co-debtors in respect of liabilities of the joint estate was brought about by *Nedbank v Van Zyl* [91].

See also the note on *Nedbank v Van Zyl*.

meenskaplike skulde (47) maar daar is ook al gesê dat die gades afsonderlike skuldenaars bly al moet die skuld uit die gemeenskaplike boedel betaal word tensy die gade wat die skuld aangegaan het voldoende afsonderlike bates het om die skuld te betaal (sien byvoorbeeld *Santam Versekeringsmaatskappy Bpk v Roux* 1978 2 SA 856 (A)). Na die beslissing in *Nedbank Van Zyl* [91] is dit duidelik dat die gades medeskuldenaars is ten opsigte van skulde wat die gemeenskaplike boedel bind.

Sien ook die aantekening by *Nedbank v Van Zyl*.

[91] NEDBANK v VAN ZYL

1990 2 SA 469 (A)

Wife married in community of property cannot stand surety for debts owed by her husband

In September 1980 the respondent, Mrs Van Zyl, entered into a written contract of suretyship with the appellant in terms of which she bound herself to the appellant as surety and co-principal debtor for the repayment on demand of all moneys owed by her husband, Mr Van Zyl, to the appellant on overdraft then and from time to time thereafter. At the time of the execution of this contract Mr and Mrs Van Zyl were married in community of property, but in 1982 they were divorced. During 1984 Mr Van Zyl defaulted on his obligations to the appellant and all the appellant's endeavours to recover the amount owing to it from Mr Van Zyl were fruitless. The appellant then instituted action against the respondent claiming payment of the outstanding amount together with interest and costs. The appellant sought to hold the respondent liable solely on the basis of the deed of suretyship. In the court *a quo* it was held that the deed of suretyship was a nullity and the appellant's claim was dismissed. The appellant's appeal to the Appellate Division was unsuccessful.

'n Vrou wat binne gemeenskap van goed getroud is, kan nie vir haar man se skuld borg staan nie

In September 1980 het die respondent, mev Van Zyl, 'n skriftelike borgkontrak met die appellant aangegaan ingevolge waarvan sy haar teenoor laasgenoemde as borg en medehoofskuldenaar verbind het vir die terugbetaling op aanvraag van enige geldsom wat haar man, mnr Van Zyl, toe en daarna op 'n oortrokke rekening aan die appellant verskuldig mag wees. Ten tyde van die aangaan van hierdie kontrak was mnr en mev Van Zyl binne gemeenskap van goed getroud, maar in 1982 is hulle geskei. Gedurende 1984 het mnr Van Zyl versuim om sy verpligtinge teenoor die appellant na te kom en al die appellant se pogings om die verskuldigde bedrag van hom te verhaal was vrugteloos. Die appellant het toe die respondent vir die uitstaande bedrag plus rente en koste gedagvaar. Die appellant het sy eis teen die respondent uitsluitlik op die borgkontrak gebaseer. Die hof *a quo* het beslis dat die borgkontrak nietig was en die eis is van die hand gewys. Die appellant se appèl na die Appèlhof was onsuksesvol.

CORBETT CJ: [473] One of the crucial issues which arises on appeal is whether a wife married in community of property can validly enter into a contract in terms of which she stands surety for a monetary obligation undertaken by her husband. There are two conflicting decisions on this point. In *Reichmans (Pty) Ltd v Ramdass* 1985 (2) SA 111 (D) FRIEDMAN J held that such a deed of suretyship was valid; and in the unreported case of *Volkskas Bpk v Van Heerden*, decided on 20 May 1985 in the Cape Provincial Division, ROSE-INNES J held that it was not. In the present case ROUX J [in the court *a quo*] preferred to follow the decision, and reasoning, in *Volkskas Bpk v Van Heerden*.

Fundamental to the decision in the latter case were the propositions that a person cannot stand surety for his own obligation; and that if he purports to do so the resulting transaction is a nullity. There is authority to support these propositions. The obligations of a surety are essentially accessory in nature, in the sense that they are grafted onto a principal obligation and without a principal obligation they can have no separate existence. The definition of a contract of suretyship given in Caney *The Law of Suretyship* 3rd ed at 27 reads as follows:

> 'Suretyship is an accessory contract by which a person (the surety) undertakes to the creditor of another (the principal debtor), primarily that the principal debtor, who remains bound, will perform his obligation to the creditor and, secondarily that if and so far as the principal debtor fails to do so, he, the surety, will perform it or, failing that, indemnify the creditor' . . .

Of course, this is not to say that the principal obligation must be in existence at the time when the contract of suretyship is entered into . . . [A] suretyship [474] may be contracted with reference to a principal obligation which is to come into existence in the future, in which event the obligation of the surety does not arise until the principal obligation has been contracted. In the meanwhile it is, as Van der Keessel (*Praelectiones* 3.3.24) puts it, '*in pendenti*'. (See also *Digest* 5.1.35.)

One of the consequences of the accessory nature of a suretyship obligation is that it must relate to a principal obligation *owed by another*. This is reflected in *Caney's* definition and the principle may be traced back to Roman law. [See] *Digest* 46.1.21 . . .

[475] Modern South African writers also accept that under our law it is essential to the existence of a suretyship that there be a principal obligation in terms whereof someone other than the surety is the debtor; and that a person cannot stand as surety for his own debt (see De Wet and Yeats *Kontrakteg en Handelsreg* 4th ed at 345; Joubert (ed) *Law of South Africa* vol 26 para 153; Caney *The Law of Suretyship* 3rd ed at 27–8, 174; Wessels *Law of Contract in South Africa* 2nd ed paras 2624, 4368; Van Jaarsveld *Suid-Afrikaanse Handelsreg* 3rd ed at 760). It may be argued that the corollary to this would seem to be that a contract, intended by the parties to constitute a suretyship, in terms of which a person purports to stand surety for a principal obligation owed by himself, is a nullity (see *Law of South Africa* vol 26 para 153); cf *Croxon's Garage (Pty) Ltd v Olivier* 1971 (4) SA 85 (T) at 88A–C. In *Standard Bank of SA Ltd v Lombard and Another* 1977 (2) SA 808 (W) at 813F–H, and in the *Reichmans* case *supra* at 114E, it was accepted or assumed that a person cannot validly stand as surety for his own debt. In *Litecor Voltex (Natal) (Pty) Ltd v Jason* 1988 (2) SA 78 (D) DIDCOTT J expressed doubts as to the correctness of a classification of invalidity, but went on to say (at 81B):

> 'To guarantee the payment of your own debt is a futile exercise, to say the least, neither underwriting nor reinforcing the obligation to pay it that rests on you in any event. Failing the basic test for a suretyship, it does not amount to such. Nor does it accomplish anything else. It is not worth, in short, the paper on which it is written.'

It seems to me that, whatever the precise terminology should be, an undertaking in a contract whereby a person purports to stand as surety for his own debt is not a legally enforceable one.

In the present case the respondent bound herself in terms of the contract as surety *and* co-principal debtor ('borg en medehoofskuldenaar'). It is clear, however, that this undertaking as co-principal debtor did not in any way change the purported nature of the contract, viz one of suretyship, the [476] effect of such an undertaking merely being a renunciation of the benefits of excussion and division (see *Neon and Cold Cathode Illuminations (Pty) Ltd v Ephron* 1978 (1) SA 463 (A) at 471D-E).

The next question is whether a contract whereby a woman married in community of property purports (with her husband's assistance) to stand surety for an obligation undertaken by her husband amounts to standing surety for one's own debt.

The legal position in regard to contractual debts incurred by husband and wife where they are married to one another in community of property was authoritatively stated by this Court in *De Wet NO v Jurgens* 1970 (3) SA 38 (A) as follows (at 47D-F) [90].

> 'Dit blyk duidelik dat die man en die vrou se skulde gemeenskaplike skulde is wat uit die gemeenskaplike boedel betaalbaar is. Hulle is dus eintlik medeskuldenaars. Dit is wel waar dat die man gewoonweg verantwoordelik is vir die betaling van skulde, maar dit beteken nie dat net hy skuldenaar is nie. Betalings word van hom geëis omdat hy in beheer van die boedel is, en hy word in die Hof aangespreek omdat, behalwe in sekere uitsonderingsgevalle, slegs hy voor die Hof gedaag kan word. Wanneer hy skulde betaal, betaal hy dit uit die gemeenskaplike boedel, en wanneer hy 'n vonnisskuld nie betaal nie, word eksekusie teen die bates in die gemeenskaplike boedel gehef.'

On the facts of this case it is not necessary to consider what the position is with regard to so-called 'private debts' (see Lee and Honoré *Family, Things and Succession* 2nd ed (paras 82-4)).

If the principles enunciated in *De Wet NO v Jurgens* (*supra*) be applied in the present case, then it is clear that on 10 September 1980, when the suretyship contract was signed, the principal debt, viz the amount owed or to be owed to appellant on overdraft, was the joint obligation of Van Zyl and respondent. Moreover, although the suretyship was entered into by respondent alone as surety . . ., the suretyship obligation which she thus purported to incur would, if valid, likewise become a joint obligation owed by Van Zyl and herself. There was thus at the time of signature of the suretyship a complete identity of surety and principal debtor: the purported effect of the transaction was to make respondent and Van Zyl co-sureties of the overdraft obligation in respect of which they were co-debtors. It was consequently a clear case of persons standing surety for their own debt and, in my view, in the light of the principles expounded above, the suretyship was unenforceable when entered into.

The position is, of course, complicated by the fact that at the time when appellant instituted action against respondent (in March 1985) respondent was no longer married to Van Zyl, their marriage having been dissolved by divorce on 25 May 1982. Although the evidence on the point is not clear, it seems probable that as at the date of divorce Van Zyl's current account with appellant was overdrawn.

Upon divorce the community of property and of debts subsisting between Van Zyl and respondent was terminated and respondent became endowed with full legal capacity. Each became entitled to half the joint estate, such as it was, and the assets thereof were divided by agreement between them. Debts incurred as joint liabilities during the marriage and [477] unpaid as at the dissolution of the marriage remained exigible from the former parties to the marriage. In Lee and Honoré (*op cit* para 97) it is stated that such a debt may be enforced by the creditor concerned for the whole amount outstanding against the estate of the spouse who incurred it and for half the amount against the estate of the other spouse; and that the original debtor who has paid the whole amount has a *regressus pro semisse* against the other spouse because the debt was a joint one. As the learned author of this section (Prof *AH van Wyk*) indicates, however, the position is not altogether clear, particularly in the light of our case law. But I do not find it necessary in present circumstances to express any view as to the precise nature of the post-nuptial liability of the spouses for community debts. What is of significance is the fact that as at the date of dissolution of the marriage the amount owing to appellant on overdraft remained a joint liability of the parties; and that thereafter all subsequent amounts advanced by appellant to Van Zyl on overdraft constituted his own separate liability.

I would again emphasise that at no time did appellant seek to recover the amount owed on overdraft (as at 23 October 1984) from respondent on the basis of her liability for the joint debts of the community (at the time of the dissolution); and that the present claim is based entirely on the contract of suretyship.

The questions which now arise are how, if at all, the termination of the marriage and the consequent dissolution of the community of property and debts between Van Zyl and the respondent affected the position; and whether under such changed circumstances respondent became liable on the suretyship for the outstanding amount of Van Zyl's overdraft. The suretyship is in the widest possible terms. The relevant portion reads:

> 'Vir die verlening deur Nedbank Bpk (hierna "die genoemde Bank") van sekere bank-fasiliteite aan Petrus Gideon van Zyl ... (hierna genoem die "genoemde skuldenaar") garandeer en verbind ek ... die ondergetekende ... Magrieta van Zyl my ... sowel gesamentlik as afsonderlik ... as borg en medehoofskuldenaar ... vir die terugbetaling op aanvraag van enige geldsom of geldsomme wat die genoemde skuldenaar ... nou of hierna van tyd tot tyd aan genoemde Bank ... skuldig mag wees ... hetsy die skuld voortspruit uit geld wat reeds voorgeskiet is of hierna voorgeskiet sal word ...'

Accordingly it might be contended that as there is no limitation as to the duration and applicability of the surety's undertaking it covers overdraft obligations (to the appellant) incurred by Van Zyl after the divorce; and that *qua* such future obligations the suretyship was valid and enforceable.

The chief obstacle in the path of this line of argument is that proof that the amount of R15 213,61 constituted a post-nuptial overdraft obligation is totally lacking. As I have indicated, it is probable that at the time of the divorce Van Zyl's current account was overdrawn, possibly in an amount at least equivalent to the amount of appellant's claim; but appellant made no attempt either in the pleadings or the evidence at the trial or in the course of argument before us to establish precisely what the overdraft amount was at the time of the divorce or to show that, according to a correct process of appropriation or allocation of deposits (cf *Trust Bank of Africa Ltd v Senekal* 1977 (2) SA 587 (W); Paget's *Law of Banking* 9th ed at 118ff); the debit balance existing at the time of divorce had been wholly [478] liquidated by 23 October 1984, when the claim was computed ... Thus, even if the claim could in law be based upon the validity of the suretyship insofar as it related to the post-nuptial obligations of Van Zyl to appellant's bank, it must fail for want of a proven factual foundation.

Finally, I must refer to the decision in the *Reichmans* case *supra*. In that case FRIEDMAN J was confronted with a factual situation similar to the present one. The main differences were that (*a*) in that case the wife, who stood surety, owned a valuable piece of immovable property which she had acquired by way of inheritance and which did not form part of the joint estate, and (*b*) husband and wife were still married to one another at the time when the creditor sued the wife (defendant) on the deed of suretyship. It was argued on behalf of the defendant that she was in effect standing surety for herself and that this was something which in law created a nullity.

FRIEDMAN J rejected this argument and gave judgment for the plaintiff. He assumed in favour of the defendant that one cannot stand surety for oneself (see at 114E). His further reasoning may be summarised as follows:

(1) It does not follow from the fact that the joint estate may be liable for the payment of any debt incurred by the wife under the suretyship that she is standing surety for herself: her husband, not she, is the principal debtor.

(2) The rights and obligations of the wife under the deed of suretyship differ in certain respects from those of the principal debtor.

(3) The suretyship agreement could survive the dissolution of the marriage, upon which there would be a total separation of identity between surety and principal debtor.

(4) The joint estate is not the only source out of which the wife's indebtedness to the creditor can and need necessarily be met, eg where the wife has assets falling outside the community.

With respect, I am not able to agree with this reasoning. As to (1), it seems to me that it is incorrect to say that the husband is the principal debtor. Husband and wife are in truth joint debtors with regard to the [479] principal debt, even though it may contractually have been incurred by him. As to (2), the rights and obligations under the suretyship are also those of both husband and wife, owed jointly. As I have indicated, the point made under (3) may, given the proper facts, be sound in the sense that the suretyship is enforceable in respect of post-nuptial obligations, but I fail to see the relevance of this in a case where the marriage has not been dissolved or where the obligations are incurred *stante matrimonio*. And as to (4), the fact that the wife may have assets outside the community, which is not pertinent in the present case, does not seem to me to alter the basic identity between surety and principal debtor.

FRIEDMAN J also referred by way of analogy to the following remarks of BOTHA J in the *Standard Bank* case *supra* at 813F–H (a case concerned with whether a partner could validly bind himself as a surety for the debts of the partnership):

'In the next place counsel for the defendant submitted that, since a partnership was not a legal *persona* separate from the individual partners, partners could not validly bind themselves as sureties for the partnership, because they would in effect be standing in as sureties for themselves. I was not referred to any authority for the proposition that partners could not validly bind themselves individually as sureties for partnership debts. (Cf Caney on *Suretyship* 2nd ed at 48.) In matters of practice and procedure, the law does to some extent recognise the existence of a partnership as an entity in itself, albeit not as an entity endowed with legal personality. Thus a creditor of the partnership is obliged during the subsistence of the partnership to sue all the partners together for payment of the partnership debts and execution must first be levied on partnership assets before the assets of individual partners may be attached in execution. I can see no reason in principle why partners should not bind themselves to a partnership creditor in such a way that each partner is individually liable *in solidum* to the creditor for payment of the whole of the partnership debts, even during the subsistence of the partnership. This, I conceive, was plainly the object sought to be achieved by means of the documents in question in this case. I can see no reason why the documents should not be valid and operative as such, even if it is to be assumed that they do not qualify as suretyships *stricto sensu*, a matter on which I need not express any firm opinion.'

And it is to be noted that in *Du Toit en 'n Ander v Barclays Nasionale Bank Bpk* 1985 (1) SA 563 (A) at 575F–G, this Court confirmed these views. I do not think that the partnership analogy is a valid one. Unlike a partnership, there is no basis for saying that the law, to any extent, recognises the relationship of marriage in community 'as an entity in itself'; nor do the features of the law of partnership emphasised in this quotation from the judgment in the *Standard Bank* case find any parallel in marriage in community.

I accordingly agree with the conclusion reached by the Court *a quo*. The appeal is dismissed with costs.

HEFER JA; NESTADT JA; FH GROSSKOPF JA and NICHOLAS AJA concurred.

Note

The view in respect of the nature of the liability of spouses for joint debts which was expressed in *De Wet v Jurgens* [90] was confirmed and applied in *Nedbank v Van Zyl*. The court held that spouses who are married in community of property are co-debtors in respect of liabilities that bind the joint estate. Applying this rule, the court held that the principal debt (the debt to the bank in respect of the overdraft) was the joint obligation of the spouses. By entering into the suretyship the wife had therefore attempted to stand surety for her own debt. The court accordingly declared the deed of suretyship to be unenforceable.

The court correctly rejected the decision in *Reichmans (Pty) Ltd v Ramdass* 1985 2 SA 111 (D) where it was held that a wife married in community of property can stand surety for debts of the joint estate. In *Reichmans* the court decided that in standing surety for the liabilities of the joint estate the wife was not standing surety for her own debts. This decision was based on the reasoning that the husband, not the wife, was the principal debtor and that the rights and obligations of the surety and those of the principal debtor were not the same. The judge further stated that a suretyship agreement might well survive the dissolution of the marriage and that there would then no longer be "any form of identity between surety and principal debtor". In that case the wife's liability as surety would not be co-extensive with her liability as co-owner of the joint estate. In deciding that the wife could stand surety for debts of the joint estate the court also relied on the fact that she had assets which did not fall into the joint estate. The court considered that these assets could be attached in execution.

See also the note on *De Wet v Jurgens* [90].

Aantekening

Die mening oor die aard van die gades se aanspreeklikheid vir gemeenskaplike skulde wat die hof in *De Wet v Jurgens* [90] uitgespreek het, is in *Nedbank v Van Zyl* bevestig en toegepas. Die hof het beslis dat gades wat binne gemeenskap van goed getroud is medeskuldenaars is van die gemeenskaplike boedel se skulde. Die hof het hierdie reël toegepas en bevind dat die hoofskuld (die skuld aan die bank met betrekking tot die oortrokke bankrekening) die gemeenskaplike skuld van die gades was. Deur die borgkontrak aan te gaan, het die vrou dus gepoog om vir haar eie skuld borg te staan. Die hof het gevolglik verklaar dat die borgkontrak onafdwingbaar was.

Die hof het heeltemal tereg die beslissing in *Reichmans (Pty) Ltd v Ramdass* 1985 2 SA 111 (D) verwerp. In daardie saak is beslis dat 'n vrou wat binne gemeenskap van goed getroud is wel borg kan staan vir skulde van die gemeenskaplike boedel. In *Reichmans* het die hof beslis dat die vrou nie borg gestaan het vir haar eie skulde deur borg te staan vir skulde van die gemeenskaplike boedel nie. Hierdie beslissing is gebaseer op die argument dat die man, en nie die vrou nie, die hoofskuldenaar was en dat die regte en verpligtinge van die borg en dié van die hoofskuldenaar nie dieselfde was nie. Die hof het verder verklaar dat dit goed moontlik is dat 'n borgkontrak kan bly voortbestaan na die ontbinding van die huwelik en dat daar dan nie meer "any form of identity between surety and principal debtor" sal wees nie. Dan sou die vrou se aanspreeklikheid as borg nie meer saamval met haar aanspreeklikheid as mede-eienaar van die gemeenskaplike boedel nie. Vir sy beslissing dat die vrou borg kan staan vir skulde van die gemeenskaplike boedel het die hof verder gesteun op die feit dat die vrou bates gehad het wat buite die gemeenskaplike boedel geval het. Die hof het gemeen dat daar op hierdie bates beslag gelê kon word en dat dit in eksekusie verkoop kon word.

Sien ook die aantekening by *De Wet v Jurgens* [90].

[92] TOMLIN V LONDON AND LANCASHIRE INSURANCE CO LTD

1962 2 SA 30 (D)

Delictual liability *inter se* of spouses married in community of property

A husband and wife, married in community of property with retention of the marital power, were involved in a motor accident in which the wife sustained personal injuries. The collision was caused by the negligence of her husband and the third party. The husband (plaintiff) instituted action against the insurer of the car driven by the third party. The plaintiff claimed damages for himself in his personal capacity and, as administrator of the joint estate, he claimed damages for his wife. In reconvention, the insurer (defendant) claimed, *inter alia*, that, as the plaintiff was also negligent in causing the accident, he should be ordered to contribute to the amount of damages to be awarded to his wife. The plaintiff excepted to the claim in reconvention on the grounds that he was married to his wife in community of property and that no delictual claim could therefore lie between them. On behalf of the defendant it was argued that section 2 of the Matrimonial Affairs Act 37 of 1953, which limits the husband's marital power over certain movable properties of his wife, enabled the wife to claim delictual damages from her husband. The exception was upheld.

Onderlinge deliktuele aanspreeklikheid van gades getroud binne gemeenskap van goed

'n Man en vrou, wat binne gemeenskap van goed met behoud van die maritale mag getroud was, was in 'n motorbotsing betrokke waarin die vrou liggaamlike beserings opgedoen het. Die botsing is veroorsaak deur die nalatigheid van haar man en die derde party. Die man (eiser) het aksie ingestel teen die versekeraar van die motor wat deur die derde party bestuur is. Die eiser het skadevergoeding vir hom in sy persoonlike hoedanigheid geëis en, as administrateur van die gemeenskaplike boedel, het hy skadevergoeding vir sy vrou geëis. In rekonvensie het die versekeraar (verweerder) onder andere geëis dat die eiser beveel moes word om 'n bydrae te maak tot die bedrag skadevergoeding wat aan sy vrou uitbetaal moes word aangesien hy bydraend nalatig was in die veroorsaking van die ongeluk. Die eiser het eksepsie aangeteken teen die eis in rekonvensie op grond daarvan dat hy en sy vrou binne gemeenskap van goed getroud was en dat daar dus geen deliktuele eis tussen hulle kon bestaan nie. Namens die verweerder is aangevoer dat 'n vrou ingevolge artikel 2 van die Wet op Huweliksaangeleenthede 37 van 1953, wat die man se maritale mag oor sekere roerende eiendom van sy vrou beperk, wel bevoeg is om op grond van delik skadevergoeding van haar man te eis. Die eksepsie is gehandhaaf.

CANEY J: [32] The question then is how, if at all, Act 37 of 1953 has affected the situation when the marriage is with community of property. That was the issue argued before me . . . The following are the provisions of the statute particularly relevant:

"2. (1) No husband shall be entitled, without his wife's written consent—

(a) ....

(b) to receive any compensation awarded to the wife in respect of personal injuries sustained by her or to take possession of any such compensation received by her.

2 (6) Every wife shall be entitled, without the assistance of her husband–

(a)   ....

(b)   to receive or sue for any compensation, deposit, dividend or proceeds referred to in para (b), (c) or (d) of sub-sec (1)."

To Mr *Didcott's* [for the plaintiff] contention that the latter provision could not be interpreted as creating a new cause of action, Mr *Shaw* [for the defendant] answered that there was no need for a new cause of action: para (b) of sec 2(1) must be read in the light of the other paragraphs – (a), relating to the wife's remuneration for services, the counterpart of which is para (a) of sec 6(1), entitling a wife to sue her employer for such remuneration; (c) relating to deposits in Post Office Savings Bank and building societies and in savings accounts of banking institutions and (d) relating to shares in building societies and the dividends on and proceeds of them, the counterparts of (c) and (d) being contained in para (b) of sec 6(1), quoted above. The effect was to remove the bar to action by a wife married with community; whereas in the past, when her husband owed her salary or wages or became liable to her in damages for personal injuries or in respect of the matters contained in paras (c) or (d), she could not sue him (although he was indebted to her), now she could do so. The present legislation did not, the argument ran, confer a new cause of action on her but removed procedural difficulties and altered the common law effects of a marriage with community. The procedural difficulties were a wife's inability to sue alone, unassisted by her husband (save in matrimonial actions) and the fact that if the husband sued for her or assisted her he would be bringing action against [33] himself. Now a wife could sue unassisted because of the provisions of sec 2(6). The other alteration which, the argument ran, made the difference was that the proceeds of the action would no longer fall under the administration of the husband because of the provisions of sec 2(1). This, Mr *Shaw* argued, was the essential aspect of the matter; it was this which made possible and effectual an action to enforce her rights, an action which would previously have been ineffectual because the proceeds would not merely fall into the joint estate but be under his administration.

I am not able to accede to this argument. It postulates an unenforceable legal obligation, a ghost elusive to the grasp, not because of its nature but for lack of procedure to reach it and because, if grasped, it will dissolve itself. I cannot accept that the law's ingenuity would not have devised means to enable a wife to pursue a remedy if she had a right. In my judgment, *not the husband's power of administration, but the existence by law of a joint estate was and is* at common law *the obstacle to an action between spouses married with community of property* [our emphasis], an insuperable obstacle in so far as one claims from the other money or assets out of the joint estate, for . . . neither has a separate estate and what he or she recovers from the other comes out of the joint estate and falls back instantly into the joint estate . . .

Clearly sec 2 does not operate to exclude from a joint estate the assets or moneys concerned in any of the paragraphs of sub-secs (1) and (6); these relieve a wife in some degree of her husband's marital power and confer upon her some contractual power and a *locus standi in judicio* in the cases indicated. The common law obstacle to a wife suing her husband for damages for personal injury consequently remains; what she recovers from him as administrator of the joint estate would instantly fall back into that estate. Mr *Shaw* argued that, [34] although the damages recovered by a wife out of the joint estate remained in the joint estate, yet she had the administration of what was recovered, by reason of sec 2(1)(b), and so for practical purposes this was not in the joint estate unless creditors exercised their rights in respect of it. He said that when the marriage comes to an end and the joint estate is dissolved, appropriate adjustments could be made. This appears to me, however, to be artificial and impractical. A marriage may last many years and it is not, in the nature of things, usual for husband and wife to keep an accounting of their affairs *inter se*. In the course of years the amount of damages would be swallowed up in their transactions. It does not appear to me that there was an existing cause of action, previously unenforceable, but now made enforceable by the provisions of the legislation.

This brings me to a consideration of the language of the two provisions in order to ascertain whether the legislation intended now to create and confer such a right of action or otherwise what its intention was . . .

[CANEY J studied the language of the provisions and proceeded:]

These considerations convince me, on examination of the language, that para (*b*) of sub-sec (6), in entitling a wife to sue unassisted for an award of compensation, does not entitle her to sue her husband for damages as compensation for personal injuries sustained by her as a result of negligence on his part.

Further, it is clear, I consider, that no new cause of action was created by the provisions under discussion . . .

[35] The . . . exception succeeds . . .

Note

The general rule is that spouses who are married in community of property cannot claim delictual damages from each other. This was the position in the common law and it is still the position. The abolition of the marital power did not alter the position. As was emphasised in this case (33), the reason for this incapacity is the existence of the joint estate: where one spouse institutes an action for a delict committed against him by the other spouse, the compensation awarded to the injured spouse is taken from the joint estate and then falls back into the joint estate (see also *Rohloff v Ocean Accident and Guarantee Corporation Ltd* [93]). The payment of compensation is therefore nothing more than giving with the one hand and taking back with the other. Awarding damages is therefore pointless.

However, where one of the spouses and a third party are joint wrongdoers the situation is somewhat different. A statutory provision has amended the general rule in this regard. Section 2 of the Apportionment of Damages Act 34 of 1956 provides that if a spouse is injured as a result of the combined wrongdoing of the other spouse and a third party, the injured spouse may claim the full amount of damages from the third party but the third party then has a right of recourse against the spouse who contributed to the injury (see also *SA Onderlinge Brand- en Algemene Versekerings-maatskappy Bpk v Van den Berg* 1976 1 SA 602 (A)).

Aantekening

Die algemene reël is dat gades wat binne gemeenskap van goed getroud is geen deliktuele eise teen mekaar kan instel nie. Dit was die posisie in die gemenereg en is steeds die posisie. Die afskaffing van die maritale mag het nie die posisie verander nie. Soos wat in die onderhawige saak beklemtoon is (33), is die rede vir hierdie onbevoegdheid die bestaan van die gemeenskaplike boedel: waar een gade 'n deliktuele aksie teen die ander instel, word die skadevergoeding wat aan die benadeelde toegeken word uit die gemeenskaplike boedel geneem en dit val weer daarin terug (sien ook *Rohloff v Ocean Accident and Guarantee Corporation* [93]). Die betaling van die skadevergoeding beteken dus niks anders nie as om met die een hand te gee en met die ander te neem. Om skadevergoeding toe te ken, is dus sinloos.

Waar een van die gades en 'n derde party egter mededaders is, is die situasie ietwat anders. Die algemene reël is in hierdie verband deur 'n statutêre bepaling gewysig. Artikel 2 van die Wet op die Verdeling van Skadevergoeding 34 van 1956 bepaal dat indien die gade benadeel word as gevolg van 'n delik wat gesamentlik deur die ander gade en 'n derde gepleeg word, die benadeelde gade die volle bedrag van sy skade van die derde party kan verhaal maar die derde party het dan 'n verhaalsreg teenoor die gade wat medeverantwoordelik vir die skade was (sien ook *SA*

The position regarding non-patrimonial damages resulting specifically from physical injury has also been changed by statute. Section 18(*b*) of the Matrimonial Property Act 88 of 1984 provides that a spouse "may recover from the other spouse damages, other than damages for patrimonial loss, in respect of bodily injuries suffered by him and attributable either wholly or in part to the fault of that spouse." Any amount thus recovered by the injured spouse will fall outside the joint estate (section 18(*a*) of the Matrimonial Property Act). It is regrettable that the legislature did not extend sections 18(*a*) and (*b*) to all delictual claims between spouses married in community of property. The spouses would then have been able to freely institute delictual claims against each other and the injured spouse would have been able to retain the delictual damages as his separate property.

In the case of spouses who are married out of community of property the joint estate forms no obstacle to the granting of actions between the spouses because there is no joint estate. Spouses married out of community of property can therefore freely institute delictual actions against each other (*Rohloff v Ocean Accident and Guarantee Corporation Ltd* [93]).

In this regard it is interesting to note the decision in *C v C* 1958 3 SA 547 (SR) in passing. In this case the court held that spouses who are married out of community of property cannot sue each other with the *actio iniuriarum* (action for injury to a personality right) as "actions based on *iniuria* are essentially of a personal character . . . and they are more likely to cause ill-feeling and resentment and to disrupt family life than other forms of civil actions" (552). It is submitted that this distinction is untenable (see also Hahlo 1959 *SALJ* 6) and that the decision is incorrect. (See also Scholtens 1959 *SALJ* 205; Boberg 1960 *SALJ* 260; Gordon 1962 *SALJ* 249; De Villiers 1972 *THRHR* 175; Boberg 1984 *SALJ* 613.)

It should be noted that section 2 of the Matrimonial Affairs Act 37 of 1953 was repealed by section 10 of the General Law Fourth Amendment Act 132 of 1993.

Onderlinge Brand- en Algemene Versekeringsmaatskappy Bpk v Van den Berg 1976 1 SA 602 (A)).

Die posisie rakende nie-vermoënsregtelike vergoeding wat spesifiek uit liggaamlike besering voortspruit, is ook statutêr verander. Artikel 18(*b*) van die Wet op Huweliksgoedere 88 van 1984 bepaal dat 'n gade "op die ander gade vergoeding, uitgesonderd vergoeding vir vermoënskade, [kan] verhaal ten opsigte van liggaamlike beserings deur hom opgedoen en wat in die geheel of gedeeltelik aan die skuld van daardie gade te wyte is." Enige bedrag wat aldus verhaal word, val buite die gemeenskaplike boedel (artikel 18(*a*) van die Wet op Huweliksgoedere). Dit is jammer dat die wetgewer nagelaat het om artikels 18(*a*) en (*b*) uit te brei na alle deliktuele eise tussen gades wat binne gemeenskap van goed getroud is. Sodoende sou die gades in staat gewees het om vrylik deliktuele aksies teen mekaar in te stel en die benadeelde gade sou die deliktuele skadevergoeding as sy afsonderlike eiendom kon behou.

In die geval van gades wat buite gemeenskap van goed getroud is, vorm die gemeenskaplike boedel geen struikelblok teen die toestaan van aksies tussen die gades nie aangesien daar geen gemeenskaplike boedel is nie. Gades wat buite gemeenskap van goed getroud is, kan dus vrylik deliktuele aksies teen mekaar instel (*Rohloff v Ocean Accident and Guarantee Corporation Ltd* [93]).

In dié verband kan terloops verwys word na die beslissing in *C v C* 1958 3 SA 547 (SR). In hierdie saak is beslis dat gades wat buite gemeenskap van goed getroud is mekaar nie met die *actio iniuriarum* (aksie op grond van krenking van 'n persoonlikheidsreg) kan aanspreek nie aangesien "actions based on *iniuria* are essentially of a personal character . . . and they are more likely to cause ill feeling and resentment and to disrupt family life than other forms of civil actions" (552). Daar word aan die hand gedoen dat hierdie onderskeid onhoudbaar is (sien ook Hahlo 1959 *SALJ* 6) en dat die beslissing verkeerd is. (Sien ook Scholtens 1959 *SALJ* 205; Boberg 1960 *SALJ* 260; Gordon 1962 *SALJ* 249; De Villiers 1972 *THRHR* 175; Boberg 1984 *SALJ* 613.)

Let op dat artikel 2 van die Wet op Huweliksaangeleenthede 37 van 1953 herroep is deur artikel 10 van die Vierde Algemene Regswysigingswet 132 van 1993.

[93] Rohloff v Ocean Accident and Guarantee Corporation Ltd

1960 2 SA 291 (A)

Delictual liability *inter se* of spouses married out of community of property	**Onderlinge deliktuele aanspreeklikheid van gades getroud buite gemeenskap van goed**
The appellant, who was married out of community of property, sued the insurer of her husband for damages as a result of injuries she sustained when the car in which she and her husband were travelling, collided with a wagon. The collision was caused by her husband's negligence. In the court *a quo* the action was dismissed. The appellant appealed against that decision and her appeal succeeded.	Die appellant, wat buite gemeenskap van goed getroud was, het haar man se versekeraar aangespreek vir skadevergoeding op grond van beserings wat sy opgedoen het toe die motor waarin sy en haar man gereis het met 'n wa gebots het. Die ongeluk was te wyte aan haar man se nalatigheid. In die hof *a quo* is die eis van die hand gewys. Die appellant het teen hierdie uitspraak geappelleer en haar appèl het geslaag.

MALAN JA: [297] The legal issue . . . is whether a wife, who is married out of community of property, is entitled to sue her husband for damage suffered by her as a result of his negligence . . .

The action in the present case is one for damages for personal injuries caused by negligence and is based on the *actio legis Aquiliae* in its developed form. The question which arises is whether in our law delictual actions lie between spouses married by antenuptial contract with the marital power excluded.

There is a singular dearth of authority on the subject and only a few recognised Roman-Dutch commentators deal with the problem and then only in a perfunctory manner. This may be ascribed to the fact that in Holland during the sixteenth and seventeenth centuries marriages were, as a general rule, contracted in community of property and the wife [298] almost invariably occupied a subordinate position in the household which was, especially in relation to the business and financial side of the establishment, dominated by the husband . . .

[MALAN JA analysed a number of texts on Roman and Roman-Dutch law and concluded that Roman law provided an answer to the problem at hand. He proceeded:]

[301] The only restrictions placed upon actions between husband and wife under Roman law were . . . confined to actions which rendered the unsuccessful defendant *turpis* [disgraceful] or *infamis* [of bad name]. Although under Roman law recovery of damages arising from the commission of a criminal act was not allowed because it was said that the injured party should be satisfied with the penalty allowed by law, under present-day law no such restriction is recognised and a criminal act gives rise to both criminal and civil proceedings.

It is clear on the authorities cited that actions between spouses during the subsistence of marriage were prohibited only by reason of the consequences which flowed from condemnation. Family honour was jealously guarded and prohibition was absolute only in cases where loss of honour or reputation was involved . . .

I have come to the conclusion that as the restrictions referred to above have fallen into disuse and have at no time been recognised in our law, actions both *ex contractu* and *ex delicto* are competent between spouses.

I now proceed to approach the problem from a different standpoint. It is trite law that a woman married by antenuptial contract, excluding the marital power and community of property, is *sui juris* and may enter into contractual relationship with her husband and others without his consent. She acquires rights thereunder and may maintain actions even against the husband and such actions are not confined to disputes arising purely out of the matrimonial state.

It has been contended, however, that although contractual relationship between spouses married out of community of property founds a cause of action, such action may not be instituted during the subsistence of the marriage. I am aware of no authority for this proposition. The enforcement of rights under any valid contract, immediately upon the arrival of the date stipulated for fulfilment of obligations thereunder, is an obvious and necessary remedy and is recognised under any system of law worthy of the name.

[302] The postponement of the enforcement of rights acquired by one spouse against the other until dissolution of the marriage is a denial of elementary justice and may in a large number of cases be tantamount to a deprivation of a right of action altogether. It is quite conceivable that in many cases dissolution of marriage might take place many years after the cause of action had arisen when evidence in support of the claim may no longer be available.

There appears to me to be no valid reason to withhold a similar right from the wronged spouse in the case of delict. If the right to sue during the subsistence of the marriage in the case of contract is conceded, it is illogical and manifestly unjust to withhold such right in the case of delict. The wrong caused by breach of contract usually involves less serious consequences to the innocent party than the commission of a delict and there is a greater justification for granting an immediate remedy to a spouse upon whom serious bodily injury has been inflicted, or who has been grossly defamed, than in the case of a breach of contract which may involve a paltry sum of money.

The denial of a right of action arising *ex delicto* will lead to absurd results. For instance, a spouse may, as the complainant, set criminal proceedings in motion, and may even institute a private prosecution, against the other but would be debarred from being the plaintiff in an action for damages based on precisely the same wrongs complained of in the criminal case. In effect the role of a spouse as complainant in a criminal case is not very different from that of plaintiff in a civil action.

As regards the contention that even if it is conceded that actions arising *ex delicto* are permissible such actions should not be instituted *stante matrimonio*, there appears to me no difference in principle in this respect between actions based on contract and those based on delict, and the aggrieved spouse suing in delict has, in my opinion, the right to institute proceedings as soon as a cause of action arises. In addition, the action should not be restricted to the recovery of damages for patrimonial loss. The *actio utilis Legis Aquiliae* was allowed in certain instances under the Roman law and, in modern practice, damages of all kinds, flowing directly from the commission of a delict, are awarded as between strangers and I can see no acceptable reason for not applying the same principle in actions between spouses.

It is said, however, that public policy demands that actions between husband and wife should be barred during the subsistence of the marriage because such litigation will cause disharmony in the household and because any existing estrangement between them will be intensified. It is obviously in the public interest that the unity of the family should be preserved but I cannot agree that withholding the right of redress from an injured spouse will be conducive to the attainment of that end. The denial to a spouse of a right open to a stranger will, in my opinion, have the very opposite effect. While redress is denied, the injured party will labour under a sense of injustice and frustration and such denial will, in most cases, promote the harbouring of bitterness and resentment. The breach will be widened and ultimate reconciliation and resumption of harmonious relationship rendered more difficult.

[303] On the other hand the granting of a remedy in addition to the recognised ones of judicial separation and criminal prosecution, will operate as a wholesome corrective for past wrongs and a salutary deterrent for the future. It will, moreover, bring relief to the injured feelings of the aggrieved party and will be of particular value in cases where no criminal act has been committed and insufficient ground for judicial separation exists.

Experience teaches that, in the ordinary course, spouses living together in reasonable harmony do not institute actions against each other, no matter what the nature of the dispute or how serious it may be. Neither spouse will be prepared to expose their private life to the public gaze and run the risk of having their differences blazoned abroad. As a general rule, recourse is had to law only if the rupture is both of an aggravated nature and of long standing. It is frequently the climax of an accumulation of a long series of wrongs which have made further living together unendurable.

I am of the opinion that permitting the additional remedy especially in the case of assault by the husband upon the wife, will be in the public interest. The assault may be of a serious nature and the wife may, with good reason, consider the laying of a criminal charge or the institution of proceedings for judicial separation as being against her own interests and/or those of the children or of future family relationship. She will otherwise, to all intents and purposes, be deprived of all right of redress and the disharmony might well continue indefinitely and do irreparable harm.

It is obvious that the prosecution of one spouse at the instance of another may have far-reaching effects not only upon the preservation of the marriage but also upon the individual members of the family and should be discouraged. To grant the proposed alternative remedy will in many cases be in the interests of all concerned. Again, in theory judicial separation is sometimes regarded as the ideal solution, but in practice it succeeds in rare instances only.

In so far as public interest is concerned actions arising *ex contractu* and *ex delicto* appear to me to be indistinguishable and the arguments pro and con must strike both equally. I have not heard it suggested that permitting the action *ex contractu* offends against public policy.

This view finds support in recent Union legislation which gives expression to public policy in this connection. The Matrimonial Causes Act, 37 of 1953, extends the rights and privileges of women married in community of property. It limits the husband's powers in respect of the wife's movable and immovable property and creates a separate estate which she is entitled to protect by action even against the husband without his consent. In addition, opinion both in England and America in favour of allowing actions *ex delicto* between spouses is gaining in volume.

The *una caro* – unity of flesh – concept has, without doubt and quite legitimately exercised, and still exercises, a very great influence on the moral and religious life in a very large number of civilised countries, but as a legal concept it is unrealistic and illogical and can have no place in our law...

[304] I have considered all the available authorities with care and have come to the conclusion that actions *ex delicto* are, in our law, permitted *stante matrimonio* between spouses

married out of community of property with exclusion of the marital power...

The appeal succeeds...

VAN BLERK JA; BEYERS JA and HOLMES AJA concurred.

Note

Although this case does not belong under the heading "marriage in community of property", it is included here to facilitate comparison between delictual liability of spouses married in community of property and delictual liability of spouses married out of community of property.

See further the note on *Tomlin v London and Lancashire Insurance Co Ltd* [92]. Judicial separation no longer exists in our law. See the note on *Calitz v Calitz* [19].

Aantekening

Alhoewel hierdie saak nie tuishoort onder die opskrif "die huwelik binne gemeenskap van goed" nie, word dit hier bespreek ten einde 'n vergelyking van die deliktuele aanspreeklikheid van gades getroud binne gemeenskap van goed en die deliktuele aanspreeklikheid van gades getroud buite gemeenskap van goed te vergemaklik.

Sien verder die aantekening by *Tomlin v London and Lancashire Insurance Co Ltd* [92]. Geregtelike skeiding bestaan nie meer in ons reg nie. Sien die aantekening by *Calitz v Calitz* [19].

[94] MAURY (EDMS) BPK H/A FRANELLE GORDYN BOUTIQUE V ERASMUS

1988 2 SA 314 (O)

Liability for unpaid joint debts at the dissolution of the joint estate

During the existence of her marriage, which was in community of property, the defendant, who was subject to the marital power, bought curtains from the plaintiff. She had her husband's consent to buy the curtains and accordingly bound the joint estate for payment of the debt. When the marriage was later dissolved by divorce, the debt for the curtains had not yet been fully met. The divorce order included an order for forfeiture of benefits against the husband. After the divorce the plaintiff sued the defendant for an amount of R497,55 which was still owing on the curtains. The plaintiff averred that the defendant's husband was insolvent and could not be excussed. The court *a quo* decided that a wife's liability only arose after her ex-husband had been excussed and the plaintiff's claim was accordingly rejected. The

Aanspreeklikheid vir gemeenskaplike skulde wat by ontbinding van die gemeenskaplike boedel nog uitstaande is

Gedurende die bestaan van haar huwelik wat binne gemeenskap van goed en met insluiting van die maritale mag was, het die verweerderes gordyne by die eiser gekoop. Sy het haar man se toestemming gehad om die gordyne te koop en het dus die gemeenskaplike boedel vir betaling van die skuld gebind. Toe die huwelik later deur egskeiding ontbind is, was die volle bedrag van die skuld nog nie betaal nie. Die egskeidingsbevel het 'n verbeuringsbevel teen die man ingesluit. Na die egskeiding het die eiser die verweerderes aangespreek vir die betaling van R497,55 wat nog op die gordyne verskuldig was. Die eiser het beweer dat die verweerderes se man insolvent was en nie uitgewin kon word nie. Die hof *a quo* het beslis dat 'n vrou se aanspreeklikheid eers ontstaan na-

plaintiff appealed against this decision and his appeal was upheld.

dat haar man uitgewin is en die eiser se eis is gevolglik van die hand gewys. Die eiser het teen hierdie beslissing geappelleer en sy appèl was suksesvol.

SMUTS R: [318] Ek behandel vervolgens die vraag of verweerderes se aanspreeklikheid vir helfte van die bedrag verskuldig op die koopprys van die gordyne afhanklik was van bewys dat eiser gepoog het maar nie in staat was om die verskuldigde bedrag van haar eggenoot te verhaal nie. Die landdros het beslis, op gesag van Hahlo *The South African Law of Husband and Wife* 4de uitg op 434; *Rautenbach v Groenewald* 1911 TPD 1148; *Stevenson v Alberts* 1912 CPD 698 en *Thom v Worthmann NO and Another* 1962 (4) SA 83 (N) dat uitwinning van die man 'n voorvereiste was vir aanspreeklikheid deur verweerderes vir helfte van die tans verskuldigde bedrag van R995,10. Die passasie uit prof *Hahlo* se werk, waarop die landdros staatgemaak het, lui soos volg:

> "Moreover, in modern law the creditor may not proceed for half of the debt against the wife before her husband has been excussed."

Hierdie sienswyse word herhaal op 377 van die 5de uitgawe. In beide uitgawes word hierdie woorde voorafgegaan deur die volgende:

> "The old rules relating to the payment of debts after dissolution of the marriage, which in the case of the dissolution of the marriage by death have become somewhat transformed as a result of the replacement of the Roman-Dutch system of universal succession by an English-inspired system of administration of estates, still apply in full vigour where the marriage is dissolved by divorce. As far as postnuptial liabilities are concerned, creditors whose claims have not been met out of the joint estate before division of the assets may proceed for the whole of their [319] claims against the husband (who, if he pays such a debt in full, has a right of recourse for half against his former wife) or for half against the wife . . ."

Die stelling op 434 van die 4de uitgawe waarop die landdros staatgemaak het, kom ook voor op 250 van die genoemde uitgawe en moet saamgelees word met wat dit voorafgaan op 249. Daar word die volgende gesê:

> "As a rule, postnuptial debts bind both spouses personally and have to be paid out of the joint estate. In old law, in the event of the marriage being dissolved by death or divorce, creditors could proceed for the full amount of their claims against the husband (or his heirs), as the former administrator of the community. If the husband (or his heirs) paid the claim in full, he had a right of recourse *pro semisse* against the wife (or her heirs). Alternatively, the creditors could sue the wife (or her heirs) for half. Where the debt was one for which the wife had validly pledged her personal credit during the marriage – for instance, where she had contracted as a public trader – the creditor, instead of proceeding against the husband (or his heirs), could elect to claim payment in full from the wife (or her heirs), who then had a right of recourse *pro semisse* against the husband (or his heirs)."

Op 250 word dan gesê dat:

> "All this is still the law, though our Courts have held that before a creditor may proceed for half against the wife (or her estate) he must excuss the husband (or his estate)."

As gesag vir hierdie stelling word in die voetnoot verwys na *Sichel v De Wet* (1885) 5 EDC 58; *Faure v Divisional Council of Tulbagh* (1890) 8 SC 72; *Rautenbach v Groenewald* (*supra*) en *Stevenson v Alberts* (*supra*). In die voetnoot word die mening uitgespreek dat "presumably no excussion of the husband is necessary where he is out of the jurisdiction or insolvent."

In die 5de uitgawe word die menings wat op 249 en 250 van die 4de uitgawe uitgespreek is wesenlik herhaal op 183. Met betrekking tot die stelling dat 'n skuldeiser wat teen die eggenote wil optree om helfte van 'n skuld van die gesamentlike boedel te verhaal, word daar, benewens die beslissings waarna verwys word in die 4de uitgawe en wat ek hierbo aangehaal het, verwys as gesag na *Blatchford v Blatchford's Executors* (1861) 1 EDC 365 op 368; *Liquidators of Union Bank v Kiver* (1891) 8 SC 146; *Moore and Co v Smuts* (1906) 10 HCG 84; *Valashiya v Arnot* 1922 EDL 162 en *Thom v Worthmann NO and Another* 1962 (4) SA 83 (N) op 88. Ek dink egter nie dat dit die bedoeling was dat al hierdie beslissings beskou moet word as gesag vir genoemde stelling nie. Sommige daarvan het nie betrekking daarop nie en is blykbaar aangehaal as gesag vir die stelling dat die gemeenregtelike aanspreeklikheid van 'n eggenoot vir na-huwelikse skulde, soos deur die geleerde outeur uiteengesit op 249 van die 4de uitgawe en 183 van die 5de uitgawe, tans nog die geldende regsposisie is waar die partye onder die ou bedeling met betrekking tot gemeenskap van goedere getroud is.

Namens eiser het mnr *Geldenhuys* aangevoer dat die beslissings waarop prof *Hahlo* staatmaak vir die stelling dat uitwinning van die man nodig is voor die vrou aanspreeklik is om helfte van die skuld wat aangegaan is tydens die bestaan van die gemeenskaplike boedel te betaal, slegs betrekking het op gevalle waar die man oorlede is tydens die bestaan van die huwelik. Dit is aangevoer dat hulle nie gesag is vir die gevolgtrekking [320] dat waar die huwelik ontbind word deur 'n bevel van egskeiding die man ook eers uitgewin moet word nie. Indien die beslissings waarop die geleerde outeur staatmaak bestudeer word, dan kom dit my voor dat hierdie betoog gegrond is.

[SMUTS R het die betrokke beslissings bespreek en vervolg:]

[322] Nie een van die beslissings waarna verwys word deur *Hahlo* was gevolglik 'n geval waar die aanspreeklikheid van 'n geskeide vrou ter sprake was nie. Daar is egter wel twee beslissings te vinde waarin 'n geskeide vrou gedagvaar was vir 'n skuld van die gemeenskaplike boedel en in geeneen daarvan is dit van die eiser verlang dat hy eers die man moes dagvaar of bewys dat hy insolvent was nie. Die eerste hiervan is [323] *Grassman v Hoffman* (1885) 3 SC 282 . . . Die indruk wat hierdie uitspraak skep, is . . . dat dit nie as noodsaaklik beskou [word] dat die man in 'n geval van egskeiding eers uitgewin moet word nie. Die tweede beslissing wat handel met 'n geskeide vrou is die van *Copeland and Creed v Ditton* (1895) 9 EDC 123 waarin uitspraak gegee is in 1895. Mevrou Ditton het tydens die bestaan van 'n huwelik in gemeenskap van goedere met Griffiths huishoudelike benodigdhede gekoop by die eiser vir £8,3,10 gedurende die tydperk Maart tot Augustus 1891. In 1893 is die huwelik ontbind deur egskeiding. Toe sy gedagvaar is, het sy 'n eksepsie opgewerp en aangevoer dat Griffiths en nie sy gedagvaar behoort te gewees het omdat sy nie *locus standi* gehad het nie. Uit die getuienis wat gelei is ter ondersteuning van die eksepsie het dit nie geblyk of enige bevel gemaak is tydens die egskeiding met betrekking tot die gemeenskaplike goedere nie en of daar wel enige sodanige goedere bestaan het nie. Die eksepsie is gehandhaaf maar 'n appèl teen die beslissing van die laerhof het geslaag en vonnis is verleen ten gunste van die eiser in die bedrag £4,1,11 synde helfte van die bedrag verskuldig toe die huwelik beëindig is. Namens mev Ditton is aangevoer dat Griffiths eers gedagvaar moes gewees het en met verwysing na *Faure v Divisional Council of Tulbagh* (*supra*) is betoog dat dit beweer en bewys moes gewees het dat stappe gedoen is teen die persoon wat die beheer oor die gemeenskaplike boedel uitgeoefen het. Die Hof het met betrekking tot hierdie betoog die opmerking gemaak dat daar geen getuienis was dat daar 'n bestuurder van die gesamentlike boedel was nie of dat daar enige boedel was wat bestuur kon word nie. Van hierdie opmerking kan nie

met enige sekerheid afgelei word of die Hof sou saamgestem het met die betoog indien dit wel bewys was dat daar 'n [324] gesamentlike boedel was wat nog deur die man beheer is nie. Dit kan moontlik slegs beteken dat die Hof die mening toegedaan was dat dit nie nodig was om hierdie punt te beslis nie omdat die nodige getuienis dat daar wel 'n gesamentlike boedel was, ontbreek het. Aan die ander kant mag dit wees dat die argument byval gevind het. Al wat duidelik is, is dat die Hof tevrede was dat in die afwesigheid van sodanige getuienis dit nie nodig was vir die eiser om die man te dagvaar en uit te win alvorens hy aksie teen die vrou ingestel het nie.

Uit bogaande ontleding van die beslissings blyk dit dat daar geen saak te vinde is voor 1965 waar dit beslis is dat in 'n geval van 'n egskeiding uitwinning van die man of bewys van sy insolvensie nodig is voor dit van die vrou geëis kan word dat sy helfte van die skuld van die voormalige gemeenskaplike boedel moet betaal nie. (Ek sal later handel met *Bredenkamp v Comax Wholesalers (Pty) Ltd and Others* 1965 (2) SA 876 (K) waar wel aanvaar is dat dit nodig is.) Die gemene reg het nie so 'n voorwaarde gestel nie. (*Grotius* 1.5.22; 2.11.17; *Voet* 23.2.52 en 80; 42.1.33; Groenewegen *ad Cod* 4.12.1; Van Leeuwen *Cens For* 1.4.23.20; *Roomsch Hollandsch Recht* 5.3.13; Van der Keessel *Theses Selectae* Th 225; *Van der Linden* 1.3.7). Blykbaar as gevolg van die aanvaarding van die Engelse stelsel van boedeladministrasie en die aanstelling van 'n eksekuteur om die boedel te beredder na die dood van 'n eggenoot of eggenote [in die geval waar die huwelik deur die dood ontbind word], is aanvaar dat 'n skuldeiser eers sy eis aan die eksekuteur moet rig en slegs indien die skuld nie deur laasgenoemde betaal is nie, kan die weduwee gedagvaar word vir helfte van die skuld. Hierdie beginsel is waarskynlik ingevoer op grond van billikheidsoorwegings soos blyk uit die reeds aangehaalde woorde van DE VILLIERS HR in *Faure v Divisional Council of Tulbagh (supra)* waar gesê word dat:

"It is quite possible, for aught that appears to the contrary, that the executors may have sufficient assets of the joint estate to pay the plaintiff's claim in which case it would be manifestly unjust that the defendant's wife should be called upon to pay her half-share of the claim."

In die geval van egskeiding word die wyse waarop die gesamentlike boedel, wat bestaan het tot op datum van uitvaardiging van 'n egskeidingsbevel, verdeel en beredder moet word nie statutêr gereël soos in die geval van ontbinding deur dood nie. Tensy die partye ooreenkom dat 'n ontvanger aangestel word by wie eise ingedien kan word, is daar nie 'n persoon soortgelyk aan 'n eksekuteur wat eise teen die vorige gesamentlike boedel kan ontvang en uitbetaal nie. Die egteliede kan onmiddellik die bates van die gesamentlike boedel onder mekaar verdeel of dit kan by ooreenkoms gereël word dat die vrou die hele boedel behou as haar eie . . .

Alhoewel die beginsel toegepas in die bogemelde beslissings, waar die Howe te doen gehad het met huwelike wat deur die dood van die man ontbind is, ook aanwending kan vind in die geval van egskeiding waar die boedelbates nog in die besit van 'n ontvanger of die man is en die gedeelte waarop die vrou geregtig is kragtens 'n hofbevel of 'n ooreenkoms tussen die partye nog nie aan haar oorhandig is nie, kan daardie beginsel nie outomaties toegepas word op alle gevalle waar 'n huwelik deur egskeiding [325] ontbind is nie omdat die basiese feite waarop die beginsel gebaseer is, mag ontbreek. Dit mag wel wees dat dit van 'n skuldeiser verlang kan word dat hy die man dagvaar en uitwin waar hy of 'n ontvanger nog in besit van al die boedelbates is, maar daar bestaan geen rede waarom dit van hom verlang moet word waar die vrou in besit is van al die boedelbates of van meer as die helfte daarvan nie. Voordat die beginsel dat die man eers uitgewin moet word, toegepas kan word ten opsigte van 'n geskeide vrou sal sy moet beweer en bewys dat die boedelbates nog in die besit van 'n ontvanger of haar eggenoot is. Dit kan nie van die skuldeiser verwag word om te bewys dat die vrou reeds haar gedeelte van die boedelbates

ontvang het nie. Hy sal gewoonlik nie kennis dra van die tersaaklike feite nie. In die onderhawige geval is geen sodanige bewys gelewer nie. Die getuienis dui inteendeel daarop dat verweerderes die oorgrote gedeelte van die gesamentlike boedel, indien nie selfs die hele boedel nie, besit. Toe die huwelik ontbind is, is op aansoek van verweerderes – wat eiseres in daardie geding was – beveel dat die voordele van die huwelik in gemeenskap deur haar man verbeur word ... Haar getuienis skep ... die indruk dat sy besit geneem het van die hele gesamentlike boedel. Daar is sekerlik geen rede om te dink dat haar man in besit daarvan is nie.

Die beginsel wat toegepas is in die beslissings wat hierbo behandel is, kan gevolglik nie toegepas word in hierdie geval nie omdat dit nie bewys is dat verweerderes se man in besit van die boedelbates is nie. Ek het vroeër hierin verwys na *Bredenkamp v Comax Wholesalers (Pty) Ltd and Others*. In daardie saak het CORBETT R verwys na die siening van Hahlo soos uitgespreek op 240 en 421 van die 2de uitgawe van *Law of Husband and Wife* en wat dieselfde is as die mening wat ek aangehaal het uit die 4de en 5de uitgawes. Na aanleiding daarvan sê die geleerde Regter dan op 879A–B die volgende:

> "Thus the position appears generally to be this: that, where in pursuance of an order of divorce a division of the joint estate has taken place, a creditor whose claim arose during the course of the marriage may claim the whole of his debt from the husband and failing payment by the husband may claim half thereof from the wife, his right to claim this half-share from the wife being dependent upon excussion of the husband having taken place."

Die gronde waarop die Hof uitspraak gegee het teen die skuldeiser in die *Bredenkamp*-saak was egter dat beslaglegging op die bates van 'n geskeide vrou nie kon geskied op grond van 'n vonnis wat *teen haar man* verkry is *na die huwelik reeds ontbind was* nie. [Ons kursivering.]

Volgens die uitspraak is dit die punt wat deur die applikante, die vrou, se advokaat beredeneer is. Dit is nie duidelik of die vraag of die man eers uitgewin moes word, geargumenteer is nie. Die opmerkings van CORBETT R wat ek hierbo aangehaal het was blykbaar *obiter* aangesien die aansoek op die ander punt beslis is.

[326] Na my mening moet die appèl gevolglik slaag ...

MALHERBE R het saamgestem.

Note

This case provides clear authority for the statement that a wife who incurred a debt through which she bound the joint estate can be sued for the full amount of that debt after the dissolution of the joint estate by divorce without her ex-husband first being excussed. This would at least be the position if there is some evidence that she has most of the assets of the dissolved joint estate in her possession.

Since both spouses now have the capacity to bind the joint estate (because the marital power has been abolished) the same should apply, *mutatis mutandis*, if the husband incurred the debt.

The position regarding the payment of contractual debts incurred during the existence of the marriage and which are still due at dissolution

Aantekening

Hierdie saak bied duidelike gesag vir die stelling dat 'n vrou wat 'n skuld aangegaan het waardeur sy die gemeenskaplike boedel gebind het, na ontbinding van die gemeenskaplike boedel deur egskeiding aangespreek kan word vir betaling van die volle skuld sonder dat haar man eers uitgewin is. Dit sal ten minste die posisie wees waar daar getuienis is dat die meeste van die bates van die ontbinde gemeenskaplike boedel in haar besit is.

Aangesien albei gades nou die bevoegdheid het om die gemeenskaplike boedel te bind (omdat die maritale mag afgeskaf is), behoort dieselfde posisie, *mutatis mutandis*, te geld indien die man die skuld aangegaan het.

Die posisie rakende die betaling van kontraktuele skulde wat gedurende die bestaan van die hu-

of the joint estate is therefore that the debt can be claimed in full from the spouse who originally incurred the debt (irrespective of whether that spouse was the husband or the wife), or else half of the debt can be claimed from that spouse and the other half from the other spouse (Barnard, Cronjé and Olivier 212).

welik aangegaan is en wat nog by ontbinding van die gemeenskaplike boedel uitstaande is, is dus dat die skuld in sy geheel verhaal kan word van die gade wat daardie skuld oorspronklik aangegaan het (dit maak geen verskil of dit die man of die vrou was nie) of andersins kan die helfte van die skuld van daardie gade verhaal word en die ander helfte van die ander gade (Barnard, Cronjé en Olivier 218).

Administration of the joint estate

The requirement of joint consent
Protection of the spouses

Beheer oor die gemeenskaplike boedel

Die vereiste van gesamentlike toestemming
Beskerming van die gades

The requirement of joint consent

Die vereiste van gesamentlike toestemming

[95] KOTZÉ V OOSTHUIZEN

1988 3 SA 578 (K)

Fulfilment of the consent requirement in terms of section 15 of the Matrimonial Property Act 88 of 1984 in transactions in a deceased estate

The executor of the deceased estate of a husband whose marriage in community of property was subject to the Matrimonial Property Act 88 of 1984, sold certain immovable property of the deceased estate without complying with the requirements of section 15 of the act. This section deals with the requirement that a spouse who is married in community of property must obtain the consent of the other spouse for certain transactions that he wishes to enter into. The executor raised a special plea in which the issue arose whether he (the executor) could have sold the immovable property without complying with the formalities prescribed by section 15. The court found that the provisions of section 15 were inapplicable and rejected the special plea.

Nakoming van die toestemmings-vereiste ingevolge artikel 15 van die Wet op Huweliksgoedere 88 van 1984 by transaksies in verband met 'n bestorwe boedel

Die eksekuteur van die bestorwe boedel van 'n man wat binne gemeenskap van goed in-gevolge die Wet op Huweliksgoedere 88 van 1984 getroud was, het onroerende eiendom uit die bestorwe boedel verkoop sonder om aan die bepalings van artikel 15 van die wet te voldoen. Hierdie artikel handel oor die vereiste dat 'n gade wat binne gemeenskap van goed getroud is die toestemming van die ander gade moet verkry indien hy sekere transaksies wil aangaan. Die eksekuteur het 'n spesiale pleit geopper waarin die vraag ontstaan het of hy (die eksekuteur) die on-roerende eiendom kon verkoop sonder dat daar voldoen is aan die formaliteitsvereistes wat artikel 15 voorskryf. Die hof het bevind dat artikel 15 nie van toepassing was nie en het die spesiale pleit van die hand gewys.

CONRADIE R: [579] Die wetsbepalings wat betoog word van toepassing te wees, is dié vervat in art 15(2), (4) en (5). Paragrawe (a) en (b) van subart (2) van art 15, altans vir sover hulle bepalings hier ter sake is, bepaal dat 'n gade nie sonder die skriftelike toe-stemming van die ander gade onroerende goed wat deel van die gemeenskaplike boedel uitmaak, mag vervreem of 'n kontrak ter vervreemding daarvan mag sluit nie. Die toestemming moet ingevolge subart (5) ten opsigte van elke kontrak of vervreemding afsonderlik gegee word en moet deur twee bevoegde getuies geattesteer word. Toestemming kan egter ook by wyse van ratifikasie binne 'n redelike tyd verleen word tensy dit vir die registrasie van 'n akte in 'n akteskantoor vereis word. So bepaal subart (4) van art 15.

Die persoon wat toestemming tot die vervreemding of die kontrak ter vervreemding moet verkry, is 'n gade. Die uitdrukking 'gade' beteken myns insiens 'n lewende gade. 'n Dooie gade is geen gade meer nie. Die eksekuteur is nie die gade van die langslewende eggenote nie. Dit was nog nooit die struktuur van boedelbereddering in ons reg dat die eksekuteur die *alter ego* of selfs die regsopvolger van die oorledene was nie. Hy is *ex lege* die beredderaar van die boedel . . .

Artikel 15 is ingevoer hoofsaaklik om beskerming te verleen aan vrouens wie se mans onder die vroeëre huweliksgoederebedeling hulle alleenseggenskap oor die gemeenskaplike boedel misbruik het, byvoorbeeld deur bates van die gemeenskaplike boedel op 'n wyse aan te wend wat moreel onregverdigbaar maar tog regtens geoorloof was. Die vrou se bevoegdheid om in te gryp ten einde haar belange te beskerm, was vantevore bedroewend beperk. Die bepalings van die artikel is nie ingevoer om teen wanadministrasie van die gemeenskaplike boedel deur eksekuteurs te waak nie . . .

Artikel 15 vaardig voorskrifte uit met betrekking tot die gemeenskaplike boedel. Hierdie begrip word in art 1 omskryf as 'die gemeenskaplike boedel van 'n man en 'n vrou wat in gemeenskap van goed getroud is.' Die definisie veronderstel, myns insiens, dat die huwelik nog bestaan. 'n Bestorwe gemeenskaplike boedel is nie een wat deur die omskry-wing [580] gedek word nie. So 'n boedel kon dus nie in art 15 bedoel word nie. Die gemeenskaplike boedel word deur die dood van een van die gades beëindig en indien dit die bedoeling van die Wetgewer sou gewees het om by die bepalings van hierdie artikel te betrek ook die boedels van persone wat binne gemeenskap van goed getroud was, maar wie se gemeenskap deur die dood van een van die partye ontbind is, dan sou ek verwag het dat die Wetgewer in duidelike taal so sou sê.

Vir die redes wat ek hierbo aangestip het, moet die verweerder se spesiale pleit na my mening van die hand gewys word.

Protection of the spouses   Beskerming van die gades

[96] NEL V COCKCROFT

1972 3 SA 592 (T)

During the subsistence of the marriage, the wife has no action where the husband has fraudulently alienated assets of the joint estate

While the parties were still married in community of property, the husband alienated certain immovable property to a third party. The question arose as to whether the wife could institute an action to recover the property for the joint estate while the marriage still subsisted. The court held that she could not.

'n Vrou het nie 'n aksie gedurende die bestaan van die huwelik waar die man bates van die gemeenskaplike boedel op bedrieglike wyse vervreem het nie

Terwyl die partye nog binne gemeenskap van goed getroud was, het die man sekere onroerende goed aan 'n derde vervreem. Die vraag het ontstaan of die vrou gedurende die bestaan van die huwelik 'n aksie kon instel om die goed vir die gemeenskaplike boedel terug te verkry. Die hof het beslis dat sy dit nie kon doen nie.

DE WET AJ: [594] In regard to the competence of a wife to bring an action of the nature I am here concerned with, the leading authority appears to be *Voet*, 23.2.54. I repeat the translation of this passage contained in the judgment of DE VILLIERS, J, in *Pickles v Pickles*, 1947 (3) SA 175 (W) at p 178. It reads as follows:

"It is the truer opinion that amongst the people of Holland and amongst neighbouring nations a donation given by the husband, although immoderate and although savouring of lavishness and prodigality, is upheld, so as to occasion a loss to the wife. For if the wife is liable to loss through the husband's squandering his estate in debauchery and gambling, much more ought she to be liable on account of donations which he has made through extravagance and without a sufficient good consideration. For the destruction of the patrimony occasioned by prostitutes is far more grievous to the wife and more dishonourable to the husband than the loss arising from an excessive donation made without proper consideration. Unless it appears that a husband who was thrifty enough in other respects, and not given to useless extravagance, acted with liberality at the last moment of his life so as to commit a fraud upon his wife or upon her heir, and without any other probable reason for his gift. If, for instance, he gave a considerable part of his patrimony to his own nearest relations, such as children by a former marriage or others, or if he bestowed the gift upon a stranger at a time when his wife was ill, or at the point of death, or supposing that there were other circumstances from which a presumption of fraud was quite clear. In such cases it is right that the wife or her heirs should be relieved. And upon the dissolution of the marriage the wife or her heirs first deduct (from the estate) so much as was unreasonably consumed in liberality, or if after the payment of the debts there is not enough left, then the wife or her heirs can have recourse to the *actio Pauliana* in order to revoke the donation so far as the wife has been thereby defrauded." . . .

It seems clear that according to *Voet* an action of this nature can only be brought after the dissolution of a marriage or possibly after an order for judicial separation or of "boedelskeiding". An order of this nature [595] relates to a division of the joint estate which only takes place after dissolution of the marriage. In the present case the wife in effect sues on behalf of the joint estate citing her husband as a defendant. This in my opinion cannot be allowed on principle.

Hahlo, *Husband and Wife,* 3rd ed, p 156, appears to me to state the position correctly. The learned author says:

"Though the husband may freely make donations out of the joint estate to third persons, he must not do so in deliberate fraud of his wife or her heirs. If he does, the wife (or her estate) has a right of recourse against him (or his estate) on dissolution of the marriage. Where necessary, she (or her estate) may proceed with the *actio Pauliana utilis* directly against the third party for the gift or its value."

None of the authorities quoted by the author as far as I have been able to ascertain put the matter as clearly as does *Voet,* but I can find no authority to the effect that the wife can institute the *actio Pauliana utilis* while the marriage subsists.

Van der Keessel, *Praelectiones* (Pretoria University edition and translation), says at p 261:

"Onder toelaatbare vervreemding moet 'n skenking van die vrou se goed wat tot benadeling van haar gedoen is, nie ingesluit word nie; ten aansien van so 'n skenking moet die vrou in elke geval deur die man of sy erfgenaam skadeloos gestel word, of as dit nie kan nie moet die *actio Pauliana* aan haar toegestaan word."

Voet, 23.2.54, is cited as one of the authorities with apparent approval. At pp 267 and 269 *ibid* cases are cited under six heads when a wife married in community of property has *locus standi* to bring an action. It is significant that an action of the nature now before me is not mentioned.

In van Bijnkershoek, *Observationes Tumultuariae,* vol III, Obs 2326, the case is considered of a woman who claimed maintenance *pendente lite,* and also that her husband should be ordered to furnish an inventory of the joint estate and a statement of account. There appears to have been some difference of opinion between the *Senatores,* but the author is clearly of opinion that the latter claim could not succeed during the subsistence of the marriage. It seems to me *a fortiori* that the claim in the present case cannot succeed while the marriage subsists.

I have found only two cases where the *actio Pauliana* has been brought in our Courts. In *Davis v Trustee of Minors Brisley*, 18 SC 407, the action was recognized but failed because fraud was not proved. The action was brought after the husband had died, and, in *Pretorius v Pretorius and Another,* 1948 (1) SA 250 (AD), the action likewise was recognised but failed. Here the action was brought after the parties had been divorced. In *Ex parte van Kraayenburg,* 1946 TPD 686, a wife sought *venia agendi* to proceed against a third party who was alleged to have commited a fraud to the prejudice of the joint estate.

MALAN, J, says at p 689:

> "It is said that, on the authority of *Voet,* this action does not lie until after the dissolution of marriage, that it does not admit of *rei vindicatio,* and that the wife's remedy is purely a money claim against a third party after the joint estate has been divided and the husband's estate has been excussed. There is considerable authority pointing in the opposite direction, but to determine this question at this stage would be merely to give an academic decision on the point of law and this, in my opinion, is undesirable. The question should, in [596] my view, be determined only after pleadings have been drawn and the point crisply raised on the facts as pleaded."

RABIE, J, took up the same attitude when the question came before him in the present case, but the matter is now specifically raised for the determination of this Court. Both counsel inform me that they have not been able to trace any of the "considerable authority pointing in the opposite direction" mentioned by MALAN, J, nor have I been able to find any such authority . . .

[In the result the wife was unsuccessful.]

Note

In the past, the *actio Pauliana utilis* was usually invoked by the wife in a marriage in community of property where she was subject to the marital power. The action was, however, not restricted to marriages in which the marital power operated. (If it were so restricted, it would have lost all significance when the marital power was abolished completely by the General Law Fourth Amendment Act 132 of 1993.) Nor is it, it is submitted, restricted to marriages in community of property. It can be invoked by either spouse in any marriage.

For it to have real application for a spouse who has suffered as a result of a fraudulent transaction by the other spouse, it ought to be available during the subsistence of the marriage and not, as was held in *Nel v Cockcroft,* only after dissolution of the marriage. It is submitted that the criticism of *Nel v Cockcroft* in *Reyneke v Reyneke* [97] is justified. In the latter case JONES J stated (930–931) that it is "illogical to give a wife [or a husband] the right to recover community assets from a transferee who takes in bad faith, with full knowledge of the fraud, but to delay her [or his] ability to enforce that right until dissolution of the joint estate. This may take place many years later. The right may be useless by then.

Aantekening

In die verlede was dit gewoonlik die vrou wat binne gemeenskap van goed getroud was en aan die maritale mag van haar man onderworpe was wat haar op die *actio Pauliana utilis* beroep het. Die aksie is egter nie beperk tot huwelike waarin die maritale mag gegeld het nie. (Indien dit so was, sou die aksie alle betekenis verloor het toe die Vierde Algemene Regswysigingswet 132 van 1993 die maritale mag geheel en al afgeskaf het.) Daar word aan die hand gedoen dat dit ook nie tot huwelike binne gemeenskap van goed beperk is nie. Enige gade in enige huwelik kan hom of haar daarop beroep.

Om werklik betekenis te hê vir 'n gade wat benadeel is deur 'n bedrieglike transaksie wat die ander gade aangegaan het, behoort die aksie gedurende die bestaan van die huwelik beskikbaar te wees en nie, soos wat in *Nel v Cockcroft* beslis is, slegs na ontbinding van die huwelik nie. Daar word aan die hand gedoen dat die kritiek teen *Nel v Cockcroft* wat in *Reyneke v Reyneke* [97] geopper is, geregverdig is. In laasgenoemde saak het JONES R verklaar (930–931) dat dit onlogies is "to give a wife [of 'n man] the right to recover community assets from a transferee who takes in bad faith, with full knowledge of the fraud, but to delay her [of sy] ability to enforce that right

The law gives ... an immediate right in the form of an interdict to prevent the transfer in the first place pending proceedings for division of the joint estate ..., and even for a final interdict where no proceedings are pending ... Why should it ... not allow a remedy against a fraudulent or quasi-fraudulent transferee immediately upon transfer?"

until dissolution of the joint estate. This may take place many years later. The right may be useless by then. The law gives ... an immediate right in the form of an interdict to prevent the transfer in the first place pending proceedings for division of the joint estate ..., and even for a final interdict where no proceedings are pending ... Why should it ... not allow a remedy against a fraudulent or quasi-fraudulent transferee immediately upon transfer?"

[97]   REYNEKE V REYNEKE

1990 3 SA 927 (E)

A wife is not entitled to maintenance where her husband had fraudulently alienated the assets of the joint estate

The appellant (wife) was married to the respondent (husband) in community of property. The respondent became unable to work and as a result of this he received a lump sum disability payment from his employers. He deliberately impoverished himself and the joint estate by spending a portion and giving away the balance of this money to his daughters from a previous marriage. This was done with the fraudulent intention of frustrating his wife's claim for maintenance. She thereupon sued him for maintenance in the maintenance court. The magistrate found that she was in need of support but that her husband could not provide maintenance for her as he had insufficient means to support himself. Consequently the magistrate made no order for maintenance in her favour. She appealed against this decision. The appeal was dismissed.

'n Vrou is nie geregtig op onderhoud waar haar man die bates van die gemeenskaplike boedel bedrieglik vervreem het nie

Die appellant (vrou) was binne gemeenskap van goed met die respondent (man) getroud. Die respondent het onbevoeg geraak om te werk en as gevolg van sy ongeskiktheid het sy werkgewers 'n enkelbedrag aan hom uitbetaal. Hy het homself en die gemeenskaplike boedel opsetlik verarm deur 'n gedeelte van hierdie bedrag te spandeer en die res aan sy dogters uit 'n vorige huwelik te gee. Hy het dit gedoen met die bedrieglike opset om sy vrou se onderhoudseis in die wiele te ry. Sy vrou het hom in die onderhoudshof om onderhoud gedagvaar. Die landdros het bevind dat sy onderhoud nodig gehad het maar dat haar man dit nie aan haar kon verskaf nie aangesien hy onvoldoende middele gehad het om homself te onderhou. Die landdros het gevolglik nie 'n onderhoudsbevel in haar guns toegestaan nie. Sy het teen die beslissing geappelleer. Die appèl is van die hand gewys.

JONES J: [928] At first glance the issue is simple. Maintenance is awarded where there is a duty of support. This arises (i) where there is the necessary relationship by blood or marriage between the parties; (ii) where the applicant is in need of support; and (iii) where the respondent is able to provide it (*Oberholzer v Oberholzer* 1947 (3) SA 294 (O)).

In this case the parties are married to each other in community of property. The magistrate correctly found on the facts that the wife is in need of support. He also found that the husband, who lives apart from his wife and who receives a disability grant because he cannot work, has insufficient means to support himself. This finding is not challenged on appeal. It leads irresistibly to the conclusion that the husband is not able to provide maintenance for his wife. The first two requirements are established, but not the third. Hence the magistrate's decision in terms of s 5(4)(c) of the Maintenance Act 23 of 1963 to make no order for maintenance in the wife's favour.

On the face of it the magistrate's decision is correct. But he also found as a fact that the husband had deliberately impoverished himself and the joint estate by spending portion and giving away the balance of the lump sum disability payment which he received from his employers when he became unable to work. This was done with the fraudulent intention of [929] frustrating his wife's claim for maintenance. The question before us on appeal is whether this makes any difference; whether the husband should have been ordered to make regular maintenance payments which he cannot afford on the ground that he acted *in fraudem uxoris* [in fraud of his wife] . . .

The point is a novel one. Counsel were not able to refer to any authority for ordering an indigent husband to pay maintenance to his wife. Nobody appears to have thought of giving a wife a remedy *in the form of a maintenance order* where the husband has fraudulently divested the joint estate of its assets in order to defeat her claim. But Mr *Pickering* [for the appellant] argues that in justice, logic and good sense she should be given this' remedy. She has a right to maintenance from her husband which she would have had no difficulty in enforcing but for her husband's fraud. *Ubi jus ibi remedium* [where there is a right there is a remedy]. If no remedy has hitherto been given by the authorities, ancient or modern, a common law remedy can and should be given by extending or adapting an appropriate remedy which the law already gives in an analogous situation. The analogous remedies which should be extended and adapted, according to Mr *Pickering,* are the wife's action under the *actio Pauliana utilis* to recover assets belonging to the joint estate which have fraudulently been disposed of to a third party, and the wife's right of recourse against her husband for maladministration of the joint estate. Both are available where the husband has acted *in fraudem uxoris.* Mr *Pickering* argues that by extending and combining them or by extending the *actio Pauliana utilis,* and extending and adapting the wife's right of recourse, the Courts can order an indigent husband to pay maintenance to his wife. This is done by ascribing to him the means to do so, or, to put it differently, by placing him notionally in the position in which he would have been if he had not committed the fraud . . .

[930] Our law gives a number of remedies to a wife married in community of property whose husband deals fraudulently with the joint estate. Some of them are cold comfort in this case. It is too late for an interdict, whether final or *pendente lite.* An action for division of the joint estate, whether at common law or under s 20 of the Matrimonial Property Act 88 of 1984 is unlikely to produce any material benefit, although it may become necessary to sue for division as a prerequisite to another remedy. The *actio Pauliana utilis* was a remedy whereby creditors could recover from third parties assets fraudulently disposed of by the debtor in order to defeat the creditor's claims. It was extended and adapted in Roman-Dutch law to give a similar remedy to a wife married in community of property where a husband disposes of assets in the joint estate to a third party *in fraudem uxoris.* In *Nel v Cockcroft and Another* 1972 (3) SA 592 (T) [96] it was held, on the authority of *Voet* and *Van der Keessel,* that this remedy is not available to the wife while the marriage still subsists, or at any rate, while the joint estate remains undivided. If this is correct, the remedy is unlikely to afford any relief of substance to the appellant. Similarly the' wife's right of recourse against her husband on dissolution of the joint estate is likely to be an empty remedy. As far as I am aware these are the only remedies which the law

has up to now given to a person in the appellant's position. This is why Mr *Pickering* argues that the *actio Pauliana utilis* and the right of recourse should be extended to enable the maintenance court to make a valid and enforceable maintenance order against the husband; only an order for maintenance is likely to be of any benefit to the wife in the circumstances of this case.

In summary Mr *Pickering's* argument is that because there is a right to maintenance there must be a remedy. The remedy is an award of maintenance arising out of the wife's right of recourse against her husband. This right is secondary to her *actio Pauliana utilis* against her husband's daughters by a previous marriage, who are the persons to whom he donated the joint estate assets. The wife's *actio Pauliana utilis* is presently available against the daughters, so the argument runs, *Nel v Cockcroft and Another (supra)* being wrongly decided; insofar as it relates to the assets fraudulently disposed of, the right of recourse against the husband is also presently available; this right includes a right to maintenance on the basis rather that the husband should recover or be deemed to have recovered the assets fraudulently disposed of or that he be deemed not to have disposed of them and therefore to have means. See *Dawe v Dawe* 1980 (1) SA 141 (Z) which holds that:

> 'Generally speaking, a person cannot embark upon a course of conduct or voluntarily assume financial responsibilities which will inevitably render it difficult or even impossible for him to meet existing obligations to a former wife and children of that marriage, and then invoke such consequences as justification for a variation of an existing maintenance order.'

There may be substance in Mr *Pickering's* criticism of *Nel v Cockcroft (supra)*. It seems to me illogical to give a wife the right to recover community assets from a transferee who takes in bad faith, with full knowledge of the fraud, but to delay her ability to enforce that right until [931] dissolution of the joint estate. This may take place many years later. The right may be useless by then. The law gives the wife an immediate right in the form of an interdict to prevent the transfer in the first place pending proceedings for division of the joint estate (see for example *Mundy v Mundy* 1946 WLD 280; *Pickles v Pickles* 1947 (3) SA 175 (W); *Laws v Laws and Others* 1972 (1) SA 321 (W)), and even for a final interdict where no proceedings are pending (*Cullammah v Munean and Others* 1941 NPD 163). Why should it also not allow a remedy against a fraudulent or quasi-fraudulent transferee immediately upon transfer?

As far as I can establish, *Nel v Cockcroft* has not been referred to in any of the cases. Its correctness has not been questioned. Nor has it been approved. But in dealing with a right of action between spouses married out of community of property, MALAN JA in *Rohloff v Ocean Accident and Guarantee Corp Ltd* 1960 (2) SA 291 (A) [93] spells out a strong policy guideline against delaying the enforcement of the right. He says at 302A:

> 'The postponement of the enforcement of rights acquired is a denial of elementary justice and may in a large number of cases be tantamount to a deprivation of a right of action altogether. It is quite conceivable that in many cases dissolution of the marriage might take place many years after the cause of action has arisen when evidence in support of the claim may no longer be available.'

In my view this reasoning applies *a fortiori* where the right is against a third party. Whatever justification there is for delaying enforcement of a right against a husband until dissolution of the marriage or dissolution of the joint estate, it would hardly apply to the enforcement of a right against a third party, provided that the wife has or can get *locus standi*. Further, there is modern authority which is incompatible with *Nel v Cockcroft*. MALAN J in *Ex parte Van Kraayenburg; Ex parte Ahlers NO* 1946 TPD 686 refers at 689 to a 'considerable body of authority pointing in the opposite direction' to the view expressed by *Voet*, although he did not specify what it is because he considered that this was unnecessary for the purposes of the proceedings before him. His conclusion presupposes that the wife may sue *stante matrimonio*. It is disapproved in *Nel v Cockcroft*. In *Laws v Laws* (supra at 323A–325E) MARGO J formulates the principle in terms of which suggest the prior dissolution of the marriage or the joint estate is not a requirement for the enforcement of the remedy. The result of the decision in *Tel Peda Investigation Bureau (Pty) Ltd v Laws (1)*; *Laws v Laws and Another (2)* 1972 (2) SA 1 (T) also suggests that the remedy can be enforced before dissolution. In a thesis submitted by AH van Wyk to the University of Leiden in 1976 entitled *The Power to Dispose of Assets of the Universal Matrimonial Community of Property* . . . the author includes a survey of Roman-Dutch and modern South African authorities and writers on the wife's *actio Pauliana utilis*. He comes to the conclusion that *Voet's* opinion, which is the basis of *Nel v Cockcroft*, runs counter to other Roman-Dutch authorities, notably *Rodenburg*, who state the principle in the same terms as MARGO J in *Laws v Laws* (supra). In a closely reasoned argument he comes to the conclusion that the wife's primary remedy is the right to recover assets from a transferee who takes with knowledge of the fraud, that this remedy is available before dissolution of the joint estate, and hence that *Nel v Cockcroft* does not correctly reflect the Roman-Dutch [932] or modern South African law on the point. He correctly points out that questions of the marital power and the wife's *locus standi* during the subsistence of the marriage are practical difficulties readily capable of resolution. *AH van Wyk's* analysis of the old authorities may not be correct. In the 1972 *Annual Survey of South African Law* at 121 CP Joubert considers that the judgment in *Nel v Cockcroft* is well founded on Roman-Dutch law, but he too dislikes the result and proposes legislative correction. In the light of the above, and in view of modern legal and social thinking on the wife's rights *vis-à-vis* the joint estate as evidenced for example by the changes brought about by the Matrimonial Property Act of 1984, another Court may consider that a departure from *Nel v Cockcroft* is justified.

Mr *Pickering's* first point may therefore have substance. But I am unable to see how it affords a solid foundation for the rest of his argument. Assume that a wife married in community has a primary right of action to recover joint estate assets fraudulently made over to third parties, and that she is able to exercise it immediately for the benefit of the joint estate, and thus for her own benefit. It does not follow from this that her secondary right of recourse against her husband, which differs in character, can also be exercised immediately. It also does not follow that this right of recourse can take the form of an award of monthly maintenance, which again differs in character.

Whatever the position may be regarding the enforcement of rights of action by spouses married out of community of property, I fail to see how a wife married in community of property can enforce a right of recourse against her husband in respect of community property until such time as the community is dissolved. I know of no case where a declaratory order has been issued in these circumstances. It is not possible to make an order capable of execution. The parties were married in 1981. The wife is subject to her husband's marital power. She has no separate estate. Neither has her husband. She has not been given special powers of control and administration of any part of the joint estate. In principle and in logic she cannot now exercise a right of recourse against her husband because whatever is recoverable can only come out of the joint estate and will fall back into it. Mr *Pickering* argues that the right of recourse following upon a fraudulent donation distinguished this case from that, for example, of maladministration by an unwise investor against whom no immediate right of recourse would be possible, if, indeed, there is any right of recourse at all. I do not see how the husband's fraud can alter the position. There cannot be an enforceable right of recourse whether for fraud or for any other cause, until the wife has a separate estate into which the proceeds of the exercise of her right of recourse can be paid. This can only happen when the joint estate is divided. It is *then* that a right of recourse against the husband's half can be exercised. For this reason alone it is not possible by reason of the husband's fraud to adapt or extend or modify the common law remedies in the manner suggested by Mr *Pickering*. They are inappropriate for this purpose.

There is another reason why Mr *Pickering's* argument must fail. As Mr *Dugmore* [for the respondent] points out, one of the fundamental principles for an award of maintenance is an ability to pay on the part of the spouse from whom [933] maintenance is claimed. This is a factual matter. As VAN DEN HEEVER J (as he then was) put it in *Oberholzer v Oberholzer (supra* at 297):

> ' . . . (T)he duty to maintain is facultative: it depends upon the reasonable requirements or needs of the party claiming it and the ability of the party from whom it is claimed to furnish it.'

On the facts of this case the husband lacks the ability to furnish support. It is not the proper function of the Courts in extending or modifying an analogous remedy in order to afford an otherwise remediless party with relief to overlook one of the fundamental principles applicable to that relief. Mr *Dugmore* is in my view correct that this Court would encroach upon the province of the Legislature: it would in fact have to change the legal requirements for a maintenance order if it were to accept Mr *Pickering's* suggestion. It is no answer to use the device of fictionally attributing to the husband means which he no longer has. This is because the whole basis of maintenance awards depends upon reality. The factual need to be supported and the factual ability to furnish it are as crucial to the duty of support as the relationship between the parties. The Courts cannot by fiction attribute to a person the means to provide support with any greater justification than they can by fiction attribute to the parties the relationship necessary for a duty of support. It comes down to this, that the duty to provide support is not an absolute duty and the right to receive maintenance is not an unqualified right. The wife has no right to receive maintenance unless her husband is in a financial position to provide it. This distinguishes the right to claim maintenance from the right to recover debts, or the wife's right to recover community assets, or her right of recourse against her husband's half of the joint estate, none of which depend upon an ability to pay. The right to maintenance is therefore entirely different in nature. In my view this makes it impossible to extend another remedy into the field of maintenance, which is unique.

Part of Mr *Pickering's* argument is that the conclusion to which I have come allows the husband to get away with his fraud. But this is not really so. My decision is simply that on a proper application of the principles which apply in maintenance court inquiries, the wife is not entitled to an order for maintenance. The remaining remedies, for what they are worth, and also the laws relating to insolvency, for what they are worth, remain available. It is one of the stark realities of life that legal remedies can only be turned to benefit if the judgment debtor is not a man of straw. It is this reality which produces hardships, rather than the law allowing a party to get away with fraud.

In the result the appeal is dismissed . . .

KANNEMEYER JP concurred.

Note

It is submitted that the decision in this case is correct. First, as JONES J pointed out, one spouse in a marriage in community of property cannot sue the other during the subsistence of the community for "whatever is recoverable can only come out of the joint estate and will fall back

Aantekening

Daar word aan die hand gedoen dat die beslissing in hierdie saak korrek is. Eerstens het JONES R heeltemal tereg uitgewys dat een gade in 'n huwelik binne gemeenskap van goed nie die ander gade gedurende die bestaan van die gemeenskap kan dagvaar nie want "whatever is recoverable

into it" (932). Secondly, the court was correct in rejecting the claim for a maintenance order on the basis of inability to pay – it makes no sense to issue an order against somebody who has no means of complying with that order.

See also the note on *Nel v Cockcroft* [96].

can only come out of the joint estate and will fall back into it" (932). Tweedens was die hof ook heeltemal korrek deur die aansoek om 'n onderhoudsbevel van die hand te wys op grond van onvermoë om te betaal – dit maak immers geen sin om 'n bevel uit te reik teen iemand wat nie daaraan kan voldoen nie.

Sien ook die aantekening by *Nel v Cockcroft* [96].

The marriage out of community of property

Requirements for the creation of a valid antenuptial contract
Termination, cancellation and amendment of the antenuptial contract
Marriage settlements

Die huwelik buite gemeenskap van goed

Vereistes vir die totstandkoming van 'n geldige huweliksvoorwaardeskontrak
Beëindiging, kansellasie en wysiging van die huweliksvoorwaardeskontrak
Huweliksbevoordelings

Requirements for the creation of a
valid antenuptial contract

Vereistes vir die totstandkoming van 'n
geldige huweliksvoorwaardeskontrak

[98] Ex parte Spinazze

1985 3 SA 650 (A)

**Requirements for the creation of a
valid antenuptial contract**

In May 1957 Mr and Mrs Spinazze executed
an antenuptial contract in Turin, Italy. The
antenuptial contract was signed before and
attested by the British vice-consul in Turin,
who was not a qualified notary public. The
antenuptial contract excluded community of
property and of profit and loss as well as the
husband's marital power. Shortly after entering into marriage the couple settled in
South Africa where the antenuptial contract
was registered. After the husband's death a
dispute arose as to whether the spouses were
married in or out of community of property.
According to Italian law the antenuptial contract was invalid and of no force whatsoever
as all the formalities prescribed by Italian
law had not been complied with. Neither
did the antenuptial contract comply with the
formal requirements for the creation of a
foreign antenuptial contract in terms of South
African law, namely that it should have been
attested by a notary public or that it should
have been otherwise entered into in accordance with the law of the place of execution
(section 87(2) of the Deeds Registries Act 47
of 1937). In terms of South African law the
contract would be valid *inter partes* but would
be invalid as against any person who was not
a party to the contract. The court had to
decide whether Italian or South African law
governed the position in order to establish
whether any effect could be given to the
terms of the antenuptial contract. The court
a quo held that the spouses were married out
of community of property in so far as the
surviving spouse was concerned but married
in community of property as far as other
persons were concerned. The executors of the

**Die vereistes vir die totstandkoming
van 'n geldige huweliksvoorwaardeskontrak**

In Mei 1957 het mnr en mev Spinazze 'n
huweliksvoorwaardeskontrak in Turyn, Ita-
lië, gesluit. Die kontrak is voor die Britse
visekonsul in Turyn onderteken en is ook
deur hom geattesteer. Hy was egter nie 'n
gekwalifiseerde notaris nie. Die huweliksvoorwaardeskontrak het gemeenskap van
goed en van wins en verlies en die man se
maritale mag uitgesluit. Kort na huweliksluiting het die paartjie hulleself in Suid-
Afrika gevestig en ook die huweliksvoorwaardeskontrak hier laat registreer. Na die
man se dood het 'n dispuut ontstaan of die
gades binne of buite gemeenskap van goed
getroud was. Ingevolge die Italiaanse reg was
die huweliksvoorwaardeskontrak ongeldig
en was dit sonder enige krag aangesien al
die formaliteitsvoorskrifte wat deur die Italiaanse reg voorgeskryf is, nie nagekom is
nie. Die huweliksvoorwaardeskontrak het
ook nie voldoen aan die formaliteitsvereistes
wat deur die Suid-Afrikaanse reg gestel word
vir die totstandkoming van 'n geldige buitelandse huweliksvoorwaardeskontrak nie,
naamlik dat die kontrak deur 'n notaris geattesteer moet word of dat dit andersins geldig
moet wees ingevolge die reg van die plek
van verlyding (artikel 87(2) van die Registrasie van Akteswet 47 van 1937). Ingevolge
die Suid-Afrikaanse reg sou die kontrak wel
inter partes geldig wees maar sou dit ongeldig
wees teenoor enigeen wat nie 'n party tot
die kontrak was nie. Die hof moes beslis of
die Italiaanse of Suid-Afrikaanse reg die posisie reël sodat bepaal kon word of enige
gevolg gegee kon word aan die bepalings van
die huweliksvoorwaardeskontrak. Die hof *a*

estate appealed against this decision and claimed an order that the marriage was in community of property. They based the appeal on the principle of Private International Law that the formal validity of a contract is to be determined in accordance with the *lex loci contractus* (law of the place where the contract was executed). They argued that, as the agreement between the spouses was invalid in terms of Italian law, it could not be held to be valid in South Africa. The appeal was dismissed.

quo het beslis dat die gades buite gemeenskap van goed getroud was vir sover dit die langslewende gade aanbetref maar dat hulle binne gemeenskap van goed getroud was vir sover dit ander persone betref. Die eksekuteurs van die boedel het teen hierdie beslissing geappelleer en het 'n bevel gevra dat die huwelik binne gemeenskap van goed was. Hulle het die appèl gebaseer op die beginsel van Internasionale Privaatreg wat bepaal dat die formele geldigheid van 'n kontrak bepaal moet word volgens die *lex loci contractus* (reg van die plek waar die kontrak gesluit is). Hulle het aangevoer dat, aangesien die ooreenkoms tussen die gades ingevolge die Italiaanse reg ongeldig was, dit nie geldig kon wees in Suid-Afrika nie. Die appèl is van die hand gewys.

CORBETT JA: [655] The central issue in this appeal is the formal validity of the antenuptial contract entered into between Mr and Mrs Spinazze in Turin, Italy, in May 1957; and, as I shall show, this in turn would seem to depend upon whether in terms of our rules of private international law relating to choice of law the formal validity of this contract is governed exclusively by Italian domestic law or whether it may, alternatively, be adjudged by the formal requirements for antenuptial contracts laid down by South African domestic law.

The position under Italian domestic law appears to be clear ...

[656] [T]he antenuptial contract was null and void and of no force or effect, either *inter partes* or as against third parties if adjudged by the formal requirements of Italian law ...

I turn now to South African law ...

[657] Sections 86 and 87(1) and (2) of the [Deeds Registries] Act, as they were when the antenuptial contract in issue in this case was executed (in 1965 s 87 was substantially amended by s 30 of Act 87 of 1965), read as follows:

"86 An antenuptial contract executed before and not registered at the commencement of this Act or executed after the commencement of this Act, shall be registered in the manner and within the time mentioned in s 87, and unless so registered shall be of no force or effect as against any person who is not a party thereto.

87 (1) An antenuptial contract executed in the Union shall not be registered unless it has been attested by a notary public and unless it has been tendered for registration in a Deeds Registry within two months after the date of its execution or within such extended period as the Court may on application allow.

(2) An antenuptial contract executed outside the Union shall not be registered unless it has been attested by a notary public or has been otherwise entered into in accordance with the law of the place of execution and unless it has been tendered for registration in a Deeds Registry within six months after the date of its execution or the commencement of this Act, whichever may be the later date, or within such extended period as the Court may on application allow."

[658] It is clear that in terms of s 86 of the Act an antenuptial contract not registered in the manner and within the time mentioned in s 87 is of no force or effect against any person who is not a party thereto. Having regard, however, to the common law and legislative background to the Act ... an antenuptial contract which has not been so registered is valid and effective as between the parties thereto. (See Hahlo *Law of Husband and Wife* 5th ed (1985) at 261–2.) Indeed, it seems likely (though it is not necessary to decide this point and though ss 86 and 87 deal with written antenuptial contracts – see the use of the word "executed" in the English text and "onderteken" in the Afrikaans (signed) text) that even a verbal antenuptial contract, if properly proved, would have such validity *inter partes:* see *Pollard and Pollard v Registrar of Deeds* 1903 TS 353 at 356–7; *Fisher v Malherbe and Rigg and Another* (supra at 19) [1912 WLD 15]; *Ex parte Kloosman et Uxor* 1947 (1) SA 342 (T) at 347; Hahlo (*op cit* at 261–2). The effect of registration is to give notice to the world of the existence of the antenuptial contract and thereby to bind persons who are not parties thereto, including creditors: see *Kloosman's* case at 347; *Johnson and Another v Registrar of Deeds* 1931 CPD 228 at 231.

As to the manner and time of registration, s 87 distinguishes between antenuptial contracts executed in South Africa (ss (1)) and those executed outside South Africa (ss (2)). For the sake of brevity I shall refer to these, respectively, as "domestic" and "foreign" antenuptial contracts. As the antenuptial contract in question falls into the latter category, I concentrate on ss (2). This subsection lays down as alternative prerequisites for the registration of a foreign antenuptial contract (i) that it should have been attested by a notary public, or (ii) that it should have been otherwise entered into in accordance with the law of the place of execution. As regards the first of these alternatives, the term "notary public" in relation to a document executed outside South Africa is defined in s 102 of the Act to mean "A person practising as such in the place where the document is executed". In the instant case it is common cause that the antenuptial contract entered into between Mr and Mrs Spinazze in Turin did not comply with either of those prerequisites. It is clear that the British vice-consul in Turin was not a person practising as a notary public in Italy ...

Consequently the antenuptial contract was not attested by a notary public in terms of s 87(2). Furthermore, it is clear from what has been stated above in regard to the requirements of Italian law relating to the execution of antenuptial contracts that this antenuptial contract was not entered into in accordance with the law of the place of execution. It follows that the antenuptial contract, as a foreign contract, did not satisfy the formal requirements for registration laid down by s 87(2) of the Act and originally ought not to have been registered.

If ... the formal validity of the antenuptial contract in general be adjudged by domestic South African law, then, having regard to the principles stated above, it seems clear that it was valid and enforceable [659] *inter partes,* but, not having been validly registered, it was of no force or effect as against any person not a party thereto. This is in contrast to the position under Italian domestic law, which would hold the antenuptial contract to be null and void and of no force or effect, either *inter partes* or as against third parties. Consequently the question is whether a South African Court, when seized with the issue as to what must be characterised as the formal validity of such an antenuptial contract, should have regard to Italian domestic law or South African domestic law ...

[CORBETT JA discussed the relevant principles of our Private International Law and concluded that South African law should apply in this instance. He proceeded:]

[665] I hold that the antenuptial contract in question is not vitiated by reason of the fact that it did not comply, when executed, with the imperative formal requirements of Italian law ...

It follows that the Court *a quo* was correct in refusing to make an order declaring that the marriage which formerly subsisted between Mrs Spinazze and the deceased was one in community . . .

[666] The appeal is dismissed . . .

CILLIÉ JA; HOEXTER JA; HEFER JA and VIVIER AJA concurred.

Note

In this case the Appellate Division confirmed the line of cases in which it was held that an antenuptial contract which does not comply with the formal statutory requirements is valid only *inter partes* (*Steytler v Dekkers* (1872) 2 Roscoe 102; *Aschen's Executrix v Blythe* (1886) 4 SC 136; *Pollard v Registrar of Deeds* 1903 TS 353; *Ex parte Kloosman* 1947 1 SA 342 (T)). The formal requirements are aimed at providing a measure of publicity to the provisions of the antenuptial contract so that third parties, such as creditors, can determine the spouses' matrimonial property regime. If the antenuptial contract does not comply with the formal requirements the third parties are in no position to do this and they are thus at a disadvantage. Since the formal requirements are set in order to protect third parties, it follows that an antenuptial contract which does not comply with the formal requirements should not be valid as against any person who was not a party to that antenuptial contract. (Also see Joubert 1982 *De Jure* 70.)

On *Ex parte Spinazze* see also Faul 1985 *TSAR* 338; Boberg 1986 *BML* 229.

Aantekening

In hierdie saak het die Appèlafdeling die reeks sake bevestig waarin beslis is dat 'n huweliksvoorwaardeskontrak wat nie aan die formaliteitsvereistes voldoen nie, slegs *inter partes* geldig is (*Steytler v Dekkers* (1872) 2 Roscoe 102; *Aschen's Executrix v Blythe* (1886) 4 SC 136; *Pollard v Registrar of Deeds* 1903 TS 353; *Ex parte Kloosman* 1947 1 SA 342 (T)). Met die formele vereistes word daar beoog om 'n mate van publisiteit aan die bepalings van die huweliksvoorwaardeskontrak te verleen sodat derdes, byvoorbeeld skuldeisers, kan vasstel wat die gades se huweliksgoederebedeling is. Indien die huweliksvoorwaardeskontrak nie aan die formaliteitsvoorskrifte voldoen nie, kan derdes dit nie doen nie en verkeer hulle dus in 'n minder gunstige posisie. Aangesien die formaliteitsvoorskrifte gestel word om derdes te beskerm, volg dit dat 'n huweliksvoorwaardeskontrak wat nie aan die formaliteitsvereistes voldoen nie, geen krag moet hê teenoor enigiemand wat nie 'n party tot daardie huweliksvoorwaardeskontrak was nie. (Sien ook Joubert 1982 *De Jure* 70.)

Oor *Ex parte Spinazze* sien ook Faul 1985 *TSAR* 338; Boberg 1986 *BML* 229.

Termination, cancellation and amendment of the antenuptial contract

Beëindiging, kansellasie en wysiging van die huweliksvoorwaardeskontrak

[99]   Ex parte Dunn

1989 2 SA 429 (NK)

Rectification of an antenuptial contract

The applicants agreed to make the accrual system applicable to their marriage. Due to a *bona fide* error the antenuptial contract excluded the accrual system. The error was in no way due to the applicants or their attorney. The spouses applied to the court for

Rektifikasie van 'n huweliksvoorwaardeskontrak

Die applikante het ooreengekom dat die aanwasbedeling op hulle huwelik van toepassing sou wees. As gevolg van 'n *bona fide* fout het die huweliksvoorwaardeskontrak die aanwasbedeling uitgesluit. Die fout was nie aan

rectification of their antenuptial contract. Their application was granted.

die applikante of hulle prokureur toe te skryf nie. Die gades het by die hof aansoek gedoen om rektifikasie van hulle huweliksvoorwaardeskontrak. Die aansoek is toegestaan.

ERASMUS R: [431] Die huweliksvoorwaardeskontrak wat verly en geregistreer is, bepaal verkeerdelik dat die aanwasbedeling "uitdruklik uitgesluit word" in plaas daarvan dat dit volgens die applikante se ooreenkoms op hulle "huwelik van toepassing sal wees". Dit is dus duidelik dat die huweliksvoorwaardeskontrak nie die ware ooreenkoms tussen die applikante weerspieël nie.

Dit is 'n algemene beginsel van ons gemene reg dat 'n huweliksvoorwaardeskontrak, sodra dit geregistreer is, nie *inter partes* gewysig kan word nie. "It is perfectly clear that an antenuptial contract once entered into and registered is final . . ." *Vide: Ex parte De Zwaan and Another* 1909 TS 676 op 676-7 per WESSELS R; *Ex parte Venter et Uxor* 1948 (2) SA 175 (O) op 179; *Ex parte Nathan Woolf et Uxor* 1944 OPD 266 op 269; en *Union Government (Minister of Finance) v Larkan* 1916 AD 212.

> "The effect of registration is to give notice to the world of the antenuptial contract and thereby to bind persons who are not parties thereto, including creditors . . ."

(*Per* CORBETT AR in *Ex parte Spinazze and Another NNO* 1985 (3) SA 650 (A) op 658 A [98].)

> " . . . to give effect to a state of affairs that has existed since the inception of the marriage . . ."

(*Per* PRICE R in *Ex parte Kloosman et Uxor* 1947 (1) SA 342 (T) op 347). Dit is dus te verstane dat applikante wil hê dat hulle huweliksvoorwaardeskontrak die juiste posisie aangaande die basis waarop hulle met mekaar in die huwelik bevestig is, moet reflekteer.

Dit is geykte reg dat

> " . . . a contract, like an account, can be revised or rectified on the ground of mistake . . ."

Per KOTZE AR in *Weinerlein v Goch Buildings Ltd* 1925 AD 282 op 297 want selfs

> "the Romans did not allow the true agreement between the parties to be prejudiced by a slip of the pen or other inaccurate expression".

(*Per* DE VILLIERS AR supra op 289.)

In *Ex parte Venter et Uxor* 1948 (2) SA 175 (O) beslis DE BEER R op 179 dienaangaande:

> "It would seem that the power of the Court to authorise the revocation or alteration is strictly limited to those cases where the marriage has been dissolved or where the terms appearing in the antenuptial contract do not give effect to the true agreement between the parties: *Ex parte Joannou et Uxor* 1942 TPD 193; *Ex parte Kopp et Uxor* 1945 TPD 410 and *Ex parte Woolf et Uxor (supra)*."

Na verlyding en registrasie van die huweliksvoorwaardeskontrak is dit aan die applikante se prokureur versend. By ontvangs daarvan het hy dit nagegaan, die foutiewe inhoud daarvan opgemerk, en dit teruggestuur met die versoek dat dit reggestel word. Volgens die stukke aan my voorgelê, blyk dit dat die foutiewe weergawe van die applikante se ooreenkoms in hulle huweliksvoorwaardeskontrak waarskynlik sy oorsprong het in applikante se prokureur se korrespondente se kantoor. Van die applikante en hulle prokureur se kant gesien, is ek tevrede dat hulle heeltemal *bona fide* is en dat hulle geensins bygedra het tot die foutiewe opstelling van [die] bepaling . . . in die huweliksvoorwaardeskontrak nie. Hulle skriftelike [432] opdrag . . . was glashelder. BARRY R (soos hy toe was) sê dienaangaande in *Ex parte Joannou et Uxor (supra)*:

> "In the present case there was admittedly a prior agreement and the antenuptial contract does not give effect to that agreement. The only respect in which the present case

differs from *Ex parte Mouton* [1929 TPA 406] is that the attorneys instead of the applicants made a mistake ... It is, however, a distinction without a difference."

Die Registrateur van Aktes, Noord-Kaapse Afdeling, maak in sy verslag die volgende opmerking:

"Die Registrasie van Aktes Wet 47 van 1937 maak nie voorsiening vir die wysiging van die terme van 'n huweliksvoorwaardeskontrak nie maar heelwat voorbeelde is in gewysde sake gevind waar sodanige bevel wel toegestaan is."

Dit is nou wel so dat gemelde Wet nie voorsiening maak vir die wysiging van die terme van die huweliksvoorwaardeskontrak nie, maar die applikante is, soos reeds aangedui, geregtig op regstelling (rektifikasie) van hulle kontrak; en waar daar 'n reg is, is daar 'n remedie (*ubi ius ibi remedium*). *Vide: Minister of the Interior and Another v Harris and Others* 1952 (4) SA 769 (A) op 781; *Rex v Stamp* 1879 Kotzé 63; *Kinkead, Reid and Co v Johannesburg Chamber of Mines* (1894) 1 OR 139 op 146; *Rosenbaum v Margolis* 1944 WLD 147 op 156. "(A)nd the real question is therefore the nature of the remedy and not whether a remedy exists." (Ek kursiveer). *Vide* Herbstein en Van Winsen *The Civil Practice of the Superior Courts in South Africa* 3de uitg op 1.

Dit is ook so dat

"(j)ustice may sometimes be better served by denying a remedy than by granting one (cf *Ex parte Minister of Native Affairs: In re Yako v Beyi* 1948 (1) SA 388 (A) at 399–400)"

(per SCHREINER AR in *Union Government v Ocean Accident and Guarantee Corporation Ltd* 1956 (1) SA 577 (A) op 584F–H).

Ek is egter van mening dat die onderhawige geval by uitstek een is waar geregtigheid vereis dat die applikante gehelp moet word.

Dit word gelas:

1. Dat die applikante gemagtig word om 'n notariële akte te verly en registreer waarkragtens ... die aanwasbedeling op hulle huwelik van toepassing sal wees ...

Note	Aantekening
Prior to their marriage the parties may change the provisions of their antenuptial contract as often as they like. As soon as the marriage has been solemnised, however, the antenuptial contract becomes immutable. The provisions of the antenuptial contract will thereafter only be amended or changed if	Die partye kan die bepalings van hulle huweliksvoorwaardeskontrak voor hulle troue wysig so veel as wat hulle wil. Sodra die huwelik egter gesluit is, word die huweliksvoorwaardeskontrak onveranderbaar. Die bepalings van die huweliksvoorwaardeskontrak sal daarna net verander kan word indien
(i) the court orders rectification thereof,	(i) die hof rektifikasie daarvan beveel,
(ii) the court orders an alteration or revocation of the contract for good cause (the court in the Orange Free State uses this power only where it concerns the amendment of a trust – see for example *Ex parte Venter* 1948 2 SA 175 (O)),	(ii) die hof op grond van 'n goeie rede wysiging of herroeping van die kontrak beveel (die Oranje-Vrystaatse hof wend hierdie bevoegdheid slegs aan met betrekking tot die wysiging van 'n trust – sien byvoorbeeld *Ex parte Venter* 1948 2 SA 175 (O)),
(iii) the spouses draw up a joint will in which the provisions of the antenuptial contract are varied (see Hahlo 273 277–281 in this regard).	(iii) die gades 'n gesamentlike testament opstel waarin die bepalings van die huweliksvoorwaardeskontrak gewysig word (sien in verband hiermee Hahlo 273 277–281).
The court will order rectification of an antenup-	Die hof sal rektifikasie van 'n huweliksvoor-

tial contract if the spouses can convince it that the terms of the antenuptial contract do not give effect to the true agreement between the parties, for example, where the antenuptial contract incorrectly describes the property to be settled on the wife (*Ex parte Kilroe* 1945 GW 27) or where the accrual system was excluded while the spouses intended to include it as happened in the case under discussion.

In terms of section 21(1) of the Matrimonial Property Act 88 of 1984 all spouses may apply to court for leave to change their matrimonial property system. As the application in *Dunn* was brought to court after the coming into operation of the Matrimonial Property Act, the spouses could also have used section 21(1) of this act to apply to court for authorisation to change their matrimonial property system to include the accrual system. On applications in terms of section 21(1) see further the next chapter, which deals with alteration of the matrimonial property system.

waardeskontrak beveel indien die gades die hof kan oortuig dat die bepalings van die kontrak nie die ware ooreenkoms tussen die partye weergee nie, byvoorbeeld waar 'n huweliksvoorwaardeskontrak die eiendom wat aan die vrou oorgedra moet word verkeerd beskryf (*Ex parte Kilroe* 1945 GW 27), of waar die aanwasbedeling uitgesluit is terwyl die gades bedoel het om dit in te sluit soos wat in die onderhawige saak gebeur het.

Ingevolge artikel 21(1) van die Wet op Huweliksgoedere 88 van 1984 mag alle gades by die hof om wysiging van hulle huweliksgoederebedeling aansoek doen. Aangesien die aansoek in *Dunn* na die inwerkingtreding van die Wet op Huweliksgoedere gedoen is, kon die gades ook van artikel 21(1) van hierdie wet gebruik gemaak het om by die hof aansoek te doen dat hulle huweliksgoederebedeling gewysig word om die aanwasbedeling in te sluit. Oor aansoeke ingevolge artikel 21(1) sien verder die volgende hoofstuk, wat handel oor wysiging van die huweliksgoederebedeling.

[100]   EX PARTE COETZEE

1984 2 SA 363 (W)

Cancellation of an antenuptial contract

The applicants were married out of community of property in 1982. On the day of their marriage they entered into an antenuptial contract and the contract was registered subsequently. The applicants applied to court for an order cancelling the contract. They averred that they had concluded the contract reluctantly and purely as a result of pressure exerted by the wife's father who threatened to deny them access to his home if they married in community of property. The applicants were young and inexperienced and the pressure exercised by the father together with the advice of a minister of religion who urged them to marry out of community of property to preserve the family peace had led to their entering into the antenuptial contract. This decision threat-

Kansellasie van 'n huweliksvoorwaardeskontrak

Die applikante is in 1982 buite gemeenskap van goed getroud. Hulle het op dieselfde dag as wat hulle getroud is 'n huweliksvoorwaardeskontrak gesluit en die kontrak is later geregistreer. Die applikante het by die hof om kansellasie van die kontrak aansoek gedoen. Hulle het beweer dat hulle onwillig was om die kontrak te sluit en dit bloot gedoen het as gevolg van druk wat uitgeoefen is deur die vrou se vader wat gedreig het om hulle sy huis te belet indien hulle binne gemeenskap van goed sou trou. Die applikante was jonk en die druk vanaf die vader tesame met advies van 'n predikant wat hulle aangeraai het om buite gemeenskap van goed te trou ten einde die vrede in die gesin te bewaar, het veroorsaak dat hulle die huwe-

ened the happiness of their marriage. The application was granted.

liksvoorwaardeskontrak gesluit het. Hierdie besluit het hulle huweliksgeluk bedreig. Die aansoek is toegestaan.

COETZEE R: [366] Die Hof het . . . wye magte om toe te laat dat 'n voorhuwelikse kontrak na die huwelik gekanselleer word, alhoewel hierdie mag baie selde gebruik word en dit baie duidelik slegs onder besondere omstandighede vir goeie rede wel gebruik word. Kyk Hahlo *The Law of Husband and Wife* 3de uitg op 302. Hier sê die geleerde skrywer dat die sake waarin die wysiging of kansellasie van 'n voorhuwelikse kontrak deur die Hof beveel word in twee kategorieë val, naamlik:

1. Waar die terme van die voorhuwelikse kontrak nie uitdrukking gee aan die ware ooreenkoms tussen die partye nie en die Hof rektifikasie daarvan beveel.

2. Waar "good cause" vir die wysiging of kansellasie bestaan.

In die huidige geval is daar geen kwessie van rektifikasie nie en kan die aansoek slegs slaag onder die hoof "goeie rede". In hierdie verband is daar 'n verskil van mening tussen verskeie van die Afdelings van die Hooggeregshof. In die Oranje-Vrystaatse Provinsiale Afdeling word die houding ingeneem dat die mag van die Hof om 'n voorhuwelikse kontrak te laat wysig beperk is tot rektifikasie en dat die Hof geen inherente jurisdiksie het om 'n wysiging toe te laat "for good cause" nie. Kyk *Ex parte Nathan Woolf* 1944 OPD 266 en *Ex parte Venter et Uxor* 1948 (2) SA 175 (O). In Transvaal en in die Kaapse Provinsiale Afdelings word egter aanvaar dat hierdie beperking in die Oranje-Vrystaat te eng is en word dit nie nagevolg nie. Dat volgens die Transvaalse siening die Hof die fundamentele mag het om 'n voorhuwelikse [367] kontrak te kanselleer, blyk uit *Ex parte Orchison* 1952 (3) SA 66 (T) op 80H en 81G. Hierdie was 'n uitspraak van die Volhof van hierdie Afdeling en die vraag is dus eintlik wat "goeie rede" beteken en of dit in 'n besondere geval bestaan of nie.

Dat hierdie mag een is wat nie maklik of gou aangewend word nie, blyk uit 'n aantal sake. Kyk veral *Ex parte Kopp et Uxor* 1945 TPD 410 wat ook 'n uitspraak van die Volhof was. In hierdie geval het die voorhuwelikse kontrak 'n *donatio propter nuptias* [skenking met die oog op 'n huwelik] van vaste eiendom bevat. Tydens sluiting van die kontrak het die applikante nie besef dat hereregte betaalbaar was binne ses maande vanaf die skenking nie en het beweer dat, indien hulle daarvan geweet het, hulle nie daardie kontrak in daardie vorm sou aangegaan het nie. Die verlof om te rektifiseer is geweier in die Hof *a quo* en op appèl is dit besluit dat die appellante nie geregtig is op regshulp nie aangesien die vrou se motief om toe te stem tot die terugtrekking van die donasie, die bevoordeling van haar man was. Boonop sou die terugtrekking van die donasie die fiskus benadeel, wat 'n krediteur was ten opsigte van die bedrag van hereregte. Daar is dus nie toegegee aan die appellante se versoek dat hulle voorhuwelikse kontrak gekanselleer moet word nie.

Daar is skynbaar geen gerapporteerde saak waar omstandighede soos in die huidige geval ter sprake gekom het in hierdie verband nie. Maar ek dink dat hierdie omstandighede wel beskou kan word as goeie of voldoende rede vir die aanwending van die Hof se mag om die voorhuwelikse kontrak tersyde te stel. Hier is klaarblyklik die geluk van 'n huwelik moontlik op die spel. Dit mag eienaardig klink, maar dit is tog denkbaar dat huweliksmaats sulke sterk beginsels oor hierdie dinge daarop nahou, dat 'n huwelikslewe in 'n vir hulle onaanvaarbare regime, hulle ongelukkig kan stem en bydra tot 'n verbrokkeling van die huwelik. Dit is iets wat natuurlik die Hof sal noop om ver te gaan om bystand te verleen om dit te vermy, of ten minste te vertraag, ter bevordering van die openbare belang.

Die verhaal van die applikante klink heeltemal oortuigend veral aangesien hulle die moeite gedoen het om twee predikante spesiaal daaroor te raadpleeg wat vir my 'n aanduiding is hoe ernstig hierdie saak vir hulle is. Boonop, toe hulle wel die voorhuwelikse kontrak aangegaan het en die beste onder die omstandighede van 'n slegte saak moes maak het hulle ten minste die maritale mag uitgesluit. Insiggewend ook is dat hulle nie enige voorsiening hoegenaamd gemaak het vir donasies of selfs eers ten opsigte van trougeskenke nie wat baie gebruiklik is. Dit is vir my 'n aanduiding dat ek hulle ernstig kan opneem wanneer hulle sê dat hierdie 'n baie vername komponent is in hulle benadering tot 'n gelukkige huwelik. Hulle het knaend probeer om binne gemeenskap van goedere te trou en ek meen dit sou verstandig wees om nie in hierdie jong huwelikspaar se weg nog verdere dorings te plaas nie.

Ek staan dus die aansoek toe en beveel dat die voorhuwelikse kontrak gekanselleer moet word. Dit word egter nie nietig *ab initio* verklaar nie, met die gevolg dat die gemeenskap van goedere en van wins en verlies 'n aanvang neem slegs vanaf datum van hierdie bevel.

Note

This case was decided before the commencement of the Matrimonial Property Act 88 of 1984. It is submitted that circumstances such as those of this case would be considered sound reason for purposes of an application in terms of section 21(1) of the act (see also Barnard, Cronjé and Olivier 229).

In respect of applications in terms of section 21(1) see the next chapter, which deals with alteration of the matrimonial property system.

Aantekening

Hierdie saak is beslis voordat die Wet op Huweliksgoedere 88 van 1984 in werking getree het. Daar word aan die hand gedoen dat omstandighede soos dié wat in hierdie saak aanwesig was 'n goeie rede vir 'n aansoek ingevolge artikel 21(1) van die wet sou daarstel (sien ook Barnard, Cronjé en Olivier 235).

Oor aansoeke ingevolge artikel 21(1) sien die volgende hoofstuk, wat handel oor wysiging van die huweliksgoederebedeling.

Marriage settlements   **Huweliksbevoordelings**

[101]   CUMMING V CUMMING

1984 4 SA 585 (T)

Validity of a reversion clause regarding marriage settlements in an antenuptial contract

The applicant and her husband were married out of community of property. Their antenuptial contract included a clause which provided that the marriage settlements made in favour of the applicant would revert back to her husband in the event of the spouses' separation, judicial or otherwise, irrespective of who was responsible for the separation. The spouses were then divorced and the applicant claimed ejectment of her ex-husband from the matrimonial home. She based her claim, *inter alia*, on the fact that she was the reg-

Geldigheid van 'n terugvalklousule met betrekking tot huweliksbevoordelings in 'n huweliksvoorwaardeskontrak

Die applikant en haar man was buite gemeenskap van goed getroud. Hulle huweliksvoorwaardeskontrak het 'n bepaling bevat ingevolge waarvan die huweliksbevoordelings aan die vrou na die man sou terugval indien die gades geregtelik of andersins sou skei, ongeag van wie vir die skeiding verantwoordelik was. Die gades is toe geskei en die applikant het aansoek gedoen om 'n bevel dat haar gewese man uit die huis gesit word waarin hulle gedurende die huwelik gewoon het. Sy het haar eis onder andere daarop ge-

istered owner of the house and that the reversion clause in the antenuptial contract was
invalid as it was *contra bonos mores*. The respondent counterclaimed a declaratory order
that the house which he had donated to his
wife had reverted back to him when the
spouses were divorced and that the property
had to be registered in his name. The court
a quo held that the reversion clause was not
contra bonos mores and that it was enforceable
by the husband. The applicant appealed
against this decision but her appeal was
dismissed.

baseer dat sy die geregistreerde eienaar van
die huis was en dat die terugvalklousule ongeldig was aangesien dit *contra bonos mores*
was. In 'n teeneis het die respondent aansoek
gedoen om 'n verklarende bevel dat die huis
wat hy aan sy vrou geskenk het, met hulle
egskeiding na hom teruggeval het en dat die
eiendom in sy naam geregistreer moes word.
Die hof *a quo* het beslis dat die terugvalklousule nie *contra bonos mores* was nie en wel
deur die man afgedwing kon word. Die applikant het teen hierdie beslissing geappelleer maar haar appèl is van die hand gewys.

LE ROUX J: [589] [T]he only true issue is whether the reversionary clause is void as
being *contra bonos mores*. In this regard it was argued that the law looks favourably upon
the institution of marriage and would, on grounds of public policy, refuse to enforce
contracts which are prejudicial to the continuance of the marriage, which impair the
sanctity of its solemn obligations, which weaken the loyalty which one spouse owes the
other, or which erode any of the cornerstones of the institution of marriage. Proceeding
from this premise, it was submitted that the general purpose of a marriage settlement
effected by the husband on the wife is to provide the family with financial security both
during its existence and after a divorce. This purpose would be negated, according to the
argument, if a condition of the kind under discussion was sanctioned . . .

Whilst there is no difficulty in accepting the principles and lofty ideals expressed in the
preamble, the general application contended for, and more especially the attempt to apply
it to the settlement in question, fails lamentably. In the first place (as was pointed out
by MELAMET J in the court *a quo*) there is no duty on a party to an antenuptial contract
to make any settlement in favour of the other party. If [590] he chooses to do so, he is
surely at liberty to limit the value and extent of the donation in any way he sees fit.
Should he elect to donate to his future wife a house for a fixed period of time, I can see
no objection thereto . . . The submission [on behalf of the applicant] in my view loses
sight of the essential point that a donor may make his gift as large or as small as he
chooses, and once the other party assents thereto, the agreement becomes binding provided
it is not against public policy to enforce it. Certainly there is no support for the submission
that any settlement in an antenuptial contract must endure during the marriage and after
a divorce, or that public policy requires that such donations should serve as some kind
of financial security for a divorced wife.

This brings me to the second leg of counsel's submission on the issue of public policy.
He submits that the condition attached to the settlement may have the effect of encouraging
divorce for pecuniary benefit, because it offers the respondent an inducement to act in
such a way that continued co-habitation becomes intolerable. Any act aimed at the en-
couragement of divorce is contrary to public policy, and any donation which contemplates
or negotiates with a view to the dissolution of the marriage should not be countenanced,
according to the argument. The condition in question, so it is submitted, has a tendency
to induce, promote or leave unpenalised a course of conduct inconsistent with the marriage
tie. Reliance is placed for this submission on *Kuhn v Karp* 1948 (4) SA 825 (T); *Barclays
Bank DC & O NO v Anderson and Others* 1959 (2) SA 478 (T) and *Ex parte Isaacs* 1964 (4)
SA 606 (GW).

Kuhn v Karp (supra) may confidently be described as the *locus classicus* in our case law on the extent and application of the doctrine of public policy to contractual provisions. As was pointed out by ROPER J in his concise but admirable resumé of the law on the subject, the principle (of the vitiation of a contract on the grounds of public policy) is not to be applied "rigidly, without regard to the facts of the particular case and heedless of all other possible considerations that may affect the interests of the community" (at 828). He referred with approval to the *dictum* of LORD ATKIN in *Fender v St John-Mildmay* 1938 AC 1 (HL) at 12, to the following effect:

"... the doctrine should only be invoked in clear cases in which the harm to the public is substantially incontestable and does not depend upon the idiosyncratic inferences of a few judicial minds. I think that this should be regarded as the true guide. In popular language, following the wise aphorism of SIR GEORGE JESSEL cited above, the contract should be given the benefit of the doubt."

The balance to be struck between harm to the community arising [591] from a possible impairment of some of the incidences of marriage and the enforcement of a contract freely and solemnly entered into between "men of full age and competent understanding" is fully dealt with by WILLIAMSON AJ (as he then was) in the same judgment. The same learned Judge had occasion some ten years later to deal with a similar argument in regard to a will in *Barclays Bank DC & O NO v Anderson and Others (supra)*. In his judgment he stressed the rule that a mere *tendency* to disrupt a marriage relationhip is not enough. At 486C–E the following appears:

"Opinions as to what may reasonably develop as the result of a particular condition in a bequest might vary considerably with different individuals. Mere 'tendency' seems to me, after careful consideration, to be an unsatisfactory test for the purpose. If the object of a particular provision is to interfere with or disrupt a marital relationship there can be no doubt that the provision should be regarded as *contra bonos mores*. A condition which is calculated inevitably to lead to an infringement of the sanctity of a marriage relationship may be taken as having been intended to have that effect. But in my opinion, a condition or provision in a will which is not inserted for the purpose of causing any interference in the marital relationship of any persons but for some other legal purpose, is quite valid even though there may exist a tendency for disruption to arise in such relationship as a consequence thereof." ...

In applying these principles to the instant case, I can find no error in the approach or reasoning of the learned Judge *a quo*. The obvious intention of a provision of this nature would seem to be to offer an inducement to preserve the marriage tie rather than to dissolve it. The only possible problem area arises from the words –

"from whatever cause and irrespective of who was responsible for same",

when referring to divorce as the trigger for the reversion of the settlement. The mere fact that a husband donates a house to his wife for the duration of their marriage cannot be said to have the object of interfering with the marital relationship. The suggestion that he could now act with impunity in a manner calculated to break up that relationship in order to recover this donation is indeed far-fetched and "fanciful", as the learned Judge *a quo* expressed it. No doubt, should a husband act with this deliberate intention, a wife would have her remedies at law if she were able to prove a calculated course of conduct of this nature. But to say that the condition would inevitably lead to this result is not only absurd but ignores the obvious and desirable result of keeping the marriage tie intact. In my view the appellant has not shown that enforcement of the condition would lead inevitably to a result which is contrary to the public interest. Even if a tendency may be said to exist, in theory, on the wording of the condition that an undesirable result might ensue, the contract and its obvious intention should "be given the benefit of the doubt" . . .

[593] I would dismiss the appeal . . .

GORDON J and HUMAN AJ concurred.

Note

The parties to an antenuptial contract are free to make any stipulation in that contract as long as it is not *contra bonos mores* or contrary to the law or the nature of marriage. For example a stipulation which provides that the spouses do not have to live together or do not have to be faithful to each other will be *contra bonos mores* and contrary to the nature of marriage and will be void (see also *Van Oosten v Van Oosten* 1923 CPD 409). We agree with LE ROUX J in the case under discussion that the reversion clause in the antenuptial contract was not *contra bonos mores* and that it could therefore be enforced against the applicant.

On this case see further Sinclair and Kaganas 1984 *Annual Survey* 103–105; Lupton 1985 *BML* 173.

Aantekening

Die partye by 'n huweliksvoorwaardeskontrak kan enige bepaling in daardie kontrak insluit mits die bepaling nie *contra bonos mores* of strydig met die reg of die aard van die huwelik is nie. 'n Bepaling wat byvoorbeeld bepaal dat die gades nie saam hoef te woon of trou aan mekaar hoef te wees nie, sal *contra bonos mores* en strydig met die aard van die huwelik wees en sal dus nietig wees (sien ook *Van Oosten v Van Oosten* 1923 KPA 409). Ons stem saam met LE ROUX R se standpunt in die onderhawige saak dat die terugvalklousule in die huweliksvoorwaardeskontrak nie *contra bonos mores* was nie en dat dit dus teen die applikant afgedwing kon word.

Sien verder oor hierdie saak Sinclair en Kaganas 1984 *Annual Survey* 103–105; Lupton 1985 *BML* 173.

Alteration of the matrimonial property system

Section 21(1) of the Matrimonial Property Act
Extra-judicial amendment

Wysiging van die huweliksgoederebedeling

Artikel 21(1) van die Wet op Huweliksgoedere
Buitegeregtelike wysiging

Section 21(1) of the Matrimonial
Property Act

Artikel 21(1) van die Wet op
Huweliksgoedere

[102] EX PARTE ENGELBRECHT

1986 2 SA 158 (NK)

Application in terms of section 21(1) of the Matrimonial Property Act 88 of 1984 to alter the matrimonial property regime

The applicants were married in community of property in 1980. Before their marriage the spouses agreed that they would be married out of community of property with exclusion of the marital power. However, they had not entered into an antenuptial contract as they thought that it would be sufficient if they simply told the marriage officer of their intention. When the marriage officer told them that such a declaration of intent would not be sufficient they decided to go ahead with the marriage as all the wedding arrangements had already been made and they did not want to disappoint their guests. Their intention was always, however, to be married out of community of property with exclusion of the marital power. The spouses subsequently approached the supreme court for an order in terms of section 21(1) of the Matrimonial Property Act 88 of 1984 which would permit them to change their matrimonial property regime to one which excluded community of property and the marital power. The court allowed their application.

Aansoek ingevolge artikel 21(1) van die Wet op Huweliksgoedere 88 van 1984 om die huweliksgoederebedeling te verander

Die applikante is in 1980 binne gemeenskap van goed getroud. Hulle het voor die huwelikssluiting ooreengekom om buite gemeenskap van goed met uitsluiting van die maritale mag te trou. Hulle het egter geen huweliksvoorwaardeskontrak aangegaan nie omdat hulle gemeen het dat dit voldoende sou wees om net die huweliksbevestiger van hulle voorneme in kennis te stel. Toe die huweliksbevestiger hulle inlig dat so 'n mededeling nie voldoende sou wees nie, het hulle besluit om nogtans met die huweliksseremonie voort te gaan aangesien al die huweliksreëlings reeds getref was en hulle nie hulle gaste wou teleurstel nie. Hulle bedoeling was egter deurgaans om buite gemeenskap van goed met uitsluiting van die maritale mag te trou. Die gades het later die hooggeregshof genader om 'n bevel ingevolge artikel 21(1) van die Wet op Huweliksgoedere 88 van 1984 ten einde hulle huweliksgoederebedeling te verander na een wat gemeenskap van goed en die maritale mag uitsluit. Die hof het die aansoek toegestaan.

STEENKAMP R: [160] Die magtiging om die huweliksgoederebedeling na die sluiting van 'n huwelik te verander spruit voort uit die bepalings van art 21(1) van die Wet op Huweliksgoedere 88 van 1984, wat soos volg bepaal:

"'n Man en vrou, hetsy hulle voor of na die inwerkingtreding van hierdie Wet in die huwelik getree het, kan gesamentlik by 'n Hof aansoek doen om verlof om die huweliksgoederebedeling, met inbegrip van die maritale mag, wat op hul huwelik van toepassing is, te verander, en die Hof kan, indien hy oortuig is dat:

(a) daar gegronde rede vir die voorgenome verandering bestaan;

(b) aan al die skuldeisers van die gades voldoende kennis van die voorgenome verandering gegee is; en

(c) geen ander persoon deur die voorgenome verandering benadeel sal word nie, gelas dat daardie huweliksgoederebedeling nie meer op hul huwelik van toepassing sal wees nie en hulle magtig om 'n notariële kontrak te sluit waardeur hul toekomstige huweliksgoederebedeling gereël word op die voorwaardes wat die Hof goedvind."

"Gegronde rede", of "sound reasons" soos dit in die Engelse teks voorkom, moet uitgelê word volgens die woorde se gewone grammatiese betekenis soos dit deurgaans in die hele Wet gebruik word. Volgens die *Afrikaanse Woordeboek* Deel III beteken "gegrond" die volgende:

"Op goeie grond, redes steunende; grondig, geregverdig; geldig; juis."

Na my mening beteken "gegronde rede" feite wat oortuigend, geldig en verankerd aan die werklikheid is. Vgl *Oatorian Properties (Pty) Ltd v Maroun* 1973 (3) SA 779 (A) op 785.

Of 'n rede gegrond is, sal natuurlik afhang van die feite en omstandighede van elke saak. In hierdie saak kan die feit dat die partye voor die huwelik ooreengekom het om met mekaar buite gemeenskap van goedere met die uitsluiting van maritale mag, te trou, en deurgaans hierdie bedoeling in die werklikheid met die administrasie van hulle afsonderlike boedels gehandhaaf het, as 'n gegronde rede beskou word.

Die tweede applikant word ook deur haar huidige regstatus gekortwiek en dit is belangrik dat sy die nodige regsbevoegdheid kry om die roerende [161] en onroerende goedere wat sy van haar vorige eggenoot voorwaardelik geërf het, te administreer. Hierdie benadering en verligting wat aangevra is, strook met die bedoeling van die Wetgewer in Wet 88 van 1984. Geen persoon kan ook benadeel word deur die aangevraagde regshulp nie . . .

Vir bogemelde redes is die regshulp . . . toegestaan.

Note

It is impossible to give a comprehensive list of circumstances which would constitute "sound reasons" for the purposes of section 21(1) of the Matrimonial Property Act 88 of 1984. Whether sound reasons exist will depend on the facts of each case. From the decided cases it would, however, appear as though the courts readily grant an application under section 21(1) of the act, unless the reasons advanced for the changes are frivolous or capricious (see also Hahlo 283). In *Engelbrecht's* case "sound reasons" for a change in the matrimonial property system of spouses are defined as facts which are convincing, valid and anchored in reality (160). Sonnekus (*Family Law Service* par B11) submits that the mere fact that the parties are going to all the trouble involved in having their property regime changed would probably be sufficient reason in itself, provided that all the requirements regarding the protection of the interests of third parties are met.

See also *Ex parte Krös* [103]; *Ex parte Oosthuizen* [104]; *Ex parte Lourens* [105].

Aantekening

Dit is onmoontlik om 'n volledige lys te verskaf van omstandighede wat as "gegronde rede" vir die doeleindes van artikel 21(1) van die Wet op Huweliksgoedere 88 van 1984 beskou sal word. Of 'n gegronde rede bestaan, sal van die feite van elke saak afhang. Uit die sake wat in hierdie verband beslis is, wil dit egter voorkom of die howe 'n aansoek ingevolge artikel 21(1) van die wet geredelik sal toestaan, mits die redes wat vir die verandering aangevoer word nie beuselagtig of onbeduidend is nie (sien ook Hahlo 283). In *Engelbrecht* se saak word "gegronde rede" vir 'n verandering in die gades se huweliksgoederebedeling gedefinieer as feite wat "oortuigend, geldig en verankerd aan die werklikheid is" (160). Sonnekus (*Family Law Service* par B11) doen aan die hand dat die blote feit dat die gades al die moeite doen om hulle huweliksgoederebedeling te verander waarskynlik op sigself 'n voldoende rede sal wees mits al die vereistes rakende die beskerming van die belange van derdes nagekom word.

Sien ook *Ex parte Krös* [103]; *Ex parte Oosthuizen* [104]; *Ex parte Lourens* [105].

[103] Ex parte Krös

1986 1 SA 642 (NK)

Application in terms of section 21(1) of the Matrimonial Property Act 88 of 1984 to alter the matrimonial property regime with retrospective effect

The applicants applied in terms of section 21(1) of the Matrimonial Property Act 88 of 1984 for their matrimonial property regime to be changed from a marriage in community of property to one out of community of property with retrospective effect. They were married in 1982 and one child was born of the marriage. The wife also had a child of her first marriage which was lawfully adopted by her present husband. An ante-nuptial contract in which the proposed future matrimonial property regime was set out was attached to the application. As reasons for the proposed change the applicants mentioned that they had been ignorant about the legal position when they entered into the marriage and that they had not sought legal advice on the implications and consequences of a marriage in community of property. If they had known the implications and consequences they would not have married in community of property. The wife was the mother of two children while her husband was the natural father of only one of the children, and because of the marriage in community of property she could not be certain that her children would benefit from the assets that she had brought into the joint estate. She intended to leave one-third of the assets which she had brought into the marriage to her husband and the balance to the children. This she could not do if the matrimonial property regime was not changed. Furthermore the husband intended to start his own business which could jeopardise the assets the wife had brought into the joint estate since they would be liable to attachment should the business fail. Notice of the

Aansoek ingevolge artikel 21(1) van die Wet op Huweliksgoedere 88 van 1984 om die huweliksgoederebedeling terugwerkend te verander

Die applikante het ingevolge artikel 21(1) van die Wet op Huweliksgoedere 88 van 1984 aansoek gedoen dat die huweliksgoederebedeling van hulle huwelik verander word van 'n huwelik binne gemeenskap van goed na een buite gemeenskap van goed met terugwerkende krag. Hulle is in 1982 getroud en een kind is uit die huwelik gebore. Die vrou het ook 'n kind uit haar eerste huwelik gehad wat wettig deur haar huidige man aangeneem is. 'n Huweliksvoorwaardeskontrak waarin die beoogde toekomstige huweliksgoederebedeling uiteengesit is, is by die aansoek aangeheg. As redes vir die beoogde verandering het die applikante aangevoer dat hulle onkundig was omtrent die regsposisie toe hulle die huwelik aangegaan het en dat hulle nie regsadvies ingewin het oor die implikasies en gevolge van 'n huwelik binne gemeenskap van goed nie. As hulle van die implikasies en gevolge bewus was, sou hulle nooit binne gemeenskap van goed getrou het nie. Die vrou was die moeder van twee kinders terwyl haar man die natuurlike vader van net een van die kinders was. As gevolg van die huwelik binne gemeenskap van goed kon sy nie seker wees dat haar kinders voordeel sou trek uit die goed wat sy in die gesamentlike boedel ingebring het nie. Sy was van voorneme om 'n derde van die goed wat sy in die huwelik ingebring het aan haar man na te laat en die res aan haar kinders. Dit kon sy nie doen as die huweliksgoederebedeling nie verander sou word nie. Verder het die man beoog om sy eie sakeonderneming te begin wat die bates wat die vrou in die huwelik ingebring het in gevaar kon stel aangesien sodanige bates vir beslaglegging

proposed change was given to the only creditor who had no objection thereto. The registrar of deeds was of the opinion that section 21(1) of the act did not make provision for the change with retrospective effect. The application was granted.

vatbaar sou wees indien die onderneming sou misluk. Die partye se enigste skuldeiser is kennis gegee van die beoogde verandering en hy het geen beswaar daarteen geopper nie. Die registrateur van aktes was van mening dat artikel 21(1) nie vir 'n verandering met terugwerkende krag voorsiening maak nie. Die aansoek is toegestaan.

[Die registrateur van aktes het betwis dat die huweliksgoederebedeling met terugwerkende krag verander kan word. BASSON R verwys hierna en gaan dan voort:]

BASSON R: [644] Op navraag noem die Registrateur dat hy hoofsaaklik steun op die woord "toekomstige" in art 21(1) vir sy siening dat dit nie terugwerkend kan wees nie. Hy vestig ook die aandag daarop dat in art 21(2)(b) bepaal word dat die bepalings van hoofstuk 1 geld vanaf die datum van die sluiting van die gades se huwelik of vanaf die datum van die verlyding van die betrokke notariële kontrak na gelang die gades in daardie kontrak verklaar. In art 21(2)(b) word dus aan die partye die keuse gegee om die aanwasbedeling terugwerkend van toepassing te maak . . .

[645] Na my mening moet daar nie te veel klem op die woord "toekomstige" gelê word nie. In art 21(1) word verwys na twee bedelings: (1) die ou of bestaande bedeling en (2) die nuwe of toekomstige bedeling. Die Wetgewer kon net so wel die woord "nuwe" in plaas van "toekomstige" gebruik het. Ek meen dus dat daar nie uit die woord "toekomstige" afgelei kan word dat so 'n verandering nie met terugwerkende krag verander kan word nie.

In art 21(2)(a) word bepaal dat in gegewe gevalle die partye die bepalings van hoofstuk 1 (die aanwasbedeling) op hul huwelik van toepassing kan maak deur die verlyding en registrasie in 'n registrasiekantoor binne twee jaar na die inwerkingtreding van die Wet van 'n notariële kontrak met daardie strekking. Artikel 21(2)(b) gee aan die eggenote 'n keuse. Hulle kan ooreenkom dat die aanwasbedeling sal geld vanaf die datum van die sluiting van hul huwelik of vanaf die datum van die verlyding van die betrokke notariële kontrak.

In art 21(2)(d) word bepaal dat by die toepassing van art 4(1) die aanvang van die betrokke huwelik geag word die datum bedoel in art 21(2)(b) te wees.

Artikel (4)(1)(a) lees soos volg:

> [646] "Die aanwas van 'n gade se boedel is die bedrag waarmee die netto waarde van sy boedel by die ontbinding van sy huwelik die netto waarde van sy boedel by die aanvang van daardie huwelik oorskry."

As daar nie in art 21(2)(b) spesifiek bepaal is dat die aanwasbedeling (hoofstuk 1) vanaf die datum van die verlyding van die kontrak van toepassing gemaak kan word nie, sou daar met groot krag geargumenteer kon word dat so 'n bepaling nie in die kontrak opgeneem kon word nie omdat dit in stryd met art 4(1) sou wees.

Na my mening sou die aanwasbedeling gegeld het vanaf die aanvang van die huwelik, dws met terugwerkende krag as 'n aansoek ingevolge art 21(2)(a) geslaag het. Hierdie noodwendige gevolg word afgeweer as die gades besluit dat die aanwasbedeling slegs geld vanaf die datum van verlyding van die betrokke notariële kontrak.

Uit bogenoemde is dit duidelik dat ek nie die Registrateur se sienswyse deel nie.

Daar is nog drie aspekte wat ek graag wil noem:

1. Die hele opset van die Wet op Huweliksgoedere, so lyk dit vir my, is om weg te doen met die onbuigsaamheid wat voorheen bestaan het. As die Hof nie by magte is om

die huweliksgoederebedeling met terugwerkende krag te verander nie, is ons weer terug by 'n onbuigsame stelsel.

2. Artikel 17(5) van genoemde Wet bepaal:

"Waar 'n skuld van 'n gemeenskaplike boedel verhaalbaar is, kan die gade wat die skuld aangegaan het of albei gades gesamentlik daarvoor aangespreek word, en waar 'n skuld vir benodigdhede vir die gesamentlike huishouding aangegaan is, kan die gades gesamentlik of afsonderlik daarvoor aangespreek word."

Die gevaar bestaan dus dat op bates wat (sê) die vrou in die huwelik ingebring het beslag gelê kan word, as 'n besigheid wat die man begin, sou misluk.

In so 'n geval is dit seker redelik om te verwag dat die vrou die goedere wat sy ingebring het sal wil beskerm. Dit is myns insiens ook 'n gegronde rede vir die verandering van die huweliksgoederebedeling soos in art 21(1)(a) bedoel.

As die Hof verbied word om die voorgenome verandering terugwerkend van krag te maak word hierdie bedoeling van die gades gefrustreer of verydel. Ek glo nie dat die Wetgewer so 'n gevolg beoog het nie.

3. Die verdere vraag ontstaan wat met die bestaande gemeenskaplike boedel gedoen moet word. As dit nie verdeel word nie sal daar drie boedels wees: die gesamentlike boedel; die man se afsonderlike boedel wat ontstaan na die verandering en die vrou se afsonderlike boedel wat na die verandering ontstaan.

Die Wetgewer skryf nie voor hoe so 'n verdeling moet geskied nie. (Vergelyk hiermee art 20 waar die Wetgewer sekere voorskrifte oor verdeling gee en magtiging om die huweliksgoederebedeling te verander.) As die Wetgewer so 'n verdeling deur die Hof beoog het, waarom is daarvoor nie voorsiening gemaak nie?

Maar as die Hof tog 'n verdeling moet maak, sal dit moet wees "op die voorwaardes wat die Hof goed vind". En wat sal dan in die Hof se pad staan om dit te doen soos die gades in hierdie geval vra en om die bedeling terugwerkend te maak vanaf die datum van huweliksluiting?

[647] Na my mening kan die huweliksgoederebedeling derhalwe met terugwerkende krag verander word.

Ek is tevrede dat daar gegronde redes vir die voorgenome verandering bestaan en dat daar ook voldoen is aan die bepalings van art 21(1)(b).

Dit blyk ook nie dat enige persoon deur die voorgenome verandering benadeel sal word nie. In die bevel sal ook voorsiening gemaak word om die regte van bestaande krediteure te beskerm . . .

Note

It should, first of all, be borne in mind that it is no longer possible to introduce the accrual system without approaching the court by means of the registration of a notarial contract in terms of section 21(2) of the Matrimonial Property Act 88 of 1984. For whites, coloureds and Asians this possibility fell away on 1 November 1988 and for blacks, on 2 December 1990.

The decision in Ex parte Krös must be contrasted with the decision in Ex parte Oosthuizen [104] where it was held that retrospective alteration of the matrimonial property system is impermissible.

Aantekening

Daar moet eerstens in gedagte gehou word dat dit nie meer moontlik is om die aanwasbedeling sonder tussenkoms van die hof op 'n huwelik van toepassing te maak deur 'n notariële kontrak ingevolge artikel 21(2) van die Wet op Huweliksgoedere 88 van 1984 te registreer nie. Vir blankes, kleurlinge en Asiërs het die moontlikheid op 1 November 1988 verval en vir swart persone op 2 Desember 1990.

Die beslissing in Ex parte Krös moet gekontrasteer word met die uitspraak in Ex parte Oosthuizen [104] waar beslis is dat terugwerkende wysiging

The decision in *Oosthuizen* is based on a strict interpretation of the wording of the act and is therefore probably the correct decision. But the decision in *Krös*, although not really in accordance with the wording of the act, is probably more in keeping with the intention of the legislature. BASSON J's argument (646) that the legislature wanted to create flexibility is not unconvincing and if the intention of the legislature was to create flexibility, retrospective changes ought to be permitted.

On *Krös* see further Labuschagne 1991 *TSAR* 516 and Van Schalkwyk 1991 *De Jure* 351. On *Oosthuizen* see further Sonnekus 1991 *THRHR* 133; Labuschagne 1991 *TSAR* 516; Van Schalkwyk 1991 *De Jure* 351.

van die huweliksgoederebedeling ontoelaatbaar is. Die uitspraak in *Oosthuizen* is gebaseer op 'n streng uitleg van die bewoording van die wet en is gevolglik waarskynlik die korrekte beslissing. Maar die beslissing in *Krös* is, alhoewel dit miskien nie in ooreenstemming met die bewoording van die wet is nie, waarskynlik meer in ooreenstemming met die bedoeling van die wetgewer. BASSON R se argument (646) dat die wetgewer buigsaamheid wou skep, is heeltemal oortuigend en indien die wetgewer buigsaamheid wou skep, behoort terugwerkende wysigings toegelaat te word.

Oor *Krös* sien verder Labuschagne 1991 *TSAR* 516 en Van Schalkwyk 1991 *De Jure* 351. Oor *Oosthuizen* sien verder Sonnekus 1991 *THRHR* 133; Labuschagne 1991 *TSAR* 516; Van Schalkwyk 1991 *De Jure* 351.

---

[104]   EX PARTE OOSTHUIZEN

1990 4 SA 15 (OK)

Application in terms of section 21(1) of the Matrimonial Property Act 88 of 1984 to alter the matrimonial property regime with retrospective effect

The applicants were married in community of property. They now applied in terms of section 21(1) of the Matrimonial Property Act 88 of 1984 for their matrimonial property regime to be altered from community of property to separation of property with retrospective effect. The application was accompanied by a draft notarial contract which the parties wished to have registered as an antenuptial contract. In other words, the parties did not apply for postnuptial registration of an antenuptial contract but they wished to obtain the same result by making use of section 21(1). They specifically wished their future matrimonial regime to have retrospective effect. The application was dismissed.

Aansoek ingevolge artikel 21(1) van die Wet op Huweliksgoedere 88 van 1984 om die huweliksgoederebedeling terugwerkend te verander

Die applikante was binne gemeenskap van goed getroud. Hulle het nou ingevolge artikel 21(1) van die Wet op Huweliksgoedere 88 van 1984 aansoek gedoen dat hulle huweliksgoederebedeling verander word van binne gemeenskap van goed na buite gemeenskap van goed met terugwerkende krag. Die aansoek was vergesel van 'n konsep notariële kontrak wat die partye as 'n huweliksvoorwaardeskontrak wou laat registreer. Die partye het met ander woorde nie aansoek gedoen om die nahuwelikse registrasie van 'n huweliksvoorwaardeskontrak nie maar hulle wou dieselfde resultaat bereik deur van artikel 21(1) gebruik te maak. Hulle het uitdruklik versoek dat hulle toekomstige huweliksgoederebedeling terugwerkende krag moes hê. Die aansoek is van die hand gewys.

ERASMUS R: [16] [D]ie applikante verlang dat hul toekomstige huweliksgoederebedeling met terugwerkende krag sal geld, sodat die konsep notariële kontrak dieselfde krag en uitwerking as 'n voorhuwelikse kontrak sal hê. Die vraag wat ontstaan is: het die Hof die bevoegdheid om ingevolge art 21(1) sodanige terugwerkendheid te gelas?

Retrospektiewe toepassing van art 21(1) was pertinent ter sprake in *Ex parte Krös en 'n Ander* 1986 (1) SA 642 (NK) [103]. In 'n aansoek om verlof om 'n huweliksgoederebedeling te verander, het die konsep notariële kontrak bepaal dat die ooreenkoms 'terugwerkend van krag sal wees vanaf huweliksluiting van die partye'. In sy verslag het die Registrateur van Aktes die mening uitgespreek dat art 21(1) nie vir die terugwerkende krag voorsiening maak nie. In sy uitspraak het Basson R die tersake bepalings in die volle samehang van die Wet ontleed, en tot die gevolgtrekking geraak dat 'n huweliksgoederebedeling wel met terugwerkende krag verander kan word. Mnr *Eksteen* [vir die applikant] steun sterk op die oortuigingskrag van dié vonnis.

Artikel 21(1) het die gemenereg gewysig. Voorheen moes voornemende huwelikspartye vóór hul huwelik oor hul huweliksgoederebedeling besluit, waarna die posisie onveranderbaar finaal was. Die vergunning dat hul met magtiging van die Hof 'n voorhuwelikse kontrak nahuweliks kon registreer (en steeds kan doen), is nie soseer 'n uitsondering op die reël nie, [17] maar eerder 'n prosedure waardeur gades kondonasie van nie-nakoming van registrasievereistes kon verkry. Die onderliggende rede vir die aandrang op finaliteit, meen ek, was sekerheid. Die bepalings van art 21(1) moet derhalwe vertolk word teen die agtergrond van die wetsuitlegbeginsel dat tensy die teendeel blyk, word vermoed dat die Wetgewer die bestaande reg nie meer wil wysig as nodig nie. Die bewoording van die artikel is die sterkste aanduiding of die Wetgewer sodanige wysiging bedoel al dan nie. Dit lui soos volg:

'21. *Verandering van huweliksgoederebedeling*

(1) 'n Man en vrou, hetsy hulle voor of na die inwerkingtreding van hierdie Wet in die huwelik getree het, kan gesamentlik by 'n Hof aansoek doen om verlof om die huweliksgoederebedeling, met inbegrip van die maritale mag, wat op hul huwelik van toepassing is, *te verander*, en die Hof kan, indien hy oortuig is dat—

(a) daar gegronde rede vir die voorgenome verandering bestaan;

(b) aan al die skuldeisers van die gades voldoende kennis van die voorgenome verandering gegee is; en

(c) geen ander persoon deur die voorgenome verandering benadeel sal word nie, *gelas* dat daardie huweliksgoederebedeling *nie meer* op hul huwelik van toepassing *sal wees nie en* hulle *magtig* om 'n notariële kontrak te sluit waardeur hul *toekomstige* huweliksgoederebedeling gereël word op die voorwaardes wat die Hof goedvind.'

(Ek het sekere sleutelwoorde kursiveer.)

Die wyse waarop die Hof 'n huweliksgoederebedeling 'verander' behels twee handelinge. *Eerstens*, gelas die Hof dat die bestaande huweliksgoederebedeling *nie meer* van toepassing *sal wees nie*, dit is *ex nunc* (datum van bevel) en nie *ex tunc* (huweliksdatum) nie. Die gebruik van die toekomstige tyd van die werkwoord beteken dat die bestaande bedeling nie terugwerkend ongedaan gemaak word nie. *Tweedens*, magtig die Hof die sluiting van 'n notariële kontrak waardeur die gades se *toekomstige* huweliksgoederebedeling gereël word. Die gebruik van die woord 'toekomstige' is *prima facie* onbestaanbaar met retrospektiewe vervanging. In *Krös* se saak bespreek die geleerde Regter nie die voormelde gebruik van die woorde 'nie meer . . . van toepassing sal wees nie', maar wel 'toekomstige'. Hy verklaar in die verband soos volg:

'Na my mening moet daar nie te veel klem op die woord "toekomstige" gelê word nie. In art 21(1) word verwys na twee bedelings: (1) die ou of bestaande bedeling en

(2) die nuwe of toekomstige bedeling. Die Wetgewer kon net so wel die woord "nuwe" in plaas van "toekomstige" gebruik het. Ek meen dus dat daar nie uit die woord "toekomstige" afgelei kan word dat so 'n verandering nie met terugwerkende krag verander kan word nie.'

Die feit van die saak is egter dat die Wetgewer nie die woorde 'nuwe bedeling' gebruik nie (ook nie 'ou bedeling' nie), maar wel die woorde 'toekomstige huweliksgoederebedeling'. Die wetgewende mag kon baie maklik die woord 'toekomstige' weggelaat het. Die feit dat dit nie gedoen is nie, dui daarop dat dit doelbewustelik aangewend is om 'n spesifieke betekenis oor te dra.

Elders, waar die Wetgewer die bepalings van die Wet met terugwerkende krag beklee, is die bewoording uitdruklik te dien effekte. Kyk art 22:

'22. *Skenkings tussen gades toelaatbaar*

Behoudens die bepalings van die Insolvensiewet 24 van 1936, is geen transaksie voor of na die inwerkingtreding van hierdie Wet uitgevoer nietig of vernietigbaar slegs omdat dit op 'n skenking tussen gades neerkom nie.'

[18] Kyk ook art 21(2)(*b*):

'Die bepalings van hoofstuk I (aanwasbedeling) geld in so 'n geval vanaf die datum van die sluiting van die gades se huwelik of vanaf die datum van die verlyding van die betrokke notariële kontrak na gelang die gades in daardie kontrak verklaar.'

Daar is binne die vier hoeke van art 21(1) klaarblyklik geen aanduiding te vind dat die Wetgewer bedoel het om die Hof te beklee met die bevoegdheid om 'n bestaande huweliksgoederebedeling met terugwerkende krag te verander nie: trouens, die teendeel blyk daaruit. Die artikel moet egter met inagneming van die algemene oogmerke van die Wet asook aanverwante wetgewing, as geheel vertolk word. In *Krös* se saak *supra* op 646D stel Basson R sy siening in die verband soos volg:

'Die hele opset van die Wet op Huweliksgoedere, so lyk dit vir my, is om weg te doen met die onbuigsaamheid wat voorheen bestaan het. As die Hof nie by magte is om die huweliksgoederebedeling met terugwerkende krag te verander nie, is ons weer terug by 'n onbuigsame stelsel.'

Wet 88 van 1984 het die huweliksbestel van alle huwelike wat ná 1 November 1984 (die datum van invoering) gesluit is, ingrypend verander. Ten einde egpare wat voor die inwerkingtrede van die Wet getrou het, tegemoet te kom, is 'n eenvoudige prosedure geskep waardeur hulle hul huwelik in ooreenstemming met die nuwe bedeling kon bring. Binne 'n grasietydperk van twee jaar kon hulle, bloot deur 'n notariële kontrak te verly, die aanwasbedeling op hul huwelik laat geld (art 21(2) gelees met hoofstuk I); die maritale mag afskaf (art 25(2) gelees met hoofstuk II); en die vrou dieselfde bevoegdheid met betrekking tot die gemeenskaplike boedel as die van die man verleen (art 25(2), gelees met hoofstuk III). Dit is opvallend dat hul nie op dié wyse hul huwelik van in na buite gemeenskap van goed (of andersom) kon omskep nie. Dit is voorts opvallend dat slegs die aanwasbedeling op dié wyse retrospektief kon geld (art 21(2)(*b*)). Dit is een van die kardinale beginsels by uitleg van Wette dat tensy die teendeel blyk, word vermoed dat die Wetgewer alleen toekomstige aangeleenthede tref (LC Steyn *Die Uitleg van Wette* 5de uitg op 82–97). In *Principal Immigration Officer v Purshotam* 1928 AD 435 word daar verwys na 'the rule that statutes regulate future conduct and are construed as operating only on cases or facts which come into existence after they were passed . . .' Die vraag is hier nie soseer of die Wet direkte retrospektiewe werking het nie, maar eerder of die Wet die verlede indirek raak deur die Hof te magtig om 'n bevel met retrospektiewe krag uit te reik. Na my oordeel geld die beswaar teen retrospektiewe werking van wetgewing ook in die geval. Terugwerkendheid beteken ondermeer 'van krag wees oor 'n voorafgaande tydperk' (*HAT*). Die terugwerkende bevel wat die partye aanvra, soos ook die in *Krös* se saak, gee voor om die aard van gedane sake te verander. Maar die verlede kan nie verander word nie. *Steyn* (aw op 82) stel dit pittig soos volg:

'Dit sou tevergeefs wees om te gebied dat iets in die verlede gedoen moet word, want die aard van die saak laat dit nie toe nie. Die verlede laat hom nie terugroep nie. So ook is dit nutteloos om te verbied dat iets in die verlede gedoen word, want as dit nie reeds gedoen is nie, kan dit nie meer in die verlede gedoen word nie, en as dit reeds gedoen is, kan die verbod niks daaraan verander nie. Dieselfde geld wat betref 'n wet wat toelaat dat iets gedoen word. Om vir die verlede iets toe te [19] laat, sou belaglik wees. Iets wat nie reeds gedoen is nie, kan nie [in] die verlede toegelaat word nie, en verlof om te doen, kan nie toegestaan word vir iets wat reeds gedoen is nie.'

Ten einde die regsaard van vergange se sake te verander, moet daar van fiksie gebruik gemaak word: byvoorbeeld, 'n regshandeling deur 'n vrou getroud in gemeenskap van goed en onderhewig aan die maritale mag van haar man, word geag verrig te gewees het deur die vrou getroud buite gemeenskap van goed en nie onderhewig aan die maritale mag nie. Die bevel wat die applikante aanvra, soos ook die in *Krös* se saak uitgereik, is nie beperk tot die posisie van die gades *inter se* nie, maar raak ook ander met wie hul sake gedoen het. Daar is kennelik veel ruimte vir probleme waar daar terugwerkend verander word aan gades se beskikkings- en handelingsbevoegdhede. En alle probleme kan nie vermy word deur die gebruiklike toevoeging tot die bevel van die woorde 'dat bestaande skuldeisers se regte nie daardeur geraak word nie'. Dit is derhalwe sinvol dat die Wetgewer, met twee uitsonderings, nie die terugwerkende verandering van die aard van gedane regshandelinge toelaat nie. Dié twee uitsonderings, hierbovermeld, is skenkings tussen gades en die voorsiening dat hul die aanwasbedeling binne twee jaar na die in-werkingtreding van die Wet op hul huwelik van toepassing kon gemaak het.

Beide uitsonderings het betrekking hoofsaaklik op die gades se posisie onderling en in beide gevalle maak die Wet uitdruklik voorsiening vir die beskerming van die regte van derdes.

Dit volg nie dat egmaats nie 'n onbillike of onbevredigende bateposisie kan regstel nie. Hulle kan ooreenkom nes hulle wil, maar binne die raamwerk van die Wet. Niks verhinder hul om by omskepping van hulle huwelik in gemeenskap van goed na een van buite gemeenskap van goed, onderling 'n ongelyke boedelverdeling te beding nie. Dit kan selfs so gereël word om tussen hulle dieselfde posisie te bewerkstellig as sou hul aanvanklik buite gemeenskap van goed met mekaar getrou het. Dit beteken egter nie dat die besware teen 'n terugwerkende bevel bloot akademies is nie. Ek het reeds na die probleme met betrekking tot die regte van buitestaanders verwys. Verdere probleme kan ontstaan. Allerlei implikasies met betrekking tot oordrag van vaste eiendom en skenkingsformaliteite, asook moontlike betaling van hereregte en skenkingsbelasting kan voortvloei uit die verskil tussen enersyds 'n Hofbevel wat gelas dat 'n huweliksgoederebedeling terugwerkend ver-ander word, en andersyds wat bepaal dat die verandering vanaf datum van die bevel geld ofskoon die partye die gemeenskaplike boedel onderling verdeel op die basis as sou die verandering terugwerkend geld.

Om voormelde redes is ek van oordeel dat die Hof nie bevoeg is om ingevolge art 21(1) van Wet 88 van 1984 'n bevel uit te reik wat voorgee om van terugwerkende krag te wees, in die volle sin van die begrip, soos in die vonnis in *Krös* se saak nie.

Die Hof weier derhalwe om enige bevel te maak, maar verleen aan die applikante verlof om op dieselfde stukke, aangevul waar nodig en behoorlik gewysig, die Hof weer om 'n bevel te nader.

Note

See the note on *Ex parte Krös* [103].

Aantekening

Sien die aantekening by *Ex parte Krös* [103].

[105]   EX PARTE LOURENS

1986 2 SA 291 (C)

Application in terms of section 21(1) of the Matrimonial Property Act 88 of 1984 to alter the matrimonial property regime

In this case five applications were made in terms of section 21(1) of the Matrimonial Property Act 88 of 1984 to alter the matrimonial property regime. All the applications were incomplete in one respect or another. The court set out guidelines as to the procedure to be followed in such cases.

Aansoek ingevolge artikel 21(1) van die Wet op Huweliksgoedere 88 van 1984 om die huweliksgoederebedeling te verander.

In hierdie saak is daar vyf aansoeke ingevolge artikel 21(1) van die Wet op Huweliksgoedere 88 van 1984 gedoen om die huweliksgoederebedeling te verander. Al die aansoeke was in een of ander opsig onvolledig. Die hof het sekere riglyne neergelê met betrekking tot die prosedure wat in sodanige gevalle gevolg moet word.

MARAIS J: [292] It seemed desirable to have some uniformity regarding the procedure to be followed because there are likely to be a number of these applications in future ...

The factors which I take into account in deciding upon the procedure to be followed are these. Firstly, there are the explicit requirements of s 21(1). Plainly these must be satisfied. Secondly, costly procedural steps should be avoided if this can be done without prejudice to anybody's legitimate interests. Thirdly, subject to the qualifications mentioned later herein, applications should be brought in the Court in the area of [293] jurisdiction in which the couple are domiciled and ordinarily reside. With these objects in view, the following guidelines should be adhered to, save in exceptional circumstances:

Notice

Notice of the application must be given to the Registrar of Deeds in terms of s 97(1) of the Deeds Registries Act 47 of 1937. The draft notarial contract which it is proposed to register must be annexed to the application. Notice of intention to make the application must also be published in the *Government Gazette* and *Die Burger* and *Cape Times* newspapers [this will, of course, only apply for the Cape] at least two weeks before the date on which the application will be heard. The date upon which the application will be heard must be specified in the published notice and anyone who wishes to object to the proposed change, or to make any representations in that regard, must be told that this can be done by writing to the Registrar of the Court and sending a copy to the applicants' attorney, or by appearing in Court on the day of the hearing. The published notice must also contain a statement that the application and the contract which it is proposed to register are available for inspection at the office of the Registrar of the Court and at the office of the applicants' attorney. In addition, at least two weeks' prior notice of the application must be given by certified post to all creditors, whether actual or contingent. A list of such creditors, verified by affidavit, shall be included in the application and proof that such notice has been given to them must be provided by an affidavit to which are annexed the relevant certificates of posting. If any material change in the parties' financial position occurs before the application is heard, a supplementary affidavit reflecting such change must be filed.

Financial Position of the Parties

Sufficient information regarding the assets and liabilities of the couple concerned must be set out in the application to enable the Court to judge whether or not there are sound reasons for the proposed change and whether or not any other person will be prejudiced by the proposed change. It should also be stated whether or not either of the applicants has been sequestrated in the past and, if so, when, and in what circumstances. The case number of any rehabilitation application must be furnished. It should also be stated whether or not there are any pending legal proceedings in which any creditor is seeking to recover payment of any alleged debt due by the couple or either of them.

Sound Reasons

Sound reasons cannot be defined exhaustively and in advance. However, care must be taken to motivate fully the proposed change in the existing matrimonial property system.

Absence of Prejudice

Applicants must explain why no other person will be prejudiced by the proposed change. In any event, the order sought, and the contract which it is proposed to register, shall contain a provision which preserves the rights of pre-existing creditors.

Domicile and Residence

The application must disclose where the parties are domiciled and, if they are not resident there when the application is made, where they are [294] resident. If there has been a recent change in domicile or residence it should be disclosed so that the Court can consider whether the application has been brought in the appropriate *forum* and/or whether or not additional notice of the application should be given ... Where the order sought is confined to altering the matrimonial property system, and not the marital power, it may be that it is not essential to apply to the Court in whose area of jurisdiction the parties are domiciled and that other Courts may enjoy jurisdiction but ordinarily the application should be brought in the Court in whose area of jurisdiction the parties are domiciled and ordinarily resident.

There may be other problems which arise when such applications are brought and they will have to be solved as and when they do. For the moment the guidelines I have mentioned should be followed. I should add that the procedure to be followed in cases of this kind has been discussed with all the other Judges of this Division and, I am authorised by them to say that, save for the question of what publication should be required, in regard to which there is no clear *consensus*, the guidelines which I have laid down, carry their broad approval ...

Note

This case deals only with the procedure to be followed when application is brought in terms of section 21(1) of the Matrimonial Property Act 88 of 1984 to alter the matrimonial property regime.

The procedural requirements laid down in this case for the Cape Provincial Division have also been adopted in the Orange Free State Provincial Division in *Ex parte Le Roux; Ex parte Von Berg*

Aantekening

Hierdie saak het net te doen met die prosedure wat gevolg moet word as ingevolge artikel 21(1) van die Wet op Huweliksgoedere 88 van 1984 aansoek gedoen word om die huweliksgoedere-bedeling te verander.

Die prosedure-vereistes wat in hierdie saak neergelê is vir die Kaapse Provinsiale Afdeling is ook in die Oranje Vrystaatse Provinsiale Afdeling aanvaar in *Ex parte Le Roux; Ex parte Von Berg*

1990 2 SA 70 (O). In this regard see also *Ex parte Coertzen* 1986 2 SA 108 (O). Here the notification to the creditors did not contain the date on which the application was to be brought. The court held solely on this ground that the application could not be granted because it could prejudice a creditor who wishes to object in the preparation of his case. The court further held that, in terms of section 21(1)(c), it must be satisfied that no other person will be prejudiced by the proposed change and to protect such person as well as creditors who inadvertently had not been given notice, a rule *nisi* must be issued and published in a newspaper.

1990 2 SA 70 (O). Sien in hierdie verband ook *Ex parte Coertzen* 1986 2 SA 108 (O). In hierdie saak het die kennisgewing aan die krediteure nie die datum vermeld waarop die aansoek gedoen sou word nie. Die hof het beslis dat die aansoek bloot op grond hiervan nie toegestaan kan word nie aangesien dit 'n skuldeiser wat beswaar wil maak in die voorbereiding van sy saak mag benadeel. Die hof het verder beslis dat dit ingevolge artikel 21(1)(c) oortuig moet wees dat geen ander persoon deur die voorgenome verandering benadeel sal word nie, en om sodanige persone te beskerm, asook skuldeisers wat per abuis nie kennis gegee is nie, moet 'n bevel *nisi* uitgereik word wat in 'n koerant gepubliseer moet word.

Extra-judicial amendment

Buitegeregtelike wysiging

[106]   HONEY V HONEY

1992 3 SA 609 (W)

Informal variation of matrimonial property regime not permitted

The parties to this action were married out of community of property. Prior to their marriage they concluded an antenuptial contract which was duly registered in the deeds registry. Apart from the normal clauses excluding community of property, this contract provided that the marriage would be subject to the accrual system. A few years after their marriage they entered into a further agreement. This contract was notarially executed, but not registered in the deeds registry and not entered into with leave of the court as provided for in section 21(1) of the Matrimonial Property Act 88 of 1984. The latter agreement purported to exclude the accrual system from the marriage as from the date of the marriage. It further listed the respective assets of the parties. Subsequently the wife sued her husband for divorce and, relying on the postnuptial contract, claimed an order that she was entitled to retain as her sole and absolute property the assets listed

Informele wysiging van huweliksgoederebedeling is ontoelaatbaar

Die partye in hierdie saak was buite gemeenskap van goed getroud. Hulle het voor hulle huweliksluiting 'n huweliksvoorwaardeskontrak aangegaan welke kontrak in die akteskantoor geregistreer is. Afgesien van die gewone klousules wat gemeenskap van goed uitgesluit het, het hierdie kontrak bepaal dat die huwelik aan die aanwasbedeling onderworpe sou wees. 'n Paar jaar na huweliksluiting het die partye 'n verdere kontrak aangegaan. Hierdie kontrak is notarieel verly maar nie in die akteskantoor geregistreer nie en ook nie met goedkeuring van die hof gesluit soos wat artikel 21(1) van die Wet op Huweliksgoedere 88 van 1984 bepaal nie. Die partye het met laasgenoemde ooreenkoms beoog om die aanwasbedeling vanaf sluiting van die huwelik uit te sluit. Die kontrak het verder aangedui welke bates aan elke gade behoort het. Die vrou het haar man later om 'n egskeiding gedagvaar en op die nahuwelikse kontrak gesteun vir haar eis om 'n bevel

as hers in this contract. At the time of the divorce the accrual in her estate was larger than the accrual in the defendant's estate. The defendant maintained that the postnuptial contract was void *ab initio*, alternatively that it was voidable, and based his claim to share in his wife's accrual on the antenuptial contract. The court held that the postnuptial contract was void and unenforceable as between the parties *inter se*.

dat die bates wat in die kontrak as hare aangedui word uitsluitlik aan haar behoort. Ten tyde van die egskeiding was die aanwas in haar boedel groter as dié in die verweerder se boedel. Die verweerder het beweer dat die nahuwelikse kontrak *ab initio* nietig was, en in die alternatief dat dit vernietigbaar was. Hy het sy eis op die huweliksvoorwaardeskontrak gebaseer. Die hof het beslis dat die nahuwelikse kontrak nietig was en nie tussen die partye afgedwing kon word nie.

DU PLESSIS J: [611] In terms of our common law, subject to an exception to which reference will be made later, parties to a marriage cannot by postnuptial agreement change their matrimonial property system. In *Union Government (Minister of Finance) v Larkan* 1916 AD 212 at 224 INNES CJ phrased the rule thus:

> 'Apart from statute, then, community once excluded cannot be introduced, and once introduced, cannot be excluded, nor can an antenuptial contract be varied by a postnuptial agreement between the spouses, even if confirmed by the death of one of them. The only exception to the rule is afforded by an underhand deed of separation either ratified, or entitled at the time to ratification under a decree of judicial separation.'

(See also *Ex parte Smuts* 1914 CPD 1034 at 1037; *Ex parte Venter et Uxor* 1948 (2) SA 175 (O) at 179; *Ex parte Nathan Woolf et Uxor* 1944 OPD 266 at 269; *Edelstein v Edelstein NO and Others* 1952 (3) SA 1 (A) at 15G [33]; *Ex parte Dunn et Uxor* 1989 (2) SA 429 (NC) at 431B–D [99].)

Counsel for both parties to the present action accepted the existence of the common-law rule as premise.

On behalf of the plaintiff Mr *Nugent* submitted that the reason for the rule was to be found in the fact that, by common law, donations between spouses were prohibited: a postnuptial contract purporting to vary the matrimonial property system of the parties invariably amounts to a donation in some form or another, so the argument went, and because donations were prohibited therefore a variation of the antenuptial contract would be void. Section 22 of the Act now, however, provides as follows:

> 'Subject to the provisions of the Insolvency Act 24 of 1936, no transaction effected before or after the commencement of this Act is void or voidable merely because it amounts to a donation between spouses.'

This being the position, the argument proceeded, the *ratio* for the voidness of a postnuptial contract varying the matrimonial property system has fallen away, at least as far as the parties *inter partes* are concerned. It therefore follows that the present postnuptial contract is valid and enforceable as far as the parties themselves are concerned, although it might not be valid and enforceable as far as third parties are concerned.

(In support of his argument Mr *Nugent, inter alia,* relied upon an unpublished article by Dr K [Douglas 1991 *De Rebus* 205]. A copy of this article has been made available to the Court and reference will be made to the article as 'the unpublished article'.

The Act itself in my view provides the answer to Mr *Nugent's* argument. Section 2 of the Act provides as follows:

> 'Every marriage out of community of property in terms of an antenuptial contract by which community of property and community of profit and loss are excluded, which

is entered into after the commencement of this Act, is subject to the accrual system specified in this chapter, except insofar as that system is expressly excluded by the antenuptial contract.'

This section makes it clear in so many words that the accrual system can, when the parties are married out of community of property and with the exclusion of the community of profit and loss, only be excluded by antenuptial contract.

[612] Mr *Nugent*, however, submitted that s 2 is no obstacle to his argument, his argument being that the present postnuptial contract is only valid *inter partes:* s 2 does not affect the present issue because that section only regulates the parties' matrimonial property system *vis-à-vis* third parties.

The argument cannot, in my view, on an interpretation of s 2, be upheld. It must be kept in mind that the term 'antenuptial contract' is not synonymous with the term 'duly registered antenuptial contract'. An antenuptial contract is valid between the parties and *inter partes* regulates their matrimonial property system even if it is not registered. (See *Ex parte Spinazze and Another NNO* 1985 (3) SA 650 (A) at 656D–658D [98]; see also s 86 of the Deeds Registries Act 47 of 1937; Joubert 'Informele en Ongeregistreerde Huwe-liksvoorwaardekontrakte' (1982) 16 *De Jure* (vol I) 70 at 74 and further.) A duly registered antenuptial contract on the other hand regulates the parties' matrimonial property system also as regards third parties. In s 2, the Legislature does not deal only with registered antenuptial contracts but, with presumed knowledge of the status of an antenuptial contract, refers to 'an antenuptial contract' without qualification. If the intention in s 2 was to deal only with the parties' position *vis-à-vis* third parties, the reference would have been to a duly registered antenuptial contract.

The answer to Mr *Nugent's* thorough argument may, however, not be as simple, and I deem it necessary also to deal with the argument relating to the reason for the rule against postnuptial amendments to antenuptial contracts.

The common-law authorities that I have consulted in most instances discuss the question whether parties may change the matrimonial property system from one in community of property to one out of community of property separately from the other question whether parties can by postnuptial contract amend or cancel an antenuptial contract. As will be seen later in this judgment, the authorities relied upon by Mr *Nugent* invariably deal with instances where parties married in community of property endeavoured to change to out of community of property. I shall, however, assume that there in fact is only one rule, namely the rule as formulated by INNES CJ in the *Larkan* case *supra*. (See also De Groot *Inleidinge* 2.12.5.) I might add that the passages quoted hereunder are, except for *De Groot*, those that deal with the ability postnuptially to amend or cancel an antenuptial contract.

With the possible exception of Van der Linden *Koopmanshandboek* 1.3.5, the common-law authorities regard the rule that the matrimonial property system is immutable as a substantive rule with a separate existence and not as a mere application of the rule prohibiting donations between spouses. (See *Voet* (*Gane's* translation) 23.4.60; Groenewegen *De Leg Abr Ad C.* 4.29.11; Van Leeuwen *RHR* 4.24.12; Cos *Rechtsgeleerde Verhandelingen over Huwelykze Voorwaarden* at 55 para III; Arntzenius *Inst* 2.4.10 (translation by *FP van den Heever* at 147–8).) MAASDORP JA in *Larkan's* case *supra* at 231 also deals with the question whether the rule referred to above is a mere application of the prohibition against donations between spouses in the following manner.

'It is said by the writers that during marriage community of property cannot be altered by contract, because that would create a gift between the spouses, but that [613] does not place an extinction of community of property in the same position as a gift. There are, in law, special rules affecting community of property, and other rules affecting gifts.'

It is true that most of the authorities quoted give the prohibition of donations between spouses as a reason for the rule, but most of them also give other, differing reasons as well. De Groot *Inleidinge* 2.12.5 states the general rule only, and gives no reasons save that, once the marriage has been solemnised, the law of the land takes effect and the parties cannot change it *inter vivos*.

The rule being a substantive rule for which different reasons are given cannot be regarded as having been abrogated by the repeal of one of the reasons given by the authorities for its existence. [Douglas] (in the unpublished article) analyses the common-law authorities, categorises the reasons furnished by them for the rule and then argues that, but for the protection of creditors, all the other reasons for the rule are either of historic interest, are not of application to marriages out of community of property or had been repealed or became obsolete. The argument has much to commend itself in logic, but the mere fact that there are authors who give reasons that are not dealt with by [Douglas] illustrates the danger of such logic. (See *De Groot* (*loc cit*); *Arntzenius* (*loc cit*); HDJ Bodenstein 'The Validity of Pacts between Husband and Wife' (1917) 34 *SALJ* 11 at 16–28.)

Mr *Nugent* also relied on various decisions of our Courts as authority for the proposition that the prohibition against donations between spouses is in fact the only reason for the immutability of spouses' matrimonial property system.

In *Union Government (Minister of Finance) v Larkan* (*supra* at 220) INNES CJ does refer to the prohibition against donations between spouses as a reason for the rule, and says that therefore the rule

'was *largely* affected in the Netherlands by the further question whether the law regulating the transaction absolutely prohibited donations between spouses'.

(My italicising.) I do not read the learned Chief Justice at all as suggesting that the rule can be regarded as a mere application of the rule against donations between spouses. (See in this regard also the passage from the judgment of MAASDORP JA quoted above.)

In his formulation of the rule (the one quoted above) INNES CJ refers to an exception to the general rule that the matrimonial property system cannot be changed by postnuptial contract – if the parties were entitled at the time of the agreement to a decree of judicial separation, they could *inter partes* divide the common estate. (See in this regard also *Voet* 24.2.19 and *De Groot* 3.21.11. See also *Scheltinga se dictata oor De Groot* as edited by De Vos and Visagie and published by *Lex Patria* publishers in 1986 at 425.)

Mr *Nugent* relied on *Ziedeman v Ziedeman* (1838) 1 Menzies 238 as authority for the proposition that a postnuptial contract is effective *inter partes* provided it does not amount to a prohibited donation. *Ziedeman's* case, however, is no more than an application of the exception referred to by INNES CJ and does not assist the plaintiff in the present case.

Pugh v Pugh 1910 TPD 792 also dealt with a notarial deed of separation and similarly does not assist the plaintiff.

[614] Mr *Nugent* further relied on the case of *Coulthard v Coulthard* 1922 WLD 13 where the learned Judge said the following at 16–17:

'The law laid down in *Ziedeman v Ziedeman* ... is as follows: All contracts which spouses may lawfully and effectually enter into with each other *before marriage* may lawfully and effectually be entered into by them *stante matrimonio* insofar as regards and concerns themselves provided always that such contract be not of a nature as to constitute, either directly or indirectly, a deed of donation from one spouse to the other. From which follows the corollary: A contract entered into between spouses whereby the one only receives from the other what that other was legally bound to grant and no more is a valid contract between the parties.'

What was said in *Ziedeman's* case is clearly *obiter* as that case dealt with the exception to the general rule that I have referred to. In any event, as far as the statement relates to a postnuptial contract purporting to amend the parties' matrimonial property system, it is not in accordance with authorities quoted above. *Coulthard's* case itself was decided on two principles: the contract in question did not contain a provision for separation *a mensa et thoro* and therefore did not fall under the exception referred to above. The second principle upon which *Coulthard's* case was decided was purely that the contract under consideration in fact amounted to a donation between spouses and was therefore void. The case is not authority for the general proposition that as long as it does not contain a prohibited donation, the parties can validly by postnuptial contract change the matrimonial property system.

In *Ex parte Marx et Uxor* (2) 1936 CPD 499 the Court had to decide whether parties could postnuptially alter their marriage from one in community of property to one out of community of property. JONES J (with whom DAVIS J concurred) does refer to *Larkan's* case *supra* and said that in that case it was decided that parties who are married in community of property cannot by postnuptial agreement change to a marriage out of community of property 'for the very simple reason that according to our law a change from a communal marriage to a marriage out of community amounts to a donation between the spouses'. The Court, however, does not go into the question whether the contract then under consideration in fact did amount to a donation or not, and simply found that the contract is void. This case too does not afford authority for the proposition advanced by Mr *Nugent*.

It is therefore concluded that the mere repeal of the prohibition against donations between spouses did not automatically abrogate the rule that parties may not postnuptially amend an antenuptial contract whether such amendment is intended to have effect *inter partes* only or not.

The following order is therefore made:

The contract between the parties dated 8 September 1989 and purporting to vary their antenuptial contract is void and unenforceable as between the parties *inter se* ...

Note

The decision in this case is not supported. Firstly, DU PLESSIS J's reliance on section 2 of the Matrimonial Property Act 88 of 1984 in holding that the postnuptial contract between the spouses was void is, it is submitted, incorrect. Section 2 deals only with the position when the spouses are entering into an antenuptial contract – in terms of section 2 they may at that stage exclude the accrual system from their marriage by having an express clause to that effect included in their antenuptial contract. The section clearly does not deal with postnuptial exclusions of or alterations to the accrual system. (See also Van Schalkwyk 1993 *De Jure* 215 218–220.)

Secondly, although DU PLESSIS J is correct in holding that "the rule that the matrimonial prop-

Aantekening

Die uitspraak in hierdie saak word nie ondersteun nie. Eerstens word aan die hand gedoen dat DU PLESSIS R verkeerd is om hom op artikel 2 van die Wet op Huweliksgoedere 88 van 1984 te beroep as gesag vir sy beslissing dat die nahuwelikse kontrak tussen die gades nietig is. Artikel 2 handel slegs oor die posisie wanneer die gades 'n huweliksvoorwaardeskontrak aangaan – ingevolge artikel 2 kan hulle op daardie stadium die aanwasbedeling uitsluit deur 'n uitdruklike bepaling te dien effekte in hulle huweliksvoorwaardeskontrak te laat inskryf. Die artikel het duidelik nie met nahuwelikse uitsluitings van of wysigings aan die aanwasbedeling te doen nie. (Sien ook Van Schalkwyk 1993 *De Jure* 215 218–220.)

erty system is immutable [is] a substantive rule with a separate existence and not ... a mere application of the rule prohibiting donations between spouses" (612), his finding that this rule renders the postnuptial contract between the spouses void both as against third parties and as between the spouses is not supported. That changes by the spouses *inter se* to the matrimonial property system cannot bind third parties is clear. But why should spouses who are married out of community of property not be permitted to enter into a contract which is binding only as between themselves, simply because that contract may have an effect on their matrimonial property system? Why, for example, should a spouse who is married out of community of property not be permitted to donate an amount to his or her spouse which is equal to the accrual benefit? (Such a donation would have the effect of cancelling the accrual system. See also Douglas 1991 *De Rebus* 221 222 who criticises the judgment and points out that, if the judgment in *Honey* is correct, such a donation would be invalid even as between the spouses if it is expressed as an amount equal to the accrual benefit.) Surely there is no reason thus to limit the principle of freedom to contract and the spouses' contractual capacity. If the contract is binding only as between the spouses no third party can be prejudiced by it, and thus the rule that the matrimonial property system is immutable still applies in respect of third parties.

On *Honey* see also Sonnekus 1992 *TSAR* 683 who supports the decision.

Tweedens, alhoewel DU PLESSIS R heeltemal korrek is dat "the rule that the matrimonial property system is immutable [is] a substantive rule with a separate existence and not ... a mere application of the rule prohibiting donations between spouses" (612), word sy bevinding dat hierdie reël tot gevolg het dat die nahuwelikse kontrak tussen die gades sowel teenoor derdes as tussen die gades onderling nietig is, nie ondersteun nie. Dit is duidelik dat veranderings wat die gades onderling aan hulle huweliksgoederebedeling aanbring nie derdes kan bind nie. Maar waarom moet gades wat buite gemeenskap van goed getroud is, verbied word om 'n kontrak aan te gaan wat net hulle bind bloot omdat daardie kontrak 'n effek op hulle huweliksgoederebedeling kan hê? Waarom mag 'n gade wat buite gemeenskap van goed getroud is byvoorbeeld nie 'n bedrag wat gelyk is aan die reg op aanwas aan sy of haar gade skenk nie? (So 'n kontrak sal die effek hê dat die aanwasbedeling gekanselleer word. Sien ook Douglas 1991 *De Rebus* 221 222 wat die uitspraak kritiseer en daarop wys dat, indien die uitspraak in *Honey* korrek is, so 'n skenking selfs tussen die gades onderling nietig sal wees indien dit uitgedruk word as 'n bedrag wat gelyk is aan die reg op aanwas.) Daar is tog sekerlik geen rede om die beginsel van kontrakteervryheid en die gades se handelingsbevoegdheid op die wyse te beperk nie. Indien die kontrak slegs tussen die gades onderling geldig is, kan geen derde daardeur benadeel word nie en gevolglik sal die beginsel dat die huweliksgoederebedeling onveranderbaar is steeds ten opsigte van derdes geld.

Oor *Honey* sien ook Sonnekus 1992 *TSAR* 683 wat die uitspraak steun.

The grounds for divorce

Irretrievable breakdown – section 4
Mental illness or continuous unconsciousness – section 5
Divorce in terms of Jewish ecclesiastical law

Die egskeidingsgronde

Onherstelbare verbrokkeling – artikel 4
Geestesongesteldheid of voortdurende bewusteloosheid – artikel 5
Egskeiding ingevolge Joodse kerkreg

Irretrievable breakdown – section 4   Onherstelbare verbrokkeling – artikel 4

[107] SCHWARTZ V SCHWARTZ

1984 4 SA 467 (A)

Irretrievable breakdown of a marriage

The appellant (husband) and the respondent were happily married until the respondent became aware of her husband's extra-marital relationship with another woman. The appellant subsequently left the matrimonial home, went to live with his mistress (Miss Lintvelt) and instituted an action for divorce on the ground of the irretrievable breakdown of the marriage. When the matter was heard the respondent admitted that the marriage relationship had broken down but denied that the breakdown was irretrievable and that there was no reasonable prospect of the restoration of a normal marital relationship between the spouses. She testified that she still loved her husband and was prepared to take him back. The court *a quo* held that the appellant had not proved that his marriage had irretrievably broken down and that a divorce could therefore not be granted. He appealed against this decision and the appeal was upheld.

Onherstelbare verbrokkeling van 'n huwelik

Die appellant (man) en die respondent was gelukkig getroud totdat die respondent agtergekom het dat haar man in 'n buite-egtelike verhouding met 'n ander vrou betrokke was. Die appellant het later die gemeenskaplike huishouding verlaat, by sy minnares (mej Lintvelt) gaan woon en 'n egskeidingsgeding teen sy vrou aanhangig gemaak. Die respondent het tydens die verhoor erken dat die huweliksverhouding verbrokkel het maar het ontken dat die verbrokkeling onherstelbaar was en dat daar geen redelike vooruitsig was dat 'n normale huweliksverhouding tussen die partye herstel kon word nie. Sy het getuig dat sy nog lief was vir haar man en bereid was om hom terug te neem. Die hof *a quo* het beslis dat die appellant nie bewys het dat sy huwelik onherstelbaar verbrokkel het nie en dat 'n egskeidingsbevel gevolglik nie toegestaan kon word nie. Hy het teen hierdie uitspraak geappelleer en die appèl was suksesvol.

CORBETT JA: [473] Section 3(*a*) of the [Divorce] Act, read with s 4, introduced a "no-fault" criterion for the grant of a decree of divorce, viz irretrievable breakdown of the marriage. The Court may grant a decree of divorce on this ground if it is satisfied, as an objective fact, that the marriage relationship between the parties to the marriage has reached such a state of disintegration that there is no reasonable prospect of the restoration of a normal marriage relationship between them. Section 4(2) specifies certain facts or circumstances which the Court may accept as proof of the irretrievable breakdown of a marriage, but the subsection makes it clear that this list does not exclude any other facts or circumstances which may be indicative of the irretrievable breakdown of the marriage ...

It was submitted by respondent's counsel that s 4(1) confers a discretion on the Court; and that inasmuch as the Court *a quo* exercised a discretion in reaching the decision it did, this Court should not readily interfere with the exercise of that discretion. Reference was made in this connection to the decision of the Full Bench of the Orange Free State Provincial Division in the case of *Smit v Smit* 1982 (4) SA 34 (O) [110].

The submission is, in my opinion, not well-founded. In the first place, I am not convinced that s 4(1) does confer upon the Court the kind of discretion contemplated by counsel's submission. It is true that s 4(1) is couched in permissive terms. It provides that a Court "may grant a decree of divorce" (Afrikaans text: "kan 'n egskeidingsbevel . . . verleen"). It does not necessarily follow, however, that the Legislature intended to confer a discretion on the Court. Section 4(1) is clearly an empowering section: it confers legislatively a power which the Court did not previously enjoy. A statutory enactment conferring [474] a power in permissive language may nevertheless have to be construed as making it the duty of the person or authority in whom the power is reposed to exercise that power when the conditions prescribed as justifying its exercise have been satisfied. Whether an enactment should be so construed depends on, *inter alia*, the language in which it is couched, the context in which it appears, the general scope and object of the legislation, the nature of the thing empowered to be done and the person or persons for whose benefit the power is to be exercised . . . As was pointed out in the *Noble & Barbour* case *supra* [*Noble & Barbour v South African Railways and Harbours* 1922 AD 527], this does not involve reading the word "may" as meaning "must". As long as the English language retains its meaning "may" can never be equivalent to "must". It is a question whether the grant of the permissive power also imports an obligation in certain circumstances to use the power.

Section 4(1) empowers the Court to grant a decree of divorce on the ground of the irretrievable breakdown of the marriage "if it is satisfied that . . .", and then follows a specified state of affairs which is in effect the statutory definition of irretrievable breakdown. Clearly satisfaction that this state of affairs exists is a necessary prerequisite to the exercise by the Court of its power to grant a decree of divorce on this ground. But once the Court is so satisfied, can it, in its discretion, withhold or grant a decree of divorce? It is difficult to visualize on what grounds a Court, so satisfied, could withhold a decree of divorce. Moreover, had it been intended by the Legislature that the Court, in such circumstances, would have a residual power to withhold a decree of divorce, one would have expected to find in the enactment some more specific indication of this intent and of the grounds upon which this Court might exercise its powers adversely to the plaintiff. In *Smit's* case *supra* it seems to be suggested that, notwithstanding the fact that a marriage has broken down irretrievably, the Court may refuse a decree of divorce in order to exercise the power granted to it in terms of s 4(3) of the Act, ie to postpone the proceedings in order that the parties may attempt a reconciliation (see at 41H–42A). The prerequisite to the exercise of the power contained in s 4(3) is that it must appear to the Court that there is a reasonable possibility that the parties may become reconciled through marriage counsel, treatment or reflection. If there is this reasonable possibility, can it be said that the marriage has broken down irretrievably? And conversely if the marriage is found to have broken down irretrievably, can such a reasonable possibility exist? It seems to me that there is much to be said for the view that these concepts, ie irretrievable breakdown and the reasonable possibility of reconciliation, are mutually contradictory and that the existence of the power conferred by s 4(3) does not necessarily indicate a residual discretion vested in the Court by s 4(1).

[475] In *Smit's* case *supra* at 42A s 6(1) is also referred to, apparently in support of the thesis that the Court enjoys a discretion under s 4(1). Section 6(1) provides that a decree of divorce "shall not be granted" until the Court is satisfied that the provisions made or contemplated with regard to the welfare of any minor or dependent child of the marriage are satisfactory or are the best that can be effected in the circumstances. And in order to satisfy itself in this regard the Court is empowered by s 6(2) to cause any investigation which it may deem necessary to be carried out. Section 6(1) thus requires, in imperative terms, that the Court should be satisfied in regard to these matters concerning minor or dependent children before it grants a decree of divorce. The power of the Court to grant a decree of divorce on the ground of irretrievable breakdown of the marriage (and on the other grounds stated in s 3) is thus qualified, or made subject to, the Court being

satisfied as to the matters referred to in s 6(1); but I do not read s 6(1) as conferring, or substantiating the existence of, a discretion under s 4(1).

It is not necessary, however, to decide the question as to whether the Court enjoys a discretion under s 4(1) since the point does not really arise in this case. Although the trial Judge did not refer specifically to the provisions of ss 3 and 4 of the Act, as I read his judgment, he found that there had not been an irretrievable breakdown in the marriage, or at any rate that irretrievable breakdown had not been proved. The necessary prerequisite to the exercise of the Court's power to grant a decree of divorce was, therefore, absent. There was no question of the Court, having found irretrievable breakdown, exercising a discretion. For this reason alone counsel's submission is ill-founded.

The main issue on appeal was whether the trial Judge's finding in regard to irretrievable breakdown was justified by the evidence. In determining whether a marriage has reached such a state of disintegration that there is no reasonable prospect of the restoration of a normal marriage relationship between the parties it is important to have regard to what has happened in the past, ie the history of the relationship up to the date of trial, and also to the present attitude of the parties to the marriage relationship as revealed by the evidence at the trial.

[CORBETT JA discussed the facts of the case including the history of the marriage up to the date of the trial and the spouses' attitude to the marriage relationship. He proceeded:]

[478] The question is whether the marriage between appellant and respondent has reached such a state of disintegration that there is no reasonable prospect of the restoration of a normal marriage relationship between them. Looking at the facts objectively I am of the opinion that the question must be answered in the affirmative. At the time of the trial the parties had been living apart for three years and the relationship between appellant and Miss Lintvelt had been in existence for five-and-a-half years. Appellant evinced at the trial a determination to obtain a divorce, if possible, and to marry Miss Lintvelt. The suggestion that he was being coerced into this attitude and was not a free agent – an issue upon which the Court *a quo* made no definite finding – seems far-fetched and contrary to the probabilities. There is no doubt that irretrievable breakdown can come about as a result of the conduct and attitude of one of the parties to a marriage, and despite the wish of the other to perpetuate a marriage relationship (see eg *Kruger v Kruger* 1980 (3) SA 283 (O)); and it seems to me that this is such a case.

The trial Judge found that the appellant was "passing through a period of uncertainty" and that his behaviour in Court was "an indication of abject misery with no true desire of breaking total relation with the defendant (respondent)". It is not clear what the basis for these findings was. The learned Judge stated that even after appellant's infatuation with Miss Lintvelt he did not break off total connection with the respondent and that, when appellant reached the stage of stating that he no longer loved the respondent, he was "most unconvincing, almost apologetic in saying so"; and he also referred to the substantial allegations made in the appellant's particulars of claim which "he was unable to prove".

It is true that after meeting Miss Lintvelt appellant did not "break off total connection" with respondent, but persons in that kind of situation very often do not . . .

[479] The fact that appellant was "almost apologetic" in saying that he no longer loved the respondent and that he did not attempt to support most of the allegations in his statement of claim do not, in my view, establish uncertainty on his part. Appellant . . . clearly still admired and respected respondent and did not wish unduly to hurt her. In the circumstances, and knowing that she professed still to love him, it would not be surprising if he were diffident about denying love for her; and for the same reasons it is understandable that he did not seek to substantiate many of the hurtful allegations con-

tained in his particulars of claim, even if he were in a position to do so. It must be accepted that appellant did present a picture of "abject misery" in the witness-box and while sitting in Court, but it does not necessarily follow that he had no true desire to become divorced. Obviously he was "torn between two duties", as he put it, and from the practical and common sense points of view there were many good reasons why he should give up Miss Lintvelt and return to the respondent. But human emotions do not always respond to the dictates of practicality and common sense. And appellant chose Miss Lintvelt and the path of divorce. His chosen path was nevertheless calculated to cause him much heartache, as obviously it did.

It was argued on behalf of the respondent that the denial of a divorce order would result in the termination of the relationship between appellant and Miss Lintvelt and in the resumption of married life between appellant and respondent; and that, therefore, the breakdown was not irretrievable. I do not think that it is legitimate or indeed logical to determine whether or not a marriage has broken down irretrievably by reference to what would or might occur if and after a decree of divorce has been refused on the ground that irretrievable breakdown has not been established ...

I feel constrained to differ from the conclusion of the trial Judge ...

[480] [T]he appellant did establish that his marriage to respondent had broken down irretrievably and ... he was entitled to a decree of divorce ... [481] [T]he appeal is allowed ...

KOTZÉ JA and JOUBERT JA concurred.

Note

It should be noted that the Appellate Division was of the opinion that the word "may" in sections 3 and 4 of the Divorce Act 70 of 1979 did not confer a discretion on the courts to refuse a divorce if irretrievable breakdown of the marriage had been proved. Although this remark was only made *obiter* it was approved of and applied by the Appellate Division in *Levy v Levy* 1991 3 SA 614 (A), and the view expressed in *Smit v Smit* [110] (where the court accepted the existence of such a discretion) was rejected. For a more detailed discussion of the question whether the courts do have such a discretion, see Barnard, Cronjé and Olivier (254–255) and Van Wyk (1979 *De Rebus* 636–637). See also Van der Vyver and Joubert (654–655) and Hahlo (345–347).

The second very important point dealt with in this case is concerned with the method the court employed to establish whether the parties' marriage had indeed broken down irretrievably. The court viewed the situation from a subjective as well as an objective point of view. In terms of the subjective approach the attitude of the spouses is considered while the objective approach concentrates on the facts and circumstances of the particular marriage. For a more detailed discussion of this subject, see Barnard and Van Aswegen

Aantekening

Let daarop dat die Appèlafdeling van mening was dat die woord "kan" in artikels 3 en 4 van die Wet op Egskeiding 70 van 1979 nie 'n diskresie aan die howe verleen om 'n egskeidingsbevel te weier as onherstelbare verbrokkeling van die huwelik bewys is nie. Alhoewel hierdie opmerking *obiter* gemaak is, is dit goedgekeur en toegepas deur die Appèlhof in *Levy v Levy* 1991 3 SA 614 (A), en is die standpunt wat in *Smit v Smit* [110] uitgespreek is (naamlik dat sodanige diskresie wel bestaan) verwerp. Sien Barnard, Cronjé en Olivier (262–263) en Van Wyk (1979 *De Rebus* 636–637) vir 'n meer diepgaande bespreking van die vraag of die howe sodanige diskresie het al dan nie. Sien ook Van der Vyver en Joubert (654–655) en Hahlo (345–347).

Die tweede baie belangrike aspek wat in hierdie saak ter sprake gekom het, het te doen met die metode wat die hof aangewend het om te bepaal of die partye se huwelik inderdaad onherstelbaar verbrokkel het. Die hof het die situasie vanuit 'n subjektiewe sowel as 'n objektiewe oogpunt beskou. Ingevolge die subjektiewe benadering word die houdings van die partye in ag geneem terwyl die objektiewe benadering op die feite en omstandighede van die spesifieke huwelik gerig is. Vir 'n meer volledige bespreking van hierdie

(1981 *THRHR* 199); Barnard, Cronjé and Olivier 257 *et seq.*

See also *Swart v Swart* [108] and *Naidoo v Naidoo* [109].

onderwerp, sien Barnard en Van Aswegen (1981 *THRHR* 199); Barnard, Cronjé en Olivier 265 ev.

Sien ook *Swart v Swart* [108] en *Naidoo v Naidoo* [109].

[108]   SWART V SWART

1980 4 SA 364 (O)

Irretrievable breakdown of a marriage

On 25 April 1979 the plaintiff left the spouses' joint household after the defendant had allegedly assaulted her the previous evening. The parties had only been married for a short time. The plaintiff and the defendant each claimed a divorce order. They agreed that the marriage had broken down irretrievably. The dispute between them was really concerned with whether the defendant had to pay any maintenance to the plaintiff. As maintenance the plaintiff claimed an amount for day to day expenses as well as payment of her medical expenses. The court granted a divorce order to the plaintiff and found that she was entitled only to payment of her medical expenses.

Onherstelbare verbrokkeling van 'n huwelik

Die eiseres het op 25 April 1979 die gades se gemeenskaplike huishouding verlaat nadat die verweerder haar na bewering die vorige aand aangerand het. Die gades was net vir 'n kort rukkie getroud. Die eiseres en die verweerder het albei om 'n egskeidingsbevel aansoek gedoen. Hulle was dit eens dat hulle huwelik onherstelbaar verbrokkel het. Die geskil tussen hulle het eintlik daaroor gegaan of die verweerder enige onderhoud aan die eiseres moes betaal. Die eiseres het 'n bedrag onderhoud vir haar daaglikse uitgawes geëis asook dat die verweerder haar mediese onkoste moes betaal. Die hof het die egskeidingsbevel aan die eiseres toegestaan en bevind dat sy slegs op betaling van haar mediese onkoste geregtig was.

FLEMMING R: [367] [Die ... Regter het die getuienis onder die volgende hoofde behandel: die bestaande of verwagte vermoëns van die partye; die partye se onderskeie verdienvermoëns; hulle finansiële behoeftes en verpligtinge; die ouderdom van die partye; die duur van die huwelik; die lewenspeil van die partye; en die gedrag van die partye [en] het toe soos volg voortgegaan:]

Artikel 7(2)

Die partye het aansienlik verskil omtrent die klem wat verskillende oorwegings moet ontvang en in verband daarmee omtrent die korrekte benadering tot art 7(2) ...

In heelwat gevalle kan die aandrang dat bepaalde gedrag in ag geneem word – bv dat eiseres se vertrek op 25 April 1979 die *consortium* beëindig het en dus in ag geneem moet word – nie gehandhaaf word nie omdat dit onvanpas is volgens die Wet. Hierdie gevolgtrekking moes gemotiveer word.

(*a*) Die maatstaf omtrent "gedrag":

Die regsband tussen eggenote wat as 'n "huwelik" bekend staan kan ontbind of beëindig word maar dit kan nie verbrokkel nie. Klaarblyklik het art 3 en gevolglik ook art 7 van die Wet . . . die onderlinge *verhouding* tussen die eggenote in gedagte, nl daardie wederkerige reaksie en gesamentlike onderneming wat gevind word wanneer op verskille, probleme en mekaar se optrede gereageer word in 'n gesindheid wat positief is omtrent oorlewing van die huweliksverhouding. Hinderlike dinge sal bv in so 'n gesindheid bespreek, aanvaar, gewysig of vergewe word. Sulke optrede spruit normaalweg uit liefde [368] wat gewoonlik die grondslag is van veral wedersydse agting, lojaliteit en vertroue. So 'n huwelik is na buite kenbaar in gedraginge soos oa die behoefte aan mekaar se samewoning, onselfsug- tigheid, ens. 'n Huwelik, en daarom ook die "huwelik" wat die Wet in gedagte het, kan egter sonder een of meer van die eienskappe bestaan wat as kenmerkend beskryf sou kon word. Vir 'n bepaalde indiwidu kan 'n gegronde en selfs gelukkige huweliksverhouding bestaan waarvoor hand en tand geveg sal word, ondanks gedraginge wat vir ander mense onuithoudbaar sou wees. Die eggenote kan 'n "huwelik" handhaaf al ontbreek die seksuele aspek daarvan (miskien meestal na 'n ongeluk of by ouer mense); al slaap hulle apart of woon hulle nie saam nie (miskien meestal met 'n rede soos dat die man in aanhouding is); of al het 'n eggenoot uit ondervinding geleer dat die ander eggenoot nie vertrou of gerespekteer kan word nie.

Die verbrokkeling van 'n huwelik is eweneens onvoorspelbaar en ondefinieerbaar . . .

Wat duidelik is, is dat gedrag wat in een huwelik verbrokkeling veroorsaak, dit by 'n ander huwelik nie doen nie. Soms is dit 'n geval dat skade aan die verhouding tog gedoen word wat daarenteen nie onmiddellik herken word nie of eers in samehang met ander gebeure 'n verbrokkelende uitwerking het. Terwyl 'n verlating of owerspel verbrokkeling kan veroorsaak, is dit in ander gevalle bloot 'n simptoom van verbrokkeling wat reeds begin het. Ek meen dus dat vroegstens gesê kan word dat verbrokkeling aanwesig is wanneer een van die eggenote nie langer 'n huweliksverhouding met die ander eggenoot wil handhaaf nie. Die vraag na die rede vir daardie besluit sal dan ontstaan. Die antwoord op daardie vraag mag die gedrag van een of beide partye betrek. Indien wel, sal oorweeg moet word of daardie gedrag (of die afwesigheid van sulke gedrag) . . . 'n effek op die uiteindelike Hofbevel het.

Die volgende implikasies omtrent hantering van die feite skyn . . . te volg:

(1) Die verbrokkeling van die huwelik en die redes daarvoor is nie objektief meetbaar nie en skep feitelike vrae. Omtrent die onherstelbaarheid van die verbrokkeling sou objektiewe waarskynlikhede in verband met die bepaalde partye en hul omstandighede tog 'n rol vervul sodat die objektiewe karigheid en oorkombaarheid van die redes waarom op die aanvra van egskeiding besluit is, 'n oortuiging mag bevorder dat die huwelik gered mag word.

(2) Vir sover onderhoud tussen die partye in gedrang kom:

   (a) moet 'n geheelbeeld deurgaans voor oë gehou word en daarvolgens sover moontlik deurgedring word na die gedrag, indien enige, wat werklik veroorsakend van die verbrokkeling was. Die totaliteitsbenadering is veral van belang omdat 'n gedraging van enige party selde losgemaak kan word van wat voorheen al plaasgevind het, die verhouding wat reeds tussen die partye ontwikkel het, en elk se ondervinding van die ander se temperament, reaksies, voorkeure, vrese, ens.

   (b) Nadat regtens relevante gedrag aldus bepaal is, bepaal 'n objektiewe maatstaf, naamlik billikheid, welke van daardie gedrag 'n invloed by die onderhoudkwessie moet hê.

(3) [369] Wanneer die erns van gedrag beoordeel word, volg dit hoofsaaklik uit (1) hierbo dat dit nie volgens die aard van die gedrag in die abstrak bepaal moet word nie maar volgens die mate waartoe dit tot die uiteindelike verbrokkeling bygedra het deur afbrekend in te werk op voortsetting van, of ontwikkeling van 'n gesonde eggenote-

verhouding. Dit gaan dus om die verwytbaarheid van veroorsaking van verbrokkeling en die gevolglike verlies van onderhoud binne die huweliksverband. Die toedeling daarvan sal slegs toevallig kan saamval met die graad van morele afkeurenswaardigheid van 'n bepaalde insident of bepaalde insidente van gedrag.

Daar is verdere redes vir so 'n beoordeling van die belang van gedrag. Art 7(2) noem gedrag in 'n verband met die eindresultaat, nl verbrokkeling van die huwelik en nie "met betrekking tot insidente wat in die loop van die huwelik voorgekom het" nie. Die Wetgewer sou boonop sekere realiteite besef het. Eerstens, kan gedrag wat min inherente afkeurenswaardigheid het, 'n drastiese aftakelende effek hê op 'n bepaalde huweliksverhouding ...

Daarenteen kan gedrag wat moreel as ernstig afkeurenswaardig beskou moet word, soos, bv, aanranding of owerspel, volgens die feite geen effek op die huwelik hê nie. Tweedens, kan bybring van oorwegings van morele erns in die abstrak tot 'n realisties-foutiewe resultaat lei. 'n Geregshof sou kwalik kon sê dat aanranding op dieselfde vlak staan as onwilligheid om enige gesprek te voer. Tog kan laasgenoemde die huwelik totaal verongeluk of juis oa die aanranding uitgelok het. Derdens, bring beoordeling van die afkeurenswaardigheid van 'n bepaalde optrede of aantal optredes amper onaf-wendbaar die aanleidende gebeure en ander verduidelikings ter sprake wat die on-dersoek eerder sou uitbrei as inkort, selfs tot op die terrein van die gedragsielkunde. Terwyl billikheid nie net een party en die verstaanbaarheid van sy gedrag betrek nie maar ook die inslag van die Hof se besluit op die teenparty, is die waarskynliker benadering die eenvoudiger vraag ... na hoe billik dit is dat die gedrag van die betrokke party (en die ander party) 'n invloed op die onderhoudsbevel moet hê. Dit is vir daardie doel onnodig om die skakerings van veroordeelbaarheid van elke insident te onderneem en voldoende om die gedrag as geheel aan te slaan ...

Die submissie is voor die Hof geplaas dat gedrag alleen as faktor kan funksioneer indien dit "ernstig" is ...

[370] Die bewoording van art 7(2) dui nie aan dat slegs ernstige gedrag van belang is nie. Deur die bewoording word trouens 'n kontras geskep met die bewoording van art 9. Art 9 skep 'n onderskeid tussen *aanleidende* "omstandighede" en "wangedrag" maar wat laas-genoemde betref is net "wesenlike" wangedrag relevant. Volledigheidshalwe moet genoem word dat art 10 verwys na "gedrag vir sover dit ter sake is" terwyl "gedrag", miskien omdat 'n huwelik sonder vasstelbare rede of om ander redes as die partye se beheerbare gedrag kan verbrokkel, nie 'n onontbeerlike faktor vir 'n egskeidingsbevel is nie.

Wyer oorwegings ... [is eerstens] die onwenslikheid daarvan dat die partye die onaan-genaamheid en koste van 'n ondersoek na "skuld" moet ondergaan slegs om 'n geskil omtrent onderhoud te besleg ... Hierdie wenslikheidsoorweging wat in die billikhede teenoorwegings vind, kan nie wysigende uitleg regverdig nie. Tweedens is die gevoel skynbaar dat dit verkeerd sou wees om 'n ondersoek na skuld by die agterdeur in te laat nadat die Wet "skuld uitgeskakel het". Alhoewel dit korrek voorkom dat nie-verwytbare gedrag nie as 'n faktor sal funksioneer nie, en al word veronderstel dat 'n ondersoek van "gedrag" gelykgestel moet word aan 'n opweging van "skuld", bewys die Wet nie die premise dat gedrag voortaan irrelevant is nie. Skuld of gedrag is bloot nie meer 'n voorvereiste of 'n beletsel vir die maak van 'n egskeidingsbevel of 'n onderhoudsbevel nie. In aansluiting by die opvatting dat meestal beide eggenote skuld het aan die ver-brokkeling van 'n huwelik, is 'n meer vloeibare en gevolglik 'n billiker situasie geskep. Die bestaan of omvang van 'n onderhoudsbevel kan nou nouer saamloop met elk van die partye se skuld maar omdat ander faktore ook van belang is, sal dit nie noodwendig of selfs gewoonlik saamval nie ...

[372] Hierdie Hof moet dus ... besluit wat in al die omstandighede billik is waarby die gedrag van die partye in aanmerking geneem kan word sonder om ten koste van billikheid 'n beperking in te lees ...

[FLEMMING R het toe die getuienis ontleed en bevind dat geeneen van die partye se gedrag "obvious and gross" was nie. Die gades se gedrag kan egter, volgens die regter, juridies relevant wees sonder om noodwendig "obvious and gross" te wees. FLEMMING R vervolg:]

[375] [Ek meen] dat dit in belang van duidelikheid in hierdie geval toelaatbaar is om rekenkundige uitdrukking te gee aan die Hof se bevindinge met betrekking tot gedrag omdat dit die mees grafiese wyse is waarop dit aangedui kan word. Op daardie grondslag kan gesê word dat verweerder in die omgewing van [376] 60 persent van die verwytbare gedrag aan die dag gelê het, hoewel dit so hoog as twee-derdes mag wees. Indien gelet moet word op die balans van morele skuld by afsonderlike insidente sou verweerder se later gedrag meebring dat soveel as 80 persent van die blaam na sy kant moet gaan. Ek meen dat selfs dan, verweerder se gedrag nie "obvious and gross" sou wees ... nie ...

Uit hoofde van die taak wat aan hierdie Hof opgedra is, volg dit nie sonder meer dat genoemde beskouings oor die partye se gedrag wel 'n invloed sal hê op die bevel wat gemaak word nie. Die billikhede sal bepaal of dit wel die geval is.

By die vraag omtrent welke onderhoudsbevel, indien enige, billik is, verkies ek om die saak te benader aan die hand van twee navrae, nl of in al die omstandighede dit reg en billik is dat eiseres vir onderhoud na verweerder kan kyk, en, tweedens, hoeveel die onderhoud nou of in die toekoms moet bedra. Hierdie benadering het die voordeel dat dit die soeklig ook werp op die belangrike teenkant van die eerste vraag, nl of dit in die omstandighede billik is dat eiseres op haar eie vermoëns aangewese is afgesien van die feit dat sy tans voldoende in haar behoeftes kan sorg. As dit onbillik sou wees dat eiseres geen reg op finansiële bystand het nie, is haar huidige selfversorgendheid in dié opsig 'n toevalligheid dat dit bloot die huidige uitval van finansiële berekenings is wat op 'n negatiewe antwoord dui. Die finansiële posisie kan wesenlik verander. Ondanks die kritiek op die maak van "nominale" onderhoudsbevele (vgl, bv, 1980 *THRHR* 56) sou ek hier bereid wees om 'n "nominale" onderhoudsbevel te maak, nie ten einde 'n leemte in die Wet aan te vul of 'n reg op wysiging te verleen wat die Wet nie beoog nie, maar om te bevestig dat dit reg en billik is dat eiseres nie op haarself aangewese is nie maar terselfdertyd te toon dat die uitval van die samelopende oorwegings wat op die oomblik heers, is dat die omvang van haar aanspraak op die huidige en in die onmiddellike toekoms nul is. Eiseres, soos ander persone, kan oorval word deur siekte, verminking of totale verlies van bates weens brand of die maak van 'n swak belegging.

Ek meen gevolglik dat die Hof 'n wye diskresie het ... Tweedens maak die noodsaak aan billikheid dit onmoontlik om af te lei dat enige van die toelaatbare oorwegings altyd oorheersende gewig moet dra ...

[378] Op die vraag of dit billik is dat eiseres ten volle op haarself aangewese is selfs ondanks buitengewone finansiële krisis, staan as gewigtige negatiewe faktor die oorweging dat die verbrokkeling van die huwelik tot so 'n groot mate deur verweerder se optrede veroorsaak is. Ten aansien van die gewone dag tot dag onderhoud is daar egter verskeie oorwegings wat genoem moet word. Op die voorgrond staan dat hier 'n huwelik van korte duur was; dat dit deurleef is deur partye wat geeneen hul jeuglewe of toekoms-vooruitsigte vir mekaar opgeoffer het nie; dat eiseres self substansiële veroorsakende gedrag getoon het ongeag of verweerder se latere en ernstiger gedrag daaruit gegroei het – moontlik net gedeeltelik – of nie. In verband met laasgenoemde en alhoewel dit onnodig is om daarop te steun en derhalwe om daaromtrent te beslis, sou dit miskien korrek wees om te sê dat die partye ewe onverantwoordelik was om so kort na ontmoeting tot

huweliksluiting oor te gaan. Van aanmerklike belang is dat eiseres met 'n na-belaste inkomste van feitlik R9 900 as sy nie 'n diensbetrekking beklee nie, in staat is om goed genoeg te leef. Die langertermyn werking van inflasie sal deels gekompenseer word deur mindere behoeftes aan, bv, sportdeelname, klerasie, ens, die neem van 'n kleiner woonstel en mindere vervoerbehoeftes maar terwyl sy werk kan sy selfs spaar vir aanvulling van lewensbehoeftes in die toekoms.

Op 'n geheelbeeld meen ek dat, alhoewel verweerder onderhoud maklik genoeg sou kon betaal, hy nie daardie aanvullende lewensmiddele moet verskaf wat die element van gerief of selfs luukse tot eiseres se leefwyse toevoeg nie en . . . meen ek dat verweerder nie 'n betaling ten aansien van die dag tot dag onderhoud moet maak nie.

Die mediese koste is een item waarby juis onvoorspelbaarheid voorspelbaar is. In die omstandighede, of verweerder se finansies ookal hanteer word as 'n positiewe faktor of bloot as iets wat nie negatief teen so 'n bevel weeg nie, meen ek dat verweerder die snykant van daardie risiko moet stomp maak. Die bevel daaromtrent is nie bedoel as 'n "nominale" onderhoudsbevel of as 'n kapstok vir 'n wysigingsaansoek nie maar bloot omdat dit billik geag word dat die besondere risiko afgeweer word . . .

[380] Ten gunste van eiseres word:

1. 'n Egskeidingsbevel toegestaan op grond van onherstelbare verbrokkeling van die huwelik.

2. Verweerder gelas om ten aansien van eiseres se mediese kostes, die fooie en uitgawes van enige geregistreerde praktisyn asook die koste van enige item of diens op aanwysing van so 'n praktisyn aangeskaf (met insluiting deurgaans van fisioterapie, bloedoortappings, prosteses, radiologiese ondersoeke en patalogiese ondersoeke) vir sover dit op eiseres se eie versorging betrekking het aan eiseres te vergoed tot op 50 persent daarvan met dien verstande dat die koste daaraan wat opgeloop word terwyl eiseres 'n pasiënt in 'n hospitaal is asook die volle verblyfkostes verskuldig aan sodanige inrigting tot op 100 persent daarvan, aan eiseres vergoed word . . .

Note

In this case the subjective and objective approaches to establish whether a marriage had irretrievably broken down, were applied in a slightly different way from that in which they were applied in *Schwartz v Schwartz* [107] and subsequently in *Naidoo v Naidoo* [109].

In the case under discussion the subjective element was considered in order to establish whether the spouses' marriage had broken down: "Die verbrokkeling van die huwelik en die redes daarvoor is nie objektief meetbaar nie" (368), and the objective approach was used only to determine whether such breakdown was irretrievable: "Omtrent die onherstelbaarheid van die verbrokkeling sou objektiewe waarskynlikhede in verband met die bepaalde partye in hulle omstandighede tog 'n rol vervul sodat die objektiewe karigheid en oorkombaarheid van die redes waarom op die aanvra van egskeiding besluit is, 'n oortuiging mag bevorder dat die huwelik gered mag word" (368). In the *Schwartz* case, on the other hand,

Aantekening

In hierdie saak is die subjektiewe en objektiewe benaderings om vas te stel of 'n huwelik onherstelbaar verbrokkel het op 'n ietwat ander manier toegepas as wat in *Schwartz v Schwartz* [107] en later in *Naidoo v Naidoo* [109] gedoen is.

In die onderhawige saak is die subjektiewe element in ag geneem ten einde te bepaal of die gades se huwelik verbrokkel het: "Die verbrokkeling van die huwelik en die redes daarvoor is nie objektief meetbaar nie" (368), en die objektiewe element is in ag geneem slegs om te bepaal of sodanige verbrokkeling onherstelbaar was: "Omtrent die onherstelbaarheid van die verbrokkeling sou objektiewe waarskynlikhede in verband met die bepaalde partye in hulle omstandighede tog 'n rol vervul sodat die objektiewe karigheid en oorkombaarheid van die redes waarom op die aanvra van egskeiding besluit is, 'n oortuiging mag bevorder dat die huwelik gered mag word" (368). In die *Schwartz*-saak daarenteen is die subjektiewe en objektiewe elemente skyn-

the subjective and objective approaches were apparently considered together: "In determining whether a marriage has reached such a state of disintegration that there is no reasonable prospect of the restoration of a normal marriage relationship between the parties it is important to have regard to what has happened in the past, ie the history of the relationship up to the date of the trial, and also to the present attitude of the parties to the marriage relationship" (475). In *Naidoo v Naidoo* [109] the court expressly held that the test to be applied "is both subjective and objective" (367).

Barnard and Van Aswegen (1981 *THRHR* 201) correctly argue that the balance between the subjective and objective elements of the test should always be retained. It is submitted that the correct approach would be the one which was applied in *Schwartz v Schwartz* [107] and *Naidoo v Naidoo* [109], in other words to use both the objective and subjective approaches, not only to establish whether the marriage relationship had broken down but also to determine whether such breakdown is irretrievable.

In respect of the court's role in determining whether a marriage has broken down irretrievably, mention must also be made of *Vermeulen v Vermeulen; Buffel v Buffel* 1989 2 SA 771 (NC). In this case BUYS J correctly explained that the breakdown of a marriage is a process which takes place over a period of time. It usually does not occur overnight. In respect of the irretrievability of the breakdown BUYS J incorrectly stated that the breakdown becomes irretrievable only when the court declares it to be irretrievable. He said (776): "Die verbrokkelingsproses duur voort totdat 'n Hof bevind dat daardie verbrokkeling onherstelbaar is ... Die verbrokkeling is *eers onherstelbaar as 'n Hof* na aanhoor van die getuienis *oortuig is* 'dat die huweliksverhouding ... so 'n toestand van verbrokkeling bereik het dat daar geen redelike vooruitsig op die herstel van 'n normale huweliksverhouding' bestaan nie" (our emphasis). It is submitted that this is incorrect. The court does not cause the breakdown to become irretrievable by deciding that the marriage has broken down irretrievably; the court merely confirms an existing position, namely that the marriage has broken down irretrievably.

baar saam oorweeg: "In determining whether a marriage has reached such a state of disintegration that there is no reasonable prospect of the restoration of a normal marriage relationship between the parties it is important to have regard to what has happened in the past, ie the history of the relationship up to the date of the trial, and also to the present attitude of the parties to the marriage relationship" (475). In *Naidoo v Naidoo* [109] het die hof uitdruklik beslis dat die toets wat toegepas moet word "both subjective and objective" is (367).

Barnard en Van Aswegen (1981 *THRHR* 201) voer tereg aan dat 'n balans altyd gehandhaaf moet word tussen die subjektiewe en objektiewe elemente van die toets. Ons wil aan die hand doen dat die benadering wat in *Schwartz v Schwartz* [107] en *Naidoo v Naidoo* [109] toegepas is korrek is, naamlik dat sowel die objektiewe as die subjektiewe benadering gebruik moet word, nie alleen om te bepaal of die huweliksverhouding verbrokkel het nie, maar ook om vas te stel of sodanige verbrokkeling onherstelbaar is.

Die saak van *Vermeulen v Vermeulen; Buffel v Buffel* 1989 2 SA 771 (NK) moet ook genoem word in verband met die rol wat die hof speel om te bepaal of 'n huwelik onherstelbaar verbrokkel het. In hierdie saak het BUYS R heeltemal korrek verduidelik dat die verbrokkeling van 'n huwelik 'n proses is wat oor 'n tydperk plaasvind. Dit gebeur gewoonlik nie oornag nie. In verband met die onherstelbaarheid al dan nie van die verbrokkeling het BUYS R verkeerdelik gesê dat die verbrokkeling eers onherstelbaar word wanneer die hof beslis dat dit onherstelbaar is. Hy het gesê (776): "Die verbrokkelingsproses duur voort totdat 'n Hof bevind dat daardie verbrokkeling onherstelbaar is ... Die verbrokkeling is *eers onherstelbaar as 'n Hof* na aanhoor van die getuienis *oortuig is* 'dat die huweliksverhouding ... so 'n toestand van verbrokkeling bereik het dat daar geen redelike vooruitsig op die herstel van 'n normale huweliksverhouding' bestaan nie" (ons beklemtoning). Dit word aan die hand gedoen dat die stelling verkeerd is. Die hof veroorsaak nie die onherstelbare verbrokkeling van die huwelik deur te beslis dat dit onherstelbaar verbrokkel het nie; die hof bevestig bloot 'n bestaande posisie, naamlik dat die huwelik onherstelbaar verbrokkel het.

Another case in which the court took the wrong view of irretrievable breakdown is *Coetzee v Coetzee* 1991 4 SA 702 (C). Here the parties had been unhappily married right from the start. At the time the wife applied for a divorce, the parties were still living together and were still having sexual intercourse, but the wife consented to sexual intercourse merely because she feared her husband, who threatened her with physical violence. She testified that she no longer loved her husband and that there was no prospect whatsoever of saving their marriage. Her husband was a rude, lazy person who was often without a job, sometimes because he stopped working for no good reason. Despite the dismal situation in which the wife found herself VAN DEN HEEVER J refused to grant her a divorce. The judge held that, for the court to be able to hold that a marriage has broken down there must be some proof that the marital relationship has deteriorated. She further held that if the marriage had been dismal from the start and had not deteriorated a divorce cannot be granted. Surely this is incorrect. If, at the time when the divorce order is sought the parties are, or even only one of them is convinced that there is no prospect of a normal marital relationship, then a divorce ought to be granted.

The second important aspect of *Swart v Swart* concerns the court's view on the role which conduct plays with regard to awarding maintenance. The court attaches much weight to conduct as a factor to be considered when the court exercises its discretion to award maintenance at divorce. According to the court's approach the conduct need not be obvious and gross before it can be considered; the court can pay attention to any conduct which it deems to be judicially relevant. Such judicially relevant conduct will have an influence on the eventual order which the court makes only if this would be equitable. Barnard and Van Aswegen (1981 *THRHR* 202) are of the opinion that this will have the same effect as requiring that the conduct be obvious and gross since equity was the underlying principle of the obvious-and-gross requirement.

See also Sinclair 1981 *SALJ* 90–94.

With regard to maintenance at divorce see also the chapter below on maintenance.

As far as FLEMMING J's remarks on nominal

maintenance are concerned (376), see *Nel v Nel* [126] and *Portinho v Portinho* [127].

Wat FLEMMING R se opmerkings oor nominale onderhoud betref, sien *Nel v Nel* [126] en *Portinho v Portinho* [127].

[109]   NAIDOO V NAIDOO

1985 1 SA 366 (T)

Irretrievable breakdown of a marriage

The plaintiff applied for an order of divorce. She was not sure what her husband's (defendant's) attitude to continuing with the marriage was but she did not wish to continue with it. Her husband had stopped working, he smoked dagga, refused to talk to the spouses' children and has physically threatened the plaintiff. The spouses were still cohabiting and they still had sexual intercourse. The plaintiff only consented to sexual intercourse because the defendant accused her of having an adulterous affair when she refused to have sexual intercourse with him and on occasion the defendant had threatened to hit her if she did not consent. The court granted the divorce order.

Onherstelbare verbrokkeling van 'n huwelik

Die eiseres het om 'n egskeidingsbevel aansoek gedoen. Sy was nie seker wat haar man (verweerder) se houding oor voortsetting van die huwelik was nie, maar sy was nie bereid om daarmee voort te gaan nie. Haar man het opgehou werk, dagga gerook, geweier om met hulle kinders te praat en het gedreig om die eiseres fisies aan te rand. Die partye het nog saamgewoon en het steeds geslagsgemeenskap gehad. Die eiseres het bloot tot geslagsgemeenskap toegestem omdat die verweerder haar van owerspel beskuldig het as sy geweier het om geslagsgemeenskap met hom te hê en by geleentheid het hy gedreig om haar te slaan indien sy nie toestem nie. Die hof het die egskeidingsbevel toegestaan.

MARGO J: [366] What the plaintiff has to establish is that the marriage has broken down irretrievably and not merely that she is unhappily married. In terms of s 4(1) of the Divorce Act, the Court must be satisfied that the marriage relationship between the parties has reached such a state of [367] disintegration that there is no reasonable prospect of the restoration of a normal marriage relationship between them. In terms of s 4(2), the Court may be so satisfied by proof of any facts or circumstances which may be indicative of the irretrievable breakdown of the marriage.

The test of irretrievable marriage breakdown is considered by some to be subjective and by others to be objective. See *Swart v Swart* 1980 (4) SA 364 (O) at 368-369 [108]; *Singh v Singh* 1983 (1) SA 781 (C) at 785-786 [113] and Hahlo and Sinclair on *The Reform of the SA Law of Divorce* at 33.

In my view, the test is both subjective and objective. It is subjective in that different individuals may react differently to a given situation. To one person certain circumstances may be wholly destructive of the conjugal relationship, while to a less sensitive person similar circumstances may evoke no such response. The test is also subjective in that, although the marriage may have broken down irretrievably for the plaintiff, the defendant may wish at all costs to preserve it. The test is objective in that, in terms of s 4(1) of the Act, the Court must be satisfied that irretrievable marriage breakdown has in fact occurred. The plaintiff's *ipse dixit* that the marriage has broken down irretrievably must therefore have some factual bases in events or conduct which show that, for him or her at least, the marriage relationship has reached such a state of disintegration that there is no reasonable prospect of the restoration of a normal marriage relationship.

Where, as in this case, the evidence is that the spouses have continued to cohabit, to share the same bed, and to enjoy frequent and regular sexual intercourse, that would tend to negative the assertion that irretrievable marriage breakdown has occurred. However, such circumstances are not necessarily conclusive and must be considered not *in vacuo*, but together with the rest of the evidence as a whole.

The plaintiff in this case has voluntarily submitted to sexual intercourse, save on the one occasion when, she says, the defendant threatened her. Nevertheless, in his approach to the sexual relationship the defendant has not shown affection and consideration, but has humiliated the plaintiff. Moreover, other elements of a normal marriage have crumbled. The defendant does not support his family. He has rejected his children, and they have been taken to live with the plaintiff's mother. The defendant smokes dagga and he refuses to change his ways. In these circumstances I think that the plaintiff has established her case . . .

The marriage is dissolved . . .

Note

See the notes on *Schwartz v Schwartz* [107] and *Swart v Swart* [108].

Aantekening

Sien die aantekeninge by *Schwartz v Schwartz* [107] en *Swart v Swart* [108].

Mental illness or continuous unconsciousness – section 5

Geestesongesteldheid of voortdurende bewusteloosheid – artikel 5

[110] SMIT V SMIT

1982 4 SA 34 (O)

The connection between sections 4 and 5 of the Divorce Act 70 of 1979

The appellant applied for a divorce order in terms of section 4 of the Divorce Act 70 of 1979. At the time of the application his wife (respondent) had been physically disabled for six and a half years. She had been in an institution for infirm persons for about five and a half years. In his evidence the appellant at no time alleged that he no longer loved his wife. He relied on the fact that, as a consequence of her condition, he could lay claim to virtually no *consortium* privileges and, according to him, no real marital relationship existed between them any more and there was no prospect of the restoration of a normal marital relationship. In the court *a quo*

Die verband tussen artikels 4 en 5 van die Wet op Egskeiding 70 van 1979

Die appellant het aansoek gedoen om 'n egskeidingsbevel ingevolge artikel 4 van die Wet op Egskeiding 70 van 1979. Ten tyde van die aansoek was sy vrou (respondent) reeds ses en 'n half jaar fisies erg verswak. Sy was vir omtrent vyf en 'n half jaar reeds in 'n inrigting vir verswakte persone. Die appellant het nêrens in sy getuienis beweer dat hy nie meer vir sy vrou lief was nie. Hy het gesteun op die feit dat daar, as gevolg van sy vrou se toestand, vir hom feitlik geen voordele uit die *consortium* voortgevloei het nie en dat daar, volgens hom, geen ware huweliksverhouding meer tussen hom en sy vrou bestaan het nie. Verder het daar ook

the application was rejected. The appellant appealed to the full bench against this decision. His appeal was allowed.

geen moontlikheid bestaan dat 'n normale huweliksverhouding weer herstel sou kon word nie. Die hof *a quo* het die aansoek van die hand gewys. Die appellant het na die volbank geappelleer en sy appèl het geslaag.

KOTZÉ WN R: [37] BRINK R se uitspraak [in die hof *a quo* (*Smit v Smit* 1982 1 SA 606 (O))] opper eerstens bedenkinge oor die vraag of daar nie 'n kurator-*ad-litem* vir respondente aangestel moes gewees het nie. Tweedens spreek hy – klaarblyklik met die onderskeiding tussen "onmoontlikwording" en "onmoontlikmaking" van 'n huwelik wat deur Olivier, Barnard en Cronjé *Die Suid-Afrikaanse Persone en Familiereg* 2de uitg te 279 en 283 voorgestaan word as agtergrond – die mening uit dat die Wetgewer, indien dit sy bedoeling was om fisiese ongesteldheid 'n egskeidingsgrond te maak, dit so uitdruklik in art 5 van die Wet op Egskeiding 70 van 1979 (hierna die Wet genoem) sou bepaal het. Derdens wens hy te verskil van die opmerkings gemaak deur COETZEE R in *Dickinson v Dickinson* 1981 (3) SA 856 (W) te 860C–E en kom hy tot die slotsom dat die Wetgewer ook nie bedoel het om onder art 4 van die Wet verbrokkeling van die huwelik weens fisiese ongesteldheid, as egskeidingsgrond in te sluit nie. Laastens gee [38] hy die volgende, klaarblyklik as alternatief bedoelde rede, vir sy bevel aan:

> "Ek mag net meld dat, indien ek verkeerd is en die Wetgewer bedoel het dat 'n verbrokkeling ten gevolge van 'n fisiese ongesteldheid, soos die onderhawige, wel 'n grond vir 'n egskeiding kan wees, ek nie tevrede is dat daar inderdaad so 'n verbrokkeling bewys is nie. Die eiser sê nêrens dat hy verweerderes nie meer lief het of nie meer enige toegeneentheid teenoor haar het nie. Sy getuienis kom net daarop neer dat, vanweë die verweerderes se toestand, daar nou al ses en 'n half jaar lank geen huwelik meer bestaan nie en dat hy en sy dogters die sorg van 'n lewensmaat en 'n moeder, waarop hulle normaalweg sou kon aanspraak maak, moet ontbeer."

Ek voel myself verplig om, met respek, te verskil van BRINK R se slotsom sowel as die grootste gedeelte van die argumente wat deur hom geopper is ...

Daar bestaan geen regverdiging vir die standpunt wat deur *Olivier, Barnard en Cronjé* (*supra*) voorgestaan word, te wete dat dit die bedoeling van die Wetgewer was om in art 4 van die Wet met "onmoontlikmaking" en in art 5 van die Wet met "onmoontlikwording" van 'n huwelik te handel nie.

Artikel 3 van die Wet bepaal dat 'n huwelik deur 'n Hof ontbind kan word (slegs) op grond van:

> "(*a*) die onherstelbare verbrokkeling van die huwelik soos in art 4 beoog;
>
> (*b*) die geestesongesteldheid of die voortdurende bewusteloosheid, soos in art 5 beoog, van 'n party by die huwelik."

Hieruit blyk dit dat dit die duidelik uitgesproke bedoeling van die Wetgewer was dat 'n huwelik ontbind kan word, òf op grond van die geestesongesteldheid, of voortdurende bewusteloosheid weens fisiese ongesteldheid van 'n verweerder soos voorsien in art 5 ... òf op grond van onherstelbare verbrokkeling van die huwelik, weens welke ander rede ookal, soos voorsien in art 4. Met ander woorde, die bedoeling wat art 5 onderlê was nie om in hierdie artikel alle gevalle van sogenaamde "onmoontlikwording" te betrek nie, maar slegs om daardie twee gevalle wat daarin genoem word, te betrek. Dit sal opgelet word dat beide hierdie gevalle handel met mense wat nie 'n sinvolle mening of houding kan uitspreek of handhaaf nie en dat daar juis, na my mening, weens hierdie rede vir hierdie gevalle besondere bepalings nodig was ...

Die feit dat art 5(2) praat van 'n verweerder wat "weens fisiese ongesteldheid in 'n toestand van voortdurende bewusteloosheid verkeer" kan ook geensins tot die slotsom lei dat alle gevalle waar fisiese ongesteldheid teenwoordig is nou by implikasie onder art 5 betrek word [39] nie. Die sleutelwoorde in art 5(2) is "voortdurende bewusteloosheid", wat 'n gevolg soortgelyk aan geestesongesteldheid waarmee art 5(1) handel bewerkstellig, soos verder ook duidelik uit die bewoording van arts 3(b) en 9(2) blyk.

'n Geval soos die onderhawige waar fisiese ongesteldheid, maar nie voortdurende bewusteloosheid nie, teenwoordig is, ressorteer dus nie, en behoort ook nie, onder art 5 van die Wet te ressorteer nie. Vir hierdie rede is dit dan nie nodig om standpunt in te neem oor die vraag wat in *Dickinson v Dickinson (supra)* en *Krige v Smit NO* 1981 (4) SA 409 (K) ter sprake was nie. Dit kan ingesien word dat die argument geopper kan word dat dit 'n eiser nie mag vrystaan om die beskermingsmaatreëls wat deur bogemelde arts 5(1), 5(2), 5(3), 5(4) en 9(2) vir geestesongesteldes en bewusteloses geskep word deur sy keuse van prosedure (verwysende na art 4 en 5 onderskeidelik) te omseil waar hy juis, in woorde van die Wet, *op grond van* die geestesongesteldheid en bewusteloosheid op 'n egskeidings-bevel aanspraak maak nie (vergelyk Midgley "The Divorce Act: Reconsideration Necessary" 1982 *SALJ* te 22 en verder). Maar so 'n argument sal glad nie in 'n geval soos die onderhawige van toepassing wees nie. Hier word juis nie *op grond van* geestesongesteldheid of bewusteloosheid vir 'n egskeidingsbevel gevra nie en daar bestaan geen toestand wat sodanige beskermingsmaatreëls nodig maak nie.

Dit volg uit die voorgaande dat ek, met groot respek, van BRINK R se gevolgtrekking, te wete dat daar waarde geheg moet word aan die feit dat 'n geval soos die onderhawige nie spesifiek deur die Wetgewer onder art 5, of waar ookal, genoem word nie, moet verskil . . .

Die volgende vraag is of daar nie aan appellant, uit hoofde van die bepalings van art 4 van die Wet, 'n egskeiding toegestaan behoort te gewees het nie en by beantwoording van hierdie vraag is dit nodig dat daar na die bepalings van art 4(1) en 4(3) gekyk moet word . . .

[KOTZÉ WN R het die betrokke bepalings aangehaal en vervolg:]

Om te bepaal wanneer 'n huwelik so 'n toestand van verbrokkeling bereik het dat daar geen redelike vooruitsig op die herstel van 'n normale [40] huweliksverhouding bestaan nie . . . bly maar steeds net 'n feitelike vraag wat deur die Regter op die getuienis voor hom beslis moet word.

Dit spreek vanself dat die redes wat die onherstelbare verbrokkeling ten grondslag lê legio kan wees en dat die feite en omstandighede wat in arts 4(2)(a) tot (c) genoem word blote voorbeelde van feitekomplekse wat mag ontstaan daarstel en nie uitputtend is nie. Die argumente wat voor hierdie Hof aangevoer is, het verwys na subjektiewe en objektiewe elemente en maatstawwe wat in hierdie verband genoem word (vgl bv Barnard en Van Aswegen: Vonnisse 1981 *THRHR* te 200 en verder; Van Wyk: Vonnisse 1980 *THRHR* te 432) maar kategorisering en etikettering kan, na my mening, nie veel hulp verleen wanneer dit in praktyk, by beslissing van die feitelike vraag hierbo gestel, kom nie. Wat duidelik is, is dat geen egskeiding verleen sal word as een van die partye nie daarvoor vra nie en dit is dus vanselfsprekend dat dit onontbeerlik vir 'n egskeiding is dat minstens een van die huwelikspartye van voorneme moet wees "om nie die *status quo* langer te aanvaar nie" soos deur VAN DEN HEEVER R in *Krige v Smit NO (supra* te 414D) gestel word. Daar sal dus altyd by minstens een (en meestal altwee) van die partye 'n subjektiewe bedoeling om te skei teenwoordig wees. So 'n subjektiewe bedoeling opsigself sal nie tot verkryging van die egskeidingsbevel kan lei nie want voorvereiste is dat die Hof, op waarskynlikhede, oortuig moet wees dat die huwelik onherstelbaar verbrokkel is. Die faktore wat sodanige oortuiging kan bewerkstellig is nie definieerbaar nie en moet vanselfsprekenderwys uiteenlopend van aard wees. Dit kan wees dat een van die partye, sonder oënskynlike regverdiging, so vasbeslote is om nie met die huwelik voort te gaan nie dat dit, met of sonder in agneming van tydsverloop, die Hof oortuig dat daar geen redelike vooruitsig op 'n normale huweliksverhouding bestaan nie (vgl *Kruger v Kruger* 1980 (3) SA 283 (O), 'n beslissing van BRINK R). Andersinds kan dit wees dat een of beide partye se gedrag of ander uitings van hulle persoonlikhede, met of sonder inwerking van omringende omstandighede of gedrag van andere, die nodige bewys daarstel. Of dit kan wees dat blote omstandighede buite beheer, skuld of toedoen van die partye hierdie gevolg kan bewerkstellig . . .

In die onderhawige geval is dit bewys dat daar vir die afgelope paar jaar geen *consortium* tussen die partye bestaan het nie en dat dit op waarskynlikhede nooit, ooit weer sal bestaan nie . . . [41] Appellant het . . . gesê dat die huwelik, wat hom betref, tot niet is en dat daar glad geen moontlikheid bestaan om 'n normale huwelikslewe voort te sit nie. Hierdie uitgesproke woord toon aan dat daar in appellant se gemoed geen begeerte tot voortsetting van die huwelik is nie terwyl die getuienis omtrent respondente se fisiese toestand bewys dat daar geen redelike vooruitsig op die herstel van 'n normale huweliksverhouding bestaan nie en of appellant vir respondente nou lief het of nie, of sê dat hy haar liefhet of nie, kan nie daaraan verander dat onherstelbare verbrokkeling as egskeidingsgrond, soos vereis deur art 4, bewys is nie.

Laastens kom ek nou by die vraag of hierdie Hof, synde 'n Hof van appèl, nie van inmenging weerhou is deur die feit dat die Wet 'n diskresie aan die Verhoorregter verleen het nie. Op die vraag of 'n Regter 'n diskresie het om 'n egskeiding toe te staan of te weier bestaan daar by teoretici nie eensgesindheid nie en, sover ek weet, het geen beslissing nog hierop standpunt ingeneem nie . . .

Dit is my beskeie mening dat dit nie ontken kan word dat die Wet wel 'n diskresie aan die Hof verleen nie. Afgesien daarvan dat arts 4 en 5 van die Afrikaanse, synde die getekende, teks onderskeidelik bepaal dat 'n egskeiding op grond van onherstelbare verbrokkeling en geestesongesteldheid of voortdurende bewusteloosheid verleen *kan* word sê art 3 ook duidelik:

> " 'n Huwelik kan deur 'n Hof deur 'n egskeidingsbevel ontbind word en die enigste gronde waarop so 'n bevel verleen kan word, is . . ."

Hiermee word nie bedoel dat 'n egskeidingsbevel na willekeur toegestaan of geweier kan word nie. Enersyds is dit duidelik uit die gebruik van die woorde "enigste gronde", hierbo aangehaal, dat 'n egskeidingsbevel slegs maar op die gronde genoem in arts 4 en 5, en op geen ander gronde of oorwegings nie, toegestaan mag word. Andersyds, meen ek, behoort 'n Hof ook nie op arbitrêre wyse 'n egskeidingsbevel te weier as die gronde genoem in arts 4(1) en 5(1) en (2) bewys is nie.

Wanneer 'n bevel wel geweier kan word en die geding, bv, uitgestel kan word, is wanneer dit, volgens oordeel van die Hof, blyk dat daar, nieteenstaande die ingetrede feit van onherstelbare verbrokkeling, tog nog 'n redelike moontlikheid van versoening . . . bestaan . . . [42] Ook wanneer die egskeidingsbegerige party of partye nie behoorlike voorsiening vir die welsyn van hul minderjarige of afhanklike kinders gemaak het nie (vgl art 6(1)). Of die diskresie wyer as dit strek is vir die onderhawige doeleindes nie nodig om te beslis nie . . .

Uit die voorgaande volg dit dat die beslissing van BRINK R nie gehandhaaf kan word nie . . .

KLOPPER RP en DE WET R het saamgestem.

Note

If a person wants to divorce his unconscious or mentally ill spouse the question arises whether

Aantekening

Indien 'n persoon van sy geestesongestelde of bewustelose gade wil skei, ontstaan die vraag of die

the divorce application can be made only in terms of section 5 of the Divorce Act 70 of 1979 or whether the application can also be made in terms of section 4. In other words the question is whether the requirements of section 5 must always be complied with where one of the spouses is mentally ill or unconscious, or whether the plaintiff has a choice whether to use section 4 or section 5.

This problem has come before our courts on a number of occasions and conflicting judgments have been delivered. In *Dickinson v Dickinson* 1981 3 SA 856 (W) the plaintiff's wife had been committed as a mental patient for more than two years and the plaintiff sued for divorce in terms of section 4. The court held that section 4 could be applied. It was further found that the marriage had broken down irretrievably but the court refused to grant the divorce because the summons had not been duly served on the defendant.

In *Krige v Smit* 1981 4 SA 409 (C) the plaintiff's husband had been in a state of semi-consciousness for nearly two years. She sued him for divorce in terms of section 4 and alternatively in terms of section 5. The court issued a divorce order in terms of section 4 but tried to give section 5 its own place and function. The court found that section 5 facilitates the onus of proof which rests on the plaintiff by specifying all the elements which have to be proved. The section also facilitates the task of the court since the court need only look for the presence or absence of the factors mentioned in section 5 and need not engage in an enquiry into the facts and the possibility of the spouses' marital relationship being restored.

The wide interpretation in *Dickinson v Dickinson* and *Krige v Smit* was rejected by the court *a quo* in *Smit v Smit* 1982 1 SA 606 (O). The court held that in cases where one spouse is mentally ill or unconscious, a divorce can only be granted in terms of section 5. On appeal to the full bench this decision was reversed in *Smit v Smit*, that is the case under discussion. In *Ott v Raubenheimer* [111], where the defendant was also mentally ill, the court granted a divorce order in terms of section 4.

From the case law it therefore appears that in cases where the defendant is mentally ill or unconscious, the plaintiff can employ section 4 of the Divorce Act to obtain a divorce order. Whether he can rely on section 4 only where

egskeidingsaansoek net ingevolge artikel 5 van die Wet op Egskeiding 70 van 1979 gedoen kan word en of hy ook van artikel 4 gebruik kan maak. Met ander woorde die vraag is of daar altyd aan die vereistes van artikel 5 voldoen moet word indien een van die gades geestesongesteld of bewusteloos is en of die eiser 'n keuse het om òf artikel 4 òf artikel 5 te gebruik.

Hierdie probleem het al verskeie keer in die howe ter sprake gekom en botsende beslissings is in die verband gelewer. In *Dickinson v Dickinson* 1981 3 SA 856 (W) was die eiser se vrou reeds vir meer as twee jaar as geestesongestelde pasiënt in 'n inrigting opgeneem. Die eiser het 'n egskeidingsaksie ingevolge artikel 4 ingestel. Die hof het beslis dat artikel 4 wel aangewend kan word. Daar is verder bevind dat die huwelik onherstelbaar verbrokkel het maar die hof het geweier om die egskeiding toe te staan aangesien die dagvaarding nie behoorlik op die verweerder beteken is nie.

In *Krige v Smit* 1981 4 SA 409 (K) het die eiseres se man al vir amper twee jaar lank in 'n half bewustelose toestand verkeer. Sy het hom ingevolge artikel 4 en in die alternatief ingevolge artikel 5 om 'n egskeiding gedagvaar. Die hof het 'n egskeidingsbevel ingevolge artikel 4 uitgereik maar het probeer om 'n eie plek en funksie aan artikel 5 toe te ken. Die hof het beslis dat artikel 5 die bewyslas wat op die eiser rus, verlig deur al die elemente te spesifiseer wat bewys moet word. Die artikel vergemaklik ook die hof se taak aangesien die hof bloot moet let op die aan- of afwesigheid van die faktore wat in die artikel genoem word en nie 'n ondersoek hoef te loods na die feite en die moontlikheid of die gades se huweliksverhouding herstel kan word nie.

Die wye interpretasie wat in *Dickinson v Dickinson* en *Krige v Smit* gevolg is, is deur die hof *a quo* in *Smit v Smit* 1982 1 SA 606 (O) verwerp. Die hof het beslis dat in gevalle waar een van die gades geestesongesteld of bewusteloos is, 'n egskeiding net ingevolge artikel 5 verleen kan word. In appèl na die volbank is hierdie beslissing omvergewerp in *Smit v Smit*, dit is die saak onder bespreking. In *Ott v Raubenheimer* [111], waar die verweerder ook geestessiek was, het die hof weer eens 'n egskeidingsbevel ingevolge artikel 4 verleen.

Uit die regspraak blyk dus dat die eiser artikel 4 van die Wet op Egskeiding kan gebruik om 'n egskeidingsbevel te verkry in gevalle waar die

the requirements of section 5, such as the lapsing of the prescribed time limit or the institution-alising of the mental patient, have not been complied with, or whether he has a choice even if the situation falls within the ambit of section 5 is not yet clear.

Barnard, Cronjé and Olivier (262-264) and Barnard (67) are apparently of the opinion that where all the elements of section 5 are present, the plaintiff would only be able to employ section 5 and would not be able to make use of section 4. Hahlo (351) is of a different opinion. He states that "[w]henever a spouse is mentally ill or continuously unconscious within the meaning of s 5, the likelihood is that the marriage will also have broken down irretrievably within the meaning of s 4 . . . [E]ven where the breakdown of a marriage was due to mental illness or continuous unconsciousness, a decree of divorce can be granted on the grounds of irretrievable marriage breakdown under s 4."

In this regard see further Barnard, Cronjé and Olivier 262-264; Barnard 65-67; Van der Vyver and Joubert 667; Hahlo 351; Midgley 1982 *SALJ* 22; Van Loggerenberg 1982 *THRHR* 174; Scott 1982 *Obiter* 20; Zaal 1983 *SALJ* 114; Barnard 1983 *THRHR* 354; Schäfer 1984 *THRHR* 299; Hoexter 1984 *De Rebus* 354.

See *Schwartz v Schwartz* [107]; *Swart v Swart* [108] and *Naidoo v Naidoo* [109] with regard to the objective and subjective approaches to determine whether a marriage has broken down irretrievably.

With regard to the statements by KOTZÉ AJ (41-42) on the possibility of the court having a discretion to refuse a divorce order where one of the grounds for obtaining a divorce has been proved, see *Schwartz v Schwartz* [107].

verweerder geestesongesteld of bewusteloos is. Dit is nog onseker of hy slegs op artikel 4 kan steun indien nie aan al die vereistes van artikel 5, soos die verloop van die voorgeskrewe tydperke of die opname van die geestesongestelde pasiënt, voldoen is nie en of hy 'n keuse het, selfs indien die situasie ten volle binne die omvang van artikel 5 val.

Barnard, Cronjé en Olivier (270-272) en Barnard (67) is skynbaar van mening dat die eiser nie kan kies om artikel 4 te gebruik indien al die elemente van artikel 5 teenwoordig is nie maar dat hy van artikel 5 gebruik sal moet maak. Hahlo (351) huldig 'n ander mening. Hy sê dat "[w]henever a spouse is mentally ill or continuously unconscious within the meaning of s 5, the likelihood is that the marriage will also have broken down irretrievably within the meaning of s 4 . . . [E]ven where the breakdown of a marriage was due to mental illness or continuous unconsciousness, a decree of divorce can be granted on the ground of irretrievable marriage breakdown under s 4."

Sien in die verband verder Barnard, Cronjé en Olivier 270-272; Barnard 65-67; Van der Vyver en Joubert 667; Hahlo 351; Midgley 1982 *SALJ* 22; Van Loggerenberg 1982 *THRHR* 174; Scott 1982 *Obiter* 20; Zaal 1983 *SALJ* 114; Barnard 1983 *THRHR* 354; Schäfer 1984 *THRHR* 299; Hoexter 1984 *De Rebus* 354.

Sien *Schwartz v Schwartz* [107]; *Swart v Swart* [108] en *Naidoo v Naidoo* [109] in verband met die objektiewe en subjektiewe benaderings om te bepaal of 'n huwelik onherstelbaar verbrokkel het.

Met betrekking tot KOTZÉ WN R se stellings (41-42) rakende die moontlike bestaan van 'n judisiële diskresie om 'n egskeidingsbevel te weier waar een van die egskeidingsgronde bewys is, sien *Schwartz v Schwartz* [107].

[111]   OTT v RAUBENHEIMER

1985 2 SA 851 (O)

The connection between sections 4 and 5 of the Divorce Act 70 of 1979

The plaintiff instituted a divorce action in terms of section 4 of the Divorce Act 70 of

Die verband tussen artikels 4 en 5 van die Wet op Egskeiding 70 van 1979

Die eiser het ingevolge artikel 4 van die Wet op Egskeiding 70 van 1979 'n aansoek om

1979 against his wife who had been certified mentally ill in terms of the Mental Health Act 18 of 1973 for a period of nearly two years (since 18 May 1983). The defendant had already been institutionalised on 4 March 1983. From the evidence of a psychiatrist it appeared that it was highly unlikely that the defendant would ever be discharged from the institution. The spouses were very happily married until the defendant's mental condition started deteriorating by the middle of 1980. The court granted the claim.

egskeiding teen sy vrou aanhangig gemaak. Sy was vir 'n ononderbroke tydperk van byna twee jaar (sedert 18 Mei 1983) ingevolge die Wet op Geestesgesondheid 18 van 1973 as geestesongesteld gesertifiseer. Die verweerderes is reeds op 4 Maart 1983 in 'n inrigting opgeneem. Uit die getuienis van 'n psigiater het geblyk dat dit hoogs onwaarskynlik was dat die verweerderes ooit weer uit die inrigting ontslaan sou word. Die partye was baie gelukkig getroud totdat die verweerderes se geestestoestand teen ongeveer die middel van 1980 begin versleg het. Die hof het die eiser se aansoek om egskeiding toegestaan.

LICHTENBURG R: [855] Op die ... getuienis van die psigiater en op eiser se getuienis is ek oortuig dat dit op 'n oorwig van waarskynlikhede bewys is dat die onderhawige huwelik onherstelbaar verbrokkel het en is ek oortuig dat die huweliksverhouding tussen eiser en die pasiënt so 'n toestand van verbrokkeling bereik het dat daar geen redelike vooruitsig op die herstel van 'n normale huweliksverhouding tussen hulle bestaan nie. Daar is dus voldoen aan die vereistes van art 4(1) van die Wet. 'n Egskeiding moet derhalwe toegestaan word (sien *Schwartz v Schwartz* 1984 (4) SA 467 (A) op 473F–475C [107]), tensy die eiser se skuldoorsaak beperk is tot art 5 van die Wet en hy derhalwe nie op art 4 van die Wet mag steun nie. Dit is duidelik dat, indien art 5 die onderhawige geval dek ter uitsluiting van art 4, die eiser nie tans 'n egskeiding kan verkry nie omdat die tydperk van twee jaar wat in art 5(1)(*a*) bepaal word as die minimum tydperk waartydens die pasiënt ingevolge die Wet op Geestesgesondheid 18 van 1973 aaneenlopend aangehou was, nog nie verstryk het nie en daar ook nie die getuienis van twee psigiaters aangevoer was nie (soos bedoel deur art 5(1)(*b*)). In elk geval, soos reeds gemeld, het eiser sy eis nie op art 5 gefundeer nie.

Artikel 3 van die Wet bepaal dat die enigste gronde waarop 'n huwelik deur 'n egskeidingsbevel ontbind mag word is die onherstelbare verbrokkeling van die huwelik, soos in art 4 beoog, of die geestesongesteldheid of die voortdurende bewusteloosheid van 'n party, soos in art 5 beoog. 'n Blote letterlike vertolking van die Wet lei nie daartoe dat die een grond die ander uitsluit as beide gronde bestaan nie want art 4 is nie aan art 5 onderhewig gestel nie en art 5 kwalifiseer ook nie art 4 nie en bepaal nie dat art 5 aangewend *moet* word in gevalle wat sowel onder art 5 asook onder art 4 tuisgebring kan word nie as daar sowel die in art 5 vereiste geestesongesteldheid (plus geen redelike vooruitsig op genesing daarvan nie) asook onherstelbare verbrokkeling aanwesig is. In feitlik alle gevalle waar daar ongeneeslike geestesongesteldheid teenwoordig is sal daar egter ook *ipso facto* onherstelbare verbrokkeling bewys kan word, en die vraag wat derhalwe ontstaan is of 'n eiser in so 'n geval 'n keuse het met betrekking tot sy skuldoorsaak tussen art 4 en art 5. Hierdie vraag is bevestigend beantwoord in *Dickinson v Dickinson* 1981 (3) SA 856 (W) op 860C–F. Ter ondersteuning van daardie standpunt kan ook verwys word na *Krige v Smit NO* 1981 (4) SA 409 (K) op 414C–D en 415H–416B, [856] wat egter *obiter* is met betrekking tot die onderhawige vraag aangesien art 5 in daardie geval nie van toepassing was nie; sien op 416C. 'n *Obiter dictum* in *Smit v Smit* 1982 (4) SA 34 (O) op 39B–D [110] skyn daarop te dui dat so 'n keuse nie behoort te bestaan nie, maar die betrokke uitlating het die vraagstuk beslis nie opgelos wat hierdie Afdeling betref nie ...

Die getuienis in die onderhawige saak bewys presies dieselfde as dié in die *Dickinson*-saak, naamlik dat die oorsaak van die verbrokkeling geheel-en-al die pasiënt se sielsiekte was, of, anders gestel, dat die huweliksverhouding nie sou verbrokkel het nie indien die pasiënt geen geestesongesteldheid opgedoen het nie. Daar was dus geen verbrokkeling vóórdat die pasiënt geestesgebrekkig geraak het nie en 'n betoog dat die verbrokkeling reeds ingetree het en derhalwe bestaan het vóórdat die pasiënt sielsiek geword het, sou dus nie kon opgaan nie. Dit is egter ook duidelik dat . . . [daar] reeds verbrokkeling van die huwelik [was] lank voordat die pasiënt op 18 Mei 1983 gesertifiseer was, soos bedoel in art 5(1)(*a*)(i) van die Wet, en derhalwe is eiser geregtig om op sodanige verbrokkeling as skuldoorsaak te steun en hoef hy nie op die pasiënt se geestesongesteldheid binne die raamwerk van art 5 staat te maak nie. Die feit dat die verbrokkeling wat reeds bestaan het vóórdat die pasiënt gesertifiseer was, sy regstreekse oorsprong in haar sielsiekte gehad het, is egter onsaaklik want al wat moet bewys word is die objektiewe feit van onherstelbare verbrokkeling van die huwelik (sien *Schwartz* se saak *supra* op 473E [107]), en daardie feit het eiser bewys binne die raamwerk van art 4, wat die enigste artikel is waaronder hy sy eis kon formuleer, want die fondament vir 'n eis onder art 5 bestaan nog nie omdat die tydperk van twee jaar na die pasiënt se sertifisering nog nie verstryk het nie. Die feit dat eiser se eis, ná verloop van dié in art 5(1)(*a*) bepaalde tydperk van minstens twee jaar aaneenlopende aanhouding in 'n inrigting vir sielsiekes, ook onder art 5(1)(*a*)(i) ingestel sal kan word, ontneem hom in 'n geval soos die onderhawige waar daar reeds verbrokkeling bestaan het vóór sertifisering, [857] nie van sy reg om ingevolge art 4 te eis nie. Inteendeel, dit is die enigste remedie wat hy het totdat daar aan die vereistes van art 5 voldoen is . . .

[858] Derhalwe word . . . 'n [e]gskeidingsbevel . . . toegestaan . . .

Note	Aantekening
See the note on *Smit v Smit* [110].	Sien die aantekening by *Smit v Smit* [110].

Divorce in terms of Jewish ecclesiastical law	Egskeiding ingevolge Joodse kerkreg

[112]   RAIK V RAIK

1993 2 SA 617 (W)

Enforcement of an agreement to grant a "get"	Afdwinging van 'n ooreenkoms om 'n "get" te verleen
The parties had married according to Jewish ecclesiastical law and in compliance with South African law. The marriage broke down and the wife (plaintiff) sued the husband for divorce in terms of section 4 of the Divorce Act 70 of 1979. It was clear that the parties' marriage had broken down irretrievably. In addition to an order for divorce the wife claimed, *inter alia*, an order compelling her husband to grant her a "get" (Jewish ecclesiastical divorce). It appeared that, although the husband had, in the parties' "ketubah"	Die partye is ooreenkomstig Joodse kerkreg en die Suid-Afrikaanse reg getroud. Hulle huwelik het verbrokkel en die vrou (eiseres) het die man ingevolge artikel 4 van die Wet op Egskeiding 70 van 1979 vir 'n egskeiding gedagvaar. Dit was duidelik dat die huwelik onherstelbaar verbrokkel het. Benewens die egskeidingsbevel het die vrou onder andere aansoek gedoen om 'n bevel wat haar man sou dwing om aan haar 'n "get" (Joodse kerklike egskeiding) te verleen. Dit het geblyk dat, alhoewel die man in die partye se "ke-

(premarital agreement), agreed to grant his wife a "get" should their marriage break down, he had subsequently indicated that he was unwilling to do so. The court had to decide whether the agreement to grant a "get" was enforceable. It held that it was enforceable and issued an order for specific performance, compelling the husband to do everything in his power to ensure that a "get" was obtained.

tubah" (voorhuwelikse ooreenkoms) toegestem het om aan sy vrou 'n "get" te verleen indien hulle huwelik sou verbrokkel, hy later te kenne gegee het dat hy dit nie gaan doen nie. Die hof moes beslis of die ooreenkoms om 'n "get" te verleen afdwingbaar is. Die hof het beslis dat dit wel afdwingbaar is en het 'n bevel vir spesifieke nakoming uitgereik wat die man verplig het om alles in sy vermoë te doen om te verseker dat die vrou 'n "get" bekom.

COETZEE J: [624] I have been referred to a very learned article by Mr Nathan Segal of the Johannesburg Bar entitled 'Enforcement of Agreement to Grant a Get or Jewish Ecclesiastical Bill of Divorce' (1988) 105 *SALJ* 97. It would be necessary for me to quote fairly extensively from this article, because it sets out the position clearly (at 99–100):

> [625] 'Marriage in Jewish law takes place in two stages: first the betrothal, and thereafter the nuptials. In modern practice both stages take place consecutively in the same ceremony beneath a bridal canopy. Certain benedictions are recited, which constitute the betrothal. The groom, with the consent of the bride and in the presence of two competent witnesses, presents the bride with a ring and pronounces the formula: "Behold, thou art betrothed unto me, with this ring, in accordance with the law of Moses and Israel". The ketubah or antenuptial contract is read out. This sets out the obligations of the husband towards his wife. It may also deal with other issues, such as a dowry or marriage settlement. The nuptial ceremony follows. Seven benedictions are recited. The bride and bridegroom then spend a few minutes in private to symbolise the consummation of the marriage.
>
> The legal requirement for a valid marriage is that the requisite formalities should take place before the necessary witnesses. In practice a Rabbi officiates. This is to ensure that the necessary legal formalities are complied with. His function is merely supervisory, and his presence is not an essential legal requirement. The point to be noted is that the marriage is not a sacrament but takes place by virtue of the consent of the parties.
>
> Just as marriage is not a sacrament, and takes place by consent, so are the parties entitled to terminate the marriage by mutual consent without requiring the permission of any third party. The procedure for a divorce requires the husband to deliver a get or bill of divorce to his wife in the presence of two witnesses. The get is couched in a prescribed form. The essence of it is that the wife is released from the marriage in accordance with the law of Moses and Israel. Again, the consent of clergy is not a prerequisite. However, the laws relating to the granting of a get are intricate, and it is necessary in practice for a Jewish Ecclesiastical Court or Beth Din to officiate at the granting of the get to ensure that the procedures are properly complied with. For example, the bill of divorce must be written out by hand in the correct calligraphy by a qualified scribe.
>
> In practice this service is provided in Southern Africa by the Beth Din of Johannesburg. The Beth Din fixes a time for the ceremony and arranges for a scribe and witnesses to be present. The husband must appear and instruct the scribe to prepare the get. The document must be drafted in the proper form. The scribe commences work, which lasts about an hour. The wife must then appear, and the get is presented to her. The Beth Din then retains the original document in its records.'

Further, at 100–1:

> 'The necessity for a get arises out of the provisions of Jewish law. A woman is not regarded as divorced until she receives a get, even if the marriage has been dissolved by the civil court. Until a get is granted (or the husband dies), the woman remains a married woman in the eyes of the law. If she should form an intimate relationship with another man, she (and he) will be guilty of adultery, which is a very serious offence. Further, any child born of such a union will be illegitimate. The technical term for such a child is a mamzer. The mamzer is subject to the severest disabilities, far more stringent than those applying to an illegitimate child under the civil law. A mamzer, while Jewish, may never marry a partner who is of legitimate birth.

> The result of these restrictions is that an observant Jewish woman who is divorced by the civil court but does not receive a get is consigned to a life of permanent widowhood. She can have no prospects of remarrying, but must remain in limbo until her "husband" dies or agrees to grant her a get.

> It has been known to happen that an embittered husband has refused to grant his wife a get; or that he has demanded exorbitant payment before agreeing to do so. This causes a problem of tragic dimensions for the wife, to which there is no ready solution. In times when the Beth Din had authority to execute its rulings, it [626] would inflict corporal punishment to persuade the recalcitrant husband to grant a get. In the State of Israel the authorities will imprison such a husband until he consents to grant the get. No such solution is available in the Republic. It is against this background that one approaches the problem of the husband who consents to grant a get and then retracts.'

I must add that, in my view, from what I have seen before me, the defendant is the embittered husband who is refusing to grant his wife a 'get'.

Reference is made to the case of *Berkowitz v Berkowitz* 1956 (3) SA 522 (SR) [where the court refused to enforce an agreement to grant a "get"] This, I am told, is the only reported case, and it is the only case which I have been referred to, that dealt with this problem. It is dealt with by *Segal* in his article and more specifically at 98. Then, quite rightly, the judgment of MURRAY CJ is criticised by *Nathan Segal* at 103. It is pointed out that there are three factors involved which go to the root of the matter.

1. The undertaking to grant a 'get' cannot be described as 'of an intimate personal character concerned entirely with religious formalities'. It is stated, again correctly, that one is concerned rather with legal formalities relating to a legal system which is binding on the conscience of the parties, or at least on that of the wife. The husband consented to be married in accordance with the provisions of Jewish law. He also consented expressly in the divorce agreement to be divorced on the same basis (these were the facts in *Berkowitz*). The nature of the undertaking does not appear to detract from the general rule that undertakings should be kept.

2. *Segal* said that objection was raised that the wife seeks specific performance under circumstances in which the Court cannot supervise the grant of the get by the Beth Din. As Coetzee J has demonstrated in *Ranch International Pipelines (Transvaal) (Pty) Ltd v LMG Construction (City) (Pty) Ltd; LMG Construction (City) (Pty) Ltd v Ranch International Pipelines (Transvaal) (Pty) Ltd and Others* 1984 (3) SA 861 (W) at 880 the absence of supervision by a Court does not preclude it from granting an order for specific performance.

3. The objection is that MURRAY CJ acted on the premise that the Beth Din grants a 'get' in the same way as a civil Court grants a decree of divorce. As *Segal* sets out, the 'get' is in fact granted by the husband and not by the Beth Din. It seems, as *Segal*

suggests, the Court in Southern Rhodesia was probably not addressed on that issue. *Segal* makes the point that it is true that husbands would be unable to grant a 'get' without the assistance of the Beth Din, but he goes on to say that it is inconceivable that the Beth Din, which is painfully aware of the problem, would withhold its assistance. If the Beth Din, he says, should nevertheless for some unforseeable reason refuse to assist, the husband would certainly not be in contempt of the order directing him to grant a 'get', and commital proceedings brought against him for contempt would be unsuccessful.

The objections which *Segal* has raised in respect of that judgment are in my view valid. I do not consider MURRAY CJ's judgment to be correct.

Attention is also drawn to the practice, apparently in the Witwatersrand [627] Local Division, where some Judges strike out of settlement agreements the undertaking by the husband to get a get.

It is clear that the defendant and the plaintiff were married according to the law of Moses and Israel. This carries in Jewish law certain obligations. I find that there is too much to be said against the judgment of MURRAY CJ, and I do not intend to follow it. I am of the view, and clearly so on the evidence before me, that the defendant is that type of person who is embittered who will resort to extortion and who will not grant his wife a 'get' unless there is an order compelling him to do so. But clearly, if the spouses promised each other in the 'ketubah' that they intend that on the breakdown it will be dissolved according to Jewish law, an order should be made compelling the defendant to give his wife a get. This was also held to be the position in New York in the case of *Avitzur v Avitzur* 449 NYS 2d 83. The Court of Appeals concluded:

'The present case can be decided solely upon the application of neutral principles of contract law, without reference to any religious principle. Consequently, defendant's objections to enforcement of his promise to appear before the Beth Din, based as they are upon the religious origin of the agreement, pose no constitutional barrier to the relief sought by the plaintiff. The fact that the agreement was entered into as part of a religious ceremony does not render it unenforceable. The Courts may properly enforce so much of this agreement as is not in contravention of law or public policy. In short the relief sought by plaintiff in this action is simply to compel defendant to perform a secular obligation to which he contractually bound himself.'

The parties to the agreement to grant a 'get' must be held thereto. Public policy in my view demands that this agreement be enforced. An embittered husband must not be allowed to blackmail his wife before consenting to go to the Beth Din for the 'get'. I have no doubt that the Court must come to the wife's assistance and in a marriage like the present grant the order for specific performance ...

[Accordingly the defendant was] [629] ordered to do all things as may be reasonably necessary to ensure that a 'get' or a bill of divorce in accordance with the Jewish law is granted under the supervision of the Jewish Ecclesiastical Court or the Beth Din of Johannesburg ...

Note	Aantekening
The decision in this case is welcomed because it relieves the difficult position in which a Jewish wife finds herself if her husband refuses to grant her a "get". Because of the unenviable position a Jewish wife finds herself in if a "get" is not granted, it seems only fair that her husband should	Die uitspraak in hierdie saak word verwelkom omdat dit erkenning verleen aan die moeilike posisie waarin 'n Joodse vrou haarself bevind indien haar man weier om 'n "get" aan haar te verleen. As gevolg van die onbenydenswaardige posisie waarin 'n Joodse vrou haar bevind indien

be held to his undertaking to grant his wife a "get" should their marriage break down.

The South African Law Commission in its recent *Working Paper 45* Project 76 *Jewish Divorces* 27 November 1992 also recognised the difficult position in which Jewish wives find themselves if a "get" is not obtained. It recommended that a new section 5A be inserted into the Divorce Act 70 of 1979. The proposed section provides that if it appears to a court in divorce proceedings that, despite the granting of a decree of divorce, the spouses will be bound by their religion to have their marriage dissolved in terms of the requirements of that religion before they or any one of them will, in terms of their religion, be free to remarry, the court may refuse to grant a decree of divorce. If it appears to the court that the spouses cannot succeed in removing the religious barrier to remarriage the court may, having regard to the personal circumstances of each spouse and to public policy, make any order that it finds just.

'n "get" nie verkry word nie, lyk dit niks minder as billik nie dat haar man verplig moet word om sy ooreenkoms na te kom om 'n "get" aan sy vrou te verleen indien hulle huwelik sou verbrokkel.

Die Suid-Afrikaanse Regskommissie het in sy onlangse *Werkstuk 45* Projek 76 *Joodse Egskeidings* 27 November 1992 ook die benarde posisie erken waarin Joodse vrouens hulle bevind indien 'n "get" nie verleen word nie. Die Regskommissie het aanbeveel dat 'n nuwe artikel 5A in die Wet op Egskeiding 70 van 1979 ingevoeg word. Die voorgestelde artikel bepaal dat indien dit vir 'n hof in 'n egskeidingsgeding blyk dat, selfs al word 'n egskeidingsbevel uitgereik, die gades deur hulle geloof verplig word om hulle huwelik ooreenkomstig hulle geloof te laat ontbind voordat hulle, of enigeen van hulle, ingevolge hulle geloof in staat sal wees om weer te trou, die hof kan weier om 'n egskeidingsbevel uit te reik. Indien dit vir die hof blyk dat die gades nie daarin kan slaag om die beletsel op hertroue wat ingevolge hulle geloof bestaan te verwyder nie, kan die hof met inagneming van die persoonlike omstandighede van elk van die gades en van die openbare belang enige bevel uitreik wat hy billik ag.

Forfeiture of patrimonial benefits

Requirements for forfeiture of benefits
What can be forfeited?

Verbeuring van vermoënsregtelike voordele

Vereistes vir verbeuring van voordele
Wat kan verbeur word?

Requirements for forfeiture of benefits   Vereistes vir verbeuring van voordele

[113]   SINGH V SINGH

1983 1 SA 781 (C)

Forfeiture of patrimonial benefits

The plaintiff (husband) and the defendant (wife) were married in community of property. It was alleged that their marriage had broken down irretrievably and that there was no prospect of its resumption. The plaintiff alleged that this was, *inter alia*, due to the defendant's desertion, her improper intimate relations with other men and neglecting her duties as a wife and mother. In view of all this the plaintiff, *inter alia*, applied for divorce and for forfeiture of the benefits of the marriage in community of property. The defendant denied the plaintiff's allegations. She stated that the breakdown of the marriage was due to the plaintiff's repeated assaults, threats to kill her, use of abusive language and inadequate maintenance for her. In a counterclaim she, *inter alia*, applied for divorce and division of the joint estate. The plaintiff was successful.

Verbeuring van vermoënsregtelike voordele

Die eiser (man) en die verweerderes was binne gemeenskap van goed getroud. Daar is aangevoer dat hulle huwelik onherstelbaar verbrokkel het en dat daar geen vooruitsig was dat dit weer hervat sou kon word nie. Die eiser het beweer dat dit onder andere die gevolg was van die feit dat die verweerderes die huis verlaat het, dat sy onbehoorlik intieme verhoudings met ander mans gehad het en dat sy nie haar verpligtinge as vrou en moeder nagekom het nie. In die lig hiervan het die eiser onder andere om 'n egskeiding en verbeuring van die voordele van die huwelik binne gemeenskap van goed aansoek gedoen. Die verweerderes het die eiser se bewerings ontken. Sy het beweer dat die verbrokkeling van die huwelik die gevolg was van die eiser se herhaalde aanrandings, dreigemente om haar te vermoor, sy gebruik van skeltaal en onvoldoende onderhoud vir haar. In 'n teeneis het sy onder andere aansoek gedoen om 'n egskeiding en verdeling van die gemeenskaplike boedel. Die eiser was suksesvol.

BAKER J: [785] This case is a case about money, and nothing else. The cat-and-dog life of the parties is proved beyond any doubt whatsoever; there is no doubt that the marriage is a disaster. This appears from the evidence of almost all the witnesses . . .

Plaintiff wants forfeiture; defendant wants division; that is what the four-day wrangle in Court was about. It therefore becomes necessary to deal briefly with the law regarding the two matters:

  (i) the factors relevant to the actual divorce; and

  (ii) the factors involved in a claim for forfeiture, division, maintenance and costs.

<u>As to (i):</u>

It seems to be plain that today, in the eyes of the Legislature, fault is irrelevant in considering whether or not a divorce should be granted.

> "The Divorce Act revolutionizes the South African law of divorce by replacing fault with failure, matrimonial offence with marriage breakdown as the main ground of divorce."

(Hahlo and Sinclair *The Reform of the South African Law of Divorce* published in 1980 at 1 of the introduction; s 3(*a*) of the Divorce Act 70 of 1979; *Hahlo and Sinclair* at 21–39 of the main text.)

Irretrievable breakdown may be proved in any number of ways: by proof of defendant's adultery, as happened here, coupled with the fact that plaintiff finds this irreconcilable with a continued marriage relationship (s 4(2)(*b*)); or proof of living apart for a year or more (s 4(2)(*a*)) – the living apart need not amount to malicious desertion by defendant, as was the case formerly (*Hahlo and Sinclair* at 24); in short, "any facts or circumstances which may be indicative of the irretrievable breakdown of a marriage . . ." (s 4(2)). Malicious desertion by defendant, which overlapped the admitted adultery by her, would clearly be such a fact or circumstance (*Hahlo and Sinclair* (*ibid* at 24 *ad* n 65–29)) . . .

[786] In the present instance there can be no doubt that both parties regard the marriage as done with and both wish it to be formally terminated.

As to (ii):

> Fault remains a factor in deciding whether to order forfeiture, or division, maintenance, and costs (*Hahlo and Sinclair* "Introduction" at 1 note 2 and main text at 20, referring to s 7(2) (maintenance for one spouse), s 9(1) (forfeiture) and s 10 (costs)):

> " . . . the Act specifies the situations in which conduct (or misconduct) may be taken into account: when deciding . . . maintenance . . . forfeiture . . . and . . . costs."

I now refer very briefly to the statutory provisions in the above connections . . .

I refer to the three abovementioned matters in the order in which they are mentioned in the Act.

(*a*) Maintenance for defendant:

The Act, s 7(2), provides that, in the absence of a consent paper in respect of maintenance of one spouse by the other, it may, having regard to the existing or prospective means of each of the parties, their respective earning capacities, financial needs and obligations, the age of each of the parties, the duration of the marriage, the standard of living of the parties prior to the divorce, their conduct in so far as it may be relevant to the breakdown of the marriage, and any other factor which in the opinion of the Court should be taken into account, make an order which the Court finds just in respect of the payment of maintenance by the one party to the other for any period until the [787] death or remarriage of the party in whose favour the order is given, whichever event may first occur.

Under s 9(1) of the Act the fault (misconduct) relevant to the breakdown of the marriage must be "substantial misconduct"; but under s 7(2) this conduct (misconduct) can be any conduct which has caused or contributed to the breakdown of the marriage. In practice this will probably be adultery, desertion, and/or cruelty (*Hahlo and Sinclair* at 45).

It follows that s 7(2), in regard to questions of maintenance, perpetuates the guilt factor (the learned authors at 45, last paragraph, use the word "reintroduces"; with the greatest respect, "perpetuates" is perhaps closer to the mark). At 46–47 there is a discussion of what sort of misconduct is to be had regard to by the Court seized of the case. Although the learned authors accept that:

> "It would outrage one's sense of justice if a man who by gross maltreatment of his wife has caused the breakdown of the marriage were to be awarded maintenance against her, because she happens to be well off whereas he is not",

they add one proviso: the misconduct of the "guilty" spouse must be "gross" before the Court should take it into account as the factor which has led to the disintegration of the marriage . . .

I accept for present purposes that the misconduct must be "gross" – eg adultery by the defendant irreconcilable (in plaintiff's honest view) with the continuance of the marriage. I would put malicious desertion upon almost the same footing; it is not so heinous an "offence" as adultery, so let us accord it rather less weight . . .

It remains to be seen whether defendant's conduct during the marriage is "gross" enough to disentitle her to maintenance, or whether this case is merely one of many in which both parties have contributed to the breakdown of the marriage, and the Court should allow defendant a fair sum in maintenance . . .

[788] (*b*) Forfeiture of benefits:

Section 9(1) of the Act provides for forfeiture of the patrimonial benefits of the marriage, either wholly or in part, when a divorce is granted on the ground of irretrievable breakdown, if the Court is satisfied that, if forfeiture be *not* ordered, the one party will in relation to the other be unduly benefited. The factors to be considered are the duration of the marriage, the circumstances which gave rise to its breakdown and any substantial misconduct on the part of either of the parties. The Courts now possess a discretionary power which they previously did not have, but they cannot order a redistribution of capital and property, as the Courts of Holland in the 17th and 18th centuries enjoyed, and which English Courts now have; our Courts' power is confined to patrimonial benefits . . .

[BAKER J referred to Hahlo and Sinclair's (51–52) criticism of section 9(1). These authors, *inter alia*, state that "forfeiture of benefits is logically predicated upon guilt and does not, therefore, fit into a divorce system which is based on marriage breakdown." BAKER J proceeded:]

[789] The trouble with s 9(1) is no concern of this Court. The learned authors' criticism is probably sound; I think it is; but that is a matter for the Legislature to consider. In the meantime this Court may order forfeiture of the patrimonial benefits upon the old grounds of adultery and/or malicious desertion.

(*c*) Costs:

Section 10 of the Act provides that:

> "In a divorce action the court shall not be bound to make an order for costs in favour of the successful party, but the court may, having regard to the means of the parties, and their conduct in so far as it may be relevant, make such order as it considers just, and the court may order that the costs of the proceedings be apportioned between the parties."

This plainly gives the Court a wide discretion in the matter. Once again, the conduct of the parties must be taken into account . . .

[BAKER J again referred to Hahlo and Sinclair and proceeded:]

The learned authors suggest that "conduct" may include conduct after separation but before divorce. This may be so, though as the main ground for divorce these days is breakdown, it may be argued that only conduct leading to such breakdown is to be considered. I agree with their next suggestion, that conduct in the course of the proceedings may lead to an adverse order for costs; the Court has had that discretion for generations, anyway.

I turn to deal with the evidence on the various issues.

[BAKER J then dealt with the evidence and continued as follows:]

To sum it up in broad terms, the evidence of plaintiff and his witnesses contains little that is improbable. The witnesses corroborate each other. No damage was done to them by defendant's counsel. The evidence of defendant, and her witnesses, *per contra*, is not very impressive and contains several contradictions and improbabilities, in particular the defendant's sudden burst of mother-love for the two boys.

[790] I proceed to deal with the various prayers set out in the pleadings. The prayer of plaintiff (in convention) for an order of divorce will be granted and the similar prayer of defendant (plaintiff in reconvention) will be refused – assuming that refusal is necessary . . .

Forfeiture *versus* division of the assets of the parties: This is the real issue in this case, as said earlier. Forfeiture of the benefits derived by a party from having married in community of property can be ordered either wholly or in part. (Section 9(1); Hahlo in *Husband and Wife* 4th ed at 435 last paragraph and 438 second paragraph.) The rider means that the "guilty" party forfeits what he or she would have derived by virtue of having married in community, and does not any longer extend as far as forfeiture of what that party may have contributed to the marriage (*Hahlo* at 438 *ad* note 70, 435 para 3). The wife who has been ordered to forfeit the benefits will therefore retain what she has contributed to the common estate; this is not forfeitable in modern law (*Hahlo* at 438 *ad* note 70). These contributions are those made before, at, or during the marriage (*Gates v Gates* 1940 NPD 361 at 364 para 2). The *onus* of establishing their respective contributions rests upon the respective spouses. (*Gates'* case *supra* at 365.) In the present instance defendant has done very little to establish her contribution save to show that she looked after the children when they needed looking after, kept house, helped to build it in the first place (to a very small extent), and contributed some uncertain sums of money at various times towards food. The . . . defendant was allowed to obtain a sworn valuation of the plaintiff's house at her own expense on condition that such valuation should not be conclusive proof of the value of the residence nor be binding on plaintiff . . . She did not do so. It might at least have served as a starting point for an inquiry. Plaintiff, on the other hand, established that he paid for the plot and the building of the house and maintained the family for 22 years. The sum total of the estate is this house plus the furniture I have mentioned elsewhere; whether plaintiff has a savings account or other monetary capital or indeed any other form of capital at all is unclear. In these circumstances I consider that the best course I can follow, rough and ready though it may be . . . is to follow the *Gates* solution, and attempt an allocation myself. This may save the parties expense in the long run. SELKE J in that case said at 365:

"Where, as in most cases, the sum total of the joint estate represents simply the sum total of the values of the contributions, then the whole estate is divisible in the proportions represented by the values thus established."

Near the bottom of the same page the learned Judge said:

[791] "In practice it is in most cases obviously impossible to arrive at an accurate present valuation of the contributions made from time to time by the parties to the estate throughout their married life, because, amongst other reasons, it is not normally the practice of spouses to keep accurate accounts as between themselves."

His Lordship went on to enunciate the well-established principle that a housewife and mother is entitled to credit for managing the joint household, performing the usual household duties, and caring for the children;

"these services have a very real and substantial value which may well, and usually does, exceed the bare cost of her maintenance"

(at 365–366). In view of the sparseness of the evidence as to both parties' contributions the best I can do is to follow the *Gates* example and assess the respective contributions myself . . .

I intend to order forfeiture, because the defendant's misconduct with Bennett [with whom she had committed adultery] was "substantial", in my opinion, and outweighs the fact that the duration of the marriage was 20 years (I leave out the time from the date of desertion to the trial). The third consideration enjoined upon the Court, namely the circumstances which gave rise to the breakdown, involves fault and responsibility (*Hahlo and Sinclair* (*op cit* at 52 line 5)). It overlaps the misconduct factor in so far as the adultery and desertion are concerned, and is neutral in so far as the quarrelling, arguing and recriminating are concerned, for I consider the blame for this should be apportioned 50/50. I consider that division would unduly benefit defendant, and she is not in my opinion entitled to it. I do, however, consider that she is entitled to salvage something from the wreck of her marriage, even though she is largely responsible for it. Where the Court considers that one spouse in a marriage in community of property ought to receive more than the other, it can be achieved by means of a forfeiture order (*Hahlo and Sinclair* at 53 lines 9–10). I assess, as best I can on the scanty evidence, that defendant is entitled to 20 per cent of the joint estate, ie the value of the house and furniture, and plaintiff to 80 per cent. The resemblance to the *Gates* apportionment is coincidental.

Maintenance has already been mentioned . . . I do not consider that defendant ought to receive maintenance from plaintiff even though such an order would be competent under s 7(2) of the Act . . .

Note

Since the inception of the Divorce Act 70 of 1979 our divorce law is no longer based on the fault principle but on the irretrievable breakdown of the marriage. As far as granting of the divorce order is concerned fault is irrelevant but it remains a factor in deciding whether to order forfeiture of benefits, division of the estate, maintenance, or costs. As far as these matters are concerned the importance of matrimonial misconduct has also been reduced by the Divorce Act. In *Singh's* case the "guilty" spouse was, however, no better off that she would have been under the old dispensation (Sinclair 1983 *SALJ* 172). BAKER J found that her conduct was gross enough to disentitle her to maintenance. He also ordered forfeiture as he found that her misconduct was substantial and that it outweighed the fact that the marriage had lasted for twenty-two years. But the court did not consider the defendant's age or her need for maintenance after the dissolution of the marriage. In order to come to a decision the court should take these criteria into account in terms of section 7(2) of the Divorce Act, but none of the factors mentioned in section 7(2) was considered (Sinclair 1983 *Annual Survey* 98 and 1983 *SALJ* 169). Furthermore in *Koza v Koza* 1982 3 SA 462 (T) it was held that a person claiming forfeiture "should plead the necessary facts to support that claim and formulate a proper prayer in the pleadings to define the nature of the relief sought." In this case the required details were not forthcoming and the

Aantekening

Sedert die inwerkingtreding van die Wet op Egskeiding 70 van 1979 is ons egskeidingsreg nie meer op die skuldbeginsel gebaseer nie maar op die onherstelbare verbrokkeling van die huwelik. By die verlening van die egskeiding speel skuld nie meer 'n rol nie maar dit is wel nog van belang by beslissing van die vraag of verbeuring van voordele, verdeling van die boedel, onderhoud of koste toegestaan moet word. Ook wat hierdie aangeleenthede betref, is die belang van wangedrag gedurende die huwelik deur die Wet op Egskeiding verminder. In die *Singh*-saak was die "skuldige" gade egter niks beter daaraan toe as wat sy ingevolge die ou bedeling sou gewees het nie (Sinclair 1983 *SALJ* 172). BAKER R het bevind dat haar wangedrag so erg was dat sy nie op onderhoud geregtig was nie. Hy het verder ook verbeuring van voordele gelas aangesien hy van mening was dat haar wangedrag wesenlik was en dat dit swaarder geweeg het as die feit dat die huwelik twee en twintig jaar geduur het. Die hof het egter nie die verweerderes se ouderdom of haar behoefte aan onderhoud na ontbinding van die huwelik in ag geneem nie. Ten einde tot 'n beslissing te kom, moet die hof hierdie kriteria ingevolge artikel 7(2) van die Wet op Egskeiding in ag neem, maar nie een van die faktore wat in artikel 7(2) genoem word, is oorweeg nie (Sinclair 1983 *Annual Survey* 98 en 1983 *SALJ* 169). Verder is in *Koza v Koza* 1982 3 SA 462 (T) beslis dat 'n persoon wat verbeuring van voordele eis "should plead the necessary facts to

court had to decide the matter on rather scanty evidence (see also Sinclair 1983 *SALJ* 171).

This case should be compared with *Swart v Swart* [108] where a partially guilty spouse who had deserted her husband was awarded maintenance.

support that claim and formulate a proper prayer in the pleadings to define the nature of the relief sought." In hierdie saak, daarenteen, was die nodige besonderhede nie voor die hof nie en moes die hof die aangeleentheid maar op karige getuienis beslis (sien ook Sinclair 1983 *SALJ* 171).

Hierdie saak moet vergelyk word met *Swart v Swart* [108] waar onderhoud toegestaan is aan 'n vrou wat gedeeltelik skuldig was en haar man verlaat het.

[114]   WIJKER V WIJKER

1993 4 SA 720 (A)

Forfeiture of patrimonial benefits

The appellant and the respondent (wife) had been married in community of property for some 35 years. During the subsistence of their marriage the wife had started and run a successful business as an estate agent. Initially half the shares in the estate agency had been held by the appellant and half by the respondent. The appellant subsequently transferred his shares to the respondent so that she could obtain a tax benefit. The spouses agreed that the appellant could have his shares back if and when he wanted them. When the appellant asked for the return of his shares, the respondent refused to return them because she did not have a high regard for the appellant's financial ability and was afraid that he would use the shares to further his own interest. The respondent's persistent refusal to return the shares caused the appellant to institute a divorce action. In a counter-claim the respondent claimed a forfeiture order against the appellant (then the plaintiff) in respect of his shares in the estate agency and certain assets purchased with the income derived from the company. In the court *a quo* a divorce order was granted against the respondent and a forfeiture order was made against the appellant. The appellant appealed against the forfeiture order, *inter*

Verbeuring van vermoënsregtelike voordele

Die appellant en die respondent (vrou) was vir ongeveer 35 jaar binne gemeenskap van goed getroud. Gedurende die bestaan van die huwelik het die vrou 'n suksesvolle besigheid as eiendomsagent op die been gebring en ook self bestuur. Aanvanklik het die appellant en die respondent elkeen die helfte van die aandele in die besigheid besit. Die appellant het later sy aandele aan die respondent oorgedra ten einde haar in staat te stel om 'n belastingvoordeel te verkry. Die gades het ooreengekom dat die appellant sy aandele te eniger tyd sou kon terug kry wanneer hy hulle wou hê. Toe die appellant die respondent egter om teruggawe van sy aandele vra, het sy geweier om hulle terug te gee omdat sy nie veel vertroue in die appellant se finansiële vernuf gehad het nie en omdat sy bang was dat hy die aandele vir eie gewin sou gebruik. Die respondent se volgehoue weiering om die aandele terug te gee, het daartoe gelei dat die appellant 'n egskeidingsaksie ingestel het. In 'n teeneis het die respondent aansoek gedoen om 'n verbeuringsbevel teen die appellant (toe die eiser) met betrekking tot sy aandele in die eiendomsagentskap en sekere bates wat met die inkomste van die maatskappy gekoop is. In

alia, on the ground that forfeiture could not have been decreed because the trial court had made no finding of substantial misconduct on his part. The appellant also alleged that the trial court misdirected itself in blaming him for the breakdown of the marriage and in considering that it was unfair for him to share in the business which his wife had made successful. The Appellate Division considered the requirements for an order for forfeiture and the approach to be adopted when dealing with an appeal against an order for forfeiture. It held that the forfeiture order should not have been made and accordingly upheld appellant's appeal.

die hof *a quo* is 'n egskeidingsbevel teen die respondent toegestaan en is 'n verbeuringsbevel teen die appellant verleen. Die appellant het teen die verbeuringsbevel geappelleer onder andere op grond daarvan dat verbeuring nie toegestaan moes gewees het nie omdat die hof *a quo* geen bevinding met betrekking tot wesenlike wangedrag aan sy kant gemaak het nie. Die appellant het ook beweer dat die hof *a quo* gefouteer het deur hom te blameer vir die verbrokkeling van die huwelik en deur te bevind dat dit onregverdig sou wees indien hy sou deel in die onderneming wat deur sy vrou opgebou is. Die Appèlafdeling het gekyk na die vereistes vir die verlening van 'n verbeuringsbevel en ook oorweging geskenk aan die benadering wat 'n appèlhof moet volg wanneer dit 'n appèl teen 'n verbeuringsbevel aanhoor. Die hof het beslis dat die verbeuringsbevel nie uitgereik moes gewees het nie en het gevolglik die appèl gehandhaaf.

VAN COLLER AJA: [726] The respondent's claim for a forfeiture order was based on the provisions of s 9(1) of the Divorce Act 70 of 1979 ('the section') which reads as follows:

'When a decree of divorce is granted on the ground of the irretrievable breakdown of a marriage the Court may make an order that the patrimonial benefits of the marriage be forfeited by one party in favour of the other, either wholly or in part, if the Court, having regard to the duration of the marriage, the circumstances which gave rise to the breakdown thereof and any substantial misconduct on the part of either of the parties, is satisfied that, if the order for forfeiture is not made, the one party will in relation to the other be unduly benefited.'

The learned trial Judge referred to the long duration of the marriage. As regards the circumstances which gave rise to the breakdown of the marriage, he concluded that the main cause of the breakdown of the marriage was the fact that the appellant could not get the shares back from the respondent. The learned trial Judge [HEYNS J] expressed surprise at the appellant's explanation that he considered the respondent's refusal as a breach of trust. He was not impressed by the moral tone adopted by the appellant, which he considered to be insincere. Other significant findings made by the learned trial Judge with regard to the appellant's conduct are that nobody forced him to transfer the 50 shares to the respondent; that he did so from considerations which he did not explain to the Court and that he was bound by his own decision. HEYNS J emphasised the fact that it was the appellant who initiated the divorce proceedings after he had already threatened to do so in 1985. He stated in the judgment that the divorce action was a calculated step by the appellant to obtain half of the shareholding of the company which the respondent was not prepared to give to him. That part of the judgment dealing with the cause of the breakdown of the marriage concludes as follows:

'On what principle of fairness can he be heard to say that he wants half a share of the shareholding of the company, which would result in him being able to have a half share in all the profits that the company makes? It seems to me that his attitude is that because I am married to Mrs Wijker, she must give me a half share in this company, although she is the person who works hard and conducts the affairs of the company.'

The learned trial Judge had not made any findings with regard to the third factor mentioned in the section, namely substantial misconduct. He [727] did not refer to any such conduct and he made the following concluding remarks with regard to the three factors referred to in the section:

'Bearing these considerations in mind, I find that on a balance of probabilities, I am satisfied that if an order of forfeiture is not made as asked by Mrs Wijker, Mr Wijker will in relation to Mrs Wijker be unduly benefited. He will share in the company and its assets whilst he made hardly any contribution towards its management and administration and so did not help it to earn its profits. As I have already said, he has during the subsistence of the marriage enjoyed the financial advantages from the income which Mrs Wijker earned from the company, but apparently he is not satisfied with that. He wants to hold half of the shares of the company in his own name.'

Before dealing with the merits of the appeal, it is necessary to consider the approach that should be adopted on appeal in this matter. Counsel for the respondent contended that the decision that the appellant would be unduly benefited had been reached in the exercise of a judicial discretion. The power of this Court to interfere with this decision, according to this argument, is limited and it can only do so if the discretion of the Court *a quo* is shown to have been unjudicial in one or more of the respects mentioned in *Ex parte Neethling and Others* 1951 (4) SA 331 (A) at 335D–E. I cannot agree with this contention.

It is obvious from the wording of the section that the first step is to determine whether or not the party against whom the order is sought will in fact be benefited. That will be purely a factual issue. Once that has been established the trial Court must determine, having regard to the factors mentioned in the section, whether or not that party will in relation to the other be unduly benefited if a forfeiture order is not made. Although the second determination is a value judgment, it is made by the trial Court after having considered the facts falling within the compass of the three factors mentioned in the section. In dealing with the manner in which an appeal in an unfair labour practice dispute should be approached, EM GROSSKOPF JA made the following remarks in *Media Workers Association of South Africa and Others v Press Corporation of South Africa Ltd* ('Perskor') 1992 (4) SA 791 (A) at 800C–G:

'However, as I stated above, the word discretion is used here in a wide sense. Henning "Diskresie-uitoefening" in 1968 *THRHR* 155 at 158 quotes the following observation concerning discretionary powers:

" '(A) truly discretionary power is characterised by the fact that a number of courses are available to the repository of the power' (Rubinstein *Jurisdiction and Illegality* (1956) at 16)."'

The essence of a discretion in this narrower sense is that, if the repository of the power follows any one of the available courses, he would be acting within his powers, and his exercise of power could not be set aside merely because a Court would have preferred him to have followed a different course among those available to him. I do not think the power to determine that certain facts constitute an unfair labour practice is discretionary in that sense. Such a determination is a judgment made by a Court in the light of all relevant considerations. It does not involve a choice between permissible alternatives. In respect of such a judgment a Court of appeal may, in principle, well come to a different conclusion from that reached by the Court *a quo* on the merits of the matter.'

These remarks are in my view of equal application in this matter. To determine whether a party would be unduly benefited, a trial Court would [728] certainly not be exercising a discretion in the narrower sense. Here too no choice between permissible alternatives is involved. In considering the appeal this Court is therefore not limited by the principles set out in *Ex parte Neethling (supra)* and it may differ from the Court *a quo* on the merits. It is only after the Court has concluded that a party would be unduly benefited that it is empowered to order a forfeiture of benefits, and in making this decision it exercises a discretion in the narrower sense. It is difficult to visualise circumstances where a Court would then decide not to grant a forfeiture order. This discretionary power may be more apparent than real but it is not an issue in this appeal and no more need be said about it.

I now turn to consider the merits of the appeal. Mr *Van der Merwe*, who appeared on behalf of the appellant, advanced three arguments in support of his contention that the appeal should be upheld. He firstly submitted that because no finding of substantial misconduct on the part of the appellant had been made, forfeiture could not have been decreed. His second contention related to the extracts from the judgment quoted above and to the blameworthy conduct of the appellant referred to by the learned trial Judge. Mr *Van der Merwe* submitted that the Court *a quo* misdirected itself in blaming the appellant for the breakdown of the marriage and in taking into account that it was unfair that the appellant should share in a company which the respondent made successful. Mr *Van der Merwe's* third argument was that it was not possible on the evidence to find that the respondent had in fact contributed more to the common estate than the appellant, or, if so, to what extent. The evidence with regard to the value of the parties' respective contributions is certainly not satisfactory and the third argument is not without merit. In view of the conclusion to which I have come with regard to the second argument it is not necessary to deal any further with this contention. It will be assumed in favour of the respondent that the respondent had in fact contributed more to the common estate than the appellant. It is strictly speaking also not necessary to deal with the first argument but in view of conflicting decisions on that issue I propose to do so.

In support of his first argument, Mr *Van der Merwe* relied on *Matyila v Matyila* 1987 (3) SA 230 (W) where it was held that if a party failed to prove substantial misconduct, forfeiture could not be decreed. VAN ZYL J, with whom O'DONOVAN AJ concurred, held all three factors to which a Court must have regard should be alleged and proved and said the following at 234G:

'On a proper interpretation of this section, it would appear that all three factors should in fact be both alleged and proved. There is no indication that the Court may have reference to only the one or the other. Had the section read differently insofar as there was a reference to "any other factor which may be relevant" or had the word "or" or some similar word indicating alternative possibilities been used, then Mr *Wepener's* argument may hold water.'

This judgment was apparently not brought to the attention of KRIEGLER J when he decided the matter of *Klerck v Klerck* 1991 (1) SA 265 (W). In that case counsel on behalf of the plaintiff argued that not only was substantial misconduct a precondition to the granting of a forfeiture order, but that all [729] three factors mentioned in the section were preconditions. In rejecting this argument KRIEGLER J dealt fully with the wording and context of the section and said the following at 269D-G:

'Bowendien, en laastens, meen ek dat die interpretasie waarvoor mnr *Kruger* betoog [that is that all three factors had to be present]; geweld doen aan die woorde van die subartikel soos hulle daar staan. Dit is wel so dat die drietal faktore gekoppel word deur die koppelwoord "en". 'n Mens kan jou egter nie blindstaar op daardie koppelwoord nie. Wat die Wetgewer duidelik met sy woordkeuse aandui, is dat die Hof die drie genoemde faktore in ag moet neem. Ek weet van geen taalkundige manier om drie faktore te noem wat saam in een verband genoem word, anders as om hulle met 'n "en" te koppel nie. Die Wetgewer wou juis nie die koppelwoord "of" gebruik nie omdat hy aan die Hof die opdrag wou gee om breed en wyd te kyk na die drie kategorieë faktore. *Non constat* [(it is not evident)] egter, dat as een van hulle ontbreek, die diskresie te niet gaan. As dit die bedoeling van die Wetgewer was, dan kon daardie bedoeling baie maklik deur ander woordkeuse so uitgespel gewees het.

Myns insiens is die duidelike betekenis van die woorde wat the Wetgewer gebruik het dat ek myself moet afvra of daar *in casu* onbehoorlike bevoordeling van die eiseres sal wees indien daar nie 'n verbeuringsbevel gemaak word nie. Ten einde daardie vraag te beantwoord, moet ek kyk na die duur van die huwelik, die verbrokkelingsomstandighede en, indien teenwoordig, wesenlike wangedrag aan die kant van óf eiseres, óf verweerder, óf albei.'

I am in full agreement with these passages and in my judgment LEVESON J in *Binda v Binda* 1993 (2) SA 123 (W) correctly held that the decision in *Matyila v Matyila (supra)* was clearly wrong. The context and the subject-matter make it abundantly clear that the Legislature could never have intended that the factors mentioned in the section should be considered cumulatively. As was pointed out by LEVESON J in *Binda v Binda (supra* at 126A–B) the following statement by INNES CJ in *Barlin v Licensing Court for the Cape* 1924 AD 472 is apposite also with regard to the interpretation of the section here in issue:

'Now the words "and" and "or" are sometimes inaccurately used; and there are many cases in which one of them has been held to be the equivalent of the other. Much depends on the context and the subject-matter. I cannot think that in this instance the Legislature intended to make these provisions cumulative.'

Mr *Van der Merwe's* first argument can therefore not be upheld.

The second and main argument on behalf of the appellant relates to the two overriding considerations which persuaded HEYNS J that the appellant would be unduly benefited should a forfeiture order not be granted. Although he found that the main cause for the breakdown of the marriage was the fact that the appellant could not get his shares back, he also found that it was brought about solely by the appellant and burdened him with all the blame. Secondly, the extracts from his judgment referred to above, clearly indicate that the learned trial Judge was strongly influenced by what he found as a fact, namely that should a forfeiture order not be made, the appellant would share in the company and its assets while having made hardly any contribution towards its management and administration, which he considered to be unfair. I have little doubt that notwithstanding the introduction into our law of the 'no fault' principle to divorce, a party's misconduct may be taken into account in considering the circumstances which gave rise to the breakdown of the marriage. The words 'the [730] circumstances which gave rise to the breakdown' of the marriage are words of wide import and as KRIEGLER J also pointed out in *Klerck v Klerck (supra)* this factor has been stated in broad terms. The fact that substantial misconduct has been included as a third factor does not in my opinion exclude a consideration of misconduct as a circumstance which gave rise to the breakdown of the marriage. Substantial misconduct may include conduct which has nothing to do with the breakdown of a marriage and may for that and other reasons have been included as a separate factor. Too much importance should, however, not be attached to misconduct which is not of a serious nature. In regard to a Court's assessment of a party's misconduct as a relevant factor under ss (2) and (3) of s 7 of the Divorce Act 70 of 1979, BOTHA JA made the following remarks in *Beaumont v Beaumont* 1987 (1) SA 967 (A) at 994D–E [117]:

'... (I)n my opinion the Court is entitled, in terms of the wide words of para (d) of ss (5) that I have quoted, to take a party's misconduct into account even when only a redistribution order is being considered under ss (3), and where no maintenance order under ss (2) is made. But I should add at once that I am convinced that our Courts will adopt a conservative approach in assessing a party's misconduct as a relevant factor, whether under ss (2) or ss (3).'

And at 994I *in fin*–995A he said the following:

'In many, probably most, cases, both parties will be to blame, in the sense of having contributed to the breakdown of the marriage (see per LORD DENNING in *Wachtel's* case *supra* at 835g [*Wachtel v Wachtel* [1973] 1 All ER 829 (CA)]. In such cases, where there is no conspicuous disparity between the conduct of the one party and that of the other, our Courts will not indulge in an exercise to apportion the fault of the parties, and thus nullify the advantages of the "no fault" system of divorce.'

These remarks apply with equal validity when a Court, in considering the circumstances which gave rise to the breakdown of the marriage, also assesses a party's misconduct as a relevant factor.

HEYNS J, however, in taking the appellant's conduct into account as one of the factors which contributed to the breakdown of the marriage, misdirected himself. The finding that the appellant transferred the shares out of considerations which he did not explain, is factually incorrect. It is common cause that the appellant transferred the shares at the auditor's suggestion to enable the respondent to obtain certain income tax benefits. The learned trial Judge then went on to say that the appellant had by his own decision transferred the shares and was bound thereby. This is not quite correct and does not put the facts in a true and correct perspective. It was clearly not the intention that the respondent should keep the shares on a permanent basis. There was an undertaking that the appellant could have an option to buy the shares back. Even if the respondent was initially prepared to grant an option, she later refused to do so. The conclusion that the appellant was insincere in regarding the respondent's refusal as a breach of trust was clearly founded on a wrong premise. It seems to me that in putting all the blame on the appellant, the trial Court has also been guilty of a one-sided approach. No criticism has been levelled at the respondent who, in November 1990, wrote to the appellant and gave him three weeks to think about his demands and to make a choice between her and the shares. This letter reveals an uncompromising attitude and is [731] something like an ultimatum. The respondent was not really justified in refusing to return the shares and her reasons for doing so were not convincing. She was not prepared to give the shares back even if it resulted in a divorce. On the other hand, the appellant was not prepared to abandon his claim to the shares and sued for divorce in order to get them. The conduct of the appellant and that of the respondent with regard to the shares issue was equally unrelenting, and in considering the circumstances which led to the breakdown of the marriage it was wrong to put all the blame on the appellant.

The only remaining factor which persuaded the Court *a quo* to grant the forfeiture order is that it was considered unfair that the appellant should share in the company and its assets while he had made hardly any contribution towards its management, administration and profit-making. The finding that the appellant would be unduly benefited if a forfeiture order was not made, was therefore based on a principle of fairness. It seems to me that the learned trial Judge, in adopting this approach, lost sight of what a marriage in community of property really entails. HR Hahlo in *The South African Law of Husband and Wife* 5th ed at 157–8 describes community of property as follows:

'Community of property is a universal economic partnership of the spouses. All their assets and liabilities are merged in a joint estate, in which both spouses, irrespective of the value of their financial contributions, hold equal shares.'

The fact that the appellant is entitled to share in the successful business established by the respondent is a consequence of their marriage in community of property. In making a value judgment this equitable principle applied by the Court *a quo* is not justified. Not only is it contrary to the basic concept of community of property, but there is no provision in the section for the application of such a principle. Even if it is assumed that the appellant made no contribution to the success of the business and that the benefit which he will receive will be a substantial one, it does not necessarily follow that he will be unduly benefited. Compare *Engelbrecht v Engelbrecht* 1989 (1) SA 597 (C) at 601F–G. The benefit that will be received cannot be viewed in isolation, but in order to determine whether a party will be unduly benefited the Court must have regard to the factors mentioned in the section. In my judgment the approach adopted by the Court *a quo* in concluding that the appellant would be unduly benefited should a forfeiture order not be granted was clearly wrong.

It is plain on the evidence that a forfeiture order should not have been granted. The marriage lasted for a very long time, approximately 35 years. The appellant was the only breadwinner of the family over a period of almost 20 years and he rendered more than adequate support to the children and to the respondent. It was only after the respondent's business was successfully established that she also started to contribute to the expenses of the joint household. Initially the appellant assisted the respondent in the estate agency business. When it became successful he did not rest on his laurels but continued with his own employment and he also started a business. If this business was not a very successful one it does not appear to have been due to a lack of interest or application on the part of the appellant and it is in any event not really relevant. The marriage was [732] reasonably happy until 1983 and it can be accepted that the parties became estranged mainly as a result of the fact that the respondent became successful in business. It seems that the appellant found it difficult to cope with this situation and this was probably one of the circumstances which gave rise to the breakdown of the marriage. The appellant's conduct can certainly not be ignored but it must be assessed with all the other circumstances. One must also bear in mind that the final breakdown came as a result of the shares issue and on this issue the respondent's conduct was certainly not beyond reproach. Having regard to all the circumstances and to the fact that no substantial misconduct has been proved against the appellant it cannot, in my judgment, be concluded that the appellant will be unduly benefited should an order of forfeiture, as claimed by the respondent, not be made. The appeal must therefore succeed . . .

JOUBERT JA and EKSTEEN JA concurred.

Note

This case at long last settled the dispute about whether the three factors set out in section 9(1) of the Divorce Act 70 of 1979 must all be present before an order for forfeiture can be granted and particularly whether substantial misconduct is a prerequisite for the making of a forfeiture order.

In *Matyila v Matyila* 1987 (3) SA 230 (W) it was held that all three factors must be alleged and proved and that a forfeiture order cannot be made in the absence of proof of substantial misconduct.

In *Engelbrecht v Engelbrecht* 1989 1 SA 597 (C) the court referred to *Matyila v Matyila* and to *Singh v Singh* [113] in respect of the view that substantial

Aantekening

Hierdie saak het uiteindelik die dispuut opgelos oor die vraag of die drie faktore wat in artikel 9(1) van die Wet op Egskeiding 70 van 1979 genoem word almal teenwoordig moet wees voordat 'n verbeuringsbevel uitgereik kan word, en in die besonder of wesenlike wangedrag 'n vereiste is voordat 'n verbeuringsbevel verleen kan word.

In *Matyila v Matyila* 1987 (3) SA 230 (W) is beslis dat al drie faktore beweer en bewys moet word en dat 'n verbeuringsbevel nie uitgereik kan word indien wesenlike wangedrag nie bewys is nie.

In *Engelbrecht v Engelbrecht* 1989 1 SA 597 (K) het die hof na *Matyila v Matyila* en *Singh v Singh* [113]

misconduct must be proved. It was stated, however, in an *obiter dictum*, that the legislature did not intend misconduct to be more important than any of the other factors which are to be considered when the court has to decide whether or not to make an order for forfeiture. The court warned that if too much emphasis was placed on misconduct the advantages of the no-fault divorce law would be lost.

In *Klerck v Klerck* 1991 (1) SA 265 (W) the decision in *Matyila* was not referred to, apparently because it had not been brought to the attention of the judge. The court held in *Klerck* that the legislature did not intend that the three factors all had to be present and that they had to be viewed cumulatively. The legislature intended only that those factors that are present must be given consideration.

The next decision to deal with the three factors listed in section 9(1) was *Binda v Binda* 1993 (2) SA 123 (W). The court held that the decision in *Matyila v Matyila* was clearly wrong in so far as it held that substantial misconduct was an essential requirement for an order of forfeiture. In *Binda* the court held that the legislature required each of the three factors to be given due and proper weight in assessing whether a party had been benefited unduly but that these factors were not cumulative in the sense that they all had to be present before a forfeiture order could be made.

In *Wijker v Wijker* the Appellate Division held, in respect of the issue whether substantial misconduct is a prerequisite for an order for forfeiture, that the context and subject-matter of section 9(1) make it abundantly clear that the legislature never intended that the three factors mentioned in section 9(1) should be considered cumulatively. The Appellate Division approved of the decision in *Klerck v Klerck* and also confirmed the rejection in *Binda v Binda* of the decision in *Matyila v Matyila*.

The decision in *Wijker* is important in another respect: It set out the approach which a court of appeal must follow when hearing an appeal in respect of an order for forfeiture of patrimonial benefits. It held that the decision whether a party would be unduly benefited is not reached merely in the exercise of a judicial discretion, with which the court of appeal can interfere only if the discretion is unjudicially exercised. The Appellate

verwys in verband met die standpunt dat wesenlike wangedrag bewys moet word. Die hof het egter in 'n *obiter dictum* verklaar dat die wetgewer nie bedoel het dat wangedrag belangriker is as enige van die ander faktore wat oorweeg moet word wanneer die hof besluit of 'n verbeuringsbevel uitgereik moet word nie. Die hof het gemaan dat indien te veel klem gelê word op wangedrag die voordele van die geen-skuld egskeidingsreg tot niet sal gaan.

In *Klerck v Klerck* 1991 (1) SA 265 (W) is daar nie na die beslissing in *Matyila* verwys nie, oënskynlik omdat die beslissing nie onder die aandag van die regter gebring is nie. In *Klerck* het die hof beslis dat die wetgewer nie bedoel het dat al drie die faktore aanwesig moet wees en dat hulle kumulatief oorweeg moet word nie. Die wetgewer het net bedoel dat die faktore wat aanwesig is, oorweeg moet word.

Die volgende beslissing wat oor die drie faktore in artikel 9(1) gehandel het, was *Binda v Binda* 1993 (2) SA 123 (W). Die hof het beslis dat die uitspraak in *Matyila v Matyila* duidelik verkeerd was vir sover daar beslis is dat wesenlike wangedrag 'n onontbeerlike vereiste vir 'n verbeuringsbevel is. In *Binda* het die hof beslis dat die wetgewer vereis dat elk van die drie faktore behoorlike oorweging moet geniet wanneer die hof besluit of 'n party onbehoorlik bevoordeel is maar dat hierdie faktore nie kumulatief is in die sin dat hulle almal teenwoordig moet wees voordat 'n verbeuringsbevel uitgereik mag word nie.

In *Wijker v Wijker* het die Appèlafdeling met betrekking tot die vraag of wesenlike wangedrag 'n vereiste is vir 'n verbeuringsbevel beslis dat die konteks en inhoud van artikel 9(1) dit baie duidelik maak dat die wetgewer nooit bedoel het dat al drie die faktore wat in artikel 9(1) genoem word kumulatief aanwesig moet wees nie. Die Appèlafdeling het die beslissing in *Klerck v Klerck* goedgekeur en ook die verwerping in *Binda v Binda* van die beslissing in *Matyila v Matyila* bevestig.

Die beslissing in *Wijker* is ook in 'n ander verband van belang: Dit het die benadering uiteengesit wat 'n appèlhof moet volg wanneer dit 'n appèl in verband met 'n verbeuringsbevel aanhoor. Die hof het beslis dat die beslissing of 'n party onbehoorlik bevoordeel word nie op 'n blote judisiële diskresie berus nie. Met sodanige diskresie kan die appèlhof slegs inmeng indien die dis-

Division held that in determining whether an order for forfeiture should be made the court should first determine whether or not the party against whom the order is sought will in fact be benefited if the order is not made. That, the Appellate Division held, is a purely factual issue. Once it is determined that that party will benefit, the court must determine whether there will be undue benefit. Although this will involve a value judgment, the value judgment is made after having considered the three factors mentioned in section 9(1). The court therefore does not merely exercise a judicial discretion. (See also *Engelbrecht v Engelbrecht* where it was held that it must first be proved what the nature and extent of the benefit is. Only once that has been proved will the court consider whether the benefit is an undue one. It will do so by taking the three factors listed in section 9(1) into consideration.)

It is also important to note that the court stated that the introduction of no-fault divorce did not do away with misconduct as a factor to be considered when forfeiture of benefits is at issue. (See also *Singh v Singh* [113].) The Appellate Division held that misconduct can be considered because it falls within the ambit of "the circumstances which gave rise to the break-down" as contemplated in section 9(1). The fact that "substantial misconduct" has been included as a separate factor in section 9(1) does not exclude consideration of misconduct as a circumstance which gave rise to the breakdown of the marriage. "Substantial misconduct may include conduct which has nothing to do with the breakdown of a marriage and may for that and other reasons have been included as a separate factor" (730). On the facts of the case the Appellate Division found that the trial court had misdirected itself in taking into account the appellant's conduct as one of the factors which contributed to the breakdown of the marriage.

Lastly, the court's decision that sight must not be lost of what the matrimonial property system which operates in the marriage entails, is important. The court held that, in finding that it would be unfair to allow the appellant to share in his wife's estate agency, the judge in the court *a quo* lost sight of what community of property entails. That the appellant is entitled to share in his wife's business is a consequence of commu-

kresie onbehoorlik uitgeoefen is. Die Appèlafdeling het beslis dat, wanneer besluit word of 'n verbeuringsbevel uitgereik moet word, die hof eerstens moet bepaal of die party teen wie die bevel uitgereik staan te word inderdaad bevoordeel sal word indien die bevel nie uitgereik word nie. Dit, het die Appèlafdeling beslis, is 'n bloot feitevraag. Sodra vasgestel is dat die betrokke party bevoordeel sal word, moet die hof bepaal of daar 'n onbehoorlike bevoordeling sal wees. Alhoewel dít 'n waarde-oordeel behels, word hierdie waarde-oordeel gemaak na inagneming van die drie faktore wat in artikel 9(1) genoem word. Die hof oefen gevolglik nie bloot 'n judisiële diskresie uit nie. (Sien ook *Engelbrecht v Engelbrecht* waar beslis is dat daar eerstens bewys moet word wat die aard en omvang van die bevoordeling is. Eers nadat dit vasgestel is, sal die hof bepaal of die bevoordeling onbehoorlik is. Dit sal die hof doen deur die drie faktore in artikel 9(1) in ag te neem.)

Dit is ook belangrik om daarop te let dat die hof gesê het dat die invoering van die geen-skuld egskeidingsreg nie beteken dat wangedrag glad nie 'n faktor is wat by oorweging van 'n verbeuringsbevel in ag geneem word nie. (Sien ook *Singh v Singh* [113].) Die Appèlafdeling het beslis dat wangedrag wel in ag geneem kan word omdat dit binne die omvang val van "die omstandighede wat tot die verbrokkeling ... aanleiding gegee het", soos bedoel in artikel 9(1). Die feit dat "wesenlike wangedrag" as 'n aparte faktor in artikel 9(1) ingesluit word, beteken nie dat wangedrag as 'n omstandigheid wat aanleiding gegee het tot die verbrokkeling van die huwelik nie oorweeg moet word nie. "Substantial misconduct may include conduct which has nothing to do with the breakdown of a marriage and may for that and other reasons have been included as a separate factor" (730). Op grond van die feite van die saak het die Appèlafdeling beslis dat die hof *a quo* gefouteer het deur die appellant se wangedrag in ag te neem as een van die faktore wat gelei het tot die verbrokkeling van die huwelik.

Laastens beslis die hof dat die betekenis van die betrokke huweliksgoederebedeling wat in die huwelik geld nie uit die oog verloor moet word nie. Die hof het beslis dat die hof *a quo* gefouteer het deur te bevind dat dit onbillik sou wees om die appellant toe te laat om te deel in sy vrou se eiendomsagentskap. Sodoende het die hof *a quo* uit die oog verloor wat gemeenskap van goed

nity of property. The court held that section 9 does not provide for the application of the principle of fairness in order to deviate from the nature of community of property. In this respect the decision in *Engelbrecht v Engelbrecht* 1989 1 SA 597 (C) must also be noted. Here the court held that the starting point in an application for forfeiture must be that the parties must be held to their antenuptial undertakings. In this case, as in *Wijker,* the parties were married in community of property. The court stated (601) that: "Toe die appellante en die respondent in die huwelik getree het, was dit op die grondslag dat hulle uitdruklik of stilswyend ooreenkom dat elkeen mede-eienaar van die ander se goed word. Mede-eienaarskap van die ander gade se goed is 'n reg wat elk van die egliede by die huweliksluiting verwerf. Tensy die partye ... presies gelyke bydraes tot die [gemeenskaplike] boedel gemaak het, sal die een wat minder bygedra het by ontbinding van die huwelik bo die ander bevoordeel word as verbeuring nie beveel word nie. Dit is 'n onafwendbare gevolg van die partye se huweliksgoederebedeling. Die Wetgewer gee dan ook nie aan die groter bydraer die geleentheid om hom hieroor te bekla nie. Hy kan hom slegs oor *onbehoorlike* bevoordeling bekla" (our emphasis).

behels. Dat die appellant in sy vrou se besigheid kan deel, is 'n gevolg van gemeenskap van goed. Die hof het beslis dat artikel 9 nie bepaal dat die beginsel van billikheid gebruik kan word om af te wyk van die aard van gemeenskap van goed nie. In hierdie verband moet ook gelet word op die uitspraak in *Engelbrecht v Engelbrecht* 1989 1 SA 597 (K). Hier het die hof beslis dat die uitgangspunt by die besluit of 'n verbeuringsbevel uitgereik moet word, moet wees dat gades gebonde gehou moet word aan hulle voorhuwelikse ooreenkomste. In hierdie saak, soos in *Wijker,* was die partye binne gemeenskap van goed getroud. Die hof het verklaar (601): "Toe die appellante en die respondent in die huwelik getree het, was dit op die grondslag dat hulle uitdruklik of stilswyend ooreenkom dat elkeen mede-eienaar van die ander se goed word. Mede-eienaarskap van die ander gade se goed is 'n reg wat elk van die egliede by die huweliksluiting verwerf. Tensy die partye ... presies gelyke bydraes tot die [gemeenskaplike] boedel gemaak het, sal die een wat minder bygedra het by ontbinding van die huwelik bo die ander bevoordeel word as verbeuring nie beveel word nie. Dit is 'n onafwendbare gevolg van die partye se huweliksgoederebedeling. Die Wetgewer gee dan ook nie aan die groter bydraer die geleentheid om hom hieroor te bekla nie. Hy kan hom slegs oor *onbehoorlike* bevoordeling bekla" (ons beklemtoning).

What can be forfeited?

Wat kan verbeur word?

[115]   WATT V WATT

1984 2 SA 455 (W)

Forfeiture of patrimonial benefits

The plaintiff (husband) and first defendant (wife) were married to each other out of community of property. During the course of the marriage the plaintiff donated a house to the first defendant. In a joint application they applied for certain questions of law to be decided before evidence was led in the action. For purposes of arguing the questions of law the parties agreed upon the following facts:

Verbeuring van vermoënsregtelike voordele

Die eiser (man) en die eerste verweerderes was buite gemeenskap van goed met mekaar getroud. Die eiser het gedurende die huwelik 'n huis aan die eerste verweerderes geskenk. Hulle het gesamentlik aansoek gedoen dat sekere regsvrae beslis moes word voordat getuienis in die saak gelei word. Vir doeleindes van beredenering van die regsvrae het die partye oor die volgende feite ooreengekom:

(a) that the plaintiff alone had contributed the purchase price of the property as well as all amounts expended on improvements to the property.

(b) that the value of the property had escalated since it was registered in the name of the first defendant.

The court had to decide whether the house was a patrimonial benefit of the marriage as contemplated in section 9(1) of the Divorce Act 70 of 1979 and was therefore subject to a possible forfeiture. If the answer was no, the court was asked to rule on whether any contributions made by the plaintiff referred to in (a) above were patrimonial benefits of the marriage as contemplated in section 9(1) of the Divorce Act and therefore subject to a possible forfeiture; and whether the escalation in value of the property could be the subject of a separate claim and if so whether the amount of such escalation in value was a patrimonial benefit of the marriage as contemplated in section 9(1) of the Divorce Act and therefore subject to a possible forfeiture.

The plaintiff contended that the answers to these questions were affirmative while the first defendant contended that the answers were negative. The court held that the property, the plaintiff's contributions and the escalation in the value of the property were not patrimonial benefits of the marriage.

(a) dat die eiser alleen vir betaling van die koopprys van die eiendom en verbeteringe daaraan verantwoordelik was.

(b) dat die waarde van die eiendom vermeerder het sedert dit in die naam van die eerste verweerderes geregistreer is.

Die hof moes beslis of die huis ingevolge artikel 9(1) van die Wet op Egskeiding 70 van 1979 'n vermoënsregtelike voordeel van die huwelik was wat dus moontlik verbeur sou kon word. As hierdie vraag negatief beantwoord sou word, is die hof gevra om te beslis oor die vraag of enige bydraes deur die eiser, waarna hierbo in (a) verwys is, ingevolge artikel 9(1) van die Wet op Egskeiding vermoënsregtelike voordele van die huwelik was wat moontlik verbeur sou kon word; en of die waardevermeerdering van die eiendom die voorwerp van 'n aparte eis kon vorm, en indien wel, of sodanige waardevermeerdering ingevolge artikel 9(1) van die Wet op Egskeiding 'n vermoënsregtelike voordeel van die huwelik was wat moontlik verbeur sou kon word.

Die eiser het aangevoer dat die antwoorde op hierdie vrae bevestigend was terwyl die eerste verweerderes beweer het dat die vrae ontkennend beantwoord moes word. Die hof het beslis dat die eiendom, die eiser se bydraes en die waardevermeerdering van die eiendom nie vermoënsregtelike voordele van die huwelik was nie.

MELAMET J: [457] Section 9(1) of the Divorce Act 70 of 1979 provides:

"(1) When a decree of divorce is granted on the ground of irretrievable breakdown of a marriage the Court may make an order that the patrimonial benefits of the marriage be forfeited by one party in favour of the other, either wholly or in part, if the Court, having regard to the duration of the marriage, the circumstances which gave rise to the breakdown thereof and any substantial misconduct on the part of either of the parties, is satisfied that, if the order for forfeiture is not made, the one party will in relation to the other be unduly benefited." . . .

[460] I am of the opinion that the effect of an order for forfeiture on divorce in a marriage by antenuptial contract, prior to the present Act [ie the Divorce Act 70 of 1979], was only that the guilty spouse forfeits the benefits which have accrued to him under the contract as well as those which are to accrue in the future.

In this connection I refer also to Hahlo and Sinclair *The Reform of the SA Law of Divorce*

at 51; *Lee and Honore* [*Family, Things and Succession*] at 143); Sinclair "Financial Provisions on Divorce" (1981) 98 *SALJ* 469 at 471; Van Wyk 43 (1980) *THRHR* 429 at 433.

Counsel for plaintiff did not dispute the above to be the common law but contended that the position had been changed, substantially, by s 9 of the Divorce Act which is set out above. Counsel for the first defendant, on the other hand, contended that only limited change had been brought about by the section, namely that it conferred a discretion on the Court to order forfeiture on the application of the innocent spouse; under common law the innocent spouse had a right to such an order, and the Court could now order a partial forfeiture whereas previously it could order only complete forfeiture. There is authority for the contention advanced on behalf of the first defendant. *Rousalis v Rousalis* 1980 (3) SA 446 (C) at 450; *Singh v Singh* 1983 (1) SA 781 (C) at 788–789 [113]. The latter case is based on the views expressed in *Hahlo and Sinclair* (*supra* at 51–52). As set out above, it was contended on behalf of the plaintiff, that the situation had been altered substantially by s 9 of the Divorce Act and not only to the limited extent contended for on behalf of first defendant. It is contended on behalf of the plaintiff that, having granted a decree of divorce on the grounds that the marriage is irretrievably broken down, a Court will pose the question: are there any patrimonial benefits of the marriage? And, if there are such benefits, then the Court will pass on to consider whether one party will be unduly benefited if an order for forfeiture of the benefits, either in whole or partially, is not made. In considering whether a party will be so unduly benefited, the Court will have regard to the duration of the marriage, the circumstances which gave rise to the breakdown of the marriage and any substantial misconduct on the part of either of the parties. It is only then that the fault on the part of either of the parties becomes relevant and subject to consideration.

It was contended, on behalf of the plaintiff, that the ownership of the asset is not a criterion nor is the question whether the marriage is [461] one in or out of community of profit. On the above contention it makes no difference on divorce whether the marriage was in or out of community of property. It is contended that for the limited purpose of deciding on proprietary consequences of the marriage on divorce, the Legislature intended to treat both classes of marriage on the same basis and do away with the distinction.

The above contentions assume that patrimonial benefits of the marriage are the same irrespective of how the parties were married. It is clear that s 9 can only become operative if there are patrimonial benefits of the marriage in existence at the time of the divorce. For purposes of the judgment, I shall assume, without deciding the issue, that a patrimonial benefit is a benefit in respect of property which is capable of pecuniary assessment as contended for on behalf of the plaintiff. It is not patrimonial benefits, *simpliciter*, but patrimonial benefits of the marriage.

I was referred to the definition of the word "of" in the *Shorter Oxford English Dictionary* and it was contended that the apposite meaning was that "indicating means or instrument". The meaning indicating the origin or source would appear to me to be the applicable meaning. I am of the opinion that the more correct meaning is the benefits arising on the marriage. The phrase "of the marriage" is the traditional phrase that appears in the Roman-Dutch authorities and which has a particular meaning. Those are the benefits which arise on the marriage of the parties. Those benefits are determined on the marriage and I am in agreement with the *dicta* of VAN DEN HEEVER J in *Rousalis v Rousalis* (*supra* at 450E)

"that the patrimonial benefits of a marriage out of community are fixed at marriage by the terms of the parties' antenuptial contract".

It is to be noted that the Legislature has used the old expressions in the Divorce Act. On this basis, on divorce, in a marriage by antenuptial contract, the benefits fixed in the

antenuptial contract are those which come under consideration. On divorce, in a marriage within community of property, the pecuniary benefits which flow from such marriage come under consideration. Section 9, in my view, does not and could not have been intended to have the effect on divorce of empowering the Court to order a redistribution of property irrespective of whether the marriage was in or out of community of property.

It was contended on behalf of the plaintiff that the gift of the house by the plaintiff to the first defendant during the marriage was a benefit which arises from the marriage. It is submitted that the benefit derives because first defendant is married to the plaintiff and but for the marriage he would not have given it to her. I am of the opinion that the benefits which are liable to be forfeited are those which are derived either by virtue of the legal effect of the marriage in community of property or by virtue of a provision made in an antenuptial contract. This accords with the Roman-Dutch law authorities and the decided cases prior to the Divorce Act. A gift during marriage does not fall under these headings, and it is something which flows from the relationship developed between the parties subsequent to the marriage – as such it is not a benefit of the marriage. If the relationship [462] was not good, I should imagine that the plaintiff would not have made the gift. The marriage led to the relationship but it is the subsequent relationship which is the cause of the gift and not the marriage itself.

The gift of the house by the plaintiff to the defendant was not made in terms of the antenuptial contract governing the marriage between the parties and was made subsequently during the existence of the marriage. In my opinion, it is not a patrimonial benefit of the marriage and does not fall to be dealt with in terms of s 9 of the Divorce Act.

The contributions were all made subsequent to the marriage and by the same reasoning these would also not be patrimonial benefits of the marriage.

In view of my finding that the property is not a patrimonial benefit of the marriage, it follows that any escalation in the value of such property is also not a patrimonial benefit of the marriage.

In the result, I uphold the contentions of the first defendant and dismiss those of the plaintiff . . .

Note

This case deals with the question of whether patrimonial benefits of a marriage out of community of property which may be forfeited, are limited to benefits conferred in the antenuptial contract or whether benefits acquired during the subsistence of the marriage are also subject to forfeiture. The court was of the opinion that the patrimonial benefits of a marriage out of community of property are fixed at marriage by the terms of the parties' antenuptial contract. This accords with the weight of Roman Dutch authority. The views of the old authorities have been followed in a number of cases (see for example *Dawson v Dawson* (1892) 9 SC 446; *Celliers v Celliers* 1904 TS 926; *Ferguson v Ferguson* 1906 EDC 218; *Kilroe v Kilroe* 1928 WLD 112; *Swil v Swil* 1978 1 SA 790 (W); *Rousalis v Rousalis* 1980 3 SA 446 (C)). In other cases it was, however,

Aantekening

Hierdie saak het te doen met die vraag of die vermoënsregtelike voordele van 'n huwelik buite gemeenskap van goed wat verbeur kan word, beperk is tot die voordele wat in die huweliksvoorwaardeskontrak verleen is en of voordele wat gedurende die bestaan van die huwelik verkry is ook vir verbeuring vatbaar is. Die hof was van mening dat die vermoënsregtelike voordele van 'n huwelik buite gemeenskap van goed by huweliksluiting in die partye se huweliksvoorwaardeskontrak vasgelê word. Dit is in ooreenstemming met die opvattings van die meerderheid van die Romeins-Hollandse skrywers. Die menings van die ou skrywers is ook dikwels deur die howe gevolg (sien byvoorbeeld *Dawson v Dawson* (1892) 9 SC 446; *Celliers v Celliers* 1904 TS 926; *Ferguson v Ferguson* 1906 OD 218; *Kilroe v Kilroe* 1928 WPA 112; *Swil v*

held that benefits obtained during the subsistence of the marriage were also subject to forfeiture (*Kohn v Kohn* 1914 WLD 9; *Martin v Martin* 1925 EDL 264; *Bhengu v Bhengu* 1949 4 SA 22 (N)). In *Watt's* case MELAMET J, however, found that none of these cases were based on authority.

Hahlo (1984 *SALJ* 456) criticises the decision in *Watt's* case. He is of the opinion that the word "marriage" is ambiguous. It may mean the ceremony itself or the relationship established by it. He argues that the phrase "benefits of the marriage" should be interpreted as benefits which flow from the marriage as a continuing relationship since this is more in accordance with the natural meaning of the words. This would mean that benefits acquired during the subsistence of the marriage would also be liable to forfeiture. This interpretation was applied in respect of a marriage in community in *Persad v Persad* [116], where the court held that a tenancy acquired during the marriage was a benefit which could be forfeited.

Sinclair and Kaganas (1984 *Annual Survey* 110 *et seq*) differ from Hahlo. They suggest that in this context the word "marriage" means matrimonial property system. The implication of this is that only benefits derived from the proprietary system are liable to forfeiture. In a marriage out of community of property only benefits contained in the antenuptial contract will therefore be subject to forfeiture. In terms of section 9 of the Matrimonial Property Act 88 of 1984, benefits that flow from the accrual system will also be liable to forfeiture but this act was not yet in operation when the decision under discussion was handed down. According to Sinclair and Kaganas the decision in *Watt's* case was correct (112–113).

Hahlo's criticism was levelled *inter alia* at the fact that this decision further curtails the already limited powers of our courts in comparison to the far-reaching discretionary powers of the English courts in respect of the division of property on divorce. Hahlo's comment was, however, written prior to the amendment of section 7 of the Divorce Act 70 of 1979 by section 36 of the Matrimonial Property Act. This section empowers the court, in certain specified circumstances, where the parties are married out of community of property, to make an order that assets belonging to one of the spouses, be transferred to the other

Swil 1978 1 SA 790 (W); *Rousalis v Rousalis* 1980 3 SA 446 (K)). In ander sake is egter beslis dat voordele wat gedurende die bestaan van die huwelik verkry is ook verbeur kan word (*Kohn v Kohn* 1914 WPA 9; *Martin v Martin* 1925 OD 264; *Bhengu v Bhengu* 1949 4 SA 22 (N)). In *Watt* se saak het MELAMET R egter bevind dat nie een van hierdie sake op gesag gebaseer is nie.

Hahlo (1984 *SALJ* 456) het die beslissing in *Watt* se saak gekritiseer. Hy is van mening dat die woord "huwelik" dubbelsinnig is. Dit kan òf die seremonie self beteken, òf die verhouding wat daaruit voortspruit. Hy voer aan dat die frase "voordele van die huwelik" geïnterpreteer moet word as voordele wat uit die huwelik as 'n voortdurende verhouding voortspruit aangesien dit meer in ooreenstemming met die natuurlike betekenis van die woorde is. Dit sou beteken dat voordele wat gedurende die bestaan van die huwelik verkry word ook verbeur kan word. Hierdie siening is toegepas ten opsigte van 'n huwelik binne gemeenskap in *Persad v Persad* [116], waar die hof beslis het dat die regte wat ontstaan ingevolge 'n huurkontrak wat gedurende die bestaan van die huwelik gesluit is, voordele is wat verbeur kan word.

Sinclair en Kaganas (1984 *Annual Survey* 110 ev) verskil met Hahlo. Hulle doen aan die hand dat die woord "huwelik" in hierdie verband die huweliksgoederestelsel beteken. Die implikasie hiervan is dat net voordele verbeur kan word wat uit die huweliksgoederestelsel verkry word. In 'n huwelik buite gemeenskap van goed sal dus net voordele wat in die huweliksvoorwaardeskontrak verleen is, verbeur kan word. Ingevolge artikel 9 van die Wet op Huweliksgoedere 88 van 1984 is die reg om in die aanwas van die ander gade se boedel te deel ook 'n voordeel wat verbeur kan word maar hierdie wet was nog nie in werking toe die onderhawige saak beslis is nie. Volgens Sinclair en Kaganas was die beslissing in *Watt* se saak korrek.

Hahlo se kritiek was onder andere gemik teen die feit dat hierdie beslissing die reeds beperkte bevoegdheid van ons howe nog verder beperk in vergelyking met die verreikende diskresionêre bevoegdheid wat die Engelse howe in verband met die verdeling van goedere by egskeiding het. Hahlo se kommentaar is egter geskryf voor die wysiging van artikel 7 van die Wet op Egskeiding 70 van 1979 deur artikel 36 van die Wet

spouse. (See in this regard the chapter on redistribution of assets.)

Before the commencement of the Matrimonial Property Act in 1984, a prohibition existed on donations between spouses married out of community of property. In terms of section 22 of this act such donations are, however, now allowed (see further in this regard Barnard, Cronjé and Olivier 199-200).

It is further evident from this case that although divorce is no longer based on fault, fault is still important as far as forfeiture (and maintenance) is concerned. (See *Singh v Singh* [113]; *Wijker v Wijker* [114] and Sinclair and Kaganas 1984 *Annual Survey* 111.)

op Huweliksgoedere. Ingevolge hierdie artikel verkry die hof die bevoegdheid om waar die partye buite gemeenskap van goed getroud is, in bepaalde omstandighede, te gelas dat bates van die een party aan die ander een oorgedra moet word. (Sien in die verband die hoofstuk oor herverdeling van bates.)

Voor die inwerkingtreding van die Wet op Huweliksgoedere in 1984 het 'n skenkingsverbod tussen gades getroud buite gemeenskap van goed bestaan. Ingevolge artikel 22 van hierdie wet is sodanige skenkings egter nou wel toelaatbaar (sien in hierdie verband verder Barnard, Cronjé en Olivier 204-205).

Dit is uit hierdie saak verder duidelik dat alhoewel egskeiding nie meer op skuld gebaseer is nie, skuld nog by verbeuring van voordele (en onderhoud) van belang is. (Sien *Singh v Singh* [113]; *Wijker v Wijker* [114] en Sinclair en Kaganas 1984 *Annual Survey* 111.)

[116] PERSAD V PERSAD

1989 4 SA 685 (D)

Forfeiture of patrimonial benefits

The plaintiff successfully sued the defendant for divorce on the ground of irretrievable breakdown. In addition she applied for an order for forfeiture of benefits in respect of a lease which had been concluded between her husband and a city council. The lease was in respect of a house which was administered by the city council in terms of a municipal housing scheme. The house had served as the spouses' matrimonial home. Throughout the twelve year period during which the spouses lived in it, plaintiff had paid the rental of the house as well as all household expenses. Her husband had contributed nothing to either the rental or the household expenses. Though able to work, he never sought employment. In the opinion of the court, he was "[i]dle and dissolute, a layabout and a drunkard, he sponged on his wife and lived off her industry" (686). The court had to

Verbeuring van vermoënsregtelike voordele

Die eiseres was suksesvol met haar egskeidingseis op grond van onherstelbare verbrokkeling teen haar man. Sy het verder aansoek gedoen om 'n bevel vir verbeuring van voordele ten opsigte van 'n huurooreenkoms wat haar man met 'n stadsraad gesluit het. Die huurooreenkoms was ten opsigte van 'n huis wat die stadsraad ingevolge 'n munisipale behuisingskema beheer het. Die huis was die gades se gemeenskaplike woning. Gedurende die twaalf jaar wat die gades in die huis gewoon het, het die eiseres die huur van die huis asook alle huishoudelike uitgawes betaal. Haar man het geen bydrae gemaak tot die huur van die huis of die huishoudelike uitgawes nie. Alhoewel hy in staat was om te werk, het hy nooit werk gesoek nie. Volgens die hof was hy "[i]dle and dissolute, a layabout and a drunkard, he sponged on

decide whether it could order the city council to transfer all the rights, title and interest in the lease to the plaintiff. The court held that the tenancy was a patrimonial benefit of the marriage which could be forfeited by the husband and ordered the city council to transfer the tenancy from the husband to the wife.

his wife and lived off her industry" (686). Die hof moes beslis of dit die stadsraad kon beveel om alle regte, titel en belang ingevolge die huurooreenkoms aan die eiseres oor te dra. Die hof het beslis dat die huurooreenkoms 'n vermoënsregtelike voordeel van die huwelik was wat deur die man verbeur kon word en het die stadsraad beveel om die huurooreenkoms van die man aan die vrou oor te dra.

DIDCOTT J: [687] The question boiled down to this. Did the tenancy amount to a patrimonial benefit of the marriage? I had no doubt that, if it did and its forfeiture was therefore competent, the conditions thus prescribed for the grant of the relief were all met.

The conclusion to which I came was that the question should be answered in the affirmative. The tenancy seemed to me, in the first place, to have been a benefit derived from the marriage, and accordingly a benefit of the marriage. An asset of the joint estate, it was acquired during the marriage. It was acquired for the purposes of the marriage, for the purposes of the matrimonial home that was needed because of the [688] marriage. And for those purposes it was used throughout the marriage. It could never have been obtained, what was more, but for the marriage. For, in conformity with the policy of the housing scheme, the second defendant would not otherwise have granted it. [(The policy of the city council was to enter into a lease agreement only if the property was to be occupied by a family unit. The agreement was entered into with the head of the family.)] The benefit ranked, I thought in the second place, as a patrimonial one. I took no account of the possibility that a by-product of the tenancy might turn out to be the opportunity for an advantageous purchase, since nothing stronger had emerged than a hope that the opportunity would arise. The tenancy itself, however, did not strike me as worthless. Its value would have been much greater, to be sure, had it enjoyed both an assignability and a contractually settled duration of longer than a month at a time. It would then have had a distinct market value. But it was worth something to the joint estate, I believed, without those attributes and that enhanced value. So much appeared to be illustrated by the following hypothetical situations that occurred to me. Had the act of a third party made the house temporarily uninhabitable in circumstances rendering him liable for the consequences, and necessitating the hire while it remained in that state of alternative accommodation outside the housing scheme, loss recoverable from him would have been suffered, consisting of the expense thus incurred which was proved by evidence along the lines of that heard in this case, evidence establishing that the other accommodation had cost more than the rent saved and that, though legally terminable earlier, the tenancy was likely in fact to have lasted for the period in question. Then one imagined a notice given by the second defendant which terminated the tenancy, and its demolition of the house before the month expired, indeed the very next day. The extra expense of accommodation found elsewhere for the rest of the month could likewise have been recovered, this time from it. What all this went to show was some measurable value attaching to the right of occupation, and therefore to the tenancy which engendered it. Such was no doubt a good deal lower, on the other hand, than the total amount of rent paid by the plaintiff over the 12 years while it had run.

Since granting the order, and while writing this judgment, I have come across a couple of reported cases, *Ex parte De Beer* 1952 (3) SA 288 (T) and *Steenberg v Steenberg* 1963 (4)

SA 870 (C), which I cite in conclusion. Both were decided before the current legislation was enacted and had to do with forfeitures of benefits decreed under the common law. And their facts were not on all fours with those of the present matter. Neither, one thus sees, is directly in point. The analogies seem sufficient, even so, for the decisions that were reached then to lend some support to the view now taken by me.

The applicant in the first case, who had already been awarded a divorce and an order declaring her husband to have forfeited the benefits of their marriage in community of property, sought and obtained a rule *nisi* calling on him to show cause why a further order should not ensue which gave effect to the forfeiture by requiring the transfer to her of immovable property that was registered in his name, but had been bought during the marriage and become an asset of the joint estate. The report does not indicate whether the rule was subsequently confirmed. The relief for which it provided was held at the time to be warranted, however, on the evidence presented by the applicant. This showed that her husband's [689] employment had been irregular and his support of the family meagre; that she had consequently had to work; that the purchase of the property had been financed by a loan covering the full price; that she had paid every instalment of capital and interest that was payable under the mortgage bond securing the repayment of the loan; and that the property had in addition been maintained and improved at her cost alone. She obviously had no prospect of reimbursement by him for all or any of this expenditure. He was probably penniless and could not be traced anyhow. ROPER J felt satisfied in the circumstances that she was entitled to the property itself, saying (at 289H–290C):

> 'It seems clear... that an order for forfeiture of benefits is designed to protect the right of a plaintiff to his or her separate contributions to the property of the marriage, and that these include ... acquisitions made as a result of industry, economy or investment ... where it can be shown that ... the defendant's contribution towards the joint household was insufficient to allow of any such acquisitions, so that they must have resulted from the plaintiff's effects alone.'

The decision was followed in the second case, also concerning a marriage in community of property, when the wife was granted a decree of divorce, an order for forfeiture of benefits and, under that heading, a more specific one entitling her to the rights derived by her husband from a hire-purchase agreement which he had signed, and to the transfer of the property bought by him in terms of it. The evidence proved that she had paid all the instalments and he had contributed nothing to them.

The first difference which I have noted between those two cases and this, the difference between the adjudication under the common law and one governed by the Divorce Act, seems not to matter now. For, as I understand the statute, it left untouched the concept of a forfeiture of benefits, when it dealt at all events with marriages in community of property, not altering what was then envisaged or encompassed by the notion in the eyes of the common law, but merely defining and adumbrating the circumstances in which the Court was empowered to order a forfeiture.

More material, superficially at any rate, is the second difference. In each of the other cases the wife had paid for the acquisition of the property. She had paid in effect the price for the property, or the part of it to have become payable. Here, by comparison, the plaintiff did not pay for the acquisition of the tenancy. Nothing had to be paid for its acquisition. And her payments had nothing to do with its acquisition. They had a lot to do, however, with its preservation. For, had she not paid the rent, nobody else in all probability would have done so. And then it would inevitably have been terminated. I see no reason in principle why payments preserving an asset of the joint estate should be distinguished in a case like the present from those made in other situations for its acquisition. But for them, in each situation, the joint estate does not have the asset when it comes to be liquidated. As the result of them, in each situation, it does. In the one the asset itself may be declared forfeited in lieu of the cash equivalent to the amount paid, once there is none available because the coffers are bare. That surely goes for the other as well. The difference between them therefore strikes me in the end as unimportant.

Note	Aantekening
See the note on *Watt v Watt* [115].	Sien die aantekening by *Watt v Watt* [115].

Redistribution of assets in terms of section 7(3) of the Divorce Act 70 of 1979

Herverdeling van bates ingevolge artikel 7(3) van die Wet op Egskeiding 70 van 1979

Redistribution of assets in terms of
section 7(3) of the Divorce Act 70 of
1979

Herverdeling van bates ingevolge
artikel 7(3) van die Wet op Egskeiding
70 van 1979

[117]   BEAUMONT V BEAUMONT

1987 1 SA 967 (A)

Redistribution order in terms of section 7(3) of the Divorce Act 70 of 1979

The appellant (husband) and the respondent (wife) were married in 1964. Before entering into marriage they entered into an antenuptial contract excluding community of property and of profit and loss. At the time of entering into marriage the spouses had no assets. Twenty years later the appellant sued the respondent for divorce. At that stage the appellant had an estate of R450 000 and the respondent had only R10 000. During the existence of the marriage the respondent had kept house for her husband and children and fulfilled all the tasks of a wife and mother. She also assisted her husband in his business without receiving any remuneration for her assistance. When the appellant instituted divorce proceedings against the respondent, she counterclaimed redistribution of assets in terms of section 7(3) of the Divorce Act 70 of 1979. The court a quo granted the respondent's claim and awarded her R150 000 of the appellant's estate as well as maintenance. The appellant appealed against this order but his appeal was unsuccessful.

Herverdelingsbevel ingevolge artikel 7(3) van die Wet op Egskeiding 70 van 1979

Die appellant (man) en die respondent (vrou) is in 1964 getroud. Voordat hulle in die huwelik getree het, het hulle 'n huweliksvoorwaardeskontrak aangegaan ingevolge waarvan gemeenskap van goed en van wins en verlies uitgesluit is. Ten tyde van die huweliksluiting het die gades geen bates gehad nie. Twintig jaar later het die appellant die respondent om 'n egskeiding gedagvaar. Op daardie stadium het die appellant 'n boedel van R450 000 gehad en die respondent het slegs R10 000 gehad. Gedurende die bestaan van die huwelik het die respondent huisgehou vir haar man en kinders en al die take van 'n moeder en huisvrou verrig. Sy het ook haar man in sy besigheid bygestaan sonder om ooit enige vergoeding daarvoor te ontvang. Toe die appellant die aksie om egskeiding ingestel het, het die respondent 'n teeneis ingestel om herverdeling van bates ingevolge artikel 7(3) van die Wet op Egskeiding 70 van 1979. Die hof a quo het die respondent se eis toegestaan en aan haar R150 000 van die appellant se bates sowel as onderhoud toegeken. Die appellant het teen hierdie bevel geappelleer maar die appèl was onsuksesvol.

[BOTHA JA quoted section 7 of the Divorce Act 70 of 1979 in full and proceeded:]

BOTHA JA: [987] Subsection (1) does not apply in the present case, since the parties did not enter into any agreement as contemplated therein . . .

Subsection (2) was amended in 1984 by the addition to the matters . . . as considerations to which a Court must have regard in applying it, of a further factor to be taken into account, viz "an order in terms of ss (3)". The amendment established an interrelationship between ss (2) and (3). The nature, extent and effect of that interrelationship will be examined later in this judgment . . . At this stage I would merely point to the very wide discretion which the subsection confers upon a Court in deciding upon "an order which the Court finds just ...", which is underscored by the words "and any other factor which in the opinion of the Court should be taken into account"...

Subsection (3) introduced an entirely novel concept into this branch of our law: the power of a Court under certain circumstances to order the transfer of assets of the one spouse to the other. An order in terms of ss (3) may conveniently be referred to as a redistribution order. The creation of a power enabling a Court to make a redistribution order was obviously a reforming and remedial measure ... What the measure was designed to remedy is trenchantly demonstrated by the facts of the present case: the inequity which could flow from the failure of the law to recognise a right of a spouse upon divorce to claim an adjustment of a disparity between the respective assets of the spouses which is incommensurate with their respective contributions during the subsistence of the marriage to the maintenance or increase of the estate of the one or the other.

Subsection (3) contains in itself a number of prerequisites that must be satisfied before an order can be made in terms of it, apart from those which are incorporated in it by reference to ss (4). The marriage must have been [988] entered into before the coming into operation of the 1984 Act. That requirement is satisfied in the present case ...

The marriage must have been entered into in terms of an antenuptial contract excluding community of property and of profit and loss and any form of accrual sharing. In the present case the parties' antenuptial contract was in a standard form, expressly excluding community of property and of profit and loss. As mentioned earlier, KRIEGLER J [in the court *a quo*] found that it was inconsistent with any accrual sharing. It was rightly not contended that this finding was not justified or that this requirement of the subsection was not satisfied. As KRIEGLER J pointed out (at 175B), the possibility of making a redistribution order was created concomitantly with the introduction of a system of accrual sharing in chap I of the 1984 Act. The Legislature could not have intended an express exclusion of the type of accrual sharing envisaged in the 1984 Act to be a prerequisite for the application of ss (3), introduced by the same Act. Consequently the express exclusion of community of property and of profit and loss in a pre-1984 standard form of antenuptial contract must be taken to embrace an implied exclusion of "accrual sharing in any form", sufficient for the purposes of ss (3). Next, the subsection requires an "application" to be made for a redistribution order. Since only a "Court granting a decree of divorce" is empowered to make such an order, the contemplated "application" will, in practice, take the form of a claim put forward in the pleadings in the action. This was done in the present case ...

The presence in this case of the requirement that there must be no agreement between the parties as to the division of their assets has already been noted. On satisfaction of the requirements laid down in ss (3) itself and those incorporated by reference to ss (4), the Court may order the transfer of such assets or such part of the assets of the one spouse to the other "as the Court may deem just" ... The Legislature clearly intended to confer a very wide discretion upon a Court exercising its jurisdiction under ss (3). This is highlighted by the provisions of ss (5), to which reference will be made presently.

Subsection (4), in the words of KRIEGLER J (at 175B-C), "contains two conjoined jurisdictional preconditions to the exercise of the discretion". The one is a contribution by the one spouse to the estate of the other ... The other is that the Court must be satisfied that, by reason of such a contribution, it would be "equitable and just" to make a redistribution order. The first requirement involves a purely factual finding. The second involves the exercise of a purely discretionary judgment in equity. It is certainly a very prominent and important feature of ss (4) that ultimately, when once the factual requirements of ss (3) and (4) are satisfied, the [989] determination of whether or not a redistribution order is to be made at all is entrusted by the Legislature to the wholly unfettered discretionary judgment of the Court as to whether it would be equitable and just to do so.

Subsection (5) prescribes the considerations which the Court must take into account in the determination of the assets or part of the assets to be transferred in terms of a redistribution order. First and foremost is the contribution by the one spouse to the estate of the other, by which is obviously meant the nature and extent of the contribution. Next to be considered, in terms of para (a), are the existing means and obligations of the parties ... Para (b) refers to any donation made by one party to the other during the subsistence of the marriage or which is owing and enforceable in terms of their antenuptial contract. These facts are of no real consequence in the present case ... Paragraph (c) refers to any forfeiture order made under s 9 of the Act or under any other law. This plays no role in the present case. Lastly, para (d) mentions "any other factor which should in the opinion of the Court be taken into account". It is this feature of ss (5), coupled with the paucity of the considerations mentioned in the preceding paras (a)–(c), to which I referred earlier as highlighting the very wide discretion which a Court is given in the exercise of its power to make a redistribution order ...

[BOTHA JA then made a few general remarks which included his response to the husband's counsel's request that he lay down guidelines as to how section 7(3) should be applied. He proceeded:]

[990] I do not believe that any attempt to formulate guidelines outside the wide criteria mentioned by the Legislature itself would be a useful, or even a feasible, exercise. The truth of the matter is that there is such an infinite variety of circumstances under which ss (3) falls to be applied that any attempt to lay down guidelines as to the manner in which the Court's discretion is to be exercised is likely to increase uncertainty rather than to reduce it. On the other hand, guidelines laid down by the Courts may result in a rigidity of approach displacing the flexibility envisaged by the Legislature itself.

[BOTHA JA discussed the application of the one-third guideline in English law as applied in *Wachtel v Wachtel* [1973] 1 All ER 829 (CA) in which LORD DENNING advocated the allocation of one-third of the family assets to the spouse with fewer assets as a starting point. He proceeded:]

[991] It seems to me fair to say that LORD DENNING's attempt to establish a guideline in the form of a one-third starting point has created more problems than it resolved, and although an obituary may be inappropriate as yet, it is likely that this guideline will eventually come to nought. In our legislation the feature of overriding importance in the exercise of the Court's discretion as to what proportion of assets is to be transferred in terms of ss (3) is the Court's assessment of what would be "just", having regard to the factors mentioned specifically and to "any other factor which should in the opinion of the Court be taken into account". This power has to be exercised in widely divergent circumstances, as is illustrated by comparing the facts of the present case with those in the other cases decided under the new legislation and reported up to date – see *Van Gysen v Van Gysen* 1986 (1) SA 56 (C), *MacGregor v MacGregor* 1986 (3) SA 644 (C) and *Kroon v Kroon* 1986 (4) SA 616 (E) [123]. The Legislature has seen fit to confer a wide discretion upon the Courts, and the flexibility in the application of ss (3) thus created ought not, in my judgment, to be curtailed by placing judicial glosses on the subsection in the form of guidelines as to the determination of what would be a just redistribution order.

In the present case, however, the arguments addressed to us have raised a number of questions of principle relating to the interpretation and manner of application of ss (2), (3) and (4), which require to be answered.

The first matter I propose to discuss is the interrelationship between ss (2) and (3). I said earlier that such an interrelationship was established by the introduction into ss (2), in 1984, of a reference to an order under ss (3), as one of the matters to which regard must be had in deciding upon an order in terms of ss (2) ...

[992] I cannot imagine that the Legislature could have intended ... to require the Court to shut its eyes to the possibility of making an order in terms of ss (2) when considering what order to make in terms of ss (3). If the Court should find, for whatever reason ... that an order in terms of ss (2) is necessary in order to do justice between the parties, it is clear, in my view, that such an order would qualify to be taken into account under the wide terms of para (d) of ss (5) in determining the nature or extent of a redistribution order which is to be made in terms of ss (3) ...

Arising from and related to the interrelationship between ss (2) and (3) there are two further matters which were raised in argument before us and which may conveniently be discussed at this stage. The first is the so-called 'clean break' principle and the second the role of the 'misconduct' of either of the parties. I shall deal with each of these matters in turn.

With regard to the 'clean break' principle ... [993] there is no doubt in my mind that our Courts will always bear in mind the possibility of using their powers under the new dispensation in such a way as to achieve a complete termination of the financial dependence of the one party on the other, if the circumstances permit. The last-mentioned qualification is, of course, very important; I shall return to it in a moment. The advantages of achieving a 'clean break' between the parties are obvious; I do not think they need be elaborated upon. The manner of achieving such a result is, of course, by making only a redistribution order in terms of ss (3) and no maintenance order in terms of ss (2). What I have said earlier with regard to the Court taking an overall view, from the outset, of the possibility of making an order or orders under either ss (2) or ss (3) or both, does not mean that the Court will not consider specifically the desirability in any case of making only a redistribution order and awarding no maintenance, having regard particularly to the feasibility of following such a course. With regard to the latter and to the qualification I stressed a moment ago ("if the circumstances permit"), there will no doubt be many cases in which the constraints imposed by the facts (the financial position of the parties, their respective means, obligations and needs, and other relevant factors) will not allow justice to be done between the parties by effecting a final termination of the financial dependence of the one on the other. In the end everything will depend on the facts and the Court's assessment of what would be just ...

With regard to the role of the 'misconduct' of the parties, counsel for the appellant pointed to the fact that the parties' "conduct in so far as it may be relevant to the break-down of the marriage" was mentioned in ss (2) as one of the factors to be taken into account in deciding upon a maintenance order, but that there was no corresponding provision in ss (3) and (5) in relation to a redistribution order. Counsel argued that after the introduction into our law of the 'no fault' principle in regard to divorce, by the Divorce Act of 1979, the Legislature must have intended that 'fault' or [994] 'misconduct' should play no role at all in connection with the making of redistribution orders in terms of ss (3) ...

[I]n my opinion the Court is entitled, in terms of the wide words of para (d) of ss (5) that I have quoted, to take a party's misconduct into account even when only a redistribution order is being considered under ss (3), and where no maintenance order under ss (2) is made. But I should add at once that I am convinced that our Courts will adopt a conservative approach in assessing a party's misconduct as a relevant factor, whether under ss (2) or ss (3) ... In many, probably most cases, both parties will be to blame, in the sense of having contributed to the break-down of the marriage ... In such cases, where there is no conspicuous disparity between the conduct of the one party and that of the other, our Courts will not indulge in an exercise to apportion the fault of the parties, and thus [995] nullify the advantages of the 'no fault' system of divorce. But in the present case the misconduct was found to have existed on the part of the appellant only, and it was found to have been "certainly gross and prolonged". Upon that footing KRIEGLER J was fully justified in taking it into account as a relevant factor, as he did . . .

[996] I turn now to the next aspect of the legislative provisions that requires examination. It is the manner in which the Legislature, in ss (4), has circumscribed the nature of the contribution which the one party is required to have made to the estate of the other, as a prerequisite for the issuing of a redistribution order. In the argument of counsel for the appellant this aspect of the legislation assumed great importance . . . It rested on the premise that under our common law the spouses owe a reciprocal duty of support to each other. Typically, it was said, it is the husband who, out of his income, provides his wife and family with support, and in return, the wife's primary duty is to perform her traditional role as wife and mother by managing the household and looking after the children of the marriage. So far so good. The crux of the argument then was that the Legislature could not have intended a contribution by either spouse, made purely in the discharge of the common law duty of support as described above, to qualify as a contribution which entitled the spouse making it to claim 'compensation' for it in the form of a redistribution order. Something more was required: a contribution which exceeded the bounds of the duty of support which existed *ex lege*, which went beyond the call of duty, as it were . . .

In terms of ss (4), what is required is that the claimant for a redistribution order must have

> "contributed directly or indirectly to the maintenance or increase of the estate of the other party during the subsistence of the marriage, either by the rendering of services, or the saving of expenses which would otherwise have been incurred, or in any other manner."

In these words one searches in vain for any suggestion of a qualification of the nature of the contribution required, in the sense contended for by counsel. To read the words used by the Legislature subject to the restriction contended for, would compel one to import into the subsection a notion which is simply not to be found there, and for the implication of which I can find no warrant whatever. Counsel relied strongly on an article by Prof JC Sonnekus, 'Egskeiding en Kwantifisering van die Bydrae tot die Ander Gade se Boedel – Artikel 7(3)–(5) van die Wet op Egskeiding 70 van 1979', in 103 (1986) *SALJ* 367. In that article Prof *Sonnekus* propounds the theory that only a contribution which exceeds that which a spouse is required to make by virtue of the common law duty of support (ie what is referred to as a "meer-bydrae") is relevant for the purposes of ss (4) . . . With respect to the [997] learned author, I have carefully studied the arguments advanced by him in support of his theory, and having done so, I have no hesitation in firmly rejecting it . . .

Our legislation . . . refer[s] specifically to contributions made "directly *or indirectly* . . . by the *rendering of services*, or the *saving of expenses* . . . or *in any other manner*". In my view there can be no doubt that the plain meaning of these words is so wide that they embrace the performance by the wife of her ordinary duties of 'looking after the home' and 'caring for the family'; by doing that, she is assuredly rendering services and saving expenses which must necessarily contribute indirectly to the maintenance or increase of the husband's estate . . .

[BOTHA JA then dealt with the attack by counsel for the husband on the judgment of KRIEGLER J in the court *a quo*. He found that KRIEGLER J had exercised his discretion properly and held:]

[1002] In my judgment, there are no grounds in the present case upon which this Court could interfere with the orders made by the Court *a quo* . . .

The appeal is dismissed . . .

TRENGOVE JA; VILJOEN JA and BOSHOFF AJA concurred. Due to temporary indisposition JACOBS JA could not participate in the delivery of the judgment.

Note

This case is the first Appellate Division decision on the redistribution of assets in terms of sections 7(3) to (6) of the Divorce Act 70 of 1979.

The first important point that the court made is concerned with whether one third of the matrimonial property should be transferred to the spouse with the smaller estate if a redistribution of assets is ordered. The decision of the court *a quo* in the *Beaumont* case (1985 4 SA 171 (W)) was the first reported case in which section 7(3) was applied. In that decision the court referred to the one-third "rule" which is often applied in English law. According to this "rule" the court awards one third of the total value of the spouses' assets to the spouse with the smaller estate on divorce unless there are other factors which indicate that a different division should be made. The court *a quo* expressed the opinion that this "rule" could also be of use to South African courts and applied it to the case before it.

Before the Appellate Division's decision in the *Beaumont* case was reported, the one-third "rule" was dealt with in two other reported cases. In the first, *Van Gysen v Van Gysen* 1986 1 SA 56 (C), the wife had contributed to the growth of the spouses' assets during the existence of the marriage in a one-third versus two-thirds relationship to her husband. On divorce the wife claimed a redistribution of assets. The court emphasised that the one-third "rule" could only serve as a starting point and that it should not be viewed as a hard and fast rule. Taking into consideration the spouses' contributions to the various assets which each of them owned at the time of divorce, the court held that each spouse should retain his or her own assets and that no further division should take place. This order had the same effect as a one-third versus two-thirds division of the spouses' assets.

Aantekening

Hierdie saak is die eerste Appèlhofuitspraak oor die herverdeling van bates ingevolge artikels 7(3) tot (6) van die Wet op Egskeiding 70 van 1979.

Die eerste belangrike aspek wat in hierdie uitspraak na vore gekom het, handel oor die vraag of een derde van die huweliksbates by die herverdeling van die goedere aan die gade met die kleinste boedel oorgedra moet word. Die uitspraak van die hof *a quo* in die *Beaumont*-saak (1985 4 SA 171 (W)) was die eerste gerapporteerde beslissing oor die toepassing van artikel 7(3). In daardie beslissing het die hof verwys na die een derde-"reël" wat dikwels in die Engelse reg aanwending vind. Ooreenkomstig hierdie "reël" ken die hof by egskeiding een derde van die totale waarde van die gades se bates toe aan die gade met die kleinste boedel, tensy daar ander faktore is wat daarop dui dat 'n ander verdeling gemaak moet word. Die hof *a quo* het die mening gehuldig dat hierdie "reël" ook vir die Suid-Afrikaanse reg van nut kon wees en het dit toe ook toegepas.

Voor die Appèlhofuitspraak in die *Beaumont*-saak gerapporteer is, het die een derde-"reël" in twee ander sake ter sprake gekom. In *Van Gysen v Van Gysen* 1986 1 SA 56 (K) het die vrou gedurende die bestaan van die huwelik in 'n verhouding van een derde teenoor haar man se twee derdes bygedra tot die groei van die gades se bates. By egskeiding het die vrou 'n herverdeling van die bates geëis. Die hof het beklemtoon dat die een derde-"reël" slegs as 'n uitgangspunt gebruik kon word en dat dit nie as 'n vaste reël beskou moes word nie. Die hof het die gades se onderskeie bydraes tot die bates wat elkeen by egskeiding gehad het, in ag geneem en beslis dat elkeen sy eie bates moes behou en het geen verdere verdeling van bates beveel nie. Hierdie bevel het dieselfde uitwerking gehad as wat 'n verdeling van een derde teenoor twee derdes sou gehad het.

The other case was *MacGregor v MacGregor* 1986 3 SA 644 (C). In this case the wife had a far larger estate at the time of the divorce than her husband had. At the time of divorce the husband claimed redistribution of assets. During the existence of the marriage both spouses had contributed to the growth of the spouses' assets. On the facts of the case the court awarded one third of the spouses' total assets to the husband. Although no mention was made of the one-third "rule" or of either of the two earlier reported decisions which dealt with this "rule", it appears as though the court did in fact apply it.

From the Appellate Division's decision in *Beaumont v Beaumont* it is clear that the one-third "rule" has found no favour with our highest court. The Appellate Division expressly rejected the suggestion that there should be guidelines, such as the one-third starting point, for the exercise of the court's discretion in terms of section 7(3). The Appellate Division correctly held that the court's discretion should not be limited by laying down guidelines and that the facts of the case together with all the considerations that the court deems to be relevant, should determine the outcome of each case.

The second important point on which the Appellate Division expressed its opinion, relates to whether the awarding of maintenance should be considered completely separately from the issue of redistribution of assets in terms of section 7(3) of the Divorce Act. In the decision of the court *a quo* in the *Beaumont* case, it was held that the transfer of assets in terms of section 7(3) must be considered together with the question regarding maintenance, in other words the court held that there is an interrelationship between section 7(3) and section 7(2). This point was confirmed by the Appellate Division and has also been followed in *Archer v Archer* [121]; *Kretschmer v Kretschmer* [120]; *Kroon v Kroon* [123]; *Kritzinger v Kritzinger* [118] and *Katz v Katz* [119].

Thirdly the court considered the "clean break" principle. (This matter partly overlaps with point two relating to the interrelationship between sections 7(2) and 7(3).) The court correctly pointed out that the "clean break" principle is not foreign to our law and that it is something to be strived for "if the circumstances permit" (993). The latter qualification is most important. The "clean break" principle cannot be used in all divorce

Die ander saak was *MacGregor v MacGregor* 1986 3 SA 644 (K). In hierdie saak het die vrou ten tyde van die partye se egskeiding 'n veel groter boedel as haar man gehad. By egskeiding het die man 'n herverdeling van bates gevra. Gedurende die bestaan van die huwelik het albei partye tot hulle bates bygedra. Op grond van die feite van die saak het die hof een derde van die gades se totale bates aan die man toegeken. Alhoewel daar nêrens in die saak melding gemaak is van die een derde-"reël" of die twee sake waarin die aangeleentheid vroeër ter sprake gekom het nie, wil dit tog voorkom asof die hof die reël in elk geval toegepas het.

Uit die Appèlhof se uitspraak in *Beaumont v Beaumont* blyk dit dat die een derde-"reël" nie byval gevind het by ons hoogste hof nie. Die Appèlhof het die voorstel uitdruklik verwerp dat daar riglyne, soos die een derde-reël, moet bestaan waarvolgens die hof sy diskresie ingevolge artikel 7(3) moet uitoefen. Die Appèlhof het heeltemal tereg beslis dat die hof se diskresie nie aan bande gelê moet word deur die daarstel van riglyne nie en dat die feite van die saak tesame met al die oorwegings wat die hof as relevant beskou die deurslag moet gee.

Die tweede belangrike aangeleentheid waaroor die Appèlhof 'n mening uitgespreek het, het te doen met die vraag of die toekenning van onderhoud heeltemal afsonderlik van die herverdeling van bates ingevolge artikel 7(3) van die Wet op Egskeiding beskou moet word. Die hof *a quo* in die *Beaumont*-saak het beslis dat die oordrag van bates ingevolge artikel 7(3) tesame met die kwessie van onderhoud oorweeg moet word, met ander woorde die hof het beslis dat daar 'n onderlinge verhouding tussen artikel 7(3) en artikel 7(2) bestaan. Hierdie aangeleentheid is deur die Appèlhof bevestig en is ook gevolg in *Archer v Archer* [121]; *Kretschmer v Kretschmer* [120]; *Kroon v Kroon* [123]; *Kritzinger v Kritzinger* [118] en *Katz v Katz* [119].

In die derde plek het die hof oorweging geskenk aan die "skoon breuk"-beginsel ("clean break principle"). (Hierdie aangeleentheid oorvleuel gedeeltelik met die tweede aspek wat hierbo bespreek is, naamlik die onderlinge verhouding tussen artikels 7(2) en 7(3).) Die hof het tereg daarop gewys dat die "skoon breuk"-beginsel nie vreemd is aan ons reg nie en dat uitvoering daaraan gegee kan word "if the circumstances permit" (993).

actions – only if the spouses' financial position is such that both of them would have sufficient means to make a living, can a "clean break" be considered. This approach is realistic and was also adopted in *Katz v Katz* where the court held that a "clean break" could only be achieved if the spouses were or at least one of them was sufficiently well off to enable the court to make a distribution which would place the poorer spouse "in a financial position to maintain herself or himself" (11). (See also *Archer v Archer* [121] and *Kretschmer v Kretschmer* [120].)

Another important point which the court dealt with relates to the role which the spouses' conduct plays in determining the redistribution of assets on divorce. In this regard the court held that conduct can be a relevant consideration in the exercise of the court's discretion on the re-distribution order. However, the court further held that a conservative approach to misconduct should be adopted (994). Misconduct should not be considered "where there is no conspicuous disparity between the conduct of the one party and that of the other" (994). (See further *Kritzinger v Kritzinger* [118]; *Archer v Archer* [121]; *Kretschmer v Kretschmer* [120].)

The last very important point of the Appellate Division's decision in the case under discussion deals with the description of the nature of the contribution which would entitle the applicant to a redistribution of assets. The court correctly interpreted section 7(4) in such a way that any contribution which a spouse makes is sufficient to be considered as a contribution in terms of the section. Even if, for example, the wife only performed "her ordinary duties of 'looking after the home' and 'caring for the family' " (997) this will constitute a contribution. (In this regard see further *Kritzinger v Kritzinger; Katz v Katz* and *Kretschmer v Kretschmer.*)

See further Hahlo 384; Van der Vyver and Joubert 670; Barnard, Cronjé and Olivier 275 *et seq*; Sinclair 47-55; Sonnekus 1985 *De Rebus* 327; 1985 *TSAR* 342; 1986 *SALJ* 367; 1987 *THRHR* 331; 1988 *TSAR* 120; Dillon 1986 *CILSA* 271; Heaton 1987 *THRHR* 103; Joubert 1987 *De Jure* 369; Van Wyk 1988 *THRHR* 228.

Laasgenoemde kwalifikasie is baie belangrik. Die "skoon breuk"-beginsel kan nie in alle egskeidingsgedinge toegepas word nie – slegs indien die gades se finansiële posisie sodanig is dat elke gade voldoende bates het om hom in staat te stel om 'n bestaan te maak, kan 'n "skoon breuk" oorweeg word. Hierdie benadering is realisties en is ook in *Katz v Katz* toegepas waar die hof beslis het dat 'n "skoon breuk" slegs bewerkstellig kan word indien die gades, of ten minste een van hulle, ryk genoeg is om dit vir die hof moontlik te maak om 'n bevel uit te reik wat die armer gade sou plaas "in a financial position to maintain herself or himself" (11). (Sien ook *Archer v Archer* [121] en *Kretschmer v Kretschmer* [120].)

'n Ander belangrike aangeleentheid waaraan die hof aandag gegee het, handel oor die rol wat die gades se gedrag by die herverdeling van bates speel. In hierdie verband het die hof beslis dat gedrag wel 'n relevante oorweging by die herverdeling van bates kan wees. Die hof het egter verder beslis dat die hele aangeleentheid van gedrag versigtig benader moet word (994). Wangedrag behoort nie oorweeg te word nie "where there is no conspicuous disparity between the conduct of the one party and that of the other" (994). (Sien verder *Kritzinger v Kritzinger* [118]; *Archer v Archer* [121]; *Kretschmer v Kretschmer* [120].)

Die laaste belangrike aspek van die Appèlhof se uitspraak in die onderhawige saak handel oor die beskrywing van die aard van die bydrae wat die applikant op 'n herverdeling van bates geregtig sou maak. Heeltemal tereg het die hof artikel 7(4) op so 'n wyse uitgelê dat enige bydrae wat 'n gade gedurende die bestaan van die huwelik gemaak het voldoende is om as 'n bydrae ingevolge die artikel oorweeg te word. Selfs indien die vrou byvoorbeeld slegs "her ordinary duties of 'looking after the home' and 'caring for the family' " (997) nagekom het, sal dit as 'n bydrae kwalifiseer. (Sien in hierdie verband verder *Kritzinger v Kritzinger; Katz v Katz* en *Kretschmer v Kretschmer.*)

Sien verder Hahlo 384; Van der Vyver en Joubert 670; Barnard, Cronjé en Olivier 284 ev; Sinclair 47-55; Sonnekus 1985 *De Rebus* 327; 1985 *TSAR* 342; 1986 *SALJ* 367; 1987 *THRHR* 331; 1988 *TSAR* 120; Dillon 1986 *CILSA* 271; Heaton 1987 *THRHR* 103; Joubert 1987 *De Jure* 369; Van Wyk 1988 *THRHR* 228.

[118] KRITZINGER V KRITZINGER

1989 1 SA 67 (A)

Redistribution order in terms of section 7(3) of the Divorce Act 70 of 1979

The appellant (wife) and the respondent (husband) were married out of community of property in 1967. The appellant was the managing director of Clicks and the respondent was a legal adviser to Mobil Oil in Cape Town. At some point during the existence of the spouses' marriage the respondent was offered a post at the headquarters of Mobil Oil in New York but he declined the offer because it would be detrimental to the appellant's business career. The appellant earned twice as much as the respondent and she had contributed twice as much as the respondent to the acquisition, improvement and maintenance of the parties' matrimonial home. Both parties contributed to their joint living expenses. In 1985 the appellant sued the respondent for divorce. At that stage the appellant's estate was worth approximately R690 000 and the respondent's estate was worth approximately R275 000. The appellant claimed, *inter alia*, transfer to her of R109 000 which represented half of the net value of the spouses' matrimonial home, which was registered in the respondent's name. She based her claim on section 7(3) of the Divorce Act 70 of 1979 and alleged that the sum of R109 000 represented her contribution towards the acquisition, improvement and maintenance of the matrimonial home as well as her contribution towards payment of the mortgage bond instalments on the home. The respondent denied that it would be just and equitable to transfer any of his assets to the appellant. He counter-claimed for a divorce and alleged that the irretrievable breakdown of the marriage was due to the appellant's committing adultery with a certain Mr Green. The respondent further claimed transfer of R200 000 of the appellant's assets to him. He alleged that he

Herverdelingsbevel ingevolge artikel 7(3) van die Wet op Egskeiding 70 van 1979

Die appellant (vrou) en die respondent (man) is in 1967 buite gemeenskap van goed getroud. Die appellant was die besturende direkteur van Clicks, en die respondent was 'n regsadviseur by die Mobil-oliemaatskappy in Kaapstad. Op 'n stadium gedurende die bestaan van die huwelik is die respondent 'n pos by Mobil se hoofkantoor in New York aangebied maar hy het die aanbod van die hand gewys op grond daarvan dat dit nie in belang van die appellant se loopbaan sou wees nie. Die appellant het twee keer soveel as die respondent verdien en sy het twee keer soveel as die respondent bygedra tot die verkryging, verbetering en onderhoud van die partye se gemeenskaplike woning. Albei partye het tot die gesin se uitgawes bygedra. In 1985 het die appellant die respondent om 'n egskeiding gedagvaar. Op daardie stadium was die appellant se boedel omtrent R690 000 werd en die respondent s'n R275 000. Die appellant het onder andere geëis dat R109 000 aan haar oorgedra moes word. Dit het die helfte van die waarde van die gesin se gemeenskaplike woning verteenwoordig. Die huis was in die naam van die respondent geregistreer. Sy het haar eis op artikel 7(3) van die Wet op Egskeiding 70 van 1979 gebaseer en beweer dat die bedrag van R109 000 haar bydrae tot die verkryging, verbetering en instandhouding van die gemeenskaplike woning sowel as haar bydrae tot afbetaling van die verbandpaaiemente op die huis verteenwoordig het. Die respondent het ontken dat dit billik en regverdig sou wees om enige van sy bates aan die appellant oor te dra. In 'n teeneis het hy aansoek om egskeiding gedoen en beweer dat die onherstelbare verbrokkeling van die huwelik aan die appellant se owerspel met ene mnr Green te wyte was.

was entitled to such a transfer as he had contributed indirectly to the maintenance or increase of the appellant's estate by not settling overseas and thus forfeiting promotion in order to further the appellant's career in South Africa. He further alleged that his contribution enabled the appellant to acquire shares in Clicks and Clickden which increased the value of her estate with approximately R600 000. The court a quo dismissed the appellant's claim for transfer of assets and allowed the respondent's counterclaim for transfer of R200 000 to him. The appellant appealed against this decision and the appeal was upheld.

Die respondent het verder geëis dat R200 000 van die appellant se bates aan hom oorgedra moes word. Hy het aangevoer dat hy op hierdie bedrag geregtig was aangesien hy indirek tot die groei of instandhouding van die appellant se boedel bygedra het deurdat hy nie na die buiteland verhuis het nie en sodoende sy bevordering opgeoffer het sodat die appellant se loopbaan in Suid-Afrika bevorder kon word. Hy het verder beweer dat sy bydrae die appellant in staat gestel het om aandele in Clicks en Clickden te verkry wat tot gevolg gehad het dat die waarde van haar boedel met omtrent R600 000 verhoog het. Die hof a quo het die appellant se eis vir oordrag van bates verwerp en dié respondent se teeneis vir oordrag van R200 000 toegestaan. Die appellant het teen hierdie beslissing geappelleer en die appèl is gehandhaaf.

MILNE JA: [76] The trial Court seems to have reached [its] conclusion in the following manner. In the first place it did not deal separately with the claim and counterclaim, but adopted an overall or globular approach. It then found that:

(a) it was the appellant's fault that the marriage came to an end;
(b) in subordinating his prospects of advancement with Mobil Oil to the appellant's prospects of advancement with Clicks, the respondent made a contribution, as contemplated in s 7(4) of the Act, to the increase of the appellant's estate;
(c) since 'no figure can be put on defendant's sacrifice', it was impossible to say that one spouse had contributed more than the other;
(d) it was impossible 'to put a price on her blameworthiness in bringing the marriage to an end';
(e) having regard to the existing means and obligations of the parties, the duration of their marriage, their way of life and the objectives they pursued over the years 'it seems . . . that it can fairly be said that the parties are entitled to share equally'. [The spouses' assets totalled approximately R1 million. By awarding R200 000 of the wife's assets to the respondent the court a quo in effect divided the spouses' assets in half – each spouse ended up with approximately R500 000.]

This appears to me, with all due respect, to be an imprecise and faulty method of dealing with the claims (even assuming, for the moment, the correctness of the factual findings of the trial Court). The judgment appears to be based upon a finding that the parties

'effectively pooled their resources. Although they were married de jure out of community of property by antenuptial contract, as between themselves they were de facto married in community of property for the house was always "ours" and not "his" and the shares were never regarded as her exclusive property.'

The trial Judge also found

'that where spouses intend that all they acquired during their marriage should be regarded as their common property, a unique form of partnership does effectively come into existence'.

[77] It is, no doubt, correct that during the marriage each of the parties contributed to their joint living expenses ... also ... both parties put a substantial sum of money into the acquisition, maintenance and improvement of the home. It is true, furthermore, that every marriage is a partnership in one sense of the word. The spouses live together and contribute ... to each other's physical and mental well-being. They may, furthermore, agree that they will pool their resources. Such an arrangement, unless it has the requisites of a legal partnership ... is not irrevocable, and may be resiled from at any time. Only if the requisites of a partnership are present and it is intended by the parties that there will be a universal partnership could it be said that, in a sense, although parties were married *de jure* out of community of property they were *de facto* married in community – although even in these circumstances this would be an imprecise description.

It does not follow that where some of the income (not all) goes into a common home, the parties intend there to be a partnership in the legal sense, even in respect of that home; counsel for the respondent expressly disavowed any suggestion that there was a partnership in the legal sense between the parties ... Even if it was correct to say that there was a partnership in some vague general sense, there is no warrant whatsoever for saying that it is fair or appropriate to divide the joint net assets of the parties equally, regardless of their respective known and unequal contributions. Even in the case of the dissolution of a legal partnership, the dissolution takes into account the respective contributions of each of the partners, unless it is impossible to say that one has contributed more than the other ...

It was argued by the respondent's counsel that the trial Court's approach was not really based upon the finding that the parties were '*de facto* married in community of property'. It is possible that the passages from the judgment cited above were intended merely to support the proposition that a contribution need not be '... measured in terms exclusively or even primarily confined to money provided, or property delivered or services rendered ...' in order to qualify as a contribution within the meaning of s 7(3) of the Act. I am not confident that this is so, but, assuming that this submission is correct, I am nevertheless satisfied that the trial Court misdirected itself in yet another respect, in that it adopted the globular approach already referred to. There is nothing in the section which authorises such an approach ...

[78] Where, as here, a claim in convention invoking the provisions of ss (3) is answered by a claim in reconvention also relying on such provisions the claims are, in [79] law, separate claims ... There may, possibly, be cases where the facts relevant to both claims are so inextricably interrelated that a globular approach is the only possible one, but, save in such circumstances, the claims must, at least initially, be considered separately. It may well occur that where, as here, there are conflicting claims under s 7(3), the Court would consider the practical effect of giving judgment on the claim in convention upon the financial position of the defendant, and the practical effect of giving judgment on the claim in reconvention upon the financial position of the defendant in reconvention, before finally formulating its order or orders. This appears to have been done in *Van Gysen v Van Gysen* (... at 66) [1986 1 SA 56 (C)]. It might well occur, furthermore, that judgment upon the claim in convention would be wholly or partly extinguished, by way of set-off, by the judgment on the counterclaim or *vice versa*; but that does not mean that the Court is not obliged to consider such claims separately on their merits. The trial Court, in fact, never applied its mind to the appellant's claim in this manner, and this Court is accordingly at large to make its own findings on the merits or demerits of the parties' respective claims ...

[MILNE JA then proceeded to deal with the grounds upon which the respondent submitted that the appellant's claim for transfer of R109 000 should fail. He rejected the argument that the respondent's contribution to the spouses' matrimonial home exceeded the appellant's contribution. He proceeded:]

I deal now with the question of fault. The learned trial Judge regarded [80] the nature of 'this particular marital relationship' as being 'of prime significance in resolving the proprietary claims'.

In *Beaumont v Beaumont* (. . . at 994D) [117] BOTHA JA expressed the view that, by virtue of the wide import of the wording of para *(d)* of ss (5) of s 7 of the Act,

'. . . the Court is entitled . . . to take a party's misconduct into account even when only a redistribution order is being considered under ss (3), and where no maintenance order under ss (2) is made'.

Although this opinion was avowedly *obiter*, no attack on it was made in this Court and I respectfully agree with it. BOTHA JA, however, went on to say, firstly 'I am convinced that our Courts will adopt a conservative approach in assessing a party's misconduct as a relevant factor whether under ss (2) or ss (3)' and, secondly . . . that the Courts are to consider 'the conduct of each of the parties if that conduct is such that it would in the opinion of the Court be inequitable to disregard it'. The judgment then goes on at 994I:

'In many, probably most, cases both parties will be to blame, in the sense of having contributed to the breakdown of the marriage . . . In such cases, where there is no conspicuous disparity between the conduct of the one party and that of the other, our Courts will not indulge in an exercise to apportion the fault of the parties, and thus nullify the advantages of the "no fault" system of divorce.'

The facts in *Beaumont's* case were that misconduct existed on the part of the appellant only, and that such misconduct was 'certainly gross and prolonged'. Despite this, the Court took such misconduct into account only in allowing the scales of justice to be tipped in favour of the respondent where the facts were not altogether clear or certain, and where the areas of uncertainty were not due to any remissness on the part of the respondent in placing available information before the Court.

The learned trial Judge . . . did not have the benefit of this Court's judgment in the *Beaumont* case when he delivered judgment in this case [the Appellate Division's decision in *Beaumont* had not yet been reported] and, had he done so, I doubt whether he would have given the appellant's 'fault' the weight that he clearly did.

In any event the evidence does not justify his finding that, in effect, the appellant was solely to blame for the marriage coming to an end. Even if it is correct that it was her 'fault' in the sense that her adultery or, more correctly, her intention to marry Mr Green, was the immediate cause of the marriage coming to an end, it is quite clear, on the facts, that the respondent was by no means free from blame, nor could it conceivably be said that any relevant misconduct on the part of the appellant was either gross or prolonged . . .

[MILNE JA discussed the evidence regarding the spouses' sexual problems and proceeded:]

[83] Putting the respondent's case at its highest I do not think that it can be said that there is a 'conspicuous disparity of fault between the conduct of the one party and that of the other'. In these circumstances I think the learned trial Judge erred in regarding fault as a significant factor, and all the more so in regarding it as being '. . . of prime significance in resolving the proprietary claims . . .'. With regard to contention (*c*) [the contention that the respondent contributed to the growth in the appellant's estate by not settling overseas], this argument proceeds on the basis that the respondent's conduct constituted a 'contribution' within the meaning of s 7(3). For reasons which are set out later in this judgment I have come to the conclusion that it did not, and this contention accordingly falls away . . .

As the trial Court failed to exercise its judicial discretion properly in considering the appellant's claim, this Court is at large to exercise its own discretion . . . I have no doubt that it is just and equitable to grant judgment for the appellant on the claim in convention in the amount of R109 000 . . .

[84] I deal now with the respondent's claim in reconvention. Before dealing with the legal question of whether the respondent's conduct could constitute a contribution within the meaning of ss (4) I think it is necessary to consider precisely what that conduct was. The trial Judge found that the respondent

> '. . . did indeed sacrifice his future career and prospects upon the altar of her advancement with Clicks, and I am satisfied that it was indeed a sacrifice which the defendant made' . . .

That is not the basis upon which the respondent himself put the claim. What the respondent said was that the decision 'not to go the Mobil route' was '. . . a decision that was taken after discussion as to what was in our joint best interests' . . .

[85] What he is saying is that he decided that it was in their *joint financial* interest not to take the overseas posting . . .

[MILNE JA further analysed the evidence of the respondent and reached the conclusion that the respondent might well have over-estimated his prospects of promotion. MILNE JA proceeded:]

[86] The respondent is, so it seems to me, caught on the horns of a dilemma. If, in fact, his prospects were really as rosy as those painted by him and his counsel, then he simply made a bad error of judgment in deciding to stay where he was, and cannot expect to be compensated for his error by the appellant. If, however, his prospects were not nearly as rosy as those suggested on his behalf, then he has not, in fact, made the sacrifice which it is suggested he made. On the contrary he has profited from the decision to remain in South Africa by enjoying the very high standard of living which his wife's earnings made possible during the past eight to nine years. It becomes apparent that what the respondent was really seeking to do was to claim damages for loss of his wife's contribution to their combined earning power, due to the breaking up of their marriage, which he alleges was her fault. There is, of course, no warrant for such a claim . . .

On the facts . . . I am not satisfied that the respondent 'gave up' anything, still less that he 'sacrificed' his career.

In any event, I consider that for the reasons that follow, the conduct pleaded by the respondent did not constitute a contribution within the meaning of ss (4).

Counsel for the respondent relied heavily upon the remarks in *Beaumont's* case (*supra* at 996H) where BOTHA JA said with reference to the provisions of ss (4) 'in these words one searches in vain for any suggestion of a qualification of the nature of the contribution required in the sense contended for by counsel'. There, of course, the Court was considering the submission of counsel that the Legislature could not have intended a contribution by either spouse made solely in the discharge of a common law duty of support, to qualify as a contribution which entitled the spouse [87] making it to claim 'compensation' in the form of a redistribution order. The Court found there was nothing in the words used to indicate that the Legislature intended that qualification. That is quite a different question from the problem that arises in this case . . . In the case before us, so the appellant's counsel argued, the respondent did nothing – he could not be said to have contributed to the maintenance of or an increase in the estate of the other party 'by merely not earning'. In other words, the submission was that all the respondent did was to fail to prevent the appellant from increasing her estate. The validity of this point depends upon what the Legislature meant in ss (4) when it used the words

'... contributed directly or indirectly to the maintenance or increase of the estate of the other party during the subsistence of the marriage, either by the rendering of services or the saving of expenses which would otherwise have been incurred or in any other manner'.

The words used are certainly of wide meaning but that does not make them of unlimited meaning. One must look at the ordinary grammatical meaning of the words used, and what is more, the particular context within which they are used. The first (non-obsolete) definition of the word 'contribute' in the *Oxford English Dictionary* is 'to give or pay jointly with others; to furnish to a common fund' (vol II at 924 of the 1961 ed). The dictionary includes, as a figurative meaning, 'to give or furnish along with others towards bringing about a result; to lend (effective agency or assistance) to a common result or purpose'. (I stress the word *effective* in that definition.) Black's *Law Dictionary* defines 'contribute' as follows: 'to lend assistance or aid or give something to a common purpose; to have a share in any act or effect; to discharge a joint obligation'. It goes on to say that when applied to negligence it

'signifies causal connection between injury and negligence which transcends and is distinguished from negligent acts or omissions which play so minor a part in producing injury that law does not recognise them as legal causes'

(at 297 (5th ed)). The Afrikaans version of the Act (which is the signed version, both in the case of the original Act and in the case of the amending Act which introduced the relevant subsections) uses the following words: 'Direk of indirek bygedra het tot die instandhouding of groei in die boedel van die ander party', and respondent's counsel relied upon the second meaning given by *HAT* at 124-5, namely 'saamhelp, help' (the first meaning is 'iets skenk'), and the second meaning given in *Die Afrikaanse Woordeboek* at 564, namely 'iets wat meehelp tot bevordering van 'n bepaalde of gemeenskaplike saak' (the first meaning is 'wat as skenking gegee word, dikw i/d vorm van geld'). There does not appear to be any significant difference between the English and the Afrikaans versions. This legislation is dealing with the financial position of the parties and, *prima facie*, therefore, with contributions of a financial nature. In *Beaumont's* case *supra* at 987 BOTHA JA, having said that the creation of a power enabling a Court to make a redistribution order was a reforming and remedial measure, went on to say:

[88] 'What the measure was designed to remedy is trenchantly demonstrated by the facts of the present case: the inequity which could flow from the failure of the law to recognise a right of a spouse upon divorce to claim an adjustment of a disparity between the respective assets of the spouses which is incommensurate with their respective contributions during the subsistence of the marriage to the maintenance or increase of the estate of the one or the other.'

I am inclined to agree with the opening submissions of counsel for the respondent in the *Beaumont* case (as reported at 978E–G) as to the reasons for the introduction of this power, but, clearly, if a husband's claim falls within the provisions of the Act, he is just as much entitled to an order as the wife. But as the legislation is dealing with the financial position of the parties, what was clearly envisaged was some positive act by means of which one spouse puts something into the maintenance or increase of the estate of the other spouse – whether by way of money or property, labour or skill. It does not envisage a mere refraining from a particular activity or course of conduct. It was submitted that the inclusion of 'the saving of expenses which would have otherwise been incurred' indicated that a positive act was not necessary. This is not necessarily so. For example, if a spouse was to spend money or time or labour in cultivating vegetables for the family that would constitute a positive action which would have the effect of saving expenses. It is conceivable, however, that a spouse may refrain from expenditure which in the circumstances of the parties is reasonable (for example, the employment of a domestic servant), and that this could constitute a saving of expenses amounting to a contribution within the meaning of the section. On the other hand to refrain from employing a domestic servant would entail many positive acts. Such a situation could be put positively or negatively. Thus one may say 'refrain from employing a domestic servant' or do 'domestic work'; 'refrain from buying clothes' or 'make clothes oneself to effect a saving'. The negative generally entails a positive. Refraining from extravagance, for example, would not fall within the meaning of the subsection, being purely negative. The words 'expenses which would otherwise have been incurred' implies necessary or at least reasonable expenditure in the particular circumstances. It seems to me that it is prerequisite to a successful claim under this subsection that the claimant must show, on a balance of probabilities, that the conduct relied upon as a contribution in fact *caused* the alleged maintenance or increase of the other spouse's estate. To borrow from the language of causation used in negligence cases, the conduct must be the *causa causans*, and not merely the *causa sine qua non*, of the alleged maintenance or increase. If the appellant had not been married, or had married some other man, there is no reason to suppose that she would not have accumulated exactly the same estate. The respondent contributed nothing in the form of money, property, work, time or skill – or, indeed, any form of activity, whatsoever, to the increase of the appellant's estate.

I must say, furthermore, that I am inclined to think that it was never contemplated by the Legislature that the sacrifice by one of the spouses of a more lucrative career which was *not* accompanied by the rendering of service or the saving of expenses which would otherwise have been incurred, or some other factor for which a value in money can reasonably be ascertained, would be capable of constituting such a contribution. [89] Divorce is a distressingly common feature of contemporary life in South Africa and, if a claim could be made for giving up a career to the parties' common benefit, there would be few marriages between parties of any real economic substance where such a claim would not be made. I find it difficult to consider upon what conceptual basis such a claim would be formulated in terms of money unless the conduct under consideration was capable of being so evaluated. For example, in *Beaumont's* case the wife contributed her services in various ways which are apparent from the judgment of the trial Court, and a value could be put upon those services. Suppose, however, that a young woman who is half-way through her medical degree marries a politician, and decides not to pursue that degree in order to assist her husband socially in his public life; is she to be compensated if the marriage comes adrift for giving up her degree and her medical career? If so, upon what monetary basis? Or let us suppose that both parties have qualified as medical practitioners, and the wife is offered an overseas course lasting six months to a year, the result of which, it is shown on a balance of probabilities, would have been to place her on the specialist register in a particularly lucrative field, and she declines to take up the scholarship because they make a joint decision that she will remain with her husband in South Africa where his career is; if the marriage breaks down and a divorce ensues, is she to be compensated for the career she would have had, had she taken up the scholarship? The kind of difficulty which would be involved in acceding to claims of this nature is well illustrated by the fact that the respondent's counsel found it quite impossible to indicate any basis at all upon which it would be proper to evaluate the respondent's claim. The trial court found that '. . . no figure can be put on defendant's sacrifice . . .' and this must generally be the case where, during the course of the marriage one of the spouses has given up a more lucrative career, or given up a career.

The respondent accordingly failed to establish that he contributed to the maintenance or increase of the appellant's estate. This renders it unnecessary to consider whether, in calculating whether it would be just or equitable to make a redistribution order in favour of the respondent, it would be necessary to take into account that the appellant, in order to provide funds to improve the home, sold shares at a much lower price than she would have received had she sold them at the date of the trial.

The appeal is accordingly upheld ...

CORBETT JA and NICHOLAS AJA concurred.

Note

The first important point made by the court was that a claim and counterclaim for the redistribution of assets should generally not be considered by means of a globular approach. The two claims should be considered separately to ensure that each claim gets the attention it deserves. There may be "cases where the facts relevant to both claims are so inextricably interrelated that a globular approach is the only possible one, but, save in such circumstances, the claims must, at least initially, be considered separately" (79).

Secondly the court emphasised that each marriage is a partnership of a kind but this does not mean that a marriage has the same consequences as those of a partnership in the legal sense. The spouse who avers that a partnership in the legal sense has come into operation between the spouses will have to prove this and the mere fact that both spouses contributed to the common household will not constitute sufficient proof (77). (See also *Katz v Katz* [119]; *Mühlmann v Mühlmann* 1984 3 SA 102 (A) and *Van Gysen v Van Gysen* 1986 1 SA 56 (C).)

The third point which should be noted deals with the role that fault plays in relation to the redistribution of assets. In the case under discussion the Appellate Division referred to *Beaumont v Beaumont* [117] and accepted that fault could be considered in deciding whether a redistribution order should be granted. The facts of the present case did not, however, indicate that there was a "conspicuous disparity of fault" between the spouses and therefore fault could not be regarded as a significant factor.

As regards the nature of the contribution which could be considered in terms of section 7(3) and 7(4) of the Divorce Act 70 of 1979, it must be noted that the Appellate Division in the case under discussion required a causal connection between the applicant's conduct and the growth or maintenance of the other spouse's estate (88). The court further stated that normally only a positive act would constitute a contribution. To merely

Aantekening

Die eerste belangrike punt wat die hof geopper het, is dat 'n eis en teeneis om die herverdeling van bates gewoonlik nie saam beskou moet word nie. Die twee eise behoort apart beoordeel te word sodat elkeen die aandag kan geniet wat dit verdien. Daar mag gevalle wees "where the facts relevant to both claims are so inextricably interrelated that a globular approach is the only possible one, but, save in such circumstances, the claims must, at least initially, be considered separately" (79).

Tweedens het die hof beklemtoon dat elke huwelik in 'n sekere sin 'n vennootskap is maar dat dit nie beteken dat 'n huwelik dieselfde gevolge het as wat 'n vennootskap regtens het nie. Die gade wat beweer dat 'n vennootskap regtens ontstaan het, sal dit moet bewys en die blote feit dat beide gades tot die gemeenskaplike huishouding bygedra het, sal nie as voldoende bewys aanvaar word nie (77). (Sien ook *Katz v Katz* [119]; *Mühlmann v Mühlmann* 1984 3 SA 102 (A) en *Van Gysen v Van Gysen* 1986 1 SA 56 (K).)

Derdens moet gelet word op die rol wat gedrag speel met betrekking tot die herverdeling van bates. In die saak onder bespreking het die Appèlafdeling na *Beaumont v Beaumont* [117] verwys en aanvaar dat gedrag wel 'n oorweging kan wees wanneer 'n beslissing oor 'n herverdelingsbevel gemaak moet word. Die feite van die onderhawige saak het egter nie daarop gedui dat daar 'n "conspicuous disparity of fault" tussen die gades was nie en dus kon gedrag nie as 'n relevante faktor in ag geneem word nie.

Wat die aard van die bydrae betref wat ingevolge artikels 7(3) en 7(4) van die Wet op Egskeiding 70 van 1979 oorweeg kan word, moet daarop gelet word dat die Appèlafdeling in die onderhawige saak vereis het dat daar 'n kousale verband moet bestaan tussen die optrede van die applikant en die groei of instandhouding van die ander gade se boedel (88). Die hof het verder verklaar dat dit gewoonlik slegs 'n positiewe optrede sal wees wat as 'n bydrae sal kwalifiseer. Om niks te doen

refrain from action would therefore not qualify as a contribution to the growth or maintenance of the other spouse's estate.

Lastly it should be noted that the remedy afforded by section 7(3) of the Divorce Act cannot be applied in such a way as to award a spouse damages for the loss of the other spouse's contribution to the spouse's combined earning power where the other spouse caused the breaking up of the marriage (86). See also Sinclair 1989 *SALJ* 249 and Clark and Van Heerden 1989 *SALJ* 243.

nie sal dus nie 'n bydrae tot die groei of instandhouding van die ander gade se boedel uitmaak nie.

Laastens moet daarop gelet word dat die remedie wat ingevolge artikel 7(3) verleen word nie op so 'n wyse aangewend mag word dat skadevergoeding aan 'n gade toegeken word vir die verlies van die ander gade se bydrae tot die gades se gesamentlike verdienvermoë waar die ander gade die verbrokkeling van die huwelik veroorsaak het nie (86). Sien ook Sinclair 1989 *SALJ* 249 en Clark en Van Heerden 1989 *SALJ* 243.

[119] KATZ V KATZ

1989 3 SA 1 (A)

Redistribution order in terms of section 7(3) of the Divorce Act 70 of 1979

The appellant (husband) and the respondent (wife) were married out of community of property in 1964. In September 1986 the respondent instituted a divorce action against the appellant. She claimed, *inter alia*, the selling price of the spouses' matrimonial home (± R278 000) which had been registered in her name, maintenance and the transfer of one half of the appellant's assets to her in terms of section 7(3) of the Divorce Act 70 of 1979. At the time of the divorce in August 1987 the appellant's estate was valued at R7 539 200 while the respondent, apart from the house, only had R26 000 in a savings account. The appellant made a "clean break" settlement offer to the respondent in which he undertook to pay her R750 000. The respondent did not accept this. In the court *a quo* the appellant was ordered to pay the selling price of the house as well as R3 500 000 (approximately half of the value of his estate) to the respondent. The court decided on this division because it had reached the conclusion that throughout the marriage there had been a universal partnership between the parties in which they held equal shares and that

Herverdelingsbevel ingevolge artikel 7(3) van die Wet op Egskeiding 70 van 1979

Die appellant (man) en die respondent (vrou) is in 1964 buite gemeenskap van goed getroud. In September 1986 het die respondent 'n egskeidingsaksie teen die appellant aanhangig gemaak. Sy het onder andere geëis dat die verkoopprys van die gades se gemeenskaplike woning (± R278 000), wat in haar naam geregistreer was, aan haar betaal word. Verder het sy onderhoud sowel as oordrag van die helfte van die appellant se bates ingevolge artikel 7(3) van die Wet op Egskeiding 70 van 1979 geëis. Ten tyde van die egskeiding in Augustus 1987 het die appellant 'n boedel ter waarde van R7 539 200 gehad terwyl die respondent benewens die huis net R26 000 in 'n spaarrekening gehad het. Die appellant het 'n "skoon breuk"-skikkingsaanbod aan die respondent gemaak waarin hy aangebied het om R750 000 aan haar te betaal. Die respondent het dit nie aanvaar nie. In die hof *a quo* is die appellant beveel om die verkoopprys van die huis sowel as R3 500 000 (omtrent die helfte van die waarde van sy boedel) aan die respondent te betaal. Die hof het op die verdeling besluit

they should therefore share equally in the division of the estate. The appellant appealed against this decision. He did not object to the part of the order relating to the payment of the selling price of the house to the respondent. He only objected to the amount of R3 500 000 that he was to transfer to the respondent. He argued that it "should be reduced substantially to reflect a transfer by the appellant to the respondent of an amount which the Court deems just and equitable in terms of s 7 of the [Divorce] Act". The appeal was successful.

aangesien dit tot die gevolgtrekking geraak het dat daar vir die hele duur van die huwelik 'n universele vennootskap tussen die gades bestaan het waarin hulle gelyke aandele gehad het en dat hulle dus gelykop moes deel. Die appellant het teen hierdie beslissing appèl aangeteken. Hy het nie beswaar gemaak teen die gedeelte van die hofbevel waarin hy beveel is om die verkoopprys van die huis aan die respondent te betaal nie. Hy het slegs beswaar gemaak teen die bedrag van R3 500 000 wat hy aan die respondent moes oordra. Hy het geredeneer "that it should be reduced substantially to reflect a transfer by the appellant to the respondent of an amount which the Court deems just and equitable in terms of s 7 of the [Divorce] Act". Die appèl het geslaag.

MILNE JA: [6] The finding that the net assets of the appellant at the date of conclusion of the trial were R7 539 200 was not challenged, and appears to be correct. The appellant's counsel initially contended that, on a proper reading of s 7, it was necessary to determine the parties' assets at the date when they separated, namely in September 1986, but he abandoned this contention in argument. In my view it is quite clear that the Court, in making an order in terms of s 7(3), is required to have regard, so far as that is practicable, to the assets and liabilities of the parties as at the date of the order. Subsection (2), which deals with the payment of maintenance, requires the Court to have regard to '... the existing or prospective means of each of the parties, their respective earning capacities, financial needs and obligations ...'. Subsection (3), which deals with a redistribution order, requires the Court to consider the provisions of ss (4), (5) and (6) before making an order in terms of ss (3). Subsection (5) expressly refers in subpara (a) to 'the existing means and obligations of the parties'. There is nothing to indicate that the Legislature had in mind any date other than the date of the Court's order and, indeed, if the original contention of the appellant were to succeed, it could give rise to highly anomalous consequences.

Despite the submissions of the respondent's counsel to the contrary, it is quite clear that the trial Court arrived at the conclusion that it was just and equitable to award the respondent R3,5 million on the basis that a [7] universal partnership in equal shares existed between the parties throughout the marriage, and on no other basis ... The learned Judge dealt at length in his judgment with a letter which the appellant wrote to the respondent on 11 November 1978 ... In this letter the appellant said '... I have always considered our marriage a universal partnership...' The trial Court found that certain statements in that letter were the truth, '... and that a universal partnership existed between the parties at the time of the marriage and during the marriage'. He then went on to say, 'I find that this was an equal affair'. At a later stage in his judgment, after dealing with the factors to be taken into account in making an order under s 7(3) of the Act, the learned Judge says:

'I am of the view that the parties should share equally. I find as a fact that the parties at all times intended that their assets during the marriage belonged to both equally.

The letter of 11 November 1978 corroborates the plaintiff's version as to "what is mine is yours and what is yours is mine". The defendant's denial of this attitude is rejected. The redistribution order I make will reflect this position.'

In adopting this approach it is plain that the trial Court misdirected itself. In the first place the respondent's case was not based upon a claim for distribution of the assets of an equal partnership. It was based upon the provisions of s 7(3) of the Act. That is clear from the pleadings and the evidence, and, indeed, it was common cause between counsel at the hearing of the appeal. Secondly, it is quite clear from the respondent's evidence that there never was a legal partnership between them, and the respondent's counsel conceded as much in argument. Even if spouses agree to pool their resources such an agreement, unless it has the requisites of a legal partnership, is not irrevocable and may be resiled from at any time. *Kritzinger v Kritzinger* 1989 (1) SA 67 (A) at 77C–E [118] . . .

Furthermore, in the instant case the only properties that were 'acquired by the joint endeavours and out of the joint resources of the spouses during marriage' were the three matrimonial homes, namely the properties at Glenhazel, Waverley and Melrose, and it is the Melrose [8] property which the respondent claimed as her sole property, and the entire proceeds of which were separately awarded to her in the trial Court's order.

On the facts of this case it certainly cannot be said that a legal partnership existed; still less a universal partnership, and even less a partnership in equal shares . . .

[10] Since this finding [that there was an equal partnership] coloured the whole approach of the learned trial Judge this Court is now free to consider the matter afresh.

I think it must be borne in mind that the respondent not only claimed a redistribution order in terms of s 7(3) of the Act, but also a maintenance order in terms of ss (2). These two subsections refer to a variety of matters which are to be taken into account when orders under them are sought. Some of these factors are to be found in both subsections, eg ss (2) refers to the means and obligations of the parties as does ss (5)(a) which, together with ss (4), lays down matters which must be taken into account by a Court making an order under ss (3) in addition to those set out in ss (3) itself. There are, of course, clear differences between these two subsections. It is a prerequisite to the grant of an order under ss (3) that the spouse seeking such an order has made a contribution of the nature described in ss (4). No such contribution is required under ss (2). The two subsections are, however, interrelated, because one of the matters required to be taken into account when considering the grant of a maintenance order is 'an order in terms of ss (3)'. What is more, it is clear that in the *Beaumont* case . . . at 992E–F [117] read with the passage cited above this Court decided that the Legislature intended the Court to be able to take

[11] '. . . an overall view, from the outset, of how justice could best be achieved between the parties in the light of possible orders under either ss (2) or ss (3) or both subsections, in relation to the means and obligations, and the needs of the parties, and all the other relevant factors'.

When a Court makes an order for maintenance in terms of s 7(2) it may have regard to the factors there set out, including 'an order in terms of ss (3) and any other factor which in the opinion of the Court should be taken into account'. There is nothing in ss (5) which specifically provides that in the determination of the assets to be transferred as contemplated in ss (3), regard may be had to the fact that no order is being made in terms of ss (2). Nevertheless, such regard is not excluded. (See ss (5)(d)). In terms of the decision in *Beaumont's* case *supra* the 'clean break' concept is not foreign to our law. It is obvious that a 'complete termination of the financial dependence of one party on the other' cannot be achieved so long as there is to be an order for the periodical payment of maintenance. It follows that it will frequently (one may almost say generally) be necessary, if a clean break is to be achieved, that the amount of the determination should be at least such that the spouse concerned will be in a financial position to maintain herself or himself. In such circumstances a Court will ordinarily take into account the spouse's maintenance needs.

I have already referred to the trial Court's findings as to the capital sum required to provide the respondent with a new town house and a new motor car, and as to what sum she would reasonably require to maintain herself. On the basis of these findings and on the basis of a calculation contained in a document which formed part of the agreed bundle of documents, the amount needed to maintain the respondent would be in the vicinity of R500 000. This is on the assumption that the R300 000 needed for the house and car and incidental expenses would be provided for by the amount of the net proceeds of the Melrose home together with the respondent's R26 000 invested in a savings account. The calculation referred to indicated that R500 000 would purchase an annuity which would provide a monthly income of approximately R6 000 per month.

The respondent's claim was, however, not confined to one for maintenance. The trial Court found that the respondent had, indeed, contributed to the increase or maintenance of the appellant's estate, and that she had done so in various ways. For the sake of convenience these may be divided into three broad categories. The first consisted of contributions made by the respondent's parents. The second consisted of contributions to the matrimonial home made directly by the respondent. The third consisted of her indirect contributions in the shape of her 'services' as a wife.

I exclude from the first category any contribution by the respondent's parents to the acquisition of the matrimonial homes of the parties ...

[MILNE JA then mentioned the contributions made by the respondent's parents such as donations of trousseau, curtains and holiday accommodation. He proceeded:]

[12] I am not certain that these contributions constitute contributions by the respondent within the meaning of ss (3). They were certainly contributions made for the benefits of the family, but were probably made mainly on account of the love and affection which the respondent's parents had for the respondent. Possibly they were also made out of affection for the appellant. Assuming, without deciding, that they do constitute contributions within the meaning of the subsection, I do not think that they should play a material part in arriving at the value of the respondent's contributions. I say this because the contribution which the appellant made to the respondent's estate was at least equal in value to the contributions made to his estate by the respondent's parents. I refer here to the increase in the respondent's estate caused by the appellant's conduct in enhancing the value of the matrimonial homes of the parties which were the respondent's property ...

[13] Before dealing with the value of the respondent's 'services' as a wife, I should refer to the argument of the respondent's counsel that the respondent had also contributed to the increase in the appellant's estate with regard to his property dealing. There can be no doubt that the appellant's large estate at the time of the trial came into being because the appellant made money out of property dealings, and then, at the right time, sold his total property portfolio for approximately R3 000 000 and put all his money into the stock market which then rose spectacularly. At the time of the trial the stock market was just about at its peak before the crash of October 1987. It ... was his money and not hers that went into his property portfolio and property developments ...

There is no doubt that it was, to an overwhelming degree, the appellant's own energy, ability, knowledge and courage that enabled him to make extremely profitable investments in property, and even more profitable investments in the stock market ...

True, the respondent has some recollection of the properties being purchased, as she was kept generally informed in regard to what was happening, and perhaps it is fair to say that the appellant used her on some occasions as a 'sounding board' in respect of his proposed investments. It is clear however that, as contended by appellant's counsel, the respondent played no role in the decisions to acquire any assets which constituted the [14] appellant's property portfolio, and later his share portfolio. She took no part in the business of running the properties or realising them.

The respondent must therefore rely upon the performance by her of 'services' as a wife in order to establish that she contributed to the maintenance or increase of the appellant's estate. Her role in the marriage was confined to the traditional one of being wife, mother and manageress of the household. This role is rather more fully described in the respondent's pleadings as follows:

> 'Throughout their marriage, plaintiff afforded defendant moral support in respect of all his undertakings and ventures, and was a dutiful and loyal wife to defendant and mother to the children. At defendant's insistence plaintiff was totally and actively involved in the running of the home and the caring for the children and defendant. At his insistence she was always home when the children returned from school and personally supervised their extra-mural activities, both educational, sporting and social. In order to free defendant on weekends to enable him to attend to his weekend activities, plaintiff was obliged to bear the entire burden of attending to the children's weekend social and sporting activities. Plaintiff attended to all defendant's personal needs, even to the extent of purchasing his toiletries and always being at home when he returned from work. Whenever required to, she accompanied him to social functions and entertained business associates by holding numerous dinner parties and Christmas parties for defendant's staff, clients and business associates. Plaintiff assumed total responsibility for the running of the home and attended to the needs of the children so as to leave defendant completely free to further his career, investment and other interests.'

I doubt whether it can accurately be said that it was 'at defendant's insistence' that the respondent undertook what was primarily a domestic role, and furthermore the pleading omits to state that the parties had three servants and 'all of the accoutrements of a comfortable home'. The respondent had regular holidays and overseas trips, she acquired jewellery and furs and her own estate was substantially improved by the appellant's efforts. I refer here to the efforts he made, which were successful, to increase the value of the matrimonial home which was hers. It is also the case that the appellant encouraged the respondent to pursue her own occupations, and she did at various times work for an auditor, for ten months as a real estate agent during which time she earned some R16 000 (which she retained to spend as she wished), as was the case with her earnings as a public relations officer for an aerobics establishment. She was encouraged to attend university, and other courses, and these courses were paid for by the appellant. Furthermore, it was clear that, when Christmas parties were held for the appellant's staff, caterers were called in to assist. Nevertheless, in my view, the trial Court was right in holding that:

> 'Throughout the years the plaintiff ... assisted defendant by rendering him services in his home. In pursuit of his practice and his property speculation, he relied on her implicitly to keep the home fires burning and he lived in great comfort.'

There is no evidence which enables one to put a money value on these services. Nor is there evidence that if the respondent had not performed them the appellant would have employed someone to perform them, nor as to what it would have cost to employ such a person. In *Kretschmer v Kretschmer* 1989 (1) SA 566 (W) [120] FLEMMING J appears to have thought that [15] such evidence was a prerequisite to a finding that the plaintiff in that case had made a contribution within the meaning of ss (3) and (4) of s 7. (At 580H–

581C). What is more, he appears to have thought that the spouse seeking to prove a contribution would have to prove that the contribution exceeded '... the amount of the duty to contribute to own support'. (At 579C–582E).

It seems to me, with respect, that this reasoning involves a confusion between the jurisdictional facts which have to be proved before a Court can make an order in terms of s 7(3) and the manner in which the Court is to exercise that power once it is established. Before the Court can make an order in terms of ss (3) it must be established (a) that the party seeking such an order has made a contribution; (b) that such a contribution has increased or maintained the other party's estate; and (c) that it would be just and equitable to make such an order because of (a) and (b). It does not follow that the manner in which the Court is to arrive at what is just and equitable is limited to what has been contributed. In the first place this is not what the section says. In the second place this Court in *Beaumont's* case *supra* has held quite clearly that this is not what the section means ...

I return therefore to the question as to the evaluation of the wife's 'services'. This is a difficult task. I have already dealt in detail with the nature and extent of the respondent's contribution to the appellant's estate. The following are also factors which I regard as relevant: [16]

(a) The net value of the appellant's assets at the time when the Court *a quo* made its order was R7 539 200 (excluding the value of his share in the legal practice).

(b) The net value of the respondent's assets at that time (excluding household furniture and fittings, clothing, jewellery and furs) was R26 000 and in terms of the Court's order she was to receive a further R278 000 being the net proceeds of the Melrose property and it was common cause that this part of the order would stand.

(c) While it is reasonably *possible* that the respondent may take up some occupation which would provide some income it is reasonable to proceed on the basis that she probably will not. In the first place, on the evidence she is not qualified for any particular profession, occupation or job. Secondly, she is no longer a young woman and apart from brief periods when she worked as an estate agent and later as a public relations officer she did not have a job of any kind during the marriage.

(d) The appellant has a substantial legal practice and is obviously highly successful in the investment field, and is more likely than not to continue to be successful.

(e) The marriage had its ups and downs and ... each of the spouses committed adultery, but they had three children who are now grown up and the marriage lasted some 23 years.

(f) The appellant has always provided satisfactorily for the maintenance of the children, and will continue to do so.

(g) On the facts of this case there is not such a conspicuous disparity of fault between the conduct of the appellant and that of the respondent in bringing the marriage relationship to an end as to warrant this being taken into account, even on the very limited basis that it was taken into account in *Beaumont's* case at 995E–J [117] ...

[T]he sum of R500 000 would purchase the respondent an annuity which would provide her with approximately R6 000 per month for the rest of her life. This is, however, an unrealistic calculation since it fails to take into account the effect of inflation. For some years, the annual rate of inflation in the Republic has been substantial and there does not appear to be any ground for believing that it is likely to decrease appreciably in the foreseeable future. What is more, the Republic is subject to artificial pressures in the form of sanctions which have an effect on the economy. Interest rates have fluctuated very considerably over the past few years. In these circumstances it is difficult for the average person to invest safely and at the same time receive a reasonable return while avoiding the ravages of inflation. Furthermore, the calculation referred to does not take into account the tax which the respondent would have to pay on the R6 000 per month.

[17] In the light of all the circumstances I consider that, on the facts of this particular case (and I stress that I am laying down no principle nor even a general guide) it would be just and equitable to make a redistribution order which would, so far as is reasonably practicable, enable the respondent to maintain the same standard of living as the parties enjoyed when the marriage broke up. This order is intended, again so far as is practicable, to give the respondent financial security for the rest of her life. What is more, it is intended to be sufficient to cater for the respondent paying for expert advice on her investments on a continuing basis, and even to cater for occasional losses on investments. It is only possible to proceed on this relatively generous basis because the appellant has a very large estate. This may seem anomalous because, in the case of the person of average means and even more so in the case of a poor person, the spouse may actually have worked a great deal harder and had a much more demanding married life than the respondent; yet because of the limited nature of the other spouse's resources, be entitled to very limited maintenance, and in the case of a poor person to virtually nothing. This is, in the nature of things, unavoidable and, in any event, it is no more anomalous than taking into account the standard of living of the parties prior to the divorce which ss (2) expressly enjoins the Court to do when making a maintenance order. It is not possible to make anything like a precise calculation, partly because of the difficulty in putting a money value on the respondent's services and partly because of the impossibility of forecasting what interest rates are likely to be during future years. In the light of all the factors I have referred to I have come to the conclusion that it would be just and equitable to make a redistribution order in favour of the respondent in the sum of R1,5 million . . .

CORBETT CJ; HOEXTER JA; NESTADT JA and NICHOLAS AJA concurred.

Note

In this case, as in *Beaumont v Beaumont* [117], the Appellate Division emphasised that any contribution to the increase or maintenance of the other spouse's estate can qualify as a contribution in terms of section 7(4), provided of course that the other statutory requirements are also complied with. The Appellate Division further made it quite clear that it is not a prerequisite that the contribution must be of such a nature that a monetary value could be placed upon it (14). This *dictum* overruled *Kretschmer v Kretschmer* [120], which appears to have required that a monetary value be placed upon the contribution. The Appellate Division overruled the decision in *Kretschmer v Kretschmer* on another point as well. The Appellate Division held that it is not, as was held in the *Kretschmer* case, necessary for the applicant to prove that his contribution entailed more than a contribution to his own support (15). In this respect the *Katz* case also conforms with the decision in *Beaumont v Beaumont*.

Aantekening

In hierdie saak het die Appèlafdeling, net soos in *Beaumont v Beaumont* [117], beklemtoon dat enige bydrae tot die groei of instandhouding van die boedel van die ander gade as 'n bydrae ingevolge artikel 7(4) kan kwalifiseer mits natuurlik ook aan die ander statutêre vereistes voldoen word. Die Appèlafdeling het dit verder ook baie duidelik gestel dat dit geen voorvereiste is dat 'n geldwaarde op die bydrae geplaas moet kan word voordat dit in ag geneem kan word nie (14). Met hierdie uitspraak is *Kretschmer v Kretschmer* [120], wat skynbaar wel vereis het dat 'n geldwaarde op die betrokke bydrae geplaas moet kan word, verwerp. Die Appèlhof het die uitspraak in *Kretschmer v Kretschmer* ook in 'n ander opsig verwerp. Die Appèlafdeling het beslis dat dit nie, soos wat in die *Kretschmer*-saak beslis is, nodig is dat die applikant moet bewys dat sy bydrae meer behels het as bloot 'n bydrae tot sy eie onderhoud nie (15). Die *Katz*-uitspraak is ook in hierdie opsig in ooreenstemming met *Beaumont v Beaumont*.

Concerning the Appellate Division's decision in the case under discussion, it should also be borne in mind that the date on which the value of the spouses' assets and liabilities should be calculated for purposes of a possible redistribution of assets, is the date of the making of the court order (6).

On the interrelationship between sections 7(2) and 7(3) and the "clean break" principle see the note on *Beaumont v Beaumont* [117]. See further *Kritzinger v Kritzinger* [118]; *Kretschmer v Kretschmer* [120] and *Archer v Archer* [121].

Dit is verder belangrik om in gedagte te hou dat die Appèlhof in die onderhawige saak beslis het dat die datum vir die berekening van die waarde van die gades se bates en laste met die oog op 'n moontlike herverdelingsbevel, die datum van die hofbevel is (6).

Sien ook die aantekening by *Beaumont v Beaumont* [117] in verband met die onderlinge verhouding tussen artikels 7(2) en 7(3) en die "skoon breuk"-beginsel. Sien verder *Kritzinger v Kritzinger* [118]; *Kretschmer v Kretschmer* [120] en *Archer v Archer* [121].

[120]   KRETSCHMER V KRETSCHMER

1989 1 SA 566 (W)

Redistribution order in terms of section 7(3) of the Divorce Act 70 of 1979

The plaintiff and the defendant were married to each other out of community of property in 1972. Their marriage broke down irretrievably and the plaintiff sued the defendant for divorce. She was granted a decree of divorce and was awarded the custody of the two minor children born of the marriage. The defendant was further ordered to pay maintenance to the plaintiff in respect of the children. The dispute between the parties mainly concerned financial matters. The court had to determine which amounts, if any, were payable to the plaintiff as maintenance or otherwise. During the marriage the plaintiff, who was an artist, held an exhibition of her paintings in New York which incurred a loss. The loss gave the defendant a rebate on his income tax of R33 000. During the marriage the plaintiff had committed adultery but at the trial it was agreed that the parties had equal fault in regard to the breakdown of the marriage. The court ordered the defendant to pay the plaintiff R33 000 and to pay an insurance company, nominated by the plaintiff, in respect of a single premium policy towards a retirement

Herverdelingsbevel ingevolge artikel 7(3) van die Wet op Egskeiding 70 van 1979

Die eiseres en die verweerder is in 1972 buite gemeenskap van goed met mekaar getroud. Hulle huwelik het onherstelbaar verbrokkel en die eiseres het die verweerder om 'n egskeiding gedagvaar. Die egskeiding is toegestaan en bewaring van die twee minderjarige kinders wat uit die huwelik gebore is, is ook aan die eiseres toegeken. Die verweerder is verder gelas om aan die eiseres onderhoud vir die kinders te betaal. Die geskil tussen die partye het eintlik oor geldelike aangeleenthede gehandel. Die hof moes beslis oor watter bedrae, indien enige, aan die eiseres as onderhoud of andersins betaal moes word. Gedurende die huwelik het die eiseres, wat 'n skilder was, 'n uitstalling van haar skilderye in New York gehou wat op 'n verlies uitgeloop het. Die verlies het egter daartoe gelei dat die verweerder R33 000 minder inkomstebelasting betaal het. Die eiseres het gedurende die huwelik owerspel gepleeg maar tydens die verhoor is ooreengekom dat die partye ewe veel skuld aan die verbrokkeling van die huwelik gehad het. Die hof het die verweerder gelas om R33 000 aan die eiseres te betaal. Ten einde 'n skoon

annuity or endowment policy contracted for by the plaintiff, an amount of R20 000 as maintenance to the plaintiff on a clean break basis.

breuk tussen die partye te bewerkstellig, is die verweerder verder gelas om as onderhoud R20 000 te betaal aan 'n versekeringsmaatskappy wat deur die eiseres aangewys moes word ten opsigte van 'n enkelpremie-polis wat die eiseres moes sluit ten opsigte van 'n uittredingsannuïteit of 'n uitkeringspolis.

FLEMMING J: [568] The object is firstly to attend to the question whether there is any increase in defendant's estate which has anything to do with plaintiff, and what the potential extent is of any such increase . . .

[FLEMMING J set out the parties' assets and then turned to their conduct in regard to the breakdown of the marriage:]

[575] When the hearing of the matter commenced, plaintiff's attitude was conveyed by her counsel as being that an investigation into 'conduct' would not be of any importance in this case and will not affect the decision of any of the debated issues. Defendant's counsel insisted that 'conduct' is relevant. The attention thereafter given to 'conduct' is due to this divergence of attitude. It was not specified what conduct is relevant for what purpose. The Divorce Act 70 of 1979 refers to 'conduct insofar as it may be relevant' in respect of costs (s 10); 'conduct insofar as it may be relevant to the breakdown of the marriage' in regard to maintenance; 'substantial misconduct' (s 9) but no reference to 'conduct' is made at all with regard to transfer of assets.

Where 'conduct' was separately attended to, it was done in the sense of investigating blame, not in the abstract but in regard to the breakdown of the marriage or in regard to the breakdown becoming irretrievable. At the end of the case plaintiff's counsel submitted that the parties had equal fault. Defendant's counsel had by then probably accepted a similar assessment . . .

[576] Broadly speaking the parties were different persons and it took time to show this up and to prove that neither the bond of marriage, nor the children, nor the highs of purchasable pleasures could hold them together. I am not convinced that defendant did not care. To the extent that he may have come across as having that attitude, he probably intended no more than conveying that plaintiff is making more of specific aspects than he thought justified. On other aspects it is not possible to reach a conclusion in favour of the one party or the other . . . or to ascertain as a matter of regular consistent attitude, what the correct interpretation of attitude was. Broadly speaking there is nothing to point a finger against the one rather than against the other. More pertinently, even if there is some difference, the conduct in regard to breakdown does not deserve to alter the view of appropriateness which would have prevailed if none of the parties is to blame in applying s 7(2).

I do, however, believe that the conduct which s 7(3) encompasses without any mention thereof is not the yardstick of s 7(2) or 9 or 10. Reprehensible conduct which is causative of the very crisis between the parties may play a role in applying s 7(3). Cf *Beaumont v Beaumont* 1987 (1) SA 967 (A) [117]. But that is so only if and to the extent of that factor being a factor 'which should in the opinion of the Court be taken into account'. For reasons which I will state more fully, such misbehaviour should generally be taken into account only if it does affect the equity relevant to requiring a party to part with an asset which is the property of no one other than himself, and for which parting with there is no legal basis except if the Court finds it equitable. There are accordingly other aspects of 'conduct' which to my mind should play a role in applying s 7(3) in this case. I will eventually summarise the most important thereof . . .

[577] It is necessary to bear in mind the standard of living of the parties for the purposes of assessing maintenance payable in terms of s 7(2). The scale of living also has an impact in other directions. It affects the probabilities of a 'contribution' by plaintiff. It also encompasses elements of conduct of the parties which should in this case be borne in mind in applying s 7(5) . . .

[579] *About the applicable scope of s 7(3)*

Before summarising the aspects already dealt with and stating conclusions in that regard, it is convenient to deal with two factors which the Court is obliged to bear in mind. There is no statutory definition of the role which they are supposed to play or may be permitted to play. Section 7(5)(*a*) refers to the 'existing means and obligations' of the parties. Section 7(5)(*d*) mentions 'any other factor which should in the opinion of the Court be taken into account'. Parliament has made those factors relevant in a context where the very making of an order is not permissible at all unless the equity of the order arises by virtue of a specific fact. Section 7(4) prohibits an order for the transfer of assets unless the order is equitable and just

> '*by reason of* the fact that the party . . . contributed . . . to the increase of the estate of the other party'

(or to his maintenance). It was probably not intended that, once the Court has overcome the prohibition of s 7(4), the Court may under s 7(5) introduce any factor whatsoever, irrespective of its lack of bearing upon the consideration that the governing yardstick for the equity of depriving a party of his exclusive property is whether the other party 'contributed'.

Quite apart from the wording and the indications given thereby, the object of s 7(3) is also something less than an authority to create an accrual system whenever it would have been sensible for the parties, in the interests of one or both, to change their financial relationship in terms of s 21 of the Matrimonial Property Act 88 of 1984. There is no free discretion to look at what accrued without scrutiny of what contributions each of the parties made and with what effect. Section 7(3) was introduced for the situation where the facts fall short of a legal basis of recovery (such as enrichment, gifts made on a supposition, tacit partnership, duly created accrual property system), but it is recognisably unfair if the one party is to be left without any recompense for his causation of recognisable benefits to the other party.

It follows that s 7(3) does not create a free judicial discretion to create a system of accrual-sharing which the parties themselves did not create. It would require particular facts to dictate equities which justify a literal equal sharing in all accruals. No other fixed proportion is fitting unless the equities attached to the particular contributions justify it. Neither is it a free discretion in the name of general fairness, because the content of what a party 'contributed' and the circumstances surrounding that is dominant. The mere fact that defendant is a rich man or that there is a disparity [580] between the estate of the two spouses, does not create authority to tag on additional amounts to what was 'contributed'. The 'means and obligations' of the parties may well affect the appropriate order in other directions, eg making no adjustment in favour of the contributing party because of decimation of the losing party's estate by business developments beyond his control.

Section 7(3) is also not a whip for punishment. Imagine a 20-year marriage where it is known that the parties contributed exactly equally little (or much) to the accrual in both their estates and wherein both had equal (or no) blame until the last month before divorce when the defendant committed adultery, abandoned the common home and whatever else one wants to add to make his conduct 'gross and prolonged' or to create a 'conspicuous disparity between the conduct of the one party and that of the other' in regard to the breakdown of the marriage. I cannot see that the fault in the last month which is unrelated to any financial factors is a 'factor which should . . . be taken into account' in my opinion. It should not lead to an order about assets which would have been unjustified if blame remained exactly equal. The illustration represents a situation where the most serious and reprehensible behaviour is irrelevant to the accrual of assets or expenditure on maintenance or the equities surrounding those events. Whether the keeping in the background of conduct which causes the breakdown of the marriage but *no alteration* of equities affecting financial events amounts to 'a conservative approach in assessing a party's misconduct' (*Beaumont v Beaumont* 1987 (1) SA 967 (A) at 994E [117]), or whether it represents a divergence from the *obiter dicta* in the said decision in regard to conduct, it is my view that equities under s 7(3) cannot be created merely because some conduct happened to be the outstanding or direct cause of the irretrievability of breakdown of the marriage. If then defendant is correct that plaintiff's adultery was the major factor in the irretrievability of the marriage, it does not reduce the fairness of an order in terms of s 7(3) by virtue of the equities which arose before the time when she so misbehaved.

Section 7(3) is not an action for damages suffered as a result of a lost opportunity to build up an own estate. Even if it had been, plaintiff as a woman remaining unmarried would have used most of her own income on her own maintenance. She would probably have had a smaller net estate than she now has. Also if she had married a different man.

Section 7(3) does not import an implied condition into the behaviour of the parties to the effect that what is done as marriage partner without financial expenditure will be paid for in the event of a divorce ensuing. There is no justification for reasoning that, simply because specific behaviour would have cost money if performed by an outside party, monetary value should be placed thereon for the purposes of s 7(3). Accordingly neither party can claim, unless further facts are proved, that because they drove children to school, it represents a contribution to maintenance or to the other party's estate.

Linked to what has just been said, s 7(3) merely takes knowledge of what happened and does not create a fiction about what might have been. If plaintiff had been a chef, she could have charged for preparing meals for defendant's business associates. She was in fact not involved in that [581] capacity but as a partner to the marriage. Capacity together with motive, manner and effect are of great importance. If plaintiff collected the eggs from the hens or groomed their dogs, that is what she did as wife without making a 'contribution'. It may be different if she collected all the eggs of an egg-producing venture and someone sold them for defendant's benefit. Her efforts would then have saved the expenditure of someone's labour. Similarly the mere dressing and tending to her children is, at least where this is not done in order to save the expenditure, in contrast with doing the work of a nanny which the parties in their position would have been expected to have employed. The point is that not every activity which can notionally be obtained as a paid-for service can be claimed to represent something by which a party 'contributed' to maintenance or to an increase in net estate.

Two last observations remain before the facts are more pertinently dealt with. The parties lived together before their marriage. It is not inconceivable that plaintiff 'contributed' in that period. There is no evidence to prove that and the statute renders reference permissible only to what was contributed 'during the subsistence of the marriage'. Secondly, the sheer unfairness of destroying all hope of an order in terms of s 7(3) by the simple expedient of granting the order 'in favour of' a defendant (in this case it would be a mere choice but in other cases such an order may be made appropriate by other facts and despite the defendant being the party who benefited by contributions), may create room for the view that a Court may grant an order in favour of both parties. Because an order only in favour of defendant was not sought, I will grant the order in favour of plaintiff so that she resultantly 'is the party in whose favour the order is granted'.

The salient points in applying s 7(3)

The gist of plaintiff's evidence on non-expenditure contributions is summarised by para 3(*a*)(vi) of the plaintiff's particulars for trial purposes. It commences with the statement that 'plaintiff ran, looked after and maintained the common home with the assistance of a domestic, cared for the children, transported the children to and fro',

and continues with other exertions which will be familiar to a housewife-mother who is married to a businessman, ending by referring to tidying up defendant's personal effects. Those are the alleged 'contributions'. In subpara (vii) she sets out her 'services' as also being 'duties of a housekeeper, chauffeur, gardener, nanny, tour guide, cook, hostess and attendant at a dog kennel'. In the last subparagraph the 'expenses allegedly saved which would otherwise have been incurred' are said to be:

> 'Save to state that it involved the cost of employing persons to carry out the services referred to in subpara (vii) above the remaining information requested is not needed for the purposes of preparing for trial.'

Oral evidence elaborated and added but did not change the substance of these allegations. The basis or context was not altered.

Unless some contribution by her to her *own* maintenance which is really overall being provided to some extent by the other party is erroneously [582] equated with a contribution to the other party's maintenance, no such contribution was proved. On the facts of this case it is impossible to say that the extent of plaintiff's additions to the pool of joint maintenance contributed to the maintenance *of defendant*. There is no reason to think that the amount of the duty to contribute to own support was exceeded.

In regard to the possibility that plaintiff 'by rendering of services ... contributed to an increase' in defendant's estate, I have made various observations. I add that such services as plaintiff rendered not for the pursuit of her own preferences (social, painting, caring for the children) but for the partial or full benefit of defendant (if that be so, the taking of children to school, supervising gardening, preparing meals for business contacts, etc) did not serve as a reason why expenditure or debt was not incurred or to assist in the acquisition or retention of an asset. (The statute may refer to services rendered in that *household* or in connection therewith and thus exclude the efforts towards export of paintings. I will therefore consider that as a contribution to the estate in 'any other manner'.)

Although the efforts of the plaintiff were notionally capable of being a contribution 'by ... the saving of expenses', the behaviour of caring for the household, repairing clothes, etc do not in fact have the necessary causative link to cognisable receipt of maintenance or to increases in defendant's estate. The plaintiff's efforts outside the household did save the expense of payments to the Receiver of Revenue. It seems fair and correct to have regard to the extent of the saving (R33 000), at least in the circumstances of such a disparity between the assets of the parties, rather than to take account only of the lower expenditure (R18 000) by plaintiff.

In regard to increases in the net estate which were contributed to 'in any other manner' I accordingly turn mainly to the consequences of money expended by plaintiff. On the evidence the amount which on probability had to be expended in cash to get defendant's estate to the point where it now stands is on a level which he could achieve without a contribution from plaintiff despite high living standards ...

I have considered this field in its widest sense, eg looking for obtaining a discount on a purchase to the benefit of defendant's estate. The cash flow calculations prove she was substantially unable to have contributed from her funds to the building up of defendant's estate.

The 'existing means and obligations' of the parties does not, despite the large estate of defendant, justify adding to what plaintiff in fact 'contributed', all the more if account is taken of other counterweighing considerations such as donations. Nor does it provide reason, because of donations received or otherwise, why a lesser amount than the actual contribution should be paid.

The balance of donations which includes carpets, furs, clothing, jewellery and the Mercedes Benz has favoured plaintiff substantially to such an extent that I felt obliged to consider seriously whether it does not fully outweigh the equity of ordering any transfer of assets to plaintiff. I have concluded that gifts in this case should be mere past history. Not only were they given with the idea that they need not be made good monetarily, but the overall picture is that cutting back on the restitution of the tax rebates will operate to increase the need for maintenance of the children [583] and affect the scale on which defendant himself wants them to live. There is no reason to think that defendant wants the used furs or gifts back . . .

In respect of 'other factors' some conclusions about the atmosphere surrounding the behaviour of the parties have been stated, eg that there is no sign of plaintiff adjusting her manner of living or spending with an object (or with the planned result) of increasing defendant's assets or decreasing his burdens, excluding of course what has been discussed, eg in terms of adding to the general household kitty. I find it necessary to rely on the fact that plaintiff has, apart from donations, gained the advantages of a very high standard of living generally at the expense of defendant's estate. What I should mention is that the fairness of striving for a greater equalisation between the two spouses is greatly reduced by a noticeable amount of levelling having taken place. One need only look at plaintiff's clothing, furniture, jewellery and car to notice that her estate has progressed well since the marriage. The assets which defendant on the other hand owns are his not only despite free spending and high living, but despite some financed progress for the plaintiff.

Insofar as plaintiff did buy 'something for the household' from her own money or her personal allowance from defendant, or insofar as her efforts which she perceived as taking up three-quarters of her day did 'contribute', eg towards the saving of an expense, it seems to be balanced by a combination of factors. Defendant probably also had some non-expenditure exertions in fetching children, arranging repairs to lawn-mowers, etc. Defendant gave plaintiff a monthly allowance and also a substantial balance of donations. She has the use of some household goods which she took with her but are not hers.

In the result the order regarded as appropriate in terms of s 7(3) is for the payment of R33 000.

Note

In the first place it is important to note that the decision in this case was partially overruled by the Appellate Division decision in *Katz v Katz* [119]. In that case the Appellate Division rejected some of the statements as to the nature of a contribution which qualifies as a contribution in terms of section 7(4) of the Divorce Act 70 of 1979. See in this regard the note on *Katz v Katz*.

The statements of the court in *Kretschmer's* case relating to the role that a spouse's misconduct

Aantekening

Dit is eerstens belangrik om daarop te let dat die beslissing in hierdie saak gedeeltelik verwerp is deur die Appèlhofuitspraak in *Katz v Katz* [119]. In daardie saak het die Appèlafdeling sommige van die stellings rakende die aard wat 'n bydrae moet hê om te kan kwalifiseer as 'n bydrae ingevolge artikel 7(4) van die Wet op Egskeiding 70 van 1979 verwerp. Sien in hierdie verband die aantekening by *Katz v Katz*.

Die stellings wat in die onderhawige saak gemaak

could play with regard to sections 7(3) to 7(6) are interesting. The court expressed its agreement with the *dictum* in *Beaumont v Beaumont* [117] that conduct can be a relevant consideration when the court exercises its discretion regarding the redistribution of assets. The court, however, in the case under discussion, emphasised that the redistribution of assets is not a punitive measure (580). The court further limited the conduct which it would consider to that which affects "the equity relevant to requiring a party to part with an asset which is the property of no one other than himself, and for which parting with there is no legal basis except if the Court finds it equitable" (576). The court also expressed the opinion that such equity "cannot be created merely because some conduct happened to be the outstanding or direct cause of the irretrievability of breakdown of the marriage" (580). From this statement as well as an earlier statement that "[r]eprehensible conduct which is causative of the very crisis between the parties may play a role in applying s 7(3)" (576) it can be deduced that the court will only consider conduct that pertains to the irretrievable breakdown of the marriage. Other conduct will not be considered.

As regards the "clean break" principle see the note on *Beaumont v Beaumont* [117]. See further *Kritzinger v Kritzinger* [118] and *Archer v Archer* [121].

is met betrekking tot die rol wat 'n gade se wangedrag in verband met artikels 7(3) tot 7(6) kan speel, is interessant. Die hof het saamgestem met die *dictum* in *Beaumont v Beaumont* [117] dat gedrag 'n relevante oorweging kan wees wanneer die hof sy diskresie in verband met die herverdeling van bates uitoefen. Die hof het egter in die onderhawige saak klem daarop gelê dat die herverdeling van bates nie 'n strafmaatreël is nie (580). Verder het die hof die gedrag wat in ag geneem sal word, beperk tot gedrag wat 'n invloed het op "the equity relevant to requiring a party to part with an asset which is the property of no one other than himself, and for which parting with there is no legal basis except if the Court finds it equitable" (576). Die hof het ook die mening uitgespreek dat sodanige "equity" "cannot be created merely because some conduct happened to be the outstanding or direct cause of the irretrievability of breakdown of the marriage" (580). Uit hierdie stelling asook 'n vroeëre stelling dat "[r]eprehensible conduct which is causative of the very crisis between the parties may play a role in applying s 7(3)" (576), kan afgelei word dat die hof slegs gedrag wat 'n invloed op die verbrokkeling van die huwelik gehad het in aanmerking sal neem. Ander gedrag sal nie oorweeg word nie.

Sien ook die aantekening by *Beaumont v Beaumont* [117] in verband met die "skoon breuk"-beginsel. Sien verder *Kritzinger v Kritzinger* [118] en *Archer v Archer* [121].

[121] ARCHER V ARCHER

1989 2 SA 885 (E)

Redistribution order in terms of section 7(3) of the Divorce Act 70 of 1979

The plaintiff wife (respondent) and the defendant (appellant) were married out of community of property in 1972. At the time of the marriage the appellant was only earning a half-day salary because his health was such that he could not cope with a full-day job. He suffered from a lung condition for which part of the treatment required was the use

Herverdelingsbevel ingevolge artikel 7(3) van die Wet op Egskeiding 70 van 1979

Die eiseres (respondent) en die verweerder (appellant) is in 1972 buite gemeenskap van goed getroud. Ten tyde van die huweliksluiting het die appellant net 'n halfdagsalaris verdien aangesien sy gesondheid sodanig was dat hy nie 'n vol dag se werk kon verrig nie. Hy het aan 'n longkwaal gely waarvoor hy onder andere die middel bekend as Valium

of a drug known as Valium, to which the appellant became addicted. The respondent was also working at the time. The parties subsequently moved from Durban to Cape Town. The respondent once again took up employment and gave her salary to the appellant to be used for housekeeping. The appellant did not work during this time and had no other income. In due course the appellant recovered sufficiently to take up employment again. The couple then moved to East London where both of them were employed. The respondent gave up her employment when she fell pregnant in 1976. This pregnancy terminated in a miscarriage but she stayed home and gave birth to twin girls in 1977 and to a boy in 1979. While the children were still very small the respondent went to work again on a part-time basis. During this time all her earnings went into the household. In 1982 she stopped working altogether. In the meantime the appellant had become involved in property development and had built up a considerable estate of almost one and a half million rand, while the respondent's assets amounted to almost R200 000. With regard to the marriage itself the court found that the respondent loved, cared for and assisted the appellant. In the words of the court she "was everything, a breadwinner, a friend, a lover, a servant, a housekeeper and mother." The appellant on the other hand testified that he had never loved his wife. He did not tell her before the marriage that he did not love her, but during the marriage he told respondent that he did not love her and never had. He resented the presence of the children because the respondent had to spend time with them in caring for them and rearing them. It also irritated him that the respondent became overweight after the birth of the children. Eventually the parties drifted apart and the appellant left the common home. After he had left the common home the appellant began a relationship with another woman and the relationship ultimately developed into an

moes gebruik waaraan hy verslaaf geraak het. Die respondent het ook op hierdie stadium gewerk. Die partye het toe van Durban na Kaapstad verhuis. Die respondent het weer eens begin werk en haar salaris aan die appellant gegee om vir die huishouding gebruik te word. Die appellant het nie op hierdie stadium gewerk nie en ook geen ander inkomste gehad nie. Met verloop van tyd het die appellant sodanig herstel dat hy weer kon begin werk. Die partye het na Oos-Londen verhuis waar albei gewerk het. Die respondent het in 1976 opgehou om te werk toe sy swanger geraak het. Hierdie swangerskap het egter in 'n miskraam geëindig. Sy het nietemin by die huis gebly en in 1977 aan tweelingdogtertjies geboorte geskenk en in 1979 aan 'n seuntjie. Terwyl die kinders nog baie klein was, het die respondent weer op 'n deeltydse basis begin werk. Gedurende hierdie tydperk het haar hele verdienste in die huishouding ingegaan. In 1982 het sy heeltemal opgehou om te werk. Die appellant het in die tussentyd by eiendomsontwikkeling betrokke geraak en 'n aansienlike vermoë van byna een-en-'n half miljoen rand opgebou, terwyl die respondent se bates byna R200 000 bedra het. Met betrekking tot die huwelik self het die hof bevind dat die respondent die appellant liefgehad het, vir hom gesorg het en hom gehelp het. Sy was in die woorde van die hof "everything, a breadwinner, a friend, a lover, a servant, a housekeeper and mother." Die appellant, aan die ander kant, het getuig dat hy nooit vir sy vrou lief was nie. Hy het nooit voor die huwelik vir haar gesê dat hy haar nie lief het nie maar gedurende die huwelik het hy dit wel vir haar gesê asook dat hy haar nooit liefgehad het nie. Hy kon die kinders se teenwoordigheid nie verdra nie omdat die respondent tyd aan hulle moes bestee ten einde vir hulle te sorg en hulle op te voed. Dit het hom ook geïrriteer dat die respondent na die kinders se geboorte oorgewig geraak het. Die partye het uiteindelik van mekaar verwyderd geraak en die appellant het die ge-

adulterous one. With full knowledge of the appellant's adulterous relationship the respondent offered forgiveness and invited him back to the matrimonial home, but he declined this offer. It was evident that the marriage had broken down irretrievably and the respondent sued the appellant for divorce in the court *a quo*. She was granted a decree of divorce and custody of the three minor children was also awarded to her. The appellant was further ordered to pay maintenance to the respondent for herself and the children, and, in terms of section 7(3) of the Divorce Act 70 of 1979, he was ordered to pay the plaintiff the sum of R3 700. The appellant appealed against that part of the order which ordered him to pay maintenance to the respondent and the respondent cross-appealed against that part of the order in which she was only awarded R3 700. The full bench ordered the appellant to pay the respondent R300 000 in terms of section 7(3) of the Divorce Act. This amount was to be paid in three instalments. Pending payment of the total amount the appellant was ordered to pay maintenance to the respondent but no further order as to maintenance was made.

meenskaplike huishouding verlaat. Nadat hy die huis verlaat het, het hy in 'n verhouding met 'n ander vrou betrokke geraak wat op die ou end 'n owerspelige verhouding geword het. Terwyl sy ten volle van die appellant se owerspelige verhouding bewus was, het die respondent aangebied om hom te vergewe en hom genooi om terug te keer huis toe, maar hy het die aanbod van die hand gewys. Dit was duidelik dat die huwelik onherstelbaar verbrokkel het en die respondent het die appellant in die hof *a quo* om 'n egskeiding gedagvaar. Die egskeiding is toegestaan en bewaring van die drie minderjarige kinders is ook aan haar toegeken. Die appellant is verder gelas om aan die respondent onderhoud vir haar en die kinders te betaal, en hy is verder gelas om ingevolge artikel 7(3) van die Wet op Egskeiding 70 van 1979 R3 700 aan die respondent te betaal. Die appellant het teen die gedeelte van die bevel geappelleer wat hom beveel het om onderhoud aan die respondent te betaal, en in 'n teenappèl het die respondent geappelleer teen die gedeelte van die bevel waarin net R3 700 aan haar toegeken is. Die volbank het die appellant gelas om R300 000 ingevolge artikel 7(3) van die Wet op Egskeiding aan die respondent te betaal. Hierdie bedrag moes in drie paaiemente betaal word. Hangende betaling van die volle bedrag moes die appellant onderhoud aan die respondent betaal maar geen verdere onderhoudsbevel is gemaak nie.

LUDORF J: [891] It was on the facts which I have endeavoured to summarise above that the learned trial Judge made the orders referred to.

In so doing the Court exercised a discretion conferred upon it in very wide terms and this Court will not interfere with that order unless it is satisfied that the Court *a quo* misdirected itself or exercised its discretion improperly. See *Beaumont v Beaumont* 1987 (1) SA 967 (A) at 1002B–C [117] . . .

[892] When dealing with the question of misconduct (which was termed 'fault') in relation to maintenance in terms of s 7(2) of the Act [ie the Divorce Act 70 of 1979] the learned trial Judge found the following:

'As to fault in relation to the break-up of the marriage between the parties, I am unable to come to a firm conclusion. Defendant denies that "the other woman" was the cause of his leaving plaintiff and it seems as if the marriage between the parties had been in some difficulty for some years before they separated. Plaintiff herself referred to a crisis point during 1981 when they sought aid to try and save the marriage. Regrettably it seems that each of the parties wanted and expected too much of the other, with the result that the parties drifted further apart and I do not consider that there is anything to be gained by trying to put too fine a point on the individual complaints of the parties.

Plaintiff was prepared to try and continue with the marriage, whereas defendant ultimately was not. To that extent only is the ultimate break-up of the marriage due to the conduct of defendant, but this can have no great bearing on the maintenance payable by defendant to plaintiff.'

With this conclusion I am regrettably not in agreement. I can find no justification for limiting the enquiry with regard to fault to the aspect concerning 'the other woman', as the learned Judge seems to have done, nor do I believe that the facts as they emerge from the evidence warrant the finding that:

'Plaintiff was prepared to try and continue with the marriage whereas defendant ultimately was not. To that extent *only* is the ultimate break-up of the marriage due to the conduct of the defendant . . .'

(My emphasis.)

In making that finding it is obvious that the learned Judge must have overlooked the fact that it was the appellant who married respondent for convenience and who, having regained his health and achieved his wealth, discarded her after he had utilised respondent during her best years. It was he who hurt his wife deeply by informing her after the marriage that he never loved her in the first place. It was he who admittedly was resentful of sharing his wife's attention with his own children. It was he who was not prepared to accept his wife when she became overweight as a result of bearing his children, despite the fact that it was the very wife whom he spurned who was his crutch both morally and financially in his early years when he was a hopeless, ailing and penurious addict. Finally, it was he who declined his wife's generous offer of forgiveness and continuation of the marriage.

It is clear that it was this misconduct which I have described (not necessarily exhaustively) which caused the breakdown of the marriage and [893] that responsibility for the breakdown rests firmly and surely upon the appellant. The misconduct was gross and it would most certainly in my judgment be 'inequitable to disregard it'. It was also in my view disproportionate to the misconduct, if any, of the respondent. In fact, I believe that the evidence fails to reveal misconduct of any note on her part.

In this regard I would refer to the *dicta* of BOTHA JA in *Beaumont's* case *supra* at 993H *et seq*.

In my judgment the finding of the Court *a quo* to which I have referred is clearly erroneous, constituting a misdirection of the kind entitling this Court to adjudicate afresh on the evidence as if it were itself the Court of first instance, and to exercise its own discretion with regard to an order in terms either of s 7(2) or s 7(3), or both.

I point out that, although s 7(3) does not in its own terms explicitly include a reference to misconduct, it does include explicit reference to ss (5), which by clear implication empowers the Court to consider and weigh misconduct in the exercise of its discretion when making an order in terms of s 7(3). See *Beaumont's* case (*supra* at 993I) . . .

With regard to the inter-relationship between s 7(2) and s (7)3 it is true that there is an absence of reference in ss (3) and ss (5) to any order made in terms of ss (2), while ss (2) includes a reference to any order made in terms of ss (3) as material to be considered and weighed when considering an order in terms of ss (2). This does not mean, however, that the Court was intended by the Legislature to be restricted to a consideration first (and in isolation) of any order in terms of ss (3) before turning to a [894] consideration of any order in terms of ss (2). See *Beaumont's* case *supra* at 991I – 992F. The proper approach as set out by the learned Judge of Appeal is to take an overall view

> 'from the outset of how justice could best be achieved between the parties in the light of possible orders under either ss (2) or ss (3) or both subsections in relation to the means and obligations and the needs of the parties and all the other relevant factors'.

Furthermore, as was pointed out in the judgment at 993B:

> 'Our Courts will always bear in mind the possibility of using their powers under the new dispensation in such a way as to achieve a complete termination of the financial dependence of the one party on the other, if the circumstances permit. The last-mentioned qualification is, of course, very important.'

In the light of the above I turn now to consider which order or orders it would in the circumstances be 'equitable and just' to make.

The Court is only empowered to make an order in terms of ss (3) (transfer of assets) if it

> '. . . is satisfied that it is equitable and just by reason of the fact that the party in whose favour the order is granted contributed directly or indirectly to the maintenance or increase of the estate of the other party during the subsistence of the marriage, either by the rendering of services or the saving of expenses which would have otherwise been incurred, or in any other manner'.

(Subsection (4) of s 7 of the Act.)

It is common cause, and correctly so in my judgment, that respondent has made a contribution of the kind contemplated in the subsection and, as I understand it, that she would be entitled to a transfer of assets in her favour. It is argued, however, that she is already in possession of assets to the value of R200 000 to which the appellant lays no claim and that those assets are to be regarded as having been received by the respondent and are sufficient. She is, so it is argued, in the circumstances not entitled to more, especially so in the event of an adequate maintenance award.

In the present matter the estate concerned is considerable in extent. It would, other requirements being satisfied, permit of division into portions being economically viable in the sense that such portions would be capable each of providing adequately by way of maintenance for the owner of such portion. Moreover, the nature of appellant's business is such that the separate sectional title units, being independent units, permit of transfer out of his estate without affecting the essence or continuance of his enterprise, nor its profitability or potential for future profitability. Certainly the transfer out of his estate of such units would have the result of a diminution of his estate, quantitatively speaking, but that fact would represent only a 'setback' which would be capable of correction. One is, so to speak, not depriving the journeyman of his lathe but only of some of the fruits of his labour which he would be capable of replacing with further and, if needs be, intensified labour. (I should, however, not be understood to hold that a Court may not so deprive a party.)

Quite apart from the above consideration, it seems to me that in the light of appellant's conduct during the marriage, more particularly his attitude towards respondent as evidenced by such conduct, and his relationship with the lady with whom he is living, it would be desirable to [895] exercise my discretion so as to bring about a 'clean break' between the parties and to render the respondent financially independent from the appellant.

The parties are agreed that, if the Court were to order the transfer of assets in terms of s 7(3), such order should be for the transfer of a sum of money in lieu of assets rather

than the assets themselves which would entail administrative and other practical difficulties. It seems to me that there can in present circumstances be no objection to such a
course, and I adopt it.

In my judgment the appellant should be ordered to transfer an amount of R300 000 to
the respondent and no order should be made in terms of s 7(2) in respect of maintenance ...

[LUDORF J held that, in terms of section 7(6) of the Divorce Act, the sum of R300 000
was to be paid in three instalments. Pending payment of the total amount, the defendant
was ordered to pay maintenance to the plaintiff.]

MULLINS J and KROON J concurred.

Note

It should be noted that the court is not bound to
order the transfer of a specific asset or specific
assets to the successful applicant for a redistribution order. The court may order that a sum of
money be transferred in lieu of the asset or assets.

See further the note on *Beaumont v Beaumont* [117]
on how the courts assess the conduct of the parties
as a relevant factor in terms of section 7(3) of
the Divorce Act 70 of 1979, the interrelationship
between sections 7(2) and 7(3) of the Divorce Act
as well as the "clean break" principle. See also
Kritzinger v Kritzinger [118]; *Katz v Katz* [119] and
Kretschmer v Kretschmer [120].

Aantekening

Let daarop dat die hof nie verplig is om te beveel
dat 'n bepaalde bate of bepaalde bates oorgedra
moet word aan die suksesvolle applikant wat om
'n herverdelingsbevel aansoek doen nie. Die hof
kan ook beveel dat 'n som geld in die plek van
die bate of bates oorgedra word.

Sien verder die aantekening by *Beaumont v Beaumont* [117], ten opsigte van die howe se beoordeling van die gedrag van die partye as 'n relevante
faktor ingevolge artikel 7(3) van die Wet op Egskeiding 70 van 1979, die onderlinge verhouding
tussen artikels 7(2) en 7(3) van die Wet op Egskeiding en die "skoon breuk"-beginsel. Sien verder *Kritzinger v Kritzinger* [118]; *Katz v Katz* [119]
en *Kretschmer v Kretschmer* [120].

Maintenance of the spouses

Maintenance *pendente lite*
The factors which are considered when a maintenance order
is to be made – section 7(2)
Token maintenance
The rescission, suspension or variation of maintenance orders
The termination of maintenance orders

Onderhoud van die gades

Onderhoud *pendente lite*
Die faktore wat by die verlening van 'n onderhoudsbevel in
ag geneem word – artikel 7(2)
Nominale onderhoud
Die intrekking, opskorting of wysiging van onderhoudsbevele
Die beëindiging van onderhoudsbevele

Maintenance *pendente lite*   Onderhoud *pendente lite*

[122]   NILSSON V NILSSON

1984 2 SA 294 (C)

Maintenance for a spouse *pendente lite*	Onderhoud vir 'n gade *pendente lite*
The applicant (wife) and the respondent were married on 20 January 1982. The applicant left the common home on 14 July 1983. It was common cause between the parties that their marriage had irretrievably broken down. The applicant instituted divorce proceedings against the respondent and also claimed interim maintenance from him. She averred that her husband caused the breakdown of the marriage. The respondent agreed to a divorce being obtained but opposed the applicant's claim for maintenance. He contended that the applicant had deserted him and that he needed all his income for his own maintenance. He was eighty-five years old, almost totally blind, bedridden and in need of assistance day and night. The court refused to make any order as to maintenance but left it to be determined at the trial.	Die applikant (vrou) en die respondent is op 20 Januarie 1982 getroud. Die applikant het die gemeenskaplike huishouding op 14 Julie 1983 verlaat. Die partye was dit eens dat hulle huwelik onherstelbaar verbrokkel het. Die applikant het 'n egskeidingsgeding teen die respondent aanhangig gemaak en ook tussentydse onderhoud van hom geëis. Sy het beweer dat haar man die oorsaak van die huweliksverbrokkeling was. Die respondent het saamgestem dat 'n egskeiding toegestaan moes word maar het die applikant se eis om onderhoud teengestaan. Hy het beweer dat sy vrou hom verlaat het en dat hy al sy inkomste vir sy eie onderhoud nodig gehad het. Hy was vyf en tagtig jaar oud, omtrent heeltemal blind, bedlêend en het dag en nag hulp nodig gehad. Die hof het geweier om 'n onderhoudsbevel uit te reik maar het dit gelaat om by die verhoor beslis te word.

VAN DEN HEEVER J: [295] The only reason I reserved judgment in this Rule 43 application is because law and fairness should if possible run hand-in-hand. It seems unfair that a woman of 78 should on the strength of a marriage contracted on 20 January 1982 to an 85-year old which came to an end when she left the common home on 14 July 1983, be entitled, without enquiry into the merits of their matrimonial dispute, to a contribution towards costs and maintenance *pendente lite*. If that is indeed the legal position in regard to such an application *pendente lite* then obviously the law must be applied.

Primarily Rule 43 was envisaged to provide temporary assistance for women, who had given up careers or potential careers for the sake of matrimony with or without maternity, until such time as at a trial and after hearing evidence maintenance claims and, if children had been born, custody claims could be properly determined. It was not created to give an interim meal-ticket to women who quite clearly at the trial would not be able to establish a right to maintenance. The grey area between the two extremes causes problems.

[297] Section 7(2) of the Divorce Act 70 of 1979 provides that:

"In the absence of an order made (by agreement between the parties) with regard to the payment of maintenance by the one party to the other, the Court may, having regard to the existing or prospective means of each of the parties, their respective earning capacities, financial needs and obligations, the age of each of the parties, the duration of the marriage, the standard of living of the parties prior to the divorce, their conduct in so far as it may be relevant to the breakdown of the marriage, and any other factor which in the opinion of the Court should be taken into account, make an order which the Court finds just in respect of the payment of maintenance by the one party to the other for any period until the death or remarriage of the party in whose favour the order is given, whichever may first occur."

A proper weighing of all these factors is important to counterbalance the inherent immorality that could follow were the sole or even the main criterion for a claim for maintenance to be the plaintiff's need or ability to maintain herself. Had the Legislature intended to preserve the common law and limit maintenance in accordance with a wife's ability to maintain herself (cf Professor Andreas van Wyk *THRHR* vol 43 (1980) at 433) the Divorce Act could encourage immorality in many ways. It could then be the middle-aged libertine's charter of freedom. A man could throw out the woman who had shared his bed, ran his home, and reared his children, after twenty years or so, replacing her with something younger and prettier, and claim that his wife is not entitled to maintenance because during twenty years of minding his home and family she had also earned money outside that home (which she had, as in law and duty bound, contributed towards the maintenance of the home and its inhabitants) and could now that the children were off her hands work that much harder. On the other hand it would be equally unjust that an indigent woman unable to earn much money could marry a wealthy man, walk out of her wifely duties and try to use him as a meal-ticket for life. In short, where an order of divorce is now obtainable without regard to fault, the Courts can and should use s 7 to ensure that, where there can be no equitable division of capital assets because there was no community nor sufficient antenuptial settlements to ensure fairness, the parties are treated fairly *vis-à-vis* one another. One of the factors that must be considered in quantifying a woman's claim to maintenance is what she herself put into the marriage, whether in cash or in kind (tolerance, patience, frugality, etc, etc). I do not suggest, any more than the Legislature did, that such contribution is more than one of many factors to be considered. It could also operate in favour of a husband, in changing social circumstances. I can think of no reason why a blameless husband who has sacrificed his own career advancement and along with it income and pension benefits, in favour of his wife's, should not be entitled to a contribution towards his maintenance from her, merely because he would not starve without. It is quite possible to sketch the pattern of a marriage without the nit-picking feared by Hahlo and Sinclair in their *Reform of the South African Law of Divorce* at 46–7.

The shorter the duration of a marriage, the more important the conduct of the parties within the relationship – their respective "guilt" or "innocence" – would ordinarily be in relation to the question whether maintenance should be paid at all, outside of cases where the [298] marriage itself resulted in a loss: for example because of loss of previous alimony or a usufruct or perhaps of other marriage prospects, or by reason of resignation from employment. (The examples are not intended to be exhaustive).

[VAN DEN HEEVER J made no order as to maintenance but left it to be determined at the trial.]

Note

In this case the marriage had lasted for less than two years and the applicant had suffered no loss as a result of the marriage. Moreover she had been able to maintain herself before the marriage. In these circumstances it was not considered fair towards her husband to award her maintenance *pendente lite*.

Aantekening

In hierdie saak het die huwelik minder as twee jaar geduur en die applikant het geen verlies as gevolg daarvan gely nie. Verder was sy voor die huwelik daartoe in staat om haarself te onderhou. In hierdie omstandighede is dit nie as billik teenoor haar man beskou om onderhoud *pendente lite* aan haar toe te staan nie.

The factors which are considered when a maintenance order is to be made – section 7(2)

Die faktore wat by die verlening van 'n onderhoudsbevel in ag geneem word – artikel 7(2)

[123] KROON V KROON

1986 4 SA 616 (EC)

Maintenance for a spouse upon divorce

The plaintiff (wife) and defendant (husband) were married out of community of property in 1965. The plaintiff now sued the defendant, *inter alia*, for divorce and maintenance. The spouses had three minor children of schoolgoing age. The children attended private schools as day pupils and lived with their mother in the spouses' matrimonial home. The house was registered in the plaintiff's name. The house, which was described as being in the "luxury" class, was worth, at a conservative estimate, R125 000. The defendant was living in a town house which he had bought and which was worth approximately R70 000. The plaintiff claimed maintenance from the defendant for herself at the rate of R1 000 per month and for each of the children at the rate of R500 per month. She also wanted such maintenance to be increased annually, on the anniversary date in each year of the decree of divorce, in accordance with the inflation rate as measured by the consumer price index. The plaintiff further claimed an order that the defendant pay all the schooling and other educational expenses of the children, including the expenses for their possible tertiary education, as well as all their medical and dental expenses. She also claimed sole and exclusive ownership of all the movable assets which she had in her possession, with the exception of the defendant's personal property. The defendant agreed to pay all the educational, medical and dental expenses of the children and he also agreed to the plaintiff's acquiring sole and exclusive ownership of all the movable assets she had in her possession, with the exclusion of his personal property. The

Onderhoud vir 'n gade na egskeiding

Die eiseres en die verweerder is in 1965 buite gemeenskap van goed getroud. Die eiseres het die verweerder nou onder andere om 'n egskeiding sowel as vir onderhoud gedagvaar. Die gades het drie kinders van skoolgaande ouderdom gehad. Die kinders het privaatskole bygewoon en het saam met hulle moeder in die gesin se woning gewoon. Die huis was in die naam van die eiseres geregistreer. Die huis, wat as luuks beskryf is, was volgens 'n konserwatiewe skatting R125 000 werd. Die verweerder het in 'n meenthuis gewoon wat hy gekoop het en wat omtrent R70 000 werd was. Die eiseres het R1 000 per maand onderhoud vir haar en R500 per maand vir elk van die kinders geëis. Sy het ook gevra dat die onderhoud jaarliks op die datum waarop die egskeidingsbevel verleen is, verhoog moes word in ooreenstemming met die inflasiekoers soos gemeet aan die verbruikersprysindeks. Die eiseres het verder ook aansoek gedoen om 'n bevel dat die verweerder al die skool- en ander onkoste verbonde aan die opvoeding van die kinders, insluitende die onkoste verbonde aan moontlike tersiêre opleiding, sowel as al hulle mediese en tandheelkundige onkoste moes betaal. Sy het ook die alleeneiendomsreg geëis van al die roerende goed wat sy in haar besit gehad het, met die uitsondering van die verweerder se persoonlike besittings. Die verweerder het ingestem om al die onkoste verbonde aan die kinders se opvoeding asook hulle mediese en tandeelkundige onkoste te betaal en hy het ook ingestem dat die eiseres alleeneiendomsreg kon verkry van al die roerende bates wat sy in haar besit gehad het, met die uitsondering van sy persoonlike be-

defendant also agreed to pay maintenance to the plaintiff and the children but asked the court to decide on the *quantum* thereof. The defendant further lodged a counterclaim in which he asked the court to order the plaintiff to transfer an undivided half-share of the spouses' matrimonial home to him or, alternatively, to sell the home and to pay one half of the proceeds of the sale of the property to him. The court rejected the counterclaim and ordered the defendant to pay maintenance to the plaintiff and the children but at a lesser rate than that claimed by the plaintiff. The court order was framed in such a way as to oblige the plaintiff to sell the spouses' matrimonial home in order to increase her means.

sittings. Die verweerder het ook ingestem om onderhoud vir die eiseres en die kinders te betaal maar hy het die hof versoek om die bedrag van die onderhoud te bepaal. Die verweerder het verder in 'n teeneis aansoek gedoen om 'n bevel dat die eiseres 'n onverdeelde halwe aandeel van die gade se gemeenskaplike woning aan hom oordra of, in die alternatief, dat sy die woning verkoop en die helfte van die verkoopprys aan hom oordra. Die hof het die teeneis van die hand gewys en die verweerder beveel om onderhoud aan die eiseres en die kinders te betaal maar op 'n laer skaal as waarop die eiseres aangedring het. Die hofbevel is op so 'n manier geformuleer dat die eiseres verplig was om die gades se gemeenskaplike woning te verkoop om sodoende haar finansiële posisie te verbeter.

BAKER J: [617] In her statement of claim plaintiff alleged that the marriage relationship between the parties had reached such a state of disintegration that there was no reasonable prospect of the restoration of a normal marriage relationship between them. The details are not important. There is no evidence of conduct on either side that can be described as "obvious and gross" (see *Wachtel v Wachtel* [1973] 1 All ER 829 (CA)). The plaintiff no longer wants to continue the marriage and that is sufficient "breakdown" to warrant a divorce (*Swart v Swart* 1980 (4) SA 364 (O) [108]). Fault is not relevant to the divorce itself (*ibid*) and, although the conduct of the parties is relevant to questions of maintenance (*ibid*; and *Singh v Singh* 1983 (1) SA 781 (C) [113]), the important question in settling the maintenance is what is fair in all the circumstances and the Court should not engage in raking up the *minutiae* of ancient domestic grievances (Hahlo *The South African Law of Husband and Wife* 5th ed at 361; *Trippas v Trippas* [1973] 2 WLR 585 (CA) at 595 [1973] 2 All ER 1 at 9h–i).

In the circumstances a divorce was granted at the end of the hearing on 11 April 1985 . . .

[621] What the Court now has to do is to decide the proprietary aspects of this case, for that is all that remains unsettled. The dispute is no longer matrimonial but patrimonial. The law to be applied is s 7 of the Divorce Act 70 of 1979 . . .

[622] By and large . . . the dispute centres upon the matter of maintenance and relates only indirectly to the division of assets. Section 7(3) has an application which is only peripheral to the main issue, which falls under s 7(2).

In regard to the matter of maintenance in this case all the factors set out in s 7(2) of the Act have some relevance . . .

[BAKER J then dealt with the relevant factors, including the ages of the parties and the duration of the marriage, the standard of living of the parties before divorce and the absence of conduct on the part of either spouse that had to be considered. As far as the plaintiff's contribution to the home was concerned, BAKER J concluded that:]

[624] her monetary contribution to the house and its erection nearly twenty years ago may be estimated at about R7 000. What is of far greater significance is her non-monetary contribution as mother, wife and housewife . . .

[BAKER J then dealt with the existing means of the parties:]

Plaintiff has no means in the sense of a regular income. But she does have a property registered in her name which is too big for herself and three children, one of whom will in the normal course be leaving home in the coming year, unless he enters the local university as a day-student, in which case he will require housing for several years to come. Whether the eldest offspring leaves home or not, the present house is too much of a luxury for defendant to have to maintain after divorce. The plaintiff must sell it and rent or buy a smaller house, preferably a so-called town house, ie a house without a garden to keep up. And if the present property can be sold and some part of the proceeds be used to produce income, that part represents "means" in my opinion.

"Means of support" is an expression covering not only income but property that can be used to produce income (cf *Slabbert v Harmse* 1923 CPD 187 at 190 where WATERMEYER J said it was "some available property or right, by the use of which support can be procured". This opinion was followed in *Price v Price* 1948 (1) SA 518 (SR) at 521, in a similar case. The respondent had £400 in cash and "by means of that sum she can procure her own support". So for the purpose of that case "means" included property as opposed to current income: it was the "means" of producing income – or more accurately, support. See also *Van Wyk v Van Wyk* 1959 (3) SA 223 (T) at 225–6, where BOSHOFF J followed *Slabbert v Harmse* on this point. *Slabbert v Harmse* seems to have been approved in Natal as well (see *Steinmann v Steinmann* 1948 (3) SA 930 (N) at 934).

Apart from the house (which as I have suggested is potentially partly "means") the plaintiff has a car worth about R7 000 and furniture insured for R34 000. These things cannot be regarded as "means". They are capital assets needed for her own use and that of the children. They are what the English Courts used to call "family assets", acquired by one or both of the parties, for the use and benefit [625] of the family as a whole; and in English law when a marriage comes to an end these capital assets have to be divided (*Rayden [on Divorce] (op cit* at 750 para 19)). The matrimonial home was and is a "family asset" . . . I deal with the house in more detail below.

As far as concerns the other "family assets" we can leave plaintiff in possession of her car and furniture, for defendant has already agreed to let her keep every movable asset in her possession and in the house except his personal belongings (which he has already removed to his own new small town house).

Defendant's existing means are derived from two sources. He has now a salary and an allowance (having been elevated to the Bench in an acting capacity prior to the hearing of this matter) and he has a certain private income from a family trust and certain shares, and a small income from certain "growth funds". In addition he has now the free use of a motor car supplied and maintained by the taxpayers of this country . . .

[BAKER J then investigated the value of these sources of income and concluded that the total value of the defendant's income was R83 793 (which amount included the children's income derived from dividends and interest). BAKER J then detailed amounts which had to be deducted from the defendant's total income, such as tax payments, and proceeded:]

[626] This is the amount which defendant at present has left, ie R7 128 by way of "invisible" income [the value of the use of a motor car] and R26 897 to spend.

Plaintiff admitted that her claim for maintenance . . . was beyond defendant's capability . . . She was asked by his counsel how she proposed to solve that problem. One solution was to send the two younger children to Government schools, which would cost only R400 per annum in fees as opposed to R11 000 per annum at the private schools presently attended by them . . . The only other solution she could suggest was that defendant should have his retirement annuities converted into paid-up sums and thereby stop paying the premiums. This would result in a saving of R9 985 per annum . . . Defendant's solution is that plaintiff should sell the house and rent or buy something smaller and less expensive to maintain. He also suggests that plaintiff should secure employment and thereby augment her maintenance paid by him . . .

[The court then dealt with the possible solutions and rejected the first two suggested by the plaintiff. BAKER J then discussed the third solution, namely that the big house should be sold and a smaller residence be bought. The balance of the proceeds of the sale could then be used to generate income or the entire proceeds could be used to generate income and a smaller residence could be rented. In this regard BAKER J proceeded:]

[628] Plaintiff did not adduce any compelling reason for saddling defendant with the cost of retaining the big house. She merely said that the children would object to being uprooted from the house; that they played in the garden; used the pool; entertained their friends at home; and it was all part of their way of life. None of this impresses. We are not dealing with six-year-olds who are usually confined to home and in whose case a garden is a good place to be in. We are dealing with a boy of 14 or 15 and a girl of 13 or so, who will be less and less inclined to remain home. They do not need a garden or a large house with a "family room" such as the big house contains. I agree with counsel that these children, particularly as they are apparently intelligent above the average, will adapt to a new house very quickly. As Mr *Mostert* [for the defendant] pointed out, the real problem with the children is that their parents have separated; the problem is not the new home; it is the separation of the parents that has to be adapted to.

I can see no valid objections to plaintiff's moving into a three-bedroomed flat at R600 per month. It will not harm the children.

The alternative is (having sold the big house for the same sum as before, viz R125 000) to buy a house or flat, also of three bedrooms, similar to defendant's duplex and for the same price, R70 000. This would leave her with R55 000. Let us call it R50 000, to be on the safe side. The tax on the income is under R700. This would leave her with R10 000 or so [per annum].

Finally, said counsel for the defendant, if defendant succeeds in his counterclaim for half the value of the house, he and plaintiff will receive R62 500 each. At 20% that will yield R12 500 per annum. The tax on this is about R985, leaving R11 515 per annum or R960 per month in round figures. Once again plaintiff could maintain herself on this – though after paying R400 or R600 rent there would not be much left. This last exercise is therefore rather pointless. We must bear in mind that the claims for maintenance in the declaration postulate the retention of the big house to live in.

Fourth solution: Secure employment, if possible, to augment maintenance from defendant:

This is obviously only a partial solution, and nobody would expect plaintiff to maintain herself entirely from her own earnings . . .

[BAKER J dealt with the defendant's means and concluded that he had assets of R182 325. BAKER J then proceeded to look at the prospective means of the parties:]

[629] There is no evidence that plaintiff is likely to acquire any property that can be used to "produce or procure" income within the meaning of the language of WATERMEYER J in *Slabbert v Harmse*. But there is a property which she has already in that she is the registered owner thereof, ie the former matrimonial home of the parties to which I have already referred as "the big house" . . .

The question of getting rid of the big house was one of the barriers in the way of a settlement of this case. As indicated earlier, it is in essence joint property, a family asset in English terminology, despite its registration in the name of plaintiff. The fact that plaintiff has the sole right of possession because she is the legal, ie registered, owner (see

Hahlo at 386 para IV) is irrelevant: defendant put far more money into the property than plaintiff did and, if that were the sole issue in this case, his counterclaim would succeed; for where spouses have pooled resources towards the creation of a matrimonial home on the understanding that it should belong to them jointly, as was the position here, the transfer thereof into the name of the wife makes her the legal owner but the spouses *inter se* are joint owners (*Hahlo* at 290 *ad* note 32; *Rayden* at 750 para 19 and at 751 para 20; *De Jager v De Jager* (CPD, 26 April 1985 not reported)). To grant or, for that matter, to refuse the counterclaim would in effect be to make an order in terms of s 7(3) of the Divorce Act 1979, as amended. Alternatively the Court could, in an appropriate case, act under s 9 of the Act and order a forfeiture (this is *not* an appropriate case for resort to s 9, in my opinion).

In *Beaumont v Beaumont (supra)* [1985 4 SA 171 (W)] KRIEGLER J said that the fact that he was going to make an order for maintenance was a factor in deciding how much of the husband's property should be transferred to the wife: the bigger the transfer, the smaller the maintenance (I might mention that in *Higgo v Higgo* (WLD, 25 March 1983, *per* COETZEE J) the entire estate was split fifty-fifty and no maintenance was allowed, the yield from the 50% share of the assets being [630] sufficient to generate all the maintenance that the wife might need). Both these cases support my view, and Mr *Mostert's* submission, that, if this Court orders the defendant's share of the property to be transferred to plaintiff (ie if the Court dismisses the counterclaim), the maintenance which defendant would have had to pay in the absence of a property transfer would fall to be reduced. The one balances the other. If assets are transferred and are capable of generating maintenance, the actual cash sum of maintenance to be paid by defendant may be reduced. In this case, since the plaintiff and the children need a home, the counterclaim will be dismissed ... Since it was accepted that plaintiff would buy a suitable place for about R70 000 (as defendant did), she would have about R50 000 to R62 500 over, which can produce a useful income. It would be only fair to defendant to make due allowance for that ...

[631] As far as concerns defendant, there is no evidence as to his prospective means (eg inheritances or anything else). All that can be said is that during the next twenty-five years or so he will, as a judge, be given the occasional salary increase. In addition he will in the normal course receive a pension and the customary retirement gratuity. The two last-mentioned items are of no relevance to the matter of present maintenance and therefore need not be taken into account now ...

[BAKER J then discussed the respective earning capacities of the parties:]

We can dispose of defendant's earning capacity first. Since he is now an acting Judge of the Supreme Court and I am informed will in all probability be confirmed as a permanent one, he is debarred fom taking any other employment ... so we may assume that his earning capacity will be that of a Judge. Ownership of shares can hardly be said to fall under the definition of "earning capacity"; it falls rather under the heading of "existing means". I have already listed this share income under "existing means" ...

[BAKER J then analysed the evidence on the plaintiff's earning capacity and proceeded:]

In short, I doubt whether this lady is employable at all, especially after nearly twenty years of absence from the market place. Bridegrooms must take their brides as they find them; and if they marry wives who probably cannot obtain or retain employment they are not entitled to expect a Court to attribute a notional earning capacity to those wives upon divorce. In a case recently decided in the WLD the wife was much the same age as plaintiff in this case, had been married for much the same length of time, had spent her whole married life at home and in her husband's office helping him for many hours a day as well as running the house; and yet, despite her ability to do various useful work of an unskilled nature, was not attributed any notional earning capacity (see *Beaumont v Beaumont (supra)*).

Apart from the above considerations we have the following views [632] of the English Court of Appeal on the subject: When the Court is called upon to consider the earning capacity of a divorced woman in assessing maintenance there is no general rule that can be followed. Each case must be decided on its own facts (*Rose v Rose* [1950] 2 All ER 311 (CA)). In that case the woman was 41 years of age, had no training for any work, had been married for 20 years, had not worked during that period, and had a child of four and a half years to look after. After the divorce she had worked for a short time in the kitchen of a school owned by a friend. The Judge *a quo* had attributed a notional earning capacity to her and had based his calculation on the husband's earnings plus that notional figure. The Court of Appeal held that in the circumstances there was no earning capacity to be taken into account. LORD DENNING held that as a rule such notional capacity should only be attributed to a woman who does in fact earn; or who is young and has no children and obviously ought to go out and work in her own interest but does not; or who has worked regularly during her married life and might reasonably be expected to work after divorce. Except for those cases it did not, as a rule, lie in the mouth of a wrong-doing husband to say that the ex-wife ought to go out to work simply to relieve him from paying maintenance. That expression of opinion was uttered 35 years ago when fault was an important factor in the reasoning of the Court in maintenance matters. SOMERVELL and DENNING LLJ were both insistent on the fault aspect. The law has changed since then, in regard to the importance of fault as *Wachtel's* case has shown; and the argument involving the infant of four and a half years is not relevant to the present case; but the other factors in *Rose v Rose* still apply, viz the age of the wife, the length of the marriage, her absence from the work-scene for years, and her lack of any marketable skills. As *Sinclair* has shown with a wealth of illustration from other jurisdictions, the Courts do not today distribute maintenance with any degree of liberality to women who can and ought to work after divorce (Sinclair *Reform of the SA Law of Divorce* at 47–48; see also *Hahlo (op cit* at 363–4)) but that argument can hardly apply here.

As far as our law is concerned, the position is that no maintenance will be awarded to a woman who can support herself (*Hahlo (op cit* at 361 *ad* n 45)); but in the instant case there is no positive evidence that plaintiff can support herself even to a limited extent. Present prospects of employment in this country for unqualified women in their middle forties are depressing. *Hahlo* at 364 observes that "rehabilitative" maintenance may be awarded to middle-aged women who have for years devoted themselves full-time to the management of the household and the care of the children of the marriage; it is awarded for a period sufficient to tide them over while being trained or retrained for a job or a profession . . . But that postulates a woman who can be trained or retrained. In the present case the plaintiff's history shows small indication of such an [633] ability.

In the circumstances no notional earning capacity will be attributed to plaintiff . . .

[BAKER J then proceeded to discuss the financial needs and obligations of the parties and concluded:]

The expression ["the financial needs and obligations of the parties"] means what one would think it means in everyday parlance, ie how much money does each party need for day-to-day living, and how much of the income or resources of each has to be spent for some obligatory purpose?

In the case of plaintiff, she needs a certain sum to provide for the normal living requirements of herself and the children. She has no "obligations" outside of that.

In the case of defendant, he also needs an adequate sum to live on and to maintain his status as a Judge of the Supreme Court. But he does have "obligations" as has already been pointed out. Those fall to be deducted from his gross income before this Court can attempt to allot maintenance to plaintiff out of what is left . . .

[BAKER J then discussed:]

Any other factor which in the opinion of the Court should be taken into account:

The only "other factors" which might conceivably be relevant are:

(a) the Judge's pension . . .;

(b) the Judge's retirement gratuity . . .;

(c) the Judge's widow's pension . . .; and [634]

(d) the Judge's widow's gratuity payable to her if her husband dies before he can be paid his gratuity, if any . . . (ie the widow is paid the gratuity *vice* the Judge).

The Judge's pension will be income and, if at his retirement his ex-wife still needs maintenance, it will be a source thereof. We need pay no further attention to it. The Judge's gratuity will be a capital gain which will become the Judge's personal property if he is alive to receive it. As the parties were married out of community of property the ex-wife has no entitlement to that gratuity anyway. It might conceivably be the subject of an order under s 7(3) of the Divorce Act as amended by the 1984 Act, but does not seem to me to be relevant to the present claim for maintenance. The widow's pension stands on a rather different footing. If a Judge were to die the day after his permanent appointment to the Bench his widow would receive a pension of not less than three quarters of 40% of his salary at that date . . . Had the parties here jogged along till death did them part and not the Divorce Court, plaintiff would have been entitled to a pension of at least R19 800 per annum or R1 650 per month. That prospect is now lost . . . The widow's possible pension and/or gratuity . . . do not, I think, fit into the sphere of the maintenance claimed in this action though they may, and I think do, fall to be considered in any claim for redistribution of property . . .

[BAKER J then analysed the evidence on the needs of the plaintiff and proceeded to make his order. He ordered the defendant to pay maintenance for the children at the rate of R200 per child per month, and to pay their school expenses, the cost of tertiary education and their medical and dental expenses. The defendant was further ordered to pay maintenance to the plaintiff at the rate of R1 000 per month for approximately four months from the date of the order. Thereafter the defendant had to pay the plaintiff R650 per month. The order was framed in this way so as to "force" the plaintiff to sell the big house and to use the proceeds of the sale to obtain some income for herself. The Court refused to link the maintenance order to the consumer price index as requested by the plaintiff, but instead provided that the maintenance shall increase proportionately to each rise in the defendant's salary.]

Note

This case addresses a number of important points. Firstly, it is important to note the court's emphasis of the fact that the parties' conduct is irrelevant as to the granting of a divorce order but that it can be relevant for purposes of deciding on the maintenance issue (617). (With regard to the relevance of conduct for the financial consequences of divorce, see also *Swart v Swart* [108]; *Singh v Singh* [113]; *Beaumont v Beaumont* [117]; *Katz v Katz* [119]; *Kretschmer v Kretschmer* [120].)

Aantekening

Hierdie saak is in verskeie opsigte van belang. Dit is eerstens belangrik om te let op die sterk klem wat die hof gelê het op die feit dat die partye se gedrag irrelevant is vir doeleindes van die verlening van 'n egskeidingsbevel maar dat dit wel relevant kan wees met betrekking tot die vraag of 'n onderhoudsbevel toegestaan moet word (617). (Sien verder *Swart v Swart* [108]; *Singh v Singh* [113]; *Beaumont v Beaumont* [117]; *Katz v Katz* [119]; *Kretschmer v Kretschmer* [120] met betrekking

Another very important point relates to the way in which the eventual order of the court was framed. The order was framed in such a way as to place indirect, but very strong, pressure on the plaintiff to sell the matrimonial home and thus to acquire additional means of income for herself. It is submitted that this was a fair order in the light of the specific circumstances of the case.

The court's views on the earning capacity of the wife and the possibility of awarding rehabilitative maintenance perhaps form the most important part of the judgment: no notional earning capacity will be attributed to a woman (or a man, for that matter) who does not have the necessary skills that will enable her to be trained or retrained for a job, occupation or profession after her divorce (631). Only if she can be trained or retrained will some earning capacity be attributed to her. From the court's judgment it is clear that her age and the duration of her absence from the market place will be very important considerations. If, however, it is likely, in the light of all relevant considerations, that she can be trained or retrained, and that she therefore is able to provide her own support, or at least to contribute to it, the court will consider the possibility of awarding only rehabilitative maintenance to her (632). Such rehabilitative maintenance will support her for a period of time which will enable her to be trained or retrained. This interpretation of the law conforms with the position in the Anglo-American jurisdictions. It is submitted that this is the correct view. The facts of the case should, however, be determinative. Where the husband is, for example, a very wealthy man this could have an influence on the court's decision and the court could award the ex-wife substantially more than only rehabilitative maintenance despite the fact that she can be retrained – see in this regard *Grasso v Grasso* [124] and *Pommerel v Pommerel* [125].

With regard to the interrelationship between sections 7(2) and 7(3) of the Divorce Act 70 of 1979, see the note on *Beaumont v Beaumont* [117].

With regard to the court's remarks on the possibility of pension interests or rights being considered in maintenance awards, the provisions of the Divorce Amendment Act 7 of 1989 should be borne in mind. In terms of section 2 of this

tot die rol wat gedrag speel by die finansiële gevolge van egskeiding.)

'n Ander baie belangrike aangeleentheid is die wyse waarop die hofbevel geformuleer is. Die hofbevel is so geformuleer dat daar op 'n indirekte wyse baie sterk druk op die eiseres geplaas is om die gemeenskaplike woning te verkoop ten einde sodoende vir haar 'n addisionele bron van inkomste te skep. Daar word aan die hand gedoen dat dit, in die lig van die omstandighede van die spesifieke geval, 'n billike bevel was.

Die hof se mening oor die verdienvermoë van die vrou en die moontlikheid van rehabilitatiewe onderhoud vir haar is moontlik die belangrikste gedeelte van die hof se uitspraak: geen denkbeeldige verdienvermoë sal aan 'n vrou (of 'n man) toegeken word indien sy nie die nodige vaardighede het wat haar geskik maak vir opleiding of heropleiding vir 'n werk, beroep of professie na haar egskeiding nie (631). Slegs indien sy opgelei of heropgelei kan word, sal 'n denkbeeldige verdienvermoë aan haar toegeken word. Uit die hof se uitspraak is duidelik dat haar ouderdom en die tydperk van haar afwesigheid uit die arbeidsmark baie belangrike oorwegings sal wees. Indien dit egter, in die lig van alle relevante oorwegings, waarskynlik is dat sy opgelei of heropgelei kan word en dat sy dus in staat sal wees om in haar eie onderhoudsbehoeftes te voorsien, of gedeeltelik daarin te kan voorsien, sal die hof die verlening van 'n rehabilitatiewe onderhoudsbevel oorweeg (632). Sodanige rehabilitatiewe onderhoud sal aan haar onderhoud verskaf vir 'n tydperk wat haar in staat sal stel om opgelei of heropgelei te word. Hierdie uitleg van die regsposisie is in ooreenstemming met die posisie in die Anglo-Amerikaanse lande. Daar word aan die hand gedoen dat dit die korrekte uitleg is. Die feite van die saak sal egter bepalend wees. Indien die man byvoorbeeld baie welgesteld is, kan dit 'n invloed hê op die hof se bevel en kan die hof beslis dat die vrou geregtig is op veel meer as bloot rehabilitatiewe onderhoud ten spyte van die feit dat sy heropgelei kan word – sien in hierdie verband *Grasso v Grasso* [124] en *Pommerel v Pommerel* [125].

Sien die aantekening by *Beaumont v Beaumont* [117] met betrekking tot die onderlinge verhouding tussen artikels 7(2) en 7(3) van die Wet op Egskeiding 70 van 1979.

act, section 7 of the Divorce Act was amended so that a person's pension interests can be taken into account upon divorce.

Met betrekking tot die hof se opmerkings oor die moontlikheid dat pensioenregte of -belange oorweeg kan word by die maak van onderhoudsbevele, moet die bepalings van die Wysigingswet op Egskeiding 7 van 1989 in gedagte gehou word. Artikel 2 van hierdie wet het artikel 7 van die Wet op Egskeiding gewysig sodat 'n persoon se pensioenbelange nou by egskeiding in ag geneem kan word.

[124]   GRASSO V GRASSO

1987 1 SA 48 (C)

Maintenance for a spouse upon divorce

The plaintiff (wife) and defendant's marriage had irretrievably broken down. The plaintiff claimed a divorce, custody of the two minor children born of the marriage and maintenance for herself and the two children. In a counterclaim the defendant, *inter alia*, claimed transfer of the parties' matrimonial home and the return of a BMW motor car. The house was registered in the plaintiff's name. The main issue between the parties, however, was whether the plaintiff was entitled to maintenance. The plaintiff was a primary school teacher by profession but she did not work prior to the divorce. On the opening day of the trial the defendant made an offer of settlement in which he, *inter alia*, consented to the grant of a decree of divorce and to an order in terms of which the plaintiff was awarded custody of the two minor children. He further offered to pay maintenance for each of them in the sum or R300 per month as well as maintenance for the plaintiff in the sum of R600 per month until her death, remarriage or 30 June 1986, whichever occurred first. The plaintiff could retain the BMW car, certain specified jewellery and she was to have first choice of the furniture up to half its value. The common home was to be sold and the net proceeds to be dealt with on the following basis, viz each

Onderhoud aan 'n gade na egskeiding

Die eiseres en die verweerder se huwelik het onherstelbaar verbrokkel. Die eiseres het 'n aksie ingestel vir egskeiding, bewaring van die twee minderjarige kinders wat uit die huwelik gebore is en onderhoud vir haar en die twee kinders. In 'n teeneis het die verweerder onder andere registrasie van die partye se huis in sy naam en die teruggawe van 'n BMW-motor geëis. Die huis was in die eiseres se naam geregistreer. Die werklike geskilpunt tussen die partye was egter die vraag of die eiseres op onderhoud geregtig was. Die eiseres was 'n laerskoolonderwyseres maar sy het nie voor die egskeiding gewerk nie. Op die openingsdag van die verhoor het die verweerder 'n skikkingsaanbod gemaak waarin hy onder andere toegestem het dat 'n egskeidingsbevel verleen word en dat die bewaring van die twee minderjarige kinders aan die eiseres toegestaan word. Hy het verder aangebied om R300 per maand onderhoud vir elkeen van hulle te betaal asook onderhoud vir die eiseres van R600 per maand tot haar dood, hertroue of 30 Junie 1986, wat ook al die eerste mag gebeur. Die eiseres kon die BMW-motor en sekere gespesifiseerde juweliersware behou en sy het eerste keuse gehad ten opsigte van die meubels tot die helfte van die waarde daarvan. Die gesin se huis moes verkoop word en uit

party was to receive R10 000 in cash and the balance was to be held in trust, of which the two children were to be the beneficiaries. The plaintiff declined to accept this offer. The court granted a decree of divorce and awarded the custody of the two minor children to the plaintiff. It was further held that the plaintiff could retain the house and the car. The defendant was further ordered to pay maintenance for the plaintiff at the rate of R1 500 per month and R450 per month for each of the two minor children.

die netto opbrengs daarvan moes hulle elkeen R10 000 in kontant ontvang en die res moes in trust belê word met die kinders as begunstigdes. Die eiseres het geweier om die aanbod te aanvaar. Die hof het die egskeiding toegestaan en bewaring van die twee kinders aan die eiseres verleen. Daar is verder beslis dat die eiseres die motor en die huis kon behou. Die verweerder is verder gelas om R1 500 per maand onderhoud aan die eiseres en R450 per maand vir elk van die twee kinders te betaal.

BERMAN J: [52] Before turning to a consideration of the various matters to which a Court is enjoined, in terms of s 7(2) of the Divorce Act 1979, to have regard if it is to make an award of maintenance to a spouse upon divorce, it seems to me to be necessary to make certain preliminary remarks as to the general approach which should be adopted in a matter such as this. Mr *Van der Berg* (who appeared for defendant) made much of the truism that upon divorce 'everybody suffers, the innocent as well as the guilty'. To whatever extent this may be so, and it no doubt is in so far as the emotional and psychological effect divorce has on the husband, wife and their children are concerned, none the less the trauma of divorce does not need to extend to material matters, where the necessary financial means are readily available. Where money is no object, there is no reason why a wife, on becoming an ex-wife, should not, in appropriate circumstances, continue to enjoy the same standard of living and the same good things in life she did whilst the marriage subsisted – and certainly the same applies to the minor children born to the parties. Furthermore, the tendency in England for Courts, in assessing the *quantum* of maintenance to be paid by one spouse to the other upon divorce, to lay stress on the aspects of need, contribution and practicality, and to have less regard to the issue as to where the fault lay in the break-up of the marriage, might not apply in this jurisdiction. In setting forth, in s 7(2) of the Divorce Act 1979, the various factors to which the Court is to have regard when considering the payment of maintenance upon divorce, no particular stress was laid on any one or more of these factors, and they are not listed in any particular order of importance or of greater or lesser relevance. The proper approach, it seems to me, is to consider each case on its own merits in the light of the facts and circumstances peculiar to it and with regard to those factors set out in this particular section of the Divorce Act – which list of factors is clearly not exhaustive of what the Court is to have regard to in deciding what maintenance (if any) is to be paid upon divorce by one spouse to the other, for the Court is free to have regard to any other factor which, in its opinion, ought to be taken into account in coming to a fair and just decision. Nor is the Court in any way inhibited in its task by the applicability of the so-called 'one-third rule', see Hahlo *South African Husband and Wife* 5th ed at 361; it is, at best, a starting point to be reverted to in cases where this would be appropriate; see eg *Beaumont v Beaumont* [1985 4 SA 171 (W)]. It is against this background that I now turn to a consideration of each of the factors mentioned in s 7(2) of the Divorce Act 1979 in the light of the facts found in the instant case . . .

[BERMAN J considered the age of the parties and the duration of the marriage and concluded:]

[53] In all these circumstances she would be entitled to more by way of maintenance than a wife in a marriage of short duration would be – someone who for a few brief years

had kept house and shared a husband's bed. See *Rousalis v Rousalis* 1980 (3) SA 446 (C) at 450 H . . .

[BERMAN J then turned to the conduct of the parties:]

Were this nothing more than a case where the parties found themselves to be incompatible (as the parties here certainly were) the weighing-up of fault in a balance between them in an attempt to assess whether defendant's side of the scale is weighted down more heavily than plaintiff's would be an unrewarding exercise. Where, however, the misconduct of one of the parties is gross, fault not unnaturally assumes greater relevance. See *Singh v Singh* 1983 (1) SA 781 (C) [113] . . .

[T]his marriage, from its very inception, never prospered; it might conceivably have limped along as all too many unhappy marriages do – and in the instant case through [54] plaintiff's efforts alone, but for defendant's adulterous relationship with Ms Bennington . . .

Whatever matrimonial sins defendant may have committed over the years they were, to plaintiff, as nothing compared to her husband's persistent adultery . . .

That plaintiff was prepared to consider and to attempt a reconciliation reflects only credit on her . . .

There was in fact no reconciliation ever effected between the parties, [55] nor – for that matter – did defendant ever have any genuine desire for one. His conduct in this regard, if anything, aggravated the situation as it was when and after his affair with his mistress became known to plaintiff, and gave his gross misconduct an added cruel twist. This misconduct on defendant's part must inevitably play no small part in deciding whether or not he should be ordered to pay maintenance to plaintiff . . .

[BERMAN J then referred to the high standard of living that the parties maintained and proceeded:]

It was defendant's case that this house was donated by him to plaintiff and he purported to revoke this gift and as we have seen he claimed its return by way of his counterclaim. I am satisfied that the registration of the house in plaintiff's name was no gesture of beneficence made by defendant to plaintiff, motivated by a sense of liberality or generosity on his part. The present home in which plaintiff is still residing with her two children is hers because – as already stated – defendant caused transfer of the plot on which it was erected to be passed by the seller into plaintiff's name and he built the house thereon because he intended to provide her (and the children) with a home of their own in substantiation of what he perceived his duty to be – though, strictly speaking, the transaction was a donation . . .

The position is the same with the BMW motor car. This vehicle was not lent to plaintiff nor did defendant ever have the intention of donating it to her in fulfilment of some sense of liberality on his part. Plaintiff was given the car specifically for 'family use', viz for fetching and carrying the children from and to school and the extra-mural activities in which they participated by way of taking part in what is known in families with school-going children as a 'lift-club', and to enable her to do her shopping and generally for her personal use. A 'second' motor car, ie one for the wife's exclusive use, is nowadays no longer regarded as a luxury for a man of means, as defendant has been for some years, and in so far as his claim to ownership of the BMW motor car is concerned, I propose treating it as I have the family home . . .

[56] It may well be, and it has been stated (see eg *Hahlo* (*op cit* at 361)), that a divorced wife cannot expect to enjoy the same standard of living which she had before divorce, because the divorced husband has two homes to maintain where formerly he had only one. Where, however, as here, no economy need be practised by the divorced husband

(for – as will be shown later in this judgment – defendant is a man of substance who can well afford to maintain two homes to the same standard at which he previously maintained the common home) there is no reason why plaintiff and the minor children should not continue to live every bit as well as they have done in recent years. As will be seen, there is no good reason why plaintiff should not keep her house (and her car) and enjoy in the future the same high standard of living as that for which she and defendant had striven from the inception of the marriage and had latterly achieved ...

[BERMAN J then discussed the existing and prospective means of the parties:]

Plaintiff has no regular income. Besides the house, the BMW car and household furniture and appliances, she has no property. The question of taking up employment is dealt with hereunder, but, this apart, she is wholly dependent upon defendant.

Defendant on the other hand is a man of very considerable means ...

[After listing all the defendant's assets BERMAN J proceeded:]

[57] Defendant – on this unchallenged evidence – is thus not merely a man of substance, but, to put not too fine a point on it, he is a rich man. In addition his business, or businesses, are flourishing and there is nothing to indicate that he will suffer any financial setback in the future. Furthermore, there was no suggestion throughout the hearing that defendant could not afford to meet plaintiff's demands – his attack on them was directed to her need therefor and was at no time based on any alleged inability to pay ...

[BERMAN J then considered the earning capacity of the parties:]

It seems to me that defendant, being the wealthy person he is, will continue to be in receipt of a substantial income from his business and his property dealings. It was plaintiff's earning capacity and thus the contribution this would make to her personal maintenance that was put in issue by defendant, for he insisted that she resume her profession by July 1986 at the latest, and it is to a consideration of this issue, viz is she to work or not?, which was hotly debated, than I now turn.

That plaintiff is a qualified primary school teacher has already been mentioned; also that she worked during the subsistence of the marriage, albeit for two brief periods and not during the last six or seven years. Must she, because of this (or for any other reason) have resort to her professional qualifications and now seek employment as a teacher, and thus contribute, in part at least, towards her own support? Now, it has been said that:

> 'In days gone by when, except among the poorer classes, women did not go out to work for a living, a married woman who was not wealthy in her own right was financially totally dependent on her husband. It was only fair, therefore, that, if her marriage was dissolved on account of his misconduct, he should be obliged to maintain her until her death or re-marriage.

> But the picture has changed. Women today have the same educational and vocational opportunities as men. Increasing numbers are working for a living. Many go on working after they are married. With the emergence of the 'working wife' and the equalisation of the sexes, the economic dependence of the wife upon the husband is slowly coming to an end and, as a result, the idea that marriage ought to provide a woman with a 'bread-ticket' for life is on its way out ...

> Middle-aged women who have for years devoted themselves full-time to the management and care of the children of the marriage, are awarded 'rehabilitative maintenance' for a period sufficient to enable them to be trained or re-trained for a job or profession. 'Permanent maintenance' is reserved for the elderly wife who has been married to her husband for a long time and is too old to earn her own living and unlikely to re-marry.

These trends are more pronounced in America and Europe than in South Africa. With the replacement of the guilt principle with the break-down principle, they are likely to become accentuated.'

See Hahlo and Sinclair *The Reform of the South African Law of Divorce* (1980) at 33.

[58] Now, I am by no means entirely satisfied that what the authors of the passage quoted above say with regard to the entitlement of a divorced wife, who did not work during her marriage but who devoted herself to the running of her home and the raising of her children, to no more than 'rehabilitation maintenance' is at the present time of application in this country or as yet reflects the state of affairs here, for we in South Africa live in a unique society where the non-working wife is the norm in upper middle-class (and certainly in the case of wealthy) families, with the working wife on their social and ecnonomic level a relative rarity. There is little, if any, doubt in my mind that, where the divorced husband (and particularly one whose misconduct has caused the breakdown of the marriage) can easily afford to have his ex-wife not go out to work and where she did not work prior to divorce, but devoted herself instead to her home and to the upbringing of her children, he should be required to see to it that such state of affairs continues – to revert to the truism that on divorce all concerned must suffer, then pursuing this policy reduces the suffering. Nor is adopting such a policy to be depreciated as 'old fashioned' or as being 'out of date' or 'out of line with the *mores* of present-day society', for it is certainly in the best interests of the minor children of the broken home, which is a matter of primary importance and concern. Charges of indolence were levelled at plaintiff by Mr *Van der Berg* because of her reluctance to take up teaching once more, but I reject them as unwarranted. What the authors have said in the passage quoted above may well be true of childless couples, or where the husband does not earn enough to maintain, after divorce, two separate homes so as to permit his former wife (and the mother of his children) to be at home all day – in such cases payment of 'rehabilitation maintenance' may, or perforce must, be resorted to, but then of necessity and not because it is in the best interests of all concerned.

In the instant case defendant can well afford to pay sufficient maintenance to maintain his wife and children according to the standard they were accustomed to before divorce. Plaintiff did not work prior to the dissolution of the marriage and it is manifestly in the best interests of the parties' two school-going children that they remain and are brought up in the same milieu as had existed over the past few years. Whatever plaintiff's ability to earn her own living or to contribute towards her personal maintenance may be, for the foreseeable future this falls to be disregarded, more particularly as all the other factors mentioned in s 7(2) of the Divorce Act 1979 are favourable to plaintiff in her claim for maintenance.

[BERMAN J considered the financial needs and obligations of the parties. He then referred to the fact that the court is enjoined to have regard, in considering a claim for maintenance for a divorced spouse, in addition to those factors specifically referred to in s 7(2) of the Divorce Act to any other factor which in the opinion of the court should be taken into account:]

[60] No evidence was led of any other factor which counsel urged me to take into account, but I have nevertheless consciously taken into account that a high rate of inflation is one of the facts of life in South Africa today, and that there is no reason to believe that it will be brought down appreciably (if at all) in the years to come. When I say that I have taken inflation (and thus the probable decrease in the value of money in the future) into account I mean thereby that I have deliberately refrained from making any allowance therefor, . . . because I consider it undesirable to inhibit plaintiff in any way from seeking

increases in maintenance from time to time because of the ravages of inflation thereon or if there is other sufficient reason therefor.

It seems to me that the most sensible course to follow is to make an overall award for the support of plaintiff and the two children, and then to make an apportionment between the three of them. Following this course I come to the view, in the light of plaintiff's evidence as to her needs and those of the children, that a globular amount of R2 400 a month, apart from the payment of the children's medical and like expenses is in all the circumstances a fair, proper and adequate award, and that it should be apportioned as to R1 500 per month for plaintiff, and R450 per month for each child – this apart from continuing payment for the children's medical expenses, and with provision for the continuation of maintenance in the event of either child (or both children) studying after attaining majority . . .

Note

The world-wide trend today is to break away from the idea that marriage entitles a woman to lifelong maintenance (Sinclair 1983 *SALJ* 169; Van Zyl 1984 *Codicillus* 13; Sonnekus 1988 *TSAR* 440 *et seq*). It is suggested that this trend will continue despite decisions such as the one handed down in *Grasso's* case, where BERMAN J rejected the husband's offer to pay his wife maitenance for a period in order to enable her to resume her profession. However, this case illustrates that each case will have to be considered on its own merits.

This case is criticised by Sonnekus (1988 *TSAR* 440 *et seq*). He expresses the opinion that the whole question of maintenance must be removed from the fields of family law and the law of succession: "Slegs in uitsonderingsgevalle kan die verantwoordelikheid afgeskuif word op 'n ander draagkragtige. Indien daardie versorgingspligtige die *ex* gade is, behoort sy verantwoordelikheid tydsbegrens te wees. Daarna behoort die staat die verantwoordelikheid oor te neem" (450). (See further Sonnekus 1989 *TSAR* 202.) This suggestion has far-reaching implications and at this stage it is uncertain whether it will ever be accepted in South Africa.

Note that there is no indication in the case why the applicant did not apply for a redistribution order in terms of section 7(3) of the Divorce Act 70 of 1979 (see also Sonnekus 1988 *TSAR* 450).

See also *Kroon v Kroon* [123]; *Pommerel v Pommerel* [125]; Sinclair 1983 *Acta Juridica* 75; Van Wyk 1979 *De Rebus* 637–638; Joubert 1980 *De Jure* 80; 1984 *De Jure* 350.

Aantekening

Daar bestaan vandag 'n wêreldwye tendens om weg te breek van die opvatting dat 'n huwelik 'n vrou op lewenslange onderhoud geregtig maak (Sinclair 1983 *SALJ* 169; Van Zyl 1984 *Codicillus* 13; Sonnekus 1988 *TSAR* 440 ev). Daar word aan die hand gedoen dat hierdie tendens sal voortduur ten spyte van 'n beslissing soos dié in die *Grasso*-saak waar BERMAN R die man se aanbod verwerp het om vir 'n tydperk onderhoud aan sy vrou te betaal ten einde haar in staat te stel om haar beroep weer voort te sit. Hierdie saak toon egter aan dat elke saak op sy eie meriete beoordeel sal moet word.

Hierdie saak word deur Sonnekus gekritiseer (1988 *TSAR* 440 ev). Hy is van mening dat die hele aangeleentheid van onderhoud uit die gebied van die familiereg en die erfreg weggeneem moet word: "Slegs in uitsonderingsgevalle kan die verantwoordelikheid afgeskuif word op 'n ander draagkragtige. Indien daardie versorgingspligtige die *ex* gade is, behoort sy verantwoordelikheid tydsbegrens te wees. Daarna behoort die staat die verantwoordelikheid oor te neem" (450). (Sien verder Sonnekus 1989 *TSAR* 202.) Hierdie voorstel het ingrypende implikasies en op hierdie stadium is dit onseker of dit ooit in Suid-Afrika aanvaar sal word.

Let daarop dat daar geen aanduiding in die saak is waarom die applikant nie om 'n herverdelingsbevel ingevolge artikel 7(3) van die Wet op Egskeiding 70 van 1979 aansoek gedoen het nie (sien ook Sonnekus 1988 *TSAR* 450).

Sien ook *Kroon v Kroon* [123]; *Pommerel v Pommerel* [125]; Sinclair 1983 *Acta Juridica* 75; Van Wyk 1979 *De Rebus* 637–638; Joubert 1980 *De Jure* 80; 1984 *De Jure* 350.

[125] POMMEREL V POMMEREL

1990 1 SA 998 (E)

Maintenance for the spouse upon divorce

When the appellant (husband) and respondent were divorced, the appellant was ordered to pay maintenance for the respondent in the sum of R750 per month and for each of his two children in the sum of R325 per month. The respondent then applied in terms of section 4(1)(b) of the Maintenance Act 23 of 1963 for an increase in the existing maintenance to R1120 per month for herself and to R510 per month for each child. The magistrate made an order increasing the existing amounts to R1 000 for the respondent and R450 per month for each child. The appellant appealed against this order. The main argument on his behalf was that the respondent was capable of working and contributing from her salary to her own and her children's maintenance, and that she could not escape these maintenance obligations by declining to work. The court found that no grounds had been made out for interfering with the magistrate's order. Consequently the appeal was dismissed.

Onderhoud vir die gade na egskeiding

Toe die appellant (man) en die respondent geskei is, is die appellant gelas om R750 per maand onderhoud vir die respondent te betaal en R325 per maand vir elk van sy twee kinders. Die respondent het later ingevolge artikel 4(1)(b) van die Wet op Onderhoud 23 van 1963 aansoek gedoen dat die bestaande onderhoud verhoog word na R1 120 per maand vir haar en na R510 per maand vir elke kind. Die landdros het gelas dat die onderhoud verhoog moes word na R1 000 vir die respondent en na R450 per maand vir elke kind. Die appellant het teen hierdie bevel geappelleer. Die belangrikste argument wat namens hom aangevoer is, was dat die respondent in staat was om te werk en dat sy uit haar salaris tot haar eie onderhoud sowel as dié van haar kinders kon bydra, en dat sy nie hierdie onderhoudsverpligtinge kon ontsnap deur te weier om te werk nie. Die hof het bevind dat daar geen gronde aangetoon is op grond waarvan met die landdros se bevel ingemeng kon word nie en die appèl is gevolglik van die hand gewys.

MULLINS J: [1001] I revert ... to the main argument for appellant before this Court, namely whether account should not be taken of respondent's ability to work, and that she should from her own income contribute towards the maintenance of herself and her children ...

The question whether respondent should work or not was first raised in questions to her by the magistrate. She stated that it was in the interests of her children that she stay at home and care for her children, who she described as going through a disturbing and stressful time in their lives. Apparently there is a pending dispute relating to appellant's access to the children. However, respondent says she intends to seek mornings only work in about two years' time, when her youngest daughter is in standard 1. She does not at present consider a crèche as a substitute for a mother, especially as her daughters are used to having their mother around.

Respondent stated that she previously worked as a dictaphone typist and secretary, but that for most of the period of her marriage she did not work, and she was therefore presently continuing both life style and standard of living to which she and the children were accustomed. She was cross-examined by appellant, during a lengthy and competent cross-examination, on her failure to obtain employment, but her attitude remained as set out above ...

[1002] Much reliance was placed, before us in argument, on the statement appearing in Hahlo *South African Law of Husband and Wife* 5th ed at 361 that 'no maintenance will be awarded to a wife who is able to support herself, nor can a wife expect to enjoy after the divorce the same standard of living that she had as a married woman'. Mr *Eksteen* [for the appellant] asked us to hold that this was a principle of law applicable in every case. The first portion of this statement was quoted with approval in *Kroon v Kroon* 1986 (4) SA 616 (E) at 632H [123]. In my view this statement requires qualification, and cannot as it stands be regarded as a hard and fast principle of our law applicable to all cases.

The aforementioned statement in *Hahlo* is probably correct where an ex-wife is *in fact* able to support herself, because she is *in fact* earning sufficient for her support, or *in fact* has assets that she can support herself from the income therefrom. This is a very different matter, however, from the notional employability of the woman concerned.

If it is alleged that she should be able to support herself from employment, or otherwise through her own efforts, then the question of the reasonableness of her decision not to work must be considered. In deciding the question of reasonableness, many factors come into play – her age, state of health, qualifications, when she was last employed, the length of the marriage, the standard of living of the parties during marriage, her commitment to the care of young children, and others. For present purposes I omit any question of fault in relation to the divorce, although s 7(2) of the Divorce Act 70 of 1979 envisages this as a possible additional factor.

Secondly a wife *should* in my view be able to expect the same standard of living that she had as a married woman. In most cases it may not be possible to achieve this goal, and of course a husband should be entitled to the same expectation, but in the final result it is a question of balancing up the needs of both parties and making an equitable distribution of the available income . . .

[1003] It is not necessary for the purposes of this judgment to consider whether the *dictum* that 'no maintenance will be awarded to a wife who is able to support herself' would relieve a husband, who was well able to afford to maintain his former wife, from doing so merely and exclusively because she was able to maintain herself from earning her own income. See *Grasso v Grasso* 1987 (1) SA 48 (C) [124]. A woman's ability to earn income does not *per se*, in my view, disentitle the Court from ordering her former husband to pay her maintenance.

In my view there can in no case be a simple answer. By entering into a marriage, both parties not only alter their personal status, but also their social and economic regime. During the marriage, living conditions and ways and standards of life are built up by reason of the marriage, their cohabitation, the birth of children and other factors which, when the marriage ends in divorce, are very different from what they would have been had the parties remained single.

Social conditions and changes such as the emancipation of women, their increasing role in the labour market, the acceptability of divorce, and other factors, come into play in the readjustment which divorce necessitates. Legal changes such as the elimination of fault or guilt as a ground for divorce are also important. The 'clean break' principle is also increasingly finding favour in Courts here and overseas . . .

[1004] I know of no authority which requires a mother to go to work to maintain herself where it is reasonable that she should stay at home to care for her children and where her former husband is able to maintain her and the children of the marriage without her working. Apart from the bald suggestion that the children could go to a crèche, appellant has not refuted respondent's reasons for wishing to remain at home for the sake of the children, at least for the next two years. I find her reasons to be reasonable and satisfactory, despite Mr *Eksteen's* strenuous arguments to the contrary. Appellant, by fathering the children, has brought about this situation, and in my view cannot therefore on that ground escape his liability to maintain the respondent.

As already mentioned, s 7(2) of the Divorce Act gives the Court the widest discretion to take into account numerous factors, some of which I have referred to above, and any other factor which in the opinion of the Court should be taken into account. In my view the same factors may be taken into account in deciding whether to vary a maintenance order, even where the application is before a magistrate. Even if there is a duty on a magistrate or the maintenance officer to determine the earning capacity of an ex-wife (see *Buch v Buch* 1967 (3) SA 84 (T)), the magistrate's failure to do so in the present case cannot affect the outcome.

The period of two years before the respondent starts working, as she expects to do, is a sufficiently long time to justify an increase being ordered at this stage . . .

No grounds have been made out for interfering with the order of the magistrate. The appeal is dismissed . . .

JONES J concurred.

Note

It is true, as Hahlo 361 says, that maintenance will not be awarded to a wife (or husband) who can support herself (or himself) and that a spouse cannot expect to enjoy the same standard of living after divorce as that which he or she enjoyed during marriage. However, as was held in the case under discussion, this is not "a hard and fast principle of our law applicable to all cases" (1002). The court must in each case consider the possibility that a spouse (usually the wife) who is not currently working may be able to work – that is, the notional employability of the spouse must be considered (see also *Kroon v Kroon* [123]). But the mere fact that the unemployed spouse could possibly work does not mean that he or she must find employment. In considering the spouse's employability, the court must decide whether it is reasonable for the unemployed spouse to stay at home instead of working outside the home. When the court decides on the reasonableness of a decision not to work it has to take many factors into account. These factors include the spouse's "age, state of health, qualifications, when she [or he] was last employed, the length of the marriage, the standard of living of the parties during marriage, her [or his] commitment to the care of young children, and others" (1002). Each case will therefore be decided on its own facts. What is a reasonable decision to stay at home for one spouse may be an unreasonable decision for another. For example, where the husband cannot afford to pay much maintenance to his wife after divorce and she is well-qualified to work, she can

Aantekening

Dit is waar, soos wat Hahlo 361 sê, dat onderhoud nie toegeken sal word aan 'n vrou (of 'n man) wat haarself (of homself) kan onderhou nie, en dat 'n gade nie kan verwag om dieselfde lewenstandaard na egskeiding te handhaaf as wat hy of sy gedurende die huwelik gehandhaaf het nie. Maar, soos wat in die onderhawige saak beslis is, is hierdie reël nie "a hard and fast principle of our law applicable to all cases" (1002) nie. Die hof moet in elke geval oorweging skenk aan die moontlikheid dat 'n gade (gewoonlik die vrou) wat nie werk nie, wel in staat kan wees om te werk – dit wil sê, die denkbeeldige geskiktheid van die gade om te werk ("notional employability") moet oorweeg word (sien ook *Kroon v Kroon* [123]). Die blote feit dat die nie-werkende gade moontlik kan werk, beteken egter nie dat hy of sy werk moet soek nie. Wanneer die hof die gade se geskiktheid om te werk oorweeg, moet hy beslis of dit redelik is van die nie-werkende gade om tuis te bly in plaas van om werk te soek. Om te bepaal of die besluit om nie te werk nie redelik is al dan nie, moet verskeie faktore in ag geneem word. Die faktore sluit in die gade se "age, state of health, qualifications, when she [of hy] was last employed, the length of the marriage, the standard of living of the parties during marriage, her [of sy] commitment to the care of young children, and others" (1002). Elke saak moet dus op sy eie feite beslis word. Wat in die een geval 'n redelike besluit mag wees om tuis te bly, mag in 'n ander geval onredelik wees. Byvoorbeeld, indien 'n man nie kan be-

probably not reasonably expect to stay at home. But if there is no shortage of funds and the wife is taking care of the spouses' small children, it may well be that her decision not to work will be reasonable (see for example *Grasso v Grasso* [124]).

Similarly, in respect of maintenance of the same standard of living, Hahlo's statement does not apply in all cases. As was held in the case under discussion, where one spouse is able to support the other in the same standard of living, that spouse can be ordered to pay sufficient maintenance to the other to enable him or her not to lower his or her standard of living – see also *Grasso v Grasso*.

On the clean break principle see the note on *Beaumont v Beaumont* [117].

kostig om na egskeiding veel onderhoud aan sy vrou te betaal nie en sy goed gekwalifiseer is om te werk, kan sy waarskynlik nie redelikerwys verwag om tuis te bly nie. Maar as daar geen gebrek aan middele is nie en die vrou na die gades se klein kindertjies moet omsien, sal haar besluit om nie te werk nie, heel moontlik redelik wees (sien byvoorbeeld *Grasso v Grasso* [124]).

Met betrekking tot die handhawing van dieselfde lewenstandaard geld Hahlo se stelling ook nie in alle gevalle nie. Soos wat in die onderhawige saak beslis is, kan 'n gade wat daartoe in staat is om die ander gade te onderhou sodat hy of sy dieselfde lewenstandaard kan handhaaf, beveel word om soveel onderhoud te betaal dat die ander gade nie sy of haar lewenstandaard hoef te verlaag nie – sien ook *Grasso v Grasso*.

In verband met die skoon breuk-beginsel sien die aantekening by *Beaumont v Beaumont* [117].

Token maintenance   **Nominale onderhoud**

[126]   NEL V NEL

1977 3 SA 288 (O)

Token maintenance

The plaintiff claimed maintenance to the amount of R5 per month from her husband when she divorced him. She later indicated that she would even be satisfied with R1 per month. At the time of the application she was able to support herself but she claimed the amount to make provision for future occurrences. The court rejected her claim.

Nominale onderhoud

Die eiseres het onderhoud ten bedrae van R5 per maand van haar eggenoot geëis toe sy van hom geskei het. Sy het later aangedui dat sy selfs met net R1 per maand tevrede sou wees. Ten tyde van die aansoek was sy in staat om haarself te onderhou maar sy het die bedrag geëis om voorsiening te maak vir latere gebeurlikhede. Die hof het haar eis van die hand gewys.

SMUTS R: [289] Ek stem saam met Mnr. *Hancke* [namens die eiseres] dat eiseres nie hoef te bewys dat sy behoeftig is voor onderhoud aan haar toegeken sal word nie . . . Die vraag is gevolglik of eiseres geregtig is op 'n toekenning van 'n nominale bedrag onderhoud om haar [290] in staat te stel om op 'n latere stadium aansoek te kan doen om 'n vermeerderde bedrag onderhoud. In *Ford v Ford and Another*, 1965 (1) SA 264 (D), is so 'n toekenning gemaak; in *Lincesso v Lincesso*, 1966 (1) SA 747 (W), het VIEYRA, R, geweier om 'n nominale bedrag onderhoud toe te ken. *Willis v Willis*, 1963 (2) PH B21 (SR), en *Van Jaarsveld v Van Jaarsveld*, 1961 (2) PH B25 (SR), is voorbeelde van gevalle waar nominale toekennings gemaak is waar die eiseres haarself kon onderhou op datum van die egskeiding maar dit voorsienbaar was dat sy in die toekoms onderhoud sou benodig. In die *Van Jaarsveld* saak was die eiseres middeljarig en in *Willis v Willis* was die eiseres 62 jaar oud en haar huwelik met die verweerder het reeds agt jaar geduur. In die *Lincesso* saak, *supra*, het VIEYRA, R, geweier om 'n nominale bedrag onderhoud toe te ken omdat, na sy mening, geen saak hoegenaamd daarvoor uitgemaak is nie. VIEYRA, R, het myns insiens nie beslis dat so 'n toekenning in geen omstandighede geregverdig kan word nie. Die geleerde Regter sê die volgende op bl. 750:

> "I can, however, imagine that in some instances the Court will be justified in granting a token payment, but because that is all that in the circumstances is justifiable and not merely because of an altruistic motive to circumvent the omissions of the Legislature: see eg *Ford's* case".

Na my mening kan die Hof 'n nominale bedrag onderhoud toeken wat tot gevolg sal hê dat 'n eiseres op 'n later geleentheid aansoek sal kan doen om 'n vermeerderde bedrag onderhoud, indien daar rede is om te glo dat sy in die toekoms waarskynlik onderhoud gaan benodig en dit bewys is dat dit in die omstandighede van die saak reg en billik is dat die verweerder dan voorsiening behoort te maak vir onderhoud vir haar, al is die eiseres in staat om haarself te onderhou op die datum waarop ontbinding van die huwelik beveel word.

In die onderhawige saak is ek egter van mening dat 'n saak nie uitgemaak is vir die toekenning van 'n nominale bedrag onderhoud nie. Die huwelik tussen die partye was maar van baie korte duur. Vir slegs 10 maande het eiseres en verweerder saamgewoon as man en vrou. Geen kinders is gebore uit die huwelik nie. Hierdie is gevolglik nie 'n geval waar eiseres baie jare van haar lewe bestee het aan versorging van 'n gemeenskaplike huishouding en die kinders van die partye nie. Eiseres is nog 'n jong vrou. Daar is geen suggestie dat haar gesondheid swak is nie. Alhoewel eiseres sê dat sy onderhoud eis met die oog op toekomstige gebeurlikhede, is daar geen gronde waarop bevind kan word dat daar enige waarskynlikheid bestaan dat sy in die voorsienbare toekoms nie vir haarself sal kan sorg nie. Namens eiseres is verder aangevoer dat verweerder geen beswaar teen so 'n toekenning geopper het nie aangesien hy nie die saak verdedig nie. Die feit dat hy nie verdedig nie kan egter nie beskou word as 'n toestemming tot die toekenning van R5 of 'n nominale bedrag as onderhoud nie...

Na my mening is daar nie 'n saak vir toekenning van R5 per maand of selfs vir 'n nominale bedrag as onderhoud uitgemaak nie...

Note

It is important to note that the court did not reject the plaintiff's claim on the ground that it could not issue orders for nominal maintenance but because of lack of sufficient proof to justify the making of such an order. See further the note on *Qoza v Qoza* [128].

Aantekening

Dit is belangrik om daarop te lei dat die hof nie die eiseres se eis verwerp het omdat dit van mening was dat dit nie bevele vir nominale onderhoud mag uitreik nie maar omdat daar nie voldoende getuienis was om die toestaan van so 'n bevel te regverdig nie. Sien verder die aantekening by *Qoza v Qoza* [128].

[127] PORTINHO V PORTINHO

1981 2 SA 595 (T)

Token maintenance

The plaintiff in an uncontested divorce action sued her husband for divorce and claimed

Nominale onderhoud

Die eiseres het in 'n onbestrede egskeidingsaksie onderhoud ten bedrae van R1 per jaar

maintenance at the rate of R1 per year from him. The only real issue was whether an award of token maintenance could be made. The court rejected the claim.

van haar man geëis. Die enigste werklike geskilpunt was of 'n bevel vir die betaling van nominale onderhoud toegestaan kon word. Die hof het die eis van die hand gewys.

VAN DIJKHORST J: [595] Counsel for the plaintiff contended that a token award of maintenance for the plaintiff should be made to preserve her right to maintenance. I queried the correctness of this approach.

[596] A wife had at common law no right to maintenance upon divorce. *Schultz v Schultz* 1928 OPD 155; *R v Blundell* 1943 TPD 146; *Strauss v Strauss* 1974 (3) SA 79 (A) at 93H. Such right to maintenance was created by the Legislature in the Matrimonial Affairs Act 37 of 1953 . . .

This provision was generally interpreted to mean that the innocent plaintiff was not by reason thereof now entitled to claim maintenance as of right, but that the Court was given a general discretion . . .

In *Hossack v Hossack* 1956 (3) SA 159 (W) at 165B–F LUDORF J stated that maintenance is not to be granted as a matter of course . . .

It was generally accepted by the Courts that this discretion should not be too readily exercised. See Hahlo *The South African Law of Husband and Wife* 3rd ed at 439 and cases cited in the footnotes.

The contention of counsel for the plaintiff that she has a right to maintenance upon divorce which right should be kept alive by means of a token award is therefore without foundation in the common law or in the legislation preceding the Divorce Act 70 of 1979. Neither does s 7 thereof, which contains the relevant provisions, alter the position . . .

[597] Should token maintenance then be awarded to a plaintiff who has no need for maintenance, just to provide for the contingency that she might need sustenance in future? Two cases are apposite. In *Ford v Ford and Another* 1965 (1) SA 264 (D) MILNE JP awarded token maintenance to a plaintiff who did not need it, because he deemed it just. In *Lincesso v Lincesso* 1966 (1) SA 747 (W) VIEYRA J declined to follow this case . . .

In my view it is unsatisfactory for the Courts to employ gimmicks to create rights which the Legislature in its wisdom has now twice omitted to bring into being. It surely must have been aware of the decision in *Lincesso's* case. If it is deemed in the public interest that divorced parties who upon divorce are both financially independent should for years to come be tied together by an unbreakable bond in the form of a contingent right to claim maintenance, then the Legislature should intervene. I am not convinced of the wisdom thereof.

In my view the test to be applied is whether on the probabilities maintenance is or will be needed. If the answer is positive the considerations set out in s 7(2) come into play. If on the probabilities it is not shown that maintenance is or will be needed no award thereof (whatever its size) can be made. A token award where no maintenance is needed is therefore not envisaged in the Act.

In the instant case no proof has been adduced that on the probabilities maintenance will be required in future. I therefore refuse to award token maintenance to the plaintiff . . .

Note

See the note on *Qoza v Qoza* [128].

Aantekening

Sien die aantekening by *Qoza v Qoza* [128].

[128]   Qoza v Qoza

1989 4 SA 838 (C)

Token maintenance	Nominale onderhoud

Token maintenance

In an undefended action for divorce the plaintiff (wife), *inter alia*, claimed token maintenance for herself in the sum of R1 per month. The parties were married in community of property and one minor child was born of the marriage. The evidence revealed that the breakdown of the marriage was caused by the actions of the defendant. The plaintiff was still a young woman and she was neither sickly nor ill. She earned an income of R247 per month and there was no evidence before the court that her employment was of a temporary nature only, or that she might find herself unemployed in future. As far as the financial needs of the plaintiff were concerned the evidence showed that she was self-sufficient and that she did not require any maintenance from the defendant. The defendant earned an income of approximately R125 per week. The court found that the plaintiff did not prove that she would require maintenance for herself in future and refused to make an order for token maintenance in her favour.

Nominale onderhoud

In 'n onbestrede egskeidingsaksie het die eiseres onder andere R1 nominale onderhoud per maand vir haarself geëis. Die partye was binne gemeenskap van goed getroud en een kind is uit die huwelik gebore. Die getuienis het aangetoon dat die verbrokkeling van die huwelik aan die verweerder se gedrag toe te skryf was. Die eiseres was nog jonk en sy was nie siek of sieklik nie. Sy het R247 per maand verdien en daar was geen getuienis voor die hof dat sy net tydelik in diens geneem is of dat sy in die toekoms werkloos sou raak nie. Vir sover dit die finansiële behoeftes van die eiseres aangegaan het, was dit uit die getuienis duidelik dat sy selfonderhoudend was en dat sy nie enige onderhoud van die verweerder nodig gehad het nie. Die verweerder het ongeveer R125 per week verdien. Die hof het bevind dat die eiseres nie bewys het dat sy in die toekoms vir haarself onderhoud sou benodig nie en het geweier om 'n bevel vir nominale onderhoud uit te reik.

LIEBENBERG AJ: [840] After hearing the evidence in the matter I confronted Mr *Quinn* for the plaintiff with the question whether in the circumstances of this case I should grant an order in terms of the plaintiff's prayer for maintenance for herself at the rate of R1 per month. The maintenance prayed for has become commonly known as token maintenance.

I was referred by Mr *Quinn* to three decisions on this point. They are *Portinho v Portinho* 1981 (2) SA 595 (T) [127], *Ford v Ford and Another* 1965 (1) SA 264 (D) and *Brink v Brink* 1983 (3) SA 217 (D). Mr *Quinn* argued that the decisions in the two Natal cases should be followed by me and not the decision of VAN DIJKHORST J in the *Portinho* case.

The main considerations on which the decision of VAN DIJKHORST J in the *Portinho* case was based appear from the report to be as follows:

  (a)   a wife at common law had no right to maintenance on divorce;

  (b)   in terms of s 10 of the Matrimonial Affairs Act 37 of 1953 the Court was given a discretion to grant maintenance to an innocent spouse on divorce;

  (c)   it was generally accepted by the Court that this discretion should not be too readily exercised;

(*d*) s 7(2) of the Divorce Act 70 of 1979 also grants the Court a discretion to award maintenance to a plaintiff and does also not create a right to maintenance in favour of a plaintiff;

(*e*) '... the test to be applied is whether on the probabilities maintenance is or will be needed. If the answer is positive the considerations set out in ss (2) come into play. If on the probabilities it is not shown that maintenance is or will be needed no award thereof (whatever its size) can be made' (at 597H);

(*f*) 'a token award where no maintenance is needed is therefore not envisaged in the Act' (at 597H).

In regard to (*e*) and (*f*) above I do not understand VAN DIJKHORST J to have stated that no token award is competent. I understand him to say that a token award can be made, provided that the evidence shows on the probabilities that maintenance will be needed in future. This also appears to be how MILNE J understood it in *Brink v Brink* (*supra* at 218H). In *Ford v Ford* (*supra* at 265D–266A) MILNE JP (as he then was) considered this question in the light of the provisions of s 10(1)(*a*) of the Matrimonial Affairs Act 37 of 1953. In making an award for token maintenance he expressed himself as follows (at 265G–266A of the report):

'It is clear from these cases and from *Van Deventer v Van Deventer and Another* 1962 (3) SA 969 (N) at 975 (in none of which was it apparently contended that a token payment might be ordered where there was no present need of maintenance on the part of the innocent spouse), that s 10(1)(*a*) of Act 37 of 1953 confers a discretion upon the Court and, whilst it is true that an innocent spouse having a good ground of action for divorce is not obliged to bring that action and may, in order to ensure that she will have some source of income in the future in case her present circumstances should change for the worse, elect to remain married to the guilty spouse, I deem it just, in this case, that I should make an order for a token payment of maintenance to be made by the first defendant to the plaintiff so that, [841] if her financial situation should deteriorate, she will not have lost recourse to her erstwhile husband for relief, for under the section the order may be varied on good cause shown.'

I do not understand MILNE JP to have stated any more than: (1) that a token award for maintenance is competent in the exercise of the Court's discretion; and (2) that in the circumstances of that case he found it just for such an order to be made. What the circumstances in that case were which persuaded him to make the order he however did not state.

In *Brink v Brink* (*supra*) MILNE J held that he was bound to follow the decision in *Ford v Ford* because, though that decision was open to criticism, he was not prepared to say that it was wrongly decided.

At 219E the learned Judge made the following statement regarding the decision in *Ford's* case:

'In that case it had been conceded by counsel for the plaintiff that the plaintiff was not, at the time when the matter was heard, in need of a contribution from the first defendant for her maintenance, and *the sole basis upon which the claim for a token award was said to be just was that there was no power vested in the Court to order maintenance to be paid after a divorce, and it was only the Court granting the divorce that had the power to make an order for maintenance.*' (My italicising.)

It appears that it is correct to say that the state of our law since the enactment of the Matrimonial Affairs Act in 1953 has been that the Court granting a divorce and only that Court can make an order that maintenance be paid by one spouse to the other after the dissolution of their marriage. Should that Court therefore find that although the one spouse does not need maintenance from the other at the time the order is made but finds that on a balance of probabilities it has been shown that such a need will arise at some future time, then the only manner in which provision can be made for the payment of maintenance at such future time is to make a token award when the divorce order is granted. In my view this is how the judgment in *Ford's* case must be understood. I therefore find myself in respectful disagreement with the interpretation of the judgment in *Ford's* case by MILNE J as expressed in the words italicised by me and if that interpretation is to be regarded as correct then I am in respectful disagreement with that finding in *Ford's* case.

In an apparent attempt to show that there may be limits to the mere granting of token maintenance in all cases MILNE J in *Brink's* case remarked as follows at 220E–G:

'In my view it does not follow that, because, in the majority of cases, the Court would almost always be justified in granting an order for token maintenance on the basis upon which it was granted in *Ford's* case, the Court would not be acting in accordance with the wishes of the Legislature if it were to grant such orders. It will not be so in every case. There may well be circumstances where it is perfectly clear that the respective financial positions of the parties is such that there will never be any circumstances in which it will be probable that the plaintiff will seek an increase in the amount of maintenance from a token award to a substantial award. There may be particular circumstances advanced by a defendant or by a plaintiff, which would either make the award unjust or just.'

It seems that the limiting factors which prompted the use of the word 'almost' in the beginning of the above quotation are those mentioned in the last two sentences thereof.

[842] I understand the above *dictum* of MILNE J to mean that in view of the fact that only the Court granting the divorce can make a maintenance order in favour of a spouse, such an order (I suppose, if claimed) will be granted unless circumstances are proved which show that it will probably not be needed or which render it unjust. This seems to me with respect to be a wrong approach. It does not require a consideration by the Court of the factors referred to in s 7(2) of the Divorce Act 70 of 1979 in order to exercise its discretion whether to grant a maintenance order or not. This to me seems to be in conflict with the approach envisaged by s 7(2). It also has inherent in it a real danger of an injustice resulting from its application as the order may be granted without any consideration of the circumstances of the case whatsoever.

I am also in respectful disagreement with the test adopted by VAN DIJKHORST J in *Portinho's* case (at 597H) and set out in (e) above. It seems to me that the approach adopted by Hahlo and Sinclair *The Reform of the South African Law of Divorce* at 45 is the correct one. This approach requires the Court to consider the factors referred to in s 7(2) in order to decide, firstly, whether maintenance is to be paid at all (in other words whether a need for maintenance exists) and, if so, by whom to whom; secondly, the amount to be paid and thirdly the period for which maintenance is to be paid. This approach, which I adopt, will in my view eliminate the unjust results which may result from the approach adopted in *Brink's* case.

Mr *Quinn* argued that even if I hold that a need for future maintenance must be proved before token maintenance is awarded then such a need has been shown in this case. He argued that this need is apparent from the following:

(i) Plaintiff's only source of income is that derived from her employment and if she were to become ill and unable to work she would have no source of income.

(ii) The effects of inflation may result in her requiring maintenance from defendant in future.

(iii) The fact that if she is awarded the custody of the child, childhood illnesses may probably set in which may oblige her to be absent from work.

(iv) Because the maintenance was prayed for in the summons and there is no defence the award of token maintenance should be made even if no evidence is adduced.

I will deal with the points made in (i) and (ii) above together.

In respect of point (ii) Mr *Quinn* relied on a passage in the judgment of MILNE J in *Brink's* case appearing at 220G–H where he says the following:

'Having regard to the depressing rise in the cost of living, at least in the past 10 or 12 years, it does not seem unrealistic to say that where a young woman is divorced from her husband and both of them are wage-earners or capable of earning a living, there is, at the lowest, a very distinct possibility that the wife may, in future, require maintenance from her husband and that it would be a recognition of the economic history of the Republic and, indeed, of the Western world over the past ten years to make provision for such a contingency.'

Mr *Quinn* argued that I should take judicial notice of the effects of inflation. If I am entitled to do so then I must of course also take into [843] account that inflation will affect the defendant as well and therefore will affect his ability to pay maintenance. It also seems to me to be equally notorious that as inflation continues to erode the value of money the emoluments of employees are increased from time to time to counteract the effects thereof. Without evidence therefor to show how these various factors will affect the position of the respective parties, I am of the view that I cannot take the effects of inflation into account when considering a claim for the token maintenance.

I am further of the view that grounds (i) and (ii) can in any event not be regarded as valid grounds for awarding token maintenance. If they should be so regarded it would mean that a wife who is a party to a divorce action is entitled to an order for token maintenance in all cases where both spouses are working persons. It is difficult to imagine such a marriage to which these factors will not apply. This, however, would have the effect that in all such cases the wife will, as it were, be entitled to a free policy against normal risks of life with the husband as the insurer.

Divorce puts an end to the reciprocal duty of support that existed between the spouses. (Hahlo *The South African Law of Husband and Wife* 5th ed at 354). Only in terms of the Act can an order be made for maintenance of the one spouse by the other. (See above.) Maintenance, however, will not be granted to a woman who can support herself. *Kroon v Kroon* 1986 (4) SA 616 (E) at 632H [123].

I must therefore with VAN DIJKHORST J in *Portinho's* case question the wisdom of keeping two divorced persons bonded together, possibly for life, by a token maintenance order made merely to provide for speculative possibilities. Such an order where no future need for maintenance has been proved on a balance of probabilities does not seem to me to accord with justice. A divorced spouse capable of self-support can be expected to make his or her own provisions against the normal risks of life and for retirement etc. Compare *Nel v Nel* 1977 (3) SA 288 (O) [126]; *Hurn v Hurn* 1978 (3) SA 252 (E).

Ground (iii) above also does not seem to me to be a valid one. If the defendant is ordered to pay maintenance for the child and the child should need any special care due to a childhood illness, the plaintiff may, instead of giving up her work, apply for increased maintenance for the child to enable her to provide the special care and still continue with her employment. No evidence has been placed before me to show that the child is suffering from any condition which may require plaintiff in future to look after it on a full-time basis.

As to ground (iv). Although the fact that the defendant does not defend the action may be a factor to take into account when considering whether to grant an order for token maintenance or not, it is in my view not a consideration which on its own will entitle a plaintiff to such an order. It seems to me that the only assistance a plaintiff can derive from such a fact is that the evidence adduced by such plaintiff will stand uncontested.

That the discretion given to the Court in terms of s 7(2) must be judicially exercised seems to be clear. This means that there must be some grounds for the exercise of the discretion. See Claassen *Dictionary of Legal Words and Phrases* vol 2 at 298.

[844] Mr *Quinn* conceded, correctly in my view, that save for the grounds set out in (i), (ii), (iii) and (iv) above there are no other circumstances in this case which can support the granting of a token award of maintenance. He further conceded that plaintiff has not been shown to be a sickly or ill person.

In my view plaintiff has not proved that, on a balance of probabilities, she will require maintenance for herself in future and I refuse to make an order for token maintenance in her favour . . .

Note

In the case under discussion LIEBENBERG AJ reconciled the conflicting judicial statements about whether nominal (or token) maintenance could and should be ordered. He correctly held, *inter alia*, that *Portinho v Portinho* [127] did not hold that such orders cannot be made. The court in *Portinho* merely held that an order for nominal maintenance ought not readily to be made – it should only be made if a need for it has been proved on a balance of probabilities.

In the case under discussion the court concluded that our law provides that "the Court granting a divorce and only that Court can make an order that maintenance be paid by one spouse to the other after the dissolution of their marriage. Should that Court therefore find that although the one spouse does not need maintenance from the other at the time the order is made but finds that on a balance of probabilities it has been shown that such a need will arise at some future time, then the only manner in which provision can be made for the payment of maintenance at such future time is to make a token award when the divorce is granted" (841). This test is, broadly speaking, in conformity with that set out in *Portinho*, but the court in *Qoza* criticised the way in which the test was formulated in *Portinho*. In the latter case it was held that it first had to be determined whether maintenance is or will probably be needed. Once the probabilities have shown that maintenance is or will be needed, the factors in section 7(2) of the Divorce Act 70 of 1979 come into play. In *Qoza* it was held that the first

Aantekening

In die onderhawige saak het LIEBENBERG Wn R die botsende uitsprake oor die vraag of nominale onderhoud toegeken kan en behoort te word met mekaar versoen. Hy het, onder andere, tereg beslis dat daar nie in *Portinho v Portinho* [127] beslis is dat sulke bevele nie uitgereik kan word nie. Die hof het bloot in *Portinho* beslis dat 'n bevel vir nominale onderhoud nie geredelik uitgereik moet word nie – dit moet slegs gedoen word indien bewys is dat sodanige bevel op grond van 'n oorwig van waarskynlikheid nodig is.

In die onderhawige saak het die hof tot die gevolgtrekking gekom dat ons reg bepaal dat "the Court granting a divorce and only that Court can make an order that maintenance be paid by one spouse to the other after the dissolution of their marriage. Should that Court therefore find that although the one spouse does not need maintenance from the other at the time the order is made but finds that on a balance of probabilities it has been shown that such a need will arise at some future time, then the only manner in which provision can be made for the payment of maintenance at such future time is to make a token award when the divorce is granted" (841). Hierdie toets is, in die algemeen gesproke, in ooreenstemming met die toets wat in *Portinho* neergelê is, maar in *Qoza* het die hof die wyse waarop die toets in *Portinho* geformuleer is, gekritiseer. In laasgenoemde saak is beslis dat daar eerstens bepaal moet word of onderhoud nodig is, of waarskynlik later nodig sal word. As dit waarskynlik is dat onderhoud nodig is of nodig sal word, kom

step is to consider the factors in section 7(2). These factors must be considered "in order to decide, firstly, whether maintenance is to be paid at all (in other words whether a need for maintenance exists) and, if so, by whom to whom; secondly, the amount to be paid and thirdly the period for which maintenance is to be paid" (842).

It is important to note that an order for token maintenance will not be awarded simply to protect a spouse against the normal risks of life or to provide for the eventuality of illness of a child for whom the spouse cares.

See also *Nel v Nel* [126].

die faktore in artikel 7(2) van die Wet op Egskeiding 70 van 1979 in die prentjie. In *Qoza* is beslis dat die eerste stap is om die faktore in artikel 7(2) te oorweeg. Hierdie faktore moet oorweeg word "in order to decide, firstly, whether maintenance is to be paid at all (in other words whether a need for maintenance exists) and, if so, by whom to whom; secondly, the amount to be paid and thirdly the period for which maintenance is to be paid" (842).

Dit is belangrik om daarop te let dat 'n bevel vir nominale onderhoud nie uitgereik sal word bloot om 'n gade teen die normale risiko's van die lewe te beskerm of om voorsiening te maak vir die moontlikheid dat 'n kind wat deur die gade versorg word, siek kan word nie.

Sien ook *Nel v Nel* [126].

The rescission, suspension or variation of maintenance orders

Die intrekking, opskorting of wysiging van onderhoudsbevele

[129]   RUBENSTEIN V RUBENSTEIN

1992 2 SA 703 (W)

A maintenance court has the power to vary a maintenance order issued in terms of section 7(1) or section 7(2) of the Divorce Act 70 of 1979

When the parties were divorced in 1977 they concluded an agreement in terms of which the respondent undertook to pay maintenance to the appellant. This agreement was made an order of court. In 1983 the appellant successfully applied to the maintenance court for an increase in the maintenance, but when she applied for a further increase in 1990, the magistrate held that the maintenance court had no jurisdiction to vary the order. He distinguished between the position where an agreement between the parties with regard to the payment of maintenance by the one party to the other is made an order of court in terms of section 7(1) of the Divorce Act 70 of 1979, and where the court orders the payment of maintenance in terms of sec-

'n Onderhoudshof het die bevoegdheid om 'n onderhoudsbevel te wysig wat ingevolge artikel 7(1) of artikel 7(2) van die Wet op Egskeiding 70 van 1979 uitgereik is

Toe die partye in 1977 geskei is, het hulle 'n ooreenkoms aangegaan waarin die respondent onderneem het om onderhoud aan die appellant te betaal. Hierdie ooreenkoms is 'n bevel van die hof gemaak. In 1983 het die appellant suksesvol in die onderhoudshof om verhoging van die onderhoud aansoek gedoen, maar toe sy in 1990 om 'n verdere verhoging aansoek doen, het die landdros beslis dat die onderhoudshof nie jurisdiksie het om die bevel te wysig nie. Hy het onderskei tussen die geval waar die partye ooreengekom het dat die een party aan die ander onderhoud sal betaal en sodanige ooreenkoms ingevolge artikel 7(1) van die Wet op Egskeiding 70 van 1979 'n bevel van die hof

tion 7(2) of the act, that is where there is no agreement between the parties. The magistrate held that where there is a contractual obligation on a party to pay maintenance, he is not "legally liable to maintain" in terms of section 4(1) of the Maintenance Act 23 of 1963. Consequently the maintenance court did not have jurisdiction to vary the order. On appeal this decision was reversed.

gemaak is, en die geval waar die hof die betaling van onderhoud ingevolge artikel 7(2) van die wet gelas, dit wil sê waar daar geen ooreenkoms tussen die partye is nie. Die landdros het beslis dat 'n party op wie 'n kontraktuele verpligting rus om onderhoud te betaal nie ingevolge artikel 4(1) van die Wet op Onderhoud 23 van 1963 "regtens verplig" is om onderhoud te betaal nie. Gevolglik het die onderhoudshof nie jurisdiksie om die bevel te wysig nie. 'n Appèl teen hierdie beslissing het geslaag.

McCREATH J: [711] The magistrate has referred to various provisions of Act 23 of 1963 [the Maintenance Act] and of the Divorce Act 70 of 1979. He has also quoted extensively from the case law, particularly decisions prior to the latter Act having come into operation. Reference is also made to other authorities. The magistrate's reasoning is founded principally on the distinction drawn in earlier decisions between the position of a guilty spouse against whom the innocent spouse obtained on divorce an order for the payment of maintenance and that of the innocent spouse who consented to an order for the payment of maintenance to the guilty spouse.

On this basis the magistrate sought to draw a distinction between a person 'legally obliged' to pay maintenance and one who is under a 'contractual obligation' to do so. The ultimate conclusion of the magistrate is stated in the following terms:

> 'Wanneer al die faktore soos paragraafsgewys hierbo uiteengesit in ag geneem word, dui dit dan slegs in een rigting, naamlik dat die bepalings van die Wet op Onderhoud 23 van 1963 nie betrekking het op gevalle waar 'n "onderhoud" by wyse van 'n skikkingsakte beding is nie.'

In the recently reported case of *Jerrard v Jerrard* 1992 (1) SA 426 (T), a Full Bench of two Judges of this Division came to the same conclusion as the learned magistrate albeit along a somewhat different line of reasoning.

It is true, as pointed out by the magistrate and also in *Jerrard's* case, that divorce puts an end to the reciprocal duty of support that existed between the spouses during the marriage insofar as that duty is dependent on the common law. It is also true that ss (1) and (2) of s 7 of the Divorce Act of 1979 confer a discretion on the Court granting a divorce in regard to the making of an order for the payment of maintenance by the one party to the other. Subsection (1) provides for the situation where there is a maintenance provision in the written agreement between the parties. Subsection (2) relates to cases where the Court, in the absence of any such agreement, considers it just to order the payment of maintenance, regard being had to the factors mentioned in the subsection.

The question which arises is the effect of any order made in terms of s 7 and more particularly whether it falls within the ambit of the Maintenance [712] Act of 1963 for purposes of any variation thereof. A maintenance order is defined in Act 23 of 1963 as any order

> '(f)or the periodical payment of sums of money towards the maintenance of any person made by any court (including the Supreme Court of South Africa) in the Republic and, except for the purposes of s 11, includes any sentence suspended on condition that the convicted person make periodical payments of sums of money towards the maintenance of any other person'.

The definition is made subject to the qualification 'unless the context otherwise indicates.'

In *Jerrard's* case at 429F–G the following is said:

'In this regard it must be borne in mind that in respect of both a complaint in terms of s 4(1)(*a*) and 4(1)(*b*) of Act 23 of 1963 and the investigation and the institution of an inquiry in respect thereof, there is a specific reference to the words "any person legally liable to maintain". In regard to the enquiry itself and the power to make orders (s 5 of Act 23 of 1963), where no maintenance order is in force, there is a specific reference in s 5(4) of Act 23 of 1963 to any person proved to be legally liable to maintain, while in the case where the maintenance order is in force, the aforesaid words are specifically incorporated by reference in s 5(4)(*b*) of Act 23 of 1963.'

The Court went on to hold (at 430B) that

'no valid reason can be advanced why the said words "legally liable" should be given an extended meaning so as to include the discretionary orders made in terms of s 7(1) and 7(2) of Act 70 of 1979, both of which orders do not relate to a person legally liable to maintain'.

I am unable to agree with this conclusion. Section 7 of Act 70 of 1979 is designed to perpetuate, in the circumstances described in ss (1) and (2) thereof, the duty of one spouse to contribute towards the maintenance of the other.

The order made by the Court granting the divorce creates a legal duty to maintain which is in substitution for the common-law duty previously existing. I find it difficult, with respect, to appreciate how it can be said that a person who is obliged in terms of any valid order of the Supreme Court to pay maintenance is not 'a person legally liable to maintain'. There is nothing in the provisions of Act 23 of 1963 to warrant the exclusion of a person thus obliged. That this is the position has also been accepted either expressly or by implication in cases such as *Havenga v Havenga* 1988 (2) SA 438 (T) [134] and *Strime v Strime* 1983 (4) SA 850 (C).

It matters not whether the order is made in terms of ss (1) or (2). The absence of any distinction is emphasised by the fact that s 8 of the same Act makes provision for the rescission or variation of a maintenance order if the court finds that there is sufficient reason therefor. It is clear that s 8 refers to all orders made in terms of the Divorce Act of 1979. The order presently under consideration was made prior to the commencement of Act 70 of 1979. However, ss (3) of s 8 of that Act makes it clear that a maintenance order given by a Court in a divorce action before the commencement of the Act may also be rescinded or varied.

Finally, it is necessary to deal with a finding by HEYNS J in his concurring judgment in *Jerrard's* case that only a Division of the Supreme Court may rescind, suspend or vary an order granted under Act 70 of 1979. With respect, I cannot agree. Section 8, read with the definition of [713] 'court' in s 1, confers jurisdiction on the Divisions of the Supreme Court in the circumstances stated in s 8. Nowhere in that section or elsewhere in the Act is it provided that such jurisdiction is restricted to Divisions of the Supreme Court. The jurisdiction conferred on magistrates' courts in terms of the Maintenance Act 23 of 1963 is in my judgment left undisturbed by Act 70 of 1979.

In the result . . . [t]he appeal is upheld . . .

Note

It is submitted that the decision in this case is correct and that the decision in *Jerrard v Jerrard* 1992 1 SA 426 (T) is wrong. The decision in

Aantekening

Daar word aan die hand gedoen dat hierdie beslissing korrek is en dat die beslissing in *Jerrard v Jerrard* 1992 1 SA 426 (T) verkeerd is. Die be-

Rubenstein was followed by the Cape Provincial Division in *Davis v Davis* 1993 1 SA 621 (C).

It should be noted that if a maintenance court varies a maintenance order made by the supreme court, the order of the maintenance court replaces the order of the supreme court, which ceases to be of force: *Purnell v Purnell* 1993 2 SA 662 (A).

Although the maintenance court has the power to vary an order made by the supreme court it is not clear whether the reverse applies, that is, whether the supreme court has the power to vary an order made by a maintenance court. In *Steyn v Steyn* 1990 2 SA 272 (W) it was held that the supreme court does not have the power to vary an order made by a maintenance court, except by way of review or appeal. This judgment conflicts with *Sher v Sher* 1978 4 SA 728 (W) where it was held that an application for the variation of an order made by a maintenance court can be brought in the supreme court.

slissing in *Rubenstein* is in *Davis v Davis* 1993 1 SA 621 (K) deur die Kaapse Provinsiale Afdeling nagevolg.

U moet daarop let dat, indien 'n onderhoudshof 'n onderhoudsbevel wat deur die hooggeregshof gemaak is, wysig die bevel van die onderhoudshof die van die hooggeregshof vervang en dat die bevel van die hooggeregshof ophou om van krag te wees: *Purnell v Purnell* 1993 2 SA 662 (A).

Alhoewel die onderhoudshof die bevoegdheid het om 'n bevel te wysig wat deur die hooggeregshof gemaak is, is dit nie duidelik of die omgekeerde geld nie. Dit is met ander woorde onduidelik of die hooggeregshof die bevoegdheid het om 'n bevel van die onderhoudshof te wysig. In *Steyn v Steyn* 1990 2 SA 272 (W) is beslis dat die hooggeregshof nie die bevoegdheid het om 'n bevel van die onderhoudshof te wysig nie, behalwe by wyse van hersiening of appèl. Hierdie uitspraak bots met *Sher v Sher* 1978 4 SA 728 (W) waarin beslis is dat 'n aansoek om wysiging van 'n bevel van die onderhoudshof wel in die hooggeregshof gedoen kan word.

[130] SCHUTTE V SCHUTTE

1986 1 SA 872 (A)

A non-variation clause in a maintenance agreement is valid

The appellant and the respondent were divorced in 1984. At the time of their divorce they entered into a deed of settlement in which the appellant undertook to pay the respondent R1 000 per month as maintenance until her death or remarriage. They agreed further that this amount would not be subject to increase or decrease (clause 2.1) except in so far as provided for in the agreement. The court which granted the divorce incorporated the agreement in its order with the exclusion of clause 2.1. The appellant appealed against this decision to the Appellate Division. The Appellate Division held that a waiver of this nature was valid.

'n Geen-wysigingsklousule in 'n onderhoudsooreenkoms is geldig

Die appellant en die respondent is in 1984 geskei. Ten tyde van hulle egskeiding het hulle 'n skikkingsooreenkoms aangegaan waarin die appellant onderneem het om R1 000 per maand onderhoud aan die respondent te betaal tot haar dood of hertroue. Hulle het verder ooreengekom dat hierdie bedrag nie aan verhoging of verlaging onderworpe sou wees nie (klousule 2.1) behalwe vir sover as wat in die ooreenkoms daarvoor voorsiening gemaak is. Die hof wat die egskeiding toegestaan het, het die ooreenkoms by sy bevel ingelyf met die uitsluiting van klousule 2.1 Die appellant het teen hierdie beslissing na die Appèlhof geappelleer. Die Appèlhof het beslis dat 'n afstanddoening van hierdie aard geldig was.

VAN HEERDEN AR: [879] Die vraag wat dus in hierdie appèl beantwoord moet word, is of die partye tot 'n egskeidingsaksie geldiglik kan afstand doen van die bevoegdheid om ingevolge art 8(1) van die Wet op Egskeiding 70 van 1979 die Hof in die toekoms te nader om intrekking, wysiging of opskorting (hierna bloot 'n wysiging genoem) van 'n onderhoudsbevel. 'n Soortgelyke vraag het al in 'n hele aantal gewysdes ter sprake gekom in verband met die voorganger van art 8(1) van Wet 70 van 1979, nl art 10(1) van die Wet op Huweliksaangeleenthede 37 van 1953. Gerieflikheidshalwe verwys ek voortaan na die twee Wette as die 1953 Wet en die 1979 Wet.

'n Sistematiese bespreking van alle tersaaklike gewysdes is te vind in die uitspraak van DIDCOTT R in *Claassens v Claassens* 1981 (1) SA 360 (N), en dit sou onnodige herhaling meebring om weer eens na almal te verwys. 'n Aantal algemene opmerkings is egter aangewese. Soos tereg aangetoon deur DIDCOTT R (op 362–3) is uitsprake waarin aanvaar is dat 'n afstanddoening deur 'n vrou van *enige* aanspraak op onderhoud nie teen die openbare beleid indruis nie (sien bv *Swart v Swart* 1960 (4) SA 621 (K)), nie direk ter sake nie. Soos later sal blyk, kon 'n vrou haar nie na verlening van 'n egskeidingsbevel op die wysigingsbevoegdhede van 'n Hof ingevolge art 10(1) van die 1953 Wet beroep nie indien by ontbinding van die huwelik geen onderhoudsbevel gemaak is nie. Haar toekomstige regsposisie is dus bepaal deur die feit dat sy nie op onderhoud aanspraak gemaak het nie en dat 'n dusdanige bevel derhalwe nie verleen is nie. In so 'n geval was 'n afstanddoening deur haar met betrekking tot toekomstige onderhoud daarom 'n nuttelose oortolligheid. 'n Vraag wat nie in enige van die betrokke gewysdes ontstaan het nie, en wat klaarblyklik ook nie in die onderhawige geval opduik nie, is of dit 'n vrou, wat in 'n skikkingsakte afstand gedoen het van 'n aanspraak op onderhoud, vrystaan om voor ontbinding van die huwelik haar onderneming te repudieer en die Hof te versoek om wel onderhoud aan haar toe te ken.

In sake waarin aanvaar is dat 'n vrou aan wie ingevolge 'n skikkingsakte wel onderhoud deur haar man betaal sou word, afstand kon doen van die bevoegdheid om later ooreenkomstig art 10(1) van die 1953 Wet 'n verhoging van die ooreengekome bedrag aan te vra, is bevind dat sodanige afstanddoening (hierna bloot 'n afstanddoening genoem) nie [880] teen die openbare beleid indruis nie. Sien bv *Grgin v Grgin* 1960 (1) SA 824 (W), *Van Rensburg v Van Rensburg* 1978 (1) SA 436 (T) en die *Claassens*-saak *supra*. 'n Teenoorgestelde siening is egter gehuldig in *Copelowitz v Copelowitz and Others NO* 1969 (4) SA 64 (K); *Cilliers v Cilliers* 1977 (1) SA 561 (O), en in *Jones v Jones* 1963 (2) SA 193 (SR), waarin Rhodesiese wetgewing met dieselfde strekking as art 10(1) van die 1953 Wet ter sprake was. En in *Knight v Knight* 1967 (1) SA 40 (K), is *obiter* bedenkinge oor die geldigheid van 'n afstanddoening uitgespreek.

In laasgenoemde vier sake is klem gelê òf op die afkeurenswaardigheid van 'n ooreenkoms wat daarop gerig is om 'n Hof se bevoegdhede lam of aan bande te lê, òf op die meer algemene oorweging dat die situasie waarin 'n vrou weens 'n afstanddoening uiteindelik hulpbehoewend mag wees, in stryd met die openbare belang is. Hierdie oorwegings is in 'n breedvoerige uitspraak in die *Claassens*-saak deur DIDCOTT R onder die loep geneem. Na my mening is die kardinale vraag egter of die Wetgewer beoog het dat 'n Hof se wysigingsbevoegdhede ingevolge art 10(1) van die 1953 Wet en art 8(1) van die 1979 Wet nie by wyse van 'n kontraktuele bepaling uitgeskakel of beperk mag word nie. In hierdie verband is dit nodig om te let nie net op die bewoording van die betrokke bepalings en die samehang waarin dié verskyn nie, maar ook op die Wetgewer se versuim om vir bepaalde situasies statutêr voorsiening te maak. Slegs op hierdie wyse kan bepaal word of prof *Hahlo* dit reg gehad het toe hy met verwysing na 'n Hof se wysigingsbevoegdhede volgens art 10(1) van die 1953 Wet in 1960 *SALJ* op 271 geskryf het:

"To hold that the parties by their agreement can deprive the Court of these powers, or that the Court itself may surrender them, is contrary to the letter and spirit of s 10."

Soos aangetoon in *Strauss v Strauss* 1974 (3) SA 79 (A) op 93-4, was die heersende opvatting voor die inwerkingtreding van die 1953 Wet dat 'n Hof nie bevoeg was nie om die skuldige eggenoot te beveel om na egskeiding onderhoud aan die onskuldige te betaal. In sommige Afdelings was die Howe egter bereid om 'n ooreenkoms van die eggenote rakende onderhoud 'n bevel van die Hof te maak, maar soms is vereis dat sodanige ooreenkoms in die algemeen die vermoënsregte van die partye moes reguleer. Die Wetgewer het klaarblyklik hierdie toedrag van sake onbevredigend gevind en daarom in art 10(1) van die 1953 Wet soos volg bepaal:

"Die Hof wat 'n egskeiding toestaan kan, ondanks die ontbinding van die huwelik –

(a) die bevel teen die skuldige eggenoot gee vir die onderhoud van die onskuldige eggenoot, vir enige tydperk tot die dood of hertroue van die onskuldige eggenoot, na gelang die een of die ander eerste gebeur, wat die Hof billik ag; of

(b) 'n ooreenkoms tussen die eggenote vir die onderhoud van een van hulle, 'n bevel van die Hof maak,

en enige bevoegde Hof kan, by bewys van voldoende rede (wat 'n ander rede dan die geldelike vermoë van die een of ander van die onderskeie eggenote kan wees) so 'n bevel intrek, opskort of wysig."

Die heersende regsposisie is dus ingrypend verander. Eerstens kon 'n Hof 'n onderhoudsbevel ten gunste van die onskuldige eggenoot toestaan. Tweedens kon 'n ooreenkoms vir die onderhoud van een van die [881] eggenote, ook die skuldige een, 'n bevel van die Hof gemaak word (*Strauss*-saak *supra* op 95). En derdens het 'n "bevoegde" Hof die kompetensie verkry om 'n bevel betreffende onderhoud in te trek, op te skort of te wysig.

Na woordlui kon die bevoegdhede waarvoor paras (a) en (b) voorsiening gemaak het slegs by die toestaan van 'n egskeiding, en nie daarna nie, uitgeoefen word. Die bevoegdhede is immers verleen aan die Hof "wat 'n egskeiding toestaan" ("[t]he Court granting a divorce", volgens die getekende Engelse teks). Hoewel hy toegegee het dat 'n letterlike vertolking van art 10(1) gelei het tot die gevolgtrekking dat 'n onderhoudsbevel nie na ontbinding van 'n huwelik verleen kon word nie, het prof *Hahlo* aanvanklik gepleit dat die Engelse teks uitgelê moes word as "the Court which granted a divorce": 1958 *SALJ* op 205. Syne was egter 'n stem roepende in die woestyn en in 'n hele reeks gewysdes is aanvaar dat 'n onderhoudsbevel nie ingevolge art 10(1) na egskeiding gemaak kon word nie. Sien bv *Ex parte Stein and Another* 1960 (1) SA 782 (T); *Ford v Ford and Another* 1965 (1) SA 264 (D); *Lincesso v Lincesso* 1966 (1) SA 747 (W); *Nel v Nel* 1977 (3) SA 288 (O) [126]; *Zeeman v Zeeman* 1979 (2) SA 223 (K), en die *Knight-* en *Cilliers*-sake *supra*. Prof *Hahlo* het dan ook self later 'n ander mening gehuldig, en hoewel hy nog aangevoer het dat art 10(1) vir twee vertolkings vatbaar was, het hy die Howe se interpretasie as die juiste een aanvaar. Raadpleeg die derde uitgawe van sy *The South African Law of Husband and Wife* op 440.

Na my mening was die woordwysigende uitleg wat prof *Hahlo* aanvanklik verkies het, nie houdbaar nie. Daar is trouens oorwegings wat aandui dat die frase "[d]ie Hof wat 'n egskeiding toestaan" sy normale betekenis gedra het. Eerstens het die gebruik van die woorde "skuldige eggenoot" en "onskuldige eggenoot" in para (a), en van die woord "eggenote" in para (b), veronderstel dat die partye getroud sou wees tot op die stadium dat 'n onderhoudsbevel verleen is. Tweedens moet die frase gekontrasteer word met "enige bevoegde Hof" waaraan die bevoegdheid toegeken is om sodanige bevel *na* verlening daarvan in te trek, op te skort of te wysig. En derdens was 'n vertolking waarvolgens die Hof wat 'n egskeiding toegestaan *het* die bevoegdhede vervat in paras (a) en (b) kon uitoefen nouliks te rym met die klaarblyklike bedoeling dat 'n onderhoudsbevel ten tyde van die ontbinding van die huwelik verleen kon word. Soos hieronder sal blyk, geld enige twyfel wat mag bestaan het aangaande die vertolking van art 10(1) in elk geval nie ten opsigte van die trefwydte van art 7 van die 1979 Wet wat in die onderhawige geval van toepassing is nie.

Laasgenoemde artikel lui soos volg:

"(1) 'n Hof wat 'n egskeidingsbevel verleen, kan in ooreenstemming met 'n skriftelike ooreenkoms tussen die partye 'n bevel gee met betrekking tot die verdeling van die bates van die partye of die betaling van onderhoud deur die een party aan die ander.

(2) By ontstentenis van 'n bevel gegee kragtens subart (1) met betrekking tot die betaling van onderhoud deur een party aan die ander kan die Hof, met inagneming van die bestaande of verwagte vermoëns van elk van die partye, hulle onderskeie ver-dienvermoëns, finansiële behoeftes en verpligtinge, die ouderdom van elk van die partye, die duur van die huwelik, die lewenspeil van die partye voor die egskeiding, hulle gedrag vir sover dit op die verbrokkeling van die huwelik betrekking het, en enige ander faktor wat na [882] die oordeel van die Hof in aanmerking geneem behoort te word, 'n bevel gee wat die Hof billik ag met betrekking tot die betaling van onderhoud deur die een party aan die ander vir enige tydperk tot die dood of hertroue van die party ten gunste van wie die bevel gegee is, na gelang die een of die ander eerste plaasvind."

Opgelet sal word dat art 7(2) wyer strek as art 10(1)(a) van die 1953 Wet insoverre ingevolge laasgenoemde 'n onderhoudsbevel slegs ten gunste van die onskuldige eggenoot gemaak kon word. So 'n bevel kan volgens art 7(2) ook verleen word ten gunste van 'n eggenoot wat "skuldig" is in die sin dat hy of sy uitsluitlik of grotendeels vir die verbrokkeling van die huwelik verantwoordelik was. Vir huidige doeleindes is die be-langrike feit egter dat die bevoegdhede waarvoor art 7 voorsiening maak, toegesê word aan 'n Hof "wat 'n egskeidingsbevel verleen". Hierdie frase verskil stilisties ietwat van dié vervat in art 10 van die 1953 Wet en wat hierbo bespreek is, maar inhoudelik is daar geen onderskeid nie. Die Wetgewer moes bewus gewees het van die vertolking wat die Howe konsekwent aan laasgenoemde frase geheg het, en moes dus beoog het dat die ooreenstemmende frase in art 7 van die 1979 Wet dieselfde betekenis sou dra.

Dit volg dus dat 'n onderhoudsbevel nie ingevolge art 7 van die 1979 Wet na ontbinding van 'n huwelik verleen kan word nie. Hierdie konsekwensie is van kardinale belang omdat slegs 'n onderhoud*bevel* volgens art 8(1) van daardie Wet ingetrek, gewysig of opgeskort kon word. Indien daar dus nie by ontbinding van die huwelik 'n onderhouds-bevel verleen is nie, kan art 8(1) nie toegepas word nie. Bepaaldelik is 'n Hof nie bevoeg om 'n onderneming betreffende die betaling van onderhoud, ten aansien waarvan geen bevel gemaak is nie, te wysig nie.

In die lig van die trefwydte van arts 7 en 8(1) van die 1979 Wet, wat vir huidige doeleindes nie van dié van art 10(1) van die 1953 Wet verskil nie, moet nou getrag word om die bedoeling van die Wetgewer aangaande die al of nie geldigheid van 'n afstanddoening vas te stel. Ten einde herhaling te vermy, verwys ek voortaan meestal slegs na die posisie van die vrou hoewel 'n onderhoudsbevel klaarblyklik ook ten gunste van 'n man gemaak kan word, en 'n wysiging van so 'n bevel tot voordeel van òf die een òf die ander van die voormalige gades kan strek.

'n Oorweging wat geopper word ter onderskraging van die standpunt dat 'n afstanddoening nietig is, is dat art 8(1), net soos die ooreenstemmende bepaling van die 1953 Wet, op die Wetboek geplaas is omdat nòg die Hof nòg die partye ten tyde van die toestaan van 'n egskeiding met enige mate van sekerheid kan bepaal wat die toekomstige lewensbe-hoeftes van die een party, en die ander se vermoë om daaraan te voldoen, sal wees. So bv kan, strydig met die verwagtinge wat by die ontbinding van die huwelik gekoester is, die vrou se eie inkomste aangrypend verminder, of kan sy as gevolg van siekte ens aansienlike addisionele onkoste oploop. In sodanige gevalle sou dit strydig met die openbare belang wees, so word aangevoer, indien 'n Hof as gevolg van 'n afstanddoening nie die onderhoudsbevel wat voorheen verleen is, kan wysig nie, met die gevolg dat die hulpbehoewende vrou dan moontlik op liefdadigheid of Staatsbystand aangewese is.

Ek meen egter nie dat uit die patroon van die tersaaklike bepalings van òf die 1953 Wet òf die 1979 Wet 'n algemene besorgdheid aan die kant van [883] die Wetgewer oor die toekomstige behoeftes van voormalige gades af te lei is nie. 'n Vrou wat om een of ander rede nie ten tyde van die egskeiding onderhoud aangevra het nie, met die gevolg dat 'n bevel nie verleen is nie, kan glad nie daarna op onderhoud aanspraak maak nie. Die vrou wat wel 'n onderhoudsbevel aangevra het maar dit nie verkry het nie omdat sy na die Hof se oordeel nie bystand benodig het of waarskynlik in die toekoms sou benodig nie, bevind haar in dieselfde bootjie. En die vrou wat op betaling van onderhoud geregtig geword het ingevolge 'n kontraktuele bepaling wat nie by die egskeidingsbevel ingelyf is nie, kan nie ingevolge art 8(1) van die 1979 Wet daarna verhoogde onderhoud verkry nie. In al drie bogenoemde gevalle kan die vrou se finansiële posisie na die egskeiding weens onvoorsiene omstandighede net soseer versleg as dié van die vroulike gade wat wel 'n onderhoudsbevel verkry het, maar die 1979 Wet (net soos die 1953 Wet) verleen nie aan 'n Hof die bevoegdheid om eersgenoemde te hulp te kom nie. Dit kon dus nie 'n beleidsoorweging van die Wetgewer gewees het dat 'n geskeide vrou na ontbinding van die huwelik in beginsel op onderhoud, of verhoogde onderhoud, aanspraak moet kan maak nie, of dat, in die woorde van DIDCOTT R in die *Claassens*-saak op 370, "divorcees should not, as a class, become a financial burden on the community".

'n Afstanddoening is in die reël vervat in 'n skikkingsooreenkoms wat vir betaling van onderhoud voorsiening maak en wat bestem is om 'n bevel van die Hof gemaak te word. Aldus wil die partye meebring dat nieteenstaande die verlening van 'n onderhoudsbevel die ooreengekome onderhoud nie in die toekoms aan wysiging ingevolge art 8(1) van die 1979 Wet onderworpe sal wees nie. Op die keper beskou, kan hulle egter presies dieselfde resultaat bereik deur die bepaling betreffende afstanddoening weg te laat en net nie te vra dat hul ooreenkoms by die egskeidingsbevel ingelyf moet word nie. Dit is immers nouliks denkbaar dat 'n Hof uit eie beweging 'n onderhoudsbevel sal maak ten gunste van 'n party wat dit juis nie wil hê nie. Dit val dus nie in te sien nie waarom die Wetgewer sou beoog het dat bloot omdat so 'n bevel ooreenkomstig 'n skikkingsakte wel aangevra en verleen is, die bepalings van art 8(1) onverbiddelik van toepassing moet wees . . .

[884] Ek kom derhalwe tot die gevolgtrekking dat die afstanddoening vervat in die onderhawige skikkingsooreenkoms nie nietig is nie. Duidelikheidshalwe dien daarop gewys te word dat die afstanddoening albei partye bind in die sin dat die ooreengekome onderhoud "nie aan verhoging of verlaging" onderworpe is nie. Dit is natuurlik moontlik dat 'n afstanddoening betrekking kan hê op die bevoegdheid van slegs een van die partye tot 'n egskeidingsaksie om die Hof later ingevolge art 8(1) van die 1979 Wet te nader, soos bv wanneer slegs die vrou se bevoegdheid om na egskeiding verhoogde onderhoud aan te vra, uitgesluit word. Hierbo het ek daarop gewys dat die partye die bepalings van die subartikel as 't ware kan omseil deur geen bevel aan te vra nie met betrekking tot 'n onderneming om onderhoud te betaal. Hulle kan egter nie bloot kontraktueel, dws by ontstentenis van 'n onderhoudsbevel, die resultaat bereik dat slegs een van hulle by magte is om 'n wysiging van die ooreengekome onderhoud ingevolge art 8(1) te verkry nie. Die vraag of 'n eensydige afstanddoening geldig is, ontstaan egter nie in hierdie appèl nie en ek spreek geen mening daaroor uit nie.

Die appèl slaag en die bevel verleen deur die Verhoorhof word deur die volgende vervang:

"Die huweliksband tussen die partye word ontbind en die ooreenkoms tussen die partye ingehandig en gemerk 'B' word 'n bevel van die Hof gemaak."

JANSEN AR; JOUBERT AR; HEFER AR en CILLIÉ WN AR het saamgestem.

Note

Before the decision in *Schutte's* case the decisions of our courts on the effect of a non-variation clause in a maintenance agreement between the parties were by no means harmonious. On the one hand it was held that it was against public policy to allow either spouse to waive his or her right to apply for rescission, suspension or variation of the order, because the aim of such a clause was to interfere with the court's powers of variation conferred upon it by the legislature (section 8 of the Divorce Act 70 of 1979, formerly section 10 of the Matrimonial Affairs Act 37 of 1953). See in this regard, for example, *Jones v Jones* 1963 2 SA 193 (SR); *Copelowitz v Copelowitz* 1969 4 SA 64 (C); *Cilliers v Cilliers* 1977 1 SA 561 (O). In *Grgin v Grgin* 1960 1 SA 824 (W); *Van Rensburg v Van Rensburg* 1978 1 SA 436 (T) and *Claassens v Claassens* 1981 1 SA 360 (N), on the other hand, it was held that waivers of this nature do not infringe public policy and that they are valid and binding. *Schutte's* case has now brought certainty in this respect.

It is suggested that the courts will not be deprived of their jurisdiction in cases where there has been fraud or duress (Bedil 1986 *Annual Survey* 98).

The provision in *Schutte's* case was binding on both parties in the sense that they agreed that the maintenance was not subject to any increase or decrease. The court did not express itself on the question of whether a unilateral renunciation would be valid, for example, when only the wife's right to seek increased maintenance after divorce was excluded. See in this regard *Polliack v Polliack* [131]. See also *Luttig v Luttig* [132].

Aantekening

Voor die beslissing in die *Schutte*-saak was die beslissings van ons howe oor 'n geen-wysigings-klousule in 'n onderhoudsooreenkoms tussen die partye geensins eenvorming nie. Aan die een kant is beslis dat dit teen die openbare beleid is om 'n gade toe te laat om van sy of haar bevoegdheid afstand te doen om aansoek te doen om intrekking, opskorting of wysiging van die bevel, aangesien sodanige klousule ten doel het om in te meng met die wysigingsbevoegdheid van die hof wat deur die wetgewer aan hom verleen is (artikel 8 van die Wet op Egskeiding 70 van 1979, voorheen artikel 10 van die Wet op Huweliksaangeleenthede 37 van 1953). Sien in hierdie verband byvoorbeeld *Jones v Jones* 1963 2 SA 193 (SR); *Copelowitz v Copelowitz* 1969 4 SA 64 (K); *Cilliers v Cilliers* 1977 1 SA 561 (O). In *Grgin v Grgin* 1960 1 SA 824 (W); *Van Rensburg v Van Rensburg* 1978 1 SA 436 (T) en *Claassens v Claassens* 1981 1 SA 360 (N), daarenteen, is beslis dat 'n afstanddoening van hierdie aard nie teen die openbare belang indruis nie maar dat dit geldig en bindend is. *Schutte* se saak het nou duidelikheid in die verband gebring.

Daar word aan die hand gedoen dat die howe se bevoegdheid nie uitgesluit sal word in gevalle waar daar bedrog of dwang teenwoordig was nie (Bedil 1986 *Annual Survey* 98).

Die bepaling in *Schutte* se saak het albei partye gebind in die sin dat die onderhoud nie aan verhoging of verlaging onderworpe was nie. Die hof het hom nie uitgespreek oor die vraag of eensydige afstanddoening geldig sou wees nie, byvoorbeeld as net die vrou se bevoegdheid uitgesluit word om na die egskeiding om verhoogde onderhoud aansoek te doen. Sien in die verband *Polliack v Polliack* [131]. Sien ook *Luttig v Luttig* [132].

[131] POLLIACK V POLLIACK

1988 4 SA 161 (W)

A non-variation clause in a maintenance agreement is valid

The appellant (wife) and the respondent were divorced in 1977. An agreement concluded

'n Geen-wysigingsklousule in 'n onderhoudsooreenkoms is geldig

Die appellant (vrou) en die respondent is in 1977 geskei. 'n Ooreenkoms tussen die partye

by the parties was made an order of the court. In this agreement the respondent undertook to pay the appellant R500 per month as maintenance. It was further agreed that the sum of R500 would be increased at a maximum of 7½% per annum. The agreement concluded with the following paragraph:

"(f) *General*. This agreement is in full and final settlement of all property and other issues and claims between the plaintiff and the defendant emanating from their marriage and the dissolution thereof, and that after a final decree of divorce has been granted and this agreement being made an order of Court, neither the plaintiff nor the defendant will have any further claims against each other except as provided for herein."

The appellant then sought an order in the magistrate's court increasing the sum of maintenance payable in terms of the supreme court order. The magistrate held that the agreement precluded such an application. The appellant appealed against this decision. The appeal was dismissed.

is 'n bevel van die hof gemaak. Ingevolge die ooreenkoms het die respondent onderneem om R500 onderhoud per maand aan die appellant te betaal. Daar is verder ooreengekom dat die bedrag van R500 met 'n maksimum van 7½% per jaar verhoog sou word. Die ooreenkoms het met die volgende paragraaf afgesluit:

"(f) *General*. This agreement is in full and final settlement of all property and other issues and claims between the plaintiff and the defendant emanating from their marriage and the dissolution thereof, and that after a final decree of divorce has been granted and this agreement being made an order of Court, neither the plaintiff nor the defendant will have any further claims against each other except as provided for herein."

Die appellant het toe in die landdroshof aansoek gedoen om verhoging van die bedrag onderhoud wat ingevolge die bevel van die hooggeregshof betaalbaar was. Die landdros het beslis dat die ooreenkoms sodanige aansoek verhoed het. Die appellant het teen hierdie beslissing geappelleer. Die appèl is van die hand gewys.

ROUX J: [162] The right of an ex-spouse to seek a monetary increase or decrease of an order of this type was enacted initially in s 10(1) of Act 37 of 1953 and is now found in s 8(1) of the Divorce Act 70 of 1979. For the present enquiry, these two sections are similar. The debate that has existed as to whether the parties could lawfully waive reliance on the sections or whether the parties could enter into a valid contract excluding the operation of the section is now settled by the Appellate Division. See *Schutte v Schutte* 1986 (1) SA 872 (A) [130]. Such a contract is lawful and enforceable by the ex-spouse opposing reliance by his former spouse on the section in question. However, as I understand counsel for the appellant, a distinction must be drawn, so it is submitted, between a contract excluding the operation of this section and what is termed 'a unilateral waiver by one of the parties'. It is not disputed that *Schutte's* case covers a contract. It is submitted that the question of a unilateral waiver was left open by the Appellate Division. Indeed, it appears that it was in fact left open. I assume that the argument is based upon the following passage in *Schutte's* case at 884: . . .

[ROUX J quoted from *Schutte's* case and proceeded:]

[163] The answer to counsel's submission seems to be threefold: first, we are here dealing with a contract between the parties and the whole issue of unilateral waiver does not in my judgment really arise. Secondly, if it is competent, not unlawful and not *contra bonos mores* for two persons to contract out of and not rely upon the aforesaid s 8(1), why should it be incompetent, unlawful and *contra bonos mores* for one or three persons to do exactly

the same thing? No logic or public interest is offended if, in one agreement, a husband undertakes not to apply for a decrease of maintenance payable by him while a wife retains the right to rely on s 8(1). Thirdly, waiver stands exactly on the same footing as election. See, for example, *Moyce v Estate Taylor* 1948 (3) SA 822 (A) at 829. I must make reference to the manifestation of waiver because it has been argued in this case that it is possible that the appellant could lead evidence to show that she was not aware of the right she is alleged to have waived. I do not think that that submission is tenable and, bearing in mind the Appellate Division's approach to waiver and election, I feel the words of LORD BLACKBURN in *Scarf v Jardine* (1882) 51 LJ QB 612 at 621 are particularly apposite. I may point out that this passage of LORD BLACKBURN'S judgment has been quoted with approval for many years in our Courts.

The learned Judge said the following:

'Where a party in his own mind has thought that he would choose one of two remedies, even though he has written it down in a memorandum, or has indicated it in some other way, that alone will not bind him. But so soon as he is not only determined to follow one of his remedies but has communicated it to the other side, in such a way as to lead the opposite party to believe that he has made that choice, he has completed his election and can go no further. And whether he intended it or not, if he has done an unequivocal act, I mean an act which would be justifiable, if he had elected one way and would not be justifiable if he had elected the other way, the fact of his having done that unequivocal act, as to the knowledge of the persons concerned, is an election.'

In my view the act of the present appellant in concluding this agreement in the terms in which it is couched has clearly indicated what her election was and that election, in my judgment, was not to rely upon the provisions of s 8(1).

If the concluding words of para (*f*) of the agreement we are considering, namely

'neither the plaintiff, nor the defendant will have any further claims against each other excepting as provided for herein',

have reference to para (*c*) of the agreement which I have quoted, then they have both made their election not to rely on s 8(1). Put otherwise they have, to use the words if apposite, 'unilaterally waived' such rights as they had.

I have no difficulty in understanding and interpreting the agreement under consideration. Paragraph (*c*)(*a*)(i) fixes the initial sum of maintenance, namely R500 per month. Paragraph (*c*)(ii)(*aa*) determines the maximum yearly increase of the maintenance, namely 7½% per annum. It fixes the sum payable monthly in such a year.

Paragraph (*c*)(ii)(*bb*) determines the minimum increase per annum. This is fixed by reference to the consumer price index therein named. Again, this could fix the sum of maintenance payable monthly.

In my judgment, the purpose of these paragraphs was to obviate any future applications to court. To ensure that no court would in future vary their bargain and to express their common intention, para (*f*) of the agreement was included. Nothing can be more explicit than the choice of the following words, which I again quote:

'(N)either the plaintiff nor the defendant will have any further claims against each other, excepting as provided for herein.'

Accepting the fault of being repetitive, the parties excluded the Court's intervention and contractually created their own formula whereby the payment of maintenance was to be increased in the years following 1977. In my judgment the magistrate's reasons and findings are sound, and I would dismiss the appeal ...

VAN NIEKERK J concurred.

Note

Schutte v Schutte [130] concerned an agreement between the parties that the maintenance agreed upon was not subject to increase or decrease. The court did not express itself on the question of whether a unilateral renunciation would be valid. In *Polliack's* case ROUX J was of the opinion that there was also a contract between the parties so that the question of unilateral waiver did not really arise. He did, however, express the opinion that "if it is competent, not unlawful and *contra bonos mores* for two persons to contract out of and not rely upon . . . s 8(1) [of the Divorce Act 70 of 1979], why should it be incompetent, unlawful and *contra bonos mores* for one or three persons to do exactly the same thing?" (163). It cannot be said that this matter has been finally decided, but in terms of this view it would seem as though a unilateral waiver would also be valid.

Aantekening

Schutte v Schutte [130] het te doen gehad met 'n ooreenkoms tussen die partye dat die onderhoud waarop ooreengekom is nie aan verhoging of verlaging onderworpe sou wees nie. Die hof het hom nie uitgespreek oor die vraag of eensydige afstanddoening ook geldig sou wees nie. In *Polliack* se saak was ROUX R van mening dat daar ook 'n kontrak tussen die partye was sodat die probleem van eensydige afstanddoening nie werklik ter sprake gekom het nie. Hy het egter die mening uitgespreek dat "if it is competent, not unlawful and *contra bonos mores* for two persons to contract out of and not rely upon . . . s 8(1) [of the Divorce Act 70 of 1979], why should it be incompetent, unlawful and *contra bonos mores* for one or three persons to do exactly the same thing?" (163). Daar kan nie gesê word dat die finale woord oor hierdie aangeleentheid gespreek is nie maar in die lig van hierdie mening wil dit voorkom of eensydige afstanddoening ook geldig sou wees.

[132]   LUTTIG V LUTTIG

1994 1 SA 523 (O)

Presumption against waiver of right to apply for variation of maintenance which was agreed on in consent paper

The appellant (husband) and respondent were divorced in 1992. The spouses had entered into an agreement and the consent paper was incorporated in the divorce order. In the consent paper the husband undertook to pay maintenance to his wife, which maintenance was to increase annually in accordance with the consumer price index. In clause 8 the agreement provided that:

> "Die partye erken en verklaar dat na ondertekening hiervan hulle geen verdere eise van welke aard ookal wedersyds teenoor mekaar het nie, behalwe vir die bepalings hiervan en dat hierdie ooreenkoms hulle onderlinge geskille skik en afhandel."

Thereafter the appellant applied to the maintenance court for a reduction of the main-

Vermoede teen afstanddoening van die reg om aansoek te doen om wysiging van onderhoud waarop in skikkingsakte ooreengekom is

Die appellant (man) en die respondent is in 1992 geskei. Die partye het 'n skikkingsooreenkoms aangegaan wat by die egskeidingsbevel ingelyf is. In die skikkingsooreenkoms het die man onderneem om onderhoud aan die vrou te betaal, welke onderhoud jaarliks aangepas sou word in ooreenstemming met die verbruikersprysindeks. Die ooreenkoms het in klousule 8 soos volg bepaal:

> "Die partye erken en verklaar dat na ondertekening hiervan hulle geen verdere eise van welke aard ookal wedersyds teenoor mekaar het nie, behalwe vir die bepalings hiervan en dat hierdie ooreenkoms hulle onderlinge geskille skik en afhandel."

Die appellant het daarna by die onderhouds-

tenance. As a point in limine the respondent argued that the existing maintenance could not be reduced because clause 8 contains a waiver which excludes reduction. The maintenance court accepted respondent's point in limine. The appellant appealed against this to the supreme court. On appeal it was argued on behalf of the appellant that clause 8 does not constitute a waiver. The court accepted appellant's argument and the appeal was allowed.

hof aansoek gedoen om verlaging van die onderhoud. Die respondent het as 'n punt in limine geargumenteer dat die bestaande onderhoudsbevel nie verlaag kon word nie omdat klousule 8 van die skikkingsooreenkoms verlaging uitgesluit het. Die onderhoudshof het die respondent se argument in limine gehandhaaf. Die appellant het hierteen na die hooggeregshof geappèlleer. In appèl is namens die appellant aangevoer dat klousule 8 nie op 'n afstanddoening neerkom nie. Die hof het die appellant gelyk gegee en die appèl is gehandhaaf.

HANCKE R: [525] Mnr *Danzfuss*, wat namens die appellant opgetree het, het betoog dat die bewoording van die akte van dading [skikkingsakte] nie neerkom op 'n afstanddoening nie. In ieder geval, volgens sy betoog, was die partye nie geregtig om die hof se bevoegdhede ingevolge art 4 van die Wet op Onderhoud in te perk of te ontneem nie aangesien dit strydig sou wees met openbare beleid.

Dit blyk nou aanvaarde reg te wees dat 'n skikkingsooreenkoms wat voorsiening maak vir die betaling van 'n bepaalde bedrag onderhoud, onderworpe aan 'n klousule dat dit *nie* onderworpe is aan 'n verhoging of verlaging nie, geldig en afdwingbaar is. In *Schutte v Schutte* 1986 (1) SA 872 (A) [130] [526] verklaar VAN HEERDEN AR op 883F–G die volgende:

'Aldus wil die partye meebring dat nieteenstaande die verlening van 'n onderhoudsbevel die ooreengekome onderhoud nie in die toekoms aan wysiging ingevolge art 8(1) van die 1979 Wet onderworpe sal wees nie. Op die keper beskou, kan hulle egter presies dieselfde resultaat bereik deur die bepaling betreffende afstanddoening weg te laat en net nie te vra dat hul ooreenkoms by die egskeidingsbevel ingelyf moet word nie. Dit is immers nouliks denkbaar dat 'n Hof uit eie beweging 'n onderhoudsbevel sal maak ten gunste van 'n party wat dit juis nie wil hê nie. Dit val dus nie in te sien nie waarom die Wetgewer sou beoog het dat bloot omdat so 'n bevel ooreenkomstig 'n skikkingsakte wel aangevra en verleen is, die bepalings van art 8(1) onverbiddelik van toepassing moet wees.'

Die vraag of 'n eensydige afstanddoening geldig is, is in hierdie saak oopgelaat.

In *Polliack v Polliack* 1988 (4) SA 161 (W) [131] verklaar ROUX R op 163D die volgende:

'... (I)f it is competent, not unlawful and not *contra bonos mores* for two persons to contract out of and not rely upon the aforesaid s 8(1), why should it be incompetent, unlawful and *contra bonos mores* for one or three persons to do exactly the same thing? No logic or public interest is offended if, in one agreement, a husband undertakes not to apply for a decrease of maintenance payable by him while a wife retains the right to rely on s 8(1).'

Die reg van 'n voormalige eggenoot of eggenote om 'n geldelike verhoging of verlaging aan te vra word gefundeer in beide art 4(1)(*b*) van die Wet op Onderhoud 23 van 1963 asook art 8 van die Wet op Egskeiding 70 van 1979. Laasgenoemde Wet magtig 'n Hooggeregshof om 'n onderhoudsbevel (of 'n bevel met betrekking tot die bewaring van, of voogdy oor, of toegang tot 'n kind) in te trek, op te skort of te wysig, terwyl art 4, saamgelees met art 5, van die Wet op Onderhoud aan die onderhoudshof bevoegdheid verleen om 'n bestaande onderhoudsbevel te vervang of op te hef. In wese verleen gemelde

artikels dieselfde magte aan genoemde howe, ten opsigte van die wysiging van onderhoud.

Mnr *Van Rhyn,* wat namens die respondente verskyn het, het betoog dat die bewoording van klousule 8 van die akte van dading wyd genoeg is om die appellant te verhinder om nou aansoek te doen vir 'n vermindering van onderhoud. In hierdie verband het mnr *Van Rhyn* op die *Polliack*-beslissing gesteun alwaar klousule 8 van die huidige akte van dading ooreengestem het met die bewoording van die akte van dading in genoemde beslissing.

In the *Polliack*-beslissing *supra* het die voormalige eggenote 'n *verhoging* van onderhoud gevorder waar daar reeds 'n meganisme daargestel was om met verhogings te handel. Die geleerde Regter verklaar dan ook die volgende op 164E:

'Accepting the fault of being repetitive, the parties excluded the Court's intervention and contractually created their own formula whereby the payment of maintenance was to be increased in the years following 1977.'

In die huidige saak word die respondente se tempo van verhoging ook uitdruklik gereël, maar swyg die akte van dading ten opsigte van 'n *vermindering* van die onderhoud ingeval van byvoorbeeld die appellant se onvermoë om dit te betaal. Gemelde beslissing is dus onderskeibaar van die huidige feitekompleks.

[527] Die algemene beginsel is dat partye gebonde gehou word aan die terme soos vervat in 'n kontrak. 'n Party tot 'n kontrak kan hom nie later daarop beroep dat die terme waarop vroeër ooreengekom is, hom nou benadeel nie. So ook kan 'n afstanddoening bindend op die partye wees deurdat die gewone kontraktuele beginsels daarop van toepassing is. *Van Rensburg v Van Rensburg* 1978 (1) SA 436 (T) te 440B; *Claassens v Claassens* 1981 (1) SA 360 (N) te 373A–C.

Ons reg erken egter 'n vermoede teen afstanddoening en 'n hof sal nie maklik aanvaar dat iemand afstand gedoen het van regte nie. *Hepner v Roodepoort-Maraisburg Town Council* 1962 (4) SA 772 (A) te 778; *Borstlap v Spangenberg en Andere* 1974 (3) SA 695 (A) te 704G.

Daar dien ook gelet te word op die *aard* van 'n onderhoudsbevel wat dit onderskei van 'n gewone skuldverpligting. Eerstens, geniet dit geprivilegieerde status, aangesien dit gevorder kan word van die opbrengs van pensioen, jaargeld en gratifikasie en vir hierdie doel kan op sulke gelde beslag gelê word. (Vergelyk art 11(2)(*d*) van die Wet op Onderhoud.) Tweedens, kan dit nie sedeer word of deur skuldvergelyking vereffen word nie. *Greathead v Greathead* 1946 TPD 404 te 411; *Tregoning v Tregoning* 1914 WLD 95 te 96. Derdens, beëindig 'n insolvensie nie 'n onderhoudsplig of selfs die betaalbaarheid van agterstallige onderhoud nie. (Mars *The Law of Insolvency in South Africa* 8ste uitg te 311, 334.) Vierdens, bevat die Wet op Wederkerige Afdwinging van Onderhoudsbevele 80 van 1963 uitsonderlike maatreëls. Vyfdens, is daar 'n strafsanksie aan verbonde indien 'n onderhoudspligtige nie sy onderhoudsverpligtinge nakom nie.

Uit die voorgaande is dit dus duidelik dat 'n onderhoudsbevel nie alleen wye sivielregtelike implikasies vir die onderhoudspligtige inhou nie, maar ook gepaard gaan met 'n strafsanksie in sekere omstandighede. Dit is teen hierdie agtergrond wat beslis moet word of klousule 8 van die akte van dading 'n afstanddoening daarstel ten opsigte van die appellant.

In die lig van die voorgaande is ek van mening dat, alvorens 'n afstanddoening van 'n persoon se reg om 'n hof te nader om vermindering van onderhoud te eis, gekonstrueer sal word, sal, in die afwesigheid van 'n uitdruklike afstanddoening, 'n duidelike en ondubbelsinnige bewoording te dien effekte geverg word.

Mnr *Van Rhyn* het, getrou aan die tradisie van die advokatuur, ons tereg verwys na 'n beslissing wat ongunstig is vir sy saak, naamlik *Davis v Davis* 1993 (1) SA 621 (K). In genoemde saak het daar 'n sogenaamde klousule 10 voorgekom wat tot die effek was dat die akte van dading 'n finale beslegting van alle geskilpunte was en dat hulle geen verdere

eise oor en weer teen mekaar sou hê nie. KING R verklaar op 626C–F, onder andere, die volgende:

'That a provision in a consent paper whereby the parties agree that the maintenance to be paid by the one to the other "is not subject to any increase or reduction" is not void and can be incorporated in a Court order in terms of s 7 of Act 70 of 1979 is clear . . .

However, the onus is on the party relying on a waiver or abandonment of a right, here a statutory right, by the other party . . .

I am doubtful whether on a proper interpretation of clause 10 it can be said that the parties intended to introduce a waiver of the right to exercise the statutory right [528] to apply for a rescission, suspension or variation of clauses 2 and 3 of the consent paper (s 8 of Act 70 of 1979) or a substitution thereof (s 5(4)(b) of Act 23 of 1963). Clause 10 records that the consent paper constitutes a settlement of the issues between the parties – these were custody of the children and access to them, maintenance for the children and for respondent, the proprietary consequences and costs. These were the issues and it is in respect of these issues that competing claims were being made.'

Op dieselfde bladsy word teenoor G–H die volgende verklaar:

'Clause 10 would in my view have had to have been far more specific in its terminology before it could be taken to have precluded the parties from exercising the continuing statutory right to apply to the court for an increase or decrease, as the case may be, of the right to receive or obligation to pay maintenance.'

Ek stem met eerbied saam met bogemelde beslissing.

Alhoewel klousule 8 van die akte van dading se woorde 'geen verdere eise van welke aard ookal wedersyds teenoor mekaar het nie . . .' seer sekerlik wyd bewoord is, kan dit net sowel slaan op vermoënsregtelike vorderings, maar nie noodwendig op die inhoud van die onderhoudsbevel nie. In die afwesigheid van 'n uitdruklike of duidelike bepaling in hierdie verband is ek van mening dat die landdros fouteer het deur te bevind dat klousule 8 wyd genoeg bewoord is om 'n afstanddoening aan die kant van die appellant te konstrueer.

In die lig van die slotsom hierbo bereik, is dit nie nodig om met die ander aspekte te handel wat deur mnr Danzfuss in betoog geopper is nie.

Gevolglik slaag die appèl . . . en word die saak na die onderhoudshof terugverwys om die ondersoek voort te sit op die basis dat die beswaar in limine van die hand gewys word.

CILLIÉ R het saamgestem.

Note

As was pointed out in the case under discussion, it is clear from cases like Schutte v Schutte [130] that spouses can validly waive their right to apply for variation of maintenance. In Polliack v Polliack [131] it was held that even a unilateral waiver could be valid. The importance of the case under discussion lies in its emphasis that the court will not lightly find that a party has waived his or her rights. The court held that our law recognises a presumption against waiver and that this presumption will only be rebutted if there is an express waiver or if there is " 'n duidelike en

Aantekening

In die onderhawige saak is daarop gewys dat dit uit sake soos Schutte v Schutte [130] duidelik is dat gades geldiglik afstand kan doen van hulle reg om aansoek te doen om wysiging van onderhoud. In Polliack v Polliack [131] is beslis dat selfs 'n eensydige afstanddoening geldig kan wees. Die belang van die onderhawige saak is daarin geleë dat dit klem lê op die feit dat die hof nie ligtelik sal bevind dat 'n party van sy of haar regte afstand gedoen het nie. Die hof het beslis dat ons reg 'n vermoede teen afstanddoening erken en dat hierdie vermoede slegs weerlê word indien daar 'n

ondubbelsinnige bewoording te dien effekte" (527).

See also *Davis v Davis* 1993 1 SA 621 (C) where it was held that the *onus* is on the party relying on a waiver. In *Davis*, as in *Luttig*, the husband had agreed to pay maintenance to his wife, which maintenance would be increased annually in accordance with the consumer price index. The parties had acknowledged that their consent paper "constitutes a full and final settlement of the issues between them including but not limited to their proprietary rights and that neither party thereto shall have any other claim or claims against the other save and except for the fulfilment of the terms of this agreement". The court held that this clause did not constitute a waiver of the right to apply for rescission, suspension or variation of the maintenance order.

uitdruklike afstanddoening is of indien daar " 'n duidelike en ondubbelsinnige bewoording te dien effekte" (527) is.

Sien ook *Davis v Davis* 1993 1 SA 621 (K) waarin beslis is dat die *onus* rus op die party wat hom of haar op die afstanddoening beroep. In *Davis*, soos in *Luttig*, het die man ooreengekom om onderhoud aan sy vrou te betaal, welke onderhoud jaarliks in ooreenstemming met die verbruikersprysindeks verhoog sou word. Die partye het bepaal dat hulle skikkingsakte "constitutes a full and final settlement of the issues between them including but not limited to their proprietary rights and that neither party thereto shall have any other claim or claims against the other save and except for the fulfilment of the terms of this agreement". Die hof het beslis dat hierdie klousule nie beteken het dat die partye afstand gedoen het van hulle reg om aansoek te doen om die intrekking, opskorting of wysiging van die onderhoudsbevel nie.

[133]   REID V REID

1992 1 SA 443 (E)

Maintenance for the spouse upon divorce – variation of maintenance order

When the appellant and the respondent were divorced in 1987 they entered into a consent paper in which the appellant, *inter alia*, undertook to pay R1 700 per month to his former wife. Two years later the appellant applied to a maintenance court for his total maintenance obligations towards the respondent to be consolidated into a single amount of R400 per month. The maintenance court reduced the original amount of R1 700 per month to R950 per month, the other obligations remaining unchanged. The appellant then appealed against this order to the supreme court, contending that the existing order was to be varied, firstly because he had agreed to an unjust settlement of his divorce action, and secondly because his fi-

Onderhoud vir die gade na egskeiding – wysiging van onderhoudsbevel

Toe die appellant en die respondent in 1987 geskei is, het hulle 'n skikkingsooreenkoms aangegaan waarin die appellant onder andere onderneem het om R1 700 per maand aan sy gewese vrou te betaal. Twee jaar later het die appellant by 'n onderhoudshof aansoek gedoen dat al sy onderhoudsverpligtinge teenoor die respondent in 'n enkele bedrag van R400 per maand gekonsolideer word. Die onderhoudshof het die oorspronklike bedrag van R1 700 per maand na R950 per maand verminder, terwyl die appellant se ander verpligtinge onveranderd gebly het. Die appellant het teen hierdie bevel na die hooggeregshof geappelleer. Hy het aangevoer dat die bestaande bevel gewysig moes word, eerstens omdat die skikkingsooreenkoms waartoe hy ten tyde van sy egskeiding ingestem

nancial situation had substantially deteriorated since the divorce. The appeal was
dismissed.

het onregverdig teenoor hom was, en tweedens omdat sy finansiële posisie sedert sy egskeiding drasties versleg het. Die appèl is van
die hand gewys.

ERASMUS J: [445] (a) The unjust settlement

In terms of s 8(1) of the Divorce Act 70 of 1979, a maintenance order made in terms of
the Act may at any time be varied if the court finds that there is sufficient reason therefor.
In general a court will only order variation of an existing maintenance order when there
has been a change [446] in the conditions that existed when the order was made and that
it would be unfair that the order should stand in its original form (*Roos v Roos* 1945 TPD
84 at 88; *Hancock v Hancock* 1957 (2) SA 500 (C) at 501H; *Levin v Levin* 1984 (2) SA 298
(C) at 303D–H). Any change in the circumstances, income, needs and obligations of one
of the ex-spouses may be a sufficient reason for ordering variation of the earlier order
(Hahlo *The South African Law of Husband and Wife* 5th ed at 365). Appellant was entitled
to rely, as he did, on his altered financial position. The question which required some
consideration is to what extent if at all does the alleged unjust settlement agreement
constitute part of the 'sufficient reason' for variation.

The nature of the enquiry into maintenance at divorce differs from that of the subsequent
enquiry into variation. At divorce the Court embarks on a wide-ranging enquiry into
the circumstances set out in s 7(2) of the Divorce Act. These are the existing or prospective
means of each of the parties, their respective earning capacities, financial needs and
obligations, the age of each of the parties, the duration of the marriage, the standard of
living of the parties prior to the divorce, their conduct insofar as it may be relevant to
the breakdown of the marriage and any other factor which in the opinion of the Court
can be taken into account. The Court then makes the maintenance order which it finds
'just'. When it comes to variation, the emphasis is on the subsequent change in the parties'
income, needs and financial obligations. *Hahlo* (*op cit* at 365) states that it is not necessary
to show a change in circumstances before variation may be obtained. The learned author
then continues to state:

'In *Beneke* the fact that "the order of Court was consequent upon an agreement which
was ill-considered having regard to the financial position of the (husband) at the time,
the (wife) well knowing that a second marriage would be set up within a very short
space of time" was taken into consideration by the Court in reducing the amount of
maintenance payable by the husband. And if the amount payable by the husband can
be decreased on the ground that in his eagerness to obtain release from the matrimonial
tie he undertook an obligation which was too heavy for him, the opposite also must
hold true: his ex-wife must be able to obtain an upward variation if she agreed initially
to an amount which, having regard to the circumstances of the spouses at the time,
was unduly small.'

The Court in *Beneke v Beneke* 1965 (1) SA 855 (T) did not furnish reasons for stating that
the fact of a bad bargain could constitute 'good cause' in terms of the then relevant s 10(1)
of the Matrimonial Affairs Act 37 of 1953. The other case relied upon by the learned
author, *Stone v Stone* 1966 (4) SA 98 (C), concerned variation of an order of judicial
separation. WATERMEYER J, who delivered the judgment, cautioned (at 103D) that
the Court was not dealing with a case of maintenance for a divorced wife. The learned
Judge then stated that a wife who made a bad bargain might well succeed in persuading
the Court to increase the amount, even though the circumstances had not changed since
the agreement was made. The Court added that 'some practical limit' had to be placed
upon the theoretical right to approach the Court *ad infinitum* in the hope of coming before
a more benign Judge. Both *Beneke* and *Stone* were decided before the new Divorce Act.

[447] On the other hand, *Hahlo* points out at 365 that, as CLAASSEN J in *Pieterse v Pieterse* 1965 (4) SA 344 (T) at 345F 'rightly stressed', 'a man who has solemnly entered into an agreement must, as far as possible, be held to his agreement'. It goes further than an agreement: an order of Court is involved. In making an order for maintenance on divorce, the Court has regard to all the circumstances mentioned in s 7(2) of the Divorce Act in deciding what constitutes a 'just amount'. Where the parties enter into a consent paper they arrive at a settlement on these issues. They agree on what constitutes a just maintenance order on the basis of the factors mentioned in s 7(2). When the consent paper is then made an order of Court, *res judicata* is established on the just amount payable as maintenance. A Court may order variation of its own order only on the limited grounds available at common law or in terms of Uniform Rule of Court 42(1). Section 8(1) relaxes the principle of the immutability of judgments. On the canon of construction that an Act of Parliament is to be interpreted in such a way as to accord with existing law, s 8(1) should be construed so as to affect the operation of *res judicata* as little as possible. To allow an ex-spouse freely to attack the justness of the divorce order could open a door to abuse of the Court process. A litigant who finds himself in difficulties in a divorce could agree to an unfavourable settlement in the knowledge that he could later, under the guise of the variation, undo the settlement agreement. Apart from the objections in principle, it is from a practical point of view highly undesirable that a court (not being a Court of appeal) should rule on the correctness or justness of another court's order. Such an enquiry would require evidence as to all the factors relevant to the previous order. As the instant case demonstrates, this could lead to a lengthy rehash of the divorce. The court could find it difficult to decide what motivated the parties to sign a settlement agreement; or to identify and define all the factors relevant to the justness of the order.

There are, it appears, obvious and grave objections, both in principle and from a practical point of view, against allowing an applicant in a s 8(1) variation enquiry not only to reopen the divorce action, but also to raise the considerations which influenced the parties to sign the consent paper. The Legislature, in the interest of flexibility of justice, probably did not shut the door entirely to such a course. On the other hand, an applicant cannot, I think, have *carte blanche* to ventilate the divorce proceedings. In *Stone (supra)* the Court spoke of 'a practical limit'. In my view such limit will be laid down effectively by requiring an applicant to show special circumstances before a court will permit him to question the justness of the existing maintenance order.

I find that none of the factors placed before the maintenance court in regard to the existing divorce order constitutes special circumstances.

(b) The changed circumstances

The position of an ex-husband who remarries was stated by OGILVIE THOMPSON J (as he then was) as follows in the oft-quoted passage from *Hancock v Hancock (supra)* at 502H–503D):

> 'Where the former guilty spouse's financial position has, since the date of maintenance order, deteriorated as a result of circumstances beyond his control – eg illness – the Court will manifestly be more favourably disposed towards granting a reduction of the maintenance previously ordered than it will be [448] if the deterioration of his financial position has been brought about as a result of the "guilty spouse's" voluntary action or inaction. The situation which in practice frequently presents itself in applications for reduction is where the husband has remarried and then finds himself unable to implement both his existing legal obligations to his former spouse and what he conceives to be his duty to himself and to his present wife and family: the *de facto* situation thus created almost invariably renders it a difficult task for the Court both to have regard to the realities of the situation, and, at the same time, to do justice

between all concerned. On the one hand, the Court cannot overlook that, with full knowledge of his obligations to his first wife, the husband has taken upon himself additional obligations by again venturing into matrimony: the Court cannot countenance an attempt by the guilty husband of a former marriage to depreciate the payment to his former wife by the amount he is spending to "feather another nest" (see *Jacobs v Jacobs* 1955 (1) SA 235 (W) at 238). On the other hand, the Court must also look to what the result of declining to vary the existing maintenance order is likely to be. A rigid and uncompromising rule that the rights of the first wife are to be regarded as absolutely preferent might perhaps in a sense be logical enough; but that, if indeed not directly contrary to the contemplation of the Act, would certainly in some cases lead to great hardship, particularly where children of the second marriage have to be supported. Considerations such as these may sometimes render it necessary for the Court to cut down the maintenance payable to a former spouse even though the Court *ceteris paribus* would prefer to see that maintenance remain unreduced.'

See also *Hahlo* (*op cit* at 366); *Wilson v Wilson* 1981 (2) SA 536 (Z) at 539C. In *Dawe v Dawe* 1980 (1) SA 141 (ZR) at 144B the Court stated, in my view correctly, that a court must scrutinise an application (for variation) to ascertain whether a party in divorce proceedings had not agreed to pay maintenance to the 'innocent' party with the mental reservation that after the divorce was granted an application would be made to reduce the amount of maintenance agreed upon because of the financial consequences of the remarriage. It seems probable from the evidence that at the time of the divorce appellant contemplated remarriage to his present wife. He therefore signed the consent paper with the knowledge that his obligations would increase in the near future. In regard to the position of the respondent, the maintenance court found guidance from the judgment in *Loubser v Loubser* 1958 (4) SA 680 (C) at 684F–G:

'In my opinion a divorced wife in whose favour such a maintenance order has been made is entitled, particularly when the custody of a minor child or children has in addition been awarded to her, to an expectation of reasonable stability as regards the monthly income of her new household, so as to enable her to plan ahead and even to effect such savings as may be prudent and reasonable with a view to the future of herself and the child or children; and she would be deprived of this most important benefit if some change or changes in the relative financial position of the parties were too readily to be acceded to as justification for a complete revision of the maintenance arrangements.'

It is clear from the manner in which the maintenance court dealt with the issues that the presiding officer understood and endeavoured to apply the legal principles applicable in the event of remarriage of an ex-husband . . .

[449] In regard to variation for 'good cause' in terms of s 10(2) of Act 37 of 1953 (now repealed) O'HAGAN J stated in *Whiteley v Whiteley* 1959 (2) SA 148 (E) at 149E that the Court exercises a 'discretionary power' which will be dictated by considerations of fairness and justice. In *Engelbrecht v Engelbrecht* 1989 (1) SA 597 (C) at 603G–H, it was stated (in a judgment of the Full Court) that a court exercises discretionary powers in regard to the making of a maintenance order and that the competence of a Court of appeal to interfere with such discretionary power is limited. These principles apply likewise where a variation for 'sufficient reason' in terms of s 8(1) is the subject of an appeal. The maintenance court dealt with all factual issues fully and carefully. While I do not necessarily agree with its [450] every assessment and calculation, I cannot find that in the final analysis it exercised its discretion otherwise than judicially.

At the end of its exercise, the maintenance court achieved a position where appellant could with prudence and thrift come out on his income; while the respondent, although

in reduced circumstances, was left better off than appellant. Counsel for appellant attacks this, what he calls 'totally disproportionate distribution of income'. He contends that from the expenses allowed, it appears that the respondent will enjoy a significantly higher standard of living than the appellant and his family ... It is however not the function of the maintenance court in varying an existing maintenance order to achieve parity between the parties. The starting point is the existing order. Section 7(2) does not enjoin the Supreme Court to establish financial equality between the parties at divorce. The Court is required to make the order which it finds 'just' in respect of payment of maintenance having regard to a whole number of considerations. Any one or more of these considerations could result in disparity: for example, the parties' 'conduct as far as it may be relevant to the breakdown of the marriage'. In *Beaumont v Beaumont* 1985 (4) SA 171 (W) at 184E–F, KRIEGLER J remarked that although a Court should not under the guise of maintenance impose a purely penal sanction for a party's misconduct, the length of the marriage and the conduct of the parties are relevant factors in the assessment of maintenance. Such assessment is no simple task, as appears from the judgment of FLEMMING J in *Swart v Swart* 1980 (4) SA 364 (O) [108]. On the appellant's case, the existing order brought about disparity between the parties. Insofar as he now seeks to correct the disparity, he is attempting to do in an indirect manner what he is unable to achieve directly, viz vary the existing order on the basis that it was unjust as at the time it was made. If the Supreme Court maintenance order resulted in disparity, such disparity should as far as possible be perpetuated.

Supervening events have increased the disparity. Appellant's income has fallen, and by remarrying and by adopting his wife's child he has increased his financial burden. He aggravated his position in other respects: in 1988 he purchased his present wife a holiday shack for R50 000; he assisted his wife in purchasing their matrimonial home; he paid for landscaping of the garden; he replaced major items of furniture at considerable cost; he bought a boat and rubber dinghy for between R7 000–R8 000. The maintenance court considered all these factors fully.

In all the circumstances of the matter, I am not persuaded that the maintenance court erred in the exercise of its discretion. I therefore find that the appeal cannot succeed.

JANSEN J concurred.

Note

It is important to note that a court which is approached for a variation of an existing maintenance order will only consider the justness of the existing order if there are special circumstances. The court will not replace the existing order merely because its result is (or seems) unfair towards one party. In the case under discussion the court went so far as to hold that if the existing order resulted in disparity between the ex-spouses "such disparity should as far as possible be perpetuated" (450). The reason why the court will not consider the justness of the existing order is that it does not have all the facts before it which were presented when the existing order was made.

The section of the judgment dealing with the position when the maintenance debtor remarries (448) is also important. It indicates that, as a

Aantekening

Dit is belangrik om daarop te let dat 'n hof wat genader word om 'n bestaande onderhoudsbevel te wysig, die billikheid van die bestaande bevel slegs sal oorweeg indien daar spesiale omstandighede aanwesig is. Die hof sal nie die bestaande bevel vervang bloot omdat die gevolg van die bevel onbillik teenoor die een party is (of skyn te wees) nie. In die onderhawige saak het die hof so ver gegaan om te beslis dat indien die bestaande bevel ongelykheid tussen die gewese gades tot gevolg het, "such disparity should as far as possible be perpetuated" (450). Die rede waarom die hof nie die billikheid van die bestaande bevel sal oorweeg nie is omdat die hof nie al die feite voor hom het wat ten tyde van die uitreiking van die bestaande bevel voor die hof was nie.

Die gedeelte van die uitspraak wat handel oor

general rule, in respect of maintenance, the courts place the first wife in a stronger position than the second wife.

In the case under discussion it was stated further that the court will generally vary a maintenance order only if there are changed circumstances. In respect of changed circumstances see also *Havenga v Havenga* [134].

die posisie wanneer die onderhoudspligtige hertrou, (448) is ook belangrik. Dit dui aan dat die howe, as 'n algemene reël, die eerste vrou met betrekking tot onderhoud in 'n sterker posisie plaas as die tweede vrou.

In die onderhawige saak is verder verklaar dat die hof gewoonlik net 'n onderhoudsbevel sal wysig as daar veranderde omstandighede aanwesig is. In verband met veranderde omstandighede sien ook *Havenga v Havenga* [134].

[134] HAVENGA V HAVENGA

1988 2 SA 438 (T)

Maintenance upon divorce – deed of settlement – grounds for rescission or variation

The marriage of the appellant (wife) and the respondent (husband) was dissolved in 1986. The parties entered into a deed of settlement which was made an order of the court. In terms of clause 5 of this agreement the respondent, pending the decision of a maintenance court, agreed to pay interim maintenance to the appellant in the amount of R400 per month. They agreed further that both parties would be entitled, in terms of sections 4 and 5 of the Maintenance Act 23 of 1963, to apply to a maintenance court for a maintenance order and that it would not be necessary for them to prove any change in circumstances before such an application could be made. Soon after the decree of divorce had been granted, the respondent applied to the maintenance court for the maintenance order to be set aside. This was opposed by the appellant. The magistrate refused to hear the matter as he was of the opinion that a maintenance court could only vary an existing order of the supreme court if there was a material change in circumstances. The magistrate was further of the opinion that clause 5 of the agreement was directly in conflict with the provisions of

Onderhoud na egskeiding – skikkingsooreenkoms – gronde vir opheffing of wysiging

Die appellant (vrou) en die respondent (man) se huwelik is in 1986 ontbind. 'n Skikkingsooreenkoms wat die partye aangegaan het, is by die hofbevel ingelyf. Ingevolge klousule 5 van hierdie ooreenkoms het die respondent, hangende die beslissing van 'n onderhoudshof, ingestem om tussentydse onderhoud van R400 per maand aan die appellant te betaal. Die partye het verder ooreengekom dat albei partye daarop geregtig sou wees om ingevolge artikels 4 en 5 van die Wet op Onderhoud 23 van 1963 'n aansoek om onderhoud by die onderhoudshof in te dien, en dat dit nie vir hulle nodig sou wees om enige verandering van omstandighede te bewys alvorens sodanige aansoek gedoen kon word nie. Pas nadat die egskeiding toegestaan is, het die respondent by die onderhoudshof aansoek gedoen om opheffing van die onderhoudsbevel. Dit is deur die appellant teengestaan. Die landdros het geweier om die aangeleentheid aan te hoor aangesien hy van mening was dat 'n onderhoudshof net 'n bestaande bevel van die hooggeregshof kon wysig as daar 'n wesenlike verandering in die omstandighede plaasgevind het. Die landdros was verder van mening dat klousule 5 van

sections 4 and 5 of the Maintenance Act as it was aimed at evading these provisions. As a result of the magistrate's views, the respondent applied to the supreme court for the deletion of clause 5. This application was granted as the court was of the opinion that the order of the court was frustrated because the maintenance court could not determine the maintenance. It was further ordered that the deletion should not prejudice any claim to maintenance that the appellant might have. The appellant appealed against this decision to the full bench. The appeal was successful.

die ooreenkoms lynreg in stryd met die bepalings van artikels 4 en 5 van die Wet op Onderhoud was aangesien dit gepoog het om hierdie bepalings te omseil. Op grond van die landdros se standpunt het die respondent by die hooggeregshof aansoek gedoen om skrapping van klousule 5. Hierdie aansoek is toegestaan aangesien die hof van mening was dat die hofbevel verydel is aangesien die onderhoudshof nie die onderhoud kon vasstel nie. Daar is verder gelas dat die skrapping nie die aanspraak op onderhoud wat die appellant mag hê, moes benadeel nie. Die appellant het teen hierdie beslissing na die volbank geappelleer. Die appèl was suksesvol.

HARMS R: [442] Alvorens met die uitspraak van die Hof *a quo*, die landdros se siening en die advokate se betoë gehandel word, is dit nodig om op sekere aspekte van die reg op onderhoud tussen egliedere te let:

(a) *stante matrimonio* is sowel die Hooggeregshof as die onderhoudshof bevoeg om 'n onderhoudsbevel ten gunste van een eggenoot teen die ander eggenoot te gee;

(b) so 'n bevel kan deur enigeen van hierdie howe van tyd tot tyd gewysig word;

(c) die Hooggeregshof is bevoeg om tesame met 'n egskeidingsbevel 'n onderhoudsbevel ten gunste van een van die voormalige eggenotes toe te staan (art 7 van die Wet op Egskeiding 70 van 1979); dit kan geskied deur 'n ooreenkoms tot 'n Hofbevel te verhef;

(d) [443] so 'n bevel is vatbaar vir wysiging of herroeping deur òf die Hooggeregshof òf die onderhoudshof (art 8 van die Wet op Egskeiding; arts 4 en 5 van die Wet op Onderhoud);

(e) indien die Hooggeregshof nie by die toestaan van die egskeiding 'n onderhoudsbevel in terme van art 7 van die Wet op Egskeiding verleen nie, is geen hof daarna bevoeg om so 'n bevel te verleen nie (*Schutte v Schutte* 1986 (1) SA 872 (A) [130]);

(f) die onderhoudsbevel in terme van art 7 kan voorwaardelik of vir 'n termyn of vir 'n onbepaalde tydperk wees;

(g) geen Hof het die bevoegdheid om sy bevoegdheid om onderhoudsbevele te gee, te delegeer nie.

Teen hierdie agtergrond betoog die respondent se advokaat dat die partye verkeerdelik gemeen het dat die onderhoudshof 'n oorspronklike onderhoudsbevel in 'n egskeidingsgeding kan maak. In die lig van daardie geloof het die partye 'n ooreenkoms gesluit waarvolgens die onderhoudshof die bevel sal maak. Die dispuut is met ander woorde vir die onderhoudshof voorbehou. Daar is volgens die betoog dus geen onderhoudsbevel gemaak deur die Hof wat die egskeidingsbevel verleen het nie. Omdat die appellante die ooreenkoms gesluit het aan die hand van regsadvies is haar dwaling nie *iustus* nie en is sy nie geregtig op 'n regstelling van die bevel nie.

Dit is so dat klousule 5.1 die indruk skep dat die partye die beslissing van die kwessie van onderhoud vir die onderhoudshof wou voorbehou. Dit is so dat die partye graag die aangeleentheid in die onderhoudshof wou uitspook en nie die Hooggeregshof met die

probleem wou belas nie. Waarskynlik wou die partye hulself nie met die addisionele regskoste belas nie. Al hierdie feite beteken egter nie dat klousule 5 in sy geheel gelees nie 'n ooreenkoms tot betaling van onderhoud daarstel nie. Inderdaad skep hierdie klousule 'n onmiddellike verpligting om onderhoud te betaal. Hierdie verpligting duur onbepaald voort. Enigeen van die partye is egter, volgens die ooreenkoms, geregtig – en nie verplig nie – om 'n aansoek in terme van arts 4 en 5 van die Wet op Onderhoud aan die onderhoudshof te rig. So 'n aansoek deur die respondent kan slegs wees vir 'n vermindering van die betalingsverpligting van R400 per maand. 'n Aansoek deur die appellante is nie nodig om die betaling van die R400 te bevestig nie. Indien 'n party nie die onderhoudshof nader nie bly die betalingsverpligting voortbestaan soos ooreengekom. So ook as 'n aansoek om verhoging of vermindering onsuksesvol sou wees. Opgesom: klousule 5 skep 'n onderhoudsverpligting onderhewig aan 'n ontbindende voorwaarde. Dit bly steeds 'n onderhoudsverpligting vervat in 'n onderhoudsbevel uitgereik saam met 'n egskeidingsbevel. Die betoog dat klousule 5 nie 'n geldige onderhoudsbevel is nie, moet dus verwerp word.

Om terug te keer na die uitspraak van die Hof *a quo*. Soos reeds gesê, is klousule 5 deurgehaal omdat die bevel gefrustreer is. Hiermee word oënskynlik bedoel dat die uitvoering van die bevel onmoontlik geword het aangesien die landdros nie die bevoegdheid het om die ondersoek te behartig nie. 'n Hof het die bevoegdheid om 'n hofbevel tersyde te stel wat onmoontlik geword het en hierdie beginsel geld ook waar die hofbevel 'n skikkingsooreenkoms van die partye bekragtig het. *Rossouw v Haumann* 1949 (4) SA 796 (K). Indien die uitgangspunt van die Hof *a quo* juis is dat [444] die onderhoudshof nie die bevoegdheid gehad het om die aangeleentheid te verhoor nie, is dit 'n regsonbevoegdheid wat van meet af aan bestaan het. Klousule 5 het dus van die begin af 'n regtens onmoontlike prosedure geskep. Dit is dus nie 'n geval van onmoontlikwording nie maar van 'n onmoontlikheid *ab initio*.

Daar is ernstige probleme met dié benadering van die Hof *a quo*. Ten eerste, indien 'n wesenlike term van 'n ooreenkoms onmoontlik is, verval die hele ooreenkoms en nie net die regte en verpligtinge wat deur daardie term geskep is nie. Dit sou beteken dat die hele skikkingsooreenkoms 'n nietigheid is. Die feit dat die ooreenkoms in 'n hofbevel vervat is, moet daartoe lei dat die hofbevel in sy geheel 'n nietigheid moet wees. *Rossouw v Haumann (supra* op 801). Dit is ondenkbaar dat die egskeidingsbevel sonder 'n ooreenkoms gegee sou gewees het. Dit is verder ondenkbaar dat die partye die saak sou geskik het sonder om klousule 5 in die kontrak in te sluit.

Die tweede probleem het betrekking op 'n hof van eerste instansie se bevoegdheid om 'n gedeelte van 'n ander hof van eerste instansie se bevel deur te haal op grond daarvan dat dit op 'n juridies ongegronde basis gegee is. *Firestone SA (Pty) Ltd v Gentiruco AG* 1977 (4) SA 298 (A). Artikel 8 van die Wet op Egskeiding gee wel aan 'n hof van eerste instansie die bevoegdheid om 'n 'onderhoudsbevel' in te trek of te wysig. Dit voorveronderstel 'n geldige onderhoudsbevel. Waar die onderhoudsbevel na bewering 'n nietigheid is, is art 8 nie van toepassing nie. Dit is ook twyfelagtig of die jurisdiksionele feit vir die toepassing van art 8 teenwoordig is. Daar moet voldoende rede wees vir die wysiging of vervanging van die onderhoudsbevel. Dit voorveronderstel ten minste feite wat nie voor die eerste hof was nie. Dit kan nooit op regsgronde slaan nie.

Ten derde, indien die uitgangspunt was dat mens met 'n gemeenregtelike tersydestelling te doen het, is die remedie *restitutio in integrum. Childerley Estate Stores v Standard Bank of SA Ltd* 1924 OPD 163. Deur een klousule van die ooreenkoms deur te haal, word restitusie nie bewerkstellig nie. Restitusie kan alleen plaasvind indien die hele ooreenkoms deurgehaal word.

Al wat dan oorbly, is Hofreël 42(1)(*c*) wat die Hof bevoegdheid gee om in geval van 'n gemeenskaplike fout 'n bevel te wysig of te herroep. Die ironie is dat juis die huidige

respondent (die aansoeker) se advokaat nou betoog dat regshulp op grond van dwaling uitgeskakel is omdat dit 'n regsdwaling is waaraan die partye hulself skuldig gemaak het en dus nie 'n *iustus error* is nie. Ten spyte van hierdie betoog skyn dit of hierdie reël die respondent die enigste moontlike remedie gebied het. Die vraag of hierdie reël wel aangewend kon word, hoef egter nie besleg te word nie aangesien respondent nie in sy vestigende verklaring 'n saak vir verligting in terme van die reël probeer uitmaak het nie. Daar kan mee volstaan word deur daarop te wys dat die toepassing van die reël nie beteken dat die Hof *a quo* klousule 5 moes deurgehaal het nie. Die Hof moes homself teruggeplaas het in die skoene van die Verhoorhof en moes dan oorweeg het watter bevel in die plek van klousule 5 geplaas moes word om geregtigheid tussen die partye te laat geskied. Die Hof *a quo* wou dit bereik deur te gelas dat sy bevel nie appellante se regte op onderhoud sal benadeel nie. In die lig [445] van die uitspraak in die *Schutte*-saak *supra* kon die Hof *a quo* dit nie bewerkstellig nie. Die deurhaling van klousule 5 sou appellante se aanspraak op onderhoud permanent beëindig. Daarbenewens kan 'n bevel gebaseer op 'n ooreenkoms tog nie gerektifiseer word op 'n wyse wat nie met die partye se gemeenskaplike bedoeling ooreenkom nie.

Dit laat die vraag of die landdros in sy siening korrek was. Artikel 4(1) van die Wet op Onderhoud maak voorsiening vir 'n ondersoek in 'n onderhoudshof indien daar 'gegronde redes bestaan vir die vervanging of opheffing van 'n onderhoudsbevel'. Na oorweging van die getuienis kan die hof volgens art 5(4)(*b*) 'n bevel uitvaardig ter vervanging van die onderhoudsbevel of hy kan die onderhoudsbevel ophef. Die betrokke klousule 5 van die ooreenkoms wat bevestig is in 'n Hofbevel is in die lig van wat hierbo gesê is 'n onderhoudsbevel vir doeleindes van hierdie Wet.

As algemene uitgangspunt kan dit gestel word dat in die afwesigheid van 'n wesenlike verandering van omstandighede daar nie gegronde redes kan bestaan vir die vervanging of opheffing van 'n onderhoudsbevel nie. Veranderde omstandighede is egter nie 'n statutêre voorvereiste nie. Daar kan omstandighede wees waar daar gegronde redes is vir die vervanging of opheffing van 'n onderhoudsbevel sonder dat daar 'n wesenlike verandering van omstandighede plaasgevind het. (Die omgekeerde is ook waar. Die teenwoordigheid van veranderde omstandighede beteken nie noodwendig dat daar gegronde rede vir 'n wysiging is nie.) So 'n geval kan 'n geval wees waar 'n voorlopige of tydelike reëling ter betaling van onderhoud in 'n hofbevel opgeneem is. Deur as voorvereiste te stel dat daar 'n wesenlike verandering van omstandighede moet wees alvorens hy die saak kan aanhoor, het die landdros homself verkeerdelik jurisdiksie ontsê. Aangesien die aan- of afwesigheid van veranderde omstandighede nie 'n statutêre jurisdiksionele feit is nie, is die partye ten volle bevoeg om ooreen te kom dat hierdie praktyksvereiste nie op hulle van toepassing sal wees nie. Vgl *Verryne v Van Zyl and Another* 1963 (1) SA 592 (T).

Die houding van die landdros dat klousule 5 neerkom op 'n omseiling van die statutêre bepalings van die Wet op Onderhoud kan eweneens nie onderskryf word nie. Wat die landdros in effek gedoen het, was om 'n oordeel uit te spreek oor die korrektheid van 'n hofbevel wat deur 'n hoër Hof toegestaan is. Die landdros het nie daardie bevoegdheid nie.

Die landdros het ook gefouteer deur sy standpunte aan die partye oor te dra en dan om te weier om met die verrigtinge voort te gaan. Die landdros is verplig om 'n ondersoek te hou soos voorgeskryf deur arts 4 en 5 nadat 'n onderhoudsbeampte 'n ondersoek in sy hof ingestel het. Hy moes aan die einde van die verrigtinge geoordeel het of daar gegronde redes aangetoon is vir die vervanging of opheffing van die onderhoudsbevel. Daar is niks in die Wet of die reëls uitgevaardig kragtens art 15 van die betrokke Wet wat die prosedure magtig wat die landdros gevolg het nie.

Hiermee word nie te kenne gegee dat daar inderdaad gegronde redes vir 'n wysiging van die toegekende onderhoud is nie. Dit is 'n aangeleentheid wat die onderhoudshof moet bepaal.

Hieruit volg dit dat die prosedure deur die partye in klousule 5 van die ooreenkoms voorsien, nie 'n onmoontlike prosedure is nie. Waar die landdros geweier het om sy funksies na te kom, moes die respondent by wyse van 'n hersieningsaansoek hom verplig het om sy funksies na behore [446] uit te oefen. Die remedie wat die respondent gevolg het was gevolglik onvanpas en moes die aansoek in die Hof *a quo* van die hand gewys gewees het met koste. Aangesien die landdros nie 'n bevel gemaak het nie en nie *functus officio* is nie, kan die respondent weer sy ondersoek laat plaas vir verhoor...

In die lig van voorgaande behoort die appèl... te slaag en die bevel van die Hof *a quo* gewysig word om te lees: 'Aansoek van die hand gewys...'

ELOFF ARP en LEVESON R het saamgestem.

Note

In this case the court was of the opinion that it was not necessary for the parties to prove any change in circumstances for a variation in the maintenance order (see also Hahlo 365). Van der Vyver and Joubert (681), on the other hand, submit that the court will vary the order if there has been a change in circumstances. Although it appears that a change in circumstances is not a necessary requirement before the court can be approached for a variation, it must be conceded that there will normally be a change in the circumstances of the parties on account of which they approach the court for a variation in the order. (See also *Reid v Reid* [133].)

Aantekening

In hierdie saak was die hof van mening dat dit nie vir die partye nodig was om veranderde omstandighede te bewys ten einde 'n wysiging van die onderhoudsbevel te verkry nie (sien ook Hahlo 365). Van der Vyver en Joubert (681) voer egter aan dat die hof die bevel sal wysig as daar 'n verandering in die omstandighede was. Alhoewel dit wil voorkom asof veranderde omstandighede nie 'n noodsaaklike vereiste is voor die hof om 'n wysiging genader kan word nie, moet toegegee word dat daar normaalweg 'n verandering in die partye se omstandighede sal wees op grond waarvan hulle die hof om 'n wysiging sal nader. (Sien ook *Reid v Reid* [133].)

[135] SCHLESINGER V SCHLESINGER

1968 1 SA 699 (W)

Cancellation of a maintenance order

When the marriage between the applicant and respondent was dissolved the applicant undertook to pay maintenance to the respondent until she remarried or died. The respondent subsequently started cohabiting with one Dry. The applicant applied to court to have the agreement by which he undertook to pay maintenance cancelled. The court rejected the application.

Kansellasie van 'n onderhoudsbevel

Toe die huwelik tussen die applikant en respondent ontbind is, het die applikant onderneem om onderhoud aan die respondent te betaal tot by haar hertroue of dood. Die respondent het daarna met ene Dry begin saamwoon. Die applikant het die hof genader om 'n bevel dat die ooreenkoms opgehef word ingevolge waarvan hy onderneem het om onderhoud te betaal. Die hof het die aansoek van die hand gewys.

NICHOLAS J: [700] Clearly an irregular association such as that between the respondent and Dry cannot be regarded as a marriage. Nor in my view is there any room for the implication of a term that maintenance should cease to be payable if the respondent should live in concubinage. In *Parkes v Parkes,* 1932 SR 72 RUSSEL, CJ, said at p 74:

> "In this case the order was made by consent, and it specifically says that maintenance is to cease on the respondent's remarriage. Can it be said that it is a matter of necessary implication that maintenance is to cease equally on her ceasing to live chastely. I do not think it can. The maxim *inclusio unius exclusio alterius* would forbid it. The considerations that might apply to a maintenance order during judicial separation do not apply here."

That case was approved in *Watson v Watson,* 1959 (1) SA 185 (N), and in *Hughes NO v The Master and Another,* 1960 (4) SA 936 (C), where HERBSTEIN, J, said at p 941:

> "If the deceased did not make the right to maintenance dependent on second respondent leading a chaste life there is no reason why this Court should vary the agreement to include such a term."

At the hearing of the application, other grounds were submitted for the grant of the order sought.

It was argued in the first place that the fact that the respondent had lived with Dry as man and wife for nearly two years constituted "good cause" in terms of sec. 10 of the Matrimonial Affairs Act, 37 of 1953, entitling the Court to vary the agreement which had been made an order of Court.

"Good cause" as used in sec. 10 is not really capable of definition, but must depend upon the particular circumstances of each case . . .

[701] In *Watson v Watson, supra,* MILNE, J, said at p 189:

> "Mr *Feetham* has urged that it would be unfair to require a husband to go on paying alimony to a woman who has ceased to be his wife when she is living in adultery, and more particularly if the situation be such that it ought to be inferred that she is living in adultery instead of re-marrying, with the object of preventing the suspensive condition in the agreement from becoming operative. I must say that it seems to me that, if it could be shown that the respondent in this case was living in adultery with van Rensburg, although she is now *prima facie* free to marry again, and that an operative reason for not marrying van Rensburg is that by marrying him she will forfeit her right to maintenance because of the terms of the agreement, it would be good cause for the rescission of the maintenance order, at any rate in the absence of some very special circumstances."

In argument in this case, counsel for the applicant contended that an operative reason why the respondent did not marry Dry was that by marrying him she would have forfeited her right to maintenance because of the terms of the agreement. There is no evidence to support that contention, nor was it even put forward in the applicant's affidavit . . .

In any event, the circumstances of this case are such that in my view the respondent's conduct in living with Dry does not constitute "good cause", for a variation of the maintenance clause of the agreement . . .

It is clear . . . that the applicant connived at the respondent's relationship with Dry, and that by agreeing to para. (*c*) in the circumstances he led the respondent to believe that he would not rely on the respondent's living with Dry as a ground for seeking a reduction of maintenance. That being so, he cannot in my view be permitted to rely on that as ground for the relief sought, at any rate without informing the respondent that he would

do so if she persisted in the irregular relationship. Cf *Garlick Ltd v Phillips,* 1949 (1) SA 121 (AD) at pp 131–133 . . .

[702] The application fails . . . and it is dismissed . . .

Note

Although it was decided in this case that a husband could not have his obligation to support terminated or reduced merely on the ground that his ex-wife was living with another man, this decision should not be interpreted as laying down a general principle, If, for example, the ex-wife takes up living with a man and decides not to marry him purely because such a marriage would result in the loss of her claim for maintenance against her ex-husband, the court might well hold that she is no longer entitled to maintenance if the man with whom she is living can support her. (See also Hahlo 367 and *Owen-Smith v Owen-Smith* 1982 1 SA 511 (Z).) It would, however, depend on the facts of the case.

A husband's obligation to pay maintenance to his ex-wife will, however, be terminated if she starts living with another man and the maintenance order provides for such a contingency (*Drummond v Drummond* 1979 1 SA 161 (A)).

Note that section 8 of the Divorce Act 70 of 1979 has replaced section 10 of the Matrimonial Affairs Act 37 of 1953. The provisions of section 8 are, however, similar to those contained in section 10 of the Matrimonial Affairs Act.

Aantekening

Alhoewel in hierdie saak beslis is dat 'n man se verpligting om onderhoud aan sy gewese vrou te betaal nie beëindig of verminder word bloot omdat sy met 'n ander man saamwoon nie, kan nie gesê word dat hierdie saak 'n algemene beginsel neerlê nie. As 'n geskeide vrou byvoorbeeld met 'n man saamwoon en besluit om nie met hom te trou nie bloot omdat sodanige huwelik tot gevolg sal hê dat sy haar eis om onderhoud teen haar gewese man verloor, is dit goed moontlik dat die hof mag beslis dat sy nie langer op onderhoud geregtig is as die man met wie sy saamwoon haar kan onderhou nie. (Sien ook Hahlo 367 en *Owen-Smith v Owen-Smith* 1982 1 SA 511 (Z).) Alles sal egter van die feite van die besondere saak afhang.

'n Man se verpligting om onderhoud aan sy gewese vrou te betaal word egter wel beëindig as sy met 'n ander man saamwoon en die onderhoudsbevel vir sodanige gebeurlikheid voorsiening maak (*Drummond v Drummond* 1979 1 SA 161 (A)).

Let daarop dat artikel 10 van die Wet op Huweliksaangeleenthede 37 van 1953 vervang is deur artikel 8 van die Wet op Egskeiding 70 van 1979. Die bepalings van artikel 8 is egter soortgelyk aan dié van artikel 10 van die Wet op Huweliksaangeleenthede.

The termination of maintenance orders

Die beëindiging van onderhoudsbevele

[136]   HODGES V COUBROUGH

1991 3 SA 58 (D)

Transmissibility of the liability to pay maintenance to the estate of the maintaining party

When the applicant and her former husband (Mr Hodges) were divorced the court awarded her maintenance under section 7(2) of the Divorce Act 70 of 1979. The order did not specify the duration that the maintenance

Oordraagbaarheid van die verpligting om onderhoud te betaal op die boedel van die onderhoudspligtige party

Toe die applikant en haar vorige man (mnr Hodges) geskei is, het die hof onderhoud aan haar toegestaan ingevolge artikel 7(2) van die Wet op Egskeiding 70 van 1979. Die bevel het nie aangedui hoe lank die onderhoud

was to be paid. On the death of Mr Hodges the executor of his estate in the accounts provided for the payment of some arrear maintenance to the applicant. No allowance was made for subsequent maintenance as the executor was of the opinion that the applicant's right to such had expired on the death of her former husband. She then lodged an objection to the accounts with the master of the supreme court. It was overruled and she applied to the court for a declaratory order holding the estate liable to maintain her until she died or remarried. The application was dismissed.

betaal moes word nie. Na die dood van mnr Hodges het die eksekuteur van sy boedel in sy rekeninge voorsiening gemaak vir die betaling van agterstallige onderhoud aan die applikant. Daar is geen voorsiening vir toekomstige onderhoud gemaak nie aangesien die eksekuteur van mening was dat die applikant se reg op verdere onderhoud by die dood van haar vorige man verval het. Sy het toe by die meester van die hooggeregshof beswaar teen die rekeninge aangeteken. Die beswaar is verwerp en sy het by die hof aansoek gedoen om 'n verklarende bevel dat die boedel aanspreeklik is om haar te onderhou tot haar dood of hertroue. Die aansoek is van die hand gewys.

DIDCOTT J: [61] Two distinct questions were debated when the present case got argued. They were these. Did BROOME J [presiding judge at the divorce proceedings] have the power to make an order for maintenance lasting longer than the life of Hodges and burdening the estate? And, if so, did he exercise that power? The formulation of the questions suggests that an answer to the first which was given in the negative would dispose decisively of the matter. But it would not. For, if BROOME J had in truth no such power, the notional possibility nevertheless remains that he mistakenly thought he possessed it. And, if in his mistaken belief he purported then to exercise the power, the error could have been corrected only by the Court hearing an appeal against his decision, in the event of such. I certainly cannot review the decision now. This does not mean, however, that the first question is irrelevant. The [62] answer to it has a bearing all the same on the second question, on the inherent likelihood or otherwise that BROOME J intended in fact to hold the estate liable.

Section 7 of the Divorce Act must therefore be examined straight away. It provides that:

'(1) A Court granting a decree of divorce may, in accordance with a written agreement between the parties, make an order with regard to . . . the payment of maintenance by the one party to the other.

(2) In the absence of an order made in terms of ss (1) . . . the Court may . . . make an order which the Court finds just in respect of the payment of maintenance by the one party to the other for any period until the death or remarriage of the party in whose favour the order is given, whichever event may first occur' . . .

The argument of the applicant's counsel was a simple one, based on a strictly literal interpretation of ss (2), and it went thus. Maintenance could be awarded for any period that lasted no longer than but ended with the death or remarriage of the party maintained, whichever occurred earlier. No other limitation was placed on the period. The death of the maintaining party was not, in particular, mentioned. Maintenance could accordingly be awarded for a period that outlasted the life of the maintaining party, provided of course that in the meantime the party maintained had neither died nor remarried . . .

Counsel's reading of the subsection made sense, to be sure, when the wording was viewed in isolation. But it overlooked a factor which gets the matter in perspective and puts another complexion on things, once account is taken of such. I allude to the common law lying in the background.

The gist of that, in the days when it alone counted, was the following. The duty of support which each spouse owed to the other, and consequently the liability for maintenance that depended on and gave effect to the duty, were incidents of their matrimonial relationship. The [63] termination of the relationship by either death or divorce left the duty with no remaining basis and brought it in turn to an end. Maintenance that was payable after a divorce could not therefore be claimed successfully or granted competently, unless an agreement providing for its payment had been concluded between the parties which placed the award on a contractual footing, one untouched by the dissolution of the marriage. Difficulties arose even then. In some Divisions, though not others, the Courts looked askance at such agreements, suspecting collusion on the question of fault which at the time had so much to do with the cause of action for divorce, or regarding promises to pay maintenance for its own sake as offences against public policy because they tended, it was thought, to encourage divorce. Strategies were required to avoid those snags, provisions for maintenance being linked with overall settlements of property and presented as part and parcel of them.

The situation was believed to be unsatisfactory. Section 10(1) of the Matrimonial Affairs Act 37 of 1953 remedied it, proclaiming that:

'The Court granting a divorce may, notwithstanding the dissolution of the marriage –

(a) make such order against the guilty spouse for the maintenance of the innocent spouse for any period until the death or until the remarriage of the innocent spouse, whichever event may first occur, as the Court may deem just; or

(b) make any agreement between the spouses for the maintenance of one of them an order of court . . .'

So from then onwards agreements for the payment of maintenance after divorce could be made orders of Court with no fuss or bother. And, in the absence of an agreement, the Court could compel the guilty party to pay it, whether he liked that or not.

A statutory exception was thus engrafted onto the rule of common law that the duty of support ended whenever the matrimonial relationship did. The exception concerned and affected, however, only those cases where the relationship was terminated by divorce. The rule continued to operate without qualification once death put paid to the relationship.

So much was demonstrated ten years later when *Glazer v Glazer NO* 1963 (4) SA 694 (A) got decided, the Court holding that a widowed spouse had no good claim for maintenance against the estate of the deceased one . . .

Section 10(1) of the Matrimonial Affairs Act was repealed after 16 further years by s 18 of the Divorce Act and replaced simultaneously by ss 7(1) and 7(2) of that statute, the respective and current counterparts of its paras (b) and (a). The later provisions diverged from the earlier in dropping the distinction drawn between guilt and innocence, one that served no purpose once fault had fallen away when it came to divorces, and in identifying a number of factors which were deemed to be relevant to [64] grants of maintenance. Otherwise, however, the scheme remains the same. Section 7(2) does not differ from s 10(1)(a), in particular, on the duration of the maintenance that may be ordered. Section 10(1)(a) also allowed such 'for any period until the death or . . . remarriage' of the party maintained. It too said nothing about the death of the maintaining party. Its meaning on the point in issue was exactly the one, we accordingly see, which s 7(2) now happens to bear.

Like the Matrimonial Affairs Act, the Divorce Act did not touch the common law's denial to widowed spouses of the right to receive maintenance from the estates of their deceased partners, a topic hardly on its agenda. Legislative intervention in that area took 11 more years to ensue. It occurred when the Maintenance of Surviving Spouses Act 27 of 1990 was duly passed, entitling widows and widowers in some circumstances to be so maintained.

That this was by no means the situation when either the Matrimonial Affairs Act or the Divorce Act went through Parliament has a strong bearing, I believe, on the interpretation of s 10(1)(a) of the former and s 7(2) of the latter. For it seems scarcely likely that Parliament intended to place divorced persons whose erstwhile spouses had died in a position much better than that occupied by widowed ones, giving them rights against the estates of people no longer married to them at the time of death which widowed spouses did not enjoy against the estates of those to whom they were then still married. Even fainter does the likelihood seem of its having had that in mind, yet chosen the wording which it used. Had it meant something so surprising, something so startling, it would surely have spelt out the meaning. It would hardly have left such to be conveyed by the sidewind of generally worded provisions which, while accommodating the idea linguistically, dealt with it obliquely and elliptically.

Do those provisions, the provisions of ss 10(1)(a) and 7(2), lend themselves to an alternative construction that avoids so incongruous a result? I think they do. The factors limiting the period for which maintenance might be awarded were not defined exhaustively, according to the interpretation that strikes me, so as to encompass every circumstance affecting its duration that was on the cards. Only the circumstances peculiar to the party maintained were mentioned, the circumstances of that party's remarriage and of that party's death. That the death of the maintaining party would likewise put an end to the maintenance was taken quite for granted. What Parliament therefore had in mind, when it spoke of any period until the death or remarriage of the party maintained, was any such period that happened to run during the lifetime of the maintaining party. And the qualification was implicit in what it actually said.

I do not consider it fanciful or unrealistic to impute to Parliament this train of thought. It knew something, one supposes after all, about the nature of the obligation to pay maintenance which arose by operation of law, as distinct from contractually. Such is not your ordinary sort of debt which, as a matter of course, passes to the debtor's estate on his death. It has been variously described as a 'debt *sui generis*', as 'not a debt' really, and as 'a special kind of obligation', the descriptions coming respectively from the judgments given by GREENFIELD J in *AF Philip & Co (Pvt) Ltd [65] and Others v Adie NO and Others* 1970 (4) SA 251 (R) (at 257G), by BRISTOWE J in *Tregoning v Tregoning* 1914 WLD 95 (at 96), and by GREENBERG JP in *R v Blundell* 1943 TPD 146 (at 150). The obligation is not discharged or reduced, for instance, by its set-off against a debt which the party maintained owes to the maintaining party, since the provision of maintenance is its specific and sole purpose. I refer here to the case of *Tregoning* (at 96), to *Schierhout v Union Government (Minister of Justice)* 1926 AD 286 (at 291), to *Williams v Carrick* 1938 TPD 147 (at 156), and to *Hodd v Hodd; D'Aubrey v D'Aubrey* 1942 NPD 198 (at 207). From those four cases we also learn that the corresponding right to receive maintenance cannot be ceded or otherwise alienated. Nor by the same token can the obligation be assigned or delegated. The reason is that, like the right, it has a character distinctly personal to the individual to whom it attaches, one that tells too against its transmission to the estate of anybody who dies bearing it. So do two further considerations. Maintenance is payable by and large from the income of the party paying it, and its rate is normally fixed in relation to that. But the income of most people consists mainly of what they earn by working, which stops as soon as they die. That is the first point. The second is the difficulty experienced in the administration of the estate if it has to meet the liability for maintenance. Money must then be put aside for that purpose, whether the fund is kept in the estate or, in order to obviate the indefinite delay in its winding up which the retention of such would involve, settled in advance on the person concerned under

some arrangement that gets reached. The calculation of the amount is guesswork, however, once contingencies like the person's death, remarriage and changing circumstances necessarily enter the reckoning. The same problems are encountered, it is true, whenever an estate finds itself having to maintain a child of the deceased or, in terms of a contract or will requiring it to do so, a divorced spouse. But children present a special and exceptional case, as we have seen already. And those whose contracts or wills enjoin their estates to pay maintenance seem likelier than not to have spared a thought and made provision for the way in which effect is given to their directions. That trouble came with some of the territory may not therefore have struck Parliament as a reason strong enough for spreading it elsewhere, let alone to the new area, and a vast one, of maintenance orders granted against people who were less attuned on the whole to the need for management in their affairs.

Something which I have not overlooked tends admittedly to militate against the interpretation that occurs to me. It is this. Parliament must have appreciated that the liability for maintenance could never survive the death of the party maintained, since so much at least went without saying. Yet it referred specifically to that event, not taking for granted the result which I have suggested it did by its silence on the death of the maintaining party. Perhaps, however, the difference in treatment is explained by the necessity it felt to cater for the other event mentioned which had to do with the party maintained, the one of remarriage. It may then have chosen simply to complete that side of the picture.

The applicant's counsel relied heavily on the decisions given in *Colly v Colly's Estate* 1946 WLD 83, *Owens v Stoffberg NO and Another* 1946 CPD [66] 226 and *Hughes NO v The Master and Another* 1960 (4) SA 936 (C). Each of those cases concerned an agreement for the payment of maintenance after divorce, which had been made an order of Court when the divorce was obtained. The estate of the maintaining party, who had died in the meantime, was held liable in each to continue paying. Two of the agreements had required the man to maintain the woman 'until her death or remarriage'. He had undertaken in the third to do so 'until her remarriage or death'. Such words were construed in each case to mean that, in spite of his earlier death, the obligation ran till she either died or remarried. In none was sufficient reason found for the implication that it lasted no longer than his lifetime. The judgments supplied weighty authority, counsel contended, for the proposition that the selfsame interpretation should now be placed on the comparable wording of the legislation. I disagree.

The field of contract is very different from the one where the present case lies. Everybody may bind his estate, by contract no less firmly than by will, to pay maintenance after his death. And he may settle the maintenance on whomsoever he chooses, on his current wife, a former wife, a mistress, an employee or anyone else. Whether in a given instance that result has been produced, whether the liability which was incurred survives the death of the person who assumed it and passes to his estate, depends of course on the terms of the contract, on their true meaning. And that goes too for the kind of contract in question, an agreement between spouses which is made an order of Court on their divorce. So, like the legislation whenever its meaning is sought, the agreement must be interpreted. By no means is the enquiry the same, however, since the objects of the exercise differ. The intention which has to be ascertained in the one case is that of Parliament, legislating in general terms and with general effect. In the other it is the intention of private individuals, minding their own business and dealing solely with that. They have no occasion to reckon with the common law. They have no reason to worry about issues of policy. Nor do they care a fig if the party who is maintained under their arrangements turns out to be better off than somebody else's widow. Then there is a further consideration, a rule governing contractual obligations which has no counterpart in the area of those generated statutorily.

The rule lays down that the estate of each party to a contract is liable when he dies to perform every obligation incurred by him in terms of it which he, if alive, would have had to fulfil. For he is deemed to have undertaken such on behalf of his estate as well as himself. The rule is subject to a couple of exceptions. It does not apply to any contract that provides otherwise, expressly or impliedly. Nor does it operate when the performance required was the sort appropriate to the deceased alone, a performance geared for instance to his personal skill or knowledge or to a relationship of personal confidence. The obligation is then extinguished by his death. That does not go, however, for the payment of maintenance. The party who bears the obligation may not normally rid himself of it or shift it to a third person. But nothing prevents him from performing the obligation, from effecting all payments, through the agency of another, his bank let us say. So the rule covers such a case, unless it falls within the first exception. It is therefore unhelpful, I believe, to compare the wording of [67] the legislation with that of the agreements examined in the three judgments cited. The differences between the settings are too pronounced, too important. How I would have construed agreements like those, had I been set the task, is a question which I neither need to nor shall discuss. It suffices for present purposes to state merely that, in my opinion, the cases are clearly distinguishable from the one we now have.

That this might well be thought so was said, however, not to matter. I had no option, counsel suggested, but to follow suit all the same in interpreting the legislation. The reason lay, he argued, in the endorsement which the construction that found favour on those occasions must be assumed to have received from Parliament when it legislated subsequently, echoing the words of the agreements. My attention was drawn in that regard to *Copelowitz v Copelowitz and Others NO* 1969 (4) SA 64 (C), a case bearing scant resemblance to this one. It revolved around an agreement that had been made an order of Court on the divorce of the parties to it, in terms of which the husband had promised to maintain the wife and committed his estate unequivocally to continue doing so after his death. Such having ensued, an order was sought against the estate for an increase in the maintenance which it had become liable to pay. VAN ZIJL J, who heard the application, considered much more than the narrow issue thus presented, surveying the whole area of maintenance and in the process casting his eye over the part of it that concerns me now. In a passage that discussed the Matrimonial Affairs Act, but s 10(1)(a) rather than s 10(1)(b) under which the maintenance happened to have been awarded, he said (at 69H–70A):

'The question now arises whether at the time of the trial . . . the Court can order the guilty spouse to pay maintenance after his . . . death. Section 10(1)(a) of the Act says that the Court may order the guilty spouse to pay maintenance for the innocent spouse "for any period until the death or until the remarriage of the innocent spouse, whichever event may first occur". Unless the period imposed by the Court is "for the lifetime of the guilty spouse", the question can always be posed whether such an order means that the guilty spouse must continue to pay maintenance after his death. Had it not been for the decisions in *Colly v Colly's Estate* . . . and *Owens v Stoffberg NO and Another* . . . I would without hesitation have held that an order in . . . the above terms came to an end on the death of the guilty spouse.'

He considered, however, that those decisions and their aftermath had altered the picture significantly. The reason he gave for thinking so (at 70H–71A) was this:

'The Legislature knew that the Courts had interpreted the words "until the death or remarriage" of the creditor spouse as binding the debtor spouse and his estate, and in these circumstances the question must be asked: did the Legislature not use the same words because it intended the same result? Though s 10(1)(a) makes a change in the substantive law of marriage, the change is stated in the form in which the Court's order shall be made. The change is stated in words which the draftsman appears to have borrowed from the practice, and to which the Courts have given a definite meaning. The inference is almost irresistible that the draftsman must have had both *Colly's* and *Owens'* cases before him, and that he used the same words because he intended the same result: to bind the guilty spouse's estate.'

His discussion of the point concluded on the following note (at 71H):

[68] 'Finally I must state that I am and have always been of opinion that both *Colly's* and *Owens'* cases were wrongly decided. An enquiry into this aspect is, however, as far as the intention of the Legislature is concerned, quite irrelevant. The question is not whether the cases were rightly or wrongly decided, but whether they were followed when s 10 of the Matrimonial Affairs Act was drafted.'

The inference that Parliament meant the legislation to be construed in accordance with the two decisions had been strengthened, counsel maintained, by its repetition in the Divorce Act of the same wording when it must have been well aware of the importance attached on the *Copelowitz* occasion to its choice of such the first time. Again, however, I find myself disagreeing.

The canon of construction which VAN ZIJL J had in mind, and counsel urged me to observe, is a familiar one both here and elsewhere. It has been expressed thus:

'(I)f an Act of Parliament uses the same language which was used in a former Act of Parliament referring to the same subject, and passed with the same purpose and for the same object, the safe and well-known rule of construction is to assume that the Legislature, when using well-known words upon which there have been well-known decisions, uses those words in the sense which the decisions have attached to them'...

A long line of cases in this country testifies to the acceptance of the principle by us too, the leading one being *Ex parte Minister of Justice; In re R v Bolon* 1941 AD 345 (at 359–60). What we notice, however, from the decisions on the point, English and South African alike, is this. The presumption harks back to the interpretation of an earlier statute. I was referred to no judgment other than the *Copelowitz* one, and despite a [69] thorough search I have managed to find none but that, in which the construction placed previously on a contract rather than a statute was thought suitable or sufficient for the purposes of the presumption. There are sound reasons, I believe furthermore, why the rule should not be extended in any such direction, when we come at all events to the present issue. They consist of the basic differences which I have noted already between the two enquiries, contractual and statutory. In that respect, I therefore consider, the *Copelowitz* judgment should not be followed.

Something else from which I beg to differ, I should add, was said then by VAN ZIJL J (at 71C–E). It went thus:

'If it were not the intention to bind the guilty spouse's estate we would have the extraordinary position that, when the Court in terms of s 10(1)(a) orders the guilty spouse to pay maintenance to the innocent spouse until the latter's death or remarriage, the obligation to pay maintenance terminates on the death of the guilty spouse, but that when the Court orders in terms of a consent paper that the guilty spouse shall pay maintenance until the death or remarriage of the innocent spouse, the obligation to pay maintenance continues after the death of the guilty spouse and terminates only on the death or remarriage of the innocent spouse.'

I do not, on the other hand, find it extraordinary that Parliament should have empowered the Courts to sanction agreements burdening estates with maintenance, yet balked at their foisting the liability on the estates of those who had never consented to the imposition.

The conclusion I accordingly reach is that s 7(2) of the Divorce Act does not empower the Court to grant an order for the payment of maintenance which survives the death of the maintaining party and binds his estate.

Perhaps, however, I am wrong in taking that definite view. If so, I feel, the problems are such that I can with safety go the length of regarding the existence of the power as highly doubtful at least. Experience shows, what is more, that the doubts are hardly mine alone. Since the Matrimonial Affairs Act was passed in 1953, after all, awards of maintenance running into hundreds of thousands must have been made throughout the land in the absence of agreement. Countless people on the paying side must have died by now. Yet I know of no single case of that kind in which the contention has previously been advanced that any of their estates happened to be liable. The lack of such for almost 40 years tells against a widespread belief in the transmissibility of the obligation. It suggests rather an assumption to the contrary which appears to have been pretty universal.

All this, to my mind, has a bearing on the next question I must answer, the one to which I now come, concerning the apparent intention of BROOME J when he ordered Hodges to pay the applicant maintenance. For, in those circumstances of uncertainty, I cannot conceive of the possibility that he felt confident about his power to hold the estate liable for it, that he decided in fact to hold the estate liable for it, without having required the point to be argued fully. Nor can I imagine for a moment his having meant that result when he contended himself with an order like the one he granted, one failing manifestly to express any such intention. He would surely have made his meaning clear, had anything of the sort been envisaged. I do not even believe that counsel who appeared in the divorce trial had any thought of seeking an order which bound the estate. Nobody [70] wanting a rder with that effect would have formulated the claim in the way he did. I find the inference to be inescapable that the liability of the estate was an idea which neither occurred to him nor entered the mind of BROOME J.

No attempt to gainsay that was made in argument. Instead, the applicant's counsel tried to persuade me that it was by the way. What mattered, so he suggested, was this. BROOME J had not limited the period during which the maintenance would be payable. He must therefore be taken to have meant it to endure for the maximum spell that was on the cards, whatever such happened to be. Otherwise he would have exercised his power not to the full, but partially. And nothing indicated an intention on his part to do that. It followed that, if he was empowered to award maintenance outlasting the life of Hodges, I must suppose him to have done no less. I see things differently. I shall assume, for the purposes of the argument, that he possessed the power in question. His possession of it did not mean, however, that its exercise by him was obligatory or ensued automatically. Indeed, he was not authorised to exercise it unless he had satisfied himself that an order binding the estate would meet the requirements of justice which were contemplated by s 7(2). And, before he could determine that, he needed to know how matters would probably stand once Hodges was dead. He had to know what the 'prospective means' of each side were likely then to be, as the subsection put it. He had virtually no evidence on the point. He was given no inkling, in particular, of the amount of income that would still be earned, in contrast with the part which would lapse. Without such information he was in no position to conclude that an award burdening the estate would be just. And I have no reason to think that he did.

In all the circumstances, I consider, it is quite fanciful to impute to BROOME J the intention of saddling the estate with the liability for maintenance which Hodges incurred.

The application, in my opinion, must therefore fail. It is dismissed . . .

Note

The answer to the question of whether a maintenance debtor's estate is liable for the maintenance of the spouse from whom the deceased maintenance debtor had been divorced depends on whether the maintenance order giving rise to the maintenance obligation was made in terms of section 7(1) or in terms of section 7(2) of the Divorce Act 70 of 1979. If the maintenance obligation derives from a settlement agreement which was incorporated into the divorce order in terms of section 7(1) of the Act, the wording of the agreement will determine whether the duty to maintain continues after the death of the maintenance debtor. If the agreement of settlement provides for continuation of the maintenance obligation after the death of the maintenance debtor the obligation clearly continues. And the obligation also continues where the agreement is silent, for a presumption in favour of continuation applies (Joubert 1980 *De Jure* 80 94–95). However, as was held in the case under discussion, where the duty to pay maintenance derives from an order made by the court in terms of section 7(2) of the Act the obligation to maintain his or her divorced spouse comes to an end when the maintenance debtor dies.

On *Hodges* see also De Jong 1992 *THRHR* 151.

Aantekening

Die antwoord op die vraag of 'n onderhoudspligtige se boedel aanspreeklik is vir die onderhoud van 'n persoon van wie die oorlede onderhoudspligtige geskei is, hang daarvan af of die onderhoudsbevel waaruit die onderhoudsplig voortspruit ingevolge artikel 7(1) of ingevolge artikel 7(2) van die Wet op Egskeiding 70 van 1979 uitgereik is. Indien die onderhoudsplig voortspruit uit 'n skikkingsakte wat ingevolge artikel 7(1) by die egskeidingsbevel ingelyf is, sal die bewoording van die akte bepaal of die onderhoudsplig bly voortduur na die dood van die onderhoudspligtige. Indien die skikkingsakte bepaal dat die onderhoudsplig na die dood van die onderhoudspligtige voortduur, bly dit vanselfsprekend voortbestaan. Die verpligting bly ook voortbestaan indien die akte swyg, aangesien daar 'n vermoede ten gunste van die voortbestaan van die verpligting geld (Joubert 1980 *De Jure* 80 94–95).

Uit die onderhawige saak blyk egter duidelik dat indien die onderhoudsplig voortspruit uit 'n hofbevel wat ingevolge artikel 7(2) van die Wet uitgereik is, kom die plig om onderhoud vir sy of haar geskeide gade te betaal by die dood van die onderhoudspligtige tot 'n einde.

Oor *Hodges* sien ook De Jong 1992 *THRHR* 151.

The interests of the children

The family advocate
Custody and access
Maintenance

Die belange van die kinders

Die gesinsadvokaat
Bewaring en toegang
Onderhoud

The family advocate   **Die gesinsadvokaat**

[137]   TERBLANCHE V TERBLANCHE

1992 1 SA 501 (W)

Applicability of the Mediation in Certain Divorce Matters Act 24 of 1987 where application for custody *pendente lite* is brought under Rule 43 of the Uniform Rules of Court

The wife (respondent in the present application) sued her husband for divorce and also claimed custody of the children born of the marriage. Her husband (applicant in the present application) responded with an application in terms of Rule 43 of the Uniform Rules of Court, claiming interim custody of the children subject to the respondent's reasonable right of access to them. The court referred the matter to the family advocate, and accepted the report of the family advocate in which it was recommended that the custody of the children should be awarded to the respondent *pendente lite*, subject to the applicant's right of reasonable access to them.

Toepaslikheid van die Wet op Bemiddeling in Sekere Egskeidingsaangeleenthede 24 van 1987 waar ingevolge Reël 43 van die Eenvormige Hofreëls aansoek gedoen word om bewaring *pendente lite*

Die vrou (respondent in die huidige aansoek) het haar man om 'n egskeiding gedagvaar en ook aansoek gedoen dat die bewaring van die kinders wat uit die huwelik gebore is aan haar toegeken word. Hierop het haar man (applikant in die huidige aansoek) geantwoord met 'n aansoek ingevolge Reël 43 van die Eenvormige Hofreëls waarin hy om tussentydse bewaring van die kinders aansoek gedoen het onderworpe aan die respondent se reg van redelike toegang. Die hof het die aangeleentheid na die gesinsadvokaat verwys en het die verslag van die gesinsadvokaat aanvaar waarin aanbeveel is dat die bewaring *pendente lite* van die kinders aan die respondent toegeken moes word onderworpe aan die applikant se reg van redelike toegang.

VAN ZYL J: [502] O'DONOVAN AJ [who heard the application in terms of Rule 43] referred the matter to the Family Advocate with the request that an enquiry be conducted and a report furnished in regard to the interim custody of the children. This referral runs counter to ... *Davids v Davids* [1991 4 SA 191 (W)] ... The learned Judge held in the [*Davids* case] that a Rule 43 application could not be referred to the Family Advocate in terms of s 4 of the Mediation in Certain Divorce Matters Act 24 of 1987. The *ratio* for this decision was, briefly, that the said section provides only that a Family Advocate may furnish a report and recommendations at the trial of a divorce action or at the hearing of an application for variation, rescission or suspension of an order relating to the custody or guardianship of, or access to, a child made in terms of the Divorce Act 70 of 1979. Since a Rule 43 application is neither a trial nor a hearing in this sense, the Family Advocate has no powers in regard thereto. Only a legislative amendment could bestow such powers on the Family Advocate ...

Despite the fact that, in the present matter, the applicant did not object to the referral thereof to the Family Advocate ... Mr *Prendini* has argued, on behalf of the applicant, that the decision of CLOETE AJ [in *Davids v Davids*] is binding on this Court and that the report and recommendations of the Family Advocate, which have been placed before me, should be ignored ...

After careful consideration of the Judge's reasons for his decisions [ie the decision of CLOETE AJ in *Davids v Davids* 1991 4 SA 191 (W)] I have, with respect, come to the conclusion that the judgment contains a number of serious misdirections and is clearly wrong, so that this Court is not bound by it. This conclusion is based on the following considerations.

It is true that s 4 of Act 24 of 1987 defines the powers and duties of the Family Advocate as relating to the trial of a divorce action or the hearing of an application for the variation, rescission or suspension of an order concerning the custody or guardianship of, or access to, a minor or dependent child. It would appear, however, that the learned Judge lost sight of the definition of 'divorce action' in s 1(1)(ii)(a) of the Divorce Act of 1979, namely that it includes

> '(a)n application *pendente lite* for an interdict or for the interim custody of, or access to, a minor child of the marriage concerned, or for the payment of maintenance'.

[503] This definition is expressly incorporated in s 1 of Act 24 of 1987, in which it is provided that any word or expression in such Act has the meaning attached thereto in the Divorce Act of 1979, unless the context in which it appears indicates otherwise. It follows that an interim application as envisaged in Rule 43 is included in the concept of 'divorce action' in s 4 of Act 24 of 1987, there being no indication that a different meaning should be attached to it.

Even if the said decision should bear the restricted meaning propounded by CLOETE AJ, the learned Judge failed to give due consideration to Rule 43(5) which provides, *inter alia*, that the Court may 'make such order as it thinks fit to ensure a just and expeditious decision'. The power of a Court to make such an order is unqualified and unrestricted, provided that it is directed at achieving 'a just and expeditious decision' on the facts and issues before it. If the Family Advocate is able to assist the Court in coming to such a decision a referral of the matter to the Family Advocate for enquiry, report and recommendation would be an eminently suitable and proper order to make in terms of Rule 43(5). Indeed, a failure to do so may, in the circumstances of the case in issue, be unwise and may even give rise to a result which is neither just nor expeditious. In this regard it should be borne in mind that the Family Advocate is invariably a qualified lawyer with sufficient experience and expertise to enable him or her to give the Court extremely valuable assistance in coming to a decision.

Furthermore, the Family Advocate has been introduced into the South African legal system with the primary purpose of identifying and establishing what is in the best interests of the child, or children, concerned. This appears from the preamble to Act 24 of 1987, where the aim of the Act is described as including the safeguarding of the interests of minor or dependent children. Section 4 of the Act likewise contains several references to the function and duty of the Family Advocate to enquire into, report on, and make recommendations regarding the welfare and interests of such children. The Family Advocate is particularly well equipped to perform such functions and duties, having at his or her disposal a whole battery of auxiliary services from all walks of life, including family counsellors appointed in terms of the Act and who are usually qualified social workers, clinical psychologists, psychiatrists, educational authorities, ministers of religion and any number of other persons who may be cognisant of the physical and spiritual needs or problems of the children and their parents or guardians, and who may be able to render assistance to the Family Advocate in weighing up and evaluating all relevant facts and circumstances pertaining to the welfare and interests of the children concerned ...

[504] Counsel informed me that they have accepted the Family Advocate's recommendation that interim custody of the children be awarded to the respondent, subject to certain

qualifications set out in a draft order prepared by them. I am satisfied that the said order makes adequate provision for the interim situation . . .

An order is made in terms of the draft order.

Note

It is submitted that the decision in the *Terblanche* case is correct.

Aantekening

Daar word aan die hand gedoen dat die beslissing in die *Terblanche*-saak korrek is.

[138]   VAN VUUREN V VAN VUUREN

1993 1 SA 163 (T)

Circumstances under which the family advocate ought to investigate the matter in terms of section 4(1) or (2) of the Mediation in Certain Divorce Matters Act 24 of 1987

Upon their divorce the parties entered into an agreement in terms of which, *inter alia*, the parties' children would spend certain weekends and school holidays with their father. The court had difficulties with the agreement, *inter alia* because of the father's alcohol problem, and postponed the case for a day. The next day the plaintiff requested that the case be postponed indefinitely and that the family advocate be ordered to investigate the matter. The court postponed the case and ordered the family advocate to investigate the matter of access to the children and of who should have custody of the children.

Omstandighede waaronder die gesins-advokaat die aangeleentheid kragtens artikel 4(1) of (2) van die Wet op Bemiddeling in Sekere Egskeidings-aangeleenthede 24 van 1987 behoort te ondersoek

Ten tyde van hulle egskeiding het die partye 'n ooreenkoms aangegaan waarin daar onder andere ooreengekom is dat die partye se kinders sekere naweke en skoolvakansies by hulle vader sou deurbring. Die hof het probleme met die skikkingsakte ondervind, onder andere vanweë die vader se alkoholprobleem, en het die saak vir 'n dag uitgestel. Die volgende dag het die eiseres gevra dat die saak onbepaald uitgestel word en dat die gesinsadvokaat beveel word om die aangeleentheid te ondersoek. Die hof het die saak uitgestel en die gesinsadvokaat beveel om die aangeleentheid rakende toegang tot die kinders asook wie bewaring van die kinders moet hê, te ondersoek.

DE VILLIERS R: [165] 'n Verteenwoordiger van die Gesinsadvokaat het op die skik-kingsakte geskryf 'Kennis geneem', maar daar is ongelukkig versuim om die bewerings in para 6.2 van eiseres se besonderhede van eis of die inligting wat ingevolge die regulasies aan die Gesinsadvokaat voorsien is in ag te neem.

In gemelde paragraaf van die besonderhede van eis word, onder andere, gemeld dat verweerder sterk alkoholiese drank in oormaat neem en dat die verweerder die eiseres by verskeie geleenthede ernstig aangerand het.

In die vorm wat eiseres ingevolge reg 2 van die betrokke regulasies aan die Gesinsadvokaat voorsien het, word die volgende vermeld:

'Daar word gevra dat respondent huidiglik die reg van redelike toegang kry in teenwoordigheid van die applikant gesien in die lig van die respondent se ernstige drankprobleem.'

Daar is egter nie in die bedes van die besonderhede van eis gevra dat die verweerder se toegang tot die kinders op grond van sy oormatige gebruik van drank in enige opsig beperk behoort te word nie. Gesien eiseres se bewerings in gemelde vorm behoort so 'n beperking, myns insiens, aangevra te gewees het. Geen getuienis is voor my geplaas om aan te dui waarom die eiseres so drasties haar mening verander het dat sy nou selfs bereid is dat die kinders vir naweke en vakansies na verweerder gaan nie.

Daar is ook geen brief op die lêer waarin die Gesinsadvokaat die eiseres se prokureurs waarsku om in hierdie verband 'n toepaslike wysiging van die bedes van haar besonderhede van vordering aan te bring nie. Sulke briewe word, myns insiens tereg, gewoonlik in sulke gevalle deur die Gesinsadvokaat aan die eiseres se prokureurs geskryf na aanleiding van die inhoud van die besonderhede van vordering.

[166] Dit is heilsame praktyk omdat die eiseres se regsverteenwoordigers daarop kan reageer, indien hulle meen dat die feite dit regverdig, deur 'n toepaslike bede in verband met toegang deur die verweerder aan te bring.

Terloops kan ek daarop wys dat partye en hulle regsverteenwoordigers, na my oordeel, heeltemal te min gebruik maak van die bevoegdheid wat art 4(1) van die Wet op Bemiddeling in Sekere Egskeidingsaangeleenthede 24 van 1987 aan hulle verleen, om die Gesinsadvokaat na aanvang van huwelikslitigasie te vra om ondersoek in te stel en 'n verslag uit te bring oor aangeleenthede rakende die welsyn van kinders.

Indien dit in die onderhawige geval na instel van die aksie gedoen is, sou so 'n verslag waarskynlik al lankal gereed gewees het en sou die partye en hul regsverteenwoordigers dit tydens hulle skikkingsonderhandelinge in ag kon geneem het om te sorg dat die skikkingsakte in ooreenstemming is met die belange van die kinders.

Die vorms van die Gesinsadvokaat maak voorsiening dat die eiser (applikant) kan vra dat die Gesinsadvokaat ingevolge art 4(1) van die Wet ondersoek instel na enige bepaalde aangeleentheid rakende die welsyn van die betrokke kinders. Dit is ook meermale in belang van die kinders dat aangeleenthede wat hulle welsyn raak so spoedig moontlik deur die Gesinsadvokaat ondersoek behoort te word.

Waar die partye tot 'n huweliksgeding nie self die Gesinsadvokaat vra om 'n aangeleentheid te ondersoek nie, kan die Gesinsadvokaat ingevolge art 4(2) van die Wet die Hof vra om magtiging om so 'n ondersoek in te stel. Dit word in baie gevalle gedoen.

Ek meen dat die Gesinsadvokaat dit ook in die onderhawige geval behoort te gedoen het. Soos aangedui, het dit uit eiseres se vorm ingevolge reg 2 en eiseres se besonderhede van vordering geblyk dat hier ernstige probleme ten opsigte van toegang sou bestaan.

Vir leiding van die Gesinsadvokaat in hierdie verband kan enkele ander gevalle vermeld word waar die Hof, na my oordeel, genader behoort te word vir 'n bevel ingevolge gemelde art 4(2):

(a)   waar dit blyk dat daar 'n voorneme is om jong kinders nie onder die beheer en toesig van hulle moeder te plaas nie;

(b)   waar daar 'n voorneme is om kinders van mekaar te skei deur beheer en toesig van, sê, een van die kinders aan een ouer en die ander aan 'n ander ouer toe te wys;

(c)   waar daar 'n voorneme is dat die beheer en toesig van 'n kind aan iemand anders as sy ouers toegewys word;

(*d*) waar daar 'n voorneme is om 'n reëling te tref ten opsigte van beheer en toesig of toegang wat *prima facie* nie in belang van die kind is nie.

Natuurlik moet die Hof nog steeds in elke geval wat ingevolge art 4(2) voor hom geplaas word, beoordeel of 'n ondersoek gemagtig behoort te word.

Ek wil hier byvoeg dat die Gesinsadvokaat se verslae, oor die algemeen, van besonder groot hulp is omdat die ondersoeke waarop die verslag gebaseer word, en die verslae self, deeglik deur onafhanklike en goed gekwalifiseerde persone gedoen word. In huweliks- gedinge waar daar [167] dikwels hewige feitegeskille is, is sulke onafhanklike inligting en menings klaarblyklik van groot hulp.

Natuurlik moet die Gesinsadvokaat se verslag, en die ondersoeke waarop dit gebaseer is, nog steeds met 'n kritiese oog deur die Hof evalueer word.

Die verslag en aanbevelings van die Gesinsadvokaat stel ook dikwels die Hof in staat om te beoordeel of 'n skikkingsooreenkoms wat die partye aangegaan het in belang van die kinders is, al dan nie.

Dit is welbekend dat, omdat so 'n skikking ook finansiële geskille tussen die partye bylê, die een party soms onbehoorlike druk op die ander party te pas mag bring om toegewings ten opsigte van of die beheer en toesig oor die kinders, of sy toegang tot die kinders, te maak.

Veral tydens die huidige swak finansiële toestand, is dit ongelukkig 'n sterk versoeking, veral by 'n party wat geldelik in 'n swakker posisie staan as die ander eggenoot, om toegewings ten opsigte van die kinders te maak as teenprestasie vir 'n gunstige skikking van finansiële aangeleenthede. Die partye se regsverteenwoordigers behoort hiervoor op hulle hoede te wees en hulle nie leen tot sulke wanpraktyke nie. Hulle plig as amptenare van die Hof is om in die eerste plek om te sien na die belange van die kinders.

In die onderhawige geval, blyk dit uit eiseres se getuienis dat sy glad nie gelukkig is met die bepalings in die skikkingsakte dat die kinders vir naweke en vakansies na die ver- weerder gaan nie. Waarom haar regsverteenwoordigers onder hierdie omstandighede haar adviseer het om toe te stem tot die reëlings oor toegang is vir my duister. Ek sal egter in hulle guns aanneem dat dit *bona fide* geskied het in 'n poging om die saak geskik te kry. Dit kom my egter voor dat die belange van die kinders nie eerste gestel is nie. Juis daarom is dit wenslik dat die Gesinsadvokaat nagaan of die toegangsreëlings vervat in die skikkingsakte in belang van die kinders is al dan nie.

Indien daar in die onderhawige geval, na beskikbaarstelling van die verslag, 'n geskil oor die beheer en toesig van die kinders of die toegang van die verweerder sou ontstaan, sou die verweerder natuurlik die geleentheid gegee moet word om die saak te verdedig, indien dit nie onderling ooreengekom sou word nie.

Note

This case is important, firstly, because it contains guidelines about when a family advocate ought to report about the arrangements regarding the children.

Secondly, the warning to legal representatives to guard against concessions being made in respect of the children by the financially weaker party in order to get a financially improved settlement should be noted.

Aantekening

Eerstens is hierdie saak van belang omdat dit riglyne bevat omtrent wanneer 'n gesinsadvokaat die reëlings in verband met die kinders behoort te ondersoek.

Tweedens moet gelet word op die waarskuwing aan regsverteenwoordigers om te waak daarteen dat die finansieel swakkere partye toegewings maak ten opsigte van die kinders as teenprestasie vir 'n gunstiger finansiële skikking.

Finally, the court's comments in respect of the family advocate should be noted. Even though the family advocate in the case under discussion neglected to investigate the matter when an investigation was necessary, the judge was nevertheless generally positive about the family advocate and the manner in which the family advocate fulfils his or her role. In *Whitehead v Whitehead* 1993 3 SA 72 (SE) BURGER AJ was critical of the family advocate who appeared in the particular case. The judge said that he was disappointed with the attitude of the family advocate and her adviser because they had made an unbalanced recommendation and created the impression that they had taken a decision and that they wanted to prescribe to the court. BURGER AJ emphasised that the function of the family advocate is to assist the court by placing facts and considerations before it.

Laastens moet gelet word op die hof se opmerkings ten opsigte van die gesinsadvokaat. Alhoewel die gesinsadvokaat in die saak onder bespreking versuim het om 'n ondersoek in te stel terwyl sodanige ondersoek nodig was, was die regter nietemin oor die algemeen positief oor die gesinsadvokaat en die wyse waarop die gesinsadvokaat sy of haar rol vervul. In *Whitehead v Whitehead* 1993 3 SA 72 (SOK) was BURGER Wn R krities oor die gesinsadvokaat wat in die betrokke saak opgetree het. Die regter het gesê dat hy teleurgesteld was met haar en haar raadgewer se houding omdat hulle 'n ongebalanseerde aanbeveling gemaak het en die indruk geskep het dat hulle 'n besluit geneem het en aan die hof wou voorskryf. BURGER Wn R het beklemtoon dat die gesinsadvokaat se funksie is om die hof behulpsaam te wees deur feite en oorwegings voor die hof te lê.

Custody and access   **Bewaring en toegang**

[139]   FRENCH V FRENCH

1971 4 SA 298 (W)

Tests to be applied in determining what is in the best interests of a child when a custody order is varied

When the parties were divorced custody of their minor child, Dominique, was awarded to the father. A few years later the mother applied to the court for an order awarding custody of the child to her. The order was granted.

Toetse wat aangewend moet word om te bepaal wat in die beste belang van 'n kind is wanneer 'n bewaringsbevel gewysig word

Toe die partye geskei is, is bewaring van hulle minderjarige kind, Dominique, aan die vader toegeken. 'n Paar jaar later het die moeder by die hof aansoek gedoen dat bewaring van die kind aan haar toegeken word. Die bevel is toegestaan.

FS STEYN J: [298] Before drawing any conclusions from the available evidence, I wish to indicate the principles which in my view bear on the question, what would be in the child's best interests.

In respect of a young child its sense of security should be preserved and protected above all. The child must feel that it is welcome, wanted and loved. This is the principle underlying the decisions that children should not be uprooted excepting for sound reasons, and in this connection I refer to the tenor of the judgment in *Cook v Cook*, 1937 AD [299] 154, and specially at pp 161 and 162, and to the matter of *Fletcher v Fletcher*, 1948 (1) SA 130 (AD), and especially at pp 137 and 146.

This principle that the sense of security of a child should be preserved, was applied when deciding the rights of access of a mother in the matter of *Myers v Leviton*, 1949 (1) SA 203 (T), where MR JUSTICE PRICE stated at p 214:

> "There is no person whose presence and natural affection can give a child the sense of security and comfort that a child derives from his own mother – an important factor in the normal psychological development of a healthy child."

The same principle is the basis of the strong tendency to prefer the mother's rights of custody as was decided in *Fortune v Fortune* 1955 (3) SA 348 (AD), and which was applied in *Tromp v Tromp* 1956 (4) SA 738 (N), where I wish to quote from p 746 where the learned JUDGE HENOCHSBERG, said:

> "In the light of the foregoing, as it was conceded that appellant was entitled to day to day custody of the children and as the parties are living apart, the interests of the children will, in general, on that concession be best served by their being left with their mother, unless factors are averred which outweigh the consideration of benefit arising from the companionship, care and ability to satisfy the day to day needs which a mother is able to give to young daughters of that age."

After applying the primary test how the sense of security of a child will be best preserved, the suitability of the proposed custodian parent is to be tested by enquiring into his or her character – that is laid down in *Fletcher v Fletcher*, and I refer again to pp 146 and 147 of this matter – and by enquiring into the religion and language in which the children are to be brought up. These are factors to be considered and were referred to in *Tromp v Tromp* above and in the matter of *Hassan v Hassan* 1955 (4) SA 388 (D), and generally the fitness of the proposed custodian to guide the moral, cultural and religious development of the child, as was summarised in *Kallie v Kallie* 1947 (2) SA 1207 (SR), and referred to at p 1208. Certain disqualifications relating to the exercise of custody must thereafter be considered. A custodian parent likely to frustrate the access of the other parent, will be viewed with a measure of disfavour, as was indicated in the old decision of *Mitchell v Mitchell* 1904 TS 128, and I refer to p 132.

Even when the suitability of the proposed custodian parent is settled and the psychological security of the child is ensured, material considerations relating to the child's well-being will also be considered. That was introduced in *Katzenellenbogen v Katzenellenbogen and Joseph* 1947 (2) SA 528 (W), and in *Goodrich v Botha* 1954 (2) SA 540 (AD).

Finally the wishes of the child will be taken into account – with young children as a constituent element in the enquiry where they will attain a sense of security, and with more mature children a well informed judgment, albeit a very subjective judgment, of what the best interests of the child really demand.

Judging from the history of this case and the evidence of Drs Apter and Jeppe, the evidence of Mrs French, and even the evidence of the defendant, as well as the statements of Dominique to me, I have no doubt that Dominique can only attain some sense of security after years of an emotionally divided life, torn by conflict, by being [300] placed in the custody of her mother, under actual day to day physical care and control of her mother . . .

Note

The test in determining any matter involving the custody of or access to a child is the best interests of the child. What would be in the best interests of a particular child in a particular case would depend on the circumstances of that case. It is

Aantekening

Die toets in enige aangeleentheid rakende die bewaring van of toegang tot 'n kind is die beste belang van die kind. Wat in 'n besondere geval in die beste belang van 'n besondere kind sal wees, sal afhang van die omstandighede van daardie

impossible to give a list of all the factors which must be considered when the court has to decide on the best interests of a child. The case under discussion lists some of the most important factors which are to be taken into account. They include the preservation and protection of the child's sense of security (that is, in effect, the retention of the *status quo*), the fitness of the person in whose custody the child is to be placed or who is to have access to the child, the material welfare of the child and the child's wishes.

That the wishes of the child should be considered once the child is of a suitable age is a principle which is widely accepted. In *Greenshields v Wyllie* 1989 4 SA 898 (W), however, FLEMMING J declined to give much weight to the views of children aged twelve and fourteen. His reasons for doing so were that "[c]hildren come into storms, they come into upheavals" and that "the Courts know that children grow up, that their perspectives change, that their needs change" (899).

saak. Dit is onmoontlik om 'n lys te gee van al die faktore wat oorweeg moet word wanneer 'n hof oor die beste belang van 'n kind moet besluit. Die saak onder bespreking bevat 'n aantal van die belangrikste faktore wat in ag geneem moet word. Hulle sluit in die handhawing en beskerming van die kind se gevoel van sekuriteit (dit beteken maar eintlik die handhawing van die *status quo*), die geskiktheid van die persoon in wie se bewaring die kind geplaas staan te word of wat toegang tot die kind wil hê, die finansiële welvaart van die kind, en die kind se wense.

Dat die wense van die kind in ag geneem moet word sodra die kind 'n gepaste ouderdom bereik het, is 'n beginsel wat algemeen aanvaar word. In *Greenshields v Wyllie* 1989 4 SA 898 (W), het FLEMMING R egter nie veel gewig geheg aan die standpunte van kinders van twaalf en veertien nie. Sy redes was dat "[c]hildren come into storms, they come into upheavals" en dat "the Courts know that children grow up, that their perspectives change, that their needs change" (899).

[140]   KASTAN V KASTAN

1985 3 SA 235 (C)

Joint custody of children

At the time of their divorce the parents of three young children applied to have a consent paper, in terms of which they agreed to exercise joint custody over their children, incorporated in the court's divorce order. The parents did not agree as to who would be the custodian of the children should joint custody not be allowed. The court granted the application.

Gesamentlike bewaring van kinders

Ten tyde van hulle egskeiding het die ouers van drie jong kinders aansoek gedoen dat 'n skikkingsooreenkoms, waarin hulle ooreengekom het om die bewaring van hulle kinders gesamentlik uit te oefen, deur die hof by die egskeidingsbevel geïnkorporeer word. Die ouers het nie ooreengekom oor wie die bewaring van die kinders sou hê as gesamentlike bewaring nie toegestaan sou word nie. Die hof het die aansoek toegestaan.

KING AJ: [236] Section 6(3) of the Divorce Act 70 of 1979 is very wide in its terms and certainly allows for an order of this nature. Its very wideness seems to me to be a recognition by the Legislature that pre-eminently matters involving the regulation of the lives of young children should be left to the discretion of the Court as upper guardian and that that discretion should, as far as possible, be free and unfettered. It is a discretion which must be exercised within the framework of one guiding rule. It must be exercised so as best to promote the welfare and advance and protect the interests of young children.

Orders for joint custody are rare. Such few examples as can be gleaned from the law reports would seem to point emphatically in a direction away from orders of this nature and the reason for this, I would think is clear. Custody of children involves day to day decisions and also decisions of longer and more permanent duration involving their education, training, religious upbringing, freedom of association and generally the determination of how best to ensure their good health, welfare and happiness. To leave decisions of this nature to the joint decision of parents who are no longer husband and wife could be courting disaster, particularly where the divorce has been preceded by acrimony and disharmony between the parents. It is because of my concern at these inherent risks that I requested counsel to place some evidence before me ...

[KING AJ then referred to the evidence of two expert witnesses and proceeded:]

Both these gentlemen are persuaded that in the particular circumstances of this case it will be in the best interests of the children for an order in the terms as set out in the agreement to be made by the Court.

The factors which have influenced them in arriving at this conclusion and which influence me in my decision to accept their recommendation may briefly be stated as follows: Both the parties are experienced and competent parents. All three of the children are equally bonded to both their parents. They love their parents very much. Both parents reciprocate this love. The children, young as they are, have expressed their satisfaction with and approval of this arrangement. It has removed from their young minds and hearts the fear that they would lose a parent. Both parents are willing to accept this arrangement and what, of course, is more important, are determined to make it work because they both recognise that it is in their children's interest. In the almost six months [237] since the divorce the parties have established a far better relationship between themselves. The animosities which had previously existed and which the pending litigation had exacerbated have largely subsided. The parties are conciliatory and compromising towards each other. In fact, over the period since the divorce the children have experienced a relationship vis-à-vis their parents not essentially dissimilar to what is now envisaged and it has proved beneficial to them.

The alternative to an acceptance of the proposed arrangement is protracted litigation which can only have a destructive and polarising effect on the parties with a correspondingly adverse effect on the children.

The prognosis is good, according to the experts. They have told me that this sort of arrangement is being resorted to with greater frequency overseas, more particularly in the United States of America and the United Kingdom, with marked success and that joint custody of children is more and more being regarded by experts in the field as a means of ensuring the continued relationship of both parents with their children.

In all the circumstances I am satisfied that in this particular case it is in the interests of these children that I should make an order in terms of the consent paper and I do so.

Note

This is the first reported South African case in which joint custody of their children was awarded to divorced parents. The decision is welcomed heartily but it cannot be denied that the awarding of joint custody is fraught with dangers. Therefore an order for joint custody should only be made in exceptional circumstances. See further Spiro 1981 THRHR 163; Joubert 1986 De Jure 353;

Aantekening

Hierdie is die eerste gerapporteerde Suid-Afrikaanse saak waarin gesamentlike bewaring van hulle kinders aan geskeide ouers toegeken is. Die beslissing word van harte verwelkom maar daar kan nie ontken word nie dat die verlening van gesamentlike bewaring met baie probleme gepaard gaan. Sodanige bevel behoort dus net in buitengewone omstandighede toegestaan te word.

Schäfer 1987 *SALJ* 149. See also *Schlebusch v Schlebusch* [141] and *Venton v Venton* [142].

Sien verder Spiro 1981 *THRHR* 163; Joubert 1986 *De Jure* 353; Schäfer 1987 *SALJ* 149. Sien ook *Schlebusch v Schlebusch* [141] en *Venton v Venton* [142].

[141]   SCHLEBUSCH V SCHLEBUSCH

1988 4 SA 548 (E)

Joint custody of children

The plaintiff (father), in an undefended divorce action, applied to have a consent paper which provided, *inter alia*, for joint custody over the spouses' children, incorporated into the divorce order. The consent paper further provided that if the court should refuse an order for joint custody, custody should go to the plaintiff. The spouses had four minor children, ranging from thirteen to twenty years of age. The eldest child was at the Technikon in Bloemfontein while the other children were all at school in Lady Grey. The spouses agreed that the children would reside with the plaintiff. The plaintiff was a farmer who lived ten kilometres outside Lady Grey. The defendant was a nursing sister who lived in Lady Grey but spent every alternate week in Zastron (which was some eighty kilometres away). The children saw their mother regularly during the weeks when she was not in Zastron. The plaintiff and the defendant had parted about three months before the court case was heard but, according to the plaintiff, they were not on bad terms with each other. On being questioned on the matter the plaintiff stated that, if there was a dispute regarding the children, his decision would prevail. The court refused the application for joint custody.

Gesamentlike bewaring van kinders

Die eiser (vader) het in 'n onbestrede egskeidingsgeding gevra dat 'n 'n skikkingsooreenkoms, wat onder andere vir gesamentlike bewaring van die gades se kinders voorsiening gemaak het, by die egskeidingsbevel geïnkorporeer word. Die skikkingsooreenkoms het verder bepaal dat die eiser bewaring van die kinders sou hê indien die hof sou weier om gesamentlike bewaring toe te ken. Die gades het ooreengekom dat die kinders by die eiser sou inwoon. Die gades het vier minderjarige kinders gehad waarvan die ouderdom tussen dertien en twintig jaar gewissel het. Die oudste kind het in Bloemfontein aan die Technikon gestudeer terwyl die ander kinders almal in Lady Grey op skool was. Die eiser het tien kilometer buite Lady Grey geboer. Die verweerderes was 'n verpleegster wat in Lady Grey gewoon het maar elke tweede week in Zastron (wat omtrent tagtig kilometer ver was) deurgebring het. Die kinders het hulle moeder gereeld gesien in die tye wat sy nie op Zastron was nie. Die eiser en verweerderes het mekaar omtrent drie maande voor die aanhoor van die hofsaak verlaat maar volgens die eiser was hulle nie kwaaivriende nie. Toe hy daaroor uitgevra is, het die eiser gesê dat sy besluit deurslaggewend sou wees indien daar enige dispuut met betrekking tot die kinders sou ontstaan. Die hof het die aansoek om gesamentlike bewaring van die hand gewys.

MULLINS J: [549] It is, I think, clear that as a general rule, Courts in South Africa have not in the past been in favour of making joint custody orders. As stated by Hahlo in *The South African Law of Husband and Wife* 5th ed at 392:

'There is nothing to preclude the Court in a proper case from awarding joint custody of the minor to its parents, though in practice, it is rarely, if ever, done in South Africa.'

In *Heimann v Heimann* 1948 (4) SA 926 (W), MURRAY J stated that it was desirable that there should be one parent directly responsible for the child, and he accordingly refused to make an order for joint custody.

[550] The traditional viewpoint in regard to the placing of children in the custody of a single parent or individual was expressed in *Whitely v Leyshon* 1957 (1) PH B9 (D), where it was held by JAMES J that:

'In cases of this sort, as in all cases in which the welfare of a child was in issue, the factor which most predominantly concerned the Court was the true interests of the child. It was in the shadow of this great principle that questions such as the rights of a custodian parent to direct the day to day life of a child and the rights of non-custodian parents to reasonable access must be considered. The rule that gave the custodian parent the right to direct the whole life of the child and deal with such matters as his education, health and associations was merely an off-shoot from the principle that the Court was concerned primarily with the true interests of the child, it being recognised that it was in the child's interests that it should know that there was one definite person who in the last instance controlled it and who made not only the long range decisions concerning its future, but also the day to day decisions relating to its food, clothes, conduct and friends. It was because of this that the Courts had always been loath to put the non-custodian parent in a position where he could dispute or undermine the authority of the custodian parent; for a child must know where he stood.'

While not dealing specifically with joint custody, the merits of a situation where a single parent is entrusted with the rights and powers envisaged by the concept of custody in our law are set out in detail in *Marais v Marais* 1960 (1) SA 844 (C). See also Hahlo (*op cit* at 402).

In *Edwards v Edwards* 1960 (2) SA 523 (D), JANSEN J was even more emphatic (at 524 F) that 'it is plain that an agreement of this nature should not be made an order of Court'. He expressed the view that it was a 'legal impossibility that the legal custody of a child could be shared equally between two individuals'. I assume the learned Judge was there referring to two individuals who were not married to each other. In that case a joint custody order had been made at the time that the parents were divorced. Some three years later a dispute arose as to which school the child should attend. JANSEN J was no doubt influenced in his strong condemnation of the granting of joint custody by the fact that one of the very dangers inherent in such an order, namely a dispute as to a vital decision concerning the child's welfare, had in fact arisen. Such a situation would be unlikely to arise where it depended on a single, rather than a joint decision.

Despite the weight of the aforementioned authorities, the concept of joint custody is by no means dead. Issues such as this thrive in the modern nutrient of a social change, sexual equality and the rapid spread of influences from overseas countries, especially through academic channels. The overseas influence was mentioned by KING AJ in *Kastan v Kastan* 1985 (3) SA 235 (C) [140], in which case, after hearing evidence of a psychiatrist and of a clinical psychologist, he made an order for joint custody. Without suggesting that the learned Judge in that case took the easy way out, it is nevertheless significant that the parties had not agreed (as in the instant case) on who should be the custodian parent if a joint custody order were refused. The Court appears (at 237B) to have viewed with dismay the fact that:

> 'The alternative to an acceptance of the proposed arrangement is protracted litigation which can only have a destructive and polarising effect on the parties with a correspondingly adverse effect on the children.'

[551] I emphasise that in the present case I too do not take the easy way out of awarding the custody to plaintiff merely because the parties have provided me with that alternative in their consent paper . . .

Apart from the fact that *Kastan's* case is apparently the first reported judgment in which reasons for awarding joint custody are given, I do not regard it as in any way a departure from existing principles. KING AJ in fact emphasises that such orders are rare, and recognised the inherent risks in such an order, in the following passage (at 236D–F):

> 'Orders for joint custody are rare. Such few examples as can be gleaned from the law reports would seem to point emphatically in a direction away from orders of this nature and the reason for this, I would think, is clear. Custody of children involves day to day decisions and also decisions of longer and more permanent duration involving their education, training, religious upbringing, freedom of association and generally the determination of how best to ensure their good health, welfare and happiness. To leave decisions of this nature to the joint decision of parents who are no longer husband and wife could be courting disaster, particularly where the divorce has been preceded by acrimony and disharmony between the parents.' . . .

[I]t was at the learned Judge's request that . . . expert evidence . . . was placed before the Court, and which was to the effect that it would be in the interests of the children to grant an order of joint custody.

This is a far cry from suggesting that this is a decision which in any way marks a departure from existing principles, or is a stepping stone to the granting in the future of joint custody at the mere request of the parties. The law must of course recognise new and sometimes radical social and sociological trends and changes in our complicated modern society. There are constant changes in various aspects of law as affecting the family, in which many facets of social, economic and technological development play a part. Cf *Marais's* case *supra* at 847H–848A.

Nevertheless the interests of the child still remain paramount in deciding questions of custody after divorce. Judges claim no expert knowledge which excludes the possibility of a wrong decision in determining custody issues. Furthermore, the views of the parents themselves and the children must be given due weight. However, at the risk of being labelled a legal traditionalist (see Professor *Schäfer's* article [1987 *SALJ* 149] at 154), I view with concern any trend towards the granting of joint custody orders.

While there may in rare cases be a continuing situation where joint decision-making is possible and where the children continue, even years after a divorce, to regard their parents with equal affection and loyalty, such a Utopian state of affairs rarely in practice exists. While 'parents are [552] forever' (to use Professor *Schäfer's* phrase) in a purely biological sense, I cannot agree that the awarding of joint custody will, or is even likely to, ensure 'a continuing relationship between the child and both its parents, so that it need not feel deserted, abandoned or rejected by the absent (*sic*) parent'.

After all, modern children are also aware of the consequences of divorce. It no longer carries the social stigma of earlier generations, and is often welcomed by children as affording relief from unendurable tension and domestic strife. Any sensible child today, even while retaining undiminished affection and loyalty for both parents, would appreciate that their divorce necessarily involves change in domestic control and discipline. If after divorce disputes arise as to matters such as maintenance, access and control, a joint custody order is not likely to avoid such a situation, as occurred in *Edward's* case *supra*.

Nor do I agree with the other 'obvious additional advantages' of a joint custody order. It does not seem to me that such an order will reduce or eliminate the kidnapping of children or improve parental co-operation. In fact, a joint custody order is more likely to encourage a tug-of-war between the parents if, as so frequently happens, one or both the parents remarry or if one moves to another town. It is the attitude of the parents that will achieve the most beneficial relationship between both parents and the child, not the form of the Court's order . . .

In the light of the views I have expressed above, this evidence is insufficient to satisfy me that I should accede to the request for joint custody. The interests of the children clearly require that they remain with the plaintiff, and their relationship with their mother need in no way be disturbed by awarding their custody to the plaintiff. I am not prepared to make paras 1 and 2 of the consent paper an order of Court . . .

Note

It is evident from the decision in this case that although the awarding of joint custody is not ruled out altogether, it will not be granted lightly by the courts. See also *Pinion v Pinion* 1994 2 SA 725 (D) where the court refused to grant an order for joint custody even though the relationship between the parents was good.

On *Schlebusch v Schlebusch* see further Schoeman 1989 *THRHR* 462. See also *Kastan v Kastan* [140] and *Venton v Venton* [142].

Aantekening

Dit is uit die beslissing in hierdie saak duidelik dat alhoewel die verlening van gesamentlike bewaring nie geheel en al uitgesluit is nie, die howe dit nie ligtelik sal toestaan nie. Sien ook *Pinion v Pinion* 1994 2 SA 725 (D) waar die hof geweier het om gesamentlike bewaring te gelas selfs al was die verhouding tussen die ouers goed.

Oor *Schlebusch v Schlebusch* sien verder Schoeman 1989 *THRHR* 462. Sien ook *Kastan v Kastan* [140] en *Venton v Venton* [142].

[142]   VENTON V VENTON

1993 1 SA 763 (D)

Joint custody of children

In divorce proceedings between the parties the father was the plaintiff. The parties wished to apply for an order for joint custody of their two small boys but as they were advised that joint custody orders had never been made in Natal, the father claimed that custody of the children should be awarded to him alone. The judge stated that the advice which the parties had received was wrong but that it explained why they had not applied for joint custody. Both parents were sensible and responsible people, the relationship between them was an exceptionally good

Gesamentlike bewaring van kinders

In 'n egskeidingsgeding tussen die partye was die vader die eiser. Die partye wou aansoek doen dat die bewaring van hulle twee klein seuntjies aan hulle gesamentlik toegeken word, maar aangesien hulle geadviseer is dat 'n bevel vir gesamentlike bewaring nog nooit in Natal verleen is nie, het die vader versoek dat bewaring van die kinders aan hom alleen toegeken word. Die regter het daarop gewys dat die advies wat die partye ontvang het verkeerd was maar dat dit verklaar het waarom hulle nie vir gesamentlike bewaring aansoek gedoen het nie. Albei ouers was ver-

one and the reports of the family advocate, family counsellor and a clinical psychologist unanimously recommended an award of joint custody. A decree of divorce was granted and the parents were appointed as the joint custodians of their children.

standige en verantwoordelike mense, die verhouding tussen hulle was besonder goed en die gesinsadvokaat, gesinsraadgewer en kliniese sielkundige het eenparig aanbeveel dat gesamentlike bewaring aan die ouers toegeken word. Die hof het 'n egskeidingsbevel verleen en gesamentlike bewaring van die kinders aan die ouers toegeken.

DIDCOTT J: [763] What I was told went thus. [The parties] had parted five months [before their divorce action was heard], with no acrimony or animosity on either side. Their marriage had lasted for 11 years. But in the end it had failed. Of that they [764] were both convinced. Neither blamed the other. Pursuing different careers and interests, they had simply drifted apart and gone on their own separate ways. The plaintiff and the children had remained in the house that was formerly the matrimonial home. The youngsters had therefore continued to live in the environment and atmosphere to which they were accustomed. The defendant had moved to a flat nearby. Her working hours were flexible. Every afternoon she met the elder boy at the school which he attended, taking him home and staying there for a couple of hours with him and his brother, whose schooling had not yet begun. In addition they often spent nights at her flat and weekends in her company. The plaintiff employed a trustworthy nursemaid, who looked after the younger boy during the other's absence at school and the two of them whenever both were at home but neither parent was present. All these arrangements had worked well, and the parties intended to stick to them . . .

Requests for joint custody are rare, in Natal at least and presumably elsewhere too. The reason seems obvious. The personal circumstances of parents who live separately are seldom conducive to the request. Nor is it ordinarily compatible with their ruptured relationship. I was therefore not surprised when counsel cited only three reported occasions on which joint custody had ever been claimed in South Africa. The cases were *Heimann v Heimann* 1948 (4) SA 926 (W), *Kastan v Kastan* 1985 (3) SA 235 (C) [140] and *Schlebusch v Schlebusch* 1988 (4) SA 548 (E) [141].

The *Heimann* and *Schlebusch* claims failed. The earlier matter came before MURRAY J. He delivered no judgment. As far as I can tell from the cryptic report of the case, however, his decision turned on its own facts, [765] which made it an inappropriate one, in his estimation, for an award of joint custody. MULLINS J heard the later case. A judgment was written by him which dealt in detail with the topic of joint custody. It is clear from what he had to say (at 551I–J) that he was not enamoured of the idea, viewing 'with concern' the trend towards it which he perceived and postulating 'a Utopian state of affairs' as the condition for its acceptance. But in the end he too disposed of the claim on the facts of the case. Neither decision lends support to the notion that, in principle and irrespective of the circumstances, joint custody is unobtainable and should never be decreed.

That is not how matters stand indeed, according to the judgment given by KING AJ in the case of *Kastan*. He looked at s 6(3) of the Divorce Act 70 of 1979, which provides that:

'A Court granting a decree of divorce may, in regard to . . . the custody . . . of . . . a minor child of the marriage, make any order which it may deem fit. . . .'

The power bestowed was wide enough, he held (at 236C), to cover an order for joint custody. It was one, he added (at 236D) which had always to be exercised

'... so as best to promote the welfare and advance and protect the interests of young children'.

Joint custody was fraught with risks and rarely awarded, he then remarked, for reasons which he explained by saying (at 236E-F):

'Custody of children involves day to day decisions and also decisions of longer and more permanent duration involving their education, training, religious upbringing, freedom of association and generally the determination of how best to ensure their good health, welfare and happiness. To leave decisions of this nature to the joint decision of parents who are no longer husband and wife could be courting disaster, particularly where the divorce has been preceded by acrimony and disharmony between the parents.'

He nevertheless granted an order for joint custody, having come to the conclusion in the special circumstances of the case that his doing so would best serve the interests of the children concerned.

A fourth reported case must be mentioned as well, the one of *Edwards v Edwards* 1960 (2) SA 523 (D) which JANSEN J decided. It was not a matter where joint custody was claimed. The parties were divorced already. No order for the custody of their minor son had been made at the time. They had agreed, however, that his custody would be 'shared equally' between them. A dispute about his schooling had arisen, which the Court was requested to and did determine. The judgment is not, one thus sees, directly in point. But JANSEN J passed some remarks which touch cases of the present kind. They concerned the agreement to share custody. And they went thus (at 524F-H):

'It is plain that an agreement of this nature should not be made an order of Court. In this regard I refer to the case of *Heimann v Heimann* ..., where MURRAY J refused to make a similar agreement in respect of custody an order of Court. It seems to me a legal impossibility that the legal custody of a child could be shared equally between two individuals. The legal custody involves the privilege and responsibility of taking certain decisions in regard to, for example, the education of the child. It would seem that such a decision should appertain to a single individual. If the responsibility is shared between two individuals there is the continuing possibility of a deadlock arising over every triviality.'...

[766] The question that arises is whether the passage, especially its first and third sentences, told both then and now, because of its local provenance, against any such award here. For, if joint custody is truly 'a legal impossibility', s 6(3) does not empower the Court to grant that, wide though its terms may otherwise be. The question should be answered, I believe, in the negative. The case was decided on the footing that the agreement had amounted in the circumstances to a merely private arrangement with no legal effect on the custody of the boy. It was therefore unnecessary for JANSEN J to consider the situation that would have arisen had a judicial order been obtained or sought which purported to give effect to the agreement. Nor were his comments on that situation ingredients of his reasoning which led to the conclusion reached on the case as it stood. I construe them, it follows, as *obiter dicta* which are not binding. And, with due deference, I disagree with them. For I do not see why joint custody should be regarded as a 'legal impossibility'. The difficulties raised by JANSEN J do not strike me as reasons for taking that view. Instead they suggest that joint custody may well be a practical impossibility. So, of course, it usually is. Everything depends, however, on the particular circumstances of each individual matter. Joint custody will not be awarded unless they satisfy the Court that no practical impossibility of any consequence seems likely to ensue. And, if some unforeseen trouble happens to develop after the grant of the order and a dispute erupts over it, that will hardly be a calamity. The Court will simply have to be approached to resolve the dispute, as JANSEN J was.

I thus feel free to state, as I do, that I fully agree with KING AJ when it comes to the way in which cases of this sort ought to be tackled. I too consider that the Court has the power to award joint custody, that the power should be cautiously used in view of the obvious pitfalls, but that its exercise is required once the interests of the child or children appear to call clearly for such. The advantages and disadvantages of joint custody were canvassed by Professor Ivan Schäfer in his discussion of the topic which was published in (1987) 104 *South African Law Journal* 149 (at 158–60). Conditions thought to favour its award were listed by him (at 160–1), and in *The Law of Custody* by Hoffman and Pincus (at 53). Neither inventory is exhaustive. Nor are there any hard and fast rules, except for the 'one guiding rule', as KING AJ called it (at 236D), the rule governing all questions of custody, the rule that the interests of the child or children are paramount. And those must always be assessed with reference to the particular circumstances of the case.

Some of the circumstances which entered the reckoning in the present matter emerged at the trial and were mentioned at the beginning of this judgment. The rest I learnt from the reports I received subsequently, which were thorough, incisive and most illuminating. I am grateful to the Family Advocate and to her collaborators for the assistance that I got from them. She and the counsellor, a duly qualified social worker, had interviewed the parties twice. The first interview had taken place in their office. The second had been held at the plaintiff's home, which struck them as satisfactory. On that occasion they had spoken to the nursemaid [767] as well and formed a favourable impression of her. They had also observed each child in his natural habitat and in the company of his parents. They had then visited and inspected the defendant's home, finding it to be a suitable 'granny flat', to describe it colloquially, which opened onto a garden. A third interview with the parties had been conducted by the counsellor in his office. He had set each of them the task of writing an essay which answered a wide variety of pertinent questions posed by him. Both tasks had been performed excellently. Finally, and on the strength of his own interview with the parties, the psychologist had assessed their personalities, their emotional equipment and their intellectual calibres. The product of all this work was a clear picture, the salient features of which I shall now sketch.

The plaintiff and the defendant were sensible, mature, responsible and temperamentally stable people. The relationship between them was a remarkably good one for a couple whose marriage had collapsed. They respected, trusted and remained fond of each other. Throughout their cohabitation they had shared the duties of parenthood, co-operating amicably and constructively on every matter that concerned the children. With similar outlooks and values, they had usually seen eye to eye in such areas as routine, discipline, hygiene, upbringing and education. Compromise rather than altercation had been their way of coping with any difference of opinion that happened to arise. None of that had changed since they parted. They were acutely conscious of the need to render their parting as painless to the children as it could be. To that end each took care to say nothing to either boy or in his presence which might be understood as criticism or disparagement of the other. Indeed, they made a point of praising one another in front of the children. The danger inherent in the situation that the boys might try to exploit it by manipulating them was one to which they were alert and for which they felt prepared. They were committed to the experiment of joint custody and dedicated to its success. In effect they had acted as joint custodians ever since their separation. And they planned to continue doing so, even if they were not appointed as such. The children appeared to have adapted themselves well to their altered pattern of life, and to be happy and contented.

I was not sure whether that state of affairs ranked as a Utopian one. But I certainly thought that it made the prospects for joint custody look pretty good on the present occasion. And that was sufficient to persuade me, in all the circumstances of the case, that the interests of the children called clearly for such an award.

Note

See the notes on *Kastan v Kastan* [140] and *Schlebusch v Schlebusch* [141].

Aantekening

Sien die aantekeninge by *Kastan v Kastan* [140] en *Schlebusch v Schlebusch* [141].

Maintenance   **Onderhoud**

[143] HERFST V HERFST

1964 4 SA 127 (W)

Maintenance for children upon divorce

When the parties were divorced an agreement between them regarding the payment of maintenance by the respondent for the applicant and a minor child born of the marriage was made an order of court. The applicant now, *inter alia,* applied for an increase in the maintenance for the child as well as for certain arrear maintenance. The arrear maintenance was claimed because the applicant contended that she was during the period for which she claimed it, irregularly employed. She maintained that the respondent was legally liable for the whole of the child's maintenance during that period but that he only paid the amount which he normally contributed. The court ordered the increase of the maintenance for the child from R30 to R45 but refused an order for the payment of arrear maintenance.

Onderhoud vir kinders na egskeiding

Ten tyde van die partye se egskeiding het hulle 'n ooreenkoms aangegaan met betrekking tot die betaling van onderhoud deur die respondent aan die applikant vir haar en hulle minderjarige kind. Die ooreenkoms is 'n bevel van die hof gemaak. Die applikant het nou onder andere aansoek gedoen om verhoging van die onderhoud vir die kind asook vir sekere agterstallige onderhoud. Die agterstallige onderhoud is geëis omdat die applikant aangevoer het dat sy gedurende die tydperk waarvoor sy dit geëis het nie gereeld werk gehad het nie. Sy het beweer dat die respondent gedurende daardie tydperk regtens aanspreeklik was vir al die kind se onderhoud, maar dat hy net die bedrag betaal het wat hy normaalweg bygedra het. Die hof het gelas dat die onderhoud vir die kind van R30 tot R45 verhoog word maar het geweier om 'n bevel vir die betaling van agterstallige onderhoud uit te reik.

TROLLIP J: [130] The crisp legal and factual problem raised by this claim is whether, because the order of Court fixing maintenance for the child was duly honoured by the respondent during that period, the applicant is nevertheless entitled to be re-imbursed for this additional amount of R90.

Mr *Wulfsohn,* for the applicant, relied on *Farrell v Hankey,* 1921 TPD 590, and *Woodhead v Woodhead,* 1955 (3) SA 138 (SR). He rightly conceded, however, that in neither of those cases was there an order of Court regulating maintenance but he sought to extend the principles laid down by them to such a case as the present.

The general principles are that a child of divorced parents is entitled to be maintained by them, and they are correspondingly obliged to provide it with everything that it reasonably requires for its proper living and upbringing according to their means, standard of living and station in life. That obligation attaches to both parents jointly, but *inter se,* their respective shares of that obligation are apportioned according to the financial resources and circumstances of each of them. Usually that apportionment is effected on or after the divorce by a maintenance order made by a Court after it has investigated the child's needs and the parents' means and circumstances. In the absence, however, of such an order, if the one parent incurs any liability or expenditure for the proper maintenance of the child, he or she is entitled to recover, or to be indemnified for, the appropriate share thereof due by the other parent, the amount of which in the absence of agreement will be determined by the Court. In such a case the bar to the recovery of arrear maintenance as such embodied in the maxim of the common law that "a person does not live nor has to be maintained in arrear" (*Voet* 2.15.14, *Gane* vol 1 p 457); *Oberholzer v Oberholzer,* 1947 (3) SA 294 (O) at p 298; *R v van den Berg,* 1957 (4) SA 204 (O); *Spiro, Parent and Child,* 2nd ed p 256; Hahlo, *Husband and Wife,* 2nd ed pp 103/4) does not operate because the claim is not strictly for arrear maintenance but for the indemnification by one joint debtor for the expenditure or indebtedness actually incurred at the time the need therefor arose by the other joint debtor. That is the effect of *Farrell's* and *Woodhead's* cases. When an order is made by a Court for maintenance the rate is generally fixed on the basis of the needs of the child and the respective means and circumstances of the parents as they exist at that time, and perhaps also as far as they can then be reasonably foreseen, and the respective liability of the parents *inter se* for maintaining the child on that basis would therefore usually be regulated by that order of Court (see *Kemp v Kemp,* 1958 (3) SA 736 (D) at p 738 A–B; *Patrikios v Patrikios,* 1953 (3) SA 252 (SR)). An order, however, only operates as between the parties and is not binding on the child whose legal entitlement to proper maintenance is not thereby circumscribed (*Spiro, supra,* pp 270, 272; *Fillis v Joubert Park Private Hospital (Pty) Ltd.,* 1939 TPD 234; *Patrikios'* case, *supra*). The child may become entitled to some individual or non-recurring or other item of maintenance which is not covered, nor was intended to be covered, by the order, but with [131] which it has to be provided (eg medical or other treatment, funds to litigate with, etc); and as the obligation to provide all maintenance rests upon the parents jointly, there is no reason why the parent who actually incurs the liability or expense in providing the item should not, despite the existence of the order, recover the due proportionate share of such liability or expense from the other parent, in terms of *Farrell's* and *Woodhead's* cases. QUÉNET, J, (as he then was) reached a similar conclusion in *Patrikios'* case, *supra,* at pp 255/6, with which I respectfully agree. See too *Hahlo, supra,* at p 466.

I would, however, repeat and emphasise here that the item of maintenance in question must have been reasonably required by the child for its due living and upbringing in the sense mentioned above – that is fundamental to any liability attaching to the one parent to indemnify the other therefor . . .

Mr *Wulfsohn,* however, submitted in the alternative that the Court's power under sec 10(1) of the Matrimonial Affairs Act, 37 of 1953, to vary the present order could, and in this case should, be exercised retrospectively . . .

I shall assume in favour of the applicant that a variation of an order increasing the amount of maintenance can under sec 10(1) of the Act be antedated (cf *Fluxman v Fluxman,* 1958 (4) SA 409 (W)) but it is clear that such power should be very sparingly exercised (*ibid,* pp 413/4) not only because of the possible effect on the payer's financial arrangements where, as here, his means are limited (*Strauss v Strauss and Another,* 1962 (3) SA 639 (O) at p 642A) but especially because of the well-established tenet of the common law previously mentioned: . . . [a person does not live nor has to be maintained in arrear] (see the authorities quoted above) . . .

[TROLLIP J then analysed the facts and proceeded:]

[132] In my view, therefore, no case has been made out by the applicant to vary the present order retrospectively or otherwise to re-imburse the applicant in respect of past

maintenance. There are some observations which I would like to make for the assistance of the parties in approaching the problems of maintenance in the future. Firstly, the applicant cannot expect that either she or the child can or must be maintained at the same rate or according to the same standard as would have prevailed if the parties had not been divorced; it is usually one of the unfortunate consequences of the breaking up of the joint household that that rate or standard of living must inevitably be diminished where the parties are not affluent. Secondly, if the information placed by the parties before the Court about their present respective monthly expenses is correct, it is clear that both of them are living beyond their means; but that is no answer to their providing the child with its reasonable requirements of maintenance. The latter must always rank high on their respective lists of priorities in regard to outgoings and they must accordingly modify their expenditure on other items, even if it is necessary to diminish their own rate and standard of living for the purpose. Thirdly, it is possible, as Mr. *Merber*, for the respondent, suggested, that the applicant's idea of what the appropriate rate and standard of living is for her and the child has been conditioned by her well-off days when she was with Olivetti. As she is no longer earning that high income she must cut her coat according to her cloth presently available . . .

The order of the Court is that . . . the agreement between the parties which was made an order of this Court . . . is varied by the maintenance for the child mentioned therein being increased with effect from July, 1964, to R45 per month. Save as aforesaid the applicant's claims are dismissed . . .

Note

This case sets out some of the most important general principles applicable to the maintenance of a child of divorced parents. These are: Firstly, both parents are obliged to maintain their child after divorce, each according to his or her means and circumstances. Upon divorce the court usually apportions the duty between the parents by ordering the non-custodian parent to make a financial contribution to the child's support. But even in the absence of a court order both parents remain liable. If one parent provides the child with maintenance in excess of that for which that parent is liable, he or she has a right to be indemnified by the other parent. However, as was emphasised in *Zimelka v Zimelka* 1990 4 SA 303 (W), the mere fact that both parents are obliged to contribute to the support of their child does not mean that the custodian parent is in each case entitled to claim a monetary contribution from the non-custodian parent. If the non-custodian parent does not have the means to make a significant financial contribution the court will not order that parent to do so. "[T]he *order* of maintenance is ancillary to the *duty* to maintain. It does not follow that because there is a duty, *ergo*, there must be an award against the non-custodian parent" (306).

Aantekening

Hierdie saak sit sommige van die belangrikste algemene beginsels ten opsigte van die onderhoud van 'n kind van geskeide ouers uiteen. Eerstens is albei ouers verplig om hulle kind na die egskeiding te onderhou, elkeen ooreenkomstig sy of haar vermoëns en omstandighede. Ten tyde van die egskeiding beveel die hof gewoonlik hoe die verpligting tussen die ouers verdeel moet word deur die ouer wat nie bewaring van die kind het nie te beveel om 'n finansiële bydrae tot die kind se onderhoud te maak. Maar selfs indien daar geen hofbevel is nie, bly albei ouers aanspreeklik. Indien die een ouer meer onderhoud aan die kind verskaf as wat hy of sy verplig is om te doen, het hy of sy 'n reg om deur die ander ouer vergoed te word. Maar, soos wat in *Zimelka v Zimelka* 1990 4 SA 303 (W) beklemtoon is, beteken die blote feit dat albei ouers verplig is om by te dra tot die onderhoud van hulle kind nie dat die ouer wat bewaring van die kind het in iedere geval geregtig is op 'n geldelike bydrae van die ander ouer nie. Indien die ouer wat nie bewaring het nie, nie oor die vermoë beskik om 'n beduidende finansiële bydrae te maak nie, sal die hof nie daardie ouer daartoe verplig nie. "[T]he *order* of maintenance is ancillary to the *duty* to maintain. It does not follow that because there is a duty,

Secondly, the child must be provided with "everything that it reasonably requires for its proper living and upbringing according to their means, standard of living and station in life" (130). This includes food, clothing, medical and dental services, schooling and, if the circumstances of the family permit it, tertiary education.

The court also pointed out that after divorce "it is usually one of the unfortunate consequences of the breaking up of the joint household that that rate [the rate of maintenance] or standard of living must inevitably be diminished where the parties are not affluent" (132). In respect of the standard of living after divorce see also *Grasso v Grasso* [124] and *Pommerel v Pommerel* [125].

Note that section 8 of the Divorce Act 70 of 1979 has replaced section 10 of the Matrimonial Affairs Act 37 of 1953. The provisions of section 8 are similar to those contained in section 10 of the Matrimonial Affairs Act.

ergo, there must be an award against the non-custodian parent" (306).

Tweedens, moet die kind voorsien word van "everything that it reasonably requires for its proper living and upbringing according to their means, standard of living and station in life" (130). Dit sluit in voedsel, kleding, mediese en tandheelkundige dienste, skoolopleiding en, indien die omstandighede van die gesin dit toelaat, tersiêre opleiding.

Die hof het ook daarop gewys dat na egskeiding "it is usually one of the unfortunate consequences of the breaking up of the joint household that that rate [die mate waarvolgens onderhoud verskaf word] or standard of living must inevitably be diminished where the parties are not affluent" (132). In verband met die lewenstandaard na egskeiding sien ook *Grasso v Grasso* [124] en *Pommerel v Pommerel* [125].

Let daarop dat artikel 10 van die Wet op Huweliksaangeleenthede 37 van 1953 vervang is deur artikel 8 van die Wet op Egskeiding 70 van 1979. Die bepalings van artikel 8 is soortgelyk aan dié van artikel 10 van die Wet op Huweliksaangeleenthede.

Parental power

Protection of parental authority against interference by
third parties
Custody
The duty of support

Ouerlike gesag

Beskerming van ouerlike gesag teen inmenging
deur derdes
Bewaring
Die onderhoudsplig

Protection of parental authority against interference by third parties

Beskerming van ouerlike gesag teen inmenging deur derdes

[144]   L v H

1992 2 SA 594 (E)

Parental authority over a pregnant daughter of eighteen – father of the unborn child interdicted from having contact with the daughter

The applicant was the father of an eighteen year old daughter, K. She was pregnant and the respondent was the father of the unborn child. The applicant obtained a rule *nisi* in order to restrain the respondent from contacting his daughter. He alleged that his daughter was very immature, that the respondent had a tremendous influence over her and that their relationship was severely prejudicial to her future and interests. The court confirmed the rule *nisi*, in other words the respondent was interdicted from having contact with the daughter.

Ouerlike gesag oor 'n swanger dogter van agtien – vader van die ongebore kind verbied om kontak met die dogter te hê

Die applikant se dogter, K, was agtien jaar oud. Sy was verwagtend en die respondent was die vader van die ongebore kind. Die applikant het 'n bevel *nisi* verkry ten einde die respondent te verbied om kontak met sy dogter te hê. Hy het beweer dat sy dogter baie onvolwasse was, dat die respondent 'n geweldige invloed oor haar uitgeoefen het en dat hulle verhouding baie nadelig vir haar toekoms was. Die hof het die bevel *nisi* bekragtig, met ander woorde die respondent is verbied om kontak met die dogter te hê.

ZIETSMAN AJP: [596] I have no doubt that the applicant, as K's guardian, was at all relevant times, and still is, exercising his parental power and control over K who lives on the farm with her parents. As her guardian, the applicant was and is entitled to determine with whom she may associate, and he has decided that she may not associate with the respondent. I further have no doubt that K and the respondent were at all relevant times aware of the applicant's wishes and instructions and that they disregarded them, and intend to disregard them in the future if the rule *nisi* in this case is not confirmed.

There is authority in our law dealing with this type of situation. In the case of *Meyer v Van Niekerk* 1976 (1) SA 252 (T) COETZEE J refused a similar application where the applicant's daughter, who had formed a relationship with a divorced man, was 20 years old. COETZEE J seemed to doubt whether any application could be granted preventing a third person from contacting a minor child where the third person was not doing anything against the wishes of the minor child. He conceded that such an [597] application could possibly be granted in the case of a totally immature child. In the case in question the applicant's daughter was 20 years old and she had been sent from Pretoria to Port Elizabeth to attend the university there, and there may in that case have been good reasons to conclude that the applicant had relinquished his parental power to dictate his daughter's choice of associates.

Meyer's case is commented on in the Full Bench decision of *Coetzee v Meintjies* 1976 (1) SA 257 (T). Here also a similar application was dismissed. In this case the minor child was a son who in eight months' time would reach majority, and he was living away from his parental home. The following appears from the judgment at 262B-F.

'Wanneer ons te doen het met 'n jong kind is dit onteenseglik deel van die ouerlike gesag om te beslis met wie die kind vriendskaplik mag omgaan en waar die kind sy of haar tyd mag deurbring. Iemand wat hom daarmee bemoei maak inbreuk op die ouerlike gesag en dit sal 'n *injuria* wees wat deur middel van 'n interdik afgeweer kan word . . .

Die bevoegdheid om op te tree teen 'n buitestaander wat inbreuk maak op ouerlike gesag hoef nie beperk te word tot die "heel onontwikkelde jong kind" nie. Die uitgangspunt is nie die ouderdom of ontwikkelingspeil van die kind nie, maar wel die mate waarin die ouer sy gesag teenoor hom in stand gehou of laat vaar het. Ons het te doen met 'n *injuria* teenoor die ouer deurdat sy ouerlike gesag geminag word. Melius de Villiers, *Injuries,* stel dit aldus op bl 67:

"In the next place an injury may be inflicted upon a father through his sons and daughters whilst still being under his paternal power, they being regarded as one person with him."

Waar egter die ouer self die omvang van sy gesag verklein deur die kind uit die huis te laat gaan universiteit toe, waar hy vanselfsprekend sy eie vriende en vriendinne mag kies, is daar van inbreuk op sy gesag wat vriende betref geen sprake meer nie. Hy het self die betrokke gedeelte daarvan laat vaar, nl om te bepaal met wie sy kind mag omgaan. In sulke omstandighede kan daar geen *injuria* wees nie.'

With one reservation which I have it seems to me, with respect, that the position is correctly stated in the passage which I have quoted. The reservation I have concerns the statement that where a minor child leaves home to attend a university the guardian parent loses his right to determine the child's choice of associates. I am not sure that this will necessarily always be the case. However, this is not a question with which I need concern myself in the present application since K is still living with her parents.

In the case of *Gordon v Barnard* 1977 (1) SA 887 (C) a similar application was successful. The applicant's daughter was 18 years of age and although she had been working for nearly three years she resided with her parents. The applicant obtained an interdict preventing a married man of 29 years from communicating with his daughter until she reached the age of majority. It was decided in this case that the following three critical questions need to be asked and answered in such a case, namely: (1) is the parental power and control over the child extant? (2) if so, what is the extent and content of that power and control? and (3) is such power as the parent is exercising reasonably exercised?

The most recent reported case on the subject is the case of *H v I* 1985 (3) SA 237 (C). Here a similar application in respect of a 17-year-old daughter was also successful. The Court, in granting the application, held [598] that the applicant had established (a) that his daughter was immature and gullible; (b) that further association with the respondent, a 23-year-old man, was adverse to her interests; (c) that the applicant had not waived or abandoned his parental right to interfere with his daughter's choice of associates; and (d) that the respondent had knowingly defied the applicant's parental authority, and wished to persist therein.

In her judgment VAN DEN HEEVER J at 244-5 questions the correctness of two statements made by HIEMSTRA J in the case of *Coetzee v Meintjies (supra)*. One of the statements she questions is the statement that where a minor child leaves home in order to attend a university in another town the guardian parent loses his right to determine the child's choice of associates. I have already expressed my own doubts about this statement being necessarily correct in all cases, and I agree with what is stated by VAN DEN HEEVER J on the subject at 244-5 of her judgment. I also agree with her criticism of the other statement made by HIEMSTRA J, namely that where a natural guardian is fulfilling his functions there is no room for interference therewith by the Court in its capacity as upper guardian of the child. VAN DEN HEEVER J gives an example of a situation where the Court surely would refuse to uphold the wishes of the natural guardian. This position is, I think, met by the third requirement listed in the case of *Gordon v Barnard (supra)*. This is that the Court must be satisfied that the power exercised by the natural guardian is being exercised in a reasonable manner. Provided this is the case the Court, in my opinion, should, and will, uphold the wishes and decision of the natural guardian who is properly fulfilling his functions as such.

In the present case the applicant has, in my opinion, established the fact that he has at no stage relinquished his parental power and control over his daughter K. He has at all times exercised full control over her and he was and is entitled to determine the persons with whom she can associate. He has also established the fact that the respondent was and is aware of the fact that the applicant does not approve of the respondent's relationship with his daughter and that the applicant requires him to end that relationship. It is clear from the papers also that the respondent is bent upon disregarding the applicant's wishes and in undermining his parental authority, and that if not prevented he will continue to do so in the future.

The question still to be determined is whether the applicant is exercising his authority in a reasonable manner.

The respondent and K are both 18 years of age. K has passed her matriculation examination. The respondent has left school after passing standard 8. The respondent intends working as an apprentice mechanic. The respondent alleges that he and K wish to get married. The applicant states that the respondent will be in no position to maintain a wife and a child and he states that there is little chance of a marriage between them being a success. It cannot be said that he does not have grounds for his misgivings. The applicant goes on to say that his daughter is immature and not ready for marriage at this stage.

Regarding the respondent as a person, the applicant alleges that he is emotionally unstable, that he has an uncontrollable temper and that it is common knowledge that he has been admitted to hospital on two occasions for apparently taking an overdose of drugs. In reply to this allegation the [599] respondent denies that he is emotionally unstable or that he has an uncontrollable temper, but he admits that he has been treated in hospital on two occasions for taking an overdose of drugs. The respondent gives no further information or explanation of this fact. He does not say what drugs he took, and why he took them, and he does not say whether he still takes drugs. The applicant alleges in his replying affidavit that it is common knowledge that subsequent to the institution of this application the respondent has spent time in a psychiatric hospital in Queenstown. This allegation was made after the respondent had filed his affidavit, but he has not asked for leave to file any further affidavits to deal with the allegation and he has not asked that the applicant's allegation be struck from the record.

There are other allegations made by the applicant which are denied by the respondent and which are confirmed by the applicant in his replying affidavit and in certain other affidavits filed by him. One of these allegations, which is denied by the respondent, is that he has assaulted K. It is, however, not necessary to deal with these matters.

I am satisfied, on the undisputed facts, that it cannot be said that the applicant's exercise of his parental power and control over K, and his insistence that the respondent should not communicate with her, is unreasonable.

In my opinion the applicant has established all of the requirements necessary to justify the order which he seeks.

There is one problem which has caused me much concern and that is the fact of the unborn child. If a child is born, it will be illegitimate which means that the respondent, as father, will have very limited rights in respect of the child and the child will suffer the consequences of illegitimacy. The respondent alleges that he wishes to marry K. If he does so the child will be legitimised. If I confirm the rule *nisi* in this case I may thereby prevent the child's parents from marrying each other. My order will not prevent them from getting married when they reach the age of majority, but it will prevent them from seeing each other freely, and perhaps from getting to know each other better between now and the time when they turn 21. This could condemn the child to permanent illegitimacy, which may not be the case if the rule *nisi* is discharged. Is this a consideration which should be taken into account? In the case of *H v I* (*supra*) a child was conceived but an abortion had been obtained and the problem therefore no longer existed. In none of the other cases was there the complication of a child born or to be born.

I have come to the conclusion that the fact of the child to be born should not have a bearing on my decision. There is no guarantee at this stage that a child will be born although the likelihood exists that this will happen. There is also no guarantee that the respondent and K will in fact get married if the rule *nisi* is discharged. A marriage between the two of them is a possibility that the applicant himself has considered, and it is his opinion that such a marriage will severely prejudice his daughter and will have very little prospect of being successful or permanent. His misgivings are not based on flimsy grounds.

My conclusion is that the applicant has satisfied the requirements for the relief which he seeks and that the rule ought to be confirmed, and I [600] accordingly make an order confirming para 1(*a*) and (*b*) of the rule *nisi* dated 19 December 1990. The respondent is interdicted and restrained from in any manner whatsoever communicating with, and/or contacting, KL save through her father or his attorney and/or from assaulting KL and/or abducting her or aiding and abetting her to abscond from her parental home until such time as she shall have obtained the age of majority . . .

Note

By virtue of parental authority, a parent may dictate with whom his or her child may associate. This aspect of parental authority, like any other aspect thereof, can be enforced as against third parties. A third party can for example, as happened in the case under discussion, be prohibited from having contact with the child. Such a prohibition will be enforced by the court if it is reasonable. (See also *Meyer v Van Niekerk* 1976 1 SA 252 (T); *Coetzee v Meintjies* 1976 1 SA 257 (T); *Gordon v Barnard* 1977 1 SA 887 (C); *H v I* 1985 3 SA 237 (C).) Where, however, the parent has relinquished the right to determine with whom his or her child may associate an interdict will not be granted (*Meyer v Van Niekerk*). The facts of each case will determine whether the parent still has the right to determine with whom the child may associate and whether his or her refusal that the child associates with a particular person is reasonable.

Aantekening

As deel van ouerlike gesag mag 'n ouer bepaal met wie sy of haar kind mag omgaan. Hierdie aspek van die ouerlike gesag, soos enige ander aspek daarvan, kan teen derdes afgedwing word. 'n Derde kan byvoorbeeld, soos wat in die onderhawige saak gebeur het, verbied word om kontak met die kind te hê. Sodanige verbod sal deur die hof afgedwing word as dit redelik is. (Sien ook *Meyer v Van Niekerk* 1976 1 SA 252 (T); *Coetzee v Meintjies* 1976 1 SA 257 (T); *Gordon v Barnard* 1977 1 SA 887 (K); *H v I* 1985 3 SA 237 (K).) Waar die ouer egter die bevoegdheid prysgegee het om te bepaal met wie die kind mag assosieer, sal 'n interdik nie uitgereik word nie (*Meyer v Van Niekerk*). Die feite van elke saak sal bepaal of die ouer nog die reg het om te bepaal met wie die kind mag omgaan en of sy of haar weiering dat die kind met 'n betrokke persoon assosieer redelik is.

Custody   Bewaring

[145] PETERSEN V KRUGER

1975 4 SA 171 (K)

The right of a natural parent to have custody of his or her child	**Die natuurlike ouer se reg op die bewaring van sy of haar kind**

A child was born to both the applicants and the defendants on the same day and in the same hospital. The name of the applicants' child was Dawid and that of the defendants' Monray. It later became clear to the applicants that the child that was handed to them in the hospital as their child, was in fact not their natural child. Blood tests carried out on both children as well as on the applicants and the defendants proved that the applicants were in fact the parents of the child that was handed to the defendants. The applicants claimed the return of their child, who was then about two years of age. The claim was granted.

'n Kind is op dieselfde dag en in dieselfde hospitaal vir sowel die applikante as die respondente gebore. Die applikante se kind se naam was Dawid en dié van die respondente Monray. Dit het later geblyk dat die kind wat in die hospitaal aan die applikante as hulle eie oorhandig is nie hulle natuurlike kind was nie. Bloedtoetse wat op albei kinders sowel as op die applikante en die verweerders uitgevoer is, het getoon dat die applikante in werklikheid die ouers was van die kind wat aan die respondente gegee is. Die applikante het aansoek gedoen dat hulle kind, wat toe omtrent twee jaar oud was, aan hulle oorhandig word. Die eis is toegestaan.

VAN WINSEN WN RP: [173] Die eerste vraag wat in hierdie saak ontstaan is: wat is die regte van die ouerpaar ten opsigte van 'n kind uit hul huwelik gebore? By die beantwoording van hierdie vraag is dit in die omstandighede van hierdie saak onnodig om tussen die regte van die ouers onderling te onderskei.

Dit lê aan die grondslag van ons regstelsel dat, onderhewig aan sekere beperkinge, die reg van beheer en toesig oor 'n kind aan sy natuurlike ouers toekom. As voorbeeld van gewysdes waarin hierdie reg erken word volstaan ek met 'n verwysing na sake soos bv. *Calitz v Calitz*, 1939 AD 56 [19]; *Van der Westhuizen v Van Wyk and Another*, 1952 (2) SA 119 (GW); *Rowan v Faifer*, 1953 (2) SA 705 (E); *Short v Naisby*, 1955 (3) SA 572 (D); [174] *September v Karriem*, 1959 (3) SA 687 (C); en *Kaiser v Chambers*, 1969 (4) SA 224 (C). Die beperkinge hierbo na verwys vloei voort uit die gesag aan die Hof as oppervoog van alle kinders verleen om, waar die belange van 'n kind dit vereis, die ouerlike regte ten opsigte van sy kind in te kort. Die omstandighede waaronder 'n Hof hom geroepe sou voel om met die ouerlike reg van beheer en toesig in te meng bestaan waar die uitoefening van sodanige regte die lewe, gesondheid of sedes van die kind in gevaar kon stel. (Kyk bv *Calitz v Calitz, supra* op bl 63; *Bam v Bhabha*, 1947 (4) SA 798 (AD); *Van der Westhuizen v Van Wyk and Another, supra* op bl 120. Uit latere gewysdes (bv *Short v Naisby, supra* op bl 575; en *September v Karriem, supra* op bl 689) blyk dat die gesag van die Hof om met die ouers se regte ten opsigte van hul kind in te meng nie beperk is tot die genoemde drie gronde nie; enige grond wat op die welsyn van die kind betrekking het kan as rede vir die Hof se inmenging dien. By 'n Hof weeg die belange van die kind die swaarste, maar die regte van die ouers moet nie buite rekening gelaat word nie.

Ek gaan nou oor om te handel met die vraag of daar 'n wesenlike rede bestaan om te dink dat die verlening aan mnr en mev Petersen [die applikante] van hul regte van beheer en toesig oor Dawid vir sy welsyn nadelig sal wees. Dit gaan in hierdie verband in die eerste instansie oor die bevoegdheid van die aansoekdoeners om sodanige regte uit te oefen, en die geskiktheid van die familie omgewing, beide op materiële, sowel as sedelike, vlak, waarheen Dawid verplaas sal moet word as die aansoek toegestaan word. In die tweede plaas vereis dit die opweeg teen mekaar van beide die onmiddellike en toekomstige voordele en nadele wat so 'n stap vir Dawid inhou.

Laat ek dit nou onmiddellik boekstaaf dat beide mnr en mev Kruger [die respondente] op my 'n goeie indruk gemaak het. Op die oog af is geen fout te vind met hul as persone of met hul familieverband, en ek is daarvan oortuig dat hul tot op die hede vir Dawid goed opgepas het en hom behoorlik grootgemaak het. Die indruk wat ek het is dat hul hom innig lief het en dat as Dawid by hul moet bly hul pligsgetrou vir hom sal sorg. Dit is egter met die geskiktheid van die Petersens en hul huisgesin wat die Hof by hierdie saak veral te doen het.

[VAN WINSEN WN RP het die getuienis ontleed en soos volg voortgegaan:]

Daar moet ten opsigte van hierdie aspek van die saak ten slotte opgemerk word dat die Petersen huisgesin in 'n goeie buurt en in 'n behoorlike ruim huis woon en dat weens mnr. Petersen se goeie verdienste mev. Petersen in staat gestel is om heeldag by die huis te kan bly om vir die kinders te sorg. Die sedelike en godsdienstige peil van die huisgesin is ook goed. Die gevolgtrekking waartoe ek kom is dus dat die persoonlike eienskappe van Dawid se biologiese ouers, hul familielewe, hul huislike omstandighede, hul sedes en waardes geen bedreiging vir Dawid se welsyn inhou nie.

Die volgende vraag is of die oorgaan van Dawid na die beheer en toesig van sy natuurlike ouers – hoe geskik hul ookal mag wees – 'n bedreiging vir sy sielkundige welsyn inhou. Dat dit 'n ontwrigting in sy lewe sal veroorsaak – en ook in dié van Monray as hy na sy natuurlike ouers gaan – is nie te betwyfel nie. Hoe skadelik en hoe blywend die uitwerking hiervan op hom gaan wees is nie maklik om met presiesheid te bepaal nie. Die sielkundige getuienis was nie in alle opsigte in hierdie verband eensluidend nie.

[VAN WINSEN WN RP het die getuienis verder ontleed en soos volg voortgegaan:]

[175] Ek is met mnr. *Marais*, wat namens die aansoekdoeners opgetree het, dit eens waar hy sê dat die gevolge van die nie-toestaan van die aansoek 'n tersaaklike oorweging by die beslissing van die saak is. Dit daar gelaat dat die weiering van die aansoek etlike lastige ongerymdhede op privaatregtelike gebied ten opsigte van beide kinders sal mee-bring, is dit veral belangrik om nie uit die oog te verloor nie dat, gelet op die rugbaarheid wat hierdie saak in die pers geniet het, dit nie moontlik sal wees om die kinders uiteindelik te beskerm teen die wete dat hul nie by hul natuurlike ouers woon nie. Dit sou klaarblyklik 'n nadelige uitwerking op Dawid hê veral as dié ongerymdheid, sowel as die feit dat sy voorkoms anders is as dié van sy "broers" en "susters", deur ander kinders uitgebuit word en hy daaroor geterg word.

Ek is nie oortuig dat Dawid enige permanente skade sal ly as gevolg van die toestaan van die aansoek nie. Dit blyk uit [die] getuienis dat Dawid 'n "well-adjusted and happy child" is met geen emosionele probleme nie. Word hy oorgeplaas na 'n gunstige omgewing waar hy seer seker die liefdevolle versorging van twee verantwoordelike ouers sal geniet vind ek dit moeilik om te dink dat hy daardeur enige permanente skade sal ly . . .

Ek verwys na enkele sake waar kinders vir 'n geruime tydperk uit die sorg van hul ouers verkeer het, en waar die Hof nogtans gelas het dat hul na hul ouers moet teruggaan. Ek doen dit nie omdat die feite van een saak noodwendig in 'n ander deurslaggewend is nie, maar om aan te toon watter oorwegings die Howe in sodanige sake *nie* bereid was nie om as goeie rede (good cause) te beskou vir die ontneem van die natuurlike ouers van hul regte van beheer en toesig oor hul kinders. In *Bam v Bhabha* het die Hof besluit dat 'n dogter van sewe jaar oud wat feitlik haar hele lewe lank by haar grootouers gewoon

het na haar moeder moet terugkeer waar die Hof oortuig was dat laasgenoemde die kind behoorlik sou versorg.

In die saak van *Horsford v De Jager and Another*, 1959 (2) SA 152 (N), het jong kinders vir 'n tydperk van vyf en 'n half jaar weg van hul moeder met hul oom en sy vrou gewoon. Die kinders was by laasgenoemde gelukkig. Alhoewel die Hof van mening was dat die kinders 'n "considerable emotional upset" sou ondervind as gevolg van die feit dat hul in die sorg van hul moeder geplaas sou word is haar aansoek nogtans toegestaan ...

[176] Ek noem die gewysdes om die algemene rigsnoer aan te dui wat die Howe gevolg het in gevalle waar die voordele, stoflik sowel as geestelik, wat die kind by die pleegouers geniet het, min of meer gelyk opweeg teen dié wat die kind by sy natuurlike ouers sal kan geniet en waar hul gemeen het dat die oorplanting nie blywende sielkundige skade aan die kind sal veroorsaak nie ...

Om bogemelde oorwegings kom ek tot die gevolgtrekking dat die aansoek toegestaan moet word. Ek meen egter dat dit raadsaam sal wees om op hierdie tydstip geen uitvoerende bevel in verband met die aangeleentheid te maak nie. Ek sou graag wil sien dat die partye in oorleg met hul regsadviseurs en die sielkundige deskundiges weë oorweeg om uitvoering aan die Hof se bevel te gee. Dit is belangrik dat die oorgaan van Dawid na sy ouers bewerkstellig moet word op so 'n wyse wat vir hom die mins skadelik sal wees. Daarbenewens moet Monray se posisie ernstige oorweging geniet om te sien of sy aanvaarding deur sy eie ouers, in soverre dit vir hom voordelig beskou is, nie bewerkstellig kan word nie ...

Die hof se bevel is derhalwe dat die aansoek toegestaan word ...

Note

This case clearly illustrates the strength of the right of a natural parent to have custody of his or her child.

Aantekening

Hierdie saak illustreer duidelik hoe sterk die reg van 'n natuurlike ouer op die bewaring van sy of haar kind is.

[146]   DU PREEZ V CONRADIE

1990 4 SA 46 (B)

Delegation by a parent of his right to chastise his children

When the applicant and his former wife (second respondent) were divorced the custody of the two minor children born of the marriage was awarded to his wife. She later married the first respondent. The applicant averred that his daughter had informed him telephonically that the first respondent had assaulted her and her brother and that such assault was of a serious nature. He visited her the next day and, according to him, found her to be very emotional. He further noticed marks on her body which he claimed were

Delegasie van sy tugtigingsbevoegdheid deur 'n ouer

Toe die applikant en sy vorige vrou (tweede respondent) geskei is, is die bewaring van die twee kinders wat uit die huwelik gebore is aan sy vrou toegeken. Sy is later met die eerste respondent getroud. Die applikant het aangevoer dat sy dogter hom telefonies meegedeel het dat die eerste respondent haar en haar broer aangerand het en dat die aanranding van 'n ernstige aard was. Hy het haar die volgende dag besoek en volgens hom was sy baie ontsteld. Hy het ook sekere merke aan haar liggaam opgemerk en het beweer

caused by the first respondent in his assault on her. As a result thereof he caused her to be medically examined and the doctor diagnosed the abrasions and marks on her body as the type that is consistent with the use of bare hands and a leather belt. The applicant contended further that the children's mother associated herself with the first respondent's conduct towards the children and at times she incited the first respondent to assault the children and that she also participated in the assaults. The applicant's allegations relating to the assault on the children had been denied by the first and second respondents. The applicant applied for an order that the first respondent be prohibited from assaulting or molesting the children or from inflicting any corporal punishment on them, and that the second respondent be prohibited from assaulting the children. The court held that the children's mother may delegate the right of chastisement (including the right to administer corporal punishment) to the children's stepfather, but he may not exceed the bounds of reasonableness and moderation in chastising the children.

dat dit deur die eerste respondent veroorsaak is toe hy die kind aangerand het. As gevolg hiervan het hy haar medies laat ondersoek en die dokter was van mening dat die skaafplekke en merke op haar liggaam ooreengekom het met dié wat gewoonlik deur die gebruik van kaal hande en 'n leergordel veroorsaak word. Die applikant het verder beweer dat die kinders se moeder haar met die eerste respondent se optrede teenoor die kinders vereenselwig het en hom by tye aangehits het om die kinders aan te rand en ook daaraan deelgeneem het. Die eerste en tweede respondent het die applikant se bewerings omtrent die aanranding op die kinders ontken. Die applikant het aansoek gedoen om 'n bevel wat die eerste respondent verbied om die kinders aan te rand, te molesteer of om hulle lyfstraf toe te dien, en wat die tweede respondent verbied om die kinders aan te rand. Die hof het beslis dat die kinders se moeder haar tugtigingsbevoegdheid (insluitende die reg om lyfstraf toe te dien) aan die kinders se stiefvader mag delegeer, maar dat hy die bevoegdheid te alle tye op 'n beheerste en redelike wyse moet uitoefen.

FRIEDMAN J: [51] A. <u>Rights of parents relating to parental authority</u>

It is settled law that parents have the right and power to administer punishment to their minor children for the purpose of correction and education.

In order to achieve this object parents have the right to chastise their children. The chastisement must be moderate and reasonable, even when it takes the form of corporal punishment, which in turn must be restrained and tenable. See *R v Le Maitre and Avenant* 1947 (4) SA 616 (C); *R v Muller* 1948 (4) SA 848 (O); *Hiltonian Society v Crofton* 1952 (3) SA 130 (A); *R v Scheepers* 1915 AD 337 at 338; *R v Jacobs* 1941 OPD 7; *R v Roux* 1932 OPD 59 at 61; *R v Liebenberg* 1917 OPD 67 at 69; *R v Theron and Another* 1936 OPD 166 at 176 and *S v Lekgathe* 1982 (3) SA 104 (B) at 109A. See also Snyman *Criminal Law* at 107; JC van der Walt *Delict: Principles and Cases* at 47; Boberg *The Law of Persons and the Family* at 464–6; Spiro *The Law of Parent and Child* 3rd ed at 83.

In *Germani v Herf and Another* 1975 (4) SA 887 (A) it was held that a custodian is entitled to use reasonable force to compel an unwilling or recalcitrant child to submit to the non-custodian parent's right of access. Furthermore, the custodian parent can also ask the non-custodian parent to use reasonable force to compel an unwilling child to submit to the non-custodian parent's rights of access.

Even while the child is temporarily under the control of the non-custodian parent pursuant to a right of access, the parental authority revives, and the non-custodian parent in these circumstances can use reasonable force to correct or discipline the child should it be necessary.

To be justifiable the punishment must be equitable and fair.

In determining the reasonableness of the punishment the following circumstances must be considered. This list is not exhaustive:

(i) the nature of the offence;

(ii) the condition of the child, physically and mentally; [52]

(iii) the motive of the person administering the punishment;

(iv) the severity of the punishment, ie degree of force applied;

(v) the object used to administer punishment;

(vi) the age and sex of the child;

(vii) the build of the child.

See *R v Schoombee* 1924 TPD 481 at 483; *R v Theron* (*supra* at 176); *Hiltonian Society v Crofton* (*supra* at 134); R v Jacobs (*supra* at 10); and *Tshabalala v Jacobs* 1942 TPD 310 at 313.

In *R v Janke & Janke* 1913 TPD 382 at 385–6, MASON J said:

'The general rule adopted both by the Roman, the Roman-Dutch law and the English law is that a parent may inflict moderate and reasonable chastisement on a child for misconduct provided that this is not done in a manner offensive to good morals or for other objects than correction and administration ... The presumption is that such punishment has not been dictated by improper motives and the court will not lightly interfere with the discretion of parents or those empowered with a similar authority ... The character of the offence, the amount of punishment inflicted, the bodily and mental condition of the child, the nature of the instrument used and the objects, purposes and motives of the person inflicting chastisement are all matters which have to be considered. A nervous or highly sensitive child may, for instance, be seriously affected by a whipping which would be harmless in the case of a more robust constitution. And where the object of the whipping is not really for the purposes of correction or by way of admonition or instruction or the proper vindication of authority (see *Voet* 47.10) those guilty of such conduct may be held liable to the law ...'

It must also be emphasised that a parent who exceeds the bounds of moderation, or who acts from improper or ulterior motives, or from a sadistic propensity, may well face civil and criminal liability.

B. Delegation of the right to chastise

May a parent delegate the right to chastise to another person? It is accepted that by common law persons in *loco parentis,* such as housemasters, principals and teachers, have the power to chastise, and administer punishment to pupils who are under their control and care. This is done in order to maintain discipline and control of misbehaving pupils. As in the case of parents it must take the form of moderate chastisement, and is subject to the same limitations.

A teacher or housemaster or principal of a school has the right to inflict moderate and reasonable corporal punishment, not only as a result of delegation by the parent, but also in his/her own right. See *R v Roux* 1939 OPD 59 at 61; *R v Le Maitre and Avenant* (*supra*); *R v Muller* (*supra*); *Hiltonian Society v Crofton* (*supra*); *R v Scheepers* (*supra*); and *R v Jacobs* (*supra*).

For the purposes of this judgment I have not considered, nor is it necessary to consider, the limitation on the teacher's authority in this respect by various legislative enactments.

On the authorities that I have cited, I come to the conclusion that a parent does have the right to delegate the authority to chastise a child to a person in *loco parentis,* subject to the conditions that I have specified.

On the basis of the aforegoing there seems to be no reason why a parent or a person in *loco parentis* may not delegate the actual administration of corporal punishment to another person. See JC van der Walt *Delict:* [53] *Principles and Cases* at 47; *Tshabalala v Jacobs (supra)*; *R v Le Maitre and Avenant (supra)*. It also appears that a parent may delegate the right of chastisement and the decision whether and how to chastise. See Snyman *Criminal Law* at 107.

This being the case, the parent can only delegate such rights as he or she has, and nothing more. Consequently the person to whom the right of chastisement is delegated has not a greater or more extensive right than the parent has.

In the instant matter the second respondent has the right, as custodian parent, to chastise her children, the concomitant of which is also to inflict moderate and reasonable corporal punishment on them to maintain authority and discipline, subject to the limitations mentioned.

Concerning the first respondent, the second respondent may delegate this right to him, which he may only exercise on the same terms and conditions as the first respondent. His position at common law would be no different to that of a teacher.

He is the head of the household and unless he is party to or assists the second respondent to maintain discipline in the home, the children may well find themselves in an atmosphere where there is no aim, direction or purpose in their upbringing.

Nowadays it is more important in a society where permissiveness is escalating for children to be inculcated with a respect for discipline and authority, and generally instruction and guidelines for correct and proper behaviour.

If the second respondent enlists the assistance of the first respondent for these purposes, it is his duty to support and assist her. Hy may not, however, exceed the limit of his rights, nor mete out a greater degree or nature of punishment than the circumstances require. On no account is he, however, to exceed the bounds of reasonableness and moderation in chastising the children, by way of administering corporal punishment. I must assume in his favour that he is not, nor will he be, actuated by improper motives. Conversely the applicant as the natural father, and non-custodian parent, has also the same right and authority while the children are with him . . .

In order to regularise the position between the parties and the children, and inasmuch as the Court is the upper guardian of minors, it is necessary to adjust and regulate the conduct of the respondents concerning their authority to discipline the children.

Accordingly I order

(a) the second respondent has the right and power to chastise the minor children, the said chastisement must be moderate and reasonable and includes the right to impose moderate and reasonable corporal punishment;

(b) the first respondent may exercise the same rights as the second respondent if requested to do so by the second respondent, subject [54] to the same limitation, or if he is in a position of *loco parentis* during the temporary absence of the second respondent, again subject to the same condition;

(c) neither respondent shall molest the children or exceed the bounds of moderate and reasonable chastisement in the disciplining and correction of the children . . .

Note

Part of parental authority, and in particular of custody, is the right to chastise the child. This includes the right to inflict corporal punishment

Aantekening

Deel van ouerlike gesag, en in die besonder van bewaring, is die bevoegdheid om die kind te tugtig. Dit sluit die bevoegdheid om lyfstraf toe te

on the child. The case under discussion neatly sets out the principles regulating chastisement.

dien in. Die onderhawige saak sit die beginsels rakende tugtiging netjies uiteen.

The duty of support

Die onderhoudsplig

[147]   GLIKSMAN V TALEKINSKY

1955 4 SA 468 (W)

The duty of a parent to support his major child

The applicant was a widow who had six children ranging in age from eight months to eleven years. She claimed £176 per month as maintenance from her father (respondent) who offered to pay her £90 per month. Her father was well off and was financially able to support her. During her marriage the applicant and her husband had a high standard of living but their financial situation later deteriorated to such an extent that the husband was declared insolvent. Her husband died while still insolvent and the applicant was left without any means to support herself and her children. The court ordered the respondent to pay the applicant £90 per month as a contribution towards her maintenance.

Die onderhoudsplig van 'n ouer teenoor sy meerderjarige kind

Die applikant was 'n weduwee met ses kinders, wie se ouderdomme gewissel het van agt maande tot elf jaar. Die applikant het onderhoud ten bedrae van £176 per maand van haar vader (respondent) geëis. Hy het aangebied om £90 per maand aan haar te betaal. Haar vader was 'n vermoënde man wat finansieel daartoe in staat was om haar te onderhou. Gedurende haar huwelik het die applikant en haar man 'n hoë lewenstandaard gehandhaaf maar hulle finansiële posisie het later dermate verswak dat die man insolvent verklaar is. Die man het gesterf terwyl hy nog insolvent was en die applikant is agtergelaat sonder die middele om aan haar en haar kinders se onderhoudsbehoeftes te kon voldoen. Die hof het die respondent beveel om £90 per maand aan die applikant as 'n bydrae tot haar onderhoud te betaal.

WILLIAMSON J: [469] It is clear that the respondent is legally liable to provide maintenance for the support of his daughter if she is in want and if he is in a position to supply her with the means of livelihood. This legal position has not been disputed on his behalf; it has not been contended that there is no legal liability; and the fact that there is presently a legal liability on him to contribute something has to an extent been recognised by him, because he has in fact paid the applicant, since her husband's death an amount of £75 a month. In addition he has made other small contributions to her welfare, both in cash and in kind, the exact amount of which is in dispute, and he has since offered to pay her the sum of £90 a month. It is submitted by counsel for the respondent that £90 is a proper amount in law to cover the liability of the respondent to contribute towards his daughter's support and the support of his six grandchildren.

In an application of this nature the *onus* is quite clearly upon the applicant to show that she needs support, and I think, also, to show the amount of support that she requires. A child, when it becomes of age, should normally be in a position to provide for himself or herself. In the case of a married woman, of course, she usually acquires other means of support in that she can look to her husband for support. In the case of a woman who finds herself in the position in which the applicant now is, a widow with six small children, she must still show that she is not able to support herself. *Prima facie* she shows it here by the mere fact that she has no assets, has no income and has six small children to look after. She does not deal with the question as to whether she can earn a living, and perhaps she should have dealt with that matter in the petition, because the liability on the father to support her only arises when it is shown that she cannot support herself, she being a major who should be able to provide for herself in [470] normal circumstances. But I think it can be taken here that it is shown that the applicant at the moment is not able to support herself and that something is required to assist her; that fact, as I have said, is really recognised by the attitude of the respondent himself.

The real difficulty is the basis upon which the applicant is entitled to support. It is stated generally that a parent's duty to support a child is to provide maintenance for the child in accordance with the means, position and status of the parent. This statement, which is to be found in a number of reported cases, has always been made in connection with the case of a minor child requiring support; in the case of a person who has acquired a separate position in life and made a separate home this statement, in my view, requires some qualification. A child who is a major and who has gone out into the world and established his or her own home and mode of life is not entitled to come back to the parent at any time in life and say, "I am your child and when I lived with you as a minor I lived in a rich home where I had everything provided, and in as much as you are still rich and able to support me on the same basis, the legal position is that what you must pay me must be decided in accordance with your station in life, your standard of living and your means". In my view the parent's means are a factor to be taken into consideration, but it is not the only factor; the child's position in life and its standard of living are of equal importance.

I think that what must be considered is, what would be a reasonable amount to keep this child (and in this case also her children) in such a condition that she and they will not want, taking into consideration her status both as given by her father and as acquired later in life when she got married, and taking into consideration the father's means and position. I do not think there is a duty upon the father to supply sufficient means to enable his daughter to live upon exactly the same scale that she might be able to live if the father supplied her with everything he could supply her with. It has been said that "maintenance means support beyond want and all that is beyond that is left to paternal affection". That statement is probably too broad and, in my view, cannot be applied strictly to these circumstances. I do not think the father's liability here to support his daughter and her children is confined to just lifting her above the barest want. "Want" is a relative term, and I think it must, in each case, be determined with reference to the circumstances of the person concerned, what he or she has been accustomed to and what he or she can reasonably now live on. The applicant may have been accumstomed to live on £500 a month when her husband was alive; she may have been accustomed to live on considerably in excess of the £176 which she now claims; she may feel that she would like to live in the same sort of way, have the same sort of clothes, incur the same sort of expenses and send her children to the same sort of school; but that I do not think is her right. The fact that she cannot satisfy her wishes in these respects would not mean she is in want, even taking into consideration the different factors I have mentioned above. She is entitled to get the necessaries of life taking into consideration the proper facts, such as her accustomed mode of living, her position and the means and position [471] of her parent; but she cannot claim the luxuries that may have attended that previous scale of living. Any luxuries she may have previously enjoyed may be very much desired by her and could possibly be easily supplied by her parent; but they are not items which she is entitled in law to demand that her father shall supply...

[WILLIAMSON J analysed the facts of the case in order to establish what amount the applicant needs and proceeded:]

I have come to the conclusion ... that a woman in the position of the applicant can be kept free from want and can live free from distress upon a scale that is related to her position in life and to what she has been accustomed, but without any extravagance and with considerably more economy than the applicant has been exercising or is apparently prepared to exercise, upon a sum of £120 a month.

In my view such a sum is the sum which, for the moment leaving out other means, the father in all the circumstances would be legally liable to contribute. The applicant would not be able to keep up anything like the standard to which she has been trained or to which she has been accustomed; but to keep her children upon a proper basis in the circumstances, she would not manage upon a sum less than £120 a month.

Now, at the present time she is receiving a sum of £30 a month as a result of contributions by her sister and her brother. The papers make it clear that those contributions are at the moment only temporary and may be withdrawn. But while the applicant is receiving that £30 a month, in my view, the amount of £90 offered by the respondent is enough to cover his legal liability in relation to the applicant. I appreciate that it will require an effort on the part of the applicant, and possibly re-adjustment in certain respects, but I think the total of £120 which she will have from her father, her brother and sister, which represents the legal liability of her father or the family to contribute towards her maintenance, must be made to cover her and her children's [472] wants. She may be able to adopt other ways to find additional income. I can see no reason why if she engages a servant and hires a house with possibly another servant to look after the children, – some of the children are at school – she should not, with her education, earn money herself as well.

That means that the offer that has been made by the respondent is, in my view, a proper offer.

But I would like to say that my view is that the sum that should be contributed by the father, if applicant has no other means, is the sum of £120 a month, and I feel the parties should not be put to greater expense in further applications if the brother and sister are no longer going to continue with their contributions towards the maintenance of the applicant. I think it will be in the interests of all parties if my views in this respect are made known. I feel that any deficiency below the sum of £120 a month income should be made good by the father over and above the £90 which I think he should presently contribute. I also feel that if there are unforeseen expenditures, such as unexpectedly high doctors' or chemists' bills or dentists' bills, then it may be the duty of the father to make even further advances. The accident of sickness or ill-health is a matter which may create a different position at any moment and which may increase the father's liability. I feel that he should bear in mind that the view of the Court is that he should see that his daughter gets £120 a month at least for her general living expenses and for the expenses of her children ...

In the result I order that the respondent pays his daughter the sum of £90 a month as a contribution towards her maintenance ...

Note

A parent's duty to support his child continues for as long as that child is unable to support itself and is in need of maintenance and the parent is able to pay such maintenance (Spiro 392; Boberg

Aantekening

'n Ouer se onderhoudsplig teenoor sy kind duur voort vir solank as wat die kind nie in staat is om homself te onderhou nie, hy onderhoud benodig en sy ouer in staat is om die onderhoud

249 261 264; Barnard, Cronjé and Olivier 312; Van der Vyver and Joubert 630). The duty does not necessarily come to an end when the child reaches the age of majority (Spiro 402; Boberg 264; Barnard, Cronjé and Olivier 312).

If, however, a court orders one parent to pay maintenance for a child to the other parent, for example at the time of the parents' divorce, such an order will lapse when the child becomes a major. Upon attaining majority the child's parent can no longer claim maintenance on its behalf. As from then on the child must itself institute the claim for maintenance (*Smit v Smit* 1980 3 SA 1010 (O); Van der Vyver and Joubert 632).

The scope of the support to which a major child is entitled was set out in the case under discussion. From this judgment it would appear that a child who is a major is not entitled to maintenance on the same scale as a minor child of the same parents would be (see also *In re Estate Visser* [148]; Spiro 402; Boberg 265; Van der Vyver and Joubert 630-632). According to this judgment a major child is entitled to receive the necessities of life, taking into consideration all relevant facts such as the means and position of the parent and the mode of living to which the child has been accustomed. The child would be entitled to more than the bare necessities of life. It would not, however, be able to claim the luxuries of life which it may previously have had, even if those luxuries could be supplied by the parent. Spiro (402) suggests that the proper test to determine the *quantum* of maintenance should be the standard of living of the parent. Spiro is thus of the opinion that the same test should be applied to determine the amount of maintenance payable for a child who is a major as that which is applied to determine the *quantum* of maintenance payable to a minor child. (See further Spiro 397-402; Boberg 254-267; Barnard, Cronjé and Olivier 313-314; Van der Vyver and Joubert 630-632.)

(See Spiro 398; Van Zyl *Family Law Service* par C9 and Boberg 259-260 in connection with the question whether a child is entitled to claim university or other tertiary education. See also *Smit v Smit* 1980 3 SA 1010 (O) and *Mentz v Simpson* 1990 4 SA 455 (A).)

See also the note on *In re Estate Visser* [148].

te verskaf (Spiro 392; Boberg 249 261 264; Barnard, Cronjé en Olivier 322; Van der Vyver en Joubert 630). Die plig eindig nie noodwendig wanneer die kind meerderjarig word nie (Spiro 402; Boberg 264; Barnard, Cronjé en Olivier 322).

Indien 'n hof egter 'n bevel uitgereik het ingevolge waarvan die een ouer van 'n kind onderhoud vir die kind aan die ander ouer moet betaal, byvoorbeeld ten tyde van die egskeiding van die ouers, sal daardie bevel beëindig word wanneer die kind meerderjarig word. Die ouer van die kind kan dan nie meer namens hom onderhoud eis nie. Van daardie tydstip af moet die kind self onderhoud eis (*Smit v Smit* 1980 3 SA 1010 (O); Van der Vyver en Joubert 632).

Die omvang van die onderhoud waarop 'n meerderjarige kind geregtig is, is in die onderhawige geval uiteengesit. Uit hierdie beslissing wil dit voorkom asof die meerderjarige kind nie op dieselfde onderhoud geregtig is as waarop 'n minderjarige kind van dieselfde ouers geregtig is nie (sien ook *In re Estate Visser* [148]; Spiro 402; Boberg 265; Van der Vyver en Joubert 630-632). Volgens hierdie uitspraak is die meerderjarige kind geregtig op noodsaaklikhede, met inagneming van al die relevante feite soos die vermoë en status van die ouer en die lewenstandaard waaraan die kind vroeër gewoond was. Die kind sal geregtig wees op meer as net dit wat onontbeerlik is om aan die lewe te bly. Die kind sal egter nie die luukse kan eis waaraan hy vroeër gewoond mag gewees het nie, selfs nie eers indien die ouer in staat sou wees om dit aan hom te verskaf nie. Spiro (402) doen aan die hand dat die toets vir bepaling van die *quantum* van onderhoud die lewenstandaard van die ouer behoort te wees. Hy redeneer dus dat dieselfde toets aangewend behoort te word om die omvang van die onderhoud te bepaal as wat aangewend word om te bepaal hoeveel onderhoud aan 'n minderjarige kind betaal moet word. (Sien verder Spiro 397-402; Boberg 254-267; Barnard, Cronjé en Olivier 324; Van der Vyver en Joubert 630-632.)

(Sien Spiro 398; Van Zyl *Family Law Service* par C9 en Boberg 259-260 oor die vraag of 'n kind daarop geregtig is om 'n universiteits- of ander tersiêre opleiding te eis. Sien ook *Smit v Smit* 1980 3 SA 1010 (O) en *Mentz v Simpson* 1990 4 SA 455 (A).)

Sien ook die aantekening by *In re Estate Visser* [148].

[148]   IN RE ESTATE VISSER

1948 3 SA 1129 (K)

A minor is entitled to support out of its parent's estate

The applicant's deceased husband (the testator) was the father of six minor children, namely Christoffel (aged twenty), Delicia (nearly eighteen years old), Maria (nearly fourteen years old), John (approximately ten years old), Hendrik (nine years old) and Marie-Reinet (two years old). The five first-mentioned children were born of a previous marriage of the testator and Marie-Reinet was born of the marriage between the applicant and the testator. In his will the testator provided that a farm called Vissershoek should go to his eldest son, Christoffel. Christoffel had to pay £5 000 for his inheritance into the testator's estate. The will also provided that Christoffel could pass a mortgage bond for this amount over the farm. The other children of his first marriage were appointed as the beneficiaries of certain life insurance policies. In a further clause of the will the testator appointed his children, with the exception of Christoffel, as the heirs of the remainder of his estate. All the parties to the matter agreed that Marie-Reinet was also included in this bequest. The first and final liquidation and distribution account in the estate gave £23 891 as the amount available for distribution amongst the heirs. However, this amount included the value of Christoffel's inheritance. There were insufficient funds in the estate to pay out the beneficiaries. The applicant consequently applied to have *curatores ad litem* appointed for the children and she further applied for an order that the amounts required for the maintenance and education of the children

'n Minderjarige is geregtig op onderhoud uit sy oorlede ouer se boedel

Die applikant se oorlede man (die erflater) was die vader van ses minderjarige kinders naamlik Christoffel (twintig jaar oud), Delicia (amper agtien jaar oud), Maria (amper veertien jaar oud), John (omtrent tien jaar oud), Hendrik (nege jaar oud) en Marie-Reinet (twee jaar oud). Die eersgenoemde vyf kinders is gebore uit 'n vorige huwelik van die erflater en Marie-Reinet is gebore uit die huwelik tussen die applikant en die erflater. In sy testament het die erflater bepaal dat 'n plaas met die naam Vissershoek na sy oudste seun, Christoffel, moes gaan. Christoffel moes £5 000 vir sy erfporsie aan sy vader se boedel betaal. Die testament het ook daarvoor voorsiening gemaak dat Christoffel 'n verband van £5 000 oor die plaas kon registreer. Die ander kinders uit sy vorige huwelik is as die bevoordeeldes ingevolge sekere lewenspolisse aangewys. In 'n verdere klousule het die erflater sy kinders met die uitsondering van Christoffel as die erfgename van die restant van sy boedel aangestel. Al die partye in die saak was dit eens dat Marie-Reinet ook in die restant van die boedel kon deel. Ingevolge die eerste en finale likwidasie- en distribusierekening van die erflater se boedel was £23 891 vir verdeling onder die erfgename beskikbaar maar hierdie bedrag het die waarde van die bemaking aan Christoffel ingesluit. Daar was nie genoeg geld in die boedel om die erfgename uit te betaal nie. Die applikant het toe aansoek gedoen om die aanstelling van *curatores ad litem* vir die kinders en dat die bedrae wat vir die onderhoud en opvoeding van die kinders

first be paid out of the estate before any distribution in terms of the will took place. In accordance with a court order one *curator ad litem* was appointed for Christoffel and another was appointed for the other children. The court ordered the curators, *inter alia,* to establish, and report to the court, how much money would be required for the maintenance and education of the five youngest children and how these amounts could be obtained. All efforts to come to an agreement on these matters failed and the court was asked to decide the issues. The court ordered that a bond of £5 000 be passed over the farm Vissershoek and that that amount be paid into the testator's estate in accordance with his will. The court further ordered that maintenance be paid out of the testator's estate to each of his three youngest children until each turned nineteen years. The court also issued an order that the amounts payable as maintenance first be discharged out of the inheritances that the children were each to receive. The court furthermore ordered that a fund of up to £1 000 be created out of the money in the testator's estate for payment of the medical and other unforeseen expenses of the five youngest children.

benodig sou word eers uitbetaal moes word voordat enige verdeling van die bates ingevolge die testament sou plaasvind. Ingevolge 'n hofbevel is een *curator ad litem* vir Christoffel aangestel en 'n ander *curator ad litem* vir die ander kinders. Die hof het die kurators onder andere opdrag gegee om vas te stel en aan die hof verslag te doen hoeveel geld vir die onderhoud en opvoeding van die vyf jongste kinders nodig sou wees en op welke wyse hierdie bedrae verkry kon word. Alle pogings om oor hierdie aangeleenthede tot 'n vergelyk te kom, het misluk en die hof is gevra om oor die aangeleenthede te beslis. Die hof het beveel dat 'n verband van £5 000 oor die plaas Vissershoek geregistreer moes word en dat die bedrag aan die erflater se boedel betaal moes word ooreenkomstig die bepalings van die erflater se testament. Die hof het verder beveel dat onderhoud uit die erflater se boedel betaal moes word aan elk van sy drie jongste kinders totdat elkeen die ouderdom van negentien jaar bereik het. Die hof het verder beveel dat die bedrae wat vir die kinders se onderhoud nodig was eers gedelg moes word uit die erfporsies wat elke kind sou ontvang. Verder het die hof beveel dat 'n fonds van tot £1 000 uit die erflater se boedel in die lewe geroep moes word vir die betaling van mediese en ander onvoorsiene koste vir die vyf jongste kinders.

OGILVIE THOMPSON WN R: [1133] Afgesien van die bogemelde bemakings in hul vader se testament, besit geen een van die onmondiges enige iets behalwe dat die kinders van die eerste huwelik uit die boedel van hulle oorlede moeder elkeen by hulle respektiewe mondigwording 'n bedrag van £269 erf. Daar sy die stiefmoeder van hierdie laasgenoemde kinders is, is petisionaresse nie regsaanspreeklik om hulle te onderhou nie. (*Voet* (25.3.10); *Jacobs v Cape Town Municipality* (1935, CPD 474).) Verder, wat betref haar aanspreeklikheid om haar eie kind (Marie-Reinet) te onderhou, blyk dit uit die inligting tans voor die hof dat die middele wat petisionaresse besit skaars genoeg is om haarself te onderhou.

Die eerste regspunt wat beslis moet word is: is die erflater se boedel vir die onderhoud van sy onmondige kinders regsaanspreeklik? In *Ex parte Estate Pitt-Kennedy* (1946, NPD 776 te b 779) het CARLISLE R gesê:

"It is settled, see *Goldman's* case (1937, WLD 64), that the estate of the deceased father is always liable for the maintenance of his minor children and that such maintenance is a debt resting on the estate which must be satisfied before any payments of legacies are made."

Uit die terme van die bo-aangehaalde bevel van STEYN, R in die onderhawige saak blyk dit dat hy ook hierdie aanspreeklikheid van 'n vader se boedel as vaste reg beskou het. Mnr *Van Wyk* [die *curator ad litem* vir Christoffel] het egter in sy argument namens die minderjarige Christoffel hierdie stelling sterk betwis, en 'n beslissing daaromtrent moet derhalwe gegee word. Die aanspreeklikheid van 'n vader, gedurende sy leeftyd, om sy kinders te onderhou is natuurlik buite twyfel. Hierdie aanspreeklikheid spruit, volgens *Dig* (25.3.5 (2)): *ex aequitate caritateque sanguinis* [uit billikheid en toegeneentheid tussen bloedverwante]. Dieselfde begrip word in *Dig* (25.3.5 (15)) deur die woorde *ex ratione pietatis* [uit liefde], en in *Dig* (25.3.5 (16)) deur die woorde *ratione naturali* [op grond van die natuur], meegedeel. *Voet* (25.3.4) praat van . . . "*alimenta ex contractu vel legato an vero ex sola pietate et concurrente legis praecepto* . . ." [die onderhoudsplig ontstaan uit 'n kontrak of 'n bemaking of inderdaad uit blote liefde en toepaslike regsbeginsels]. Dit is in 'n hele paar sake bevestig dat hierdie verpligting *ex pietate* of *jure naturali* nog die basis is van die aanspreeklikheid vir onderhoud wat wedersyds tussen ouer en kind in ons reg vandag bestaan (sien bv *In re Knoop* (9 SC 198); *Waterson v Maybery* [1134] (1934, TPD 210 te b 214)). Daar is egter min Romeins-Hollandse autoriteit omtrent die vraag of 'n vader se boedel nog aanspreeklik vir die onderhoud van sy kinders bly. *Voet* (25.3.18 en 23.2.82) ontken dat so 'n aanspreeklikheid bestaan en sê dat die aanspreeklikheid vir onderhoud kom tot 'n einde met die dood van die vader. *Groenewegen* (*De Legibus Abrogatis ad Digest* (34.1.15)) sê presies die teenoorgestelde . . . *Groenewegen* se mening is deur DE VILLIERS HR en WESSELS R respektiewelik in *Carelse v Estate de Vries* (23 SC 532 te b 537) en in *Spies' Executors v Beyers* (1908, TS 473 te b 480) beslis aanvaar: en daarna het 'n hele reeks sake dieselfde koers ingeslaan (sien bv *Ritchken's Executors v Ritchken* (1924, WLD 17); *Davis' Tutor v Estate Davis* (1925, WLD 168); *Ex parte Burstein* (1941, CPD 87 te b 92) en *Ex parte Estate Pitt-Kennedy* (*supra*)). Afgesien van die feit dat dit in die belang van vastigheid in die reg klaarblyklik wenslik is om hierdie sake te volg, meen ek – met respek – dat hierdie beslissings volkome in ooreenstemming is met die bogemelde beginsel van aanspreeklikheid *ex pietate* of *jure naturali*; want, in die woorde van DE VILLIERS HR in *Carelse v de Vries* (*supra*) te b 537,

"were the rule otherwise an unnatural father possessed of ample means might bequeath all his property to strangers and leave his own legitimate offspring unprovided for and a burden on the rest of the community."

. . . Mnr *van Wyk* het onder meer geargumenteer dat aanspreeklikheid om onderhoud te betaal kan nie tereg 'n skuld ("a debt") genoem word nie; dat Wet 23 van 1874 (K) ['n ou Kaapse wet wat testamente gereël het] volkome vryheid van erflating bewerkstellig het; en dat om die erflater se boedel aanspreeklik te hou vir die onderhoud van sy kinders sou derhalwe op 'n verandering van sy testament neerkom: en in die verband het hy *Shearer v Shearer's Executors* (1911, CPD 813 te b 820) aangehaal. Dit is wel waar dat 'n kind se eis vir onderhoud nie met 'n krediteur kan kompeteer nie: maar meeste van die sake wat so 'n [1135] eis as 'n "debt" beskrywe het, het dit ook duidelik gemaak dat alle gewone skulde eers betaal moet word alvorens die eis vir onderhoud in ag geneem kan word. Die juiste posisie m.i. is dat 'n eis vir onderhoud as 'n skuldvordering *sui generis* beskou moet word wat nie met gewone krediteure kan kompeteer nie, maar wat, in 'n gewone saak, 'n voorkeur bo erfgename en legate geniet (*cf Beaton v Beaton's Trustee* (*supra* te bbl 191 en 193) [1935 SC 187]). Aangaande die argument wat op die vryheid van erflating gebaseer is, die kind se eis vir onderhoud (wat, soos ek hierbo gemeld het, *ex pietate, debito naturali*, gespruit het, en nie uit die *legitim* [legitieme porsie] nie) het m.i. na die afskaffing van die *legitim* nog onaangetas voortbestaan. Vryheid van erflating bedoel dat 'n kind geen aanspraak het om enige deel van sy ouer se boedel *ex testamento* te verkry nie: maar daardie vryheid van erflating kan nie aangeroep word nie om die erflater se verpligting om sy kinders te onderhou te ontduik nie. Dit is nie 'n kwessie van verandering van die testament nie: die Hof beskerm slegs die regte van die kinders ...

Mnr *van Wyk* se betoog moet derhalwe verwerp word. My beslissing is dat die erflater se boedel aanspreeklik is vir die onderhoud van sy kinders. Soos ek alreeds gemeld het, kan die oorblywende eggenote, onder die omstandighede van die onderhawige saak, nie as aanspreeklik vir onderhoud beskou word nie. Dit is derhalwe onnodig om enige mening uit te spreek oor die vraag of – en, indien wel, op watter basis – aanspreeklikheid om behoeftige kinders te onderhou tussen die oorblywende eggenoot en die afgestorwe eggenoot se boedel verdeel moet word ...

Mnr *van Wyk* se tweede hoof-argument het oor *quantum* gegaan. Hy het betoog dat die onderhoud vasgestel moet word met verwysing na 'n blote bestaan, en nie met verwysing na wat die kinders in die verlede geniet het nie. Ek kan nie met hierdie argument saamstem nie. Afgesien van die feit dat die Hof hier met egte [binne-egtelike] kinders, en nie met onegte [buite-egtelike] kinders, te doen het (sien *Carelse v de Vries* (*supra* te b 538)), is dit duidelik dat

> "support (*alimenta*) includes not only food and clothing in accordance with the quality and condition of the persons to be supplied, but also lodging and [1136] care in sickness – see *Voet* (25.3.4); van Leeuwen, *Cens For* (1.10.5); Brunneman in *Codicem* (5–25)" –

per TINDALL, AR, in *Oosthuizen v Stanley* (1938, AD te b 328); (sien ook *van Leeuwen Roomsch-Hollandsche Recht* 1.13.8 en *Scott v Scott* (1946, WLD 99)).

Die "quality and condition" van kinders wat onderhoud nodig het moet in groot mate met verwysing na die stand van hulle ouers en die betrokke familie beslis word ... van Leeuwen *Cens For* (1.10.5); ... (Kersteman *Aanhangsel sv* "onderhoud" b 975). "The term necessity has a relative meaning – relative to the party who makes the claim" – (*Fraser* (*supra*, b 691) [Parent and Child 2e uitg].) Hierdie beginsel geld m.i. ook vir 'n onderhoudseis teen 'n vader se boedel. Die maatstaf is deur DE WAAL, R in *Davis' Tutor v Estate Davis* (*supra* te b 173) toegepas, en na my oordeel is dit die korrekte maatstaf. Mnr *van Wyk* het geargumenteer dat daar 'n vader nie gedurende sy leeftyd deur die Hof gedwing kan word om sy kinders na die mate van sy rykdom te onderhou en op te voed nie, behoort die Hof dit nie na die vader se dood te doen nie. Gestel dat (teenstrydig met wat deur *Voet* in 25.3.4 (*Kersteman* b 971) aangedui is) die eerste deel van hierdie stelling juis is, stem ek saam met Mnr *van Zyl* [die *curator ad litem* vir die ander kinders] dat die twee gevalle verskil: in eersgenoemde is dit die vader se diskresie en in die tweede gebruik die Hof sy eie diskresie ...

Wanneer 'n eis vir onderhoud teen 'n boedel beslis word moet elke saak dus op sy eie meriete behandel word (*cf Oosthuizen v Stanley* (*supra* te b 328)). In die onderhawige saak is daar m.i. geen rede waarom die Hof, in die berekening van die onderhoud waarop die kinders geregtig is, nie die maatstaf van die familiestand sou toepas nie.

Die volgende vraag is of die kinders se kapitaal, in teenstelling met die rente daarop, by die berekening van die onderhoud waarop hulle geregtig is, in ag geneem moet word. Mnr *van Zyl* het betoog dat net die inkomste van die kinders, en nie hulle kapitaal [1137] nie, vir hulle onderhoud gebruik mag word ...

Een van die vereistes van 'n eis vir onderhoud is dat die eiser homself nie kan onderhou nie. (*Waterson v Maybery* (*supra* te b 215)). In die woorde van SUTTON, R (met betrekking tot die omgekeerde, maar andersins dieselfde, stelling) in *Jacobs v Cape Town Municipality* (*supra* te b 479) [1935 CPD 474]:

> "The liability only exists under two conditions that the parent cannot support himself and that the child has sufficient means to do so."

Sien ook *Oosthuizen v Stanley* (*supra* te bbl 328 en 331). Ek is nie met enige beslissing bekend wat hierdie beginsel tot inkomste beperk. As 'n kind kapitaal het, dan kan hy hom daaruit onderhou. Dit sou m.i. onregverdig wees om te beslis dat 'n minderjarige wat kapitaal besit hoef nie van daardie geld vir sy onderhoud te gebruik nie, vernaamlik wanneer, soos in die onderhawige saak, daardie kapitaal afkomstig is van die persoon wie se boedel nou vir onderhoud aanspreeklik gehou word. My beslissing is dus dat die kapitaal wat die kinders van die erflater sal ontvang, vir hulle onderhoud gebruik moet word . . .

Ek kom nou by die vasstelling van die bedrag van onderhoud waarop die kinders geregtig is. Mnr *van Zyl* het betoog dat die familie behoort as 'n eenheid beskou te word, en dat die Hof 'n globale bedrag per jaar vir die groep kinders behoort toe te staan, wat geleidelik met die sterfte van kinders en na mate hulle selfonderhoudend word, verminder kan word. Hierdie beginsel is soms gerieflik wanneer die kinders almal saamwoon (en besuinigings [1138] in verband met sekere items soos huurgeld, bediendes, loon ens kan dus gemaak word): maar dié omstandighede geld egter nie hier nie daar die kinders hulle vir die grootste gedeelte van die jaar weg van die huis in verskillende kosskole bevind. Onder die omstandighede van die onderhawige saak behoort die Hof na my oordeel – behalwe wat die hiernagenoemde gebeurlikheidsfonds betref – die kinders se onderhoud afsonderlik te bepaal. Verder, volgens my mening, behoort die Hof die bedrag per kind per maand vas te stel, want so 'n beslissing sal praktiese administrasie grootliks vereenvoudig. Die kinders is geregtig op onderhoud vanaf die datum van hulle vader se dood. Die Hof moet beslis hoe lank hierdie onderhoud moet voortduur. Volgens my oordeel is dit verkieslik om hierdie termyn met betrekking tot ouderdom liewer as – soos deur mnr *van Winsen* namens die petisionaresse betoog – met betrekking tot matrikulasie, vas te stel. Na deeglike oorweging het ek tot die gevolgtrekking gekom dat die Hof behoort soos deur mnr *van Zyl* betoog en deur die Meester in sy behulpsame verslag goedgekeur – hierdie ouderdom op 19 jaar vas te stel. Die kinders behoort almal in staat te wees om voor daardie ouderdom te matrikuleer; en hulle sal ook die voordele van die hiernagenoemde gebeurlikheidsfonds geniet. Petisionaresse se aanspraak dat onderhoud ook vir opvoeding na Seniorsertifikaat aan die kinders toegestaan behoort te word, kan m.i. nie onder die omstandighede van hierdie saak slaag nie.

Die bepaling van die bedrae van maandelikse onderhoud moet noodwendig ietwat arbitrêr wees. Verskeie bedrae is deur die Advokate aan die hand gedoen en ek het hulle argumente deeglik oorweeg. Alles in ag geneem – vernaamlik die ondervinding van onlangse jare in verband met die onderhoud van die kinders en die familiestand – is ek die mening toegedaan dat dit billik is om £12 10s per maand (die bedrag deur die Meester vir seuns aanbeveel) vas te stel. In die geval van Marie-Reinet sal die bedrag kleiner moet wees terwyl sy nog jonk is. Ek bepaal dit op £6 per maand totdat sy haar agste verjaarsdag bereik. Daarna is sy m.i. ook op £12 10s per maand geregtig. Die uitwerking van die voorgaande beslissings sal wees dat die twee oudste dogters (Delicia en Maria) nie onderhoud uit die boedel sal kry nie, want die geld wat hulle nou, volgens hulle vader se testament, gaan kry sal oorgenoeg wees vir hulle benodigdhede totdat hulle onderskeidelik die ouderdom van 19 jaar bereik.

[1139] Mnr *van Winsen* se voorstel van 'n gebeurlikheidsfonds deur die Meester beheer om buitengewone mediese en soortgelyke onkoste te dek was deur die ander Advokate goedgekeur, en ek is die mening toegedaan dat die Hof behoort hierdie voorstel te aanvaar. Uit die autoriteite wat ek hierbo aangehaal het is dit duidelik dat "onderhoud" mediese onkoste insluit. Deur middel van so 'n gebeurlikheidsfonds word 'n mate van sekuriteit teen siekte verkry, wat moontlik belangrike hulp aan een of meer van die minderjariges kan verleen. Dit is dus in beginsel slegs 'n vermeerdering van die hoeveelheid van onderhoud toegestaan. Ek meen ook dat, ondanks die bepaling, vir maandelikse onderhoudsdoeleindes, van die ouderdom van 19 jaar, die voorstel dat die omtrek van hierdie gebeurlikheidsfonds tot die ouderdom van 21 verleng word kan onder die omstandighede van hierdie saak as billik beskou word... Myns insiens moet die fonds gebruik word, onderhewig aan die Meester se beheer, om onkoste te betaal wat, direk of indirek, deur die gesondheid van enige een van die minderjariges veroorsaak is:... Die voorgestelde maksimum bedrag van hierdie fonds (dws £1 000) kom my as 'n billike bedrag voor.

Die boedel se aanspreeklikheid moet op die huidige stadium vasgestel word (*vide de Klerk v Rowan* (1922, EDL 338) en *Davis' Tutor v Estate Davis (supra)*). In plaas van die eksekutrise te beveel om 'n bedrag te belê wat die vereiste onderhoud sal lewer (soos in *Davis' Tutor v Estate Davis (supra)* geskied het), sal dit m.i. onder die omstandighede van die onderhawige saak meer prakties wees om die erfgenaam Christoffel met hierdie verpligting te belas. Hy het die grootste deel van die boedel – insluitende die waardevolle plaas – geërf: en dus is die posisie van die boedel en sy posisie feitlik dieselfde. Volgens die inligting voor die Hof, was die gemiddelde netto inkomste van hierdie plaas al vir jare tussen £1 500 en £2 000 p.a. Christoffel behoort dus uit die inkomste van die plaas sonder moeilikheid voorsiening vir die onderhoud van sy jongere broers en half-suster te kan maak, vernaamlik as die eerste betalings van onderhoud uit die minderjariges se erfporsies geskied. Mnr *van Wyk* het as kurator-ad-litem ten volle [1140] saamgestem dat dit in Christoffel se belange sou wees om die verpligting vir onderhoud op hierdie manier aan te neem; en hy het namens Christoffel toegestem dat 'n bevel in dier voege gemaak sou word...

Note

Visser's case was strongly criticised by Beinart (1958 *Acta Juridica* 92) who showed that the decision was based on a mistaken reading of Groenewegen. Nevertheless, the case has subsequently been followed by our courts and the Appellate Division has since in *Glazer v Glazer* 1963 4 SA 694 (A) held that it is too late to reverse the decision as it has become settled law. (See also Boberg 279–280 in this regard.)

Three important aspects of the parental duty of support were dealt with in this case, namely the basis, the scope and the duration of the duty.

Firstly, it should be noted that the duty of a parent to support his child arises out of the special relationship between parent and child. As Spiro (385) puts it: "The duty of parents to support their children arises *ex jure naturae et sanguinis* or out of a sense of dutifulness or *ex ratione pietatis* or *ex officio pietatis* or *ex natura necessitatis*, in short, out of a natural affection flowing from the *nexus sanguinis*... The duty is not based on an implied contract nor on the parental power as such and may be said to exist by operation of law." (See also Barnard, Cronjé and Olivier 311; Van der Vyver and Joubert 627; Boberg 254.)

Secondly, attention should be paid to the scope of the parental duty of support. Both parents are legally obliged to support their children whether

Aantekening

Die *Visser*-saak is heftig gekritiseer deur Beinart (1958 *Acta Juridica* 92) wat aangetoon het dat die beslissing gebaseer is op 'n verkeerde uitleg van Groenewegen. Die saak is nogtans deur die howe nagevolg en die Appèlafdeling het sedertdien in *Glazer v Glazer* 1963 4 SA 694 (A) beslis dat dit te laat is om die uitspraak omver te werp aangesien dit nou al gevestigde reg geword het. (Sien ook Boberg 279–280 in hierdie verband.)

Drie belangrike aspekte in verband met die ouerlike onderhoudsplig is in hierdie saak aangeraak, naamlik die basis, die omvang en die duur van hierdie plig.

Eerstens moet daarop gelet word dat die onderhoudsplig van 'n ouer teenoor sy kind uit die spesiale verhouding tussen ouer en kind ontstaan. Spiro (385) stel dit soos volg: "The duty of parents to support their children arises *ex jure naturae et sanguinis* or out of a sense of dutifulness or *ex ratione pietatis* or *ex officio pietatis* or *ex natura necessitatis,* in short, out of a natural affection flowing from the *nexus sanguinis*... The duty is not based on an implied contract nor on the parental power as such and may be said to exist by operation of law." (Sien ook Barnard, Cronjé en Olivier 321; Van der Vyver en Joubert 627; Boberg 254.)

Tweedens moet aandag geskenk word aan die

the children are legitimate or illegitimate (see for example *Hartman v Krogscheepers* 1950 4 SA 421 (W); *Herfst v Herfst* 1964 4 SA 127 (W) [143]; *Van der Harst v Viljoen* 1977 1 SA 795 (C); *Jodaiken v Jodaiken* 1978 1 SA 784 (W)). The scope of the duty of support will be determined by the circumstances of the case and will depend on the social standing and financial position of the parents (see for example *Ncubu v National Employers General Insurance Co Ltd* 1988 2 SA 190 (N); Boberg 259 and the discussion by Spiro 397–398).

The duty to support a child may also extend to a major child. In such a case the scope of the duty will be determined by taking into consideration the child's previous standard of living (in this regard, see the note on *Gliksman v Talekinsky* [147]).

The parental duty of support begins at the child's birth and continues until the child can support himself. As appears from the case under discussion, the duty of a parent to support his child is not concomitant with parental power. Even after the parent's parental power over his child has come to an end, for example through the death of the parent or the majority of the child, the duty of support may still continue (see also, *inter alia,* *Gliksman v Talekinsky; Carelse v Estate De Vries* (1906) 23 SC 532; *Spies' Executors v Beyers* 1908 TS 473; *Goldman v Executor Estate Goldman* 1937 WLD 64; *Hoffman v Herdan* 1982 2 SA 274 (T); *Ex parte Jacobs* 1982 2 SA 276 (O)). On the other hand, the duty of support can come to an end before parental power comes to an end. For example if a newborn baby inherits a large sum of money, the child will be supported out of his inheritance and his parents will not be liable to support him.

It further appears from *Visser's* case that if a child is entitled to an inheritance from its parent and the inheritance is large enough to enable the child to support himself out of the inheritance, the child will be required to do so. The child will then not be able to claim maintenance from that parent's estate (also see *Ex parte Jacobs* 1950 2 PH M26 (O); *Christie v Estate Christie* 1956 3 SA 659 (N); *Ex parte Zietsman: In re Estate Bastard* 1952 2 SA 16 (C); *Lotz v Boedel Van der Merwe* 1958 2 PH M16 (O)).

It should further be noted that the child's claim to be supported out of his deceased parent's estate

omvang van die ouerlike onderhoudsplig. Albei ouers is regtens verplig om hulle kinders te onderhou, ongeag of daardie kinders nou binne- of buite-egtelik is (sien byvoorbeeld *Hartman v Krogscheepers* 1950 4 SA 421 (W); *Herfst v Herfst* 1964 4 SA 127 (W) [143]; *Van der Harst v Viljoen* 1977 1 SA 795 (K); *Jodaiken v Jodaiken* 1978 1 SA 784 (W)). Die omvang van die onderhoudsplig word bepaal deur die omstandighede van elke besondere geval en sal van die sosiale stand en finansiële posisie van die ouers afhang (sien byvoorbeeld *Ncubu v National Employers General Insurance Co Ltd* 1988 2 SA 190 (N); Boberg 259 en die bespreking deur Spiro 397–398).

'n Ouer kan ook verplig wees om sy meerderjarige kind te onderhou. In sodanige geval sal die vorige lewenstandaard van die kind in ag geneem word om die omvang van die onderhoudsplig te bepaal (sien in hierdie verband die aantekening by *Gliksman v Talekinsky* [147]).

Die ouerlike onderhoudsplig neem 'n aanvang by die geboorte van die kind en duur voort totdat die kind homself kan onderhou. Soos uit die onderhawige saak blyk, hang die ouer se onderhoudsplig nie direk saam met sy ouerlike gesag nie. Die ouer se onderhoudsplig kan bly voortbestaan selfs nadat sy ouerlike gesag beëindig is, byvoorbeeld deur die dood van die ouer of die mondigwording van die kind (sien byvoorbeeld ook *Gliksman v Talekinsky; Carelse v Estate De Vries* (1906) 23 SC 532; *Spies' Executors v Beyers* 1908 TS 473; *Goldman v Executor Estate Goldman* 1937 WPA 64; *Hoffmann v Herdan* 1982 2 SA 274 (T); *Ex parte Jacobs* 1982 2 SA 276 (O)). Aan die ander kant, kan die onderhoudsplig tot 'n einde kom voordat die ouerlike gesag beëindig word. Indien 'n pasgebore baba byvoorbeeld 'n groot som geld erf, sal die kind uit sy erfenis onderhou word en sal sy ouers nie teenoor hom onderhoudspligtig wees nie.

Dit blyk verder uit die *Visser*-saak dat 'n kind wat geregtig is op 'n erflating uit sy ouers se boedel homself uit daardie erfenis sal moet onderhou indien dit groot genoeg is daarvoor. Die kind sal dan nie 'n onderhoudseis teen die ouer se boedel hê nie (sien ook *Ex parte Jacobs* 1950 2 PH M26 (O); *Christie v Estate Christie* 1956 3 SA 659 (N); *Ex parte Zietsman: In re Estate Bastard* 1952 2 SA 16 (K); *Lotz v Boedel Van der Merwe* 1958 2 PH M16 (O)).

enjoys preference over the claims of heirs and legatees but not over creditors (see *Davis' Tutor v Estate Davis* 1925 WLD 168; *Ex parte Zietsman: In re Estate Bastard; Barnard v Miller* 1963 4 SA 426 (C)).

Some uncertainty exists as to whether the estate of the deceased parent is proportionately liable to support the child if the child's other parent is able to support the child fully. (See in this regard Barnard, Cronjé and Olivier 313; Van der Vyver and Joubert 628; Boberg 287; Van Zyl *Family Law Service* par C21.)

'n Mens moet verder daarop let dat die kind se onderhoudseis teen sy oorlede ouer se boedel voorrang geniet bo die eise van erfgename en legatarisse maar nie bo skuldeisers nie (sien *Davis' Tutor v Estate Davis* 1925 WPA 168; *Ex parte Zietsman: In re Estate Bastard; Barnard v Miller* 1963 4 SA 426 (K)).

Daar bestaan onsekerheid oor die vraag of die boedel van 'n oorlede ouer proporsioneel aanspreeklik is vir die onderhoud van die kind indien die kind se ander ouer in staat is om die kind ten volle te onderhou. (Sien in hierdie verband Barnard, Cronjé en Olivier 323; Van der Vyver en Joubert 628; Boberg 287; Van Zyl *Family Law Service* par C21.)

Bibliography/Bibliografie

Barnard AH *Die Nuwe Egskeidingsreg* Butterworths, Durban 1979.

Barnard AH *The New Divorce Law* Butterworths, Durban 1979 (translation by J Church).

Barnard AH, Cronjé DSP and Olivier PJJ *The South African Law of Persons and Family Law* 3 ed by DSP Cronjé, Butterworths, Durban 1994.

Barnard AH, Cronjé DSP en Olivier PJJ *Die Suid-Afrikaanse Persone- en Familiereg* 3e uitg deur DSP Cronjé, Butterworths, Durban 1994.

Bekker PM *Die Aksie weens Seduksie* Proefskrif, Unisa 1977.

Boberg PQR *The Law of Persons and the Family* Juta, Cape Town Wynberg Johannesburg 1977.

Christie RH *The Law of Contract in South Africa* 2 ed Butterworths, Durban 1991.

Corbett MM, Hahlo HR, Hofmeyr G and Kahn E *The Law of Succession in South Africa* Juta, Cape Town Wetton Johannesburg 1980.

Davel T *Skadevergoeding aan Afhanklikes by die Dood van 'n Broodwinner* Digma-Publikasies, Roodepoort 1987.

De Groot H *Inleidinge tot de Hollandsche Rechts-geleerdheid* met Aantekeningen van SJ Fockema Andreae, 3e uitg deur LJ van Apeldoorn, S Gouda Quint, Arnhem 1926.

De Wet JC en Yeats JP *Die Suid-Afrikaanse Kontraktereg en Handelsreg* 3e uitg Butterworths, Durban 1964.

De Wet JC en Van Wyk AH *Die Suid-Afrikaanse Kontraktereg en Handelsreg* bd 1 *Kontraktereg* 5e uitg Butterworths, Durban 1992.

Grotius See De Groot H.

Hahlo HR *The South African Law of Husband and Wife* 4 ed (1975); 5 ed Juta, Cape Town Wetton Johannesburg 1985.

Hahlo HR and Kahn E *The South African Legal System and its Background* Juta, Cape Town Wynberg Johannesburg 1968.

Hahlo HR and Kahn E *The Union of South Africa The Development of its Laws and Constitution*, Stevens & Son Limited, London, Juta, Cape Town 1960.

Hahlo HR and Sinclair JD *The Reform of the South African Law of Divorce* Juta, Cape Town Wetton Johannesburg 1980.

Heaton J *The Meaning of the Concept "Best Interests of the Child" as Applied in Adoption Applications in South African Law* LL M Dissertation, Unisa 1988.

Hutchison Dale, Van Heerden Belinda, Visser DP and Van der Merwe CG *Wille's Principles of South African Law* 8 ed Juta, Cape Town Wetton Johannesburg 1991.

Jordaan RA en Davel CJ *Personereg – Bronnebundel* Juta, Kaapstad Wetton Johannesburg 1992.

Kahn E *The South African Law of Domicile of Natural Persons* Juta, Cape Town Wynberg Johannesburg 1972.

Lee and Honoré *Family, Things and Succession* 2 ed by HJ Erasmus, CG van der Merwe and AH van Wyk, Butterworths, Durban Pretoria 1983.

Schäfer ID (Editor) *Family Law Service* Butterworths, Durban.

Sinclair JD *An Introduction to the Matrimonial Property Act 1984* Juta, Cape Town Wetton Johannesburg 1984.

Sinclair JD *Inleiding tot die Wet op Huweliksgoedere 1984* Juta, Kaapstad Wetton Johannesburg 1984 (vertaling deur C Visser).

Sonnekus JC *Die Privaatregtelike Beskerming van die Huwelik* Proefskrif, Dutch Efficiency Bureau Pijnacker, Leiden 1976.

South African Law Commission *Report on Marriages and Customary Unions of Black Persons* Project 51 October 1986.

South African Law Commission *Report on Domicile* Project 60 March 1990.

South African Law Commission *Working Paper 41* Project 63 *Review of the Law of Insolvency: Voidable Dispositions and Dispositions that may be set aside and the Effect of Sequestration on the Spouse of the Insolvent* 1991.

South African Law Commission *Working Paper 45* Project 76 *Jewish Divorces* 27 November 1992.

South African Law Commission *Working Paper 44* Project 79 *A Father's Rights in respect of his Illegitimate Child* 1993.

Spiro E *Law of Parent and Child* 4 ed Juta, Cape Town Wetton Johannesburg 1985.

Suid-Afrikaanse Regskommissie *Verslag oor Huwelike en Gebruiklike Verbindings van Swart Persone* Projek 51 Oktober 1986.

Suid-Afrikaanse Regskommissie *Verslag oor Domisilie* Projek 60 Maart 1990.

Suid-Afrikaanse Regskommissie *Werkstuk 41* Projek 63 *Hersiening van die Insolvensiereg: Vervreemdings wat Nietig is of tersyde gestel kan word en die uitwerking van Sekwestrasie op die Insolvent se Gade* 1991.

Suid-Afrikaanse Regskommissie *Werkstuk 45* Projek 76 *Joodse Egskeidings* 27 November 1992.

Suid-Afrikaanse Regskommissie *Werkstuk 44* Projek 79 *'n Vader se Regte ten opsigte van sy Buite-egtelike kind* 1993.

Van den Heever FP *Breach of Promise and Seduction in South African Law* Juta, Cape Town Wynberg Johannesburg 1954.

Steyn LC *Die Uitleg van Wette* 4e uitg Juta, Kaapstad Wynberg Johannesburg Durban 1974.

Van der Keessel DG *Theses Selectae Juris Hollandici et Zelandici* F Muller, Amsteodami 1860.

Van der Merwe NJ en Rowland CJ *Die Suid-Afrikaanse Erfreg* 6e uitg JP van der Walt & Seun, Pretoria 1990.

Van der Vyver JD en Joubert DJ *Persone- en Familiereg* 3e uitg Juta, Kaapstad Wetton Johannesburg 1991.

Van Leeuwen *Censura Forensis* S Luchtmans en C Haak, Lugduni in Batavis 1741.

Van Leeuwen *Het Rooms-Hollands-Regt* met Aantekeninge van CW Decker, J Ten Houten, deel I 1780, deel II Amsteldam 1783.

Voet J *Commentarius ad Pandectas* J Verbessel, Lugduni Batavorum 1698–1704.

Wille's Principles of South African Law See Hutchison Dale, Van Heerden Belinda, Visser DP and Van der Merwe CG.

Yeats JP *Die Algehele Huweliksgemeenskap van Goedere,* Proefskrif, Stellenbosch.

Table of Cases/Vonnisregister

Where a page number appears in **bold** it indicates that the case is discussed
'n Bladsynommer in **vet gedruk**, dui daarop dat die betrokke vonnis bespreek word